Marketing AN INTRODUCTION

Canadian Edition

Gary Armstrong
University of North Carolina

Philip Kotler
Northwestern University

Peggy H. Cunningham
Queen's University

Peter Mitchell
British Columbia Institute of Technology

PEARSON
Prentice
Hall

Toronto

To my wife, Lynda

National Library of Canada Cataloguing in Publication

Marketing: An Introduction/Gary Armstrong…[et al] _
Canadian ed.

Includes index.
ISBN 0-13-039127-1

     1. Marketing. I. Armstrong, Gary

HF5415.A75 2004   658.8   C2002-905287-4

ISBN 0-13-039127-1

Vice President, Editorial Director: Michael J. Young
Senior Acquisitions Editor: Kelly Torrance
Marketing Manager: Deborah Meredith
Senior Developmental Editor: Suzanne Schaan
Production Editor: Judith Scott
Copy Editor: Dawn Hunter
Production Coordinator: Janette Lush
Page Layout: Carol Anderson
Permissions and Photo Research: Amanda McCormick and Lisa Brant
Interior Design: Julia Hall
Cover Art: Julia Hall

Excerpt from "In the Aisles: Housewares—Little Guys vs. Mass Merchant," by Vicky Sanderson
Hardware Merchandising, 1 February, 2002, reprinted by permission of Vicky Sanderson,
writer; Norco Company profile at http://www.norco.com/profile/index.htm reprinted by permission of Norco Performance Bikes; Table 4-1 Canada's Population Trends based on Table:
Statistics Canada, 2001 Census Analysis Series A-A Profile of the Canadian Population: Where
we Live. Cat no. 96F0030XIE010012001 http://geodepot.statcan.ca/Diss/Highlights/Table_e.pdf;
Major Stages of the Business Buying Process in Relation to Major Buying Situations, adapted
from Patrick J. Robinson, Charles W. Faris, and Yoram Wind, *Industrial Buying and Creative
Marketing*, Boston: Allyn and Bacon, 1967:14; WestJet Annual Report 2001, 20 March 2002,
accessed online at www.westjet.com, May 2002, courtesy of WestJet; Case 11 adapted from
"Sound Strategy" from *INC: The Magazine for Growing Companies* by Welles, Edward O.
Copyright 1991 by Bus Innovator Group Resources/INC. Reproduced with permission of Bus
Innovator Group Resources/INC via Copyright Clearance Centre; Excerpts from *Fortune
Magazine* article "They all want to be like Mike," by Marc Gunther, Monday, 21 July, 1997
Fortune Magazine reprinted with permission of *FORTUNE Magazine*; Ben & Jerry's Mission
Statement reproduced by permission of Ben & Jerry's www.benjerry.com/mission.html.

Statistics Canada information is used with the permission of the Minister of Industry, as
Minister responsible for Statistics Canada. Information on the availability of the wide range of
data from Statistics Canada can be obtained from Statistic Canada's Regional Offices, its World
Wide Web site at http://www.statcan.ca, and its toll-free access number 1-800-263-1136.

  3 4 5   08 07 06 05 04
Printed and bound in the USA.

BRIEF CONTENTS

Contents

ABOUT THE AUTHORS

Gary Armstrong is Crist W. Blackwell Distinguished Professor of Undergraduate Education in the Kenan-Flagler Business School at the University of North Carolina at Chapel Hill. He holds undergraduate and masters degrees in business from Wayne State University in Detroit, and he received his Ph.D. in marketing from Northwestern University. Dr. Armstrong has contributed numerous articles to leading business journals. As a consultant and researcher, he has worked with many companies on marketing research, sales management, and marketing strategy. But Professor Armstrong's first love is teaching. His Blackwell Distinguished Professorship is the only permanent endowed professorship for distinguished undergraduate teaching at the University of North Carolina at Chapel Hill. He has been very active in the teaching and administration of Kenan-Flagler's undergraduate program. His administrative posts include Chair of the Marketing Faculty, Associate Director of the Undergraduate Business Program, Director of the Business Honors Program, and others. He works closely with business student groups and has received several campus-wide and Business School teaching awards. He is the only repeat recipient of school's highly regarded Award for Excellence in Undergraduate Teaching, which he has received three times.

Philip Kotler is S. C. Johnson & Son Distinguished Professor of International Marketing at the Kellogg Graduate School of Management, Northwestern University. He received his master's degree at the University of Chicago and his Ph.D. at M.I.T., both in economics. Dr. Kotler is author of *Marketing Management: Analysis, Planning, Implementation, and Control* (Prentice Hall), now in its eleventh edition and the world's most widely used marketing textbook in graduate schools of business. He has authored seventeen other successful books and has written over 100 articles in leading journals. He is the only three-time winner of the coveted Alpha Kappa Psi award for the best annual article in the Journal of Marketing. Dr. Kotler's numerous major honors include the Paul D. Converse Award given by the American Marketing Association to honor "outstanding contributions to science in marketing" and the Stuart Henderson Britt Award as Marketer of the Year. He was named the first recipient of two major awards: the Distinguished Marketing Educator of the Year Award given by the American Marketing Association and the Philip Kotler Award for Excellence in Health Care Marketing presented by the Academy for Health Care Services Marketing. He has also received the Charles Coolidge Parlin Award, which each year honors an outstanding leader in the field of marketing. In 1995, he received the Marketing Educator of the Year Award from Sales and Marketing Executives International. Dr. Kotler has served as chairman of the College on Marketing of the Institute of Management Sciences (TIMS) and a director of the American Marketing Association. He has received honorary doctoral degrees from Stockholm University, the University of Zurich, Athens University of Economics and Business,

DePaul University, the Cracow School of Business and Economics, Groupe H.E.C. in Paris, and the University of Economics and Business Administration in Vienna. He has consulted with many major U.S. and foreign companies in the areas of marketing strategy and planning, marketing organization, and international marketing. He has travelled extensively throughout Europe, Asia, and South America, advising and lecturing companies about global marketing opportunities.

Peggy Cunningham is Associate Professor of Marketing at Queen's University School of Business. She received her undergraduate degree from Queen's University, completed her MBA at the University of Calgary, and earned her Ph.D. in marketing from Texas A&M University. She is the Co-Chair of the E-Commerce Research Group and the Head of the new MBA program for students with undergraduate business degrees. She has considerable international experience and has been a visiting professor at universities and government training programs in France, Germany, China, the UK, and the U.S. Her prior industry experience and current consulting practice help her to bring the perspective of the practitioner to the study of marketing. She conducts research in the fields of e-commerce, marketing ethics, strategic alliances, and cause-related marketing. Her work is published in a number of journals including the *Journal of the Academy of Marketing Science*. She is a devoted teacher who tries to inspire her students to realize their full and unique potential. In recognition of these efforts, she has received several teaching and service awards including the Frank Knox award for teaching excellence, a Queen's campus-wide award granted by undergraduate students. She was named as the Academy of Marketing Science Outstanding Teacher in 2001. She has applied her love of teaching to a wide range of courses including marketing management and strategy, principles of marketing, services marketing, international marketing, marketing ethics, and Customer Relationship Management.

Peter Mitchell is an instructor in the Marketing Management Faculty at the British Columbia Institute of Technology (BCIT), in Burnaby, B.C. He has an Honours Degree in Business Administration, an Advanced Graduate Diploma in Management and is completing a Master's Degree in Online Education. Before embarking on his current academic career, he spent 30 years in senior marketing management positions through to chief executive roles with major international organizations including Southam, Nabisco Brands and Pepsi. Immediately prior to joining BCIT in his current role, he was President and a shareholder in a specialized business-to-business distribution company in Vancouver, B.C. His teaching career includes 10 years of teaching in BCIT's School of Business's extensive part-time-studies program. He moved to a full-time teaching position in September of 1998.

PREFACE

The goal of this book is to help students master the basic concepts and practices of modern marketing in an enjoyable and practical way. Achieving this goal involves a constant search for the best balance among the "three pillars" that support the text—theories and concepts, practices and applications, and pedagogy. *Marketing: An Introduction* provides the most authoritative and up-to-date coverage of marketing theory and concepts, brings the theory to life with real examples of marketing practices, and presents both theory and practice in a way that makes them easy and enjoyable to learn.

Marketing: An Introduction, focuses on pedagogy—providing an effective *teaching and learning tool*. This exciting teaching and learning thrust comes to life through a short, lively design that features a set of "Road to Marketing" learning aids that begin students on their marketing journey. To help students learn, link, and apply important marketing concepts more effectively, *Marketing: An Introduction*, is filled with "road map" learning tools throughout each chapter. These pedagogical guides help students by:

- challenging them to stop and think at important junctures in their journey
- previewing chapter material
- reviewing and linking key chapter concepts
- providing practical Internet and marketing-application exercises through which students apply newly-learned marketing concepts in realistic situations

The result is an enhanced learning experience for the student.

STARTING DOWN THE ROAD TO MARKETING

Marketing is the business function that identifies customer needs and wants; determines which target markets the organization can serve best; and designs appropriate products, services, and programs to serve these markets. However, marketing is much more than just an isolated business function—it is a philosophy that guides the entire organization. The goal of marketing is to create customer satisfaction profitably by building value-laden relationships with important customers. The marketing department cannot accomplish this goal by itself. To provide superior value to customers, it must team up closely with other departments in the company and partner with other organizations throughout its entire value-delivery system. Thus, marketing calls upon everyone in the organization to "think customer: and to do all they can to help create and deliver superior customer value and satisfaction.

Marketing is all around us, and we all need to know something about it. Marketing is used not only by manufacturing companies, wholesalers, and retailers, but by all kinds of individuals and organizations. Lawyers, accountants, and doctors use marketing to manage demand for their services. So do museums and performing arts groups. No politician can get the needed votes, and no resort the needed tourists, without developing and carrying out marketing plans.

People throughout these organizations need to know how to define and segment a market and how to position themselves strongly by developing products and services that satisfy the needs of chosen target segments. They must know how to price their offerings to make them attractive and affordable, and how to choose and manage intermediaries to make their products available to customers. They need to know how to advertise and promote products so customers will know about them and want them. Clearly, marketers need a broad range of skills in order to sense, serve, and satisfy consumer needs.

Students also need to know marketing in their roles as consumers and citizens. Someone is always trying to sell us something, so we need to recognize the methods they use. And when students enter the job market, they must do "marketing research" to find the best opportunities and the best ways to "market themselves" to prospective employers. Many will start their careers with marketing jobs in sales, retail, advertisement, research, or one of a dozen other marketing areas.

MARKETING: AN INTRODUCTION—A NEW LEARNING APPROACH

Our goal with *Marketing: An Introduction* is to create an effective teaching and learning environment. Most students learning marketing want a broad picture of marketing's basics. They want to know about important marketing principles and concepts and how these concepts are applied in actual marketing management practice. However, they don't want to drown in a sea of details, or to be overwhelmed by marketing's nuances and complexities. Instead, they want a text that guides them effectively and efficiently down the road to learning marketing in an easy-to-grasp, lively, and enjoyable way.

Marketing: An Introduction serves all of these important needs of beginning marketing students. The book is complete, covering all of the important principles and concepts that the marketer and consumer need to know. Moreover, it takes a practical, marketing-management approach—concepts are applied through countless examples of situations in which well known and little known companies assess and solve their marketing problems.

Marketing: An Introduction makes the teaching and learning of marketing easy, effective, and enjoyable. The "Road to Marketing" aids help students to learn, link, and apply important concepts. The length makes it manageable for beginning marketing students to cover the subject during a given semester. Its approachable writing style and level are well suited to the beginning marketing student. A lively design, the abundant use of illustrations, and New Directions boxes help bring life to the marketing journey.

Marketing: An Introduction tells the stories that reveal the drama of modern marketing:

- **Mountain Equipment Coop**'s customer-focused marketing strategy, dedicated not only to commercial success but also to environmental and social causes

- **Tim Hortons**' consistent product and positioning strategy throughout its history
- **Canadian Tire**'s powerful "click-and-mortar" model that combines traditional retailing and e-tailing
- **Procter & Gamble**'s use of segmentation, targeting, and positioning
- **WestJet**'s successful "less for less" strategy
- **Intrawest**'s exciting integration of product and service
- **Roots**' lifestyle marketing that captures customers' way of looking at the world

These and dozens of other examples and illustrations throughout each chapter reinforce key concepts and bring marketing to life.

TAXIGUY Comprehensive Case and Marketing Plan

From our eye-catching cover to the comprehensive case in the text, students are introduced to Justin Raymond's TAXIGUY, the small Canadian company that made it *big*. The comprehensive case examines the development of the company and looks at how it created a relationship with Molson as part of Molson's responsible drinking campaign. Students then are invited to read TAXIGUY's marketing plan, which has been annotated to serve as a model and teaching tool. The TAXIGUY story has it all, from strong co-branding and partnership between a start-up entrepreneur and a leading national company to an inside look at a successful value-delivery network and socially responsible marketing.

CONTENT AND ORGANIZATION

As we enter the twenty-first century, the major marketing developments can be summed up in a single theme: *connectedness*. Rapidly changing computer, information, communication, and transportation technologies are making the world a smaller place. Now, more than ever before, we are all connected to each other and to things near and far in the world around us. Moreover, we are connecting in new and different ways. *Marketing: An Introduction* reflects the major trends and forces that are impacting marketing in this new, connected millennium. It offers coverage on:

Customers: connecting more selectively, more directly, and for life:

- *Relationship marketing*—developing profitable customers and capturing customer lifetime value by building value-laden customer relationships.
- *Delivering superior customer value, satisfaction, and quality*—attracting, keeping, and growing customers by developing market-centred strategies and "taking care of the customer."
- *Connecting technologies*—employing the Internet and other information, computer, communications, and transportation technologies to connect directly with customers and to shape marketing offers tailored to their needs.

Marketing partners: connecting inside and outside the company to jointly bring more value to customers:

- *The company value chain*—connecting inside the company to create cross-functional, customer-focused teamwork and integrated action.
- *Value-delivery networks*—connecting with partners outside the company to create effective supply chains.

The world around us:

- *Global marketing*—connecting globally with customers and marketing partners. This book offers integrated chapter-by-chapter coverage plus a full chapter focusing on global marketing considerations.
- *Marketing ethics, environmentalism, and social responsibility*—reexamining connections with social values and responsibilities. This book offers integrated chapter-by-chapter coverage plus a full chapter on social responsibility and marketing ethics.
- *Broadened connections*—the increasing adoption of marketing by nonprofit and government organizations.

Chapter 1 introduces and integrates these important themes to set the stage at the beginning of the course. The chapter concludes with a section on the challenges and opportunities marketers will face in the new, connected millennium. Chapter 3, Marketing in the Internet Age, assesses the impact of the Internet and other technologies on marketing. Recent technological advances, including the explosion of the Internet, have created an Internet age, which is having a dramatic impact on both buyers and the marketers who serve them. To thrive in this new Internet age—even to survive—marketers must rethink their strategies and practices. This chapter introduces the exciting new strategies and tactics that firms are applying in order to prosper in today's high-tech environment. The chapter explores major forces shaping the Internet age; major e-commerce and e-marketing developments in B2C, B2B, C2C, and C2B domains; and strategies and tactics for setting up a successful e-commerce presence.

Related topics are covered throughout the other chapters, with material on everything from Internet research and the virtual reality displays that test new products to the high-tech approaches of the e-commerce marketers who sell them. Students will learn about the wonders of new marketing technologies, from the Internet, database marketing, customer relationship marketing, and Web-based marketing research to mass customization, Internet business-to-business purchasing networks, Web-based personal selling, and technological advances in marketing logistics. The Companion Website for the text provides Web-based exercises that guide students through the fascinating world of marketing and the Internet.

Additional coverage of up-to-date trends and concers includes customer management and assessing customer value, brand equity and brand management, value propositions and positioning, experiences marketing, the new direct marketing model, "markets-of-one" marketing, internal and online marketing databases, Internet and online marketing research, cross-functional partnering and supply chain management, business-to-business marketing on the Internet, value pricing, integrated marketing communications, diversity, environmental sustainability, international marketing strategy, and much more.

LEARNING AIDS

The following "Road to Marketing" learning devices dispersed at critical points throughout the chapter help students to learn, link, and apply major concepts as they progress through their journey toward learning marketing.

Looking Ahead A section at the beginning of each chapter briefly previews chapter concepts, links them with previous chapter concepts, outlines chapter learning objectives, and introduces the chapter-opening vignette.

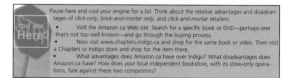

Looking Ahead
Ready to travel on? In the first chapter, you learned the core concepts and philosophies of marketing. Next, you'll investigate marketing's role in the broader organization and the specifics of the marketing process. First, marketing urges a whole-company philosophy that puts customers at the centre. Then, marketers work with other company functions to design strategies for delivering value to carefully targeted customers and to develop marketing mixes—comprising product, price, distribution, and promotion tactics—to carry out these strategies profitably. Chapters 1 and 2 will fully introduce you to the basics of marketing, the decisions marketing managers make, and where marketing fits into an organization. After that, we'll look at the environments in which marketing operates.

After studying this chapter, you should be able to
1. explain companywide strategic planning and its four steps
2. discuss how to design business portfolios and develop growth strategies
3. explain functional planning strategies and assess marketing's role in strategic planning

You Are Here "Concept checks" inserted at key points in each chapter help students ensure that they are grasping and applying key concepts and

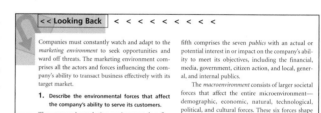

Pause here and cool your engine for a bit. Think about the relative advantages and disadvantages of *click-only*, *brick-and-mortar only*, and *click-and-mortar* retailers.
• Visit the Amazon.ca Web site. Search for a specific book or DVD—perhaps one that's not too well known—and go through the buying process.
• Now visit www.chapters.indigo.ca and shop for the same book or video. Then visit a Chapters or Indigo store and shop for the item there.
• What advantages does Amazon.ca have over Indigo? What disadvantages does Amazon.ca have? How does your local independent bookstore, with its store-only operations, fare against these two competitors?

linkages. This feature consists of a brief statement and a few concept and application questions.

Looking Back A summary of key concepts at the end of each chapter reviews chapter concepts and the chapter objectives.

<< Looking Back < < < < < < < < <

Companies must constantly watch and adapt to the *marketing environment* to seek opportunities and ward off threats. The marketing environment comprises all the actors and forces influencing the company's ability to transact business effectively with its target market.

1. Describe the environmental forces that affect the company's ability to serve its customers.

fifth comprises the seven *publics* with an actual or potential interest in or impact on the company's ability to meet its objectives, including the financial, media, government, citizen action, and local, general, and internal publics.

The *macroenvironment* consists of larger societal forces that affect the entire microenvironment—demographic, economic, natural, technological, political, and cultural forces. These six forces shape

Mastering Marketing The multimedia tool that means business. This technologically innovative CD-ROM uses video and interactive exercises to actively engage students in learning core marketing concepts. Exercises at the end of each chapter in the text direct students to the CD-ROM.

Mastering Marketing

The Mastering Marketing CD-ROM included with this book uses a fictional Internet company, CanGo, to examine the ideas presented in the text. Explore the videos and interactive exercises on the CD-ROM, and consider the questions that appear in the Mastering Marketing section at the end of each chapter.

Beyond creating short-term transactions, marketers need to build long-term relationships with valued customers, distributors, dealers, and suppliers. Cite three examples from CanGo of relationship marketing with customers, distributors, dealers, or suppliers. Be specific in your comments.

Navigating the Key Terms A list of the chapter's key terms helps students review the chapter content. Definitions are provided in an end-of-book glossary.

Navigating the Key Terms

Business portfolio, p. 53
Business unit strategy, p. 47
Corporate strategic planning, p. 47
Diversification, p. 59
Functional strategy, p. 48
Growth-share matrix, p. 55
Market development, p. 59

Marketing control, p. 71
Marketing implementation, p. 69
Marketing mix, p. 64
Marketing process, p. 61
Marketing strategy, p. 68
Mission statement, p. 51
Portfolio analysis, p. 54

Concept Check

Fill in the blanks and then check your answers.

1. _____ is the process of developing and maintaining a strategic fit between the organization's goals and capabilities and its changing marketing opportunities.

2. A _____ is a statement of the organization's purpose—what it wants to accomplish in the larger environment.

3. Management should avoid making its mission too narrow or too broad. According to this section of the text, missions should be _____, _____, fit the

6. Once a company has classified its SBUs, the company must determine what role each will play in the future. The company may choose one of four strategies. These strategies are to _____, _____, _____, or _____ the SBU.

7. When the marketing manager considers growth strategies, _____ would be chosen if the goal of the company wants to make more sales to current customers without changing products.

8. When each department within a firm carries out

Discussing the Issues

1. Define strategic planning. List and briefly describe the four steps of the strategic-planning process.

2. In a series of job interviews, you ask three recruiters to describe the missions of their companies. One says, "to make profits." Another says, "to create customers." The third says, "to fight world hunger." Analyze and discuss what these mission statements tell you about each company. Which appears to be more *market oriented*? Explain and justify.

3. An electronics manufacturer obtains the semi-

should the parent company do with this SBU?

4. Beyond evaluating current businesses, designing the business portfolio involves finding businesses and products the company should consider in the future. Using the product–market expansion grid, illustrate the process that a company can use to evaluate a portfolio. Pick an example for your demonstration that is different from the one used in the text. Be sure your example covers all cells.

5. To succeed in today's marketplace, companies must be customer centred. Explain how (a)

Concept Check and Discussing the Issues

These questions help students keep track of and apply what they've studied in the chapter.

MAP 6 Marketing Applications

Performance review is one of the most critical stages in a business buying process. Perhaps nowhere is this more important than in the highly competitive aircraft manufacturing business. Whether the planes are large or small, once a purchase is made, the buyer is tied to the manufacturer for a long time for service and parts requirements. "Air wars" are currently being fought between Europe's Airbus Industrie and America's Boeing. To a lesser extent, the same competitive conflict exists in the smaller personal and corporate aircraft market between Cessna and Lear

Jet. Who will eventually win these dramatic competitive struggles is literally "up in the air." Note: for additional information, see **www.airbus.com, www.boeing.com, www.cessna.textron.com,** and **www.learjet.com.**

Thinking Like a Marketing Manager

1. Apply either of the above two competitive situations to Figure 6-6 and demonstrate the critical factors that might be present in a business buying situation.

MAP-Marketing Applications

Interesting case histories, real-life situations, and timely descriptions of business situations put students in the place of a

marketing manager so they can make real marketing decisions.

Digital Map

 Visit our Web site at **www.pearsoned.ca/armstrong** for online quizzes, Internet exercises, and more!

Digital MAP

Students are directed to the Companion

Website, where exercises and resources guide them through the fascinating real world of marketing and the Internet.

ADDITIONAL LEARNING AIDS

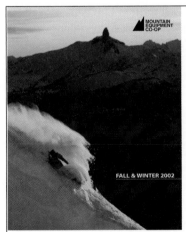

FALL & WINTER 2002

You've finally made it through university and you're about to realize a long-held dream—back-

The MEC logo on packs and clothing has come to state "I am Canadian" almost as much as a replica of the Canadian flag. In fact, few companies or brands are as associated with being Canadian as MEC. How has such a young company, born in 1970, developed this level of brand identity, especially since MEC prides itself on shunning such traditional tactics as mass media advertising? Its history is novel, to say the least. MEC's founders began by first recognizing unmet needs in a particular marketplace and then working to fill those needs. In the late 1960s, a small group of students from the University of British Columbia, with a passion for climbing and hiking, discovered that Vancouver had no mountaineering stores. To get the equipment they needed, people were forced to travel to the top supplier of gear at the time, REI in Seattle. However, Canada Customs agents were becoming increasingly tough on people who sometimes "forgot" to declare their American purchases. Storm-bound on Mt. Baker one week-

Chapter-Opening Vignettes

Each chapter starts with a dramatic marketing story that introduces the chapter material and arouses student interest.

New Directions Boxes

Additional examples and important information are highlighted in boxes throughout the text.

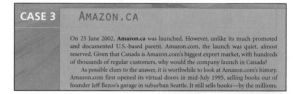

New Directions 3-2 >> The New World of E-Mail Marketing

E-mail is *the* hot new marketing medium. In ever-larger numbers, e-mail ads are popping onto our computer screens and filling up our e-mailboxes. What's more, they're no longer just the quiet, plain-text messages of old. The new breed of e-mail ad is designed to command your attention—loaded with glitzy features such as animation, interactive links,

sales and marketing research firm, estimates that permission e-mail campaigns typically achieve 10 percent to 15 percent click-through rates. That's good when compared with the 0.5 percent to 2 percent average response rates for traditional direct mail.

E-mail success stories abound. *Business Week* offers these:

Video Cases

Every chapter is supplemented with a video case that can be accessed on the CD accompanying the text.

Cases

Every chapter ends with a case that challenges students to apply marketing principles to companies in real situations.

CASE 3 AMAZON.CA

On 25 June 2002, **Amazon.ca** was launched. However, unlike its much promoted and documented U.S.-based parent, Amazon.com, the launch was quiet, almost reserved. Given that Canada is Amazon.com's biggest export market, with hundreds of thousands of regular customers, why would the company launch in Canada?

As possible clues to the answer, it is worthwhile to look at Amazon.com's history. Amazon.com first opened its virtual doors in mid-July 1995, selling books out of founder Jeff Bezos's garage in suburban Seattle. It still sells books—by the millions.

TAXIGUY Comprehensive Case and Marketing Plan

The TAXIGUY case integrates concepts from throughout the text, and the annotated marketing plan provides a real-life example of marketing planning in action and serves as a model for students.

Glossary

At the end of the book, an extensive glossary provides quick reference to the key terms found in the book.

Marketing Arithmetic

This appendix provides additional, practical information for students.

Indexes

Author, company and subject indexes reference all information and examples in the book.

A TOTAL TEACHING AND LEARNING PACKAGE

A successful marketing course requires more than a well written book. Today's classroom requires a dedicated instructor and a fully-integrated teaching system. A total package of teaching and learning supplements extends this edition's emphasis on effective teaching and learning. The following aids support *Marketing: An Introduction.*

For the Instructor

New! Pearson's MarketShare Website (www.pearsoned.ca/MarketShare). Visit MarketShare to discover the only one-stop information portal and meeting place developed for all Canadian Marketing instructors. Browse Virtual Libraries for most major courses in the undergraduate curriculum, spice up your lectures with additional media and news stories, visit the calendar of upcoming events, join in the online discussion of the latest hot topic with your peers, or add your name to our "Who's Who" list of Marketing instructors in Canada.

Instructor's Resource Manual and FACTS guide (ISBN 0-13-120457-2). This highly praised teaching guide contains chapter-by-chapter teaching strategies, outlines, interactive assignments, class projects, and answers to end-of-chapter questions and applications. Throughout, this guide places special emphasis on media supplements such as PowerPoint slides and Web resources, cross-referencing other supplements to do the work for you.

Test Item File (ISBN 0-13-120460-2). This test bank has been carefully tested and revised based on user feedback. The test bank includes up to 85 multiple choice and 35 true/false questions per chapter, together with essay and application questions. All questions are graded for difficulty, are labelled "recall" or "applied," include page references, and cite the chapter objective tested.

Pearson TestGen. The Pearson TestGen is a special computerized version of the Test Item File that enables instructors to view and edit the existing questions, add questions, generate tests, and print the tests in a variety of formats. Powerful search and sort functions make it easy to locate questions and arrange them in any order desired. TestGen also enables instructors to administer tests on a local area network, have the tests graded electronically, and have the results prepared in electronic or printed reports. Available on the Instructor's Resource CD (see below), the Pearson TestGen is compatible with PC or Macintosh systems.

PowerPoint Express and Extendit! Slides. Two sets of PowerPoint slides are available with this edition. PowerPoint Extendit! presentations include up to 25 slides per chapter with Weblinks and attention-grabbing video clips embedded into key slides. This set of lecture aids follows the chapter outline and also offers additional material from outside the text. PowerPoint Express slideshows are shorter and more basic, aimed at instructors who like to customize more. Both sets of PowerPoint files can be accessed on the Instructor's Resource CD (see below) or through the Companion Website.

Colour Transparencies (ISBN 0-13-121746-1). PowerPoint slides and text figures are available to qualified adopters as full-colour acetates.

Instructor's Resource CD (ISBN 0-13-120459-9). This handy resource provides one source for all your supplement needs. The CD-ROM contains the entire Instructor's Resource Manual and FACTS Guide, TestGen software loaded with the complete Test Item File, and PowerPoint Slides.

Companion Website (www.pearsoned.ca/armstrong). This Web resource provides instructors with a complete array of teaching material including downloadable versions of the Instructor's Resource Manual and PowerPoint slides and a Syllabus Builder to help plan your course. Also included is an interactive and exciting online Student Study Guide, plus great resources such as current events and Internet exercises.

CBC and On Location Videos (0-13-139811-3). This video library provides 16 segments (one per chapter), including topical coverage from CBC's *Venture, Marketplace,* and *Undercurrents,* as well as On Location segments created specifically for use with Pearson's Marketing texts. These videos, along with related cases, can also be accessed through the Companion Website or the Media Companion CD-ROM provided with the text. Contact your Pearson sales representative for details about the videotapes.

The Bessies (ISBN 0-13-121578-7). The Television Bureau of Canada annually recognizes excellence in Canadian television advertising with The Bessies awards program. Copies of the 2001 and 2002 show reels have been made available by the Television Bureau to instructors using *Marketing: An Introduction.* These tapes feature the best in recent advertising for Canadian companies for Canadian audiences. Please contact your Pearson sales representative for details. These videos are subject to availability. For further information about The Bessies or to inquire about the Television Bureau of Canada's library of nearly 30 000 commercials, please contact The Television Bureau of Canada, at 160 Bloor Street East, Suite 1005, Toronto, ON, M4W 1B9 (416-923-8813) or visit their website at www.tvb.ca.

Marketing: An Introduction 2003 Video Library (ISBN 0-13-035398-1). This set of three videotapes offers custom videos shot on location at leading companies, including companies such as *Exclusively Weddings* (segmentation and targeting), *Clarins* (distribution), and *American Standard* (integrated marketing communications). A video guide with cases is available on the Companion Website. These videotapes are available in Canada by special request through your Pearson sales representative.

ADvertising ADventure CD (0-13-140314-1). This CD-ROM contains a whole host of award-winning ads for use in the classroom. This supplement is available to qualified adopters through your Pearson sales representative.

Pearson Custom Publishing (www.prenhall.com/custombusiness). Pearson Custom Publishing can provide you and your students with texts, cases, and articles to enhance your course. Choose material from Darden, Ivey, Harvard Business School Publishing, NACRA, and Thunderbird to create your own custom casebook. Contact your Pearson sales representative for details.

Online Learning Solutions. Pearson Education Canada supports instructors interested in using online course management systems. We provide text-related content in WebCT and Blackboard. To find out more about creating an online course using Pearson content in one of these platforms, contact your Pearson sales representative.

New! Instructor's ASSET. Pearson Education is proud to introduce Instructor's ASSET, the Academic Support and Service for Educational Technologies. ASSET is the first integrated Canadian service program committed to meeting the customization, training, and support needs for your course. Ask your Pearson sales representative for details!

Your Pearson Sales Representative. Your Pearson rep is always available to ensure you have everything you need to teach a winning course. Armed with experience, training, and product knowledge, your Pearson rep will support your assessment and adoption of any of the products, services, and technology outlined here to ensure our offerings are tailored to suit your individual needs and the needs of your students. Whether it's getting instructions on TestGen software or specific content files for your new online course, your Pearson Sales Representative is there to help.

For the Student

Online Study Guide and Companion Website (www.pearsoned.ca/armstrong). Part of this text's integrated package is an interactive and exciting Study Guide, including multiple choice, true/false, and short essay questions with hints and answers that direct them to specific text pages for reinforcement. Students can read about the latest marketing issues "In the News" or use the Internet exercises to explore and deepen their knowledge. Other online resources include links to streaming videos and accompanying cases, lecture notes in PowerPoint, a "Careers in Marketing" section, sample marketing plans, and an unbeatable Virtual Library for Introductory Marketing.

Included with this textbook!

Mastering Marketing CD-ROM. Linked to this book via end of chapter material, this self-paced, interactive software helps reinforce marketing principles by linking theory to practice. It features 12 video episodes, bringing key marketing concepts to life. Students watch as employees at CanGo, a fictional Internet company, are faced with various realistic marketing issues. Interactive exercises accompany each video segment, challenging students to analyze the issue and develop new marketing strategies.

Included with this textbook!

Media Companion CD-ROM. This CD-ROM offers 16 video segments and cases (one per chapter). The videos include topical segments from CBC's *Venture*, *Marketplace*, and *Undercurrents*, as well as On Location segments created specifically for use with Pearson's Marketing texts.

Included with this textbook!

Marketing Plan Pro CD-ROM (0-13-065436-1). Available at a modest extra charge in a value-package, this highly acclaimed software enables students to build a marketing plan from scratch. Marketing Plan Pro also includes sample marketing plans.

The Marketing Plan: A Handbook with CD-ROM by Marian Burke Wood (0-13-175947-7). This brief paperback, which includes Marketing Plan Pro software (described above), is the ideal companion for any course in which students will create a marketing plan.

Strategy Magazine. Students can log in to www.strategymag.com/studentpromo and receive access for one year to past and current article searches on www.strategymag.com, a powerful research tool.

Acknowledgments

I would like to recognize the support and encouragement of my wife, Lynda, during the preparation of this book. The support and guidance of Jeff Collier, Senior Sales and Editorial Representative for Pearson Education, provided the incentive and opportunity to get involved in this Canadian Edition.

We could not have provided the important insight into the entrepreneurial environment without the considerable contribution and support from Justin Raymond, the founder of TAXIGUY, and Nathalie Masse from Molson. Scott McGillivray (University of Regina) formalized and annotated the marketing plan provided by TAXIGUY. Martha McEnally (University of North Carolina, Greensboro) wrote the original On Location cases, which have been adapted here for the Canadian market.

The dedicated team from Pearson Education—Kelly Torrance (Senior Acquisitions Editor), who identified the need and potential and championed this project from its inception, and Suzanne Schaan (Senior Developmental Editor), who was responsible for overseeing the project and keeping the author on track—were invaluable in this project coming to a successful completion. Thanks are also due to Judith Scott (Production Editor) and Dawn Hunter (Copy Editor), who ably handled the details of the manuscript, and Julia Hall (Assistant Art Director), who provided a terrific design and came up with the innovative cover concept. Deborah Meredith has brought a lot of enthusiasm to the project as Marketing Manager.

No new product comes to market without a rigorous vetting process, and for this I must acknowledge the reviewers who provided insight throughout the writing process to bring draft material in line with teaching and learning requirements. Reviewers for this Canadian edition included the following:

Deborah Andrus, *University of Calgary*

Denton Anthony, *St. Francis Xavier University*

Bryan Barbieri, *Concordia University*

Brad Davis, *Wilfrid Laurier University*

Webb Dussome, *University of Alberta*

Ian A. Fisher, *Sheridan College*

Gordon Fullerton, *Saint Mary's University*

C. Shannon Goodspeed, *Mount Royal College*

Derek N. Hassay, *University of Calgary*

D.G. Brian Jones, *University of Prince Edward Island*

Shirley Litchi, *Wilfrid Laurier University*

Marni Matheson, *Northern Alberta Institute of Technology*

Jean-Paul Olivier, *Red River College*

Nancy Ryan, *Humber College*

Murray Sang, *Concordia University*

Harvey Skolnick, *Sheridan College*

Maxwell Winchester, *University College of the Fraser Valley*

Peter Yannopoulos, *Brock University*

Finally, I wish to thank Philip Kotler, Gary Armstrong, and Peggy Cunningham; I can only hope that I have done justice to their original material in the preparation of this book.

Peter Mitchell
British Columbia Institute of Technology

The Pearson Education Canada **COMPANION WEBSITE**

A Great Way to Learn and Instruct Online

The Pearson Education Canada Companion Website is easy to navigate and is organized to correspond to the chapters in this textbook. Whether you are a student in the classroom or a distance learner you will discover helpful resources for in-depth study and research that empower you in your quest for greater knowledge and maximize your potential for success in the course.

Companion
Website

[www.pearsoned.ca/armstrong]

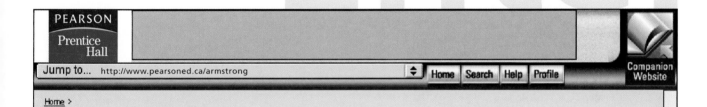

PEARSON
Prentice Hall

Jump to... http://www.pearsoned.ca/armstrong   Home | Search | Help | Profile

Companion
Website

Home >

PH Companion Website

Marketing: An Introduction, Canadian Edition
by Armstrong, Kotler, Cunningham, and Mitchell

Student Resources

The modules in this section provide students with tools for learning course material. These modules include:

- PowerPoint Lecture Slides
- Glossary
- Self-Tests, including multiple choice, true and false, and essay questions
- Internet Exercises
- Video Cases
- Company Weblinks
- In the News Exercises

In the quiz modules, students can send answers to the grader and receive instant feedback on their progress through the Results Reporter. Coaching comments and references to the textbook may be available to ensure that students take advantage of all available resources to enhance their learning experience.

Instructor Resources

The modules in this section provide instructors with additional teaching tools. Downloadable PowerPoint Presentations, Electronic Transparencies, and an Instructor's Manual are just some of the materials that may be available in this section.

1 >> Marketing in a Changing World: Creating Customer Value and Satisfaction

Looking Ahead

You're about to begin an exciting journey toward learning about marketing. To make sure we are travelling in the right direction, we'll first define marketing and its key concepts. Then, you'll make pit stops to learn about the various philosophies that guide marketing management and the challenges that marketers face. The goal of marketing is to create profitable customer relationships by delivering superior value to customers. Understanding these basic concepts, and forming your own ideas about what they mean to you, will give you a solid foundation for all that follows.

After studying this chapter, you should be able to

1. define marketing and discuss its core concepts

2. explain the relationships among customer value, satisfaction, and quality

3. define marketing management and understand how marketers manage demand and build profitable customer relationships

4. compare the five marketing management philosophies

5. analyze the major challenges facing marketers in the new "connected" world

Our first stop is Mountain Equipment Co-op, a successful organization that applies basic marketing concepts daily. It is a co-op and is therefore member owned. Although this type of organization differs from a for-profit company owned by shareholders, it is an excellent example of how to apply a long-term, customer-focused marketing strategy within an organizational mission dedicated not only to commercial success, but also to environmental and social causes.

FALL & WINTER 2002

The MEC logo on packs and clothing has come to state "I am Canadian" almost as much as a replica of the Canadian flag. In fact, few companies or brands are as associated with being Canadian as MEC. How has such a young company, born in 1970, developed this level of brand identity, especially since MEC prides itself on shunning such traditional tactics as mass media advertising? Its history is novel, to say the least. MEC's founders began by first recognizing unmet needs in a particular marketplace and then working to fill those needs. In the late 1960s, a small group of students from the University of British Columbia, with a passion for climbing and hiking, discovered that Vancouver had no mountaineering stores. To get the equipment they needed, people were forced to travel to the top supplier of gear at the time, REI in Seattle. However, Canada Customs agents were becoming increasingly tough on people who sometimes "forgot" to declare their American purchases. Storm-bound on Mt. Baker one weekend in the spring of 1970, the six original members of MEC developed the founding concept.

You've finally made it through university and you're about to realize a long-held dream—backpacking through Asia. But now you aren't so sure about this adventure. Your travel buddy backed out at the last minute, and you've just landed in the crowded Bangkok Airport only to discover that no one speaks English. You are almost ready to climb back on a flight home when you turn around and see a stranger elbowing her way through the crowd wearing a backpack with the distinctive Mountain Equipment Co-op (MEC) logo. A fellow Canadian for sure, looking just as lost as you, but perhaps the two of you can work together through airport maze. Maybe this trip won't be too bad after all.

Simply filling a need didn't make MEC what it is today; it was the fact that MEC filled this need in a distinctive fashion. First, rather than being a traditional retailer, MEC is a cooperative, which means that Mountain Equipment Co-op is member owned. It has had a narrow and focused approach since the beginning: MEC provides products and services for self-propelled, wilderness-oriented recreational activities. It prides itself on offering the lowest reasonable price on its products and on offering informative, helpful service.

Although MEC is a retailer that survives by promoting "consumption," it does so in an environmentally responsible manner. One of its environmental initiatives is MEC's Ecological Footprint Calculator. The co-op developed this educational tool to encourage members to think about the sustainability of their day-to-day life choices. It is intended to provoke thought and discussion about social values and thoughtful consumption. MEC also encourages its members to use their gear for its full lifetime. To help them do this, MEC has member education programs on the use and care of its products. It has a product repair program and a gear reuse program in addition to its recycling and donation programs for equipment that members no longer want or need. MEC is also working to expand its rental programs for those who need gear only occasionally.

Although MEC certainly focused on customer needs, quality products, and outstanding service, it grew to realize that many stakeholder groups were critically connected to its long-term success. It is a values-led organization that knows the power of having a motivated network of top-quality suppliers. MEC is energized by its employees, and it is committed to people and their communities, not just to a financial bottom line. This orientation is exemplified in its statement of values:

- We conduct ourselves ethically and with integrity.

- We show respect for others in our words and actions.

- We act in the spirit of community and co-operation.

- We respect and protect our natural environment.

- We strive for personal growth, continual learning and adventure.

MEC also knows that simply working to make a one-time sale to a customer isn't enough. Developing lifelong relationships with its members has been another touchstone of the cooperative. As part of its vision, MEC sets the goal of having its members purchase most of their equipment for outdoor activities from MEC. It sends members catalogues twice a year. Each is filled with high-quality information and product listings. MEC also sends out newsletters and increasingly relies on its Web site and e-commerce capabilities to maintain links with people who have paid $5 for their lifetime memberships.

These relationships are critical, since MEC has no doubt that its best marketers are the members themselves. Member-generated word-of-mouth communication has helped the company to grow—and grow it has. The six-member organization has become more than a million strong and its annual sales are in excess of $154 million. MEC currently operates stores in Vancouver, Edmonton, Calgary, Winnipeg, Toronto, Ottawa, and Halifax. Each store remains committed to MEC's guiding principle to contribute beyond their commercial mandate and be a positive force for change and social and environmental responsibility.[1]

Many factors contribute to making a business successful. However, today's successful companies at all levels have one thing in common—like MEC, they are strongly customer focused and heavily committed to marketing. These companies are dedicated to understanding and satisfying the needs of customers in well-defined target markets. They motivate everyone in the organization to produce superior value for their customers, leading to high levels of customer satisfaction.

WHAT IS MARKETING?

Marketing, more than any other business function, deals with customers. Creating customer value and satisfaction is at the heart of modern marketing thinking and practice. Although we will explore detailed definitions of marketing later in this chapter, perhaps the simplest definition is this one: *Marketing is the delivery of customer satisfaction at a profit.* The twofold goal of marketing is to attract new customers by promising superior value and to keep and increase the purchases by current customers by delivering satisfaction.

Wal-Mart became the world's largest retailer and *Marketing Magazine*'s 1999 Canadian Marketer of the Decade by delivering on its promise: "Always low prices—always." Dell leads the personal computer industry in Canada by consistently keeping its promise to "be direct," making it easy for customers to design their own computers and have them delivered quickly to their doorsteps. Ritz-Carlton promises—and delivers—truly "memorable experiences" for its hotel guests. And Coca-Cola, long the world's leading soft drink, delivers on the simple but enduring promise that with Coca-Cola, "life tastes good." These and other highly successful companies know that if they take care of their customers, then market share and profits will follow.

Sound marketing is critical to the success of every organization—large or small, for-profit or nonprofit, domestic or global. Large for-profit firms such as Canadian Tire, IBM, and Marriott use marketing. Small companies such as Obsolete Automotive in Point Edward, Ontario, a supplier to vintage British Sports car enthusiasts, also use marketing, but so do nonprofit organizations such as the Canadian Wildlife Fund, universities, colleges, hospitals, museums, symphony orchestras, and even churches. Moreover, marketing is practised not only in North America, but also in the rest of the world. Most countries in South America, Western Europe, and Asia have well-developed marketing systems. Even in Eastern Europe and other parts of the world where marketing long had a bad name, dramatic political and social changes have created new opportunities for marketing. Business and government leaders in most of these nations are eager to learn everything they can about modern marketing practices.

You already know a lot about marketing—it's all around you. You see the results of marketing in the abundance of products in a shopping mall. You see marketing in the advertisements that fill your TV, spice up your magazines, stuff your mailbox, or enliven your Web pages. At home, at school, where you work, and where you play, you are exposed to marketing in almost everything you do. Yet, there is much more to marketing than meets the consumer's eye. Behind it is a massive network of people and activities competing for your attention and purchasing dollars.

This book will give you a more complete and formal introduction to the basic concepts and practices of marketing. In this chapter, we begin by defining marketing and its core concepts, describing the major philosophies of marketing thinking and practice, and discussing some of the major challenges marketers face.

MARKETING DEFINED

What does the term *marketing* mean? Many people think of marketing only as selling and advertising. And no wonder—every day we are bombarded with television commercials, newspaper ads, direct-mail campaigns, sales calls, and Internet pitches. However, selling and advertising are only the tip of the marketing iceberg. Although they are important, they are only two of many marketing functions and are often not the most important ones.

Today, marketing must be understood not in the old sense of making a sale—"telling and selling"—but in the new sense of *satisfying customer needs.* If the marketer does a good job of understanding consumer needs; develops products that provide superior value; and prices, distributes, and promotes them effectively, these products will sell very easily. Thus, selling and advertising are only part of a larger "marketing mix"—a set of marketing tools that work together to affect the marketplace.

We define **marketing** as a social and managerial process whereby individuals and groups obtain what they need and want through creating and exchanging products and value with others.[2] To explain this definition, we will examine the following important terms: *needs, wants,* and *demands; products, services,* and *experiences; value, satisfaction,* and *quality; exchange, transactions,* and *relationships;* and *markets.* Figure 1-1 shows that these core marketing concepts are linked, with each concept building on the one before it.

Marketing A social and managerial process by which individuals and groups obtain what they need and want through creating and exchanging products and value with others.

Needs, Wants, and Demands

The most basic concept underlying marketing is that of human needs. Human **needs** are states of felt deprivation. They include basic *physical* needs for food, clothing, warmth, and safety; *social* needs for belonging and affection; and *individual* needs for knowledge and self-expression. These needs were not invented by marketers; they are a basic part of human makeup.

Need A state of felt deprivation.

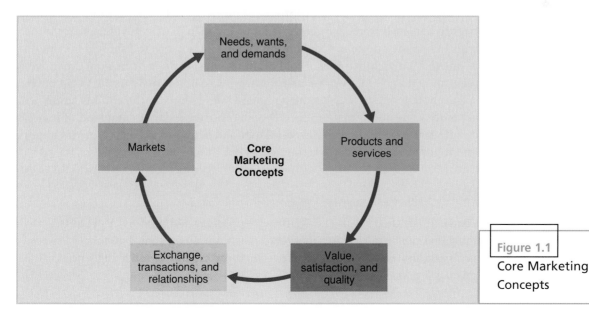

Figure 1.1

Core Marketing Concepts

Want The form taken by a human need as shaped by culture and individual personality.

Wants are the form human needs take as they are shaped by culture and individual personality. A Canadian *needs* food but *wants* a hamburger, poutine, and a soft drink. A person in Mauritius *needs* food but *wants* a mango, rice, lentils, and beans. Wants are shaped by an individual's society and are described in terms of objects that will satisfy needs.

People have almost unlimited wants but limited resources. Thus, they want to choose products that provide the most value and satisfaction for their money. When backed by buying power, wants become **demands**. Consumers view products as bundles of benefits and choose products that give them the best bundle for their money. A Honda Civic means basic transportation, affordable price, and fuel economy; a Lexus means comfort, luxury, and status. Given their wants and resources, people demand products with the benefits that add up to the most satisfaction.

Demands Human wants that are backed by buying power.

Outstanding marketing companies go to great lengths to learn about and understand their customers' needs, wants, and demands. They conduct research about consumer likes and dislikes. They analyze customer inquiry, warranty, and service data. They observe customers using their products and competing ones and train salespeople to watch for unfulfilled customer needs.

In these outstanding companies, people at all levels—including top management—stay close to customers. For example, top executives from Wal-Mart spend two days each week visiting stores and mingling with customers. For years, one of Home Depot's cofounders spent 25 percent of his time out in the stores meeting with customers and trying to understand them better. And it's not only the large companies that are learning to stay close to their customers.

Corrina Kroeker, the buyer for the housewares section of the Homestead True Value in Winkler, Manitoba, stays in close contact with her customers and the competition. "There's such a difference between our service and the mass merchant. My husband [Dave, the store's manager] and I often walk through big box stores or call one for a price check. I get off the phone and wonder to myself if the manager knows how the salespeople speak to customers."[3]

Kroeker believes that good product knowledge keeps her customers coming back to her small store. "I recently had a young man in here buying a mixer for his wife. I knew the one he was looking at wouldn't be suitable, so I showed him another one that I myself had used. I told him that while it was a little more expensive, I really thought it would work better for her. I wasn't purposely trying to get him to spend more money. I was just being honest, and I think in the end his family will get more value out of that product. People relate these days to that kind of logic."[4]

Wal-Mart
www.walmart.com

Understanding customer needs, wants, and demands in detail provides important input for designing marketing strategies.

Products, Services, and Experiences

Products Anything that can be offered to a market for attention, acquisition, use, or consumption that might satisfy a want or need. They include physical objects, services, persons, places, organizations, and ideas.

People satisfy their needs and wants with products and services. A **product** is anything that can be offered to a market to satisfy a need or want. The concept of *product* is not limited to physical objects—anything capable of satisfying a need can be called a product.

Products do not have to be physical objects. Here the product is an idea: Smoking harms you and others.

In addition to tangible goods, products include **services**, which are activities or benefits offered for sale that are essentially intangible and do not result in the ownership of anything.

More broadly defined, products include other entities such as *experiences, persons, places, organizations, information,* and *ideas.* For example, by orchestrating several services and goods, companies can create, stage, and market brand experiences. Attending a Nickelback concert is an experience, so is going to the Art Gallery of Ontario, riding on a Harley-Davidson, visiting Indigo or Canadian Tire, or surfing Sony's playstation.com Web site. In fact, as products and services increas-

Services Any activities or benefits that one party can offer to another that are essentially intangible and do not result in the ownership of anything. Examples include banking, airlines, hotels, tax preparation, and home repair services.

ingly become commodities, experiences have emerged for many firms as the next step in differentiating the company's offer.

"What consumers really want is products, communications, and marketing campaigns that dazzle their senses, touch their hearts, and stimulate their minds," declares one expert. "They want products, communications, and marketing campaigns to deliver an experience."[5]

In recent years, for example, a rash of theme stores and restaurants have burst onto the scene, offering much more than just merchandise or food. Stores such as Virgin Mega Store draw consumers in by offering fun activities, such as promotional events (sometimes featuring live artists), and listening stations to allow customers to preview the latest CDs.

At theme restaurants such as the Hard Rock Cafe, the food is secondary to what's known as "eatertainment." Much of the attraction of Hard Rock Cafes is the rock and roll paraphernalia on display and the entertainment offered. In Nike's first Niketown Store in Chicago, customers played basketball on a court in the store to test out different styles of footwear. At Tom Lee Music in Vancouver, all the major instrument groups have their own area in the store. For example, the guitar department presents its instruments in a "displayed to be played" fashion (only collectibles and custom models require assistance from a product specialist). The acoustic guitars are presented in three unique showrooms, with climate-controlled environments that are decorated in rustic woods throughout. More than a hundred guitars are within reach, and customers can play whatever they want to ensure they've found the right guitar. The amplifier displays are integrated within the guitar display so that customers can freely move from one amplifier to another.

Thus, the term *product* includes more than just the physical properties of a good or service. It also includes a brand's *meaning* to consumers. Coca-Cola means much more to consumers than just something to drink—it has become a global icon with a rich tradition and meaning. Nike is more than just shoes—it's what the shoes do for you and where they take you. The familiar Nike swoosh stands for high sports performance, famous athletes, and a "Just Do It!" attitude (see New Directions 1-1).

The term *product* also includes more than just goods or services. Consumers decide which events to experience, which entertainers to watch on television, which places to visit on vacation, which organizations to support through contributions, and which ideas to adopt. To the consumer, these things are all products. If the term *product* does not seem to fit, we could substitute other terms such as *satisfier, resource,* or *marketing offer.*

Many sellers make the mistake of paying more attention to the specific products they offer than to the benefits produced by these products. They see themselves as selling a product rather than fulfilling a need. A manufacturer of quarter-inch (6-mm) drill bits may think that the customer needs a drill bit, but what the customer *really* needs is a quarter-inch (6-mm) hole. These sellers may suffer from "marketing myopia"—they are so taken with their products that they focus only on existing wants and lose sight of underlying customer needs.[6] They forget that a product is only a tool to solve a consumer problem. These sellers will have trouble if a new product comes along that serves the customer's need better or less expensively. The customer with the same *need* will *want* the new product.

Virgin Online
www.virgin.com

Nike Canada
www.nike.com/canada

Tom Lee Music Canada
www.tomleemusic.ca

New Directions 1-1 >> Nike: It's Not So Much the Shoes as Where They Take You!

The power of the Nike swoosh speaks loudly of Nike's superb marketing skills. The ever-present symbol has come to stand for all that Nike means to those who wear it all around the world.

The swoosh is everywhere! Try counting the swooshes you see when you read the sports pages, watch a pickup basketball game, or tune into a televised golf match. Nike has built the ubiquitous swoosh into one of the world's best-known brand symbols. And the swoosh has come to stand for all the things that Nike means to those who wear it all around the world.

The power of its brand and logo speaks loudly of Nike's superb marketing skills. The company's strategy of building superior products around popular athletes and its classic "Just Do It!" ad campaign have forever changed the face of sports marketing. Nike spends hundreds of millions of dollars each year on big-name endorsements, splashy promotional events, and attention-grabbing ads. Over the years, Nike has associated itself with some of the biggest names in sports: Michael Jordan, Tiger Woods, Pete Sampras, Bruny Surin, Mark Boswell, and Simon Whitfield. It also works to promote sport at a more grassroots level. For example, Nike Canada has partnered with the Association for Advancement of Women and Sport and Physical Activity (CAAWS) in their Girls@Play program. Thus, no matter what your sport, chances are good that one of your favourite athletes wears the Nike swoosh.

Nike knows, however, that good marketing is more than just promotional hype and promises—it is also the consistent building of strong relationships with customers that are based on real value. Nike's initial success resulted from the technical superiority of its running and basketball shoes, which pitched to serious athletes who were frustrated by the lack of innovation in athletic equipment. To this day, Nike leads the industry in research and development spending.

But Nike gives its customers more than just good athletic gear. Beyond shoes, apparel, and equipment, Nike markets a way of life, a sports culture, a "Just do it" attitude. That's the real meaning of Nike to its customers. Says Phil Knight, Nike's founder and chief executive, "Basically, our culture and our style is to be a rebel." The company was built on a genuine passion for sports, a maverick disregard for convention, hard work, and serious sports performance. Anyone at Nike will tell you, Nike is athletes, athletes are sports, *Nike is sports*.

The strong relationships between customers and Nike's brand have paid off handsomely for the company. During the decade ending in 1997, Nike's worldwide revenues grew at an incredible annual rate of 21 percent; annual return to investors averaged 47 percent. In the mid-1990s, Nike leveraged its brand strength, moving aggressively into new product categories, sports, and regions of the world. Its sports apparel business grew explosively; the company slapped its familiar swoosh logo on everything from sunglasses and soccer balls to batting gloves and hockey sticks. Nike invaded a dozen new sports, including baseball, golf, ice and street hockey, inline skating, wall climbing, and hiking.

In the late 1990s, however, Nike stumbled and its sales slipped. Many factors contributed to the company's sales woes. The whole industry suffered a setback as the "brown shoe" craze for hiking and outdoor shoe styles ate into the athletic sneaker business. Competition improved: A revitalized Adidas saw its North American sales surge as Nike's sales declined. To make matters worse, college and university students on many campuses protested against Nike for its alleged exploitation of child labour in Asia and its commercialization of sports.

But Nike's biggest obstacle may be its own incredible success—it may have overswooshed North America. The brand suffered from brand backlash, and the swoosh became too common to be cool. According to one analyst, "When Tiger Woods made his debut in Nike gear, there were so many logos on him that he looked as if he'd got caught in an embroidering machine." A Nike executive admits, "There has been a little bit of backlash about the number of swooshes that are out there." Moreover, with sales of more than U.S $9 billion, Nike has moved from maverick to mainstream. Today, rooting for Nike is like rooting for Microsoft.

To address these problems, Nike has returned to the basics—focusing on innovation, developing new product lines, creating subbrands, and focusing once again on product performance. The sports giant is also trimming its costs, including substantial cutting of its formerly lavish advertising budget.

Despite the recent difficulties, Nike still dominates the athletic shoe market. It captures a 42 per-

cent market share in the United States and more than 25 percent abroad. Competitors can hope that Nike's slump will continue, but few are counting on it. Most can only sit back and marvel at Nike's marketing prowess. One market analyst comments, "Nike remains one of the great American brands, as well known around the world as Coke or McDonald's."

Still, to stay on top, Nike will have to find new ways to deliver the kind of quality, innovation, and value that built the brand so powerfully in the past. No longer the rebellious, anti-establishment upstart, huge Nike must continually reassess and rekindle its meaning to customers. Says Knight, "Now that we've [grown so large], there's a fine line between being a rebel and being a bully. [To our customers,] we have to be beautiful as well as big."

Sources: Quotes from Bill Saporito, "Can Nike Get Unstuck?" *Time*, 30 March 1998:48–53; CAAWS Press Release, "Symposium Provides Strong Recommendations on Gender Equity in Sport," Thornhill, Ontario, 20 May 1999; Jolie Solomon, "When Cool Goes Cold," *Newsweek*, 30 March 1998:36–37; Jerry Edgerton, "Can Nike Still Play Above the Rim?" *Money*, May 1999:48; and Louise Lee, "Can Nike Still Do It?" *Business Week*, 21 February 2000:121–128. Also see Nike Press Release, "Four Athletes to Be Honored as Nike World Headquarters Expansion Nears Completion of Second Phase," accessed online at **www.nikebiz.com**, 12 June 2001; and Douglas Robson, "Just Do…Something," *Business Week*, 2 July 2001:70–71.

Value, Satisfaction, and Quality

Consumers usually face a broad array of products and services that might satisfy a given need. How do they choose among these many products and services? Consumers make buying choices based on their perceptions of the value that various products and services deliver.

Customer value The difference between the values the customer gains from owning and using a product and the costs of obtaining the product.

Customer Value **Customer value** is the difference between the values the customer gains from owning and using a product and the costs of obtaining the product. For example, Purolator customers gain several benefits. The most obvious are fast and reliable package delivery. Purolator employs more than 13 000 people across Canada and boasts an extensive network that delivers more packages to destination points in Canada than any other courier.

Purolator
www.purolator.ca

However, when using Purolator, customers also may receive some status and image values. Using Purolator can make both the package sender and the receiver feel more important. When deciding whether to send a package via Purolator, customers will weigh these and other values against the money, effort, and psychic costs of using the service. Moreover, they will compare the value of using Purolator against the value of using other shippers—Canada Post, Loomis, or FedEx—and select the one that gives them the greatest delivered value.

Customers often do not judge product values and costs accurately or objectively. They act on *perceived* value. For example, does Purolator really provide faster, more reliable delivery? If so, is this better service worth a higher price than competitors charge? Canada Post offers its Xpresspost service with one- to two-day delivery, and its prices are lower than Purolator's. However, judging by Purolator's strong market position, most consumers prefer Purolator's products and services over those of Canada Post's Xpresspost.

Customer Satisfaction **Customer satisfaction** depends on a product's perceived performance in delivering value relative to a buyer's expectations. If the product's performance falls short of the customer's expectations, the buyer is dissatisfied. If performance matches expectations, the buyer is satisfied. If performance exceeds expectations, the buyer is delighted. Outstanding marketing companies go out of their way to keep their customers satisfied. Satisfied customers make repeat purchases, and they tell others about their good experiences with the product. The key is to match customer expectations with company performance. Smart companies aim to *delight* customers by promising only what they can deliver, and then delivering *more* than they promise.[7] Customer expectations are based on past buying experiences, the opinions of friends, and marketer and competitor information and promises. Marketers must be careful to set the right level of expectations. If they set expectations too low, they may satisfy those who buy but fail to attract enough buyers. If they raise expectations too high, buyers will be disappointed.

Today's most successful companies are raising expectations—and delivering performance to match. These companies embrace *total customer satisfaction*. For example, Honda claims that "[o]ne reason our customers are so satisfied is that we aren't." Such companies track customer expectations, perceived company performance, and customer satisfaction.

However, although the customer-centred firm seeks to deliver high customer satisfaction relative to its competitors, it does not attempt to *maximize* customer satisfaction. A company can always increase customer satisfaction by lowering its price or increasing its services, but this may result in lower profits. Thus, the purpose of marketing is to generate customer value profitably. This requires a very delicate balance: The marketer must continue to generate more customer value and satisfaction but not "give away the house."

Quality Quality has a direct impact on product or service performance; thus, it is closely linked to customer value and satisfaction. In the narrowest sense, quality is defined as "freedom from defects." But most customer-centred companies go beyond this narrow definition of quality. Instead, they define quality in terms of customer satisfaction. For example, the vice president of quality at Motorola, a company that pioneered total quality efforts, says that "quality has to do something for the customer.... Our definition of a defect is 'if the customer doesn't like it, it's a defect.'"[8] Similarly, the National Quality Institute in Canada has as its primary aim to "understand, meet and strive to exceed the needs of customers."[9]

This focus on the customer suggests that quality begins with customer needs and ends with customer satisfaction. The fundamental aim of today's *total quality*

Canada Post
www.mailposte.ca

Customer satisfaction The extent to which a product's perceived performance in delivering value matches a buyer's expectations.

National Quality Institute
www.nqi.ca

movement has become *total customer satisfaction.* To accomplish this, marketers must deliver marketing quality as well as product and service quality. They must set and meet high standards for each marketing activity—marketing research, sales training, advertising, customer service, and others.

Exchange, Transactions, and Relationships

Exchange The act of obtaining a desired object from someone by offering something in return.

Marketing occurs when people decide to satisfy needs and wants through exchange. **Exchange** is the act of obtaining a desired object from someone by offering something in return. Exchange is only one of many ways that people can obtain a desired object. For example, hungry people could find food by hunting, fishing, or gathering fruit. They could beg for food or take food from someone else. Or they could offer money, another good, or a service in return for food.

As a means of satisfying needs, exchange has much in its favour. People do not have to prey on others, depend on donations, or have the skills to produce every necessity for themselves. They can concentrate on making things that they are good at making and trade them for needed items made by others. Thus, exchange allows a society to produce much more than it would with any alternative system.

Transaction A trade between two parties that involves at least two things of value, agreed-on conditions, a time of agreement, and a place of agreement.

Since exchange is the core concept of marketing, a transaction is marketing's unit of measurement. A **transaction** is a trade of values between two parties: One party gives X to another party and gets Y in return. For example, you pay Sears $350 for a television set. This is a classic *monetary transaction,* but not all transactions involve money. In a *barter transaction,* you might trade your old refrigerator for a neighbour's secondhand television set.

In the broadest sense, the marketer tries to bring about a response to some offer. The response may be more than simply buying or trading goods and services. A political candidate, for instance, wants votes, a church wants membership, and a social action group wants idea acceptance. Marketing consists of actions taken to obtain a desired response from a target audience toward some product, service, idea, or other object.

Relationship marketing The process of creating, maintaining, and enhancing strong, value-laden relationships with customers and other stakeholders.

Today, marketers are focusing less on single transactions and more on the larger idea of **relationship marketing**. Increasingly, the focus of marketing is shifting from trying to maximize the profit on each individual transaction to building mutually beneficial relationships with consumers and other parties. In fact, marketers need to build long-term relationships with valued customers, distributors, dealers, and suppliers. They want to establish strong economic and social connections by promising and consistently delivering high-quality products, good service, and fair prices. The goal is to retain customers and increase their business with the company. Good relationships with customers begin with delivering superior value.

Ultimately, a company wants to build a unique company asset called a *marketing network.* A marketing network consists of the company and all its supporting stakeholders: customers, employees, suppliers, distributors, retailers, ad agencies, and others with whom it has built relationships. Increasingly, competition is not between companies but rather between whole networks, with the prize going to the company that builds the better network. The operating principle is simple: Build a good network of relationships with key stakeholders and profits will follow.

Relationship marketing is oriented toward the long term. The goal is to deliver long-term value to customers, and the measures of success are long-term customer satisfaction and retention. Beyond offering consistently high value and satisfaction, marketers can use several specific marketing tools to develop stronger bonds with consumers. First, a company might build value and satisfaction by adding *financial benefits* to the customer relationship. For example, Air Canada offers frequent-flyer programs, Marriott Hotels give room upgrades to their frequent guests, and supermarkets such as Safeway and Overwaitea give preferred-customer discounts through extensive use of loyalty programs. In these cases, the emphasis is on "share of customer" rather than "share of market," the traditional approach of many marketers.

Second, a company can add *social benefits* as well as financial benefits. Here, the company works to increase its social bonds with customers by learning individual customer's needs and wants and then personalizing its products and services. For example, Ritz-Carlton Hotels employees treat customers as individuals, not as nameless, faceless members of a mass market. Whenever possible, they refer to guests by name and give each guest a warm welcome every day. They record specific guest preferences in the company's customer database, which holds more than 500 000 individual customer preferences and is accessible by all hotels in the worldwide Ritz chain. A guest who requests a foam pillow at the Ritz in Montreal will be delighted to find one waiting in the room when he or she checks into the Atlanta Ritz months later.[10]

To build better relationships with its customers, Saturn developed its now-famous "Saturn Reunions." In 1995, Saturn invited Canadian owners and their families to drive-in movies to see *Apollo 13*. The event was highly successful, and Saturn wanted to capitalize on the community spirit the event created. Saturn marketing vice president Chuck Novak asked himself, "How can we reflect our commitment to Saturn communities?" Saturn staff, car owners, and interested community members now construct playgrounds across the country, with more than 50 built so far. Because many Saturn owners have families with young children, Saturn's community efforts focus on things that enhance children's quality of life. Playgrounds aren't the only community need Saturn addresses, however. Its retailers are the eyes and ears of the company and when a community need arises, they let Saturn know. For example, Saturn helped plant trees in areas hard hit by the 1997 ice storm in eastern Ontario and Quebec; in North Bay, Saturn helped raise funds for a new heart-monitoring unit in a local hospital.[11]

A third approach to building customer relationships is to add *structural ties* as well as financial and social benefits. For example, a business marketer might supply customers with special equipment or computer linkages that help them manage their orders or customer service. Dell Computer, for instance, creates personalized Web sites for its large commercial customers—called Premier Pages—that provide all the information and support the customer would need. The company's purchasing managers, information technology people, and individual employees can log onto the company's Premier Page, build their own computers within preset specifications, receive price quotes based on prenegotiated pricing agreements, place an order, and have network-ready machines delivered within days. The site

Relationship marketing: Saturn builds lasting relationships with customers. Many dealers post photos of customers in their service areas to help employees link customers with their cars. "Hey you" is not the most endearing greeting, especially to someone who took the time to shop at your dealership and who spent hard-earned money on one of your cars.

also supplies tailored technical support, diagnostic tools, and other features to suit the customer's special needs. Many larger customers set up multiple Dell Premier Pages, reflecting different purchasing agreements in different divisions. To date, Dell has set up roughly 15 000 such Web pages.[12]

Relationship marketing means that marketers must focus on managing their customers as well as their products. At the same time, they don't want relationships with every customer. In fact, there are undesirable customers for every company. The objective is to determine which customers the company can serve most effectively relative to competitors. In some cases, companies may even want to "fire" customers who are too unreasonable or who cost more to serve than they are worth. Ultimately, marketing is the art of attracting, keeping, and growing *profitable customers*.

Markets

Market The set of all actual and potential buyers of a product or service.

The concepts of exchange and relationships lead to the concept of a market. A **market** is the set of actual and potential buyers of a product. These buyers share a particular need or want that can be satisfied through exchanges and relationships. Thus, the size of a market depends on the number of people who exhibit the need, have resources to engage in exchange, and are willing to offer these resources in exchange for what they want.

Originally, the term *market* stood for the place where buyers and sellers gathered to exchange their goods, such as a village square. Economists use the term *market* to refer to a collection of buyers and sellers who transact in a particular product class, as in the housing market or the grain market. Marketers, however, see sellers as constituting an industry and the buyers as constituting a market.

Modern economies operate on the principle of division of labour, whereby each person specializes in producing something, receives payment, and buys needed things with this money. Thus, modern economies abound in markets. Producers go to resource markets (raw material markets, labour markets, money markets), buy resources, turn them into goods and services, and sell them to intermediaries, who sell them to consumers. The consumers sell their labour and receive income to pay for goods and services. The government is another market that plays several roles. It buys goods from resource, producer, and intermediary markets, it pays them, it taxes these markets (including consumer markets), and it returns needed public services. Thus, each nation's economy and the whole world economy consist of complex, interacting sets of markets that are linked through exchange processes.

Marketers are keenly interested in markets. Their goal is to understand the needs and wants of specific markets and to select the markets that they can serve best. In turn, they can develop products and services that will create value and satisfaction for customers in these markets, resulting in sales and profits for the company.

Marketing

The concept of markets brings us full circle to the concept of marketing. Marketing means managing markets to bring about exchanges and relationships for the purpose of creating value and satisfying needs and wants. Thus, we return to our definition of marketing as a process by which individuals and groups obtain what they need and want by creating and exchanging products and value with others.

Exchange processes involve work. Sellers must search for buyers, identify their needs, design good products and services, set prices for them, promote them, and store and deliver them. Activities such as product development, research, communication, distribution, pricing, and service are core marketing activities. Although we normally think of marketing as being carried on by sellers, buyers also carry on marketing activities. Consumers do marketing when they search for the goods they need at prices they can afford. Company purchasing agents do marketing when they track down sellers and bargain for good terms.

Figure 1-2 shows the main elements in a modern marketing system. Usually, marketing involves serving a market of end users in the face of competitors. The company and the competitors send their respective products and messages to consumers either directly or through marketing intermediaries to end users. All the components of the system are affected by major environmental forces (demographic, economic, physical, technological, political–legal, social–cultural).

Each party in the system adds value for the next level. Thus, a company's success depends not only on its own actions, but also on how well the entire system serves the needs of final consumers. Zellers cannot fulfill its promise of low prices unless its suppliers provide merchandise at low costs. And Ford cannot deliver high-quality service to car buyers unless its dealers provide outstanding service.

MARKETING MANAGEMENT

We define **marketing management** as the analysis, planning, implementation, and control of programs designed to create, build, and maintain beneficial exchanges with target buyers so as to achieve organizational objectives. Thus, marketing management involves managing demand, which in turn involves managing customer relationships.

Marketing management
The analysis, planning, implementation, and control of programs designed to create, build, and maintain beneficial exchanges with target buyers so as to achieve organizational objectives.

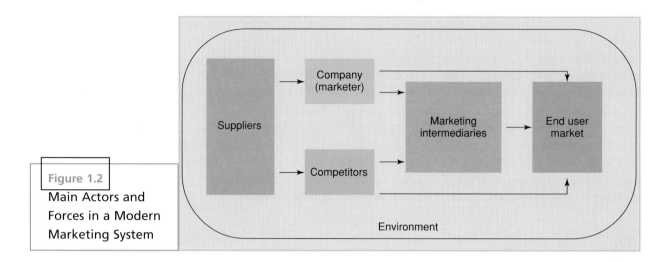

Figure 1.2

Main Actors and Forces in a Modern Marketing System

Time for a breather! You have read a great deal of material, and it's time to reflect. What have you learned so far about marketing? For the moment, set aside the more formal definitions we've examined and try to develop your own understanding of marketing.

- In *your own words,* what is marketing? Write down your definition. Does your definition include such key concepts as customer value and relationships?
- What does marketing mean to you? How does it affect your daily life?
- What brand of athletic shoes did you purchase last? Describe your relationship with Nike, Reebok, Adidas, or the company that made the shoes you purchased.

Demand Management

Some people think of marketing management as finding enough customers for the company's current output, but this view is too limited. The organization has a desired level of demand for its products. At any time, there may be no demand, adequate demand, irregular demand, or too much demand, and marketing management must find ways to deal with these different demand states. Marketing management is concerned not only with finding and increasing demand, but also with changing or even reducing it.

For example, Banff National Park is overcrowded in the summer, power companies struggle to meet demand during peak usage periods, and expressways in big cities are clogged with traffic during rush hours, causing city councils to actively promote the use of public transit. In these and other cases of excess demand, **demarketing** may be required to reduce demand temporarily or permanently. The aim of demarketing is not to destroy demand, but to reduce or shift it.[13] Thus, marketing management seeks to affect the level, timing, and nature of demand in a way that helps the organization achieve its objectives. Simply put, marketing management is *demand management.*

Demarketing Marketing to reduce demand temporarily or permanently—the aim is not to destroy demand, but to reduce or shift it.

Service providers such as BC Hydro demarket by providing consumers with practical ways to reduce the amount of electricity they use.

Building Profitable Customer Relationships

Managing demand means managing customers. A company's demand comes from two groups: new customers and repeat customers. Traditional marketing theory and practice focused on attracting new customers and making the sale. Today, however, the emphasis is shifting. Beyond designing strategies to *attract* new customers and create *transactions* with them, companies now are going all out to *retain* current customers and build lasting customer *relationships*.

Why the new emphasis on keeping customers? In the past, companies facing an expanding economy and rapidly growing markets could practise the "leaky-bucket" approach to marketing. Growing markets meant a plentiful supply of new customers. Companies could keep filling the marketing bucket with new customers without worrying about losing old customers through holes in the bottom of the bucket. However, companies today face new marketing realities. Changing demographics, a slow-growth economy, more sophisticated competitors, and overcapacity in many industries all mean that there are fewer new customers to go around. Many companies now are fighting for shares of flat or fading markets. Thus, the costs of attracting new customers are rising. In fact, it costs five times as much to attract a new customer as it does to keep a current customer.[14] Companies have also discovered that losing a customer means losing not only a single sale, but also a lifetime's worth of purchases and referrals. For example, the *customer lifetime value* of a Taco Bell customer exceeds $16 000. For General Motors or Ford, the customer lifetime value might well exceed $470 000. Thus, working to keep profitable customers makes good economic sense.[15] The key to customer retentions is superior customer value and satisfaction. With this in mind, many companies are going to extremes to keep their customers satisfied. (See New Directions 1-2.)

New Directions 1-2 >> Customer Relationships: Keeping Customers Satisfied

Delighted customers come back again and again. American Express loves to tell stories about how its people have rescued customers from disasters ranging from civil wars to earthquakes, no matter what the cost.

At some companies, exceptional value and customer service are more than a set of policies or actions—they are a companywide attitude.

Some companies go to extremes to coddle their customers. Consider the following examples:

- Lexus Canada recently ran an advertisement recounting the tale of how it had delighted one of its customers. Lexus went to great lengths to get a car key to a driver who had lost his keys while fishing on Lake Kenogami, north of Regina. Not only did the local dealer replace the key, but it also booked a charter flight for the driver, since he had missed the once-a-week plane because of the mishap.
- An American Express cardholder fails to pay more than $5000 of his September bill. He explains that during the summer he had purchased expensive rugs in Turkey. When he got home, appraisals showed that the rugs were worth half of what he'd paid. Rather than ask questions or demand payment, the American Express representative notes the dispute, asks for a letter summarizing the appraisers' estimates, and offers to help solve the problem. Until the conflict is resolved, American Express doesn't ask for payment.
- A frustrated homeowner faces a difficult and potentially costly home plumbing repair. He visits the nearby Home Depot store, prowls the aisles, and picks up an armful of parts and supplies—$67 worth in all—that he thinks he'll need to do the job. However, before he gets to the checkout, a Home Depot salesperson heads him off. After some coaxing, the salesperson convinces the do-it-yourselfer that there's a simpler solution to his repair problem. The cost: $5.99 and a lot less trouble.

Keeping customers satisfied involves more than simply opening a complaints department, smiling a lot, and being nice. Companies that do the best job of taking care of customers set high customer service standards and often make seemingly outlandish efforts to achieve them. At these companies, exceptional value and service are more than a set of policies or actions—they are a companywide attitude, an important part of the overall company culture.

American Express loves to tell stories about how its people have rescued customers from disasters ranging from civil wars to earthquakes, no matter what the cost. The company gives cash rewards of up to $1000 to "Great Performers." Four Seasons Hotels, long known for its outstanding service, tells its employees the story of Ron Dyment, a doorman in Toronto, who forgot to load a departing guest's briefcase into his taxi. The doorman called the guest, a lawyer in Washington, DC, and learned that he desperately needed the briefcase for a meeting the following morning. Without asking for approval from management, Dyment hopped on a plane and returned the briefcase. The company named Dyment Employee of the Year. There's no simple formula for taking care of customers, but neither is the process a mystery. According to the president of L.L. Bean, "A lot of people have fancy things to say about customer service…but it's just a day-in, day-out, ongoing, never-ending, unremitting, persevering, compassionate type of activity." For the companies that do it well, it's also very rewarding.

Sources: Bill Kelley, "Five Companies That Do It Right—and Make It Pay," *Sales and Marketing Management*, April 1988:57–64; Patricia Sellers, "Companies That Serve You Best," *Fortune*, 31 May 1993:74–88; Rahul Jacob, "Why Some Customers Are More Equal Than Others," *Fortune*, 19 September 1994:215–224; Brian Silverman, "Shopping for Loyal Customers," *Sales and Marketing Management*, March 1995:96–97; and Howard E. Butz, Jr., and Leonard Goodstein, "Measuring Customer Value: Gaining the Strategic Advantage," *Organizational Dynamics*, Winter 1996:63–77.

Marketing Management Practice

All kinds of organizations use marketing, and they practise it in widely varying ways. Many large firms apply standard marketing practices in a formalized way. However, other companies use marketing in a less formal and orderly fashion. A recent book, *Radical Marketing,* praises companies such as Harley-Davidson, Virgin Atlantic Airways, and Boston Beer for succeeding by breaking many of the rules of marketing.[16] Instead of commissioning expensive marketing research, spending huge sums on mass advertising, and operating large marketing departments, these companies stretch their limited resources, live close to their customers, and create more satisfying solutions to customer needs. They form buyers' clubs, use creative public relations, and focus on delivering high-quality products and winning long-term customer loyalty. It seems that not all marketing must follow in the footsteps of marketing giants such as Procter & Gamble.

In fact, marketing practice often passes through three stages: entrepreneurial marketing, formulated marketing, and intrepreneurial marketing.

1. *Entrepreneurial marketing:* Most companies are started by individuals who live by their wits. They visualize an opportunity and knock on every door to gain attention. Two young entrepreneurs from Winnipeg using their grandmother's recipe for "Clodhoppers," a chocolate and nut mixture, founded a major confectionery company called Krave's Candy. They went to trade shows and knocked on the doors of large retailers such as Wal-Mart and Zellers to get their new product on store shelves. They invested in eye-catching packaging to help move product off shelves. They received awards as one of Canada's fastest growing companies and they were featured on *Venture.* Television coverage and other free publicity were important because the company simply couldn't initially afford advertising. The founders relied on the positive publicity to increase their presence in the market.

   Today, Clodhoppers are sold by many of Canada's major retailers, such as Canada Safeway stores, Overwaitea, Costco in Western Canada, Shoppers Drug Mart, Sobey's, Wal-Mart, Zellers, and Loblaws. The candy is given to passengers on Air Canada flights and you can even order Clodhoppers in a Blizzard at your local Dairy Queen. The company even makes it product available to fundraisers so they can raise support for their causes through door-to-door sales.

Krave's Candy
www.kraves.com

2. *Formulated marketing:* As small companies achieve success, they inevitably move toward more formulated marketing. Take the case of Gap Adventure Tours: After 10 years of offering small group adventure holidays to less travelled places, Toronto-headquartered Gap Adventure Tours found itself at a crossroads. Although sales revenues had climbed to $70 million, it faced increased competition. It was also having trouble managing its supplier relationships and reservation system. To help overcome these problems, it hired its first professional marketer, Dave Bowen, who saw the challenge as bringing corporate discipline and a better market orientation to the small energetic firm. Dave first focused on market segmentation and better target marketing. Gap had to change the way it looked at customers and realize that it couldn't satisfy everybody. Dave also had a nose for inefficiencies. He worked to revamp the reservation system and added visual and verbal clarity to Gap's promotional brochures. Since demand had grown, functional stovepipes were producing more and more inefficiencies, so Dave worked to better link supply chain management with operations and marketing. Although there was some resistance to change, Gap is now trekking on toward smoother operations.[17]

3. *Intrepreneurial marketing:* Many large and mature companies get stuck in formulated marketing, poring over the latest Nielsen numbers, scanning market research reports, and trying to fine-tune dealer relations and advertising messages. These companies sometimes lose the marketing creativity and passion that they had at the start. They need to reestablish within their companies the entrepreneurial spirit and actions that made them successful. They need to encourage more initiative and "intrepreneurship" at the local level. Their brand and product managers need to get out of the office, start living with their customers, and visualize new and creative ways to add value to their customers' lives.

The bottom line is that effective marketing can take many forms. A constant tension exists between the formulated side of marketing and the creative side. It is easier to learn the formulated side of marketing, which will occupy most of our attention in this book. But we will also see how real marketing creativity and passion operate in many companies—whether small or large, new or mature—to build and retain success in the marketplace.

MARKETING MANAGEMENT PHILOSOPHIES

We describe marketing management as carrying out tasks to achieve desired exchanges with target markets. What *philosophy* should guide these marketing efforts? What weight should be given to the interests of the organization, customers, and society when these interests conflict?

The Production Concept, Product Concept, and Selling Concept

Production concept The idea that consumers will favour products that are available and highly affordable and that management should therefore focus on improving production and distribution efficiency.

Some managers follow a **production concept** believing consumers will favour products that are available and highly affordable.

Gap Adventure Tours
www.gap.ca

Other sellers follow the **product concept**, which holds that consumers will favour products that offer the most in quality, performance, and innovative features. Thus, an organization should devote energy to making continual product improvements. Such manufacturers believe that if they can build a better mousetrap, the world will beat a path to their door.[18] But they are often rudely awakened. Buyers may well be looking for a better solution to a mouse problem but not necessarily for a better mousetrap. The solution might be a chemical spray, an exterminating service, or something that works better than a mousetrap. Furthermore, a better mousetrap will not sell unless the manufacturer designs, packages, and prices it attractively, places it in convenient distribution channels, brings it to the attention of people who need it, and convinces buyers that it is a better product.

Still other organizations adhere to a **selling concept**—a philosophy that consumers will not buy enough of the organization's products unless it undertakes a large-scale selling and promotion effort.

Most firms practise the selling concept when they have overcapacity. Their aim is to sell what they make rather than make what the market wants. Such marketing carries high risks. It focuses on creating sales transactions rather than on building long-term, profitable relationships with customers. It assumes that customers who are coaxed into buying the product will like it. Instead, many are dissatisfied since products pushed in this way rarely meet their needs. Most studies show that dissatisfied customers do not buy again. Worse yet, the average dissatisfied customer tells 10 others about his or her bad experiences, whereas the average satisfied customer tells only three others about a good experiences.[19]

Instead of following these more limiting philosophies, we suggest that firms should follow a marketing or societal marketing concept.

The Marketing Concept

The **marketing concept** holds that achieving organizational goals depends on determining the needs and wants of target markets and delivering the desired satisfaction more effectively and efficiently than competitors do. The marketing concept has been stated in colourful ways, such as "Reliability is our service" (Canpar), "We make it happen for you" (Marriott), "To fly, to serve" (British Airways), and "We're not satisfied until you are" (GE).

The selling concept and the marketing concept are sometimes confused. Figure 1-3 compares the two concepts. The selling concept takes an *inside-out* perspective. It starts with the factory, focuses on the company's existing products, and calls for heavy selling and promotion to obtain profitable sales. It focuses primarily on customer conquest—getting short-term sales with little concern about who buys or why.

In contrast, the marketing concept takes an *outside-in* perspective. The marketing concept starts with a well-defined market, focuses on customer needs, coordinates all the marketing activities affecting customers, and makes profits by creating long-term customer relationships based on customer value and satisfaction. Thus, under the marketing concept, customer focus and value are the *paths* to sales and profits. In the words of one Ford executive, "If we're not customer driven, our cars won't be either."

Product concept The idea that consumers will favour products that offer the most quality, performance, and features and that the organization should therefore devote its energy to making continual product improvements.

Selling concept The idea that consumers will not buy enough of the organization's products unless the organization undertakes a large-scale selling and promotion effort.

Marketing concept The marketing management philosophy that holds that achieving organizational goals depends on determining the needs and wants of target markets and delivering the desired satisfactions more effectively and efficiently than competitors do.

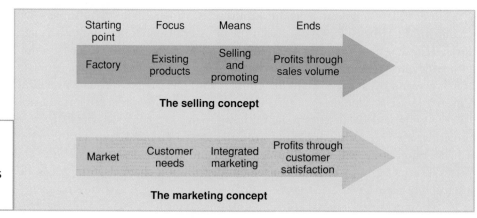

Starting point	Focus	Means	Ends
Factory	Existing products	Selling and promoting	Profits through sales volume

The selling concept

Market	Customer needs	Integrated marketing	Profits through customer satisfaction

The marketing concept

Figure 1.3

The Selling and Marketing Concepts Contrasted

L.L. Bean
www.llbean.com

Many successful and well-known companies have adopted the marketing concept. Procter & Gamble, Bombardier, Fido, Wal-Mart, Marriott, Mountain Equipment Co-op, and Dell Computer follow it faithfully. The goal is to build customer satisfaction into the very fabric of the firm. L.L. Bean, the highly successful catalogue retailer, was founded on the marketing concept. In 1912, in his first circulars, L.L. Bean included the following notice: "I do not consider a sale complete until goods are worn out and the customer still is satisfied. We will thank anyone to return goods that are not perfectly satisfactory.… Above all things we wish to avoid having a dissatisfied customer."

Today, L.L. Bean dedicates itself to giving perfect satisfaction in every way. To inspire its employees to practise the marketing concept, L.L. Bean has for decades displayed posters around its offices that proclaim the following:

What is a customer? A customer is the most important person ever in this company—in person or by mail. A customer is not dependent on us, we are dependent on him. A customer is not an interruption of our work, he is the purpose of it. We are not doing a favor by serving him, he is doing us a favor by giving us the opportunity to do so. A customer is not someone to argue or match wits with—nobody ever won an argument with a customer. A customer is a person who brings us his wants—it is our job to handle them profitably to him and to ourselves.

People at L.L. Bean practise the marketing concept in everything they do every day.

In contrast, many companies claim to practise the marketing concept but do not. They have the *forms* of marketing, such as a marketing vice president, product managers, marketing plans, and marketing research, but this does not mean that they are market-focused and customer-driven companies. The question is whether they are finely tuned to changing customer needs and competitor strategies. Formerly great companies—General Motors, Sears, Eaton's—all lost substantial market share or, in the case of Eaton's, went out of business because they failed to adjust their marketing strategies to the changing marketplace.

Implementing the marketing concept often means more than simply responding to customers' stated desires and obvious needs. *Customer-driven* companies research current customers to learn about their desires, gather new product and service ideas, and test proposed product improvements. Such customer-driven marketing usually works well when a clear need exists and when customers know what they want. In many cases, however, customers *don't* know what they want or even what is possible. For example, 20 years ago, how many consumers would have thought to ask for cellular telephones, fax machines, home copiers, 24-hour Internet brokerage accounts, DVD players, or handheld global satellite positioning systems?

Such situations call for *customer-driving marketing*—understanding customer needs even better than customers themselves do and creating products and services that will meet existing and latent needs now and in the future. As Sony's visionary leader Akio Morita puts it: "Our plan is to lead the public with new products rather than ask them what kinds of products they want. The public does not know what is possible, but we do." And according to an executive at 3M, a company known for its customer-driving innovativeness, "Our goal is to lead customers where they want to go *before* they know where they want to go."[20]

The Societal Marketing Concept

The **societal marketing concept** holds that the organization should determine the needs, wants, and interests of target markets. It should then deliver superior value to customers in a way that maintains or improves the consumer's *and society's* well-being. The societal marketing concept is the newest of the five marketing management philosophies.

The societal marketing concept questions whether the pure marketing concept is adequate in an age of environmental problems, resource shortages, rapid population growth, worldwide economic problems, and neglected social services. It asks whether the firm that senses, serves, and satisfies individual short-term wants is always doing what's best for consumers and society in the long run.

Companies embracing this concept include Canada's 900 credit unions and *caisses populaires* and such firms as the Upper Canada Brewing Company, which has saved $20 000 per year by following the "3Rs" philosophy of reduce, recycle, and reuse. Imperial Oil is another company that firmly believes in "doing well by doing good." The firm has been one of Canada's leading corporate donors for over 80 years. It recently developed the Esso Kids Program, whereby the company supports more than 200 activities, ranging from promoting childhood safety and injury prevention, through helping teenage parents raise their children and funding postsecondary education, to supporting children's sporting activities such as swimming and hockey. Consumers have responded strongly to Imperial's efforts, and the firm believes that giving consumers additional reasons to buy Esso products will help to build customer loyalty and relationships in an industry characterized by heavy brand-switching.[21]

Societal marketing concept The idea that the organization should determine the needs, wants, and interests of target markets and deliver the desired satisfaction more effectively and efficiently than do competitors in a way that maintains or improves the consumer's and society's well-being.

According to the societal marketing concept, the pure marketing concept overlooks possible conflicts between consumer *short-run wants* and consumer *long-run welfare.*

Consider the fast-food industry. Most people see today's giant fast-food chains as offering tasty and convenient food at reasonable prices. Yet many consumer and environmental groups have voiced concerns. Critics point out that hamburgers, fried chicken, French fries, and most other foods sold by fast-food restaurants are high in fat and salt. The products are wrapped in convenient packaging, but that packaging leads to waste and pollution. Thus, in satisfying consumer wants, the highly successful fast-food chains may be harming consumers' health and causing environmental problems.

Such concerns and conflicts led to the societal marketing concept. As Figure 1-4 shows, the societal marketing concept calls on marketers to balance three considerations in setting their marketing policies: company profits, consumer wants, and society's interests. Originally, most companies based their marketing decisions largely on short-run company profit. Eventually, they began to recognize the long-run importance of satisfying consumer wants, and the marketing concept emerged. Now, many companies are beginning to think of society's interests when making their marketing decisions.

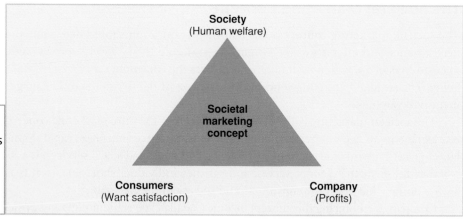

Figure 1.4

Three Considerations Underlying the Societal Marketing Concept

Let's slow down for a moment and give you a chance develop your *own* thoughts about marketing and marketing management.

• In *your own words,* what is marketing management, and what does it seek to accomplish?

• What marketing management philosophy appears to guide Nike? How does this compare with the marketing philosophy that guides Johnson & Johnson? Can you think of another company guided by a very different philosophy? Is marketing management philosophy best for all companies?

MARKETING CHALLENGES IN THE NEW CONNECTED WORLD

In this first decade of the twenty-first century, dramatic changes are occurring in the marketing arena. Richard Love of Hewlett-Packard observes, "The pace of change is so rapid that the ability to change has now become a competitive advantage." Technological advances, rapid globalization, and continuing social and economic shifts are all causing profound changes in the marketplace. As the marketplace changes, so must those who serve it.

This decade's major marketing developments can be summed up in a single theme: *connectedness.* Now, more than ever before, we are all connected to each other and to things near and far in the world around us. Moreover, we are connecting in new and different ways. Where it once took weeks or months to travel across Canada, we can now travel around the globe in only hours or days. Where it once took days or even weeks to receive news about important world events, we now see them as they are occurring through live satellite broadcasts. Where it once took days or weeks to correspond with others in distant places, they are now only moments away by phone or the Internet.

In this section, we examine the major trends and forces that are changing the marketing landscape and challenging marketing strategy in this new, connected environment. As shown in Figure 1-5 and discussed in the following pages, sweep-

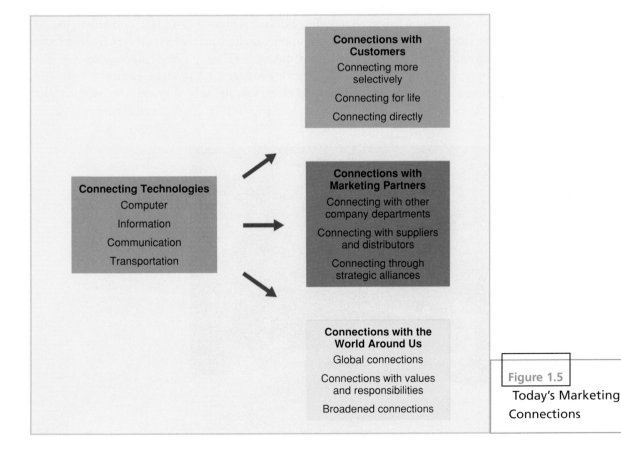

Figure 1.5

Today's Marketing Connections

ing changes in connecting technologies are causing marketers to redefine how they connect with the marketplace—with customers, with marketing partners inside and outside the company, and with the world around them. We first look at the dramatic changes that are occurring in the connecting technologies. Then, we examine how these changes are affecting marketing connections.

Technologies for Connecting

The major force behind the new connectedness is technology. Explosive advances in computer, telecommunications, information, transportation, and other connecting technologies have created a new economy. The technology boom has created exciting new ways to learn about and track customers, create products and services tailored to meet customer needs, distribute products more efficiently and effectively, and communicate with customers in large groups or one to one. For example, through videoconferencing, marketing researchers at a company's headquarters in Toronto can look in on focus groups in Vancouver or Paris without ever stepping onto a plane. With only a few clicks of a mouse button, a direct marketer can tap into online data services to learn anything from what car you drive through what you read to what flavour of ice cream you prefer.

Using today's powerful computers, marketers create detailed databases and use them to target individual customers with offers designed to meet their specific needs and buying patterns. With a new wave of communication and advertising tools—ranging from cellular phones, fax machines, CD-ROMs, and interactive TV to video kiosks at airports and shopping malls—marketers can zero in on selected customers with carefully targeted messages. Through electronic commerce, customers can design, order, and pay for products and services without ever leaving home. Then, through the marvels of express delivery, they can receive their purchases in less than 24 hours. From virtual reality displays that test new products to

Through videoconferencing, marketing researchers can easily consult with their partners worldwide.

online virtual stores that sell them, the technology boom is affecting every aspect of marketing.

The Internet Perhaps the most dramatic new technology driving the connected age is the Internet. The Internet is a vast and burgeoning global web of computer networks with no central management or ownership. Today, the Internet links individuals and businesses of all types to each other and to information all around the world.

The Internet has been hailed as the technology behind the new economy. It allows anytime, anywhere connections to information, entertainment, and communication. Companies are using the Internet to build closer relationships with customers and marketing partners and to sell and distribute their products more efficiently and effectively. Beyond competing in traditional marketplaces, companies now have access to exciting new market*spaces.*

Internet usage surged in the 2000s with the development of the user-friendly World Wide Web. A 2002 *Canadian Netizens* study by NFO CFgroup, a marketing and social research company, showed Internet penetration in Canada at 67 percent of the population aged 18 years and older, up from 63 percent only a year previous.[22] The Internet is truly a global phenomenon—the number of Internet users worldwide is expected to approach 1 billion by 2004.[23] This growing and diverse Internet population means that all kinds of people are now going to the Web for information and to buy products and services. Notes one analyst, "In just [a few short years], the Net has gone from a playground for nerds to a vast communications and trading center where…people swap information and do deals around the world.… [More and more] companies have hung www.shingle.com atop their digital doorways with the notion that being anywhere on the Net means selling virtually everywhere."[24]

Companies of all types are now attempting to snare new customers on the Web. Many traditional brick-and-mortar companies have now become "click-and-mortar" companies, venturing online in an effort to attract new customers and build stronger relationships with existing ones. The Internet also spawned an entirely new breed of "click-only" companies—the so-called dot-coms. During the Web frenzy of the late 1990s, dot-coms popped up everywhere, selling everything from books, toys, and CDs to furniture, home mortgages, and 50-kg bags of dog food via the Internet. The frenzy cooled during the "dot-com meltdown" of 2000, when many poorly conceived e-tailers and other Web start-ups went out of business. Today, despite its turbulent start, online consumer buying is growing at a healthy rate, and many of the dot-com survivors face promising futures. For example, in 2001, Canadian companies received $10.4 billion in customer orders over the Internet, up 43.4 percent from 2000, according to the *Survey of Electronic Commerce and Technology*. The percentage of businesses that reported selling goods and services online rose marginally to 7 percent from 6 percent.[25]

If consumer e-commerce looks promising, business-to-business e-commerce is booming. Global business-to-business transactions online are expected to reach $3.6 trillion in 2003, compared with only $107 billion in consumer purchases. By 2005, more than 500 000 businesses will engage in e-commerce as buyers, sellers, or both.[26] Most major businesses have set up shop on the Web. Large companies such as PWC Sierra, Crystal Decisions, Telus, Research In Motion, IBM, Dell, and many others have moved quickly to exploit the power of the Internet.

NFO CFgroup
www.nfocfgroup.com

This move to create marketing synergy with advancing technology includes numerous Canadian organizations such as Atlantic Blue Cross, Bombardier Recreational Products, Clearwater Fine Foods, and even small organizations such the Dragonfly Toy Company.

Thus, changes in connecting technologies are providing exciting new opportunities for marketers. We will explore the impact of the new economy in more detail in Chapter 3. For now, we'll look at the ways these technological changes affect how companies connect with their customers, marketing partners, and the world around us.

Connections with Customers

The most profound new developments in marketing involve the ways in which today's companies are connecting with their customers. Yesterday's companies focused on mass marketing at arm's length. Today's companies are selecting their customers more carefully and building lasting and direct relationships with these carefully targeted customers.

Connecting with More Carefully Selected Customers Few firms today still practise true mass marketing—selling in a standardized way to any customer who comes along. Today, most marketers realize that they don't want to connect with just *any* customers. Instead, most are targeting fewer, more profitable customers. (See New Directions 1-3).

New Directions 1-3 >>   Customer Profitability: Calculating the Costs

All customers are created equal—right? Wrong! Whereas traditional marketing involved casting a wide net to capture as many customers as possible, today's companies now focus on keeping and growing only the most profitable customers they already have. "They are aggressively mining their vast databases to weed out losers, or at least to charge them more, and to target the best customers for pampering," says Rick Brooks of the *Wall Street Journal.*

Some industries have long favoured profitable customers over others. For example, airlines, credit card companies, and hotels provide special services for their "premier" or "platinum" customers. And recent advances in technology now allow companies to assess the value of every customer more precisely and weed out the less profitable ones.

Customer profitability is generally calculated as follows: Customer Revenue − Customer Costs = Customer Profit Contribution

After their contribution is calculated, customers are then ranked from highest to lowest in profitability. This analysis allows management to develop strategies directed at specific customer groups and target markets and to balance the investment needed to attract and retain profitable customers. For example, for Thomas Cook Travel, differentiating between best and worst customers required a huge change in the company's culture. Agents had always been coached to deliver top-level service to everyone. Realizing that such an attitude just isn't profitable anymore, the agency divided its customers into A's (those generating $750 or more in annual revenues), B's (those generating $250 to $749), and C's (those generating less than $250). It found that 80 percent of its customers were C's. "It's not that you don't want them, it's just that you differentiate," says Wendy White, marketing manager for Thomas Cook Travel Canada. "You still deliver professional service," she observes, "but not every client requires—or deserves—two hours' worth of service to purchase an airline ticket."

The travel agents at Thomas Cook now know which customers deserve the full treatment and which ones don't. When C clients demand time-consuming services—for example, asking an agent to research a trip that they aren't positive they want to take—they are now asked for a $25 deposit. Serious clients pay up; the fee will go toward their booking cost. If they aren't serious and won't pay, it frees the agent to deal with more profitable A and B clients. Agents also receive a quarterly printout from a database that lists the company's top 500 clients and the revenue each generates. It helps agents look for missed sales opportunities and "get a handle on the target and their needs," White explains. The change in focus has been lucrative for Thomas Cook Travel, resulting in 20 percent growth in the company's A-level and B-level clients.

This sorting process, of course, has many risks. For one, future profits are hard to predict. A high-school student on his or her way to a Queen's MBA and a plum job on Bay Street might be unprofitable now but worth courting for the future. So might an unprofitable customer who suddenly inher-

its a lot of money. "That shabby-looking guy might actually be or become an eccentric billionaire. But as a result of using this technology, do you give him the bum's rush?" asks one analyst.

Analyst Erika Rasmusson summarizes: "All men may be created equal, but increasingly, all customers are not.... Learning where your customers rank in terms of profitability is the future of business, and companies that are doing it now have a distinct advantage over their competitors. Call it *selective* relationship management—companies need to pick wisely which customers they're going to have relationships with—and what kind of relationships."

Sources: Examples adapted from Rick Brooks, "Unequal Treatment: Alienating Customers Isn't Always a Bad Idea, Many Firms Discover," *Wall Street Journal*, 7 January 1999:A1; and Erika Rasmusson, "Wanted: Profitable Customers," *Sales and Marketing Management*, May 1999:28–34. Also see Peter Cockburn, "CRM for Profit," *Telecommunications*, December 2000:89–93; Joseph A. Ness, Michael J. Schrobeck, Rick A. Letendre, and Willmar J. Douglas, "The Role of ABM in Measuring Customer Value," *Strategic Finance*, March 2001:32–37; and Joseph A. Ness, Michael J. Schrobeck, Rick A. Letendre, and Willmar J. Douglas, "The Role of ABM in Measuring Customer Value—Part 2," *Strategic Finance*, April 2001:44–49.

Canada has become a mosaic of diverse ethnic, cultural, and social groups. Although these diverse groups have mixed, they maintain diversity by keeping and valuing important differences. Moreover, customers themselves are connecting in new ways to form "consumer communities" in which buyers connect with each other through common interests, situations, and activities.

The greater diversity and new consumer connections have meant greater market fragmentation. In response, most firms have moved from mass marketing to segmented marketing, in which they target carefully chosen submarkets or even individual buyers. One-to-one marketing has become the order of the day for some marketers. They build extensive customer databases containing rich information on individual customer preferences and purchases. Then, they mine these databases to gain insights by which they can "mass-customize" their offerings to deliver greater value to individual buyers.

At the same time that companies are finding new ways to deliver more value to customers, they are also beginning to assess carefully the value of customers to the firm. They want to connect only with customers who they can serve *profitably*. Once they identify profitable customers, firms can create attractive offers and special handling to capture these customers and earn their loyalty.

Connecting for a Customer's Lifetime Just as companies are being more selective about which customers they choose to serve, they are serving those they choose in a deeper, more lasting way. In the past, many companies focused on finding *new customers* for their products and closing *sales* with them. In recent years, this focus has shifted toward keeping *current customers* and building lasting customer *relationships*. Increasingly, the goal is shifting from making a profit on each sale to making long-term profits by managing the lifetime value of a customer.

As businesses do a better job of keeping old customers, competitors find it increasingly difficult to acquire new customers. As a result, marketers now spend less time figuring out how to increase share of market and more time trying to increase share of customer. They offer greater variety to current customers and train employees to cross-sell and up-sell to market more products and services to existing customers. For example, Amazon.com began as an online bookseller but now offers music, videos, gifts, toys, consumer electronics, home improvement items, and an online auction. In addition, based on each customer's purchase history, the company recommends related books, CDs, or videos that might be of interest. In this way, Amazon.com captures a greater share of each customer's leisure and entertainment budget.

Connecting Directly Beyond connecting more deeply with their customers, many companies are also connecting more *directly*. In fact, direct marketing is booming. Virtually all products are now available without going to a store—by telephone, mail-order catalogues, kiosks, and e-commerce. For example, customers surfing the Web can view pictures of almost any product, read the specs, shop among online vendors for the best prices and terms, speak with online vendors' shopping consultants, and place and pay for their orders—all with only a few mouse clicks. Business-to-business purchasing over the Internet has increased even faster than online consumer buying. Business purchasing agents routinely shop on the Web for items ranging from standard office supplies to high-priced, high-tech computer equipment.

Tilley Endurables
www.tilley.com

Some companies sell *only* via direct channels—firms such as ING Bank, Dell Computer, Grocery Gateway, Lands' End, and 1-800-Flowers, to name only a few. Other companies use direct connections to supplement their other communications and distribution channels. For example, Tilley Endurables sells their unique adventure clothing through their own retail outlets and through mail-order. However, Tilley uses its Web site not only to sell clothes, but also to build customer relationships by providing travel tips.

Similarly, you can't buy crayons from the Crayola Web site; however, you can find out how to remove crayon marks from your new carpeting or freshly painted walls.

Lands' End
www.landsend.com

Direct marketing is redefining the buyer's role in connecting with sellers. Instead of being the targets of a company's one-way marketing efforts, customers have now become active participants in shaping the marketing offer and process. Many companies now let customers design their own desired products online. For example, most shoppers at the Lands' End site can build a virtual model with their own hair colour, height, and shape. They then visit an online dressing room, where they can try clothes on the model to see how they would look in them. The site also gives buyers tips on how best to dress given their individual body types.

Some marketers have hailed direct marketing as the "marketing model of the new millennium." They envision a day when all buying and selling will involve direct connections between companies and their customers. Others, although agreeing that direct marketing will play a growing and important role, see it as just one more way to approach the marketplace. We will take a closer look at the world of direct marketing in Chapter 14.

Kraft Canada is at the forefront when it comes to using customer information to connect more directly with the carefully selected customers it hopes to keep for a lifetime. Kraft's aim is to provide total solutions to consumers' meal problems as the foundation for its relationship building efforts. Although Kraft brands are incorporated into many of the solutions, other products and information provided are often beyond the Kraft brand portfolio. Kraft has done this so well that *Marketing Magazine* included Kraft in its annual top-ten list of Marketers That Matter. To develop better relationships with Canadian consumers, Kraft had to work to better understand the dilemmas busy working families face each day in preparing school lunches, family meals, and special occasion dinners. And Kraft wants to partner with its consumers to find solutions to these problems. Under its new customer relationship marketing (CRM) initiatives, Kraft is increasingly becoming a service provider that helps consumers shop more efficiently, prepare meals quickly with simple ingredients, and impress guests with that special dinner—right down to which wine to buy. Although Kraft certainly doesn't sell Kraft Dinner online, it does give consumers a wealth of information on meal and snack preparation on its Web site and in its *What's Cooking* magazine it mails to its key customers. Both vehicles focus on providing food solutions, which is at the heart of Kraft's strategy: "Family. Food. Simple."

Connections with Marketing Partners

In these connected times, major changes are occurring in how marketers connect with others inside and outside the company to jointly bring greater value to customers.

Although Kraft doesn't sell its dinners online, the company's Web site provides food solutions as a strategy to develop better relationships with its customers.

Connecting Inside the Company Traditionally, marketers have tried to understand customer needs and represent the customer to different company departments, which then act on these needs. The old thinking was that marketing is done only by marketing, sales, and customer support people. However, in today's connected world, every functional area can interact with customers, especially electronically. Marketing no longer has sole ownership of customer interactions. The new thinking is that every employee must be customer focused. David Packard, cofounder of Hewlett-Packard, wisely said, "Marketing is far too important to be left only to the marketing department."

Today's forward-looking companies are reorganizing to align better with customer needs. Rather than letting each department go its own way, firms are linking all departments in the cause of creating customer value. Rather than assigning only sales and marketing people to customers, they are forming cross-functional customer teams. For example, Procter & Gamble assigns "customer development teams" to each of its major retailer accounts. These teams—consisting of sales and marketing people, operations and logistics specialists, market and financial analysts, and others—coordinate the efforts of many P&G departments to help the retailer be more successful.

Connecting with Outside Partners Rapid changes are also occurring in how marketers connect with their suppliers, channel partners, and even competitors. Most companies today are networked companies, relying heavily on partnerships with other firms.

Supply Chain Management Marketing channels consist of distributors, retailers, and others who connect the company to its buyers. The *supply chain* describes a longer channel, stretching from raw materials through components to final products that are carried to final buyers. For example, the supply chain for personal computers consists of suppliers of computer chips and other components, the computer manufacturer, and the distributors, retailers, and others who sell the computers to businesses and final customers. Each member of the supply chain creates and captures only a portion of the total value generated by the supply chain.

Through *supply chain management,* many companies today are strengthening their connections with partners all along the supply chain. They know that their fortunes rest not only on how well they perform, but also on how well their entire supply chain performs against competitors' supply chains. Rather than treat suppliers as vendors and distributors as customers, a company treats both as partners in delivering consumer value. For example, Wal-Mart works with suppliers such as Procter & Gamble, Rubbermaid, and Black & Decker to streamline logistics and reduce joint distribution costs, resulting in lower prices to consumers.

Strategic Alliances Beyond managing the supply chain, today's companies are also discovering that they need *strategic* partners if they hope to be effective. In the new, more competitive global environment, going it alone is going out of style. *Strategic alliances* are booming across the entire spectrum of industries and services. For example, Dell Computer recently ran advertisements describing how it partnered with Microsoft and Intel to provide customized e-business solutions. Companies need to give careful thought to finding partners who might complement their

strengths and offset their weaknesses. Well-managed alliances can have a huge impact on sales and profits. A recent study found that one in every four dollars earned by the top one thousand North American companies flows from alliances, which is double the rate in the early 1990s.

Strategic alliances: Dell recently ran ads telling how it partners with Microsoft and Intel to provide customized e-business solutions.

Connections with the World Around Us

As they are redefining their relationships with customers and partners, marketers are also taking a fresh look at the ways in which they connect with the broader world around them. Here we look at trends toward increasing globalization, more concern for social and environmental responsibility, and greater use of marketing by nonprofit and public sector organizations.

Global Connections In an increasingly smaller world, many marketers are now connected *globally* with their customers and marketing partners. The world economy has undergone radical change during the past two decades. Geographical and cultural distances have shrunk with the advent of jet planes, fax machines, world satellite television broadcasts, global Internet hookups, and other technical advances. This shrinkage has allowed companies to greatly expand their geographical market coverage, purchasing, and manufacturing. The result is a vastly more complex marketing environment for both companies and consumers.

Today, almost every company, large or small, is touched in some way by global competition—from the neighbourhood florist that buys its flowers from Mexican nurseries to the Canadian manufacturer that competes in its home markets with giant Japanese rivals, from the fledgling Internet retailer that finds itself receiving orders from all over the world to the large North American consumer goods producer that introduces new products into emerging markets abroad.

North American firms have been challenged at home by the skillful marketing of European and Asian multinationals. Companies such as Toyota, Nestlé, Sony, and Samsung have often outperformed their North American competitors. Similarly, Canadian companies in a wide range of industries have found new opportunities abroad. Bombardier, Nortel, SNC Lavalin, Alcan, Magna International, McCain Foods, and dozens of other Canadian companies have developed truly global operations, making and selling their products worldwide.

Today, companies are not only trying to sell more of their locally produced goods in international markets, they also are buying more supplies and components abroad. For example, Alfred Sung, one of Canada's top fashion designers, may choose cloth woven from Australian wool with designs printed in Italy. He will design a dress and e-mail the drawing to a Hong Kong agent, who will place the order with a Chinese factory. Finished dresses will be air-freighted to Montreal and New York, where they will be redistributed to department and specialty stores throughout North America.

Thus, managers in countries around the world are increasingly taking a global, not just local, view of the company's industry, competitors, and opportunities. They are asking: What is global marketing? How does it differ from domestic marketing? How do global competitors and forces affect our business? To what extent should we "go global?" Many companies are forming strategic alliances with foreign companies, even competitors, who serve as suppliers or marketing partners. Winning companies in the next century may well be those that have built the best global networks.

Connections with Our Values and Social Responsibilities

Marketers are reexamining their connections with social values and responsibilities and with the planet that sustains us. As worldwide consumerism and environmentalism movements mature, today's marketers are being called on to take greater responsibility for the social and environmental impact of their actions. Corporate ethics and social responsibility have become hot topics in almost every business arena, from the corporate boardroom to the business school classroom. Few companies can ignore the renewed and very demanding environmental movement.

The social responsibility and environmental movements will place even stricter demands on companies in the future. Some companies resist these movements, budging only when forced by legislation or consumer outcries. More forward-looking companies, however, readily accept their responsibilities to the world around them. They view socially responsible actions as an opportunity to do well by doing good—to profit by serving the best long-run interests of their customers and communities. Some companies, such as Mountain Equipment Co-op, the Royal Bank, and VanCity Credit Union, are building social responsibility and action into their mission statements.

VanCity Credit Union
www.vancity.com

For example, VanCity's Web site states, "As a community-based and member-owned financial institution, VanCity is committed to doing business in a way that contributes to the social, economic, and environmental well-being of the communities in which we operate."

Broadening Connections

Many different kinds of organizations are using marketing to connect with customers and other important constituencies. In the past, marketing has been most widely applied in the for-profit business sector. Recently, however, marketing also has become a major part of the strategies of many nonprofit organizations, such as universities, hospitals, museums, symphony orchestras, and even churches.

According to the Canadian Centre for Philanthropy, Canada has more than 80 000 registered charities and nonprofit organizations. These range from small community-based organizations such as the Brockville Volunteer Firefighters Association to large national charities such as the United Way and the Heart and Stroke Foundation. With cutbacks in government funding, competition for donors is intensifying and nonprofit organizations are adopting more marketing practices. For example, some are building alliances. Witness the birth in 1998 of the Girl Child Network, a joint initiative funded by World Vision Canada, Foster Parents Plan of Canada, Christian Children's Fund of Canada, and Save the Children. The four organizations shared costs on a mass-market advertising campaign to address global issues that specifically affect young girls: child prostitution, child labour, and female genital mutilation.

The Arthritis Society, Care Canada, and other charities are turning to the data-mining techniques and donor lifetime value analysis used by for-profit firms. Kelly Ducharme, database manager at Care Canada's Ottawa headquarters, notes that data mining is becoming a trend since it helps nonprofits target their fundraising efforts while providing donors with more accountability.

Care has been able to segment its 160 000-name donor base into a descending scale according to the period during which the person made their last donation. They found that only 25 percent gave in the past 18 months, so rather than swallowing the massive mailing costs incurred with blanket mailings, Care targeted only those who passed the "recency" test. Response rates from its latest campaigns have been as high as 9 percent, compared with the 4 percent average for most nonprofit campaigns. Keeping donors active is as important for nonprofits as it is for firms to retain their customers. Experts note that it costs about $13 a name to acquire a new donor, so many nonprofits are starting to realize that it's cheaper to get incremental revenue out of an existing donor than to try to find a new one.[27]

Even government agencies are showing an increased interest in marketing. The Canadian Army has a marketing plan to attract recruits; Transport Canada has a program to discourage drunk driving; and Health and Welfare Canada has long-standing social marketing campaigns to discourage smoking, excessive drinking, and drug use. Even once-stodgy Canada Post has developed innovative marketing programs to increase use of its priority mail services. Thus, it seems that every type of organization can connect through marketing. The continued growth of nonprofit and public-sector marketing presents new and exciting challenges for marketing managers.

The New Connected World of Marketing

Smart marketers of all kinds are taking advantage of new opportunities for connecting with their customers, their marketing partners, and the world around them. Table 1-1 compares the old marketing thinking to the new. The old marketing thinking saw

Table 1-1   Marketing Connections in Transition

The Old Marketing Thinking	The New Marketing Thinking
Connections with Customers	
Be sales and product centred	Be market and customer centred
Practise mass marketing	Target selected market segments or individuals
Focus on products and sales	Focus on customer satisfaction and value
Make sales to customers	Develop customer relationships
Get new customers	Keep old customers
Grow share of market	Grow share of customer
Serve any customer	Serve profitable customers, "fire" losing ones
Communicate through mass media	Connect with customers directly
Make standardized products	Develop customized products
Connections with Marketing Partners	
Leave customer satisfaction and value to sales and marketing	Enlist all departments in the cause of customer satisfaction and value
Go it alone	Partner with other firms
Connections with the World Around Us	
Market locally	Market locally *and* globally
Assume profit responsibility	Assume social and environmental responsibility
Marketing for profits	Marketing for nonprofits
Conduct commerce in market*places*	Conduct e-commerce in market*spaces*

marketing as little more than selling or advertising. It viewed marketing as customer acquisition rather than customer care. It emphasized trying to make a profit on each sale rather than trying to profit by managing customer lifetime value. And it concerned itself with trying to sell products rather than to understand, create, communicate, and deliver real value to customers.

Fortunately, old marketing thinking is now giving way to newer ways of thinking. Today's smart marketing companies are improving their customer knowledge and customer connections. They are targeting profitable customers and finding innovative ways to capture and keep these customers. They are forming more direct connections with customers and building lasting customer relationships. Using more targeted media and integrating their marketing communications, they are delivering meaningful and consistent messages through every customer contact. They are employing more technologies such as videoconferencing, sales automation software, and the Internet, intranets, and extranets. They view their suppliers and distributors as partners, not adversaries. In sum, today's companies are forming new kinds of connections for delivering superior value to their customers.

We will explore all these developments in more detail in later chapters. For now, we must recognize that marketing will continue to change dramatically. Today's connected world offers many exciting opportunities for forward-thinking marketers.

<< Looking Back < < < < < < < < <

Now that we've introduced you to marketing, let's review the material. So far, we've examined the basics of what marketing is, the philosophies that guide it, and the challenges it faces in the new connected world.

Today's successful companies—whether large or small, for-profit or nonprofit, domestic or global—share a strong customer focus and a heavy commitment to marketing. Many people think of marketing as only selling or advertising. But marketing combines many activities—marketing research, product development, distribution, pricing, advertising, personal selling, and others—designed to sense, serve, and satisfy consumer needs while meeting the organization's goals. Marketing seeks to attract new customers by promising superior value and to keep and grow current customers by delivering satisfaction.

Marketing operates within a dynamic global environment. Rapid changes can quickly make yesterday's winning strategies obsolete. In the next century, marketers will face many new challenges and opportunities. To be successful, companies will have to be strongly market focused.

1. Define marketing and discuss its core concepts.

Marketing is a social and managerial process whereby individuals and groups obtain what they need and want by creating and exchanging products and value with others. The core concepts of marketing are *needs, wants,* and *demands; products, services,* and *experiences; value, satisfaction,* and *quality; exchange, transactions,* and *relationships;* and *markets. Wants* are the form assumed by human needs when shaped by culture and individual personality. When backed by buying power, wants become *demands.* People satisfy their needs, wants, and demands with products and services. A *product* is anything that can be offered to a market to satisfy a need, want, or demand. Products also include *services* and other entities such as *experiences, persons, places, organizations, information,* and *ideas.*

2. Explain the relationships among customer value, satisfaction, and quality.

In deciding which products and services to buy, consumers rely on their perception of relative value. *Customer value* is the difference between the value the customer gains from owning and using a product and the cost of obtaining and using the product. *Customer satisfaction* depends on a product's perceived performance in delivering value relative to a buyer's expectations. Customer satisfaction is closely linked to *quality,* leading many companies to adopt *total quality* practices. Marketing occurs when people satisfy their needs, wants, and demands through *exchange.* Beyond creating short-term transactions, marketers need to build long-term relationships with valued customers, distributors, dealers, and suppliers.

3. Define marketing management and understand how marketers manage demand and build profitable customer relationships.

Marketing management is the analysis, planning, implementation, and control of programs designed to create, build, and maintain beneficial exchanges with target buyers so as to achieve organizational objectives. It involves more than simply finding enough customers for the company's current output. Marketing is at times also concerned with changing or even reducing demand. Managing demand means managing customers. Beyond designing strategies to *attract* new customers and create *transactions* with them, today's companies are focusing on *retaining* current customers and building lasting relationships through offering superior customer value and satisfaction.

4. Compare the five marketing management philosophies.

Marketing management can be guided by five different philosophies. The *production concept* holds that consumers favour products that are available and highly affordable; management's task is to improve production efficiency and bring down prices. The *product concept* holds that consumers favour products that offer the most in quality, performance, and innovative features; thus, little promotional effort is required. The *selling concept* holds that consumers will not buy enough of the organization's products unless it undertakes a large-scale selling and promotion effort. The *marketing concept* holds that achieving organizational goals depends on determining the needs and wants of target markets and delivering the desired satisfactions more effectively and efficiently than competitors do. The *societal marketing concept* holds that generating customer satisfaction *and* long-run societal well-being are the keys to both achieving the company's goals and fulfilling its responsibilities.

5. Analyze the major challenges facing marketers in the new "connected" world.

Dramatic changes in the marketplace are creating many marketing opportunities and challenges. Major marketing developments can be summed up in a single theme: *connections*. The explosive growth in connecting technologies—computer, information, telecommunications, and transportation technologies—has created an exciting new economy, filled with new ways for marketers to learn about and serve consumers, in large groups or one to one. Marketers are rapidly redefining how they connect with their customers, with their marketing partners, and with the world around them. They are choosing their customers more carefully and developing closer, more direct, and lasting connections with them. Realizing that going it alone is going out of style, marketers are connecting more closely with other company departments and with other firms in an integrated effort to bring more value to customers. They are taking a fresh look at the ways in which they connect with the broader world, resulting in increased globalization, growing attention to social and environmental responsibilities, and greater use of marketing by nonprofit and public-sector organizations. The new, connected millennium offers exciting possibilities for forward-thinking marketers.

Navigating the Key Terms

Customer satisfaction, **p. 11**
Customer value, **p. 10**
Demands, **p. 6**
Demarketing, **p. 16**
Exchange, **p. 12**
Market, **p. 14**
Marketing concept, **p. 21**
Marketing management, **p. 15**
Marketing, **p. 5**
Need, **p. 5**

Product concept, **p. 21**
Production concept, **p. 20**
Products, **p. 6**
Relationship marketing, **p. 12**
Selling concept, **p. 21**
Services, **p. 7**
Societal marketing concept, **p. 23**
Transaction, **p. 12**
Want, **p. 6**

Concept Check

Fill in the blanks and then check your answers.

1. _____ is a social and managerial process whereby individuals and groups obtain what they need and want through creating and exchanging products and value with others.

2. Today, marketing must be understood not in the old sense of making a sale—"telling and selling"—but in the new sense of _____.

3. The concept of _____ is not limited to physical objects—anything capable of satisfying a need can be called a _____.

4. _____ is the difference between the values the customer gains from owning and using a product and the costs of obtaining the product.

5. Smart companies aim to _____ customers by promising only what they can deliver and delivering more than they promise.

6. The goal of _____ is to deliver long-term value to customers, and the measures of success are long-term customer satisfaction and retention.

7. A _____ is the set of actual and potential buyers of a product.

8. Most companies are started by individuals who live by their wits. This would be an example of _____ marketing.

9. There are five alternative concepts under which organizations conduct their marketing activities: they are the _____, _____, _____, _____, and _____ concepts.

10. "We make it happen for you," "To fly, to serve," "We're not satisfied until you are," and "Let us exceed your expectations" are all colourful illustrations of the _____ concept.

11. The major force behind the new connectedness in the "connected" world is _____.

Concept Check Answers: 1. Marketing; 2. satisfying customer needs; 3. product; product; 4. Customer value; 5. delight; 6. relationship marketing; 7. market; 8. entrepreneurial; 9. production; product; selling; marketing; societal marketing; 10. marketing; 11. technology.

Discussing the Issues

1. What is marketing?

2. Discuss the concept of customer value and its importance to successful marketing. How are the concepts of customer value and relationship marketing linked?

3. Identify the single biggest difference between the marketing concept and the production, product, and selling concepts. Discuss which concepts are easier to apply in the short run. Which concept offers the best long-run success potential? Why?

4. According to economist Milton Friedman, "Few trends could so thoroughly undermine the very foundations of our free society as the acceptance by corporate officials of a social responsibility other than to make as much money for their stockholders as possible." Do you agree or disagree with Friedman's statement? What are some of the drawbacks of the societal marketing concept?

5. The major marketing developments in this new millennium can be summed up in a single theme: *connectedness*. Explain what "connectedness" is and how marketers can apply it to customers, marketing partners, and the world around us.

 **Mastering Marketing**

The Mastering Marketing CD-ROM included with this book uses a fictional Internet company, CanGo, to examine the ideas presented in the text. Explore the videos and interactive exercises on the CD-ROM, and consider the questions that appear in the Mastering Marketing section at the end of each chapter.

Beyond creating short-term transactions, marketers need to build long-term relationships with valued customers, distributors, dealers, and suppliers. Cite three examples from CanGo of relationship marketing with customers, distributors, dealers, or suppliers. Be specific in your comments.

 Check out the enclosed Video case CD-ROM, or our Companion Website at www.pearsoned.ca/armstrong, to view a CBC video segment and case for this chapter.

 **Marketing Applications**

Using the MAP Feature

The best way to become a good marketing decision maker is to practise marketing decision making. In MAP (marketing application) stops at the end of each chapter, you will find interesting case histories, real-life situations, or timely descriptions from business articles that illustrate specific chapter subjects. At each MAP stop, you will be asked to make marketing decisions as if you were the marketing manager of the company in question. Here's your first MAP Stop—have fun on your journey!

MAP Stop

One of the most loyal but yet hard-to-reach markets among Gen Y teens is the skateboarder market. Of all the clothing and tennis shoe manufacturers, only California-based Vans, Inc. has really been successful. Vans has figured out that skateboarding has come a long way from the days when a kid made a board by nailing a pair of roller-skates to the bottom of a wooden plank. By pioneering thick-soled, slip-on sneakers that can absorb the shock of 1-m to 1.5-m leaps, Vans has remained "cool" with the skateboard crowd. The problem is, how can Vans grow its market when the target audience is part of an outlaw culture that has been banned from most modern malls

and shopping centres? Vans believes that branching out into elaborate skateboard parks (eight have opened at the very malls that have banned skateboarders), designing clothing lines, and manufacturing snowboard boots will be the strategies that will serve them well in the next decade. Using its own branded 140 retail stores (as well as a number of independents), Vans has carved out a 1-percent to 2-percent share of the giant sneakers market in the United States.

In Canada, Vans has targeted independent retailers that cater to their youthful and adventurous target market, such as Antisocial, Comor Sports, Pacific Snowboarder, and Snowcovers in Vancouver, Mike E's Skateboard Shop, Sporting Life, and Olly Shoes in Toronto, and Spin, Diz, Street and Snow, and Underworld Skate Shop in Montreal.

Though not exactly a Nike (which owns more than 50 percent of this lucrative market), Vans is betting its future on a plan that will position them in the growing number of Xtreme sports. However, one area that Vans is avoiding is inline skating, since most Vans loyalists and skateboard enthusiasts consider this a sport for "wimps." Therefore, it appears that the main guiding principle for Vans' strategic positioning in the future will be to remain authentic and loyal to their roots.

Thinking Like a Marketing Manager

1. What elements of the marketing concept does Vans appear to be applying with their strategies?

2. Go to a retail outlet that carries Vans, or go online to **www.vans.com**, and review their product lines. What seem to be the advantages and the disadvantages of products they carry? After considering Vans' target market and its outlaw image, what do you think would be the best way to reach this target market in Canada? Is Vans on the right track in using a highly focused distribution strategy with independent retailers or should it consider the U.S. concept of Vans branded retail outlets?

3. It has been reported that Vans is now attempting to reach the female market with its clothing line. Present three relationship- or value-oriented strategies that you believe might help it to accomplish this goal.

4. Keeping in mind the marketing concept, relationship marketing, and customer value, design a strategy to help Vans enter the snowboard market with its new line of snowboard boots. How will industry leader Burton Snowboards, **www.burton.com** likely react to Vans' entry and strategy? How would you deal with this reaction? Present your strategy and ideas to the class.

Digital Map

Visit our Web site at **www.pearsoned.ca/armstrong** for online quizzes, Internet exercises, and more!

CASE 1 GROCERY GATEWAY www.grocerygateway.com

"Everyone has better things to do in life than shop for groceries," states Grocery Gateway's Web site.

The company's founder, Bill Di Nardo, created the concept with some friends in 1996. "A bunch of us piled into my basement and started mapping out all the amazing and wonderful opportunities the Internet might provide. We drew some radical conclusions, put a business plan together, visited some folks in the U.S. to see what they were up to, and decided we were on to something," recalls Di Nardo.

The idea was simple: people in the Toronto area could order their groceries over the Internet and have them delivered right to the counter tops in their kitchens with a smile.

However, unlike most e-commerce businesses, the idea behind Grocery Gateway (GG), was to control every stage of the transaction with their customers. From the outset, the focus was on providing and owning the infrastructure, an approach unprecedented in Canadian e-commerce. For example, the company strategy was always to have a single, dedicated warehouse location that would allow for improved inventory control. In addition, this would allow GG to optimize the use of their customized delivery trucks. As Di Nardo states, "We didn't want to have to rely on anyone else to ship our products."

Today, GG, controls every stage of the e-commerce transaction. Once customers place orders on the Web site, GG's staff picks, packs, and delivers the order directly to the customers' door. "That kind of face-to-face relationship is to key to our strategy of friendly, personal service and makes our customers more comfortable with adopting an e-commerce solution" adds Di Nardo.

Di Nardo was relying on his knowledge of some fundamental consumer trends, one of which is that consumers are busy, and, more specifically, dislike wasting their time bumping carts with other shoppers in supermarket aisles.

Although the original concept was to use the Internet exclusively, the company realized that if they were to truly be customer service responsive, then they would have to consider customer requests for changes in placing orders. As a result, Grocery Gateway has recently fallen back on existing technology to service their clients: the telephone! GG has recently added telephone-ordering capability for consumers and is supporting this mode of ordering with a printed catalogue. A spokesperson for GG indicated that the addition of telephone service was targeted at "those [consumers] who don't have a computer or aren't comfortable using one to purchase items online."

Today, Grocery Gateway receives approximately one thousand orders a day and services these orders from a 23 000-m^2 fulfillment centre in Mississauga, Ontario. This facility integrates some of the most advanced inventory management technology in the world and acts as a head office.

Although Grocery Gateway has seen its sales grow six-fold, the company is still not generating a profit. Recently, the company increased its minimum order size from $45 to $60 to improve profitability.

However, Webvan Group, a California-based online grocer, filed for bankruptcy protection in mid-2001, on the heels of other failed U.S.-based online grocers such as Streamline.com and Shoplink.com in Boston and Cozmo in New York.

Does Grocery Gateway have a chance of survival? Industry watchers believe that if GG maintains the focus on efficiency and customer service, and resists the temptation to expand beyond the Toronto and area base, until it is profitable, then there is hope for success.

One new and interesting challenge that GG will have to deal with, however, is Loblaws, one of Ontario's largest supermarket bricks-and-mortar chains. It has recently begun testing its own Internet grocery service.

Questions:

1. How does the Internet illustrate the marketing concept in action?

2. Explain how traditional supermarkets, department stores, and discounters create value for consumers.

3. How do Internet sellers such as Grocery Gateway, Indigo.ca, and canadiantire.ca create value for their consumers?

4. How does Grocery Gateway exemplify the new model for connecting with customers as explained in this chapter?

Sources: D. Calleja, "Now We're in Business," *Canadian Business*, December 2000:118–126; R. Razel, "Food for Thought," *Canadian Business*, May 2001:88; "Toronto's Grocery Gateway and Orbis Team up for Efficiency," *Modern Materials Handling*, July 2001:G28; "What's Old Is New at Online Supermarket," Canadian Press, Mississauga, ON, 13 October 2001, Item Number CX 2001286U7812.

2 >> Strategic Planning and the Marketing Process

Looking Ahead

Ready to travel on? In the first chapter, you learned the core concepts and philosophies of marketing. Next, you'll investigate marketing's role in the broader organization and the specifics of the marketing process. First, marketing urges a whole-company philosophy that puts customers at the centre. Then, marketers work with other company functions to design strategies for delivering value to carefully targeted customers and to develop marketing mixes—comprising product, price, distribution, and promotion tactics—to carry out these strategies profitably. Chapters 1 and 2 will fully introduce you to the basics of marketing, the decisions marketing managers make, and where marketing fits into an organization. After that, we'll look at the environments in which marketing operates.

After studying this chapter, you should be able to

1. explain companywide strategic planning and its four steps
2. discuss how to design business portfolios and develop growth strategies
3. explain functional planning strategies and assess marketing's role in strategic planning
4. describe the marketing process and the forces that influence it
5. list the marketing management functions, including the elements of a marketing plan

Calgary-based WestJet has done what other giant airlines thought impossible—it remains consistently profitable and it doesn't have a mountain of debt. How has it managed these rare feats? By constantly and unrelentingly following a strategy of cost leadership that allows it to offer the lowest prices in the Canadian skies. The result of this strategy can be seen by comparing WestJet's cost per available seat mile (ASM)[1] with that of Air Canada. WestJet's cost per ASM is about $0.141, while Air Canada's is $0.176. Low costs also translate into higher revenue per ASM. WestJet earns $0.160 per ASM, while Air Canada earns $0.148. To keep its costs low, WestJet flies one type of aircraft, the Boeing 737. Having only one type of aircraft lowers the costs of training and maintenance and allows bulk purchase efficiencies. WestJet also keeps a grip on its marketing costs. It uses a ticketless software system for its bookings and it uses low-cost media such as newspapers, radio, and outdoor advertisements to carry its message of friendly, low-cost service.

WestJet's record of profitability is especially amazing when you consider the turbulence that characterizes the airline industry in Canada and worldwide. The number of mergers and alliances is increasing. Rising fuel prices and a slowing economy are making profitability a challenge for all high flyers. Price wars are rampant and deregulation has shaken up the industry. In Canada, Air Canada joined the Star Alliance and bought Canadian Airlines. Canada 3000 purchased Royal Airlines but had to declare bankruptcy following the 11 September 2001 crisis. Roots Air briefly took flight but quickly discovered that beavers really weren't meant to fly.

WestJet is a relative newcomer to the airline industry. It was founded in February 1996 with only three planes and 220 employees. By year-end 2002, WestJet operated 36 aircraft and served more than 21 cities in Canada. In the third quarter of 2002, it had net earnings of $23.1 million. Since 1996, WestJet has grown steadily and has caused ticket prices to plunge by as much as 70 percent in every market it has entered. Its entrepreneurial founders, Clive Beddoe, Mark Hill, Tim Morgan, and Donald Bell, designed their new airline using United States–based Southwest Airlines as their model. Like Southwest, WestJet enjoys an image of unconventionality: Its flight attendants tell corny jokes and organize in-flight toilet-paper-rolling contests. But more important, just like Southwest, it is one of the few airlines in the world to have a record of profitability despite such crises as the tragedy of September 11.

Before starting their airline, WestJet's founders did their homework. They analyzed hundreds of other airlines and the dynamics of the airline industry. Their analysis of the Canadian marketplace revealed that the needs of a significant portion of the Canadian market were not being met. All Canadian competitors were look-alikes. As WestJet's marketing vice president Bill Lamberton noted, "Air Canada and Canadian were Tweedledum and Tweedledee, offering the same products. We have consistently offered a no-frills service and consumers can clearly see the difference."

In addition to its low cost strategy, the new airline selected markets and competitors carefully. Rather than attacking its major competitors head on and relying on business travellers to ensure profitability, WestJet began by specializing in serving what it calls "VFR customers" in Western Canada (people who are visiting friends and relatives). It saw its main competitor as the family car and realized that if it could offer low airfares, people would choose to fly rather than drive to visit friends and family.

Another key to WestJet's success is its corporate culture. As founder Clive Beddoe notes, "We empower employees and push the decision making down [the corporate structure]. We try to make it a fun environment, to encourage people to be a bit bizarre and off the wall." To illustrate this culture, he tells the story of the employee in the airline's maintenance hangar who uses a unicycle to get around the giant space. Beddoe regards his employees as his partners. Informality also marks the culture. Everybody calls Beddoe, who is the CEO and president, Clive. "If they don't, they know I'll fire them," he jokes. To reinforce the airline's low-cost strategy, his own office is simply furnished and the entrance to the executive suite bears the self-deprecating sign "Big Shots." WestJet's employees respond enthusiastically to this culture and consistently give that extra effort that keeps customers walking through its gates. Beddoe believes his people are his most important marketing tool. "We built this company on low fares and quality of service. Our 'oh my gosh!' fares got people on board, but it's our people and the quality of their service that keep them coming back."

WestJet is now becoming a true national rival of Air Canada's. After Air Canada purchased Canadian Airlines in 1999, WestJet saw an opportunity to grow and decided to extend its successful low-fare airline across Canada. Using Hamilton as its hub, it began offering flights to cities in Eastern Canada. In May 2002, the airline made a major competitive move and began flying into Toronto's Pearson Airport, Air Canada's power base. Not to be outdone, Air Canada countered by having its new no-frills airline, Zip, establish operations on WestJet's western doorstep. It will be interesting to watch this war in the skies unfold.

WestJet's strategy and success haven't gone unnoticed. In 2000, WestJet's four founders were honoured with The Ernst & Young Entrepreneur of the Year Award. In 2001, Clive, Don, Mark, and Tim received an International Entrepreneurship award for Outstanding Teamwork in Monaco.[2]

In this chapter, we look first at the organization's overall strategic planning. Next, we discuss marketing's role in the organization as defined by that strategic plan. Finally, we explain the marketing management process—the process that marketers undertake to carry out their role in the organization.

STRATEGIC PLANNING

Many companies operate without formal plans. In new companies, managers are sometimes so busy they have no time for planning. In small companies, managers sometimes think that only large corporations need formal planning. In mature companies, many managers argue that they have done well without formal planning and that therefore it cannot be too important. They may resist taking the time to prepare a written plan. They may argue that the marketplace changes too quickly for a plan to be useful, that it would end up collecting dust.

Granted, planning is not much fun, and it takes time away from doing. Yet companies must plan. As someone said, "If you fail to plan, you are planning to fail."[3] Formal planning yields many benefits for all types of companies, large and small, new and mature.

The process of planning can be as important as the plans that emerge. Planning encourages management to think systematically about what has happened, what is happening, and what might happen to the company. It forces them to sharpen the company's objectives and policies, leads to better coordination of company efforts, and provides clearer performance standards for control. The argument that planning is less useful in a fast-changing environment makes little sense. In fact, the opposite is true: Sound planning helps the company to anticipate and respond quickly to changes and to prepare better for sudden developments.

Companies usually prepare annual plans, long-range plans, and strategic plans. The annual and long-range plans deal with the company's current businesses and how to keep them going. In contrast, the strategic plan involves adapting the firm to take advantage of opportunities in its constantly changing environment.

We define **strategic planning** as the process of developing and maintaining a strategic fit between the organization's goals and capabilities and its changing marketing opportunities. Various types of strategic plans are developed to guide different levels of business. Since many firms are diversified and compete in multiple markets, they organize themselves into strategic business units. A **strategic business unit (SBU)** is an identifiable unit within a larger company with its own profit and loss responsibility. An SBU may have one or more divisions and product lines. For example, Bayer AG, the giant German chemical company, operates in six major sectors. In the health-related products sector, it has six SBUs: ethical products, self-medication, consumer products, diagnostic products, hospital products, and biotechnological products.

Given that Bayer operates several business units in six industry sectors, it has a complex portfolio of businesses to manage. Thus, its strategic planning takes place at different levels of the organization.[4] It does **corporate strategic planning**. This plan sets the mission for the firm as a whole and addresses two major questions: What businesses should we be in? How should we integrate these businesses?

Strategies are also developed by each business unit. Although the corporate strategy is the glue that holds the firm together, the **business unit strategy** determines how the unit will compete in its given business and how it will position itself among its competitors. The business unit strategy maps out resource allocation decisions among the different business functions and the best means of integrating the various functions. For example, it determines the proportion of resources going

Strategic planning The process of developing and maintaining a strategic fit between the organization's goals and capabilities and its changing marketing opportunities.

Strategic business unit (SBU) An identifiable unit within a larger company with its own profit and loss responsibility; it may have one or more divisions and product lines.

Corporate strategic planning Setting the mission for a firm as a whole.

Business unit strategy Strategy that determines how the unit will compete in its given business and how it will position itself among its competitors.

to such things as research and development, product design, operations, human resources, information technology, and marketing.

Functional strategy
Strategy that deals with questions of how the function can best support the business unit strategy.

Finally, each functional area (marketing, human resources, operations, and so on) within each business unit develops its own **functional strategy**. A functional strategy deals with questions of how the function can best support the business unit strategy. For example, if the business unit strategy sets an objective of gaining market share in its business arena, then the marketing strategy will outline the various action plans needed to help the business achieve its aim. It might describe how improvements in product quality, additional channels of delivery such as the Internet, and a new communication campaign will help the unit achieve its objective.

Figure 2-1 shows the steps in strategic planning and the relationship among the corporate strategic plan, the strategic business unit, and the marketing plans. Corporate strategic planning sets the stage for the rest of the firm's planning efforts. The corporate plan contains a clear statement of the company's mission. This mission then is turned into detailed supporting objectives that guide the whole company. Next, head office decides what portfolio of businesses and products is best for the company and how much support to give each. In turn, each business and product unit must develop detailed marketing and other departmental plans that support the companywide plan. Thus, marketing planning occurs at the business unit, product, and market levels. It supports company strategic planning with more detailed planning for specific marketing opportunities.[5]

Strategic Planning and Small Business

Many discussions of strategic planning focus on large corporations with many divisions and products. However, small businesses also can benefit greatly from sound strategic planning. Although most small ventures start out with extensive business and marketing plans to attract potential investors, strategic planning often falls by the wayside once the business gets going. Entrepreneurs and presidents of small companies are more likely to spend their time "putting out fires" than planning. But what does a small firm do when it finds that it has taken on too much debt, when its growth is exceeding production capacity, or when it's losing market share to a competitor with lower prices? Strategic planning can help small business managers anticipate such situations and determine how to prevent or handle them. The King's Medical Company example and New Directions 2-1 illustrate how small companies have used very simple strategic planning tools to chart their course.

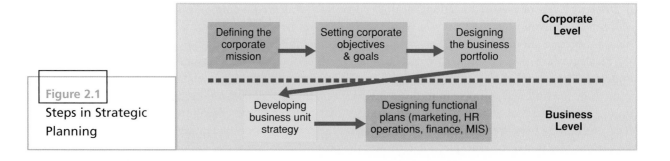

Figure 2.1

Steps in Strategic Planning

King's Medical Company is an example of how one small company uses very simple strategic planning tools to chart its course every three years. King's Medical owns and manages magnetic resonance imaging (MRI) equipment—million-dollar-plus machines that produce X-ray-type pictures. Strategic planning has been the key to this small company's very rapid growth and high profit margins. As the company's cofounder claims: "A lot of literature says there are three critical issues to a small company: cash flow, cash flow, cash flow. I agree those issues are critical, but so are three more: planning, planning, planning."[6] King's Medical's planning process, which hinges on an assessment of the company, its place in the market, and its goals, includes the following steps:

1. Identify the major elements of the business environment in which the organization has operated over the past few years.

2. Describe the mission of the organization in terms of its nature and function for the next two years.

3. Explain the internal and external forces that will affect the mission of the organization.

4. Identify the basic driving force that will direct the organization in the future.

5. Develop a set of long-term objectives that will identify what the organization will become in the future.

6. Outline a general plan of action that defines the logistical, financial, and personnel factors needed to integrate the long-term objectives into the whole organization.[7]

Small, single-unit businesses will have only a corporate strategic plan and functional plans. Larger, multi-unit businesses will have a corporate plan, plans for each business unit, and plans for each functional unit. These different types of planning efforts are described in the next sections.

New Directions 2-1 >> Strategic Planning for Small Business Growth

Small businesses are responsible for much of the growth in the Canadian business sector. In recognition of this trend, the Canadian government has begun to focus more on helping entrepreneurs. *A Guide for Canadian Small Business* can be found on the Canada Customs and Revenue Agency's Web site at **www.ccra-adrc.gc.ca**. As a recent article on Canada's best-managed private companies noted, strategic planning is as important for small, private firms as it is for their much larger rivals. "We found that the winning companies all have a clear vision and a strategic direction…they were always focused. They recognize that they have a competitive advantage and are exploiting it." Two other factors—communicating corporate vision and enhancing employee morale—added to their success. The strategies of many small Canadian businesses are illustrated in the video cases that follow each chapter. Examples of other award-winning small Canadian businesses are given below.

Sabian Ltd.
Meductic, New Brunswick
Business: Musical cymbals
Employees: 100
Annual sales: $20 million

SABIAN is one of the percussion industry's greatest success stories. Located is rural New Brunswick, in less than twenty years this innovative

cymbal company became the world's single largest producer of cymbals for drummers and percussionists. Big-name clients include Phil Collins, Dave Weckl, Evelyn Glennie, and drummers with The Barenaked Ladies, Red Hot Chili Peppers, Disturbed, Incubus, and other major groups. The SABIAN name and its ringed logo pattern (representing the rings of a cymbal) is everywhere. This award-winning company produces ten cymbal series plus metal percussives, which are exported to approx. 120 countries. Understanding the market and its customers is at the heart of SABIAN'S strategy.

Knowing the market and the customer for this specialized product is at the heart of the company's strategy. The company must be highly customer focused since, according to former company president Bill Jildjian, "Each musician decides which product is best suited to expressing him- or herself. In that respect it's more of a collaboration than a business deal."

Source: "Banging the Drum in New Brunswick," *Financial Post*, 14 December 1996:42.

Mascoll Beauty Supply Ltd.
Toronto, Ontario
Business: Beauty   products   for   African-Canadians

Employees: 25
Annual sales: Unknown

Beverley Mascoll established her business with $700, an idea, industry experience, and the trunk of her car. Beginning her firm with one product line—a hair relaxer she packaged at her kitchen table—she has developed her company into one that now sells more than 3000 items. From the earliest days, she understood the power of niche marketing based on personal service. She offered a unique benefit in Canada. No other company was marketing beauty products designed specifically for black women. Yet, Mascoll knew that black women spend six times more on hair care and cosmetics than do Caucasian women. Furthermore, they don't scrimp on these products, even when times are bad. Consequently, she discovered a recession-proof business. She also found a market where she could ride a growth wave.

When she started her business, fewer than 50 000 black people lived in Canada. Since then, that number has grown ten-fold. Mascoll also understood that few beauticians knew how to treat "black hair." Thus, part of her strategy was to train her customers. She brought the hottest styles to Canada and invited people to demonstrations, thereby creating demand for her products. Today, Mascoll is not only successful, but is also dedicated to giving back to her community. She has worked with Dalhousie University in Halifax to establish the first black history professorship chair in Canada and recently founded the Beverley Mascoll Community Foundation, a philanthropic organization that offers scholarships to deserving students, supports community work, and funds a summer camp for sick children.

Source: Margaret Cannon, "Looking Good, Doing Good," *Report on Business*, December 1996:99–104.

Defining the Company's Business and Mission

An organization exists to accomplish something. At first, it has a clear purpose or mission, but over time, its mission may become unclear as the organization grows, adds new products and markets, or faces new conditions in the environment. When management senses that the organization is drifting, it must renew its search for purpose. It is time to ask: What is our business? Who is the customer? What do consumers value? What should our business be? These simple-sounding questions are among the most difficult the company will ever have to answer. Successful companies continually raise these questions and answer them carefully and completely.

1 We've been on a roll for 67 years.

2 Now we've popped up with **another big idea.** It's an ingenious dispensing system that pops up strips of tape – pre-cut, one at a time, right into your hand. New Scotch™ Pop-up Tape Strips make gift wrapping easier, especially when you've got your hands full. We're making tape even more handy, because we make the leap *from need to...*

3M *Innovation*

© 3M 1997   78-6900-8329-6(1171)ii   *For more information, call 1-800-3M-HELPS, or Internet: http://www.3M.com*

> **Company mission:** 3M does more than just make adhesives, scientific equipment, health care, and communications products. It solves people's problems by putting innovation to work for them.

Many organizations develop formal mission statements that answer these questions. A **mission statement** is a statement of the organization's purpose—what it wants to accomplish in the larger environment. A clear mission statement acts as an "invisible hand" that guides people in the organization.

Traditionally, companies have defined their businesses in product terms ("We manufacture furniture") or in technological terms ("We are a chemical-processing firm"). But mission statements should be *market oriented* (see New Directions 2-2). Products and technologies eventually become outdated, but basic market needs can last forever. A market-oriented mission statement defines the business in terms of satisfying basic customer needs. For example, 3M does more than just make adhesives, scientific equipment, and health care products. It solves people's problems by putting innovation to work for them. Cantel doesn't merely sell cellular phones, it is in the communications business. Likewise, eBay's mission isn't simply to hold online auctions. Instead, it connects individual buyers and sellers in "the world's online marketplace," a unique Web community in which they can shop, have fun, and get to know each other, for example, by chatting at the eBay Café.[8] Table 2-1 provides several other examples of product-oriented versus market-oriented business definitions.

> **Mission statement** A statement of the organization's purpose—what it wants to accomplish in the larger environment.

Table 2-1 Market-Oriented Business Definitions

Company	Product-Oriented Definition	Market-Oriented Definition
M·A·C Cosmetics	We make cosmetics.	We sell lifestyle and self-expression; tolerance of diversity, and a platform for the outrageous.
Zellers	We run discount stores.	We offer products and services that deliver superior value to Canadians.
Canadian Tire	We sell tools and home improvement items.	We provide advice and solutions that transform people into do-it-yourselfers.

Norco
www.norco.com

Management should avoid making its mission too narrow or too broad. A pencil manufacturer that says it is in the communication equipment business is stating its mission too broadly. A mission should be *realistic*. WestJet would be deluding itself if it adopted the mission to become the world's largest airline. A mission should also be *specific*. Many mission statements are written for public relations purposes and lack specific, workable guidelines. Too often, companies develop mission statements that look much like this tongue-and-cheek version:

We are committed to serving the quality of life of cultures and communities everywhere, regardless of sex, age, sexual preference, religion, or disability, whether they be customers, suppliers, employees, or shareholders—we serve the planet—to the highest ethical standards of integrity, best practice, and sustainability, through policies of openness and transparency vetted by our participation in the International Quality Business Global Audit forum, to ensure measurable outcomes worldwide....[9]

Such generic statements sound good but provide little real guidance or inspiration. In contrast, Celestial Seasonings' mission statement is very specific: "Our mission is to grow and dominate the U.S. specialty tea market by exceeding consumer expectations with the best tasting, 100 percent natural hot and iced teas, packaged with Celestial art and philosophy, creating the most valued tea experience...."[10]

Missions should fit the *market environment*. McDonald's could probably enter the solar energy business, but that would not take advantage of its core competence—providing low-cost food and fast service to large groups of customers.

Finally, mission statements should be *motivating*. A company's mission should not be stated as the desire to increase sales or profits—profits are only a reward for undertaking a useful activity. A company's employees need to feel that their work is significant and that it contributes to people's lives. One study found that "visionary companies" set a purpose beyond making money. Andyne Computing Limited, one of Canada's most successful software companies, captures its aspirations for the future in its mission statement: "Our mission is to be a world leader in providing information access and decision support for informed business decisions."[11]

New Directions 2-2 >>   **Norco: Performance Is Their Mission**

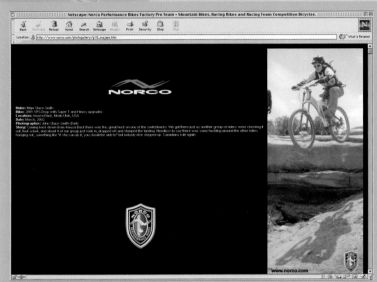

Quality:
Continually bettering our standards for performance and safety.

Dedication to Service:
Building a strong team to do what it takes to meet internal and external Customer needs.

Innovation:
Developing new products and new ways of doing business.

Fiscal Responsibility:
Managing our resources wisely, with a vision committed to long term growth and stability

Our Customers:
We will be the number one supplier to our customers, partnering with them in the adventure of cycling.

Our Products:
We will be an industry leader in developing and delivering innovative performance products.

Our People:
People are our greatest asset. We will provide a rewarding and challenging environment where our employees and the company can grow together on a progressive basis.

Our Profitability:
We will maintain the financial stability of the company and ensure an adequate return on investment for our shareholders.

Source: Norco's Company Profile, accessed online at **www.norco.com/profile/index.htm**, 26 September 2002.

Norco, a British Columbia–based manufacturer and marketer of performance bikes with an international reputation, has developed an extensive expression of company mission and values that includes customers, employees, and stakeholders.

Our Mission
We are dedicated to building rewarding, long-term relationships with our Customers, our Employees, and our Suppliers. We are driven by our customers to supply innovative cycle products and outstanding service and marketing support that will promote their growth and success.

Our Values
Respect and Integrity: Dealing fairly, openly and honestly with our Employees, our Customers, and our Suppliers.

DESIGNING THE BUSINESS PORTFOLIO

Guided by the company's mission statement and objectives, management now must plan its **business portfolio**—the collection of businesses and products that compose the company. The best business portfolio is the one that best fits the company's strengths and weaknesses to opportunities in the environment. The company must (1) analyze its *current* business portfolio and decide which businesses

Business Portfolio The collection of businesses and products that compose the company.

should receive more, less, or no investment, and (2) develop growth strategies for adding *new* products or businesses to the portfolio.

Analyzing the Current Business Portfolio

Portfolio analysis A tool management uses to identify and evaluate the businesses that compose the company.

Gemeral Electric
www.ge.com/canada

The major activity in strategic planning is business **portfolio analysis**, whereby management identifies and evaluates the businesses that compose the company. The company will want to put strong resources into its more profitable businesses and scale down or drop its weaker ones. An excellent example is General Electric. Through skillful management of its portfolio of businesses, General Electric has grown into one of the world's largest and most profitable companies. Over the past two decades, GE has shed many low-performing businesses, such as air conditioning and housewares. It kept only those businesses that could be number one or number two in their industries. At the same time, it acquired profitable businesses in broadcasting (NBC Television), financial services (Kidder, Peabody Investment Bank), and several other industries. GE now operates 49 business units selling an incredible variety of products and services—from consumer electronics, financial services, and television broadcasting to aircraft engines, plastics, industrial power, and a global Internet trading network. Superb management of this diverse portfolio has earned GE shareholders a 29 percent average annual return over the past 10 years.[12]

Management's first step is to identify the company's strategic business units (SBU). Remember, an SBU is a unit of the company that has a separate mission and objectives and that can be planned independently from other company businesses. An SBU can be a company division, a product line within a division, or sometimes a single product or brand.

The next step in business portfolio analysis calls for management to assess the attractiveness of its various SBUs and decide how much support each deserves. In some companies, this is done informally. Management looks at the company's collection of businesses or products and judges how much each SBU should contribute and receive. Other companies use formal portfolio-planning methods.

The business portfolio: Through skillful management of its portfolio of businesses, General Electric has grown into one of the world's largest and most profitable companies.

The purpose of strategic planning is to find ways that the company can best use its strengths to take advantage of attractive opportunities. Most standard portfolio-analysis methods evaluate SBUs on two important dimensions: (1) the attractiveness of the SBU's market or industry and (2) the strength of the SBU's position in that market or industry. The best-known portfolio-planning method was developed by the Boston Consulting Group, a leading management consulting firm.

Boston Consulting Group
www.bcg.com

The Boston Consulting Group Approach Using the Boston Consulting Group (BCG) approach, a company classifies all its SBUs according to the **growth-share matrix** shown in Figure 2-2. On the vertical axis, *market growth rate* provides a measure of market attractiveness. On the horizontal axis, *relative market share* serves as a measure of company strength in the market. By dividing the growth-share matrix as indicated, four types of SBUs can be distinguished:

Growth-share matrix A portfolio-planning method that evaluates a company's strategic business units in terms of their market growth rate and relative market share. SBUs are classified as stars, cash cows, question marks, or dogs.

- *Stars.* Stars are high-growth, high-share businesses or products. They often need heavy investment to finance their rapid growth. Eventually their growth will slow down, and they will turn into cash cows.

- *Cash cows.* Cash cows are low-growth, high-share businesses or products. These established and successful SBUs need less investment to hold their market share. Thus, they produce a lot of cash that the company uses to pay its bills and to support other SBUs that need investment.

- *Question marks.* Question marks are low-share business units in high-growth markets. They require a lot of cash to hold their share, let alone increase it. Management has to think hard about which question marks it should try to build into stars and which it should phase out.

- *Dogs.* Dogs are low-growth, low-share businesses and products. They may generate enough cash to maintain themselves but do not promise to be large sources of cash.

The 10 circles in the growth-share matrix represent a company's 10 current SBUs. The company has two stars, two cash cows, three question marks, and three

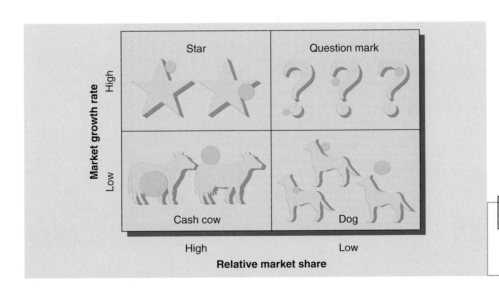

Figure 2.2

The BCG Growth-Share Matrix

dogs. The areas of the circles are proportional to the SBU's dollar sales. This company is in fair shape, although not in good shape. It wants to invest in the more promising question marks to make them stars and to maintain the stars so that they will become cash cows as their markets mature. Fortunately, it has two good-sized cash cows whose income helps finance the company's question marks, stars, and dogs. The company should take some decisive action concerning its dogs and its question marks. The picture would be worse if the company had no stars, if it had too many dogs, or if it had only one weak cash cow.

Once it has classified its SBUs, the company must determine what role each will play in the future. One of four strategies can be pursued for each SBU. The company can invest more in the business unit to *build* its share. Or it can invest just enough to *hold* the SBU's share at the current level. It can *harvest* the SBU, milking its short-term cash flow regardless of the long-term effect. Finally, the company can *divest* the SBU by selling it or phasing it out and using the resources elsewhere.

As time passes, SBUs change their positions in the growth-share matrix. Each SBU has a life cycle. Many SBUs start out as question marks and move into the star category if they succeed. They later become cash cows as market growth falls, then finally die off or turn into dogs toward the end of their life cycle. The company needs to add new products and units continually so that some of them will become stars and, eventually, cash cows that will help finance other SBUs.

Problems with Matrix Approaches The BCG method and other formal methods revolutionized strategic planning. However, such approaches have limitations. They can be difficult, time consuming, and costly to implement. Management may find it difficult to define SBUs and measure market share and growth. In addition, these approaches focus on classifying *current* businesses but provide little advice for *future* planning. Management must still rely on its own judgment to set the business objectives for each SBU, to determine what resources each will be given, and to figure out which new businesses should be added.

Despite such problems, and although many companies have dropped formal matrix methods in favour of more customized approaches that are better suited to their situations, most companies remain firmly committed to strategic planning. It can help management to understand the company's overall situation, to see how each business or product contributes, to assign resources to its businesses, and to orient the company for future success.

Developing Growth Strategies in the Age of Connectedness

Beyond evaluating current businesses, designing the business portfolio involves finding businesses and products the company should consider in the future. Companies need growth if they are to compete more effectively, satisfy their stakeholders, and attract top talent. "Growth is pure oxygen," states one executive. "It creates a vital, enthusiastic corporation where people see genuine opportunity.... In that way, growth is more than our single most important financial driver; it's an essential part of our corporate culture." At the same time, a firm must be careful not to make growth itself an objective. The company's objective must be "profitable growth."

Marketing has the main responsibility for achieving profitable growth for the company. Marketing must identify, evaluate, and select market opportunities and lay down strategies for capturing them. One useful device for identifying growth opportunities is the **product–market expansion grid**,[13] shown in Figure 2-3. We apply it here to Tim Horton's (see New Directions 2-3).

Product–market expansion grid A portfolio-planning tool for identifying company growth opportunities through market penetration, market development, product development, or diversification.

	Existing products	New products
Existing markets	1. Market penetration	3. Product development
New markets	2. Market development	4. Diversification

Figure 2.3

The Product–Market Expansion Grid

New Directions 2-3 >> Tim Horton's: Where Things Are Really Perking

Canadians, it appears, *always have time for Tim Horton's*. Generations of competitors have come and gone, but none have managed to defeat Tim Horton's, headquartered in Oakville, Ontario. In fact, it has become a Canadian icon. The doughnut chain's long-running "Roll up the Rim to Win" promotion has become a beloved part of Canadian slang, and scenes in Tim Horton's are shown weekly on the comedy news show *This Hour Has 22 Minutes*. The dominance of the chain can be seen in these facts: One of every three cups of coffee sold in Canada comes from Tim Horton's, and each and every day Canadians dunk more than three million doughnuts. It is one of Canada's largest employers, with more than 42 000 people on the payroll. The firm has been remarkably successful in the past few years. Sales increased by 10.4 percent in 1998, on top of an 8 percent increase a year earlier.

As impressive as these figures are, one has to wonder how Tim Horton's has achieved this success, offering such standard products as coffee and baked goods. Horton's strategy is deceptively simple. First, it has followed one consistent product and positioning strategy throughout its history. Its promise of "Always Fresh"

Tim Hortons doesn't advertise until it has enough outlets in a region to justify the expense. It knows advertising has more impact when people can see its outlets in their daily travels.

is never broken. Next, it builds outlets in focal areas until they reach a large enough critical mass to justify advertising. As Patti Jameson, director of corporate communications, notes, "Advertising is a lot more relevant to people when they actually see the stores on the street." Having the physical presence of a retail outlet made brand messages more relevant and meaningful.

Horton's spends about $3 million a year on advertising, which has been important to its growth strategy. Throughout much of the 1990s, the chain's ads focused on its new products—bagels, sandwiches, and soup—to get consumers to see Tim Horton's as more than a doughnut shop. New products also increased revenues for both the corporation and its franchisees. Advertising served to build the brand message that Horton's is "relaxed, caring, friendly, and honest."

To further strengthen the equity of the brand, "feel-good advertising" followed the more traditional product advertising. The True Stories campaign (by Toronto agency Enterprise Advertising), which was launched in 1997, worked to build an emotional connection between Horton's and its customers. For example, musician Natalie MacMaster told viewers about her first cup of coffee—from Tim Horton's, of course. Another ad featured the crew of the *HMCS Toronto* and described how much they missed Tim's coffee while they were stationed in the Persian Gulf. Another ad even featured a four-legged customer, Sammi, a golden retriever, who picks up her owner's coffee from the drive-through.

Given Tim Horton's track record, it's hard to imagine how it could expand any further. There seems to be an outlet on the corner of every major intersection. This is not surprising, given that the chain boasts more than 1700 Canadian outlets. Yet even an institution needs to be willing to change and grow. And change is exactly what Horton's has done

in recent years. In a bid to broaden its appeal and attract more women and young people, the chain has recently branched out into new product lines, such as iced cappuccino. It also retooled its lunchtime offerings last fall, offering Tim's Own brand of soups and sandwiches.

The firm isn't about to stop there. Tim Horton's plans to open between 170 and 175 new locations across Canada. It is also using the clout of its partner-owner, Wendy's, to tap into the U.S. market. Since Horton's believes that the breakfast category is underdeveloped in the United States and that Americans are poorly served by current "morning destinations," it sees tremendous opportunity south of the border. "In the U.S., they don't have high expectations for morning destinations…. People will grab a coffee from a gas station in the morning, [but] we're promising that consistent experience. No one else is really doing everyday morning coffee and baked goods very well." Two television spots and a series of radio ads each will portray Tim Horton's as the real reason morning people are so chipper. The tag line is: "Morning people. Where do they come from?" Although success in the highly competitive U.S. market is far from guaranteed, if the history of professional hockey offers any indication, then Americans may also soon be claiming this Canadian institution as their own.

Sources: Natalie Bahadur, "Tim Horton's Plans Aggressive Roll-Out," *Strategy*, 29 March 1999:7; Lesley Daw, "More Than Just a Doughnut Shop," *Marketing Magazine* (Online edition), 27 December 1999; Scott Gardiner, "In Praise of Saint Timmy," *Marketing Magazine* (Online edition), 21 August 2000; Laura Pratt, "Roll up the Rim Major Player for Tim Horton's," *Strategy*, 22 May 2000:22; Craig Saunders, "Tim Horton's Issues Wakeup Call," *Strategy*, 14 February 2000:25; Sinclair Stewart, "Top Client, Retail–Restaurants: Tim Horton's Brews up Fresh Ideas," *Strategy*, 2 August 1999:7; Sinclair Stewart, "Tim Horton's Brews New U.S. Campaign," *Strategy*, 27 September 1999:3.

Market penetration A strategy for company growth by increasing sales of current products to current market segments without changing the product.

Tim Horton's strategy is deceptively simple and has long been founded on **market penetration**. It works to open a critical mass of outlets in a geographic region, and then it supports them with advertising. Increased awareness and the building of strong brand equity in turn builds requests for new franchises—this is how Tim Horton's plans to continue expansion in both Quebec and Western Canada. It also works to train people who come into Tim Horton's first thing in the morning for coffee and breakfast to return several times during the rest of the day. To that end, Horton's routinely upgrades and refurbishes its outlets, adding double drive-throughs and establishing satellite outlets in settings like hospitals and retail stores—bringing the restaurant to the consumer instead of the other way around. "Wherever you are," says one top manager, "there's a coffee and a donut waiting for you."

Second, Tim Horton's management focuses on **product development**—offering modified or new products to current markets. Horton's introduced bagels, sandwiches, and soup to get consumers to see it as more than a doughnut shop.

Third, the firm explores possibilities for **market development**—identifying and developing new markets for its current products. It has recently moved south of the border, opening 116 outlets in the northern United States.

Tim Horton's could also consider **diversification**. It could start up or buy businesses outside its current products and markets. For example, like Loblaws, it could begin offering financial services. It could leverage its strong brand name onto products like sportswear that fits with its friendly, relaxed image. However, it must take care: Companies that diversify too broadly into unfamiliar products or industries can lose their market focus.

Planning Cross-Functional Strategies

The company's strategic plan establishes what kinds of businesses the company will be in and its objectives for each. Then, within each business unit, more detailed planning must take place. The major functional departments in each unit—marketing, finance, accounting, purchasing, manufacturing, information systems, human resources, and others—must work together to accomplish strategic objectives.

Marketing's Role in Strategic Planning Much overlap exists between overall company strategy and marketing strategy. Marketing looks at consumer needs and the company's ability to satisfy them; these same factors guide the company's overall mission and objectives.

Marketing plays a key role in the company's strategic planning in several ways. First, marketing provides a guiding *philosophy*—the marketing concept—that suggests company strategy should revolve around serving the needs of important consumer groups. Second, marketing provides *inputs* to strategic planners by helping to identify attractive market opportunities and by assessing the firm's potential to take advantage of them. Finally, within individual business units, marketing designs *strategies* for reaching the unit's objectives. Once the unit's objectives are set, marketing's task is to carry them out profitably.

Marketing and the Other Business Functions Customer value and satisfaction are important ingredients in the marketer's formula for success. However, as we noted in Chapter 1, marketing alone cannot produce superior value for customers. *All* departments must work together in this important task. Each company department can be thought of as a link in the company's **value chain**;[14] that is, each department carries out value-creating activities to design, produce, market, deliver, and support the firm's products. The firm's success depends not only on how well each department performs its work, but also on how well the activities of various departments are coordinated.

For example, Wal-Mart's goal is to create customer value and satisfaction by providing shoppers with the products they want at the lowest possible prices.

Product development A strategy for company growth by offering modified or new products to current market segments.

Market development A strategy for company growth by identifying and developing new market segments for current company products.

Diversification A strategy for company growth by starting up or acquiring businesses outside the company's current products and markets.

Value chain The series of departments that carry out value-creating activities to design, produce, market, deliver, and support a firm's products.

Marketers at Wal-Mart play an important role. They learn what customers need and want and stock the store's shelves with the desired products at unbeatable low prices. They prepare advertising and merchandising programs and assist shoppers with customer service. Through these and other activities, Wal-Mart's marketers help deliver value to customers. However, the marketing department needs help from the company's other departments. For example, Wal-Mart's ability to offer the right products at low prices depends on the purchasing department's skill in tracking down the needed suppliers and buying from them at low cost. Similarly, Wal-Mart's information systems department must provide fast and accurate information about which products are selling in each store. And its operations people must provide effective, low-cost merchandise handling.

A company's value chain is only as strong as its weakest link. Thus, success depends on how well each department performs its work of adding value for customers and on how well the activities of various departments are coordinated. At Wal-Mart, if purchasing can't wring the lowest prices from suppliers or if operations can't distribute merchandise at the lowest costs, then marketing can't deliver on its promise of lowest prices.

> Creating value for buyers is much more than a "marketing function"; rather, [it's] analogous to a symphony orchestra in which the contribution of each subgroup is tailored and integrated by a conductor—with a synergistic effect. A seller must draw upon and integrate effectively…its entire human and other capital resources.[15]

Marketing and Its Partners in the Marketing System In its search for competitive advantage, the firm needs to look beyond its own value chain and into the value chains of its suppliers, distributors, and, ultimately, customers. More companies today are partnering with the other members of the marketing system to improve the performance of the entire customer **value delivery network**.

For example, Magna International provides many of the components of the Ford Explorer SUV. Seats, metal underbody stampings and assemblies, front and

---

Value delivery network The network made up of the company, suppliers, distributors, and ultimately customers who partner with one another to improve the performance of the entire system.

Magna International
www.magnaint.com

The value chain: Wal-Mart's ability to offer the right products at low prices depends on the contributions from people in all of the company's departments—marketing, purchasing, information systems, and operations.

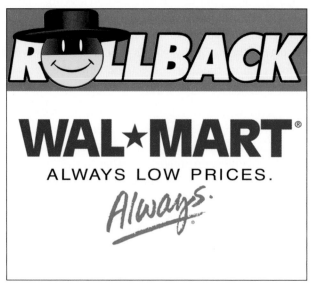

rear door panels, fuel filter, door latches, radiator assemblies, and various engine components are designed, manufactured, and delivered according to Ford's (the customer) requirements. This is one way to create customer value—by actually partnering with organizations. A company can also partner by performing all functions. Magna Steyr, one of Magna's European Divisions, contracts with organizations to perform complete niche vehicle assembly. Magna Steyr recently partnered with BMW to develop and manufacture the new BMW X3 Sports Activity Vehicle. Engineers from the BMW Group worked out the detailed vehicle concept and forwarded it to Magna Steyr Engineering for series development. Magna Steyr Fahrzeugtechnik in Graz, Austria, then took over production.[16]

This is a good place to pause for a moment to think about and apply what you've read in the first part of this chapter.
- Why are we talking about companywide strategic planning so early in a marketing text? What *does* strategic planning have to do with marketing?
- What are Norco's mission and strategy? What role does marketing play in helping Norco to accomplish this mission and strategy?
- What roles do other functional departments play, and how can Norco marketers work more effectively with these other functions to maximize overall customer value?

THE MARKETING PROCESS

The strategic plan defines the company's overall mission and objectives. Within each business unit, marketing plays a role in helping to accomplish the overall strategic objectives. Marketing's role and activities in the organization are shown in Figure 2-4, which summarizes the entire **marketing process** and the forces influencing company marketing strategy.

Target consumers are in the centre. The goal is to build strong and profitable connections with these consumers. The company first identifies the total market, then divides it into smaller segments, selects the most promising segments, and focuses on serving and satisfying these segments. It designs a marketing mix made up of factors under its control—product, price, place, and promotion. To find the best marketing mix and put it into action, the company engages in marketing analysis, planning, implementation, and control. Through these activities, the company watches and adapts to the actors and forces in the marketing environment. We will now look briefly at each element in the marketing process. In later chapters, we will discuss each element in more depth.

Marketing process The process of (1) analyzing marketing opportunities, (2) selecting target markets, (3) developing the marketing mix, and (4) managing the marketing effort.

Connecting with Consumers

To succeed in today's competitive marketplace, companies must be customer centred, winning customers from competitors, then keeping and growing them by delivering greater value. But before it can satisfy consumers, a company must first understand their needs and wants. Thus, sound marketing requires a careful analysis of consumers. Companies know that they cannot connect profitably with all consumers in a given market—at least not all consumers in the same way. There are

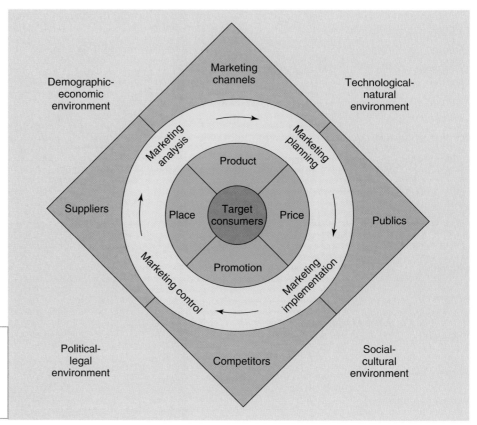

Figure 2.4

Factors Influencing Company Marketing Strategy

too many different kinds of consumers with too many different kinds of needs. Some companies are in a better position to serve certain segments of the market. Thus, each company must divide up the total market, choose the appropriate segments, and design strategies for profitably serving those chosen segments better than its competitors do. This process involves three steps: *market segmentation, market targeting,* and *market positioning.*

Terry Ortt, president of Canada's Journey's End Corp., understands the need for this type of information. Although conventional wisdom suggested that Journey's End customers were mainly businesspeople on two-day trips, after digging through 10 million guest registration cards, Ortt discovered that this was a misconception. Forty-five percent of Journey's End guests were people visiting cities from rural areas. Understanding the value of this information, Ortt developed a sophisticated database to track guests' needs and wants—from the time they request wake-up calls to what they eat for breakfast. The power of a database lies in its ability to track customers' actual behaviour rather than their intentions or what they say they do. This information allows the firm to provide the unique services demanded by individual guests, reward them for repeat visits and multiple-night stays, and target promotional information on specials to each guest by name.[17]

Market Segmentation The market consists of many types of customers, products, and needs, and the marketer has to determine which segments offer the best opportunity for achieving company objectives. Consumers can be grouped and served in various ways based on geographic, demographic, psychographic, and behavioural factors. The process of dividing a market into distinct groups of buyers with different needs, characteristics, or behaviour who might need separate products or marketing mixes is called **market segmentation**.

Every market has segments, but not all ways of segmenting a market are equally useful. For example, Tylenol would gain little by distinguishing between male and female users of pain relievers if both respond the same way to marketing efforts. A **market segment** consists of consumers who respond in a similar way to a given set of marketing efforts. In the car market, for example, consumers who choose the biggest, most comfortable car regardless of price make up one market segment. Another segment is customers who care mainly about price and operating economy. It would be difficult to make one model of car that was the first choice of every consumer. Companies are wise to focus their efforts on meeting the distinct needs of one or more market segments.

Market segmentation Dividing a market into distinct groups with distinct needs, characteristics, or behaviour that might need separate products or marketing mixes.

Market segment A group of consumers who respond in a similar way to a given set of marketing efforts.

Market Targeting After a company has defined market segments, it can enter one or many segments of a given market. **Market targeting** involves evaluating each market segment's attractiveness and selecting one or more segments to enter. A company should target segments in which it can profitably generate the greatest customer value and sustain it over time. A company with limited resources might decide to serve only one or a few special segments or "market niches." This strategy limits sales but can be very profitable. Or a company might choose to serve several related segments—perhaps those with different kinds of customers but with the

Market targeting The process of evaluating each market segment's attractiveness and selecting one or more segments to enter.

Positioning: Bentley promises "shameless luxury." In contrast, Toyota promises that, with its excellent mileage, "it's not you. It's the car." Such deceptively simple statements form the backbone of a product's marketing strategy.

same basic wants. Or a large company might decide to offer a complete range of products to serve all market segments.

Most companies enter a new market by serving a single segment, and if this proves successful, they add segments. Large companies eventually seek full market coverage. They want to be the General Motors of their industry. GM says that it makes a car for every "person, purse, and personality." The leading company normally has different products designed to meet the special needs of each segment.

Market Positioning   After a company has decided which market segments to enter, it must decide what positions it wants to occupy in those segments. A product's *position* is the place the product occupies in consumers' minds relative to competitors. If a product is perceived to be exactly like another product on the market, consumers have no reason to buy it.

Market positioning
Arranging for a product to occupy a clear, distinctive, and desirable place relative to competing products in the minds of target consumers.

Market positioning is arranging for a product to occupy a clear, distinctive, and desirable place relative to competing products in the minds of target consumers. Thus, marketers plan positions that distinguish their products from competing brands and give them the greatest strategic advantage in their target markets. For example, the Ford Taurus is "built to last"; Chevy Blazer is "like a rock"; and Saturn is "a different kind of company, different kind of car." Lexus avows "the passionate pursuit of excellence," Jaguar is positioned as "the art of performance," and Mercedes says, "In a perfect world, everyone would drive a Mercedes." Toyota's economical Echo states, "it's not you. It's the car"; while the luxurious Bentley promises "handcrafted...shameless luxury." Such deceptively simple statements form the backbone of a product's marketing strategy.

In positioning its product, the company first identifies possible competitive advantages on which to build the position. To gain competitive advantage, the company must offer greater value to chosen target segments, either by charging lower prices than competitors do or by offering more benefits to justify higher prices. But if the company positions the product as *offering* greater value, it must then *deliver* that greater value. Thus, effective positioning begins with actually *differentiating* the company's marketing offer so that it gives consumers more value than they are offered by the competition. Once the company has chosen a position, it must take strong steps to deliver and communicate that position to target consumers. The company's entire marketing program should support the chosen positioning strategy.

When Cadbury's Canadian division launched a new chocolate bar, Time Out, it used an integrated, multimedia campaign. Its positioning statement for the product could have been written as follows: For time-pressed adults (the target market) who need an energy boost (statement of need), Time Out (the brand) is the chocolate bar (product category) that offers the perfect way to take a break (key benefit or reason to buy). Unlike rich, heavy chocolate bars (competitive offerings), our product is a light wafer snack with a chocolate wave (statement of differentiation).

Developing the Marketing Mix

Marketing mix The set of controllable tactical marketing tools—product, price, place, and promotion—that the firm blends to produce the response it wants in the target market.

Once the company has decided on its overall competitive marketing strategy, it is ready to begin planning the details of the marketing mix, one of the major concepts in modern marketing. The **marketing mix** is the set of controllable, tactical mar-

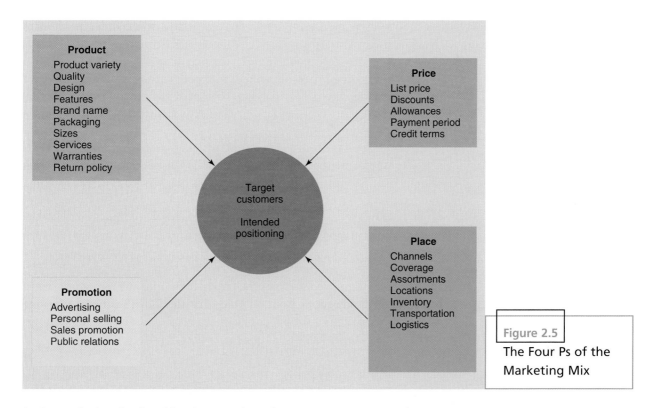

Product
Product variety
Quality
Design
Features
Brand name
Packaging
Sizes
Services
Warranties
Return policy

Price
List price
Discounts
Allowances
Payment period
Credit terms

Target
customers

Intended
positioning

Promotion
Advertising
Personal selling
Sales promotion
Public relations

Place
Channels
Coverage
Assortments
Locations
Inventory
Transportation
Logistics

Figure 2.5
The Four Ps of the
Marketing Mix

keting tools that the firm blends to produce the response it wants in the target market. The marketing mix consists of everything the firm can do to influence the demand for its product. The many possibilities are collected into four groups of variables known as the "four Ps": *product, price, place,* and *promotion.*[18]

Product is the goods-and-services combination the company offers to the target market. Thus, a Ford Taurus product consists of nuts and bolts, spark plugs, pistons, headlights, and thousands of other parts. Ford offers several Taurus styles and dozens of optional features. The car comes fully serviced and with a comprehensive warranty that is as much a part of the product as the tailpipe.

Price is the amount of money customers must pay to obtain the product. Ford calculates suggested retail prices that its dealers can charge for each Taurus. But Ford dealers rarely charge the full sticker price. Instead, they negotiate the price with each customer, offering discounts, trade-in allowances, and credit terms to adjust for the current competitive situation and to bring the price into line with the buyer's perception of the car's value.

Place includes company activities that make the product available to target consumers. Ford maintains a large body of independently owned dealerships that sell the company's many different models. Ford selects its dealers carefully and supports them strongly. The dealers keep an inventory of Ford automobiles, demonstrate them to potential buyers, negotiate prices, close sales, and service the cars after the sale.

Promotion is the activities that communicate the merits of the product and persuade target customers to buy it. Ford spends more than $850 million worldwide annually on advertising to tell consumers about the company and its many products. Dealership salespeople assist potential buyers and persuade them that Ford is the best car for them. Ford and its dealers offer special promotions—sales, cash rebates, low financing rates—as added purchase incentives.

An effective marketing program blends all elements of the marketing mix into a coordinated plan designed to achieve the company's marketing objectives by delivering value to consumers. The marketing mix constitutes the company's tactical tool kit for establishing strong positioning in target markets.

Some critics feel that the four Ps may omit or underemphasize some important activities. For example, they ask, "Where are services?" Just because they don't start with a P doesn't justify omitting them. The answer is that services, such as banking, airline, and retailing services, are products too. We might call them *service products*. "Where is packaging?" the critics might ask. Marketers would answer that they include packaging as just one of many product decisions. As Figure 2-5 suggests, many marketing activities that might appear to be left out of the marketing mix are subsumed under one of the four Ps. The issue is not whether there should be four, six, or ten Ps but what framework is most helpful in designing marketing programs.

Another concern, however, is valid. It holds that the four Ps concept takes the seller's view of the market, not the buyer's view. From the buyer's viewpoint, in this age of connectedness, the four Ps might be better described as the four Cs.[19]

4Ps	4Cs
Product	Customer solution
Price	Customer cost
Place	Convenience
Promotion	Communication

Thus, although marketers see themselves as selling products, customers see themselves as buying value or solutions to their problems. And customers are interested in more than just the price; they are interested in the total costs of obtaining, using, and disposing of a product. Customers want the product and service to be as conveniently available as possible. Finally, they want two-way communication. Marketers would do well to first think through the four Cs and then build the four Ps on that platform.

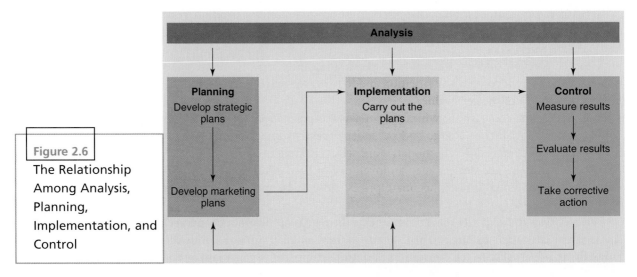

Figure 2.6

The Relationship Among Analysis, Planning, Implementation, and Control

MANAGING THE MARKETING EFFORT

The company wants to design and put into action the marketing mix that will best achieve its objectives in its target markets. Figure 2-6 shows the relationship among the four marketing management functions—*analysis, planning, implementation,* and *control.* The company first develops overall strategic plans, then translates these companywide strategic plans into marketing and other plans for each division, product, and brand. Through implementation, the company turns the plans into actions. Control consists of measuring and evaluating the results of marketing activities and taking corrective action where needed. Finally, marketing analysis provides the information and evaluations needed for all the other marketing activities.

Marketing Analysis

Managing the marketing function begins with a complete analysis of the company's situation. The company must analyze its markets and marketing environment to find attractive opportunities and to avoid environmental threats. It must analyze company strengths and weaknesses, as well as current and possible marketing actions, to determine which opportunities it can best pursue. Marketing provides input to each of the other marketing management functions.

Marketing Planning

Through strategic planning, the company decides what it wants to do with each business unit. Marketing planning involves deciding on marketing strategies that will help the company reach its overall strategic objectives. A detailed marketing plan is needed for each business, product, or brand. What does a marketing plan look like? Our discussion focuses on product or brand plans.

Table 2-2 outlines the major sections of a typical product or brand plan. The plan begins with an executive summary, which quickly overviews major assess-

Marketers must continually plan their analysis, implementation, and control of activities.

Table 2-2   Contents of a Marketing Plan

Section	Purpose
Executive summary	Presents a brief summary of the main goals and recommendations of the plan for management review, helping top management to find the plan's major points quickly. A table of contents should follow the executive summary.
Current marketing situation	Describes the target market and the company's position in it, including information about the market, product performance, competition, and distribution. this section includes •· A *market description* that defines the market and major segments, reviews customer needs, and outlines factors in the marketing environment that may affect customer purchasing. •· A *product review* that shows sales, prices, and gross margins of the major products in the product line. •· A review of *competition* that identifies major competitors and assesses their market positions and strategies for product quality, pricing, distribution, and promotion. •· A review of *distribution* that evaluates recent sales trends and other developments in major distribution channels.
Threat and opportunity analysis	Assesses major threats and opportunities that the product may face, helping management to anticipate important positive or negative developments that may affect the firm and its strategies.
Objectives and issues	States the marketing objectives that the company would like to attain during the plan's term and discusses key issues that will affect their attainment. For example, if the goal is to achieve a 15 percent market share, the key issue is how market share can be increased.
Marketing strategy	Outlines the broad marketing logic by which the business unit hopes to achieve its marketing objectives and the specifics of target markets, positioning, and marketing expenditure levels. It outlines specific strategies for each marketing mix element and explains how each responds to the threats, opportunities, and critical issues spelled out earlier in the plan.
Action program	Indicates how marketing strategies will be turned into specific action programs that answer the following questions: *What* will be done? *When* will it be done? *Who* is responsible for doing it? *How much* will it cost?
Budgets	Details a supporting marketing budget that is essentially a projected profit-and-loss statement. It shows expected revenues (forecast number of units sold and the average net price) and expected costs (of production, distribution, and marketing). The difference is the projected profit. Once approved by higher management, the budget is the basis for materials buying, production scheduling, personnel planning, and marketing operations.
Controls	Outlines the controls that will be used to monitor progress and allow higher management to review implementation results and spot products that are not meeting their goals.

ments, goals, and recommendations. The main section of the plan presents a detailed analysis of the current marketing situation as well as potential threats and opportunities. It next states major objectives for the brand and outlines the specifics of a marketing strategy for achieving them.

A **marketing strategy** is the marketing logic whereby the company hopes to achieve its marketing objectives. It consists of specific strategies for target markets,

Marketing strategy The marketing logic by which the business unit hopes to achieve its marketing objectives.

positioning, the marketing mix, and marketing expenditure levels. In this section, the planner explains how each strategy responds to the threats, opportunities, and critical issues spelled out earlier in the plan. Additional sections of the marketing plan lay out an action program for implementing the marketing strategy, along with the details of a supporting *marketing budget*. The last section outlines the controls that will be used to monitor progress and take corrective action.

A sample marketing plan for TAXIGUY, Inc., is included in Appendix I. TAXIGUY provides consumers with toll-free access to taxi services across Canada, and its "Operation Ossifer" involves sponsorship from Molson as part of Molson's responsible drinking and driving campaign.

Marketing Implementation

Planning good strategies is only part of successful marketing. A brilliant marketing strategy counts for little if the company fails to implement it properly. **Marketing implementation** is the process that turns marketing *plans* into marketing *actions* to accomplish strategic marketing objectives. Implementation involves daily and monthly activities that effectively put the marketing plan to work. Whereas marketing planning addresses the *what* and *why* of marketing activities, implementation addresses the *who, where, when,* and *how.*

Many managers think that "doing things right" (implementation) is as important as, or even more important than "doing the right things" (strategy). The fact is that both are critical to success.[20] However, companies can gain competitive advantages through effective implementation. One firm can have essentially the same strategy as another, yet win in the marketplace through faster or better execution. Still, implementation is difficult—it is often easier to create good marketing strategies than it is to carry them out.

In an increasingly connected world, people at all levels of the marketing system must work together to implement marketing plans and strategies. At Black & Decker, for example, marketing implementation for the company's power tool products requires daily decisions and actions by thousands of people both inside and outside the organization. Marketing managers make decisions about target segments (Black & Decker brand for the do-it-yourself or home segment and DeWalt Tools for the professional segment), branding, packaging, pricing, promoting, and distributing. They connect with people elsewhere in the company to get support for their products and programs. They talk with engineering about product design, with manufacturing about production and inventory levels, and with finance about funding and cash flows. They also connect with outside people, such as advertising agencies to plan ad campaigns and the media to obtain publicity support. The sales force urges Home Hardware, Rona-Revy, Home Depot, Wal-Mart, and other retailers to advertise Black & Decker products, provide ample shelf space, and use company displays.

Successful marketing implementation depends on how well the company blends its people, organizational structure, decision and reward systems, and company culture into a cohesive action program that supports its strategies. At all levels, employees must have the needed skills, motivation, and personal characteristics. The

Marketing implementation The process that turns marketing strategies and plans into marketing actions to accomplish strategic marketing objectives.

Black & Decker
www.blackanddecker.
com

company's formal organizational structure plays an important role in implementing marketing strategy; so do its decision and reward systems. For example, if a company's compensation system rewards managers for short-run profit results, they will have little incentive to work toward long-run market-building objectives.

Finally, to be successfully implemented, the firm's marketing strategies must fit with its company culture, the system of values and beliefs shared by people in the organization. A study of the most successful companies found that these companies have almost cultlike cultures built around strong, market-oriented missions. At companies such as Wal-Mart, Microsoft, Nordstrom, Citicorp, Procter & Gamble, Walt Disney, and Hewlett-Packard, "employees share such a strong vision that they know in their hearts what's right for their company."[21]

Marketing Department Organization

The company must design a marketing department that can carry out marketing strategies and plans. If the company is very small, one person might do all the marketing work—research, selling, advertising, customer service, and other activities. As the company expands, a marketing department organization emerges to plan and carry out marketing activities. In large companies, this department contains many specialists. Thus, Black & Decker has product and market managers, sales managers and salespeople, market researchers, advertising experts, and other specialists.

Modern marketing departments can be arranged in several ways. The most common form of marketing organization is the *functional organization* in which different marketing activities are headed by a functional specialist—a sales manager, advertising manager, marketing research manager, customer service manager, new-product manager. A company that sells across the country or internationally often uses a *geographic organization* in which its sales and marketing people are assigned to specific countries, regions, and districts. Geographic organization allows salespeople to settle into a territory, get to know their customers, and work with a minimum of travel time and cost.

Companies with many very different products or brands often create a *product management organization*. Using this approach, a product manager develops and implements a complete strategy and marketing program for a specific product or brand. Product management first appeared at Procter & Gamble in 1929. A new company soap, Camay, was not doing well, and a young P&G executive was assigned to give his exclusive attention to developing and promoting this product. He was successful, and the company soon added other product managers.[22] Since then, many firms, especially consumer products companies, have set up product management organizations. However, recent changes in the marketing environment have caused many companies to rethink the role of the product manager. Many companies are finding that today's marketing environment calls for less brand focus and more customer focus. They are shifting toward *customer equity management*—moving away from managing just product profitability and toward managing *customer* profitability.[23]

For companies that sell one product line to many different types of markets and customers that have different needs and preferences, a *market or customer man-*

agement organization might be best. A market management organization is similar to the product management organization. Market managers are responsible for developing marketing strategies and plans for their specific markets or customers. This system's main advantage is that the company is organized around the needs of specific customer segments.

Large companies that produce many different products flowing into many different geographic and customer markets usually employ some *combination* of the functional, geographic, product, and market organization forms. This ensures that each function, product, and market receives its share of management attention. However, it can also add costly layers of management and reduce organizational flexibility. Still, the benefits of organizational specialization usually outweigh the drawbacks.

Marketing Control

Because many surprises occur during the implementation of marketing plans, the marketing department must practise constant marketing control. **Marketing control** involves evaluating the results of marketing strategies and plans and taking corrective action to ensure that objectives are attained.

Figure 2-7 shows the four steps involved in marketing control. Management first sets specific marketing goals. It then measures its performance in the marketplace and evaluates the causes of any differences between expected and actual performance. Finally, management takes corrective action to close the gaps between its goals and its performance. This step may require changing the action programs or even changing the goals.

Operating control involves checking ongoing performance against the annual plan and taking corrective action when necessary. Its purpose is to ensure that the company achieves the sales, profits, and other goals set out in its annual plan. It also involves determining the profitability of different products, territories, markets, and channels.

Strategic control involves looking at whether the company's basic strategies are well matched to its opportunities. Marketing strategies and programs can quickly become outdated, and each company should periodically reassess its overall approach to the marketplace. A major tool for such strategic control is a **marketing audit**. The marketing audit is a comprehensive, systematic, independent, and periodic examination of a company's environment, objectives, strategies, and activities to determine problem areas and opportunities. The audit provides good input for a plan of action to improve the company's marketing performance.[24] The marketing audit covers *all* major marketing areas of a business, not just a few trouble spots. It assesses the marketing environment, marketing strategy, marketing organization, marketing systems,

Marketing control The process of measuring and evaluating the results of marketing strategies and plans, and taking corrective action to ensure that objectives are achieved.

Marketing audit A comprehensive, systematic, independent, and periodic examination of a company's environment, objectives, strategies, and activities to determine problem areas and opportunities and to recommend a plan of action to improve the company's marketing performance.

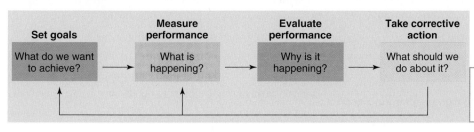

Set goals	Measure performance	Evaluate performance	Take corrective action
What do we want to achieve?	What is happening?	Why is it happening?	What should we do about it?

Figure 2-7

The Control Process

marketing mix, and marketing productivity and profitability. The audit is normally conducted by an objective and experienced outside party. The findings may come as a surprise—and sometimes as a shock—to management. Management then decides which actions make sense and how and when to implement them.

The Marketing Environment

Managing the marketing function would be hard enough if the marketer had to deal only with the controllable marketing mix variables. But the company operates in a complex marketing environment, consisting of uncontrollable forces to which the company must adapt. The environment produces both threats and opportunities. The company must carefully analyze its environment so that it can avoid the threats and take advantage of the opportunities.

The company's marketing environment includes forces close to the company that affect its ability to serve consumers, such as other company departments, channel members, suppliers, competitors, and the public. It also includes broader demographic and economic forces, political and legal forces, technological and ecological forces, and social and cultural forces. To connect effectively with consumers, others in the company, external partners, and the world around them, marketers need to consider all these forces when developing and positioning its offer to the target market. The marketing environment is discussed more fully in Chapter 4.

<< Looking Back   <   <   <   <   <   <   <   <   <

What have you learned so far? To this point, we've defined marketing and its core concepts and philosophies, examined marketing's role in an overall company strategy, overviewed the key elements of the marketing process, and outlined the major marketing management functions. You've had a pretty good overview of the fundamentals of marketing. In later chapters, we'll expand on these fundamentals.

Strategic planning sets the stage for the rest of the company's planning. Marketing contributes to strategic planning, and the overall plan defines marketing's role in the company. Although formal planning offers a variety of benefits to companies, not all companies use it or use it well. Although many discussions of strategic planning focus on large corporations, small business also can benefit greatly from sound strategic planning.

1. **Explain companywide strategic planning and its four steps.**

Strategic planning involves developing a strategy for long-run survival and growth. It consists of four steps: defining the company mission, setting objectives and goals, designing a business portfolio, and developing functional plans. *Defining a clear company mission* begins with drafting a formal mission statement, which should be market oriented, realistic, specific, motivating, and consistent with the market environment. The mission is then transformed into detailed *supporting goals and objectives* to guide the entire company. Based on those goals and objectives, head office designs a *business portfolio,* deciding which businesses and products should receive more or fewer resources. In turn, each business and product unit must develop detailed marketing plans in line with the companywide plan. Comprehensive and sound marketing plans support company strategic planning by detailing specific opportunities.

2. Discuss how to design business portfolios and develop growth strategies.

Guided by the company's mission statement and objectives, management plans its *business portfolio,* or the collection of businesses and products that make up the company. To produce a business portfolio that best fits the company's strengths and weaknesses to opportunities in the environment, the company must analyze and adjust its *current* business portfolio and develop growth strategies for adding *new* products or businesses to the portfolio. The company might use a formal portfolio-planning method like the *BCG growth-share matrix.* But many companies are now designing more customized portfolio-planning approaches that better suit their unique situations. The *product–market expansion grid* suggests four possible growth paths: market penetration, market development, product development, and diversification.

3. Explain functional planning strategies and marketing's role in strategic planning.

Once strategic objectives have been defined, management must prepare a set of *functional plans* that coordinates the activities of the marketing, finance, operations, and other departments. A company's success depends on how well each department performs its customer value-adding activities and on how well the departments work together to serve the customer. Each department has a different idea about which objectives and activities are most important. The marketing department stresses the consumer's point of view, whereas the operations department may be more concerned with reducing production costs. To best accomplish the firm's overall strategic objectives, marketing managers must understand other functional managers' points of view.

Marketing plays an important role throughout the strategic planning process. It provides *inputs* to strategic planning concerning attractive market possibilities, and marketing's customer focus serves as a guiding *philosophy* for planning. Marketers design *strategies* to help meet strategic objectives and pre-

pare programs to carry them out profitably. Marketing also plays an integrative role to help ensure that departments work together toward the goal of delivering superior customer value and satisfaction.

4. Describe the marketing process and the forces that influence it.

The *marketing process* matches consumer needs with the company's capabilities and objectives. Consumers are at the centre of the marketing process. The company divides the total market into smaller segments, selecting the segments it can best serve. It then designs a *marketing mix* to differentiate its marketing offer and position this offer in selected target segments. The marketing mix consists of product, price, place, and promotion decisions.

5. List the marketing management functions, including the elements of a marketing plan.

To find the best mix and put it into action, the company engages in marketing analysis, planning, implementation, and control. The main components of a *marketing plan* are the executive summary, current marketing situation, threats and opportunities, objectives and issues, marketing strategies, action programs, budgets, and controls. Planning good strategies is often easier than carrying them out. To be successful, companies must also be effective at *implementation*—turning marketing strategies into marketing actions.

Much of the responsibility for implementation goes to the company's marketing department. Modern marketing departments can be organized in one or a combination of ways: *functional marketing organization, geographic organization, product management organization,* or *market management organization.* Marketing organizations carry out *marketing control,* both operating control and strategic control. They use *marketing audits* to determine marketing opportunities and problems and to recommend short-run and long-run actions to improve overall marketing performance. Through these activities, the company watches and adapts to the marketing environment.

Navigating the Key Terms

Business portfolio, **p. 53**

Business unit strategy, **p. 47**

Corporate strategic planning, **p. 47**

Diversification, **p. 59**

Functional strategy, **p. 48**

Growth-share matrix, **p. 55**

Market development, **p. 59**

Market penetration, **p. 58**

Market positioning, **p. 64**

Market segment, **p. 63**

Market segmentation, **p. 63**

Market targeting, **p. 63**

Marketing audit, **p. 71**

Marketing control, **p. 71**

Marketing implementation, **p. 69**

Marketing mix, **p. 64**

Marketing process, **p. 61**

Marketing strategy, **p. 68**

Mission statement, **p. 51**

Portfolio analysis, **p. 54**

Product development, **p. 59**

Product–market expansion grid, **p. 57**

Strategic business unit (SBU), **p. 47**

Strategic planning, **p. 47**

Value chain, **p. 59**

Value delivery network, **p. 60**

Concept Check

Fill in the blanks and then check your answers.

1. _____ is the process of developing and maintaining a strategic fit between the organization's goals and capabilities and its changing marketing opportunities.

2. A _____ is a statement of the organization's purpose—what it wants to accomplish in the larger environment.

3. Management should avoid making its mission too narrow or too broad. According to this section of the text, missions should be _____, _____, fit the _____ _____, and be _____.

4. A business portfolio is the collection of businesses and products that make up the company. The best business portfolio is the one that _____ _____.

5. A company can classify all its SBUs according to a growth-share matrix. Four types of SBUs can usually be identified. The _____ are low-growth, high-share businesses or products. They produce a lot of cash that is used to support other SBUs.

6. Once a company has classified its SBUs, the company must determine what role each will play in the future. The company may choose one of four strategies. These strategies are to _____, _____, _____, or _____ the SBU.

7. When the marketing manager considers growth strategies, _____ would be chosen if the goal of the company wants to make more sales to current customers without changing products.

8. When each department within a firm carries out value-creating activities to design, produce, market, deliver, and support the firm's products, the department can be thought of as a link in the company's _____.

9. _____ is the process of dividing a market into distinct groups of buyers with different needs, characteristics, or behaviour who might require separate products or marketing mixes.

10. The four Ps of the marketing mix are _____, _____, _____, and _____.

11. The four marketing management functions are _____, _____, _____, and _____.

12. A _____ is the marketing logic whereby the company hopes to achieve its marketing objectives.

Concept Check Answers: 1. Strategic planning; 2. mission statement; 3. realistic, specific, market environ-ment, and motivating; 4. best fits the company's strengths and weaknesses to opportunities in the environment; 5. cash cows; 6. build, hold, harvest, or divest; 7. market penetration; 8. value chain; 9. Market segmentation; 10. product, price, place, and promotion; 11. analysis, planning, implementation, and control; 12. marketing strategy.

Discussing the Issues

1. Define strategic planning. List and briefly describe the four steps of the strategic-planning process.

2. In a series of job interviews, you ask three recruiters to describe the missions of their companies. One says, "to make profits." Another says, "to create customers." The third says, "to fight world hunger." Analyze and discuss what these mission statements tell you about each company. Which appears to be more *market oriented?* Explain and justify.

3. An electronics manufacturer obtains the semiconductors it uses in production from a company-owned subsidiary that also sells to other manufacturers. The subsidiary is smaller and less profitable than competing producers, and its growth rate has been below the industry average during the past five years. Define which cell of the BCG growth-share matrix this strategic business unit would fall into. Explain your choice. What should the parent company do with this SBU?

4. Beyond evaluating current businesses, designing the business portfolio involves finding businesses and products the company should consider in the future. Using the product–market expansion grid, illustrate the process that a company can use to evaluate a portfolio. Pick an example for your demonstration that is different from the one used in the text. Be sure your example covers all cells.

5. To succeed in today's marketplace, companies must be customer centred. Explain how (a) Cantel, (b) the Toronto Blue Jays, and (c) Mountain Equipment Co-op can use the processes of market segmentation, marketing targeting, and marketing positioning to become more customer centred. Suggest a "new" position for each organization and explain and justify the position you have suggested.

 Mastering Marketing

Building strategy is one of the most important tasks to be undertaken by the marketing manager. Using the product–market expansion grid shown in Figure 2-3 show how the products currently being produced might fit this grid. Next, suggest future product expansion using the grid cells. Justify your expansion alternative(s). Be specific in your comments.

Check out the enclosed Video case CD-ROM, or our Companion Website at www.pearsoned.ca/armstrong, to view a CBC video segment and case for this chapter.

MAP 2 Marketing Applications

Using his "Nothing but Net" philosophy, Oracle Corp. founder and CEO Larry Ellison has just about owned the Internet database management and corporate software business since Oracle's inception. However, change may be in the air. Even though his verbal wars with longtime nemesis Microsoft are famous and have grabbed the most headlines, his toughest war is about to be fought and his toughest competitor is knocking on Oracle's door. Who is this new rival? Big Blue—IBM! This sleeping giant has suddenly awakened and is hungry.

According to industry analysts, Oracle's corner on the very lucrative business market (estimated to be U.S. $80 billion) seems ripe for the taking. With stakes such as these, both of these industry giants are gearing up for battle. Each uses a different set of strategic tools. Oracle's strategy is to offer customers a complete and tightly integrated package of software that will fill all management needs. Using almost the reverse approach, IBM is backing what they call a "best-of-breed" approach in which they stitch together a quilt of business software programs from various companies, including themselves. Minor competitors are anxiously watching to see which approach industry will favour. If IBM wins, more business and applications may be available for all. Oracle's turnkey operation closes some of those doors.

IBM seems to be exploiting an Oracle weakness—it competes against many of its own partners in the database business. IBM presents itself as a neutral, noncompeting alternative. Even though Oracle is ahead at this point, IBM seems to have momentum on its side. To offset this momentum, Oracle has speeded up introduction of new products and applications and is raising doubt about IBM's credibility and intentions as a neutral, noncompeting partner. As both of these fierce competitors raise their battle flags, a similar battle cry seems to be coming from both camps—Charge!

Thinking Like a Marketing Manager

1. After visiting the Web sites for both IBM at **www.ibm.com/ca/** and Oracle at **www.oracle.ca**, write out what you perceive to be the mission, goals, or objectives for both organizations. How do these missions, goals, or objectives match their recent competitive moves?

2. After reading about the new products being offered by both companies in the business software and database management markets, construct a product–market expansion grid to indicate the direction each company seems to be taking.

3. Use outside sources to explore the personalities and careers of IBM's CEO Louis V. Gerstner, Jr., and Oracle's Lawrence J. Ellison. What insight does this give you into the strategies being used in this corporate struggle? What vulnerabilities are present? How could these be exploited by either party?

4. Pick one of the two combatants. Write a marketing strategy for your chosen company that will carry the firm toward 2010. Be sure to use the steps found in Figure 2-1 and the factors shown in Figure 2-4 in constructing your strategy. Report your ideas in class.

Digital Map

Visit our Web site at **www.pearsoned.ca/armstrong** for online quizzes, Internet exercises, and more!

CASE 2 TRAP-EASE: THE BIG CHEESE OF MOUSETRAPS

One April morning, Martha House, president of Trap-Ease, entered her office in Moncton, New Brunswick. She paused for a moment to contemplate the Ralph Waldo Emerson quotation that she had framed and hung near her desk: "If a man [can] make a better mousetrap than his neighbor . . . the world will make a beaten path to his door." Perhaps, she mused, Emerson knew something that she didn't. She had the better mousetrap—Trap-Ease—but the world didn't seem all that excited about it.

Martha had just returned from the National Hardware Show in Toronto. Standing in the trade show display booth for long hours and answering the same questions hundreds of times had been tiring. Yet, this show had excited her. Each year, National Hardware Show officials hold a contest to select the best new product introduced at the show. Of the more than 300 new products introduced at that year's show, her mousetrap had won first place. Such notoriety was not new for the Trap-Ease mousetrap. *Canadian Business* magazine had written an article about the mousetrap, and the television show *MarketPlace* and trade publications had featured it. Despite all this attention, however, the expected demand for the trap had not materialized. Martha hoped that this award might stimulate increased interest and sales.

A group of investors who had obtained worldwide rights to market the innovative mousetrap had formed Trap-Ease in January. In return for marketing rights, the group agreed to pay the inventor and patent holder, a retired rancher, a royalty fee for each trap sold. The group then hired Martha to serve as president and to develop and manage the Trap-Ease organization.

The Trap-Ease, a simple yet clever device, is manufactured by a plastics firm under contract with Trap-Ease. The trap consists of a square, plastic tube measuring about 15 cm long and 4 cm square. The tube bends in the middle at a 30-degree angle, so that when the front part of the tube rests on a flat surface, the other end is elevated. The elevated ends holds a removable cap into which the user places bait (cheese, dog food, or some other tidbit). A hinged door is attached to the front end of the tube. When the trap is "open," this door rests on two narrow "stilts" attached to the two bottom corners of the door.

The trap works with simple efficiency. A mouse, smelling the bait, enters the tube through the open end. As it walks up the angled bottom toward the bait, its weight makes the elevated end of the trap drop downward. This elevates the open end, allowing the hinged door to swing closed, trapping the mouse. Small teeth on the ends of the stilts catch in a groove on the bottom of the trap, locking the door closed. The mouse can be disposed of live, or it can be left alone for a few hours to suffocate in the trap.

Martha believed that the trap had many advantages for the consumer when compared with traditional spring-loaded traps or poisons. It appeals to consumers who want a humane alternative to spring traps. Furthermore, with Trap-Ease, consumers can avoid the unpleasant mess they encounter with the violent spring-loaded traps—there are no clean-up problems. Finally, the consumer can reuse the trap or simply throw it away.

Martha's early research suggested that women were the best target market for the Trap-Ease. Men, it seems, were more willing to buy and use the traditional, spring-loaded trap. The targeted women, however, did not like the traditional trap. They often stay at home and take care of their children. Thus, they want a means of dealing with the mouse problem that avoids the unpleasantness and risks that the standard trap creates in the home.

To reach this target market, Martha decided to distribute Trap-Ease through national grocery, hardware, and drug chains such as Safeway, Zellers, Canadian Tire, and Shoppers Drug Mart. She sold the trap directly to these large retailers, avoiding any wholesalers or other intermediaries.

The traps sold in packages of two, with a suggested retail price of $2.99. Although this price made the Trap-Ease about five times more expensive than smaller, standard traps, consumers appeared to offer little initial price resistance. The manufacturing cost for the Trap-Ease, including freight and packaging costs, was about 31 cents per unit. The company paid an additional 8.2 cents per unit in royalty fees. Martha priced the traps to retailers at $1.49 per unit and estimated that, after sales and volume discounts, Trap-Ease would realize net revenues from retailers of $1.29 per unit.

To promote the product, Martha had budgeted approximately $60 000 for the first year. She planned to use $50 000 of this amount for travel costs to visit trade shows and to make sales calls on retailers. She would use the remaining $10 000 for advertising. Because the mousetrap had generated so much publicity, however, she had not felt the need to do much advertising. Still, she had placed advertising in *Chatelaine* and in other home magazines. Martha was the company's only salesperson, but she intended to hire more salespeople soon.

Martha had initially forecast Trap-Ease's first-year sales at 500 000 units. By the end of April, however, the company had sold only a few thousand units. Martha wondered whether most new products got off to such a slow start, or whether she was doing something wrong. She had detected some problems, although none seemed overly serious. For one, there had not been enough repeat buying. For another, she had noted that many of the retailers kept their sample mousetraps on their desks as conversation pieces—she wanted the traps to be used and demonstrated. Martha wondered whether consumers were buying the traps as novelties rather than as a solution to their mouse problems.

Martha knew that the investor group believed that Trap-Ease had a once-in-a-lifetime chance with its innovative mousetrap. She sensed the group's impatience. She had budgeted approximately $150 000 in administrative and fixed costs for the first year (not including marketing costs). To keep the investors happy, the company needed to sell enough traps to cover those costs and make a reasonable profit.

In the first few months, Martha had learned that marketing a new product is not an easy task. For example, one national retailer had placed a large order with instructions that the order was to be delivered to the loading dock at one of its warehouses between 1:00 and 3:00 p.m. on a specified day. When the truck delivering the order had arrived late, the retailer had refused to accept the shipment. The retailer had told Martha it would be a year before she got another chance. Perhaps, Martha thought, she should send the retailer and other customers a copy of Emerson's famous quotation.

Questions

1. Martha and the Trap-Ease investors believe they face a once-in-a-lifetime opportunity. What information do they need to evaluate this opportunity? How do you think the group would write its mission statement? How would you write it?

2. Has Martha identified the best target market for Trap-Ease? What other market segments might the firm target?

3. How has the company positioned the Trap-Ease relative to the chosen target market? Could it position the product in other ways?

4. Describe the current marketing mix for Trap-Ease. Do you see any problems with this mix?

5. Who is Trap-Ease's direct competition? Who are indirect competitors?

6. How would you change Trap-Ease's marketing strategy? What kinds of control procedures would you establish for this strategy?

3 >> Marketing in the Internet Age

Looking Ahead

It's time to shift gears. In the first two chapters, you learned about the basic concepts of marketing, marketing strategies, and the marketing process for bringing value and satisfaction to targeted consumers. However, marketing strategy and practice have undergone dramatic change during the past decade. Major technological advances, including the explosion of the Internet, have had a major impact on buyers and the marketers who serve them. To thrive in this new Internet age—even to survive—marketers must rethink their strategies and adapt them to today's new Internet environment.

After studying this chapter, you should be able to

1. identify the major forces shaping the Internet age

2. explain how companies have responded to the Internet and other powerful new technologies with e-business strategies, and explain how these strategies have resulted in benefits to both buyers and sellers

3. describe the four major e-commerce domains

4. discuss how companies conduct e-commerce to profitably deliver more value to customers

5. summarize the promises and challenges that e-commerce presents for the future

Our first stop on this leg of the journey is at Canadian Tire. This Canadian institution resisted the Internet for some time, but in 2000, it launched an online version of its catalogue. Since then, the popularity of Canadian Tire Online has exploded, moving the company from a traditional "bricks-and-mortar" marketer to a "click-and-mortar" marketer.

Canadian Tire's familiar red and white signs with the green maple leaf have been a part of the Canadian landscape since 1922. The company has 450 stores across Canada and 200 gas stations, some in tandem with Canadian Tire stores, some as stand-alone operations.

Canadian Tire has long offered a traditional bricks-and-mortar retail environment and catalogue shopping, and in 2000, the company launched Canadian Tire Online, taking the company into the e-tailing business.

Canadian Tire was criticized for its late entry to Internet retailing, but its strategy was to learn from others' mistakes. As a result, Canadian Tire avoided the problems experienced by retailers that failed to develop a workable online strategy. But eventually, staying offline was even riskier than going online. Canadians were rapidly discovering the wonders of the Web, and e-commerce offered real convenience and selection advantages for customers. If Canadian Tire didn't take advantage of these new economy opportunities, its competitors would.

Just one year after its launch, Canadian Tire's Web site was recording two million visits to the site in a month, including more than one million unique visitors. Canadian Tire Online is now one of the top three e-commerce sites in Canada.

To ensure the its e-commerce initiatives continue to meet consumer needs, Canadian Tire Online has further developed its Web store's capabilities and service features. In 2001, it introduced a line of "Available Only Online" products, including higher-end appliances and new categories of electronic products such as digital cameras and MP3 players. Licensed clothing, luggage, and an extended collection of power tools are now also part of this category, which has been expanded to include more than one thousand items.

Recently, Canadian Tire Online was completely redesigned to make shopping faster, better, and easier for customers. Major enhancements to the site include the following:

- Information about the Item of the Week and Hot Deals of the Week is available on the home page.

- A new delivery cost calculator enables customers to determine delivery costs before beginning the checkout process. Delivery costs can be calculated as soon as an item is added to the shopping cart and recalculated as additional items are added.

- A more comprehensive list of product categories is available within the Around the House, Workshop, Sports & Recreation,

Garden & Patio, and Automotive departments, making it faster and easier to browse and shop.

- The number of products available online has more than doubled during the past year to more than 14 000 items, including 1000 available only online.

In addition, Canadian Tire's unique eFLYER has been fully integrated with the Web store, allowing eFLYER subscribers to shop directly from their eFLYER. Users can sign up to receive weekly e-mails featuring information about weekly specials and promotions on the site, and the home page has a quick link to the eFLYER Weekly Specials.

By melding the Net and non-Net worlds, Canadian Tire follows the powerful new "click-and-mortar" model of retailing—a robust two-tiered system of serving consumers. The model recognizes that, most of the time, customers can visit a local store, but occasionally they will prefer the convenience and different selection afforded by the Web.

In Chapter 1, we discussed sweeping changes in the marketing landscape that are affecting marketing thinking and practice. Recent technological advances, including the widespread use of the Internet, have created what some call a new economy. Although debate about the nature of—and even the existence of—such a new economy has been widespread in recent years, few would disagree that the Internet and other powerful new connecting technologies are having a dramatic effect on marketers and buyers. Many standard marketing strategies and practices of the past— mass marketing, product standardization, media advertising, store retailing, and others—were well suited to the so-called old economy. These strategies and practices will continue to be important in the new economy; however, marketers will also have to develop new strategies and practices better suited to today's new environment.

In this chapter, we first describe the key forces shaping the new Internet age. Then we examine how marketing strategy and practice are changing to meet the requirements of this new age.

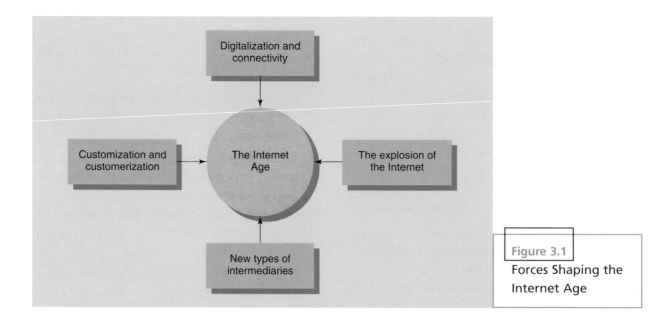

Figure 3.1

Forces Shaping the Internet Age

Major Forces Shaping the Internet Age

Many forces play major roles in reshaping the world economy, including technology, globalization, environmentalism, and others. Here we discuss four specific forces that underlie the new Internet age (see Figure 3-1): (1) digitalization and connectivity, (2) the Internet explosion, (3) new types of intermediaries, and (4) customization and customerization.

Digitalization and Connectivity

Many appliances and systems in the past—ranging from telephone systems, wristwatches, and musical recordings to industrial gauges and controls—operated on analogue information. Analogue information is continually variable in response to physical stimuli. Today, a growing number of appliances and systems operate on *digital information,* which comes as streams of zeros and ones, or *bits.* Text, data, sound, and images can be converted into *bitstreams.* A computer can manipulate bits in thousands of applications. Software consists of digital content for operating systems, games, information storage, and other applications.

In today's world of digitized information, *connectivity* through a telecommunications network is essential. Much of the world's business is carried out over networks that connect people and companies. **Intranets** are networks that connect people within a company to each other and to the company network. **Extranets** connect a company with its suppliers and distributors. And the **Internet**, a vast public web of computer networks, connects users of all types all around the world to each other and to an amazingly large information repository. The Internet makes up one big information highway that can dispatch bits at incredible speeds from one location to another.

Intranet A network that connects people within a company to each other and to the company network.

Extranet A network that connects a company with its suppliers and distributors.

Internet A vast public web of computer networks that connects users of all types all around the world to each other and to a large information repository. The Internet is an information highway that can dispatch bits at incredible speeds from one location to another.

The Internet Explosion

With the creation of the World Wide Web and Web browsers in the 1990s, the Internet was transformed from a mere communication tool into a revolutionary technology. During the final decade of the twentieth century, the number of Internet users worldwide grew to almost 400 million. By early 2001, Internet penetration in Canada had reached 69 percent of the population 18 years of age and older. Although the dot-com crash in 2000 led to cutbacks in technology spending, research suggests that the growth of Internet access among the world's citizens will continue to explode. The number of Web surfers worldwide is expected to approach 1 billion by 2004.

This explosive worldwide growth in Internet usage forms the heart of the so-called new economy. The Internet has been *the* revolutionary technology of the new millennium, empowering consumers and businesses alike with blessings of connectivity. For nearly every new economy innovation to emerge during the past decade, the Internet has played a starring—or at the very least a strong supporting—role. The Internet enables consumers and companies to access and share unprecedented amounts of information with just a few mouse clicks. To be competitive in today's marketplace, companies must adopt Internet technology or risk being left behind.

New Types of Intermediaries

New technologies have led thousands of entrepreneurs to launch Internet companies—the so-called dot-coms. The amazing success of early Internet-only companies, such as AOL, Amazon.com, Yahoo, eBay, E*Trade, and dozens of others, worried many established manufacturers and retailers. For example, Compaq Computer, which sold its computers only through retailers, worried when Dell Computer grew faster by selling online. Toys "R" Us worried when eToys lured toy buyers to the Web. Established store-based retailers of all kinds—from bookstores, music stores, and florists to travel agents, stockbrokers, and car dealers—began to doubt their futures as competitors sprung up selling their products and services via the Internet. Store-based retailers feared, and rightly so, being *disintermediated* (being cut out) by this new type of intermediary, the e-tailer.

The formation of new types of intermediaries and new forms of channel relationships caused existing firms to reexamine how they served their markets. At first, the established *brick-and-mortar* firms—such as IBM, Canadian Tire, and the traditional banks and brokerage houses—dragged their feet, hoping that the assaulting *click-only* firms would falter or disappear. Then they wised up and started their own online sales channels, becoming *click-and-mortar* competitors. Ironically, many click-and-mortar competitors have become stronger than the click-only competitors that pushed them reluctantly onto the Internet. TD Waterhouse is a good example. In fact, although some click-only competitors like ING Direct are surviving and even prospering in today's marketplace, many once-formidable dot-coms—such as Furniture.com, eToys, Pets.com, Garden.com, and Mothernature.com—have failed in recent years in the face of poor profitability and plunging stock values.

Customization and Customerization

The old economy revolved around *manufacturing companies* that mainly focused on standardizing their production, products, and business processes. They invested large sums in brand building to tout the advantages of their standardized market offerings. Through standardization and branding, manufacturers hoped to increase demand and take advantage of economies of scale. As a key to managing their assets, they set up command-and-control systems that would run their businesses like machines.

In contrast, the new economy revolves around *information businesses.* Information has the advantages of being easy to differentiate, customize, personalize, and dispatch at incredible speed over networks. With rapid advances in Internet and other connecting technologies, companies have grown skilled at gathering information about individual customers and business partners (suppliers, distributors, retailers). In turn, they have become more adept at individualizing their products and services, messages, and media. Dell Computer, for example, lets customers specify exactly what they want in their computers and delivers customer-designed units in only a few days. On its Reflect.com Web site, Procter & Gamble allows people to create their own makeup by answering sets of questions. It then formulates a unique mix of P&G products (various Oil of Olay items for example) for each person. *Customization* differs from *customerization*. Customization involves taking the initiative to customize the market offering. A restaurant server takes a customer's order for a salad with more broccoli, no cheese, and dressing on the side and the restaurant *customizes* the salad for the customer. In **customerization**, the company leaves it to individual customers to design the offering. For example, jeans customers may take their own measurements and add specific features that they want in their jeans, such as colourful patches. Restaurant customers go to a salad bar and *customerize* their salads by choosing the exact salad ingredients they want. Such companies have become facilitators and their customers have moved from being consumers to being *prosumers*.[1] ("Prosumers" was a word coined by Alvin Toffler in his book *The Third Wave*. It is a contraction of "consumer" and "producer" and refers to those product categories and consumer purchasing behaviours that combine producing and consuming at purchase. An example is purchasing a Dell Computer, where each machine is custom made for each order.)

Customerization Leaving it to individual customers to design the marketing offering, which allows customers to be *prosumers* rather than just consumers.

MARKETING STRATEGY IN THE INTERNET AGE

Conducting business in the new Internet age requires a new model for marketing strategy and practice. According to one strategist: "Sparked by new technologies, particularly the Internet, the corporation is undergoing a radical transformation that is nothing less than a new industrial revolution.… To survive and thrive in this century, managers will need to hard-wire a new set of rules into their brains. The twenty-first-century corporation must adapt itself to management via the Web."[2] Another suggests that the Internet is "revolutionizing the way we think about…how to construct relationships with suppliers and customers, how to cre-

Customerization: At Reflect.com, people formulate their own beauty products. It offers "one-of-a-kind products for a one-of-a-kind you." More than 650 000 people visit the site each month.

ate value for them, and how to make money in the process; in other words, [it's] revolutionizing marketing."[3]

Some strategists envision a day when all buying and selling will involve direct electronic connections between companies and their customers. The new model will fundamentally change customers' notions of convenience, speed, price, product information, and service. This new consumer thinking will affect every business. Comparing the adoption of the Internet and other new marketing technologies to the early days of the airplane, Amazon.com CEO Jeff Bezos says, "It's the Kitty Hawk era of electronic commerce." Even those offering more cautious predictions agree that the Internet and e-business will have a tremendous impact on business strategies.

The fact is that today's economy requires a mixture of old economy and new economy thinking and action. Companies need to retain most of the skills and practices that have worked in the past, but they will also need to add major new competencies and practices, if they hope to grow and prosper in the new environment. Marketing should play the *lead role* in shaping new company strategy.

E-Business, E-Commerce, and E-Marketing in the Internet Age

E-business The use of electronic platforms—intranets, extranets, and the Internet—to conduct a company's business.

E-business involves the use of electronic platforms—intranets, extranets, and the Internet—to conduct a company's business. The Internet and other information and computer technologies have greatly increased the ability of companies to do business faster, more accurately, and over a wider range of time and space. Countless companies have set up Web sites to inform consumers about and promote their products and services. They have created intranets to help employees communicate with each other and access information in the company's computers. They have set up extranets with their major suppliers and distributors to facilitate information exchange, orders, transactions, and payments. Companies such as Cisco, Microsoft, and Oracle run almost entirely as e-businesses in which memos, invoices, engineering drawings, sales and marketing information—virtually everything—travel over the Internet instead of on paper.[4]

E-commerce Buying and selling processes supported by electronic means, primarily the Internet.

E-commerce is more specific than e-business. Whereas e-business includes all electronics-based information exchanges within or between companies and customers, e-commerce involves buying and selling processes supported by electronic means, primarily the Internet. *E-markets* are "market*spaces*," rather than physical "market*places*," in which sellers offer their products and services online, and buyers search for information, identify what they want, and place orders using credit cards or other means of electronic payment.

E-marketing The "e-selling" side of e-commerce, including company efforts to communicate about, promote, and sell products and services over the Internet.

E-commerce includes *e-marketing* and *e-purchasing* (*e-procurement*). **E-marketing** is the "e-selling" side of e-commerce. It consists of company efforts to communicate about, promote, and sell products and services over the Internet. Thus, Amazon.ca, Schwab.ca, and Dell.ca conduct e-marketing at their Web sites. The other side of e-marketing is e-purchasing, the "e-buying" side of e-commerce. It consists of companies purchasing goods, services, and information from online suppliers. In business-to-business buying, e-marketers and e-purchasers come together in huge e-commerce networks. For example, Global eXchange Services (GXS) operates one of the world's largest transaction management infrastructures for business-to-business e-commerce networks. More than 100 000 trading partners in 58 countries—including giants such as General Electric, Eastman Kodak, DaimlerChrysler, J.C. Penny, Sara Lee, and Unilever—use the GXS network to complete some 1 billion transactions each year, accounting for $1 trillion worth of goods and services.[5]

**Global eXchange Services
www.gxs.com**

A recent Canadian survey by Deloitte Consulting (which is soon changing its name to Braxton) found that 78 percent of responding companies are planning to take advantage of *collaborative commerce* to improve their interactions with both suppliers and customers. Collaborative commerce is a way of using technology to allow "entire value chains to share decision making, workflow, capabilities, and information with each other."[6]

E-commerce and the Internet bring many benefits to both buyers and sellers. Let's review some of these major benefits.

Benefits to Buyers

Internet buying benefits both final buyers and business buyers in many ways. It is *convenient*: customers don't have to battle traffic, find parking spaces, and trek through stores and aisles to find and examine products. They can comparison shop by browsing through catalogues or surfing Web sites. Direct marketers never close their doors. Buying is *easy* and *private*: Customers encounter fewer buying hassles and don't have to face salespeople or open themselves to persuasion and emotional pitches. Business buyers can learn about and buy products and services without waiting for and spending time with salespeople.

In addition, the Internet often provides buyers with greater *product access and selection*: the world's the limit for the Web. Unrestrained by physical boundaries, cybersellers can offer an almost unlimited selection. Compare the incredible selections offered by Web merchants such as Indigo.ca or eVineyard to the more meagre assortments of their counterparts in the brick-and-mortar world.

Beyond a broader selection of sellers and products, e-commerce channels also give buyers access to a wealth of comparative *information*, information about companies, products, and competitors. Good sites often provide more information in more useful forms than even the most solicitous salesperson can. For example, Amazon.com offers top-10 product lists, extensive product descriptions, expert and user product reviews, and recommendations based on customers' previous purchases.

Finally, online buying is *interactive* and *immediate*. Buyers often can interact with the seller's site to create exactly the configuration of information, products, or services they want, and then order or download them on the spot. Moreover, the Internet gives consumers a greater measure of control. "The Internet will empower consumers like nothing else ever has," notes one analyst. "Think about this: Already 16 percent of car buyers shop online before showing up at a dealership, and they

Internet buying is easy and private: Final consumers can shop the world from home with few hassles; business buyers can learn about and buy products and information without tying up time with salespeople.

aren't comparing paint jobs—they're arming themselves with information on dealer costs.... The new reality is consumer control."[7]

Benefits to Sellers

E-commerce also yields many benefits to sellers. First, the Internet is a powerful tool for *customer relationship building*. Because of its one-to-one, interactive nature, the Internet is an especially potent marketing tool. Companies can interact online with customers to learn more about their specific needs and wants. In turn, online customers can ask questions and volunteer feedback. Based on this ongoing interaction, companies can increase customer value and satisfaction through product and service refinements. One expert concludes: "Contrary to the common view that Web customers are fickle by nature and will flock to the next new idea, the Web is actually a very sticky space in both business-to-consumer and business-to-business spheres. Most of today's online customers exhibit a clear [tendency] toward loyalty."[8]

The Internet and other electronic channels yield additional advantages, such as *reducing costs* and *increasing speed and efficiency*. E-marketers avoid the expense of maintaining a store and the accompanying costs of rent, insurance, and utilities. E-tailers such as Amazon.com reap the advantage of a negative operating cycle: Amazon.com receives cash from credit card companies just one day after customers place an order. It can hold on to the money for 46 days until it pays suppliers, the book distributors, and publishers.

By using the Internet to link directly to suppliers, factories, distributors, and customers, businesses such as Dell Computer and General Electric are wringing waste out of the system and passing savings on to customers. Because customers deal directly with sellers, e-marketing often results in lower costs and improved efficiencies for channel and logistics functions such as order processing, inventory handling, delivery, and trade promotion. Finally, communicating electronically often costs less than communicating on paper through the mail. For instance, a company can produce digital catalogues for much less than the cost of printing and mailing paper ones.

E-marketing also offers greater *flexibility*, allowing the marketer to make ongoing adjustments to its offers and programs. For example, once a paper catalogue is mailed to final consumer or business customers, the products, prices, and other catalogue features are fixed until the next catalogue is sent. However, an online catalogue can be adjusted daily or even hourly, changing product assortments, prices, and promotions to match changing market conditions.

Finally, the Internet is a truly *global* medium that allows buyers and sellers to click from one country to another in seconds. The GXS network, for example, provides business buyers with immediate access to suppliers in 58 countries, ranging from the United States and the United Kingdom to Hong Kong and the Philippines. A Web surfer from Paris or Istanbul can access an online Canadian Tire catalogue as easily as someone living in Toronto, Ontario, the retailer's hometown. Thus, even small e-marketers find that they have ready access to global markets.

Let's reflect on this new Internet age. What, specifically, does the Internet age mean in *your* life?

- Look back through the major forces shaping the Internet Age and write down some specific ways that these forces have affected your everyday life.

- How often and in what ways do you use the Internet to research and buy products? How has the Internet changed what and how you buy?

- Go to the Web, visit **www.SonyStyle.ca**, and have a look around. How does such a site benefit consumers like you? How does it benefit Sony?

E-COMMERCE DOMAINS

The four major e-marketing domains are shown in Figure 3-2 and discussed below: B2C (business to consumer), B2B (business to business), C2C (consumer to consumer), and C2B (consumer to business).

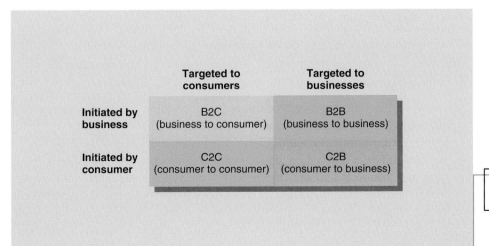

	Targeted to consumers	Targeted to businesses
Initiated by business	B2C (business to consumer)	B2B (business to business)
Initiated by consumer	C2C (consumer to consumer)	C2B (consumer to business)

Figure 3.2

Marketing Domains

B2C (Business to Consumer)

B2C (business to consumer) e-commerce The online selling of goods and services to final consumers.

The popular press has paid the most attention to **B2C** (**business-to-consumer**) **e-commerce**—the online selling of goods and services to final consumers. Despite some gloomy predictions, online consumer buying continues to grow at a healthy rate. Although we have the positive experiences associated with Canadian Tire's entrance into e-commerce, we also have the Holt Renfrew experience, where the decision was made to discontinue its e-commerce site. The decision to discontinue its involvement in e-tailing was based on the realization that high-end fashion is better suited to a storefront, bricks-and-mortar strategy. Successes and failures will continue in the B2C environment, but studies suggest that B2C sales in Canada will reach $18 billion by 2004. The largest categories of consumer online spending include travel services, clothing, computer hardware and software, consumer electronics, books, music and videos, health and beauty, home and garden, flowers and gifts, sports and fitness equipment, and toys.[9]

Online Consumers When people envision the typical Internet user, some still mistakenly envision a pasty-faced computer nerd or "cyberhead." Others envision a young, techy, upscale male professional. Such stereotypes are outdated. As increasingly more people find their way onto the Internet, the cyberspace population is becoming more mainstream and diverse. "The Internet was, at first, an elitist country club reserved only for individuals with select financial abilities and technical skills," says an e-commerce analyst. "Now, nearly every socioeconomic group is aggressively adopting the Web."[10]

Thus, increasingly, the Internet provides e-marketers with access to a broad range of demographic segments. For example, home Internet access for blue-collar workers is growing faster than for any other occupational group, surging 52 percent in just the past year. One study of Internet "newbies"—those who started using the Internet in the past year—found that 71 percent had no postsecondary degree, 65 percent earned less than $50 000 a year, and only 25 percent were younger than 30.

These days, everybody's logging on…. Doral Main, a 51-year-old mother of two and office manager saves precious time by shopping the Internet for greeting cards and getaways. Her Net-newbie father, Charles, 73, goes online to buy supplies for his wood-carving hobby. Even niece Katrina, 11, finds excitement on the Web, picking gifts she wants from the Disney.com site. "It's addictive," Main says of the Internet. [Indeed,] the Web isn't mostly a hangout for techno-nerds anymore.[11]

Growing Internet diversity continues to open new e-commerce targeting opportunities for marketers. For example, the Web now reaches consumers in all age groups. Seventy-four percent of Canadians between the ages of 12 and 18 have access to the Internet. Forty-four percent of this same group spend more than an hour per day connected to the Internet, and the average Canadian family with Internet access spends more than 32 hours per week online.[12] The Microsoft Network site carries Disney's Daily Blast, which offers kids games, stories, comic strips with old and new Disney characters, and current events tailored to preteens. Nickelodeon offers a full slate of games based on favourite Nickelodeon characters.

Nickelodeon
www.nick.com

Although Internet users are still younger on average than the population as a whole, 48 percent of consumers aged 45 to 54 and 34 percent of consumers aged 55 to 64 have Internet access. In fact, a recent NFO WorldGroup study suggests that this age group is showing faster penetration growth than all younger age groups. To help online marketers to better target their customers, Internet research companies now segment the increasingly diverse Web population by needs and interests. For example, Harris Interactive has labelled a segment it calls cyberchondriacs, the roughly 100 million North Americans who go online for health care information. Slightly older than the general population, typically they or someone else in their family has a medical condition. They view the Internet as a kind of mobile medical library and log on to dig out the latest research and treatments for a specific malady. Pharmaceutical firms such as Pfizer Canada and GlaxoSmithKline Inc. have launched Web sites to market their prescription drugs directly to these cyberchondriacs, hoping to spur them to ask their doctors for the medication by brand name. "The Internet is the mother of all customizers," observes a Harris executive. "You can customize a product to a 36-year-old…diabetic with red hair. And you can do it in a way that you could never do with traditional media."[13]

Internet consumers differ from traditional offline consumers in their approaches to buying and in their responses to marketing. The exchange process in the Internet age has become more customer initiated and customer controlled. People who use the Internet place greater value on information and tend to respond negatively to messages aimed only at selling. Whereas traditional marketing targets a somewhat passive audience, e-marketing targets people who actively select which Web sites they will visit, what marketing information they will receive about which products and services, and under what conditions. Marketers and their representatives are held at bay until customers invite them to participate in the exchange. Even after marketers enter the exchange process, customers define what information they need, what offerings they are interested in, and what prices they are willing to pay. Thus, the new world of e-commerce requires new marketing approaches.

This is especially important because Canadians are still reluctant to move to the e-commerce purchasing model. A Statistics Canada survey showed that only 18.4 percent of Internet users had ordered and paid for goods online. The main reasons cited for this relatively low participation rate were (1) security concerns (orders being manipulated or intercepted) and (2) privacy (confidential information being transmitted). This information reveals a marketing challenge for those companies involved in e-commerce.[14]

B2C Web Sites Consumers can buy almost anything online. The Internet is most useful for products and services when the shopper wants greater ordering convenience or lower costs. The Internet also provides value to buyers looking for information about differences in product features and value. However, consumers find the Internet less useful when buying products that must be touched or examined in advance. Still, even here there are exceptions. For example, who would have thought that people would order expensive computers from Dell without seeing and trying them first? People now go online to order a wide range of goods: lobster and other premium seafoods from Clearwater Fine Foods, groceries from Grocery Gateway, books or CDs from Indigo, clothing from Tilley Endurables, an airline ticket from WestJet, home mortgages from

Point2 Used Iron
www.point2usediron.
com

ING Direct, and even used heavy equipment. If you need a bulldozer, for example, simply go to the site "where man meets machine," at Point2 Used Iron.

- Flower Power sells fresh flowers directly to consumers. Customers can order bouquets or plants from an online colour catalogue by phoning a toll-free number or placing orders at the Web site at www.24hrFlowerPower.com.

- At ING Direct prospective borrowers receive a high-tech, high-touch, one-stop mortgage shopping experience. At the site, customers can research a wide variety of home financing and refinancing options, apply for a mortgage, and receive quick loan approval—all without leaving home. The site provides useful interactive tools that help borrowers decide how much house they can afford, whether to rent or buy, or whether to refinance a current mortgage. Customers can receive advice by phone or by chatting online with one of ING's loan consultants.

ING Direct
www.ingdirect.ca

B2B (Business to Business)

B2B (business-to-business) e-commerce Using B2B trading networks, auction sites, spot exchanges, online product catalogues, barter sites, and other online resources to reach new customers, serve current customers more effectively, and obtain buying efficiencies and better prices.

Although the popular press has given the most attention to business-to-consumer (B2C) Web sites, consumer goods sales via the Web are dwarfed by **B2B (business-to-business) e-commerce.** Gartner Group, a major research firm on online commerce, estimates that B2B e-commerce will reach $3.6 trillion in 2003, compared with just $107 billion in B2C transactions. Gartner also estimates that by 2005, more than 500 000 enterprises will participate in e-commerce as buyers, sellers, or both.[15] These firms are using B2B trading networks, auction sites, spot exchanges, online product catalogues, barter sites, and other online resources to reach new customers, serve current customers more effectively, and obtain buying efficiencies and better prices.

Most major business-to-business marketers now offer product information, customer purchasing, and customer support services online. In a survey of 50 major Canadian companies, 90 percent of those companies had some Internet-based sales in 2002, with 36 percent indicating that their online sales would range between 21 percent and 50 percent of total sales.[16] For example, corporate buyers can visit PMC

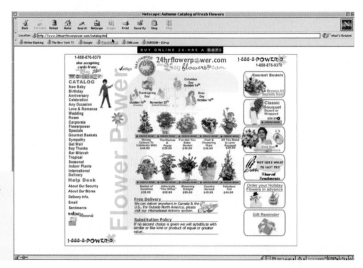

B2C e-commerce: People now go online to order a wide range of goods—from groceries to fresh flowers.

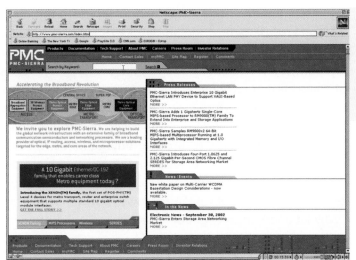

B2B e-commerce: Corporate buyers can visit PMC Sierra's Web site to learn about its products, get technical support, and find distributors worldwide.

Sierra's Web site to learn about the latest in broadband communication semi-conductors and networking processors. This site provides an online product listing with technical and application details, allows current customers to register for timely communication from the company on issues associated with product advances, provides technical support for PMC Sierra products, and directs the user to distributors that carry the PMC Sierra line of products around the world.

Much B2B e-commerce takes place in **open trading networks**—huge e-marketspaces in which buyers and sellers find each other online, share information, and complete transactions efficiently. Here are some examples of B2B trading network sites:

Open trading networks Huge e-marketspaces in which B2B buyers and sellers find each other online, share information, and complete transactions efficiently.

- PlasticsNet.com is an Internet marketplace for the plastic products industry, connecting more than 90 000 monthly visitors with more than 200 suppliers. In addition to facilitating online transactions, the site provides a supplier directory, material data sheets, an industry publication, a list of educational programs, and books and seminars relevant to the plastics industry.

- The Medical EquipNet serves as a medical equipment e-marketplace in which companies, doctors' offices, and hospitals can buy, sell, or auction off new, used, refurbished, or surplus medical equipment. Members can place classified ads or want ads, place or receive auction bids, or access medical equipment financing, shipping, repair, or installation services. To date, the site has attracted more than 4.5 million visitors.

Despite the increasing popularity of such e-marketspaces, one Internet research firm estimates that 93 percent of all B2B e-commerce is conducted through private sites. Increasingly, online sellers are setting up their own **private trading networks (PTNs)**. Whereas open trading networks such as PlasticsNet.com facilitate transactions between a wide range of online buyers and sellers, private trading networks link a particular seller with its own trading partners. Rather than simply completing transactions, PTNs give sellers greater control over product presentation and allow them to build deeper relationships with buyers and sellers by providing value-added services. As an example, take Trane Company, a maker of air-conditioning and heating systems:

Private trading networks (PTNs) B2B trading networks that link a particular seller with its own trading partners.

Since last autumn, Trane…has been red-hot with the business-to-business Internet crowd. Each of the horde of B2B [open trading] exchanges targeting the construction industry wants Trane to join. "Construction.com, MyPlant.com, MyFacility.com—we get up to five calls a week," says James A. Bierkamp, head of Trane's e-business unit. But after some consideration, Bierkamp did not see what any of those [third-party] e-marketplaces could offer that his company couldn't do itself. So in May, Trane rolled out its own private exchange, which allows its 5000 dealers to browse, buy equipment, schedule deliveries, and process warranties. The site lets Trane operate with greater efficiency and trim processing costs—without losing control of the presentation of its brand name or running the risks of rubbing elbows with competitors in an open exchange. "Why let another party get between us and our customers?" asks Bierkamp.[17]

C2C (Consumer to Consumer)

C2C (consumer-to-consumer) e-commerce
Online exchanges of goods and information between final consumers.

Much **C2C (consumer-to-consumer) e-commerce** and communication occurs on the Web between interested parties over a wide range of products and subjects. In some cases, the Internet provides an excellent means by which consumers can buy or exchange goods or information directly with one another. For example, eBay, Amazon.com Auctions, and other auction sites offer popular marketspaces for displaying and selling almost anything, from art and antiques, coins, stamps, and jewellery to computers and consumer electronics. EBay's C2C online trading community of more than 30 million registered users made more than $5 billion in trades last year. The company's Web site hosts more than two million auctions each month for items in more than one thousand categories. EBay maintains auction sites in several countries, including Canada, Japan, the United Kingdom, the United States, and Germany.

Such C2C sites give people access to much larger audiences than the local flea market or newspaper classifieds (which, by the way, are now also going online). Ask Barbara Dreschsler, a systems engineer, who has been buying and selling Beanie

C2C e-commerce: eBay offers a popular marketspace for displaying and selling almost anything.

Babies via Internet auction sites such as eBay.com and Amazon.com for more than a year. What started out as a family hobby has rapidly become a part-time business. In the first two months of this year, Dreschsler received 102 orders for Beanie Babies and other toys priced between $10 and $200. "We still call it a hobby, but we would love to do it full time," she says.[18]

In other cases, C2C involves interchanges of information through forums and Internet newsgroups that appeal to specific special-interest groups. Such activities may be organized for commercial or noncommercial purposes. *Forums* are discussion groups located on commercial online services such as Yahoo and AOL. A forum may take the form of a library, a chat room for real-time message exchanges, and even a classified ad directory. For example, Yahoo Canada Chat has thousands of chat rooms. It also provides "friends in chat lists," which alert members when their friends are online, allowing them to exchange instant messages.

Newsgroups are the Internet version of forums. However, such groups are limited to people posting and reading messages on a specified topic, rather than managing libraries or conferencing. Internet users can participate in newsgroups without subscribing. There are tens of thousands of newsgroups dealing with every imaginable topic, from healthful eating and caring for your Bonsai tree to collecting antique cars and exchanging views on the latest soap opera happenings.

C2C means that online visitors don't just consume product information—increasingly, they create it. They join Internet interest groups to share information, with the result that "word of Web" is joining "word of mouth" as an important buying influence. Word of good companies and products travels fast; word of bad companies and products travels even faster.

C2B (Consumer to Business)

The final e-commerce domain is **C2B (consumer-to-business) e-commerce.** Thanks to the Internet, today's consumers are finding it easier to contact and communicate with companies. Most companies now invite prospects and customers to send in suggestions and questions via company Web sites. Beyond this, rather than waiting for companies to send catalogues or other information, consumers can search out sellers on the Web, learn about their offers, and initiate purchases.

Using the Web, consumers can even drive transactions with businesses, rather than the other way around. For example, using Travelocity.ca, would-be buyers bid for airline tickets, hotel rooms, rental cars, and even home mortgages, leaving the sellers to decide whether to accept their offers.

C2B (consumer-to-business) e-commerce Online exchanges in which consumers search out sellers, learn about their offers, and initiate purchases, sometimes even driving transaction terms.

CONDUCTING E-COMMERCE

Companies of all types are now engaged in e-commerce. In this section, we first discuss different types of e-marketers shown in Figure 3-3. Then, we examine how companies go about conducting marketing online.

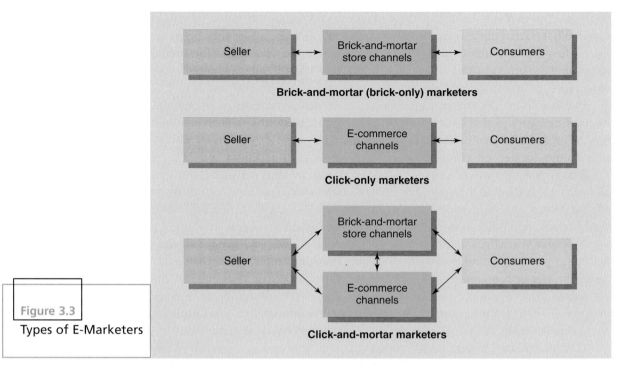

Figure 3.3

Types of E-Marketers

Click-Only versus Click-and-Mortar E-Marketers

The Internet gave birth to a new species of e-marketers—the *click-only* dot-coms—which operate only online without any brick-and-mortar market presence. In addition, most traditional brick-and-mortar companies have now added e-marketing operations, transforming themselves into *click-and-mortar* competitors.

Click-only companies The so-called dot-coms, which operate only online, without any brick-and-mortar market presence.

Click-Only Companies Click-only companies come in many shapes and sizes. They include *e-tailers*, dot-coms that sell products and services directly to final buyers via the Internet. Familiar e-tailers include Amazon.ca, CDNow, and eVineyards. The click-only group also includes *search engines* and *portals* such as Yahoo, Excite, and Go, which began as search engines and later added services such as news, weather, stock reports, entertainment, and storefronts, hoping to become the first port of entry to the Internet. *Internet service providers (ISPs)* such as HotMail, Earthlink, and AltaVista are click-only companies that provide Internet and e-mail connections for a fee. *Transaction sites,* such as auction site eBay, take commissions for transactions conducted on their sites. Various *content sites*, such as *The Globe and Mail*, TSN.ca, and Encyclopedia Britannica Online, provide financial, research, and other information. Finally, *enabler sites* provide the hardware and software that enable Internet communication and commerce.

The Globe and Mail
www.globeandmail.ca

The hype surrounding such click-only Web businesses reached astonishingly high levels during the "dot-com gold rush" of the late 1990s, when avid investors drove dot-com stock prices to dizzying heights. However, the investing frenzy collapsed in 2000 and many high-flying, overvalued dot-coms came crashing down. Even some of the strongest and most attractive e-tailers—eToys.com, Pets.com, Furniture.com, Mothernature.com, Garden.com, Eve.com, Living.com, ValueAmerica.com—filed for bankruptcy. Survivors such as Amazon.com and Priceline.com saw their stock values plunge. Notes one analyst, "Once teeming with thousands of vibrant new ideas, the consumer Net is beginning to look like the mall at midnight."[19]

Dot-coms failed for a variety of reasons. Many rushed into the market without proper research or planning, often with the primary goal of simply launching an initial public offering (IPO) while the market was hot. Many relied too heavily on spin and hype instead of developing sound marketing strategies. Flush with investors' cash, the dot-coms spent lavishly offline on mass marketing in an effort to establish brand identities and attract customers to their sites. For example, during the fourth quarter of 1999, the average e-tailer spent an astounding 109 percent of sales on marketing and advertising.[20] As one industry watcher concludes, many dot-coms failed because they "had dumb-as-dirt business models, not because the Internet lacks the power to enchant and delight customers in ways hitherto unimaginable."[21]

The dot-coms tended to devote too much effort to acquiring new customers instead of building loyalty and purchase frequency among current customers. In their rush to cash in, many dot-coms went to market with poorly designed Web sites that were complex, hard to navigate, and unreliable. When orders did arrive, some dot-coms found that they lacked the well-designed distribution systems needed to ship products on time and handle customer inquiries and problems. Finally, the ease with which competitors could enter the Web, and the ease with which customers could switch to Web sites offering better prices, forced many dot-coms to sell at margin-killing low prices.

Pets.com, the now defunct online pet store, provides a good example of how many dot-coms failed to understand their marketplaces.

From the start, Pets.com tried to force its way to online success with unbeatable low prices and heavy marketing hype. In the end, however, neither worked. During its first year of operation, Pets.com lost $61.8 million on a meager $5.8 million in sales. During that time, it paid $13.4 million for the goods it sold for just $5.8 million. Thus, for every dollar that Pets.com paid suppliers such as Ralston Purina for dog food and United Parcel Service for shipping, it collected only 43 cents from its customers. Moreover, by early spring of 1999, Pets.com had burned through more than $21 million on marketing and advertising to create an identity and entice pet owners to its site. Its branding campaign centered on the wildly popular Sock Puppet character, a white dog with black patches. Sock Puppet even made an appearance in Macy's Thanksgiving Day Parade in New York as a 36-foot-high balloon. The singing mascot was also featured in Super Bowl ads that cost Pets.com more than $2 million. At first, investors bought into Pets.com's "landgrab" strategy—investing heavily to stake out an early share, then finding ways later to make a profit. However, even though it attracted 570 000 customers, Pets.com never did figure out how to make money in a low-margin business with high shipping costs. Its stock price slid from a February 1999 high of $14 to a dismal 22 cents by the end of 2000. In early 2001, the once-bold e-tailer retired Sock Puppet and quietly closed its cyberdoors.[22]

At the same time, many click-only dot-coms are surviving and even prospering in today's marketspace. Others are showing losses today but promising profits tomorrow. Consider Earthlink.com:

Earthlink.com is an Internet service provider (ISP) that sells Internet and email connection time for a $20 monthly fee. Customer maintenance expenses amount to only $9 a month, leaving an $11 contribution margin. On average, it costs Earthlink $100 to acquire a new customer. Therefore, it takes 11 months before the company breaks even on a new customer. Fortunately, Earthlink keeps its customers for an average of 31 months. This leaves Earthlink with 20 months of net income from the average customer. At a $9 monthly contribution margin, Earthlink makes $180 (20 months × $9) on the average customer. When Sky Dayton, Earthlink's founder, was asked why Earthlink is still losing money, he answered that Earthlink is acquiring so many new customers that it will take a while for the inflow of contribution margin to cover the $100 customer acquisition.[23]

Thus, for many dot-coms, including Internet giants such as Amazon.com, the Web is still not a money-making proposition. Companies engaging in e-commerce need to describe to their investors how they will eventually make profits. They need to define a *revenue and profit model*. Table 3-1 shows that a dot-com's revenues may come from any of several sources.

Click-and-Mortar Companies Many established companies moved quickly to open Web sites providing information about their companies and products. However, most resisted adding e-commerce to their sites. They felt that this would produce *channel conflict*, in that selling their products or services online would compete with their offline retailers and agents. For example, Compaq Computer feared that its retailers would drop Compaq's computers if the company sold the same computers directly online. Merrill-Lynch hesitated to introduce online stock trading to compete with E*Trade, Charles Schwab, and other online brokerages, fearing that its own brokers would rebel. Even store-based bookseller Barnes & Noble delayed opening its online site to challenge Amazon.com.

These companies struggled with the question of how to conduct online sales without cannibalizing the sales of their own stores, resellers, or agents. However, they soon came to realize that the risks of losing business to online competitors were even greater than the risks of angering channel partners. If they didn't cannibalize these sales, online competitors soon would. Thus, many established brick-and-mortar companies are now prospering as **click-and-mortar companies**. Consider Staples/Business Depot, the $10.7 billion office-supply retailer. After just two years on the Net, Staples captured annual online sales of $512 million last year. However, it's not robbing from store sales in the process. The average yearly spending of small business customers jumps from $600 when they shop in stores to $2800 when they shop online. As a result, Staples is slowing new store openings to a trickle this year; it plans to spend $50 million on expanding its Net presence. "We're still going whole hog," says CEO Thomas Stemberg. "The payoffs are just very high."[24]

Click-and-mortar companies Traditional brick-and-mortar companies that have added e-marketing to their operations.

Table 3-1   Sources of E-Commerce Revenue

Product and service sales income	Many e-commerce companies draw a good portion of their revenues from markups on goods and services they sell online.
Advertising income	Sales of online ad space can provide a major source of revenue. At one point, Buy.com received so much advertising revenue that it was able to sell products at cost.
Sponsorship income	A dot-com can solicit sponsors for some of its content and collect sponsorship fees to help cover its costs.
Alliance income	Online companies can invite business partners to share costs in setting up a Web site and offer them free advertising on the site.
Membership and subscription income	Web marketers can charge subscription fees for use of their site. Many online newspapers (*Wall Street Journal* and *Financial Times*) require subscription fees for their online services. Auto-By-Tel receives income from selling subscriptions to auto dealers who want to receive hot car buyer leads.
Profile income	Web sites that have built databases containing the profiles of particular target groups may be able to sell these profiles if they get permission first. However, ethical and legal codes govern the use and sale of such customer information.
Transaction commissions and fees	Some dot-coms charge commission fees on transactions between other parties who exchange goods on their Web sites. For example, eBay puts buyers in touch with sellers and takes from a 1.25 percent to a 5 percent commission on each transaction.
Market research and information fees	Companies can charge for special market information or intelligence. For example, NewsLibrary charges a dollar or two to download copies of archived news stories. LifeQuote provides insurance buyers with price comparisons from approximately 50 different life insurance companies, then collects a commission of 50 percent of the first year's premium from the company chosen by the consumer.
Referral income	Companies can collect revenue by referring customers to others. Edmunds receives a "finder's fee" every time a customer fills out an Auto-By-Tel form at its Edmunds.com Web site, regardless of whether a deal is completed.

Most click-and-mortar marketers have found ways to resolve the resulting channel conflicts.[25] For example, Gibson Guitars found that although its dealers were outraged when it tried to sell guitars directly to consumers, the dealers didn't object to direct sales of accessories such as guitar strings and parts. Avon worried that direct online sales might cannibalize the business of its Avon ladies, who had developed close relationships with their customers. Fortunately, Avon's research showed little overlap between existing customers and potential Web customers. Avon shared this finding with the reps and then moved into e-marketing. As an added bonus for the reps, Avon also offered to help them set up their own Web sites. Finally, rather than only competing with its own stores, Office Depot partnered with Amazon.com for its online presence. Amazon.com routes orders for Office Depot products to existing bricks and mortar stores for fulfillment.

Click-and-mortar:
Staples/Business Depot's
Web site supplements its
brick-and-mortar opera-
tions. After two years on
the Net, Staples captured
annual online sales of
more than $500 million.

Despite potential channel conflict issues, many click-and-mortar companies are now having more online success than their click-only competitors. In fact, in a recent study of the top 50 retail sites, ranked by the number of unique visitors, 56 percent were click-and-mortar retailers, and 44 percent were Internet-only retailers.[26]

What gives the click-and-mortar companies an advantage? Established companies such as Canadian Tire, Wal-Mart, Staples/Business Depot, and the Royal Bank have known and trusted brand names and large financial resources. They have extensive customer bases, deeper industry knowledge and experience, and good relationships with key suppliers. By combining e-marketing and established brick-and-mortar operations, they can offer customers more options. For example, consumers can choose the convenience and assortment of 24-hour-a-day online shopping, 24-hour-a-day online banking, the more personal and hands-on experience of in-store shopping, or both. Customers can buy merchandise online and easily return unwanted goods to a nearby store. For example, those wanting to do business with Fidelity Investments can call a Fidelity agent on the phone, go online to the company's Web site, or visit the local Fidelity branch office. Thus, in its advertising, Fidelity can issue a powerful invitation to "call, click, or visit Fidelity Investments."

Pause here and cool your engine for a bit. Think about the relative advantages and disadvantages of *click-only*, *brick-and-mortar only*, and *click-and-mortar* retailers.
- Visit the Amazon.ca Web site. Search for a specific book or DVD—perhaps one that's not too well known—and go through the buying process.
- Now visit www.chapters.indigo.ca and shop for the same book or video. Then visit a Chapters or Indigo store and shop for the item there.
- What advantages does Amazon.ca have over Indigo? What disadvantages does Amazon.ca have? How does your local independent bookstore, with its store-only operations, fare against these two competitors?

Setting up an E-Marketing Presence

Clearly, all companies need to consider moving into e-marketing. Companies can conduct e-marketing in any of the four ways shown in Figure 3-4: creating a Web site, placing ads online, setting up or participating in Web communities, or using online e-mail or Webcasting.

Creating a Web Site For most companies, the first step in conducting e-marketing is to create a Web site. However, beyond simply creating a Web site, marketers must design attractive sites and find ways to get consumers to visit the site, stay around, and come back often.

Types of Web Sites Web sites vary greatly in purpose and content. The most basic type is a **corporate Web site**. These sites are designed to build customer goodwill and to supplement other sales channels, rather than to sell the company's products directly. For example, you can't buy ice cream at benjerrys.com, but you can learn all about Ben & Jerry's company philosophy, products, and locations; send a free e-card to a friend; subscribe to the Chunk Mail newsletter; and spend time in the Fun Stuff area, playing Scooper Challenge or Virtual Checkers.

> **Corporate Web site** A Web site designed to build customer goodwill and to supplement other sales channels, rather than to sell the company's products directly.

Corporate Web sites typically offer a rich variety of information and other features in an effort to answer customer questions, build closer customer relationships, and generate excitement about the company. They generally provide information about the company's history, its mission and philosophy, and the products and services that it offers. They might also describe current events, company personnel, financial performance, and employment opportunities. Most corporate Web sites provide entertainment features to attract and hold visitors. Finally, the site might provide opportunities for customers to ask questions or make comments by e-mail before leaving the site.

Other companies create a **marketing Web site**. These sites engage consumers in interactions that will move them closer to a direct purchase or other marketing outcome. Such sites might include a catalogue, shopping tips, and promotional features such as coupons, sales events, or contests. For example, visitors to SonyStyle.ca can search through dozens of categories of Sony products, review detailed features and specifications lists for specific items, read expert product reviews, and check out the latest hot deals. They can place an order for the desired Sony products online and pay by credit card, all with a few clicks of the mouse button. Companies aggressively promote their marketing Web sites in offline print and broadcast advertising and through "banner-to-site" ads that pop up on other Web sites.

> **Marketing Web site** A Web site that engages consumers in interactions that will move them closer to a direct purchase or other marketing outcome.

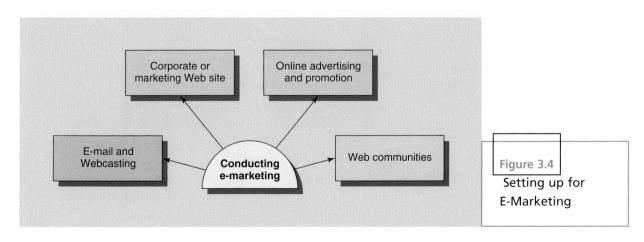

Figure 3.4
Setting up for E-Marketing

Toyota operates a marketing Web site. Once a potential customer clicks in, the carmaker wastes no time trying to turn the inquiry into a sale. The site offers plenty of useful information and a garage full of interactive selling features, such as detailed descriptions of current Toyota models and information on dealer locations and services, complete with maps and dealer Web links. Visitors who want to go further can use the Shop@Toyota feature to choose a Toyota, select equipment, and price it, then contact a dealer and even apply for credit. Or they fill out an online order form (supplying name, address, phone number, and e-mail address) for brochures and a free, interactive CD-ROM that shows off the features of Toyota models. The chances are good that before the CD-ROM arrives, a local dealer will call to invite the prospect in for a test drive. Toyota's Web site has now replaced its 800 number as the number-one source of customer leads.

B2B marketers also make good use of marketing Web sites. For example, customers visiting GE Plastics' Web site can draw on more than 1500 pages of information to get answers about the company's products anytime and from anywhere in the world. FedEx's Web site allows customers to schedule their own shipments, request package pickup, and track their packages in transit.

Designing Attractive Web Sites Creating a Web site is one thing; getting people to *visit* the site is another. The key is to create enough value and excitement to get consumers to come to the site, stick around, and come back again. This means that companies must constantly update their sites to keep them current, fresh, and exciting. Doing so involves time and expense, but the expense is necessary if the e-marketer wants to cut through the increasing online clutter. In addition, many online marketers spend heavily on good old-fashioned advertising and other offline marketing avenues to attract visitors to their sites. Says one analyst, "The reality today is you can't build a brand simply on the Internet. You have to go offline."[27]

Toyota
www.toyota.com

FedEx
www.fedex.ca

Marketing Web site: Visitors to SonyStyle.ca can search for products, check out the latest hot deals, and place orders online, all with a few clicks of the mouse.

For some types of products, attracting visitors is easy. Consumers buying new cars, computers, or financial services are usually open to information and marketing initiatives from sellers. Marketers of lower-involvement products, however, may face a difficult challenge in attracting Web site visitors. As one veteran notes, "If you're shopping for a computer and you see a banner that says, 'We've ranked the top 12 computers to purchase,' you're going to click on the banner. [But] what kind of banner could encourage any consumer to visit dentalfloss.com?"[28]

For such low-interest products, the company can create a corporate Web site to answer customer questions, build goodwill and excitement, supplement selling efforts through other channels, and collect customer feedback. For example, although Nabisco's LifeSavers Candystand Web site doesn't sell candy, it does generate a great deal of consumer excitement and sales support:

Nabisco's highly entertaining LifeSavers Candystand.com Web site, teeming with free videogames, endless sweepstakes, and sampling offers, has cast a fresh face on a brand that kid consumers once perceived as a stodgy adult confection. The Web site grabs 2.5 million visitors per month, mostly children and teenagers, and these surfers are not just passing through. They're clicking the mouse for an average 27-minute stay playing Foul Shot Shootout, Waterpark Pinball, and dozens of other arcade-style games, all while soaking in a LifeSavers aura swirling with information about products. "Our philosophy is to create an exciting online experience that reflects the fun and quality associated with the LifeSavers brands," says Silvio Bonvini, senior manager of new media at LifeSavers Company. "For the production cost of about two television spots, we have a marketing vehicle that lives 24 hours a day, seven days a week, 365 days a year." While Candystand.com has not directly sold a single roll of candy, the buzz generated by the site makes it an ideal vehicle for offering consumers their first glimpse of a new product, usually with an offer to get free samples by mail. In addition, LifeSavers reps use the site as sales leverage to help seal distribution deals when they talk with retailers. And the site offers LifeSavers an efficient channel for gathering customer feedback. Its "What Do You Think?" feature has generated 180 000 responses since the site launched in March 1997. "It's instant communication that we pass along directly to our brand people," Bonvini says. "It's not filtered by an agency or edited in any way." Comments collected from the Web site have resulted in improved packaging of one LifeSavers product and the resurrection of the abandoned flavor of another.[29]

A key challenge is designing a Web site that is attractive on first view and interesting enough to encourage repeat visits. The early text-based Web sites have largely been replaced in recent years by graphically sophisticated Web sites that provide text, sound, and animation (for examples, see SonyStyle or Nike's Web sites). To attract new visitors and to encourage revisits, suggests one expert, e-marketers should pay close attention to the seven Cs of effective Web site design:[30]

SonyStyle
www.sonystyle.ca

Nike
www.nike.ca

1. *Context:* the site's layout and design

2. *Content:* the text, pictures, sound, and video on the Web site

3. *Community:* the ways that the site enables user-to-user communication

4. *Customization:* the site's ability to tailor itself to different users or to allow users to personalize the site

5. *Communication:* the ways the site enables site-to-user, user-to-site, or two-way communication

6. *Connection:* the degree to which the site is linked to other sites

7. *Commerce:* the site's ability to enable commercial transactions

In all, a Web site should be easy to use and physically attractive. Beyond this, however, Web sites must also be interesting, useful, and challenging. Ultimately, it's the value of the site's *content* that will attract visitors, get them to stay longer, and bring them back for more.

Effective Web sites contain deep and useful information, interactive tools that help buyers find and evaluate products of interest, links to other related sites, changing promotional offers, and entertaining features that lend relevant excitement. For example, Clinique.com offers in-depth information about cosmetics, a library of beauty tips, a computer for determining the buyer's skin type, advice from visiting experts, a bulletin board, a bridal guide, a directory of new products, and pricing information. Burpee.com provides aspiring gardeners with everything they need to make this year's garden the best ever. Besides selling seeds and plants by the thousands, the site offers an incredible wealth of information resources, including a Garden Wizard (to help new gardeners pick the best plants for specific sun and soil conditions), the Burpee Garden School (online classes about plants and plant care), an archive of relevant service articles, and a chance to subscribe to an e-mail newsletter containing timely tips and gardening secrets.

Effective Web sites contain useful information, helpful tools, and entertaining features. Burpee.com provides aspiring gardeners with a wealth of resources, including the Burpee Garden School and a Garden Wizard to help them pick the best plants for specific conditions.

Periodically, a company must reassess its Web site's attractiveness and useful-ness. One way is by inviting the opinion of site design experts. But a better way is by having users themselves evaluate what they like and dislike about the site and offer suggestions for improving it. For example, Otis Elevator Company's Web site serves 20 000 registered customers, among them architects, general contractors, building managers, and others interested in elevators. The site, offered in 52 coun-tries and 26 languages, provides a wealth of helpful information, from moderniza-tion, maintenance, and safety information to drawings of various Otis models. Otis uses two sources of information to gauge satisfaction with its complex site. First, in an effort to detect potential problems, it tracks hits, time spent on the site, fre-quently visited pages, and the sequence of pages the customer visits. Second, it con-ducts quarterly phone surveys with 200 customers each in half the countries in which Otis does business. Such customer satisfaction tracking has resulted in numerous site improvements. For example, Otis found that customers in other countries were having trouble linking to the page that would let them buy an ele-vator online; now, the link is easier to find. Some customers were finding it hard to locate a local Otis office, so the company added an Office Locator feature.[31]

Placing Ads and Promotions Online E-marketers can use **online advertising** to build their Internet brands or to attract visitors to their Web sites. Here, we dis-cuss forms of online advertising promotion and their future.

Online advertising Advertising that appears while consumers are surfing the Web, including banner and ticker ads, interstitials, skyscrapers, and other forms.

Forms of Online Advertising and Promotion Online ads pop up while Internet users are surfing online. Such ads include banner ads and tickers (banners that move across the screen). For example, a Web user or ISP subscriber who is looking up air-line schedules or fares might find a flashing banner on the screen exclaiming, "Rent a car from Budget and get up to two days free!" To attract visitors to its own Web site, Lincoln sponsors Web banner ads on other sites, such as TSN, to advertise the new Navigator model. New online ad formats include skyscrapers (tall, skinny ads at the side of a Web page and rectangles (boxes that are much larger than a banner).

Interstitials are online ads that pop up between changes on a Web site. Visitors to MSNBC who visit the site's sports area might suddenly be viewing a separate window hawking wireless video cameras. Ads for Johnson & Johnson's Tylenol headache reliever pop up on brokers' Web sites whenever the stock market falls by 100 points or more. Sponsors of *browser ads* pay viewers to watch them. For exam-ple, Alladvantage.com downloads a view bar to users where ads are displayed to tar-geted users. Viewers earn 20 cents to $1 per hour in return.

MSNBC **www.msnbc.com**

Content sponsorships are another form of Internet promotion. Many compan-ies gain name exposure on the Internet by sponsoring special content on various Web sites, such as news or financial information. For example, Sportchek advertises heavily on The Sports Network (TSN) and their ads can be seen rotating through the various home pages for specific sports that TSN offers, such as the NHL, NFL, and NBA. In this case, the sponsor pays for showing the content and, in turn, receives recognition as the provider of the particular service on the Web site. Sponsorships are best placed in carefully targeted sites where they can offer relevant information or a service to the audience. In the case of Sportchek, TSN provides an excellent target audience for sports equipment and clothing.

E-marketers can go online with *microsites,* limited areas on the Web managed and paid for by an external company. For example, an insurance company might create a microsite on a car-buying site, offering insurance advice for car buyers and at the same time offering good insurance deals. Internet companies can also develop alliances and affiliate programs in which they work with other online companies to "advertise" each other. For example, AOL has created many successful alliances with other companies and mentions their names on its site. Amazon.com has more than 350 000 affiliates who post Amazon.com banners on their Web sites.

Finally, e-marketers can use **viral marketing**, the Internet version of word-of-mouth marketing. Viral marketing involves creating an e-mail message or other marketing event that is so infectious that customers will want to pass it along to their friends. Because customers pass the message or promotion along to others, viral marketing can be very inexpensive. And when the information comes from a friend, the recipient is much more likely to open and read it.

Viral marketing can be very effective. For example, e-mail provider Hotmail grew to 12 million users in 18 months by offering free e-mail—every e-mail message sent contained a Hotmail ad and tag line at the bottom. Viral marketing can also work well for B2B marketers. For example, to improve customer relationships, Hewlett-Packard recently sent tailored e-mail newsletters to customers who had registered online. The newsletters contained information about optimizing the performance of H-P products and services. Now that was good, but here's the best part: The newsletters also featured a button that let customers forward the newsletters to friends or colleagues. By clicking the button, customers entered a Web site where they could type in the friend's e-mail address and a comment, then hit send. The system inserted the message above the newsletter and e-mailed the whole thing to the friend. New recipients were then asked if they'd like to receive future H-P newsletters. In this textbook case of viral marketing, Hewlett-Packard inexpensively met its goal of driving consumers to its Web site and ultimately increasing sales. "For those on our original e-mail list, the click-through rate was 10 to 15 percent," says an H-P executive. "For those who received it from a friend or colleague, it was between 25 and 40 percent."[32]

The Future of Online Advertising Although online advertising serves a useful purpose, the Internet will not soon rival the major television and print media. Many marketers still question the value of Internet advertising as an effective tool. Costs are reasonable compared with those of other advertising media but Web surfers can easily ignore such advertising and often do. Although many firms are experimenting with Web advertising, it plays only a minor role in most promotion mixes.

As a result, online advertising expenditures still represent only a small fraction of overall advertising media expenditures. Moreover, in spite of its early promise, the growth of online advertising spending has slowed recently. According to one account,

The Internet was supposed to be the ultimate ad medium, the killer app that would eclipse newspapers, magazines, even television. But it's become increasingly clear that the online ad boom was largely a mirage, one created by the unfettered spending of the dot-coms themselves. Flush with venture funding…. Internet companies had been only too happy to ring one another's Web

Viral marketing The Internet version of word-of-mouth marketing—the creation of e-mail messages or other marketing events that are so infectious that customers will want to pass them along to their friends.

sites with flashing banners. Those days are over: After growing at a compound annual rate of 103 percent to an estimated $8 billion last year, online ad spending [this year] is expected to be completely flat.[33]

The drop-off in Web advertising has caused hard times for companies that rely on it for profits. Companies such as DoubleClick and 24/7 Media that sell ads for large groups of Web sites are struggling. Many ad-dependent sites, such as AngryMan.com and Pseudo.com, have gone out of business entirely. The nation's most heavily trafficked Web site, Yahoo, which relies on Web advertising for 90 percent of its revenue, has seen its stock price plunge from more than $250 at its peak to little more than $30 today. Facing these new realities, companies are now seeking more effective forms and uses of Web advertising and marketing (see New Directions 3-1).

Despite the recent setbacks, some industry insiders remain optimistic about the future of online advertising. "The reports of online advertising's death are not just exaggerated," says one such optimist, "they are stupendously wrong. The online advertising business has grown from next to nothing in 1994 to $8.2 billion in 2000—a new-media trajectory unmatched in the annals of advertising. Web advertising has already blown past the venerable outdoor category, which had revenues of $5 billion last year. It is breathing down the tailpipes of the cable-TV ad business."[34]

New Directions 3-1>> Online Advertising: For the Survivors, There Still Will Be Gold in Webland

To reach eyeballs without glazing them over, MyPoints.com offers surfers points and prizes for agreeing to visit companies' sites, read their ads and e-mail, or buy their products online.

Advertising was supposed to be the gold paving the Internet's busy streets. Consumers would eagerly surf, chat, and shop, and ads would pay Web companies for providing all those cool sites. In return, marketers would flash brightly colored banners at viewers, entice them to click through to their own sites, and get lots of business. But it didn't happen that way. Today, banner ad click-through rates have plummeted to a tiny 0.1 percent, ad rates may be heading from $33 per thousand-page-requests a year ago into the single digits, and ad volumes are falling. The blowout is pushing even the best-known sites down financial black holes.

What went wrong? It turns out that the Internet opened up brand-new worlds for advertisers, only they didn't see it. They tried to do what they always did—post their names in big letters, build their brands in two dimensions. But they didn't seize on the Net's potential or exploit its unique characteristics, such as the ability to target individual preferences and engage customers in interactivity. "This is the true value of what the Internet provides marketers," says Christopher Todd, analyst at Jupiter Media Metrix.

Web operators that based their businesses entirely on the expected free flow of ad dollars are learning that the hard way. "No longer can anyone in this space rely on only one revenue stream," warns John Fullmer, CEO of Internet direct marketer MyPoints.com. But those whose broader approach has kept them alive may yet reap benefits as marketers get smarter about the Net. For starters, advertising hasn't all dried up. Much of the current ad decline is due to the flameout of dot-coms that spent wildly online to build their new brands. "The kindling has been burned through," says Tim McHale, chief media officer of Tribal DDB Worldwide, whose clients include Anheuser-Busch, McDonald's, and Volkswagen. Traditional marketers may be cutting back, but they're not bailing out. A few, like IBM, are even ratcheting up their Internet ad budgets.

But this time, it will be different. It's now clear that folks are getting as good at screening out online banner ads as they are at tuning out TV commercials or flipping past glossies in a magazine. So companies are finding ways to reach eyeballs without glazing them over.

Some advertisers are ditching banner ads totally, instead using old-fashioned TV spots to drive traffic directly to their Web sites, rather than through intermediaries like portals. Other companies are signing up with sites that essentially pay consumers to engage with a mall full of marketers. At MyPoints.com, for example, surfers collect points and prizes for agreeing to visit companies' sites, read their e-mail, or buy their products online. Another tack: bidding for prime spots on search engines. By paying to top the list of results for users who search for, say, "banking" on GoTo.com, a marketer such as Citicorp ensures it is reaching live prospects. A study by researcher NPD Group Inc. shows that a top position is three times more effective than a banner ad in building brand awareness on a search-engine site.

And even though they're taking the biggest hit right now, banner ads aren't going away—just as roadside billboards didn't disappear once such alternatives as TV arrived. Web sites are now willing to offer advertisers more shapes and sizes to play with, pop-up ads are developing a following, and the roll-out of broadband will bring streaming videos with grabbier messages. And while banner ads could capture some data about clickers before, agencies are helping marketers to track customer profiles more minutely. Avenue A Inc., for example, is working with client BestBuy.com Inc. to identify whether a visitor directed to its site by a banner ad has ever visited the site before, has visited but not purchased anything, or has purchased goods there many times.

Still, plenty of pain is in store for ad buyers and sellers groping their way around this new medium. "We keep turning up evidence that this works, but we need to get through the slowdown," says Avenue A CEO Brian P. McAndrews. For the survivors, there still will be gold in Webland.

Source: Reprinted with permission from Gerry Khermouch and Tom Lowry, "The Future of Advertising," *Business Week*, 26 March 2001, p. 138.

Creating or Participating in Web Communities The popularity of forums and newsgroups has resulted in a rash of commercially sponsored Web sites called **Web communities**, which take advantage of the C2C properties of the Internet. Such sites allow members to congregate online and exchange views on issues of common interest. They are the cyberspace equivalent to a coffeehouse, a place where everybody knows your e-mail address.

For example, iVillage.com is a Web community in which women can exchange views and obtain information, support, and solutions on families, food, fitness, relationships, relaxation, home and garden, news and issues, or just about any other topic. The site draws 214 million page views per month, putting it in a league with magazines such as *Cosmopolitan*, *Glamour*, and *Vogue*. Another example is

Web communities Web sites on which members can congregate online and exchange views on issues of common interest.

Web communities: iVillage.com, a Web community for women, draws 214 million page views per month. The site provides an ideal environment for Web ads of companies such as Procter & Gamble, Kimberly Clark, Avon, and others.

MyFamily.com, which aspires to be the largest and most active online community for families in the world. It provides free, private family Web sites to which family members can connect online to hold family discussions, share family news, create online family photo albums, maintain a calendar of family events, share family history information, jointly build family trees, and buy gifts for family members quickly and easily. "People talk about forming communities on the Internet," says cofounder Paul Allen. "Well, the oldest community is the family."[35]

Visitors to these Internet neighbourhoods develop a strong sense of community. Such communities are attractive to advertisers because they draw consumers with common interests and well-defined demographics. Moreover, cyberhood consumers visit frequently and stay online longer, increasing the chance of meaningful exposure to the advertiser's message. For example, iVillage provides an ideal environment for the Web ads of companies such as Procter & Gamble, Kimberly Clark, Avon, Hallmark, and others who target female consumers. And MyFamily.com hosts The Shops@MyFamily, in which such companies as Disney, Kodak, Hallmark, Compaq, Hewlett-Packard, and Microsoft advertise and sell their family-oriented products.

Web communities can be either social or work related. One successful work-related community is @griculture Online. This site offers commodity prices, recent farm news, and chat rooms of all types. Rural surfers can visit the Electronic Coffee Shop and pick up the latest down-on-the-farm joke or join a hot discussion on controlling soybean cyst nematodes. @griculture Online has been highly successful, attracting as many as 5 million hits per month.[36]

Using E-Mail and Webcasting E-mail has exploded onto the scene as an important e-marketing tool. Jupiter Media Metrix estimates that companies will be spending $7.3 billion annually on e-mail marketing by 2005, up from $164 million in 1999.[37] To compete effectively in this cluttered e-mail environment, marketers are designing "enriched" e-mail messages—animated, interactive, and personalized messages full of streaming audio and video. Then they are carefully targeting these attention-grabbers to those who want them and will act on them. (See New Directions 3-2.)

New Directions 3-2 >> The New World of E-Mail Marketing

E-mail is *the* hot new marketing medium. In ever-larger numbers, e-mail ads are popping onto our computer screens and filling up our e-mailboxes. What's more, they're no longer just the quiet, plain-text messages of old. The new breed of e-mail ad is designed to command your attention—loaded with glitzy features such as animation, interactive links, colour photos, streaming video, and personalized audio messages.

But if you think that you're already getting too much e-mail, hang onto your mouse. Jupiter Media Metrix predicts that the number of commercial e-mail messages sent per year will increase from an already daunting 43 billion in 2000 to an inbox-busting 375 billion by 2005. And no wonder. E-mail allows marketers to send tailored messages to targeted consumers who actually want to receive them, at a cost of only a few cents per contact. Even better, they can target audiences in any country and get responses within 24 hours.

As in any other direct-marketing effort, e-mail success depends on a good customer database. Companies can obtain e-mail addresses from outside list brokers. However, the best way to build an e-mail database easily is simply to ask customers for their e-mail addresses at every point of contact. Marketers can ask for e-mail addresses on their Web sites, in their brick-and-mortar stores, via response cards sent with catalogues, during customer service calls, or even in print ads. Some marketers sponsor sign-up promotions, offering sweepstakes or prizes as incentives to customers who fork over their e-mail addresses. All of these are permission-based methods that allow customers to "opt in" or "opt out," ensuring that e-mails are sent only to customers who ask for them. "That leaves marketers largely immune from the wrath of privacy advocates and spam fighters," states *Business Week* writer Arlene Weintraub.

Another advantage of e-mail ads is that companies can track customer responses—how many people open the message, who clicks through to the Web site, and what they do when they get there. And well-designed e-mail ads really do command attention and get customers to act. ITM Strategies, a sales and marketing research firm, estimates that permission e-mail campaigns typically achieve 10 percent to 15 percent click-through rates. That's good when compared with the 0.5 percent to 2 percent average response rates for traditional direct mail.

E-mail success stories abound. *Business Week* offers these:

Zomba Recording, corporate parent of teen band 'N Sync's label Jive Records, cooked up an e-campaign that made other marketers drool. In March, 200 000 fans received a video message about the album *No Strings Attached* that allowed them to hear band members speak and to listen to a snippet of the song "Bye Bye Bye." Fans went wild: 34 percent of the e-mail recipients, whose names had been collected from the 'N Sync Web site, downloaded the video. Of those, 88 percent clicked on one of the links. Thousands forwarded the e-mail to friends. In the world of direct marketing, where a 1 percent response rate is considered acceptable, the numbers were extraordinary. *No Strings Attached* had its debut in April and sold 2.4 million copies in its first week—the biggest opening since SoundScan started tracking sales in 1991. "E-mail is a technology that kids are really into, so it was a great direct-hit way to get to them," says Jeff Dodes, vice president for new media and Internet operations at Zomba.

Kids aren't the only targets for e-mail ads. Customers of golf-supply retailer Chipshot.com—average age 41—received e-ads for a new line of clubs. The mail included streaming video and an audio message that greeted recipients using their first names. Of those who received it, 14.7 percent clicked through to the site, and 11.6 percent of them bought the clubs. "The multimedia message with animated graphics looked very attractive," says Nick Mehta, Chipshot's vice president for interactive marketing. "We saw 98 percent more revenue per customer among people who received that message versus those who got just a standard e-mail."

Still, even permission-based e-mail can be very annoying. "Even among consumers who opt in to the e-mail barrage, there's a fine line between legitimate marketing and spam," says Weintraub. "As more companies glom onto the trend, there is strong potential for a backlash." Companies crossing that fine line will quickly learn that "opting out" is only a click away for disgruntled customers. According to Weintraub, marketers are aware of the potential for irritation and are taking steps to head it off:

> Petopia.com, which mails monthly e-newsletters and personalized pet birthday messages, has set its computer system to automatically limit the number of e-mails any one customer receives in a month. Handheld-computer maker Palm Inc. has been experimenting with the length of its e-ads, and recently found that a 150-word message produced a better click-through rate than 300 words did. IKEA took an even more drastic step. In April, the furniture retailer promoted its new San Francisco store by e-mailing customers and inviting them to send virtual postcards to friends through its

site. A mind-boggling 70 000 postcards were sent in 10 days. But when a handful of recipients cried "spam!," IKEA pulled the campaign. "We only want to communicate with customers in ways that they think are appropriate," says Rich D'Amico, IKEA's manager of new business development.

Still, marketing history is full of examples of effective tactics that were taken too far, and some experts see little reason to expect that e-mail advertising will be any different. "It will be overdone," predicts the president of a firm that creates e-mail campaigns. "Brace your e-mail box for the results," adds Weintraub.

Sources: Quotes and extracts from Arlene Weintraub, "When E-Mail Ads Aren't Spam," *Business Week*, 16 October 2000, pp. 112–114. Also see Chad Kaydo, "As Good As It Gets," *Sales and Marketing Management*, March 2000, pp. 55–60; Eileen P. Gunn, "Marketers Are Keen on Enriched E-Mail," *Advertising Age*, 16 October 2000, p. S12; Dana James, "Addresses (Are) the Issue," *Marketing News,* 9 October 2000, p. 19; and Stephen J. Eustace, "The World Is Your Cybermarket," *Target Marketing*, April 2001, pp. 54–56.

E-mail is becoming a mainstay for both B2C and B2B marketers. 3Com Corporation, a B2B marketer of high-tech computer hardware, made good use of e-mail to generate and qualify customer leads for its network interface cards. The company used targeted e-mail and banner ads on 18 different computer-related Web sites to attract potential buyers to its own Web site featuring a "3Com Classic" sweepstakes—by filling out the entry form, visitors could register to win a 1959 Corvette. The campaign generated 22 000 leads, which were further qualified using e-mail and telemarketing. "Hot" leads were passed along to 3Com's inside sales force. "[Sales reps] were very skeptical," says a 3Com marketing manager, "but they were blown away by how well the contest did." Of the 482 leads given to reps, 71 turned into actual sales that totalled $2.5 million. What's more, states the manager, "Now I've got 22 000 names in my e-mail database that I can go back and market to."[38]

Companies can also sign on with any of a number of "**Webcasting**" services, which automatically download customized information to recipients' computers. An example is Internet Financial Network's Infogate, which sends up-to-date financial news, market data, and real-time stock quotes to subscribers in the financial services industry for a fee. Infogate frames the top and bottom inch of subscribers' computer screens with personalized news and other information tailored to their specific interests. Rather than spending hours scouring the Internet, subscribers can sit back while Infogate automatically delivers information of interest to their desktops.[39] The major commercial online services also offer Webcasting to their members. For example, America Online offers a feature called Driveway that will fetch information, Web pages, and e-mail-based articles on members' preferences and automatically deliver it to their computers.

Webcasting The automatic downloading of customized information to recipients' computers, creating an attractive channel for delivering Internet advertising or other information.

Also known as "push" programming, Webcasting creates an attractive channel through which online marketers can deliver their Internet advertising or other information content. For example, via Infogate, advertisers can market their products and services using highly targeted messages to a desirable segment of at-work Internet users.

As with other types of online marketing, companies must be careful that they don't cause resentment among Internet users who are already overloaded with "junk e-mail." Warns one analyst, "There's a fine line between adding value and the consumer feeling that you're being intrusive."[40] Companies must beware of irritating consumers by sending unwanted e-mail to promote their products. Netiquette, the unwritten rules that guide Internet etiquette, suggests that marketers should ask customers for permission to e-mail marketing pitches—and tell recipients how to "opt in" or "opt out" of e-mail promotions at any time. This approach, known as permission-based marketing, has become a standard model for e-mail marketing.

THE PROMISE AND CHALLENGES OF E-COMMERCE

E-commerce continues to offer great promise for the future. Its most ardent followers still envision a time when the Internet and e-commerce will replace magazines, newspapers, and even stores as sources for information and buying. However, such "dot-com fever" has cooled recently and a more realistic view has emerged. "It's time for Act II in the Internet revolution," suggests one analyst. "The first act belonged to dot-coms with big visions and small bank accounts. Now the stage will be taken by big companies that move their factories, warehouses, and customers onto the Web."[41]

To be sure, online marketing will become a successful business model for some companies—Internet firms such as Amazon.com, eBay, Yahoo, and Netscape and direct-marketing companies such as Charles Schwab and Dell Computer. Michael Dell's goal is one day "to have *all* customers conduct *all* transactions on the Internet, globally." And e-business will continue to boom for many B2B marketers, companies such as Cisco Systems, General Electric, and Hewlett-Packard.

However, for most companies, online marketing will remain just one important approach to the marketplace that works alongside other approaches in a fully integrated marketing mix. Eventually, the "e" will fall away from e-business or e-marketing as companies become more adept at integrating e-commerce with their everyday strategy and tactics. "The key question is not whether to deploy Internet technology—companies have no choice if they want to stay competitive—but how to deploy it," says business strategist Michael Porter. He continues: "We need to move away from the rhetoric about 'Internet industries,' 'e-business strategies,' and a 'new economy,' and see the Internet for what it is:…a powerful set of tools that can be used, wisely or unwisely, in almost any industry and as part of almost any strategy."[42]

Along with its considerable promise, e-commerce faces many challenges. Here are just some of the challenges that online marketers face:

- *Limited consumer exposure and buying:* Although expanding rapidly, online marketing still reaches only a limited marketspace. Moreover, in most product categories, many Web users still do more window browsing and product research than actual buying.

- *Skewed user demographics and psychographics:* Although the Web audience is becoming more mainstream, online users still tend to be somewhat more upscale and more technology oriented than the general population. This makes online marketing ideal for marketing computer hardware and software, consumer electronics, financial services, and certain other classes of products. However, it makes online marketing less effective for selling mainstream products.

- *Chaos and clutter:* The Internet offers millions of Web sites and a staggering volume of information. Thus, navigating the Internet can be frustrating, confusing, and time-consuming for consumers. In this chaotic and cluttered environment, many Web ads and sites go unnoticed or unopened. Even when noticed, marketers will find it difficult to hold consumers' attention. One study found that a site must capture Web surfers' attention within eight seconds or lose them to another site. That leaves very little time for marketers to promote and sell their goods.

- *Security:* Some consumers worry that unscrupulous snoopers will eavesdrop on their online transactions or intercept their credit card numbers and make unauthorized purchases. In turn, companies doing business online fear that others will use the Internet to invade their computer systems for commercial espionage or even sabotage. Online marketers are developing solutions to such security problems, and this has relieved most buyer fears in recent years. However, there appears to be an ongoing competition between the technology of Internet security systems and the sophistication of those seeking to break them.

- *Ethical concerns:* Privacy is a primary concern. Marketers can easily track Web site visitors, and many consumers who participate in Web site activities provide extensive personal information. This may leave consumers open to information abuse if companies make unauthorized use of the information in marketing their products or exchanging electronic lists with other companies.

Canada has recognized the potential loss of the right to privacy in the rapid growth of online commerce and information technology. Canada's Parliament passed a new law, the Personal Information Protection and Electronic Documents Act, which took effect 1 January 2001.[43] This Act (subtitled Bill C-6) stringently defines "personal information," and it requires that organizations collect personal information in a fair and lawful manner and obtain an individual's consent before usage. We have the right to decide who will see our personal information and how it will be used.

Concerns have also arisen about segmentation and discrimination online. The Internet currently serves upscale consumers well; however, poorer consumers have less access to the Internet, leaving them increasingly less informed about products, services, and prices.[44]

Despite these challenges, companies large and small are quickly integrating online marketing into their marketing strategies and mixes. As it continues to grow, online marketing will be a powerful tool for building customer relationships, improving sales, communicating company and product information, and delivering products and services more efficiently and effectively.

<< Looking Back   < < < < < < < < <

In the first two chapters, you discovered the fundamentals of marketing and marketing strategy. In this chapter, you learned about some major changes in the marketing landscape that are having an impact on marketing practice. Recent technological advances have created a new Internet age. To thrive in this new environment, marketers will have to add some Internet thinking to their strategies and tactics. This chapter introduced the forces shaping the new Internet environment and how marketers are adapting. In the next chapter, we'll look at other forces and actors affecting the complex and changing marketing environment.

1. Identify the major forces shaping the Internet age.

Four major forces underlie the Internet age: digitalization and connectivity, the explosion of the Internet, new types of intermediaries, and customization and customerization. Much of today's business operates on digital information, which flows through connected networks. Intranets, extranets, and the Internet now connect people and companies with each other and with important information. The Internet has grown explosively to become *the* revolutionary technology of the new millennium, empowering consumers and businesses alike with connectivity.

The Internet and other new technologies have changed the ways that companies serve their markets. New Internet marketers and channel relationships have arisen to replace some types of traditional marketers. The new technologies are also helping marketers to tailor their offers effectively to targeted customers or even to help customers customerize their own marketing offers. Finally, the new economy technologies are blurring the boundaries between industries, allowing companies to pursue opportunities that lie at the convergence of two or more industries.

2. Explain how companies have responded to the Internet and other powerful new technologies

with e-business strategies, and explain how these strategies have resulted in benefits to both buyers and sellers.

Conducting business in the new economy calls for a new model of marketing strategy and practice. Companies need to retain most of the skills and practices that have worked in the past. However, they must also add major new competencies and practices if they hope to grow and prosper in the new economy. E-business is the use of electronic platforms to conduct business. E-commerce involves buying and selling processes supported by electronic means, primarily the Internet. It includes e-marketing (the selling side of e-commerce) and e-purchasing (the buying side of e-commerce).

E-commerce benefits both buyers and sellers. For buyers, e-commerce makes buying convenient and private, provides greater product access and selection, and makes available a wealth of product and buying information. It is interactive and immediate and gives the consumer a greater measure of control over the buying process. For sellers, e-commerce is a powerful tool for building customer relationships. It also increases the sellers' speed and efficiency, helping to reduce selling costs. E-commerce also offers great flexibility and better access to global markets.

3. Describe the four major e-commerce domains.

Companies can practice e-commerce in any or all of four domains. B2C (business-to-consumer) e-commerce is initiated by businesses and targets final consumers. Despite recent setbacks following the "dot-com gold rush" of the late 1990s, B2C e-commerce continues to grow at a healthy rate. Although online consumers are still somewhat higher in income and more technology oriented than traditional buyers, the cyberspace population is becoming much more mainstream and diverse. This growing diversity opens up new e-commerce targeting opportunities for marketers. Today, consumers can buy almost anything on the Web. B2B (business-to-business) e-commerce dwarfs B2C e-commerce. Most businesses today operate Web sites or use B2B trading networks, auction sites, spot exchanges, online product catalogues, barter sites, or other online resources to reach new customers, serve current customers more effectively, and obtain buying efficiencies and better prices. Business buyers and sellers meet in huge marketspaces—or open trading networks—to share information and complete transactions efficiently. Or, they set up private trading networks that link them with their own trading partners.

Through C2C (consumer-to-consumer) e-commerce, consumers can buy or exchange goods and information directly from or with one another. Examples include online auction sites, forums, and Internet newsgroups. Finally, through C2B (consumer-to-business) e-commerce, consumers are now finding it easier to search out sellers on the Web, learn about their products and services, and initiate purchases. Using the Web, customers can even drive transactions with business, rather than the other way around.

4. Discuss how companies can conduct e-commerce to profitably deliver more value to customers.

Companies of all types are now engaged in e-commerce. The Internet gave birth to the *click-only* dot-coms, which operate only online. In addition, many traditional brick-and-mortar companies have now added e-marketing operations, transforming themselves into *click-and-mortar* competitors. Many click-and-mortar companies are now having more online success than their click-only competitors.

Companies can conduct e-marketing in any of four ways: creating a Web site, placing ads and promotions online, setting up or participating in Web communities, or using online e-mail or Webcasting.

The first step typically is to set up a Web site. Corporate Web sites are designed to build customer goodwill and to supplement other sales channels, rather than to sell the company's products directly. Marketing Web sites engage consumers in an interaction that will move them closer to a direct purchase or other marketing outcome. Beyond simply setting up a site, companies must make their sites engaging, easy to use, and useful to attract visitors, hold them, and bring them back again.

E-marketers can use various forms of online advertising to build their Internet brands or to attract visitors to their Web sites. Beyond online advertising, other forms of online marketing include content sponsorships, microsites, and viral marketing, the Internet version of word-of-mouth marketing. Online marketers can also participate in Web communities, which take advantage of the C2C properties of the Web. Finally, e-mail marketing has become a hot new e-marketing tool for both B2C and B2B marketers.

5. Summarize the promise and challenges that e-commerce presents for the future.

E-commerce continues to offer great promise for the future. For most companies, online marketing will become an important part of a fully integrated marketing mix. For others, it will be the major means by which they serve the market. Eventually, the "e" will fall away from e-business or e-marketing as companies become more adept at integrating e-commerce with their everyday strategy and tactics. However, e-commerce also faces many challenges. Among these are limited consumer exposure and buying, skewed user profiles, chaos and clutter, security, and ethical concerns. Despite these challenges, most companies are rapidly integrating online marketing into their marketing strategies and mixes.

Navigating the Key Terms

B2B (business-to-business) e-commerce, **p. 92**
B2C (business-to-consumer) e-commerce, **p. 90**
C2B (consumer-to-business) e-commerce, **p. 95**
C2C (consumer-to-consumer) e-commerce, **p. 94**
Click-and-mortar companies, **p. 98**
Click-only companies, **p. 96**
Corporate Web site, **p. 101**
Customerization, **p. 85**
E-business, **p. 86**
E-commerce, **p. 86**
E-marketing, **p. 86**

Extranet, **p. 83**
Internet, **p. 83**
Intranet, **p. 83**
Marketing Web site, **p. 101**
Online advertising, **p. 105**
Open trading networks, **p. 93**
Private trading networks (PTN), **p. 93**
Viral marketing, **p. 106**
Web communities, **p. 108**
Webcasting, **p. 111**

Concept Check

Fill in the blanks and then check your answers.

1. Four specific forces that underlie the new economy are _____ and _____, the explosion of the Internet, new types of intermediaries, and _____ and _____.

2. _____ connect a company with its suppliers and distributors.

3. If a new e-tailer cuts out a traditional intermediary in a channel relationship, then the traditional intermediary has been _____.

4. In _____, the company leaves it to individual customers to design the product or service offering.

5. Internet buying benefits both final buyers and sellers in many ways. It is _____; buying is _____ and _____; buyers have greater _____ and _____; channels give comparative information; and online buying is interactive and immediate.

6. _____ networks are huge e-marketspaces in which buyers and sellers find each other online, share information, and complete transactions efficiently.

7. When buyers use Travelocity.ca to bid for airline tickets and hotel rooms, they are conducting _____ e-commerce.

8. According to Figure 3-3, the three types of e-marketers are _____, _____, and _____.

9. The seven Cs of effective Web site design are _____, _____, _____, _____, communication, connection, and commerce.

10. _____ marketing involves creating an e-mail message or other marketing event that is so infectious that customers will want to pass it along to their friends.

11. _____ services automatically download customized information to a recipient's computer.

12. Online users tend to be somewhat more upscale and more technology oriented than the general population. This would be an example of the _____ challenge that online marketers face.

Concept Check Answers: 1. Digitalization and connectivity; customization and customerization; 2. Extranets; 3. Disintermediated; 4. Customerization; 5. Convenient; easy and private; product access and selection; 6. Open trading; 7. C2B (consumer-to-business); 8. Click-only; brick-and-mortar only; click-and-mortar; 9. context, content, community, customization; 10. Viral; 11. Webcasting; 12. Skewed user demographics and psychographics.

Discussing the Issues

1. Discuss how a traditional retailer or wholesaler can be *disintermediated* by the new e-tailer. Give an example to illustrate.

2. Explain and illustrate how customization differs from customerization.

3. Describe and illustrate the many benefits that e-commerce and the Internet bring to both buyers and sellers.

4. The statement has been made that all companies need to consider moving into e-marketing. List and discuss the four generally accepted ways that a company can conduct e-marketing. Pick a local retailer or service provider that has not yet moved into e-marketing and suggest how they might do this. Be specific.

5. Pick a favourite Web site and write a brief analysis of how the site rates on the seven Cs of effective Web site design. What forms of online advertising and promotion does your chosen Web site seem to be using to its advantage? How can the site be improved? Be specific.

 **Mastering Marketing**

Having an effective e-marketing presence is of primary importance in today's competitive marketplace. Explain how CanGo has or should use marketing in the wired world. Critique the organization's efforts by using the evaluation and analysis options suggested in this chapter. How effective have their efforts been to date? What suggestions would you offer to the company? Explain.

Check out the enclosed Video case CD-ROM, or our Companion Website at www.pearsoned.ca/armstrong, to view a CBC video segment and case for this chapter.

MAP 3 Marketing Applications

One of the oldest forms of marketing and promotion is word-of-mouth. In the new Internet age, word-of-mouth has become known as viral marketing. Viral marketing is really quite simple—tell a friend to tell a friend that something is hot and worth noticing. This has worked successfully with the Doom video game, *The Blair Witch Project* movie, Harry Potter books, Razor scooters, and Chrysler's PT Cruiser automobile, to name only a few. To create "buzz," the viral marketer targets a group of carefully chosen trend leaders in a community who are likely to use phone or Internet communication to spread the word about the product, event, or service. Think about it. Who do you believe most—your friends or an ad? The friends win easily. This form of messaging can also revive brands that have seen better days. Lucky Strike cigarettes, Lee jeans, and even Vespa scooters have seen increases in sales and interest as a result of such "new buzz" tactics. However, buzz-building in this technologically savvy marketplace is no easy task. In fact, it can become a public relations nightmare if the selected communicators choose to "trash" your product.

Effective viral marketing requires following a few simple rules to get just the right buzz about your product or service: (1) Identify trendsetters quickly and let them spread your message, (2) withhold supply early to simulate scarcity—everyone wants what they cannot have, (3) be authentic—no one wants a fake or to be tricked, and (4) be prepared to change quickly—every good firefighter knows when to retreat. If there is one thing that all viral marketers have learned it is this: start consumers talking and you will start selling.

Thinking Like a Marketing Manager

1. What applications can you think of for viral or buzz marketing on the Internet?

2. List three products that you have heard about from friends. Describe what you were told, how this matched ad claims, what action you took because of the information, and how likely you were to buy the products.

3. Assume you are the marketing manager for a new product to be sold primarily to consumers in your generation using the Internet. Describe how you would use viral marketing to accom-plish this. Be specific in the descriptive steps of your plan.

4. Choose an actual product and start a positive buzz about it using one of the communication methods suggested in the chapter. Keep a record of what you communicated and how you communicated the information. What were the results of your communication? What could you do to increase the effectiveness of the communication? How were "connections" made? How could an e-marketer make the same "connections"?

5. Consider the ethics of viral marketing. What could be the potential problems with the method? What cautions should be taken by an e-marketer wanting to use this technique?

Digital Map

Visit our Web site at **www.pearsoned.ca/armstrong** for online quizzes, Internet exercises, and more!

CASE 3   AMAZON.CA

On 25 June 2002, **Amazon.ca** was launched. However, unlike its much promoted and documented U.S.-based parent, Amazon.com, the launch was quiet, almost reserved. Given that Canada is Amazon.com's biggest export market, with hundreds of thousands of regular customers, why would the company launch in Canada?

As possible clues to the answer, it is worthwhile to look at Amazon.com's history. Amazon.com first opened its virtual doors in mid-July 1995, selling books out of founder Jeff Bezos's garage in suburban Seattle. It still sells books—by the millions. But it now sells products in a dozen other categories as well: from music, videos, consumer electronics, and computers to tools and hardware, kitchen and house-wares, toys, and baby products. "We have the Earth's Biggest Selection," declares the company's Web site.

In only a few short years, Amazon.com has become the best-known name on the Net. In the process, it is also rewriting the rules of marketing. "Amazon.com is blazing a trail in the world of commerce where no merchant has gone before," asserts business analyst Robert Hof. "By pioneering—and darn near perfecting—the art of selling online,…[Amazon.com has caused] a wrenching shift to a new

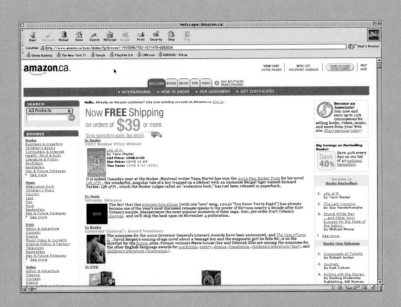

way of doing business." Its most ardent fans view Amazon.com as *the* model for new economy businesses of the twenty-first century. If any dot-com can make it, they believe, Amazon.com will.

Attracting customers and sales hasn't been a problem. In just the past two years, Amazon.com's customer base has grown more than sevenfold to 32 million customers in more than 220 countries. Sales have rocketed from a modest U.S.$15 million in 1996 to more than U.S.$3.1 billion at year-end 2001. So, what's the problem? Profits—or a lack thereof. Amazon.com's losses have mounted almost as fast as its sales, reaching more than U.S.$1.1 billion in 2000, or 40 percent of sales. Amazon.com, however, turned a modest profit in the fourth quarter of 2001 and continued to be profitable in the first quarter of 2002. Supporters attribute initial losses to high start-up costs. After all, they note, the company has started what amounts to several new businesses within only a few years.

No matter what your view of its future, there's little doubt that Amazon.com is an outstanding marketing company. To its core, the company is relentlessly customer-driven. "The thing that drives everything is creating genuine value for customers," says founder Jeff Bezos. "Nothing happens without that." A few years back, when asked when Amazon.com would start putting profits first rather than growth, Bezos replied, "Customers come first. If you focus on what customers want and build a relationship, they will allow you to make money."

The relationship with customers is the key to the company's future. Anyone at Amazon.com will tell you that the company wants to do much more than just sell books or DVDs or digital cameras. It wants to deliver a special *experience* to every customer. "The customer experience really matters," says Bezos. "We've focused on just having a better store, where it's easier to shop, where you can learn more about the products, where you have a bigger selection, and where you have the lowest prices.

You combine all of that stuff together and people say, 'Hey, these guys really get it.'"

And they do get it. Most Amazon.com regulars feel a surprisingly strong and personal relationship with the company, especially given the almost complete lack of actual human interaction. To offset the lack of human contact, Amazon.com was first to use "collaborative filtering" technology, which sifts through each customer's past purchases and the purchasing patterns of customers with similar profiles to come up with personalized site content. "We want Amazon.com to be the right store for you as an individual," says Bezos. "If we have 30 million customers, we should have 30 million stores."

The Canadian site is no different. Visitors to Amazon.ca's Web site receive a unique blend of benefits: the site is bilingual and offers a huge selection, good value, convenience, and what Amazon.com vice president Jason Kilar calls "discovery." In the book section, for example, Amazon.ca offers an easily searchable virtual selection of more than 1.5 million titles, seven and a half times more than any physical bookstore. Good value comes in the form of reasonable prices, with everyday discounts on the suggested retail price. And at Amazon.ca, it's irresistibly convenient to buy. With Amazon.ca's one-click checkout feature, you can log on, find what you want, and order with a single mouse click, all in less time than it takes to find a parking space at the local mall.

But it's the "discovery" factor that makes the Amazon.com or the Amazon.ca experience special. Once on the Web site, you're compelled to stay for a while—looking, learning, and discovering. Amazon.ca continues the concept of the online *community*, in which customers can browse for products and research purchase alternatives in books, music, and movies.

In addition to the ability to develop personalized relationships with millions of customers, selling on the Internet gives Amazon.ca some real advantages over its brick-and-mortar rivals. By selling direct to customers, Amazon.ca reaps significant cost advantages. At the Canadian site, management and transaction handling is still located in Seattle, within Amazon.com. It avoids the huge costs of building and operating stores and carrying large inventories. And whereas traditional retailers must continually build new stores to grow revenues, Amazon.ca can boost sales by simply attracting more customers to its new Web store.

Selling on the Web also presents serious challenges. Although it doesn't face store costs, Amazon.ca has had to make large initial investments in such things as computer systems, distribution centres, and customer acquisition. Perhaps more important, many people still like shopping in a real store, where they can rub elbows with other shoppers, touch and try out the merchandise, buy goods on the spot, and easily return purchases that don't work out.

Many experts predict that the future will belong to retailers who offer *both* "clicks" and "bricks," the current business model of Indigo Books and Music Inc. In fact, almost 60 percent of consumer online revenues are now captured by companies that sell both online and through traditional stores. In response to these new realities, Amazon.com is already partnering with real-world retailers. It recently teamed up with Toys "R" Us to create a co-branded toys and games Web site. Toys "R" Us handles purchasing and inventory. Amazon.ca oversees the customer experience—maintaining the Web site, filling orders, and managing customer service. Amazon.com is exploring a similar partnership with brick-and-mortar giant Wal-Mart. The Amazon.ca site has yet to promote these partnerships, preferring to focus on books, music, and DVDs, but as demand grows for the services that the Amazon.ca site offers, these partnerships will become part of the business expansion strategy.

So, what do you think? Does Amazon.ca really create superior value for customers? Will it eventually become the Wal-Mart of the Web? Or will it end up as just another dot-com has-been? Jeff Bezos, the founder and chief executive officer of Amazon.com characterized the new bilingual Canadian site as a benefit for Canadian publishers and consumers, as well as a champion for Canadian culture as a whole. "Anyone who is a proponent of Canadian culture should be ecstatic," Bezos stated in an interview. "We are going to make it available to the world."

Heather Reisman, chief executive officer of Indigo Books and Music Inc. predictably disagrees. She believes that Amazon.ca "opens the door to all kinds of things and changes the nature of the Canadian industry." Toronto retail consultant Wendy Evans, however, states that "any competition at the retail end is good in Canada," an obvious reference to Indigo's current dominant position as the major player in the Canadian industry.

It is clear that Amazon.ca will shake up the Canadian book-selling industry. The analogy in Canadian retailing would be that Indigo must feel like Zellers did when Wal-Mart said it was planning to expand into Canada.

Today's successful companies at all levels have one thing in common: Like Amazon.com and Amazon.ca, they are strongly customer focused and heavily committed to marketing. These companies share an absolute dedication to understanding and satisfying the needs of customers in well-defined target markets. They motivate everyone in the organization to produce superior value for their customers, leading to high levels of customer satisfaction. As cofounder Bernie Marcus of Home Depot asserts, "All of our people understand what the Holy Grail is. It's not the bottom line. It's an almost blind, passionate commitment to taking care of customers."

Questions

1. What are the relative advantages and disadvantages of doing business in the bricks-and-mortar retail environment?

2. What are the advantages and disadvantages of doing business strictly on the Internet?

3. Does Indigo have any competitive advantage over Amazon.ca? If so, how can it be exploited to differentiate Indigo from Amazon.ca? For example, do Canadians prefer to deal with Canadian companies? Recall that Canada is Amazon.com's largest export market.

4. As a consumer, how do you prefer to purchase books, music, and DVDs? Is your personal experience typical of consumers today? How about five years from now?

5. Put yourself in the position of senior marketing management at Indigo Books and Music Inc. What actions should Indigo take to compete effectively with Amazon.ca?

Sources: Stewart Alsop, "I'm Betting on Amazon," *Fortune,* 30 April 2001; Robert D. Hof, "Amazon.com: The Wild World of E-Commerce," *Business Week,* 14 December 1998; Kathleen Doler, "Interview: Jeff Bezos, Founder and CEO of Amazon.com Inc.," *Upside,* September 1998; Mathew Ingram, "On Balance, Amazon.ca Is Likely a Good Thing," *The Globe and Mail,* 26 June 2002, p. B12; Hollie Shaw, "Amazon.ca Takes Direct Aim at Indigo," *The Financial Post,* 25 June 2002, p. FP1; Elizabeth Church, "Amazon.ca Set to Go Today," 25 June 2002, p. B6; and "About Amazon.com," accessed online at **www.amazon.com**, July 2002.

4 >> The Marketing Environment

Looking Ahead

Now that you've seen how the new economy affects marketing strategy and practice, your marketing journey continues with a look at how to analyze marketing opportunities. In this chapter, you'll discover that marketing does not operate in a vacuum but rather in a complex and changing environment. Other *actors* in this environment—suppliers, intermediaries, customers, competitors, publics, and others—may work with or against the company. Major environmental *forces*—demographic, economic, natural, technological, political, and cultural—shape marketing opportunities, pose threats, and affect the company's ability to serve customers and develop lasting relationships with them. To understand marketing, and to develop effective marketing strategies, you must first understand the context in which marketing operates.

After studying this chapter, you should be able to

1. describe the environmental forces that affect the company's ability to serve its customers

2. explain how changes in the demographic and economic environments affect marketing decisions

3. identify the major trends in the firm's natural and technological environments

4. explain the key changes in the political and cultural environments

5. discuss how companies can react to the marketing environment

First, we'll check out a major development in the marketing environment, millennial fever, and the nostalgia boom that it has produced. Volkswagen responded with the introduction of a born-again New Beetle. As you read on, ask yourself: What makes this little car so right for the times?

As we settle in to the new millennium, social experts are busier than ever assessing the impact of a host of environmental forces on consumers and the marketers who serve them. "An old year turns into a new one," observes one such expert, "and the world itself, at least for a moment, seems to turn also. Images of death and rebirth, things ending and beginning, populate…and haunt the mind. Multiply this a thousand-fold, and you get 'millennial fever'…driving consumer behaviour in all sorts of interesting ways."

This millennial fever has hit the nation's baby boomers, the most commercially influential demographic group in history, especially hard. The oldest boomers, now in their mid-fifties, are resisting the aging process with the vigour they once reserved for antiwar protests. Other factors are also at work. Today, people of all ages seem to be overworked, overstimulated, and overloaded: many people feel overwhelmed by high-speed modems, cellular phones, and the instant nature of virtually everything in our lives. The result of this "millennial fever" is a yearning to turn back the clock, to return to simpler times. This yearning has in turn produced a massive nostalgia wave. "We are creating a new culture, and we don't know what's going to happen," explains a noted futurist. "So we need some warm fuzzies from our past." Marketers of all kinds have responded to these nostalgia pangs by recreating products and images that help take consumers back to "the good old days." Examples are plentiful: Kellogg has revived old Corn Flakes packaging and car makers have created retro roadsters such as the Porsche Boxter and Chrysler's PT Cruiser. Disney developed an entire town—Celebration, Florida— to recreate the look and feel of 1940s neighbourhoods. According to a Coca-Cola marketing executive, when the company introduced a plastic version of its famous contour bottle in 1994, sales grew by double digits in some markets.

Perhaps no company has more riding on the nostalgia wave than Volkswagen. The original Volkswagen Beetle first sputtered into North America in 1949. With its simple, bug-like design, no-frills engineering, and economical operation, the Beetle was the antithesis of Detroit's chrome-laden gas-guzzlers. Although most owners would readily admit that their Beetles were underpowered, noisy, cramped, and freezing in the winter, they saw these as endearing qualities. Overriding these minor inconveniences, the Beetle was cheap to buy and own, dependable, easy to fix, fun to drive, and anything but flashy.

During the 1960s, as young baby boomers by the thousands were buying their first cars, demand exploded and the Beetle blossomed into an unlikely icon. Bursting with personality, the understated Bug came to personify an era of rebellion against conventions. It became the most popular car in North American history, with sales peaking at 423 000 in 1968. By the late 1970s, however, the boomers had moved on, Bug mania had faded, and Volkswagen had dropped Beetle production for North America. Still, more than 20 years later, the mere mention of these chugging oddities evokes smiles and strong emotions. Almost everyone over the age of 25, it seems, has a "feel-good" Beetle story to tell.

In an attempt to surf the nostalgia wave, Volkswagen introduced a New Beetle in 1998. Outwardly, the reborn Beetle resembles the original, tapping into the strong emotions and memories of times gone by. Beneath the skin, however, the New Beetle is packed with modern features. According to an industry expert, "The Beetle comeback is...based on a combination of romance and reason—wrapping up modern conveniences in an old-style package. Built into the dashboard is a bud vase perfect for a daisy plucked straight from the 1960s. But right next to it is a high-tech multi-speaker stereo—and options like power windows, cruise control, and a power sunroof make it a very different car than the rattly old Bug. The new version...comes with all the modern features car buyers demand, such as four air bags and power outlets for cell phones. But that's not why VW expects folks to buy it. With a familiar bubble shape that still makes people smile as it skitters by, the new Beetle offers a pull that is purely emotional."

Initial advertising for the New Beetle played strongly on the nostalgia theme, while at the same time refreshing the old Beetle heritage. "If you sold your soul in the '80s," tweaked one ad, "here's your chance to buy it back." Other ads read, "Less flower, more power," and "Comes with wonderful new features. Like heat." Still another ad declared "0 to 60? Yes." The car's Web page summarizes: "The New Beetle has what any Beetle always had. Originality. Honesty. A point of view. It's an exhaustive and zealous rejection of banality. Isn't the world ready for that kind of car again?"

Volkswagen invested $840 million to bring the New Beetle to market. However, this investment has paid big dividends as demand quickly outstripped supply. Even before the first cars reached VW showrooms, dealers across the country had long waiting lists of people who'd paid for the car without ever seeing it, let alone driving it. One dealer claimed that the New Beetle was such a traffic magnet that he had to remove it from his showroom floor every afternoon at 2 p.m. to discourage gawkers and let his salespeople work with serious prospects. The dealer encountered similar problems when he took to the streets in the new car. "You can't change lanes," said the dealer. "People drive up beside you to look."

Volkswagen's initial first-year sales projections of 50 000 New Beetles in North America proved pessimistic. After only nine months, the company had sold more than 64 000 of the new Bugs in the United States and Canada. The smart little car also garnered numerous distinguished awards, including *Motor Trend*'s 1999 Import Car of the Year, *Time* magazine's The Best of 1998 Design, *Business Week*'s Best New Products, and 1999 North American Car of the Year, awarded by an independent panel of top journalists who cover the auto industry. And sales are still sizzling—the New Beetle now accounts for more than a quarter of Volkswagen's U.S. sales and has helped win VW a fivefold increase in sales since 1993. The car was selected a *Money Magazine*'s Best Car of 2001. To follow up, Volkswagen plans to introduce a reincarnation of its old cult-classic flower-power Microbus in 2003.

The New Beetle has been a cross-generational hit, appealing to more than the stereotyped core demographic target of Woodstock-recovered baby boomers. Even kids too young to remember the original Bug appear to love this new one. "It's like you have a rock star here and everybody wants an autograph," states a VW sales manager. "I've never seen a car that had such a wide range of interest, from 16-year-olds to 65-year-olds." One wait-listed customer confirms the car's broad appeal. "In 1967, my Dad got me a VW. I loved it. I'm sure the new one will take me back," says the customer. "I'm getting the New Beetle as a surprise for my daughter, but I'm sure I'm going to be stealing it from her all the time."

Millennial fever results from the convergence of a wide range of forces in the marketing environment—from technological, economic, and demographic forces to cultural, social, and political ones. Most trend analysts believe that the nostalgia craze will only grow as the baby boomers continue to mature. If so, the New Beetle, so full of the past, has a very bright future. "The Beetle is not just empty nostalgia," says Gerald Celente, publisher of *Trend Journal*. "It is a practical car that is also tied closely to the emotions of a generation." Says another trend analyst, the New Beetle "is our romantic past, reinvented for our hectic here-and-now. Different, yet deeply familiar—a car for the times."[1]

Marketing environment
The factors and forces outside marketing's direct control that affect marketing management's ability to develop and maintain successful transactions with target customers.

As noted in Chapter 1, marketers operate in an increasingly connected world. Today's marketers must connect effectively with customers, others in the company, and external partners in the face of major environmental forces that buffet all these actors. A company's **marketing environment** consists of the actors and forces outside marketing that affect marketing management's ability to develop and maintain successful relationships with target customers. The marketing environment offers both opportunities and threats. Successful companies know the vital importance of constantly watching and adapting to the changing environment.

In this new millennium, the environment continues to change at a rapid pace. For example, think about how you buy groceries today. How will your grocery buying change during the next few decades? What challenges will these changes present for marketers? Here's what two leading futurists envision for the year 2025.[2]

The New Beetle
www.vw.com/newbeetle

We won't be shopping in 21-aisle supermarkets in 2025, predicts Gary Wright, corporate demographer for Procter & Gamble in Cincinnati. He believes the growth of e-commerce and the rapid speed of the Internet will lead to online ordering of lower-priced, nonperishable products—everything from peanut butter to coffee filters. Retailers will become "bundlers," combining these orders into large packages of goods for each household and delivering them efficiently to their doorsteps. As a result, we'll see mergers between retailing and home-delivery giants—think Wal-Mart Express, a powerful combo of Wal-Mart and Federal Express. Consumers won't waste precious time searching for the best-priced bundle. Online information agents will do it for them, comparing prices among competitors.

Smart information agents also play a role in the world imagined by another futurist, Ryan Mathews. By 2025, computers will essentially be as smart as humans, he contends, and consumers will use them to exchange information with on-screen electronic agents that ferret out the best deals online. Thanks to embedded-chip technology in the pantry, products on a CHR (continuous household replenishment) list—such as paper towels and pet food—will sense when they're running low and reorder themselves automatically. If the information agent finds a comparable but cheaper substitute for a CHR product, the item will be switched instantly.

Such pictures of the future give marketers plenty to think about. A company's marketers take the major responsibility for identifying and predicting significant changes in the environment. More than any other group in the company, marketers must be the trend trackers and opportunity seekers. Although every manager in an organization needs to observe the outside environment, marketers have two special aptitudes. They have disciplined methods—marketing intelligence and marketing research—for collecting information about the marketing environment. They also spend more time in the customer and competitor environment. By conducting systematic environmental scanning, marketers can revise and adapt marketing strategies to meet new challenges and opportunities in the marketplace.

The marketing environment is made up of a *microenvironment* and a *macroenvironment*. The **microenvironment** consists of the forces close to the company that affect its ability to serve its customers—the company, suppliers, marketing channel firms, customer markets, competitors, and publics. The **macroenvironment** consists of the larger societal forces that affect the microenvironment—demographic, economic, natural, technological, political, and cultural forces. We look first at the company's microenvironment.

Microenvironment The forces close to the company that affect its ability to serve its customers—the company, suppliers, marketing channel firms, customer markets, competitors, and publics.

Macroenvironment The larger societal forces that affect the microenvironment—demographic, economic, natural, technological, political, and cultural forces.

THE COMPANY'S MICROENVIRONMENT

Marketing management's job is to attract and build relationships with customers by creating customer value and satisfaction. However, marketing managers cannot accomplish this task alone. Their success depends on other actors in the company's microenvironment—other company departments, suppliers, marketing intermediaries, customers, competitors, and various publics, which combine to make up the company's value delivery network.

The Company

In designing marketing plans, marketing management takes other company groups into account—groups such as top management, finance, research and development (R&D), purchasing, manufacturing, information technology, and accounting. All these interrelated groups form the internal environment (see Figure 4-1). Top management sets the company's mission, objectives, broad strategies, and policies. Marketing managers make decisions within the plans made by top management, and marketing plans must be approved by top management before they can be implemented.

Marketing managers must also work closely with other company departments. Finance is concerned with finding and using funds to carry out the marketing plan. The R&D department focuses on designing safe and attractive products. Purchasing worries about getting supplies and materials, whereas manufacturing is responsible for producing the desired quality and quantity of products. The information technology department maintains the data warehouse that is the lifeblood

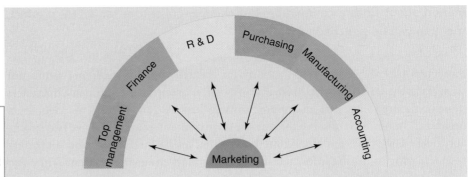

Figure 4-1

The Company's
Internal Environment

of many marketing programs. Accounting has to measure revenues and costs to help marketing know whether it is achieving its objectives. Together, all these departments have an impact on the marketing department's plans and actions. Under the marketing concept, all these functions must "think consumer," and they should work in harmony to provide superior customer value and satisfaction.

Suppliers

Suppliers are an important link in the company's overall customer value delivery system. They provide the resources needed by the company to produce its goods and services. Supplier problems can seriously affect marketing. Marketing managers must watch supply availability—supply shortages or delays, labour strikes, and other events can cost sales in the short run and damage customer satisfaction in the long run. Marketing managers also monitor the price trends of their key inputs. Rising supply costs may force price increases that can harm the company's sales volume.

Marketing Intermediaries

Marketing intermediaries
Firms that help the company to promote, sell, and distribute its goods to final buyers; they include resellers, physical distribution firms, marketing services agencies, and financial intermediaries.

Marketing intermediaries help the company to promote, sell, and distribute its goods to final buyers. They include *resellers, physical distribution firms, marketing services agencies,* and *financial intermediaries. Resellers* are distribution channel firms that help the company find customers or make sales to them. These include wholesalers and retailers, who buy and resell merchandise. Selecting and working with resellers is not easy. No longer do manufacturers have many small, independent resellers from which to choose. They now face large and growing reseller organizations. These organizations frequently have enough power to dictate terms or even to shut the manufacturer out of large markets.

Physical distribution firms help the company to stock and move goods from their points of origin to their destinations. Working with warehouse and transportation firms, a company must determine the best ways to store and ship goods, balancing factors such as cost, delivery, speed, and safety.

Marketing services agencies are the marketing research firms, advertising agencies, media firms, and marketing consulting firms that help the company target and promote its products to the right markets. When the company decides to use one of these agencies, it must choose carefully because these firms vary in creativity, quality, service, and price.

Financial intermediaries include banks, credit companies, insurance companies, and other businesses that help finance transactions or ensure against the risks associated with the buying and selling of goods. Most firms and customers depend on financial intermediaries to finance their transactions.

Like suppliers, marketing intermediaries form an important component of the company's overall value delivery system. In its quest to create satisfying customer relationships, the company must do more than just optimize its own performance; it must partner effectively with marketing intermediaries to optimize the performance of the entire system.

Customers

The company needs to study its customer markets closely. Figure 4-2 shows five types of customer markets. *Consumer markets* consist of individuals and households that buy goods and services for personal consumption. *Business markets* buy goods and services for further processing or for use in their production process, whereas *reseller markets* buy goods and services to resell at a profit. *Government markets* are made up of government agencies that buy goods and services to produce public services or transfer the goods and services to others who need them. Finally, *international markets* consist of these buyers in other countries, including consumers, producers, resellers, and governments. Each market type has special characteristics that call for careful study by the seller.

Competitors

The marketing concept states that to be successful, a company must provide greater customer value and satisfaction than its competitors do. Thus, marketers must do more than simply adapt to the needs of target consumers. They also must gain strategic advantage by positioning their offerings strongly against competitors' offerings in the minds of consumers.

No single competitive marketing strategy is best for all companies. Each firm should consider its own size and industry position compared with those of its competitors. Large firms with dominant positions in an industry can use certain strate-

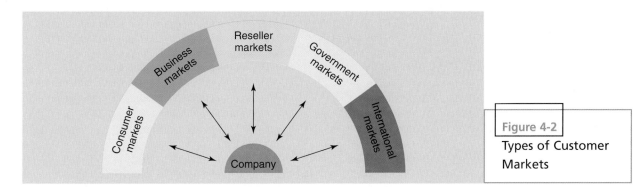

Figure 4-2

Types of Customer Markets

gies that smaller firms cannot afford. But being large is not enough. There are winning strategies for large firms, but there are also losing ones. And small firms can develop strategies that give them better rates of return than large firms enjoy.

Publics

Public Any group that has an actual or potential interest in or impact on an organization's ability to achieve its objectives.

The company's marketing environment also includes various publics. A **public** is any group that has an actual or potential interest in or impact on an organization's ability to achieve its objectives. Figure 4-3 shows seven types of publics.

1. *Financial publics* influence the company's ability to obtain funds. Banks, investment houses, and stockholders are the major financial publics.

2. *Media publics* carry news, features, and editorial opinion. They include newspapers, magazines, and radio and television stations.

3. *Government publics.* Management must consider federal, provincial, and municipal government developments. Marketers must often consult the company's lawyers on issues of product safety, truth in advertising, and other matters.

4. *Citizen-action publics.* A company's marketing decisions may be questioned by consumer organizations, environmental groups, minority groups, and others. Its public relations department can help it stay in touch with consumer and citizen groups.

5. *Local publics* include neighbourhood residents and community organizations. Large companies usually appoint a community relations officer to deal with the community, attend meetings, answer questions, and contribute to worthwhile causes.

6. *General public.* A company needs to be concerned about the general public's attitude toward its products and activities. The public's image of the company affects its buying.

7. *Internal publics* include workers, managers, volunteers, and the board of directors. Large companies use newsletters and other means to inform and motivate their internal publics. When employees feel good about their company, this positive attitude spills over to external publics.

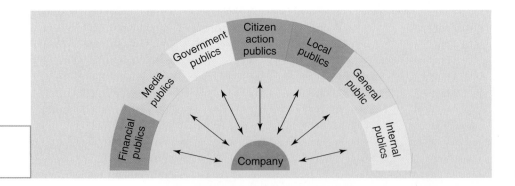

Figure 4-3

Types of Publics

A company can prepare marketing plans for these major publics as well as for its customer markets. Suppose the company wants a specific response from a particular public, such as goodwill, favourable word of mouth, or donations of time or money. The company would have to design an offer to this public that is attractive enough to produce the desired response.

THE COMPANY'S MACROENVIRONMENT

The company and all the other actors operate in a larger macroenvironment of forces that shape opportunities and pose threats to the company. Figure 4-4 shows the six major forces in the company's macroenvironment. In the remaining sections of this chapter, we examine these forces and show how they affect marketing plans.

Demographic Environment

Demography is the study of human populations in terms of size, density, location, age, gender, race, occupation, and other statistics. The demographic environment is of major interest to marketers because it involves people, and people make up markets.

Demography The study of human populations in terms of size, density, location, age, sex, race, occupation, and other statistics.

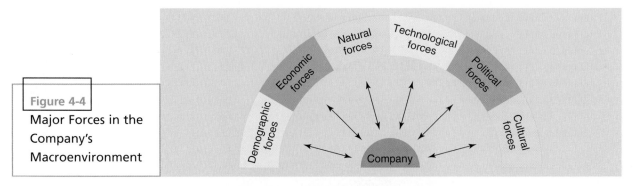

Figure 4-4

Major Forces in the Company's Macroenvironment

David Foot, an economist at the University of Toronto and author of the best-selling book *Boom, Bust & Echo: How to Profit from the Coming Demographic Shift*, believes that demographics explains about two-thirds of everything.[3] For example, how do you explain the rapid rise in the rates charged by babysitters? Easy, says Foot, when you realize that the huge pool of boomer parents relies on a relatively small pool of baby-bust teens. Foot has also shown that studying demographics helps to explain the growth of some leisure markets and the decline of others. Golf has experienced a 38 percent increase in popularity over the last 25 years, pushed by its popularity among baby-boomers.

People who study demographics assume that people do certain things and purchase certain things at certain ages. For example, people in their thirties tend to have begun their families and thus are the major purchasers of baby products. Although demographic information can be useful when it comes to predicting macro trends and purchases within a product category, marketers should use the information with some caution. According to veteran Canadian pollster Allan Gregg, demographics "can be wildly simplistic."[4] Complex factors—everything from the marketing itself to an individual's values and attitudes—influence why a person buys a particular brand within a product category. Moreover, despite the best demographic predictions, people don't always follow predictable patterns. Given an aging North American population, many predicted that people would follow a healthier lifestyle and diet. But a recent report suggests that, "when it comes to food, Canadians are tired of worrying about what's good for them."[5] Unlike with many Europeans, vegetarianism isn't a lifestyle choice for many Canadians; in fact, only 4 percent of Canadians follow this type of diet.

New studies are being done to help overcome the shortcomings of using demographics alone. National advertisers who want to know more than just the age and sex of the people who are listening to radio have access to plenty of qualitative data, thanks to research information from the Bureau of Broadcast Measurement. The latest study completed in the fall of 2001 provides information on computer ownership, leisure activities, home renovations, and mutual funds. National advertisers that require more data than basic demographics have access to many resources. One such resource was commissioned by the Canadian Radio Marketing Bureau and the Bureau of Broadcast Measurement.[6] This study will allow media buyers to understand the media habits and lifestyles of individuals and to predict what those individuals will purchase for a wide variety of products, such as cars, beer, and toothpaste.

Bureau of Broadcast Measurement www.bbm.com

Radio Marketing Bureau www.rmb.com

Statistics Canada data indicate that population growth between 2001and 2002 will increase only 0.3 percent. Since 1997, Canada's population has increased only 4 percent. This trend is expected to continue through 2006, when the total population is estimated to be 32 228 600, up from the 2002 level of 31 413 990. There are a number of reasons for the slow growth in population. One such factor is the total fertility rate (TFR), which fell to the lowest rate ever recorded in Canada of 1.55 children per woman in 1997. This low rate, combined with a decrease in immigration levels and longer life expectancies, could accelerate the aging of the Canadian population.[7]

Statistics Canada www.statcan.ca

Although Canada's population growth rate remains low, the world's population is growing at an explosive rate and will total 7.9 billion by the year 2025.[8] This population explosion has been of major concern to governments and various groups around the world, since the earth's finite resources can support a limited number of people, particularly at the living standards to which many countries aspire.

The explosive world population growth has major implications for business. A growing population means growing human needs to satisfy. Depending on purchasing power, it may also mean growing market opportunities. For example, to curb its skyrocketing population, the Chinese government passed regulations limiting families to one child each. As a result, Chinese children are spoiled and fussed over as never before. Known in China as "little emperors," Chinese children are being showered with everything from candy to computers as a result of what's known as the "six-pocket syndrome." As many as six adults—including parents, grandparents, great-grandparents, and aunts and uncles—may be indulging the whims of each child. This trend has encouraged toy companies such as Japan's Bandai Company (known for its Mighty Morphin Power Rangers), Denmark's Lego Group, and Mattel to enter the Chinese market.[9]

The world's large and highly diverse population presents both opportunities and challenges. Therefore, marketers must keep close track of demographic trends and developments in their markets, both at home and abroad—changing age and family structures, geographic population shifts, educational characteristics, and population diversity. Statistics Canada offers a wealth of information for marketers interested in demographic trends. Here, we discuss the most important demographic trends in Canada.

Changing Age Structure of the Canadian Population Canada's population was 31 413 990 in October 2002 according to Statistics Canada. As noted earlier, the single most important trend is that the population is getting *older*. The median age of the Canadian population—the point at which half of the population is younger and half is older—is now 38. Just 30 years ago, the median age was 25.[10]

During the **baby boom** that followed World War II and lasted until the early 1960s, the annual birth rate reached an all-time high. The baby boom created a huge "bulge" in age distribution—the nine million baby boomers account for almost one-third of Canada's population. And as the baby-boom generation ages, the nation's average age increases. Because of its sheer size, many major demographic and socioeconomic changes in Canada and the United States are tied to the baby-boom generation (see New Directions 4-1).

Although both Canada and the United States experienced a baby boom, Canadian marketers must recognize that our baby boom was unique. It started later

Baby boom The major increase in the annual birth rate following World War II and lasting until the early 1960s. The "baby boomers," now moving into middle age, are a prime target for marketers.

New Directions 4-1 >>   The Baby Boomers, the Generation Xers, and the Sunshine Generation

Demographics involve people, and people make up markets. Thus, marketers track demographic trends and groups carefully. The following are some of today's most important demographic groups.

The Baby Boomers

The postwar baby boom, which began in 1947 and ran through 1966, produced a population explosion. Since then, the baby boomers have become one of the largest forces shaping the marketing environment. The fact that Maureen Kempston Darkes, a 47-year-old lawyer, was recently named CEO of General Motors of Canada Ltd., is important not only because she is one of the few women to attain such a position, but also because it is an indication of the power that baby boomers, in general, are now wielding in Canadian business. The boomers have presented a moving target, creating new markets as they grew through infancy to preadolescence, teenagehood, young adulthood, and now middle age.

The baby boomers account for a third of the population but make up 40 percent of the workforce and earn more than half of all personal income. Today, the aging boomers are moving to the suburbs, settling into home ownership, and raising families. Many people who are turning 45 are reaching a milestone many find unthinkable—becoming grandparents. However, they are determined to fight the stereotypes long associated with this life cycle stage. They are more active and look and feel younger than their predecessors did. Furthermore, they prefer not to be confronted with advertising or products that address their age or label them as being old; therefore, many products are being retooled to meet their needs in a more subtle way. This group is also responsible for the explosive growth of products such as seamless bifocals, large-print books, and wrinkle-fighting creams. Since 36 percent of the people going to the movies are over the age of 40, theatres have been aggressively refurbishing. It isn't enough just to show movies that appeal to older audiences; middle-aged people demand bigger screens, more comfortable seating, and better food.

Boomers are reaching their peak earning and spending years. They constitute a lucrative market for housing, furniture and appliances, children's products, low-calorie foods and beverages, physical fitness products, high-priced cars, convenience products, and financial services.

Baby boomers cut across all lifestyles. But marketers have typically paid the most attention to the small upper crust of the boomer generation—its more educated, mobile, and wealthy segments. These segments have gone by many names. In the 1980s, they were called yuppies (young urban professionals); yummies (young upwardly mobile mommies), and dinks (dual-income, no-kids couples). In the 1990s, however, yuppies and dinks gave way to a new breed, with such names as dewks (dual earners with kids); mobys (mother older, baby younger); woofs (well-off older folks); or just plain grumpies (just what the name suggests).

The older boomers are now in their fifties; the youngest are in their thirties. Thus, the boomers are evolving from the "youthquake generation" to the "backache generation." They're slowing down, having children, and settling down. They're experiencing the pangs of midlife and rethinking the purpose and value of their work, responsibilities, and relationships. Community and family values have become more important, and staying home with the family has become their favourite way to spend an evening.

In examining the boomer market in Canada, it is significant that boomers are going from being net-borrowers to being net-savers. Many plan to retire early—almost one-third plan to stop working before they reach age 60. This has resulted in the recent phenomenal growth of Canadian mutual funds.

This increased wealth among boomers is also evident in the travel market. The generation who developed their wanderlust backpacking around Europe and Asia in their twenties now has the money to go beyond standard vacations. Although boomers often seek vacations with an environmental focus or those that promise something exotic or thrilling, they also want to be coddled with a gourmet meal at the end of the day.

{ Oh yeah. I stand around the gazebo in my underwear all the time. }

Jack Purcell
CONVERSE

Converse targets Generation Xers with this black and white ad for Jack Purcell sneakers. The ad is "soft sell" and makes fun of a favourite GenXer target—advertising itself.

Even though some markets are benefiting, others are threatened as the boomers age. Once the prime consumers of Molson and Labatt beer, boomers are moving away from beer consumption, leaving these brewers with flat or declining markets.

The Generation Xers

Marketers' focus has shifted in recent years to a new group—those born between 1965 and 1976. Six million strong in Canada and representing $140 billion in disposable income, this group represents an extremely important market. Author Douglas Coupland calls them "Generation X." Others call them baby busters, the Nexus generation, or yiffies—young, individualistic, freedom-minded, few.

Many who belong to the 25 to 36 age group hate the label Generation X. In contrast to the boomers, who were an easy group to target, defining this younger generation is difficult. Companies that want to market to them or recruit them as employees are turning to such firms as Toronto's d-Code Inc., a consulting firm that helps companies and governments appreciate what makes 18- to 34-year-olds tick. This techno-savvy generation was raised on music, television, computers, and video games. They are satisfied, independent, and optimistic. Quality of life is more important than money to those entering the workforce; longer vacations and funky office space may be more important than the signing bonus. Lacking confidence in business and educational and government institutions, this group tends to be highly self-reliant. Their confidence is reflected in their number-one career choice—becoming an entrepreneur. However, this generation is also more likely to be unemployed or underemployed. They are more accepting of change than are baby boomers, and they delay getting married, having children, and buying a home longer than do their predecessors. Only 21 percent of members of this generation plan to buy a home in the next two years.

Marketers must remember that this generation is a highly diverse group and resent being clustered into a single market. They are also highly critical of advertising and are extremely perceptive about its underlying purpose. As Eric Blais noted in *Marketing*, this is a generation "who no longer cares what McCain has done to their fries." Growing up on a diet of Saturday-morning cartoons and advertising promises that didn't deliver, they enjoy parodying advertising slogans, revelling in producing distorted advertising slogans such as "At Speedy, you're a nobody." However, Xers do share a set of influences. Increasing divorce rates and higher employment of mothers made them the first generation of latchkey kids. Whereas the boomers created a sexual revolution, the Xers have lived in the age of AIDS.

The Xers buy many products, such as sweaters, boots, cosmetics, electronics, cars, fast food, beer, computers, and mountain bikes. However, their cynicism makes them savvy shoppers. Because they often did much of the family shopping when growing up, they are experienced shoppers. Their financial pressures make them value conscious, and they like lower prices and a more functional look.

Generation Xers share new cultural concerns. They care about the environment and respond favourably to companies such as The Body Shop and Ben & Jerry's, which have proven records of environmentally and socially responsible actions.

Generation Xers will have a big impact on the workplace and marketplace of the future. They are poised to displace the lifestyles, culture, and materialistic values of the baby boomers. By the year 2010, they will have overtaken the baby boomers as a primary market for almost every product category.

The Sunshine Generation

Also labelled the echo generation (the boomers' children), the millennial generation (they will start to enter maturity after the year 2000), and Generation Y (building on the Generation X label), this generation was born between 1980 and 1995. Although the oldest members are in their twenties, the youngest are still toddlers. This group is attracting increased attention from marketers because of its impact on certain product categories. Children's movies earn the biggest dollar at the box office, and they are a major market for fashion and consumer goods.

This group has been immersed in more technology than any previous generation. They are fluent and comfortable with computer, digital, and Internet technology, earning themselves the nickname "net-gens" (or n-gens). With greater access to information, they are more aware of global issues and have a sense of themselves as part of a larger world community. This awareness has a cost, however. They believe they have a calling to fix the problems created by previous generations—significant problems such as environmental degradation, war, crime, and poverty. The archetype of this generation is Craig Kielburger, the famous teenage Canadian activist who has developed a global campaign against child labour and founded the international youth movement (Kids Can) Free the Children. How this generation will evolve remains a big question. They face a world full of questions and ambiguity about their roles as individuals, spouses, parents, workers, and consumers.

Sources: Howard Schlossberg, "Aging Baby Boomers Give Marketers a Lot of Changes to Consider," *Advertising Age,* 12 April 1993, p. 10; Campbell Gibson, "The Four Baby Booms," *American Demographics,* November 1993, pp. 36–40; Cyndee Miller, "Xers Know They're a Target Market, and They Hate That," *Marketing News,* 6 December 1993, pp. 2, 15; Jeff Giles, "Generalizations X," *Newsweek,* 6 June 1994, pp. 62–69; Nathan Cobb, "Agent X," *Boston Globe,* 28 September 1994, pp. 35, 40; Nicholas Zill and John Robinson, "The Generation X Difference," *American Demographics,* April 1995, pp. 24–39; Harvey Schacter, "Power Shift," *Canadian Business,* August 1995, pp. 20–30; Eric Blais, "Generation X: Targeting a Tough Crowd That's Not Easily Impressed," *Marketing,* 6 June 1994, pp. 13–15; Eric Beauchesne, "Generation X Not the Lost Generation: Survey," *Kingston Whig Standard,* 15 June 1997, p. 22; Christopher Harris, "Faith in Popcorn," *The Globe and Mail,* 10 May 1997, p. C10; Deborah Jones, "Here Comes the Sunshine Generation," *The Globe and Mail,* 10 May 1997, pp. D1, D2; Dorothy Lipovenko, "Growing Old Is a Baby-Booming Business," *The Globe and Mail,* 6 April 1996, pp. A1, A4; Dorothy Lipovenko, "Rich Boomers Aiming to Retire Earlier Than Parents, Poll Says," *The Globe and Mail,* 10 October 1996, p. B10; Gayle MacDonald, "The Eyes and Ears of a Generation," *The Globe and Mail,* 4 February 1997, p. B13; Leonard Zehr, "Gen-Xers Heading Home: Survey," *The Globe and Mail,* 13 February 1997, p. B9; (Kids Can) Free the Children, "About Craig," available online at **www.freethechildren.org/info/aboutcraig.html**, accessed 10 October 2002.

than the American version (1947 versus 1946) and lasted longer (the American boom ended in 1964; the Canadian boom continued until 1966). Although the American baby boom resulted in 3.5 children per family, the Canadian boom produced 4 children. Furthermore, the baby boom was not a worldwide phenomenon. Only Australia and New Zealand among the other developed countries experienced the same explosion in the birth rate. Europe had no baby boom, and in Japan, the birth rate declined during our baby boom years, which explains why these countries have a higher proportion of older people in their societies.[11]

The baby boom was followed by a "birth dearth," and by the mid-1970s the birth rate had fallen sharply. This decrease was caused by smaller family sizes, the result of the desire to improve personal living standards, the increasing number of women working outside the home, and improved birth control. Although family sizes are expected to remain smaller, the birth rate has climbed again as the baby boom generation moves through the childbearing years and creates a second but smaller "baby boomlet." Following this boomlet, however, the birth rate will again decline as we move into the twenty-first century.[12]

Figure 4-5 shows the changing age distribution of the Canadian population through 2041. The differing growth rates for various age groups will strongly affect marketers' targeting strategies. For example, the upper end of the "tween" market, the 9- to 14-year-old offspring of the baby boom generation, is 2.5 million strong. They are grabbing marketers' attention not only because of the size of this "echo boom" market, but also because of its spending power. New products are being developed just for them—GT Global Mutual Funds for Kids, Pillsbury's Pizza Pops, portable milkshakes called Milk Mania, L'Oreal Kids Shampoo and Conditioner, and Bonne Bell Lip Smackers. They're wired and media savvy, and marketers are rushing to build brand loyalty among them or to create new brands they might regard as "cool."

At the other end of the spectrum, almost 13 percent of Canadians were over age 65 in 2001, with the percentage projected to increase to 25 percent by 2031. As this group grows, so will the demand for retirement communities, quieter forms of recreation, single-portion food packaging, life care and health care services, and leisure travel.[13]

Figure 4-5

Age Projection for Canada, Provinces and Territories, 1993–2041

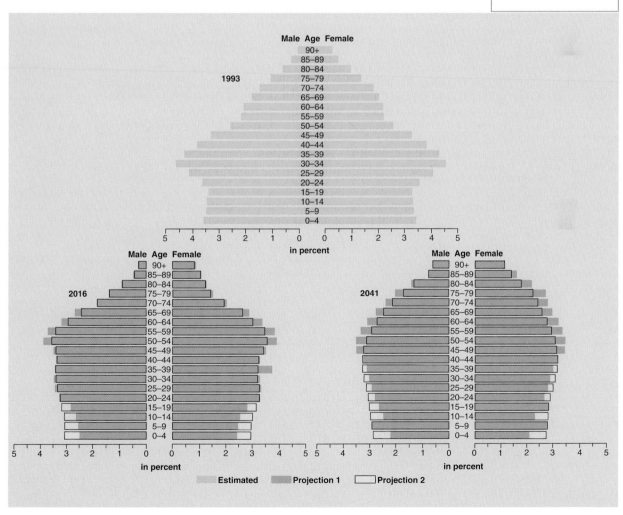

Source: Statistics Canada, Catalogue 91520 occasional, December 1994.

Seniors represent a unique marketing challenge. Many are active and well-educated and resent being classified as "elderly." Although some will have more leisure time than the rest of the population, many others plan to work beyond the traditional retirement age. Seniors value information in advertising materials and reasoned arguments instead of claims based on sex and impulse. Being avid consumers of information, seniors represent a larger than average market for books, newspapers, and magazines. They seek convenience, quality, comfort, and security in many of their purchases.

Older Canadians are wealthier than many stereotypes would have us believe: "Whoopies" (well-off older people) account for two thirds of Canada's disposable income. Many seniors are debt-free, but this fact should not be taken as an indication that they are price-insensitive. Seniors are experienced, knowledgeable, value-conscious consumers; however, they do account for almost 50 percent of the luxury car market and one third of new home sales.

Packaging is an important issue for many seniors. Although many marketers have responded to their dietary concerns by placing more details about product ingredients on labels, marketers sometimes forget that reading the small print on packages is difficult for many older consumers. Wrestling with childproof caps is a source of constant frustration for individuals whose joints are inflamed by arthritis. Some over-the-counter drug producers have responded to this concern with easy-to-open containers especially designed for this market. Similarly, cleaning products are not only being made in smaller containers to meet the needs of seniors who often live alone, but they are also being made in easier-to-handle containers. Windex, for example, now comes in a bottle with an indented neck that is easier to grip.[14]

Changing Canadian Households When the term household is used, a stereotype of the typical family living in the suburbs with its two children comes to mind. However, this stereotype is far from accurate. The 2001 census data from Statistics Canada shows that common-law and lone-parent families together make up almost 30 percent of all families in Canada, compared to 26 percent in 1996.[15]

The 2001 census is the first census to provide data on same-sex partnerships. A total of 34, 000 couples identified themselves as same-sex, common-law couples and constituted only 0.5 percent of the total. However, female same-sex partnerships indicated that they were more likely to have children, with 15 percent indicating female same-sex couples living with children vs. only 3 percent for male same-sex partnerships.

Overall, the total number of families in Canada increased to 11, 563, 000, an increase of 6.9 percent over 1996. An increase in smaller families contributed to the rise. The latest data now shows that the size of the average Canadian household has decreased to the point where there were as many households of one as there were of four. Further, from 1981 to 2001, the average Canadian household has reduced from 2.9 persons to 2.6.

Responsibility for household tasks and the care of children is also changing. Approximately 60 percent of women aged 15 and older had jobs in 2001 compared to only 42 percent in 1976. Women in the Canadian Labour Force continue to grow in importance. Growth in female employment increased 8.7 percent since 1997, while males increased only 5.9 percent.

Marriage continues to appear to be a fragile bond. At 153, 000 marriages in 2001, the number of marriages is essentially unchanged since 1997. Further, divorces continue to increase, with divorced women increasing 16.9 percent in 2001 compared to 1997. Men, who tend to remarry after divorce, now represent only 42.5 percent of all divorced people.

Canada's population continues to age, reaching an all-time median age high of 37.6 years, an increase of 2.3 years from 35.3 in 1996.

The decline in the number of births that has occurred since 1991 is a major factor behind both the record-low growth in population between 1996 and 2001, and the record increase in median age.

The nation's median age has been rising steadily since the end of the baby boom in 1996, when it was only 25.4 years.

The population aged 45 to 64 increased 36 percent between 1991 and 2001, due to the entry of the baby boomers into this group. As a result, Canada's working-age population has become more dominated by older individuals.

As further evidence of our aging population, the 2001 census showed that seniors aged 65 or over accounted for 13 percent of the nation's population in 2001, up from almost 12 percent in 1991. Projections indicate this proportion will reach 15 percent by 2011. At the other end of the age spectrum, 26 percent of the population was aged 19 or younger, down from 28 percent in 1991.[16]

Population and Growth Shifts The 2001 preliminary census data shows the total population of Canada increased by 1, 095, 000 between 1997 and 2001, a total growth rate of only 3.5 percent. As Table 4-1 shows, however, growth rates across all provinces are not uniform: the populations of Newfoundland, Saskatchewan, and the Yukon decreased from 2000 to 2001, while the populations of other provinces either stabilized or grew.[17]

Canadians are a mobile people. For more than a century, Canadians have been moving from rural to urban areas. The urban areas have a faster pace of living, more commuting, higher incomes, and greater variety of goods and services than can be found in the small towns and rural areas that dot Canada. But Canada's cities

The employment rate of women with children has grown particularly sharply in the past two decades, especially for those with preschool-aged children. One result is the growth of childcare services.

Table 4-1 Canada's Population Trends

	1997	1998	1999 thousands	2000	2001
Canada	29 987.2	30 248.2	30 499.2	30 769.7	31 081.9
Newfoundland and Labrador	554.1	545.3	540.7	537.2	533.8
Prince Edward Island	136.9	136.9	137.6	138.1	138.5
Nova Scotia	934.5	936.1	939.7	941.2	942.7
New Brunswick	754.2	753.3	754.4	755.3	757.1
Quebec	7 302.6	7 323.6	7 349.7	7 377.7	7 410.5
Ontario	11 249.5	11 387.3	11 522.7	11 685.3	11 874.4
Manitoba	1 136.6	1 137.9	1 142.4	1 146.0	1 150.0
Saskatchewan	1 022.0	1 024.9	1 025.5	1 022.0	1 015.8
Alberta	2 837.2	2 906.8	2 959.5	3 009.2	3 064.2
British Columbia	3 959.7	3 997.1	4 028.1	4 058.8	4 095.9
Yukon	32.2	31.5	31.0	30.6	29.9
Northwest Territories	41.8	41.1	41.0	40.9	40.9
Nunavut	25.9	26.4	26.9	27.4	28.2

Source: Statistics Canada, 2001 Census Analysis Series A—A Profile of the Canadian Population: Where We Live. Cat. No. 96F0030XIE010012001. Available online at <http://geodepot.statcan.ca/Diss/Highlights/Tables_e.pdf>.

are changing as well. Canadian cities are often surrounded by large suburban areas. Statistics Canada calls these combinations of urban and suburban populations "census metropolitan areas" (CMAs). About 50 percent of Canada's population lives in the top 25 CMAs. Information about CMAs is useful for marketers trying to decide which geographical segments represent the most lucrative markets for their products and which areas are most critical in terms of buying media time. Marketers also track the relative growth of these markets to see which areas are expanding and which ones are contracting.

An estimated 277 000 people moved from one province to another in 1999, while about 900 000 moved from one CMA to another within their province. The Toronto CMA recorded a net inflow of 56 600 individuals, the largest net inflow of any CMA, at 12 people per 1000 living there. Vancouver recorded the second largest net inflow of 21 610. Relative to the size of the population of the CMA, Calgary had a net inflow of 19 per 1000, the highest rate among CMAs. The Windsor CMA was a distant second, with a net inflow of 13 migrants per 1000.[18]

A Better-Educated and More White-Collar Population The Canadian population is becoming better educated. From 1986 to 1996, the number of people without any degree or certificate dropped, while the numbers completing high school or a trade college increased. The rising number of educated people will increase the demand for quality products, books, magazines, and travel. It suggests a decline in television viewing, because university-educated consumers watch less television than the population at large. The workforce is also becoming more white collar, with 28 percent of the workforce falling into that category.

Increasing Diversity Countries vary in their ethnic and racial composition. At one extreme are homogeneous countries like Japan, where almost everyone is of Japanese descent. At the other are such countries as Canada and the United States whose populations are "salad bowls" of mixed races. Anyone who has walked the streets of Vancouver, Montreal, Calgary, or Toronto will immediately understand that visible minorities in Canada are a large group. The United Nations reported that Toronto is the world's most multicultural city, and the Canadian Advertising Foundation recently predicted that the combined purchasing power of ethnic markets will soon exceed $300 billion. Many ethnic markets are growing in size. For example, the Italian, German, and Chinese markets in Canada each have populations of more than 400 000.

Nabisco is a firm that understands the power of ethnic marketing. Its product Magic Baking Powder was losing share in its traditional markets, but the firm revived its lacklustre performance when it targeted Chinese and Japanese restaurants with a sampling and promotion program for its product. Unlike baking powder's traditional market of consumers who were moving away from "scratch baking," this market valued quality baked goods. Sales in British Columbia alone increased by 14 percent as a result of this targeted sampling program.

Marketers must avoid negative stereotypes when it comes to serving ethnic markets. Seventeen percent of immigrants hold university degrees, compared with 11 percent of people born in Canada. Immigrants are also more likely to hold managerial or professional jobs and have more stable family lives than people born in Canada.

Targeting ethnic consumers involves far more than mere tokenism, many ethnic marketing specialists warn. Merely placing a person from a visible minority in an advertisement is not sufficient evidence that one is an ethnic marketer (see New Directions 4-2). Communicating in the consumer's native language is often mandatory, but marketers must also face the challenge of not alienating sophisticated second-generation individuals. The TD Bank recently demonstrated the power of providing information in potential customers' native language. The bank

Anyone who has walked the streets of Vancouver, Montreal, Calgary, or Toronto will immediately understand that visible minorities in Canada are a large group. Many firms, such as Air Canada, are recognizing racial diversity in their advertising.

launched a Chinese Green Info Line to target potential Chinese investors. More than 300 callers per month take advantage of the service, which has generated considerable investments.

New Directions 4-2 >>   Is Canada's Marketing Industry Racist?

The question of whether Canada's marketing industry is racist was posed to 21 marketing specialists. Although most respondents denied racism in Canadian marketing, they did stress that marketers should do more to reflect Canada's multicultural reality. Rather than being overtly racist, some members of the marketing community are racist by omission, claims Suzanne Keeler of the Canadian Advertising Foundation. These people just don't include people from different backgrounds on their management teams or in their advertisements. Instead of selecting people based on their individual characteristics, they make choices based on outdated stereotypes. Although many respondents noted that more and more advertisers, especially those aiming products at young people, are using people from minority populations in their ads, others, such as Deanna Dolson, advertising director of *Aboriginal Voices* magazine, claim that many advertisers haven't "opened their eyes to what native culture is."

As the importance of global marketing grows, people from different ethnic and language groups will become increasingly valuable in the roles of marketing managers, advertising creative specialists, and account executives. Today, people in charge of new product development consider the opinions of ethnic groups when developing their product concepts. Some new product categories, such as ethnic foods, depend completely on understanding ethnic target populations. B.K. Sethi, publisher of *Ethnic Food Merchandiser,* doesn't believe any marketer can afford to be racist. Liz Torlée, chairperson of the Institute of Canadian Advertising, takes a similar stance. Advertising is "an all-embracing industry, and we have to be so much in tune with consumers that we are, I hope, constantly reflecting consumers' changing attitudes."

Source: "Is Canada's Marketing Industry Racist?" *Marketing Magazine,* 3 March 1997.

The diversity in the Canadian marketplace isn't restricted to ethnic markets. People's sexual orientation is another point of diversity, and tolerance is growing of alternative lifestyles in Canada. Companies such as Labatt's, Fujifilm, TD Canada Trust, Rogers, AT&T and Hershey are sponsors of the annual Lesbian and Gay Film and Video Festival. In June each year, upward of 750 000 participants and observers are involved in the Pride Parade in Toronto. Since gay and lesbian consumers tend to be cosmopolitan and have high incomes, they are desirable target markets for everything from health and beauty products, to travel, fashion, entertainment, and financial services. Nonetheless, until recently, few national advertisers, with the exception of the large breweries, created advertisements explicitly directed at this audience. One reason is the lack of research on this market; Statistics Canada, for example, doesn't even ask about sexual orientation in its surveys. Another reason is the dearth of middle-of-the-road media directed at these consumers. Finally, some marketers fear that advertising in alternative lifestyle media or at events would cause a backlash by heterosexual consumers.

Things are changing. Several research firms, including Environics, have started gathering information on the market. A growing body of media is directed at the gay and lesbian community including electronic media, such as PrideNet. People who have experience advertising to the gay and lesbian community, such as Tom Blackmore, a partner in the Toronto-based advertising agency Robins Blackmore, says that clients who have used creative materials that are relevant to this audience have experienced remarkable successes from their campaigns. The one mistake that marketers can make with respect to this audience is doing nothing. "It is a market that people have ignored for way too long," he explains.[19]

PrideNet
www.pridenet.com

Diversity goes beyond ethnicity or sexual preferences. For example, almost 18 percent of the Canadian population has some form of disability, and this group has considerable spending power, as well as great need for tailored products and services. Not only do they value services that make daily life easier, like online grocery shopping from sites like GroceryGateway.com, but they are also a growing market for travel, sports, and other leisure-oriented products.

Economic Environment

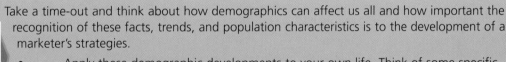

Take a time-out and think about how demographics can affect us all and how important the recognition of these facts, trends, and population characteristics is to the development of a marketer's strategies.

• Apply these demographic developments to your own life. Think of some specific examples of how the changing demographic factors affect you and your buying behaviour.

• Identify a specific company that you feel has done a good job of reacting to the shifting demographic environment—generational segments (baby boomers, GenXers, and Generation Y), the changing Canadian family, and our increasing diversity as a country. Compare this company with one that has done a poor job.

Markets require buying power as well as people. The **economic environment** consists of factors that affect consumer purchasing power and spending patterns. Nations vary greatly in their levels and distribution of income. Some countries have *subsistence economies*—they consume most of their own agricultural and industrial output. These countries offer few market opportunities. At the other extreme are *industrial economies,* which are rich markets for many different kinds of goods. Marketers must pay close attention to major economic trends and consumer spending patterns, both across and within their world markets.

Economic environment
Factors that affect consumer buying power and spending patterns.

Changes in Income In the 1980s, the economy entered its longest peacetime boom. Consumers fell into a consumption frenzy, fuelled by income growth, federal tax reductions, rapid increases in housing values, and a boom in borrowing. They bought and bought, seemingly without caution, amassing record levels of debt. "It was fashionable to describe yourself as 'born to shop…. Many…became literally addicted to personal consumption."[20]

Free spending and high expectations were dashed by the economic slowdowns in the early 1990s and 2000s. Consumers have sobered up, pulled back, and adjusted to leaner times. Value marketing became the watchword for many marketers. They looked for ways to offer today's more financially cautious buyers greater value—just the right combination of product quality and good service at a fair price.

Despite the slowdowns, median family income increased 1 percent from 1998 to 1999 to $48 600, after adjusting for inflation.

Marketers should pay attention to *income distribution* as well as average income. Income distribution in Canada is still very skewed. At the top are *upper-class* consumers, whose spending patterns are not affected by current economic events and who are a major market for luxury goods. There is also a comfortable *middle class*, which is somewhat careful about its spending but can still afford the good life some of the time. The *working class* must stick close to the basics of food, clothing, and shelter, and must try hard to save. Finally, the *underclass* (persons on welfare and some retirees) must count their pennies even when making the most basic purchases. People with Canada's lowest incomes are often found on Aboriginal reserves.[21]

The growing income divide has sent marketers in opposite directions. On one hand, they have responded with a ceaseless array of pricey, upscale products aimed at satisfying the appetites of wealthy North Americans. On the other hand, companies are now tailoring their marketing offers to two different markets—the affluent and the less affluent. For example, Walt Disney Company markets two distinct Winnie-the-Pooh bears: the original line-drawn figure appears on fine china, pewter spoons, and pricey kids' stationery found in upscale specialty and department stores, while a lower-priced cartoon-like Pooh adorns plastic key chains and polyester bed sheets and sells in Wal-Mart.[22]

Paradoxes of the New Economy   For decades, many analysts predicted that advances in technology would create a leisure generation—people who worked less and had more time to enjoy life. Although many people now have more time on their hands, few would consider themselves a leisure class. Many Canadians still rely on one, or multiple, part-time jobs. At the other end of the spectrum is the growing number of Canadians working more than 50 hours per week. Thus, although the average workweek remains at 40 hours, a growing number of people are work-

Income distribution: Walt Disney markets two distinct Pooh bears to match its two-tiered market.

ing far less, and a growing number are working far more. This polarity in terms of hours worked is the paradox of the new economy.[23]

What are the reasons for these trends? Economic necessity is a prime culprit. In the 1950s and 1960s, a family could support itself on about 48 hours of employment. Today, family members must work 65 to 72 hours, which means that both spouses must work.[24]

Marketers must target their offerings to these two very different segments. Although many people who work part time use their extra time to save money, others demand time-saving products. People at the time-pressed end of the continuum often don't even have time to eat or prepare meals. Kellogg's built an advertising campaign around this knowledge and positioned its breakfast bars as meals for people on the run. Grocery retailers are also taking notice. Since people aren't preparing meals at home the way they used to, grocers' market share is eroding. Loblaws is experimenting with a strategy to win back harried consumers. The company has created *Take Me Marché:* kiosks in some stores, offering ready-to-eat meals and take-home food for people who want to eat at home but don't have time to cook.[25]

**Loblaw Companies Ltd.
www.loblaw.com**

Changing Consumer Spending Patterns Food, housing, and transportation use up most household income (51 percent). Consumer spending patterns have changed considerably in the past 50 years. In 1947, spending on the basics (food, clothing, housing, fuel) accounted for 69 cents out of every dollar. What expenditures account for the money no longer spent on the basics? Canadians are spending more on two categories—what Statistics Canada refers to as personal goods and services; and recreation, entertainment, education, and cultural services. However, consumers at different income levels have different spending patterns. Some of these differences were noted over a century ago by Ernst Engel, who studied how people shifted their spending as their income rose. He found that as family income rises, the percentage spent on food declines, the percentage spent on housing remains constant (except for utilities such as gas, electricity, and public services, which decrease), and both the percentage spent on other categories and that devoted to savings increase. **Engel's laws** generally have been supported by later studies.

Changes in such major economic variables as income, cost of living, interest rates, and savings and borrowing patterns have a large impact on the marketplace. Companies watch these variables by using economic forecasting. Businesses do not have to be wiped out by an economic downturn or caught short in a boom. With adequate warning, they can take advantage of changes in the economic environment.

Engel's laws Differences noted more than a century ago by Ernst Engel in how people shift their spending across food, housing, transportation, health care, and other goods and services categories as family income rises.

Natural Environment

The **natural environment** has the natural resources needed as inputs by marketers or affected by marketing activities. Environmental concerns have grown steadily over the past two decades. Some trend analysts labelled the 1990s as the Earth Decade, claiming that the natural environment is the major worldwide issue facing business and the public. The Earth Day movement celebrated its 30th birthday in the year 2000; yet, in many cities around the world, air and water pollution have reached dangerous levels. World concern continues to mount over the depletion of

Natural environment The natural resources needed as inputs by marketers or affected by marketing activities.

the earth's ozone layer and the resulting "greenhouse effect," a dangerous warming of the earth. And many environmentalists fear that we soon will be buried in our own trash. Marketers should be aware of trends in the natural environment:

- *Growing shortages of raw materials.* Air and water may seem to be infinite resources, but some groups see long-run dangers. Air pollution chokes many of the world's large cities. Remember how smoke from fires in Indonesia choked the air of whole nations? Great Lakes water levels are low, causing problems in many Canadian interior port cities, and water shortages are already a big problem in some parts of the United States and the world. Renewable resources, such as forests and food, also have to be used wisely. Nonrenewable resources, such as oil, coal, and various minerals, pose a serious problem. Firms making products that require these scarce resources face large cost increases, even if the materials do remain available.

- *Increased pollution.* Industry will almost always damage the quality of the natural environment. Consider the disposal of chemical and nuclear wastes; the dangerous mercury levels in the ocean; the quantity of chemical pollutants in the soil and food supply; and the littering of the environment with non-biodegradable bottles, plastics, and other packaging materials.

- *Increased government intervention in natural resource management.* The governments of different countries vary in their concern and efforts to promote a clean environment. Some, like the German government, vigorously pursue environmental quality. When Prime Minister Jean Chrétien announced at the September 2002 Earth Summit that Parliament would vote on ratifying the Kyoto agreement by the end of the year, cries of protest were heard from Alberta politicians and the oil patch. Other governments, especially many poorer nations, do little about pollution, largely because they lack the needed funds or political will.

- *Increased environmentally sustainable strategies.* Concern for the natural environment has spawned the "green movement." Today, enlightened companies go beyond what government regulations dictate. They are developing environmentally sustainable strategies and practices in an effort to create a world economy that the planet can support indefinitely. They are responding to consumer demands with ecologically safer products, recyclable or biodegradable packaging, better pollution controls, and more energy-efficient operations. Loblaws began its G.R.E.E.N. program in 1989; today, it is one of the most successful environmental businesses in the world. More than 100 new products have been launched since the program's inception, while manufacturing changes have helped make dozens of other products environmentally friendly. Increasingly, companies are recognizing the link between a healthy economy and a healthy ecology.[26]

Technological environment: Technology is perhaps the most dramatic force shaping the marketing environment. Here a Samburu warrior in northern Kenya makes a call on a cellular phone.

Technological Environment

The **technological environment** is perhaps the most dramatic force now shaping our destiny. Technology has released such wonders as antibiotics, organ transplants, and notebook computers, and such horrors as nuclear missiles, nerve gas, and assault rifles.

The technological environment changes rapidly. Many of today's common products were not available a hundred years ago. Companies that do not keep up with technological change soon find their products outdated. And they will miss new product and market opportunities. Marketers often face the difficult task of "envisioning" markets for products and services that didn't exist just a few years ago.

The costs of researching and developing new, complex technologies are rapidly increasing. The United States leads the world in research and development (R&D) spending, but recent data suggest that it may soon lose its position to Japan or Scandinavia. Until recently, Canada hasn't had a sterling record when it comes to R&D expenditures. Canada is working to turn things around, and the government is investing heavily in research-related activities and education. Although Canada has been improving in this regard, other countries are racing ahead. Canadian firms such as IBM Canada, Bell Canada, Bombardier (transportation equipment), Pratt & Whitney Canada (the aircraft engine manufacturer), CAE Inc. (a diversified maker of electronic products), and Alcan Aluminium spend heavily on R&D to ensure they can compete internationally. Marketers in these and other firms need to understand the changing technological environment and the ways that new technologies can serve human needs. They need to work closely with R&D people to encourage more market-oriented research. They must be alert to the possible negative aspects of any innovation that might harm users or arouse opposition.

Technological environment Forces that create new technologies, in turn creating new product and market opportunities.

Political Environment

Political environment
Laws, government agencies, and pressure groups that influence and limit various organizations and individuals in a given society.

Marketing decisions are strongly affected by developments in the political environment. The **political environment** consists of laws, government agencies, and lobby groups that influence and limit various organizations and individuals in a given society.

Legislation Regulating Business Even the most liberal advocates of free-market economies agree that the system works best with at least some regulation. Well-conceived regulation can encourage competition and ensure fair markets for goods and services. Thus, governments develop *public policy* to guide commerce, by enacting laws and regulations that limit business for the good of society as a whole. Almost every marketing activity is subject to a wide range of laws and regulations.

Increasing Legislation Legislation affecting business around the world has increased steadily over the years. Canada has many laws covering such issues as competition, fair trade practices, environmental protection, product safety, truth in advertising, packaging and labelling, pricing, and other important areas (see Table 4-2). The European commission has been active in establishing a new framework of laws covering competitive behaviour, product standards, product liability, and commercial transactions for the nations of the European Community. Some countries have especially strong consumerism legislation. For example, Norway bans several forms of sales promotion—trading stamps, contests, premiums—as being inappropriate or unfair ways of promoting products. Thailand requires food processors selling national brands to market low-price brands also, so that low-income consumers can find economy brands on the shelves. In India, food companies must obtain special approval to launch brands that duplicate those already existing on the market, such as additional soft drinks or new brands of rice.

Understanding the public policy implications of a particular marketing activity is not a simple matter. For example, in Canada, many laws are created at the federal, provincial, and municipal levels, and these regulations often overlap. Moreover, regulations are constantly changing—what was allowed last year may now be prohibited, and what was prohibited may now be allowed. The North American Free Trade Agreement (NAFTA) replaced the Free Trade Agreement (FTA) in August 1992. It governs free trade among Canada, the United States, and Mexico. As trade among the three countries expands, the provisions of NAFTA will continue to be updated and amended. Marketers must work hard to keep up with changes in regulations and their interpretations.

Personal Information Protection and Electronic Documents Act
www.privcom.gc.ca/legislation/02_06_01_e.asp

Business legislation has been enacted for various reasons. The first is to *protect companies* from each other. Although business executives may praise competition, they sometimes try to neutralize it when it threatens them. So laws are passed to define and prevent unfair competition.

The second purpose of government regulation is to *protect consumers* from unfair business practices. Some firms, if left alone, would make shoddy products, lie in their advertising, and deceive consumers through their packaging and pricing. Various agencies have defined unfair business practices and enforce their regulation.

Table 4-2 Major Federal Legislation Affecting Marketing

The *Competition Act* is a major legislative act affecting the marketing activities of companies in Canada. Specific sections and the relevant areas are as follows:

- Section 34: Pricing—Forbids suppliers from charging different prices to competitors purchasing like quantities of goods (price discrimination). Forbids price-cutting that lessens competition (predatory pricing).

- Section 36: Pricing and Advertising—Forbids advertising prices that misrepresent the "usual" selling price (misleading price advertising).

- Section 38: Pricing—Forbids suppliers from requiring subsequent resellers to offer products at a stipulated price (resale price maintenance).

- Section 33: Mergers—Forbids mergers by which competition is, or is likely to be, lessened to the detriment of the interests of the public.

Other selected Acts that have an impact on marketing activities are as follows:

- *National Trade Mark and True Labelling Act*—Established the term Canada Standard, or CS, as a national trademark; requires certain commodities to be properly labelled or described in advertising for the purpose of indicating material content or quality.

- *Consumer Packaging and Labelling Act*—Provides a set of rules to ensure that full information is disclosed by the manufacturer, packer, or distributor. Requires that all prepackaged products bear the quantity in French and English in metric as well as traditional Canadian standard units of weight, volume, or measure.

- *Motor Vehicle Safety Act*—Establishes mandatory safety standards for motor vehicles.

- *Food and Drug Act*—Prohibits the advertisement and sale of adulterated or misbranded foods, cosmetics, and drugs.

- *Personal Information Protection and Electronic Documents Act*—Establishes rules to govern the collection, use, and disclosure of personal information that recognize the right of privacy of individuals. The law recognizes the needs of organizations to collect, use, and disclose personal information for appropriate purposes.

The third purpose of government regulation is to *protect the interests of society* against unrestrained business behaviour. Profitable business activity does not always create a better quality of life. Regulation arises to ensure that firms take responsibility for the social costs of their production or products.

Business executives must watch these developments of new laws and their enforcement when planning their products and marketing programs. Marketers need to know about the major laws protecting competition, consumers, and society, at the municipal, provincial, federal, and international levels.

Increased Emphasis on Ethics and Socially Responsible Actions Written regulations cannot possibly cover all potential marketing abuses, and existing laws are often difficult to enforce. However, beyond written laws and regulations, business is also governed by social codes and rules of professional ethics. Enlightened companies encourage their managers to look beyond what the regulatory system allows and simply to "do the right thing." These socially responsible firms actively seek out ways to protect the long-run interests of their customers and the environment.

Business scandals and increased concerns about the environment have created fresh interest in ethics and social responsibility. Almost every aspect of marketing involves such issues. Unfortunately, because they usually involve conflicting interests, well-meaning people can disagree about the right course of action in a particular situation. Thus, many industrial and professional trade associations have suggested codes of ethics, and many companies are developing policies and guidelines to deal with complex social responsibility issues.

The boom in e-commerce and Internet marketing has created a new set of social and ethical issues. Issues as diverse as the online sale of prescription drugs, fraudulent offers, and online gambling have troubled regulators and legitimate online marketers alike. No matter how troubling these issues appear, it is online information gathering, with and without consumers' knowledge, that has emerged as one of the most significant concerns. Not only do Web-surfers knowingly provide information when they comply with online information requests, other information is gathered by sites that use cookies and Web bugs—devices embedded in sites that track click stream data without the consumers' knowledge. Although some governments, such as the European Union and Canada, have recently passed legislation to better protect the privacy of Web users, other countries, such as the United States, have little regulation in place to protect consumers' privacy and unauthorized use of their personal information.

Protecting children and other vulnerable groups from exposure to inappropriate material is another ethical concern that has arisen with online marketing. Protecting children from explicit sexual material and restricting access to "hate" sites or adult chat rooms is an ongoing challenge since all online marketers have great difficulty determining the demographic profile of users. Take the example of eBay.com, the online auction site. It recently found itself the victim of a 13-year-old boy who'd bid on and purchased on the site more than $3 million worth of rare art works and high-priced antiques, including a bed that once belonged to Canada's first prime minister. eBay has a strict policy against bidding by anyone under 18 but works largely on the honour system. Unfortunately, this honour system did little to prevent the teenager from taking a cyberspace joyride.[27]

Cyberspace has its own examples of more typical consumer abuses. For example, although America Online has been hugely successful and is a popular online service provider, it has lost millions of dollars because of consumer complaints about unethical marketing tactics:

In 1998, America Online agreed to pay a $3.9 million penalty and revamp some of its business practices to settle deceptive-marketing complaints. In this instance, AOL failed to clearly notify consumers that the "50 free hours" in its online service's much-touted trial memberships must be used within a one-month period and that users would incur subscription fees after the first month. This was AOL's third settlement in less than two years. Previous settlements dealt with the company's data network congestion in early 1997 (due to a move to flat rate pricing that gave the company more subscriptions than it had equipment to handle) and efforts in late 1996 to switch customers to a higher-priced subscription plan. The three agreements not only cost the company $51 million in total, but also created a barrage of negative publicity that AOL had to work hard to counter.[28]

Some of the New Directions boxes found throughout this book present public policy and social responsibility issues surrounding major marketing decisions. These exhibits discuss the legal issues that marketers should understand and the common ethical and societal concerns that marketers face. In Chapter 16, we discuss a broad range of societal marketing issues in greater depth.

Cultural Environment

The **cultural environment** is made up of institutions and other forces that affect a society's basic values, perceptions, preferences, and behaviours. People grow up in a particular society that shapes their basic beliefs and values. They absorb a world view that defines their relationships with others. The following cultural characteristics can affect marketing decision making.

Cultural environment
Institutions and other forces that affect society's basic values, perceptions, preferences, and behaviours.

Persistence of Cultural Values People in a society hold many beliefs and values. Their core beliefs and values have a high degree of persistence. For example, most Canadians believe in working, getting married, giving to charity, and being honest. Although such values have been described as dull, reserved, and modest, Canadians view themselves as hard-working, generous, and sophisticated. These beliefs shape more specific attitudes and behaviours found in everyday life. *Core* beliefs and values are passed from parents to children and are reinforced by schools, churches, business, and government.

Secondary beliefs and values are more open to change. Believing in marriage is a core belief; believing that people should get married early in life is a secondary belief. Marketers have some chance of changing secondary values, but little chance of changing core values. For example, family-planning marketers could argue more effectively that people should get married later than argue that they should not get married at all.

Shifts in Secondary Cultural Values Although core values are fairly persistent, cultural swings do occur. Consider the impact of popular music groups, movie personalities, and other celebrities on young people's hair styling, clothing, and sexual norms. Marketers want to predict cultural shifts to identify new opportunities or threats, so several firms offer "futures" forecasts. For example, the Environics marketing research firm tracks such regional values as "anti-bigness," "mysticism," "living for today," "away from possessions," and "sensuousness." Such information helps marketers cater to trends with appropriate products and communication appeals. (See New Directions 4-3 for a summary of today's cultural trends.)

The major cultural values of a society are expressed in people's views of themselves and others, as well as in their views of organizations, society, nature, and the universe.

People's Views of Themselves People vary in their emphasis on serving themselves versus serving others. Some people seek personal pleasure, wanting fun, change, and escape. Others seek self-realization through religion, recreation, or the avid pursuit of careers or other life goals. People use products, brands, and services as a means of self-expression, and they buy products and services that match their views of themselves.

New Directions 4-3 >>　Regional Differences in Culture Values and Product Usage

Canadian marketers must be sensitive to the regional differences that mark the country. Recent polls have shown that people in different parts of the nation have dramatically different values and beliefs. Although it does not surprise most Canadians that Quebeckers are fiercely independent, they might be surprised at the extent to which they live for today and place a high value on enjoying life. Seventy-one percent of Quebec residents agreed with the statement "We should eat, drink, and be merry, for tomorrow we may die," while people's agreement levels from other regions of Canada ranged from 17 to 43 percent. Quebeckers are also more security conscious than other Canadians. They put greater importance on family and on the cultivation of friendships. Unlike the rest of Canada, they demonstrate a respect for authority. Picturing themselves as *au courant,* they stress fashion and being up to date on current events. Quebeckers place less importance on earning a lot of money than do people from English Canada, and they pride themselves on being more emotional than English Canadians.

Regional differences are not just limited to those between French and English Canadians: Newfoundlanders think that they are the hardest-working segment of the Canadian population, while people from British Columbia express the greatest love of reading.

These regional values often translate into different patterns of product usage. Fredericton is the capital of white bread consumption. Montrealers eat more deep brown beans than other Canadians. Consumers in Halifax drink more Diet Coke per capita than other Canadians, and people from Manitoba and Saskatchewan have the highest per capita consumption of Kellogg's Corn Flakes. People from Quebec consume more than half of all tomato juice sold in Canada, but Quebeckers are less likely to try new products, use no-name products, or make long-distance phone calls. Although marketers are often at a loss when it comes to explaining how regional values translate into different product usage patterns, marketers must still be highly sensitive to these regional differences.

Sources: Rosemary Todd, "Food for Thought," *The Globe and Mail,* 12 March 1988, p. D2; *Maclean's*/CTV Poll, "A National Mirror," *Maclean's,* 3 January 1994, pp. 12–15; "Portrait of the Quebec Consumer," *Marketing,* 22 March 1993, p. 14; "Quebec," advertising supplement to *Advertising Age,* 22 November 1993.

People's Views of Others Observers have noted a shift from a "me-society" to a "we-society" in which more people want to be with and serve others. Notes one trend tracker, "People want to get out, especially those 48 million people working out of their home and feeling a little cooped up [and] all those shut-ins who feel unfulfilled by the cyberstuff that was supposed to make them feel like never leaving home."[29] Moreover, materialism, flashy spending, and self-indulgence are being replaced by more sensible spending, saving, family concerns, and helping others. The aging baby boomers are limiting their spending to products and services that improve their lives instead of one that boost their images. This suggests a bright future for products and services that serve basic needs rather than those relying on glitz and hype. It also suggests a greater demand for "social support" products and services that improve direct communication between people, such as health clubs and family vacations.

People's Views of Organizations People have differing attitudes toward corporations, government agencies, trade unions, universities, and other organizations. Most people are willing to work for major organizations, and they expect them, in turn, to carry out society's work. In recent years, there has been a decline in organizational loyalty and a growing skepticism regarding business and political organizations and institutions. The recent failure of firms such as Enron and Worldcom have caused people to give a little less to their organizations and trust them less.

This trend suggests that organizations need to find new ways to win consumer confidence. They need to review their advertising communications to ensure that their messages are honest. They also need to review their various activities to ensure that they are perceived as good corporate citizens. More companies are linking themselves to worthwhile causes, measuring their images with important publics, and using public relations to build more positive images.

People's Views of Society People differ in their attitudes toward their society: Patriots defend it; reformers want to change it; malcontents want to leave it. People's orientation to their society influences their consumption patterns, levels of savings, and attitudes toward the marketplace.

The last decade saw an increase in consumer patriotism. Some companies such as Zellers responded with "made-in-Canada" themes and promotions. Others, such as Clearly Canadian and Upper Canada Brewing Company, made national identity part of their branding strategy. Canadians do not respond to in-your-face nationalistic appeals, but they love the quirky humour of Labatt Blue's television campaign built around the insights about Canada's future by two early voyageurs, and Molson Canadian's "I am Canadian" spots.

Clearly Canadian
www.clearly.ca

Upper Canada Brewing Company
www.uppercanada.com

People's Views of Nature People have differing attitudes toward the natural world: some feel ruled by it, others feel in harmony with it, and still others seek to master it. A long-term trend has been people's growing mastery over nature through technology and the belief that nature is bountiful. More recently, however, people have recognized that nature is finite and fragile—that it can be destroyed or spoiled by human activities.

Love of nature is leading to more camping, hiking, boating, fishing, and other outdoor activities. Business has responded by offering more hiking gear, camping equipment, better insect repellents, and other products for nature enthusiasts. Tour operators are offering more tours to wilderness areas. Food producers have found growing markets for "natural" products such as natural cereal, natural ice cream, and health foods. Marketing communicators are using appealing natural backgrounds in advertising their products.

People's Views of the Universe People vary in their beliefs about the origin of the universe and their place in it. Although many Canadians practise religion, religious conviction and practice have been dropping off gradually through the years. As people lose their religious orientation, they seek goods and experiences with more immediate satisfactions. Some futurists, however, have noted an emerging renewal of interest in religion, perhaps as part of a broader search for a new inner purpose.

Cultural environment: Love of nature is leading to more camping, hiking, boating, fishing, and other outdoor activities. Positioning Canada as a pristine wilderness and spiritual refuge appeals to both Canadian and international consumers.

You deserve another pit stop! You have now read about a large number of environmental forces. How are all of these forces linked with one another? with company marketing strategies?

• How are the major demographic forces linked with economic change? with cultural trends? How are the natural and technological environments linked? Think of an example of a company that has recognized one of these links and created an opportunity.

• Is the marketing environment uncontrollable—something the company can only prepare for and react to? Or can companies be proactive in changing environmental factors? Think of a good example that makes your point, then read on.

RESPONDING TO THE MARKETING ENVIRONMENT

Someone once observed, "There are three kinds of companies: those who make things happen; those who watch things happen; and those who wonder what's happened."[30]

Many companies view the marketing environment as an uncontrollable element to which they must adapt. They passively accept the marketing environment and do not try to change it. They analyze the environmental forces and design strategies that will help the company avoid the threats and take advantage of the opportunities the environment provides.

Other companies take an **environmental management perspective**.[31] Rather than simply watching and reacting, these firms take aggressive action to affect the publics and forces in their marketing environment. Such companies hire lobbyists to influence legislation affecting their industries and stage media events to gain favourable press coverage. They run advertorials—ads expressing editorial points of view—to shape public opinion. They file lawsuits and complaints with regula-

Environmental management perspective A management perspective in which the firm takes aggressive action to affect the publics and forces in its marketing environment rather than simply watching and reacting to them.

tors to keep competitors in line, and they form contractual agreements to better control their distribution channels.

Other companies find positive ways to overcome seemingly uncontrollable environmental constraints. Some forestry firms, including Noranda, have joined the Round Table on the Environment, a government-sponsored discussion group, to help all stakeholders affected by forestry policies better understand environmental concerns about forestry management.

Marketing management cannot always affect environmental forces. In many cases, it must settle for simply watching and reacting to the environment. For example, a company would have little success trying to influence geographic population shifts, the economic environment, or major cultural values. But whenever possible, smart marketing managers will take a *proactive* rather than a *reactive* approach to the marketing environment.

<< Looking Back   < < < < < < < < <

Companies must constantly watch and adapt to the *marketing environment* to seek opportunities and ward off threats. The marketing environment comprises all the actors and forces influencing the company's ability to transact business effectively with its target market.

1. Describe the environmental forces that affect the company's ability to serve its customers.

The company's marketing environment has five microenvironmental and six macroenvironmental components. The microenvironment consists of other actors close to the company that combine to form the company's value delivery system or that affect its ability to serve its customers. The first microenvironmental component is the company's *internal environment*—its several departments and management levels—as it influences marketing decision making. The second component consists of the *marketing channel firms* that cooperate to create value—the suppliers and marketing intermediaries, including resellers, physical distribution firms, marketing services agencies, and financial intermediaries. The third component comprises the five types of customer *markets*, including consumer, business, reseller, government, and international markets. The fourth component consists of *competitors*, and the

fifth comprises the seven *publics* with an actual or potential interest in or impact on the company's ability to meet its objectives, including the financial, media, government, citizen action, and local, general, and internal publics.

The *macroenvironment* consists of larger societal forces that affect the entire microenvironment—demographic, economic, natural, technological, political, and cultural forces. These six forces shape opportunities and pose threats to the company.

2. Explain how changes in the demographic and economic environments affect marketing decisions.

Demography is the study of the characteristics of human populations. Today's demographic environment shows a changing age structure, shifting profiles of Canadian households, geographic population shifts, a more-educated and more white-collar population, and increasing diversity. The economic environment consists of factors that affect buying power and patterns. The economic environment is characterized by lower unemployment rates and shifting consumer spending patterns. Some "financially squeezed consumers" seek greater value—just the right combination of good quality and service at a fair price. The distribution of income is also shifting, leading to a two-tiered market. Many companies now tailor their marketing offers to two different markets—the affluent and the less affluent.

3. Identify the major trends in the firm's natural and technological environments.

The natural environment shows four major trends: shortages of certain raw materials, increased costs of energy, higher pollution levels, and more government intervention in natural resource management. Environmental concerns create marketing opportunities for alert companies. The marketer should watch for four major trends in the technological environment: the rapid pace of technological change, high R&D budgets, the concentration by companies on minor product improvements, and increased government regulation. Companies that fail to keep up with technological change will miss new product and marketing opportunities.

4. Explain the key changes in the political and cultural environments.

The political environment consists of laws, agencies, and groups that influence or limit marketing actions.

The political environment has undergone three changes that affect marketing worldwide—increased legislation regulating business, strong government agency enforcement, and greater emphasis on ethics and socially responsible actions. The cultural environment is made up of institutions and forces that affect a society's values, perceptions, preferences, and behaviours. The environment shows long-term trends toward a "we-society," a return to cautious trust of institutions, increasing patriotism, greater appreciation for nature, a new spiritualism, and the search for more meaningful and enduring values.

5. Discuss how companies can react to the marketing environment.

Companies can passively accept the marketing environment as an uncontrollable element to which they must adapt, avoiding threats and taking advantage of opportunities as they arise. Or they can take an environmental management perspective, proactively working to change the environment rather than simply reacting to it. Whenever possible, companies should try to be proactive rather than reactive.

Navigating the Key Terms

Baby boom, **p. 133**
Cultural environment, **p. 151**
Demography, **p. 131**
Economic environment, **p. 143**
Engel's laws, **p. 145**
Environmental management perspective, **p. 154**
Macroenvironment, **p. 127**

Marketing environment, **p. 126**
Marketing intermediaries, **p. 128**
Microenvironment, **p. 127**
Natural environment, **p. 145**
Political environment, **p. 148**
Public, **p. 130**
Technological environment, **p. 147**

Concept Check

Fill in the blanks and then check your answers.

1. A company's _____ consists of the actors and forces outside marketing that affect marketing management's ability to develop and maintain successful relationships with target customers.

2. The _____ consists of the forces close to the company that affect its ability to serve its customers—the company, marketing channel firms, customer markets, competitors, and publics.

3. _____ _____ (such as resellers, physical distribution firms, marketing services agencies, and financial intermediaries) help the company to promote, sell, and distribute its goods to final buyers.

4. The company's marketing environment includes various publics. If a company's marketing decisions were questioned by residents of a neighbourhood or a community organization, then the company would need to develop strategies to respond to these _____ publics.

5. One distinguishing characteristic of Generation Y is their utter fluency and comfort with computer, digital, and Internet technology. For this reason, this generation has also been called _____ _____.

6. One of _____ laws is that as family income rises, the percentage spent on food declines.

7. Marketers should be aware of several trends in the natural environment. Chief among these are the _____, _____, and _____.

8. Business legislation has been enacted for a number of reasons. Chief among these are to protect _____ _____, to protect _____ _____, and to protect _____.

9. The major cultural values of a society are expressed in people's views of themselves and others. Recent studies suggest that consumers are interested in getting out more, in family concerns, and in helping others. This is evidence that our society is moving more toward a "____-society."

10. Companies that take an _____ _____ _____ take aggressive actions to affect the publics and forces in their marketing environment rather than simply watching and reacting to them.

Concept Check Answers: 1. marketing environment; 2. microenvironment; 3. Marketing intermediaries; 4. local; 5. net-gens (or n-gens); 6. Engel's; 7. growing shortages of raw materials, increased pollution, and increased government intervention in natural resource management; 8. companies from each other, consumers from unfair business practices, and the interests of society against unrestrained business behaviour; 9. we; 10. environmental management perspective.

Discussing the Issues

1. Winston Churchill was often seen in public smoking a large cigar. It became a personal "trademark." Would a prime minister be seen smoking today? Discuss how the cultural environment has changed. Considering the rash of recent court rulings and settlements concerning the tobacco industry, how might a cigarette manufacturer market its products differently to meet this new environment? What do you think are the long-term prospects for the tobacco industry?

2. McDonald's received a lot of bad press in the late 1990s, and the company wasn't as successful as it had been previously. What microenvironment and macroenvironment trends affected McDonald's throughout the 1990s? If you were in charge of marketing at McDonald's, what plans would you have made to deal with those trends?

3. Statistics Canada posts tables on its Web site at **www.statcan.ca** that outline some of its findings from the 1996 census (and will soon post findings from the 2001 census). These include tables on population projects by age group and sex, the population of census metropolitan areas (CMAs), and recent immigrants by last country of residence. Go to their Web site and choose a table that interests you. Print the table, analyze it, and describe how its information would help you design a marketing plan for a particular target audience.

4. Canada's ethnic populations are growing quickly. It is estimated that the six largest ethnic groups now encompass about 2.8 million people, almost 10 percent of the current population. What are the major challenges faced by marketers attempting to serve these populations?

5. What Canadian companies have successfully used the "green revolution" as leverage to market their products or services? Why have some of

these efforts caused controversy among consumers and environmental groups? Do you think corporations should continue to pursue green marketing? Is it a fad or a long-term trend?

6. Businesses are feeling increasing pressure to be more ethically and socially responsible. The latest areas of concern involve the Internet and e-commerce. What are the key issues regarding online ethics and social responsibilities? How should online businesses respond to these issues? Give an example of an online marketer that is not behaving responsibly. What would you propose to correct this situation?

7. Suppose that you have been assigned the task of explaining the core cultural values of people in Canada to a foreign marketer who wants to sell a new line of men's and women's clothing in this country. Identify at least six core values that you think the foreign marketer would need to understand. Explain how the marketer might apply these values.

 **Mastering Marketing**

Understanding the environment is critical for any marketing manager. An environmental management perspective can literally make or break a company. Examine each of the environments and their respective publics faced by CanGo. List the critical factors in each environments that must be proactively met by the company for its marketing plan to be implemented. Of the environments examined, which one do you think is critical to the firm's long-term success? Explain.

Check out the enclosed Video case CD-ROM, or our Companion Website at www.pearsoned.ca/armstrong, to view a CBC video segment and case for this chapter.

MAP 4 **Marketing Applications**

When Stanford University graduate students Jerry Yang and David Filo developed Yahoo!, they had little idea how far their revolutionary concept would go. Their original concept was to make "wasting time on the Internet" easier. Commercial applications came later. Today, more Internet users recognize the name Yahoo than recognize Microsoft. One reason for Yahoo's popularity is its ability to focus on people's tastes rather than on just delivering information or access to every Web site possible. Yahoo has become a full-blown package of information and services relating to health, real estate, finance, news, personalization, travel, and shopping. The major challenge now facing Yahoo is how to convince corporate North America that Yahoo constitutes an effective advertising medium. The primary future challenges will come from America Online and Microsoft.

Thinking Like a Marketing Manager

1. How will a portal site such as Yahoo affect a marketing company's technological environment?

2. Suppose you are marketing manager for a company that makes and sells consumer electronics products. After visiting Yahoo Canada at **www.yahoo.ca** and competing sites, assess Yahoo as an advertising medium for your product. What types of ads would you consider placing on such a site?

3. Given the rapid pace of change in the Internet environment, how do you think Yahoo will fare in the future? Which environmental issues are critical to Yahoo's success? If you were the marketing manager of Yahoo, what strategic alliances would you investigate?

Digital MAP
Visit our Web site at **www.pearsoned.ca/armstrong** for online quizzes, Internet exercises, and more!

CASE 4   THE NEWEST AVON LADY—BARBIE!

Selling Tradition

"Ding-dong, Avon calling." With that simple advertising message, Avon Products has spent the past 115 years building a $6 billion worldwide beauty-products business. Founded in 1886, Avon deployed an army of women to sell its products. These "Avon ladies," 40 million of them over the company's history, met with friends and neighbours in their homes, showed products, took and delivered orders, and earned sales commissions. Through direct selling, Avon bypassed the battle for retail space and attention waged by its competitors in department stores, and later in discount drug stores and supermarkets. Direct selling also offered convenience for the customer, coupled with personal beauty-care advice from a friend.

Avon's plan worked well. Most members of its up to 65 000-member Canadian and 500 000-member U.S. sales forces were homemakers who needed extra money but did not want a full-time job outside the home. They developed client lists of friends and neighbours on whom they called periodically. Customers could also call them between visits. Recruiting salespeople was easy, and a good salesperson could develop a loyal core of customers who made repeat purchases. Avon paid the salespeople a commission based on their sales, and a successful salesperson could earn an attractive income.

Times Change

However, during the 1970s and 1980s, the environment changed. First, more women found that they needed to work outside the home. As a result, when Avon ladies rang the doorbell, often no one answered. Second, many Avon ladies decided that they needed more than part-time jobs, and Avon's annual sales force turnover rates soared to more than 200 percent. Third, because of high sales force turnover, many Avon customers wanting to see a salesperson could not find one. Fourth, more competitors, such as Amway, Mary Kay Cosmetics, and Tupperware, were competing for the pool of people interested in full- or part-time direct-selling jobs. Finally, in addition to all those factors, the increasing mobility of the North American population meant that both customers and salespeople were moving. This made it difficult for salespeople to establish loyal, stable customer bases.

A New Strategy

To deal with these issues, in 1988, Avon Products recruited James E. Preston to serve as its chair and chief executive officer. Preston decided that Avon needed to overhaul its marketing strategy. First, he refocused the company on its core business—selling cosmetics, fragrances, and toiletries—and sold unrelated businesses. Next, he drastically cut prices on Avon products. Finally, he tried a new compensation program called Leadership that allowed sales representatives to earn up to 21 percent in bonuses based on the sales of new representatives they recruited. Such multilevel selling is common among direct-sales companies; however, by late 1991, Avon had killed the program, arguing that it did not fit Avon's culture.

Preston believed that Avon had left as many as 10 million former or potential customers stranded. These customers wanted to buy Avon products, but sales force turnover meant that they did not know how to find a salesperson or order products. Fourteen percent of women accounted for one-third of Avon's sales. Another 62 percent were fringe customers. These customers viewed Avon positively but did not buy regularly. Another 15 percent of women were potentially receptive to Avon but were not necessarily interested in dealing with a traditional Avon sales representative.

Therefore, Preston decided to develop another program he called Avon Select. The program featured a catalogue and toll-free telephone number that allowed direct-mail selling. Avon's research revealed that its median customer was 45 years old and had an average household income of less than $45 000. The catalogue would reach younger, higher-income customers. Preston believed that, with a catalogue, the company could cut the median customer age to 38 and increase average household income to more than $45 000. Avon supported the catalogue program by kicking off a national advertising campaign that featured the slogan "Avon—The Smartest Shop in Town." To fund the advertising, the company cut sales commissions and incentives and laid off scores of executives.

As you might imagine, all these changes created a lot of turmoil at Avon. However, Preston vowed to keep pursuing changes. To keep customers, "change we did, change we must, and change we will," Preston asserted. To make good on his promise, he launched a $45 million ad campaign in 1994 with the theme, "Just Another Avon Lady." Market research showed that, despite all Avon's changes, consumers still thought of "Ding-dong" and the Avon lady when asked what they associated with the company. Observers wondered if the use of the term "lady" in the mid-1990s would cause negative reactions among many women. After all, even Avon had avoided using the term in advertising for 20 years.

In Canada, Montreal-based Avon went beyond increased advertising. The next time an Avon representative knocks on your door, she'll come bearing more than just cosmetics. The representative will carry a new glossy women's magazine called *Confidante*. More than 300 000 copies (60 000 are in French) are being distributed across Canada. The cost of the magazine is $2.99. "It's an image-builder for us, a way for us to talk to our customers," says Lucie Brodeur, product publicity manager for Avon Canada. Although most of the magazine's ads are from Avon, the debut issues included non-competing advertisers, such as General Motors, Kellogg, Clairol, and Five Roses. In addition to the new magazine, the company is testing a new interactive kiosk called an "Interactive Makeup and Skin Care Centre" aimed at women who cringe at the thought of asking younger, more fashionable clerks for beauty advice.

The kiosk, which is reminiscent of a photo booth, also serves as a mall poster medium. Once seated inside, visitors can view video clips and receive personalized beauty advice via a bilingual touch-screen multimedia program. At the end of the presentation, the visitor is offered a free Avon sample in exchange for her name and address.

Between 1992 and 1996, Avon's sales and profits rose slowly but steadily, driven primarily by sales in international markets. Then, in late 1997, Avon announced what might be its most radical change yet. It announced that it would soon test the idea of selling its products through retail stores. Although the company had been using retail stores in some foreign markets for years, this approach would be new to the North American market. Preston argued that no matter how great Avon's products were, many customers just weren't interested in buying from Avon ladies in a one-on-one situation. To pacify the company's sales reps, Avon said it would consider giving them a share of the new business either through franchising or through referrals from the stores. It also announced that it would cut its product line by 30 percent to put its marketing resources behind fewer products, pursue the creation of global brands out of several of its skin-care and cosmetics products, and standardize its promotion efforts using the same promotions for its products around the world.

Global Reach

Avon has been working for a considerable time to transform itself into a global firm. The value of Avon's global reach and its 2.3 million sales representatives worldwide had not gone unnoticed by other firms wanting to crack international markets. Mattel, Inc. announced in 1997 that it would partner with Avon to allow its salespeople to begin selling its Barbie dolls. In a 1996 test, Avon sold $65 million worth of two versions of Barbie, including more than one million of one version in just two weeks. Andrea Jung, Avon's president of global marketing, noted, "Our powerful distribution channel combined with their powerful brand is a huge opportunity."

Companies such as Mattel are attracted to direct-sales forces such as Avon's for several reasons. In international markets, the companies do not have to wait for retailers to build stores if they use a direct-sales force. Further, in many developing economies, being a direct-sales rep may be the most attractive job for many women, thus making recruitment easy. However, there are problems. Turnover is often high, and many sales representatives are not really committed to the company. Further, many don't have formal business training or the basic skills needed to perform their duties. Finally, in some countries, such as China, the government can wrench a market away from a firm. Fearing that direct-sales efforts took advantage of Chinese consumers and that sales meetings could be used as a venue to start secret societies and sell smuggled or fake goods, the government outlawed all direct sales. Avon and other direct sellers protested the move loudly. After considerable effort, Avon eventually convinced the Chinese government to let it restart its business. Avon agreed, however, to operate as a wholesaler, selling its products to retail stores.

Today, Avon is undergoing yet another facelift and is transforming itself under its new president and chief executive officer, Andrea Jung. After a long period of rationalization and cost-cutting so that it could compete as a "lean and mean" global firm, Avon is now moving to a "buy-side" mentality and is making more long-term marketing investments. It launched a new "Let's Talk" positioning campaign, the first global branding effort the company has ever done. Go to **www.avon.ca** to see one facet of the campaign. Avon has decided to expand the use of its Internet technology to strengthen its direct selling and invigorate the brand. Although the Web site includes more product information, it won't be used to sell cosmetics directly to consumers. Avon still prefers to redirect consumers to their nearest Avon lady, showing a strong commitment to its 65 000 Canadian direct sellers. Thus, the Let's Talk campaign is just the first leg in a race to make over the cosmetic giant and wipe out its image as grandma's brand.

The Let's Talk campaign was developed after Avon consulted with marketing departments in 13 key markets, including North America, Italy, Poland, Japan, the Philippines, and Taiwan. The aim of the research was to uncover women's commonalties as well as their differences. The $132-million campaign, which accounts for a 50 percent increase in ad spending for Avon, represents women and their relationships with other women and their beauty products. The campaign also heralds Avon's entry into such new categories as hair care products and even vitamins. Avon recently announced a strategic alliance with Roche Consumer Health to develop a line of vitamins and nutritional supplements. As Avon meets the challenges of the twenty-first century, it is going to have more than just cosmetics to talk about.

Questions

1. Which actors in Avon's microenvironment and forces in the macroenvironment have been important in shaping its marketing strategies?

2. What microenvironmental and macroenvironmental factors should Avon consider as it works to expand its international marketing efforts?

3. Assess Avon's marketing strategy in North America. What marketing recommendations would you make to help Avon improve its marketing strategy on this continent?

4. Assess Avon's marketing strategy in international markets. What marketing recommendations would you make to help Avon improve its marketing strategy in international markets such as China?

Sources: Astrid Van Den Broek, "Avon Calling on Global Ad Effort to Change Its Image," *Marketing On-Line*, 26 June 2000; "Avon Gets a Green Light to Restart China Business," *WWD*, 8 June 1998, p. 27; "Avon Kiosk Doles out Beauty Advice," *Strategy*, 8 May 2000, p. 7; William J. McDonald, "The Ban in China: How Direct Marketing Is Affected," *Direct Marketing*, June 1998, p. 16; Tara Parker-Pope, "Avon Is Calling with New Way to Make a Sale," *The Wall Street Journal*, 27 October 1997, p. B1; Tara Parker-Pope and Lisa Bannon, "Avon's New Calling: Sell Barbie in China," *The Wall Street Journal*, 1 May 1997, p. B1; Yumiko Ono, "Remember the Avon Lady? She's Back," *The Wall Street Journal*, 22 January 1995; Suein L. Hwang, "Updating Avon Means Respecting History without Repeating It," *The Wall Street Journal*, 4 April 1994, p. A1.

5 >> Managing Marketing Information

Looking Ahead

In the last chapter, you learned about the complex and changing marketing environment. In this chapter, we'll look at how companies develop and manage information about important elements of the environment—about their customers, competitors, products, and marketing programs. We'll examine marketing information systems designed to give managers the right information, in the right form, at the right time to help them make better marketing decisions. We'll also take a close look at the marketing research process and at some special marketing research considerations. To succeed in today's marketplace, companies must know how to manage mountains of marketing information effectively.

After reading this chapter, you should be able to

1. explain the importance of information to the company
2. define the marketing information system and discuss its parts
3. outline the steps in the marketing research process
4. explain how companies analyze and distribute marketing information
5. discuss the special issues some marketing researchers face, including public policy and ethics issues

We'll start the chapter with a look at a classic marketing blunder—Coca-Cola's ill-considered decision some years ago to introduce New Coke. The company based its decision on substantial marketing research, yet the new product fizzled badly. As you read on, ask yourself how a large and resourceful marketing company such as Coca-Cola could make such a huge research mistake. The moral: If it can happen to Coca-Cola, it can happen to any company.

In 1985, in what has now become an all-time classic marketing tale, the Coca-Cola Company made a major marketing blunder. After 99 successful years, it set aside its long-standing rule—"Don't mess with Mother Coke"—and dropped its original formula Coke! In its place came *New Coke* with a sweeter, smoother taste.

At first, amid the introductory flurry of advertising and publicity, New Coke sold well. But sales soon went flat, as a stunned public reacted. Coke began receiving sacks of mail and more than 1500 phone calls each day from angry consumers. A group called "Old Cola Drinkers" staged protests, handed out T-shirts, and threatened a class-action suit unless Coca-Cola brought back the original formula. After only three months, the Coca-Cola Company brought original Coke back. Now called "Coke Classic," it sold side by side with New Coke on supermarket shelves. The company said that New Coke would remain its flagship brand, but consumers had a different idea. By the end of that year, Classic was outselling New Coke in supermarkets by two to one.

Quick reaction saved the company from potential disaster. It stepped up efforts for Coke Classic and slotted New Coke into a supporting role. Coke Classic again became the company's main brand and the country's leading soft drink. New Coke became the company's "attack brand"—its Pepsi stopper—and ads boldly compared New Coke's taste with Pepsi's. Still, New Coke managed only a 2 percent market share. In the spring of 1990, the company repackaged New Coke and relaunched it as a brand extension with a new name, Coke II. Today, Coke Classic captures more than 20 percent of the U.S. soft drink market; Coke II has quietly disappeared. Why was New Coke introduced in the first place? What went wrong? Many analysts blame the blunder on poor marketing research.

In the early 1980s, although Coke was still the leading soft drink, it was slowly losing market share to Pepsi. For years, Pepsi had successfully mounted the "Pepsi Challenge," a series of televised taste tests showing that consumers preferred the sweeter taste of Pepsi. By early 1985, although Coke led in the overall market, Pepsi led in share of supermarket sales by 2 percent. (That doesn't sound like much, but 2 percent of today's huge North America soft drink market amounts to more than $1.2 billion in retail sales!) Coca-Cola had to do something to stop the loss of its market share, and the solution appeared to be a change in Coke's taste.

Coca-Cola began the largest new-product research project in the company's history. It spent more than two years and $4 million on research before settling on a new formula. It conducted some 200 000 taste tests—30 000 on the final formula alone. In blind tests, 60 percent of consumers chose the new Coke over the old, and 52 percent chose it over Pepsi. Research showed that New Coke would be a winner, and the company introduced it with confidence. So what happened?

Looking back, we can see that Coke defined its marketing research problem too narrowly. The research looked only at taste; it did not explore consumers' feelings about dropping the old Coke and replacing it with a new version. It took no account of the *intangibles*—Coke's name, history, packaging, cultural heritage, and image. To many people, Coke is an institution; it represents the very fabric of the country. Coke's symbolic meaning turned out to be more important to many consumers than its taste. Research addressing a broader set of issues would have detected these strong emotions.

Coke's managers may also have used poor judgment in interpreting the research and planning strategies around it. For example, they took the finding that 60 percent of consumers preferred New Coke's taste to mean that the new product would win in the marketplace, as when a political candidate wins with 60 percent of the vote. But it

also meant that 40 percent still liked the original formula. By dropping the old Coke, the company trampled the taste buds of the large core of loyal Coke drinkers who didn't want a change. The company might have been wiser to leave the old Coke alone and introduce New Coke as a brand extension, as it later did successfully with Cherry Coke.

The Coca-Cola Company has one of the largest, best-managed, and most advanced marketing research operations in North America. Good marketing research has kept the company atop the rough-and-tumble soft drink market for decades. But marketing research is far from an exact science. Consumers are full of surprises and figuring them out can be tough. If Coca-Cola can make a large marketing research mistake, any company can.[1]

To produce superior value and satisfaction for customers, companies need information at almost every turn. As the New Coke story highlights, good products and marketing programs begin with a thorough understanding of consumer needs and wants. Companies also need an abundance of information on competitors, resellers, and other actors and forces in the marketplace.

Increasingly, marketers are viewing information not only as an input for making better decisions, but also as an important strategic asset and marketing tool. A company's information may prove to be its chief competitive advantage. Competitors can copy each other's equipment, products, and procedures, but they cannot duplicate the company's information and intellectual capital. Several companies have recently recognized this by appointing vice presidents of knowledge, learning, or intellectual capital.[2]

In today's more rapidly changing environments, managers need up-to-date information to make timely, high-quality decisions. In turn, with the recent explosion of information technologies, companies can now generate information in great quantities. In fact, today's managers often receive too much information. One study

Information overload: "In this oh so overwhelming Information Age, it's all too easy to be buried, burdened, and burned out by data overload."

found that with all the companies offering data, and with all the information now available through supermarket scanners, a packaged-goods brand manager is bombarded with one million to one *billion* new numbers each week. Another study found that, on average, North American office workers spend 60 percent of their time processing information; a typical manager reads about a million words a week. Thus, running out of information is not a problem but seeing through the "data smog" is. "In this oh so overwhelming Information Age," comments one observer, "it's all too easy to be buried, burdened, and burned out by data overload."[3]

Despite this data glut, marketers frequently complain that they lack enough information of the *right* kind. A recent survey of managers found that although half the respondents said they couldn't cope with the volume of information coming at them, two thirds wanted even more. The researcher concluded that, "despite the volume, they're still not getting what they want."[4] Thus, most marketing managers don't need *more* information, they need *better* information. Companies must design effective marketing information systems that give managers the right information, in the right form, at the right time to help them make better marketing decisions.

Marketing information system (MIS) The people, equipment, and procedures needed to gather, sort, analyze, evaluate, and distribute needed, timely, and accurate information to marketing decision makers.

A **marketing information system (MIS)** consists of people, equipment, and procedures to gather, sort, analyze, evaluate, and distribute needed, timely, and accurate information to marketing decision makers Figure 5-1 shows that the MIS begins and ends with information users—marketing managers, internal and external partners, and others who need marketing information. First, it interacts with these information users to assess *information needs*. Next, it *develops needed information* from internal company databases, marketing intelligence activities, and marketing research. Then it helps users to analyze information to put it in the right form for making marketing decisions and managing customer relationships. Finally, the MIS *distributes* the marketing information and helps managers *use* it in their decision making.

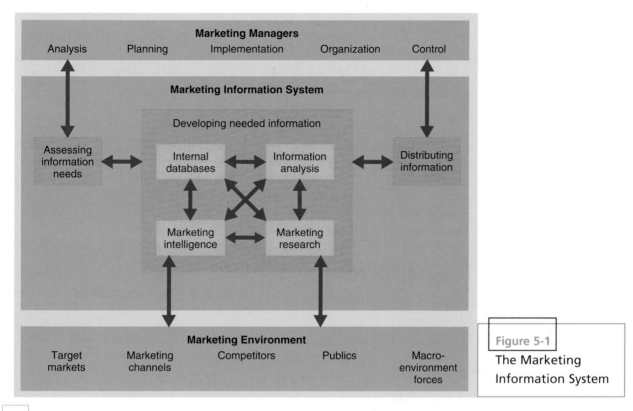

Figure 5-1

The Marketing Information System

ASSESSING MARKETING INFORMATION NEEDS

The marketing information system primarily serves the company's marketing and other managers. However, it may also provide information to external partners, such as suppliers or marketing services agencies. For example, Wal-Mart might give Procter & Gamble and other key suppliers access to information on customer buying patterns and inventory levels. In addition, important customers may be given limited access to the information system. Dell Computer creates tailored Premium Pages for large customers, giving them access to product design, order status, and product support and service information. FedEx lets customers into its information system to schedule and track shipments. In designing an information system, the company must consider the needs of all these users.

A good marketing information system balances the information users would *like* to have against what they really *need* and what is *feasible* to offer. The company begins by interviewing managers to find out what information they would like. Some managers will ask for whatever information they can get without thinking carefully about what they really need. Too much information can be as harmful as too little. Other managers may omit things they ought to know or may not know to ask for some types of information they should have. For example, managers might need to know that a competitor plans to introduce a new product during the coming year. Because they do not know about the new product, they do not think to ask about it. The MIS must monitor the marketing environment and provide decision makers with information they should have to make key marketing decisions.

Sometimes the company cannot provide the needed information, either because it is not available or because of MIS limitations. For example, a brand manager might want to know how competitors will change their advertising budgets next year and how these changes will affect industry market shares. The information on planned budgets probably is not available. Even if it is, the company's MIS may not be advanced enough to forecast resulting changes in market shares.

Finally, the costs of obtaining, processing, storing, and delivering information can mount quickly. The company must decide whether the benefits of having additional information are worth the costs of providing it, and both value and cost are often hard to assess. By itself, information has no worth; its value comes from its *use.* In many cases, additional information will do little to change or improve a manager's decision, or the costs of the information may exceed the returns from the improved decision. Marketers should not assume that additional information will always be worth obtaining. Rather, they should weigh carefully the costs of additional information against the benefits resulting from it.

DEVELOPING MARKETING INFORMATION

Marketers can obtain the needed information from *internal data, marketing intelligence,* and *marketing research.*

Internal Data

Internal databases
Electronic collections of information obtained from data sources within the company.

Many companies build extensive **internal databases**, electronic collections of information obtained from data sources within the company. Marketing managers can readily access and work with information in the database to identify marketing opportunities and problems, plan programs, and evaluate performance.

Information in the database comes from many sources. The accounting department prepares financial statements and keeps detailed records of sales, costs, and cash flows. Manufacturing reports on production schedules, shipments, and inventories. The sales force reports on reseller reactions and competitor activities. The marketing department furnishes information on customer demographics, psychographics, and buying behaviour, and the customer service department keeps records of customer satisfaction and service problems. Research studies done for one department may provide useful information for several others.

Canon Canada provides an example of how companies use their internal databases to make better marketing decisions. The company "recently introduced a 24-hour toll-free help line to help the company better understand the home-office market. Since customer service and repair capabilities are key features of Canon's large-business marketing efforts, it uses this help line to assess the effectiveness of these efforts for the relatively undeveloped home-office market."[5]

Internal databases usually can be accessed more quickly and cheaply than other information sources, but they also present some problems. Because internal information was collected for other purposes, it may be incomplete or in the wrong form for making marketing decisions. For example, sales and cost data used by the accounting department for preparing financial statements must be adapted for use in evaluating product, sales force, or channel performance. Data ages quickly; keeping the database current requires a major effort. In addition, a large company produces mountains of information, and keeping track of it all is difficult. The database information must be well integrated and readily accessible through user-friendly interfaces so that managers can find it easily and use it effectively.

Marketing Intelligence

Marketing intelligence is the systematic collection and analysis of publicly available information about competitors and developments in the marketing environment. The goal of marketing intelligence is to improve strategic decision making, assess and track competitors' actions, and provide early warning of opportunities and threats.

Competitive intelligence gathering has grown dramatically as more and more companies are now busily spying on their competitors. Techniques range from quizzing the company's own employees and benchmarking competitors' products to researching the Internet, lurking around industry trade shows, and rooting through rivals' trash bins.

Much intelligence can be collected from people inside the company—executives, engineers and scientists, purchasing agents, and the sales force. Consider this example:

While talking with a Kodak copier salesperson, a Xerox technician learned that the salesperson was being trained to service Xerox products. The Xerox employee reported back to his boss, who in turn passed the news to Xerox's intelligence unit. Using such clues as a classified ad Kodak placed seeking new people with Xerox product experience, Xerox verified Kodak's plan—code-named Ulysses—to service Xerox copiers. To protect its profitable service business, Xerox designed a Total Satisfaction Guarantee, which allowed copier returns for any reason as long as *Xerox* did the servicing. By the time Kodak launched Ulysses, *Xerox* had been promoting its new program for three months.[6]

The company can also obtain important intelligence information from suppliers, resellers, and key customers. Or it can get good information by observing competitors. It can buy and analyze competitors' products, monitor their sales, check for new patents, and examine various types of physical evidence. For example, one company regularly checks out competitors' parking lots—full lots might indicate plenty of work and prosperity; half-full lots might suggest hard times.[7]

Competitors may reveal intelligence information through their annual reports, business publications, trade show exhibits, press releases, advertisements, and Web pages. The Internet is proving to be a vast new source of competitor-supplied information. Most companies now place volumes of information on their Web sites, providing details to attract customers, partners, suppliers, or franchisees. For example, Mail Boxes Etc., a chain of mailing services, provides data on its average franchise, including floor area, number of employees, operating hours, and more—all valuable insights for a competitor.

For a fee, companies can subscribe to any of more than 3000 online databases and information search services such as Dialog, DataStar, Lexis-Nexis, Dow Jones

Marketing intelligence A systematic collection and analysis of publicly available information about competitors and developments in the marketing environment.

News Retrieval, UMI ProQuest, and Dun & Bradstreet's Online Access. Scott Hogan is a strategic market analyst with the High Performance Optical Component Solutions group at Nortel Networks in Ottawa and one of the two Chapter Chairs for the Eastern Ontario chapter of the Society of Competitive Intelligence Professionals. He takes his mantra from Frederick the Great, who said, "It is pardonable to be defeated but never to be surprised."

Professionals such as Scott see competitive intelligence (CI) as a systematic and ethical program of gathering and analyzing information. They turn data into *actionable intelligence* that managers from sales, manufacturing, R&D, marketing, and product management can use in real time to make better decisions. Actionable intelligence is information that arrives at the desk of decision makers in time for them to act on it.

CI is also value-added information analysis. For example, Scott knows it isn't enough to report on the contents of a competitor's press release. His group must interpret what the press release means for the group's competitive strategy. Scott stresses that CI is not a crystal ball or a compilation of rumours flying around the Internet. Moreover, CI is *not* industrial espionage. Espionage is the use of illegal means to gather information. Scott emphasizes that Nortel follows strict ethic codes including its own *Code of Business Conduct* and the *SCIP Code of Ethics*.[8]

CI is an early-warning tool to alter management to meet both threats and opportunities. For example, CI can help a company determine whether it wants to continue its own product development if competitors have taken the lead. CI is an ongoing process used as a means of seeing outside the organization. CI is especially important in high-tech environments, since product change is very short compared with other industries. The cycle time from product definition to product shipping is approximately 18 months and this cycle is constantly getting shorter. Furthermore, a cloud of competitors potentially lurks on every front—customers, suppliers, and partners. Since some companies have customers in more than 100 countries, they have to be aware of competitors from diverse geographies. If the scope of competition is wide, CI may have to cover a wide market segment and the deployment of internal as well as external information resources.

The growing use of marketing intelligence raises some ethical issues. Although most of the preceding techniques are legal, and some are considered shrewdly competitive, some may involve questionable ethics. Clearly, companies should take advantage of publicly available information; however, they should not stoop to spying. With all the legitimate intelligence sources now available, a company does not have to break the law or accepted codes of ethics to get good intelligence.[9]

Marketing Research

In addition to information about competitor and environmental happenings, marketers often need formal studies of specific situations. For example, Toshiba wants to know how many and what kinds of people or companies will buy its new superfast notebook computer. In such situations, marketing intelligence will not provide the detailed information needed. Managers will need marketing research.

Marketing research is the systematic design, collection, analysis, and reporting of data relevant to a specific marketing situation facing an organization. Companies use marketing research in a wide variety of situations. For example, marketing research can help marketers to assess market potential and market share; understand customer satisfaction and purchase behaviour; and measure the effectiveness of pricing, product, distribution, and promotion activities.

Some large companies have their own research departments that work with marketing managers on marketing research projects. This is how Kraft, Royal Bank, and many other corporate giants handle marketing research. In addition, these companies—like their smaller counterparts—frequently hire outside research specialists to consult with management on specific marketing problems and conduct marketing research studies. Sometimes firms simply purchase data collected by outside firms to aid in their decision making.

The marketing research process has four steps (see Figure 5-2):

1. defining the problem and the research objectives

2. developing the research plan,

3. implementing the research plan

4. interpreting and reporting the findings

Defining the Problem and the Research Objectives Marketing managers and researchers must work closely to define the problem and agree on the research objectives. The manager best understands the decision for which information is needed; the researcher best understands marketing research and how to obtain the information.

Defining the problem and the research objectives is often the hardest step in the research process. The manager may know that something is wrong, without knowing the specific causes. For example, in the classic New Coke case, Coca-Cola defined its research problem too narrowly, with disastrous results. In another example, managers of a large discount retail store chain hastily decided that falling sales were caused by poor advertising, and they ordered research to test the company's advertising. When this research showed that current advertising was reaching the right people with the right message, the managers were puzzled. It turned out that the real problem was that the chain was not delivering the prices, products, and service promised in the advertising. Careful problem definition would have avoided the cost and delay of doing advertising research.

After the problem has been defined carefully, the manager and researcher must define the research objectives. A marketing research project might have one of three types of objectives. The objective of **exploratory research** is to gather preliminary information that will help define the problem and suggest hypotheses. The objec-

Marketing research The systematic design, collection, analysis, and reporting of data relevant to a specific marketing situation facing an organization.

Exploratory research Marketing research to gather preliminary information that will help define problems and suggest hypotheses.

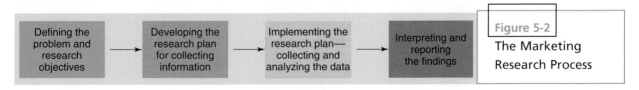

Figure 5-2

The Marketing Research Process

Descriptive research
Marketing research to better describe marketing problems, situations, or markets, such as the market potential for a product or the demographics and attitudes of consumers who buy the product.

Causal research Marketing research to test hypotheses about cause-and-effect relationships.

tive of **descriptive research** is to describe things, such as the market potential for a product or the demographics and attitudes of consumers who buy the product. The objective of **causal research** is to test hypotheses about cause-and-effect relationships. For example, would a 10 percent decrease in tuition at a private school result in an enrollment increase sufficient to offset the reduced tuition? Managers often start with exploratory research and later follow with descriptive or causal research.

The statement of the problem and research objectives guides the entire research process. The manager and researcher should put the statement in writing to be certain that they agree on the purpose and expected results of the research.

Developing the Research Plan Once the research problems and objectives have been defined, researchers must determine the exact information needed, develop a plan for gathering it efficiently, and present the plan to management. The research plan outlines sources of existing data and spells out the specific research approaches, contact methods, sampling plans, and instruments that researchers will use to gather new data.

Research objectives must be translated into specific information needs. For example, suppose Campbell decides to conduct research on how consumers of its soup would react to the introduction of the bowl-shaped plastic containers that it has used successfully for several of its other products. The containers would cost more but would allow consumers to heat the soup in a microwave oven without adding water or milk and to eat it without using dishes. This research might call for the following specific information:

- The demographic, economic, and lifestyle characteristics of current soup users (busy working couples might find the convenience of the new packaging worth the price; families with children might want to pay less and wash the pan and bowls)

- Consumer-usage patterns for soup: how much soup they eat, where, and when (the new packaging might be ideal for adults eating lunch on the go but less convenient for parents feeding lunch to several children)

- Retailer reactions to the new packaging (failure to get retailer support could hurt sales of the new package)

- Consumer attitudes toward the new packaging (the red-and-white Campbell can has become an institution—will consumers accept the new packaging?)

- Forecasts of sales of both new and current packages (will the new packaging increase Campbell's profits?)

Campbell managers will need these and many other types of information to decide whether to introduce the new packaging.

The research plan should be presented in a *written proposal*. A written proposal is especially important when the research project is large and complex or when an outside firm carries it out. The proposal should cover the management problems addressed and the research objectives, the information to be obtained, and the way the results will help management decision making. The proposal also should include research costs.

To meet the manager's information needs, the research plan can call for gathering primary data, secondary data, or both. **Primary data** consist of information collected for the specific purpose at hand. **Secondary data** consist of information that already exists somewhere, having been collected for another purpose.

Primary data Information collected for the specific purpose at hand.

Gathering Secondary Data Researchers usually start by gathering secondary data. The company's internal database provides a good starting point. However, the company can also tap a wide assortment of external information sources, including commercial data services and government sources (see Table 5-1).

Secondary data Information that already exists somewhere, having been collected for another purpose.

Table 5-1   Sources of Secondary Data

Government Publications

Statistics Canada, Demography Division provides summary data on demographic, economic, social, and other aspects of the Canadian economy and society.

Periodicals and Books

- *Canadian Markets,* produced by the Financial Post Datagroup, provides annual demographic and retail data for more than 700 Canadian urban and regional markets.

- *Scott's Directories* annually lists manufacturers, their products, and their standard industrial classification (SIC) codes, alphabetically as well as by city and region. The directory also provides the names and telephone and fax numbers of chief executives, as well as corporate information such as annual sales. Directories come in four volumes: Ontario, Quebec, Atlantic Canada, and Western Canada.

- *Canadian Trade Index* and *Fraser's Canadian Trade Directory* provide information on manufacturers of different product categories, manufacturing equipment, and supplies.

- *Standard & Poor's Industry Surveys* provide updated statistics and analyses of US industries.

- Marketing journals include the *Canadian Journal of Marketing Research, Journal of Marketing, Journal of Marketing Research, Journal of Consumer Research,* and *Journal of the Academy of Marketing Science.*

- Useful trade magazines include *Marketing, Strategy, Advertising Age, Chain Store Age, Progressive Grocer, Sales & Marketing Management,* and *Stores.*

- Useful general business magazines include *Canadian Business, The Globe and Mail Report on Business, Profit, Business Week, Fortune, Forbes,* and *Harvard Business Review.*

Commercial Data Services

These are a few of the dozens of commercial research houses selling data to subscribers:

- *ABI Inform* (1983 to present) and *Business Abstracts* (1989 to present) are examples of CD-ROM databases available in most university libraries. They contain abstracts of articles on business appearing in academic journals and the business press.

- *(PMB) Print Measurement Bureau* (Toronto) prepares product category reports that provide information about the users of more than 1000 products and services. Compares the demographic profiles of users versus nonusers, and heavy versus light users on dimensions such as age, education, marital status, income, occupation, employment status, region and city, household size, residence ownership, sex, and language. Data are also matched to location where main grocery shopping occurs and are usually gathered over two years.

- *Canadian Grocer* produces an annual *Directory of Chains* with information on head office locations, store locations, management names and functions, technologies used, buying policies, store sizes, private labels, and annual sales.

- *Card Reports* provides annual information on Canadian media types, the gross rating points (GRP) associated with each, and the costs of placing advertisements in the various media.

- *ACNielsen* (a division of D&B Marketing Information Services) provides supermarket scanner data on sales, market share, and retail prices (ScanTrack), data on household purchasing (ScanTrack National Electronic Household Panel), data on television audiences (Nielsen National Television Index), and more.

- *Information Resources, Inc.* provides supermarket scanner data for tracking grocery product movement (InfoScan) and single-source data collection (BehaviorScan).

- *The Arbitron Company* provides local market radio audience and advertising expenditure information, along with other media and ad spending data.

- *NPD Canada* offers *Consumer Panel of Canada,* a national diary panel; *Canadian Apparel Market Monitor; National Eating Trends,* which reports on in-home and out-of-home consumption behaviour; and an *OnLine Panel.*

- *Equifax Canada* is the country's largest information service, specializing in credit reports on both consumers and small businesses.

International Data

These are a few of the many sources providing international information:

- Euromonitor, www.euromonitor.com, sells a wide range of print and CD-ROM products including *European Marketing Data and Statistics, International Marketing Data and Statistics,* and *International Marketing Forecasts,* which can help marketers gain insights into international consumer markets.

- *United Nations* publications include the *Statistical Yearbook,* a comprehensive source of international data for socioeconomic indicators; the *Demographic Yearbook,* a collection of demographics data and vital statistics for 220 countries; and the *International Trade Statistics Yearbook,* which provides information on foreign trade for specific countries and commodities.

- *Europa Yearbook* provides surveys on history, politics, population, economy, and natural resources for most countries of the world, along with information on major international organizations.

- Other sources include *Political Risk Yearbook, Country Studies, OECD Economic Surveys, Economic Survey of Europe, Asian Economic Handbook,* and *International Financial Statistics.*

Internet Data Sources

- Both large and small companies have developed Web sites as a means of communicating with their customers. Many company sites provide information about the history of the company, its products, and its financial information. Marketing research company sites provide some interesting insights into Canadian consumers; the Environics site, for example, lets users classify themselves on the 3SC Social Values Monitor.

- Governments also post information on the Web; for example, the Industry Canada site provides a wealth of information about various sectors of the economy. Marketers planning to enter the U.S. market can glean background information from the U.S. Census Bureau or from American Demographics. The US government's site is designed to help small businesspeople and can be used by both Canadian and American marketers.

- At several online press services, such as Canoe, marketers can track the effectiveness of their own and other companies' public relations efforts. Ecola's 24-Hour Newsstand allows marketers to link with the Web sites of more than 2000 newspapers, journals, and computer publications.

- Publishers of marketing periodicals who post their material online can be a gold mine. Brunico Communications publishes *Strategy: The Canadian Marketing Report* online, in addition to providing it in hard-copy format. Using keywords, marketers can search all editions for articles on a wide range of topics.

- Internet search engines such as Yahoo!, Excite, Lycos, or Infoseek allow marketers to locate material on special topics. Publications such as the *Canadian Internet Directory* can facilitate the search for Canada's top Web sites.

Environics
www.environics.ca

Industry Canada
strategis.ic.gc.ca

U.S. Census Bureau
www.census.gov

American Demographics
www.demographics.com

Canoe
www.canoe.ca

Ecola's 24-Hour Newsstand
www.ecola.com/news

Strategy: The Canadian Marketing Report
www.strategymag.com

Companies can buy data reports from outside suppliers to suit a wide variety of marketing information needs. For example, two firms, Nielsen Marketing Research and Information Resources, Inc., sell data on brand shares, retail prices, percentages of stores stocking different brands, measures of trial and repeat purchasing, brand loyalty, and buyer demographics. Another firm, NPD Canada, maintains the country's longest running national diary panel, the *Consumer Panel of Canada*. It also has an *OnLine Panel*, which companies can use to get insights about Canada's Web savvy population, and compiles specialized reports such as the *Canadian Apparel Market Monitor* and the *National Eating Trends*, which reports on in-home and out-of-home consumption behaviour.

General database services such as Dialog put an incredible wealth of information at the keyboards of marketing decision makers.

Online databases
Computerized collections of information available from online commercial sources or via the Internet.

Using commercial **online databases**, marketing researchers can conduct their own searches of secondary data sources. General database services such as CompuServe, Dialog, and LEXIS-NEXIS put an incredible wealth of information at the keyboards of marketing decision makers. Beyond commercial Web sites offering information for a fee, almost every industry association, government agency, business publication, and news medium offers free information to those tenacious enough to find their Web sites. There are so many Web sites offering data that finding the right ones can become an almost overwhelming task.

Secondary data can usually be obtained faster and at a lower cost than primary data. For example, an Internet or online database search might provide all the information Campbell needs on soup usage, quickly and inexpensively. A study to collect primary information might take weeks or months and cost thousands of dollars. Secondary sources sometimes can provide data an individual company cannot collect on its own—information that either is not directly available or would be too expensive to collect. For example, it would be too expensive for Campbell to conduct a continuing retail store audit to find out about the market shares, prices, and displays of competitors' brands. But it can buy ACNielsen's Market Measurement Services such as "Market Track." These services are arguably the industry standard for measuring and understanding the performance and dynamics of consumer package good sales in Canada. Point-of-sale scanning data is captured from grocery supermarkets, drug pharmacy and mass merchandiser retail outlets. Additionally, ACNielsen collects data from convenience stores, gas/convenience outlets, variety stores, general merchandise store's, club stores, and so on. As a further information source, scanning data can be combined with ACNielsen's proprietary causal databases (pricing, display activity, cooperative advertising, media expenditures, etc.) to aid in determining various promotional influences on consumer purchasing.[10]

Secondary data can also present problems. The needed information may not exist—researchers can rarely obtain all the data they need from secondary sources. For example, Campbell will not find existing information about consumer reactions to new packaging that it has not yet placed on the market. Even when data can be found, they might not be very usable. The researcher must evaluate secondary information carefully to make certain it is *relevant* (fits research project needs), *accurate* (reliably collected and reported), *current* (up to date enough for current decisions), and *impartial* (objectively collected and reported).

Primary Data Collection Secondary data provide a good starting point for research and often help to define problems and research objectives. In most cases, however, the company must also collect primary data. Just as researchers must carefully evaluate the quality of secondary information, they also must take great care when collecting primary data to ensure that it will be relevant, accurate, current, and unbiased. Table 5-2 shows that designing a plan for primary data collection calls for decisions on *research approaches, contact methods, sampling plan,* and *research instruments.*

Research Approaches Research approaches for gathering primary data include observation, surveys, and experiments. **Observational research** involves gathering primary data by observing relevant people, actions, and situations. For example, a consumer packaged-goods marketer might visit supermarkets and observe shoppers as they browse the store, pick up products and examine packages, and make

Observational research The gathering of primary data by observing relevant people, actions, and situations.

Table 5-2 Planning Primary Data Collection			
Research Approaches	**Contact Methods**	**Sampling Plan**	**Research Instruments**
Observation	Mail	Sampling unit	Questionnaire
Survey	Telephone	Sample size	Mechanical instruments
Experiment	Personal	Sampling procedure	

actual buying decisions. Or a bank might evaluate possible new branch locations by checking traffic patterns, neighbourhood conditions, and the location of competing branches. Many companies now use *ethnographic research*—which combines intensive observation with customer interviews—to gain deep insights into how customers buy and use their products (see New Directions 5-1).

New Directions 5-1 >>   Ethnographic Research: Keeping a Close Eye on Consumers

What do customers *really* think about your product and what do they say about it to their friends? How do they *really* use it? Will they tell you? *Can* they tell you? These are difficult questions for most marketers. And too often, traditional research simply can't provide accurate answers. To get better insights, many companies are now turning to an increasingly popular research approach: ethnographic or observational research.

Ethnographic research involves sending trained observers to watch consumers in their "natural environment"—to observe up close the subtleties of how consumers use and feel about products and services.

The 60-ish woman caught on the grainy videotape is sitting on her hotel bed, addressing her husband after a long day spent on the road. "Good job!" she exults. "We beat the s—— out of the front desk and got a terrific room." No, this wasn't an RCMP sting operation. Instead, the couple was part of [an ethnographic study in which Best Western International] paid 25 over-55 couples to tape themselves on cross-country journeys. The effort convinced the hotel chain that it didn't need to boost its standard 10 percent senior citizen discount. The tapes showed that seniors who talked the hotel clerk into a better deal didn't need the lower price to afford the room; they were after the thrill of the deal. Instead of attracting new customers, bigger discounts would simply allow the old customers to

Using ethnographic research, companies observe consumers in their "natural environment." In one Best Western study, over-55 couples taped themselves on cross-country journeys, providing a wealth of consumer behaviour insights.

trade up to a fancier dinner down the street somewhere, doing absolutely nothing for Best Western.... Best Western captured such a wealth of customer behavior on tape that it has delayed its marketing plan in order to weave the insights into its core strategy. Unfortunately for seniors, that means the rooms won't be getting any cheaper.

In today's intensely competitive marketplace, holding onto customers requires more than a superficial understanding of customers' interactions with a product. "You can run a marketing campaign that might make people pick up your product the first time, but if they live with it under different conditions than the advertised benefits, it's not likely that they're going to pick it up a second time," notes an ethnographic researcher. To keep customers coming back, companies must have a deep understanding of how they feel about and interact with products and adjust their marketing offers and programs accordingly. Ethnographic research helps provide such an understanding. It combines intense observation with customer interviews to get an up-close and personal view of how people actually live with products—how they buy and use them in their everyday lives. Here's another example.

A woman is shopping for her family's meals for the week. She cruises past the poultry section, stopping only momentarily to drop a couple of packages of boneless chicken breasts into her cart. Then, the dreaded sea of red meat looms before her. Tentatively, she picks up a package of beef. "This cut looks good, not too fatty," she says, juggling her two-year-old on her hip. "But I don't know what it is. And I don't know how to cook it," she confesses. She trades it for a small package of sirloin and her regular order of ground beef. Scenes like this play out daily in supermarkets across the country. But this time, it's being captured on videotape, part of a recent ethnographic study of beef consumers for the National Cattlemen's Beef Association (NCBA) and major grocery retailers.

Knowing what consumers actually do with beef is vital to the NCBA. Even though sales of ground beef have risen in recent years, other beef products have lost ground. To get a first-hand understanding of what really goes on in consumers' minds as they shop the meat case,

NCBA researchers videotaped not only consumers' store behaviour, but also their preparation habits at home. And they interviewed consumers at each step, asking what they thought about beef, why they did or didn't select particular cuts, their thoughts on meat department layouts, how they prepared the family meal, and the availability of recipes.

The conclusion? Confusion. Although the typical shopper would initially say that she wasn't confused about buying beef, "when we went deeper, we found that she wasn't confused because she always buys the same cuts—ground beef, boneless chicken breast, maybe one steak," says Kevin Yost, NCBA's director of consumer marketing. "When you start to broaden the range [of meat selection], she has no idea what you're talking about." All of this was a revelation to the beef industry. "The first time I showed [the tapes] to a group of major retailers, they started laughing," Yost says. The retailers couldn't believe how little consumers knew about something that seemed so familiar to them. The result? Many grocers' meat cases are now being rearranged to display beef by cooking method, rather than by cuts of meat. Simple, three-step cooking instructions will soon be printed on the packages.

Ethnographic research often yields the kinds of intimate details that just don't emerge from traditional focus groups. For example, focus groups told Best Western that men decide when to stop for the night and where to stay. The videotapes showed it was usually the women. And by videotaping consumers in the shower, plumbing fixture maker Moen uncovered safety risks that consumers didn't recognize—such as some women shaving their legs while holding onto one unit's temperature control. Moen would find it almost impossible to discover such design flaws simply by asking questions.

Montreal-based Bugle Boy found that traditional focus groups fail miserably in getting the scoop on teens and GenXers. These often-cynical young people are skeptical of sales pitches and just won't speak up in a conference room with two-way mirrors. So, Bugle Boy turned to ethnographic research. It chose four young men at random, handed each of them a camcorder, and told them to document their lives. The young amateurs were given only broad categories to work with: school, home, closet, and shopping. Bugle Boy then used the videos to prompt discussions of product and lifestyle issues in free-form focus groups held in unconventional locations, such as restaurants. Says one Bugle Boy ad manager, "I think this really helped us to get a handle on what these kids do. It let us see what their lives are all about, their awareness of the Bugle Boy brand, and how they perceive the brand."

Increasingly, marketers are keeping a close eye on consumers. "Knowing the individual consumer on an intimate basis has become a necessity," says a research industry consultant, "and ethnography is the intimate connection to the consumer."

Sources: Excerpts from Kendra Parker, "How Do You Like Your Beef?" *American Demographics,* January 2000, pp. 35–37; and Gerry Khermouch, "Consumers in the Mist," *Business Week,* 26 February 2001, pp. 92–94.

Urban Outfitters, the fast-growing specialty clothing chain, prefers observation to other types of market research. "We're not after people's statements," notes the chain's president, "we're after their actions." The company develops customer profiles by videotaping and taking photographs of customers in its stores. This helps managers determine what people are actually wearing and allows them to make quick decisions about merchandise.[11]

Many companies collect data through *mechanical* observation via machine or computer. For example, Nielsen Media Research attaches *people meters* to television sets in selected homes to record who watches which programs. ACNielsen also collects *checkout scanner* data to record shoppers' purchases so that manufacturers and retailers can assess product sales and store performance. And DoubleClick, among other Internet companies, places a *cookie*—a bit of information—on consumers' hard drives to monitor their Web surfing patterns. Similarly, MediaMetrix places special software on consumers' PCs to monitor Web surfing patterns and produce ratings for top Web sites.

Observational research can obtain information that people are unwilling or unable to provide. In some cases, observation may be the only way to obtain the needed information. In contrast, some things simply cannot be observed, such as feelings, attitudes, motives, and private behaviour. Long-term or infrequent behaviour is also difficult to observe. Because of these limitations, researchers often use observation along with other data collection methods.

Survey research, the most widely used method for primary data collection, is the approach best suited for gathering *descriptive* information. A company that wants to know about people's knowledge, attitudes, preferences, or buying behaviour can often find out by asking them directly.

Some firms provide marketers with a more comprehensive look at buying patterns through **single-source data systems**. These systems combine surveys of huge consumer panels—carefully selected groups of consumers who agree to participate in ongoing research—and electronic monitoring of respondents' purchases and exposure to various marketing activities in an effort to better understand the link among consumer characteristics, attitudes, and purchase behaviour.

The major advantage of survey research is its flexibility—it can be used to obtain many different kinds of information in many different situations. However, survey research also presents some problems. Sometimes people are unable to answer survey questions, because they cannot remember or have never thought

Survey research The gathering of primary data by asking people questions about their knowledge, attitudes, preferences, and buying behaviour.

Single-source data systems Electronic monitoring systems link consumers' exposure to television advertising and promotion (using television meters) with what they buy in stores (measured using store check scanner data).

about what they do and why. People may be unwilling to respond to unknown interviewers or about subjects that they consider private. Respondents may answer survey questions even when they do not know the answer to appear smarter or more informed. Or they may try to help the interviewer by giving pleasing answers. Finally, busy people may not take the time, or they might resent the intrusion into their privacy.

Whereas observation is best suited for exploratory research and surveys for descriptive research, **experimental research** is best suited for gathering *causal* information. Experiments involve selecting matched groups of subjects, giving them different treatments, controlling unrelated factors, and checking for differences in group responses. Thus, experimental research tries to explain cause-and-effect relationships.

For example, before adding a new sandwich to its menu, McDonald's might use experiments to test the effects on sales of two different prices it might charge. It could introduce the new sandwich at one price in one city and at another price in another city. If the cities are similar, and if all other marketing efforts for the sandwich are the same, then differences in sales in the two cities could be related to the price charged.

Contact Methods Information can be collected by mail, telephone, personal interview, or online. Table 5-3 shows the strengths and weaknesses of each of these contact methods.

Mail questionnaires can be used to collect large amounts of information at a low cost per respondent. Respondents may give more honest answers to more personal questions on a mail questionnaire than to an unknown interviewer in person or over the phone. Since no interviewer is involved, one form of bias is eliminated. However, mail questionnaires are not very flexible—all respondents answer the same questions in a fixed order. Mail surveys usually take longer to complete, and the response rate—the number of people returning completed questionnaires—is often very low. Finally, the researcher often has little control over the mail questionnaire sample. Even with a good mailing list, it is hard to control *who* at the mailing address fills out the questionnaire.

Telephone interviewing is the one of the best methods for gathering information quickly, and it provides greater flexibility than mail questionnaires. Interviewers can explain difficult questions and, depending on the answers they

Experimental research
The gathering of primary data by selecting matched groups of subjects, giving them different treatments, controlling unrelated factors, and checking for differences in group responses.

Table 5-3   Strengths and Weaknesses of the Three Contact Methods

	Mail	Telephone	Personal
1. Flexibility	Poor	Good	Excellent
2. Quantity of data that can be collected	Good	Fair	Excellent
3. Control of interviewer effect	Excellent	Fair	Poor
4. Control of sample	Fair	Excellent	Fair
5. Speed of data collection	Poor	Excellent	Good
6. Response rate	Poor	Good	Good
7. Cost	Good	Fair	Poor

Source: Adapted with permission of Macmillan Publishing Company from Donald S. Tull and Del I. Hawkins, *Marketing Research: Measurement and Method,* 6th ed., Macmillan Publishing Company, 1993.

receive, skip some questions or probe on others. Response rates tend to be higher than with mail questionnaires, and interviewers can ask to speak to respondents with the desired characteristics or even by name.

However, with telephone interviewing, the cost per respondent is higher than with mail questionnaires. Also, people may not want to discuss personal questions with an interviewer. The method also introduces interviewer bias—the way interviewers talk, how they ask questions, and other differences may affect respondents' answers. Finally, different interviewers may interpret and record responses differently, and under time pressures some interviewers might even cheat by recording answers without asking questions.

Personal interviewing takes two forms—individual and group interviewing. *Individual interviewing* involves talking with people in their homes or offices, on the street, or in shopping malls. Such interviewing is flexible. Trained interviewers can guide interviews, explain difficult questions, and explore issues as the situation requires. They can show subjects actual products, advertisements, or packages and observe reactions and behaviour. However, individual personal interviews may cost three to four times as much as telephone interviews.

Group interviewing consists of inviting six to ten people to talk with a trained moderator about a product, service, or organization. Participants normally are paid a small sum for attending. The moderator encourages relaxed discussion, hoping that group interactions will bring out actual feelings and thoughts. At the same time, the moderator "focuses" the discussion—hence the name **focus group interviewing**. The comments are recorded in writing or on videotape for later study.

Focus group interviewing has become one of the major marketing research tools for gaining insight into consumer thoughts and feelings. However, focus group studies usually employ small sample sizes to keep time and costs low, and it may be hard to generalize from the results. Because interviewers have more freedom in personal interviews, the problem of interviewer bias is greater.

Today, modern communications technology is changing the way that focus groups are conducted:

Videoconferencing links, television monitors, remote-control cameras, and digital transmission are boosting the amount of focus group research done over long-distance lines. [In a typical videoconferencing system], two cameras focused on the group are controlled by clients who hold a remote keypad. Executives in a far-off boardroom can zoom in on faces and pan the focus group at will.... A two-way sound system connects remote viewers to the back-room, focus group room, and directly to the monitor's earpiece. [Recently], while testing new product names in one focus group, the [client's] creative director...had an idea and contacted the moderator, who tested the new name on the spot.[12]

Another form of interviewing is *computer-assisted interviewing*, a contact method in which respondents sit at computers, read questions on the screen, and type in their own answers while an interviewer is present. The computers might be located at a research centre, trade show, shopping mall, or retail location.

Focus group interviewing
Personal interviewing of a small group of people invited to gather for a few hours with a trained interviewer to discuss a product, service, or organization. The interviewer focuses the group discussion on important issues.

Online (Internet) marketing research Collecting primary data through Internet surveys and online focus groups.

The latest technology to hit marketing research is the Internet. Increasingly, marketing researchers are collecting primary data through **online (Internet) marketing research**—*Internet surveys, experiments,* and *online focus groups.* Online focus groups offer advantages over traditional methods:

Janice Gjersten, director of marketing for an online entertainment company, wanted to...gauge reaction to a new Web site. [She] contacted Cyber Dialogue, which provided focus group respondents drawn from its 10 000-person database. The focus group was held in an online chat room, which Gjersten "looked in on" from her office computer. Gjersten could interrupt the moderator at any time with flash e-mails unseen by the respondents. Although the online focus group lacked voice and body cues, Gjersten says she will never conduct a traditional focus group again. Not only were respondents more honest, but the cost for the online group was one third that of a traditional focus group and a full report came to her in one day, compared to four weeks.[13]

Although online research offers much promise, and some analysts predict that the Internet will soon be the primary marketing research tool, others are more cautious. New Directions 5-2 summarizes the advantages, drawbacks, and prospects for conducting marketing research on the Internet.

Which contact method is best depends on what information the researcher wants, as well as the number and types of respondents to be contacted. Advances in computers and communications have had a large impact on methods of obtaining information. Most research firms now do computer-assisted telephone interviewing (CATI). Professional interviewers call respondents around the country, often using phone numbers drawn at random. When the respondent answers, the interviewer reads a set of questions from a video screen and types the respondent's answers directly into the computer.

Online focus groups offer advantages over traditional methods, including convenience and low cost. Says ActiveGroup about its online research: "No traveling, no scheduling, no problems.

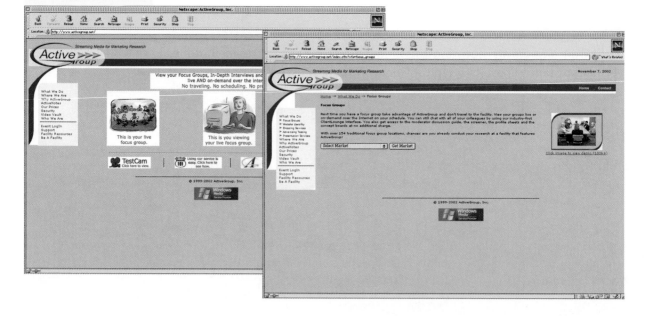

New Directions 5-2 >> Marketing Research on the Internet

Doing marketing research on the Internet is still in its infancy. But as the use of the World Wide Web and online services are becoming more habit than hype for consumers, online research has become a quick, easy, and inexpensive way to tap into their opinions. The potential of the Internet as a data collection tool is evident: not only is it unlimited by geographic boundaries, it also offers almost instant responses. People can respond to questionnaires posted on Web sites in the privacy of their own homes at any time convenient to them. Currently, only a small proportion of Canadians use the Internet. However, online users tend to be better educated, more affluent, and younger than average consumers. Most are male. These are highly important consumers to companies offering products and services online. They are also some of the hardest consumers to reach when conducting a research study. Online surveys and chat sessions (or online focus groups) often prove effective in getting elusive teen, single, affluent, and well-educated audiences to participate.

"It's very solid for reaching hard-to-get segments," says one analyst. "Doctors, lawyers, professionals—people you might have difficulty reaching because they are not interested in taking part in surveys. It's also a good medium for reaching working mothers and others who lead busy lives. They can do it in their own space and at their own convenience."

Online research isn't right for every company or product. For example, mass marketers who need to survey a representative cross-section of the population will find online research methodologies less useful. "If the target for the product or service you're testing is inconsistent with the Internet user profile, then it's not the medium to use," Jacobson points out. "Is it the right medium to test Campbell's Chunky Soup? Probably not, but if you want to test how people feel about Campbell's Web site, yes."

When appropriate, online research offers marketers two distinct advantages over traditional surveys and focus groups: speed and cost-effectiveness. Online researchers routinely field quantitative studies and fill response quotas in a matter of days. Online focus groups require some advance scheduling, but results are virtually instantaneous. Notes an online researcher, "Online research is very fast, and time is what everybody wants now. Clients want the information yesterday."

Research on the Internet is also relatively inexpensive. Participants can dial in for a focus group from anywhere in the world, eliminating travel, lodging, and facility costs, making online chats less expensive than traditional focus groups. And for surveys, the Internet eliminates most of the postage, phone, labour, and printing costs associated with other survey approaches. Moreover, sample size has little influence on costs. "There's not a huge difference between 10 and 10 000 on the Web," said Tod Johnson, head of NPD Group, a firm that conducts online research. "The cost [of research on the Web] can be anywhere from 10 percent to 80 percent less, especially when you talk about big samples."

However, using the Internet to conduct marketing research does have some drawbacks. One major problem is knowing who is in the sample. "If you can't see a person with whom you are communicating, how do you know who they really are?" asks Tom Greenbaum, president of Groups Plus. Moreover, trying to draw conclusions from a "self-selected" sample of online users, those who clicked through to a questionnaire or accidentally landed in a chat room, can be troublesome. "Using a convenient sample is a way to do research quickly, but when you're done, you kind of scratch your head and ask what it means."

To overcome such sample and response problems, NPD and many other firms that offer online services construct panels of qualified Web regulars to respond to surveys and participate in online focus groups. NPD's panel consists of 15 000 consumers recruited online and verified by telephone; Greenfield Online chooses users from its own database, then calls them periodically to verify that they are who they say they are. Another online research firm, Research Connections, recruits in advance by telephone, taking time to help new users connect to the Internet, if necessary.

Brand manager eliminates pilot costs, becomes hero

Testing new package designs online with rotating 3-D images not only saved the client expensive tooling costs but also saved time. Now manufacturers can design today and test tomorrow. Eliminating pilot costs and shortening "time to market" are just some of the many ways that Greenfield Online quantitative research beats the old-fashioned kind.

Put our expert consultants and advanced technology to work for you.

www.greenfield.com
888-291-9997

Greenfield Online
Leading the Research Revolution

+ Quantitative Studies
+ Qualitative Studies
+ Media Research
+ Self-Directed Research
+ Syndicated Studies
+ Website Evaluations

HERO

Online research has become a quick, easy, and inexpensive way to tap into consumer opinions. According to this Greenfield Online ad, it "beats the old-fashioned kind" of market research in many ways.

Even when using qualified respondents, focus group responses can lose something in the translation. "You're missing all of the key things that make a focus group a viable method," says Greenbaum. "You may get people online to talk to each other and play off each other, but it's very different to watch people get excited about a concept." Eye contact and body language are lost in the online world. And although researchers can offer seasoned moderators, the Internet format greatly restricts respondent expressiveness. Similarly, technology limits researchers' capability to show visual cues to research subjects. But just as it hinders the two-way assessment of visual cues, Web research can actually permit some participants the anonymity necessary to elicit an unguarded response. "There are reduced social effects online," Jacobson says. "People are much more honest in this medium."

Some researchers are wildly optimistic about the prospects for marketing research on the Internet; others are more cautious. One expert predicts that in the next few years, 50 percent of all research will be done on the Internet. "Ten years from now, national telephone surveys will be the subject of research methodology folklore," he proclaims. "That's a little too soon," cautions another expert. "But in 20 years, yes."

Sources: Portions adapted from Ian P. Murphy, "Interactive Research," *Marketing News,* 20 January 1997, pp. 1, 17. Selected quotations from "NFO Executive Sees Most Research Going to Internet," *Advertising Age,* 19 May 1997, p. 50. Also see Brad Edmondson, "The Wired Bunch," *American Demographics,* June 1997, pp. 10–15; Charlie Hamlin, "Market Research and the Wired Consumer," *Marketing News,* 9 June 1997, p. 6; and Mariam Mesbah, "Special Report: Research: Internet Research Holds Potential," *Strategy,* 14 April 1997, p. 40.

YOUtv
www.youtv.com

YOUtv, a young Canadian company, believed that consumers would be more open and honest in their feedback to companies if they could use video booths that they could activate by themselves. But just providing firms with this technology wasn't enough, explains Ian Chamandy, co-owner of YOUtv. The company's ability to transform the raw data into meaningful information was key when Cadbury Chocolate Canada decided to use YOUtv to search for a new couple to advertise Crispy Crunch chocolate bars.[14]

Other firms are using *computer interviewing*, in which respondents sit down at a computer, read questions from a screen, and type their own answers into the computer. Electronic focus groups, or electronic brainstorming, are becoming powerful and efficient ways for companies to gauge customer sentiments. Twelve people are invited to a lab where a researcher poses questions. Respondents enter their responses and can read other respondents' answers on a large screen. Some companies, such as Microsoft Canada, are conducting surveys using the Internet. The company received more than 55 000 responses in just over 24 hours to a survey it conducted asking about people's relationships with computers.[15]

The Royal Bank of Canada has mastered computer-assisted interviewing without making people actually use a computer. Under a large sign that asks customers to "tell us what you think," customers use a special pen to complete a questionnaire on an electronic board. The information can be downloaded directly into a database for analysis.[16] Some U.S. researchers use completely automated telephone surveys (CATS), which employ voice-response technology to conduct interviews, but the Canadian Radio-television and Telecommunication Commission has banned such devices in Canada.[17]

Sampling Plan Marketing researchers usually draw conclusions about large groups of consumers by studying a small sample of the total consumer population. A **sample** is a segment of the population selected to represent the population as a whole. Ideally, the sample should be representative so that the researcher can make accurate estimates of the thoughts and behaviours of the larger population.

Sample A segment of the population selected to represent the population as a whole

Designing the sample requires three decisions. First, *who* is to be surveyed (what *sampling unit*)? The answer to this question is not always obvious. For example, to study the decision-making process for a family automobile purchase, should the researcher interview the husband, wife, other family members, dealership salespeople, or all these? The researcher must determine what information is needed and who is most likely to have it.

Second, *how many* people should be surveyed (what *sample size*)? Large samples give more reliable results than small samples. It is not necessary to sample the entire target market or even a large portion to get reliable results, however. If well chosen, samples of less than 1 percent of a population can often give good reliability.

Third, *how* should the people in the sample be *chosen* (what *sampling procedure*)? Table 5-4 describes different kinds of samples. Using *probability samples*, each population member has a known chance of being included in the sample, and researchers can calculate confidence limits for sampling error. But when probability sampling costs too much or takes too much time, marketing researchers often take *nonprobability samples*, even though their sampling error cannot be measured. These varied ways of drawing samples have different costs and time limitations, as well as different accuracy and statistical properties. Which method is best depends on the needs of the research project.

Research Instruments In collecting primary data, marketing researchers have a choice of two main research instruments: the *questionnaire* and *mechanical devices*. The *questionnaire* is by far the most common instrument, whether administered in person, by phone, or online.

Questionnaires are very flexible—there are many ways to ask questions. *Closed-end questions* include all the possible answers, and subjects make choices among them. Examples include multiple-choice questions and scale questions. *Open-end*

Table 5-4 Types of Samples	
Probability Sample	
Simple random sample	Every member of the population has a known and equal chance of selection.
Stratified random sample	The population is divided into mutually exclusive groups (such as age groups), and random samples are drawn from each group.
	The population is divided into mutually exclusive groups (such as blocks), and the researcher draws a sample of the groups to interview.
Nonprobability Sample	
Convenience sample	The researcher selects the easiest population members from which to obtain information.
Judgment sample	The researcher uses his or her judgment to select population members who are good prospects for accurate information. The researcher finds and interviews a prescribed number of people in each of several categories.

questions allow respondents to answer in their own words. In a survey of airline users, Westjet might simply ask, "What is your opinion of Westjet Airlines?" Or it might ask people to complete a sentence: "When I choose an airline, the most important consideration is.…" These and other kinds of open-end questions often reveal more than closed-end questions, because respondents are not limited in their answers. Open-end questions are especially useful in exploratory research, when the researcher is trying to find out *what* people think but not measuring *how many* people think in a certain way. Closed-end questions provide answers that are easier to interpret and tabulate.

Researchers should also use care in the *wording* and *ordering* of questions. They should use simple, direct, unbiased wording. Questions should be arranged in a logical order. The first question should create interest if possible, and difficult or personal questions should be asked last so that respondents do not become defensive. A carelessly prepared questionnaire usually contains many errors (see Table 5-5).

Although questionnaires are the most common research instrument, *mechanical instruments* such as people meters and supermarket scanners are also used. Another group of mechanical devices measures subjects' physical responses. For example, a galvanometer measures the strength of interest or emotions aroused by a subject's exposure to different stimuli, such as an advertisement or picture. The galvanometer detects the minute degree of sweating that accompanies emotional arousal. Eye cameras are used to study respondents' eye movements to determine on what points their eyes focus first and how long they linger on a given item.

Implementing the Research Plan After developing the research plan, which includes choosing the best type of data for the plan and the best data collection method, the researcher next puts the marketing research plan into action. This involves collecting, processing, and analyzing the information. Data collection can be carried out by the company's marketing research staff or by outside firms. The data collection phase of the marketing research process is generally the most expensive and the most subject to error. The researcher should watch closely to ensure that the plan is implemented correctly and to guard against problems with con-

Table 5-5 A Questionable Questionnaire

Suppose that a summer camp director had prepared the following questionnaire to use in interviewing the parents of prospective campers. How would you assess each question?

1. What is your income to the nearest hundred dollars?
    People don't usually know their income to the nearest hundred dollars, nor do they want to reveal their income that closely. Moreover, a researcher should never open a questionnaire with such a personal question.

2. Are you a strong or a weak supporter of overnight summer camping for your children?
    What do "strong" and "weak" mean?

3. Do your children behave themselves well at a summer camp? Yes ( ) No ( )
    "Behave" is a relative term. Furthermore, are "yes" and "no" the best response options for this question? Besides, will people want to answer this? Why ask the question in the first place?

4. How many camps mailed literature to you last April? this April?
    Who can remember this?

5. What are the most salient and determinant attributes in your evaluation of summer camps?
    What are "salient" and "determinant" attributes? Don't use big words with me!

6. Do you think it is right to deprive your child of the opportunity to grow into a mature person through the experience of summer camping?
    A loaded question. Given the bias, how can any parent answer "yes"?

tacting respondents, with respondents who refuse to cooperate or who give biased answers, and with interviewers who make mistakes or take shortcuts.

Researchers must process and analyze the collected data to isolate important information and findings. They need to check data for accuracy and completeness and code it for analysis. The researchers then tabulate the results and compute averages and other statistical measures.

Interpreting and Reporting the Findings The market researcher must now interpret the findings, draw conclusions, and report them to management. The researcher should not try to overwhelm managers with numbers and fancy statistical techniques. Rather, the researcher should present important findings that are useful in the major decisions faced by management.

However, interpretation should not be left only to the researchers. They are often experts in research design and statistics, but the marketing manager knows

Mechanical research instruments: Eye cameras determine at what points respondents' eyes focus first and how long they linger on a given item.

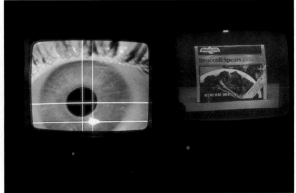

more about the problem and the decisions that must be made. The best research is meaningless if the manager blindly accepts faulty interpretations from the researcher. Similarly, managers may be biased—they might tend to accept research results that show what they expected and to reject those that they did not expect or hope for. In many cases, findings can be interpreted in different ways, and discussions between researchers and managers will help point to the best interpretations. Thus, managers and researchers must work together closely when interpreting research results, and both must share responsibility for the research process and resulting decisions.

ANALYZING MARKETING INFORMATION

Information gathered in internal databases and through marketing intelligence and marketing research usually requires more analysis, and managers may need help to apply the information to their marketing problems and decisions. This help may include advanced statistical analysis to learn more about both the relationships within a set of data and their statistical reliability. Such analysis allows managers to go beyond means and standard deviations in the data and to answer questions about markets, marketing activities, and outcomes.

Information analysis might also involve a collection of analytical models that will help marketers make better decisions. Each model represents some real system, process, or outcome. These models can help answer the questions of *what if* and *which is best.* Marketing scientists have developed numerous models to help marketing managers make better marketing mix decisions, design sales territories and sales call plans, select sites for retail outlets, develop optimal advertising mixes, and forecast new-product sales.

Customer Relationship Management (CRM)

The question of how best to analyze and use individual customer data presents special problems. In recent years, many companies have acquired or developed special software and analysis techniques, called **customer relationship management (CRM)**. The systems integrate customer information from across the firm and across its channels of delivery, analyze it in depth, and use the results to build stronger customer relationships.

Customer relationship management (CRM) Sophisticated software and analytical tools that integrate customer information from all sources, analyze it in depth, and use the results to build stronger customer relationships.

Most companies are awash in information about their customers. In fact, smart companies capture information at every possible customer *touch point.* These touch points include customer purchases, sales force contacts, service and support calls, Web site visits, satisfaction surveys, credit and payment interactions, market research studies—every contact between the customer and the company.

The trouble is that this information is usually scattered widely across the organization. It is buried deep in the separate databases, plans, and records of many different company functions and departments. CRM integrates everything that a company's sales, service, and marketing teams know about individual customers to provide a complete view of the customer relationship. It pulls together, analyzes, and provides easy access to customer information from all of the various touch

SPSS's CRM software integrates individual customer data from every touch point—from a company's call centre to its Web site—to provide a complete view of the customer relationship.

points. Companies use CRM analysis to assess the value of individual customers, identify the best ones to target, and customize their products and interactions to each customer.

CRM analysts develop *data warehouses* and use sophisticated *data mining* techniques to unearth the riches hidden in customer data. A data warehouse is a companywide electronic storehouse of customer information—a centralized database of finely detailed customer data that needs to be sifted through for gems. The purpose of a data warehouse is not to gather information—many companies have already amassed endless stores of information about their customers. Rather, the purpose is to allow managers to integrate the information the company already has. Then, once the data warehouse brings the data together for analysis, the company uses high-powered data mining techniques to sift through the mounds of data and dig out interesting relationships and findings about customers.

Companies can gain many benefits from customer relationship management. By understanding customers better, they can provide higher levels of customer service and develop deeper customer relationships. They can use CRM to pinpoint high-value customers, target them more effectively, cross-sell their company's products, and create offers tailored to specific customer requirements. Consider the case of FedEx.

FedEx recently launched a multimillion-dollar CRM initiative in an effort to cut costs, improve its customer support, and use its existing customer data to cross-sell and up-sell services to potential or existing customers. Using CRM software from Clarify Inc., the new system gives every member of FedEx's 3300-person sales force a comprehensive view of every customer, detailing each one's needs and suggesting services that might meet those needs. For instance, if a customer who does a lot of international shipping calls to arrange a delivery, a sales rep will see a detailed customer history on his or her computer screen, assess the customer's needs, and determine the most appropriate offering on the spot. Beleaguered sales reps can use such high-tech help. FedEx offers 220 different services—from logistics to transportation to customs brokerage—often making it difficult for salespeople to identify the best fit for customers. The new CRM system will also help FedEx conduct promotions and qualify potential sales leads. The Clarify software will analyze market segments, point out market "sweet spots," and calculate how profitable those segments will be to the company and to individual salespeople.[18]

CRM benefits don't come without cost or risk, not only in collecting the original customer data, but also in maintaining and mining it. North American companies will spend an estimated $25 billion to $50 billion this year on CRM software alone from companies such as Siebel Systems and Oracle.[19] And as many as half of all CRM efforts fail to meet their objectives. The most common cause of CRM failures is that companies fail to clearly define their CRM goals or that they rely too heavily on the technology alone, rather than being truly customer-centred.

But when it works, the benefits of CRM usually outweigh the costs and risks. Based on regular polls of its customers, Siebel Systems claims that customers using its CRM software report an average 16 percent increase in revenues and 21 percent increase in customer loyalty and staff efficiency.[20]

Here's a good place to pause and apply the concepts you've examined so far in this chapter.

- Think about a major purchase you've made recently. What follow up from the company where you made the purchase did you receive? If none, what customer relationship building techniques would you recommend to the company to ensure that customers are satisfied with their purchases and will buy from that company in future?
- Pick a company that we've discussed in a previous chapter, such as Canadian Tire, Mountain Equipment Co-op, Norco Bikes. Amazon.ca, or another. Does the company you chose display any customer relationship management techniques?
- Think about Dofasco, which sells its products to carmakers and other businesses that require steel, rather than to final consumers. How would Dofasco's customer relationship strategies differ from a company such as Kraft, which sells to final consumers?

DISTRIBUTING AND USING MARKETING INFORMATION

Marketing information has no value until it is used to make better marketing decisions. Thus, the marketing information system must make the information available to the managers and others who make marketing decisions or deal with customers daily. In some cases, this means providing managers with regular performance reports, intelligence updates, and reports on the results of research studies.

But marketing managers may also need nonroutine information for special situations and on-the-spot decisions. For example, a sales manager having trouble with a large customer may want a summary of the account's sales and profitability over the past year. Or a retail store manager who has run out of a best-selling product may want to know the current inventory levels in the chain's other stores. Increasingly, therefore, information distribution involves entering information into databases and making these available in a user-friendly and timely way. The CRM systems described above are valuable tools to accomplish goal.

Thanks to modern technology, today's marketing managers can gain direct access to the information system at any time and from virtually any location. While working at a home office, in a hotel room, on an airplane—anyplace where they can turn on a laptop computer and phone in—managers can obtain information from company databases or outside information services, analyze the information using statistical packages and models, prepare reports using word processing and presentation software, and communicate with others in the network through electronic communications. Such systems allow managers to get the information they need directly and quickly and to tailor it to their own needs.

OTHER MARKETING INFORMATION CONSIDERATIONS

This section discusses marketing information in two special contexts: marketing research in small businesses and nonprofit organizations, and international marketing research. To close the chapter, we look at public policy and ethics issues in marketing research.

Marketing Research in Small Businesses and Nonprofit Organizations

Just like their larger counterparts, small organizations need market information. Start-up businesses need information about their industries, competitors, potential customers, and reactions to new market offers. Existing small businesses must track changes in customer needs and wants, reactions to new products, and changes in the competitive environment.

Managers of small businesses and nonprofit organizations often think that marketing research can be done only by experts in large companies with big research budgets. Although large-scale research studies are beyond the budgets of most small businesses, many of the marketing research techniques discussed in this chapter can also be used by smaller organizations in a less formal manner and at little or no expense.

Managers of small businesses and nonprofit organizations can obtain good marketing information simply by observing things around them. For example, retailers can evaluate new locations by *observing* vehicle and pedestrian traffic. They can monitor competitor advertising by collecting ads from local media. They can evaluate their customer mix by recording how many and what kinds of customers shop in the store at different times. In addition, many small business managers routinely visit their rivals and socialize with competitors to gain insights.

Managers can conduct informal *surveys* using small convenience samples. The director of an art museum can learn what patrons think about new exhibits by conducting informal focus groups—inviting small groups to lunch and having discussions on topics of interest. Retail salespeople can talk with customers visiting the store; hospital officials can interview patients. Restaurant managers might make random phone calls during slack hours to interview consumers about where they eat out and what they think of various restaurants in the area.

Managers also can conduct their own simple *experiments*. For example, by changing the themes in regular fundraising mailings and watching the results, a nonprofit manager can find out much about which marketing strategies work best. By varying newspaper advertisements, a store manager can learn the effects of things such as ad size and position, price coupons, and media used.

Small organizations can obtain most of the secondary data available to large businesses. In addition, many associations, local media, chambers of commerce, and government agencies provide special help to small organizations. The Confederation of Independent Business represents more than 100 000 small businesses in Canada and provides advice on topics ranging from starting, financing, and expanding a small business to ordering business cards. Other excellent Web resources for small businesses include the Canada Customs and Revenue Agency's *Guide for Canadian Small Business,* which helps explain everything from setting up a business to importing and exporting regulations, and excise taxes. Industry Canada's Strategis site offers a broad range of information related to establishing and managing a small business.

There are also private companies who specialize in consulting and providing information for small businesses, much of it free. One such organization is GDSourcing. The company's Web site explains their mission clearly: "to help Canadian entrepreneurs with limited research budgets assess their market potential and performance."

Confederation of Independent Business
www.cfib.ca

Canada Customs and Revenue Agency's *Guide for Canadian Small Businesses*
www.ccra-adrc.gc.ca

Industry Canada's Strategis
strategis.ic.gc.ca

GDSourcing
www.gdsourcing.com

Industry Canada's Strategis site offers a broad range of information related to establishing and managing a small business, including market research information and links.

The business sections at local libraries can also be a good source of information. They often provide access to resources such as the *Financial Post's Canadian Markets, Scott's Directories, Standard and Poor's Industry Surveys* for U.S.-based companies, and many business periodicals. Local newspapers may provide information on local shoppers and their buying patterns. Finally, small businesses can collect a considerable amount of information at very little cost on the Internet. They can scour competitor and customer Web sites and use Internet search engines to research specific companies and issues.

In summary, secondary data collection, observation, surveys, and experiments can all be used effectively by small organizations with small budgets. Although these informal research methods are less complex and less costly, they still must be conducted carefully. Managers must think carefully about the objectives of the research, formulate questions in advance, recognize the biases introduced by smaller samples and less skilled researchers, and conduct the research systematically.[21]

INTERNATIONAL MARKETING RESEARCH

International marketing researchers follow the same steps as domestic researchers, from defining the research problem and developing a research plan to interpreting and reporting the results. However, these researchers often face more and different problems. Whereas domestic researchers deal with homogenous markets within a single country, international researchers deal with differing markets in many different countries. These markets often vary greatly in their levels of economic development, cultures and customs, and buying patterns.

In many foreign markets, the international researcher sometimes has a difficult time finding good secondary data. Whereas Canadian marketing researchers can obtain reliable secondary data from dozens of domestic research services, many countries have almost no research services at all.

Because of the scarcity of good secondary data, international researchers often must collect their own primary data. Here again, researchers face problems not found domestically. For example, they may find it difficult simply to develop good samples.

Once the sample is drawn, reaching respondents may be difficult in other parts of the world. In some countries, few people have phones; for example, there are only 32 phones per thousand people in Argentina. In other countries, like Brazil, the postal system is notoriously unreliable. In many developing countries, poor roads and transportation systems make certain areas hard to reach, making personal interviews difficult and expensive. Finally, few people in developing countries are connected to the Internet.[22]

Cultural differences from country to country cause additional problems for international researchers. Language is the most obvious obstacle. Translating a questionnaire from one language to another is anything but easy. Many idioms, phrases, and statements mean different things in different cultures. For example, a Danish executive suggests that all materials should be checked "by having a different translator put back into English what you've translated from English. You'll get the shock of your life. I remember [an example in which] 'out of sight, out of mind' had become 'invisible things are insane.'"[23]

Consumers in different countries also vary in their attitudes toward marketing research. People in one country may be very willing to respond; in other countries, nonresponse is a major problem. Customs in some countries may prohibit people from talking with strangers. In certain cultures, research questions often are considered too personal. For example, in many Latin American countries, people may feel embarrassed to talk with researchers about their choices of shampoo, deodorant, or other personal care products. Even when respondents are *willing* to respond, they may not be *able* to because of high illiteracy rates.

Despite these problems, the recent growth of international marketing has resulted in a rapid increase in the use of international marketing research. Global companies have little choice but to conduct such research. Although the costs and problems associated with international research may be high, the costs of not doing it—in terms of missed opportunities and mistakes—might be even higher. Once recognized, many of the problems associated with international marketing research can be overcome or avoided.

Public Policy and Ethics in Marketing Research

Most marketing research benefits both the sponsoring company and its consumers. Through marketing research, companies learn more about consumers' needs,

Some of the largest international research services operate in many countries. Roger Starch Worldwide provides companies with information resources "from Brazil to Eastern Europe to Cape Town to Beijing."

resulting in more satisfying products and services. A recent study conducted by the Canadian Survey Research Council found that 73 percent of Canadians liked being surveyed. Most consumers feel positively about marketing research and believe that it serves a useful purpose.[24] However, others strongly resent or even mistrust marketing research. A few consumers fear that researchers might use their findings to manipulate our buying. Others may have been taken in by previous "research surveys" that actually turned out to be attempts to sell them something. Most, however, simply resent the intrusion. They dislike mail or telephone surveys that are too long or too personal, or that interrupt them at inconvenient times.

Increasing consumer resentment has become a major problem for the research industry, leading to lower survey response rates in recent years. The research industry is considering several possible responses. One is to expand its "Your Opinion Counts" program to educate consumers about the benefits of marketing research and to distinguish it from telephone selling and database building. Another is to provide a toll-free number that people can call to verify that a survey is legitimate.

To guard against inappropriate or harmful research practices in Canada, both the Canadian Marketing Association and the Professional Marketing Research Society (PMRS) publish codes of conduct. You can read the full PMRS code on its Web site. Several principles provide the foundation of the code. First is the importance of acting professionally and ensuring that methods used to address research questions are valid and reliable. Next are principles for dealing with research subjects. Subjects are not to be exposed to any risk or harm because of their participation in the research, their voluntary cooperation for participation in the research study must be sought, and their consent attained. Both organizations' codes deal with two major concerns: (1) intrusions on consumer privacy and (2) the misuse of research findings.

Professional Marketing Research Society (PMRS) www.pmrs-aprm.com/ What/RulesA01.html?

Intrusions on Consumer Privacy Although Canadians have long been concerned with protecting their privacy, the growth in the number of people using the Internet has given more urgency to this issue. In a report released in August 1994, the Canadian privacy commissioner warned about the threat to privacy presented by the use of interactive computer technology and the ability of firms to merge databases from different businesses to cross-promote products and services. Canadian fears recently turned into a reality. When DoubleClick, a New York–based advertising firm, revealed plans to provide marketers with the names of anonymous Web surfers, there was a huge outcry on both sides of the border. David Jones, president of Electronic Frontier Canada in Kitchener, Ontario, says what made DoubleClick's practice especially dubious is that it went on without the consumer being aware of it. "There is not the usual knowledge and consent you should have when someone is collecting personal information."[25]

Canada is not alone in its concerns about privacy. In 1995, the European Union (EU) responded to this issue with its Directive on the Protection of Personal Data. The Directive establishes certain fundamentals: People must be aware that data about them are being collected and consumers have fundamental rights, including the right of access to data, the right to know where data originated, the right to have inaccurate data rectified, and the right to withhold permission for certain uses of their personal information. Another critical aspect of the directive, from a North American perspective, was that it requires non-EU countries receiving EU data to ensure that the information is adequately protected.

The U.S. and Canadian governments responded to the privacy issue differently. Quebec was the first government to establish regulations with regard to protecting privacy. Although the U.S. federal government opted to let business self-regulate with regard to privacy, the Canadian federal government passed the *Personal Information Protection and Electronic Documents Act*, Bill C-6. Effective January 2001, the public sector and interprovincial businesses now need consent to collect, use, or transfer information about an individual, or to use that information for purposes other than the original purpose for which it was collected. Moreover, every organization has to appoint a privacy officer to ensure compliance with the legislation and to field consumer inquiries and complaints. In 2004, the legislation will extend to the entire private sector.[26] In addition to the new federal legislation, the Internet Advertising and Marketing Bureau of Canada (IAMBC) will scrutinize the practices of Internet marketers.

Misuse of Research Findings Research studies can be powerful persuasion tools—companies often use study results as claims in their advertising and promotion. Today, however, many research studies appear to be little more than vehicles for pitching the sponsor's products. Few advertisers openly rig their research designs or blatantly misrepresent the findings—most abuses tend to be subtle "stretches." Consider these examples:[27]

- A study by Chrysler contends that North Americans overwhelmingly prefer Chrysler to Toyota after test driving both. However, the study included only 100 people in each of two tests. More important, none of the people surveyed owned a foreign car, so they appear to be favourably predisposed to North American produced cars.

- A poll sponsored by the disposable diaper industry asked: "It is estimated that disposable diapers account for less than 2 percent of the garbage in today's landfills. In contrast, beverage containers, third-class mail, and yard waste are estimated to account for about 21 percent of the garbage in landfills. Given this, in your opinion, would it be fair to ban disposable diapers?" Not surprisingly, 84 percent said "no."

Thus, subtle manipulations of the study's sample, or the choice or wording of questions, can greatly affect the conclusions reached. In other cases, so-called independent research studies are paid for by companies with an interest in the outcome. These are the kind of questionable practices the PMRS is on guard to prevent, since it firmly believes that such offences will undermine the credibility of the entire industry.

<< Looking Back   < < < < < < < < <

In the previous chapter, we discussed the marketing environment. In this chapter, you've studied tools used to gather and manage information that marketing managers and others can use to assess opportunities in the environment and the impact of a firm's marketing efforts. After this brief pause for rest and reflection, we'll head out again in the next chapter to take a closer look at the object of all of this activity—consumers and their buying behaviour.

In today's complex and rapidly changing environment, marketing managers need more and better information to make effective and timely decisions. This greater need for information has been matched by the explosion of information technologies for supplying information. Using today's new technologies, companies can now handle great quantities of information, sometimes even too much. Yet marketers often complain that they lack enough of the *right* kind of information or have an excess of the *wrong* kind. In response, many companies are now studying their managers' information needs, and designing information systems that help managers develop and manage market and customer information.

1. Explain the importance of information to the company.

Good products and marketing programs start with a complete understanding of consumer needs and wants. Thus, the company needs sound information to produce superior value and satisfaction for customers. The company also requires information on competitors, resellers, and other actors and forces in the marketplace. Increasingly, marketers are viewing information not only as an input for making better decisions but also as an important strategic asset and marketing tool.

2. Define the marketing information system and discuss its parts.

The *marketing information system (MIS)* consists of people, equipment, and procedures to gather, sort, analyze, evaluate, and distribute needed, timely, and accurate information to marketing decision makers. A well-designed information system begins and ends with users. The MIS first *assesses information needs,* then *develops information* from internal databases, marketing intelligence activities, and marketing research. *Internal databases* provide information on the company's own sales, costs, inventories, cash flows, and accounts receivable and payable. Such data can be obtained quickly and cheaply but often need to be adapted for marketing decisions. *Marketing intelligence* activities supply everyday information about developments in the external marketing environment. *Market research* consists of collecting information relevant to a specific marketing problem faced by the company. Lastly, the MIS *distributes information* gathered from these sources to the right managers in the right form and at the right time to help them make better marketing decisions.

3. Outline the steps in the marketing research process.

The first step in the marketing research process involves *defining the problem and setting the research objectives,* which may be exploratory, descriptive, or causal research. The second step consists of *developing a research plan* for collecting data from primary and secondary sources. The third step calls for *implementing the marketing research plan* by gathering, processing, and analyzing the information. The fourth step consists of *interpreting and reporting the findings.* Additional information analysis helps marketing managers use the information and provides them with sophisticated statistical procedures and models from which to develop more rigorous findings.

Both *internal* and *external* secondary data sources often provide information more quickly and at a lower cost than primary data sources, and they can sometimes yield information that a company cannot collect by itself. However, needed information might not exist in secondary sources, and even if data can be found, they might be largely unusable. Researchers must also evaluate secondary information to ensure that it is *relevant, accurate, current,* and *impartial.* Primary research must also be evaluated for these features. Each primary data collection method—*observational, survey,* and *experiment*—has its own advantages and disadvantages. Each of the various primary research contact methods—mail, telephone, personal interview, and online—also has its own advantages and drawbacks. Similarly, each contact method has its pluses and minuses.

4. Explain how companies analyze and distribute marketing information.

Information gathered in internal databases and through marketing intelligence and marketing research usually requires more analysis. This may include advanced statistical analysis or the application of analytical models that will help marketers make better decisions. In recent years, marketers have paid special attention to the analysis of individual customer data. Many companies have now acquired or developed special software and analysis techniques—called *customer relationship management (CRM)*—that integrate, analyze, and apply the mountains of individual customer data contained in their databases.

Marketing information has no value until it is used to make better marketing decisions. Thus, the marketing information system must make the information available to the managers and others who make marketing decisions or deal with customers. In some cases, this means providing regular reports and updates; in other cases it means making nonroutine information available for special situations and on-the-spot decisions. Thanks to modern technology, today's marketing managers can gain direct access to the information system at any time and from virtually any location.

5. Discuss the special issues some marketing researchers face, including public policy and ethics issues.

Some marketers face special marketing research situations, such as those conducting research in small business, nonprofit, or international situations. Marketing research can be conducted effectively by small businesses and nonprofit organizations with limited budgets. International marketing researchers follow the same steps as domestic researchers but often face more and different problems. All organizations need to respond responsibly to major public policy and ethical issues surrounding marketing research, including issues of intrusions on consumer privacy and misuse of research findings.

Navigating the Key Terms

Causal research, **p. 172**

Customer relationship management (CRM), **p. 188**

Descriptive research, **p. 172**

Experimental research, **p. 180**

Exploratory research, **p. 171**

Focus group interviewing, **p. 181**

Internal databases, **p. 168**

Marketing information system (MIS), **p. 166**

Marketing intelligence, **p. 169**

Marketing research, **p. 171**

Observational research, **p. 176**

Online databases, **p. 176**

Online (Internet) marketing research, **p. 182**

Primary data, **p. 173**

Sample, **p. 185**

Secondary data, **p. 173**

Single-source data systems, **p. 179**

Survey research, **p. 179**

Concept Check

Fill in the blanks and then check your answers.

1. A _____ _____ _____ consists of people, equipment, and procedures to gather, sort, analyze, evaluate, and distribute needed, timely, and accurate information to marketing decision makers.

2. The information needed by marketing managers can be obtained from _____, _____, and _____.

3. _____ _____ is a systematic collection and analysis of publicly available information about competitors and developments in the marketing environment.

4. _____ _____ can be defined as the systematic design, collection, analysis, and reporting of data relevant to a specific marketing situation facing an organization.

5. The marketing research process has four steps: _____, _____, _____, and _____.

6. A marketing research project might have any one of three types of objectives. If the objective were to gather preliminary information that would help define the problem and suggest hypotheses, the researcher would use _____ research.

7. _____ data consist of information collected for the specific purpose at hand.

8. Many companies now use _____ research, which combines intensive observation with customer interviews, to gain deep insights into how consumers buy and use their products.

9. _____ research is the approach best suited for gathering descriptive information.

10. Of the four research contact methods discussed, _____ is the only one rated as "excellent" with respect to low cost.

11. A researcher is using a _____ sample when he or she selects the easiest population members from which to obtain information.

12. _____ _____ _____ consists of sophisticated software and analytical tools that integrate customer information from all sources, analyze it in depth, and use the results to build stronger customer relationships.

Concept Check Answers: 1. Marketing information system (MIS); 2. internal data, marketing intelligence, and marketing research; 3. Marketing intelligence; 4. Marketing research; 5. defining the problem and the research objectives, developing the research plan, implementing the research plan, and interpreting and reporting the findings; 6. exploratory; 7. Primary; 8. ethnographic; 9. Survey; 10. online; 11. convenience; 12. Customer relationship management (CRM).

Discussing the Issues

1. Many companies build extensive internal databases so marketing managers can readily access and work with information to identify marketing opportunities and problems, plan programs, and evaluate performance. If you were the marketing manager for a large computer software manufacturer, what type of information would you like to have available in your internal database? Explain.

2. Marketing intelligence has become increasingly important to marketing managers, because of its ability to aid them in improving strategic decision making. What other benefits are attributed to a marketing intelligence function? Assuming that you have been hired as a consultant by a company that is developing a new highly caffeinated energy drink, what type of intelligence sleuthing tips would you offer the firm?

3. Name the type of research that would be appropriate in the following situations, and explain why:

   a. Kellogg wants to investigate the impact of young children on their parents' decisions to buy breakfast foods.

   b. Your university bookstore wants to get some insights into how students feel about the store's merchandise, prices, and service.

   c. McDonald's is considering where to locate a new outlet in a fast-growing suburb.

   d. Gillette wants to determine whether a new line of deodorant for children will be profitable.

4. Focus group interviewing is both a widely used and widely criticized research technique in marketing. List the advantages and disadvantages of focus groups. Suggest some kinds of questions that are suitable for exploration by using focus groups. How could focus group research be done via the Internet?

5. Increasingly, companies are turning to customer relationship management (CRM) as a means for integrating and applying the mountains of customer data contained in their databases. Two techniques that analysts use to aid them in applying CRM are data warehousing and data mining. Explain each term and how each is used to improve relationships and "connections." Next, assume that your local grocery store has implemented a store service card. This card allows you to receive special patronage discounts and to cash personal cheques. Beginning with the registration process for the card and moving through its final usage at the checkout stand, discuss all the types of data that could be collected on customers and how this data could eventually be used to build relationships.

 ## Mastering Marketing

Using marketing information systems, marketing intelligence, marketing research, and customer relationship management is vital to today's competitive marketing organization. Take one of the above areas and demonstrate how CanGo has used it to better understand its competitive environment and relate to its customers. Provide examples to illustrate your conclusions.

 Check out the enclosed Video case CD-ROM, or our Companion Website at www.pearsoned.ca/armstrong, to view a CBC video segment and case for this chapter.

MAP 5 Marketing Applications

The North American consumer is one of the most researched subjects in the world. Millions of dollars are spent annually to find out what you want, when you want it, and how much you will pay for it. Becoming intimate with consumers is not a luxury, it is a necessity. The desire to become a closer companion to the customer has spurred interest in ethnographic research—which combines intensive observation with customer interviews (see New Directions 5-1 for more details). However, this form of research can often be an expensive pursuit for a company.

Is there a lower cost alternative? Some in marketing believe that one of the oldest forms of research—the consumer poll—is the answer. At one time polling was expensive and often seriously inaccurate. What if the researcher could, however, get the advantages of participatory information results combined with low cost? If this were possible, it would be of great interest. Well, hold onto your questionnaires, the Internet has provided the answer—the online poll.

Although often not scientifically accurate, the online poll has become a great way to get large amounts of preferential information from an interested audience at a low cost. Trends do reveal themselves and, unlike normal polling, those who participate can be recontacted by an interested marketer because a trail is left on the Internet. Ask someone a question in a shopping mall and then he or she is gone. On the Internet this same consumer can be recontacted at a later date with a variety of messages. In fact, many do not mind the recontact at all—it is a "connection" they actually desire. Have you been polled lately? If you want to participate in our society and marketplace, isn't it about time that you were?

Thinking Like a Marketing Manager

Interested in participating in a research process yourself? Go to the following Web sites: **www.pollingreport.com**, **www.gallup.com**, and **www.cnn.com** and answer questions 1 to 4 below.

1. Which of the polls or questionnaires were the most interesting to you?

2. Which of the polls were easiest to answer?

3. Which of the polls could be tied most easily to marketing research? Why?

4. Under what circumstances are you willing to supply information to an online researcher? to a Web site? Explain.

5. The American Consumer Opinion Web site at **www.acop.com** maintains a panel of Internet users who agree to complete online surveys. Sign up and see how it works.

6. Assume that you are a marketing researcher who has just been hired to establish an online marketing poll for a product or service of your choice (your choice should not currently have an online polling mechanism). Using the product or service's Web site, construct an online poll for the company. Specify research objectives, questions for your poll, who the poll will be intended for, what you will learn from your poll, how the poll results will be fed back to those polled (if they will), and how the poll results or the poll itself will help you to gain data on and making connections with your customers or viewers. Report your results to the class.

Digital Map

Visit our Web site at **www.pearsoned.ca/armstrong** for online quizzes, Internet exercises, and more!

CASE 5 CARA OPERATIONS

Most Canadians won't recognize the company name Cara Operations. They will, however, recognize the company's brands, which include Swiss Chalet, Second Cup, and Harvey's.

Cara has a long history. Founded in 1883 as the Canadian Railway News Company, its primary business was selling newspapers and magazines. The company's name was changed to Cara in 1961. Today, Cara no longer sells newspapers and magazines, focusing instead on the food industry. The company generates almost $2 billion in sales annually and employs 38 000 people. Cara owns some of the most famous restaurant brands in Canada—Swiss Chalet, Harvey's, Kelsey's, Montana's, Outback Steakhouse, and Milestone's—competes in the specialty coffee market through the Second Cup, and is a leading provider of food services to the airline industry and merchandise concessions in travel centres such as airports.

Additionally, the company operates Summit Food Service Distributors, serving the restaurant, hotel, health care, and institutional markets in Ontario and Quebec.

Franchises are one key to Cara's success. Of Canada's 64 000 food service establishments, two thirds are independently owned and many are franchised. More than 500 franchising corporations operate 65 000 locations in Canada. You see franchises in every city across the country, in restaurants, gas stations, hardware stores, clothing stores, video outlets, and more. Franchising is Canada's fastest growing method of business expansion: In the 1990s, the average annual franchise sales growth rate exceeded 10 percent, compared with 7.4 percent for the GNP and 7.7 percent for retail sales growth. However, the Canadian franchise market is far from being fully developed.

Cara's commitment to the franchise business concept helped establish its belief that success comes from recognizing how important people are to the organization. Perhaps the company president, who is an ex-franchisee and has spent time in the trenches, influenced this vision.

The company calls all its employees, franchisees, and their staffs teammates, and they are expected to demonstrate the company's core values and principles in their daily actions and interactions. Cara's five core values centre on people, self-responsibility, integrity, passion for winning, and quality. The organization's principles, which are intended to guide teammates' behaviour, include leadership, respect, hospitality, innovation, and fun.

To keep each of Cara's restaurant brands in touch with Canada's ever-changing marketplace, the company created a branding team in 1999. This centralized group evaluated each of Cara's brands, researched consumer needs, and developed marketing strategies for each chain. Cara made an initial investment of $3 million in "brand intelligence gathering capability," which required the building of the technical infrastructure to support the company's brands. Maintaining this information system costs $1 million per year. Cara uses a marketing information system that gathers data from 21 different sources including Fasttrack, PMB reports, focus groups, studies, surveys, and 7000 consumer interviews each year. This information gives the company a way to predict trends and to develop marketing programs that will hit consumers just as the trends do.

One major revelation made through the marketing information process was that every Cara brand needed to attract younger customers. In late 2002, Cara's leading chain, Swiss Chalet, began upgrading restaurant décor, increasing the number of promotions, adding new dishes to the menu, focusing on home delivery, and increasing the interactivity of Swiss Chalet's Web site. Specifically, the number of promotions will increase from five to six. The company has run the Swiss Chalet Festive Special promotion involving a Lindt chocolate give-away for the past 15 years. This consumer promotion has always been strong, and Sandra Cimetta, marketing manager at Swiss Chalet, describes it as "getting up there in icon status, along with Tim Hortons' 'Roll Up the Rim to Win' and McDonald's Monopoly." In mid-2002, Swiss Chalet introduced a new family-targeted promotion, teaming up with Nestlé Canada's Häagen Dazs ice cream. This new promotion increased "dining room participation rates" and is replicating the success of the Festive Special promotion.

Harvey's has also been busy. It has added new menu items and relaunched its

Web site. While McDonald's promotional efforts emphasize speed of service, Harvey's continues to emphasize its food's good taste. Harvey's roots are in its cooking methodology and the way the sandwich is garnished, not in getting the consumer out as fast as possible. Harvey's was well ahead of McDonald's in meeting the needs of vegetarians, launching a vegetarian burger several years before McDonald's did.

Second Cup's marketing initiatives move in a different direction. It is increasing marketing efforts and including sponsorships in its major markets. It recently signed sponsorship agreements with the Toronto International and Calgary International Film Festivals and is moving to align coffee with music by sponsoring several jazz festivals across Canada.

Cara defines its Kelsey's Bar and Grill, Montana's Cookhouse, and Outback Steakhouse as "full-service casual" brands. Milestone's, which Cara recently purchased, is an "upscale casual" brand. Kelsey's positioning is as a neighbourhood bar and grill, and it focuses much of its marketing efforts on community events and local sponsorships. Generous portions for less money are a substantial part of its efforts to encourage word-of-mouth advertising.

Gabriel T. Tsampalieros, the chief executive officer of Cara, indicated in a *Wall Street Journal* interview that Cara plans to launch 65 restaurants each year and about 25 Second Cup locations, focusing on key geographic areas. He said Cara was cautiously looking at geographic expansion of Swiss Chalet and Montana's into the United States and at expansion of the Second Cup internationally, but not into the United States. The company will expand its internal foodservice distribution network into Western Canada to better service its restaurants and will continue building market share on the catering side. To increase efficiency, the company plans to spend money on systems upgrades and infrastructure for easier communication among its restaurants and suppliers. It will also spend significant time and money on human resource development.

With more than a century of success behind it, Cara's brands are positioned to remain category leaders in their market segments.

Sources: The Wall Street Journal, "CEO of Cara Operations Discusses Its New Focus," 15 July 2002; Sarah Dobson, "Cara's Winning Combo," *Marketing Magazine,* 28 October 2002; *The Globe and Mail Report on Business* "Snapshot," 19 September 2002.

Questions

1. What are the differences in marketing information systems between an organization that is based on franchising compared with one that is not?

2. What types of research Cara gather to provide market segmentation information to its marketing group?

3. Visit Harris Interactive's Web site at **www.harrisinteractive.com/tech/qual.asp.** On the left side of the page under Tech Edge, click on Qualitative Research. Click on View a Demo of an Online Focus Group. Where might this technique be used at Cara?

4. With Cara's intended expansion to international markets, what types of marketing information the company need to identify market segments?

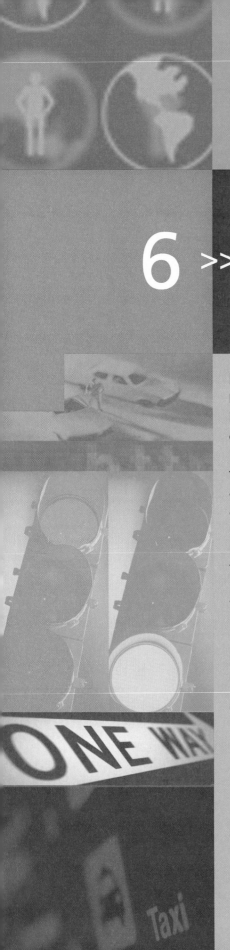

6 >> Consumer and Business Buyer Behaviour

Looking Ahead

In the previous chapter, you studied how marketers obtain, analyze, and use information to identify marketing opportunities and to assess marketing programs. In this chapter, you'll continue your marketing journey with a closer look at the most important element of the marketing environment—customers. The aim of marketing is to somehow affect how customers think about and behave toward the organization and its marketing offers. To affect the whats, whens, and hows of buying behaviour, marketers must first understand the *whys*. We look first at *final consumer* buying influences and processes and then at the buying behaviour of *business customers*. You'll see that understanding buying behaviour is an essential but very difficult task.

After studying this chapter, you should be able to

1. understand the consumer market and the major factors that influence consumer buyer behaviour
2. identify and discuss the stages in the buyer decision process
3. describe the adoption and diffusion process for new products
4. define the business market and identify the major factors that influence business buyer behaviour
5. list and define the steps in the business buying-decision process

Our first point of interest: Harley-Davidson, maker of the nation's top-selling heavyweight motorcycles. Who rides these big Harley "Hogs?" What moves them to tattoo their bodies with the Harley emblem, abandon home and hearth for the open road, and flock to Harley rallies by the hundreds of thousands? *You* might be surprised, but Harley-Davidson knows *very* well.

Few brands engender such intense loyalty as that found in the hearts of Harley-Davidson owners. "The Harley audience is granitelike" in its devotion, laments the vice president of sales for competitor Yamaha. Observes the publisher of *American Iron,* an industry publication, "You don't see people tattooing Yamaha on their bodies." And according to the president of a motorcycle research company, "For a lot of people, it's not that they want a motorcycle; it's that they want a Harley—the brand is that strong." Each year, in early March, more than 400 000 Harley bikers rumble through the streets of Daytona Beach, Florida, to attend Harley-Davidson's Bike Week celebration. Bikers from across the nation lounge on their low-slung Harleys, swap biker tales, and sport T-shirts proclaiming "I'd rather push a Harley than drive a Honda."

Riding such intense emotions, Harley-Davidson has rumbled its way to the top of the fast-growing heavyweight motorcycle market. Harley's "Hogs" capture more than one-fifth of all U.S. bike sales and more than half of the heavyweight segment. Their popularity is similar in Canada. Both the segment and Harley's sales are growing rapidly. In fact, for several years running, sales have far outstripped supply, with customer waiting lists of up to three years for popular models and street prices running well above suggested list prices. "We've seen people buy a new Harley and then sell it in the parking lot for $4000 to $5000 more," says one dealer. Between its initial public stock offering in 1986 and the year 2000, Harley-Davidson shares had split four times and were up more than 7100 percent.

Harley-Davidson's marketers spend a great deal of time thinking about customers and their buying behaviour. They want to know who their customers are, what they think, how they feel, and why they buy a Harley rather than a Yamaha or a Kawasaki or a Honda. What is it that makes Harley buyers so fiercely loyal? These are difficult

questions; even Harley owners themselves don't know exactly what motivates their buying. But Harley management puts top priority on understanding customers and what makes them tick.

Who rides a Harley? You might be surprised. It's no longer the Hell's Angels crowd—the burly, black-leather-jacketed rebels and biker chicks who once made up Harley's core clientele. Motorcycles are attracting a new breed of riders—older, more affluent, and better educated. Harley now appeals more to "rubbies" (rich urban bikers) than to rebels. The average Harley customer is a 48-year-old husband with a median household income of $94 000. Harley's big, comfortable cruisers give these new consumers the easy ride, prestige, and twist-of-the-wrist power they want and can afford.

Harley-Davidson makes good bikes, and to keep up with its shifting market, the company has upgraded its showrooms and sales approaches. But Harley customers are buying a lot more than just a quality bike and a smooth sales pitch. To gain a better understanding of customers' deeper motivations, Harley-Davidson conducted focus groups in which it invited bikers to make cut-and-paste collages of pictures that expressed their feelings about Harley-Davidsons. (Can't you just see a bunch of hard-core bikers doing this?). It then mailed out 16 000 surveys containing a typical battery of psychological, sociological, and demographic questions as well as subjective questions such as "Is Harley more typified by a brown bear or a lion?" The research revealed seven core customer types: adventure-loving traditionalists, sensitive pragmatists, stylish status seekers, laid-back campers, classy capitalists, cool-headed loners, and cocky misfits. However, all owners appreciated their Harleys for the same basic reasons. "It didn't matter if you were the guy who swept the floors of the factory or if you were the CEO at that factory, the attraction to Harley was very similar," says a Harley executive.

"Independence, freedom, and power were the universal Harley appeals."

These studies confirm that Harley customers are doing more than just buying motorcycles. They're making a lifestyle statement and displaying an attitude. As one analyst suggests, owning a Harley makes you "the toughest, baddest guy on the block. Never mind that [you're] a dentist or an accountant. You [feel] wicked astride all that power." Your Harley renews your spirits and announces your independence. As the Harley Web site's home page announces, "Thumbing the starter of a Harley-Davidson does a lot more than fire the engine. It fires the imagination." Adds a Harley dealer: "We sell a dream here. Our customers lead hardworking professional or computer-oriented lives. Owning a Harley removes barriers to meeting people on a casual basis, and it gives you maximum self-expression in your own space."

The classic look, the throaty sound, the very idea of a Harley—all contribute to its mystique. Owning this "legend" makes you a part of something bigger, a member of the Harley family. The fact that you have to wait to get a Harley makes it all that much more satisfying to have one. In fact, the company deliberately restricts its output. "Our goal is to eventually run production at a level that's always one motorcycle short of demand," says Harley-Davidson's chief executive.

Such strong emotions and motivations are captured in a classic Harley-Davidson advertisement. The ad shows a close-up of an arm, the bicep adorned with a Harley-Davidson tattoo. The headline asks, "When was the last time you felt this strongly about anything?" The ad copy outlines the problem and suggests a solution: "Wake up in the morning and life picks up where it left off. You do what has to be done. Use what it takes to get there. And what once seemed exciting has now become part of the numbing routine. It all begins to feel the same. Except when you've got a Harley-Davidson. Something strikes a nerve. The heartfelt thunder rises up, refusing to become part of the background. Suddenly things are different. Clearer. More real. As they should have been all along. The feeling is personal. For some, owning a

Harley is a statement of individuality. For others, owning a Harley means being a part of a home-grown legacy that was born in a tiny Milwaukee shed in 1903.... To the uninitiated, a Harley-Davidson motorcycle is associated with a certain look, a certain sound. Anyone who owns one will tell you it's much more than that. Riding a Harley changes you from within. The effect is permanent. Maybe it's time you started feeling this strongly. Things are different on a Harley."[1]

The Harley-Davidson example shows that many different factors affect consumer buying behaviour. Buying behaviour is never simple, yet understanding it is the essential task of marketing management. First, we explore the dynamics of final consumer markets and consumer buyer behaviour. We then examine business markets and the business buying process.

CONSUMER MARKETS AND CONSUMER BUYER BEHAVIOUR

Consumer buyer behaviour refers to the buying behaviour of final consumers, individuals and households who buy goods and services for personal consumption. All these final consumers combine to make up the **consumer market**. The Canadian consumer market comprises more than 30 million people who consume billions of dollars' worth of goods and services each year, making it a very attractive consumer market. The world consumer market comprises more than 6 *billion* people.

Consumers around the world vary tremendously in age, income, education level, and tastes. They also buy an incredible variety of goods and services. How these diverse consumers connect with each other and with other elements of the world around them affects their choices among various products, services, and companies. Here we examine the fascinating array of factors that affect consumer behaviour.

> **Consumer buyer behaviour** The buying behaviour of final consumers—individuals and households who buy goods and services for personal consumption.
>
> **Consumer market** All the individuals and households who buy or acquire goods and services for personal consumption.

Model of Consumer Behaviour

Consumers make many buying decisions every day. Most large companies research consumer buying decisions in great detail to answer questions about what consumers buy, where they buy, how and how much they buy, when they buy, and why they buy. Marketers can study actual consumer purchases to find out what they buy, where, and how much. But learning about the *whys* of consumer buying behaviour is not so easy—the answers are often locked deep within the consumer's head.

The central question for marketers is this: How do consumers respond to various marketing efforts the company might use? The starting point is the stimulus–response model of buyer behaviour shown in Figure 6-1. This figure shows that marketing and other stimuli enter the consumer's "black box" and produce certain responses. Marketing stimuli consist of the four Ps: product, price, place, and promotion. Other stimuli include major forces and events in the buyer's environment: economic, technological, political, and cultural. All these inputs enter the buyer's black box, where they are turned into a set of observable buyer responses: product choice, brand choice, dealer choice, purchase timing, and purchase amount.

The marketer wants to understand how the stimuli are changed into responses inside the consumer's black box, which has two parts. First, the buyer's characteris-

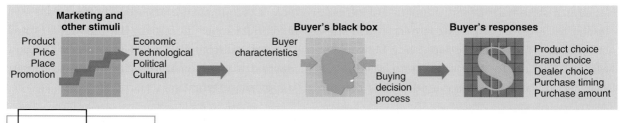

Figure 6-1

Model of Buyer Behaviour

tics influence how he or she perceives and reacts to the stimuli. Second, the buyer's decision process itself affects the buyer's behaviour. We look first at buyer characteristics as they affect buying behaviour and then discuss the buyer decision process.

Characteristics Affecting Consumer Behaviour

Consumer purchases are influenced strongly by cultural, social, personal, and psychological characteristics, shown in Figure 6-2. For the most part, marketers cannot control such factors, but they must consider them. To help you understand these concepts, we apply them to the case of a hypothetical consumer—Jennifer Wong, a 26-year-old brand manager working for a multinational packaged-goods company in Toronto. Jennifer was born in Vancouver, but her grandparents came from Hong Kong. She's been in a relationship for two years but isn't married. She has decided that she wants to buy a vehicle but isn't sure she wants to buy a car. She rode a motor scooter while attending university and is now considering buying a motorcycle—maybe even a Harley.

Cultural Factors Cultural factors exert a broad and deep influence on consumer behaviour. The marketer needs to understand the role played by the buyer's *culture, subculture,* and *social class.*

Culture The set of basic values, perceptions, wants, and behaviours learned by a member of society from family and other important institutions.

Culture Culture is the most basic cause of a person's wants and behaviour. Human behaviour is largely learned. Growing up in a society, a child learns basic values, perceptions, wants, and behaviours from the family and other important institutions.

    Maclean's 1999 and 2000 polls of Canadian values and attitudes revealed that more than 90 percent of Canadians believe that our country has a distinct culture and distinct values. Almost 80 percent of Canadians believe that our identity is based on a strong sense of our own history, rather than simply a desire not to be

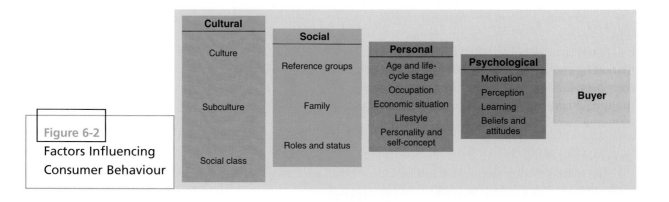

Figure 6-2

Factors Influencing Consumer Behaviour

Americans. The majority of Canadians noted that our flag, the achievements of prominent Canadians such as artists and scientists, our climate and geography, our social safety net, our international role, and our multicultural and multiracial makeup are symbols of our uniqueness. Canadians want the government to take a tough stand on law and order and see rebuilding our social institutions as a government priority. They strongly favoured investments in the CBC and our health care and education systems over tax cuts in the 2000 poll. Furthermore, we are becoming an increasingly confident and optimistic people who no longer see ourselves as boring or sexually repressed.[2]

Another recent study outlined some other basic values shared by Canadians: "Canada is a country that believes in freedom, dignity, respect, equality and fair treatment, and opportunity to participate. It is a country that cares for the disadvantaged at home and elsewhere, a country that prefers peaceful solutions to disputes. Canada is a country that, for all its diversity, has shared values."[3]

Canadians still see government as the leader in the fight to protect unique Canadian values from the inroads of American influence. Respect for diversity has also long been part of our heritage. Canada had three founding nations: Aboriginal people, England, and France. More than four million Canadians report that they can speak both English and French. The proportion of francophones who are bilingual is almost five times that of anglophones who are bilingual. Not surprisingly, Quebec has the largest number of bilingual Canadians (35 percent). New Brunswick is the second most bilingual province.[4]

Canada is becoming more multicultural and multilingual. Because of increased immigration, our population comprises a rich mix of people from around the globe (for example, Canada is home to 4.2 million Scots, 2.7 million Germans, 1.2 million Italians, 900 000 Chinese, 300 000 Russians, and 200 000 million Jamaicans). The number of visible minorities almost doubled from 1991 to 2000 and now comprises 5.7 million people (about 17.7 percent of the population). By 2016 it is estimated that the group will grow to 7.7 million people and will comprise almost a quarter of Canada's population. Today's visible minorities include Chinese (23 percent), South Asians (19 percent), blacks (19 percent), West Asians/Arabs (13 percent), Filipinos (8 percent), Southeast Asians (5 percent), Latin Americans (6 percent), and others (7 percent).[5]

Marketers are always trying to spot *cultural shifts* in order to discover new products. For example, the cultural shift toward greater concern about health and fitness has created a huge industry for health and fitness services, exercise equipment and clothing, and lower-fat and more natural foods. The shift toward informality has resulted in more demand for casual clothing and simpler home furnishings.

Subculture Each culture contains smaller **subcultures**, or groups of people with shared value systems based on common life experiences and situations. Subcultures include nationalities, religions, racial groups, and geographic regions. Many subcultures make up important market segments, and marketers often design products and marketing programs tailored to their needs. Native Canadians, ethnic consumers, and Internet user are just three of Canada's important subcultures:

1. *Native Canadians.* Native Canadians are making their voices heard both in the political arena and in the marketplace. There are 416 000 status Indians living

Subculture A group of people with shared value systems based on common life experiences and situations in Canada. When Métis, nonstatus natives, and Inuit are added to this group, the number swells to 712 000. Not only do Native Canadians have distinct cultures that influence their values and purchasing behaviour, but they have also profoundly influenced the rest of Canada through their art, appreciation of nature, and concern for the environment.

Banks have been particularly responsive to the unique needs of Aboriginal Canadians.[6] Scotiabank, for example, has maintained its relationship with First Nations people through its three on-reserve branches and 24 Aboriginal banking centres. It also uses grassroots marketing and public relations efforts, including its sponsorship of the Aboriginal Achievement Awards and 10 annual scholarships of $2500 for young Aboriginal entrepreneurs. CIBC found that cultural symbols can better link a firm with its native customers. On its Aboriginal Banking Web site, CIBC features a medicine wheel to symbolize CIBC's "holistic and integrated approach" to achieving "balance and harmony in [its] relationship with Aboriginal people." The symbol was selected as an indication of CIBC's respect for the cultural integrity and diversity of Aboriginal people in Canada.

2. *Canada's ethnic consumers.* Consumers from ethnic groups represent some of the fastest-growing markets in Canada. In Toronto, for example, close to 42 percent of the population comprises visible minorities, and its four major ethnic population groups—Chinese, Italian, Portuguese, and South Asian—account for $13 billion in consumer spending. Marketing to ethnic communities isn't just an issue for marketers working in Vancouver, Toronto, and Montreal. Even smaller centres, such as Ottawa, Edmonton, and Calgary, have growing ethnic populations. The Canadian Advertising Foundation suggests that visible minorities have as much as $300 billion in purchasing power.[7]

Specialized media have been springing up across Canada to serve these communities. Besides newspapers targeting these communities, a growing number of local multiethnic broadcasters, like Toronto-based CFMT International are being established. Several national television services are aimed at specific cultural groups, such as Black Entertainment Television, Telelatino Network, and the Asian Television Network.

Some marketers have seen the wisdom of targeting religious communities as well as visible minorities. For example, 351 705 people across Canada in 2000 identified themselves as being of Jewish ethnic origin. Hallmark Canada saw an opportunity to serve this market. Although it has offered cards for Jewish holidays for many years, it now also offers such products as Star of David cookie cutters, wooden dreidel toys, themed wrapping paper, and paper party items subbranded under its Tree of Life brand to give them a unique identity.[8]

Marketers must track evolving trends in various ethnic communities. Consider Chinese-Canadians, for example. In the past, most members of this ethnic group came from Hong Kong. Today they are arriving from Taiwan and mainland China. Why should marketers be concerned where Chinese immigrants come from? Primarily for language reasons. Although the Chinese who come from Hong Kong speak Cantonese, people from Taiwan and mainland China often speak Mandarin. Marketers must also be aware of the differences between new immigrants and those who are "integrated immigrants"—people who are second-, third-, fourth-, fifth-,

CIBC
http://www2.cibc.com/
aboriginal/home.html

and even sixth-generation Chinese-Canadians. Although marketing information often must be translated into the language of new immigrants, integrated immigrants communicate mainly in English. Although Chinese-Canadians are influenced by many of the values of their adopted country, they may also share some values rooted in their ethnic history: trust family, work hard, be thrifty, save, and have liquid and tangible goods. Air Canada used its knowledge of these values in a campaign that linked Chinese-Canadians' need for security and the desire to keep connected to their homeland with Air Canada's services.[9]

Many ethnic groups believe that they have been neglected or misrepresented by marketers. A Canadian Advertising Foundation study revealed that 80 percent of people belonging to visible minorities believed that advertising has been targeted almost exclusively at "white" people. Yet 46 percent of this group stated that they would be more likely to buy a product if its advertising featured models from visible minority populations.

Let's consider our hypothetical consumer. How will Jennifer Wong's cultural background influence her decision about whether to buy a motorcycle? Jennifer's parents certainly won't approve of her choice. Tied strongly to the values of thrift and conservatism, they believe that she should continue taking the subway instead of purchasing a vehicle. However, Jennifer identifies with her Canadian friends and

Air Canada used its knowledge of Chinese-Canadian values in a campaign that linked two symbols: Canadian maple leaves (the airline's brand symbol) and Chinese embroidery.

colleagues as much as she does with her family. She views herself as a modern woman in a society that accepts women in a wide range of roles, both conventional and unconventional. She has female friends who play hockey and rugby. Women riding motorcycles are becoming a more common sight in Toronto.

3. *Internet users.* People who "surf the Net" also have a culture that marketers ignore at their peril. Internet users have their own language, norms, values, and etiquette or "netiquette." One recent *Globe and Mail* headline claimed, "Internet has transformed life!"[10] Although this may be hyperbole, the Internet has certainly revolutionized the way we shop, communicate, and learn. One 16-year-old Ottawa teenager, for example, claimed, "I spend a lot of time on the computer talking to people. My life sort of revolves around it."

About 54 percent of Canadians used the Internet during March 2002, compared with 59 percent of Americans. The first Canadian Internet audience information and usage data from Nielsen/NetRatings indicate that, in one month, Canadian Web surfers spent nearly two hours less time online than U.S. Internet users and averaged fewer sessions and sites visited. Table 6-1 outlines the findings from the Nielsen study.[11]

Canada is number two in the world in terms of the proliferation of home computers and Internet access, trailing the United States. It is not surprising that mar-

Table 6-1	Activity for Average Internet User at Home in Canada versus the United States, March 2002	
	Canada	United States
Number of sessions per month	19	20
Number of unique sites visited	23	45
Time spent per month	9:18:28	11:02:29
Time spent during surfing session	0:29:01	0:33:30
Duration of a page viewed	0:00:50	0:00:56
Active Internet universe (had access and actually surfed)	10.0 million	105.1 million
Current Internet universe estimate (had access but did not necessarily go online)	17.0 million	167.3 million

keters are working hard to target Canadian Internet users. They must remember, however, that hard-sell marketing is definitely unacceptable on the Web, and marketers who violate this norm may be "flamed" or "mail bombed" by irate Web users.

Today's Internet users are not the stereotypical 14-year-old computer nerds, pounding away on a computer in the basement. One reason that retailers are so interested in using the Internet as a marketing channel is the compelling demographic characteristics of Internet users. First, they are above-average spenders. Internet users tend to be highly educated people in white-collar jobs who earn high incomes. In Canada, the largest group of Internet users (29 percent) fall in the 35 to 44 age group. People 25 to 35 years of age make up the next largest group (27 percent), followed by the youth market, those 18 to 24, who represent 21 percent of the Internet population. This market is highly attractive, given its technological sophistication and willingness to make Internet purchases. People aged 45 to 54 make up 15 percent of Internet users, while those over 55 constitute only 8 percent of the Internet usage group.

Historically, male Internet users have outnumbered female Internet users. Recent surveys, however, have shown that users are now equally represented between men, more closely resembling the general public.[12]

Unlike any group of consumers before them, Internet users are powerful and in control. The consumer is the one who chooses to access a Web site, and marketers must adjust to the idea that the Internet is a means of two-way communication between a customer and a vendor, not the one-way street that media advertising represents. In other words, consumers are not just listening to what the corporation wants to tell them; they're choosing the information that appeals to them. And Internet users value information.

Several articles have claimed that the Internet hasn't lived up to its promise as a marketing tool. Those who make this claim base their argument on the fact that few users actually make purchases over the Internet (even though Canadians spend $21 million annually on online purchases). However, before marketers deny the value of the Internet, they must understand how and why people use the technology. Most people who use the Internet do so for communication purposes, primarily e-mail. A third of people use it for information and reference. Ten percent use it to access online magazines.[13] The fact that many Internet users use the technology as a source of information is important for marketers, especially those selling goods and services that require extensive information searches. Auto or real estate purchases fall into this category. Purchasers of mutual funds are renowned "information hounds," who conduct extensive comparisons among competing products.

Although many consumers use the Internet in the information search stage of the purchase process, few use it in the final step in the transaction process for several reasons. People are worried about providing their credit card numbers when making an Internet purchase. Since consumers can't see or touch a product offered for sale over the Internet, they fear they will have little recourse if the product they order isn't the right one, isn't delivered, or arrives broken. Consumers also have privacy concerns: They are concerned that the information they provide when making a purchase or requesting information may be sold or given to another organization without their permission.

How does being part of the Internet generation affect Jennifer Wong and her purchase decision? Jennifer is highly computer literate. She uses a computer daily at work, carries a laptop when attending meetings, and has a computer in her apartment. One of the first things she did when considering a motorcycle purchase was to log on to the Internet. She learned a great deal simply by browsing the sites of such manufacturers as Honda, Yamaha, and Harley-Davidson. She especially liked the Harley site and the annual events listed for Harley owners. She was concerned that most of these events took place in the United States, however. Using their response button, she requested information on dealers in her area and information about specific models. Jennifer also found several chat groups and posted questions to members of these groups, especially female riders.

Social classes Relatively permanent and ordered divisions in a society whose members share similar values, interests, and behaviours.

Social Class Almost every society has some form of social class structure. **Social classes** are society's relatively permanent and ordered divisions whose members share similar values, interests, and behaviours. Social class is determined by a combination of occupation, income, education, wealth, and other variables. In some social systems, members of different classes are reared for certain roles and cannot change their social positions. In Canada, however, the lines between social classes are not fixed and rigid: People can move to a higher social class or drop into a lower one. Marketers are interested in social class because people within a given social class tend to exhibit similar buying behaviour, showing distinct product and brand preferences in areas such as clothing, home furnishings, leisure activity, and automobiles.

In 2000, Compusearch Micromarketing and Data Systems conducted a study that allowed them to develop profiles of the top five percent of the Canadian population.[14] They grouped households based on such factors as average household income, education, and house value. The resulting 12 distinct profiles allow marketers to gain insights about groups' lifestyles, geographic locations, and media habits. For example, Compusearch labelled one group "Asian Heights" after the people of Chinese origin that compose its membership. They have large families, live in heavily mortgaged homes, attend fashion shows, enjoy eating exotic foods, and love to buy home entertainment equipment. Many are two-income families who balance the stress of commuting with the stress of their managerial and white-collar jobs.

Jennifer Wong's social class may affect her motorcycle decision. As a member of the Asian Heights group, Jennifer finds herself frequently buying brand-name products that are fashionable and popular with her friends and extended family.

Social Factors A consumer's behaviour also is influenced by social factors, such as membership in *small groups* and *family*, and *social roles* and *status*.

Groups A person's behaviour is influenced by many small **groups**. Groups that have a direct influence and to which a person belongs are called *membership groups*. Some are *primary groups* with which a person has regular but informal interaction—such as family, friends, neighbours, and co-workers. A person also has less regular interaction with the more formal *secondary groups*—organizations such as religious groups, professional associations, and trade unions.

Group Two or more people who interact to accomplish individual or mutual goals.

Reference groups serve as direct (face-to-face) or indirect points of comparison or reference in forming a person's attitudes or behaviour. People often are influenced by reference groups to which they do not belong. For example, an *aspirational group* is one to which the individual wants or aspires to belong. For example, a teenage hockey player hopes to play someday for the Montreal Canadiens: He identifies with this group, although there is no face-to-face contact between him and the team. Marketers try to identify the reference groups of their target markets. Reference groups expose a person to new behaviours and lifestyles, influence the person's attitudes and self-concept, and create pressures to conform that may affect the person's product and brand choices.

The importance of group influence varies across products and brands. It tends to be strongest when the product is visible to others whom the buyer respects. Purchases of products that are bought and used privately are not much affected by group influences because neither the product nor the brand will be noticed by others. Manufacturers of products and brands subjected to strong group influence must figure out how to reach **opinion leaders**, people within a reference group who, because of special skills, knowledge, personality, or other characteristics, exert influence on others.

Opinion leader A person within a reference group who, because of special skills, knowledge, personality, or other characteristics, exerts influence on others.

Many marketers try to identify opinion leaders for their products, so that they can direct marketing efforts toward them. In other cases, they create advertisements to simulate opinion leadership, thereby reducing the need for consumers to seek advice from others. For example, the hottest trends in teenage music, language, and fashion often start in Canada in major cities, then quickly spread to more mainstream youth in the suburbs. Thus, clothing companies who hope to appeal to these fickle and fashion-conscious youth often make a concerted effort to monitor urban opinion leaders' style and behaviour. Levi-Strauss is a good example:

In recent years, Levi-Strauss has been squeezed by the competition as teens and youth flock to designer labels and more "cool" brands. To revitalize sales for its Silver Tab line of clothing, the company's ad agency sent out employees to build a network of contacts familiar with the urban scene, including club-hoppers, stylists, photographers, and disk jockeys. The agency kept a scrap-book of people and looks and separated them into "tribes" defined by the music they like, including electronica, hip-hop and rap, and retro soul music.

Its illustrated ads appealing to hip-hop and rap culture featured the statement "It's bangin', son," which means "cool," and teenagers clad in Silver Tab clothing—baggy pants, hip huggers, tiny tops—and wearing accessories such as nose rings, beepers, and chunky gold jewellery.[15]

If Jennifer Wong buys a motorcycle, both the product and the brand will be visible to others she respects. Therefore, her decision to buy the motorcycle and her brand choice may be influenced strongly by some of her groups, such as friends who belong to a weekend motorcycle club. Jennifer often feels left out when these friends leave for weekend road trips.

Family Marketers have extensively researched the family, the most important consumer buying organization in society. Since family members can have a strong influence on buyer behaviour, marketers are interested in the roles and influence of the husband, wife, and children on the purchase of different products and services.

Husband–wife involvement depends on product category and on stage in the buying process. Buying roles change with evolving consumer lifestyles. In Canada and the United States, the wife has traditionally been the main purchasing agent for the family, especially for food, household products, and clothing. But with 70 percent of women holding jobs outside the home and the willingness of husbands to do more of the family's purchasing, this is changing. For example, women buy about 45 percent of all cars and men account for about 40 percent of food-shopping dollars.[16] Many teenagers are now responsible for doing the grocery shopping. Because these roles depend on ethnicity and social classes, as always, marketers must research specific patterns in their target markets.

Changes in family buying behaviour suggest that marketers who've typically sold their products to only women or only men are now courting the opposite sex. For example, consider the hardware business:

Women now account for nearly half of all hardware-store purchases. Home improvement retailer Builders Square identified this trend early and has capitalized on it by turning what had been an intimidating warehouse into a user-friendly retail outlet. The new Builders Square II outlets feature decorator design centres at the front of the store. To attract more women to these stores, Builders Square runs ads targeting women in *Home, House Beautiful, Woman's Day,* and *Better Homes and Gardens.* The retailer even offers bridal registries. Says a marketing director at Builders Square, "It's more meaningful to them to have a great patio set or gas grill than to have fine china."[17]

Children can also have a strong influence on family buying decisions. Chevrolet recognizes these influences in marketing its Chevy Venture minivan:

In an issue of *Sports Illustrated for Kids,* which attracts mostly 8- to 14-year-old boys, the inside cover featured a brightly coloured two-page spread for the Chevy Venture to woo [what it calls] "back-seat consumers." [GM] is sending the minivan into malls and showing previews of Disney's *Hercules* on a VCR inside. "We're kidding ourselves when we think kids aren't aware of brands,"

Children can have a strong influence on family buying decisions. Chevrolet actively woos these "back-seat consumers" with carefully targeted advertising and a Chevy Venture Warner Bros. Edition, complete with a DVD player.

says [Venture's brand manager], adding that even she was surprised at how often parents told her that kids played a tie-breaking role in deciding which car to buy.[18]

In the case of expensive products and services, husbands and wives more often make joint decisions. Although Jennifer isn't married, her boyfriend will influence her choice. He purchased a motorcycle last year and really loves it. Since he rarely lets Jennifer drive it, she really relates to the slogan on the new Harley-Davidson ads, which feature women, proclaiming, "You never took a back seat before!"

Roles and Status A person belongs to many groups: family, clubs, organizations. The person's position in each group can be defined in terms of both role and status. A *role* comprises the activities that others expect from the person. Each role carries a *status* reflecting the general esteem society gives it. People often choose products that show their status in society. Jennifer occupies many roles simultaneously. In her role as a daughter, she has lower status than her parents and grandparents, so she often acquiesces to their opinions with respect to family matters. In her role as a brand manager, Jennifer has high status and assumes a leadership role in her brand group. Jennifer also wants to be a leader in her social activities and often organizes group activities. Her desire to be a leader causes her to identify with leading status brands such as Harley-Davidson.

Personal Factors A buyer's decisions also are influenced by personal characteristics such as the buyer's *age* and *life-cycle stage, occupation, economic situation, lifestyle,* and *personality* and *self-concept.*

Age and Life-Cycle Stage People change their preferences in the goods and services they buy over their lifetimes. Tastes in food, clothes, furniture, and recreation are often age related. Buying is also shaped by the stage of the *family life cycle*—the stages through which families might pass as they mature over time. Marketers often define their target markets in terms of life-cycle stage and develop appropriate products and marketing plans for each stage. Traditional family life-cycle stages include young singles and married couples with children. Today, however, marketers are increasingly catering to a growing number of alternative, nontraditional stages such as unmarried couples, singles marrying later in life, childfree couples, same-sex couples, single parents, extended parents (those with young adult children returning home), and others.

Occupation People's occupations affect the goods and services they buy. Blue-collar workers tend to buy more rugged work clothes, whereas executives buy more business suits. Marketers try to identify the occupational groups that have an above-average interest in their products and services. A company can even specialize in making products needed by a given occupational group. Thus, computer software companies will design different products for brand managers, accountants, engineers, lawyers, and doctors.

Economic Situation A person's economic situation will affect product choice. Marketers of income-sensitive goods watch trends in personal income, savings, and interest rates. If economic indicators point to a recession, marketers can take steps to redesign, reposition, and reprice their products.

Lifestyle People coming from the same subculture, social class, and occupation may have quite different lifestyles. A **lifestyle** is a person's pattern of living as expressed in his or her *psychographics*. It involves measuring consumers' major *AIO dimensions: activities* (work, hobbies, shopping, sports, social events), *interests* (food, fashion, family, recreation), and *opinions* (about themselves, social issues, business, products). Lifestyle captures something more than the person's social class or personality. It profiles a person's whole pattern of acting and interacting in the world.

Several research firms have developed lifestyle classifications. The most widely used is the SRI Consulting's *Values and Lifestyles (VALS)* typology. VALS classifies people according to how they spend their time and money. It divides consumers into eight groups based on two major dimensions: self-orientation and resources.

Lifestyle segmentation can also be used to understand Internet behaviour. Forrester developed its "Technographics" scheme, which segments consumers according to motivation, desire, and ability to invest in technology.[19] The framework splits people into 10 categories, such as

Fast Forwards: The biggest spenders on computer technology. Fast Forwards are early adopters of new technology for home, office, and personal use.

Mouse Potatoes: Consumers who are dedicated to interactive entertainment and willing to spend for the latest in "technotainment."

Handshakers: Older consumers, typically managers, who don't touch computers at work and leave that to younger assistants.

These lifestyle classifications are by no means universal—they can vary significantly among countries. Michael Adams, president of Environics Research Group

Lifestyle A person's pattern of living as expressed in his or her activities, interests, and opinions.

Ltd., wrote *Sex in the Snow: Canadian Social Values at the End of the Millennium* to capture significant psychographic changes in the Canadian marketplace. He believes that psychographic changes eclipse demographic factors among Canadians. While his classification system begins with demographic factors, he divides the Canadian population along age-based lines into three groups: those over 50, baby boomers, and Generation Xers. Furthermore, he asserts that 12 value-based "tribes" exist within these broader groups. Table 6-2 provides descriptions of these groups.

When used carefully, the lifestyle concept can help the marketer understand changing consumer values and how they affect buying behaviour.

For example, lifestyle information has helped marketers of cellular phones target consumers. Although early users of the products were often corporate executives and salespeople who used their cars as their offices, later users often bought cellular phones for quite different reasons.[20] For example, although 46 percent of Bell Mobility's customers still cite business reasons as their primary motivation for purchasing a cellular phone, 34 percent now say they bought them for safety reasons. Another 19 percent of users purchased mobile phones just for convenience.

Personality and Self-Concept Each person's distinct personality influences his or her buying behaviour. *Personality* refers to the unique psychological characteristics that lead to relatively consistent and lasting responses to one's own environment. Personality is usually described in terms of traits such as self-confidence, dominance, sociability, autonomy, defensiveness, adaptability, and aggressiveness. Personality can be useful in analyzing consumer behaviour for certain product or brand choices. For example, coffee marketers have discovered that heavy coffee drinkers tend to be high on sociability. Thus, to attract customers, Starbucks and other coffeehouses create environments in which people can relax and socialize over a cup of steaming coffee.

Many marketers use a concept related to personality—a person's *self-concept* (also called *self-image*). The basic self-concept premise is that people's possessions contribute to and reflect their identities; that is, "we are what we have." Thus, to understand consumer behaviour, the marketer must first understand the relationship between consumer self-concept and possessions. For example, the founder and

Heavy coffee drinkers tend to be high on sociability, so coffeehouses create environments in which people can relax and socialize over a cup of steaming coffee.

Table 6-2   The Social Value Groups of Canada

Groups	% Pop. & Size	Motivators	Values	Exemplar
The Elders:				
Rational Traditionalists	15% 3.5M	Financial independence, stability, and security.	Value safety, reason, tradition, and authority. Religious.	Winston Churchill
Extroverted Traditionalists	7% 1.7M	Traditional communities and institutions. Social status.	Value tradition, duty, family, and institutions. Religious.	Jean Chrétien
Cosmopolitan Modernists	6% 1.4M	Traditional institutions. Nomadic, experience seeking.	Education, affluence, innovation, progress, self-confidence, world perspective.	Pierre Trudeau
The Boomers:				
Disengaged Darwinists	18% 4.3M	Financial independence, stability, and security.	Self-preservation, nostalgia for the past.	Mike Harris
Autonomous Rebels	10% 2.4M	Personal autonomy, self-fulfillment, and new experiences.	Egalitarian, abhor corruption, personal fulfillment, education. Suspicion of authority and big government.	John Lennon
Anxious Communitarians	9% 2.1M	Traditional communities, big government, and social status.	Family, community, generosity, duty. Needs self-respect. Fearful.	Martha Stewart
The Gen-Xers:				
Aimless Dependents	8% 1.9M	Financial independence, stability, security. Fearful.	Desire for independence. Disengagement.	Courtney Love
Thrill-Seeking Materialists	7% 1.7M	Traditional communities, social status, experience-seeking.	Money, material possessions, recognition, living dangerously	Calvin Klein
Autonomous Postmaterialists	6% 1.4M	Personal autonomy and self-fulfillment.	Freedom, human rights, egalitarian, quality of life.	Bart Simpson
Social Hedonists	4$ .9M	Experience seeking, new communities.	Esthetics, hedonism, sexual freedom, instant gratification.	Janet Jackson
New Aquarians	4% .9M	Experience seeking, new communities.	Ecologism, hedonism.	Tori Amos

chief executive of Barnes & Noble, one of the largest booksellers in the United States, notes that people buy books to support their self-images:

People have the mistaken notion that the thing you do with books is read them. Wrong.... People buy books for what the purchase says about them— their taste, their cultivation, their trendiness. Their aim...is to connect themselves, or those to whom they give the books as gifts, with all the other refined owners of Edgar Allen Poe collections or sensitive owners of Virginia Woolf collections.... [The result is that] you can sell books as consumer products, with seductive displays, flashy posters, an emphasis on the glamour of the book, and the fashionableness of the bestseller and the trendy author.[21]

Jennifer Wong falls into Michael Adams's psychographic category of thrill-seeking materialists. Since she values material possessions, recognition, and the idea of living dangerously, owning a motorcycle instead of a traditional car appeals to her. Since her personality is outgoing, daring, and active, she will favour a mode of transportation that projects the same qualities.

Psychological Factors A person's buying choices are further influenced by four major psychological factors: *motivation*, *perception*, *learning*, and *beliefs* and *attitudes*.

Motivation We know that Jennifer Wong is interested in buying a motorcycle. Why? What is she *really* seeking? What *needs* is she trying to satisfy?

A person has many needs at any given time. Some are *biological*, arising from states of tension such as hunger, thirst, or discomfort. Others are *psychological*, arising from the need for recognition, esteem, or belonging. A need becomes a *motive* when it is aroused to a sufficient level of intensity. A **motive** (or *drive*) is a need that is sufficiently pressing to direct the person to seek satisfaction. Psychologists have developed theories of human motivation. Two of the most popular—the theories of Sigmund Freud and Abraham Maslow—have quite different meanings for consumer analysis and marketing.

> **Motive (drive)** A need that is sufficiently pressing to direct the person to seek satisfaction of the need.

Sigmund Freud assumed that people are largely unconscious of the real psychological forces shaping their behaviour. He saw the person as growing up and repressing many urges. These urges are never eliminated or under perfect control; they emerge in dreams, in slips of the tongue, in neurotic and obsessive behaviour, or in psychoses. Thus, Freud suggested that a person does not fully understand his or her motivations. Motivation researchers collect in-depth information from small samples of consumers to uncover the deeper motives for their product choices.

Abraham Maslow sought to explain why people are driven by particular needs at particular times. Why does one person spend much time and energy on personal safety and another on gaining the esteem of others? Maslow's answer is that human needs are arranged in a hierarchy, as shown in Figure 6-3, from the most pressing at the bottom to the least pressing at the top. They include *physiological* needs, *safety* needs, *social* needs, *esteem* needs, and *self-actualization* needs. A person tries to satisfy the most important need first. When that need is satisfied, it will stop being a motivator and the person will then try to satisfy the next most important need. For example, starving people (physiological need) will not take an interest in the latest happenings in the art world (self-actualization needs), nor in how

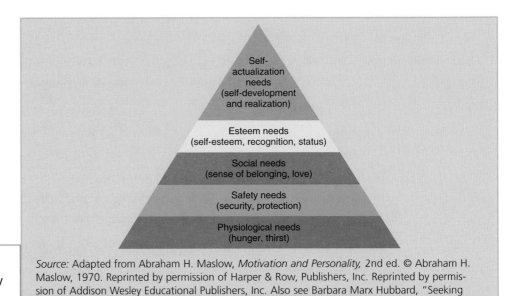

Figure 6-3

Maslow's Hierarchy of Needs

Source: Adapted from Abraham H. Maslow, *Motivation and Personality,* 2nd ed. © Abraham H. Maslow, 1970. Reprinted by permission of Harper & Row, Publishers, Inc. Reprinted by permission of Addison Wesley Educational Publishers, Inc. Also see Barbara Marx Hubbard, "Seeking Our Future Potentials," *The Futurist,* May 1998, pp. 29–32.

they are seen or esteemed by others (social or esteem needs), nor even in whether they are breathing clean air (safety needs). But as each important need is satisfied, the next most important need will come into play.

What light does Maslow's theory throw on Jennifer Wong's interest in buying a motorcycle? We can guess that Jennifer has satisfied her physiological, safety, and social needs; they do not motivate her interest in motorcycles. Her interest may come from a strong need for more esteem from others. Or it may come from a need for self-actualization—she may want to be a daring person and express herself through product ownership.

Perception A motivated person is ready to act. How the person acts is influenced by his or her own perception of the situation. We all learn by using the flow of information through our five senses: sight, hearing, smell, touch, and taste. However, we each receive, organize, and interpret this sensory information in an individual way. **Perception** is the process by which people select, organize, and interpret information to form a meaningful picture of the world.

People can form different perceptions of the same stimulus because of three perceptual processes: selective attention, selective distortion, and selective retention. People are exposed to a great amount of stimuli every day. For example, the average person may be exposed to more than 1500 ads in a single day. It is impossible for a person to pay attention to all these stimuli. *Selective attention*—the tendency for people to screen out most of the information to which they are exposed—means that marketers have to work especially hard to attract the consumer's attention.

Even noted stimuli do not always come across in the intended way. Each person fits incoming information into an existing mind-set. *Selective distortion* describes the tendency of people to interpret information in a way that will support what they already believe. Selective distortion means that marketers must try to understand the mind-sets of consumers and how these will affect interpretations of advertising and sales information.

Perception The process by which people select, organize, and interpret information to form a meaningful picture of the world.

People also will forget much of what they learn. They tend to retain information that supports their attitudes and beliefs. Because of *selective retention,* Jennifer is likely to remember good points made about Harleys and to forget good points made about competing motorcycles. Because of selective exposure, distortion, and retention, marketers have to work hard to get their messages through. This fact explains why marketers use so much drama and repetition in sending messages to their market.

Interestingly, although most marketers worry about whether their offers will be perceived at all, some consumers worry that they will be affected by marketing messages without even knowing it—through *subliminal advertising.* In 1957, a researcher announced that he had flashed the phrases "Eat popcorn" and "Drink Coca-Cola" on a screen in a New Jersey movie theatre every five seconds for 1/300th of a second. He reported that although viewers did not consciously recognize these messages, they absorbed them subconsciously and bought 58 percent more popcorn and 18 percent more Coke. Suddenly advertisers and consumer-protection groups became intensely interested in subliminal perception. People voiced fears of being brainwashed, and California and Canada declared the practice illegal. Although the researcher later admitted to making up the data, the issue has not died. Some consumers still fear that they are being manipulated by subliminal messages.

Numerous studies by psychologists and consumer researchers have *not* found a link between subliminal messages and consumer behaviour. It appears that subliminal advertising simply doesn't have the power attributed to it by its critics. Most advertisers scoff at the notion of an industry conspiracy to manipulate consumers through "invisible" messages.

Learning When people act, they learn. **Learning** describes changes in an individual's behaviour arising from experience. Learning theorists say that most human behaviour is learned. Learning occurs through the interplay of *drives, stimuli, cues, responses,* and *reinforcement.*

> **Learning** Changes in an individual's behaviour arising from experience.

We saw that Jennifer Wong has a drive for self-actualization. A *drive* is a strong internal stimulus that calls for action. Her drive becomes a motive when it is directed toward a particular *stimulus object,* in this case a motorcycle. Jennifer's response to the idea of buying a motorcycle is conditioned by the surrounding cues. *Cues* are minor stimuli that determine when, where, and how the person responds. Seeing motorcycles roaring along the Toronto streets, hearing about Harley's 75th anniversary special edition cycle, and receiving her boyfriend's support for buying her own motorcycle are all *cues* that can influence Jennifer's *response* to her interest in buying a motorcycle.

Suppose Jennifer buys a Harley. If she attends the company's weekend events, makes new friends, and simply enjoys riding the bike around Toronto, her decision will be reinforced. If she decides to upgrade from her first bike to a more upscale model, the probability is greater that she will buy another Harley.

The practical significance of learning theory for marketers is that they can build up demand for a product by associating it with strong drives, using motivating cues, and providing positive reinforcement.

Beliefs and Attitudes Through doing and learning, people acquire beliefs and attitudes. These, in turn, influence their buying behaviour. A **belief** is a descriptive

> **Belief** A descriptive thought that a person holds about something.

thought that a person has about something. These beliefs may be based on real knowledge, opinion, or faith, and may or may not carry an emotional charge.

Marketers are interested in the beliefs that people formulate about specific products and services, because these beliefs make up product and brand images that affect buying behaviour. If some of the beliefs are wrong and prevent purchase, the marketer will want to launch a campaign to correct them.

People have attitudes regarding religion, politics, clothes, music, food, and almost everything else. **Attitude** describes a person's relatively consistent evaluations, feelings, and tendencies toward an object or idea. Attitudes put people into a frame of mind of liking or disliking things, of moving toward or away from them. Attitudes are difficult to change. A person's attitudes fit into a pattern, and to change one attitude may require difficult adjustments in many others. Thus, a company should usually try to fit its products into existing attitudes rather than attempt to change attitudes. Of course, there are exceptions in which the great cost of trying to change attitudes may pay off handsomely.

Attitude A person's consistently favourable or unfavourable evaluations, feelings, and tendencies toward an object or idea.

An unspoken rule in food marketing is to avoid using newspaper ads. "Given the general standard of newsprint reproduction, that tempting plate of pasta is likely to wind up with all the appetite appeal of a used muffler." But breaking the rules helped the Quebec Milk Producers (La Fédération des Producteurs de Lait du Quebec) change the attitude of adults over 30 and get them back into the habit of drinking milk. And non-traditional, newspaper advertising proved to be the best way to reach this older target audience on a daily basis. In contrast to other newspaper advertising that tends to be visually clamorous and overloaded with information, the Quebec Milk Producers kept their ads relatively clean and uncluttered, and, thus, they gave themselves a better shot at standing out. Since adults already knew the health benefits of milk, creators of the campaign decided to take a different tack and decided to play upon the consumer's emotional connection with the product. Each ad showed milk in a simple, highly recognized receptacle—a glass, jug, carton, plastic container, and a baby bottle—on a white background. Each photo was overlaid by a catchy phrase. It was these headlines—"What your inner child is thirsting for," "Remember, you used to cry for it," "The mother of all beverages"—that made an emotional connection between these adult consumers and the product. Was the campaign a success? Not only did it win five Coq d'Or awards, it was "the first time in 25 years of working in advertising that I've ever gotten so many calls and letters from people saying they love our campaign," says Nicole Dubé, director of advertising and promotions for the milk marketers at La Fédération des Producteurs de Lait du Québec.[22]

Like the Quebec adults who changed their attitudes about drinking more milk after seeing a great ad campaign, Jennifer Wong responded to the Harley ad discussed earlier in this chapter. The headline grabbed her attention. Like the women shown in the ad photo, Jennifer "never took a back seat before." She is more inclined than ever to go and buy a Harley.

each source. Consumers should be asked how they first heard about the brand, what information they received, and what importance they placed on different information sources.

Evaluation of Alternatives We have seen how the consumer uses information to arrive at a set of final brand choices. How does the consumer choose among the alternative brands? The marketer needs to know about alternative evaluation—that is, how the consumer processes information to arrive at brand choices. Unfortunately, consumers do not use a simple and single evaluation process in all buying situations. Instead, several evaluation processes are at work.

The consumer arrives at attitudes toward different brands through some evaluation procedure. How consumers go about evaluating purchase alternatives depends on the individual consumer and the specific buying situation. In some cases, consumers use careful calculations and logical thinking. At other times, the same consumers do little or no evaluating; instead they buy on impulse and rely on intuition. Sometimes consumers make buying decisions on their own; sometimes they turn to friends, consumer guides, or salespeople for buying advice.

Suppose Jennifer has narrowed her choices to four motorcycles. And suppose that she is primarily interested in four attributes—quality, ease of handling, ergonomic design, and price. Jennifer has formed beliefs about how each brand rates on each attribute. The marketer wants to predict which motorcycle Jennifer will buy.

Clearly, if one motorcycle rated best on all the attributes, we could predict that Jennifer would choose it. But the brands vary in appeal. Some buyers will base their buying decision on only one attribute, and their choices are easy to predict. If Jennifer wants ease of handling above everything, she will buy the motorcycle that rates highest on this attribute. But most buyers consider several attributes, each with different importance. If we knew the importance weights that Jennifer assigns to each of the four attributes, we could predict her motorcycle choice more reliably.

Marketers should study buyers to determine how they actually evaluate brand alternatives. If they know what evaluative processes go on, marketers can take steps to influence the buyer's decision. Motorcycle manufacturers that want to appeal directly to female riders can design products to appeal specifically to them. Models such as Harley's Sportster 883 Hugger are lighter in weight than some of their traditional models, with higher seats and easier handling. The company has also moved away from traditional motorcycle colours to power colours such as red. At the same time, the firm has retained traditional features such as Harley's unique engine, so "the streets never sound the same."

Purchase Decision In the evaluation stage, the consumer ranks brands and forms purchase intentions. Generally, the consumer's purchase decision will be to buy the most preferred brand, but two factors can come between the purchase *intention* and the purchase *decision*. The first factor is the *attitudes of others*. If Jennifer's friends ride Honda motorcycles, chances of her buying a Harley will be reduced.

The second factor is *unexpected situational factors*. The consumer may form a purchase intention based on factors such as expected income, expected price, and expected product benefits. However, unexpected events may change the purchase intention. Jennifer may lose her job, some other purchase may become more urgent, or a friend may report being disappointed in her preferred motorcycle. Thus, preferences and even purchase intentions do not always result in actual purchase choice.

Postpurchase Behaviour The marketer's job does not end when the product is bought. After purchasing the product, the consumer will be satisfied or dissatisfied and will engage in postpurchase behaviour of interest to the marketer. What determines whether the buyer is satisfied or dissatisfied with a purchase? The answer lies in the relationship between the *consumer's expectations* and the product's *perceived performance*. If the product falls short of expectations, the consumer is disappointed; if it meets expectations, the consumer is satisfied; if it exceeds expectations, the consumer is delighted.

The larger the gap between expectations and performance, the greater the consumer's dissatisfaction. This suggests that sellers should make product claims that faithfully represent the product's performance so that buyers are satisfied. Some sellers might even understate performance levels to boost consumer satisfaction with the product. For example, Boeing's salespeople tend to be conservative when they estimate the potential benefits of their aircraft. They almost always underestimate fuel efficiency—they promise a 5 percent savings that turns out to be 8 percent. Customers are delighted with better-than-expected performance; they buy again and tell other potential customers that Boeing lives up to its promises.

Almost all major purchases result in **cognitive dissonance**, or discomfort caused by postpurchase conflict. After the purchase, consumers are satisfied with the benefits of the chosen brand and are glad to have avoided the drawbacks of the brands not bought. However, every purchase involves compromise. Consumers feel uneasy about acquiring the drawbacks of the chosen brand and about losing the benefits of the brands not purchased. Thus, consumers feel at least some postpurchase dissonance for every purchase.[23]

Why is it so important to satisfy the customer? Such satisfaction is important because a company's sales come from two basic groups—*new customers* and *retained customers*. It usually costs more to attract new customers than to retain current ones, and the best way to retain current customers is to keep them satisfied. Customer satisfaction is a key to making lasting connections with consumers—to keeping and growing consumers and reaping their customer lifetime value. Satisfied customers buy a product again, talk favourably to others about the product, pay less attention to competing brands and advertising, and buy other products from the company. Many marketers go beyond merely *meeting* the expectations of customers—they aim to *delight* the customer.

A dissatisfied consumer responds differently. Whereas, on average, a satisfied customer tells 3 people about a good product experience, a dissatisfied customer gripes to 11 people. In fact, one study showed that 13 percent of the people who had a problem with an organization complained about the company to more than 20 people.[24] Clearly, negative word of mouth travels farther and faster than positive word of mouth and can quickly damage consumer attitudes about a company and its products.

Therefore, a company would be wise to measure customer satisfaction regularly. It cannot simply rely on dissatisfied customers to volunteer their complaints when

Cognitive dissonance
Buyer discomfort caused by postpurchase conflict.

they are dissatisfied. Some 96 percent of unhappy customers never tell the company about their problem. Companies should set up systems that *encourage* customers to complain. In this way, the company can learn how well it is doing and how it can improve (see New Directions 6-1). The 3M Company claims that over two-thirds of its new-product ideas come from listening to customer complaints. But listening is not enough—the company also must respond constructively to the complaints it receives.

By studying the overall buyer decision, marketers may be able to find ways to help consumers move through it. For example, if consumers are not buying a new product because they do not perceive a need for it, marketing might launch advertising messages that trigger the need and show how the product solves customers' problems. If customers know about the product but are not buying because they hold unfavourable attitudes toward it, the marketer must find ways to either change the product or change consumer perceptions.

New Directions 6-1 >>   **Got a Problem? Just Phone, Fax, E-Mail or "Teleweb" Us!**

What should companies do with dissatisfied customers? Everything they can! Unhappy customers not only stop buying, but they can also quickly damage the company's image. Studies show that customers tell many more people about bad experiences than about good ones. However, dealing effectively with gripes can actually boost customer loyalty and the company's image. Enlightened companies don't try to hide from dissatisfied customers; they go out of their way to encourage customers to complain, then bend over backward to make disgruntled buyers happy again.

The first opportunity to handle gripes often comes at the point of purchase. Many firms teach their customer contact people how to resolve problems and defuse customer anger. However, most companies have also set up call centres and Web sites to coax out and deal with consumer problems and questions.

Today, more than two thirds of all North American manufacturers offer toll-free numbers to handle complaints, inquiries, and orders. For example, in its first 10 years, the Gerber help line (1-800-GERBER) received more than four million calls. Help line staffers, most of them mothers or grandmothers themselves, handle customer concerns and provide baby care advice 24 hours a day, 365 days a

Gerber help line staffers, most of them mothers or grandmothers themselves, handle customer concerns and provide baby care advice 24 hours a day, 365 days a year, to more than 2400 callers a day.

year, to more than 2400 callers a day. The help line is staffed by English-speaking, French-speaking, and Spanish-speaking operators, and interpreters are available for most other languages. Callers include new parents, day care providers, and even health professionals. One in five calls to the help line comes from men. Callers ask a wide variety of questions, from when to feed a baby specific foods to how to babyproof a home.

"It used to be that mom or grandmom was right around the corner to answer your baby questions," notes the manager of the Gerber help line. "But more and more, that's not the case. For new or expectant parents, it's nice to know that they can pick up the phone any time of the day and talk to someone that understands and can help."

General Electric's Answer Center may be one of the most extensive 800-number systems. It handles more than three million calls a year, only 5 percent of them complaints. At the heart of the system is a giant database that provides the centre's service reps with instant access to more than a million answers to questions about 8500 models in 120 product lines. The centre receives some unusual calls, as when a submarine crew off the Connecticut coast requested help fixing a motor. Still, according to GE, its people resolve 90 percent of complaints or inquiries on the first call, and complainers often become even more loyal customers. Although the company spends an average of $5 per call, it reaps two to three times that much in new sales and warranty savings. GE has also set up the GE Online Answer Center at **www.ge.com/oac** to help customers obtain information about its products and services, locate dealers, and get answers to frequently requested topics.

As Susan Leigh, marketing and communications manager for Bell Canada's Contact Centre Solutions Team notes, call centres themselves have evolved dramatically. Instead of just being a bank of phones staffed by people who receive complaints, they've become high-tech and high-touch operations that help companies to keep customers from defecting, lure customers from the competition, target the most profitable customers, and increase repeat customer purchases. Traditional call centres have grown into sophisticated technology-driven *contact centres* that are the hub of the enterprise and the focal point for managing customer relationships.

Today, enabled by computer-telephone integration, companies use their contact centres to leverage existing customer information to enhance, maintain, and manage customer relationships throughout their life cycles. Today's multimedia contact centres can be accessed through the Internet and a host of other vehicles—interactive video kiosks, telephone, e-mail, and fax. The idea is to make customers' interactions with companies seamless and uniform, no matter which form of communication they choose.

Integrate the telephone—long a medium for developing customer relationships—with Web technology and you have a "teleweb" connection, a powerful means of handling customer questions and concerns. This technology lets a customer browse a Web site on a PC at the same time that a customer service agent browses the site. The two can talk over a separate telephone line or an Internet connection to discuss problems or compare products. Operators can synchronize the Web screens viewed by a company's agents and their customers as they talk. The technology even lets either party draw circles around words or pictures for both to see. This may not seem like a big deal, but in discussions about a complex technological device, it helps if customer and agent are viewing a common diagram.

Bell helps its clients develop and improve their customer contact centres. Experience has shown that building a contact centre can spearhead enormous changes in the way a firm delivers its services and relates to its customers. With Bell's help, a firm's contact centre can anticipate and respond to shifts in customer needs and preferences while reducing costs and increasing revenues. Leigh notes that contact centres have become critical to customer-focused business strategies and are often the differentiating factor that allows a company to gain a significant competitive advantage. "For instance, a sudden spike in calls to a customer service number often suggests breakdowns elsewhere in the organization, perhaps in quality control, marketing, or shipping," Leigh suggests. "If companies don't bother to find out why their customer service agents are suddenly swamped, they may never address the root of the problem."

The best way to keep customers happy is to provide good products and services in the first place. Short of that, however, a company must develop a good system for ferreting out problems and connecting with customers. Such a system is much more than just unavoidable—customer happiness usually shows up on the company's bottom line. One recent study found that dollars invested in complaint-handling and customer contact systems yield an average return of between 100 and 200 percent. Maryanne Rasmussen, vice president of worldwide quality at American Express, offers this formula: "Better complaint handling equals higher customer satisfaction equals higher brand loyalty equals higher performance."

Today's business-to-business marketers, such as Bell, go out of their way to give customers every opportunity for contact. For example, Indus International, a maker of enterprise asset management software, launched CareNet, a Web site designed to boost retention by simplifying customer contact. The site lets clients access product information, pose questions to service reps, and find solutions to specific problems. Customers are also encouraged

to give feedback on the Web and post solutions to production problems. So far, Indus's clients are impressed. CareNet had 30 users in its first month, but this number jumped to 600 just 10 months later.

Sources: Quotes from Susan Leigh, "Customer Contact Centres a Tool for Growth," *Strategy,* 7 June 1999, p. D14; Ziff Communications, "On Mother's Day, Advice Goes a Long Way," *PR Newswire,* 2 May 1995; Alessandra Bianchi, "Lines of Fire," *Inc. Technology,* 1988, pp. 36–48; and Matt Hamblen, "Call Centers and Web Sites Cozy Up," *Computerworld,* 2 March 1998, p. 1. Also see Roland T. Rust, Bala Subramanian, and Mark Wells, "Making Complaints a Management tool," *Marketing Management,* Fall 1992, pp. 41–45; Tibbett L. Speer, "They Complain Because They Care," *American Demographics,* May 1996, pp. 13–14; John F. Yarbrough, "Dialing for dollars," *Sales & Marketing Management,* January 1997, pp. 60–67; Geoffrey Brewer, "The Customer Stops Here," *Sales & Marketing Management,* March 1998, pp. 31–36; and Marcia Stepanek, "You'll Wanna Hold Their Hands," *Business Week,* 22 March 1999, pp. EB30–EB31.

The Buyer Decision Process for New Products

We have looked at the stages buyers go through in trying to satisfy a need. Buyers may pass quickly or slowly through these stages, and some of the stages may even be reversed. Much depends on the nature of the buyer, the product, and the buying situation.

We now look at how buyers approach the purchase of new products. A **new product** is a good, service, or idea that is perceived by some potential customers as new. It may have been around for a while, but our interest is in how consumers learn about products for the first time and make decisions on whether to adopt them. We define the **adoption process** as "the mental process through which an individual passes from first learning about an innovation to final adoption," and *adoption* as the decision by an individual to become a regular user of the product.[25]

New product A good, service, or idea that is perceived by some potential customers as new.

Adoption process The mental process through which an individual passes from first hearing about an innovation to final adoption.

Stages in the Adoption Process Consumers go through five stages in the process of adopting a new product:

1. *Awareness:* The consumer becomes aware of the new product but lacks information about it.

2. *Interest:* The consumer seeks information about the new product.

3. *Evaluation:* The consumer considers whether trying the new product makes sense.

4. *Trial:* The consumer tries the new product on a small scale to improve his or her estimate of its value.

5. *Adoption:* The consumer decides to make full and regular use of the new product.

This model suggests that the new-product marketer should think about how to help consumers move through these stages. A manufacturer of large-screen televisions may discover that many consumers in the interest stage do not move to the trial stage because of uncertainty and the large investment. If these same consumers were willing to use a large-screen television on a trial basis for a small fee, the manufacturer should consider offering a trial-use plan with an option to buy.

Individual Differences in Innovativeness

People differ greatly in their readiness to try new products. In each product area, there are "consumption pioneers" and early adopters. Other individuals adopt new products much later. People can be classified into the adopter categories shown in Figure 6-5. After a slow start, an increasing number of people adopt the new product. The number of adopters reaches a peak and then drops off as fewer nonadopters remain. Innovators are defined as the first 2.5 percent of the buyers to adopt a new idea (those beyond two standard deviations from mean adoption time); the early adopters are the next 13.5 percent (between one and two standard deviations); and so forth.

The five adopter groups have differing values. *Innovators* are venturesome—they try new ideas at some risk. *Early adopters* are guided by respect—they are opinion leaders in their communities and adopt new ideas early but carefully. The *early majority* are deliberate—although they rarely are leaders, they adopt new ideas before the average person. The *late majority* are skeptical—they adopt an innovation only after a majority of people have tried it. Finally, *laggards* are tradition bound—they are suspicious of changes and adopt the innovation only when it has become something of a tradition itself.

This adopter classification suggests that an innovating firm should research the characteristics of innovators and early adopters and should direct marketing efforts toward them. In general, innovators tend to be relatively younger, better educated, and higher in income than later adopters and nonadopters. They are more receptive to unfamiliar things, rely more on their own values and judgment, and are more willing to take risks. They are less brand loyal and more likely to take advantage of special promotions such as discounts, coupons, and samples.

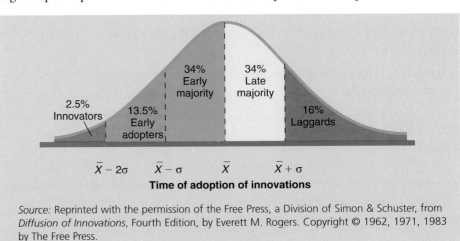

Figure 6-5

Adopter Categorization on the Basis of Relative Time of Adoptions of Innovations

Source: Reprinted with the permission of the Free Press, a Division of Simon & Schuster, from *Diffusion of Innovations*, Fourth Edition, by Everett M. Rogers. Copyright © 1962, 1971, 1983 by The Free Press.

Influence of Product Characteristics on Rate of Adoption The characteristics of the new product affect its rate of adoption. Some products catch on almost overnight (Beanie Babies), whereas others take a long time to gain acceptance (high-density television or HDTV). Five characteristics are especially important in influencing an innovation's rate of adoption. For example, consider the characteristics of HDTV in relation to the rate of adoption:

1. *Relative advantage:* The degree to which the innovation appears superior to existing products. The greater the perceived relative advantage of using HDTV—say, in picture quality and ease of viewing—the sooner such HDTVs will be adopted.

2. *Compatibility:* The degree to which the innovation fits the values and experiences of potential consumers. HDTV, for example, is highly compatible with the lifestyles found in upper-middle-class homes. However, it is not very compatible with the programming and broadcasting systems currently available to consumers.

3. *Complexity:* The degree to which the innovation is difficult to understand or use. HDTVs are not very complex and, therefore, once programming is available and prices come down, will take less time to penetrate Canadian homes than more complex innovations.

4. *Divisibility:* The degree to which the innovation may be tried on a limited basis. HDTVs are still very expensive. To the extent that people can lease them with an option to buy, their rate of adoption will increase.

5. *Communicability:* The degree to which the results of using the innovation can be observed or described to others. Because HDTV lends itself to demonstration and description, its use will spread faster among consumers.

Other characteristics influence the rate of adoption, such as initial and ongoing costs, risk and uncertainty, and social approval. The new-product marketer has to research all these factors when developing the new product and its marketing program.

Consumer Behaviour Across International Borders

Understanding consumer behaviour is difficult enough for companies marketing within the borders of a single country. For companies operating in many countries, however, understanding and serving the needs of consumers can be daunting. Although consumers in different countries may have some things in common, their values, attitudes, and behaviours often vary greatly. International marketers must understand such differences and adjust their products and marketing programs accordingly.

Sometimes the differences are obvious. For example, in Canada and the United States, where most people eat cereal regularly for breakfast, Kellogg focuses its marketing on persuading consumers to select a Kellogg brand rather than a competitor's brand. In France, however, where most people prefer croissants and coffee or no breakfast at all, Kellogg advertising simply attempts to convince people that they should eat cereal for breakfast. Its packaging includes step-by-step instructions on how to prepare cereal. In India, where many consumers eat heavy, fried breakfasts and many consumers skip the meal altogether, Kellogg's advertising attempts to convince buyers to switch to a lighter, more nutritious breakfast diet.

Often, differences across international markets are more subtle. They may result from physical differences in consumers and their environments. For example, Remington makes smaller electric shavers to fit the smaller hands of Japanese consumers and battery-powered shavers for the British market, where few bathrooms have electrical outlets. Other differences result from varying customs. In Japan, for example, where humility and deference are considered great virtues, pushy, hard-hitting sales approaches are considered offensive. Failing to understand such differences in customs and behaviours from one country to another can spell disaster for a marketer's international products and programs.

Marketers must decide on the degree to which they will adapt their products and marketing programs to meet the unique cultures and needs of consumers in various markets. On the one hand, they want to standardize their offerings to simplify operations and take advantage of cost economies. On the other hand, adapting marketing efforts within each country results in products and programs that better satisfy the needs of local consumers. The question of whether to adapt or standardize the marketing mix across international markets has created a lively debate in recent years.

Here's a good place to pause and apply the concepts you've examined in the first part of this chapter.

• Think about a specific major purchase you've made recently. What buying process did you follow? What major factors influenced your decision?

• Pick a company that we've discussed in a previous chapter—Nike, Coca-Cola, Starbucks, Wal-Mart, Volkswagen, Canadian Tire or another. Does the company you chose understand its customers and their buying behaviour?

• Think about Intel, which sells its products to computer makers and other businesses rather than to final consumers. How would Intel's marketing to business customers differ from Nike's marketing to final consumers? The second part of the chapter deals with this.

BUSINESS MARKETS AND BUSINESS BUYER BEHAVIOUR

In one way or another, most large companies sell to other organizations. Many companies, such as Alcan Aluminum, Bombardier, Nortel, Research in Motion, and countless other firms, sell *most* of their products to other businesses. Even large consumer-products companies, which make products used by final consumers, must first sell their products to other businesses. For example, Kraft Canada makes many familiar consumer products, Kraft Dinner, Post cereals, Maxwell House coffee, Jell-o, Kraft Peanut Butter and Kraft Salad Dressings to name but a few. Before these products can reach consumers, Kraft Canada must first sell their products to wholesalers and retailers that serve the consumer market and to specialized food service wholesalers for resale to restaurants.

Business buyer behaviour refers to the buying behaviour of all the organizations that buy goods and services for use in the production of other products and services that are sold, rented, or supplied to others. It also includes retailing and wholesaling firms that acquire goods for the purpose of reselling or renting them to others at a profit.

Business buyer behaviour The buying behaviour of organizations that buy goods and services for use in the production of other products and services that are sold, rented, or supplied to others.

Business Markets

The business market is *huge.* In fact, business markets involve far more dollars and items than do consumer markets. For example, think about the large number of business transactions involved in the production and sale of a single set of Michelin tires. Various suppliers sell Michelin the rubber, steel, equipment, and other goods that it needs to produce the tires. Michelin then sells the finished tires to retailers, who in turn sell them to consumers. Thus, many sets of *business* purchases were made for only one *consumer* purchase. In addition, Michelin sells tires as original equipment to manufacturers who install them on new vehicles, and as replacement tires to companies that maintain their own fleets of company cars, trucks, buses, or other vehicles.

In some ways, business markets are similar to consumer markets. Both involve people who assume buying roles and make purchase decisions to satisfy needs. However, business markets differ in many ways from consumer markets. The main differences are in *market structure and demand,* the *nature of the buying unit,* and the *types of decisions and the decision process* involved.

Market Structure and Demand The business marketer normally deals with *far fewer but far larger buyers* than the consumer marketer does. For example, when Michelin sells replacement tires to final consumers, its potential market includes the owners of the millions of cars currently in use in North America. But Michelin's fate in the business market depends on getting orders from one of only a few large automakers. Even in large business markets, a few buyers normally account for most of the purchasing.

Business markets are also *more geographically concentrated.* More than 70 percent of Canada's manufacturers are located in Ontario and Quebec and most of these are located in a section approximately 100 km north of the U.S. border extending from Quebec City to Windsor, Ontario. Further, business demand is **derived demand**—it ultimately derives from the demand for consumer goods. General Motors buys steel because consumers buy cars. If consumer demand for cars drops, so will the demand for steel and all the other products used to make cars. Therefore, business marketers sometimes promote their products directly to final consumers to increase business demand. For example, Intel's long-running "Intel Inside" advertising campaign sells personal computer buyers on the virtues of Intel microprocessors. The increased demand for Intel chips boosts demand for the PCs containing them, and both Intel and its business partners win.

Derived demand Business demand that ultimately comes from (derives from) the demand for consumer goods.

Derived demand: Intel's long-running "Intel Inside" logo advertising campaign boosts demand for Intel chips and for the PCs containing them. Now, most computer makers feature a logo like this one in their ads.

Nature of the Buying Unit Compared with consumer purchases, a business purchase usually involves *more decision participants* and a *more professional purchasing effort.* Often, business buying is done by trained purchasing agents who spend their working lives learning how to buy better. The more complex the purchase, the more likely that several people will participate in the decision-making process. Buying committees made up of technical experts and top management are common in the buying of major goods. As one observer notes, "It's a scary thought: Your customers may know more about your company and products than you do.... Companies are putting their best and brightest people on procurement patrol."[26] Therefore, business marketers must have well-trained salespeople to deal with well-trained buyers.

Types of Decisions and the Decision Process Business buyers usually face *more complex* buying decisions than do consumer buyers. Purchases often involve large sums of money, complex technical and economic considerations, and interactions among many people at many levels of the buyer's organization. Because the purchases are more complex, business buyers may take longer to make their decisions.

The business buying process tends to be *more formalized* than the consumer buying process. Large business purchases usually call for detailed product specifications, written purchase orders, careful supplier searches, and formal approval. Finally, in the business buying process, buyer and seller are often much *more dependent* on each other. Consumer marketers are often at a distance from their customers. In contrast, business marketers may roll up their sleeves and work closely with their customers during all stages of the buying process—from helping customers define problems, to finding solutions, to supporting after-sale operation. In the long run, business marketers keep a customer's sales by meeting current needs *and* by working with customers to help them succeed with their own customers.

Business Buyer Behaviour

At the most basic level, marketers want to know how business buyers will respond to various marketing stimuli. Figure 6-6 shows a model of business buyer behaviour. In this model, marketing and other stimuli affect the buying organization and produce certain buyer responses. As with consumer buying, the marketing stimuli for business buying consist of the four Ps: product, price, place, and promotion. Other stimuli include major forces in the environment: economic, technological, political, cultural, and competitive. These stimuli enter the organization and are turned into buyer responses: product or service choice; supplier choice; order quantities; and delivery, service, and payment terms. To design good marketing mix strategies, the marketer must understand what happens within the organization to turn stimuli into purchase responses.

Within the organization, buying activity has two major parts: the buying centre, comprising all the people involved in the buying decision, and the buying-decision process. The model shows that the buying centre and the buying-decision process are influenced by internal organizational, interpersonal, and individual factors as well as by external environmental factors.

The model in Figure 6-6 suggests four questions about business buyer behaviour: What buying decisions do business buyers make? Who participates in the buying process? What are the major influences on buyers? How do business buyers make their buying decisions?

Major Types of Buying Situations There are three major types of buying situations.[27] At one extreme is the *straight rebuy,* which is a fairly routine decision. At the other extreme is the *new task,* which may call for thorough research. In the middle is the *modified rebuy,* which requires some research.

In a **straight rebuy**, the buyer reorders something without any modifications. It is usually handled on a routine basis by the purchasing department. Based on past buying satisfaction, the buyer simply chooses from the various suppliers on its list. "In" suppliers try to maintain product and service quality. They often propose automatic reordering systems so that the purchasing agent will save reordering time. "Out" suppliers try to offer something new or exploit dissatisfaction so that the buyer will consider them.

Straight rebuy A business buying situation in which the buyer routinely reorders something without any modifications.

Figure 6-6

A Model of Business Buyer Behaviour

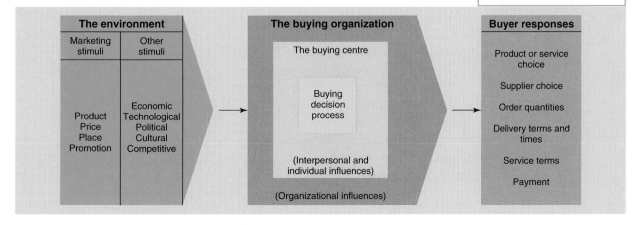

The environment		The buying organization	Buyer responses
Marketing stimuli	**Other stimuli**	**The buying centre**	Product or service choice
Product Price Place Promotion	Economic Technological Political Cultural Competitive	Buying decision process	Supplier choice
		(Interpersonal and individual influences)	Order quantities
		(Organizational influences)	Delivery terms and times
			Service terms
			Payment

Modified rebuy A business buying situation in which the buyer wants to modify product specifications, prices, terms, or suppliers.

New task A business buying situation in which the buyer purchases a product or service for the first time.

Systems selling Buying a packaged solution to a problem from a single seller, thus avoiding all the separate decisions involved in a complex buying situation.

Buying centre All the individuals and units that participate in the business buying-decision process.

In a **modified rebuy**, the buyer wants to modify product specifications, prices, terms, or suppliers. The modified rebuy usually involves more decision participants than does the straight rebuy. The in suppliers may become nervous and feel pressured to put their best foot forward to protect an account. Out suppliers may see the modified rebuy situation as an opportunity to make a better offer and gain new business.

A company buying a product or service for the first time faces a **new task** situation. In such cases, the greater the cost or risk, the larger the number of decision participants and the greater their efforts to collect information will be. The new-task situation is the marketer's greatest opportunity and challenge. The marketer not only tries to reach as many key buying influences as possible, but also tries to provide help and information.

Many business buyers prefer to buy a packaged solution to a problem from a single seller. Instead of buying and putting all the components together, the buyer may ask sellers to supply the components *and* assemble the package or system. The sale often goes to the firm that provides the most complete system meeting the customer's needs. Thus, **systems selling** is often a key business marketing strategy for winning and holding accounts.

Participants in the Business Buying Process Who does the buying of the trillions of dollars' worth of goods and services needed by business organizations? The decision-making unit of a buying organization is called its **buying centre**: all the individuals and units that participate in the business decision-making process. The buying centre includes all members of the organization who play a role in the purchase decision process. This group includes the actual users of the product or service, those who make the buying decision, those who influence the buying decision, those who do the actual buying, and those who control buying information.

The buying centre is not a fixed and formally identified unit within the buying organization. It is a set of buying roles assumed by different people for different purchases. Within the organization, the size and makeup of the buying centre will vary for different products and for different buying situations. For some routine purchases, one person—say, a purchasing agent—may assume all the buying centre roles and serve as the only person involved in the buying decision. For more complex purchases, the buying centre may include 20 or 30 people from different levels and departments in the organization.

The buying centre concept presents a major marketing challenge. The business marketer must learn who participates in the decision, each participant's relative influence, and what evaluation criteria each decision participant uses. For example, Baxter International, the large health care products and services company, sells disposable surgical gowns to hospitals. It identifies the hospital personnel involved in this buying decision as the vice president of purchasing, the operating room administrator, and the surgeons. Each participant plays a different role. The vice president of purchasing analyzes whether the hospital should buy disposable gowns or reusable gowns. If analysis favours disposable gowns, then the operating room administrator compares competing products and prices and makes a choice. This administrator considers the gown's absorbency, antiseptic quality, design, and cost, and normally buys the brand that meets requirements at the lowest cost. Finally, surgeons affect the decision later by reporting their satisfaction or dissatisfaction with the brand.

The buying centre usually includes some obvious participants who are involved formally in the buying decision. It may also involve less obvious, informal participants, some of whom may actually make or strongly affect the buying decision. Sometimes, even the people in the buying centre are not aware of all the buying participants

Major Influences on Business Buyers Business buyers are subject to many influences when they make their buying decisions. Some marketers assume that the major influences are economic. They think buyers will favour the supplier who offers the lowest price or the best product or the most service. They concentrate on offering strong economic benefits to buyers. However, business buyers actually respond to both economic and personal factors. Far from being cold, calculating, and impersonal, business buyers are human and social as well. They react to both reason and emotion.

Today, most business-to-business marketers recognize that emotion plays an important role in business buying decisions. For example, you might expect that an advertisement promoting large trucks to corporate truck fleet buyers would stress objective technical, performance, and economic factors. However, a recent ad for Volvo heavy-duty trucks shows two drivers arm wrestling and claims "It solves all your fleet problems. Except who gets to drive." It turns out that, in the face an industry-wide driver shortage, the type of truck a fleet provides can help it to

Emotions play an important role in business buying: This Volvo Truck ad mentions objective factors, such as efficiency and ease of maintenance. But it stresses more emotional factors such as the raw beauty of the truck and its comfort and roominess, features that make it more appealing to drivers.

INTRODUCING THE VOLVO 660. IT SOLVES ALL YOUR FLEET PROBLEMS. EXCEPT WHO GETS TO DRIVE.

May the best man win. We designed the new 660 to be the perfect fleet partner. Spacious and smooth handling. Efficient and easy to maintain. Built to make fleets more profitable and drivers a lot more possessive.

To find out how the Volvo 660 can help you be more successful, give us a call at 1-800-444-RSVP for a free video or visit www.volvotrucks.volvo.com.

VOLVO
Drive Smart.

attract qualified drivers. The Volvo ad stresses the raw beauty of the truck and its comfort and roominess, features that make it more appealing to drivers. The ad concludes that Volvo trucks are "built to make fleets more profitable and drivers a lot more possessive."

Figure 6-7 lists various groups of influences on business buyers—environmental, organizational, interpersonal, and individual.[28] *Environmental factors* play a major role. For example, buyer behaviour can be heavily influenced by factors in the current and expected economic environment, such as the level of primary demand, the economic outlook, and the cost of money. Another environmental factor is shortages in key materials. Many companies now are more willing to buy and hold larger inventories of scarce materials to ensure adequate supply. Business buyers also are affected by technological, political, and competitive developments in the environment. Finally, culture and customs can strongly influence business buyer reactions to the marketer's behaviour and strategies, especially in the international marketing environment (see New Directions 6-2).

Business buyer behaviour is also influenced strongly by *organizational factors*. Each buying organization has its own objectives, policies, procedures, structure, and systems, and the business marketer must understand these factors well. Questions such as these arise: How many people are involved in the buying decision? Who are they? What are their evaluative criteria? What are the company's policies and limits on its buyers?

The buying centre usually includes many participants who influence each other, so *interpersonal factors* also influence the business buying process. However, it is often difficult to assess such interpersonal factors and group dynamics. As one writer notes, "Managers do not wear tags that say 'decision maker' or 'unimportant person.' The powerful are often invisible, at least to vendor representatives."[29] Nor does the buying centre participant with the highest rank always have the most influence. Participants may influence the buying decision because they control rewards and punishments, are well liked, have special expertise, or have a special relationship with other important participants. Interpersonal factors are often very subtle. Whenever possible, business marketers must try to understand these factors and design strategies that take them into account.

Finally, business buyers are influenced by *individual factors*. Each participant in the business buying-decision process brings in personal motives, perceptions, and

Figure 6-7

Major Influences on Business Buyer Behaviour

New Directions 6-2 >>   International Marketing Manners: When in Rome, Do as the Romans Do

Picture this: Consolidated Amalgamation, Inc. thinks it's time that the rest of the world enjoyed the same fine products it has offered Canadian consumers for two generations. It dispatches vice president Harry E. Slicksmile to Europe to explore the territory. Harry stops first in London, where he makes short work of some bankers—he phones them. He handles Parisians with similar ease. After securing a table at *La Tour d'Argent*, he greets his luncheon guest, the director of an industrial engineering firm, with the words, "Just call me Harry, Jacques."

In Germany, Harry is a powerhouse. Whisking through a lavish, state-of-the-art marketing presentation, complete with flip charts and audiovisuals, he shows them that this prairie boy *knows* how to make a buck. Heading on to Milan, Harry strikes up a conversation with the Japanese businessman sitting next to him on the plane. He flips his card onto his neighbour's tray and, when the two say good-bye, shakes hands warmly and clasps the man's right arm. Later, for his appointment with the owner of an Italian packaging-design firm, our hero wears his comfy corduroy sport coat, khaki pants, and deck shoes. Everybody knows Italians are zany and laid back, right?

Wrong. Six months later, Consolidated Amalgamation has nothing to show for the trip but a pile of bills. In Europe, they weren't wild about Harry.

This hypothetical case has been exaggerated for emphasis. Businesspeople are seldom such dolts. But experts say success in international business has much to do with knowing the territory and its people. By learning English and extending themselves in other ways, the world's business leaders have met North Americans more than halfway. In contrast, North Americans too often do little except assume that others will march to their music. "We want things to be just like they are at home when we travel. Fast. Convenient. Easy. So we demand that others change," says one world trade expert. "I think more business would be done if we tried harder."

Poor Harry tried, all right, but in all the wrong ways. The English do not, as a rule, make deals over the phone as much as North Americans do. It's not so much a "cultural" difference as a difference in approach. The French neither like instant familiarity—questions about family, church, or alma mater—nor refer to strangers by their first names. "That poor fellow, Jacques, probably wouldn't show anything, but he'd recoil. He'd *not* be pleased," explains an expert on French business practices. "It's considered poor taste," he continues. "Even after months of business dealings, I'd wait for him or her to make the invitation [to use first names].… You are always right, in Europe, to say 'Mister or 'Madam.' Calling secretaries by their first names would also be considered rude: They have a right to be called by the surname. You'd certainly ask—and get—permission first."

Harry's flashy presentation would likely have been a flop with the Germans, who dislike overstatement and ostentation. According to one German expert, however, German businesspeople have become accustomed to dealing with North Americans. Although differences in body language and customs remain, the past 20 years have softened them.

When Harry Slicksmile grabbed his new Japanese acquaintance by the arm, the executive probably considered him disrespectful and presumptuous. Harry made matters worse by tossing his busi-

North American companies must help their managers to understand the needs, customs, and cultures of international business buyers. For example, the Japanese revere the business card as an extension of self and as an indicator of rank; they do not *hand* it to people, they *present* it.

ness card. The Japanese revere the business card as an extension of self and as an indicator of rank. They do not *hand* it to people, they *present* it—with both hands. In addition, the Japanese are sticklers about rank. Unlike North Americans, they don't heap praise on subordinates in a room; they will praise only the highest-ranking official present.

Hapless Harry's last gaffe was assuming that Italians are like Hollywood's stereotypes of them. The flair for design and style that has characterized Italian culture for centuries is embodied in the businesspeople of Milan and Rome. They dress beautifully and admire flair, but they blanch at garishness or impropriety in others' attire.

To compete successfully in global markets, or even to deal effectively with international firms in their home markets, North American companies must help their managers to understand the needs, customs, and cultures of international business buyers. These are additional examples of a few rules of social and business etiquette that North American managers should understand when doing business abroad:

France: Dress conservatively, except in the south where more casual clothes are worn. Do not refer to people by their first names—the French are formal with strangers. It should be noted that Europeans who speak French are more formal than their North American counterparts.

Germany: Be especially punctual. A businessperson invited to someone's home should present flowers, preferably unwrapped, to the hostess. Don't give red roses, which are only for lovers. During introductions, greet women first and wait until they extend their hands before extending yours.

Italy: Whether you dress conservatively or go native in a Giorgio Armani suit, keep in mind that Italian businesspeople are style-conscious. Make appoint-

ments well in advance. Prepare for and be patient with Italian bureaucracies.

United Kingdom: Toasts are often given at formal dinners. If the host honours you with a toast, be prepared to reciprocate. Business entertaining is done more often at lunch than at dinner.

Saudi Arabia: Although men will kiss each other in greeting, they will never kiss a woman in public. A businesswoman should wait for a man to extend his hand before offering hers. If a Saudi offers refreshment, accept—it is an insult to decline it.

India: Although businesspeople here speak English, Canadians cannot assume that doing business will be smooth sailing. India is a conservative society marked by contrasts—a peasant culture on one hand, and European-educated professionals on the other. Business deals take a long time to close and may be impossible without the assistance of an Indian agent to help firms understand India's impenetrable bureaucracy.

Japan: Don't imitate Japanese bowing customs unless you understand them thoroughly—who bows to whom, how many times, and when. It's a complicated ritual. Presenting business cards is another ritual. Carry many cards, present them with both hands so your name can be easily read, and hand them to others in order of descending rank. Expect Japanese business executives to take time making decisions and to work through all of the details before making a commitment.

Sources: Adapted from Susan Harte, "When in Rome, You Should Learn to Do What the Romans Do," *Atlanta Journal-Constitution,* 22 January 1990, pp. D1,D6. Also see Lufthansa's *Business Travel Guide/Europe;* Sergey Frank, "Global Negotiating," *Sales & Marketing Management,* May 1992, pp. 64–69; and Brian Banks, "English Too," *Canadian Business,* January 1995, pp. 20–35.

preferences. These individual factors are affected by personal characteristics such as age, income, education, professional identification, personality, and attitudes toward risk. Also, buyers have different buying styles. Some may be technical types who make in-depth analyses of competitive proposals before choosing a supplier. Other buyers may be intuitive negotiators who are adept at pitting the sellers against one another for the best deal.

The Business Buying Process Figure 6-8 shows the eight stages of the business buying process and the application of each of the eight steps to the three buying situations.[30] Buyers who face a new task buying situation usually go through all stages

Stages of the Buying Process	Buying Situations		
	New Task	Modified Rebuy	Straight Rebuy
1. Problem recognition	Yes	Maybe	No
2. General need description	Yes	Maybe	No
3. Product specification	Yes	Yes	Yes
4. Supplier search	Yes	Maybe	No
5. Proposal solicitation	Yes	Maybe	No
6. Supplier selection	Yes	Maybe	No
7. Order-routine specification	Yes	Maybe	No
8. Performance review	Yes	Yes	Yes

Source: Adapted from Patrick J. Robinson, Charles W. Faris, and Yoram Wind, *Industrial Buying and Creative Marketing,* Boston: Allyn & Bacon, 1967, p. 14.

Figure 6-8

Major Stages of the Business Buying Process in Relation to Major Buying Situations

of the buying process. Buyers making modified or straight rebuys may skip some of the stages. We will examine these steps for the typical new-task buying situation.

Problem Recognition The buying process begins when someone in the company recognizes a problem or need that can be met by acquiring a specific product or service. Problem recognition can result from internal or external stimuli. Internally, the company may decide to launch a new product that requires new production equipment and materials. Or a machine may break down and need new parts. Perhaps a purchasing manager is unhappy with a current supplier's product quality, service, or prices. Externally, the buyer may get some new ideas at a trade show, see an ad, or receive a call from a salesperson who offers a better product or a lower price. In fact, in their advertising, business marketers often alert customers to potential problems and then show how their products provide solutions.

General Need Description Having recognized a need, the buyer next prepares a general need description that describes the characteristics and quantity of the needed item. For standard items, this process presents few problems. For complex items, however, the buyer may have to work with others—engineers, users, consultants— to define the item. The team may want to rank the importance of reliability, durability, price, and other attributes desired in the item. In this phase, the alert business marketer can help the buyers define their needs and provide information about the value of different product characteristics.

Product Specification The buying organization next develops the item's technical product specifications, often with the help of a value analysis engineering team. **Value analysis** is an approach to cost reduction in which components are studied carefully to determine whether they can be redesigned, standardized, or made by less costly methods of production. The team decides on the best product characteristics and specifies them accordingly. Sellers, too, can use value analysis as a tool to help secure a new account. By showing buyers a better way to make an object,

Value analysis An approach to cost reduction in which components are studied carefully to determine whether they can be redesigned, standardized, or made by less costly methods of production.

outside sellers can turn straight rebuy situations into new task situations that give them a chance to obtain new business.

Supplier Search The buyer now conducts a supplier search to find the best vendors. The buyer can compile a small list of qualified suppliers by reviewing trade directories, doing a computer search, or phoning other companies for recommendations. Today, more and more companies are turning to the Internet to find suppliers. For marketers, this has levelled the playing field—smaller suppliers have the same advantages as larger ones and can be listed in the same online catalogues for a nominal fee:

Worldwide Internet Solutions Network, better known as WIZnet (**www.wiznet.net**) has built an "interactive virtual library of business-to-business catalogs" that is global in coverage. At last report, its database included complete specifications for more than 10 million products and services from 90,000 manufacturers, distributors, and industrial service providers. For purchasing managers, who routinely receive a foot-high stack of mail each day, much of it catalogs, this kind of one-stop shopping will be an incredible time-saver (and price saver, because it allows easier comparison shopping). More than just electronic Yellow Pages, WIZnet includes all specifications for the products right in the system and offers secure e-mail to communicate directly with vendors to ask for requests for bids or to place an order. More than 10,000 product specs are added to WIZnet per week, and its database includes catalogs from Germany, Taiwan, the Czech Republic, and other countries.[31]

The newer the buying task, and the more complex and costly the item, the greater the amount of time the buyer will spend searching for suppliers. The supplier's task is to get listed in major directories and build a good reputation in the marketplace. Salespeople should watch for companies in the process of searching for suppliers and make certain that their firm is considered.

Proposal Solicitation In the proposal solicitation stage of the business buying process, the buyer invites qualified suppliers to submit proposals. In response, some suppliers will send only a catalogue or a salesperson. However, when the item is complex or expensive, the buyer will usually require detailed written proposals or formal presentations from each potential supplier.

Business marketers must be skilled in researching, writing, and presenting proposals in response to buyer proposal solicitations. Proposals should be marketing documents, not just technical documents. Presentations should inspire confidence and should make the marketer's company stand out from the competition.

Supplier Selection The members of the buying centre now review the proposals and select a supplier or suppliers. During supplier selection, the buying centre often will draw up a list of the desired supplier attributes and their relative importance. In one survey, purchasing executives listed the following attributes as most important in influencing the relationship between supplier and customer: quality products and services, on-time delivery, ethical corporate behaviour, honest communication, and competitive prices. Other important factors include repair and servicing capabilities, technical aid and advice, geographic location, performance history, and reputation. The members of the buying centre will rate suppliers against these attributes and identify the best suppliers.

Buyers may attempt to negotiate with preferred suppliers for better prices and terms before making the final selections. In the end, they may select a single supplier or a few suppliers. Many buyers prefer multiple sources of supplies to avoid being dependent on one supplier and to allow for comparisons of prices and performance of several suppliers over time.

Order-Routine Specification The buyer now prepares an order-routine specification. It includes the final order with the chosen supplier or suppliers and lists items such as technical specifications, quantity needed, expected time of delivery, return policies, and warranties. In the case of maintenance, repair, and operating items, buyers may use *blanket contracts* rather than periodic purchase orders. A blanket contract creates a long-term relationship in which the supplier promises to resupply the buyer as needed at agreed prices for a set period. A blanket order eliminates the expensive process of renegotiating a purchase each time that stock is required. It also allows buyers to write more, but smaller, purchase orders, resulting in lower inventory levels and carrying costs. Blanket contracting leads to more single-source buying and to buying more items from that source. This practice locks the supplier in tighter with the buyer and makes it difficult for other suppliers to break in unless the buyer becomes dissatisfied with prices or service.

Performance Review In this stage, the buyer reviews supplier performance. The buyer may contact users and ask them to rate their satisfaction. The performance review may lead the buyer to continue, modify, or drop the arrangement. The seller's job is to monitor the same factors used by the buyer to make sure that the seller is giving the expected satisfaction.

We have described the stages that typically would occur in a new-task buying situation. The eight-stage model provides a simple view of the business buying-decision process. The actual process is usually much more complex. In the modified rebuy or straight rebuy situation, some of these stages would be compressed or bypassed. Each organization buys in its own way, and each buying situation has unique requirements. Different buying centre participants may be involved at different stages of the process. Although certain buying process steps usually do occur, buyers do not always follow them in the same order, and they may add other steps. Often, buyers will repeat certain stages of the process. Finally, a customer relationship might involve many different types of purchases ongoing at a given time, all in different stages of the buying process. The seller must manage the total customer relationship, not just individual purchases.

Business Buying on the Internet

Advances in information technology have changed the face of the business-to-business marketing process. As we saw in Chapter 3, increasingly, business buyers are purchasing all kinds of products and services electronically, either through electronic data interchange links (EDI) or on the Internet. Such "e-procurement" gives buyers access to new suppliers, lowers purchasing costs, and hastens order processing and delivery. In turn, business marketers are connecting with customers online to share marketing information, sell products and services, provide customer support services, and maintain ongoing customer relationships.

So far, most of the products bought by businesses through Internet connections are MRO materials—maintenance, repair, and operations. To take advantage of this, Business Depot, which operates Staples and Bureau en Gros stores across Canada, is using the Net in a bid to become a one-stop online shop for the growing small business market in Canada. The new site carries the retailer's entire catalogue of supplies, more than 5000 products plus an extended line of technology products and computer equipment. It also offers a variety of time-saving options and personalization features designed to cater primarily to business customers with fewer than four employees. The site has already exceeded the sales goals set for it three-fold, indicating that Canadian small business customers are definitely ready to shop online.

Business Depot
www.businessdepot.com

To most consumers, all the buzz about Internet buying has focused on B2C Web sites selling computers, software, clothing, books, flowers, or other retail goods. However, consumer goods sales via the Web are dwarfed by the Internet sales of business goods. In fact, B2B e-procurement now accounts for a lion's share of the dollar value of all e-commerce transactions.

The rapid-growth business-to-business e-procurement yields many benefits.[32] It shaves transaction costs and results in more efficient purchasing for both buyers and suppliers. A Web-powered purchasing program eliminates the paperwork associated with traditional requisition and ordering procedures. At National Semiconductor, for example, the $110 to $375 cost of processing each paper-based requisition has been cut to just $4.50 per electronic order. A more efficient centralized purchasing platform also saves time and money.

E-procurement reduces the time between order and delivery. The rapidly expanding use of e-purchasing, however, also presents some problems. At the same time that the Web makes it possible for suppliers and customers to share business data and even collaborate on product design, it can also erode decades-old customer–supplier relationships. Many firms are using the Web to search for better suppliers. Japan Airlines (JAL) has used the Internet to post orders for in-flight materials such as plastic cups. On its Web site, it posts drawings and specifications that will attract proposals from any firm that comes across the site, rather than from just the usual Japanese suppliers. Finally, e-purchasing can create potential security disasters. More than 80 percent of companies say security is the leading barrier to expanding electronic links with customers and partners.

>> Looking Back < < < < < < < < <

This chapter is the last of four chapters on analyzing marketing opportunities by looking closely at consumers, businesses, and their buying behaviour. The Canadian consumer market comprises more than 30 million people who consume many billions of dollars' worth of goods and services each year. The business market involves far more dollars and items than the consumer market. Final consumers and business buyers vary greatly in their characteristics and circumstances. Understanding *consumer* and *business buyer behaviour* is one of the biggest challenges marketers face.

1. Understand the consumer market and the major factors that influence consumer buyer behaviour.

The *consumer market* comprises all the individuals and households who buy or acquire goods and services for personal consumption. A simple stimulus–response model of consumer behaviour suggests that marketing stimuli and other major forces enter the consumer's "black box." This black box has two parts: buyer characteristics and the buyer's decision process. Once in the black box, the inputs result in observable buyer responses, such as product choice, brand choice, dealer choice, purchase timing, and purchase amount.

Consumer buyer behaviour is influenced by four key sets of buyer characteristics: cultural, social, personal, and psychological. Understanding these factors can help marketers to identify interested buyers and to shape products and appeals to serve consumer needs better. *Culture* is the most basic determinant of a person's wants and behaviour. People in different cultural, subcultural, and social class groups have different product and brand preferences. *Social factors*—such as small group and family influences—strongly affect product and brand choices, as do *personal characteristics,* such as age, life-cycle stage, occupation, economic circumstances, lifestyle, and personality. Finally, consumer buying behaviour is influenced by four major sets of *psychological factors*—motivation, perception, learning, and beliefs and attitudes. Each of these factors provides a different perspective for understanding the workings of the buyer's black box.

2. Identify and discuss the stages in the buyer decision process.

When making a purchase, the buyer goes through a decision process comprising need recognition, information search, evaluation of alternatives, purchase decision, and postpurchase behaviour. During *need recognition,* the consumer recognizes a problem or need that could be satisfied by a product or service. Once the need is recognized, the consumer moves into the *information search* stage. With information in hand, the consumer proceeds to *alternative evaluation* and assesses brands in the choice set. From there, the consumer makes a *purchase decision* and actually buys the product. In the final stage of the buyer decision process, *postpurchase behaviour,* the consumer takes action based on satisfaction or dissatisfaction. The marketer's job is to understand the buyer's behaviour at each stage and the influences that are operating.

3. Describe the adoption and diffusion process for new products.

The product *adoption process* comprises five stages: awareness, interest, evaluation, trial, and adoption. New-product marketers must think about how to help consumers move through these stages. With regard to the *diffusion process* for new products, consumers respond at different rates, depending on consumer and product characteristics. Consumers may be innovators, early adopters, early majority, late majority, or laggards. Each group may require different marketing approaches. Marketers often try to bring their new products to the attention of potential early adopters, especially those who are opinion leaders.

4. Define the business market and identify the major factors that influence business buyer behaviour.

The *business market* comprises all organizations that buy goods and services for use in the production of other products and services or for the purpose of reselling or renting them to others at a profit. As compared with consumer markets, business markets usually have fewer, larger buyers who are more geographically concentrated. Business demand is derived demand, and the business buying decisions usually involves more, and more professional, buyers.

Business buyers make decisions that vary with the three types of *buying situations:* straight rebuys, modified rebuys, and new tasks. The decision-making unit of a buying organization—the *buying centre*—can comprise many different persons playing many different roles. The business marketer needs to know the following: Who are the major buying centre participants? In what decisions do they exercise influence and to what degree? What evaluation criteria does each decision participant use? The business marketer also needs to understand the major environmental, organizational, interpersonal, and individual influences on the buying process.

5. List and define the steps in the business buying-decision process.

The *business buying-decision process* itself can be quite involved, with eight basic stages: problem recognition, general need description, product specification, supplier search, proposal solicitation, supplier selection, order-routine specification, and performance review. Buyers who face a new-task buying situation usually go through all stages of the buying process. Buyers making modified or straight rebuys may skip some of the stages. Companies must manage the overall customer relationship, which often includes many different buying decisions in various stages of the buying decisions process.

Advances in information technology have given birth to "e-purchasing," by which business buyers are purchasing all kinds of products and services electronically, either through electronic data interchange links (EDI) or on the Internet. Such cyberbuying gives buyers access to new suppliers, lowers purchasing costs, and hastens order processing and delivery. However, it can also erode customer–supplier relationships and create potential security problems. Still, business marketers are increasingly connecting with customers online to share marketing information, sell products and services, provide customer support services, and maintain ongoing customer relationships.

Navigating the Key Terms

New task, **p. 238**

Opinion leaders, **p. 215**

Perception, **p. 222**

Social classes, **p. 214**

Straight rebuy, **p. 237**

Subculture, **p. 209**

Systems selling, **p. 238**

Value analysis, **p. 243**

Concept Check

Fill in the blanks and then check your answers.

1. _____ refers to the buying behaviour of final consumers—individuals and households who buy goods and services for personal consumption.

2. _____ is the most basic cause of a person's wants and behaviour.

3. _____ are society's relatively permanent and ordered divisions whose members share similar values, interests, and behaviours.

4. People within a reference group who, because of special skills, knowledge, personality, or other characteristics, exert influence on others are called _____.

5. Lifestyle is a person's pattern of living as expressed in his or her psychographics. It involves measuring consumer's major *AIO* dimensions where $A =$ _____, $I =$ _____, and $O =$_____.

6. Abraham Maslow sought to explain why people are driven by particular needs at particular times. He identified five primary need categories, which include _____ needs, _____ needs, _____ needs, _____ needs, and _____ needs.

7. The buyer decision process consists of five stages: _____, _____, _____, _____, and _____.

8. Consumers go through five stages in the process of adopting a new product: _____, _____, _____, _____, and _____.

9. Five characteristics are especially important in influencing an innovation's rate of adoption. _____ is the degree to which the innovation appears superior to existing products.

10. With respect to business buying situations, there are three major types: _____, _____, and _____.

11. The decision-making unit of a buying organization is called its _____ and it includes all individuals and units that participate in the business decision-making process.

12. The eight stages of the business buying process include problem recognition, general need description, product specification, _____, _____, _____, and performance review.

Concept Check Answers: 1. Consumer buyer behaviour; 2. Culture; 3. Social classes; 4. opinion leaders: 5. activities, interests, and opinions; 6. physiological needs, safety needs, social needs, esteem needs, and self-actualization needs; 7. need recognition, information search, evaluation of alternatives, purchase decision, and postpurchase behaviour; 8. awareness, interest, evaluation, trial, and adoption; 9. relative advantage; 10. straight rebuy, modified rebuy, and new task; 11. buying centre; 12. suppliers search, proposal solicitation, supplier selection, and order-routine specification.

Discussing the Issues

1. List several factors that you could add to the model shown in Figure 6-1 to make it a more complete description of consumer behaviour. Explain your ideas and reasoning.

2. In designing the advertising for a soft drink, which would you find more helpful, information about consumer demographics or information about consumer lifestyles? Select a new soft drink on the market and give examples of how you would use each type of information.

3. Using Figure 6-4, trace a recent purchase you have made. Examine each of the five stages of the buyer decision process and detail your experiences in each stage. What could the seller have done to make your buying experience better? Did you experience any cognitive dissonance? Explain.

4. Which of the major types of business buying situations is represented by each of the following? (a) Chrysler's purchase of computers that go in cars and adjust engine performance to changing driving conditions. (b) Volkswagen's purchase of spark plugs for its line of vans. (c) Honda's purchase of light bulbs for a new Acura model.

5. Increasingly, business buyers are purchasing all kinds of products and services electronically, either through electronic data interchange links (EDI) or on the Internet. List the benefits of "cyberpurchasing" and "e-procurement." Illustrate your view with an example from the Internet.

 **Mastering Marketing**

Using the information from either Figure 6-1 or Figure 6-8, demonstrate how CanGo or its consumers are required to make buying decisions. Do you see any problems or opportunities? Discuss and explain.

Check out the enclosed Video case CD-ROM, or our Companion Website at www.pearsoned.ca/armstrong, to view a CBC video segment and case for this chapter.

MAP 6 Marketing Applications

Performance review is one of the most critical stages in a business buying process. Perhaps nowhere is this more important than in the highly competitive aircraft manufacturing business. Whether the planes are large or small, once a purchase is made, the buyer is tied to the manufacturer for a long time for service and parts requirements. "Air wars" are currently being fought between Europe's Airbus Industrie and America's Boeing. To a lesser extent, the same competitive conflict exists in the smaller personal and corporate aircraft market between Cessna and Lear Jet. Who will eventually win these dramatic competitive struggles is literally "up in the air." Note: for additional information, see **www.airbus.com**, **www.boeing.com**, **www.cessna.textron.com**, and **www.learjet.com**.

Thinking Like a Marketing Manager

1. Apply either of the above two competitive situations to Figure 6-6 and demonstrate the critical

factors that might be present in a business buying situation.

2. How would performance review be conducted in either of the above two situations? Who might be responsible for such a performance review?

3. If the review were negative, how might the selling organization overcome this difficulty?

a. Examine Figure 6-7. Which specific components might be involved in a performance review of aircraft safety?

b. Find a recent example of "air war" competitiveness and bring the example to class for discussion. How does your example relate to business-to-business marketing and business buying?

Digital Map

Visit our Web site at **www.pearsoned.ca/armstrong** for online quizzes, Internet exercises, and more!

CASE 6 LIFE TIME CUSTOMER VALUE

In the fall of 2002, Wunderman, a large global marketing services organization, announced the winners of their "Wunderman Brand Scoreboard." The agency surveyed 10 000 consumers in North America about their use of and experience with 1993 different brands in 190 product and service categories. Topping the list of favourites were Saturn, Gateway Computers, Wal-Mart, Palm, and Costco.

Daniel Morel, CEO of Wunderman, says that "companies are starting to realize that building brand loyalty has less to do with traditional brand imagery than with frequent, customized one-to-one communication and interaction with customers about their specific needs." Other conclusions drawn from this survey are that consumers are more loyal to (and willing to pay a premium price for) brands that provide a better overall experience. Consumer feedback indicated that the most important aspects of brand experience are performance, treatment of users, and community among users.

How did Saturn win over its customers? A quick review of its Web site provides some insight into the uniqueness of the Saturn experience. For example, the Web site lists Saturn's values, including its commitment to customers. These values are followed by a description of the company's distinctive "no pressure" approach to car buying, details on its 30-day money-back guarantee, and a brief commentary on the car itself that stresses quality and safety.

Articulating this kind of customer commitment in the non-luxury car market segment is unusual. Beyond its commitment to customers, Saturn's values include a commitment to excel, to teamwork, to trust and respect for the individual, and to continuous improvement.

Saturn's consultative selling process is based on its full disclosure, no-hassle philosophy. Car consultants first determine the customer's needs and then begin showing cars. Saturn provides full pricing information up front and outlines the customer's choices for acquiring the car (i.e., purchase, Smartlease, low-kilometre lease, and financing options). The company believes in "creating an atmosphere where customers can make informed decisions without high-pressure sales tactics and number games." If the customer is dissatisfied, he or she can return the car within 30 days or 2500 km (whichever comes first) for a full refund.

On the one hand, we have the Saturn experience; on the other, we have the following scenario.

At 1:30 on a wet, cold Saturday afternoon, a customer is standing in line at a fast-food restaurant with her five-year-old son. They have been standing in the line for 10 minutes, seven minutes over the industry standard for restaurants of this type. They place their orders and ask for the children's toys that usually come with this type of meal. The teenager behind the counter says that the food order will ready soon, but the restaurant is out of toys. The young child understands what "out of toys" means and immediately begins to wail. To this young consumer, this restaurant is about the toys, not the food, and its failure to supply the toy has condemned the brand.

No big deal, one grumpy child isn't going to make a difference to a large fast-food chain. Or is it? With a life expectancy of 70 years, the lifetime customer value of this child is approximately $15 000. He will not want to return to the restaurant, fearing that he will be again disappointed. In addition, in casual conversation with friends and other mothers at the boy's preschool, the mother of this child will tell them what happened. Some of those mothers will remember this and on their next shopping trip may avoid that restaurant, not wanting to deal with the potential embarrassment of a screaming child who didn't get a toy with the meal.

The fast-food restaurant will not ask this child about his disappointing experience with their company. It does not have any mechanism to measure the 10-minute wait, even though it has a service standard that is a three-minute maximum wait for an order. No one else in the company will ever know that the toy was out of stock. In fact, if the company measures only the sales numbers for the specific toy and food combination promotion, they might consider the promotion a success.

This scene is played out every day in even the largest and most sophisticated businesses. The fact is that many organizations do not place the customer first.

The economics of retaining customers over a lifetime is compelling. The Boston Consulting Group's research into purchasing patterns suggests that acquiring new customers generally costs four to ten times the margin of their first purchase. Further research indicates that truly satisfied loyal customers become brand champions and, by word of mouth, influence a significant number product purchase by others.

A model often used to measure the lifetime value of a customer is called *RFM* (recency, frequency, and monetary value). In other words, how recent was the consumers' last purchases? How often has that consumer purchased? What was the dollar value of those purchases?

A typical RFM model is based on three empirical principles:

1. Customers who purchased *recently* are more likely to buy again compared with customers who have not purchased in a while.
2. Customers who purchase *frequently* are more likely to buy again compared with customers who have made only a few purchases.
3. Customers who *spend the most money* in total are more likely to buy again.

From a company's customer history files or a database, each customer is assigned an RFM score based on each criterion. The customers with higher scores (i.e., who recently bought, buy frequently and spend the most) are usually the most profitable. These customers will also have the highest lifetime value for the company. A company must concentrate their efforts on those customers to ensure total customer satisfaction.

Even a small business can adopt the RFM model. If the company does not have the resources to track all components of RFM, it should focus on recency. Recency is the strongest predictor of repeat purchases and of response to future marketing actions. Any number of measures can be used, including purchases, Web site visits, downloads, log-ins, or virtually anything that requires customer involvement. Understanding the concept of RFM leads to a broader understanding of the customer relationship management process and a long-term profitable customer base.

Questions

1. What is an RFM system?
2. How can a company utilize its customer data in its overall marketing efforts?
3. How would Saturn go about determining the lifetime customer value for their car buyers?
4. Is there a difference in developing an RFM for a click-only business than for a traditional product or service supplier?
5. Choose a small business that you are familiar with (your local drycleaner or favourite specialty store) and develop an RFM for that business. What is that business doing now and what could it be doing better in future to retain loyal customers?

Sources: Michael Silverstein, "Creating a Flawless Brand Experience," The Boston Consulting Group, accessed online at **www.bcg.com/publications/search_view_ofas.asp?pubID=334**, 21 November 2002; "Saturn, Gateway Top Experience Brands" accessed online at **www.promom-agazine.com**, 3 November 2002; Yvette Mahieu, "Note on Customer Relationship Management,

Richard Ivey School of Business," The University of Western Ontario, Article 9B02A001; Saturn Canada Web site, accessed online at **www.saturncanada.com**, 11 November 2002.

7 >> Market Segmentation, Targeting, and Positioning for Competitive Advantage

Looking Ahead

So far in your marketing journey, you've learned what marketing is and about the complex environments in which it operates. With that as background, you're now ready to travel more deeply into marketing strategy and tactics. This chapter looks at key marketing strategy decisions in detail—how to divide markets into meaningful customer groups (market segmentation), choose which customer groups to serve (market targeting), and create marketing offers that best serve targeted customers (positioning). The chapters that follow explore in depth the tactical marketing tools—the 4Ps—through which marketers bring these strategies to life.

After studying this chapter, you should be able to

1. define the three steps of target marketing: market segmentation, market targeting, and market positioning

2. list and discuss the major levels of market segmentation and bases for segmenting consumer and business markets

3. explain how companies identify attractive market segments and choose a market-coverage strategy

4. discuss how companies position their products for maximum competitive advantage in the marketplace

Next stop: Procter & Gamble, one of the world's premier consumer goods companies. Some 99 percent of all North American households use at least one P&G brand, and the typical household regularly buys and uses from one to two *dozen* P&G brands. How many P&G products can you name? Why does this superb marketer compete with itself on supermarket shelves by marketing eight different brands of laundry detergent? The P&G story provides a great example of how smart marketers use segmentation, targeting, and positioning.

Procter & Gamble (P&G) sells seven brands of laundry detergent in Canada (Tide, Cheer, Bold, Gain, Era, and Ivory Snow). It also sells five brands each of hand soap (Ivory, Safeguard, Camay, Olay, and Zest) and shampoo (Pantene, Head & Shoulders, Pert Plus, Physique, and Vidal Sassoon); four brands of dishwashing detergent (Dawn, Ivory, Joy, and Cascade); three brands each of toilet roll and tissues (Charmin, Bounty, Puffs), floor cleaners (Mr. Clean), deodorant (Secret, Sure, and Old Spice), cosmetics (Cover Girl, Max Factor, and Olay), and skin care potions (Olay and Noxzema); and two brands each of fabric softener (Downy and Bounce) and disposable diapers (Pampers and Luvs). Moreover, P&G has many additional brands in each category for different international markets. For example, it sells 16 different laundry product brands in Latin America and 19 in Europe, the Middle East, and Africa. (See Procter & Gamble's Web site at www.pg.com for a full view of the company's impressive lineup of familiar brands.) These P&G brands compete with one another on the same supermarket shelves. But why would P&G introduce several brands in one category instead of concentrating its resources on a single leading brand? The answer lies in the fact that different people want different *mixes of benefits* from the products they buy. Take laundry detergents as an example. People use laundry detergents to get their clothes clean. But they also want other things from their detergents— such as economy, bleaching power, fabric softening, a fresh smell, strength or mildness, and lots of suds or only a few. We all want *some* of every one of these benefits from our detergent, but we may have different *priorities* for each benefit. To some people, cleaning and bleaching power are most important; to others, fabric softening matters most; still others want a mild, fresh-scented detergent. Thus, there are groups—or segments—of laundry detergent buyers, and each segment seeks a special combination of benefits.

Procter & Gamble has identified at least seven important laundry detergent segments, along with numerous subsegments, and has developed a different brand designed to meet the special needs of each. The P&G brands are positioned for different segments as follows:

- *Tide* "helps keep clothes looking like new." It's the all-purpose family detergent that is "tough on greasy stains." *Tide with Bleach* is "so powerful, it whitens down to the fibre."

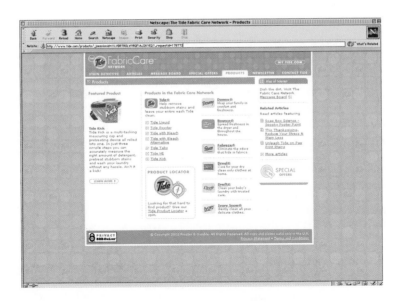

- *Cheer with Triple Color Guard* is the "colour expert." It guards against fading, colour transfer, and fuzzy buildup. *Cheer Free* is "dermatologist tested. . .[and] contains no irritating perfume or dye."

- *Bold* is the detergent with built-in fabric softener. It's "for clean, soft, fresh-smelling clothes." *Bold* liquid adds "the fresh fabric softener scent."

- *Gain*, originally P&G's "enzyme" detergent, was repositioned as the detergent that gives you clean, fresh-smelling clothes. It "cleans and freshens like sunshine. It's not just plain clean, it's Gain clean."

- *Era* has "built-in stain removers." It's "the power tool for stains."

- *Febreze Clean Wash* "doesn't just cover up odours, it truly eliminates worked in, driven in, cooked-in odours in just one wash." It's "the Cleaner Clean for where you live."

- *Ivory Snow* is "Ninety-nine and forty-four one hundredths percent pure." It "gently cleans fine washables and baby clothes… leaving them feeling soft."

Within each segment, Procter & Gamble has identified even *narrower* niches. For example, you can buy regular Tide (in powder or liquid form) or any of several formulations:

- *Tide with Bleach* helps to "keep your whites white and your colours bright," and "kills 99.9 percent of bacteria."

- *Tide Clean Rinse* "goes beyond stain removal to prevent dingy buildup on clothes."

- *Tide High Efficiency* is "formulated for high efficiency top-loading machines"—it prevents oversudsing.

- *Tide Free* "provides all the stain removal benefits without any dyes or perfumes."

- *Tide WearCare* "prevents damage to cotton clothes so they last longer."

- *Tide Rapid Action Tablets* are portable and powerful. It's Tide "all concentrated into a little blue and white tablet that fits into your pocket."

By segmenting the market and having several detergent brands, Procter & Gamble has an attractive offering for consumers in all important preference groups. As a result, P&G is really cleaning up in the $4.3 billion laundry detergent market. Tide, by itself, captures a whopping 38 percent market share. All P&G brands combined take a 57 percent share of the market—two and one-half times that of nearest rival Unilever and much more than any single brand could obtain by itself.[1]

Companies today recognize that they cannot appeal to all buyers in the marketplace, or at least not to all buyers in the same way. Buyers are too numerous, too widely scattered, and too varied in their needs and buying practices. Moreover, the companies themselves vary widely in their abilities to serve different segments of the market. Rather than trying to compete in an entire market, sometimes against superior competitors, each company must identify the parts of the market that it can serve best and most profitably.

Thus, most companies are being choosier about the customers with whom they connect. Most have moved away from mass marketing and toward *market segmentation and targeting*—identifying market segments, selecting one or more of them, and developing products and marketing programs tailored to each. Instead of scattering their marketing efforts (the "shotgun" approach), firms are focusing on the buyers who have greater interest in the values they create best (the "rifle" approach).

Market segmentation
Dividing a market into smaller groups of buyers with distinct needs, characteristics, or behaviours who might require separate products or marketing mixes.

Market targeting The process of evaluating each market segment's attractiveness and selecting one or more segments to enter.

Market positioning Arranging for a product to occupy a clear, distinctive, and desirable place relative to competing products in the minds of target consumers, formulating competitive positioning for a product, and creating a detailed marketing mix.

Figure 7-1 shows the three major steps in target marketing. The first is **market segmentation**—dividing a market into smaller groups of buyers with distinct needs, characteristics, or behaviours who might require separate products or marketing mixes. The company identifies different ways to segment the market and develops profiles of the resulting market segments. The second step is **market targeting**—evaluating each market segment's attractiveness and selecting one or more of the market segments to enter. The third step is **market positioning**—setting the competitive positioning for the product and creating a detailed marketing mix. We discuss each of these steps in turn.

MARKET SEGMENTATION

Markets consist of buyers, and buyers differ in one or more ways. They may differ in their wants, resources, locations, buying attitudes, and buying practises. Through market segmentation, companies divide large, heterogeneous markets into smaller segments that can be reached more efficiently and effectively with products and services that match their unique needs. In this section, we discuss five important segmentation topics: levels of market segmentation, segmenting consumer markets, segmenting business markets, segmenting international markets, and requirements for effective segmentation.

Levels of Market Segmentation

Because buyers have unique needs and wants, each buyer is potentially a separate market. Ideally, then, a seller might design a separate marketing program for each buyer. However, although some companies attempt to serve buyers individually, many others face larger numbers of smaller buyers and do not find complete segmentation worthwhile. Instead, they look for broader classes of buyers who differ in their product needs or buying responses. Thus, market segmentation can be carried out at several different levels. Figure 7-2 shows that companies can practise no

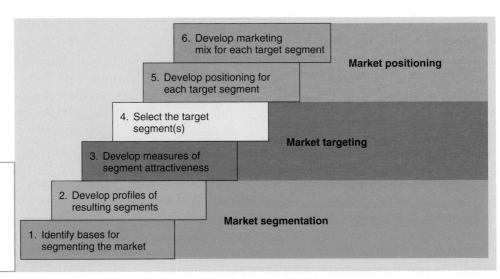

Figure 7-1

Steps in Market Segmentation, Targeting, and Positioning

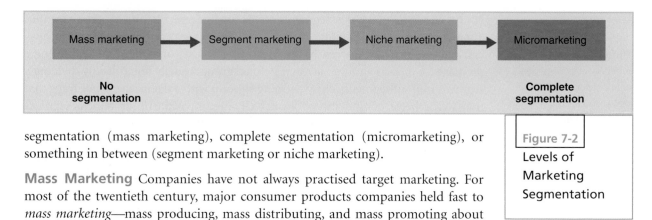

Figure 7-2

Levels of Marketing Segmentation

segmentation (mass marketing), complete segmentation (micromarketing), or something in between (segment marketing or niche marketing).

Mass Marketing Companies have not always practised target marketing. For most of the twentieth century, major consumer products companies held fast to *mass marketing*—mass producing, mass distributing, and mass promoting about the same product in about the same way to all consumers. Henry Ford epitomized this marketing strategy when he offered the Model T Ford to all buyers; they could have the car "in any color as long as it is black." Similarly, Coca-Cola at one time produced only one drink for the whole market, hoping it would appeal to everyone.

The traditional argument for mass marketing is that it creates the largest potential market, which leads to the lowest costs, which in turn can translate into either lower prices or higher margins. However, many factors now make mass marketing more difficult. For example, the Canadian mass market has slowly splintered into a profusion of smaller segments—the baby boomers, the Gen Xers, the immigrants with their specific tastes, the French-Canadians, working women, parents, Easterners and Westerners. Today, marketers find it very hard to create a single product or program that appeals to all these diverse groups.

The proliferation of distribution channels and advertising media has also made it difficult to practise "one-size-fits-all" marketing. Today's consumers can shop at megamalls, superstores, or specialty shops or through mail catalogues or virtual stores on the Internet. They are bombarded with messages delivered via media ranging from old standards such as television, radio, magazines, newspapers, and telephone to newcomers such as Web banners, fax, and e-mail. No wonder some have claimed that mass marketing is dying. Not surprisingly, many companies are retreating from mass marketing and turning to segmented marketing.

Segment Marketing A company that practises **segment marketing** isolates broad segments that make up a market and adapts its offers to more closely match the needs of one or more segments. Thus, Marriott markets to a variety of segments—business travellers, families, and others—with packages adapted to their varying needs. GM has designed specific models for different income and age groups. In fact, it sells models for segments with varied *combinations* of age and income. For instance, GM has traditionally designed its Cadillacs for older, higher-income consumers.

Segment marketing offers several benefits over mass marketing. The company can market more *efficiently*, targeting its products or services, channels, and communications programs toward only those consumers that it can serve best and most profitably. The company can also market more *effectively* by fine-tuning its products, prices, and programs to the needs of carefully defined segments. And the company may face fewer competitors if fewer competitors are focusing on this market segment.

Segment marketing
Isolating broad segments that make up a market and adapting the marketing to match the needs of one or more segment

Niche Marketing Market segments are normally large, identifiable groups within a market—for example, luxury car buyers, performance car buyers, utility car buyers, and economy car buyers. **Niche marketing** focuses on subgroups within these segments. A *niche* is a more narrowly defined group, usually identified by dividing a segment into subsegments or by defining a group with a distinctive set of traits that may seek a special combination of benefits. For example, the utility vehicles segment might include light-duty pickup trucks and sport utility vehicles (SUVs). The sport utility vehicles subsegment might be further divided into standard SUV (as served by Ford and Chevrolet) and luxury SUV (as served by Lincoln and Lexus) niches.

Whereas segments are large and normally attract several competitors, niches are smaller and normally attract only one or a few competitors. Niche marketers presumably understand their niches' needs so well that their customers willingly pay a price premium. For example, the luxurious Bentley gets a high price for its cars because its loyal buyers feel that no other automobile comes close to offering the product-service-membership benefits that Bentley does.

Niche marketing offers smaller companies an opportunity to compete by focusing their limited resources on serving niches that may be unimportant to or overlooked by larger competitors. For example, tiny Vans Inc. specializes in making thick-soled, slip-on sneakers for skateboarders that can absorb the shock of a two-metre leap on wheels. Although it captures only a point or two of market share in the overall athletic shoe market, Vans's small but intensely loyal customer base has made the company more profitable than many of its larger competitors.[2]

Large companies also serve niche markets. For example, American Express offers not only its traditional green cards but also gold cards, corporate cards, and even a black card, called the Centurian, with a $1000 annual fee aimed at a niche of "superpremium customers."[3] And Nike makes athletic gear for basketball, running, and soccer but also for smaller niches such as biking and street hockey.

Niche marketing Focusing on subsegments or niches with distinctive traits that may seek a special combination of benefits.

Vans Inc. has a small but intensely loyal customer base for its sneakers, which has made the company more profitable than many of its larger competitors.

In many markets today, niches are the norm. As an advertising agency executive observed, "There will be no market for products that everybody likes a little, only for products that somebody likes a lot." Other experts assert that companies will have to "niche or be niched."[4]

Micromarketing Segment and niche marketers tailor their offers and marketing programs to meet the needs of various market segments. At the same time, however, they do not customize their offers to each individual customer. Thus, segment marketing and niche marketing fall between the extremes of mass marketing and micromarketing. **Micromarketing** is the practice of tailoring products and marketing programs to suit the tastes of specific individuals and locations. Micromarketing includes *local marketing* and *individual marketing.*

Local Marketing **Local marketing** involves tailoring brands and promotions to the needs and wants of local customer groups—cities, neighbourhoods, and even specific stores. For example, retailers such as The Bay and Safeway routinely customize a specific store's merchandise and promotions to match its specific clientele. The Royal Bank provides different mixes of banking services in its branches depending on neighbourhood demographics. Kraft helps supermarket chains identify the specific cheese assortments and shelf positioning that will optimize cheese sales in low-income, middle-income, and high-income stores and in different ethnic communities.

Local marketing has some drawbacks. It can drive up manufacturing and marketing costs by reducing economies of scale. It can also create logistics problems as companies try to meet the varied requirements of different regional and local markets. Further, a brand's overall image might be diluted if the product and message vary too much in different localities. Still, as companies face increasingly fragmented markets, and as new supporting technologies develop, the advantages of local marketing often outweigh the drawbacks. Local marketing helps a company to market more effectively in the face of pronounced regional and local differences in demographics and lifestyles. It also meets the needs of the company's first-line customers—retailers—who prefer more fine-tuned product assortments for their neighbourhoods.

Individual Marketing In the extreme, micromarketing becomes **individual marketing**—tailoring products and marketing programs to the needs and preferences of individual customers. Individual marketing has also been labelled *one-to-one marketing, customized marketing,* and *markets-of-one marketing.*[5]

The widespread use of mass marketing has obscured the fact that for centuries consumers were served as individuals: The tailor custom-made the suit, the cobbler designed shoes for the individual, the cabinetmaker made furniture to order. Today, however, new technologies are permitting many companies to return to customized marketing. More powerful computers, detailed databases, robotic production and flexible manufacturing, and immediate and interactive communication media such as e-mail, fax, and the Internet—all have combined to foster "mass customization." *Mass customization* is the process through which firms interact one to one with masses of customers to create customer-unique value by designing products and services tailor-made to individual needs (see New Directions 7-1).

Micromarketing The practice of tailoring products and marketing programs to the needs and wants of specific individuals and local customer groups—includes *local marketing* and *individual marketing.*

Local marketing Tailoring brands and promotions to the needs and wants of local customer groups—cities, neighbourhoods, and even specific stores.

Individual marketing Tailoring products and marketing programs to the needs and preferences of individual customers.

New Directions 7-1 >> Markets of One: "Anything You Can Digitize, You Can Customize"

Imagine walking into a booth that bathes your body in patterns of white light and, in a matter of seconds, captures your exact three-dimensional form. The digitized data are then imprinted on a credit card, which you use to order customized clothing. No, this isn't a scene from the next *Star Wars* sequel; it's a peek ahead at how you will be able to buy clothing in the not-so-distant future. A consortium of more than 100 apparel companies, including Levi-Strauss, has banded together to develop body-scanning technology in the hope of making mass customization commonplace.

Although body-scanning technology and smart cards carrying customer measurements are still in development, many companies are now using existing technologies to tailor products to individual customers. Dell creates custom-configured computers, Ford lets buyers "build a vehicle" from a palette of options, and Golf to Fit crafts custom clubs based on consumer measurements and preferences. Here are some other examples of companies in the forefront of the mass customization economy.

Reflect.com is a direct-to-consumer Web site that not only allows a consumer to customize a cosmetic product's formula, scent, and packaging, but also to create an experience that reflects her needs and desires. The cyberbrand is a spin-off business founded by Procter & Gamble and it represents its first online effort at one-to-one marketing. Critical Mass, which has been winning international clients because of its ability to personalize sites, scored the $1.49 million account to build an e-commerce beauty destination when Reflect.com first launched its initial site two years ago. Creative and Web development have now been brought in-house. Reflect.com continues to be a leader in customized beauty care, having recently created its one-millionth customized product.

The Canadian Imperial Bank of Commerce uses its sophisticated database to improve customer retention. The database contains up to 150 pieces of information on each CIBC client. By looking at specific variables, the bank can differentiate between clients who intend to remain with the bank and those who are likely to switch to another provider. The bank develops scores for individual customers based on such behavioural information as whether they pay credit card bills on time and whether they transfer funds to buy registered retirement savings plans with another institution. When clients are identified as people who are likely to switch to another bank, they become the target of a new communications campaign that involves direct-mail pieces, personal calls from a bank representative, a newsletter about the benefits of one of the CIBC financial services they use, and offers of special rates on loans and mortgages.

Mattel. Since 1998, girls have been able to log onto the "My Design" page of the Barbie Web site at **www.barbie.com** and create their very own "friend of Barbie" doll. They choose the doll's skin tone, eye colour, hairstyle and hair colour, clothes, accessories, and name. They even fill out a questionnaire detailing

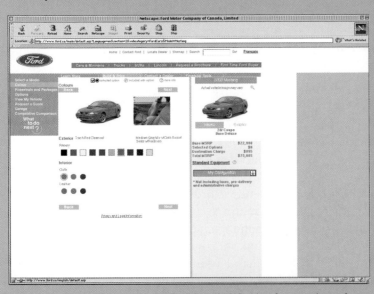

Mass customization: Ford lets buyers "build a vehicle" online from a palette of options.

their doll's likes and dislikes. When Barbie's special friend arrives in the mail, the girls find the doll's name on the packaging along with a computer-generated paragraph about her personality.

CDuctive lets customers cut their own CDs online. A customer who likes acid jazz can click on the category, see 30 titles, and sample a 45-second snatch of each. With a few keystrokes, the customer can then order a $21 CD with all the tunes he or she has selected.

Consumer goods marketers aren't the only ones going one to one. B2B marketers also provide customers with tailor-made goods, often more cheaply and quickly than it used to take to make standardized ones. Particularly for small companies, mass customization provides a way to stand out against larger competitors.

Telus, Canada's second-largest telecommunications company, sees one-to-one marketing as a core strategy for targeting small to medium-sized businesses. Telus knows that other Canadian telephone companies can offer products and services to these businesses. To make itself stand out from the crowd, Telus focuses on customer service and tailors solutions to meet small firms' unique communication needs.

Telus began targeting the small and medium-sized business market with the belief that customers wanted them to be "data-centric," but feedback made it clear that small businesses wanted more than just data services. What they wanted was a full-service provider. Telus uses behavioural segmentation and its database to develop predictive models so that it spends its marketing resources on targeting and retaining top customers. As one Telus manager notes, "It will really allow us to decide if this is a customer who we can afford to market to, and to what degree." These techniques enabled Telus to launch a personalized direct mail campaign to small business in British Columbia. This campaign was followed by telemarketing blitz. Telus was delighted that these joint efforts generated 21 percent more sales per contact than with an untargeted list. To drive home the point that Telus is clearly positioned as a full solutions provider for small and medium-sized business, the company also created three TV spots in which business people talk about what Telus is doing for them.

Two trends are behind the growth in one-to-one marketing. One is the increasing emphasis on customer value and satisfaction. Today's consumers have very high expectations and expect products and services that meet their individual needs. Yet, it would be prohibitively expensive or downright impossible to meet these individual demands if it weren't for rapid advances in new technologies. Data warehouses allow companies to store trillions of bytes of customer information. Computer-controlled factory equipment and industrial robots can now quickly readjust assembly lines. Barcode scanners make it possible to track parts and products. Most important of all, the Internet ties it all together and makes it easy for a company to interact with customers, learn about their preferences, and respond.

Indeed, the Internet appears to be the ultimate one-to-one medium. The notion of personal service on the Internet might seem like an oxymoron, but it's rapidly becoming a reality. Consider the following example.

Soon after Jeri Capozzi logged on to the online nursery Garden Escape last winter, she was hooked. It wasn't just because the World Wide Web site offered unusual plants, such as hyacinth beans, firecracker, and dog's tooth violet. It's because Garden Escape created a personal store just for her. Greeted by name on her personal Web page when she visits, Capozzi can take notes on a private online notepad, tinker with garden plans using the site's interactive design program, and get answers from the Garden Doctor. So far, [she] has spent $900 at Garden Escape and has no plans to shop at any other nursery. With service that personal, she says, "I probably will never leave."

Thus, just as mass production was the marketing principle of the last century, mass customization is becoming the marketing principle for the twenty-first century. The world appears to be coming full circle-from the good old days when customers were treated as individuals, to mass marketing when nobody knew your name, and back again. As Joseph Pine, author of *Mass Customization,* concludes, "Anything you can digitize, you can customize."

Sources: See Fawzia Sheikh, "Calgary Agency Critical Mass Hits the Big Time. . .Twice," *Marketing On-Line,* 25 October 1999; Eve Lazarus, "The Telus Target," *Marketing On-Line,* 22 May 2000; Gordon Arnaut, "Getting to Know You; Getting to Know All About You," *The Globe and Mail,* 15

February 1994, p. B27; Erick Schonfeld, "The Customized, Digitized, Have-It-Your-Way Economy," *Fortune,* 28 September 1998, pp. 115-124; Marc Ballon, "Sale of Modern Music Keyed to Customization," *Inc.,* May 1998, pp. 23, 25; Robert D. Hof, "Now It's Your Web," *Business Week,*

5 October 1998, pp. 164-176; Don Peppers, Martha Rogers, and Bob Dorf, "Is Your Company Ready for One-to-One Marketing?" *Harvard Business Review,* January-February 1999, pp. 151-160; and Otis Port, "Customers move into the driver's seat, *Business Week,* 4 October 1999, pp. 103-106.

Thus, Dell Computer delivers computers to individual customers loaded with customer-specified hardware and software. And Ritz-Carlton Hotels creates custom-designed experiences for its delighted guests:

Check into any Ritz-Carlton hotel around the world, and you'll be amazed at how well the hotel's employees anticipate your slightest need. Without ever asking, they seem to know that you want a nonsmoking room with a king-size bed, a nonallergenic pillow, and breakfast with decaffeinated coffee in your room. How does Ritz-Carlton work this magic? The hotel employs a system that combines information technology and flexible operations to customize the hotel experience. At the heart of the system is a huge customer database, which contains information about guests gathered through the observations of hotel employees. Each day, hotel staffers—from those at the front desk to those in maintenance and housekeeping—discreetly record the unique habits, likes, and dislikes of each guest on small "guest preference pads." These observations are then transferred to a corporatewide "guest preference database." Every morning, a "guest historian" at each hotel reviews the files of all new arrivals who have previously stayed at a Ritz-Carlton and prepares a list of suggested extra touches that might delight each guest. Guests have responded strongly to such markets-of-one service. Since inaugurating the guest-history system in 1992, Ritz-Carlton has boosted guest retention by 23 percent. An amazing 95 percent of departing guests report that their stay has been a truly memorable experience.[6]

Business-to-business marketers are also finding new ways to customize their offerings. For example, Becton-Dickinson, a major medical supplier, offers to customize almost anything for its hospital customers. It offers custom-designed labelling, individual packaging, customized quality control, customized computer software, and customized billing.

Segmenting Consumer Markets

There is no single way to segment a market. A marketer has to try different segmentation variables, alone and in combination, to find the best way to view the market structure. Table 7-1 outlines the major variables that might be used in segmenting consumer markets. Here we look at the major *geographic, demographic, psychographic,* and *behavioural variables.*

Table 7-1 Major Segmentation Variables for Consumer Markets	
Variable	**Typical Breakdown**
	Geographic
Region	Maritimes, Quebec, Ontario, Prairies, British Columbia, Northern Territories
City size	Less than 5000; 5000–20 000; 20 000–50 000; 50 000–100 000; 100 000–250 000; 250 000–500 000; 500 000–1 000 000; 1 000 000–4 000 000; 4 000 000 and over
Density	Urban, suburban, rural
Climate	Northern, Southern, Coastal, Prairie, Mountain
	Demographic
Age	Under 6, 6–11, 12–19, 20–34, 35–49, 50–64, 65+
Gender	Male, female
Family size	1–2, 3–4, 5+
Family life cycle	Young, single; young, married, no children; young, married, youngest child under 6; young, married, youngest child 6 or over; older, married, with children; older, married, no children under 18; older, single; same- sex partners; unmarried partners, no children; unmarried partners, with children; other
Income	Under $10 000; $10 000–15 000; $15 000–20 000; $20 000–30 000; $30 000–50 000; $50 000–75 000; $75 000 and over
Occupation	Professional and technical; managers, officials, and proprietors; clerical, sales; craftspeople, supervisors; operatives; farmers; retired; students; homemakers; unemployed
Education	Grade school or less; some high school; high school graduate; college; some university; university graduate; post-graduate
Religion	Catholic, Protestant, Jewish, Muslim, other
Ethnic origin	African-Canadian, Asian, British, French, German, Scandinavian, Italian, Latin American, Native Canadian, Middle Eastern, Japanese
	Psychographic
Lifestyle	Achievers, believers, strivers
Personality	Compulsive, gregarious, authoritarian, ambitious
	Behavioural
Purchase occasion	Regular occasion, special occasion
Benefits	Sought quality, service, economy
User status	Nonuser, ex-user, potential user, first-time user, regular user
Usage rate	Light user, medium user, heavy user
Loyalty status	None, medium, strong, absolute
Readiness state	Unaware, aware, informed, interested, desirous, intending to buy
Attitude toward product	Enthusiastic, positive, negative, hostile

Geographic segmentation Dividing a market into different geographical units such as nations, states, regions, counties, cities, or neighbourhoods.

Geographic Segmentation **Geographic segmentation** calls for dividing the market into different geographical units such as nations, regions, states, counties, cities, or neighbourhoods. A company may decide to operate in one or a few geographical areas, or to operate in all areas but pay attention to geographical differences in needs and wants.

Many companies are "regionalizing" their marketing programs—localizing their products, advertising, promotion, and sales efforts to fit the needs of individual regions, cities, and even neighbourhoods. For example, Absolut, the makers of vodka, launched a regional advertising campaign aimed at East Coast consumers.[7]

Demographic segmentation Dividing the market into groups based on demographic variables such as age, sex, family size, family life cycle, income, occupation, education, religion, race, and nationality.

Demographic Segmentation **Demographic segmentation** divides the market into groups based on variables such as age, gender, family size, family life cycle, income, occupation, education, religion, race, generation, and nationality. Demographic factors are the most popular bases for segmenting customer groups. One reason is that consumer needs, wants, and usage rates often vary closely with demographic variables. Another is that demographic variables are easier to measure than most other types of variables. Even when market segments are first defined using other bases, such as benefits sought or behaviour, their demographic characteristics must be known to assess the size of the target market and to reach it efficiently.

Age and life-cycle segmentation Offering different products to or using different marketing approaches for different age and life-cycle groups.

Age and Life-Cycle Stage Consumer needs and wants change with age. Some companies use **age and life-cycle segmentation**, offering different products to or using different marketing approaches for different age and life-cycle groups.

Geographic segmentation: Many companies are "regionalizing" their marketing programs—for example, Absolut launched a campaign aimed at East Coast consumers.

ABSOLUT EAST.

One of the largest challenges for today's marketers has been trying to determine what makes the youth market—those aged 18 to 25—tick, even though, as Edward Caffyn of Toronto-based advertising agency MacLaren McCann notes, "We've labelled them, prodded them, followed them, partied with them."[8] First, many young adults just don't like advertisers, don't want to be sold to, and don't want to be related to. Second, they defy the generalizations that marketers tend to make. Rather than falling into a well-defined, age-based segment, young adults are extremely diverse and celebrate their differences rather than their similarities. Even though they disdain advertising, they enjoy watching ads, and advertising is often a topic of conversation. But since an ad intrudes on their viewing, it must provide something to compensate for the interruption. It must amuse and entertain. It can't make the mistake of telling them what is cool or implying that if you use the advertised product, you will be cool. The youth market is too perceptive and cynical to accept that kind of pitch. Young adults want ads that tell them about the company and the product, and then leave it up to the viewer to decide whether they like you and your products. Ads that work share this common trait. Diesel Jeans creates a quirky world of its own; Molson Canadian's "I Am" campaign lays out the essence of a brand and asks the viewer to accept it or not; and Calvin Klein ads deal with people more than they do with clothes and imply, "Be who you gotta be and everything will be cool."[9]

Marketers must be careful to guard against stereotypes when using age and life-cycle segmentation. Although you might find some 70-year-olds in wheelchairs, you will find others on yachts. Becel, Canada's leading margarine, used this insight to develop its award-winning TV campaign. Similarly, whereas some 40-year-old couples are sending their children off to university, others are just beginning new families. Thus, age is often a poor predictor of a person's life cycle, health, work or family status, needs, and buying power.

Gender Gender segmentation has long been used in clothing, cosmetics, toiletries, and magazines. For example, Procter & Gamble was among the first with Secret, a brand specially formulated for a woman's chemistry, packaged and advertised to reinforce the female image. Recently, other marketers have noticed opportunities for gender segmentation. Merrill Lynch offers a *Financial Handbook for Women Investors* who want to "shape up their finances." Owens-Corning consciously aimed a major advertising campaign for home insulation at women after its study on women's role in home improvement showed that two-thirds were involved in materials installation, with 13 percent doing it themselves. Half the women surveyed compared themselves to Bob Vila, whereas less than half compared themselves to Martha Stewart. The automobile industry also uses gender segmentation extensively. Women buy half of all new cars sold and influence 80 percent of all new-car purchasing decisions. "Selling to women should be no different than selling to men," notes one analyst. "But there are subtleties that make a difference." Women have different frames, less upper-body strength, and greater safety concerns. To address these issues, automakers are designing cars with hoods and trunks that are easier to open, seat belts that fit women better, and an increased emphasis on safety features. Male car designers at Cadillac now go about their work with paper clips on their fingers to simulate what it feels like to operate buttons, knobs,

Gender segmentation
Dividing a market into different groups based on sex.

and other interior features with longer fingernails. Under the hood, yellow markings highlight where fluid fills go.[10]

Gender is also important when it comes to understanding consumer behaviour at the grocery checkout counter. Men make up 37 percent of Canada's principal grocery shoppers. These men are younger than the average grocery shopper, ranging in age from 25 to 34. They are also more likely to be professionals, business owners, or senior managers who live in Quebec or British Columbia. The factors that drive male grocery shoppers differ from those that concern women. Men are not as likely to clip coupons or buy no-name products. They seem to care little about products with environmental claims. They are less concerned about nutrition than their female counterparts, showing lower preferences for reduced-calorie or "light" products. Finally, men want convenience and are willing to pay higher prices for it.[11]

Income segmentation
Dividing a market into different income groups.

Income **Income segmentation** has long been used by the marketers of products and services such as automobiles, boats, clothing, cosmetics, financial services, and travel. Many companies target affluent consumers with luxury goods and convenience services. Stores such as Neiman Marcus mail their famous catalogue to wealthy Canadian consumers offering everything from expensive jewellery and fine fashions to glazed Australian apricots priced at $20 a pound.

At the other end of the spectrum are those with restricted income. Marketers must be aware that many low-income people are quite different from traditional stereotypes. Instead of being poorly educated, many fall into "the young and the jobless" class. The unemployment rate for people aged 15 to 24 is about 16 percent. Many of those who are employed can find only part-time work; others who have university educations are trying to repay the loans that allowed them to pursue a degree. They are often forced to return home and live with their parents. These living arrangements free them from the burden of paying rent and buying groceries, which allows them to make more eclectic purchases with their limited income,

Income segmentation: Stores such as Neiman Marcus target affluent consumers with luxury goods. To cater to its best customers, Neiman Marcus created its InCircle Rewards program, whose members must spend U.S.$3000 a year to be eligible.

often on entertainment-related products and services such as music, movies, and video games, as well as clothing.[12]

Psychographic Segmentation **Psychographic segmentation** divides buyers into different groups based on social class, lifestyle, or personality characteristics. People in the same demographic group can have very different psychographic makeups.

Lifestyle People's interest in various goods is affected by their lifestyles, and the goods they buy express those lifestyles. Marketers are increasingly segmenting their markets by consumer lifestyles, which can yield big payoffs:

Toronto-based Modrobes Saldebus Lounge Clothing Inc. was born to target the casual student lifestyle. Their comfortable, easy-care clothing has been a hit. The firm began with a single product-something every student needed-exam pants! As founder, Steve "Sal" Debus, exclaimed, "I had the idea to design these pants for student life. . .You could eat, sleep, drink, party, get up the next day and go to class in them and still look good." With little money for distribution, he went from campus to campus selling Exam Pants. His sales pitch soon had the clothing flying off the folding tables he used to display his wares. Sal promised prospective buyers that if his pants weren't the most comfortable piece of clothing they had ever owned, he would refund their money. Who could resist such an offer? Today, Modrobes sells its clothing line through 350 stores, including Athletes World as well as their own Toronto retail store. Creative new products, consumer insight, and carefully crafted advertising help Modrobes target consumers whose lifestyles match that of the founder. Not a bad model for success.[13]

Personality Marketers also have used personality variables to segment markets, giving their products personalities that correspond to consumer personalities. Successful market segmentation strategies based on personality have been used for such products as cosmetics, cigarettes, insurance, and liquor.[14]

Nokia differentiated itself by creating cellular phones in a range of colours that allowed people to express themselves through a functional product. Lillian Tepera, Nokia's marketing manager, says cellular phones are like watches: "They're there to serve a purpose, but people want something more than a grey or black rectangular box. People are looking for an expression of who they are, not just something to call their stockbroker with."[15]

Behavioural Segmentation **Behavioural segmentation** divides buyers into groups based on their knowledge, attitudes, uses, or responses to a product. Many marketers believe that behaviour variables are the best starting point for building market segments.

Occasions Buyers can be grouped according to occasions when they get the idea to buy, actually make their purchase, or use the purchased item. **Occasion segmentation** can help firms build product usage. For example, orange juice is most often consumed at breakfast, but orange growers have promoted drinking orange juice as a cool and refreshing drink at other times of the day. Some holidays, such as

Psychographic segmentation Dividing a market into different groups based on social class, lifestyle, or personality characteristics

Behavioural segmentation Dividing a market into groups based on consumer knowledge, attitude, use, or response to a product.

Occasion segmentation Dividing the market into groups according to occasions when buyers get the idea to buy, actually make their purchase, or use the purchased item.

Occasion segmentation: Altoids created a special "Love Tin"—a "curiously strong valentine."

Mother's Day, Father's Day, and Halloween were originally promoted partly to increase the sale of candy, flowers, cards, and other gifts.

Many marketers prepare special offers and ads for holiday occasions. For example, Beatrice Foods runs special Thanksgiving and Christmas ads for Reddi-wip during October and December, months that account for 30 percent of all whipped cream sales. Electronics retailer RadioShack Canada, based in Barrie, Ontario, launched a new E-Gift program in its stores for the 2000 holiday season. The E-Gifts are electronic gift certificates in denominations of $25, $50 and $100 in the form of plastic cards with magnetic strips.[16]

Benefits Sought A powerful form of segmentation is to group buyers according to the *benefits* they seek from the product. **Benefit segmentation** requires finding the major benefits people look for in the product class, the kinds of people who look for each benefit, and the major brands that deliver each benefit. One of the best examples of benefit segmentation was conducted in the toothpaste market (see Table 7-2). Research found four benefit segments: economic, medicinal, cosmetic, and taste. Each benefit group had special demographic, behavioural, and psychographic characteristics. For example, the people seeking to prevent decay tended to have large families, were heavy toothpaste users, and were conservative. Each segment also favoured certain brands. Most current brands appeal to one of these segments. For example, Crest toothpaste stresses protection and appeals to the family segment, whereas Aim looks and tastes good and appeals to children.

Companies can use benefit segmentation to clarify the benefit segment to

Benefit segmentation
Dividing the market into groups according to the different benefits that consumers seek from the product.

Table 7-2 Benefit Segmentation of the Toothpaste Market

Benefit Segments	Demographics	Behaviour	Psychographics	Favoured Brands
Economy (low price)	Men	Heavy users	High autonomy, value oriented	Brands on sale
Medicinal (decay prevention)	Large families	Heavy users	Hypochondriac, conservative	Crest
Cosmetic (bright teeth)	Teens, young adults	Smokers	High sociability, active	Aqua-Fresh, Ultra Brite
Taste (good tasting)	Children	Spearmint lovers	High self-involvement, hedonistic	Colgate, Aim

Source: Adapted from Russell J. Haley, "Benefit Segmentation: A Decision-Oriented Research Tool," *Journal of Marketing,* July 1968, pp. 30–35. Also see Haley, "Benefit Segmentation: Backwards and Forwards," *Journal of Advertising Research*, February–March, 1, 1984, pp. 19–25; and Haley, "Benefit Segmentation—20 Years Later," *Journal of Consumer Marketing,* 1984: 5–14.

which they are appealing, its characteristics, and the major competing brands. They also can search for new benefits and launch brands that deliver them.

User Status Markets can be segmented into groups of nonusers, ex-users, potential users, first-time users, and regular users of a product. Potential users and regular users may require different kinds of marketing appeals. For example, one study found that blood donors are motivated by need—understanding the need for blood and blood products within the community, and with the potential of their own need for blood in the future. Blood donors were also found to be very receptive to being telerecruited to make additional blood donations; most target markets are not receptive to telerecruiters. This suggests that social agencies should use different marketing approaches for keeping current donors and attracting new ones. A company's market position will also influence its focus. Market share leaders will focus on attracting potential users, whereas smaller firms will focus on attracting current users away from the market leader.

Usage Rate Markets can also be segmented into light-, medium-, and heavy-user groups. Heavy users are often a small percentage of the market but account for a high percentage of total consumption. Marketers usually prefer to attract one heavy user to their product or service rather than several light users. A study of branded ice cream buyers showed that heavy users make up only 18 percent of all buyers but consume 55 percent of all the ice cream sold; on average, these heavy users pack away 52 litres of ice cream a year versus only 10 litres for light users.

Despite the importance of heavy users, light users can also represent important targets, as Danone International Brands Canada Inc. found when trying to increase sales of its Lea & Perrins Worcestershire Sauce, which is used by many consumers only when making Bloody Caesars. The company placed ads in general interest and women's magazines, focusing on the "exotic" quality of the product and alerting consumers to the fact that Worcestershire sauce can also be used in everyday cooking. The success of the campaign could be measured by both the increase in sales and the number of calls to a toll-free number to order recipe books.[17]

Loyalty Status A market can also be segmented by consumer loyalty. Consumers can be loyal to brands (Tide), stores (The Bay), and companies (Ford). Buyers can be divided into groups according to their degree of loyalty. Some consumers are completely loyal—they buy one brand all the time. Others are somewhat loyal—they are loyal to two or three brands of a given product or favour one brand while sometimes buying others. Still other buyers show no loyalty to any brand. They either want something different each time they buy or they buy whatever is on sale.

A company can learn a lot by analyzing loyalty patterns in its market. It should start by studying its own loyal customers. Colgate finds that its loyal buyers are more middle class, have larger families, and are more health conscious. These characteristics identify the target market for Colgate. By studying its less loyal buyers, the company can identify which brands are most competitive with its own. If many Colgate buyers also buy Crest, Colgate can attempt to improve its positioning against Crest, possibly by using direct-comparison advertising. By looking at customers who are shifting away from its brand, the company can learn about its marketing weaknesses. As for nonloyals, the company may attract them by putting its brand on sale.

Companies need to be careful when using brand loyalty in their segmentation strategies. What appear to be brand-loyal purchase patterns may reflect little more than *habit, indifference,* a *low price,* or *unavailability* of other brands. Thus, frequent or regular purchasing may not be the same as brand loyalty, and marketers must examine the motivations behind observed purchase patterns.

Using Multiple Segmentation Bases Marketers rarely limit their segmentation analysis to only one or a few variables. Rather, they are increasingly using multiple segmentation bases in an effort to identify smaller, better-defined target groups. Thus, a bank may not only identify a group of wealthy retired adults, but also distinguish, within that group, several segments depending on their current income, assets, savings and risk preferences, and lifestyles. Companies often begin by segmenting their markets using a single base, then expand using other bases.

One of the most promising developments in multivariable segmentation is "geodemographic" segmentation. IRI Canada, a market information company, offers results from its retail-purchase checkout tracking systems to Canadian marketers. The data allow marketers to follow the purchase patterns of each store's trading area and overlays this information with geodemographic census data. Firms can then link census data with lifestyle and purchase patterns to develop estimates of market potential at the level of postal codes or neighbourhoods.

Canadian marketers know it is often essential to combine income with information on regional differences. A Print Measurement Bureau study revealed that regional differences act as powerful determinants of Canadians' behaviour and choices. When looking at the narrow segment of affluent consumers, we find not only that the concentration of this group varies by region, but also by buying and lifestyle habits. Affluent consumers living in Quebec, for example, have significantly different preferences from affluent consumers living in other provinces. High-income French-Canadians read more magazines and live in more moderately priced housing. They shop at specialty clothing stores more often and spend more on clothing and cosmetics. They are also more likely to bike, golf, swim, or ski than

Print Measurement Bureau www.pmb.ca

other affluent Canadians, who prefer to jog, garden, or visit health clubs. Although Quebec's affluent consumers don't travel as much as other high-income Canadians, they prefer Latin American destinations when they do travel. Thus, it can be seen that geodemographic segmentation provides a powerful tool for refining demand estimates, selecting target markets, and shaping promotion messages.

Segmenting Business Markets

Consumer and business marketers use many of the same variables to segment their markets. Business buyers can be segmented geographically or by benefits sought, user status, usage rate, and loyalty status. Yet, business marketers use some additional variables such as business customer *demographics* (industry, company size), *operating characteristics, purchasing approaches, situational factors,* and *personal characteristics.*[18]

By pursuing segments instead of the whole market, companies have a much better opportunity to deliver value to consumers and to receive maximum rewards for close attention to consumer needs. Thus, Hewlett-Packard's Computer Systems Division targets specific industries that promise the best growth prospects, such as telecommunications and financial services. Its "red team" sales force specializes in developing and serving these major customers, while its "blue team" telemarkets to smaller accounts and to those that don't fit neatly into the industries that H-P strategically targets.[19]

A company can also set up separate systems for dealing with larger or multiple-location customers. Steelcase, a major producer of office furniture, for example, segments customers into 10 industries, including banking, insurance, and electronics. Company salespeople work with independent Steelcase dealers to handle smaller, local, or regional customers in each segment. But since many national multiple-location customers, such as Exxon or IBM, have special needs that may go beyond the scope of individual dealers, Steelcase uses national accounts managers to help its dealer networks handle these accounts.

Within a target industry and customer size, the company can segment by purchase approaches and criteria. As in consumer segmentation, many marketers believe that buying behaviour and benefits provide the best basis for segmenting business markets.[20]

Segmenting International Markets

Few companies have either the resources or the will to operate in all, or even most, of the countries that dot the globe. Although some large companies, such as Coca-Cola and Sony, sell products in more than 200 countries, most international firms focus on a smaller set. Operating in many countries presents new challenges. Different countries, even those that are close together, can vary greatly in their economic, cultural, and political makeup. Thus, just as they do within their domestic markets, international firms need to group their world markets into segments with distinct buying needs and behaviours.

Companies can segment international markets using one or a combination of several variables. They can segment by *geographic location,* grouping countries by regions such as Western Europe, the Pacific Rim, the Middle East, or Africa. Geographic segmentation assumes that nations close to one another will have many common traits and behaviours. Although this is often the case, there are many exceptions. For example, although the United States and Canada have much in common, both differ culturally and economically from neighbouring Mexico. Even within a region, consumers can differ widely. For example, many Canadian marketers think that all Central and South American countries are the same, including their 400 million inhabitants. However, the Dominican Republic is no more like Brazil than Italy is like Sweden. Many Latin Americans don't speak Spanish, including 140 million Portuguese-speaking Brazilians and the millions in other countries who speak a variety of Indian dialects.

World markets can also be segmented based on *economic factors*. For example, countries might be grouped by population income levels or by their overall level of economic development. Some countries, such as the United States, Britain, France, Germany, Japan, Canada, Italy, and Russia, have established, highly industrialized economies. Other countries have newly industrialized or developing economies (Singapore, Taiwan, Korea, Brazil, Mexico). Still others are less developed (China, India). A company's economic structure shapes its population's product and service needs and, therefore, the marketing opportunities it offers.

Countries can be segmented by *political and legal factors* such as the type and stability of government, receptivity to foreign firms, monetary regulations, and the amount of bureaucracy. Such factors can play a crucial role in a company's choice of which countries to enter and how. *Cultural factors* can also be used, grouping markets according to common languages, religions, values and attitudes, customs, and behavioural patterns.

Segmenting international markets on the basis of geographic, economic, political, cultural, and other factors assumes that segments should consist of clusters of countries. However, many companies use a different approach called **intermarket segmentation**. Using this approach, they form segments of consumers who have similar needs and buying behaviour even though they are located in different countries. For example, Mercedes-Benz targets the world's well-to-do, regardless of their country. MTV targets the world's teenagers. One study of more than 6500 teenagers from 26 countries showed that teens around the world live surprisingly parallel lives. As one expert notes, "From Rio to Rochester, teens can be found enmeshed in much the same regimen:. . .drinking Coke,. . .dining on Big Macs, and surfin' the Net on their computers."[21] The world's teens have a lot in common: They study, shop, and sleep. They are exposed to many of the same major issues: love, crime, homelessness, ecology, and working parents. In many ways, they have more in common with each other than with their parents. MTV bridges the gap between cultures, appealing to what teens around the world have in common.[22]

Intermarket segmentation Forming segments of consumers who have similar needs and buying behaviour even though they are located in different countries

Requirements for Effective Segmentation

Clearly, there are many ways to segment a market, but not all segmentations are effective. For example, buyers of table salt could be divided into blond and brunette customers. But hair colour obviously does not affect the purchase of salt.

Furthermore, if all salt buyers bought the same amount of salt each month, believed that all salt is the same, and wanted to pay the same price, the company would not benefit from segmenting this market.

To be useful, market segments must be

- *Measurable:* The size, purchasing power, and profiles of the segments can be measured. Certain segmentation variables are difficult to measure. For example, there are 4 million left-handed people in Canada—representing 15 percent of the population. Yet few products are targeted toward this left-handed segment. The major problem may be that the segment is hard to identify and measure. There are no data on the demographics of lefties, and Statistics Canada does not keep track of left-handedness in its surveys. Private data companies keep reams of statistics on other demographic segments but not on left-handers.

- *Accessible:* The market segments can be effectively reached and served. Suppose a fragrance company finds that heavy users of its brand are single men and women who stay out late and socialize a lot. Unless this group lives or shops at certain places and is exposed to certain media, its members will be difficult to reach.

- *Substantial:* The market segments are large or profitable enough to serve. A segment should be the largest possible homogenous group worth pursuing with a tailored marketing program. It would not pay, for example, for an automobile manufacturer to develop cars especially for people whose height is less than one metre.

- *Differentiable:* The segments are conceptually distinguishable and respond differently to different marketing mix elements and programs. If married and unmarried women respond similarly to a sale on perfume, they do not constitute separate segments.

Intermarket segmentation: MTV targets teens around the world by appealing to what they have in common.

- *Actionable:* Effective programs can be designed for attracting and serving the segments. For example, although one small airline identified seven market segments, its staff was too small to develop separate marketing programs for each segment.

Time for a pit stop. How do the companies you do business with employ the segmentation concepts you're reading about here?

- Take another look at Figure 7-2. Can you identify specific companies, other than the examples already discussed, that practise each level of segmentation?
- Using the segmentation bases you've just read about, segment the Canadian automobile market. Describe each major segment and subsegment. Keep these segments in mind as you read the next section on market targeting.

MARKET TARGETING

Market segmentation reveals the firm's market segment opportunities. The firm now has to evaluate the various segments and decide how many and which ones to target. We now look at how companies evaluate and select target segments.

Evaluating Market Segments

In evaluating different market segments, a firm must look at three factors: segment size and growth, segment structural attractiveness, and company objectives and resources. The company must first collect and analyze data on current segment sales, growth rates, and expected profitability for various segments. It will be interested in segments that have the right size and growth characteristics. But "right size and growth" is a relative matter. The largest, fastest-growing segments are not always the most attractive ones for every company. Smaller companies may lack the skills and resources needed to serve the larger segments or may find these segments too competitive. Such companies may select segments that are smaller and less attractive, in an absolute sense, but that are potentially more profitable for them.

The company also needs to examine major structural factors that affect long-run segment attractiveness.[23] For example, a segment is less attractive if it already contains many strong and aggressive *competitors*. The existence of many actual or potential *substitute products* may limit prices and the profits that can be earned in a segment. The relative *power of buyers* also affects segment attractiveness. Buyers with strong bargaining power relative to sellers will try to force prices down, demand more services, and set competitors against one another—all at the expense of seller profitability. Finally, a segment may be less attractive if it contains *powerful suppliers* who can control prices or reduce the quality or quantity of ordered goods and services.

Even if a segment has the right size and growth and is structurally attractive, the company must consider its own objectives and resources in relation to that segment. Some attractive segments could be dismissed quickly because they do not mesh with the company's long-run objectives. Even if a segment fits the company's objectives, the company must consider whether it possesses the skills and resources it needs to succeed in that segment. If the company lacks the strengths needed to compete successfully in a segment and cannot readily obtain them, it should not enter the segment. Even if the company possesses the *required* strengths, it needs to employ skills and resources *superior* to those of the competition to really win in a market segment. The company should enter only segments in which it can offer superior value and gain advantages over competitors.

Selecting Market Segments

After evaluating different segments, the company must now decide which and how many segments to serve. This is the problem of *target market selection.* A **target market** consists of a set of buyers who share common needs or characteristics that the company decides to serve. Figure 7-3 shows that the firm can adopt one of three market-coverage strategies: *undifferentiated marketing, differentiated marketing,* and *concentrated marketing.*

Undifferentiated Marketing Using an **undifferentiated marketing** (or mass-marketing) strategy, a firm might decide to ignore market segment differences and go after the whole market with one offer. This mass-marketing strategy focuses on what is *common* in the needs of consumers rather than on what is *different.* The company designs a product and a marketing program that will appeal to the largest number of buyers. It relies on mass distribution and mass advertising, and it aims to give the product a superior image in people's minds. As noted earlier in the chap-

Target market A set of buyers sharing common needs or characteristics that the company decides to serve.

Undifferentiated marketing A market-coverage strategy in which a firm decides to ignore market segment differences and go after the whole market with one offer.

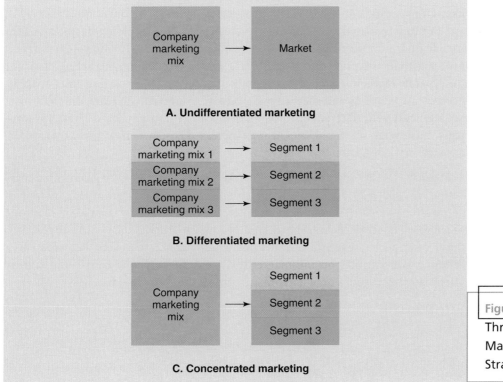

A. Undifferentiated marketing

B. Differentiated marketing

C. Concentrated marketing

Figure 7-3
Three Alternative Market-Coverage Strategies

ter, most modern marketers have strong doubts about this strategy. Difficulties arise in developing a product or brand that will satisfy all consumers. Moreover, mass marketers often have trouble competing with more focused firms that do a better job of satisfying the need of specific segments and niches.

Differentiated market- ing A market-coverage strategy in which a firm decides to target several market segments and designs separate offers for each

Cadbury Chocolate Canada **www.cadbury.chocolate. ca**

Differentiated Marketing Using a **differentiated marketing** strategy, a firm decides to target several market segments or niches and designs separate offers for each. General Motors tries to produce a car for every "purse, purpose, and personality." Nike offers athletic shoes for a dozen or more different sports, from running, fencing, and aerobics to bicycling and baseball. And Weston Foods appeals to the needs of different shopper segments with its No Frills discount stores, Extra Foods and Loblaws SuperCentres.

Cadbury Chocolate Canada changed the way chocolate bars were marketed by targeting its Mr. Big candy bars to teenagers, its Crispy Crunch bars to young adults, and its most recent offering, Time Out, to harried businesspeople. Cadbury identified a segment of the market that no other candy manufacturer was serving. By offering product and marketing variations, these companies hope for higher sales and a stronger position within each market segment. They hope that a stronger position in several segments will strengthen consumers' overall identification of the company with the product category. They also hope for more loyal purchasing, because the firm's offer better matches each segment's desires.

By offering product and marketing variations, these companies hope for higher sales and a stronger position within each market segment. Developing a stronger position within several segments creates more total sales than undifferentiated marketing across all segments. Procter & Gamble gets more total market share with its multiple brands of laundry detergents than it could with only one.

But differentiated marketing also increases the costs of doing business. A firm usually finds it more expensive to develop and produce, say, 10 units of 10 different products than 100 units of one product. Developing separate marketing plans for the separate segments requires extra marketing research, forecasting, sales analysis, promotion planning, and channel management. And trying to reach different market segments with different advertising increases promotion costs. Thus, the company must weigh increased sales against increased costs when deciding on a differentiated marketing strategy.

Concentrated marketing A market-coverage strategy in which a firm goes after a large share of one or a few submarkets

Concentrated Marketing A third market-coverage strategy, **concentrated marketing**, is especially appealing when company resources are limited. Instead of going after a small share of a large market, the firm goes after a large share of one or a few segments or niches. For example, Oshkosh Truck is the world's largest producer of airport rescue trucks and front-loading concrete mixers. Recycled Paper Products concentrates on the market for alternative greeting cards. And Clearly Canadian concentrates on a narrow segment of the soft-drink market.

Concentrated marketing: Oshkosh Truck has found its niche as the world's largest producer of airport rescue trucks and front-loading concrete mixers.

Today, the low cost of setting up shop on the Internet makes it even more profitable to serve seemingly minuscule niches. Small businesses, in particular, are realizing riches from serving small niches on the Web. Here is a "Webpreneur" who achieved astonishing results:

Whereas Internet giants like Amazon.com have yet to even realize a profit, Steve Warrington is earning a six-figure income online selling ostriches—and every product derived from them—online at **www.ostrichesonline.com**. Launched for next to nothing on the Web in 1996, Ostrichesonline.com now boasts that it sends newsletters to 27,000 subscribers and sells 17,500 ostrich products to more than 8,000 satisfied clients worldwide. The site tells visitors everything they ever wanted to know about ostriches and much, much more— it supplies ostrich facts, ostrich pictures, an ostrich farm index, and a huge ostrich database and reference index. Visitors to the site can buy ostrich meat, feathers, leather jackets, videos, eggshells, and skin care products derived from ostrich body oil.[24]

Concentrated marketing provides an excellent way for small new businesses to get a foothold against larger, more resourceful competitors. No firm knows this better than Gennum, an integrated chip manufacturer located in Burlington, Ontario. The firm has built a formidable presence in niche markets ignored by its large multinational rivals.[25] This marketing-driven company began unobtrusively by supplying the world market with integrated circuits for hearing aids. Its technologies have had a substantial influence on the miniaturization of hearing aids around the world. Ninety percent of the company's revenues come from its export markets and it has been surprisingly successful in selling chips to the Japanese, who are renowned as masters of the art.

Gennum Corporation
www.gennum.com

Through concentrated marketing, the firm achieves a strong market position because of its greater knowledge of consumer needs in the segments or niches it serves and the special reputation it acquires. It also enjoys many operating economies because of specialization in production, distribution, and promotion. If the segment is well chosen, the firm can earn a high rate of return on its investment.

At the same time, concentrated marketing involves higher-than-normal risks. The particular market segment can turn sour. Or larger competitors may decide to enter the same segment. For example, although many niche marketers, such as Jill

McDonough, a 27-year-old Calgary entrepreneur who founded Schwartzie's Bagel Noshery, have been highly successful, they always fear that this success will attract big players, like Tim Hortons, into their marketplace. If small niche players like McDonough do not have the marketing resources to compete, they are often forced to sell out to their larger competitors. For these reasons, many companies prefer to diversify in several market segments.

Choosing a Market-Coverage Strategy Companies need to consider many factors when choosing a market-coverage strategy. Which strategy is best depends on *company resources.* When the firm's resources are limited, concentrated marketing makes the most sense. The best strategy also depends on the degree of *product variability.* Undifferentiated marketing is more suited for uniform products such as grapefruit or steel. Products that can vary in design, such as cameras and automobiles, are more suited to differentiation or concentration. The *product's life-cycle stage* also must be considered.

When a firm introduces a new product, it may be practical to launch only one version, and undifferentiated marketing or concentrated marketing may make the most sense. In the mature stage of the product life cycle, however, differentiated marketing begins to make more sense. Another factor is *market variability.* If most buyers have the same tastes, buy the same amounts, and react the same way to marketing efforts, undifferentiated marketing is appropriate. Finally, *competitors' marketing strategies* are important. When competitors use differentiated or concentrated marketing, undifferentiated marketing can be suicidal. Conversely, when competitors use undifferentiated marketing, a firm can gain an advantage by using differentiated or concentrated marketing.

Socially Responsible Target Marketing

Smart targeting helps companies to be more efficient and effective by focusing on the segments that they can satisfy best and most profitably. Targeting also benefits consumers—companies reach specific groups of consumers with offers carefully tailored to satisfy their needs. However, target marketing sometimes generates controversy and concern. Issues usually involve the targeting of vulnerable or disadvantaged consumers with controversial or potentially harmful products.

For example, over the years, the cereal industry has been heavily criticized for its marketing efforts directed toward children. Critics worry that premium offers and high-powered advertising appeals presented through the mouths of lovable animated characters will overwhelm children's defences. The marketers of toys and other children's products have been similarly battered, often with good justification.

For these reasons, in 1980, the Quebec government banned all advertising to children under age 13. The other provinces follow the Code of Advertising to Children developed by a partnership between the Canadian Association of Broadcasters and the Advertising Standards Council. The code includes the stipulation that advertisements cannot directly urge children to pressure their parents to buy products. If products, such as cereals, use premiums as part of their promotion program, then the advertising must give at least as much time to the product description as it does to the premium. The code forbids the use of well-known puppets, persons, or characters (including cartoon characters) as product endorsers.[26]

Although the code has improved children's advertising on those television and radio stations licensed by the Canadian Radio-television and Telecommunications Commission (CRTC), it has not stopped the spillover advertising from the United States, where 75 percent of the advertisements seen by Canadian children originate. Although many of these ads are adapted to meet Canadian standards, others shown on American cable channels do not adhere to Canadian standards. For example, voiceovers are often added to children's commercials run in Canada giving information such as "batteries not included" or "some assembly required" since this is a Canadian, not an American, requirement.

Cigarette, beer, and fast-food marketers also have generated much controversy in recent years by their attempts to target vulnerable segments. For example, McDonald's and other chains have drawn criticism for pitching their high-fat, salt-laden fare to low-income consumers who are much more likely to be heavy consumers. R.J. Reynolds took heavy flak in 1990 when it announced plans to market Uptown, a menthol cigarette targeted toward low-income blacks. It quickly dropped the brand in the face of a loud public outcry and heavy pressure from African-American leaders.[27]

Labatt Breweries of Canada was criticized for marketing its new ice beer to young male consumers. Although young males have traditionally been the main target of many brands of beer, Labatt drew criticism because of the product's higher alcohol levels, especially in the brand extension, Maximum Ice.[28]

Women have long been concerned that they pay more for certain products and services than their male counterparts. For example, women are protesting when they are charged more than men for dry cleaning the same type of clothing. They object to paying three to four times more than men for a haircut. Research that sent white males, African-Canadian, and women to bargain for new cars at 100 dealerships revealed that white men were offered better deals when they purchased cars than were women or ethnic consumers.[29]

Although some marketers are criticized for the segments they target and for the marketing programs directed at those segments, other firms are reproached for not targeting certain groups of consumers. For example, many critics charge that the poor, who are four times less likely to buy or own a computer, have been totally left off the information highway.[30] Many firms have also been reluctant to target the gay or lesbian markets. Hiram Walker is one of the first mainstream marketers to specifically target lesbian women. Their ads for Tuaca liqueur clearly suggest that the female characters are more interested in cultivating relationships with other women, using a headline from the personal ads, "Cool girl seeks sociable silent type to share 'la dolce vita.'"[31]

Not all attempts to target children, minorities, or other special segments draw such criticism. In fact, most provide benefits to targeted consumers. For example, recent statistics reveal that women make up 42 percent of Canada's 4.5 million RRSP contributors. Although many financial institutions believe that you should reach women with your general marketing efforts, others, such as Trimark Investment Management and Altamira, are running programs with women as their

Financial institutions such as Altamira are running programs with women as their specific target, recognizing that women's needs may differ from men's.

"Money Can Not Buy Health, But I'd Settle For A Diamond Studded Rocking Chair."
~Dorothy Parker~

Altamira RRSPs
Call now: 1-800-263-7396 ext. 24

specific target. Altamira broke through the rush of RRSP advertising by using pithy quotations from notable women. These firms note that women want information, not sales pitches. Furthermore, they value financial information presented at convenient times that fit into the busy schedules inherent in two-income families, such as lunch-time financial seminars. They want advice presented in a friendly, easy-to-understand format. Whereas many male customers will not admit when they do not know something, women will ask questions about financial matters but do not want to be made to feel stupid for asking.[32]

Colgate-Palmolive's Colgate Junior toothpaste is another product targeted in a socially responsible manner. It has special features designed to get children to brush longer and more often—it's less foamy, has a milder taste, and contains sparkles, and it comes out of the tube in a star-shaped column. And some cosmetics companies have responded to the special needs of minority segments by adding products specifically designed for black, Hispanic, or Asian women. For example, M·A·C Cosmetics offers a wide range of colours that appeal to various ethnic groups.[33]

Thus, in market targeting, the issue is not really *who* is targeted but rather *how* and for *what*. Controversies arise when marketers attempt to profit at the expense of targeted segments—when they unfairly target vulnerable segments or target them with questionable products or tactics. Socially responsible marketing calls for segmentation and targeting that serve not just the interests of the company, but also the interests of those targeted.

Time to take a break and take stock.

• At the last stop, you segmented the Canadian automobile market. Now, pick two companies that serve this market and describe their segmentation and targeting strategies (oil and tire companies, for example). Can you come up with one that targets many different segments versus another that focuses on only one or a few segments?

• How does each company you chose differentiate its marketing offer and image? Has each done a good job of establishing this differentiation in the minds of targeted consumers? The final section in this chapter deals with such positioning issues.

Product position The way the product is defined by consumers on important attributes—the place the product occupies in consumers' minds relative to competing products.

POSITIONING FOR COMPETITIVE ADVANTAGE

Beyond deciding which segments of the market it will enter, the company must decide what positions it wants to occupy in those segments. A **product's position** is the way the product is *defined by consumers* on important attributes—the place the product occupies in consumers' minds relative to competing products. Positioning involves implanting the brand's unique benefits and differentiation in customers' minds. Tide is positioned as a powerful, all-purpose family detergent; Ivory Snow is positioned as the gentle detergent for fine washables and baby clothes. In the automobile market, Toyota Tercel and Subaru are positioned on economy, Mercedes and Cadillac on luxury, and Porsche and BMW on performance. Volvo positions powerfully on safety.

Consumers are overloaded with information about products and services. They cannot reevaluate products every time they make a buying decision. To simplify the buying process, consumers organize products into categories—they "position" products, services, and companies in their minds. A product's position is the complex set of perceptions, impressions, and feelings that consumers have for the product compared with competing products.

Consumers position products with or without the help of marketers. But marketers do not want to leave their products' positions to chance. They must *plan* positions that will give their products the greatest advantage in selected target markets, and they must design marketing mixes to create these planned positions.

Choosing a Positioning Strategy

Some firms find it easy to choose their positioning strategy. For example, a firm well known for quality in certain segments will go for this position in a new segment if there are enough buyers seeking quality. But in many cases, two or more firms will go after the same position. Then, each will have to find other ways to set itself apart. Each firm must differentiate its offer by building a unique bundle of benefits that appeals to a substantial group within the segment.

The positioning task consists of three steps: identifying a set of possible competitive advantages upon which to build a position, choosing the right competitive advantages, and selecting an overall positioning strategy. The company must then effectively communicate and deliver the chosen position to the market.

Identifying Possible Competitive Advantages

The key to winning and keeping customers is to understand their needs and buying processes better than competitors do and to deliver more value. To the extent that a company can position itself as providing superior value to selected target markets, it gains **competitive advantage**. But solid positions cannot be built on empty promises. If a company positions its product as *offering* the best quality and service, it must then *deliver* the promised quality and service. Thus, positioning begins with actually *differentiating* the company's marketing offer so that it will give consumers more value than competitors' offers do.

To find points of differentiation, marketers must think through the customer's entire experience with the company's product or service. An alert company can find ways to differentiate itself at every point where it comes in contact with customers.[34] In what specific ways can a company differentiate its offer from those of competitors? A company or market offer can be differentiated along the lines of *product, services, channels, people,* or *image.*

Product differentiation takes place along a continuum. At one extreme we find physical products that allow little variation: chicken, steel, aspirin. Yet even here

Competitive advantage
An advantage over competitors gained by offering consumers greater value, either through lower prices or by providing more benefits that justify higher prices.

some meaningful differentiation is possible. For example, Maple Leaf Foods claims that its Prime brand turkey is better—because it uses air not water to chill the product making the product a more tender. It also gets a price premium based on this differentiation. At the other extreme are products that can be highly differentiated, such as automobiles, commercial machinery, and furniture. Such products can be differentiated on features, performance, or style and design. Thus, Volvo provides new and better safety features; Whirlpool designs its dishwasher to run more quietly; Bose positions its speakers on their striking design characteristics. Similarly, companies can differentiate their products on such attributes as *consistency, durability, reliability,* or *repairability.*

Beyond differentiating its physical product, a firm can also differentiate the services that accompany the product. Some companies gain *services differentiation* through speedy, convenient, or careful *delivery.* For example, President's Choice Financial (operated by a member of the CIBC group of companies) has opened full-service branches in supermarkets to provide location convenience along with Saturday, Sunday, and weekday-evening hours. *Installation* can also differentiate one company from another, as can *repair* services. Many an automobile buyer will gladly pay a little more and travel a little farther to buy a car from a dealer that provides top-notch repair service. Some companies differentiate their offers by providing *customer training service* or *consulting services*—data, information systems, and advising services that buyers need. McKesson Corporation, a major drug wholesaler, consults with its 12 000 independent pharmacists to help them set up accounting, inventory, and computerized ordering systems. By helping its customers compete better, McKesson gains greater customer loyalty and sales.

Firms that practise *channel differentiation* gain competitive advantage through the way they design their channel's coverage, expertise, and performance. President's Choice Financial, in addition to location convenience also provides Internet banking services. Dell Computer and Avon distinguish themselves by their

Competitive advantage: Volvo positions powerfully on safety. When a Volvo is struck from behind, a sophisticated system "guides the front seats through an intricate choreography that supports the neck and spine while helping to reduce dangerous collision impact forces."

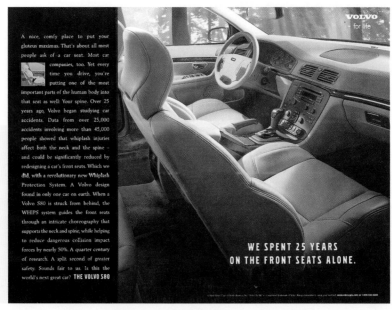

high-quality direct channels. And Science Diet pet food achieved success by going against tradition, distributing its prescription products only through veterinarians.

Companies can gain a strong competitive advantage through *people differentiation*—hiring and training better people than their competitors do. Toronto's Four Seasons Hotel is famous for its people and the service it provides to the business travellers it has targeted since the early 1970s. For years, it has set the standard for business travellers by offering state-of-the art amenities. But it is not just the hotel facilities that bring in repeat customers; it is the hotel's world-class service. For example, when a Chicago-based executive was stranded without his luggage through a flight cancellation, the hotel sent a toiletries kit to his room so he could freshen up, while hotel staff went out to purchase shirts and underwear for him. And Four Seasons employees consider it all in a day's work to fly to New York to return luggage or business papers left behind by distracted business travellers. The hotel concierge, Nancy Shulman, does everything in her power to make guests feel welcome and comfortable, including renting a chartered plane to get a first-time father home for a premature delivery or sodding a balcony to make a guest's dog feel more at home.[35]

Even when competing offers look the same, buyers may perceive a difference based on company or brand *image differentiation*. A company or brand image should convey the product's distinctive benefits and positioning. Developing a strong and distinctive image calls for creativity and hard work. A company cannot plant an image in the public's mind overnight using only a few advertisements. If The Four Seasons in Toronto means quality, this image must be supported by everything the company says and does. *Symbols*—such as the McDonald's golden arches, the Prudential rock, the Nike swoosh, the Intel Inside logo, or the Pillsbury doughboy—can provide strong company or brand recognition and image differentiation. The company might build a brand around a famous person, as Nike did with its Air Jordan basketball shoes. Some companies even become associated with colours, such as IBM (blue), Campbell (red and white), or Kodak (red and yellow). The chosen symbols, characters, and other image elements must be communicated through advertising that conveys the company or brand's personality.

Choosing the Right Competitive Advantages Suppose a company is fortunate enough to discover several potential competitive advantages. It now must choose the ones on which it will build its positioning strategy. It must decide *how many* differences to promote and *which ones*.

How Many Differences to Promote? Many marketers think that companies should aggressively promote only one benefit to the target market. Ad man Rosser Reeves, for example, said a company should develop a *unique selling proposition* (*USP*) for each brand and stick to it. Each brand should pick an attribute and tout itself as "number one" on that attribute. Buyers tend to remember number one better, especially in an overcommunicated society. Thus, Crest toothpaste consistently promotes its anticavity protection and Volvo promotes safety. A company that hammers away at one of these positions and consistently delivers on it probably will become best known and remembered for it.

Other marketers think that companies should position themselves on more than one differentiating factor. This may be necessary if two or more firms are claiming to be best on the same attribute. Today, in a time when the mass market is fragmenting into many small segments, companies are trying to broaden their positioning strategies to appeal to more segments. For example, Unilever introduced the first three-in-one bar soap—Lever 2000—offering cleansing, deodorizing, *and* moisturizing benefits. Clearly, many buyers want all three benefits, and the challenge was to convince them that one brand can deliver all three. Judging from Lever 2000's outstanding success, Unilever easily met the challenge. However, as companies increase the number of claims for their brands, they risk disbelief and a loss of clear positioning.

In general, a company needs to avoid three major positioning errors. The first is *underpositioning*—failing ever to really position the company at all. Some companies discover that buyers have only a vague idea of the company or that they do not really know anything special about it. The second error is *overpositioning*—giving buyers too narrow a picture of the company. Thus, a consumer might think that the Steuben glass company makes only fine art glass costing $1600 and up, when in fact it makes affordable fine glass starting at around $90. *Finally, companies should avoid confused positioning.*

Zellers faced an identity crisis as it struggled to ward off arch-rival Wal-Mart. Zellers went from positioning itself as the store where the "Lowest Price is the Law," to suggesting Zellers was the place "where young families shop." Next, it went to brand-building advertisements for its Martha Stewart and Gloria Vanderbilt house brands. Then there was another about-face with Zellers ads suggesting that the retailer was the place for "Everyday home fashions." It finally went back to its roots and is again stressing value with more price-promotional advertising and its Club Z loyalty program.[36]

Zellers
www.hbc.com/zellers

Which Differences to Promote? Not all brand differences are meaningful or worthwhile; not every difference makes a good differentiator. Each difference has the potential to create company costs as well as customer benefits. Therefore, the company must carefully select the ways in which it will distinguish itself from competitors. A difference is worth establishing to the extent that it satisfies the following criteria:

- *Important:* The difference delivers a highly valued benefit to target buyers.
- *Distinctive:* Competitors do not offer the difference, or the company can offer it in a more distinctive way.
- *Superior:* The difference is superior to other ways that customers might obtain the same benefit.
- *Communicable:* The difference is communicable and visible to buyers.
- *Preemptive:* Competitors cannot easily copy the difference.
- *Affordable:* Buyers can afford to pay for the difference.
- *Profitable:* The company can introduce the difference profitably.

Many companies have introduced differentiations that failed one or more of these tests. The Westin Stamford hotel in Singapore advertises that it is the world's tallest hotel, a distinction that is not important to most tourists—in fact, it turns many off. Polaroid's Polarvision, which produced instantly developed home movies, bombed too. Although Polarvision was distinctive and even preemptive, it was inferior to another way of capturing motion, namely, camcorders. When Pepsi introduced clear Crystal Pepsi some years ago, customers were unimpressed. Although the new drink was distinctive, consumers didn't see "clarity" as an important benefit in a soft drink. Thus, choosing competitive advantages upon which to position a product or service can be difficult, yet such choices may be crucial to success.

Selecting an Overall Positioning Strategy Consumers typically choose products and services that give them the greatest value. Thus, marketers want to position their brands on the key benefits that they offer relative to competing brands. The full positioning of a brand is called the brand's **value proposition**—the full mix of benefits on which the brand is positioned. It is the answer to the customer's question "Why should I buy your brand?" Volvo's value proposition hinges on safety but also includes reliability, roominess, and styling, all for a price that is higher than average but seems fair for this mix of benefits.

Figure 7-4 shows possible value propositions on which a company might position its products. In the figure, the five green cells represent winning value propositions-positioning that gives the company competitive advantage. The orange cells, however, represent losing value propositions, and the centre yellow cell represents at best a marginal proposition. In the following sections, we discuss the five winning value propositions on which companies can position their products: more for more, more for the same, the same for less, less for much less, and more for less.[37]

More for More "More for more" positioning involves providing the most upscale product or service and charging a higher price to cover the higher costs. Ritz-Carlton Hotels, Mont Blanc writing instruments, Mercedes-Benz automobiles—each claims superior quality, craftsmanship, durability, performance, or style and charges a price to match. Not only is the marketing offer high in quality, it also offers prestige to the buyer. It symbolizes status and a loftier lifestyle. Often, the price difference exceeds the actual increment in quality.

Sellers offering "only the best" can be found in every product and service category, from hotels, restaurants, food, and fashion to cars and kitchen appliances. Consumers are sometimes surprised, even delighted, when a new competitor enters

Value proposition The full positioning of a brand—the full mix of benefits on which it is positioned

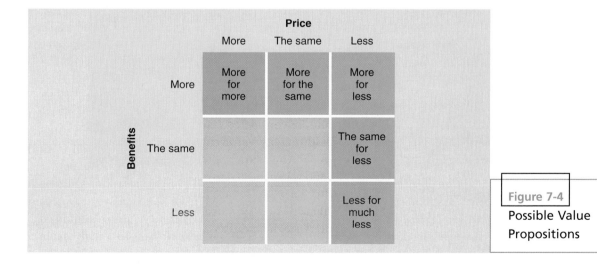

Figure 7-4

Possible Value Propositions

Before we knew it we were having Häagen~Dazs.

Fall deeply in Häagen~Dazs.

a category with an unusually high-priced brand. Starbucks coffee entered as a very expensive brand in a largely commodity category; Häagen-Dazs came in as a premium ice cream brand at a price never before charged.

Generally, companies should be on the lookout for opportunities to introduce a "much more for much more" brand in any underdeveloped product or service category. Yet "more for more" brands can be vulnerable. They often invite imitators who claim the same quality but at a lower price. Luxury goods that sell well during good times may be at risk during economic downturns when buyers become more cautious in their spending.

More for the Same Companies can attack a competitor's more for more positioning by introducing a brand offering comparable quality but at a lower price. For example, Toyota introduced its Lexus line with a "more for the same" value proposition. Its headline read: "Perhaps the first time in history that trading a U.S.$72 000 car for a U.S.$36 000 car could be considered trading up." It communicated the high quality of its new Lexus through rave reviews in car magazines, through a widely distributed videotape showing side-by-side comparisons of Lexus and Mercedes-Benz automobiles, and through surveys showing that Lexus dealers were providing customers with better sales and service experiences than were Mercedes dealerships. Many Mercedes-Benz owners switched to Lexus, and the Lexus repurchase rate has been 60 percent, twice the industry average.

Lexus Canada
www.lexuscanada.com

The Same for Less Offering "the same for less" can be a powerful value proposition—everyone likes a good deal. For example Chapters/Indigo sells the same book titles as its brick-and-mortar competitors but at lower prices, and Dell Computer offers equivalent quality at a better "price for performance." Discounts stores such as Wal-Mart and "category killers" such as Winners, Costco, Sportmart and Business Depot, use this positioning. They don't claim to offer different or better products. Instead, they offer many of the same brands as department stores and specialty stores but at deep discounts based on superior purchasing power and lower-cost operations.

Other companies develop imitative but lower-priced brands in an effort to lure customers away from the market leader. For example, Advanced Micro Devices (AMD) makes less expensive versions of Intel's market-leading microprocessor chips. Many personal computer companies make "IBM clones" and claim to offer the same performance at lower prices.

Less for Much Less A market usually exists for products that offer less and therefore cost less. Few people need, want, or can afford "the very best" in everything they buy. In many cases, consumers will gladly settle for less than optimal performance or give up some of the bells and whistles in exchange for a lower price. For example, many travellers seeking lodgings prefer not to pay for what they consider unnecessary extras, such as a pool, attached restaurant, or mints on the pillow. Motel chains such as Holiday Inn Express suspend some of these amenities and charge less accordingly. Calgary-based WestJet is another firm that understands the power of appealing to price-sensitive passengers (see New Directions 7-2).

"Less for much less" positioning involves meeting consumers' lower performance or quality requirements at a much lower price. For example, Family Dollar and Dollar General stores offer more affordable goods at very low prices. Costco warehouse stores offer less merchandise selection and consistency, and much lower levels of service; as a result, they charge rock-bottom prices.

More for Less Of course, the winning value proposition would be to offer "more for less." Many companies claim to do this. For example, Dell Computer claims to have better products *and* lower prices for a given level of performance. Procter & Gamble claims that its laundry detergents provide the best cleaning *and* everyday low prices. In the short run, some companies can actually achieve such lofty positions. For example, when it first opened for business, Home Depot had arguably the best product selection and service *and* the lowest prices compared with local hardware stores and other home improvement chains.

In the long run, companies will find it very difficult to sustain such best-of-both positioning. Offering more usually costs more, making it difficult to deliver on the "for less" promise. Companies that try to deliver both may lose out to more focused competitors.

Each brand must adopt a positioning strategy designed to serve the needs and wants of its target markets. "More for more" will draw one target market, "less for much less" will draw another, and so on. Thus, in any market, there is usually room for many different companies, each successfully occupying different positions.

New Directions 7-2 >>	WestJet: "Less for Less" Strategy at Work

History

WestJet was founded in 1996 by Clive Beddoe, Mark Hill, Tim Morgan, and Donald Bell, four Calgary entrepreneurs who saw an opportunity to provide low-fare air travel across Western Canada. By researching other successful airlines in North America—and in particular low-cost carriers—the team followed the primary examples of Southwest Airlines and Morris Air and determined that a similar concept could be successful in Western Canada.

On 29 February 1996, the airline started flight operations to Vancouver, Kelowna, Calgary, Edmonton, and Winnipeg, with 220 employees and three aircraft. Over the next three years, the company expanded, bringing more Western cities into WestJet's world—including Victoria, Saskatoon, Abbotsford/Fraser Valley, and Thunder Bay—and adding additional aircraft.

WestJet achieved a major milestone when, in July 1999, it completed its initial public offering of 2.5 million common shares. That same year also saw unprecedented change and restructuring in the airline industry in Canada, offering a window of opportunity for WestJet to expand its service across Canada. By June 2000, the company had added service to Hamilton, Moncton, and Ottawa, creating an eastern network with Hamilton as the hub.

In 2000, WestJet's four founders were honoured as the Ernst & Young Entrepreneur of the Year for Canada, in recognition of the contributions they have made to Canadian travellers and the lives of all of WestJet's people and shareholders. In 2001, Clive, Don, Mark, and Tim received an International Entrepreneurship Award for Outstanding Teamwork.

In 2001, WestJet announced further destinations, including Fort McMurray, Comox, Sault Ste. Marie, Sudbury, Thompson, and Brandon, and added its first four new-generation Boeing 737 aircraft. These are exciting times for WestJet, as it grows toward its vision of being Canada's low-air-fare leader.

Business Model

Southwest Airlines had pioneered, developed, and successfully exploited the low-fare airline model for 25 years before WestJet's creation. Southwest began in 1971 with three aircraft servicing three cities in Texas. It became known over time as an employee-oriented, somewhat irreverent, work-hard-play-hard company. It has also been the most consistently profitable airline in the world.

The actual business model differed from traditional airlines in several ways:

- Low-cost-producer strategy: From the outset, the company adopted a low-cost, no-frills strategy
- Target market focus: Price-sensitive passengers
- Single-class service focus: Short haul, point-to-point routes

Southwest's communications strategy emphasized that the airline was a complement to traditional airlines and targeted travellers who might other-

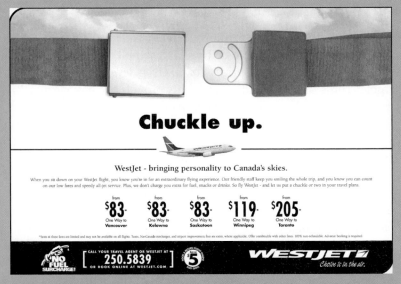

WestJet's offers a "less for less" value proposition with a dash of humour: "a low-cost, pretzel kind of carrier."

wise drive or travel by bus or train.

WestJet adopted much of Southwest's successful model, one key example being that both airlines are employee owned. The "less for less" philosophy is evident in various service choices: they offer a single class of service, without ticket offices at points other than airports; they do not offer baggage transfer services with other airlines, in-flight meals, frequent flier promotions, or special passenger privileges like business-class lounges.

The company's annual report contains the following "spirit statement" that says a great deal about the employees' focus:

At WestJet we keep the spirit alive by:
- Being successful in the air.
- Being successful on the ground.
- Celebrating new markets.
- Providing legendary service.
- Experiencing legendary growth.
- Creating internal "magic" and external "wow."

WestJet focuses on short-haul, point-to-point service. They have chosen to service both traditional and nontraditional routes where they can increase flight service frequency and where their jet service will have a competitive advantage over the regional turbo-prop planes. Although focused on minimizing costs and prices, WestJet has maintained respect for its customers and rightfully takes pride in their customer service. Once again, the annual report provides some insight on the employees' values and the company's culture:

At WestJet we have legendary values:
- We are positive and passionate about what we do.
- We take our jobs seriously, but not ourselves.
- We embrace change and innovation.
- We are friendly and caring towards our People and Customers and we treat everyone with respect.

- We provide people with the tools & training they need to do their jobs.
- We celebrate our success.
- We personify the hardworking "can do" attitude.
- We are honest, open and keep our commitments.
- We are TEAM WESTJET!

A critical element in WestJet's communications strategy is to retain the consistent image of the airline as "a low-cost, pretzel kind of carrier." Siobhan Vinish, the airline's director of public relations and communications, says, "We don't want to be perceived as another monolithic airline. Our advertising has to reinforce our image as an easygoing, fun airline,"

The Air Travel Complaints Commission began tracking complaints from air travellers in mid-2000. To the end of December 2001, 3912 complaints had been laid. Of this total, 2597 complaints had been lodged against Air Canada and their regional carriers, while only 13 had been registered against WestJet. Even considering Air Canada's dominance of the Canadian airline market, WestJet's performance in this area is testimony to their commitment to their customers and totally consistent with WestJet's values and "spirit."

WestJet is an excellent example of the success possible with the "less for less" model. In WestJet's case, "less service for less money" is defined as fewer routes and fewer amenities for a lower fare, *not* less customer service. With WestJet's focus on performance and excellent customer service, there may be an argument that this exemplifies a "more for less" strategy!

Sources: WestJet Annual Report 2001, 20 March 2002, accessed online at **www.westjet.com**, May 2002; *Southwest Airlines Fact Sheet-June 2001,* accessed online at **www.southwest.com**, May 2002; Peter Verburg, "Reach for the Bottom," *Canadian Business,* 2000; Helena Katz, "Peanuts and Pretzels Fly East," *Marketing,* 6 March 2000; Norma Ramage, "WestJet Fuels up Advertising Effort," *Marketing,* 12 March 2001.

The important thing is that each company must develop its own winning positioning strategy, one that makes it special to its target consumers. Offering only "the same for the same" provides no competitive advantage, leaving the firm in the middle of the pack. Companies offering one of the three losing value propositions—"the same or more," "less for more," and "less for the same"—will inevitably fail. Here, customers soon realize that they've been underserved, tell others, and abandon the brand.

Communicating and Delivering the Chosen Position

Once it has chosen a position, the company must take strong steps to deliver and communicate the desired position to target consumers. All the company's marketing mix efforts must support the positioning strategy. Positioning the company calls for concrete action, not just talk. If the company decides to build a position on better quality and service, it must first *deliver* that position. Designing the marketing mix—product, price, place, and promotion—involves working out the tactical details of the positioning strategy. Thus, a firm that seizes on a "more for more" position knows that it must produce high-quality products, charge a high price, distribute through high-quality dealers, and advertise in high-quality media. It must hire and train more service people, find retailers who have a good reputation for service, and develop sales and advertising messages that broadcast its superior service. This is the only way to build a consistent and believable more for more position.

Companies often find it easier to come up with a good positioning strategy than to implement it. Establishing a position or changing one usually takes a long time. In contrast, positions that have taken years to build can quickly be lost. Once a company has built the desired position, it must take care to maintain the position through consistent performance and communication. It must closely monitor and adapt the position over time to match changes in consumer needs and competitors' strategies. However, the company should avoid abrupt changes that might confuse consumers. Instead, a product's position should evolve gradually as it adapts to the ever-changing marketing environment.

<< Looking Back   < < < < < < < < <

Time to stop and stretch your legs. In this chapter, you've learned about the major elements of marketing strategy: segmentation, targeting, and positioning. Marketers know that they cannot appeal to all buyers in their markets, or at least not to all buyers in the same way. Buyers are too numerous, too widely scattered, and too varied in their needs and buying practices. Therefore, most companies today are moving away from mass marketing. Instead, they practice *target marketing*—identifying market segments, selecting one or more of them, and developing products and marketing mixes tailored to each. In this way, sellers can develop the right product for each target market and adjust their prices, distribution channels, and advertising to reach the target market efficiently.

1. Define the three steps of target marketing: market segmentation, market targeting, and market positioning.

Market segmentation is the act of dividing a market into distinct groups of buyers with different needs, characteristics, or behaviours who might require separate products or marketing mixes. Once the groups have been identified, *market targeting* evaluates each market segment's attractiveness and suggests one or more segments to enter. *Market positioning* consists of setting the competitive positioning for the product and creating a detailed marketing plan.

2. List and discuss the major levels of market segmentation and bases for segmenting consumer and business markets.

Market segmentation can be carried out at several different levels, including no segmentation (mass marketing), complete segmentation (micromarketing), or something in between (segment marketing or niche marketing). *Mass marketing* involves mass producing, mass distributing, and mass promoting about the same product in about the same way to all consumers. Using *segmented marketing,* the company tries to isolate broad segments that make up a market and adapt its offers to more closely match the needs of one or more segments. *Niche marketing* focuses on more narrowly defined subgroups within these segments, groups with distinctive sets of traits that may seek a special combination of benefits. *Micromarketing* is the practice of tailoring products and marketing programs to suit the tastes of specific individuals and locations. Micromarketing includes *local marketing* and *individual marketing.*

There is no single way to segment a market. Therefore, the marketer tries different variables to see which give the best segmentation opportunities. For consumer marketing, the major segmentation variables are geographic, demographic, psychographic, and behavioural. In *geographic segmentation,* the market is divided into different geographical units such as nations, regions, states, counties, cities, or neighbourhoods. In *demographic segmentation,* the market is divided into groups based on demographic variables, including age, gender, family size, family life cycle, income, occupation, education, religion, race, generation, and nationality. In *psychographic segmentation,* the market is divided into different groups based on social class, lifestyle, or personality characteristics. In *behavioural segmentation,* the market is divided into groups based on consumers' knowledge, attitudes, uses, or responses to a product.

Business marketers use many of the same variables to segment their markets. But business markets also can be segmented by business consumer *demographics* (industry, company size), *operating characteristics, purchasing approaches, situational factors,* and *personal characteristics.* The effectiveness of segmentation analysis depends on finding segments that are *measurable, accessible, substantial, differentiable,* and *actionable.*

3. Explain how companies identify attractive market segments and choose a market-coverage strategy.

To target the best market segments, the company first evaluates each segment's size and growth characteristics, structural attractiveness, and compatibility with company objectives and resources. It then chooses one of three market-coverage strategies. The seller can ignore segment differences (*undifferentiated marketing),* develop different market offers for several segments (*differentiated marketing),* or go after one or a few market segments (*concentrated marketing).* Much depends on company resources, product variability, product life-cycle stage, market viability, and competitive marketing strategies.

4. Discuss how companies can position their products for maximum competitive advantage in the marketplace.

Once a company has decided which segments to enter, it must decide on its *market positioning* strategy—on which positions to occupy in its chosen segments. The positioning task consists of three steps: identifying a set of possible competitive advantages upon which to build a position, choosing the right competitive advantages, and selecting an overall positioning strategy. The brand's full positioning is called its *value proposition*—the full mix of benefits upon which the brand is positioned. In general, companies can choose from one of five winning value propositions on which to position their products: more for more, more for the same, the same for less, less for much less, or more for less. They must then effectively communicate and deliver the chosen position to the market.

Navigating the Key Terms

Age and life-cycle segmentation, **p. 266**
Behavioural segmentation, **p. 269**
Benefit segmentation, **p. 270**
Competitive advantage, **p. 283**
Concentrated marketing, **p. 278**
Demographic segmentation, **p. 266**
Differentiated marketing, **p. 278**
Gender segmentation, **p. 267**
Geographic segmentation, **p. 266**
Income segmentation, **p. 268**
Individual marketing, **p. 261**
Intermarket segmentation, **p. 274**
Local marketing, **p. 261**

Market positioning, **p. 258**
Market segmentation, **p. 258**
Market targeting, **p. 258**
Micromarketing, **p. 261**
Niche marketing, **p. 260**
Occasion segmentation, **p. 269**
Product position, **p. 282**
Psychographic segmentation, **p. 269**
Segment marketing, **p. 259**
Target market, **p. 277**
Undifferentiated marketing, **p. 277**
Value proposition, **p. 287**

Concept Check

Fill in the blanks and then check your answers.

1. The first step in target marketing is _____—dividing a market into smaller groups of buyers with distinct needs, characteristics, or behaviours who might require separate products or marketing mixes.

2. According to the chapter, the three major steps in target marketing are market segmentation, _____ _____, and _____.

3. The following statements symbolize which levels of market segmentation: (a) Henry Ford offered Model Ts to customers "in any color as long as it was black." This market segmentation level equals _____ _____; (b) GM has designed specific models of cars for different income and age groups. This market segmentation level equals _____; (c) An auto insurance company sells "nonstandard" auto insurance to high-risk drivers with a record of auto accidents or drunkenness. This market segmentation level equals _____; (d) A microbrewery tailors its products and marketing programs to suit the tastes of specific individuals and locations. This market segmentation level equals _____.

4. The major variables that might be used in segmenting consumer markets include: _____, _____, _____, and _____ variables.

5. _____ segmentation divides the market into groups based on variables such as age, gender, family size, family life cycle, income, occupation, education, religion, race, and nationality.

6. Proctor & Gamble was practising _____ segmentation when they designed Secret deodorant, a brand specially formulated for a woman's chemistry, packaged and advertised to reinforce the female image.

7. There are several requirements for effective segmentation. To be useful, market segments must be _____, _____, _____ _____, _____, and _____.

8. A _____ consists of a set of buyers who share common needs or characteristics that the company decides to serve.

9. Nike is using a _____ marketing strategy when it offers athletic shoes for a dozen or more different sports, from running, fencing, and aerobics to bicycling and baseball.

10. In general, a company needs to avoid three major positioning errors: _____ positioning, _____ positioning, and _____ _____ positioning.

11. In considering which differences to promote, a difference is worth establishing to the extent that it satisfies the following criteria: important, distinctive, _____, _____, _____ _____, _____, and profitable.

12. The full positioning of a brand is called the brand's _____—the full mix of benefits on which the brand is positioned.

Concept Check Answers: 1. market segmentation; 2. market targeting, and market positioning; 3. mass marketing, segment marketing, niche marketing, and micromarketing; 4. geographic, demographic, psychographic, and behavioural; 5. Demographic; 6. gender; 7. measurable, accessible, substantial, differentiable, actionable; 8. target market; 9. differentiated; 10. under, over, confused; 11. superior, communicable, preemptive, affordable; 12. value proposition.

Discussing the Issues

1. Describe how the Ford Motor Company has moved from mass marketing to segment marketing. Do you think the company will be able to move toward niche marketing or micromarketing? If so, how? How is the company using the Internet (see **www.ford.ca**) to change its marketing segmentation approach?

2. Several years ago Sleeman's led a charge of "microbreweries" in competing with the large established Canadian brewers. What is "micromarketing" and how might it have been used by these "microbreweries?" Do you see evidence that breweries such as Sleeman's have moved to "local" or "individual" marketing? Evaluate the "micromarketing" strategies used by this industry. (For more information see **www. sleeman.com.**)

3. There are many ways to segment a market. Using the four segmentation variables shown in Table 7-1, discuss which variables would be *most important* for segmenting (a) Internet users, (b) drivers of a proposed new sports car, and (c) the adult student who returns to college to get an undergraduate degree. Explain your choices. What assumptions did you make? In each case, where would you find the information needed to segment the markets? Be creative with your research thoughts.

4. Need help with your financial planning? Software maker Intuit (see **www.intuit.com**) probably has a product just for you. The company's Quicken (financial planning software) and TurboTax (the #1 income tax preparation software), have given Intuit a strong position in the rapidly growing financial planning and services market. If the company would like to expand, which of the market-coverage strategies shown in Figure 7-3 would you suggest? Explain how the strategy you've chosen would help the company to meet strong competitive challenges from Microsoft and other software makers.

5. Collect advertisements that demonstrate the positioning of different automobile brands. Sort the various brands into categories of brands with similar positions. Using Figure 7-4, state the *value proposition* for each of the brands you surveyed. Do the advertised positions match your perceptions of where each brand belongs?

Mastering Marketing

Using the information from Figure 7-3, identify the market-coverage strategy being used by CanGo. Critique and comment on this strategy. Should a change be made? Explain. Next, using the informa-tion found in Figure 7-4, state the value proposition of CanGo's primary product line. Critique this proposition and comment. Should a change be made? Explain.

Check out the enclosed Video case CD-ROM, or our Companion Website at www.pearsoned.ca/armstrong, to view a video segment and case for this chapter.

MAP 7 Marketing Applications

Recent events suggest that marketers are increasingly moving beyond demographics in their segmentation efforts. Demographics have not been replaced but have instead been merged with psychographic and behavioural variables. For example, many companies today appear to be tailoring their products, promo-tions, and strategies to two tiers of American con-sumers. Some call this the "Tiffany/Wal-Mart" approach. In automobiles, several General Motors divisions are selling record numbers of new SUVs to "upscale" consumers (those seeking more features at higher prices). At the same time, GM's Saturn divi-sion is selling record numbers of pre-owned cars to "downscale" consumers (those seeking value and low cost). In clothing, Gap's Banana Republic stores sell "upscale" jeans for $50 or more, whereas its Old Navy stores sell "value" jeans for $20 or less. During the past decade, marketers have seen the wealthiest 5 percent of consumers grow richer while the average American's income has remained relatively stagnant.

Thinking Like a Marketing Manager

1. What other examples of two-tier marketing can you find?

2. How does a two-tier (upscale versus downscale) consumer economy affect a marketing manag-er's marketing strategy?

3. What geographic, demographic, psychographic, or behavioural variables would be most important in designing appeals for the "upscale" and "down-scale" markets found in a two-tier economy?

4. One organization that focuses on changing income and spending levels is the Canadian Association of Retired Persons (CARP). Visit the CARP Web site at **www.50plus.com** for addi-tional data. For additional insight into this mar-ket also investigate *Fifty-Five Plus* magazine at **www.fifty-five-plus.com**. What effect does a two-tier market have on seniors? Give an exam-ple of a company that seems to be approaching seniors with a two-tier market strategy.

5. Assume that you are the marketing manager for (a) a Wal-Mart store, (b) an Indigo bookseller store, and (c) a Sears department store. Design a marketing strategy for attracting (a) "upscale" con-sumers, (b) "downscale" consumers, or (c) both to your store. Can strategies for these two distinctly different markets coexist for each of these stores? Use Figure 7-4 for aid and additional information.

Digital Map

Visit our Web site at **www.pearsoned.ca/armstrong** for online quizzes, Internet exercises, and more!

CASE 7 THE ROLLING STONES: A FORTY-YEAR-OLD BRAND STILL GOING STRONG

When rock and roll first captured the hearts of teenagers in the 1950s, many believed that this new music phenomenon would be a short-lived fad. Similarly, the "British Invasion" in music that began in the early 1960s, fronted by the Beatles, was thought to be a short-term inconvenience to the North American-dominated music scene. Although rock and roll has admittedly changed, it has survived, and the members of the British Invasion continue to flourish.

The Rolling Stones is the most successful rock and roll act in history. Just like lead brands in many consumer product categories, the group has managed to thrive in a cutthroat, heavily competitive market. Since 1989, the Rolling Stones as a corporation has generated CDN$2.4 billion in revenues. This includes record sales, song rights, merchandising, sponsorship, and touring.

One of the primary reasons for the band's success has been its very clear consumer positioning. The group is not the Beatles (at the outset they were virtually Beatles opposites) or any other group of the era. Its sound is rougher and the band members look, behave, and perform differently from other bands. Consumers had to make a choice in adopting the Stones' brand of music. Broader marketing issues are at work here as well. The Stones have always differentiated themselves from other bands and other forms of entertainment. They have maintained a consistency in their product offerings, recognizing that they will appeal to certain target markets but not to all. Unlike Coca-Cola, which once saw an opportunity to become New Coke, the Rolling Stones have stayed true to their vision. Even though consumers' tastes changed over the years to folk, disco, grunge, hip-hop, and rap, the Stones took a long-term view, maintained their product standards, and have been rewarded with exceptional brand loyalty.

The core product of the Rolling Stones is their music and within the music, Keith Richards's guitar and Mick Jagger's lyrics and delivery. The brand is instantly recognizable. Long before the Nike swoosh logo was developed and implemented, the Rolling Stones lips and tongue logo was carried on everything associated with the band. The application of the logo to all brand offerings, from T-shirts and venue signage to fan club communications, provides a lesson in integrated marketing communications. This philosophy carries through to the band's marketing partnerships. The Rolling Stones recognize that they have a defined target audience and seek partnerships with organizations that will enhance their brand image. In other words, the Rolling Stones' brand activities can be integrated with other brands that have similar target audience characteristics to enhance appeal for multiple products and services.

We don't usually consider rock groups as brands. As consumers, we normally associate brands with consumer package goods such as Scope Mouthwash, Coke, and Molson Canadian. It's one of the major reasons that many consumer package goods companies call their marketing people brand managers. But branding has become more than just a process for products with physical attributes; it has become representative of consumers' experience in using an organization's product or service. Daniel Morel, the chair and global CEO of Wunderman, one of the world's largest integrated marketing solutions companies, explains it this way: "Brands are 'lived' and adapted by each customer according to [his or her] own individual 'experiences' with them. It's what we marketers do with the insights we obtain from these experiences that make the difference with our clients."

Strong brands working together in partnership can create major consumer impact. That's why the Rolling Stones have at times linked with Anheuser-Busch, Microsoft, and Sprint. In the fall of 2002, the band's Forty Licks Tour was linked with E*Trade. These multiple brand connections work synergistically in the minds of target consumers. The Rolling Stones' organization comprises four divisions or companies: Promotour, Promotone, Promopub, and Musidor. These companies are all based in the Netherlands, a tax-friendly haven for foreign bands, and handle different aspects of the band's business interests.

In 1989, Canadian promoter Michael Cohl began managing the band's shows. The concept that Cohl used bypassed the traditional method of establishing concert tours: using local promoters in individual cities that each took a cut, leaving the tour director to chase down concert proceeds.

Cohl decided that he would deal directly with venues and cut out local promoters. New revenue streams then became possible through sales of luxury boxes in arenas and stadium venues, bus tours, TV deals, and merchandising items such as T-shirts and caps. He also saw the synergies in corporate sponsorships and created cross-promotions with Volkswagen and Tommy Hilfiger.

The first tour that used this new concept was the Steel Wheels Tour of 1989. Concert ticket sales, merchandising, and sponsorship money from brewer Anheuser-Busch generated revenues of US$260 million. In 1994-95, the Voodoo Lounge Tour brought in approximately US$370 million, and in 1997-99, the Bridges of Babylon Tour yielded US$390 million. Revenue projections for the 2002-03 Forty Licks Tour are considerably lower than for previous tours, since the band will play fewer traditional stadiums and arenas, opting instead for smaller concerts, some even in large clubs. This tour will also see more sophisticated merchandising strategy offering more than 50 products. New products such as underwear from Britain's Agent Provocateur and expensive items such as shirts, jackets, and even dresses will be featured.

Although revenues might be lower than for previous tours, profitability will not be diminished. Describing the Forty Licks Tour as "the most efficient tour ever," Joe Rascoff, the band's business manager, identifies this tour's major cost-improvement strategy: When sales in the core business aren't being maximized, cut costs and boost tertiary (merchandising) revenues. "Doing fewer stadiums this time cuts costs because in previous tours we had to have three stages and three crews. This tour we have one stage and one crew." Ticket prices will vary from US$50 to US$350.

The interesting thing about the Rolling Stones is that they haven't had a new hit in years and yet their concerts consistently sell out and new material is eagerly consumed. The Forty Licks double CD launched in October 2002 contains 36 hits and 4 new songs. The four new songs were the survivors of 30 test songs that the band recorded in Paris: another testament to the band's quality control.

It will be interesting to track the sales of this new compilation. In Canada, CD sales have fallen each year since 1998: from 66.1 million units to 55.4 million in 2001, a drop of 16 percent. Is this where the 40-year-old brand clashes with new technology in the form of downloadable MP3 music, using peer-to-peer (P2P) file sharing? As always, there are opposing views on the music controversy. Some say that downloadable music has the potential to revitalize the recorded music industry. Others, the record companies and their support network (who were successful in pushing the U.S. Justice Department to shut down Napster), believe that it undermines artists' copyright protection and must be stopped. Rik Emmett, a founder of the Canadian rock group Triumph in 1975, encourages sales of his music through the Internet. He sells 12 songs for $20, and 50 percent of all his CD sales are Internet based. He believes that Internet service providers should be regulated by the Canadian government in the same way that television and radio stations and telecommunications companies are.

In a shortsighted and clumsy attempt to reduce what the Canadian Private Copyright Collective (CPCC), a recording industry coalition, deems piracy, additional taxes are now levied for all blank recordable media, CD-Rs, cassette tapes, and DVDs. The industry is now going after MP3 players, and there is a proposed per gigabyte tax for all MP3 memory purchases.

This is a new media era: MP3, gigabytes, downloads, and digital recordings versus the dinosaurs—exciting concerts with great guitar work, rolling bass lines, and just good old rock and roll. The Rolling Stones have survived everything up to now. Can they continue in light of these changes in the industry? The lyrics of their 1964 hit "Not Fade Away" come to mind.

Sources: A. Serwer, "Inside Rolling Stone Inc.," *Fortune*, 30 September 2002, pp. 58–72; B. Johnson, "Time Is on Their Side," *Maclean's*, 9 September 2002, pp. 44–47; K. Libin, "Music to Our Ears—Not," *Canadian Business*, 15 April 2002, pp. 11–12; M. Friedman, "Damage Control," *Computing Canada*, 12 April 2002, p. 30; A. Holloway, "Turning It up to 11," *Canadian Business*, 2 September 2002, pp. 71–72; Wunderman Web site, accessed online at **www.wunderman.com**, 9 November 2002.

Questions

1. What demographic and psychographic market segments are attracted to the Rolling Stones? Why?

2. Assume you are a Canadian company. How would you attempt to partner with the Rolling Stones brand during a Canadian concert tour?

3. What evaluation techniques would be useful in determining the consumer impact of a tie-in with the Rolling Stones?

4. Consider your favourite musical group. Can you define a target market for this group? What is the group's positioning?

5. Is downloadable music a threat to the recorded music industry or is it the saviour? Explain your answer.

8 >> Product and Services Strategy

Looking Ahead

Now that you've had a good look at marketing strategy, we'll journey into the marketing mix—the tactical tools that marketers use to implement their strategies. In this and the next chapter, we'll study how companies develop and manage products. Then, in the chapters that follow, we'll look at pricing, distribution, and marketing communication tools. The product is usually the first and most basic marketing consideration. How well firms manage their individual brands and their overall product and service offerings has a major impact on their success in the marketplace. We'll start with a seemingly simple question: What is a product? As it turns out, however, the answer is not so simple.

After studying this chapter, you should be able to

1. define *product* and the major classifications of products and services
2. describe the roles of product and service branding, packaging, labelling, and product support services
3. explain the decisions companies make when developing product lines and mixes
4. identify the four characteristics that affect the marketing of a service
5. discuss the additional marketing considerations that services require

First stop on this leg of the journey: resorts and vacations. Remember that seemingly simple question, what is a product? The resort and vacation industry example shows why there is no easy answer. Resorts such as Intrawest know that when people buy vacations, they buy much more than a place to get away from it all.

Some companies don't sell products, they sell experiences. Such is the case with Intrawest, a firm that defines its mission as creating "memories for our guests and staff as the best mountain, beach and resort experience...again and again." To achieve this mission, Intrawest has to rely on its employees to deliver superior service to its guests. Thus, its employees are not just highly motivated, but they are also passionate about their work. They have a sense of excitement and commitment that is so visible, it is a tangible asset to the company. This excitement is transferred to every guest. Intrawest's employees have mastered the art of integrating their product and service.[1]

Intrawest, headquartered in Vancouver, B.C., is North America's leading developer and operator of mountain "destination" resorts. The company owns and operates magnificent, award-winning ski areas: Whistler, Blackcomb, and Panorama in British Columbia; Tremblant and Mont Ste. Marie in Quebec; Blue Mountain in Ontario; Stratton in Vermont; Copper in Colorado; Mammoth in California; and Snowshoe in West Virginia. In the 1999-2000 season, Intrawest welcomed 6.2 million skiers and snowboarders at its resorts. The company builds, markets, and sells resort accommodation and real estate, mainly condominiums, at the base of each hill. But its success has as much to do with the company's focus on the customer and the experiences it creates as it does with the physical facilities. According to company officials, "What drives the mountain resort business is the quality of the experience our guests and owners come away with."[2]

However, some people, including demographer David Foot, don't believe that investing in active sports facilities is wise, since our population is aging. Statistics seem to support Foot's analysis. The number of skiers and snowboarders in Canada has declined, and the number of ski visits has dropped from a high of 21.5 million to 16 million. So why is Intrawest investing in more ski hills? The company cites two reasons for its decision. First, Intrawest knows that there is a growing vacation industry in which people come to mountain resorts not only to ski, but also to participate in various activities throughout the summer and winter. Second, Intrawest believes that demographics are on their side. Their research reveals that the average age of a person purchasing a recreational property is 50. These purchasers have sufficient disposable income to afford this type of luxury item. Since the leading edge of the baby boom group is entering their fifties, Intrawest believes that it is well positioned to take advantage of a growth market. The company also believes that this group wants recreational activities where they can bring along younger family members so they can all enjoy an activity such as skiing. Developing a love of mountains and outdoor sports in the young represents a future marketing opportunity for Intrawest.

Selling a recreational property isn't the end goal for Intrawest, however. The company stresses that selling a mountain home or renting a time-share is just the beginning, not the end of its task. It is the long-term stream of revenue received from people returning repeatedly to its resorts that makes the company profitable over the long term. Rather than relying on skiing alone, Intrawest is investing money in its properties: It is building mountain-top theatres, water parks, children's play areas, entertainment centres, and outdoor educational facilities. In other words, it is creating year-round recreational experiences that appeal to people from around the world who are interested in "destination" vacations.

Thus, Intrawest's strategic edge lies in its ability to integrate three sectors of the leisure industry: resort operations (skiing, golfing, hiking, mountain biking, retailing, dining), resort real estate development, and its vacation club (or time-share) business. Intrawest also has a network of operations from which the company achieves economies of scale: They market together, purchase together, and learn from each other.

Marketing is an important part of the company's strategy. It is investing to build equity in the brand name Intrawest. It wants the name to be synonymous worldwide with unique resort experiences in breathtaking places. Building brand equity is a costly exercise, so developing an effective and efficient marketing program is important. To accomplish its goals, Intrawest has turned to database marketing. It began to build its database with lists of season pass holders. It added the names of resort visitors, leads from consumer shows, and replies generated from cards in its advertisements. Intrawest enters lifestyle information into its database so that it can develop profiles of people who will generate the most long-term value for the firm. It can then target its marketing efforts directly at these individuals.

Although Intrawest markets its products and services primarily to baby boomers, it also understands the importance of other age groups. The company is starting to target younger people—those aged 18 to 35—who compose the largest single segment of customers for mountain resorts. These people are high-frequency guests who have more flexibility in choosing the time for their vaca-

tion than do people with school-age children. Intrawest also recognizes the importance of teenagers, who significantly influence the choice of family vacations. Teenagers drive the interest in extreme sports and represent an important group of buyers for sports gear. To appeal to these groups, Intrawest uses humour in its breakthrough advertising directed at its target audience of affluent North American, European, and Japanese consumers. Its ads also include the company's toll-free telephone number and its Web site address.

Understanding the company's target market is important. Intrawest competes not only for these customers with other mountain resorts in Canada, the United States, Europe, and Japan, but also for market share with all other leisure companies, from cruise ships to amusement parks. For this reason, Intrawest wants to offer such a variety of vacation choices within the Intrawest network that guests will return repeatedly.

Go to their Web site at www.intrawest.com. In the "About Us" section, click on the button "Our Success Formula" to see Intrawest's strategy spelled out. It has helped them generate over $1.2 billion in revenues. Having the strategic vision to integrate product and service strategies can be a powerful and profitable endeavour.[3]

Clearly, Intrawest is marketing more than just a place to ski. The company is selling experiences, and although these may be based on such physical features as magnificent mountain peaks, people keep coming back as much for the service as they do for the product. Again, we must ask, what is a product? To answer this question, we begin by explaining that companies create offerings that may be product dominated or service dominated. We suggest that the package of benefits offered to customers by many firms is a subtle mix of product and service benefits. We go on to describe ways to classify products sold to consumer and business markets. Next, we describe links between the way the product is classified and suitable marketing strategies for products in that particular classification. For product-dominated offerings, many decisions have to be made not only about product design, but also about branding, packaging, labelling, and product support services. Marketing managers must also develop product lines and product mixes. The last section of the chapter deals with the challenges associated with marketing service-dominated products. Services present special marketing challenges since they are simultaneously produced and consumed, and are intangible, perishable, and variable.

WHAT IS A PRODUCT?

A Sony CD player, a Supercuts haircut, a Céline Dion concert, a Jasper vacation, a GMC truck, H&R Block tax preparation services, and advice from an attorney are all products. We define a **product** as a cluster of benefits that can be offered to a market for attention, acquisition, use, or consumption and that might satisfy a want or need. Products include more than just tangible goods. Broadly defined, products include physical objects, services, persons, places, organizations, ideas, or mixes of these entities. Thus, throughout this text, we use the term product broadly to include any or all of these entities.

> **Product** Anything that can be offered to a market for attention, acquisition, use or consumption and that might satisfy a want or a need.

Because of their importance in the world economy, we give special attention to **services**. Services are a form of product that consist of activities, benefits, or satisfactions offered for sale that are essentially intangible and do not result in the ownership of anything. Examples are banking, hotel accommodation, tax preparation, and home repair services. We will look at services more closely at the end of this chapter.

> **Service** A form of product that consist of activities, benefits, or satisfactions offered for sale that are essentially intangible and do not result in the ownership of anything.

Products, Services, and Experiences

A company's offer to the marketplace often combines both tangible goods and intangible services. Each component can be a minor or a major part of the total offer. At one extreme, the offer may be product dominated and consist of a *pure tangible good*, such as soap, toothpaste, or salt—no services accompany the product. At the other extreme are service-dominated offerings—an intangible benefit is created for the customer but no physical product is exchanged. Examples include a doctor's exam, a university lecture, or financial services. Between these two pure extremes, however, many goods and services combinations are possible.

As products and services become more commodity-like, many companies are moving to a new level in creating value for their customers. To differentiate their offers, they are developing and delivering total customer experiences. Whereas products are tangible and services are intangible, experiences are memorable. Whereas products and services are external, experiences are personal and take place in the minds of individual consumers. Companies such as Intrawest that market experiences realize that customers are really buying much more than just products and services; they are buying what those offers will do for them—the experiences they gain in purchasing and consuming these products and services (see New Directions 8-1).

Levels of Product

Product planners need to consider the product on three levels. The most basic level is the **core product**, which addresses the question: *What is the buyer really buying?* As Figure 8-1 illustrates, the core product stands at the centre of the total product.

> **Core product** The problem-solving services or core benefits that consumers are really buying when they purchase a product.

New Directions 8-1 >>   Beyond Products and Services:
                          Welcome to the Experience Economy

In their book *The Experience Economy,* Joseph Pine and James Gilmore argue that, as products and services become less differentiated, companies are moving to a new level in creating value for customers. As the next step in differentiating their offers, beyond simply making products and delivering services, companies are staging, marketing, and delivering memorable experiences. Consider the evolution of the birthday cake:

> [In an] agrarian economy, mothers made birthday cakes from scratch, mixing farm commodities (flour, sugar, butter, and eggs) that together cost mere dimes. As the goods-based industrial economy advanced, moms paid a dollar or two to Betty Crocker for premixed ingredients. Later, when the service economy took hold, busy parents ordered cakes from the bakery or grocery store, which, at $10 or $15, cost ten times as much as the packaged ingredients. Now,…time-starved parents neither make the birthday cake nor even throw the party. Instead, they spend $100 or more to "outsource" the entire event to McDonald's, the Discovery Zone, the Rainforest Cafe, or some other business that stages a memorable event for the kids—and often throws in the cake for free. Welcome to the emerging experience economy.… From now on, leading-edge companies—whether they sell to consumers or businesses—will find that the next competitive battleground lies in staging experiences.

Experiences are sometimes confused with services, but experiences are as distinct from services as services are distinct from goods. Whereas products and services are external, experiences exist only in the mind of the individual. They are rich with emotional, physical, intellectual, or spiritual sensations created within the consumer. According to Pine and Gilmore:

> An experience occurs when a company intentionally uses services as the stage, and goods as props, to engage individual customers in a way that creates a memorable event.… To appreciate the difference between services and experiences, recall the episode of the old television show *Taxi* in which Iggy, a usually atrocious (but fun-loving) cab driver, decided to become the best taxi driver in the world. He served sandwiches and drinks, conducted tours of the city, and even sang Frank Sinatra tunes. By engaging passengers in a way that turned an ordinary cab ride into a memorable event, Iggy created something else entirely—a distinct economic offering. The experience of riding in his cab was more valuable to his customers than the service of being transported by the cab—and in the TV show, at least, Iggy's customers happily responded by giving bigger tips. By asking to go around the block again, one patron even paid more for poorer service just to prolong his enjoyment. The service Iggy provided—taxi transportation—was simply the stage for the experience that he was really selling.

Experiences have always been important in the entertainment industry—Disney has long manufactured memories through its movies and theme parks. Today, however, all kinds of firms are recasting their traditional goods and services to create experiences. For example, restaurants create value well beyond the food they serve. Starbucks patrons are paying for more than just coffee. "Customers at Starbucks are paying for staged experiences," comments one analyst. "The company treats patrons to poetry on its wallpaper and tabletops, jaunty apron-clad performers behind the espresso machine, and an interior ambience that's both cozy and slick, marked by earth tones, brushed steel, and retro music (also for sale). Few people leave without feeling a little more affluent, sophisticated, or jazzed."

Many retailers also stage experiences. Niketown stores create "shoppertainment" by offering interactive displays, engaging activities, and promotional events in a stimulating shopping environment. At Sharper Image, "people play with the gadgets, listen to miniaturized stereo equipment, sit in massage chairs, and then leave without paying for what they valued, namely, the experience." Newer Loblaws stores have the visual appeal of small town markets. In their upstairs cafés, shoppers can enjoy a cup of coffee while listening to a live string quartet one day, a country and western band the next.

Toronto-based Playdium Entertainment's 29 Canadian locations bill themselves as "entertainment centres." Although some might call them hyped up video arcades, Playdium's goal is to make game playing a rich and engaging experience, not just an addictive pastime. Much of the distinction between arcade and "entertainment centre" comes down to the way in which the experience is packaged, according to Playdium's design consultants: "We wanted to create an immersive environment." Walking into a Playdium centre is a visual experience. Graphic displays serve to heighten the energy and excitement of the place while working to guide visitors from one zone—for example, Speed, Sports, Music, Kids—to the next. "The fun of the game should start long before people start playing," the design team notes.

In San Francisco, Sony of America developed Metreon, an "interactive entertainment experience," where visitors can shop, eat, drink, play, or simply soak up the experiences (check it out at **www.metreon.com**). The huge Metreon complex features 15 theatres, including a Sony-IMAX theatre, eight theme restaurants, and several interactive attractions. Visitors can also experience any of nine interactive stores, including the flagship Discovery Channel Store. In all, Metreon offers a dazzling experience that far transcends the goods and services assortment it contains. Sony sums up the experience this way:

> Use your eyes, ears, hands, and brain…sensory overload to a phenomenal degree…. Four floors and 350 000 square feet jam-packed with ways to entertain and escape into a whole new reality. Dazzle a date. Bring wonder to your kids. Shop in amazement. Have fun with your friends. Whenever you want real entertainment, head to Metreon.

The experience economy goes beyond the entertainment and retailing businesses. All companies stage experiences whenever they engage customers in a personal, memorable way.

In the travel business, former British Airways chairman Sir Colin Marshall has noted that the "commodity mind-set" is to "think that a business is merely performing a function—in our case, transporting people from point A to point B on time and at the lowest possible price." What British Airways does, according to Sir Colin, is "to go beyond the function and compete on the basis of providing an experience." The company uses its base service (the travel itself) as the stage for a distinctive en route experience—one that attempts to transform air travel into a respite from the traveller's normally frenetic life.

Business-to-business marketers also stage experiences for their customers. For example, one computer installation and repair company has found

Marketing experiences: Sony's Metreon offers an "interactive entertainment experience: four floors and 350,000 square feet jam-packed with ways to entertain and escape into a whole new reality."

a way to turn its otherwise humdrum service into a memorable encounter. Calling itself the Geek Squad, it sends "special agents" dressed in white shirts with thin black ties and pocket protectors, carrying badges, and driving old cars. Toronto's iPIX offers virtual real estate tours to real estate agents. These tours allow agents and their clients to tour residential, rental, or even commercial properties and see multiple rooms, view interiors and exteriors, and make informed choices easily, all from the comfort of home or office, 24 hours a day, seven days a week. You can take a sample tour yourself by visiting their Web site at **www.ipix.com**.

Thus, marketers seeking new ways to bring value to customers must look beyond the goods and services they make and sell. They must find ways to turn their offers into total customer experiences. As the experience economy grows, Pine and Gilmore caution, it "threatens to render irrelevant those who relegate themselves to the diminishing world of goods and services."

Sources: Excerpts and quotes from B. Joseph Pine II and James Gilmore, "Welcome to the Experience Economy," *Harvard Business Review,* July–August 1998, pp. 97–105; Wendy Cuthbert, "Playdium Creates Order from Chaos," *Strategy,* 13 March 2000, p. 24; Wade Roush, "Now Playing: Your Business," *Technology Review,* May–June 1999, p. 96; Metreon's Web site at **www.metreon.com**, accessed September 1999; and iPix's Web site at **www.ipix.com**. Also see B. Joseph Pine and James H. Gilmore, *The Experience Economy,* New York: Free Press, 1999.

It consists of the problem-solving services or core benefits that consumers seek when they buy a product. A woman buying lipstick buys more than lip colour. Charles Revlon of Revlon recognized this early: "In the factory, we make cosmetics; in the store, we sell hope." Theodore Levitt has pointed out that buyers "do not buy quarter-inch drills; they buy quarter-inch holes." Thus, when designing products, marketers must first define the core *benefits* the product will provide to consumers.

Actual product A product's parts, quality level, features, design, brand name, packaging, and other attributes that combine to deliver core product benefits.

The product planner must next build an **actual product** around the core product. Actual products can have up to five characteristics: a *quality level, features, design,* a *brand name,* and *packaging.* For example, Sony's PlayStation is an actual product. Its brand name, software, styling, features, packaging, and other attributes have all been combined carefully to deliver the core benefit—exciting entertainment.

Augmented product Additional consumer services and benefits built around the core and actual products.

Finally, the product planner must build an **augmented product** around the core and actual products by offering additional consumer services and benefits.

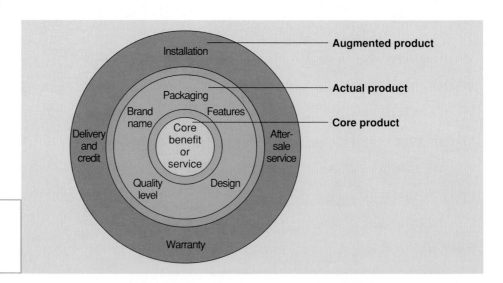

Figure 8-1

Three Levels of Product

Sony must offer more than just a videogame player. It must provide consumers with a complete solution to their entertainment needs. Thus, when consumers buy a Sony PlayStation, Sony and its dealers also might give buyers a warranty on parts and workmanship, free tips on how to maximize their game-playing experiences, quick repair services when needed, a toll-free telephone number to call if they have problems or questions, and a Web site that not only allows them to try new games, but also makes them part of the PlayStation community. To the consumer, all of these augmentations become an important part of the total product.

Therefore, a product is more than a simple set of tangible features. Consumers tend to see products as complex bundles of benefits that satisfy their needs. When developing products, marketers first must identify the *core* consumer needs the product will satisfy. They must then design the *actual* product and find ways to *augment* it to create the bundle of benefits that will best satisfy consumers.

PRODUCT CLASSIFICATIONS

Products and services fall into two broad classes based on the types of consumers that use them: (1) consumer products and (2) business products. Broadly defined, products also include other marketable entities such as experiences, organizations, persons, places, and ideas.

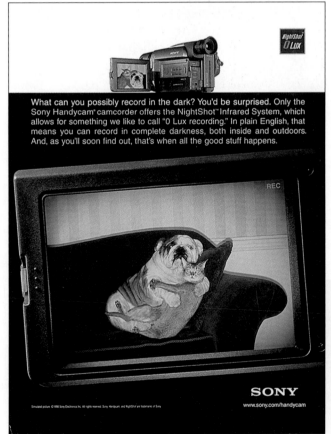

Core, actual and augmented product: Consumers perceive the Sony camcorder as a complex bundle of tangible and intangible features and services that deliver a core benefit—a convenient high-quality way to capture important moments.

Consumer Products

Consumer product
Product bought by final consumer for personal consumption.

Convenience product A consumer product that the customer usually buys frequently, immediately, and with a minimum of comparison and buying effort.

Shopping product A consumer good that the customer, in the process of selection and purchase, characteristically compares on such bases as suitability, quality, price, and style.

Consumer products are those bought by final consumers for personal consumption. Marketers usually classify these goods further based on how consumers buy them. Consumer products include convenience products, shopping products, specialty products, and unsought products. These products differ in the ways consumers buy them and therefore in how they are marketed (see Table 8-1).

Convenience products are consumer products and services that the customer usually buys frequently, immediately, and with a minimum of comparison and buying effort. Examples include soap, candy, newspapers, and fast food. Convenience products are usually low priced, and marketers place them in many locations to make them readily available when customers need them.

Shopping products are less frequently purchased consumer products and services that customers compare carefully on suitability, quality, price, and style. When buying shopping products and services, consumers spend much time and effort in gathering information and making comparisons. Examples include furniture, clothing, used cars, major appliances, and hotel and motel services. Shopping products marketers usually distribute their products through fewer outlets but provide deeper sales support to help customers in their comparison efforts.

Table 8-1 Marketing Considerations for Consumer Products

Marketing Considerations	Convenience	Shopping	Specialty	Unsought
Customer buying behaviour	Frequent purchase, little planning, little comparison or shopping effort, low customer involvement	Less frequent purchase, much planning and shopping effort, comparison of brands on price, quality, style	Strong brand preference and loyalty, special purchase effort, little comparison of brands, low price sensitivity	Little product awareness, knowledge (or if aware, little or even negative interest)
Price	Low	Higher	High	Varies
Place	Widespread in convenient locations	Selective in fewer outlets	Exclusive in only one or a few outlets per market area	Varies
Promotion	Mass promotion by the producer	Advertising and personal selling by both producer and resellers	More carefully targeted promotion by both producer and resellers	Aggressive advertising and personal selling by producer and resellers
Examples	Toothpaste, magazines, laundry detergent	Major appliances, televisions, furniture, clothing	Luxury goods, such as Rolex watches or fine crystal	Life insurance, dental services

Type of Consumer Product

Specialty products are consumer products and services with unique characteristics or brand identification for which a significant group of buyers is willing to make a special purchase effort. Examples include specific brands and types of cars, high-priced photographic equipment, designer clothes, and the services of medical or legal specialists. A Lamborghini automobile, for example, is a specialty product because buyers are usually willing to travel great distances to buy one. Buyers normally do not compare specialty products. They invest only the time needed to reach dealers carrying the wanted products.

Unsought products are consumer products that the consumer either does not know about or knows about but does not normally think of buying. Most major new innovations are unsought until the consumer becomes aware of them through advertising. Classic examples of known but unsought products and services are life insurance and blood donations to Canadian Blood Services. By their very nature, unsought products require a lot of advertising, personal selling, and other marketing efforts.

Specialty product A consumer product with unique characteristics or brand identification for which a significant group of buyers is willing to make a special purchase effort.

Unsought product A consumer product that the consumer either does not know about or knows about but does not normally think of buying.

Business Products

Business products are those purchased for further processing or for use in conducting a business. Thus, the distinction between a consumer product and a business product is based on the purpose for which the product is bought. If a consumer buys a lawn mower for use around home, the lawn mower is a consumer product. If the same consumer buys the same lawn mower for use in a landscaping business, the lawn mower is an business product.

Business product A product bought by individuals and organizations for further processing or for use in conducting a business.

The three groups of business products and services include materials and parts, capital items, and supplies and services. *Materials and parts* include raw materials and manufactured materials and parts. *Raw materials* consist of farm products (wheat, cotton, livestock, fruits, vegetables) and natural products (fish, lumber, crude petroleum, iron ore). *Manufactured materials and parts* consist of component materials (iron, yarn, cement, wires) and component parts (small motors, tires, castings). Most manufactured materials and parts are sold directly to industrial users. Price and service are the major marketing factors; branding and advertising tend to be less important.

Capital items are business products that aid in the buyer's production or operations, including installations and accessory equipment. Installations consist of major purchases such as buildings (factories, offices) and fixed equipment (generators, drill presses, large computer systems, elevators). Accessory equipment includes portable factory equipment and tools (hand tools, lift trucks) and office equipment (fax machines, desks). They have a shorter life than installations and simply aid in the production process.

The final group of business products is *supplies and services.* Supplies include operating supplies (lubricants, coal, paper, pencils) and repair and maintenance items (paint, nails, brooms). Supplies are the convenience products of the industrial field because they are usually purchased with a minimum of effort or comparison. Business services include maintenance and repair services (window cleaning, computer repair) and business advisory services (legal, management consulting, advertising). Such services are usually supplied under contract.

Organizations, Persons, Places, and Ideas

In addition to tangible products and services, in recent years marketers have broadened the concept of a product to include other "marketable entities"—organizations, persons, places, and ideas.

Organizations often carry out activities to "sell" the organization itself. *Organization marketing* consists of activities undertaken to create, maintain, or change the attitudes and behaviour of target consumers toward an organization. Both profit and nonprofit organizations practise organization marketing. Business firms sponsor public relations or corporate advertising campaigns to polish their images. Corporate image advertising is a major tool companies use to market themselves to various publics. For example, Lucent puts out ads with the tag line "We make the things that make communications work." IBM wants to establish itself as the company to turn to for "e-Business Solutions." And Ford Motor Company has "Better Ideas." Similarly, nonprofit organizations, such as churches, universities, charities, museums, and performing arts groups, market their organizations to raise funds and attract members or patrons.

People can also be marketed. *Person marketing* consists of activities undertaken to create, maintain, or change attitudes or behaviour toward particular people. All kinds of people and organizations practise person marketing. Politicians must be skillful in marketing themselves, their parties, and their platforms to get needed votes and program support. Entertainers and sports figures use marketing to promote their careers and improve their impact and incomes. Professionals such as doctors, lawyers, accountants, and architects market themselves to build their reputations and increase business. Business leaders use person marketing as a strategic tool to develop their companies' fortunes as well as their own. Businesses, charities, sports teams, fine arts groups, religious groups, and other organizations also use person marketing. Creating or associating with well-known personalities often helps these organizations achieve their goals better. That's why 12 different companies—including Nike, Buick, American Express, Disney, and Titleist—pay a combined $54 million a year to link themselves with golf superstar Tiger Woods.[4]

Place marketing involves activities undertaken to create, maintain, or change attitudes or behaviour toward particular places. Cities, provinces, regions, and even entire nations compete to attract tourists, new residents, conventions, and company offices and factories. Today, almost every city, province, and country markets its tourist attractions. Stratford, Ontario, was a little-known town with one big marketing asset—its name and a river called Avon. This became the basis for an annual Shakespeare festival, now the Stratford Festival of Canada, which put Stratford on the tourist map. Even entire nations such as Ireland, Mexico, Greece, and Indonesia have advertised themselves as good locations for business investment. For example, Ireland is an outstanding place marketer. The Irish Development Agency has convinced more than 1100 companies to locate their plants in Ireland. At the same time, the Irish Tourist Board has built a flourishing tourism business by advertising "over 11,000 places to stay and 14,000 things to do." And the Irish Export Board has created attractive markets for Irish exports.[5]

Ideas can also be marketed. In one sense, all marketing is the marketing of an idea, whether it is the general idea of brushing your teeth or the specific idea that Crest toothpastes "create smiles every day" through effective tartar control and decay prevention. Here, however, we narrow our focus to the marketing of *social ideas*, such as public health campaigns to reduce smoking, alcoholism, drug abuse, and overeating; environmental campaigns to promote wilderness protection, clean air, and conservation; and other campaigns such as family planning, human rights, and racial equality. This area has been called **social marketing**, defined by the Social Marketing Institute as the use of commercial marketing concepts and tools in programs designed to influence individuals' behaviour to improve their well-being and that of society.[6] It includes the creation and implementation of programs that seek to increase the acceptability of a social idea, cause, or practice within targeted groups. For example, YWCAs across Canada promote a "week without violence," a Calgary group called Street Teams advertises to stop child prostitution, and the United Way runs ads to show how they help people in their local communities. But social marketing involves much more than just advertising. Many public marketing campaigns fail because they assign advertising the primary role and fail to develop and use all the marketing mix tools.[7]

Social marketing The design, implementation, and control of programs that seek to increase the acceptability of a social idea, cause, or practice among a target group.

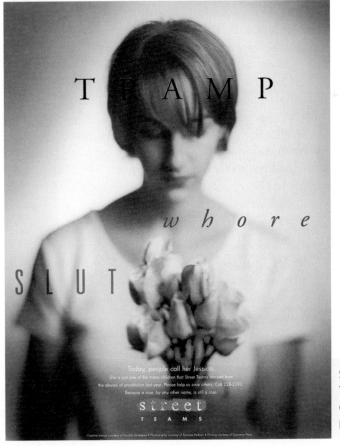

Social marketing: The Street Teams advertisement is designed to stop child prostitution.

INDIVIDUAL PRODUCT DECISIONS

Figure 8-2 shows the important decisions in the development and marketing of individual products and services. We will focus on decisions about product attributes, branding, packaging, labelling, and product support services.

Product Attributes

Developing a product or service involves defining the benefits that it will offer. These benefits are communicated and delivered by product attributes such as *quality, features,* and *style and design.*

Product quality The ability of a product to perform its functions; it includes the product's overall durability, reliability, precision, ease of operation and repair, and other valued attributes.

Product Quality **Product quality** is one of the marketer's major positioning tools. During the past two decades, a renewed emphasis on quality has spawned a global quality movement. Most firms implemented "total quality management" (TQM) programs, efforts to improve product and process quality constantly in every phase of their operations.[8]

Beyond simply reducing product defects, the ultimate goal of total quality is to improve customer satisfaction and value. For example, when Motorola first began its total quality program in the early 1980s, its goal was to drastically reduce manufacturing defects. Later, however, Motorola's quality concept evolved into one of customer-defined quality and total customer satisfaction. "Quality," noted Motorola's vice president of quality, "has to do something for the customer.... Our definition of a defect is 'if the customer doesn't like it, it's a defect.'" Similarly, Siemans defines quality this way: "Quality is when our customers come back and our products don't."[9]

As more and more companies have moved toward such customer-driven definitions of quality, their TQM programs are evolving into customer satisfaction and customer retention programs.

Thus, many companies today have turned customer-driven quality into a potent strategic weapon. They create customer satisfaction and value by consistently and profitably meeting customers' needs and preferences for quality. In fact, quality has now become a competitive necessity—in the twenty-first century, only companies with the best quality will thrive.

Product Features A product can be offered with a variety of features. A stripped-down model, one without any extras, is the starting point. The company can create higher-level models by adding more features. Features are a competitive tool for differentiating the company's product from competitors' products. Being the first producer to introduce a needed and valued new feature is one of the most effective ways to compete.

How can a company identify new features and decide which ones to add to its product? The company should periodically survey buyers who have used the prod-

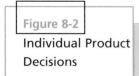

Figure 8-2

Individual Product Decisions

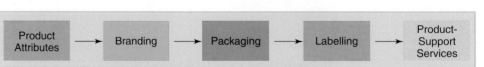

Product Attributes → Branding → Packaging → Labelling → Product-Support Services

uct and ask these questions: How do you like the product? Which specific features of the product do you like most? Which features could we add to improve the product? The answers provide the company with a rich list of feature ideas. The company can then assess each feature's value to customers versus its cost to the company. Features that customers value little in relation to costs should be dropped; those that customers value highly in relation to costs should be added.

Product Style and Design Another way to add customer value is through distinctive product style and design. Some companies have reputations for outstanding style and design, such as Black & Decker in cordless appliances and tools, Steelcase in office furniture and systems, Bose in audio equipment, and Ciba Corning in medical equipment. Design can be one of the most powerful competitive weapons in a company's marketing arsenal.

Design is a larger concept than style. Style simply describes the appearance of a product. Styles can be eye-catching or yawn producing. A sensational style may grab attention and produce pleasing aesthetics, but it does not necessarily make the product perform better. Unlike style, design is more than skin deep—it goes to the very heart of a product. Good design contributes to a product's usefulness as well as to its looks.

Good style and design can attract attention, improve product performance, cut production costs, and give the product a strong competitive advantage in the target market. For example, consider Apple's iMac personal computer:

Who said that computers have to be beige and boxy? Apple's iMac, is anything but. The iMac—which features a sleek, egg-shaped monitor and hard drive, all in one unit, in a futuristic translucent turquoise casing—redefined the look and feel of the personal computer. There's no clunky tower or desktop hard drive to clutter up your office area. There's also no floppy drive—with more and more software being distributed via CDs or the Internet, Apple thinks the floppy is on the verge of extinction. Featuring one-button Internet access, this is a machine designed specifically for cruising the Internet (that's

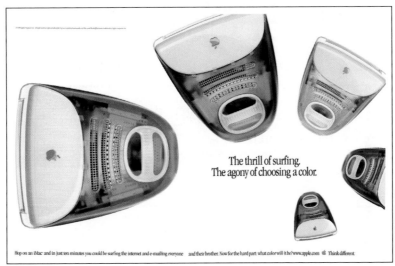

Apple's iMac redefined the look and feel of the personal computer.

what the "i" in "iMac" stands for). The dramatic iMac won raves for design and lured buyers in droves. Only one month after the iMac hit the stores, it was the number-two best-selling computer. Within a year, it had sold more than a million units, marking Apple's reemergence as a legitimate contender in the personal computer industry.[10]

Branding

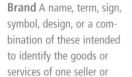

Brand A name, term, sign, symbol, design, or a combination of these intended to identify the goods or services of one seller or group of sellers and to differentiate them from those of competitors.

Perhaps the most distinctive skill of professional marketers is their ability to create, maintain, protect, and enhance brands of their products and services. A **brand** is a name, term, sign, symbol, design, or a combination of these that identifies the maker or seller of a product or service. Consumers view a brand as an important part of a product, and branding can add value to a product. For example, most consumers would perceive a bottle of White Linen perfume as a high-quality, expensive product. But the same perfume in an unmarked bottle would likely be viewed as lower in quality, even if the fragrance were identical.

Canada's *Report on Business* magazine conducted an international poll to determine what were the greatest logos of all time. Can you guess the winners? The Michelin Man took the number one spot, and the London underground logo followed as number two. In third place was a nonprofit logo, the Red Cross. The Nike swoosh, a symbol designed to convey speed and movement, grabbed fourth place, while the Volkswagen logo, the icon for the "people's car," drove into fifth spot. Canadian brand logos were among the top 50. The Esso logo was given 28th place and CN's logo took 38th spot.[11]

Branding has become so strong that today hardly anything goes unbranded. Salt is packaged in branded containers, common nuts and bolts are packaged with a distributor's label, and automobile parts—spark plugs, tires, filters—bear brand names that differ from those of the automakers. Even fruits, vegetables, and poul-

Branding has become so strong that hardly anything goes unbranded—even fruits and vegetables.

try are branded—Sunkist oranges, BC Hothouse vegetables, Chiquita bananas, Maple Leaf Prime chicken, and Butterball turkeys.

Branding helps buyers in many ways. Brand names help consumers identify products that might benefit them. Brands also tell the buyer something about product quality. Buyers who always buy the same brand know that they will get the same features, benefits, and quality each time they buy. Branding also gives the seller several advantages. The brand name becomes the basis on which a whole story can be built about a product's special qualities. The seller's brand name and trademark provide legal protection for unique product features that otherwise might be copied by competitors. And branding helps the seller to segment markets. For example, General Mills can offer Cheerios, Honey-Nut Cheerios, Wheaties, Total, Lucky Charms, and many other cereal brands, not just one general product for all consumers.

Brand Equity Brands vary in the amount of power and value they have in the marketplace. A powerful brand has high **brand equity**. Brands have higher brand equity to the extent that they have higher brand loyalty, name awareness, perceived quality, strong brand associations, and other assets such as patents, trademarks, and channel relationships.

A brand with strong brand equity is a very valuable asset. Measuring the actual equity of a brand name is difficult. However, according to one estimate, the brand equity of Coca-Cola is U.S.$110 billion, Microsoft is U.S.$103 billion, and IBM is U.S.$84 billion. Other brands rating among the world's most valuable include General Electric, Nokia, Intel, Disney, Ford, McDonald's, and AT&T. "Brand equity has emerged over the past few years as a key strategic asset," observes a brand consultant. "CEOs in many industries now see their brands as a source of control and a way to build stronger relationships with customers."[12]

Although we normally think of brand equity as something accruing to products, service companies also prize it. As Wall Street competition intensifies, financial service companies are spending millions on their brand names to attract investors. Just as Coke wants you to reach for its cans when you're thirsty, TD Evergreen and Investor's Group want you to call them when you need financial expertise. Hence, brand-building advertising by financial services companies has soared in recent years.

High brand equity provides a company with many competitive advantages. A powerful brand enjoys a high level of consumer brand awareness and loyalty. Because consumers expect stores to carry the brand, the company has more leverage in bargaining with resellers. Because the brand name carries high credibility, the company can more easily launch line and brand extensions, as when Coca-Cola leveraged its well-known brand to introduce Diet Coke or when Procter & Gamble introduced Ivory dishwashing detergent. Above all, a powerful brand offers the company some defence against fierce price competition.

Some analysts see brands as the major enduring asset of a company, outlasting the company's specific products and facilities. Yet every powerful brand really represents a set of loyal customers. Therefore, the fundamental asset underlying brand equity is customer equity. This suggests that the proper focus of marketing planning is that of extending loyal customer lifetime value, with brand management serving as a major marketing tool.[13]

Brand equity The value of a brand, based on the extent to which it has high brand loyalty, name awareness, perceived quality, strong brand associations, and other assets such as patents, trademarks, and channel relationships.

To brand or not to brand	Brand name selection	Brand sponsor	Brand strategy	Brand repositioning
Brand No brand	Selection Protection	Manufacturer's brand Private brand Licensed brand Co-branding	New brands Line extensions Brand extensions Multibrands	Brand repositioning No brand repositioning

Figure 8-3

Major Branding Decisions

Branding poses challenging decisions to the marketer. Figure 8-3 shows the key branding decisions.

Brand Name Selection A good name can add greatly to a product's success. However, finding the best brand name is a difficult task. It begins with a careful review of the product and its benefits, the target market, and proposed marketing strategies. Desirable qualities for a brand name include the following:

- It should suggest something about the product's benefits and qualities, such as DieHard, Easy-Off, Craftsman, Sunkist, Snuggles, and OFF! bug spray.

- It should be easy to pronounce, recognize, and remember. Short names help, such Tide, Aim, and Puffs. But longer ones are sometimes effective: Love My Carpet carpet cleaner, I Can't Believe It's Not Butter margarine, and President's Choice.

- It should be distinctive, such as Taurus, Kodak, Esso, Oracle.

- It should be extendable: Amazon.com began as an online bookseller but chose a name that would allow expansion into other categories.

- It should translate easily into foreign languages. Before spending U.S.$100 million to change its name to Exxon, Standard Oil of New Jersey tested several names in 54 languages in more than 150 foreign markets. It found that the name Enco referred to a stalled engine when pronounced in Japanese.

- It should be capable of registration and legal protection. A brand name cannot be registered if it infringes on existing brand names.

Once chosen, the brand name must be protected. Many firms try to build a brand name that will eventually become identified with the product category. Brand names such as Kleenex, Levi's, Jell-O, Scotch Tape, Formica, Zip-loc, and Fiberglas have succeeded in this way. However, their very success may threaten the company's rights to the name. Many originally protected brand names—such as cellophane, aspirin, nylon, kerosene, linoleum, yo-yo, trampoline, escalator, thermos, and shredded wheat—are now generic names that any seller can use.

Brand Sponsor A manufacturer has four sponsorship options. The product may be launched as a manufacturer's brand (or national brand), as when Kellogg and IBM sell their output under their own manufacturer's brand names. Or the manufacturer may sell to resellers who give it a private brand (also called a store brand or distributor brand). Although most manufacturers create their own brand names, others market licensed brands. Finally, two companies can join forces and co-brand a product.

Manufacturer's Brands versus Private Brands Manufacturers' brands have long dominated the retail scene. In recent times, however, an increasing number of retailers and wholesalers have created their own **private brands (or store brands)**. For example, Sears has created several names: DieHard batteries, Craftsman tools, Kenmore appliances, Weatherbeater paints.

Canadian Tire's private-label tires are as well known as Goodyear and Bridgestone. Private brands can be hard to establish and costly to stock and promote. However, they also yield higher profit margins for the reseller, and they give resellers exclusive products that cannot be bought from competitors, resulting in greater store traffic and loyalty.

In the so-called battle of the brands between manufacturers' and private brands, retailers have many advantages. They control what products they stock, where they go on the shelf, and which ones they will feature in local circulars. Retailers price their store brands lower than comparable manufacturers' brands, thereby appealing to budget-conscious shoppers, especially in difficult economic times. And most shoppers believe that store brands are often made by one of the larger manufacturers anyway. Most retailers also charge manufacturers **slotting fees**—payments demanded by retailers before they will accept new products and find "slots" for them on the shelves. For example, Safeway required a payment of $25 000 from a small pizza roll manufacturer to stock its new product.

As store brands improve in quality and as consumers gain confidence in their store chains, store brands are posing a strong challenge to manufacturers' brands. Consider the case of Loblaws, the Canadian supermarket chain. Its President's Choice Decadent Chocolate Chip Cookies brand is now the leading cookie brand in Canada. Loblaws' private label President's Choice cola racks up 50 percent of Loblaws' canned cola sales. Based on this success, the private label powerhouse has expanded into a wide range of food categories. For example, it now offers more than 2500 items under the President's Choice label, ranging from frozen desserts to paper, prepared foods, and boxed meats. The brand has become so popular that Loblaws now licenses it to retailers across the United States and eight other countries where Loblaws has no stores of its own. President's Choice Decadent Chocolate Chip Cookies are now sold by Jewel Food Stores in Chicago, where they are the number-one seller, beating out even Nabisco's Chips Ahoy brand. The company also offers a Web site where consumers can purchase its branded products directly.[14]

Food retailing is very concentrated in Canada. The big five retailers control more than 80 percent of sales. Thus, it is not surprising that store brands represent a powerful force in this country. Many store brands are high quality and command a significant share in their product category. Every Canadian household buys at least some store brands. One study revealed that the average Canadian consumer buys 4.6 store-branded products on each shopping trip. Some store brands appeal to value-conscious consumers who note that these brands cost 10 percent to 40 percent less than nationally branded products.[15]

The market share for private brands is expected to grow as more retailers launch and extend their lines of store brands. IGA and Food City, members of the Oshawa Group Ltd., launched 125 products under their store brand name, Our Compliments. Dominion uses the name Master Choice to identify its high-end store brands, while Safeway Canada uses Stonehenge Farms to denote its store brands. Even regional retailers have entered the fray. Selection Zel is used by

Private brand (or store brand) A brand created and owned by a reseller of a product or service.

Slotting fees Payments demanded by retailers before they will accept new products and place them on shelves.

Provigo of Quebec and Sobeys Select is used by the Nova Scotia-based retailer. Zellers, motivated by the success that supermarkets have enjoyed with private-label food and paper products, launched its own private-label line of health and beauty aids, household cleaning products, and fashion items under such names as Truly Beauty, Truly Clean, and Truly Casual. The retailer hopes the line of Truly products will generate $200 million in sales a year. Zellers is using its Canadian heritage as the foundation for its brand-building efforts.[16]

In U.S. supermarkets, private-label products account for 20 percent of U.S. supermarket sales. Private labels are even more prominent in Europe, accounting for as much as 36 percent of supermarket sales in Britain and 24 percent in France. French retail giant Carrefour sells more than 3000 in-house brands, ranging from cooking oil to car batteries.[17] Some marketing analysts predict that private brands eventually will knock out all but the strongest manufacturers' brands. We cannot assume, however, that national brands are doomed. Take the case of the "cola wars," in which Coke and Pepsi made a significant counter-attack against the private-label upstart Cott. To fend off private brands, leading brand marketers have to invest in R&D to bring out new brands, new features, and continual quality improvements. They must design strong advertising programs to maintain high awareness and preference. And they must find ways to partner with major distributors in a search for distribution economies and improved joint performance. A recent trend in branding is the move toward the creation of personal brands.[18] Although personal brands have been around for some time—consider personalized licence plates, for example—people are increasingly able to create brands uniquely their own. Canada Post offers a service that allows people to put a photo of their choice on postage stamps. Vancouver-based Urban Juice and Soda Company, bottlers of Jones Soda, has a program on its Web site to allow consumers to have the labels of their soda

Store brands: Loblaw's President's Choice store brands are so powerful that they not only dominate some categories, they are also sold under licence in nine other countries where Loblaws has no stores, including the United States.

customized with photos of their choice. People can even have cosmetics and personal hygiene products custom made and packaged by going to the Reflect.com site.

Licensing Even the Vatican engages in licensing: Heavenly images from its art collection, architecture, frescoes, and manuscripts are now imprinted on such earthly objects as T-shirts, ties, glassware, candles, and ornaments.[19]

Many companies have mastered the art of peddling their established brands and characters. For example, through savvy marketing, Warner Brothers has turned Bugs Bunny, Daffy Duck, Foghorn Leghorn, and its more than 100 other Looney Tunes characters into the world's favourite cartoon brand. The Looney Tunes licence, arguably the most sought-after nonsports licence in the industry, generates U.S.$6 billion in annual retail sales by more than 225 licensees. Warner Brothers has yet to tap the full potential of many of its secondary characters. The Tazmanian Devil, for example, initially appeared in only five cartoons. But through cross-licensing agreements with organizations such as Harley-Davidson and the NFL, Taz has become something of a pop icon.

In a real marketing coup, Quebec City-based Biscuits Leclerc licensed the whirling cartoon dervish for its Le P'tit Bonjour (Sweet Mornings) cereal. Biscuits Leclerc, an independent packaged goods manufacturer largely unknown outside the Quebec market, knew from the outset that if Le P'tit Bonjour were to stand any chance against the powerhouse brands of Kellogg, General Mills, or Post, it needed instant notoriety and it was the Taz who accomplished this task. Although several private-label cereal brands have appeared on supermarket shelves in recent years, Biscuits Leclerc is the first independent Canadian manufacturer to launch a brand of its own into this country's $862 million breakfast cereal market since 1934, when Canadian consumers were introduced to Weetabix.[20]

Co-Branding Although companies have been **co-branding** products for many years, there has been a recent resurgence in co-branded products. Co-branding occurs when two established brand names of different companies are used on the same product.

For example, in its advertising IBM Canada features companies and organizations it has helped become e-businesses. Canada Post runs an ad that features Intrawest's CEO to reinforce its claims about the power of using direct marketing. Co-branding has also become an important tool as Internet marketers work to increase the credibility of their sites. Many online marketers partner with such well-known brands as Visa, MasterCard, and E-Trust to give online consumers a greater sense of trust in their offerings.[21]

Co-branding offers many advantages. Because each brand dominates in a different category, the combined brands create broader consumer appeal and greater brand equity. Co-branding also allows a company to expand its existing brand into a category it might otherwise have difficulty entering alone. For example, by licensing its Healthy Choice brand to Kellogg, ConAgra entered the breakfast segment with a solid product. In return, Kellogg could leverage the broad awareness of the Healthy Choice name in the cereal category.

Co-branding also has limitations. Such relationships usually involve complex legal contracts and licences. Co-branding partners must carefully coordinate their advertising, sales promotion, and other marketing efforts. Finally, when co-brand-

Co-branding The practice of using the established brand names of two different companies on the same product.

ing, each partner must trust the other will take good care of its brand. As one Nabisco manager puts it, "Giving away your brand is a lot like giving away your child—you want to make sure everything is perfect."[22]

Brand Strategy A company has four choices when it comes to brand strategy (see Figure 8-4). It can introduce line extensions (existing brand names extended to new forms, sizes, and flavours of an existing product category), brand extensions (existing brand names extended to new product categories), multibrands (new brand names introduced in the same product category), or new brands (new brand names in new product categories).

Line Extensions Line extensions occur when a company introduces additional items in a given product category under the same brand name, such as new flavours, forms, colours, ingredients, or package sizes. Thus, Dannon introduced several line extensions, including seven new yogurt flavours, a fat-free yogurt, and a large, economy-size yogurt. The vast majority of all new-product activity consists of line extensions.

> **Line extension** Using a successful brand name to introduce additional items in a given product category under the same brand name, such as new flavours, forms, colours, added ingredients, or package sizes.

A company might introduce line extensions as a low-cost, low-risk way to introduce new products to meet consumer desires for variety, to use excess capacity, or simply to command more shelf space from resellers. However, line extensions involve some risks. An overextended brand name might lose its specific meaning or heavily extended brands can cause consumer confusion or frustration. For example, a consumer buying cereal at the local supermarket will be confronted by more than 150 brands, up to 30 different brands, flavours, and sizes of oatmeal alone. By itself, Quaker offers its original Quaker Oats, several flavours of Quaker instant oatmeal, and several dry cereals such as Oatmeal Squares, Toasted Oatmeal, and Toasted Oatmeal-Honey Nut. Another risk is that sales of an extension may come at the expense of other items in the line. A line extension works best when it takes sales away from competing brands, not when it cannibalizes the company's other items.

Brand Extensions A brand extension involves the use of a successful brand name to launch new or modified products in a new category. Mattel has extended its incredibly popular and enduring Barbie Doll brand into new categories ranging from Barbie home furnishings, Barbie cosmetics, and Barbie electronics to Barbie books, Barbie sporting goods, and even a Barbie band—Beyond Pink. Honda uses its company name to cover different products such as its automobiles, motorcycles, snowblowers, lawn mowers, marine engines, and snowmobiles. This allows Honda to advertise that it can fit "six Hondas in a two-car garage." Swiss Army Brand sun-

> **Brand extension** Using a successful brand name to launch a new or modified product in a new category.

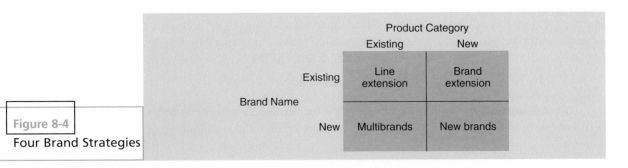

Figure 8-4
Four Brand Strategies

glasses, Disney Cruise Lines, Cosmopolitan low-fat dairy products, Century 21 Home Improvements, and Brinks home security systems are all brand extensions.

A brand extension gives a new product instant recognition and faster acceptance. It also saves the high advertising costs usually required to build a new brand name. At the same time, a brand extension strategy involves some risk. Brand extensions such as Bic pantyhose, Heinz pet food, Life Savers gum, and Clorox laundry detergent met early deaths. The extension may confuse the image of the main brand. For example, when clothing retailer Gap saw competitors targeting its value-conscious customers with Gap-like fashions at lower prices, it began testing Gap Warehouse, which sold merchandise at a cut below Gap quality and price. However, the connection confused customers and eroded the Gap image. As a result, the company renamed the stores Old Navy Clothing Company, a brand that has become enormously successful.[23]

If a brand extension fails, it may harm consumer attitudes toward the other products carrying the same brand name. Further, a brand name may not be appropriate to a particular new product, even if it is well made and satisfying—would you consider buying Esso milk or Alpo chili? A brand name may lose its special positioning in the consumer's mind through overuse. Companies that are tempted to transfer a brand name must research how well the brand's associations fit the new product.[24]

Multibrands Companies often introduce additional brands in the same category. Thus, P&G markets many different brands in each of its product categories. Multibranding offers a way to establish different features and appeal to different buying motives. It also allows a company to lock up more reseller shelf space. Or the company may want to protect its major brand by setting up flanker or fighter brands. Seiko uses different brand names for its higher-priced watches (Seiko Lasalle) and lower-priced watches (Pulsar) to protect the flanks of its mainstream Seiko brand. Finally, companies may develop separate brand names for different regions or countries, perhaps to suit different cultures or languages. Procter & Gamble dominates the North American laundry detergent market with Tide, which in all its forms captures more than a 40 percent market share. Outside North

Too many line extensions can confuse or frustrate consumers. A shopper at a local supermarket may be confronted by 30 different brands, flavours, and sizes of oat cereal alone.

America, however, P&G leads the detergent category with its Ariel brand, now Europe's number-two packaged-goods brand behind Coca-Cola.

A major drawback of multibranding is that each brand might obtain only a small market share, and none may be very profitable. The company may end up spreading its resources over many brands instead of building a few brands to a highly profitable level. These companies should reduce the number of brands they sell in a given category and set up tighter screening procedures for new brands.

New Brands A company may create a new brand name when it enters a new product category for which none of the company's current brand names is appropriate. For example, Japan's Matsushita uses separate names for its different families of products: Technics, Panasonic, National, and Quasar. Or a company might believe that the power of its existing brand name is waning and a new brand name is needed. The company may obtain new brands in new categories through acquisitions. S.C. Johnson & Son, marketer of Pledge furniture polish, Glade air freshener, Raid insect spray, Edge shaving gel, and many other well-known brands, added several new powerhouse brands through its acquisition of Drackett Company, including Windex, Drano, and Vanish toilet bowl cleaner.

As with multibranding, offering too many new brands can result in a company spreading its resources too thin. And in some industries, such as consumer packaged goods, consumers and retailers have become concerned that there are already too many brands, with too few differences among them. Thus, Procter & Gamble, Frito-Lay, and other large consumer-product marketers are now pursuing megabrand strategies—weeding out weaker brands and focusing their marketing dollars only on brands that can achieve the number-one or -two market share positions in their categories.

Building and maintaining strong brands is at the heart of successful marketing. Stop and think about all the familiar brands you encounter daily.

• List as many specific examples as you can find of each of the following: (1) brand licensing, (2) co-branding, (3) line extensions, and (4) brand extensions. Can you find a single brand that has done all of these?

• Pick and describe a familiar brand that has been widely extended. What are the benefits and dangers for this specific brand? Can you find some inappropriate brand extensions?

Packaging

Packaging The activities of designing and producing the container or wrapper for a product.

Packaging involves designing and producing the container or wrapper for a product. The package may include the product's primary container (the tube holding Colgate Total toothpaste); a secondary package that is thrown away when the product is about to be used (the cardboard box containing the tube of Colgate); and the shipping package necessary to store, identify, and ship the product (a corrugated box carrying six dozen tubes of Colgate). Labelling, printed information appearing on or with the package, is also part of packaging.

Traditionally, the primary function of the package was to contain and protect the product. In recent times, however, numerous factors have made packaging an important marketing tool. Increased competition and clutter on retail store shelves means that packages must now perform many sales tasks—from attracting attention, to describing the product, to making the sale. Companies are realizing the power of good packaging to create instant consumer recognition of the company or brand. For example, in an average supermarket, which stocks 15 000 to 17 000 items, the typical shopper passes by some 300 items per minute, and 53 percent of all purchases are made on impulse. In this highly competitive environment, the package may be the seller's last chance to influence buyers. It becomes a "five-second commercial." The Campbell Soup Company estimates that the average shopper sees its familiar red-and-white can 76 times a year, creating the equivalent of $41 million worth of advertising. The package can also reinforce the product's positioning. Coca-Cola's familiar contour bottle speaks volumes about the product inside. "Even in a shadow, people know it's a Coke," observes a packaging expert. "It's a beautiful definition of how a package can influence the way a consumer perceives a product. People taste Coke differently from a contour bottle versus a generic package."[25]

Innovative packaging can give a company an advantage over competitors. Liquid Tide quickly attained a 10 percent share of the heavy-duty detergent market, partly because of the popularity of its container's innovative drip-proof spout and cap. In contrast, poorly designed packages can cause headaches for consumers and lost sales for the company. For example, a few years ago, Planters Lifesavers Company attempted to use innovative packaging to create an association between fresh-roasted peanuts and fresh-roasted coffee. It packaged its Fresh Roast Salted Peanuts in vacuum-packed "Brik-Pacs," similar to those used for ground coffee. Unfortunately, the coffee-like packaging worked too well: Consumers mistook the peanuts for a new brand of flavoured coffee and ran them through supermarket coffee-grinding machines, creating a gooey mess, disappointed customers, and lots of irate store managers.[26]

Developing a good package for a new product requires making many decisions. First, the company must establish the packaging concept, which states what the package should be or do for the product. Should it mainly offer product protection, introduce a new dispensing method, suggest certain qualities about the product, or do something else? Decisions then must be made on specific elements of the package, such as size, shape, materials, colour, text, and brand mark. These elements must work together to support the product's position and marketing strategy. The package must be consistent with the product's advertising, pricing, and distribution.

In recent years, product safety has also become a major packaging concern. We have all learned to deal with hard-to-open "childproof" packages. And after the rash of product tampering scares during the 1980s, most drug producers and food makers are now putting their products in tamper-resistant packages. In making packaging decisions, the company also must heed growing environmental concerns and make decisions that serve society's interests as well as immediate customer and company objectives. Shortages of paper, aluminum, and other materials suggest that marketers should try to reduce packaging. Many packages end up as broken bottles and crumpled cans littering the streets and countryside. All of this packaging creates a major problem in solid waste disposal, requiring huge amounts of labour and energy.

Fortunately, many companies have gone "green." For example, S.C. Johnson repackaged Agree Plus shampoo in a stand-up pouch using 80 percent less plastic. P&G eliminated outer cartons from its Secret and Sure deodorants, saving 3.4 million pounds of paperboard per year. Tetra Pak, a major Swedish multinational company, provides an example of the power of innovative packaging that takes environmental concerns into account.

Tetra Pak
www.tetrapak.com

Tetra Pak invented an "aseptic" package that enables milk, fruit juice, and other perishable liquid foods to be distributed without refrigeration or preservatives. Not only is this packaging more environmentally responsible, it also provides economic and distribution advantages. Aseptic packaging allows companies to distribute liquid food products over a wider area without investing in refrigerated trucks and warehouses. Supermarkets can carry Tetra Pak packaged products on ordinary shelves, allowing them to save expensive refrigerator space. Tetra's motto is "a package should save more than it costs." Tetra Pak promotes the benefits of its packaging to consumers directly and even initiates recycling programs to save the environment.

Tetra Pak promotes the benefits of its packaging to consumers directly and even initiates recycling programs to save the environment.

Labelling

Labels may range from simple tags attached to products to complex graphics that are part of the package. They perform several functions. At the very least, the label identifies the product or brand, such as the name Sunkist stamped on oranges. The label might also describe several things about the product—who made it, where it was made, when it was made, its contents, how it is to be used, and how to use it safely. Finally, the label might promote the product through attractive graphics.

Labels have a long history of legal and ethical concerns. Labels have the potential to mislead customers, fail to describe important ingredients, and fail to include needed safety warnings. Labelling regulations depend on the type of product being sold. The *Consumer Packaging and Labelling Act,* which covers many nonfood products, was passed to protect consumers from labelling or packaging that is false or misleading. The *Weights and Measures Act* deals with the units of measurement on labels. The Government of Canada Web site's "Consumer Packaging and Labelling" page details the requirements for the principal display panel of prepackaged, non-food consumer products.

Consumer advocates have long lobbied for additional legislation that would require such things as open dating so that consumers can ascertain product freshness, unit pricing so that consumers can compare products in standard measurement units, and percentage labelling to reveal the percentage of ingredients such as sugar and fat. In response to these concerns, Health Canada initiated a review of its policies on nutrition labelling in 1998. The review resulted in new nutrition labelling that became mandatory on all packaged foods at the end of 2001. Labels must now be in an easy-to-read, standardized format. They provide an expanded list of ingredients including calories, fats, sodium, carbohydrate, fibre, sugar, protein, vitamin A, vitamin C, calcium, and iron. Serving size information has been made more consistent.

Health Canada's nutrition labelling
www.hc-sc.gc.ca/hppb/ nutrition/labels/e_ before.html

Product Support Services

Customer service is another element of product strategy. A company's offer to the marketplace usually includes some services, which can be a minor or a major part of the total offer. Later in the chapter, we will discuss services as products in themselves. Here, we discuss **product support services**—services that augment actual products. More and more companies are using product support services as a major tool in gaining competitive advantage.

Product support services
Services that augment actual products.

A company should design its product and support services to profitably meet the needs of target customers. The first step is to survey customers periodically to assess the value of current services and to obtain ideas for new ones. For example, Cadillac holds regular focus group interviews with owners and carefully watches complaints that come into its dealerships. From this careful monitoring, Cadillac has learned that buyers are very upset by repairs that are not done correctly the first time.

Once the company has assessed the value of various support services to customers, it must next assess the costs of providing these services. It can then develop a package of services that will both delight customers and yield profits to the company. Based on its consumer interviews, Cadillac has set up a system directly linking each dealership with a group of 10 engineers who can help walk mechanics through difficult repairs. Such actions helped Cadillac jump, in one year, from 14th to 7th in independent rankings of service.[27]

Many companies are now using the Internet and other modern technologies to provide support services that were not possible before. Using the Web, 24-hour telephone help lines, self-service kiosks, and other digital technologies, these companies are now empowering consumers to tailor their own service and support experiences. Pratt & Whitney Canada, the world's leading producer of engines for corporate jets, commuter aircraft, and helicopters, uses its Web site to provide information on engine maintenance. Air Canada provides a support Web site for its frequent flyer members: Members can book tickets, check the status of their frequent flyer accounts, and take advantage of special member fares.

Product Decisions and Social Responsibility

Product decisions have attracted much public attention. Marketers should consider carefully several public policy issues and regulations involving acquiring or dropping products, patent protection, product quality and safety, and product warranties.

Canadian manufacturers must navigate a complex web of government departments and legislation when considering their product policies. Agriculture Canada, the Canadian Food Inspection Agency, and the Consumer Products Division of Health Canada, for example, govern food and product safety. The Competition Bureau regulates many aspects of the marketing of products. The *Competition Act*'s provisions cover pricing and advertising, not just the maintenance of a competitive marketplace. When considering a merger that would give a firm access to new products, a company has to be aware that the government may invoke the Competition Act if it thinks the merger would lessen competition. Companies dropping products must be aware that they have legal obligations, written or implied, to their suppliers, dealers, and customers who have a stake in the discontinued product. Companies must also must obey patent laws when developing new products. A company cannot make its product illegally similar to another company's established product. Firms may also have to be aware of legislation controlled by Environment Canada and the Department of Transport.

Federal statutes cover product safety (except electrical equipment), competition, labelling, and weights and measures. The *Hazardous Products Act*, for example, controls the marketing of dangerous or potentially dangerous consumer and business products; the *Food and Drug Act* covers safety of cosmetics as well as food and drugs. Both acts can be found on the Canadian Department of Justice Web site. Provincial statutes deal with such matters as conditions of sale, guarantees, and licensing, as well as unfair business practices.

Consumers who have been injured by a defectively designed product can sue the manufacturer or dealer. The number of product liability suits has been increasing, and settlements often run in the millions of dollars. This, in turn, has resulted in huge increases in the cost of product liability insurance premiums. Some companies pass these higher rates along to consumers by raising prices. Others are forced to discontinue high-risk product lines.

Canadian Department of Justice
Canada.justice.gc.ca

PRODUCT LINE DECISIONS

We have looked at product strategy decisions such as branding, packaging, labelling, and support services for individual products and services. But product strategy also calls for building a product line. A **product line** is a group of products that are closely related because they function in a similar manner, are sold to the same customer groups, are marketed through the same types of outlets, or fall within given price ranges. For example, Nike produces several lines of athletic shoes, Nokia produces several lines of telecommunications products, and Nortel produces several lines of telecommunications equipment. In developing product line strategies, marketers face a number of tough decisions.

The major product line decision involves product line length—the number of items in the product line. The line is too short if the manager can increase profits by adding items; the line is too long if the manager can increase profits by dropping items. Product line length is influenced by company objectives and resources.

Product lines tend to lengthen over time. The sales force and distributors may pressure the product manager for a more complete line to satisfy their customers. Or the manager may want to add items to the product line to create growth in sales and profits. However, as the manager adds items, several costs rise: design and engineering costs, inventory costs, manufacturing changeover costs, transportation costs, and promotional costs to introduce new items. Eventually top management stops the mushrooming product line. Unnecessary or unprofitable items will be pruned from the line in a major effort to increase overall profitability. This pattern of uncontrolled product line growth followed by heavy pruning is typical and may repeat itself many times.

The company must manage its product lines carefully. It can systematically increase the length of its product line in two ways: by stretching its line upward or downward and by filling its line. Product line stretching occurs when a company lengthens its product line beyond its current range.

Many companies initially locate at the upper end of the market and later stretch their lines downward. A company may stretch downward to plug a market hole that otherwise would attract a new competitor or to respond to a competitor's attack on the upper end. Or it may add low-end products because it finds faster growth taking place in the low-end segments. Mercedes-Benz stretched downward for all these reasons.

Companies at the lower end of the market may want to stretch their product lines upward. Sometimes, companies stretch upward to add prestige to their current products. They may be attracted by a faster growth rate or higher margins at the higher end, or they may simply want to position themselves as full-line manufacturers. For example, General Electric added its Monogram line of high-quality built-in kitchen appliances targeted at the select few households earning more than $140 000 a year and living in homes valued at more than $550 000.

An alternative to product line stretching is product line filling—adding more items within the present range of the line. There are several reasons for product line filling: reaching for extra profits, satisfying dealers, using excess capacity, being the leading full-line company, and plugging holes to keep out competitors. Sony filled

Product line A group of products that are closely related because they function in a similar manner, are sold to the same consumer groups, are marketed through the same types of outlets, or fall within given price ranges.

Stretching downward: Mercedes introduced several smaller, lower-priced models, including the Smart microcompact car in a joint venture with Swatch. The "Swatchmobile" is "designed for two people and a crate of beer."

its Walkman line by adding solar-powered and waterproof Walkmans, an ultralight model that attaches to a sweatband for exercisers, the MiniDisc Walkman, the CD Walkman, and the Memory Stick Walkman, which enables users to download tracks straight from the Net. However, line filling is overdone if it results in cannibalization and customer confusion. The company should ensure that new items are noticeably different from existing ones.

PRODUCT MIX DECISIONS

Product mix (or product assortment) The set of all product lines and items that a particular seller offers for sale.

An organization with several product lines has a product mix. A **product mix (or product assortment)** consists of all the product lines and items that a particular seller offers for sale. Avon's product mix consists of four major product lines: beauty, wellness products, jewellery and accessories, and "inspirational" products (gifts, books, music, and home accents). Each product line consists of several sublines. For example, the beauty line breaks down into makeup, skin care, bath and beauty, fragrance, and outdoor protection products. Each line and subline has many individual items. Altogether, Avon's product mix includes 1300 items. In contrast, a typical Wal-mart stocks 15 000 items,, and General Electric manufactures as many as 250 000 items.

A company's product mix has four important dimensions: width, length, depth, and consistency. Product mix *width* refers to the number of different product lines the company carries. Procter & Gamble markets a fairly wide product mix consisting of many product lines, including baby care, beauty care, fabric and home care, feminine care, food and beverage, health care, and tissues and towels products. Product mix *length* refers to the total number of items the company carries within its product lines. P&G typically carries many brands within each line. For example, it sells seven laundry detergents, five hand soaps, five shampoos, and four dishwashing detergents in Canada.

Product line *depth* refers to the number of versions offered of each product in the line. Thus, P&G's Crest toothpaste comes in eight varieties, from Crest

Multicare, Crest Cavity Protection, and Crest Tartar Protection to Crest Sensitivity Protection, Crest Dual Action Whitening, and Crest Baking Soda & Peroxide Whitening formulations. (Talk about niche marketing! Remember our Chapter 7 discussion?) Finally, the *consistency* of the product mix refers to how closely related the various product lines are in end use, production requirements, distribution channels, or some other way. P&G's product lines are consistent insofar as they are consumer products that go through the same distribution channels. The lines are less consistent insofar as they perform different functions for buyers.

These product mix dimensions define the company's product strategy. The company can increase its business in four ways. It can add new product lines, thus widening its product mix. In this way, its new lines build on the company's reputation in its other lines. The company can lengthen its existing product lines to become a more full-line company. Or it can add more versions of each product and thus deepen its product mix. Finally, the company can pursue more product line consistency—or less—depending on whether it wants to have a strong reputation in a single field or in several fields.

Slow down for a minute. To get a better sense of how large and complex a company's product offering can become, investigate Procter & Gamble's product mix.

• Using P&G's Web site at **www.pg.com**, its annual report, or other sources, develop a list of all the company's product lines and individual products. What surprises you about this list of products?

• Is P&G's product mix consistent? What overall strategy or logic appears to have guided the development of this product mix?

SERVICES MARKETING

One of the major world trends in recent years has been the dramatic growth of services. As a result of rising affluence, more leisure time, and the growing complexity of products that require servicing, North America has become the world's first service economy. Services industries account for more than two thirds of Canada's GDP, almost three quarters of employment in the country, and 90 percent of new job creation.[28] In the United States, services industries account for 74 percent of national GDP and nearly 60 percent of personal consumption expenditures. In 1996 service jobs accounted for 80 of total U.S. employment. Services are growing even faster in the world economy, making up a quarter of the value of all international trade. In fact, a variety of service industries—from banking, insurance, and communications to transportation, travel, and entertainment—now accounts for more than 60 percent of the economy in developed countries around the world.[29]

Service industries vary greatly. Governments offer services through courts, employment services, hospitals, loan agencies, military services, police and fire departments, postal service, regulatory agencies, and schools. Private nonprofit organizations offer services through museums, charities, churches, foundations, and hospitals. A large number of business organizations offer services: airlines, banks, hotels, insurance companies, consulting firms, medical and law practices, entertainment companies, real estate firms, advertising and research agencies, and retailers.

Nature and Characteristics of a Service

A company must consider four special service characteristics when designing marketing programs: intangibility, inseparability, variability, and perishability. These characteristics are summarized in Figure 8-5 and discussed in the following sections.

Service intangibility
A major characteristic of services—they cannot be seen, tasted, felt, heard, or smelled before they are bought.

Service intangibility means that services cannot be seen, tasted, felt, heard, or smelled before they are bought. For example, people undergoing cosmetic surgery cannot see the result before the purchase. Airline passengers have nothing but a ticket and the promise that they and their luggage will arrive safely at the intended destination, ideally at the same time. To reduce uncertainty, buyers look for "signals" of service quality. They draw conclusions about quality from the place, people, price, equipment, and communications that they can see. Therefore, the service provider's task is to make the service tangible in one or more ways. Whereas product marketers try to add intangibles to their tangible offers, service marketers try to add tangibles to their intangible offers.

Physical goods are produced, then stored, later sold, and still later consumed. In contrast, services are first sold, then produced and consumed at the same time. **Service inseparability** means that services cannot be separated from their providers, whether the providers are people or machines. If a service employee provides the service, then the employee is a part of the service. Because the customer is also present as the service is produced, provider-customer interaction is a special feature of services marketing. Both the provider and the customer affect the service outcome.

Service inseparability
A major characteristic of services—they are produced and consumed at the same time and cannot be separated from their providers, whether the providers are people or machines.

Service variability
A major characteristic of services—their quality may vary greatly, depending on who provides them and when, where, and how.

Service variability means that the quality of services depends on who provides them as well as when, where, and how they are provided. For example, some hotels—say, Marriott—have reputations for providing better service than others. Still, within a given Marriott hotel, one registration-desk employee may be cheerful and efficient, whereas another standing just a few feet away may be unpleasant and slow. Even the quality of a single Marriott employee's service varies according to his or her energy and frame of mind at the time of each customer encounter.

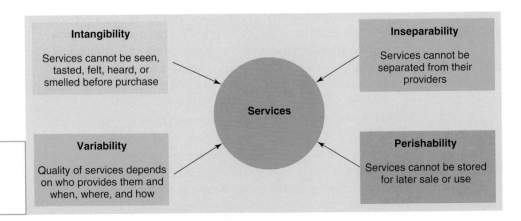

Figure 8-5
Four Service Characteristics

Intangibility
Services cannot be seen, tasted, felt, heard, or smelled before purchase

Inseparability
Services cannot be separated from their providers

Services

Variability
Quality of services depends on who provides them and when, where, and how

Perishability
Services cannot be stored for later sale or use

Service perishability means that services cannot be stored for later sale or use. Some doctors charge patients for missed appointments because the service value existed only at that point and disappeared when the patient did not show up. The perishability of services is not a problem when demand is steady. However, when demand fluctuates, service firms often have difficulties. For example, because of rush-hour demand, public transportation companies have to own much more equipment than they would if demand were even throughout the day. Thus, service firms often design strategies for producing a better match between demand and supply. Hotels and resorts charge lower prices in the off-season to attract more guests. And restaurants hire part-time employees to serve during peak periods.

Service perishability
A major characteristic of services—they cannot be stored for later sale or use.

Marketing Strategies for Service Firms

Just like manufacturing businesses, good service firms use marketing to position themselves strongly in chosen target markets. Westjet positions itself as a no-frills, airline charging very low fares. Ritz-Carlton Hotels positions itself as offering a memorable experience that "enlivens the senses, instils well-being, and fulfills even the unexpressed wishes and needs of our guests." These and other service firms establish their positions through traditional marketing mix activities.

However, because services differ from tangible products, they often require additional marketing approaches. In a product business, products are fairly standardized and can sit on shelves waiting for customers. But in a service business, the customer and frontline service employee interact to create the service. Thus, service providers must interact effectively with customers to create superior value during service encounters. Effective interaction, in turn, depends on the skills of frontline service employees and on the service production and support processes backing these employees.

The Service-Profit Chain Successful service companies focus their attention on both their customers and their employees. They understand the **service-profit chain**, which links service firm profits with employee and customer satisfaction. This chain consists of five links:[30]

Service-profit chain The chain that links service firm profits with employee and customer satisfaction.

1. Internal service quality: Superior employee selection and training, a quality work environment, and strong support for those dealing with customers, which results in…

2. Satisfied and productive service employees: More satisfied, loyal, and hard-working employees, which results in…

3. Greater service value: More effective and efficient customer value creation and service delivery, which results in…

4. Satisfied and loyal customers: Satisfied customers who remain loyal, repeat purchase, and refer other customers, which results in…

5. Healthy service profits and growth: Superior service firm performance

Therefore, reaching service profits and growth goals begins with taking care of those who take care of customers (see New Directions 8-2).

New Directions 8-2 >> Ritz-Carlton Taking Care of Those Who Take Care of Customers

CREDO

The Ritz-Carlton Hotel is a place where the genuine care and comfort of our guests is our highest mission.

We pledge to provide the finest personal service and facilities for our guests who will always enjoy a warm, relaxed yet refined ambience.

The Ritz-Carlton experience enlivens the senses, instills well-being, and fulfills even the unexpressed wishes and needs of our guests.

THREE STEPS OF SERVICE

1
A warm and sincere greeting. Use the guest name, if and when possible.

2
Anticipation and compliance with guest needs.

3
Fond farewell. Give them a warm good-bye and use their name, if and when possible.

THE EMPLOYEE PROMISE

At The Ritz-Carlton, our Ladies and Gentlemen are the most important resource in our service commitment to our guests.

By applying the principles of trust, honesty, respect, integrity and commitment, we nurture and maximize talent to the benefit of each individual and the company.

The Ritz-Carlton fosters a work environment where diversity is valued, quality of life is enhanced, individual aspirations are fulfilled, and The Ritz-Carlton mystique is strengthened.

"We Are Ladies and Gentlemen Serving Ladies and Gentlemen"

The credo and employee promise: Ritz-Carlton knows that to take care of customers, you must first take care of those who take care of customers.

Ritz-Carlton, a chain of luxury hotels renowned for outstanding service, caters to the top 5 percent of corporate and leisure travellers. The company's credo sets lofty customer service goals: "The Ritz-Carlton Hotel is a place where the genuine care and comfort of our guests is our highest mission. We pledge to provide the finest personal service and facilities for our guests who will always enjoy a warm, relaxed yet refined ambience. The Ritz-Carlton experience enlivens the senses, instils well-being, and fulfills even the unexpressed wishes and needs of our guests." The company's Web page concludes: "Here a calm settles over you. The world, so recently at your door, is now at your feet."

The credo is more than just words on paper—Ritz-Carlton delivers on its promises. In surveys of departing guests, some 95 percent report that they've had a truly memorable experience. In fact, at Ritz-Carlton, exceptional service encounters have become almost commonplace. Take the experiences of Nancy and Harvey Heffner, who stayed at the Ritz-Carlton Naples, in Naples, Florida (recently rated the best hotel in the United States, and fourth best in the world, by *Travel & Leisure* magazine): "The hotel is elegant and beautiful," Mrs. Heffner said, "but more important is the beauty expressed by the staff. They can't do enough to please you." When the couple's son became sick last year in Naples, the hotel staff brought him hot tea with honey at all hours of the night, she said. When Mr. Heffner had to fly home on business for a day and his return flight was delayed, a driver for the hotel waited in the lobby most of the night.

Such personal, high-quality service has also made the Ritz-Carlton a favourite among conventioneers. Comments one convention planner, "They not only treat us like kings when we hold our top-level meetings in their hotels, but we just never get any complaints."

In 1992, Ritz-Carlton became the first hotel company to win the Malcolm Baldrige National Quality Award. Since its incorporation in 1983, the company has received virtually every major award that the hospitality industry bestows.

More important, service quality has resulted in high customer retention: More than 90 percent of Ritz-Carlton customers return. Despite its hefty room rates, the chain enjoys a 70 percent occupancy rate, almost nine points above the industry average.

Most of the responsibility for keeping guests satisfied falls to Ritz-Carlton's customer-contact employees. Thus, the hotel chain takes great care in selecting its personnel. "We want only people who care about people," notes Patrick Mene, the company's vice president of quality. Once selected, employees are given intensive training in the art of coddling customers. New employees attend a two-day orientation, in which top management drums into them the "20 Ritz-Carlton Basics." Basic number one: "The Credo will be known, owned, and energized by all employees."

Employees are taught to do everything they can so they never lose a guest. "There's no negotiating at Ritz-Carlton when it comes to solving customer problems," says Mene. Staff members learn that anyone who receives a customer complaint owns that complaint until it's resolved (Ritz-Carlton Basic number eight). They are trained to drop whatever they're doing to help a customer—no matter what they're doing or what their department. Ritz-Carlton employees are empowered to handle problems on the spot, without consulting higher-ups. Each employee can spend up to $3000 to redress a guest grievance, and each is allowed to break from his or her routine for as long as needed to make a guest happy. "We master customer satisfaction at the individual level," adds Mene. "This is our most sensitive listening post...our early warning system." Thus, while competitors are still reading guest comment cards to learn about customer problems, Ritz-Carlton has already resolved them.

Ritz-Carlton instils a sense of pride in its employees. "You serve," they are told, "but you are not servants." The company motto states, "We are ladies and gentlemen serving ladies and gentlemen." Employees understand their role in Ritz-Carlton's success. "We might not be able to afford a hotel like this," says employee Tammy Patton, "but we can make it so people who can afford it will want to keep coming here."

And so they do. When it comes to customer satisfaction, no detail is too small. Customer-contact people are taught to greet guests warmly and sincerely, using guest names when possible. They learn to use the proper language with guests—phrases such as good morning, certainly, I'll be happy to, welcome back, and my pleasure; never Hi or How's it going? The Ritz-Carlton Basics urge employees to escort guests to another area of the hotel rather than pointing out directions, to answer the phone within three rings and with a "smile," and to take pride and care in their personal appearance. As Jorge Gonzalez, general manager of the Ritz-Carlton Naples, puts it, "When you invite guests to your house, you want everything to be perfect."

Ritz-Carlton recognizes and rewards employees who perform feats of outstanding service. Under its Five-Star Awards program, outstanding performers are nominated by peers and managers, and winners receive plaques at dinners celebrating their achievements. For on-the-spot recognition, managers award Gold Standard Coupons, redeemable for items in the gift shop and free weekend stays at the hotel. Ritz-Carlton further rewards and motivates its employees with such events as Super Sports Day, an employee talent show, luncheons celebrating employee anniversaries, a family picnic, and special themes in employee dining rooms. As a result, Ritz-Carlton's employees appear to be just as satisfied as its customers. Employee turnover is less than 30 percent a year, compared with 45 percent at other luxury hotels.

Ritz-Carlton's success is based on a simple philosophy: To take care of customers, you must first take care of those who take care of customers. Satisfied employees deliver high service value, which then creates satisfied customers. Satisfied customers, in turn, create sales and profits for the company.

Sources: Quotes from Edwin McDowell, "Ritz-Carlton's Keys to Good Service," *The New York Times,* 31 March 1993, p. D1; Howard Schlossberg, "Measuring Customer Satisfaction Is Easy to Do-Until You Try," *Marketing News,* 26 April 1993, pp. 5, 8; Ginger Conlon, "True Romance," *Sales & Marketing Management,* May 1996, pp. 85–90; and the Ritz-Carlton Hotel Company, LLC, online at **www.ritzcarlton.com**. Also see Don Peppers, "Digitizing Desire," *Forbes,* 10 April 1995, p. 76; and "Ritz-Carlton Hotels Reign in Three Categories of *Travel & Leisure's* 'World Best Awards' List," accessed online at **www.travelandleisure.com**.

All of this suggests that service marketing requires more than just traditional external marketing using the four Ps. Figure 8-6 shows that service marketing also requires internal marketing and interactive marketing. *Internal marketing* means that the service firm must effectively train and motivate its customer-contact employees and all the supporting service people to work as a team to provide customer satisfaction. For the firm to deliver consistently high service quality, marketers must get everyone in the organization to practise a customer orientation. In fact, internal marketing must precede external marketing. Ritz-Carlton orients its employees carefully, instils in them a sense of pride, and motivates them by recognizing and rewarding outstanding service deeds.

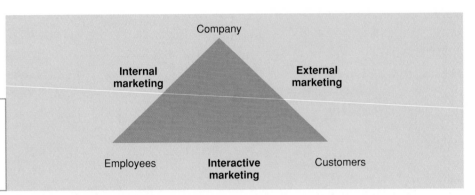

Figure 8-6
Three Types of Marketing in Service Industries

Interactive marketing means that service quality depends heavily on the quality of the buyer-seller interaction during the service encounter. In product marketing, product quality often depends little on how the product is obtained. But in services marketing, service quality depends on both the service deliverer and the quality of the delivery. Service marketers cannot assume that they will satisfy the customer simply by providing good technical service. They have to master interactive marketing skills as well. Thus, Ritz-Carlton selects only "people who care about people" and instructs them carefully in the fine art of interacting with customers to satisfy their every need.

Today, as competition and costs increase, and as productivity and quality decrease, more service marketing sophistication is needed. Service companies face three major marketing tasks: They want to increase their competitive *differentiation, service quality*, and *productivity*.

Managing Service Differentiation In these days of intense price competition, service marketers often complain about the difficulty of differentiating their services from those of competitors. To the extent that customers view the services of different providers as similar, they care less about the provider than the price.

The solution to price competition is to develop a differentiated offer, delivery, and image. The *offer* can include innovative features that set one company's offer apart from competitors' offers. Some hotels offer car rental, banking, and business centre services in their lobbies. Many airlines have introduced innovations such as in-flight movies, advance seating, air-to-ground telephone service, and frequent-flyer award programs to differentiate their offers. British Airways even offers international travellers beds and private "demi-cabins," hot showers, and cooked-to-order breakfasts.

Service companies can differentiate their service *delivery* by having more able and reliable customer-contact people, by developing a superior physical environment in which the service product is delivered, or by designing a superior delivery process. For example, many banks offer their customers Internet banking as a better way to access banking services than having to drive, park, and wait in line.

Finally, service companies also can work on differentiating their *images* through symbols and branding. The Harris Bank of Chicago adopted the lion as its symbol on its stationery, in its advertising, and even as stuffed animals offered to new depositors. The well-known Harris lion confers an image of strength on the bank. Other well-known service symbols include The Travelers' red umbrella, Merrill Lynch's bull, and Allstate's "good hands."

Managing Service Quality One of the major ways a service firm can differentiate itself is by delivering consistently higher quality than its competitors do. Unfortunately, service quality is harder to define and judge than is product quality. For instance, it is harder to get agreement on the quality of a haircut than on the quality of a hair dryer. Customer retention is perhaps the best measure of quality—a service firm's ability to hang onto its customers depends on how consistently it delivers value to them.[31]

Service companies want to ensure that customers will receive consistently high-quality service in every service encounter. However, unlike product manufacturers who can adjust their machinery and inputs until everything is perfect, service quality will always vary, depending on the interactions between employees and customers. Therefore, companies should take steps not only to provide good service every time, but also to recover from service mistakes when they do occur.[32]

The first step is to empower frontline service employees—to give them the authority, responsibility, and incentives they need to recognize, care about, and tend to customer needs. At Marriott, for example, well-trained employees are given the authority to do whatever it takes, on the spot, to keep guests happy. They are also expected to help management ferret out the cause of guests' problems and to inform managers of ways to improve overall hotel service and guests' comfort.

Top service firms also watch service performance closely, both their own and that of competitors. They also communicate their concerns about service quality to employees and provide performance feedback. At FedEx, quality measurements are everywhere. When employees walk in the door in the morning, they see the previous week's on-time percentages. Then, the company's in-house television station gives them detailed breakdowns of what happened yesterday and any potential problems for the day ahead.

INTERNATIONAL PRODUCT AND SERVICES MARKETING

International product and service marketers face special challenges. First, they must figure out what products and services to introduce and in which countries. Then, they must decide how much to standardize or adapt their products and services for world markets. On the one hand, companies would like to standardize their offerings. Standardization helps a company to develop a consistent worldwide image. It also lowers manufacturing costs and eliminates duplication of research and development, advertising, and product design efforts. On the other hand, consumers around the world differ in their cultures, attitudes, and buying behaviours. And markets vary in their economic conditions, competition, legal requirements, and physical environments. Companies must usually respond to these differences by adapting their product offerings. Something as simple as an electrical outlet can create big product problems:

Those who have traveled across Europe know the frustration of electrical plugs, different voltages, and other annoyances of international travel.... Philips, the electrical appliance manufacturer, has to produce 12 kinds of irons to serve just its European market. The problem is that Europe does not have a universal [electrical] standard. The ends of irons bristle with different plugs for different countries. Some have three prongs, others two; prongs protrude straight or angled, round or rectangular, fat, thin, and sometimes sheathed. There are circular plug faces, squares, pentagons, and hexagons. Some are perforated and some are notched. One French plug has a niche like a keyhole.[33]

Packaging also presents new challenges for international marketers. Packaging issues can be subtle. For example, names, labels, and colours may not translate easily from one country to another. A firm using yellow flowers in its logo might fare well in the United States but meet with disaster in Mexico, where a yellow flower symbolizes death or disrespect. Similarly, although Nature's Gift might be an appealing name for gourmet mushrooms in America, it would be deadly in Germany, where "gift" means *poison*. Packaging may also have to be tailored to meet the physical characteristics of consumers in various parts of the world. For instance, soft drinks are sold in smaller cans in Japan to fit the smaller Japanese hand better. Thus, although product and package standardization can produce benefits, companies must usually adapt their offerings to the unique needs of specific international markets.

Service marketers also face special challenges when going global. Some service industries have a long history of international operations. For example, the commercial banking industry was one of the first to grow internationally. Banks had to provide global services to meet the foreign exchange and credit needs of their home country clients wanting to sell overseas. In recent years, many banks have become truly global operations. Germany's Deutsche Bank, for example, has branches in 41 countries. Thus, for its clients around the world who wish to grow globally, Deutsche Bank can raise money not only in Frankfurt but also in Zurich, London, Paris, and Tokyo.

The travel industry also moved naturally into international operations. American hotel and airline companies grew quickly in Europe and Asia during the economic expansion that followed World War II. Credit card companies soon followed—the early worldwide presence of American Express has now been matched by Visa and MasterCard. Business travellers and vacationers like the convenience, and they have now come to expect that their credit cards will be honoured wherever they go.

Professional and business services industries such as accounting, management consulting, and advertising have only recently globalized.

Retailers are among the latest service businesses to go global. As their home markets become saturated with stores, North American retailers such as Wal-Mart, Kmart, Toys "R" Us, Office Depot, and Disney are expanding into faster-growing markets abroad. For example, every year since 1995, Wal-Mart has entered a new country; its international division's sales grew 40 percent last year, skyrocketing to more than $32 billion.

Service companies wanting to operate in other countries are not always welcomed with open arms. Whereas manufacturers usually face straightforward tariff, quota, or currency restrictions when attempting to sell their products in another country, service providers are likely to face more subtle barriers.

Retailers are among the latest service businesses to go global. Here, Asian shoppers buy American products in a Dutch-owned Markro store in Kuala Lumpur.

A Turkish law, for example, forbids international accounting firms from bringing capital into the country to set up offices and requires them to use the names of local partners in their marketing rather than their own internationally known company names.

Despite such difficulties, the trend toward growth of global service companies will continue, especially in banking, airlines, telecommunications, and professional services. Today service firms are no longer simply following their manufacturing customers. Instead, they are taking the lead in international expansion.

<< Looking Back   < < < < < < < < <

Time to reflect on the key concepts in this first marketing mix chapter on products and services. A product is more than a simple set of tangible features. In fact, many marketing offers consist of combinations of both tangible goods and services, ranging from pure tangible goods at one extreme to pure services at the other. Each product or service offered to customers can be viewed on three levels. The core product consists of the core problem-solving benefits that consumers seek when they buy a product. The actual product exists around the core and includes the quality level, features, design, brand name, and packaging. The augmented product is the actual product plus the various services and benefits offered with it, such as warranty, free delivery, installation, and maintenance.

1. Define product and the major classifications of products and services.

Broadly defined, a product is anything that can be offered to a market for attention, acquisition, use, or consumption that might satisfy a want or need. Products include physical objects, services, events, persons, places, organizations, ideas, or mixes of these entities. Services are products that consist of activities, benefits, or satisfactions offered for sale that are essentially intangible, such as banking, hotel, tax preparation, and home repair services.

Products and services fall into two broad classes based on the types of consumers that use them. *Consumer products*—those bought by final consumers—are usually classified according to consumer shopping habits (convenience products, shopping products, specialty products, and unsought products). *Business products*—purchased for further processing or for use in conducting a business-are classified according to their cost and the way they enter the production process (materials and parts, capital items, and supplies and services). Other marketable entities—such as organizations, persons, places, and ideas—can also be thought of as products.

2. Describe the roles of product and service branding, packaging, labelling, and product support services.

Companies develop strategies for items in their product lines by making decisions about product attributes, branding, packaging, labelling, and product support services. *Product attribute* decisions involve the product quality, features, and style and design the company will offer. *Branding* decisions include selecting a brand name, garnering brand sponsorship, and developing a brand strategy. *Packaging* provides many key benefits, such as protection, economy, convenience, and promotion. Package decisions often include designing *labels*, which identify, describe, and possibly promote the product. Companies also develop *product support services* that enhance customer service and satisfaction and safeguard against competitors.

3. Explain the decisions that companies make when developing product lines and mixes.

Most companies produce a product line rather than a single product. A *product line* is a group of products that are related in function, customer-purchase needs, or distribution channels. In developing a product line strategy, marketers face a number of tough decisions. *Line stretching* involves extending a line downward, upward, or in both directions to occupy a gap that might otherwise by filled by a competitor. In contrast, *line filling* involves adding items within the present range of the line. The set of product lines and items offered to customers by a particular seller make up the *product mix*. The mix can be described by four dimensions: width, length, depth, and consistency. These dimensions are the tools for developing the company's product strategy.

4. Identify the four characteristics that affect the marketing of a service.

As we move toward a world service economy, marketers need to know more about marketing services. Services are characterized by four key characteristics. First, services are *intangible*—they cannot be seen, tasted, felt, heard, or smelled. Services are also *inseparable* from their service providers. Services are *variable* because their quality depends on the service provider as well as the environment surrounding the service delivery. Finally, services are *perishable*. As a result, they cannot be inventoried, built up, or back ordered. Each characteristic poses problems and marketing requirements. Marketers work to find ways to make the service more tangible, to increase the productivity of providers who are inseparable from their products, to standardize the quality in the face of variability, and to improve demand movements and supply capacities in the face of service perishability.

5. Discuss the additional marketing considerations that services require.

Good service companies focus attention on both customers and employees. They understand the service-profit chain, which links service firm profits with employee and customer satisfaction. Services marketing strategy calls not only for external marketing but also for internal marketing to motivate employees and interactive marketing to create service delivery skills among service providers. To succeed, service marketers must create competitive differentiation, offer high service quality, and find ways to increase service productivity.

Navigating the Key Terms

Actual product, **p. 306**
Augmented product, **p. 306**
Brand equity, **p. 315**
Brand extension, **p. 320**
Brand, **p. 314**
Business product, **p. 309**
Co-branding, **p. 319**
Consumer product, **p. 310**
Convenience product, **p. 310**
Core product, **p. 305**
Line extension, **p. 320**
Packaging, **p. 322**
Private brand (or store brand), **p. 317**
Product line, **p. 327**
Product mix (or product assortment), **p. 328**

Product quality, **p. 312**
Product support services, **p. 325**
Product, **p. 305**
Service inseparability, **p. 330**
Service intangibility, **p. 330**
Service perishability, **p. 331**
Service variability, **p. 330**
Service, **p. 305**
Service-profit chain, **p. 331**
Shopping product, **p. 310**
Slotting fees, **p. 317**
Social marketing, **p. 311**
Specialty product, **p. 309**
Unsought product, **p. 309**

Concept Check

Fill in the blanks and then check your answers.

1. The text defines a _____ as anything that can be offered to a market for attention, acquisition, use, or consumption and that might satisfy a want or need.

2. _____ are a form of product that consist of activities, benefits, or satisfactions offered for sale that are essentially intangible and do not result in the ownership of anything.

3. Product planners need to think about products and services on three levels: the _____ product, the _____ product, and the _____ product.

4. _____ products are less frequently purchased consumer products and services that customers carefully compare on suitability, quality, price, and style.

5. Three groups of business products and services include _____ and parts, _____, and _____ and services.

6. A(n) _____ is a name, term, sign, symbol, or design, or a combination of these that identifies the maker or seller of a product or service.

7. Desirable qualities for a brand name include: (a) It should suggest something about the product's _____; (b) It should be easy to _____, _____, and _____; (c) The brand name should be _____; (d) It should be _____; and, (e) It should translate easily into foreign languages.

8. _____ occur when a company introduces additional items in a given category under the same brand name, such as new flavours, forms, colours, ingredients, or package sizes.

9. Product mix _____ refers to the number of different product lines the company carries.

10. A company must consider four special service characteristics when designing marketing programs: _____,

_____, _____,
and _____ _____.

11. A company's service-profit chain consists of five
links: Internal service quality; _____;
_____; _____; and,
healthy service profits and growth.

Concept Check Answers: 1. product; 2. Services; 3.
core, actual, and augmented; 4. Shopping; 5. materials, capital items, supplies; 6. brand; 7. benefits and
qualities; pronounce, recognize, and remember; distinctive; extendible; 8. Line extensions; 9. width; 10.
intangibility, inseparability, variability, and perishability; 11. satisfied and productive service employees;
greater service value; satisfied and loyal customers.

Discussing the Issues

1. What are the primary differences between products and services? Give illustrations of the differences that you identify. Give an original
example of a hybrid offer.

2. List and explain the core, actual, and augmented
products for educational experiences that universities offer. How are these different (if there is a
difference) from the products offered by universities? Which of these experiences (products) could
be moved online? How would these moves affect
the educational institution's marketing effort?

3. The text identifies social marketing as the use of
commercial marketing concepts and tools in
programs designed to influence individuals'
behaviour in a way that improves their well
being and that of society. Take a recent social
marketing effort, identify its intended target
market, list the primary objectives of the campaign, suggest how effectiveness could be measured, and document the overall impact of the
campaign. Critique the campaign and comment
on what you would do to improve the effort.

4. For many years there was one type of Coca-Cola,
one type of Tide, and one type of Crest (in mint
and regular). Now we find Coke in six or more
varieties; Tide in Ultra, Liquid, and Unscented
versions; and Crest Gel with sparkles for kids.
List some of the issues these brand extensions
raise for the manufacturers, retailers, and consumers. Is more always better? How does co-
branding impact the questioned brand extension? Suggest a co-branding opportunity that
you believe would make good sense from a marketing perspective.

5. Illustrate how a movie theatre can deal with the
intangibility, inseparability, variability, and perishability of the services it provides. Give specific
examples to illustrate your thoughts. How could
the movie theatre use internal and interactive
marketing to enhance the service it provides?

 Mastering Marketing

To explore the impact of products and services on
the organization, you have two assignments. First,
outline a brand extension plan for CanGo. Identify
any co-branding opportunities that you perceive
would be good long-term investments. Explain your
choices. Second, outline the service-profit chain that
seems to be in place for CanGo. What improvements
would you suggest?

 Check out the enclosed Video case CD-ROM, or our Companion Website at www.pear-
soned.ca/armstrong, to view a CBC video segment and case for this chapter.

MAP 8 Marketing Applications

Which company has the world's strongest brand? To find the answer, what questions would you ask? Is brand strength determined by sales volume, a global presence, innovation, reputation, amount of advertising, success on the Internet, positive public relations, stock value, or all of these things? Marketing managers know that strong brand equity is the key to entering new markets and successfully penetrating old ones. Brand image also shapes corporate strategy, advertising campaigns, and overall marketing effort. Alliances are encouraged or dropped based on brand reputation and confidence. Strong brands can command premium prices. Hence, the brand is a company's most important asset and profit producer. In contrast, loss of confidence in a brand, such as the recent Ford and Firestone public relations nightmare, can affect not only the companies involved but also all of the distributors, service providers, and secondary publics that are affiliated with the industry. However, when a strong brand faces difficulty, its reputation can help earn it a second chance. So, what is the world's strongest brand? According to recent studies, the vote goes to Coca-Cola, followed by Microsoft, IBM, GE, and Nokia. Were these your picks? Do you buy products from these companies? Many people around the world do.

Thinking Like a Marketing Manager

1. What makes a strong brand? How would you go about measuring brand equity?

2. What makes Coca-Cola the number one brand in the world? What characteristics do the company and its brand possess that competitors do not?

3. With all of its legal difficulties, how can Microsoft be considered the second strongest global brand? Does its status help it overcome public relations and legal problems? Explain.

4. Examine the Web sites for the listed brands: **www.cocacola.com**, **www.microsoft.com**, **www.ibm.com**, **www.ge.com**, and **www.nokia.com**. Based on your answers to question 1 above, construct a grid that evaluates each of these brands. How does your evaluation match the order suggested above?

5. Go to the Internet and examine another brand that you perceive to be a superior brand. Discuss the characteristics of the brand you value. How could its brand equity be improved?

6. Assuming that you were the marketing manager for a new dot.com startup, develop a branding strategy that would match the characteristics of "great" global brands to your enterprise. Discuss your proposal with the class.

Digital Map

Visit our Web site at **www.pearsoned.ca/armstrong** for online quizzes, Internet exercises, and more!

CASE 8 KRAVE'S CANDY COMPANY

Winnipeg-based Krave's Candy Company (discussed in Chapter 1) produces Clodhoppers, a small candy made of cashews and graham wafers in white or milk chocolate.

Started in 1995 by entrepreneurs Chris Emery and Larry Finnson, the company has already undergone a complete brand image makeover, packaging redesign, and a major international expansion in its short history. All these changes are aimed at increasing the company's sales and capturing more of the total market for boxed chocolates.

The confectionary industry is highly concentrated in Canada—the leading eight companies compose 87 percent of the value of total shipments. Further, 60 percent of industry shipments are done by foreign-controlled organizations such as Hershey Foods and Nestlé. The majority of chocolate operations in Canada are dedicated to three product categories: (1) boxed chocolates, (2) chocolate bars, and (3) seasonal novelties.

Boxed chocolates and novelty items are purchased primarily as gifts for birthdays, anniversaries, religious holidays, Valentine's Day, and Mother's Day. The chocolate bar market is highly fragmented: a 4 percent to 5 percent share of the market places a product in the top 10 brands. Firms in the chocolate industry compete on the basis of brand name, advertising, sales promotion, quality, and cost, depending on the market segment. The baby boomer segment, for example, is very quality oriented.

The Confectionary Manufacturers Association of Canada (CMAC), see **www.confectioncanada.com**, estimates that its members spend $55 million annually on advertising and sales promotion. From a consumption perspective, the CMAC estimates that the average Canadian consumes 10.3 kg of chocolate annually, with per capita annual spending on the category of $68.

The total chocolate market is valued at approximately $1.4 billion per year and the boxed chocolate segment at between $160 million and $200 million.

Despite market complexities and large multinational competitors, Krave's Candies has had considerable success. Sales are already in the millions, and the company was named one of Canada's top 10 food companies by *Food in Canada Magazine*. The key to maintaining that success will be effectively managing both the brand's identity and the company's growth through product line extensions and increased geographic distribution.

The original Clodhopper brand identity was built around the fictitious Krave family, which even has its own coat of arms. The first page of the original Krave's Web site claimed, "From their secluded castle high in the European Alps, secret recipes have been handed down from generation to generation." The family was used to help establish an image of quality for the Clodhopper product, which, according to the Krave's family tradition, was made "using only the finest ingredients from around the world." In reality, the Clodhopper product does have some family tradition behind it, since it originated with the grandmother of one of the founding partners.

Emery and Finnson learned the importance of packaging in establishing a brand identity early in the company's history. The original 300-g plastic jar that they used created shelving problems for retailers. Based on the packaging, retailers tended to place the product in the snack aisles, near the popcorn products. Since Clodhoppers were $6 a jar, the price was inconsistent with the lower-priced snacks. In addition, the plastic jar made the product look cheap and because the product settles over time, a four-centimetre gap appeared at the top of the jar, making it look half empty to consumers. Emery and Finnson repackaged the product so that it fit into the upscale boxed chocolate product category, which includes the major players in the category, Black Magic and Pot of Gold. The quality image of the candy was reinforced by using a black package with gold and red trim that included an image of the Alps (to tie in with the Krave family) in the background. Consistent with the high-quality image, a gold foil bag was used on the inside of the package, which also helped to establish the product as being appropriate as a gift. Although the new packaging helped product placement—retailers began to place it in the boxed chocolate section of stores—it did not do a good job of differentiating the product from its competitors.

Searching for a more distinctive identity, Emery and Finnson revised the entire positioning of the brand. The fictitious Krave family was replaced by the entrepreneurs themselves as the trade characters for the product. The brand was renamed Chris and Larry's Clodhoppers, and both the retro-style packaging and the Web site feature cartoon characters of Chris and Larry.

A large part of Krave's success has been its ability to sell the brand to important retailers in Canada. Clodhoppers are available in Wal-Mart, Shopper's Drug Mart, Zellers, Loblaws, and regional chains such as Sobeys, Safeway, and Save-On-Foods. However, one of the most important distribution arrangements for the future growth of Krave's is in the U.S. market. During a trade show in Toronto in 2000, Emery and Finnson met Wal-Mart U.S.A. president and CEO Lee Scott and secured a deal that expanded their distribution into Wal-Mart stores in the United States. Chris and Larry are trying to achieve a large volume in the United States through aggressive pricing. The 212-g box sells at U.S. Wal-Marts for US$1.97, compared with its Canadian retail price of CDN$5.87 for a 300-g box.

December is the most important time of the year for Krave's since 85 percent of its sales occur at this time. To reinforce the brand during the holidays, the company runs promotional sampling programs, giving away free samples to consumers in stores. In the future, Emery and Finnson would like to reduce the seasonality of the business by establishing the brand name at other times of the year. As an example of their marketing efforts, in April 2001 Dairy Queen introduced the Clodhoppers Blizzard after a successful test market.

Chris and Larry have relied on public relations more than advertising to create brand recognition and consumer positioning, partly because of their limited budget. However, recognizing the importance of consumer awareness for this product category, the company embarked on their first television campaign in May 2001.

Consistent with the company's strategy to reduce its reliance on seasonal box chocolate sales, Chris and Larry decided to launch Clodhoppers in a new line of small bags, targeted at consumers looking for a quick snack rather than a take-home product or a gift like the chocolate line.

The new line was launched in three flavours, in 45-g and 225-g packages and has gained respectable distribution by focusing on retailers that have the potential for high volume through consumers' impulse purchasing.

At this time, Chris and Larry are considering further expansion of their product line and have test formulas available on line extensions. Further, with trade restrictions reduced through the NAFTA process, Canadian chocolate manufacturers are finding that the U.S. market is a potential source of new business. Chris and Larry are evaluating the potential for further U.S. and international expansion.

Questions

1. In what product classification does the original Clodhopper's product fall? How would you classify the new snack line?

2. What distribution strategy is appropriate for Clodhopper's boxed chocolate line? for the bagged snack products?

3. Is the Clodhoppers brand name consistent with consumer expectations in the boxed chocolate category? What image does it project relative to the category leaders?

4. What further recommendations can you make in reducing the reliance on seasonal sales for the boxed chocolate product?

5. What business building programs could you recommend for (a) the current Clodhoppers product? and (b) the new line extensions in bags?

Sources: Agriculture Canada's Web site, accessed online at **www.agr.gc.ca**, 21 November 2002; Confectionary Manufacturers Association of Canada's Web site, accessed online at **www.confect-ioncanada.com**, 21 November 2002; and Krave's Web site, accessed online at **www.clodhoppers.tv**.

9 >> New Product Development and Product Life-Cycle Strategies

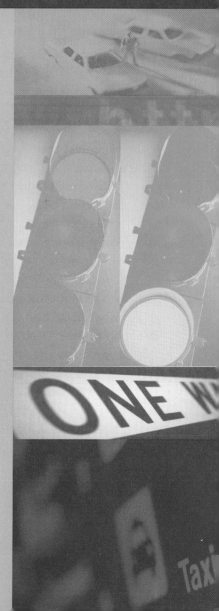

Looking Ahead

In the previous chapter, you learned about decisions that marketers make in managing individual brands and entire product mixes. In this chapter, we'll cruise on into two additional product topics: developing new products and managing products through their life cycles. New products are the lifeblood of an organization. However, new product development is risky, and many new products fail. So, the first part of this chapter lays out a process for finding and growing successful new products. Once introduced, marketers want their products to enjoy a long and happy life. In the second part of the chapter, you'll see that every product passes through several life-cycle stages and that each stage poses new challenges requiring different marketing strategies and tactics.

After studying this chapter, you should be able to

1. explain how companies find and develop new product ideas
2. list and define the steps in the new product development process
3. describe the stages of the product life cycle
4. describe how marketing strategies change during the product's life cycle

First stop: Gillette. The chances are good that you use at least one Gillette product. However, this company doesn't rest on past performance; as you'll see, it owes much of its success to a passion for innovation and new product development.

"New products!" declares Gillette's former chairman and CEO, Alfred M. Zeien, "That's the name of the game." Since Gillette's founding in 1901, its heavy commitment to innovation has kept the company razor sharp. Gillette is best known for its absolute dominance of the razor-and-blades market. However, all its divisions—Duracell batteries, Gillette toiletries and cosmetics (Right Guard, Soft & Dri), stationery products (Parker, Paper Mate, and Waterman pens), Oral-B toothbrushes, and Braun electrical appliances—share common traits: Each is profitable, fast-growing, number one worldwide in its markets, and anchored by a steady flow of innovative new product offerings. In 1998, 40 percent of Gillette's sales came from products that didn't exist five years before. "Gillette is a new product machine," said one Wall Street analyst.

New products don't just happen at Gillette. New product success starts with a companywide culture that supports innovation. Whereas many companies try to protect their successful existing products, Gillette encourages innovations that will cannibalize its established product hits. "They know that if they don't bring out a new zinger, someone else will," observed an industry consultant. Gillette also accepts blunders and dead ends as a normal part of creativity and innovation. It knows that it must generate dozens of new product ideas to get just one success in the marketplace. The company scorns what CEO Zeien calls "putting blue dots in the soap powder"—attaching superficial frills to existing products and labelling them innovations. However, Gillette strongly encourages its people to take creative risks in applying cutting-edge technologies to find substantial improvements that make life easier for customers.

New product development is complex and expensive, but Gillette's mastery of the process has put the company in a class of its own. For example, Gillette spent $275 million on designing and developing its Sensor family of razors, garnering 29 patents along the way. It spent an incredible $1.5 billion on the development of Sensor's successor, the triple-bladed Mach3, and applied for 35 more patents. Competing brands Bic and Wilkinson have managed to claim significant shares of the disposable-razor market, and Schick, Norelco, and Remington compete effectively in electric razors with Gillette's Braun unit. But Gillette, with its stunning technological superiority, operates with virtually no competition worldwide in the burgeoning cartridge-razor sector. Backed by Gillette's biggest new product launch ever, the Mach3 strengthened the company's stranglehold on this market. Within only a few months of its introduction, the new razor and blades were number-one sellers.

At Gillette, it seems that almost everyone gets involved in one way or another with new product development. Even people who don't participate directly in the product design and development are likely to be pressed into service testing prototypes. Every working day at Gillette, 200 volunteers from various departments come to work unshaven, troop to the second floor of the company's gritty South Boston manufacturing and research plant, and enter small booths with a sink and mirror. There they take instructions from technicians on the other side of a small window as to which razor, shaving cream, or aftershave to use. The volunteers evaluate razors for sharpness of blade, smoothness of glide, and ease of handling. When finished, they enter their judgments into a computer. In a nearby shower room, women perform the same ritual on their legs and underarms. "We bleed so you'll get a good shave at home," says one Gillette employee.

This type of research supported Gillette's launch of its shaving gel Satin Care into the Canadian marketplace. Aimed at women, the gel is similar to Gillette's shaving gel for men, but with a few key differences: It has distinct packaging, a scent that women find more appealing, and extra moisturizers. Although 80 percent of women shave their legs regularly, the women's market is underdeveloped. Many women still use their partner's shaving products, a trend that Gillette hopes to reverse.

Gillette also excels at bringing new products to market. The company understands that, once introduced, fledgling products need generous manufacturing and marketing support to thrive in the hotly competitive consumer products marketplace. To deliver the required support, Gillette has devised a formula that calls for R&D, capital investment, and advertising expenditures-which it refers to collectively as "growth drivers."

Gillette's Cavalcade of Sports, a made-in-Canada promotional campaign that has run annually in the August-September period since its inception in 1971, has long acted as one of these drivers. Gillette uses it as an umbrella program that unites all of its premium brands. Different brands may be played up in the promotion from year to year. Several years ago, Gillette's Sensor Excel shaving system was spotlighted. In 2000–01, attention focused on the Mach3 system and the Duracell Ultra line of batteries. Although the essential components of the Cavalcade have remained consistent from year to year, Gail MacDonald, director of promotion, sponsorship, and event marketing, knows that the secret to success for a long-running promotion is to refresh it constantly. "We have to be innovative," she says. "That's one of the reasons the Cavalcade has such great staying power." At "Sports Celebration 2000," winners were invited to an interactive sporting event at Toronto's SkyDome and received their choice of six fantasy sports trips anywhere in North America plus $25 000 in spending money. MacDonald says the company tries to offer prizes with appeal to a wide audience—not just sports enthusiasts. Gillette's retail partners such as Shoppers Drug Mart love the promotion because it brings busi-

ness into their outlets. Getting retailers involved early in the effort is another key to the Cavalcade's success. Gillette invited its retail partners to a special event at SkyDome six months in advance of the campaign roll-out to showcase the promotion and encourage retailers to buy in. It's a win-win situation, MacDonald says: The $2-million annual promotion drives sales for Gillette, and creates in-store activity for the participating retailers.

Thus, over the decades, superior new products combined with innovative marketing programs have been the cornerstone of Gillette's amazing success. The company commands the loyalty of more than 700 million shavers in 200 countries around the globe. These customers have purchased hundreds of millions of Gillette razors and billions of blades, giving Gillette more than 70 percent of the wet-shave market in North America and 72 percent of the $10.5-billion worldwide market. It's not surprising that in 1999, Gillette was named by the American Marketing Association as its New Product Marketer of the Year.[1]

Gillette is also smart enough to know that successfully adding new products to their line is not enough. For example, Gillette followed the successful Mach 3 razor for men launch with a Cool Blue handle line extension and in early 2001 launched the Venus razor for women. Not satisfied with now emerging as the dominant player in the women's wet shave category, Gillette introduced a Crystal Clear handle, based on the success of the Cool Blue handle for men. In addition, in the spring of 2002, Gillette again developed and launched improvements to the Mach 3 by adding a lubricating strip near the blades on the razor and developing a more comfortable blade for shaving in both directions. So, although new products are important to organizations such as Gillette, a process of ongoing refinement and improvement increases the potential for long-term success.[2]

The Gillette Company
www.gillette.com

As with Gillette, new products are the lifeblood of many firms, and Canadians have had a long history as inventors in this process. McIntosh apples, Pablum, frozen fish, and instant mashed potatoes are food products that all originated in Canada. Canadians are responsible for developing such sports and leisure activities as basketball, five-pin bowling, table hockey, and Trivial Pursuit. Many of these inventions spawned entire industries. The modern communications industry was born with the invention of the telephone (Alexander Graham Bell). Reginald Fessenden, born near Sherbrooke, Quebec, was known as the father of radio after he invented amplitude modulation (AM) radio and transmitted his first broadcast in 1900. Another Canadian, Charles Fenerty, with his ability to make paper from wood pulp, founded that industry. Modern air travel was made possible by another Canadian, Wallace Rupert Turnbull, who developed the variable-pitch propeller.

Dr. Cluny McPherson, of St. John's, Newfoundland, invented the gas mask used to save the lives of many allied soldiers in World War I. A quintessentially Canadian tool, the snowblower, was invented in 1925 by Quebec resident Arthur Sicard. Olivia Poole invented the Jolly Jumper, the internationally popular baby seat, in the 1950s, and Steve Pacjack of Vancouver invented the beer case with a tuck-in handle that helps you lug your beer home. Three Canadian Olympic sailors—Bruce Kirby, Hans Fogh, and Ian Bruce—designed the world-class Laser sailboat in 1970. Wendy Murphy, a medical research technician, developed the Weevac 6–so named because it can carry six wee babies. Her idea was born when she realized, during the devastation of the 1985 Mexico City earthquake, that no apparatus existed to evacuate young children. Dr. Dennis Colonello designed the Abdomenizer in 1986 while practising as a chiropractor in northern Ontario. Before you laugh, note that he has rung up more than $100 million in sales. Dr. Frank Gunston, of Brandon, Manitoba, may have been one of the most philanthropic inventors. After developing and building a total knee-joint replacement, he decided not to patent his invention. This made it freely available to manufacturers and allowed patients needing the joint to benefit quickly from the technology and walk without pain. He received the prestigious Manning Principal Award in 1989 for his efforts.[3]

A company has to be good at developing and managing new products. Every product seems to go through a life cycle—it is born, goes through several phases, and eventually dies, as newer products come along that better serve consumer needs. This product life cycle presents two major challenges. First, because all products eventually decline, the firm must be good at developing new products to replace aging ones (the problem of *new product development*). Second, the firm must be good at adapting its marketing strategies in the face of changing tastes, technologies, and competition, as products pass through life cycle stages (the problem of *product life cycle strategies*). We first look at the problem of finding and developing new products and then at the problem of managing them successfully over their life cycles.

NEW PRODUCT DEVELOPMENT STRATEGY

Given the rapid changes in consumer tastes, technology, and competition, companies must develop a steady stream of new products and services. A firm can obtain new products in two ways. One is through *acquisition*—by buying a whole company, a patent, or a licence to produce someone else's product. The other is through **new product development** in the company's own research and development department. By *new products,* we mean original products, product improvements, product modifications, and new brands that the firm develops through its own R&D efforts. In this chapter, we concentrate on new product development.

Innovation can be very risky. Texas Instruments lost a staggering $920 million before withdrawing from the home computer business. Other costly product failures from sophisticated companies include Vim Micro Liquid (Unilever), Zap Mail electronic mail (Federal Express), Polarvision instant movies (Polaroid), Crystal Pepsi (PepsiCo), Clorox detergent (Clorox Company), and McLean Burgers (McDonald's).

New products continue to fail at a disturbing rate.[4] Why do so many new products fail? There are several reasons. Although an idea may be good, the market size may have been overestimated. Perhaps the actual product was not designed as well as it should have been. Or maybe it was incorrectly positioned in the market, priced too high, or advertised poorly. A high-level executive might push a favourite idea despite poor marketing research findings. Sometimes the costs of product development are higher than expected, and sometimes competitors fight back harder than expected.

Because so many new products fail, companies are anxious to learn how to improve their odds of new product success. One way is to identify successful new products and find out what they have in common. Another is to study new product failures to see what lessons can be learned. Various studies suggest that new product success depends on developing a *unique superior product,* one with higher quality, new features, and higher value in use. Another key success factor is a *well-defined product concept* before development, in which the company carefully defines and assesses the target market, the product requirements, and the benefits before proceeding. Other success factors have also been suggested—senior management commitment, relentless innovation, and a smoothly functioning new product development process. In all, to create successful new products, a company

New product development The development of original products, product improvements, product modifications, and new brands through the firm's own R&D efforts.

must understand its consumers, markets, and competitors and develop products that deliver superior value to customers.

So companies face a problem—they must develop new products, but the odds weigh heavily against success. The solution lies in strong new product planning and in setting up a systematic *new product development process* for finding and growing new products. Figure 9-1 shows the eight major steps in this process.

Idea Generation

Idea generation The systematic search for new product ideas.

New product development starts with **idea generation**—the systematic search for new product ideas. A company typically has to generate many ideas in order to find a few good ones. According to one well-known management consultant, "For every 1,000 ideas, only 100 will have enough commercial promise to merit a small-scale experiment, only ten of those will warrant substantial financial commitment, and of those, only a couple will turn out to be unqualified successes."[5] His conclusion? "If you want to find a few ideas with the power to enthrall customers, foil competitors, and thrill investors, you must first generate hundreds and potentially thousands of unconventional strategic ideas."

Major sources of new product ideas include internal sources, customers, competitors, distributors and suppliers, and others. Using *internal sources,* the company can find new ideas through formal research and development. It can pick the brains of its executives, scientists, engineers, manufacturing, and salespeople. Some companies have developed successful "intrapreneurial" programs that encourage employees to think up and develop new product ideas. For example, 3M's well-known "15 percent rule" allows employees to spend 15 percent of their time "bootlegging"—working on projects of personal interest whether those projects directly benefit the company. The spectacularly successful Post-it notes evolved out of this program. Similarly, Texas Instruments' IDEA program provides funds for employees who pursue their own ideas. Among the successful new products to come out of the IDEA program was TI's Speak 'n' Spell, the first children's toy to contain a

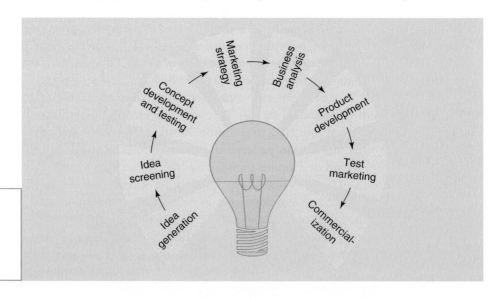

Figure 9-1

Major Stages in New Product Development

microchip. Many other speaking toys followed, ultimately generating several hundred million dollars for TI.[6]

Good new product ideas also come from watching and listening to *customers*. The company can analyze customer questions and complaints to find new products that better solve consumer problems. Company engineers or salespeople can meet with and work alongside customers to get suggestions and ideas. The company can conduct surveys or focus groups to learn about consumer needs and wants. Heinz did just that when its researchers approached children, who consume more than half of the ketchup sold, to find out what would make ketchup more appealing to them. "When we asked them what would make the product more fun," says a Heinz spokesperson, "changing the color was among the top responses." Change the colour. So, Heinz developed and launched EZ Squirt, green ketchup that comes in a soft, squeezable bottle targeted at kids. The bottle's special nozzle also emits a thin ketchup stream, "so tykes can autograph their burgers (or squirt someone across the table, though Heinz neglects to mention that)."[7]

Finally, consumers often create new products and uses on their own, and companies can benefit by finding these products and putting them on the market. Customers can also be a good source of ideas for new product uses that can expand the market for and extend the life of current products. For example, Avon capitalized on new uses discovered by consumers for its Skin-So-Soft bath oil and mois-

Avon capitalized on new uses discovered by consumers for its Skin-So-Soft bath oil and moisturizer by developing a complete line of Skin-So-Soft Bug Guard products.

turizer. For years, customers have been spreading the word that Skin-So-Soft bath oil is also a terrific bug repellent. Whereas some consumers were content simply to bathe in water scented with the fragrant oil, others carried it in their backpacks to mosquito-infested campsites or kept a bottle on the deck of their beach houses. Now, Avon offers a complete line of Skin-So-Soft Bug Guard products, including Bug Guard Mosquito Repellent Moisturizing Towelettes and Bug Guard Plus, a combination moisturizer, insect repellent, and sunscreen.[8]

Competitors are another good source of new product ideas. Companies watch competitors' ads and other communications to get clues about their new products. They buy competing new products, take them apart to see how they work, analyze their sales, and decide whether they should bring out a new product of their own. Finally, *distributors and suppliers* contribute many good new product ideas. Resellers are close to the market and can pass along information about consumer problems and new product possibilities. Suppliers can tell the company about new concepts, techniques, and materials that can be used to develop new products. Other idea sources include trade magazines, shows, and seminars; government agencies; new product consultants; advertising agencies; marketing research firms; university and commercial laboratories; and inventors.

The search for new product ideas should be systematic rather than haphazard. Otherwise, few new ideas will surface and many good ideas will sputter and die. Top management can avoid these problems by installing an *idea management system* that directs the flow of new ideas to a central point where they can be collected, reviewed, and evaluated. In setting up such a system, the company can do any or all of the following:[9]

- Appoint a respected senior person to be the company's idea manager.
- Create a multidisciplinary idea management committee consisting of people from R&D, engineering, purchasing, operations, finance, and sales and marketing to meet regularly and evaluate proposed new product and service ideas.
- Set up a toll-free number for anyone who wants to send a new idea to the idea manager.
- Encourage all company stakeholders—employees, suppliers, distributors, dealers—to send their ideas to the idea manager.
- Set up formal recognition programs to reward those who contribute the best new ideas.

The idea manager approach yields two favourable outcomes. First, it helps create an innovation-oriented company culture. It shows that top management supports, encourages, and rewards innovation. Second, it will yield a larger number of ideas among which will be found some especially good ones. As the system matures, ideas will flow more freely. No longer will good ideas wither for the lack of a sounding board or a senior product advocate.

Idea Screening

The purpose of idea generation is to create a large number of ideas. The purpose of the succeeding stages is to *reduce* that number. The first idea-reducing stage is

idea screening, which helps spot good ideas and drop poor ones as soon as possible. Product development costs rise greatly in later stages, so the company wants to go ahead only with the product ideas that will turn into profitable products. As one marketing executive suggests, "Three executives sitting in a room can get 40 good ideas ricocheting off the wall in minutes. The challenge is getting a steady stream of good ideas out of the labs and creativity campfires, through marketing and manufacturing, and all the way to consumers."[10]

Many companies require their executives to write up new product ideas on a standard form that can be reviewed by a new product committee. The write-up describes the product, the target market, and the competition. It makes some rough estimates of market size, product price, development time and costs, manufacturing costs, and rate of return. The committee then evaluates the idea against a set of general criteria. For example, at Kao Company, the large Japanese consumer-products company, the committee asks questions such as these: Is the product truly useful to consumers and society? Is it good for our particular company? Does it mesh well with the company's objectives and strategies? Do we have the people, skills, and resources to make it succeed? Does it deliver more value to customers than do competing products? Is it easy to advertise and distribute? Many companies have well-designed systems for rating and screening new product ideas.

Concept Development and Testing

An attractive idea must be developed into a **product concept**. It is important to distinguish between a product idea, a product concept, and a product image. A *product idea* is an idea for a possible product that the company can see itself offering to the market. A *product concept* is a detailed version of the idea stated in meaningful consumer terms. A *product image* is the way consumers perceive an actual or potential product.

Concept Development DaimlerChrysler is getting ready to commercialize its experimental fuel-cell-powered electric car. This car's nonpolluting fuel-cell system runs directly off liquid hydrogen, producing only water as a by-product. It is highly fuel efficient (75 percent more efficient than gasoline engines) and gives the new car an environmental advantage over standard internal combustion engine cars or even today's super efficient gasoline-electric hybrid cars. DaimlerChrysler is currently road testing its NECAR 5 (New Electric Car) subcompact prototype and plans to deliver the first fuel-cell cars to customers in 2004. Based on the tiny Mercedes A-Class, the car accelerates quickly, reaches speeds of 140 km/h, and has a 450-km driving range, giving it a huge edge over battery-powered electric cars that travel only about 130 km before needing 3 to 12 hours of recharging.[11]

DaimlerChrysler's task is one of **concept development**: it must develop this new product into alternative product concepts, find out how attractive each concept is to customers, and choose the best one. It might create the following product concepts for the fuel-cell electric car:

Concept 1 A moderately priced subcompact designed as a second family car to be used around town. The car is ideal for running errands and visiting friends.

Idea screening Screening new product ideas to spot good ideas and drop poor ones as soon as possible.

Product concept A detailed version of the new product concept stated in meaningful consumer terms.

Concept development Expanding the new product idea into various alternative forms.

DaimlerChrysler's task is to develop its fuel-cell powered electric car into alternative product concepts, find out how attractive each is to customers, and choose the best one.

Concept 2 A medium-cost sporty compact appealing to young people.

Concept 3 An inexpensive subcompact "green" car appealing to environmentally conscious people who want practical transportation and low pollution.

Concept 4 A high-end SUV appealing to those who love the space SUVs provide but lament the poor gas mileage.

Concept testing Testing new product concepts with a group of target consumers to find out whether the concepts have strong consumer appeal

Concept Testing   **Concept testing** calls for testing new product concepts with groups of target consumers. The concepts may be presented to consumers symbolically or physically. Here, in words, is concept 3: "An efficient, fun-to-drive, fuel-cell-powered electric subcompact car that seats four. This high-tech wonder runs on liquid hydrogen, providing practical and reliable transportation with virtually no pollution. It goes up to 90 miles per hour and, unlike battery-powered electric cars, it never needs recharging. It's priced, fully equipped, at $20,000."

For some concept tests, a word or picture description might be sufficient. However, a more concrete and physical presentation of the concept will increase the reliability of the concept test. Today, some marketers are finding innovative ways to make product concepts more real to consumer subjects. For example, some are using virtual reality to test product concepts. Virtual reality programs use computers and sensory devices (such as gloves or goggles) to simulate reality. A designer of kitchen cabinets can use a virtual reality program to help a customer "see" how his or her kitchen would look and work if remodelled with the company's products. Hairdressers have used virtual reality for years to show consumers how they might look with a new style. Although virtual reality is still in its infancy, its applications are increasing daily.[12]

After being exposed to the concept, consumers then may be asked to react to it by answering questions such as those in Table 9-1. The answers will help the company decide which concept has the strongest appeal. For example, the last question asks about the consumer's intention to buy. Suppose 10 percent of the consumers said they "definitely" would buy and another 5 percent said "probably." The company could project these figures to the full population in this target group to estimate sales volume. Even then, the estimate is uncertain because people do not always carry out their stated intentions.

Many firms routinely test new product concepts with consumers before attempting to turn them into actual new products. In recent polls, Nabisco's Oreo Chocolate Cones concept received a rare A+ rating, meaning that consumers think it is an outstanding concept that they would try and would buy. Glad Ovenware, Reach Whitening Tape dental floss, and Lender's Bake at Home Bagels were also big hits. Other product concepts didn't fare so well. Nubrush Anti-Bacterial Toothbrush Spray disinfectant, from Applied Microdontics, received an F. Consumers found Nubrush to be overpriced, and most don't think they have a problem with "infected" toothbrushes.

Marketing Strategy Development

Suppose DaimlerChrysler finds that concept 3 for the fuel-cell-powered electric car tests best. The next step is **marketing strategy development**, designing an initial marketing strategy for introducing this car to the market.

The *marketing strategy statement* consists of three parts. The first part describes the target market; the planned product positioning; and the sales, market share, and profit goals for the first few years:

> The target market is younger, well-educated, moderate-to-high-income individuals, couples, or small families seeking practical, environmentally responsible transportation. The car will be positioned as more economical to operate, more fun to drive, and less polluting than today's internal combustion engine or hybrid cars, and as less restricting than battery-powered electric cars, which must be recharged regularly. The company will aim to sell 100 000 cars in the first year, at a loss of not more than $15 million. In the second year, the company will aim for sales of 120 000 cars and a profit of $25 million.

Marketing strategy development Designing an initial marketing strategy for a new product based on the product concept.

Table 9-1 Questions for Fuel-Cell Electric Car Concept Test
1. Do you understand the concept of a fuel-cell-powered electric car?
2. Do you believe the claims about the car's performance?
3. What are the major benefits of the fuel-cell-powered electric car compared with a conventional car?
4. What are its advantages compared with a battery-powered electric car?
5. What improvements in the car's features would you suggest?
6. For what uses would you prefer a fuel-cell-powered electric car to a conventional car?
7. What would be a reasonable price to charge for the car?
8. Who would be involved in your decision to buy such a car? Who would drive it?
9. Would you buy such a car? (definitely, probably, probably not, definitely not)

The second part of the marketing strategy statement outlines the product's planned price, distribution, and marketing budget for the first year:

The fuel-cell-powered electric car will be offered in three colours—red, white, and blue—and will have optional air-conditioning and power-drive features. It will sell at a retail price of $20 000—with 15 percent off the list price to dealers. Dealers who sell more than 10 cars per month will get an additional discount of 5 percent on each car sold that month. An advertising budget of $20 million will be split 50–50 between national and local advertising. Advertising will emphasize the car's fun spirit and low emissions. During the first year, $100 000 will be spent on marketing research to find out who is buying the car and their satisfaction levels.

The third part of the marketing strategy statement describes the planned long-run sales, profit goals, and marketing mix strategy:

DaimlerChrysler intends to capture a 3 percent long-run share of the total auto market and realize an after-tax return on investment of 15 percent. To achieve this, product quality will start high and be improved over time. Price will be raised in the second and third years if competition permits. The total advertising budget will be raised each year by about 10 percent. Marketing research will be reduced to $60 000 per year after the first year.

Business Analysis

Business analysis A review of the sales, costs, and profit projections for a new product to find out whether these factors satisfy the company's objectives.

Once management has decided on its product concept and marketing strategy, it can evaluate the business attractiveness of the proposal. **Business analysis** involves a review of the sales, costs, and profit projections for a new product to find out whether they satisfy the company's objectives. If they do, the product can move to the product development stage.

To estimate sales, the company might look at the sales history of similar products and conduct surveys of market opinion. It can then estimate minimum and maximum sales to assess the range of risk. After preparing the sales forecast, management can estimate the expected costs and profits for the product, including marketing, R&D, operations, accounting, and finance costs. The company then uses the sales and costs figures to analyze the new product's financial attractiveness.

Product Development

Product development Developing the product concept into a physical product to ensure that the product idea can be turned into a workable product.

So far, for many new product concepts, the product may have existed only as a word description, a drawing, or perhaps a crude mock-up. If the product concept passes the business test, it moves into **product development**. Here, R&D or engineering develops the product concept into a physical product. The product development step, however, now calls for a large jump in investment. It will show whether the product idea can be turned into a workable product.

The R&D department will develop and test one or more physical versions of the product concept. R&D hopes to design a prototype that will satisfy and excite consumers and that can be produced quickly and at budgeted costs. Developing a successful prototype can take days, weeks, months, or even years. Often, products undergo rigorous functional tests to make sure that they perform safely and effectively. Here are some examples of such functional tests:[13]

A scuba-diving Barbie doll must swim and kick for 15 straight hours to satisfy Mattel that she will last at least one year. But because Barbie may find her feet in small owners' mouths rather than in the bathtub, Mattel has devised another, more tortuous test: Barbie's feet are clamped by two steel jaws to make sure that her skin doesn't crack—and choke—potential owners.

Mattel Inc.www.mattel.com

At Shaw Industries, temporary workers are paid $5 an hour to pace up and down 5 long rows of sample carpets for up to 8 hours a day, logging an average of 14 miles each. One regular reads 3 mysteries a week while pacing and shed 40 pounds in 2 years. Shaw Industries counts walkers' steps and figures that 20,000 steps equal several years of average carpet wear.

Test Marketing

If the product passes functional and consumer tests, the next step is **test marketing**, the stage at which the product and marketing program are introduced into more realistic market settings. Test marketing gives the marketer experience with marketing the product before going to the great expense of full introduction. It lets the company test the product and its entire marketing program—positioning strategy, advertising, distribution, pricing, branding and packaging, and budget levels.

Test marketing The stage of new product development in which the product and marketing program are tested in more realistic market settings.

Product testing: Shaw Industries pays temps to pace up and down five long rows of sample carpets for up to eight hours a day, logging an average of 14 miles each.

The amount of test marketing needed varies with each new product. Test marketing costs can be enormous, and it takes time that may allow competitors to gain advantages. When the costs of developing and introducing the product are low, or when management is already confident about the new product, the company may do little or no test marketing. Companies often do not test-market simple line extensions or copies of successful competitor products. For example, Procter & Gamble introduced its Folger's decaffeinated coffee crystals without test marketing, and Pillsbury rolled out Chewy granola bars and chocolate-covered Granola Dipps with no standard test market. However, when introducing a new product requires a big investment, or when management is not sure of the product or marketing program, a company may do a lot of test marketing. For instance, Lever spent two years testing its highly successful Lever 2000 bar soap before introducing it internationally. Frito-Lay did 18 months of testing in three markets on at least five formulations before introducing its Baked Lays line of low-fat snacks. And both Procter & Gamble and Unilever have spent many months testing their new Juvian and MyHome valet laundry and home fabric care services.[14]

The costs of test marketing can be high, but they are often small when compared with the costs of making a major mistake. For example, Nabisco's launch of one new product without testing had disastrous—and soggy—results:[15]

Nabisco hit a marketing homerun with its Teddy Grahams, teddy-bear-shaped graham crackers in several different flavors. So, the company decided to extend Teddy Grahams into a new area. In 1989, it introduced chocolate, cinnamon, and honey versions of Breakfast Bears Graham Cereal. When the product came out, however, consumers didn't like the taste enough, so the product developers went back to the kitchen and modified the formula. But they didn't test it. The result was a disaster. Although the cereal may have tasted better, it no longer stayed crunchy in milk, as the advertising on the box promised. Instead, it left a gooey mess of graham mush on the bottom of cereal bowls. Supermarket managers soon refused to restock the cereal, and Nabisco executives decided it was too late to reformulate the product again. So a promising new product was killed through haste to get it to market.

Recently, some marketers have begun to use interesting new high-tech approaches to test-market research, such as virtual reality and the Internet (see New Directions 9-1).

Commercialization

Commercialization
Introducing a new product into the market.

Test marketing gives management the information needed to make a final decision about whether to launch the new product. If the company goes ahead with **commercialization**—introducing the new product into the market—it will face high costs. The company will have to build or rent a manufacturing facility. And it may have to spend, in the case of a new consumer packaged good, between $16 million and $300 million for advertising, sales promotion, and other marketing efforts in the first year.

New Directions 9-1 >>   Virtual Reality Test Marketing: the Future is Now

It's a steamy summer Saturday afternoon. Imagine that you're stopping off at the local supermarket to pick up some icy bottles of your favourite sports drink before heading to the tennis courts. You park the car, cross the parking lot, and walk through the store's automatic doors. You head for aisle 5, passing several displays along the way, and locate your usual sports drink brand. You pick it up, check the price, and take it to the checkout counter. Sounds like a typical shopping experience, doesn't it? But in this case, the entire experience took place on your computer screen, not at the supermarket.

You've just experienced virtual reality—the wave of the future for test marketing and concept-testing research—courtesy of Gadd International Research. Gadd has developed a research tool called Simul-Shop, a virtual reality approach that recreates shopping situations in which researchers can test consumers' reactions to factors such as product positioning, store layouts, and package designs.

For example, suppose General Mills wants to test reactions to a new Cheerios package design and store shelf positioning. Using Simul-Shop on a standard desktop PC, test shoppers begin their shopping spree with a screen showing the outside of a grocery store. They click to enter the virtual store and are guided to the appropriate store section. Once there, they can scan the shelf, pick up various cereal packages, rotate them, study the labels—even look around to see what is on the shelf behind them. About the only thing they can't do is open the box and taste the cereal.

The virtual shopping trip includes full sound and video, along with a guide who directs users through the experience and answers their questions. Explains a Gadd's research director, "Once [users] move toward the item we want to test, [they] can look at different packaging, shelf layouts, and package colors. Depending on the activity, we can even ask users why they did what they did."

Virtual reality testing can take any of several forms. For example, Elumens has created a virtual reality amphitheatre called the VisionDome. The Dome offers 360 by 160 degrees of film projection, allowing as many as 45 people at one time to participate in a virtual reality experience. The VisionDome is like an IMAX theatre, but with one big difference—it's interactive. "When you use a computer to generate an image,…you have the advantage of making that image interactive," comments an Elumens executive. When conducting research on a car, he suggests, "We can go into a VisionDome, see that car in three dimensions, look at it from every angle, take it out for a test drive, and allow the customer to configure that car exactly the way he wants it." Caterpillar sees enormous potential for the Dome. "We can put one of our tractors in a VisionDome and actually have a customer sit in it and test it under whatever conditions they would use it for," says a Caterpillar design engineer. "The ability to immerse people in the product makes it a phenomenal [research and sales] tool."

Virtual reality as a research tool offers several advantages. For one, it's relatively inexpensive. For example, a firm can conduct a Simul-Shop study for only about $25 000, including initial programming and the actual research on 75 to 100 people. This makes virtual reality research accessible to firms that can't afford full market-testing campaigns or the expense of creating actual mock-ups for each different product colour, shape, or size. Another advantage is flexibility. A virtual reality store can display an almost infinite variety of products, sizes, styles, and flavours in response to consumers' desires and needs. Research can be conducted in almost any simulated surroundings, ranging from food store interiors and new car showrooms to farm fields or the open road. The technique also offers great interactivity, allowing marketers and consumers to work together via computer on designs of new products and marketing programs.

Finally, virtual reality has great potential for international research, which has often been difficult for marketers to conduct. With virtual reality, researchers can use a single standardized approach to evaluate products and programs worldwide. Consider the following example.

One multinational company has begun to conduct virtual-shopping studies in North and South

America, Europe, Asia, and Australia. Researchers create virtual stores in each country and region using the appropriate local products, shelf layouts, and currencies. Once the stores are online, a product concept can be quickly tested across locations. When the studies are completed, the results are communicated to headquarters electronically. The analysis reveals which markets offer the greatest opportunity for a successful launch.

Virtual reality research also has its limitations. The biggest problem: Simulated shopping situations never quite match the real thing. Observes one expert, "Just because it's technically [feasible], that doesn't mean that when you put [people] behind a computer you're going to get true responses. Anytime you simulate an experience you're not getting the experience itself. It's still a simulation."

So, what's ahead for virtual reality in marketing? Some pioneers are extremely enthusiastic about the technology—not only as a research tool but also as a place where even real buying and selling can occur. They predict that the virtual store may become a major channel for personal and direct interactions with consumers, interactions that encompass not only research but sales and service as well. They see great potential for conducting this type of research over the Internet, and virtual stores have become a reality on the Web. As one observer notes, "This is what I read about in science fiction books when I was growing up. It's the thing of the future." For many marketers, that future is already a virtual reality.

Sources: Quotes and extracts from Raymond R. Burke, "Virtual Shopping: Breakthrough in Marketing Research," *Harvard Business Review,* March–April, 1996, pp. 120–131; Tom Dellacave Jr., "Curing Market Research Headaches," *Sales and Marketing Management,* July 1996, pp. 84–85; Brian Silverman, "Get 'Em While They're Hot," *Sales and Marketing Management,* February 1997, pp. 47–48, 52; and Mike Hoffman, "Virtual Shopping," *Inc.,* July 1998, p. 88. Also see Sara Sellar, "The Perfect Trade Show Rep," *Sales and Marketing Management,* April 1999, p. 11; Christopher Ryan, "Virtual Reality in Marketing," *Direct Marketing,* April 2001, pp. 57–62; and information accessed online at **www/elumens.com/products/ visiondome.htm**, August 2001

Virtual reality: The wave of the future for marketing-testing and concept-testing research. Elumens' Vision Dome allows as many as 45 people at a time to participate in a virtual reality experience.

The company launching a new product must first decide on introduction *timing*. If DaimlerChrysler's new fuel-cell electric car will eat into the sales of the company's other cars, its introduction may be delayed. If the car can be improved further, or if the economy is down, the company may wait until the following year to launch it.

Next, the company must decide *where* to launch the new product—in a single location, a region, the national market, or the international market. Few companies have the confidence, capital, and capacity to launch new products into full national or international distribution. They will develop a planned *market rollout* over time. In particular, small companies may enter attractive cities or regions one at a time. Larger companies, however, may quickly introduce new models into several regions or into the full national market.

Companies with international distribution systems may introduce new products through global rollouts. Colgate-Palmolive used to follow a "lead-country" strategy. For example, it launched its Palmolive Optims shampoo and conditioner first in Australia, the Philippines, Hong Kong, and Mexico, then rapidly rolled it out into Europe, Asia, Latin America, and Africa. However, most international companies now introduce their new products in swift global assaults. Last year, in its fastest new product rollout ever, Colgate introduced its Actibrush battery-powered toothbrush into 50 countries in a year, generating $115 million in sales. Such rapid

Colgate
www.colgate.com

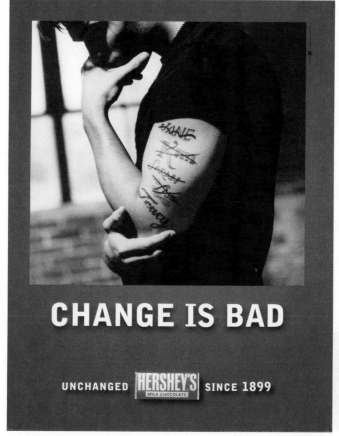

Product life cycle: Companies want their products to enjoy long and happy life cycles. Hershey's chocolate bars have been "unchanged since 1899."

worldwide expansion solidified the brand's market position before foreign competitors could react.[16]

You Are Here!

Take a break. Think about new products and how companies find and develop them.

• Suppose that you're on a panel to nominate the "best new products of the year." What products would you nominate and why? See what you can learn about the new product development process for one of these products.

• Applying the new product development process you've just studied, develop an idea for an innovative new snack food product and sketch out a brief plan for bringing it to market. Be creative and have some fun with this.

PRODUCT LIFE-CYCLE STRATEGIES

After launching the new product, management wants the product to enjoy a long and happy life. Although it does not expect the product to sell forever, the company wants to earn a decent profit to cover all the effort and risk that went into launching it. Management is aware that each product will have a life cycle, although its exact shape and length is not known in advance.

Figure 9-2 shows a typical **product life cycle (PLC)**, the course that a product's sales and profits take over its lifetime. The product life cycle has five distinct stages:

Product life cycle (PLC)
The course of a product's sales and profits over its lifetime. It involves five distinct stages: product development, introduction, growth, maturity, and decline.

1. *Product development* begins when the company finds and develops a new product idea. During product development, sales are zero and the company's investment costs mount.

2. *Introduction* is a period of slow sales growth as the product is introduced in the market. Profits are nonexistent in this stage because of the heavy expenses of product introduction.

3. *Growth* is a period of rapid market acceptance and increasing profits.

4. *Maturity* is a period of slowdown in sales growth because the product has achieved acceptance by most potential buyers. Profits level off or decline because of increased marketing outlays to defend the product against competition.

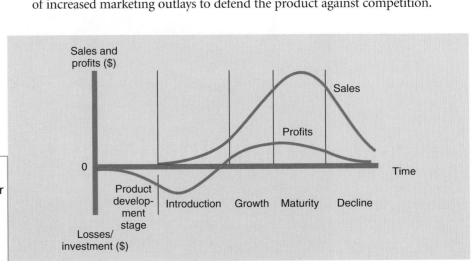

Figure 9-2

Sales and Profits over the Product's Life from Inception to Demise

5. *Decline* is the period when sales fall off and profits drop.

Not all products follow this product life cycle. Some products are introduced and die quickly; others stay in the mature stage for a long, long time. Some enter the decline stage and are then cycled back into the growth stage through strong promotion or repositioning.

The PLC concept can describe a *product class* (gasoline-powered automobiles), a *product form* (minivans), or a *brand* (the Ford Taurus). The PLC concept applies differently in each case. Product classes have the longest life cycles—the sales of many product classes stay in the mature stage for a long time. Product forms, in contrast, tend to have the standard PLC shape. Product forms such as "cream deodorants," "dial telephones," and "phonograph records" passed through a regular history of introduction, rapid growth, maturity, and decline. A specific brand's life cycle can change quickly because of changing competitive attacks and responses. For example, although laundry soaps (product class) and powdered detergents (product form) have enjoyed long life cycles, the life cycles of specific brands have tended to be much shorter. Today's leading brands of powdered laundry soap are Tide and Cheer; the leading brands 75 years ago were Fels Naptha, Octagon, and Kirkman.[17]

The PLC concept also can be applied to what are known as styles, fashions, and fads. Their special life cycles are shown in Figure 9-3. A **style** is a basic and distinctive mode of expression. For example, styles appear in homes (colonial, ranch, transitional), clothing (formal, casual), and art (realist, surrealist, abstract). Once a style is invented, it may last for generations, passing in and out of vogue. A style has a cycle showing several periods of renewed interest. A **fashion** is a currently accepted or popular style in a given field. For example, the more formal "business attire" look of corporate dress of the 1980s and early 1990s has now given way to the "business casual" look of today. Fashions tend to grow slowly, remain popular for a while, then decline slowly.

Fads are fashions that enter quickly, are adopted with great zeal, peak early, and decline very quickly. They last only a short time and tend to attract only a limited following. "Pet rocks" are a classic example of a fad. On hearing his friends complain about how expensive it was to care for their dogs, advertising copywriter Gary Dahl joked about his pet rock and was soon writing a spoof of a dog-training manual for it. Soon Dahl was selling some 1.5 million ordinary rocks at $4 a pop. Yet the fad, which broke in October 1975, had sunk like a stone by the next February. Dahl's advice to those who want to succeed with a fad: "Enjoy it while it lasts." Other examples of fads include Rubik's Cubes, lava lamps, CB radios, and scooters. Most fads do not survive for long because they normally do not satisfy a strong need or satisfy it well.[18]

The PLC concept can be applied by marketers as a useful framework for describing how products and markets work. But using the PLC concept for forecasting product performance or for developing marketing strategies presents some practical problems. For example, managers may have trouble identifying which stage of the PLC the product is in, pinpointing when the product moves into the next stage, and determining the factors that affect the product's movement through the stages. In practice, it is difficult to forecast the sales level at each PLC stage, the length of each stage, and the shape of the PLC curve.

Style A basic and distinctive mode of expression.

Fashion A currently accepted or popular style in a given field.

Fads Fashions that enter quickly, are adopted with great zeal, peak early, and decline very quickly.

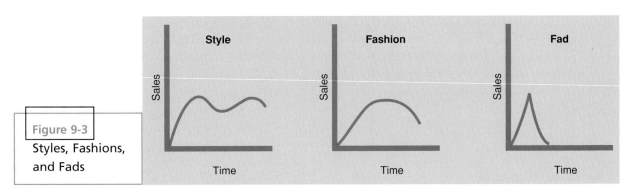

Figure 9-3

Styles, Fashions, and Fads

Using the PLC concept to develop marketing strategy also can be difficult because strategy is both a cause and a result of the product's life cycle. The product's current PLC position suggests the best marketing strategies, and the resulting marketing strategies affect product performance in later life-cycle stages. Yet, when used carefully, the PLC concept can help in developing good marketing strategies for different stages of the product life cycle.

We looked at the product development stage of the product life cycle in the first part of the chapter. We now look at strategies for each of the other life-cycle stages.

Introduction Stage

Introduction stage The product life-cycle stage in which the new product is first distributed and made available for purchase.

The **introduction stage** starts when the new product is first launched. Introduction takes time, and sales growth is apt to be slow. Well-known products such as instant coffee, frozen orange juice, and powdered coffee creamers lingered for many years before they entered a stage of rapid growth.

In this stage, as compared with other stages, profits are negative or low because of the low sales and high distribution and promotion expenses. Much money is needed to attract distributors and build their inventories. Promotion spending is relatively high to inform consumers of the new product and get them to try it. Because the market is not generally ready for product refinements at this stage, the company and its few competitors produce basic versions of the product. These firms focus their selling on those buyers who are the most ready to buy.

A company, especially the *market pioneer,* must choose a launch strategy that is consistent with the intended product positioning. It should realize that the initial strategy is just the first step in a grander marketing plan for the product's entire life cycle. If the pioneer chooses its launch strategy to make a "killing," it will be sacrificing long-run revenue for the sake of short-run gain. As the pioneer moves through later stages of the life cycle, it will have to continually formulate new pricing, promotion, and other marketing strategies. It has the best chance of building and retaining market leadership if it plays its cards correctly from the start.[19]

Growth Stage

Growth stage The product life-cycle stage in which a product's sales start climbing quickly.

If the new product satisfies the market, it will enter a **growth stage**, in which sales will start climbing quickly. The early adopters will continue to buy, and later buyers will start following their lead, especially if they hear favourable word of mouth.

Attracted by the opportunities for profit, new competitors will enter the market. They will introduce new product features, and the market will expand. The increase in competitors leads to an increase in the number of distribution outlets, and sales jump just to build reseller inventories. Prices remain where they are or fall only slightly. Companies keep their promotion spending at the same or a slightly higher level. Educating the market remains a goal, but now the company must also meet the competition.

Profits increase during the growth stage, as promotion costs are spread over a large volume and as unit manufacturing costs fall. The firm uses several strategies to sustain rapid market growth as long as possible. It improves product quality and adds new product features and models. It enters new market segments and new distribution channels. It shifts some advertising from building product awareness to building product conviction and purchase, and it lowers prices at the right time to attract more buyers.

In the growth stage, the firm faces a trade-off between high market share and high current profit. By spending a lot of money on product improvement, promotion, and distribution, the company can capture a dominant position. In doing so, however, it gives up maximum current profit, which it hopes to make up in the next stage.

Maturity Stage

At some point, a product's sales growth will slow down, and the product will enter a **maturity stage**. This maturity stage normally lasts longer than the previous stages, and it poses strong challenges to marketing management. Most products are in the maturity stage of the life cycle, and therefore most of marketing management deals with the mature product.

Maturity stage The stage in the product life cycle in which sales growth slows or levels off

The slowdown in sales growth results in many producers with many products to sell. In turn, this overcapacity leads to greater competition. Competitors begin marking down prices, increasing their advertising and sales promotions, and upping their R&D budgets to find better versions of the product. These steps lead to a drop in profit. Some of the weaker competitors start dropping out, and the industry eventually contains only well-established competitors.

Although many products in the mature stage appear to remain unchanged for long periods, most successful ones are actually evolving to meet changing consumer needs (see New Directions 9-2). Product managers should do more than simply ride along with or defend their mature products—a good offence is the best defence. They should consider modifying the market, product, and marketing mix.

In *modifying the market,* the company tries to increase the consumption of the current product. It looks for new users and market segments, as when Johnson & Johnson targeted the adult market with its baby powder and shampoo. The manager also looks for ways to increase usage among present customers. Campbell does this by offering recipes and convincing consumers that "soup is good food." Or the company may want to reposition the brand to appeal to a larger or faster-growing segment, as Arrow did when it introduced its new line of casual shirts and announced, "We're loosening our collars."

The company might also try *modifying the product*—changing characteristics such as quality, features, or style to attract new users and to inspire more usage. It

New Directions 9-2 >> Age-Defying Products or Just Skillful PLC Management?

Some products are born and die quickly. Others, however, seem to defy the product life cycle, enduring for decades or even generations with little or no apparent change in their makeup or marketing. Look deeper, however, and you'll find that such products are far from unchanging. Rather, skillful product life-cycle management keeps them fresh, relevant, and appealing to customers. Here are examples of three products that might have been only fads but instead were turned into long-term market winners with plenty of staying power.

Kraft Dinner

The Barenaked Ladies sing about it, and university students, adults, and children across Canada wolf down an incredible 246 000 boxes of KD a day. Nine out of ten Canadian households buy the product. Kraft Dinner is not only Kraft Canada's biggest business from a volume standpoint, but is also the country's number-one-selling grocery item, holding a 75 percent share of the market. Not bad for basic food that has been close to the hearts of Canadians since 1937. In fact, per capita, Canadians eat three times more Kraft dinner than their American counterparts.

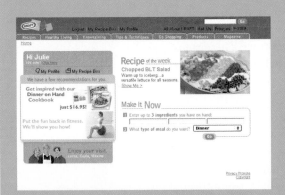

The Kraft Dinner has even managed to score in cyber-space with a site featuring games and offers.

Despite its Canadian success, senior brand manager Gannon Jones confesses that "it's a business that's been suffering over the last while." In an ever-changing market, "You can't sit back and simply expect the brand to continue to be popular without trying to keep it relevant with consumers." The very popularity of the product presents its own challenges. How, you might ask, can you get Canadians to eat even more of the stuff? The biggest danger in trying to revitalize the brand is making changes that will alienate KD's core customers, just like Coke did when it introduced New Coke.

For a period, managers of the product had become too reliant on price to drive the KD business. Today that is history. Kraft has put a lot of its market research muscle, new product development skills, and advertising shrewdness behind revitalizing the brand. Rather than just talking to kids, as had become its habit, Kraft Canada decided it needed to reconnect with adults. So, Kraft and its agency, J. Walter Thompson, asked cultural anthropologist Grant McCracken to study the brand to uncover consumer insights about KD.

This research, along with 15 000 videos of Canadians talking about why they love Kraft Dinner, revealed that everyone has their own "KD truths." Such truths could be any of those special moments we all remember about eating KD at university since it was all we could afford on our tight budgets, to eating it with our culinary-challenged dad while mom was away. The first TV spot based on these research insights was a hit. Dubbed "Laundry Night," it was targeted to young adults as well as moms. It featured a group of university-age guys filing into a laundromat, where one of them uses a washing machine to prepare KD. When another patron gives him a look, he shrugs and says, "My night to cook."

Kraft has also been busy on other fronts. The famous blue and yellow box was given a face-lift, giving the lettering a 3-D look. New product versions were developed. These include Easy Mac Macaroni & Cheese, a microwaveable, snack-size extension. Kraft called the launch of this product its biggest in

Canada in a decade. The TV campaign used to launch the product, titled "Dog Gone Girl," won praise among viewers and critics alike. It shows a young man returning home, finding nothing in his apartment but his dog. Although not overly concerned about being abandoned by his girlfriend, he is hungry and manages to make Easy Mac in the dog's dish.

The born-again brand has even managed to score in cyberspace. As *Marketing Magazine*'s digital critic notes, "I love this site. I have always thought of Kraft Dinner more as entertainment than food and that is the approach taken with this Web site. No fuzzy lifestyle shots of happy families or time-pressed yuppies, just lurid comic book pages of outrageous fun."

Beanie Babies
When Ty Inc. unleashed Beanie Babies on the market in 1993, most experts saw them as just a passing fad. Priced under $5, the tiny bean-filled creatures were designed by company founder Ty Warner as a back-to-basics toy that kids could buy with their own allowance money. Soon, however, adults began compulsively collecting the floppy little animals, and the company couldn't get them onto store shelves fast enough.

Yet Ty quickly realized that scarcity would be the key to keeping the Beanie Babies craze going—and going and going. The company became adept at maintaining consumer demand by limiting distribution to small gift and specialty stores. Each store is limited to 36 toys of each style per month. Ty also adds to the hype by regularly retiring old characters and replacing them with many new ones. There are just over 200 styles of Beanie Babies, with about 150 of them retired. Retired models fetch as much as $1000 from hard-core collectors. When new models or retirements are announced, visits to the company's Web site skyrocket. By mid-1999, the site had received almost 3 billion visits.

Thus, long after the experts would have predicted the demise of these cute little critters, avid collectors are still lining up to get their hands on new styles. In a typical scenario, Penny Madsen, who manages the gift shop in the Adventureland amusement park, says that she receives 15 or 20 calls a day asking whether the store has certain Beanies in stock. Even though Adventureland doesn't advertise its Beanie Babies, when new styles are expected,

"People will be standing outside our gate at 6 in the morning, waiting until we open at 10," says Madsen. Even more impressive, they willingly pay the $20 gate admission just to get into the gift shop.

Crayola Crayons
Over the past century, Binney & Smith's Crayola crayons have become a household staple in more than 60 countries around the world. Few people can forget their first pack of "64s"—64 beauties neatly arranged in the familiar green and yellow flip-top box with a sharpener on the back. The aroma of a freshly opened Crayola box still drives kids into a frenzy and takes members of the older generation back to some of their fondest childhood memories.

In some ways, Crayola crayons haven't changed much since 1903, when they were sold in an eight-pack for a nickel. But a closer look reveals that Binney & Smith has made many adjustments to keep the brand out of decline. The company has added a steady stream of new colours, shapes, sizes, and packages. It has gradually increased the number of colours from the original eight in 1903 (red, orange, yellow, green, blue, black, brown, and violet) to 96 in 1999. In 1962, as a result of the civil rights movement, it changed its crayon colour "flesh" to "peach"; and in 1992, it added multicultural skin tones by which "children are able to build a positive sense of self and respect for cultural diversity." Binney & Smith has also extended the Crayola brand to new markets—Crayola markers, watercolour paints, themed stamps and stickers, and stencils. The company has licensed the Crayola brand for use on everything from lunch boxes and children's apparel to house paints. Finally, the company has added several programs and services to help strengthen its relationships with Crayola customers. For example, its *Crayola Kids* magazine and Crayola Web site offer features for the children along with expert advice to parents on helping develop reading skills and creativity.

Not all of Binney & Smith's life cycle adjustments have been greeted favourably by consumers. For example, in 1990, to make room for more modern colours, it retired eight colours from the time-honoured box of 64—raw umber, lemon yellow, maize, blue grey, orange yellow, orange red, green blue, and violet blue—into the Crayola Hall of Fame. The move unleashed a groundswell of protest from loyal Crayola users, who formed such organizations as the

RUMPS—the Raw Umber and Maize Preservation Society—and the National Committee to Save Lemon Yellow. Company executives were flabbergasted: "We were aware of the loyalty and nostalgia surrounding Crayola crayons," a spokesperson says, "but we didn't know we [would] hit such a nerve." The company reissued the old standards in a special collector's tin—it sold all of the 2.5 million tins made.

Thus, Crayola continues its long and colourful life cycle. Through smart product life cycle management, Binney & Smith, now a subsidiary of Hallmark, has dominated the crayon market for almost a century. Sixty-five percent of all American children between the ages of two and seven pick up a crayon at least once a day and colour for an average of 28 minutes. Nearly 80 percent of the time, they pick up a Crayola crayon.

Sources: See John Heinzl, "Kraft Dinner Serves up a New Look," *The Globe and Mail,* 13 January 1999, p. B30; Lara Mills, "Kraft Builds Ads Around 'KD truths,'" *Marketing On-Line,* 26 April 1999; "Easy Mac Simplifies Kraft Dinner," *Marketing On-Line,* 6 September 1999; Michael Cavanaugh, "The Digital Eye," *Marketing On-Line,* 13 March 2000; Kathleen Deslauriers, "Easy Mac Stirs up Awareness," *Strategy,* 13 March 2000, p. 18; Gary Samuels, "Mystique Marketing," *Forbes,* 21 October 1996, p. 276; Carole Schmidt and Lynn Kaladjian, "Ty Connects Hot-Property Dots," *Brandweek,* 16 June 1997, p. 26; Joyce Cohen, "Fans Still Lining up to Haul in Beanie Babies," *Amusement Business,* 18 January 1999, p. 4; information accessed online at **www.ty.com**, February 2000; "Hue and Cry over Crayola May Revive Old Colors," *The Wall Street Journal,* 14 June 1991, p. B1; Margaret O. Kirk, "Coloring Our Children's World Since '03," *Chicago Tribune,* 29 October 1986, pp. 5, 1; Becky Ebenkamp, "Crayola Heritage Tack Continues with $6-7M," *Brandweek,* 1 February 1999, p. 5; information accessed online at **www.crayola.com**, February 2000; Gene Del Vecchio, "Keeping It Timeless, Trendy," *Advertising Age,* 23 March 1998, p. 24.

might improve the product's quality and performance—its durability, reliability, speed, taste. It can improve the product's styling and attractiveness. Thus, car manufacturers restyle their cars to attract buyers who want a new look. The makers of consumer food and household products introduce new flavours, colours, ingredients, or packages to revitalize consumer buying. Or the company might add new features that expand the product's usefulness, safety, or convenience. For example, Sony keeps adding new styles and features to its Walkman and Discman lines, and Volvo adds new safety features to its cars. Kimberly-Clark is adding a new twist to revitalize the product life cycle of an old standby, toilet tissue:

Almost without exception, every Canadian family knows what the paper roll next to the toilet is for, knows how to use it, and purchases it faithfully. Selling an omnipresent household item requires a vital brand that stands out at the supermarket, but how do you make toilet tissue new and exciting? Kimberly-Clark, the maker of Cottonelle and Kleenex, has the answer with an unprecedented innovation: a premoistened toilet paper called Rollwipes. Like baby wipes on a roll, the product is designed to compliment traditional toilet tissue. "In this category, your growth has to come from significant product Innovations," says a marketing director for Cottonelle. Another marketing executive agrees: "Without new products, old brands become older brands. In categories where there's basic satisfactions with the products, you still have to provide new benefits...to build brand share."[20]

Finally, the company can try *modifying the marketing mix*—improving sales by changing one or more marketing mix elements. It can cut prices to attract new users and competitors' customers. It can launch a better advertising campaign or use aggressive sales promotions—trade deals, cents-off, premiums, and contests. The company can also move into larger market channels, using mass merchandisers, if these channels are growing. Finally, the company can offer new or improved services to buyers.

Decline Stage

The sales of most product forms and brands eventually dip. The decline may be slow, as in the case of oatmeal cereal, or rapid, as in the case of phonograph records. Sales may plunge to zero, or they may drop to a low level where they continue for many years. This is the **decline stage**.

Sales decline for many reasons, including technological advances, shifts in consumer tastes, and increased competition. As sales and profits decline, some firms withdraw from the market. Those remaining may prune their product offerings. They may drop smaller market segments and marginal trade channels, or they may cut the promotion budget and reduce their prices further.

Carrying a weak product can be very costly to a firm, and not just in profit terms. There are many hidden costs. A weak product may take up too much of management's time. It often requires frequent price and inventory adjustments. It requires advertising and sales force attention that might be better used to make "healthy" products more profitable. A product's failing reputation can cause customer concerns about the company and its other products. The biggest cost may well lie in the future. Keeping weak products delays the search for replacements, creates a lopsided product mix, hurts current profits, and weakens the company's foothold on the future.

For these reasons, companies need to pay more attention to their aging products. The firm's first task is to identify those products in the decline stage by regularly reviewing sales, market shares, costs, and profit trends. Then, management must decide whether to maintain, harvest, or drop each of these declining products.

Management may decide to *maintain* its brand without change in the hope that competitors will leave the industry. For example, Procter & Gamble made good profits by remaining in the declining liquid soap business as others withdrew. Or management may decide to reposition or reformulate the brand in hopes of moving it back into the growth stage of the product life cycle. Frito-Lay did this with the classic Cracker Jack brand:

When Cracker Jack passed the 100-year-old mark, it seemed that the timeless brand was running out of time. By the time Frito-Lay acquired the classic snack-food brand from Borden Foods in 1997, sales and profits had been declining for five straight years. Frito-Lay set out to reconnect the box of candy-coated popcorn, peanuts, and a prize with a new generation of kids. "We made the popcorn bigger and fluffier with more peanuts and bigger prizes, and we put it in bags, as well as boxes," says Chris Neugent, VP-marketing for wholesome snacks for Frito-Lay. New promotional programs shared a connection with baseball and fun for kids, featuring baseball star Mark

Decline stage The product life-cycle stage in which a product's sales decline.

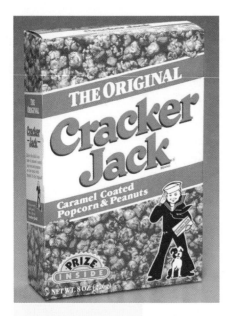

Back into the growth stage: When this timeless brand was running out of time, Frito-Lay reconnected it with a new generation of kids. Sales more than doubled during the two years following the acquisition.

McGwire, Rawlings Sporting Goods trading cards, Pokemon and Scooby Doo characters. The revitalized marketing pulled Cracker Jack out of decline. Sales more than doubled during the two years following the acquisition and the brand has posted double-digit increases each year since.[21]

Management may decide to *harvest* the product, which means reducing various costs (plant and equipment, maintenance, R&D, advertising, sales force) and hoping that sales hold up. If successful, harvesting will increase the company's profits in the short run. Or management may decide to *drop* the product from the line. It can sell it to another firm or simply liquidate it at salvage value. If the company plans to find a buyer, it will not want to run down the product through harvesting.

Table 9-2 summarizes the key characteristics of each stage of the product life cycle. The table also lists the marketing objectives and strategies for each stage.

Pause for a moment and think about some products, such as Crayola Crayons, that have been around for a long time.

• Ask a grandparent or someone else who shaved back then to compare a 1940s or 1950s Gillette razor to the most current model. Is Gillette's latest razor really a new product or just a "retread" of the previous version? What do you conclude about product life cycles?

• The Monopoly board game has been around for decades. How has Parker Brothers protected Monopoly from old age and decline (check out **www.monopoly.com**)?

Table 9-2 Summary of Product Life-Cycle Characteristics, Objectives, and Strategies

	Introduction	Growth	Maturity	Decline
Characteristics				
Sales	Low sales	Rapidly rising sales	Peak sales	Declining sales
Costs	High cost per customer	Average cost per customer	Low cost per customer	Low cost per customer
Profits	Negative	Rising profits	High profits	Declining profits
Customers	Innovators	Early adopters	Middle majority	Laggards
Competitors	Few	Growing number	Stable number beginning to decline	Declining number
Marketing Objectives	Create product and trial	Maximize market share	Maximize profit while defending market share	Reduce expenditure and milk the brand
Strategies				
Product	Offer a basic product and models	Offer product extensions, service, and warranty	Diversify brand and models	Phase out weak items
Price	Use cost-plus formula	Price to penetrate market	Price to match or best competitors	Cut price
Distribution Phase	Build selective distribution	Build intensive distribution	Build more intensive distribution	Go selective: out unprofitable outlets
Advertising	Build product awareness among early adopters and dealers	Build awareness and interest in the mass market	Stress brand differences and benefits	Reduce to level needed to retain hard-core loyals
Sales promotion	Use heavy sales promotion to entice trial	Reduce to take advantage of heavy consumer	Increase to encourage brand switching	Reduce to minimal level demand

Source: Philip Kotler, *Marketing Management: Analysis, Planning, Implementation, and Control,* 8th ed., Englewood Cliffs, NJ: Prentice-Hall, 1994, p. 365.

<< Looking Back < < < < < < < < <

Looking Back

Before we move on to the next marketing mix topic let's review the important new product and product life-cycle concepts. A company's current products face limited life spans and must be replaced by newer products. But new products can fail—the risks of innovation are as great as the rewards. The key to

successful innovation lies in a total-company effort, strong planning, and a systematic *new product development* process.

1. Explain how companies find and develop new product ideas.

Companies find and develop new product ideas from a variety of sources. Many new product ideas stem from *internal sources.* Companies conduct formal research and development, pick the brains of their employees, and brainstorm at executive meetings. By conducting surveys and focus groups and analyzing *customer* questions and complaints, companies can generate new product ideas that will meet specific consumer needs. Companies track *competitors'* offerings and inspect new products, dismantling them, analyzing their performance, and deciding whether to introduce a similar or improved product. *Distributors and suppliers* are close to the market and can pass along information about consumer problems and new product possibilities.

2. **List and define the steps in the new product development process.**

The new product development process consists of eight sequential stages. The process starts with *idea generation.* Next comes *idea screening,* which reduces the number of ideas based on the company's own criteria. Ideas that pass the screening stage continue through *product concept development,* in which a detailed version of the new product idea is stated in meaningful consumer terms. In the next stage, *concept testing,* new product concepts are tested with a group of target consumers to determine whether the concepts have strong consumer appeal. Strong concepts proceed to *marketing strategy development,* in which an initial marketing strategy for the new product is developed from the product concept. In the *business analysis* stage, a review of the sales, costs, and profit projections for a new product is conducted to determine whether the new product is likely to satisfy the company's objectives. With positive results here, the ideas become more concrete through *product development* and *test marketing* and finally are launched during *commercialization.*

3. **Describe the stages of the product life cycle.**

Each product has a *life cycle* marked by a changing set of problems and opportunities. The sales of the typical product follow an S-shaped curve made up of five stages. The cycle begins with the *product development stage* when the company finds and develops a new product idea. The *introduction stage* is marked by

slow growth and low profits as the product is distributed to the market. If successful, the product enters a *growth stage,* which offers rapid sales growth and increasing profits. Next comes a *maturity stage* when sales growth slows down and profits stabilize. Finally, the product enters a *decline stage* in which sales and profits dwindle. The company's task during this stage is to recognize the decline and to decide whether it should maintain, harvest, or drop the product.

4. **Explain how marketing strategies change during the product's life cycle.**

In the *introduction stage,* the company must choose a launch strategy consistent with its intended product positioning. Much money is needed to attract distributors and build their inventories and to inform consumers of the new product and achieve trial. In the *growth stage,* companies continue to educate potential consumers and distributors. In addition, the company works to stay ahead of the competition and sustain rapid market growth by improving product quality, adding new product features and models, entering new market segments and distribution channels, shifting advertising from building product awareness to building product conviction and purchase, and lowering prices at the right time to attract new buyers. In the *maturity stage,* companies continue to invest in maturing products and consider modifying the market, the product, and the marketing mix. When *modifying the market,* the company attempts to increase the consumption of the current product. When *modifying the product,* the company changes some of the product's characteristics—such as quality, features, or style—to attract new users or inspire more usage. When *modifying the marketing mix,* the company works to improve sales by changing one or more of the marketing mix elements. Once the company recognizes that a product has entered the *decline stage,* management must decide whether to *maintain* the brand without change, hoping that competitors will drop out of the market; *harvest* the product, reducing costs and trying to maintain sales; or *drop* the product, selling it to another firm or liquidating it at salvage value.

Navigating the Key Terms

Concept Check

Fill in the blanks and then check your answers.

1. Original products, product improvements, product modifications, and new brands that the firm develops through it own research and development efforts can all be called _____.

2. The eight steps in the new product development process are idea generation, _____, concept development and testing, _____, business analysis, _____, test marketing, and _____.

3. Major sources of new product ideas include _____, _____, _____, and distributors and suppliers.

4. A _____ is a detailed version of the idea stated in meaningful consumer terms.

5. A marketing strategy statement consists of three parts. Part one describes the target market, the planned product positioning, and the sales, market share, and profit goals for the first few years. Part two outlines the product's planned price, distribution, and marketing budget for the first year. Part three describes _____, _____, and _____.

6. _____ gives the marketer experience with marketing the product before going to the great expense of full introduction.

7. The five stages of the product life cycle (PLC) include _____, _____, _____, _____, and _____.

8. The _____ stage is a period of rapid market acceptance and increasing profits.

9. Most products are in the _____ stage of the life cycle and, therefore, most marketing management deals with this type of product.

10. In the maturity stage, "the best offence is a good defence." The marketer can consider modifying the _____, _____, or _____.

11. As compared with other stages in Table 9-2, the _____ stage is characterized as having profits that are negative because of low sales and high cost per customer.

Concept Checks Answers: 1. new products; 2. idea screening, marketing strategy, product development, commercialization; 3. internal sources, customers, competitors; 4. product concept; 5. the planned long-run sales, profit goals, and marketing mix strategy; 6. Test marketing; 7. product development, introduction, growth, maturity, and decline; 8. growth; 9. maturity; 10. market, product, or marketing mix; 11. introduction.

Discussing the Issues

1. Pick a familiar company and assume you are responsible for generating new product ideas. How you would structure your new product development process? What sources of new ideas would be most valuable? How would you stimulate the new idea development process in the organization?

2. One of the challenges faced by today's new product development manager is how to use the Internet to get new ideas from customers and competitors. Propose three ways to form relationships with consumers to encourage and get new ideas. Next, propose three ways to observe competitors to gain insight into what they are thinking and doing in the new product arena.

3. General Mills' latest entry in the highly competitive $2 billion-a-year yogurt market—a tubular yogurt called Go-Gurt—seems to be a hit with the lunchbox set. Why tubular yogurt? Children like yogurt but are not impressed with it. Some believe yogurt is "old people food." Not so with Go-Gurt (see **www.go-gurt.com**). With flavours like Chill Out Cherry and Rad Raspberry, Go-

Gurt can be eaten like regular yogurt, frozen like a frozen pop, or carried in a shirt pocket. Can this product be expanded to an adult market? Devise a plan for test marketing Go-Gurt to 25- to 45-year-old adults. What factors would be critical to your test? What types of test subjects would you want for your test? Using procedures and ideas presented in the text, evaluate the chances for success of this new adult product. Would a name change be necessary? Explain.

4. Pick a soft drink, car, fashion, food product, or electronic appliance and trace the product's life cycle. Do appropriate research to make your timeline and application as accurate as possible. Explain how you separated the stages of the product's development. Project when the product might enter a decline stage.

5. Which product life-cycle stage do you think is the most important? Which stage has the highest risk? Which stage seems to hold the greatest profit potential? Which stage needs the greatest amount of "hands-on" management? Explain your thinking behind each of your answers.

 Mastering Marketing

Examine the new product development process for CanGo. Carry the company through the new product development process for an existing product. Next, propose an innovative product for the company to consider. After reviewing the first several phases of the development process to ensure that the innovative idea has merit, propose how the product concept could be tested. What markets would be best for this testing? Explain your thinking.

 ON LOCATION

Check out the enclosed Video case CD-ROM, or our Companion Website at www.pearsoned.ca/armstrong, to view a video segment and case for this chapter.

MAP 9 Marketing Applications

What is the hottest new trend in shoes for teens? Would it be Air Jordans, soccer shoes, combat boots, or old tennis shoes? If you answered "none of the above," you were correct. The newest fad to hit teen footwear are Heelys. Heelys look like thick-soled sneakers, but they have a wheel embedded in each heel that allows them to switch (morph) from walking to skating shoes by simply shifting one's balance and weight. Texas-based Heelying Sports, Ltd., which produces these unique shoes, has venture capitalists lined up at its door. Why? Because teens are lined up in the outlets that carry the shoe. Heelying has avoided putting its product in big-box stores such as Target and has focused instead on skate, surf shops, and mall chains such as Gadzooks. All these outlets target teens and offer higher price margins. Early test marketing for the Heelys took place around malls, skate parks, college and university campuses, and amusement parks. The shoes seem to be hottest in the southwestern states of the United States and Heelying expects to ship more than a million pairs by the end of the year. Watch closely and you may soon see someone "heeling" by.

Thinking Like a Marketing Manager

1. After visiting the Heelys Web site at **www.heelys.com**, comment on the strategy devised by the company to reach its target market. What improvements are needed?

2. What stage of the product life-cycle does the product currently occupy? Using the information found in Table 9-2, comment on what the company must do to move forward to the next stage. How can Heelying Sports turn its fad into a long-term trend?

3. How has the company used the Internet to expand sales? Comment.

4. What other target markets should the company be considering? What other distribution outlets should be contacted? How could the company expand into new markets and outlets but still remain true to its core following?

5. As the new product development manager for Heelying Sport, Ltd., what new product would you advise for next year's shoe market? Explain your thinking and outline a plan for accomplishing development, testing, and introduction.

Digital Map

Visit our Web site at **www.pearsoned.ca/armstrong** for online quizzes, Internet exercises, and more!

LIFESOURCE NUTRITION: SUCCEEDING WHERE CAMPBELL SOUP FAILED

Mmm! Smart Food

How would you feel about eating a steady diet of frozen foods to improve your health? Well, that's what Campbell Soup wanted you to do when it cooked up a line of mostly frozen meals designed to reduce certain health risks such as heart disease and diabetes. Campbell introduced the product line, calling it Intelligent Quisine (IQ), in a test market in January 1997.

How IQ made it to the test market is an interesting story. In 1991, Campbell realized the soup market was mature and offered very little growth potential. As a result, the company began to beef up its research and development efforts, devoting about 1 percent of sales to R&D. A senior vice-president noted that the company's R&D efforts were guided by two objectives: "stay with the customer" and "focus on big opportunities."

While exploring diversification ideas related to its core business, CEO David W. Johnson stumbled onto the idea of "introducing the first and only meal program clinically proven to help people reduce cholesterol, blood pressure, and blood sugar." Johnson saw an explosive market potential for "functional food"—food that tasted good, was good for you, and was as effective therapeutically as a drug. Observers dubbed this type of food "nutraceuticals." Campbell thought it could offer a convenient meal program to a target market of 60 million people who suffered from a wide range of health problems like high cholesterol, high blood pressure, and hypertension. That number actually grew to 100 million when people who were at risk of getting these problems were factored in. In addition, research showed that 52 percent of the population believed food products could help reduce cancer and disease.

The company then spent two years gathering a medical advisory board that included specialists in heart disease, nutrition, and diabetes. The board also included representatives from such organizations as the American Heart Association. Campbell worked with the advisory board and conducted clinical research on 800 patients to help design the IQ products.

By 1997, Campbell had spent $55 million to develop the product line. It consisted of 41 meals, mostly frozen, that included breakfasts such as French toast or egg sandwiches, lunches such as chili or stew, and dinners such as pasta or chicken. It also included snacks such as pretzels and cookies.

During the 15-month test market, participants purchased 21 IQ meals each week for a price of about $120 per week. The participants had to agree to stick with the program for 4 to 10 weeks. With a discount, the recommended 10-week program actually cost about $1050. Consumers had to commit to eating only IQ meals and to changing other habits. With each weekly order, Campbell included printed materials that offered advice on diet, exercise, and behavioural change. Participants could also use prepaid phone cards to talk with dietitians.

Campbell decided to distribute the meals directly to consumers using UPS to make weekly deliveries of the frozen meals. The company selected direct distribution because it believed that retailers would not be able to keep the complete line of 41 meals in stock.

Campbell used television, radio, and print ads to promote the program and a toll-free number for consumers to call to place an order. The ads touted IQ's ability to reverse certain medical conditions such as high blood pressure and high blood sugar. "I ate cheesecake and my cholesterol went down 15 points," one ad proclaimed. In addition, the company had its sales representatives call on doctors and other health professionals, much as sales representatives for drug companies did.

At first glance, the test market seemed to be successful. In just 10 weeks, one consumer reported that she had lost 10 pounds and seen her cholesterol drop from 240 to 200. Another consumer had her blood sugar drop from 300 to between 110 and 135. She was even able to stop taking a prescription medication.

Overall, however, Campbell considered the test market a failure. Although the company had a sales target of 40 000 orders, fewer than 2500 people ordered just over six weeks of meals. Despite the homework that went into the project, it failed to meet Campbell's expectations. In early 1998, the company announced that it was pulling the plug on IQ. One analyst noted, "We are all waiting for the boom in nutraceuticals, but thus far there haven't been many opportunities to make money at it." Another analyst observed that it was never clear there would be a market for the product. "It never struck me as something that was very promising."

Jumping into the Soup

Just as Campbell announced its decision, LifeSource Nutrition Solutions, an Emeryville, California-based company, announced it would tackle the problem of offering nutritionally balanced meals. LifeSource is a spin-off of Age Wave, a consulting company started in 1986 by Ken Dychtwald. Age Wave specialized in advising firms on how to market to people over 50. Once Age Wave reached $15 million in revenue, Dychtwald stopped consulting and started a business incubator to create businesses that would serve the mushrooming population of people over 50. Dychtwald commented that, "The food industry has typically catered to the needs and time pressures of young adults while often neglecting the taste and nutrient needs of mature women and men."

LifeSource, which is also funded by Monsanto, operates in San Francisco and Los Angeles. In its current markets, it runs two central production kitchens where culinarians and nutritionists prepare nutraceutical foods and beverages that meet or exceed the dietary requirements of the American Heart Association, National Institutes of Health, and American Diabetes Association. Each of its 24 nutrient-rich meals, which include soups and smoothie beverages, address such common conditions as congestive heart failure, coronary artery disease, and diabetes. The company also offers free nutritional counselling and nutrition materials.

Unlike Campbell Soup, however, LifeSource conducted no clinical research to help in developing its products. The company did, however, assemble a science advisory board to make sure it understood the link between diet and health.

LifeSource's meals target customers over 50 who have risk factors for diabetes and heart disease. These people either can't or don't want to cook for themselves, or they don't have the energy or the means to get to the grocery store. Of the $1400 billion annual North American food market, only about $140 billion represents nutraceutical foods, and only about $14 billion of that amount is fortified foods (as opposed to natural fruits and vegetables). Moreover, there is a growing trend to "home meal replacements"—fully prepared foods that consumers purchase either to take home or for home delivery.

Once the company prepares the meals, it flash-freezes them in its own cold-storage facilities. Then, the company has its own fleet of vans and drivers deliver the meals. It decided on direct distribution to avoid problems with the freeze-thaw cycle. Controlling the food's temperature after production is critical to maintaining quality.

The company has not forgotten taste. Whereas a Meals-on-Wheels dinner of roast beef with red potatoes may not excite your taste buds, LifeSource's Creole cod, rice, and red chili beans, and an orange mango smoothie makes for a flashier, tastier offering. Moreover, nothing on a Meals-on-Wheels menu is fortified.

However, the average cost of a Meals-on-Wheels dinner is $7.96, with the client paying only $1.87 (welfare programs cover the balance of the cost for needy consumers). LifeSource, on the other hand, prices its dinners at $8.70 per entrée, its lunches from $4.80 to $6.30, its soups at $3.75, and its smoothies and desserts at $1.65 to $2.20. There is no delivery charge with a minimum eight-item order. People over 50, the company notes, represent only 27 percent of the population but control 70 percent of the total net worth of North American households.

LifeSource promotes its products through direct mail, direct-response advertising, and public relations. It also has a Web site at **www.lifesourcenutrition.com**, where consumers can place orders and get other valuable information about health and nutrition.

Perhaps the most important difference between IQ and the LifeSource plan is that the company has positioned its plan as giving consumers free choice. Campbell's tied its meal program to a physician network. A LifeSource spokesperson noted, "There's a customization of diets to reach individuals' health goals, and if they want to substitute 15, 20, or 50 percent of their diet, it's up to them. It's not based on clinical research—it's voluntary compliance."

A Success or Another Failure?

Will LifeSource succeed where Campbell failed? LifeSource reports that after experiencing a 50 percent reorder rate in its California markets, it is cautiously optimistic about its new products. In late 1999, it planned to expand to Seattle,

Phoenix, and Salt Lake City and roll out nationally rollout over four to seven years. Observers believe there is an opportunity for nutraceuticals and that Campbell's failure doesn't mean others will fail. However, a food industry analyst notes that, "It certainly is a niche that is extremely complex."

Questions

1. Outline Campbell Soup's marketing strategy for Intelligent Quisine and describe its new product development process. Why do you believe IQ failed?

2. Outline LifeSource Nutrition's marketing strategy for its products and describe its new product development process. How are its strategy and its new-product development process alike or different from Campbell's?

3. Do you believe there is a market for nutraceuticals? Why or why not?

4. What marketing recommendations would you make to LifeSource Nutrition to help it be successful in this market?

Sources: "Takeout Meals for Specialized Diets," *Food Management,* June 1999, p. 10; Rick Desloge, "Monsanto Puts $10 Million in Baby Boomers' Nutrition," *St. Louis Business Journal,* 4 January 1999, p. 6; Kitty Kevin, "A Golden Age for Meal Solutions," *Food Processing,* October 1998, p. 37; Jake Holden, "High-Tech Take-Out," *American Demographics,* October 1998; Claudia D. O'Donnell, "Campbell's R&D Cozies up to the Consumer," *Prepared Foods,* September 1997, p. 26; Vanessa O'Connell, "Campbell Decides Its IQ Health Meals May Be Ahead of the Curve for Foods," *The Wall Street Journal,* 27 April 1998, p. B8; Stephanie Thompson, "Eyeing an Aging America, Food Giants Broaden Inroads into Nutraceuticals," *Brandweek,* 6 January 1997, p. 8; information accessed online at **www.lifesourcenutrition.com**.

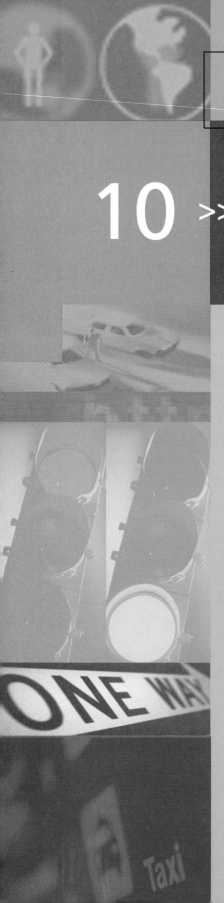

10 >> Pricing Products: Pricing Considerations and Strategies

Looking Ahead

We continue your marketing journey with a look at a second major marketing mix tool—pricing. According to one pricing expert, "If effective product development, promotion, and distribution sow the seeds of business success, effective pricing is the harvest."[1] Firms successful at the other marketing mix activities, he continues, "can still fail unless they can capture some of the value they create in the prices they earn." Yet, despite its importance, many firms do not handle pricing well. In this chapter, we'll examine factors that affect pricing decisions, general pricing approaches, and specific pricing strategies.

After studying this chapter, you should be able to

1. identify and explain the external and internal factors affecting a firm's pricing decisions
2. contrast the three general approaches to setting prices
3. describe the major strategies for pricing imitative and new products
4. explain how companies find a set of prices that maximizes the profits from the total product mix
5. discuss how companies adjust their prices to take into account different types of customers and situations
6. discuss the key issues related to initiating and responding to price changes

First stop on the pricing tour: Kellogg. For decades, Kellogg dazzled investors with its impressive market performance. However, over time, Kellogg began boosting profits by steadily raising its prices without adding real value for its customers. Consumers paid the price in the short run, but did the company pay it in the long run?

For more than eight decades, Kellogg has been hanging out with Canadians in the morning. Until recently, investment analysts saw the company as a money-making machine. Over the 1990s, annual returns to Kellogg's shareholders averaged 19 percent, with gross margins running as high as 55 percent. Over the previous 30 years, Kellogg's sales had grown at one and a half times the industry growth rate and its share of the North American cereal market had consistently exceeded 40 percent. By 2000, Kellogg had about 43 percent of the Canadian ready-to-eat cereal market by physical volume, or $550 million in terms of 1999 dollar sales. It was followed by Kraft's Post Cereals, products that held 18 percent of the market, General Mills with 17 percent market share, private label with 12 percent of the market, and Quaker Oats with 8 percent. Kellogg also holds about 42 percent of the worldwide market, with a 48 percent share in Asia and Europe and 69 percent of the Latin America marketplace. Things, it seemed, could only get better for Kellogg.

These dazzling numbers, however, hid the fact that Kellogg's cereal empire had begun to lose its lustre. Much of its recent success, especially in the United States, had come at the expense of cereal customers. Kellogg's recent gains—and those of major competitors General Mills, Post, and Quaker—had come not from innovative new products, creative marketing programs, and operational improvements that added value for customers, but rather almost entirely from price increases that padded the sales and profits of the cereal makers.

Throughout most of the 1980s and early 1990s, Kellogg had boosted profit margins by steadily raising prices on its Rice Krispies, Special K, Raisin Bran, and Frosted Flakes—often twice a year. For example, by early 1996, a 400-g box of Raisin Bran that sold for U.S.$2.39 in 1985 was going for as much as U.S.$4.00 to U.S.$5.00, but with little or no change in the costs of the materials making up the cereal or its packaging. Since World War II, no

food category has had more price increases than cereal. The price increases were very profitable for Kellogg and the other cereal companies. On average, the cereal makers were reaping more than twice the operating margins of the food industry as a whole. However, the relentless price increases became increasingly difficult for customers to swallow.

Not surprisingly, in 1994, the cereal industry's pricing policies began to backfire as frustrated consumers retaliated with a quiet fury. Cereal buyers began shifting away from branded cereals toward less expensive private-label brands; by 1995, private labels were devouring 10 percent of the North American cereal market, up from a little more than 5 percent only five years earlier. Worse, many people switched to less expensive, more portable handheld breakfast foods, such as bagels, muffins, and breakfast bars. As a result, total North American cereal sales began falling off by 3 to 4 percent a year. Kellogg's sales and profits sagged, and its North American market share dropped to 36 percent. By early 1996, after what most industry analysts viewed as years of outrageous and self-serving pricing policies, Kellogg and the other cereal makers faced a full-blown crisis.

Belated research showed that exorbitant pricing was indeed the cause of the industry's problems. "Every statistic, every survey we took only showed that our customers were becoming more and more dissatisfied." Customers were "walking down cereal aisles, clutching fistfuls of coupons and looking all over the shelves, trying to match them with a specific brand." Post Cereals was the first to boost its soggy sales by slashing an average of 20 percent off prices on its 22 cereal brands, a surprise move that rocked the industry.

At first, Kellogg, General Mills, and Quaker held stubbornly to their premium prices. However, cereal buyers began switching in droves to Post's lower-priced brands, and Post quickly stole four points from Kellogg's market share alone. Kellogg and the others had little choice but to follow Post's lead. Kellogg announced price cuts averaging 19 percent on two thirds of all brands sold in the United States, marking the start of what would become a long and costly industry price war. In recanting their previous pricing excesses, the cereal makers swung wildly in the opposite direction, caught up in layoffs, plant closings, and other cost-cutting measures and fresh rounds of price cutting. "It reminds me of one of those World War I battles where there's all this firing but when the smoke clears you can't tell who won," noted an industry analyst. In fact, it appears that nobody won, as the fortunes of all competitors suffered.

Kellogg was perhaps the hardest hit of the major competitors. Post Cereal's parent company, consumer goods powerhouse Philip Morris, owner of Kraft, derived about 2 percent of its sales and profits from cereals and could easily offset the losses elsewhere. However, Kellogg, which counted on domestic cereal sales for 42 percent of its revenues and 43 percent of its operating profits, suffered enormously. Its operating margins were halved, and even after lowering its prices, Kellogg's revenues and profits continued to decline.

Kellogg finally looked to Canada to understand how to rebuild the category. Cereal marketers in Canada and the United States had reacted very differently when faced with the price pressure presented by private-label brands. As one Canadian marketer noted, "What [the price cuts] served to do was to take money out of the category that's designed to fund new products, build advertising behind a brand-building program, and really generate news and excitement and variety within the category." Mark Childs, vice president of marketing for Kellogg Canada, based in Etobicoke, Ontario, took an approach different from his American counterparts. He began with a reevaluation of the competitive arena. Mark recognized that Kellogg's rivals included not only other packaged goods firms, but also quick-ser-

vice restaurants like Tim Hortons and McDonald's. He also quickly realized that price discounting wasn't the answer. Instead, he placed a renewed emphasis on understanding his customers and what types of products held relevance and appeal for them. To maintain its leadership position, Mark believed that Kellogg Canada had to keep the pipeline full of fresh and innovative ideas. Vector, a "meal replacement in a flaked format," developed in Canada, was the offspring of this thinking. Launched in April 1999, Vector earned both Canadian and international awards for product innovation.

It wasn't long before the U.S. marketers began following Canada's lead. Recently, Kellogg and the other cereal titans quietly began pushing ahead with modest price increases to fund the product innovation and marketing support necessary to stimulate growth in the stagnant cereal category. Today, despite its problems, Kellogg remains the industry leader. The Kellogg brand name is still one of the world's best known and most respected. Kellogg's recent initiatives to cut costs, get reacquainted with its customers, and develop innovative new products and marketing programs—all of which promise to add value for customers rather than simply cutting prices—has investors cautiously optimistic about Kellogg's future. But events of the past five years teach an important lesson. When setting prices, as when making any other marketing decisions, a company can't afford to focus just on its own costs and profits. Instead, it must focus on customers' needs and the value they receive from the company's total marketing offer. If a company doesn't give customers full value for the price they're paying, they'll go elsewhere. In this case, Kellogg stole profits by steadily raising prices without also increasing customer value. Customers paid the price in the short run—but Kellogg is paying the price in the long run.[2]

All for-profit organizations and many nonprofit organizations must set prices on their products or services. In the narrowest sense, **price** is the amount of money charged for a product or service. More broadly, price is the sum of all the values that consumers exchange for the benefits of having or using the product or service. Historically, price has been the major factor affecting buyer choice. This is still true in poorer nations, among poorer groups, and with commodity products. However, nonprice factors have become more important in buyer choice behaviour in recent decades.

Throughout most of history, prices were set by negotiation between buyers and sellers. *Fixed price* policies—setting one price for all buyers—is a relatively modern idea that arose with the development of large-scale retailing at the end of the nineteenth century. Now, a hundred years later, the Internet promises to reverse the fixed pricing trend and take us back to an era of **dynamic pricing**—charging different prices depending on individual customers and situations (see New Directions 10-1). The Internet, corporate networks, and wireless setups are connecting sellers and buyers as never before. Such Web sites as MSN eShop and PriceSCAN.com allow buyers to quickly and easily compare products and prices. Online auction sites like eBay and Amazon make it easy for buyers and sellers to negotiate prices on thousands of items—from refurbished computers to antique tin trains. At the same time, new technologies allow sellers to collect detailed data about customers' buying habits, preferences—even spending limits—so they can tailor their products and prices.[3]

Price is the only element in the marketing mix that produces revenue; all other elements represent costs. Price is also one of the most flexible elements of the marketing mix. Unlike product features and channel commitments, price can be changed quickly. At the same time, pricing and price competition are the biggest problems facing many marketing executives. Many companies do not handle

Price The amount of money charged for a product or service, or the sum of the values that consumers exchange for the benefits of having or using the product or service.

Dynamic pricing The practice of charging different prices depending on individual customers and situations.

New Directions 10-1>>   Back to the Future: Dynamic Pricing on the Web

The Internet is more than simply a new "market-space"; it's actually changing the rules of commerce. Take pricing, for example. From the mostly fixed pricing practices of the past century, the Web seems now to be taking us back—into a new age of fluid pricing. "Potentially, [the Internet] could push aside sticker prices and usher in an era of dynamic pricing," says *Business Week* writer Robert Hof, "in which a wide range of goods would be priced according to what the market will bear—instantly, constantly." Here's how the Internet is changing the rules of pricing for both sellers and buyers.

Sellers Can...
Charge lower prices and reap higher margins. Web buying and selling can result in drastically lower costs, allowing online sellers to charge lower prices and still make higher margins. "Thanks to their Internet connections, buyers and sellers around the world can connect at almost no cost—making instant bargaining [economically feasible]," observes Hof. Reduced inventory and distribution costs add to the savings. For example, by selling made-to-order computers online, Dell Computer greatly reduces inventory costs and eliminates retail markups. It shares the

savings with buyers in the form of the "lowest price per performance."

Monitor customer behaviour and tailor offers to individuals. With the help of new technologies, Web merchants can now target special prices to specific customers. For example, Internet sellers such as Amazon.com can mine their databases to gauge a specific shopper's desires, measure his or her means, instantaneously tailor products to that shopper's behaviour, and price products accordingly. However, companies must be careful in how they apply dynamic pricing. When it recently came to light that Amazon.com had been charging different prices to different customers for the same DVDs, many customers were angry. Amazon.com claims that the pricing variations were a "pure and simple price test" and stopped the practice as soon as complaints began coming in.

Change prices on the fly according to changes in demand or costs. Just ask online catalogue retailers such as Lands' End, Spiegel, or Fingerhut. With printed catalogues, a price is a price, at least until the next catalogue is printed. Online sellers, however, can change prices for specific items on a day-by-day or even hour-by-hour basis, adjusting quickly to changing costs and merchandise movement. Many B2B marketers monitor inventories, costs, and demand at any given moment and adjust prices instantly. For example, IBM automatically adjusts prices on its servers based on customer demand and product life-cycle factors. As a result, customers will find that prices change dynamically when they visit the IBM Web site on any given day. Dell also uses dynamic online pricing. "If the price of memory or processors decreases, we pass those savings along to the customer almost in real time," says a Dell spokesperson.

Both Sellers and Buyers Can...
Negotiate prices in online auctions and exchanges. Suddenly the centuries-old art of haggling is back in vogue. Want to sell that antique pickle jar that's been collecting dust for generations? Post it on eBay, the world's

The Internet is ushering in a new era of fluid pricing. MySimon is an independent site that provides product comparisons and guides and searches all merchant sites for the best prices.

biggest online flea market. Want to purchase vintage baseball cards at a bargain price? Go to Boekhout's Collectibles Mall at **www.azww.com/mall/**. Want to dump that excess inventory? Try adding an auction feature to your own Web site—Sharper Image claims it's getting 40 percent of retail for excess goods sold via its online auction site, compared with only 20 percent from liquidators.

Of the dozens of Internet auction sites, eBay and Amazon.com Auctions are the largest. eBay, which began when its owner used the Web to find a market for his girlfriend's vintage Pez dispenser collection, hosts more than 2 million auctions each month for items in more than one thousand categories, generating more than U.S.$5 billion in trades annually. Buyers like auctions because, quite simply, they like the bargains they find. Sellers like auctions because, over the Internet, the cost per transaction drops dramatically. Thus, it becomes practical—even profitable—to auction an item for mere dollars rather than thousands of dollars. For example, the seller can program its computers to accept the 3000 best bids higher than $2.10 for 3000 pieces of costume jewellery. Business marketers, whose transactions account for 68 percent of online auction sales, also use auctions to offer time-sensitive deals and gauge interest on possible price points for new products.

Buyers Can...

Get instant price comparisons from thousands of vendors. The Internet gives consumers access to reams of data about products and prices. Online comparison guides—such as CompareNet and PriceSCAN—give product and price comparisons at the click of a mouse. Other sites offer intelligent shopping agents—such as MySimon—that seek out products, prices, and reviews. MySimon www.mySimon.com, for instance, takes a buyer's criteria for a PC, camcorder, or collectible Barbie, then roots through top sellers' sites to find the best match at the best price.

Find and negotiate lower prices. With market information and access come buyer power. In addition to simply finding the vendor with the best price, customers armed with price information can often negotiate lower prices. Here are examples of both consumers and industrial buyers exercising this newfound power.

In search of the best possible deal on a Palm organizer, Stephen Manes first checked PriceSCAN.com, where he learned that buysoware.com had the high-tech gadget for only $358. Buysoware, however, was "out of stock," as was the second lowest-priced vendor, mcglen.com. Undaunted, Stephen skipped to the other end of the list were he found that PC Zone was offering the device for $449, and it was in stock. "Time to haggle," said Stephen. "I picked up the phone. In seconds, an eager salesperson quoted me the official price. 'I saw it at buy.com for $358,' I said, omitting mention of the word[s *out of stock*]. 'I don't know if I can match buy.com,' came the response. 'But we can do it for $375.'" Stephen snapped up the offer, saving himself a bundle off the store price. Business buyers have also learned the price advantages of shopping the Web. For example, hoping to save some money, United Technologies Corporation tried something new last year. Instead of the usual haggling with dozens of individual vendors to secure printed circuit boards for various subsidiaries worldwide, UTC put the contract out on FreeMarkets, an online marketplace for industrial goods. To the company's delight, bids poured in from 39 suppliers, saving UTC a cool $10 million off its initial $24 million estimate. Says a UTC executive, "The technology drives the lowest price in a hurry."

Will dynamic pricing sweep the marketing world? "Not entirely," says Hof. "It takes a lot of work to haggle—which is why fixed prices happened in the first place." However, he continues, "Pandora's E-box is now open, and pricing will never be the same. For many...products, millions of buyers figure a little haggling is a small price to pay for a sweet deal."

Sources: Quotes and extracts from Robert D. Hof, "Going, Going, Gone," *Business Week,* 12 April 1999, pp. 30–32; Robert D. Hof, "The Buyer Always Wins," *Business Week,* 22 March 1999, pp. EB26–EB28; Stephen Manes, "Off-Web Dickering," *Forbes,* 5 April 1999, p. 134; and Michael Vizard, Ed Scannell, and Dan Neel, "Suppliers Toy with Dynamic Pricing," *InfoWorld,* 14 May 2001, p. 28. Also see David Streitfeld, "On the Web, Price Tags Blur," *The Washington Post,* 27 September 2000, p. A1; and Walter Baker, Mike Marn, and Craig Zawada, "Price Smarter on the Net," *Harvard Business Review,* February 2001, pp. 122–127.

pricing well. Paul Hunt, director of the Strategic Pricing Division at The Advantage Group in Toronto, notes that the average company can increase its profitability by a whopping 25 percent to 60 percent just by improving its pricing processes. He stresses, however, that effective pricing does not mean nickel-and-diming customers; it means practising value-based pricing. When customers perceive that they are receiving superior value, they'll be willing to pay the price to get it. Hunt's research suggests that companies with successful pricing policies follow five "best practices" with regard to their pricing strategy.

1. *They develop a 1 percent pricing mindset:* Since a 1 percent difference in price can have a dramatic impact on profit, everyone in the company must understand the importance of maintaining prices and think carefully about how even short-term discounts can affect their profitability.

2. *They consistently deliver more value:* Since the most successful organizations consistently deliver more value to their customers, they are able to increase margins as a result. To deliver value, companies need insight into how their offering uniquely satisfies the customer's needs. Thus, getting close to their customers is the most critical factor in value-based pricing, since satisfied customers are profitable customers.

3. *They price strategically, not opportunistically:* Paul Hunt stresses that firms should pursue price-conscious customers only if they represent the firm's core market. This is a viable strategy only for firms like Wal-Mart with a low cost structure that enables them to compete consistently on a price platform. Otherwise, the more an organization caters to price-conscious customers to boost volume, the more it puts its core business at risk by pursuing customers who don't value the product or service more than the price.

4. *They know their competitors:* Their pricing strategy is driven by knowledge rather than fear.

5. *They make pricing a process:* Pricing should be treated as a continual process rather than a one-time event that erodes into ad hoc or "gut-feel" pricing.[4]

In addition to not following these five guidelines, other common mistakes are pricing that is too cost oriented; prices that are not revised often enough to reflect market changes; pricing that does not take the rest of the marketing mix into account; and prices that are not varied enough for different products, market segments, and purchase occasions.

In this chapter, we focus on how to set prices: the factors that marketers must consider when setting prices, general pricing approaches, pricing strategies for new product pricing, product mix pricing, price changes, and price adjustments for buyer and situational factors.

Factors to Consider When Setting Prices

A company's pricing decisions are affected by both internal company factors and external environmental factors (see Figure 10-1).[5]

Internal Factors Affecting Pricing Decisions

Internal factors affecting pricing include the company's marketing objectives, marketing mix strategy, costs, and organizational considerations.

Marketing Objectives Before setting price, the company must decide on its strategy for the product. If the company has selected its target market and positioning carefully, then its marketing mix strategy, including price, will be straightforward. For example, if General Motors decides to produce a new sports car to compete with European sports cars in the high-income segment, they might decide to charge a high price. Motel 6, Holiday Inn Express, and Comfort Inns have positioned themselves as hotels that provide economical rooms for budget-minded travellers; this position requires charging a low price. Thus, pricing strategy is largely determined by decisions on market positioning.

At the same time, the company may seek additional objectives. Common objectives include *survival, current profit maximization, market share leadership,* and *product quality leadership.* Companies set *survival* as their major objective if they are troubled by too much capacity, heavy competition, or changing consumer wants. To keep a plant going, a company may set a low price, hoping to increase demand. In the long run, however, the firm must learn how to add value that consumers will pay for or face extinction.

Many companies use *current profit maximization* as their pricing goal. They estimate what demand and costs will be at different prices and choose the price that will produce the maximum current profit, cash flow, or return on investment. Other companies want to obtain *market share leadership.* To become the market share leader, these firms set prices as low as possible.

A company might decide that it wants to achieve *product quality leadership.* This normally calls for charging a high price to cover higher performance quality and the high cost of R&D. For example, Caterpillar charges 20 percent to 30 percent more than competitors for its heavy construction equipment based on superior product and service quality. Gillette's product superiority lets it price its Mach3 razor cartridges at a 50 percent premium over its own SensorExcel and competitors' cartridges. Maytag has long built high-quality washing machines and priced them higher. Its ads use the long-running Maytag slogan "Built to last longer" and feature the Lonely Maytag Repairman (who's lonely because no one ever calls him for service). The ads point out that washers are custodians of what is often a $450 to $600 load of clothes, making Maytag washers worth the higher price tag. For instance, at nearly $1700 Maytag's Neptune, a front-loading washer without an agitator, sells for double what most other washers cost because the company's mar-

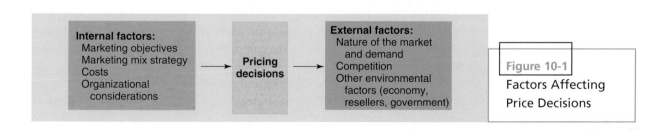

Internal factors:
  Marketing objectives
  Marketing mix strategy
  Costs
  Organizational
    considerations

Pricing decisions

External factors:
  Nature of the market
    and demand
  Competition
  Other environmental
    factors (economy,
    resellers, government)

Figure 10-1

Factors Affecting Price Decisions

keters claim that it uses less water and electricity and prolongs the life of clothing by being less abrasive.[6]

A company might also use price to attain other, more specific objectives. It can set prices low to prevent competition from entering the market or set prices at competitors' levels to stabilize the market. In doing this, however, it must be sure not to violate the laws dealing with predatory pricing or dumping. Prices can be set to keep the loyalty and support of resellers or to avoid government intervention. Prices can be reduced temporarily to create excitement for a product or to draw more customers into a retail store. One product may be priced to help the sales of other products in the company's line. Thus, pricing may play an important role in helping a company to meet its objectives at many levels.

Marketing Mix Strategy Price is only one of the marketing mix tools that a company uses to achieve its marketing objectives. Price decisions must be coordinated with product design, distribution, and promotion decisions to form a consistent and effective marketing program. Decisions made for other marketing mix variables may affect pricing decisions. For example, producers using many resellers who are expected to support and promote their products may have to build larger reseller margins into their prices. The decision to position the product on high-performance quality will mean that the seller must charge a higher price to cover higher costs.

Companies often position their products on price and then base other marketing mix decisions on the prices they want to charge. Here, price is a crucial product-positioning factor that defines the product's market, competition, and design. Many firms support such price-positioning strategies with a technique called **target costing,** a potent strategic weapon. Target costing reverses the usual process of first designing a new product, determining its cost, and then asking, "Can we sell it for that?" Instead, it starts with an ideal selling price based on customer considerations, then targets costs that will ensure that the price is met.

Target costing Pricing that starts with an ideal selling price, then targets costs that will ensure that the price is met.

The original Swatch watch provides a good example of target costing. Rather than starting with its own costs, Swatch surveyed the market and identified an unserved segment of watch buyers who wanted "a low-cost fashion accessory that also keeps time." Swatch set out to give consumers in this segment the watch they wanted at a price they were willing to pay, and it managed the new product's costs accordingly. Like most watch buyers, targeted consumers were concerned about precision, reliability, and durability. However, they were also concerned about fashion and affordability. To keep costs down, Swatch designed fashionably simpler watches that contained fewer parts and that were constructed from high-tech but less expensive materials. It then developed a revolutionary automated process for mass producing the new watches and exercised strict cost control throughout the manufacturing process. By managing costs carefully, Swatch created a watch that offered just the right blend of fashion and function at a price consumers were willing to pay. As a result of its initial major success, consumers have placed increasing value on Swatch products, allowing the company to introduce successively higher-priced designs.[7]

Other companies deemphasize price and use other marketing mix tools to create *nonprice* positions. Often, the best strategy is not to charge the lowest price, but

Target costing: By managing costs carefully, Swatch was able to create a watch that offered just the right blend of fashion and function at a price consumers were willing to pay.

rather to differentiate the marketing offer to make it worth a higher price. For example, for years Johnson Controls, a producer of climate-control systems for office buildings, used initial price as its primary competitive tool. However, research showed that customers were more concerned about the total cost of installing and maintaining a system than about its initial price. Repairing broken systems was expensive, time-consuming, and risky. Customers had to shut down the heat or air-conditioning in the whole building, disconnect many wires, and face the dangers of electrocution (or hire a maintenance company). So Johnson designed an entirely new system called "Metasys." To repair the new system, customers need only pull out an old plastic module and slip in a new one—no tools required. Metasys costs more to make than the old system, and customers pay a higher initial price, but it costs less to install and maintain. Despite its higher asking price, the new Metasys system brought in $775 million in revenues in its first year.[8]

Thus, marketers must consider the total marketing mix when setting prices. If the product is positioned on nonprice factors, then decisions about quality, promotion, and distribution will strongly affect price. If price is a crucial positioning factor, then price will strongly affect decisions made about the other marketing mix elements. But even when featuring price, marketers need to remember that customers rarely buy on price alone. Instead, they seek products that give them the best value in terms of benefits received for the price paid.

Costs Costs set the floor for the price that the company can charge for its product. The company wants to charge a price that both covers all its costs for producing, distributing, and selling the product and delivers a fair rate of return for its effort and risk. A company's costs may be an important element in its pricing strategy. Many companies work to become the "low-cost producers" in their industries. Companies with lower costs can set lower prices that result in greater sales and profits.

A company's costs take two forms, fixed and variable. *Fixed costs* (also known as overhead) are costs that do not vary with production or sales level. For example, a company must pay each month's bills for rent, heat, interest, and executive salaries, whatever the company's output. *Variable costs* vary directly with the level of production. Each personal computer produced by Compaq involves a cost of computer chips, wires, plastic, packaging, and other inputs. These costs tend to be the same for each unit produced. They are called variable because their total varies with the number of units produced. *Total costs* are the sum of the fixed and variable costs for any given level of production. Management wants to charge a price that will at least cover the total production costs at a given level of production.

The company must watch its costs carefully. If it costs the company more than its competitors to produce and sell its product, the company will have to charge a higher price or make less profit, putting it at a competitive disadvantage.

Organizational Considerations Management must decide who within the organization should set prices. Companies handle pricing in a variety of ways. In small companies, prices are often set by top management rather than by the marketing or sales departments. In large companies, pricing is typically handled by divisional or product line managers. In industrial markets, salespeople may be allowed to negotiate with customers within certain price ranges. Even so, top management sets the pricing objectives and policies, and it often approves the prices proposed by lower-level management or salespeople. In industries in which pricing is a key factor (aerospace, steel, railroads, oil companies), companies often have a pricing department to set the best prices or help others in setting them. This department reports to the marketing department or top management. Others who have an influence on pricing include sales managers, production managers, finance managers, and accountants.

External Factors Affecting Pricing Decisions

External factors that affect pricing decisions include the nature of the market and demand, competition, and other environmental elements.

The Market and Demand Whereas costs set the lower limit of prices, the market and demand set the upper limit. Both consumer and industrial buyers balance the price of a product or service against the benefits of owning it. Thus, before setting prices, the marketer must understand the relationship between price and demand for its product. In this section, we explain how the price–demand relationship varies for different types of markets and how buyer perceptions of price affect the pricing decision. We then discuss methods for measuring the price–demand relationship.

Pricing in Different Types of Markets The seller's pricing freedom varies with different types of markets. Economists recognize four types of markets, each presenting a different pricing challenge.

Under *pure competition,* the market consists of many buyers and sellers trading in a uniform commodity such as wheat, copper, or financial securities. No single buyer or seller has much effect on the going market price. A seller cannot charge more than the going price because buyers can obtain as much as they need at the going price. Nor would sellers charge less than the market price because they can sell all they want at this price. If price and profits rise, new sellers can easily enter the market. In a purely competitive market, marketing research, product development, pricing, advertising, and sales promotion play little or no role. Thus, sellers in these markets do not spend much time on marketing strategy.

Under *monopolistic competition,* the market consists of many buyers and sellers who trade over a range of prices rather than a single market price. A range of prices occurs because sellers can differentiate their offers to buyers. Either the physical product can be varied in quality, features, or style, or the accompanying services can be varied. Buyers see differences in sellers' products and will pay different prices for them. Sellers try to develop differentiated offers for different customer segments and, in addition to price, freely use branding, advertising, and personal selling to set their offers apart. Because there are many competitors in such markets, each firm is less affected by competitors' marketing strategies than in oligopolistic markets.

Under *oligopolistic competition,* the market consists of a few sellers who are highly sensitive to each other's pricing and marketing strategies. The product can

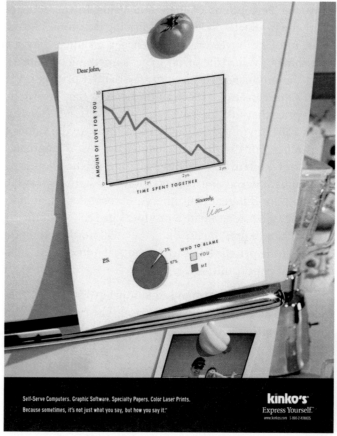

Monopolistic competition: Kinko's differentiates its offer through strong branding and advertising, reducing the impact of pricing.

be uniform (steel, aluminum) or nonuniform (cars, computers). There are few sellers because it is difficult for new sellers to enter the market. Each seller is alert to competitors' strategies and moves. If a steel company slashes its price by 10 percent, buyers will quickly switch to this supplier. The other steelmakers must respond by lowering their prices or increasing their services. An oligopolist is never sure that it will gain anything permanent through a price cut. In contrast, if an oligopolist raises its price, its competitors might not follow this lead. The oligopolist then would have to retract its price increase or risk losing customers to competitors.

In a *pure monopoly,* the market consists of one seller. The seller may be a government monopoly (Canada Post), a private regulated monopoly (a power company), or a private nonregulated monopoly (DuPont when it introduced nylon). Pricing is handled differently in each case. A government monopoly can pursue a variety of pricing objectives. It might set a price below cost because the product is important to buyers who cannot afford to pay full cost. Or the price might be set either to cover costs or to produce good revenue. It can even be set quite high to slow down consumption. In a regulated monopoly, the government permits the company to set rates that will yield a "fair return," one that will let the company maintain and expand its operations as needed. Nonregulated monopolies are free to price at what the market will bear. However, they do not always charge the full price for a number of reasons: a desire not to attract competition, a desire to penetrate the market faster with a low price, or a fear of government regulation.

Consumer Perceptions of Price and Value In the end, the consumer will decide whether a product's price is right. Pricing decisions, like other marketing mix decisions, must be buyer oriented. When consumers buy a product, they exchange something of value (the price) to get something of value (the benefits of having or using the product). Effective, buyer-oriented pricing involves understanding how much value consumers place on the benefits they receive from the product and setting a price that fits this value.

A company often finds it hard to measure the values customers will attach to its product. For example, calculating the cost of ingredients in a meal at a fancy restaurant is relatively easy. But assigning a value to other satisfactions such as taste, environment, relaxation, conversation, and status is very hard. And these values will vary both for different consumers and for different situations. Still, consumers will use these values to evaluate a product's price. If customers perceive that the price is greater than the product's value, they will not buy the product. If consumers perceive that the price is below the product's value, they will buy it, but the seller will lose profit opportunities.

Analyzing the Price–Demand Relationship Each price the company might charge will lead to a different level of demand. The relationship between the price charged and the resulting demand level is shown in the **demand curve** in Figure 10-2. The demand curve shows the number of units the market will buy in a given period at different prices that might be charged. In the normal case, demand and price are inversely related; that is, the higher the price, the lower the demand. Thus, the company would sell less if it raised its price from $P1$ to $P2$. In short, consumers with limited budgets probably will buy less of something if its price is too high.

Demand curve A curve that shows the number of units the market will buy in a given period at different prices that might be charged.

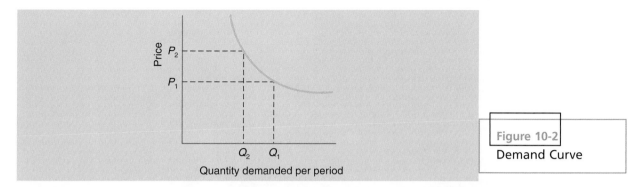

Price

P_2

P_1

Q_2 Q_1

Quantity demanded per period

Figure 10-2
Demand Curve

In the case of prestige goods, the demand curve sometimes slopes upward. Consumers think that higher prices mean more quality. For example, Gibson Guitar Corporation recently toyed with the idea of lowering its prices to compete more effectively with Japanese rivals such as Yamaha and Ibanez. To its surprise, Gibson found that its instruments didn't sell as well at lower prices. "We had an inverse [price–demand relationship]," noted Gibson's chief executive officer. "The more we charged, the more product we sold." Gibson's slogan promises: "The world's finest musical instruments." It turns out that low prices simply aren't consistent with "Gibson's century old tradition of creating investment-quality instruments that represent the highest standards of imaginative design and masterful craftsmanship."[9] Still, if the company charges too high a price, the level of demand will be lower.

Most companies try to measure their demand curves by estimating demand at different prices. The type of market makes a difference. In a monopoly, the demand curve shows the total market demand resulting from different prices. If the company faces competition, its demand at different prices will depend on whether competitors' prices stay constant or change with the company's own prices.

In measuring the price–demand relationship, the market researcher must not allow other factors affecting demand to vary. For example, if Sony increased its advertising at the same time that it lowered its television prices, we would not know how much of the increased demand was due to the lower prices and how much was due to the increased advertising. The same problem arises if a holiday weekend occurs when the lower price is set—more gift giving over the holidays causes people to buy more televisions. Economists show the impact of nonprice factors on demand through shifts in the demand curve rather than movements along it.

Price Elasticity of Demand Marketers also need to know **price elasticity**—how responsive demand will be to a change in price. If demand hardly changes with a small change in price, we say the demand is *inelastic*. If demand changes greatly, we say the demand is *elastic*.

What determines the price elasticity of demand? Buyers are less price sensitive when the product they are buying is unique or when it is high in quality, prestige, or exclusiveness. They are also less price sensitive when substitute products are hard to find or when they cannot easily compare the quality of substitutes. Finally, buyers are less price sensitive when the total expenditure for a product is low relative to their income or when the cost is shared by another party.[10]

Price elasticity A measure of the sensitivity of demand to changes in price.

The demand curve sometimes slopes upward: Gibson was surprised to learn that its high-quality instruments didn't sell as well at lower prices.

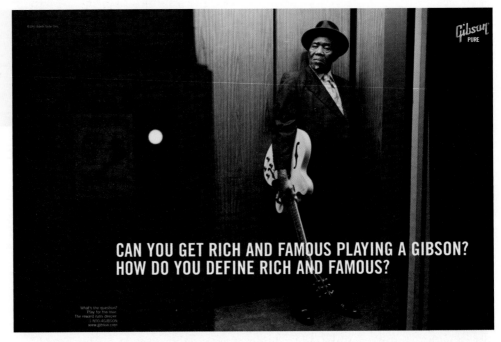

If demand is elastic rather than inelastic, sellers will consider lowering their price. A lower price will produce more total revenue. This practice makes sense as long as the extra costs of producing and selling more do not exceed the extra revenue. At the same time, most firms want to avoid pricing that turns their products into commodities. In recent years, forces such as deregulation and the instant price comparisons afforded by the Internet and other technologies have increased consumer price sensitivity, turning products ranging from telephones and computers to new automobiles into commodities in consumers' eyes. Seven Toyota dealers in southern Manitoba responded to this pressure with new pricing and sales tactics designed primarily to address the concerns of the 60 percent of car buyers who surf the Web before kicking the tires. Toyota's "product advisors" point potential customers to the Access Toyota Web site and explain that the price shown is the "drive-away" price for the vehicle selected—not the manufacturer's suggested retail price (MSRP), but a price that provides a reasonable profit for the dealer and a fair cost for the customer who buys or leases. In other words, no haggling.[11]

Marketers need to work harder than ever to differentiate their offerings when a dozen competitors are selling virtually the same product at a comparable or lower price. More than ever, companies need to understand the price sensitivity of their customers and prospects and the tradeoffs people are willing to make between price and product characteristics. In the words of marketing consultant Kevin Clancy, those who target only the price sensitive are "leaving money on the table."

Competitors' Costs, Prices, and Offers Another external factor affecting the company's pricing decisions is competitors' costs and prices and possible competitor reactions to the company's own pricing moves. A consumer who is considering the purchase of a Canon camera will evaluate Canon's price and value against the prices and values of comparable products made by Nikon, Minolta, Pentax, and others. In addition, the company's pricing strategy may affect the nature of the competition it faces. If Canon follows a high-price, high-margin strategy, it may attract competition. A low-price, low-margin strategy, however, may stop competitors or drive them out of the market.

Canon needs to benchmark its costs against its competitors' costs to learn whether it is operating at a cost advantage or disadvantage. It also needs to learn the price and quality of each competitor's offer. Once Canon is aware of competitors' prices and offers, it can use them as a starting point for its own pricing. If Canon's cameras are similar to Nikon's, it will have to price close to Nikon or lose sales. If Canon's cameras are not as good as Nikon's, the firm will not be able to charge as much. If Canon's products are better than Nikon's, it can charge more. Canon will use price to position its offer relative to the competition.

Other External Factors When setting prices, the company also must consider other factors in its external environment. *Economic conditions* can have a strong impact on the firm's pricing strategies. Economic factors such as boom or recession, inflation, and interest rates affect pricing decisions because they affect both the costs of producing a product and consumer perceptions of the product's price and value. The company must also consider what impact its prices will have on other parties in its environment. How will *resellers* react to various prices? The company should set prices that give resellers a fair profit, encourage their support, and help them to sell the product effectively. The *government* is another important external influence on pricing decisions. Finally, *social concerns* may have to be taken into account. In setting prices, a company's short-term sales, market share, and profit goals may have to be tempered by broader societal considerations.

GENERAL PRICING APPROACHES

The price the company charges will be somewhere between one that is too low to produce a profit and one that is too high to produce any demand. Figure 10-3 summarizes the major considerations in setting price. Product costs set a floor to the price; consumer perceptions of the product's value set the ceiling. The company must consider competitors' prices and other external and internal factors to find the best price between these two extremes.

Companies set prices by selecting a general pricing approach that includes one or more of these three sets of factors. We will examine the following approaches: the *cost-based approach* (cost-plus pricing, break-even analysis, and target profit pricing), the *buyer-based approach* (value-based pricing), and the *competition-based approach* (going-rate and sealed-bid pricing).

Cost-Based Pricing

The simplest pricing method is **cost-plus pricing**—adding a standard markup to the cost of the product. For example, an appliance retailer might pay a manufacturer $20 for a toaster and mark it up to sell at $30, a 50 percent markup on cost.

Cost-plus pricing Adding a standard markup to the cost of the product.

Figure 10-3	Low price				High price
Major Considerations in Setting Price	No possible profit at this price	Product costs	Competitors' prices and other external and internal factors	Consumer perceptions of value	No possible demand at this price

The retailer's gross margin is $10. If the store's operating costs amount to $8 per toaster sold, the retailer's profit margin will be $2.

The manufacturer that made the toaster probably used cost-plus pricing. If the manufacturer's standard cost of producing the toaster was $16, it might have added a 25 percent markup, setting the price to the retailers at $20. Similarly, construction companies submit job bids by estimating the total project cost and adding a standard markup for profit. Lawyers, accountants, and other professionals typically price by adding a standard markup to their costs. Some sellers tell their customers they will charge cost plus a specified markup; for example, aerospace companies price their products this way to the government.

Does using standard markups to set prices make sense? Generally, no. Any pricing method that ignores demand and competitor prices is not likely to lead to the best price. Steel manufacturer Nucor Corporation successfully uses cost-based pricing. Notes the company's general manager, "We base the price on what it costs to run the mill to capacity twenty-four hours a day." However, Nucor's very low costs allow it to charge very low prices relative to competitors. In contrast, the retail graveyard is full of merchants who insisted on using standard markups after their competitors had moved to discount pricing.[12]

Still, markup pricing remains popular for many reasons. First, sellers are more certain about costs than about demand. By tying the price to cost, sellers simplify pricing—they do not have to make frequent adjustments as demand changes. Second, when all firms in the industry use this pricing method, prices tend to be similar and price competition is thus minimized. Third, many people feel that cost-plus pricing is fairer to both buyers and sellers. Sellers earn a fair return on their investment but do not take advantage of buyers when buyers' demand becomes great.

Break-even pricing (target profit pricing) Setting price to break even on the costs of making and marketing a product, or setting price to make a target profit.

Another cost-oriented pricing approach is **break-even pricing**, or a variation called *target profit pricing*. The firm tries to determine the price at which it will break even or make the target profit it is seeking. Target pricing is used by General Motors, which prices its automobiles to achieve a 15 percent to 20 percent profit on its investment. This pricing method is also used by public utilities, which are constrained to make a fair return on their investment.

Target pricing uses the concept of a *break-even chart,* which shows the total cost and total revenue expected at different sales volume levels. Figure 10-4 shows a hypothetical break-even chart. Here, fixed costs are $300 000 regardless of sales volume, and variable costs are added to fixed costs to reach total costs, which rise with volume. The slope of the total revenue curve reflects the price of $20 per unit.

At the $20 price, the company must sell at least 30 000 units to *break even*—that is, at this level, total revenues to cover total costs. If the company wants a tar-

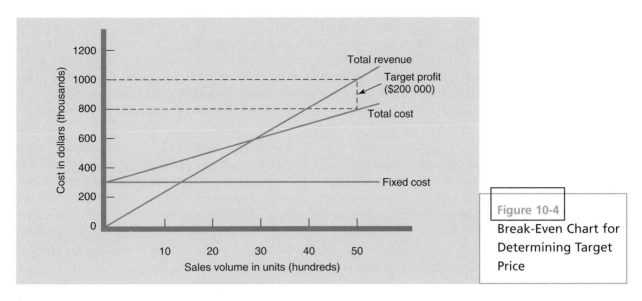

Figure 10-4

Break-Even Chart for Determining Target Price

get profit of $200 000, it must sell more than 30 000 units at $20 each. In contrast, if the company charges a higher price, say $25, it will not need to sell as many units to break even or to achieve its target profit. In fact, the higher the price, the lower the company's break-even point will be.

However, as the *price* increases, *demand* decreases, and the market may not buy even the lower volume needed to break even at the higher price. Much depends on the relationship between price and demand. For example, suppose the company calculates that given its current fixed and variable costs, it must charge a price of $30 for the product in order to earn its desired target profit. But marketing research shows that few consumers will pay more than $25. In this case, the company will have to trim its costs in order to lower the break-even point so that it can charge the lower price consumers expect.

Thus, although break-even analysis and target profit pricing can help the company to determine minimum prices needed to cover expected costs and profits, they do not take the price–demand relationship into account. When using this method, the company must also consider the impact of price on sales volume needed to realize target profits and the likelihood that the needed volume will be achieved at each possible price.

Value-Based Pricing

An increasing number of companies are basing their prices on the product's perceived value. **Value-based pricing** uses buyers' perceptions of value, not the seller's cost, as the key to pricing. Value-based pricing means that the marketer cannot design a product and marketing program and then set the price. Price is considered along with the other marketing mix variables *before* the marketing program is set.

Figure 10-5 compares cost-based pricing with value-based pricing. Cost-based pricing is product driven. The company designs what it considers to be a good product, totals the costs of making the product, and sets a price that covers costs plus a target profit. Marketing must then convince buyers that the product's value at that

Value-based pricing
Setting price based on buyers' perceptions of value rather than on the seller's cost.

price justifies its purchase. If the price turns out to be too high, the company must settle for lower markups or lower sales, both resulting in disappointing profits.

Value-based pricing reverses this process. The company sets its target price based on customer perceptions of the product value. The targeted value and price then drive decisions about product design and what costs can be incurred. As a result, pricing begins with analyzing consumer needs and value perceptions, and price is set to match consumers' perceived value.

A company using value-based pricing must find out what value buyers assign to different competitive offers. However, measuring perceived value can be difficult. Sometimes, consumers are asked how much they would pay for a basic product and for each benefit added to the offer. Or a company might conduct experiments to test the perceived value of different product offers. If the seller charges more than the buyers' perceived value, the company's sales will suffer. Many companies over-price their products, and their products sell poorly. Other companies underprice. Underpriced products sell very well, but they produce less revenue than they would have if price were raised to the perceived-value level.

During the past decade, marketers have noted a fundamental shift in consumer attitudes toward price and quality. Many companies have changed their pricing approaches to bring them into line with changing economic conditions and consumer price perceptions. According to Jack Welch, retired chairman of General Electric, "The value decade is upon us. If you can't sell a top-quality product at the world's best price, you're going to be out of the game.… The best way to hold your customers is to constantly figure out how to give them more for less."[13]

Thus, marketers increasingly have adopted **value pricing** strategies—offering just the right combination of quality and good service at a fair price. In many cases, this has involved the introduction of less expensive versions of established, brand name products. Campbell introduced its Great Starts Budget frozen-food line, Holiday Inn opened several Holiday Express budget hotels, Revlon's Charles of the Ritz offered the Express Bar collection of affordable cosmetics, and fast-food restaurants such as Taco Bell and McDonald's offer "value menus." In other cases,

Figure 10-5

Cost-Based Versus Value-Based Pricing

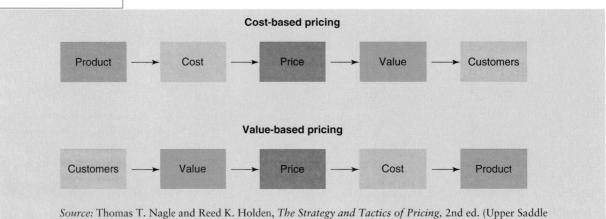

Source: Thomas T. Nagle and Reed K. Holden, *The Strategy and Tactics of Pricing,* 2nd ed. (Upper Saddle River, NJ: Prentice Hall, 1995), p. 5.

value pricing has involved redesigning existing brands to offer more quality for a given price or the same quality for less.

In many business-to-business marketing situations, the pricing challenge is to find ways to maintain the company's *pricing power*—its power to maintain or even raise prices without losing market share. To retain pricing power—to escape price competition and to justify higher prices and margins—a firm must retain or build the value of its marketing offer. This is especially true for suppliers of commodity products, which are characterized by little differentiation and intense price competition. In such cases, many companies adopt *value-added* strategies. Rather than cutting prices to match competitors, they attach value-added services to differentiate their offers and thus support higher margins.[14]

An important type of value pricing at the retail level is *everyday low pricing (EDLP)*. EDLP involves charging a constant, everyday low price with few or no temporary price discounts. In contrast, *high-low pricing* involves charging higher prices but running frequent promotions to lower prices temporarily on selected items below the EDLP level. In recent years, high-low pricing has given way to EDLP in retail settings ranging from Saturn car dealerships to upscale department stores such as Nordstrom. Retailers adopt EDLP for many reasons, the most important of which is that constant sales and promotions are costly and have eroded consumer confidence in the credibility of everyday shelf prices. Consumers also have less time

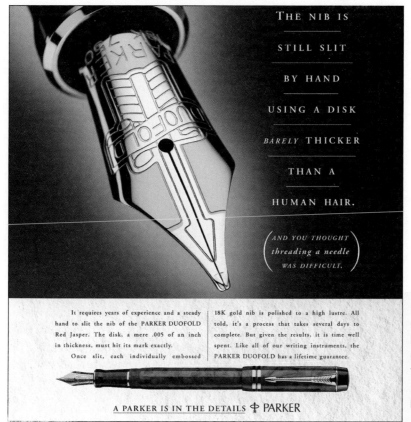

Perceived value: A less-expensive pen might write as well, but some consumers will pay much more for the intangibles. This Parker model runs about $295. Others are priced as high as $5600.

and patience for such time-honoured traditions as watching for supermarket specials and clipping coupons.

The leader of EDLP is Wal-Mart, which practically defined the concept.[15] Except for a few sale items every month, Wal-Mart promises everyday low prices on everything it sells. In contrast, Sears's attempts at EDLP in 1989 failed. To offer everyday low prices, a company must first have everyday low costs. Wal-Mart's EDLP strategy works well because its expenses are only 15 percent of sales. Sears, however, was spending 29 percent of sales to cover administrative and other overhead costs. As a result, Sears now offers everyday *fair* pricing, under which it tries to offer customers differentiated products at a consistent, fair price with fewer markdowns.

The concept of value is critical to good pricing and to successful marketing in general. Slow down for a minute and be certain that you appreciate what value really means.

- A few years ago, Buick pitched its top-of-the-line Park Avenue model as the "best car value." Does this fit with your idea of value?
- Pick two competing brands from a familiar product category (watches, perfume, consumer electronics, restaurants)—one low priced and the other high priced. Which, if either, offers the greatest value?
- Does "value" mean the same thing as "low price"? How do these concepts differ?

Competition-Based Pricing

Consumers will base their judgments of a product's value on the prices that competitors charge for similar products. One form of **competition-based pricing** is *going-rate pricing,* in which a firm bases its price largely on competitors' prices, with less attention paid to its own costs or to demand. The firm might charge the same as, more than, or less than its major competitors. In oligopolistic industries that sell a commodity such as steel, paper, or fertilizer, firms normally charge the same price. The smaller firms follow the leader: they change their prices when the market leader's prices change, rather than when their own demand or costs change. Some firms may charge a bit more or less, but they hold the amount of difference constant. Thus, minor gasoline retailers usually charge a few cents less than the major oil companies, without letting the difference increase or decrease.

Going-rate pricing is quite popular. When demand elasticity is hard to measure, firms feel that the going price represents the collective wisdom of the industry concerning the price that will yield a fair return. They also feel that holding to the going price will prevent harmful price wars.

Competition-based pricing is also used when firms *bid* for jobs. Using *sealed-bid pricing,* a firm bases its price on how it thinks competitors will price rather than on its own costs or on the demand. The firm wants to win a contract, and winning the contract requires pricing less than other firms. Yet the firm cannot set its price below a certain level. It cannot price below cost without harming its position. In contrast, the higher the company sets its price above its costs, the lower its chance of getting the contract.

Competition-based pricing Setting prices based on the prices that competitors charge for similar products.

NEW-PRODUCT PRICING STRATEGIES

Pricing decisions are subject to an incredibly complex array of environmental and competitive forces. A company sets not a single price, but rather a *pricing structure* that covers different items in its line. This pricing structure changes over time as products move through their life cycles. The company adjusts product prices to reflect changes in costs and demand and to account for variations in buyers and situations. As the competitive environment changes, the company considers when to initiate price changes and when to respond to them.

We now examine the major dynamic pricing strategies available to management. In turn, we look at *new-product pricing strategies* for products in the introductory stage of the product life cycle, *product mix pricing strategies* for related products in the product mix, *price-adjustment strategies* that account for customer differences and changing situations, and strategies for initiating and responding to *price changes.*[16]

Pricing strategies usually change as the product passes through its life cycle. The introductory stage is especially challenging. Companies bringing out a new product face the challenge of setting prices for the first time. They can choose between two broad strategies: *market-skimming pricing* and *market-penetration pricing.*

Market-Skimming Pricing

Many companies that invent new products initially set high prices to "skim" revenues layer by layer from the market. Intel is a prime user of this strategy, called **market-skimming pricing.** When Intel first introduces a new computer chip, it charges a premium price—a price that makes it *just* worthwhile for some segments of the market to adopt computers containing the chip. The new chips power top-of-the-line PCs and servers purchased by customers who just can't wait. As initial sales slow down, and as competitors threaten to introduce similar chips, Intel lowers the price to draw in the next price-sensitive layer of customers. Prices eventually bottom out at a level that makes the chip a hot mass-market processor. In this way, Intel skims a maximum amount of revenue from the various segments of the market.[17]

Market skimming makes sense only under certain conditions. First, the product's quality and image must support its higher price, and enough buyers must want the product at that price. Second, the costs of producing a smaller volume cannot be so high that they cancel the advantage of charging more. Finally, competitors should not be able to enter the market easily and undercut the high price.

Market-skimming pricing Setting a high price for a new product to skim maximum revenues layer by layer from the segments willing to pay the high price; the company makes fewer but more profitable sales.

Market-Penetration Pricing

Rather than setting a high initial price to *skim* off small but profitable market segments, some companies use **market-penetration pricing.** They set a low initial price to *penetrate* the market quickly and deeply—to attract a large number of buyers quickly and win a large market share. The high sales volume results in falling costs, allowing the company to cut its price even further. For example, Dell used penetration pricing to enter the personal computer market, selling high-quality computer products through lower-cost direct channels. Its sales soared when IBM, Compaq,

Market-penetration pricing Setting a low price for a new product to attract a large number of buyers and a large market share.

Apple, and other competitors selling through retail stores could not match its prices. Wal-Mart and other discount retailers also use penetration pricing.

Several conditions must be met for this low-price strategy to work. First, the market must be highly price sensitive so that a low price produces more market growth. Second, production and distribution costs must fall as sales volume increases. Finally, the low price must help keep out the competition, and the penetration pricer must maintain its low-price position—otherwise, the price advantage may be only temporary. For example, Dell faced difficult times when IBM and Compaq established their own direct distribution channels. However, through its dedication to low production and distribution costs, Dell has retained its price advantage and established itself as the industry's fastest-growing computer maker and number two in personal computers behind Compaq.

PRODUCT MIX PRICING STRATEGIES

The strategy for setting a product's price often has to be changed when the product is part of a product mix. In this case, the firm looks for a set of prices that maximizes the profits on the total product mix. Pricing is difficult because the various products have related demand and costs and face different degrees of competition. We now take a closer look at five product mix pricing situations: *product line pricing, optional-product pricing, captive-product pricing, by-product pricing,* and *product bundle pricing*.

Product Line Pricing

Product line pricing
Setting the price steps among various products in a product line based on cost differences among the products, customer evaluations of different features, and competitors' prices.

Companies usually develop product lines rather than single products. For example, Black and Decker makes many different lawn mowers, ranging from simple walk-behind versions priced at $259.95, $299.95, and $399.95, to elaborate riding mowers priced at $1000 or more. Each successive lawn mower in the line offers more features. Kodak offers not just one type of film but an assortment, including regular Kodak film, higher-priced Kodak Royal Gold film for special occasions, and still higher-priced Advantix APS film for Advanced Photo System cameras. It offers each of these brands in a variety of sizes and film speeds. In **product line pricing**, management must decide on the price steps to set among the various products in a line.

The price steps should take into account cost differences among the products in the line, customer evaluations of their different features, and competitors' prices. In many industries, sellers use well-established *price points* for the products in their line. Thus, men's clothing stores might carry men's suits at three price levels: $185, $285, and $385. The customer will probably associate low-quality, average-quality, and high-quality suits with the three price points. Even if the three prices are raised a little, men normally will buy suits at their own preferred price points. The seller's task is to establish perceived quality differences that support the price differences.

Optional-Product Pricing

Optional-product pricing
The pricing of optional or accessory products along with a main product.

Many companies use **optional-product pricing**—offering to sell optional or accessory products along with their main product. For example, a car buyer may choose to order power windows, cruise control, and a CD changer. Pricing these options is a sticky problem. Automobile companies have to decide which items to include in the base price and which to offer as options. At one time, General Motors' normal pricing strategy was to advertise a stripped-down model at a base price to pull people into showrooms and then devote most of the showroom space to showing option-loaded cars at higher prices. The economy model was stripped of so many comforts and conveniences that most buyers rejected it. Recently, however, GM and other carmakers have followed the example of the Japanese and German automakers and included in the sticker price many useful items previously sold only as options. The advertised price now often represents a well-equipped car.

Captive-Product Pricing

Companies that make products that must be used along with a main product are using **captive-product pricing**. Examples of captive products are razor blades, camera film, video games, and computer software. Producers of the main products (razors, cameras, video game consoles, and computers) often price them low and set high markups on the supplies. Thus, Polaroid prices its cameras low because it makes its money on the film it sells. Gillette sells low-priced razors but makes money on the replacement cartridges. U-Haul rents trucks at low rates but com-

Captive-product pricing
Setting a price for products that must be used along with a main product, such as blades for a razor and film for a camera.

Captive-product pricing: Nintendo sells game consoles at reasonable prices and makes money on video game titles.

mands high margins on accessories such as boxes, pads, insurance, and storage space rental. Nintendo sells its game consoles at low prices and makes money on video game titles. In fact, whereas Nintendo's margins on its consoles run a mere 1 percent to 5 percent, margins on its game cartridges run close to 45 percent. Video game sales contribute more than half the company's profits.[18]

In the case of services, this strategy is called *two-part pricing.* The price of the service is broken into a *fixed fee* plus a *variable usage rate.* Thus, a cellular phone company charges a monthly rate—the fixed fee—plus charges for calls beyond some minimum number—the variable usage rate. Amusement parks charge admission plus fees for food, midway attractions, and rides over a minimum. Theatres charge admission, then generate additional revenues from concessions. The service firm must decide how much to charge for the basic service and how much for the variable usage. The fixed amount should be low enough to induce usage of the service; profit can be made on the variable fees.

By-Product Pricing

By-product pricing
Setting a price for by-products to make the main product's price more competitive.

In producing processed meats, petroleum products, chemicals, and other products, there are often by-products. If the by-products have no value and if getting rid of them is costly, this will affect the pricing of the main product. Using **by-product pricing**, the manufacturer will seek a market for these by-products and should accept any price that covers more than the cost of storing and delivering them. This practice allows the seller to reduce the main product's price to make it more competitive. By-products can even turn out to be profitable. For example, many lumber mills have begun to sell bark chips and sawdust profitably as decorative mulch for home and commercial landscaping.

Sometimes, companies don't realize how valuable their by-products are. For example, most zoos don't realize that one of their by-products—their occupants' manure—can be an excellent source of additional revenue. But the Zoo Doo Compost Company has helped many zoos understand the costs and opportunities involved with these by-products. Zoo Doo licenses its name to zoos and receives royalties on manure sales. "Many zoos don't even know how much manure they are producing or the cost of disposing of it," explains president and founder Pierce Ledbetter. Zoos are often so pleased with any savings they can find on disposal that they don't think to move into active by-product sales. However, sales of the fragrant by-product can be substantial. So far, novelty sales have been the largest, with tiny containers of Zoo Doo (and even "Love, Love Me Doo" valentines) available in 160 zoo stores and 700 additional retail outlets. You can also buy Zoo Doo products online ("the easiest way to buy our crap," says Zoo Doo) or even send a friend (or perhaps a foe) a free Poopy Greeting via e-mail. For the long-term market, Zoo Doo looks to organic gardeners who buy 15 to 70 pounds of manure at a time. Zoo Doo is already planning a "Dung of the Month" club to reach this lucrative by-products market.[19]

Product bundle pricing
Combining several products and offering the bundle at a reduced price.

Product Bundle Pricing

Using **product bundle pricing**, sellers often combine several of their products and offer the bundle at a reduced price. Thus, theatres and sports teams sell season tickets at less than the cost of single tickets; hotels sell specially priced packages that include room, meals, and entertainment; computer makers include attractive software packages with their personal computers. Price bundling can promote the sales of products consumers might not otherwise buy, but the combined price must be low enough to get them to buy the bundle.[20]

PRICE-ADJUSTMENT STRATEGIES

Companies usually adjust their basic prices to account for various customer differences and changing situations. Here we examine six price-adjustment strategies: *discount and allowance pricing, segmented pricing, psychological pricing, promotional pricing, geographical pricing,* and *international pricing.*

Discount and Allowance Pricing

Most companies adjust their basic price to reward customers for certain responses, such as early payment of bills, volume purchases, and off-season buying. These price adjustments—called *discounts* and *allowances*—can take many forms.

The many forms of **discounts** include a *cash discount,* a price reduction to buyers who pay their bills promptly. A typical example is "2/10, net 30," which means that although payment is due within 30 days, the buyer can deduct 2 percent if the bill is paid within 10 days. The discount must be granted to all buyers meeting these terms. Such discounts are customary in many industries and help to improve the sellers' cash situation and reduce bad debts and credit-collection costs.

A *quantity discount* is a price reduction to buyers who buy large volumes. A typical example might be "$10 per unit for less than 100 units, $9 per unit for 100 or more units." Under provisions of Canada's Competition Act, quantity discounts must be offered equally to all customers and must not exceed the seller's cost savings associated with selling large quantities. These savings include lower selling, inventory, and transportation expenses. Discounts provide an incentive to the customer to buy more from one given seller, rather than from many different sources.

A *functional discount* (also called a *trade discount*) is offered by the seller to trade channel members who perform certain functions, such as selling, storing, and record keeping. Manufacturers may offer different functional discounts to different trade channels because of the varying services they perform, but manufacturers must offer the same functional discounts within each trade channel.

A *seasonal discount* is a price reduction to buyers who buy merchandise or services out of season. For example, lawn and garden equipment manufacturers offer seasonal discounts to retailers during the fall and winter months to encourage early ordering in anticipation of the heavy spring and summer selling seasons. Hotels, motels, and airlines will offer seasonal discounts in their slower selling periods. Seasonal discounts allow the seller to keep production steady during an entire year.

Allowances are another type of reduction from the list price. For example, *trade-in allowances* are price reductions given for turning in an old item when buying a new one. Trade-in allowances are most common in the automobile industry but are also given for other durable goods. *Promotional allowances* are payments or price reductions to reward dealers for participating in advertising and sales support programs.

Discount A straight reduction in price on purchases during a stated period.

Allowance Promotional money paid by manufacturers to retailers in return for an agreement to feature the manufacturer's products in some way.

Segmented Pricing

Companies will often adjust their basic prices to allow for differences in customers, products, and locations. In **segmented pricing**, the company sells a product or service at two or more prices, even though the difference in prices is not based on differences in costs (see New Directions 10-2).

Segmented pricing takes several forms. Under *customer-segment* pricing, different customers pay different prices for the same product or service. Museums, for example, will charge a lower admission for students and senior citizens. Under *product-form pricing*, different versions of the product are priced differently but not according to differences in their costs. For instance, Black & Decker prices its most expensive iron at $54.98, which is $12.00 more than the price of its next most expensive iron. The top model has a self-cleaning feature, yet this extra feature costs only a few more dollars to make. Using *location pricing*, a company charges different prices for different locations, even though the cost of offering each location is the same. For instance, theatres vary their seat prices because of audience preferences for certain locations, and universities charge higher tuition for foreign students. Finally, using *time pricing*, a firm varies its price by the season, the month, the day, and even the hour. Public utilities vary their prices to commercial users by time of day and weekend versus weekday. The telephone company offers lower off-peak charges, and resorts give seasonal discounts.

For segmented pricing to be an effective strategy, certain conditions must exist. The market must be segmentable, and the segments must show different degrees of demand. Members of the segment paying the lower price should not be able to turn around and resell the product to the segment paying the higher price. Competitors should not be able to undersell the firm in the segment being charged the higher price. Nor should the costs of segmenting and watching the market exceed the extra revenue obtained from the price difference. Of course, the segmented pricing must also be legal. Most important, segmented prices should reflect real differences in customers' perceived value. Otherwise, in the long run, the practice will lead to customer resentment and ill will.

Psychological Pricing

Price says something about the product. For example, many consumers use price to judge quality. A $100 bottle of perfume may contain only $3 worth of scent, but some people are willing to pay the $100 because this price indicates something special.

In using **psychological pricing**, sellers consider the psychology of prices and not simply the economics. For example, consumers usually perceive higher-priced products as having higher quality. When they can judge the quality of a product by examining it or by calling on past experience with it, they use price less to judge quality. But when they cannot judge quality because they lack the information or skill, price becomes an important quality signal.

Another aspect of psychological pricing is **reference prices**—prices that buyers carry in their minds and refer to when looking at a given product. The reference price might be formed by noting current prices, remembering past prices, or assessing the buying situation. Sellers can influence or use these reference prices when

Segmented pricing Selling a product or service at two or more prices, where the difference in prices is not based on differences in costs.

Psychological pricing A pricing approach that considers the psychology of prices and not simply the economics; the price is used to say something about the product.

Reference prices Prices that buyers carry in their minds and refer to when they look at a given product.

New Directions 10-2 >> Segmented Pricing: The Right Product to the Right Customer at the Right Time for the Right Price

Many companies would love to raise prices across the board—but fear losing business. When the Washington Opera Company, located in the U.S. capital, was considering increasing ticket prices after a difficult season, Ticket Services Manager Jimmy Legarreta decided there had to be a better way. He found one after carefully reviewing opera economics. Legarreta knew—and his computer system confirmed—that the company routinely turned away people for Friday and Saturday night performances, particularly for prime seats. Meanwhile, midweek tickets went begging.

Legarreta also knew that not all seats were equal, even in the sought-after orchestra section. So the ticket manager and his staff sat in every one of the opera house's 2200 seats and gave each a value according to the view and the acoustics. With his revenue goal in mind, Legarreta played with ticket prices until he arrived at nine levels, up from five. In the end, the opera raised prices for its most coveted seats by as much as 50 percent but also dropped the prices of some 600 seats. The gamble paid off in a 9 percent revenue increase during the next season.

Legarreta didn't have a name for it, but he was practising "segmented pricing," an approach that also has many other labels. Airlines, hotels, and restaurants call it "yield management" and practise it religiously. The airlines, for example, routinely set prices on an hour-by-hour—even minute-by-minute—basis, depending on seat availability and demand. "A business traveler who shells out $1700 for a coach seat bought at the last minute is well aware that the passenger in the next seat might have paid $300 for a ticket booked weeks in advance. while another passenger across the aisle may have scored a seat through a discount broker for, perhaps, $129," observes an industry analyst. Robert Cross, a longtime consultant to the airlines, calls it "revenue management." According to Cross, the practice ensures that "companies will sell the right product to the right consumer at the right time for the right price."

Segmented pricing and yield management aren't new ideas. For instance, Marriott Corporation used seat-of-the-pants yield-management approaches long before it installed its current sophisticated system. Back when J. W. "Bill" Marriott was a young man working at the family's first hotel, the Twin Bridges in Washington, D.C., he sold rooms from a drive-up window. As Bill tells it, the hotel charged a flat rate for a single occupant, with an extra charge for each additional person staying in the room. When room availability was tight on some nights, Bill would lean out the drive-up window and assess the cars waiting in line. If some of the cars were filled with passengers, Bill would turn away vehicles with just a single passenger to sell his last rooms to those farther back in line who would be paying for multiple occupants. He might have accomplished the same result by charging a higher rate at peak times, regardless of the number of room occupants.

Cross's underlying premise: No two customers value a product or

Segmented pricing: Not all seats in an opera house are equal. After sitting in every one of the Washington Opera House's 2200 seats, management arrived at nine pricing levels. The result: a 9 percent revenue increase.

service exactly the same way. Furthermore, the perceived value of a product results from many variables that change over time. Some of Cross's clients use sophisticated yield-management simulation models and high-powered computer systems to predict sales at different price levels. But the technique doesn't have to be rocket science. If you understand your customers' motivation for buying and you keep careful sales records, it's possible to adjust prices to remedy supply-and-demand imbalances. Legarreta, for example, ended his midweek slump by making opera affordable for more people, yet he accurately predicted that the Washington in-crowd would pay higher prices for the best weekend seats.

Probably the simplest form of segmented pricing is off-peak pricing, common in the entertainment and travel industries. Marc Epstein, owner of the Milk Street Cafe in Boston, discovered that technique more than 10 years ago, when he noticed he had lines out the door at noon but a near-empty restaurant around his 3 P.M. closing time. After some experimentation, Epstein settled on a 20 percent discount for the hours just before noon and after 2 P.M.-and he's pleased with the results. "If we didn't offer this, our overall revenue would be less," he argues. Epstein did not feel he could simultaneously raise prices during the lunch rush; instead, he has expanded the corporate-catering side of his business, where he can charge more per sandwich because "the perceived value of a catered lunch is higher."

Many other companies could conceivably segment their prices to increase revenues and profits. Cross cites examples ranging from a one-chair bar-bershop, to an accounting firm, to a health centre. But there are risks. When you establish a range of prices, customers who pay the higher ones may feel cheated. "It can't be a secret that you're charging different prices for the same service," Cross advises. "Customers must know, so they can choose when to use a service."

Even so, promotions designed to shift customer traffic to off-peak times can backfire. Rick Johnson, owner of Madison Car Wash, describes his experience with a "Wonderful Wednesday" special: "The incentive was too good. It took away from the rest of the week and made Wednesday a monster day; it was a horrible strain on my facility and my people. I played around with the discount, but it was still a problem. So I finally dropped it."

The moral of the story? You can never know too much about your customers and the different values they assign to your product or service. With that customer knowledge comes power—to make the best pricing decisions.

Sources: Portions adapted with permission from Susan Greco, "Are Your Prices Right?" *Inc.,* January 1997, pp. 88–89. Copyright 1997 by Goldhirsh Group, Inc., 38 Commercial Wharf, Boston, MA 02110. Other information from Robert G. Cross, *Revenue Management: Hard-Core Tactics for Market Domination,* New York: Broadway Books, 1998; and Joe Sharkey, "Hotels Take a Lesson from Airline Pricing," *The New York Times,* 17 December 2000, p. D3. Also see Ramarao Desiraju and Steven M. Shugan, "Strategic Service Pricing and Yield Management," *Journal of Marketing,* January 1999, pp. 44–56; and James Schembari, "More and More, We Get Less and…," *The New York Times,* 14 January 2001, p. D2.

setting price. For example, a company could display its product next to more expensive ones to imply that it belongs in the same class. Department stores often sell women's clothing in separate departments differentiated by price: Clothing found in the more expensive department is assumed to be of better quality. Companies can also influence consumers' reference prices by stating high manufacturer's suggested prices, by indicating that the product was originally priced much higher, or by pointing to a competitor's higher price.

Even small differences in price can suggest product differences. Consider a stereo priced at $300 compared to one priced at $299.95. The actual price difference is only 5 cents, but the psychological difference can be much greater. For example, some consumers will see the $299.95 as a price in the $200 range rather than the $300 range. The $299.95 will more likely be seen as a bargain price, whereas the $300

Psychological pricing: What do the prices marked on this tag suggest about the product and buying situation?

price suggests more quality. Some psychologists argue that each digit has symbolic and visual qualities that should be considered in pricing. Thus, 8 is round and even and creates a soothing effect, whereas 7 is angular and creates a jarring effect.[21]

Promotional Pricing

With **promotional pricing**, companies will temporarily price their products below list price and sometimes even below cost. Promotional pricing takes several forms. Supermarkets and department stores will price a few products as *loss leaders* to attract customers to the store in the hope that they will buy other items at normal markups. Sellers will also use *special-event pricing* in certain seasons to draw more customers. Thus, linens are promotionally priced every January to attract weary holiday shoppers back into stores.

Manufacturers will sometimes offer *cash rebates* to consumers who buy the product from dealers within a specified time; the manufacturer sends the rebate directly to the customer. Rebates have been popular with automakers and producers of durable goods and small appliances, but they are also used with consumer packaged goods. Some manufacturers offer *low-interest financing, longer warranties,* or *free maintenance* to reduce the consumer's "price." This practice has recently become a favourite of the auto industry. Or, the seller may simply offer *discounts* from normal prices to increase sales and reduce inventories.

Promotional pricing, however, can have adverse effects. Used too frequently and copied by competitors, price promotions can create "deal-prone" customers who wait until brands go on sale before buying them. Constantly reduced prices can erode a brand's value in the eyes of customers. Marketers sometimes use price

Promotional pricing
Temporarily pricing products below the list price, and sometimes even below cost, to increase short-run sales.

promotions as a quick fix instead of sweating through the difficult process of developing effective longer-term strategies for building their brands. In fact, one observer notes that price promotions can be downright addictive for both the company and the customer: "Price promotions are the brand equivalent of heroin: easy to get into but hard to get out of. Once the brand and its customers are addicted to the short-term high of a price cut it is hard to wean them away to real brand building.... But continue and the brand dies by 1000 cuts."[22]

Jack Trout, a well-known marketing author and consultant, cautions that some categories tend to self-destruct by always being on sale. Discount pricing has become routine for a surprising number of companies. Furniture, automobile tires, and many other categories of goods are rarely sold at anything near list price, and when automakers get rebate happy, the market just sits back and waits for a deal. Even Coca-Cola and Pepsi, two of the world's most popular brands, engage in regular price wars that ultimately tarnish their brand equity. Trout offers several "Commandments of Discounting," such as "Thou shalt not offer discounts because everyone else does," "Thou shalt be creative with your discounting," "Thou shalt put time limits on the deal," and "Thou shalt stop discounting as soon as you can."[23] The point is that promotional pricing can be an effective means of generating sales in certain circumstances but can be damaging if taken as a steady diet.

Here's a good place to take a rest break. Think about some of the companies and industries you deal with that are "addicted" to promotional pricing.

• Many industries have created "deal-prone" consumers through the heavy use of promotional pricing—fast food, airlines, tires, furniture, and others. Pick a company in one of these industries and suggest ways that it might deal with this problem.

• How does the concept of value relate to promotional pricing? Does promotional pricing add to or detract from customer value?

Geographical Pricing

f.o.b origin pricing A geographic pricing strategy in which goods are placed free on board a carrier and the customer pays the freight from the originating point to the required destination.

Uniform delivered pricing A geographic pricing strategy in which the company charges the same price plus freight to all customers, regardless of location

A company also must decide how to price its products for customers located in different parts of the country or the world. Should the company risk losing the business of more distant customers by charging them higher prices to cover the higher shipping costs? Or should the company charge all customers the same prices regardless of location?

As the first question implies, one option is to ask each customer to pay for shipping from the supplier's factory. This is called **f.o.b. origin pricing**, which means that the goods are placed free on board (f.o.b.) a carrier. At that point, the title and responsibility pass to the customer, who pays the freight from the factory to the destination. Although many believe this is the fairest way to assess freight charges, it means that more distant customers pay higher prices making the firm vulnerable to competitors in the customers' local area. A second option is **uniform delivered pricing**. Here, the company charges the same price to all customers, regardless of their location. It includes the average freight cost in its calculation of prices and then passes these charges along to all customers. This may make a firm's goods more expensive in its local market, but it gives the firm a better chance of winning over distant customers. Other advantages of uniform delivered pricing are that it is easy to administer and it lets the firm advertise its price nationally. **Zone pricing** is a third option that represents a compromise between f.o.b. origin pricing and uniform delivered pricing. The company sets up two or more zones. All customers within a given zone pay a single total price; the more distant the zone, the higher the price.

Zone pricing A geographic pricing strategy in which the company sets up two or more zones. All customers within a zone pay the same total price: the more distant the zone, the higher the price.

International Pricing

Companies that market their products internationally must decide what prices to charge in the different countries in which they operate. In some cases, a company can set a uniform worldwide price. For example, Bombardier sells its jetliners at about the same price everywhere, whether in the United States, Europe, or a less-developed country. However, most companies adjust their prices to reflect local market conditions and cost considerations.

The price that a company should charge in a specific country depends on many factors, including economic conditions, competitive situations, laws and regulations, and development of the wholesaling and retailing system. Consumer perceptions and preferences also may vary from country to country, calling for different prices. Or the company may have different marketing objectives in various world markets, which require changes in pricing strategy. For example, Sony might introduce a new product into mature markets in highly developed countries with the goal of quickly gaining mass-market share—this would call for a penetration-pricing strategy. In contrast, it might enter a less developed market by targeting smaller, less price-sensitive segments; in this case, market-skimming pricing makes sense.

Companies that market products internationally must decide what prices to charge in the different countries.

Costs play an important role in setting international prices. Travellers abroad are often surprised to find that goods that are relatively inexpensive at home may carry outrageously higher price tags in other countries. A pair of Levi's selling for $42 in Canada goes for about $87 in Tokyo and $122 in Paris. A McDonald's Big Mac selling for a modest $2.25 here costs $7.99 in Moscow, and an Oral-B toothbrush selling for $3.87 at home costs $15.55 in China. Conversely, a Gucci handbag going for only $95 in Milan, Italy, fetches $400 in Canada. In some cases, such *price escalation* may result from differences in selling strategies or market conditions. In most instances, however, it is simply a result of the higher costs of selling in another country-the additional costs of product modifications, shipping and insurance, import tariffs and taxes, exchange-rate fluctuations, and physical distribution.

Thus, international pricing presents some special problems and complexities. We discuss international pricing issues in more detail in Chapter 15.

PRICE CHANGES

After developing their pricing structures and strategies, companies often face situations in which they must initiate price changes or respond to price changes by competitors.

Initiating Price Changes

In some cases, the company may find it desirable to initiate either a price cut or a price increase. In both cases, it must anticipate possible buyer and competitor reactions.

Initiating Price Cuts Several situations may lead a firm to consider cutting its price. One such circumstance is excess capacity. In this case, the firm needs more business and cannot get it through increased sales effort, product improvement, or other measures. It may drop its "follow-the-leader pricing"—charging about the same price as its leading competitor—and aggressively cut prices to boost sales. But as the airline, construction equipment, fast-food, and other industries have learned in recent years, cutting prices in an industry loaded with excess capacity may lead to price wars as competitors try to hold on to market share.

Another situation leading to price changes is falling market share in the face of strong price competition. Several North American industries—automobiles, consumer electronics, cameras, watches, and steel, for example—lost market share to Japanese competitors whose high-quality products carried lower prices than did their North American counterparts. In response, North American companies resorted to more aggressive pricing action. A company may also cut prices in a drive to dominate the market through lower costs. Either the company starts with lower costs than its competitors, or it cuts prices in the hope of gaining market share that will further cut costs through larger volume. Bausch & Lomb used an aggressive low-cost, low-price strategy to become an early leader in the competitive soft contact lens market.

Initiating Price Increases A successful price increase can greatly increase profits. For example, if the company's profit margin is 3 percent of sales, a 1 percent price increase will increase profits by 33 percent if sales volume is unaffected. A major factor in price increases is cost inflation. Rising costs squeeze profit margins and lead companies to pass cost increases along to customers. Another factor leading to price increases is overdemand: When a company cannot supply all its customers' needs, it can raise its prices, ration products to customers, or both.

Companies can increase their prices in several ways to keep up with rising costs. Prices can be raised almost invisibly by dropping discounts and adding higher-priced units to the line. Or prices can be pushed up openly. In passing price increases on to customers, the company must avoid being perceived as a price gouger. Companies also need to think of who will bear the brunt of increased prices. As the Kellogg example at the beginning of the chapter suggests, customer memories are long, and they will eventually turn away from companies or even whole industries that they believe are charging excessive prices.

Wherever possible, the company should consider ways to meet higher costs or demand without raising prices. For example, it can consider more cost-effective ways to produce or distribute its products. It can shrink the product instead of raising the price, as candy bar manufacturers often do. It can substitute less expensive ingredients or remove certain product features, packaging, or services. Or it can "unbundle" its products and services, removing and separately pricing elements that were formerly part of the offer. IBM, for example, now offers training and consulting as separately priced services.

Buyer Reactions to Price Changes Whether the price is raised or lowered, the action will affect buyers, competitors, distributors, and suppliers and may interest government as well. Customers do not always interpret prices in a straightforward way. They may view a price *cut* in several ways. For example, what would you think if Sony were suddenly to cut its computer prices in half? You might think that these computers are about to be replaced by newer models or that they have some fault and are not selling well. You might think that Sony is abandoning the computer business and may not stay in this business long enough to supply future parts. You might believe that quality has been reduced. Or you might think that the price will come down even further and that it will pay to wait and see.

Similarly, a price *increase,* which would normally lower sales, may have some positive meanings for buyers. What would you think if Sony *raised* the price of its latest computer model? On the one hand, you might think that the item is very "hot" and may be unobtainable unless you buy it soon. Or you might think that the computer is an unusually good value. On the other hand, you might think that Sony is greedy and charging what the traffic will bear.[24]

Competitor Reactions to Price Changes A firm considering a price change has to worry about the reactions of its competitors as well as those of its customers. Competitors are most likely to react when the number of firms involved is small, when the product is uniform, and when the buyers are well informed.

How can the firm anticipate the likely reactions of its competitors? If the firm faces one large competitor, and if the competitor tends to react in a set way to price changes, that reaction can be easily anticipated. But if the competitor treats each price change as a fresh challenge and reacts according to its self-interest, the company will have to figure out just what makes up the competitor's self-interest at the time.

The problem is complex because, like the customer, the competitor can interpret a company price cut in many ways. It might think the company is trying to grab a larger market share, that the company is doing poorly and trying to boost its sales, or that the company wants the whole industry to cut prices to increase total demand.

When there are several competitors, the company must guess each competitor's likely reaction. If all competitors behave alike, this amounts to analyzing only a typical competitor. In contrast, if the competitors do not behave alike—perhaps because of differences in size, market shares, or policies—then separate analyses are necessary. However, if some competitors will match the price change, there is good reason to expect that the rest will also match it.

Responding to Price Changes

Here we reverse the question and ask how a firm should respond to a price change by a competitor. The firm needs to consider several issues: Why did the competitor change the price? Was it to take more market share, to use excess capacity, to meet changing cost conditions, or to lead an industrywide price change? Is the price change temporary or permanent? What will happen to the company's market share and profits if it does not respond? Are other companies going to respond? And what are the competitor's and other firms' responses to each possible reaction likely to be?

Besides these issues, the company must make a broader analysis. It has to consider its own product's stage in the life cycle, the product's importance in the company's product mix, the intentions and resources of the competitor, and the possible consumer reactions to price changes. The company cannot always make an extended analysis of its alternatives at the time of a price change, however. The competitor may have spent much time preparing this decision, but the company may have to react within hours or days. About the only way to cut down reaction time is to plan for both possible competitor's price changes and possible responses.

Figure 10-6 shows the ways a company might assess and respond to a competitor's price cut. Once the company has determined that the competitor has cut its price and that this price reduction is likely to harm company sales and profits, it might simply decide to hold its current price and profit margin. The company might believe that it will not lose too much market share, or that it would lose too much profit if it reduced its own price. It might decide that it should wait and respond when it has more information on the effects of the competitor's price change. For now, it might be willing to hold on to good customers, while giving up the poorer ones to the competitor. The argument against this holding strategy, however, is that the competitor may get stronger and more confident as its sales increase and that the company might wait too long to act.

If the company decides that effective action can and should be taken, it might make any of four responses. First, it could *reduce its price* to match the competitor's price. It may decide that the market is price sensitive and that it would lose too much market share to the lower-priced competitor. Or it might worry that recapturing lost market share later would be too hard. Cutting the price will reduce the company's profits in the short run. Some companies might also reduce their product quality, services, and marketing communications to retain profit margins, but

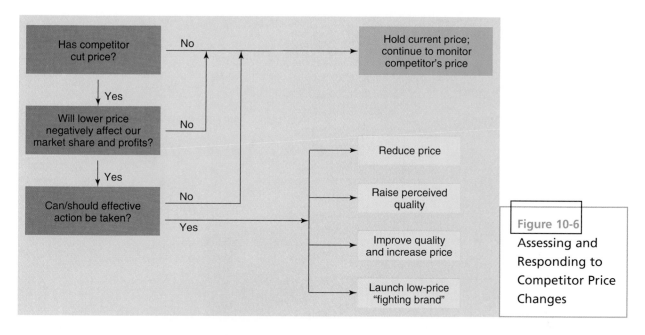

Figure 10-6

Assessing and Responding to Competitor Price Changes

this will ultimately hurt long-run market share. The company should try to maintain its quality as it cuts prices.

Alternatively, the company might maintain its price but *raise the perceived quality* of its offer. It could improve its communications, stressing the relative quality of its product over that of the lower-price competitor. The firm may find it cheaper to maintain price and spend money to improve its perceived value than to cut price and operate at a lower margin.

Or, the company might *improve quality and increase price,* moving its brand into a higher-price position. The higher quality justifies the higher price, which in turn preserves the company's higher margins. Or the company can hold price on the current product and introduce a new brand at a higher-price position.

Finally, the company might *launch a low-price "fighting brand"*—adding a lower-price item to the line or creating a separate lower-price brand. This is necessary if the particular market segment being lost is price sensitive and will not respond to arguments of higher quality. Thus, when challenged on price by store brands and other low-price entrants, Procter & Gamble turned several of its brands into fighting brands, including Luvs disposable diapers, Joy dishwashing detergent, and Camay beauty soap.

PUBLIC POLICY AND PRICING

Price competition is a core element of our free-market economy. In setting prices, companies are usually free to charge whatever prices they want. However, companies must consider broader societal pricing concerns. The most important pieces of legislation affecting pricing are the Competition Act and The Sale of Goods Act, initially adopted to promote competition and not unfairly restrain trade. Figure 10-7 shows the major public policy issues in pricing. These include potentially damag-

When challenged by store brands and other low-priced entrants, Proctor & Gamble turned LUVS disposable diapers into a "fighting brand."

ing pricing practices within a given level of the channel (price fixing and predatory pricing) and across levels of the channel (retail price maintenance, discriminatory pricing, and deceptive pricing).[25]

Pricing Within Channel Levels

Federal legislation on *price fixing* states that sellers must set prices without talking to competitors. Otherwise, price collusion is suspected. Price fixing is illegal—that is, the government does not accept any excuses for price fixing. Companies found guilty of such practices can receive heavy fines. For example, when the U.S. Justice Department found that Archer Daniels Midland Company and three of its competitors had met regularly in the early 1990s to illegally fix prices, the four companies paid more than $100 million to settle the charges.

Sellers are also prohibited from using *predatory pricing*—selling below cost with the intention of punishing a competitor or gaining higher long-run profits by putting competitors out of business. This protects small sellers from larger ones who might sell items below cost temporarily or in a specific locale to drive them out of business. The biggest problem is determining just what constitutes predatory pricing behaviour. Selling below cost to sell off excess inventory is not considered predatory; selling below cost to drive out competitors is. Thus, the same action may

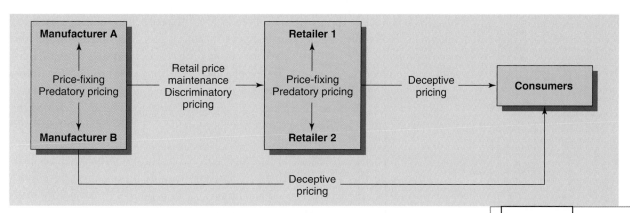

Figure 10-7

Public Policy Issues in Pricing

or may not be predatory depending on intent, and intent can be very difficult to determine or prove.

In recent years, several large and powerful companies have been accused of this practice. For example, Wal-Mart has been sued by dozens of small competitors charging that it lowered prices in their specific areas to drive them out of business. Giant Microsoft has also been a U.S. Justice Department target:

When Microsoft targets a market for domination, it frequently wins over customers with an irresistible offer: free products. In 1996, Microsoft started giving away Internet Explorer, its Web browser—and in some cases arguably even "paid" people to use it by offering free software and marketing assistance. The strategy was crucial in wresting market dominance from Netscape Communications Corporation. Netscape constantly revised its pricing structure but "better than free" is not the most appealing sales pitch. Most of Microsoft's giveaways were offered as part of its effort to gain share in the interactive corporate computing market. For instance, the company offered free Web-server software to customers who purchase the Windows NT network operating system. Netscape was selling a higher-powered version of the same software for $4,100. Although such pricing and promotion strategies might be viewed as shrewd marketing by some, competitors saw them as purely predatory. They noted that in the past, once Microsoft had use these tactics to gain a lion's share of the market, it had tended to raise prices *above* market levels. For example, the wholesale price it charged PC makers for its Windows operating system (in which is bundled the Internet Explorer) had doubled during the past seven years.[26]

Pricing Across Channel Levels

The Competition Act seeks to prevent unfair *price discrimination* by ensuring that sellers offer the same price terms to customers at a given level of trade. For example, every retailer is entitled to the same price terms from a given manufacturer, whether the retailer is Sears or the local bicycle shop. However, price discrimination is allowed if the seller can prove that its costs are different when selling to different retailers—for example, that it costs less per unit to sell a large volume of bicycles to Sears than to sell a few bicycles to a local dealer. Or the seller can discriminate in its pricing if the seller manufactures different qualities of the same product for different retailers. The seller has to prove that these differences are proportional. Price differentials may also be used to "match competition" in "good faith," provided the price discrimination is temporary, localized, and defensive rather than offensive.

Retail price maintenance is also prohibited—a manufacturer cannot require dealers to charge a specified retail price for its product. Although the seller can propose a manufacturer's *suggested* retail price to dealers, it cannot refuse to sell to a dealer who takes independent pricing action, nor can it punish the dealer by shipping late or denying advertising allowances. *Deceptive pricing* occurs when a seller states prices or price savings that mislead consumers or are not actually available to consumers. This might involve bogus reference or comparison prices, as when a retailer sets artificially high "regular" prices then announces "sale" prices close to its previous everyday prices. Such comparison pricing is widespread:

Open any newspaper and find hundreds of such promotions being offered by a variety of retailers, such as supermarkets, office supply stores, furniture stores, computer stores, appliance stores, pharmacies and drugstores, car dealers, department stores, and others. Surf the Internet and see similar price promotions. Watch the shopping channels on television and find more of the same. It seems that, today, selling prices rarely stand alone. Instead retailers are using an advertised reference price (e.g., regular price, original price, manufacturer's suggested price) to suggest that buyers will save money if they take advantage of the "deal" being offered.[27]

Such claims are legal if they are truthful. However, the Sale of Goods Act, municipal laws and the Better Business Bureau ensure that for sellers that advertise a price reduction, it is a true saving from the usual retail price. In addition, retailers are cautioned about and subject to legal penalties when falsely advertising "factory" or "wholesale" prices unless such prices are what they claim to be, and seller are warned not to advertise comparable value prices on imperfect goods.

Other deceptive pricing issues include *scanner fraud* and price confusion. The widespread use of scanner-based computer checkouts has lead to increasing complaints of retailers overcharging their customers. Most of these overcharges result from poor management—from a failure to enter current or sale prices into the system. Other cases, however, involve intentional overcharges. *Price confusion* results when firms employ pricing methods that make it difficult for consumers to understand just what price they are really paying. For example, consumers are sometimes misled regarding the real price of a home mortgage or car leasing agreement. In other cases, important pricing details may be buried in the "fine print."

Many federal and local laws regulate deceptive pricing practices. For example, automakers are required to attach a statement to new car windows stating the manufacturer's suggested retail price, the prices of optional equipment, and the dealer's transportation charges. However, reputable sellers go beyond what is required by law. Treating customers fairly and making certain that they fully understand prices and pricing terms is an important part of building strong and lasting customer relationships.[28]

<< Looking Back   < < < < < < < < <

Before you put pricing in the rear-view mirror, let's review the important concepts. *Price* can be defined as the sum of the values that consumers exchange for the benefits of having and using the product or service. It is the only marketing mix element that produces revenue; all other elements represent costs. Even so, many companies are not good at handling pricing. Pricing decisions are subject to an incredibly complex array of environmental and competitive forces.

1. **Identify and explain the external and internal factors affecting a firm's pricing decisions.**

External factors that influence pricing decisions include the nature of the *market* and *demand; competitors' costs, prices, and offers;* and factors such as *the economy, reseller needs, government actions,* and *social concerns.* The seller's pricing freedom varies with different types of markets. Ultimately, the consumer decides whether the company has set the right price. The consumer weighs the price against the perceived values of using the product—if the price exceeds the sum of the values, consumers will not buy. Therefore, *demand* and *consumer value perceptions* set the ceiling for prices. Consumers also compare a product's price to the prices of *competitors'* products. As a result, a company must learn the price and quality of competitors' offers.

Many *internal factors* influence the company's pricing decisions, including the firm's *marketing objectives, marketing mix strategy, costs,* and *organization for pricing.* Common pricing objectives include survival, current profit maximization, market share leadership, and product quality leadership. The pricing strategy is largely determined by the company's *target market* and *positioning objectives.* Pricing decisions affect and are affected by product design, dis-

tribution, and promotion decisions and must be carefully coordinated with these other marketing mix variables. *Costs* set the floor for the company's price—the price must cover all the costs of making and selling the product, plus a fair rate of return. Finally, to coordinate pricing goals and decisions, management must decide who within the organization is responsible for setting price.

2. **Contrast the three general approaches to setting prices.**

A company can select one or a combination of three general pricing approaches: the *cost-based approach* (cost-plus pricing, break-even analysis, and target profit pricing); the *value-based approach;* and the *competition-based approach.* Cost-based pricing sets prices based on the seller's cost structure, whereas value-based pricing relies on consumer perceptions of value to drive pricing decisions. Competition-based pricing involves setting prices based on what competitors are charging or are expected to charge.

3. **Describe the major strategies for pricing imitative and new products.**

Pricing is a dynamic process. Companies design a *pricing structure* that covers all their products. They change this structure over time and adjust it to account for different customers and situations. Pricing strategies usually change as a product passes through its life cycle. The company can decide on one of several price quality strategies for introducing an imitative product, including premium pricing, economy pricing, good-value pricing, or overcharging. In pricing innovative new products, it can follow a *skimming policy* by initially setting high prices to "skim" the maximum amount of revenue from various segments of the market. Or it can use *penetration pricing* by setting a low initial price to penetrate the market deeply and win a large market share.

4. **Explain how companies find a set of prices that maximizes the profits from the total product mix.**

When the product is part of a product mix, the firm searches for a set of prices that will maximize the profits from the total mix. In *product line pricing,* the company decides on price steps for the entire set of products it offers. In addition, the company must set prices for *optional products* (optional or accessory products included with the main product), *captive products* (products that are required for use of the main product), *by-products* (waste or residual products produced when making the main product), and *product bundles* (combinations of products at a reduced price).

5. **Discuss how companies adjust their prices to take into account different types of customers and situations.**

Companies apply a variety of *price-adjustment strategies* to account for differences in consumer segments and situations. One is *discount and allowance pricing,* whereby the company establishes cash, quantity, functional, or seasonal discounts, or varying types of allowances. A second strategy is *segmented pricing,* whereby the company sells a product at two or more prices to accommodate different customers, product forms, locations, or times. Sometimes companies consider more than economics in their pricing decisions, using *psychological pricing* to better communicate a product's intended position. In *promotional pricing,* a company offers discounts or temporarily sells a product below list price as a special event, sometimes even selling

below cost as a loss leader. Another approach is *geographical pricing,* whereby the company decides how to price to near and distant customers. Finally, *international pricing* means that the company adjusts its price to meet conditions and expectations in different world markets.

6. **Discuss the key issues related to initiating and responding to price changes.**

When a firm considers initiating a *price change,* it must consider customers' and competitors' reactions. There are different implications to *initiating price cuts* and *initiating price increases.* Buyer reactions to price changes are influenced by the meaning customers see in the price change. Competitors' reactions flow from a set reaction policy or a fresh analysis of each situation. There are also many factors to consider in responding to a competitor's price changes. The company that faces a price change initiated by a competitor must try to understand the competitor's intent as well as the likely duration and impact of the change. If a swift reaction is desirable, the firm should plan its reactions to different possible price actions by competitors. When facing a competitor's price change, the company might sit tight, reduce its own price, raise perceived quality, improve quality and raise price, or launch a fighting brand.

Companies are not usually free to charge whatever prices they wish. Many federal, state, and even local laws govern the rules of fair play in pricing. The major public policy issues in pricing include potentially damaging pricing practices within a given level of the channel (price fixing and predatory pricing) and across levels of the channel (retail price maintenance, discriminatory pricing, and deceptive pricing).

Navigating the Key Terms

Allowance, **p. 405**

Break-even pricing (target profit pricing), **p. 396**

By-product pricing, **p. 404**

Captive-product pricing, **p. 403**

Competition-based pricing, **p. 400**

Cost-plus pricing, **p. 395**

Demand curve, **p. 392**

Discount, **p. 405**

Dynamic pricing, **p. 383**

f.o.b. pricing, **p. 410**

Market-penetration pricing, **p. 401**

Market-skimming pricing, **p. 401**

Optional-product pricing, **p. 402**

Price elasticity, **p. 393**

Price, **p. 383**

Product bundle pricing, **p. 404**

Product line pricing, **p. 402**

Promotional pricing, **p. 409**

Psychological pricing, **p. 406**

Reference prices, **p. 406**

Segmented pricing, **p. 406**

Target costing, **p. 388**

Uniform delivered pricing, **p. 410**

Value-based pricing, **p. 397**

Zone pricing, **p. 411**

Concept Check

Fill in the blanks and then check your answers.

1. With _____ pricing, different prices are charged, depending on individual customers and situations.

2. Common objectives with respect to pricing include survival, _____, _____, and _____.

3. Economists recognize four types of markets, each presenting a different pricing challenge: _____; _____; _____; and, _____.

4. Price elasticity measures how responsive demand will be to a change in price. If demand changes greatly, we say the demand is _____.

5. The simplest pricing method is _____ where the marketer adds a standard markup to the cost of the product.

6. _____ pricing means that the marketer cannot design a product and marketing program and then set the price. Price is considered along with the other marketing-mix variables before the marketing program is set.

7. _____-based pricing is used when firms bid for jobs. A special version of this pricing form would be going-rate pricing and sealed-bid pricing.

8. If a company chooses to set a low initial price in order to go into the market quickly and deeply (to attract a large number of buyers quickly and win a large market share), the company would be using a _____ pricing strategy.

9. Examples of products that would use _____ pricing would include razor blades, camera film, video games, and computer software.

10. A typical example of a _____ discount is "2/10, net 30," which means that although payment is due within 30 days, the buyer can deduct 2 percent if the bill is paid within 10 days.

11. Consumers usually perceive higher-priced products as having higher quality. This would be a case where _____ pricing was used.

12. If a customer is asked to pay the entire cost of freight from the factory to the customer's destination (distant customers will have to pay

more), the company is most likely using the _____ pricing form of geographical pricing.

Concept Check Answers: 1. dynamic; 2. current profit maximization, market share leadership, product quality leadership; 3. pure competition, monopolistic competition, oligopolistic competition, and pure monopoly; 4. elastic; 5. cost-plus pricing; 6. Value-based; 7. Competition; 8 market-penetration; 9. captive-product; 10. cash; 11. psychological; 12. f.o.b origin.

Discussing the Issues

1. Assume you are the vice president for financial affairs at a major university. For the past three years, enrollments and revenues have declined steadily at a rate of about 10 percent per year. You are under great pressure to raise tuition to compensate for the falling revenues. However, you suspect that raising tuition might only make matters worse. What internal and external pricing factors should you consider before you make your decision? Explain.

2. Discuss the typical pricing objectives outlined in the chapter. Which of these objectives do you believe (a) is the most commonly used, (b) is the most difficult to achieve, (c) has the greatest potential for long-term growth of the organization, and (d) is most likely to be a pricing objective used by a dot-com e-commerce-oriented company? Explain.

3. After examining Figure 10-5, compare and contrast cost-based pricing and value-based pricing. What situations favour each pricing methods?

4. Which pricing strategy-market skimming or market penetration-does each of the following companies use? (a) McDonald's, (b) Samsung (televisions and other home electronics), (c) Bic Corporation (pens, lighters, razors, and related products), and (d) IBM (personal computers). Are these the right strategies for these companies? Explain.

5. Formulate rules that might govern (a) initiating a price cut, (b) initiating a price increase, (c) a negative reaction on the part of buyers to a price change by your company, (d) a competitor's response to your price change, and (e) your response to a competitor's price change. State the assumptions underlying your proposed rules.

 **Mastering Marketing**

Pricing is one of the most important and difficult decisions a firm must make. Choose a product from CanGo. (a) What pricing objective is the company using with respect to the product? Is this the correct objective? (b) Into which of the four types of economic markets does this product fit? (c) Which general pricing approach is the company using with respect to this product? Is this the best approach? (d) Would you favour market skimming or market penetration pricing for this product? Explain. (e) If a product-mix pricing strategy were to be used, which technique would be most appropriate? Explain. (f) Is a price change needed? Explain how this might be done and why the change might be necessary.

 Check out the enclosed CBC Video case CD-ROM, or our Companion Website at www.pearsoned.ca/armstrong, to view a CBC video segment and case for this chapter.

Digital Map

Visit our Web site at **www.pearsoned.ca/armstrong** for online quizzes, Internet exercises, and more!

CASE 10 PeoplePC: Is There a Free Lunch?

What's Going On?

Economists tell us that there is no such thing as a free lunch. Well, perhaps. But it certainly seems that many personal computer and Internet companies are trying to come up with one. The 22 December 1999 issue of *The Wall Street Journal* carried a full-page ad with the words "100% Off" in bold letters centred on the page. The ad from Juno Online Services went on to advise, "Starting now, Juno is offering full Internet access for free. From free Web access to premium dial-up and broadband services, everybody's getting it."

But perhaps not everyone is getting it. How can a company give away a service for which millions of people have been paying about $20 per month? What's going on? How can Juno and other companies make these offers? And what about Egreetings Network, Inc.? In 1998, when this Internet company began offering e-mail birthday cards for $0.75 to $4.50 each, only 300 000 people signed up for the service. Then, the company decided to ditch its pricing strategy and give its cards away free. By mid-1999, it had 7 million registered users. Egreetings' CEO Gordon Tucker admits, "Charging for cards was a small idea. Giving them away is a really big idea."

Giving Things Away

Is this some form of cyber-suicide? You might argue that a company giving away an electronic greeting card is not really giving away very much. But how do you explain the offer by Free-PC? The price of personal computers was already plummeting. In fact, computers priced below $1000 were accounting for the majority of sales—some were as inexpensive as $750. Then, along came Free-PC. In February 1999, the company announced that it would give away 10 000 personal computers. All that interested consumers had to do was to register at its Web site at **www.freepc.com** and provide detailed demographic information about themselves and their families including name, address, sex, age, e-mail address, marital status, makes and models of family cars, and lifestyle information from a list of 26 categories.

The company indicated it would review the applications it received and implied that it would select them to create a pool of users who would be attractive to advertisers. The company also announced that it planned to charge 200 advertisers $15 000 each for a 90-day period, a time during which Free-PC would direct their ads to the lucky 10 000. Free-PC guaranteed the advertisers one million impressions during the period. It argued that it provided real targeting using the 60 pieces of demographic data it tracked, along with response data on each variable. Moreover, advertisers could deliver media-rich ads and test different ad messages to see which got the best responses.

When Free-PC opened its Web site, more than 1.2 million people logged on and applied for the 10 000 free PCs. Applicants the company selected received a full-featured Compaq Presario Internet PC with pre-installed software and unlimited access to the Internet, which included e-mail service and technical support.

Consumers had to agree to log on to the Internet at least 10 hours per month. If customers did not live up to this commitment, FreePC would ask them to return their PCs. Whenever they surfed the Internet, consumers' monitor screens contained a bar down the right side and across the bottom, occupying about 40 percent of the screen in total, that displayed ads and other marketing messages. The company called the Free-PC network the first permission-based, one-to-one targeted marketing network. Free-PC's Web site explained that, by having so much information, "you will help us to make sure that the ads and services that appear in the small frame around the screen are relevant to you. And, just like you don't want to waste your time with meaningless ads, advertisers don't want to waste money displaying ads to people who aren't interested in their products."

Jumping on the Bandwagon

More than a dozen companies quickly jumped on the Free-PC bandwagon, with some adding new twists. Enchilada at **www.enchilada.com** threw in Internet access along with the computer to offer "the whole enchilada" for $599. The offer includes the computer and three years of Internet access. However, you have to pay extra for a monitor, warranty, and extended technical support.

InterSquid at **www.intersquid.com** offered a PC and Internet access for $45.95 per month with a 30-month commitment: Applicants had to commit to a costly credit check, or pay the total amount, about $1350, up front. MyFreePC.com at **www.myfreepc.com** provided a low-end computer and Internet access for $40.18 per month; however, people had to commit to 19 months of service and, to avoid an interest-bearing loan, pay up front.

PeoplePC

In late 1999, Nicholas Grouf, a 31-year-old Harvard MBA, launched PeoplePC and added the latest twist. PeoplePC offers a brand-name PC, such as Compaq or Toshiba, including a monitor and free Internet service through MCI Worldcom's UUNet. In addition to the computer and Internet access, PeoplePC subscribers get around-the-clock technical support and even in-home computer repair service if required. The cost is $37.43 per month for three years.

After the three-year period, PeoplePC will give you a new computer if you want to sign up again. The company planned to sign up 400 000 people in its first wave.

PeoplePC's plan differs in several ways from Free-PC's plan. PeoplePC's program requires only a minimum amount of personal information as a part of the registration process. Second, PeoplePC will not use an ad-supported business model. That is, it will not require that buyers devote some of their screen space to ads, or pledge to be online for a certain number of hours per month. Rather, PeoplePC sees itself as a membership-based model in which it will use its members' buying power to get them good deals on products and services. In a sense, the company serves as an Internet shopping club. It will earn money by getting a fee from the product or service provider whenever a PeoplePC member buys something. For example, at the PeoplePC home page, a member can click on a button marked, "Special Offers for PeoplePC Members." Offers include 5 percent off at wine.com, 10 percent off at chipshot.com, 15 percent off at Ashford.com, and a $150 sign-up bonus from E*TRADE.

PeoplePC will earn between $75 and $150 for each member who signs up with E*TRADE. That's much less than the average $600 most online brokers must spend to acquire a new customer. Moreover, the company lets each e-tailer decide how much to pay PeoplePC. Although this might seem to encourage e-tailers to take advantage of the company, Nicholas Grouf argues that the more a company pays, the harder PeoplePC will work for it. "Every company knows just how much it pays in customer acquisition costs. If it costs $1000 to get a customer, and we get just 10 percent of that for doing the same work, it's still a lucrative business." PeoplePC will also have three-year commitments from customers, allowing it to sell that receivable to a bank and get its money quickly.

To attract members, PeoplePC kicked off a $40 million multimedia promotion campaign in late 1999, starting with spots during game three of the World Series. Additional television, newspaper, and online ads that followed those spots used the tag line: "It's for people." In November 1999, the company reported that phone calls were coming in at four times the predicted rate, and it had increased the number of representatives answering phones from 100 to 500.

A Free-for-All

One observer noted, "Time and again, do-it-for-free companies are coming in and spoiling an industry for everyone else. But it's a fact on the Internet: People expect a lot of things for free. And if you don't give it away, some other start-up will." Internet companies rush to sign up large numbers of people and earn money either by selling advertising or earning fees from online vendors. One wonders what consumers expect free. Moreover, are there enough advertising revenues or indirect fees to support all these Web sites? With MP3.com giving away music, e-Fax.com giving away fax service, and Juno.com giving away Internet access, we may soon find out how much a free lunch really costs.

Questions

1. What internal and external factors affect e-commerce pricing decisions?

2. What marketing objectives and pricing approaches are PeoplePC and Free-PC pursuing?

3. What is the nature of costs for a company like PeoplePC? Which costs are fixed and which are variable? What are the implications of this cost structure?

4. How can companies like PeoplePC make offers that appear to be free or almost free? What are the true costs to the consumer?

5. What marketing recommendations would you make to PeoplePC?

Sources: "PeoplePC Energizes Personal Computer Shopping This Holiday Season," *PR Newswire,* 14 December 1999, p. 1460; Nikhil Hutheesing, "Matchmaker," *Forbes,* 15 November 1999, p. 222; "PeoplePC to Unveil Investors' Backing Totaling $65 Million," *The Wall Street Journal,* 1 November 1999, p. B13; Tobi Elkin, "Newcomer PeoplePC Rolls $40 Mil Campaign: Online Discounts and Ecard Offer Form Backbone of Trouble-Free PC-Buying Pitch," *Advertising Age,* 11 October 1999, p. 85; Cade Metz, "Nearly Free PCs," *PC Magazine,* 1 September 1999, p. 177; George Anders, "Eager to Boost Traffic, More Internet Firms Give away Services," *The Wall Street Journal,* 28 July 1999, p. A1; Makoto Ushida, "Cyberslice: Free-PC Wave Hits Japanese Shore," *Asahi Shimbun/Asahi Evening News,* 26 July 1999, p. ASAH6396762. Also see **www.freepc.com**, **www.peoplepc.com**, and **homepeoplepc.com**.

11 >> Marketing Channels and Supply Chain Management

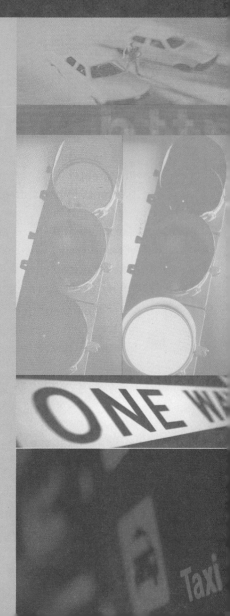

Looking Ahead

We now arrive at the third marketing mix tool: distribution. Firms rarely work alone in bringing value to customers. Instead, most are only a single link in a larger supply chain or distribution channel. As such, an individual firm's success depends not only on how well it performs, but also on how well its entire distribution channel competes with competitors' channels. For example, Ford can make the world's best cars but still will not do well if its dealers perform poorly in sales and service against the dealers of Toyota, GM, Chrysler, or Honda. Ford must choose its channel partners carefully and work with them effectively. The first part of this chapter explores the nature of distribution channels and the marketer's channel design and management decisions. We then examine physical distribution—or logistics—an area that is growing dramatically in importance and sophistication. In the next chapter, we'll look more closely at two major channel intermediaries: retailers and wholesalers.

After studying this chapter, you should be able to

1. explain why companies use distribution channels and discuss the functions these channels perform

2. discuss how channel members interact and how they organize to perform the work of the channel

3. identify the major channel alternatives open to a company

4. explain how companies select, motivate, and evaluate channel members

5. discuss the nature and importance of marketing logistics and integrated supply chain management

While your engine's warming up, we'll look at Caterpillar. You might think that Caterpillar's success, and its ability to charge premium prices, rests on the quality of the construction and mining equipment that it produces. But

Caterpillar's chair and CEO sees things differently. The company's dominance, he claims, results from its unparalleled distribution and customer support system—from the strong and caring partnerships that it has built with independent Caterpillar dealers. Read on and see why.

For more than half a century, Caterpillar has dominated the world's markets for heavy construction and mining equipment. Its familiar yellow tractors, crawlers, loaders, and trucks are a common sight at any construction area. With sales of $31 billion, Caterpillar is half again as large as its nearest competitor. It now captures more than a 35 percent share of the world's heavy construction equipment market, selling more than 300 products in nearly 200 countries.

Many factors contribute to Caterpillar's enduring success—high-quality products, flexible and efficient manufacturing, a steady stream of innovative new products, and a lean organization that is responsive to customer needs. Although Caterpillar charges premium prices for its equipment, its high-quality and trouble-free operation provide greater long-term value. Yet these are not the most important reasons for Caterpillar's dominance. Instead, Caterpillar credits its focus on customers and its corps of 211 outstanding dealers worldwide, who do a superb job of taking care of every customer need. According to former Caterpillar CEO Donald Fites:

> After the product leaves our door, the dealers take over. They are the ones on the frontline. They're the ones who live with the product for its lifetime. They're the ones customers see. Although we offer financing and insurance, they arrange those deals for customers. They're out there making sure that when a machine is delivered, it's in the condition it's supposed to be in. They're out there training a customer's operators. They service a product frequently throughout its life, carefully monitoring a machine's health and scheduling repairs to prevent costly

downtime. The customer…knows that there is a…company called Caterpillar. But the dealers create the image of a company that doesn't just stand behind its products but with its products, anywhere in the world. Our dealers are the reason that our motto—"Buy the Iron, Get the Company"—is not an empty slogan.

Caterpillar's dealers build strong customer relationships in their communities. "Our independent dealer in Novi, Michigan, or in Bangkok, Thailand, knows so much more about the requirements of customers in those locations than a huge corporation like Caterpillar could," says Fites. Competitors often bypass their dealers and sell directly to big customers to cut costs or make more profits for themselves. However, Caterpillar wouldn't think of going around its dealers. "The knowledge of the local market and the close relations with customers that our dealers provide are worth every penny," Frites asserts with passion. "We'd rather cut off our right arm than sell directly to customers and bypass our dealers."

Caterpillar and its dealers work in close harmony to find better ways to bring value to customers. A single worldwide computer network links the entire system. For example, working at their desktop computers, Caterpillar managers can check to see how many Cat machines in the world are waiting for parts. Closely linked dealers play a vital role in almost every aspect of Caterpillar's operations, from product design and delivery, to product service and support, to market intelligence and customer feedback.

In the heavy-equipment industry, in which equipment downtime can mean big losses, Caterpillar's exceptional service gives it a huge advantage in winning and keeping customers. Consider Freeport-McMoRan, a Cat customer that operates one of the world's largest copper and gold mines, 24 hours a day, 365 days a year. High in the mountains of Indonesia, the mine is accessible only by aerial cableway or helicopter. Freeport-McMoRan relies on more than 500 pieces of Caterpillar mining and construction equipment—worth several hundred million dollars—including loaders, tractors, and mammoth 240-tonne, 2000-plus-horsepower trucks. Many of these machines cost more than $1 million apiece. When equipment breaks down, Freeport-McMoRan loses money fast. Freeport-McMoRan gladly pays a premium price for machines and service it can count on. It knows that it can count on Caterpillar and its outstanding distribution network for superb support.

The close working relationship between Caterpillar and its dealers comes down to more than just formal contracts and business agreements. The powerful partnership rests on a handful of basic principles and practices:

- *Dealer profitability:* Caterpillar's rule: "Share the gain as well as the pain." When times are good, Caterpillar shares the bounty with its dealers rather than trying to grab all the riches for itself. When times are bad, Caterpillar protects its dealers. In the mid-1980s, facing a depressed global construction-equipment market and cutthroat competition, Caterpillar sheltered its dealers by absorbing much of the economic damage. It lost almost $1 billion dollars in just three years but didn't lose a single dealer. In contrast, competitors' dealers struggled and many failed. As a result, Caterpillar emerged with its distribution system intact and its competitive position stronger than ever.

- *Extraordinary dealer support:* Nowhere is this support more apparent than in the company's parts delivery system, the fastest and most reliable in the industry. Caterpillar

maintains 36 distribution centres and 1500 service facilities around the world, which stock 320 000 different parts and ship 84 000 items per day, every day of the year. In turn, dealers have made huge investments in inventory, warehouses, fleets of trucks, service bays, diagnostic and service equipment, and information technology. Together, Caterpillar and its dealers guarantee parts delivery within 48 hours anywhere in the world. The company ships 80 percent of parts orders immediately and 99 percent on the same day the order is received. In contrast, it's not unusual for competitors' customers to wait four or five days for a part.

- *Communications:* Caterpillar communicates with its dealers—fully, frequently, and honestly. According to Fites, "There are no secrets between us and our dealers. We have the financial statements and key operating data of every dealer in the world.... In addition, virtually all Caterpillar and dealer employees have real-time access to continually updated databases of service information, sales trends and forecasts, customer satisfaction surveys, and other critical data.... [Moreover,] virtually everyone from the youngest design engineer to the CEO now has direct contact with somebody in our dealer organizations."

- *Dealer performance:* Caterpillar does all it can to ensure that its dealerships are run well. It closely monitors each dealership's sales, market position, service capability, financial situation, and other performance measures. It genuinely wants each dealer to succeed, and when it sees a problem, it jumps in to help. As a result, Caterpillar dealerships, many of which are family businesses, tend to be stable and profitable. The average Caterpillar dealership has remained in the hands of the same family for more than

50 years. Some actually predate the 1925 merger that created Caterpillar.

- *Personal relationships:* In addition to more formal business ties, Cat forms close personal ties with its dealers in a kind of family relationship. Fites relates the following example: "When I see Chappy Chapman, a retired executive vice-president…, out on the golf course, he always asks about particular dealers or about their children, who may be running the business now. And every time I see those dealers, they inquire, 'How's Chappy?' That's the sort of relationship we have.…I consider the majority of dealers personal friends."

Thus, Caterpillar's superb distribution system serves as a major source of competitive advantage. The system is built on a firm base of mutual trust and shared dreams. Caterpillar and its dealers feel a deep pride in what they are accomplishing together. As Fites puts it, "There's a camaraderie among our dealers around the world that really makes it more than just a financial arrangement. They feel that what they're doing is good for the world because they are part of an organization that makes, sells, and tends to the machines that make the world work."[1]

Marketing channel decisions are among the most important decisions that management faces. A company's channel decisions are linked with every other marketing decision. The company's pricing depends on whether it uses mass merchandisers or high-quality specialty stores. The firm's sales force and advertising decisions depend on how much persuasion, training, motivation, and support the dealers need. Whether a company develops or acquires certain new products may depend on how well those products fit the capabilities of its channel members.

Companies often pay too little attention to their distribution channels, however, sometimes with damaging results. In contrast, many companies have used imaginative distribution systems to gain a competitive advantage. FedEx's creative and imposing distribution system made it the leader in the small-package delivery industry. General Electric gained a strong advantage in selling its major appliances by supporting its dealers with a sophisticated computerized order-processing and delivery system. Dell Computer revolutionized its industry by selling personal computers directly to consumers rather than through retail stores. And Charles Schwab & Company pioneered the delivery of financial services via the Internet.

Distribution channel decisions often involve long-term commitments to other firms. For example, companies such as Ford, IBM, or McDonald's can easily change their advertising, pricing, or promotion programs. They can scrap old products and introduce new ones as market tastes demand. But when they set up distribution channels through contracts with franchisees, independent dealers, or large retailers, they cannot readily replace these channels with company-owned stores or Web sites if conditions change. Therefore, management must design its channels carefully, with an eye on tomorrow's likely selling environment as well as today's.

This chapter examines four major questions concerning distribution channels: What is the nature of distribution channels? How do channel firms interact and organize to do the work of the channel? What problems do companies face in designing and managing their channels? What role do physical distribution and supply chain management play in attracting and satisfying customers? In Chapter 12, we will look at distribution channel issues from the viewpoint of retailers and wholesalers.

THE NATURE OF DISTRIBUTION CHANNELS

Most producers use intermediaries to bring their products to market. They try to forge a distribution channel—a set of interdependent organizations involved in the process of making a product or service available for use or consumption by the consumer or business user.[2]

Distribution channel A set of interdependent organizations involved in the process of making a product or service available for use or consumption by the consumer or business user.

Why Are Marketing Intermediaries Used?

Why do producers give some of the selling job to intermediaries? After all, doing so means giving up some control over how and to whom the products are sold. The use of intermediaries results from their greater efficiency in making goods available to target markets. Through their contacts, experience, specialization, and scale of operation, intermediaries usually offer the firm more than it can achieve on its own.

Figure 11-1 shows how using intermediaries can provide economies. Figure 11-1A shows three manufacturers, each using direct marketing to reach three customers. This system requires nine different contacts. Figure 11-1B shows the three manufacturers working through one distributor, which contacts the three customers. This system requires only six contacts. In this way, intermediaries reduce the amount of work that must be done by both producers and consumers.

From the economic system's point of view, the role of marketing intermediaries is to transform the assortments of products made by producers into the assortments wanted by consumers. Producers make narrow assortments of products in large quantities, but consumers want broad assortments of products in small quantities. In the distribution channels, intermediaries buy large quantities from many producers and break them down into the smaller quantities and broader assortments wanted by consumers. Thus, intermediaries play an important role in matching supply and demand.

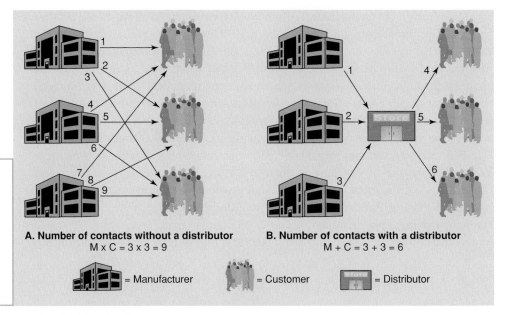

Figure 11-1

How Marketing Intermediaries Reduce the Number of Channel Transactions

A. Number of contacts without a distributor
M x C = 3 x 3 = 9

B. Number of contacts with a distributor
M + C = 3 + 3 = 6

= Manufacturer   = Customer   = Distributor

Distribution Channel Functions

The distribution channel moves goods and services from producers to consumers. It overcomes the major time, place, and possession gaps that separate goods and services from those who would use them. Members of the marketing channel perform many key functions. Some help to complete transactions:

• *Information:* Gathering and distributing marketing research and intelligence information about actors and forces in the marketing environment needed for planning and aiding exchange

• *Promotion:* Developing and spreading persuasive communications about an offer

• *Contact:* Finding and communicating with prospective buyers

• *Matching:* Shaping and fitting the offer to the buyer's needs, including activities such as manufacturing, grading, assembling, and packaging

• *Negotiation:* Reaching an agreement on price and other terms of the offer so that ownership or possession can be transferred

Others help to fulfill the completed transactions:

• *Physical distribution:* Transporting and storing goods

• *Financing:* Acquiring and using funds to cover the costs of the channel work

• *Risk taking:* Assuming the risks of carrying out the channel work

The question is not whether these functions need to be performed—they must be—but rather who will perform them. To the extent that the manufacturer performs these functions, its costs go up and its prices have to be higher. When some of these functions are shifted to intermediaries, the producer's costs and prices may be lower, but the intermediaries must charge more to cover the costs of their work. In dividing the work of the channel, the various functions should be assigned to the channel members who can perform them most efficiently and effectively to provide satisfactory assortments of goods to target consumers.

Number of Channel Levels

Distribution channels can be described by the number of channel levels involved. Each layer of marketing intermediaries that performs some work in bringing the product and its ownership closer to the final buyer is a **channel level**. Because the producer and the final consumer both perform some work, they are part of every channel. We use the number of intermediary levels to indicate the length of a channel. Figure 11-2A shows several consumer distribution channels of different lengths.

Channel 1, called a **direct marketing channel**, has no intermediary levels. It consists of a company selling directly to consumers. For example, Avon, Amway, and Tupperware sell their products door to door or through home and office sales parties; Singer sells its sewing machines through its own stores; and Dell sells computers direct through telephone selling and its Web site. The remaining channels in Figure 11-2A are **indirect marketing channels**. Channel 2 contains one intermediary level. In consumer markets, this level is typically a retailer. For example, the makers of televisions, cameras, tires, furniture, major appliances, and many other products sell their goods directly to large retailers such as Wal-Mart and Sears, which then sell the goods to final consumers. Channel 3 contains two intermediary levels, a wholesaler and a retailer. This channel is often used by small manufacturers of food, drugs, hardware, and other products. Channel 4 contains three intermediary levels. In the meatpacking industry, for example, jobbers buy from wholesalers and sell to smaller retailers who generally are not served by larger wholesalers. Distribution channels with even more levels are sometimes found, but less often. From the producer's point of view, a greater number of levels means less control and greater channel complexity.

Figure 11-2B shows some common business distribution channels. The business marketer can use its own sales force to sell directly to business customers. It can also sell to industrial distributors, who in turn sell to business customers. It can sell through manufacturer's representatives or its own sales branches to business customers, or it can use these representatives and branches to sell through industrial distributors. Thus, business markets commonly include multilevel distribution channels.

All the institutions in the channel are connected by several types of flows. These include the physical flow of products, the flow of ownership, the payment flow, the information flow, and the promotion flow. These flows can make even channels with only one or a few levels very complex.

Channel Behaviour and Organization

Distribution channels are more than simple collections of firms tied together by various flows. They are complex behavioural systems in which people and companies interact to accomplish individual, company, and channel goals. Some channel systems consist only of informal interactions among loosely organized firms; others consist of formal interactions guided by strong organizational structures.

Channel level A layer of intermediaries that performs some work in bringing the product and its ownership closer to the final buyer.

Direct marketing channel A marketing channel that has no intermediary levels.

Indirect marketing channel Channel containing one or more intermediary levels.

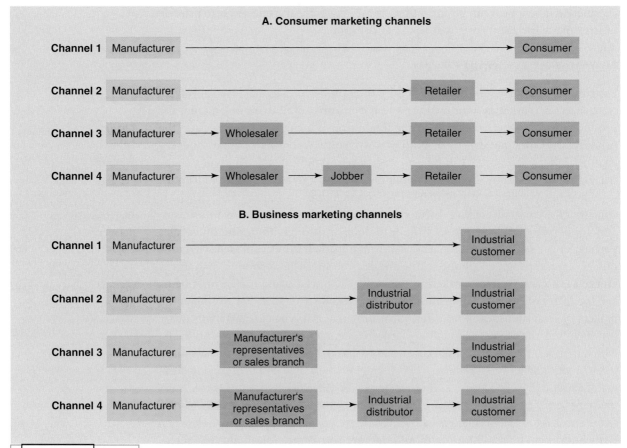

Figure 11-2

Consumer and Business Marketing Channels

Moreover, channel systems do not stand still—new types of intermediaries emerge and completely new channel systems evolve. Here we look at channel behaviour and at how members organize to do the work of the channel.

Channel Behaviour

A distribution channel comprises firms that have banded together for their common good. Each channel member depends on the others. For example, a Ford dealer depends on the Ford Motor Company to design cars that meet consumer needs. In turn, Ford depends on the dealer to attract consumers, persuade them to buy Ford cars, and service cars after the sale. The Ford dealer also depends on other dealers to provide good sales and service that will uphold the reputation of Ford and its dealer body. In fact, the success of individual Ford dealers depends on how well the entire Ford distribution channel competes with the channels of other auto manufacturers.

Each channel member plays a role in the channel and specializes in performing one or more functions. For example, IBM's role is to produce personal computers that consumers will like and to create demand through national advertising. Future Shop's role is to display these IBM computers in convenient locations, to answer buyers' questions, and to close sales. The channel will be most effective when each member is assigned the tasks it can do best.

Ideally, because the success of individual channel members depends on overall channel success, all channel firms should work together smoothly. They should understand and accept their roles, coordinate their goals and activities, and cooperate to attain overall channel goals. By cooperating, they can more effectively sense, serve, and satisfy the target market.

However, individual channel members rarely take such a broad view. They are usually more concerned with their own short-run goals and their dealings with those firms closest to them in the channel. Cooperating to achieve overall channel goals sometimes means giving up individual company goals. Although channel members are dependent on one another, they often act alone in their own short-run best interests. They often disagree on the roles each should play—on who should do what and for what rewards. Such disagreements over goals and roles generate **channel conflict**.

Horizontal conflict occurs among firms at the same level of the channel. For instance, some Ford dealers might complain about other dealers in the city who steal sales from them by being too aggressive in their pricing and advertising or by selling outside their assigned territories. Or Pizza Hut franchisees might complain about other Pizza Hut cheating on ingredients, giving poor service, and hurting the overall Pizza Hut image.

Vertical conflict, conflict among different levels of the same channel, is even more common. A recent instance took place when dealerships decided to wage war on Ford Canada:[3]

Car dealerships are among Canada's largest small businesses. Their dilemma: They depend on a single supplier for their inventory, and minor disputes are frequent. However, in an unprecedented letter written in March 2000 sent to all Ford dealers in Canada, the president of the Canadian Automobile Dealers Association lashed out at Ford Canada for its "unilateral, autocratic and confrontational" actions that pose a "threat to the Canadian dealer network." The letter was written as a result of dealer complaints that arose as a result of Ford Canada's new retail strategy called Ford Retail Networks (FRN). Ford wants to limit dealer autonomy and institute more customer-friendly sales tactics such as single-price selling. To accomplish this, Ford Canada hopes to become a 40 percent shareholder in the dealers' operations. Dealers believe they are being forced to sell out to Ford as a result of "punitive performance contracts," and as a result, dialogue between Ford and its retailers has broken down.

Some conflict in the channel takes the form of healthy competition. Such competition can be good for the channel—without it, the channel could become passive and noninnovative. But sometimes conflict can damage the channel.

If it gets out of hand, conflict can disrupt channel effectiveness and cause lasting harm to channel relationships. For the channel as a whole to perform well, each channel member's role must be specified and channel conflict must be managed. Cooperation, role assignment, and conflict management in the channel are attained through strong channel leadership. The channel will perform better if it includes a firm, agency, or mechanism that has the power to assign roles and manage conflict.

Channel conflict
Disagreement among marketing channel members on goals and roles—who should do what and for what rewards

Vertical Marketing Systems

Historically, distribution channels have been loose collections of independent companies, each showing little concern for overall channel performance. These conventional distribution channels have lacked strong leadership and have been troubled by damaging conflict and poor performance. One of the biggest channel developments has been the vertical marketing systems that have emerged over the years to challenge conventional marketing channels. Figure 11-3 contrasts the two types of channel arrangements.

A **conventional distribution channel** consists of one or more independent producers, wholesalers, and retailers. Each is a separate business seeking to maximize its own profits, even at the expense of profits for the system as a whole. No channel member has much control over the other members, and no formal means exists for assigning roles and resolving channel conflict. In contrast, a **vertical marketing system** (**VMS**) consists of producers, wholesalers, and retailers acting as a unified system. One channel member owns the others, has contracts with them, or wields so much power that they must all cooperate. The VMS can be dominated by the producer, wholesaler, or retailer. Vertical marketing systems were developed to control channel behaviour and manage channel conflict. For example, Sears buys more than 50 percent of its goods from companies that it partly or wholly owns. Bell markets telephones and related equipment through its own chain of Bell World stores. George Weston Inc., owner of Loblaws, operates a soft-drink bottling operation, an ice-cream-making plant, and a bakery that supplies stores with everything from bagels to birthday cakes.

Franchises are special types of vertical marketing systems that link several stages in the production–distribution process. Canada has more than 65 000 franchise operations (four times more per capita than the United States) that ring up more than $90 billion in sales annually. In fact, 40 percent of every dollar spent on retail items is spent at a franchise.[4] Almost every kind of business has been fran-

Conventional distribution channel A channel consisting of one or more independent producers, wholesalers, and retailers, each a separate business seeking to maximize its own profits even at the expense of profits for the system as a whole.

Vertical marketing system (VMS) A distribution channel structure in which producers, wholesalers, and retailers act as a unified system. One channel member owns the others, has contracts with them, or has so much power that they all cooperate.

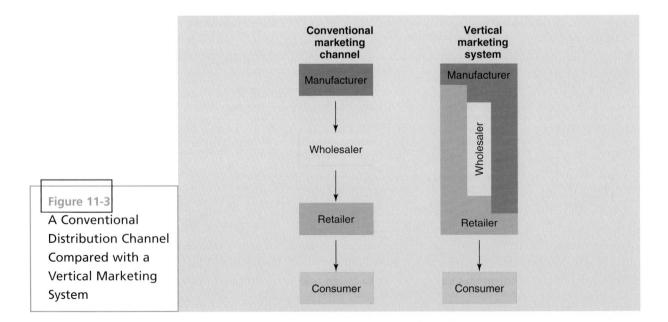

Figure 11-3

A Conventional Distribution Channel Compared with a Vertical Marketing System

chised—from motels and fast-food restaurants to dental centres and dating services, from wedding consultants and maid services to funeral homes and fitness centres.

Horizontal Marketing Systems

Another channel development is the **horizontal marketing system**, in which two or more companies at one level join together to follow a new marketing opportunity. By working together, companies can combine their capital, production capabilities, or marketing resources to accomplish more than any one company could alone. Companies might join forces with competitors or noncompetitors. They might work with each other temporarily or permanently, or they may create a separate company. Such channel arrangements also work well globally. Canada's two largest wineries, T.G. Bright & Co. Ltd. and Cartier & Inniskillin Vintners Inc., once major competitors, have merged. Together they have sales in excess of $130 million, placing them in the top 10 of North American wine marketers. Given the strength and size of large American vintners, the two formed an alliance so that they could have the economies of scale and resources necessary to export into the U.S. market.

Horizontal marketing system A channel arrangement in which two or more companies at one level join together to follow a new marketing opportunity

Forming successful horizontal marketing systems is essential in an era of global business and global travel. Air Canada is part of the Star Alliance, whose partners include United Airlines, Lufthansa, SAS, and Thai Airways International. It battles other alliances such as the one formed by American Airlines, British Airways, Japan Airlines, and Qantas. This partnership allows Air Canada to offer flights to 642 U.S. cities. It can also link the routes that the different partners fly so that passengers can have seamless travel around the world. Air Canada benefits from the marketing efforts of its partners in their home countries and bookings they make for travellers coming to Canada. These alliances improve customer satisfaction since they ensure passengers have shorter layovers, more convenient connections, and less hassle transferring their baggage.[5]

Hybrid Marketing Systems

In the past, many companies used a single channel to sell to a single market or market segment. Today, with the proliferation of customer segments and channel possibilities, more and more companies have adopted multichannel distribution systems—often called **hybrid marketing channels**. Such multichannel marketing occurs when a single firm sets up two or more marketing channels to reach one or more customer segments. The use of hybrid channel systems has recently increased significantly.

Figure 11-4 shows a hybrid channel. In the figure, the producer sells directly to consumer segment 1 using direct-mail catalogues, telemarketing, and the Internet and reaches consumer segment 2 through retailers. It sells indirectly to business segment 1 through distributors and dealers and to business segment 2 through its own sales force.

IBM uses such a hybrid channel effectively. For years, IBM sold computers only through its own sales force, which sold its large systems to business customers. However, the market for computers and information technology has now exploded into a profusion of products and services for dozens of segments and niches, ranging from large corporate buyers to small businesses to home and home office buyers. As a result, IBM has had to dramatically rethink the way it goes to market. To serve the diverse needs of the many segments, IBM added 18 new channels in fewer than 10 years. For example, in addition to selling through the vaunted IBM sales force, IBM also sells through a comprehensive network of distributors and value-added resellers, which sell IBM computers, systems, and services to a variety of special business segments. Final customers can buy IBM personal computers from specialty computer stores or any of several large retailers, including Wal-Mart, Circuit City, and Office Depot. IBM uses telemarketing to service the needs of small and medium-size business. And both business and final consumers can buy online from the company's IBM Store Web site.

Hybrid marketing channel Multichannel distribution system in which a single firm sets up two or more marketing channels to reach one or more customer segments

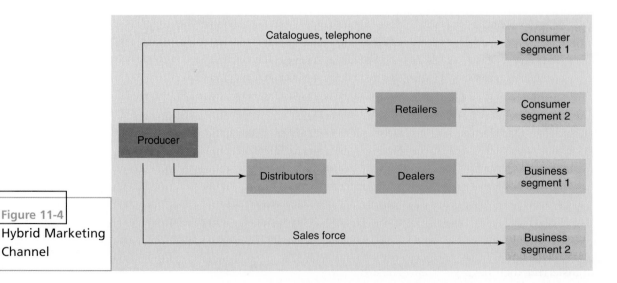

Figure 11-4
Hybrid Marketing Channel

Hybrid channels offer many advantages to companies facing large and complex markets. With each new channel, the company expands its sales and market coverage and gains opportunities to tailor its products and services to the specific needs of diverse customer segments. But such hybrid channel systems are harder to control, and they generate conflict as more channels compete for customers and sales. For example, when IBM began selling directly to customers through catalogues, telemarketing, and its own Web site, many of its retail dealers cried "unfair competition" and threatened to drop the IBM line or to give it less emphasis. Many outside salespeople felt that they were being undercut by the new "inside channels."

The IBM Store
www.can.ibm.com/store

Changing Channel Organization

Changes in technology and the explosive growth of direct and online marketing are having a profound impact on the nature and design of marketing channels. One major trend is toward **disintermediation**—a big term with a clear message and important consequences. Disintermediation means that more and more product and service producers are bypassing intermediaries and going directly to final buyers, or that radically new types of channel intermediaries are emerging to displace traditional ones.

Disintermediation The displacement of traditional resellers from a marketing channel by radical new types of intermediaries or by product and service producers going directly to final buyers.

Thus, in many industries, traditional intermediaries are dropping by the wayside. For example, companies such as Dell Computer and Westjet are selling directly to final buyers, eliminating retailers from their marketing channels. E-commerce is growing rapidly, taking business from traditional brick-and-mortar retailers. Consumers can buy books, videos, CDs, toys, consumer electronics, and other goods from Chapters/Indigo, clothes from Danier Leather or Roots, and groceries from Grocery Gateway all without ever visiting a store.

Disintermediation presents problems and opportunities for both producers and intermediaries (see New Directions 11-1). To avoid being swept aside, traditional intermediaries must find new ways to add value in the supply chain. To

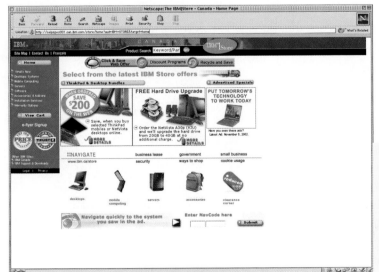

Hybrid channels: In addition to its sales force, IBM sells through distributors and value-added resellers, specialty computer stores and large retailers, telemarketing, and its IBM Store Web site.

New Directions 11-1 >> Disintermediation: A Fancy Word but a Clear Message

Bayridge Travel in Kingston, Ontario, typifies the kind of business most threatened by the advent of new marketing channels, particularly the surge in Internet selling. They fear travellers such as Canada's Internet guru Jim Carroll, who notes that, "In the last two years, I've bought some $75 000 worth of airline tickets on the Internet....By doing so directly through the Web sites of various airlines, I've cut travel agents out of several thousand dollars worth of commissions."

Thus, like other traditional travel agencies, Bayridge faces some scary new competitors: giant online travel supersites such as Expedia and Travelocity, which let consumers surf the Web for rock-bottom ticket prices. To make matters worse, the airlines themselves are opening Web sites to sell seats, not only their own, but also their competitors' seats as well. For example, visitors to the United Airlines Web site can purchase tickets on more than 500 other airlines. These new channels give consumers more choices, but they threaten the very existence of Bayridge Travel and other traditional travel agents.

Resellers in dozens of industries face similar situations as new channel forms threaten to make them obsolete. There's even a fancy 17-letter word to describe this phenomenon: *disintermediation*.

Bob Westrope, director of the electronic markets group with KPMG in Toronto, believes that disintermediation represents "a shift in the structure of our economy not seen since the dawning of the industrial age." Strictly speaking, disintermediation means the elimination of a layer of intermediaries from a marketing channel. For example, for years personal computer makers assumed that customers needed a hands-on buying experience, with lots of point-of-sale inventory and handholding sales assistance from retailers. Then, along came Dell Computer with a new distribution formula: Bypass retailers and sell made-to-order computers directly to consumers. By eliminating retailers, Dell eliminated many costs and inefficiencies from the traditional computer supply chain.

More broadly, disintermediation includes not just the elimination of channel levels through direct mar-

keting, but also the displacement of traditional resellers by radically new types of intermediaries. For example, the publishing industry had for decades assumed that book buyers wanted to purchase their books from small, intimate neighbourhood bookshops. Then, along came the book superstores— Indigo and Chapters—with their huge inventories and low prices. Disintermediation occurred as the new intermediaries rapidly displaced traditional independent booksellers. Then, most recently, Amazon.ca and the superstores' own Web sites began displacing traditional bricks-and-mortar retailers.

Disintermediation is often associated with the surge in e-commerce and online selling. In fact, the Internet is a major disintermediating force. By facilitating direct contact between buyers and sellers, the Internet is displacing channels in industries ranging from books, apparel, toys, drugs, and consumer electronics to travel, stock brokerage, and real estate services. However, disintermediation can involve almost any new form of channel competition. For example, Dell bypassed retailers through telephone and mail-order selling long before it took to the Internet.

Disintermediation works only when a new channel form succeeds in bringing greater value to consumers. Thus, if Indigo.ca weren't giving buyers greater convenience, selection, and value, it would not be able to lure customers away from traditional retailers. If Dell's direct channel weren't more efficient and effective in serving the needs of computer buyers, traditional retail channels would have little to fear. However, the huge success of these new channels suggests that they are bringing greater value to significant segments of consumers.

From a producer's viewpoint, even though eliminating unneeded intermediaries makes sense, disintermediation can be very difficult. One analyst summarizes this way:

> You thought electronic commerce would bring nothing but good news. Here at last, you reasoned, is a way to add customers, boost market share, and cut sales costs. All manufacturers have to do is set up an electronic conduit between themselves and their customers and

voilà, instant sales channel. There's just one little hitch. Those same thoughts terrify the retailers, distributors, and resellers that account for up to 90 percent of manufacturers' revenues. They fear that their role between company and customer will be rendered obsolete by the virtual marketplace. And that puts manufacturers in a bind. Either they surrender to the seductions of e-commerce and risk a mutiny from those valuable partners, or they do nothing and risk the wrath of [successful e-commerce competitors].

Dell had the advantage of starting from scratch in designing its direct channel—it didn't have to jump from one channel model to another. However, IBM and other computer producers that are already locked into traditional retail channels, disintermediation presents real problems. To compete more effectively with Dell, both Compaq (before its acquisition by Hewlett-Packard) and IBM had developed their own direct sales operations. For instance, Compaq shifted its ratio of traditional channel sales to direct sales from 98 to 2 about a year ago year ago to about 80 to 20 today, angering their channel partners. For many businesses, the major question often is not whether to move to a new, high-growth channel but how quickly and what to do with the established channels. Thus, despite the risks, most companies know that when more effective channels come along, they have no choice but to change. There is a Dell at work or in waiting in every industry, and traditional producers can't afford to wait very long to get inefficiencies out of their distribution channels.

What about traditional resellers? How can they avoid being shut-out? The answer lies in continually looking for new ways to create real customer value. Many companies threatened by Internet competitors have learned to leverage the Web to serve customers better. For example, Bayridge Travel now deemphasizes airline ticket sales and specializes in a market niche: cruises. The owner plans to do what comput-

ers can't: She will get to know her customers so well that she can provide personal advice on the cruises she books. Still, she'll use a Web site to launch this newly reformulated travel business.

Discount brokerage Charles Schwab & Company also proves the value point. Facing a horde of price-cutting e-commerce competitors who got there first—including E*Trade—Schwab jumped onto the Internet with both feet. However, instead of becoming just another no-frills Internet trading operation, Schwab has done competitors one better. It plies customers with a wealth of financial and company information, helping them to research and manage their accounts and assuming the role of investment advisor. Schwab is even teaching courses on Web trading at some of its 300 branches. Thus, rather than dragging its feet or fighting the change, Schwab embraced the new channel as a competitive opportunity. The gamble paid off handsomely. Schwab remains North America's largest discount stockbroker and ranks number one online with a 28 percent share of the online market, twice the share of nearest competitor E*Trade.

Disintermediation is a big word, but the meaning is clear. Those who continually seek new ways to add real value for customers have little to fear; those who fall behind in adding value risk being swept aside by their customers and channel partners.

Sources: Quotes from Jim Carroll, "Futures: When Old Partners Become New Competitors," *Marketing On-Line,* 22 November 1999; Rochelle Garner, "Mad as Hell," *Sales & Marketing Management,* June 1999, pp. 55–61; and Maricris G. Briones, "What Technology Wrought: Distribution Channel in Flux," *Marketing News,* 1 February 1999, pp. 3, 15. Also see "Special Report: Technology and Communications Tools for Marketers: Disintermediation: No More Middleman," *Strategy,* 1 March 1999, p. 21; Evan I. Schwartz, "How Middlemen Can Come out on Top," *Business Week,* 9 February 1998, p. ENT4-7; James Champy, "How to Fire Your Dealers," *Forbes,* 14 June 1999, p. 141; Stewart Alsop, "Is There an Amazon.com for Every Industry?" *Fortune,* 11 January 1999, pp. 159–160; and Daniel Roth, "E*Trade's Plan for World Domination," *Fortune,* 2 August 1999, pp. 95-98.

remain competitive, product and service producers must develop new channel opportunities, such as Internet and other direct channels. However, developing these new channels often brings them into direct competition with their established channels, resulting in conflict. To ease this problem, companies often look for ways to make going direct work for both the company and its channel partners.

Going direct is rarely an all-or-nothing proposition. For example, to trim costs, add business, and maintain some separability among products following the acquisition of Compaq computers, Hewlett-Packard in Canada segregated its Web site into customer groupings by product. For example, to avoid conflicts with its established reseller channels, H-P forwards all its Web orders to resellers, who complete the orders, ship the products, and get the commissions. In this way, H-P gains the advantages of direct selling but also boosts business for resellers. However, the Web site directs customers interested in Compaq computers to the Compaq Shop Online Site, where they can place an order directly without the intermediary partner's involvement.

Although this compromise system reduces conflicts, it also creates inefficiencies. "That all sounds great and everyone's happy," says a distribution consultant, "but kicking the customer over to the reseller…is a lot more expensive than letting customers order directly from the manufacturer. H-P is spending a fair chunk of change to set this up, plus the business partner still wants eight percent margins for getting the product to the customer."[6] To be truly efficient in the long run, H-P eventually will have to find ways for its resellers to add value or it will have to drop them from the direct channel.

Stop here for a moment and apply the distribution channel concepts we've discussed so far.

- Compare the Caterpillar and IBM channels. Draw a diagram that shows the types of intermediaries in each channel. What kind of channel system does each company use?
- What are the roles and responsibilities of the members in each channel? How well do these channel members work together toward overall channel success?

CHANNEL DESIGN DECISIONS

We now look at several channel decisions that manufacturers face. In designing marketing channels, manufacturers struggle between what is ideal and what is practical. A new firm with limited capital usually starts by selling in a limited market area. Deciding on the best channels might not be a problem; the problem might simply be how to convince one or a few good intermediaries to handle the line.

If successful, the new firm might branch out to new markets through existing intermediaries. In smaller markets, the firm might sell directly to retailers; in larger markets, it might sell through distributors. In one part of the country, it might grant exclusive franchises; in another, it might sell through all available outlets. Then, it might add a Web store that sells directly to hard-to-reach customers. In this way, channel systems often evolve to meet market opportunities and conditions. However, for maximum effectiveness, channel analysis and decision making should be more purposeful. Designing a channel system calls for analyzing consumer service needs, setting channel objectives and constraints, identifying major channel alternatives, and evaluating them.

Analyzing Consumer Service Needs

As noted previously, marketing channels can be thought of as customer value delivery systems in which each channel member adds value for the customer. Thus, designing the distribution channel starts with finding out what targeted consumers want from the channel. Do consumers want to buy from nearby locations or are they willing to travel to more distant centralized locations? Would they rather buy in person, over the phone, through the mail, or via the Internet? Do they value breadth of assortment or do they prefer specialization? Do consumers want many add-on services (delivery, credit, repairs, installation), or will they obtain these elsewhere? The faster the delivery, the greater the assortment provided, and the more add-on services supplied, the greater the channel's service level.

But providing the fastest delivery, greatest assortment, and most services may not be possible or practical. The company and its channel members may not have the resources or skills needed to provide all the desired services. Also, providing higher levels of service results in higher costs for the channel and higher prices for consumers. The company must balance consumer service needs not only against the feasibility and costs of meeting these needs, but also against customer price preferences. The success of off-price and discount retailing shows that consumers are often willing to accept lower service levels if this means lower prices.

Setting Channel Objectives and Constraints

Channel objectives should be stated in terms of the desired service level of target consumers. Usually, a company can identify several segments wanting different levels of channel service. The company should decide which segments to serve and the best channels to use in each case. In each segment, the company wants to minimize the total channel cost of meeting customer service requirements.

The company's channel objectives are also influenced by the nature of the company, its products, its marketing intermediaries, its competitors, and the environment. For example, the company's size and financial situation determine which marketing functions it can handle itself and which it must give to intermediaries. Companies selling perishable products may require more direct marketing to avoid delays and too much handling. In some cases, a company may want to compete in or near outlets that carry competitors' products. In other cases, producers may avoid the channels used by competitors. Avon, for example, uses door-to-door selling rather than going head to head with other cosmetics makers for scarce positions in retail stores. And Edwards Jones makes house calls seeking clients for its financial services, thus demystifying the aura of traditional stock brokerage firms. Finally, environmental factors such as economic conditions and legal constraints may affect channel objectives and design. For example, in a depressed economy, producers want to distribute their goods in the most economical way, using shorter channels and dropping unneeded services that add to the final price of the goods.

Product characteristics affect channel decisions: Fresh flowers must be delivered quickly, with a minimum of handling.

Identifying Major Alternatives

When the company has defined its channel objectives, it should next identify its major channel alternatives in terms of types of intermediaries, the number of intermediaries, and the responsibilities of each channel member.

Types of Intermediaries   A firm should identify the types of channel members available to carry out its channel work. For example, suppose a manufacturer of test equipment has developed an audio device that detects poor mechanical connections in machines with moving parts. Company executives think this product would have a market in all industries in which electric, combustion, or steam engines are made or used. The company's current sales force is small, and the problem is how best to reach these different industries. The following channel alternatives might emerge from management discussion:

- *Company sales force:* Expand the company's direct sales force. Assign outside salespeople to territories and have them contact all prospects in the area or develop separate company sales forces for different industries. Or, add an inside telesales operation in which telephone salespeople handle small or mid-size companies.

- *Manufacturer's agency:* Hire manufacturer's agents—independent firms whose sales forces handle related products from many companies—in different regions or industries to sell the new test equipment.

- *Industrial distributors:* Find distributors in the different regions or industries who will buy and carry the new line. Give them exclusive distribution, good margins, product training, and promotional support.

Number of Marketing Intermediaries   Companies must also determine the number of channel members to use at each level. Three strategies are available: intensive distribution, exclusive distribution, and selective distribution.

Producers of convenience products and common raw materials typically seek **intensive distribution**—a strategy in which they stock their products in as many outlets as possible. These goods must be available where and when consumers want them. For example, toothpaste, candy, and other similar items are sold in millions of outlets to provide maximum brand exposure and consumer convenience. Kraft, Coca-Cola, Kimberly-Clark, and other consumer goods companies distribute their products in this way.

By contrast, some producers purposely limit the number of intermediaries handling their products. The extreme form of this practice is **exclusive distribution**, in which the producer gives only a limited number of dealers the exclusive right to distribute its products in their territories. Exclusive distribution is often found in the distribution of new automobiles and prestige women's clothing. For example, Rolls-Royce dealers are rare—even large cities may have only one or two dealers. By granting exclusive distribution, Rolls-Royce gains stronger distributor selling support and more control over dealer prices, promotion, credit, and services. Exclusive distribution also enhances the car's image and allows for higher markups.

Between intensive and exclusive distribution lies **selective distribution**—the use of more than one, but fewer than all, of the intermediaries who are willing to carry a company's products. Most television, furniture, and small-appliance brands are distributed in this manner. For example, Maytag, Whirlpool, and General Electric sell their major appliances through dealer networks and selected large retailers. By using selective distribution, they do not have to spread their efforts over many outlets, including many marginal ones. They can develop good working relationships with selected channel members and expect a better-than-average selling effort. Selective distribution gives producers good market coverage with more control and less cost than does intensive distribution.

Responsibilities of Channel Members The producer and intermediaries need to agree on the terms and responsibilities of each channel member. They should agree on price policies, conditions of sale, territorial rights, and specific services to be performed by each party. The producer should establish a list price and a fair set

Intensive distribution
Stocking the product in as many outlets as possible.

Exclusive distribution
Giving a limited number of dealers the exclusive right to distribute the company's products in their territories.

Selective distribution The use of more than one, but fewer than all, of the intermediaries who are willing to carry the company's products.

Exclusive distribution: Luxury car makers sell exclusively through a limited number of dealerships. Such limited distribution enhances the car's image and generates stronger dealership support.

of discounts for intermediaries. It must define each channel member's territory, and it should be careful about where it places new resellers. Mutual services and duties need to be spelled out carefully, especially in franchise and exclusive distribution channels. For example, McDonald's provides franchisees with promotional support, a record-keeping system, training at Hamburger University, and general management assistance. In turn, franchisees must meet company standards for physical facilities, cooperate with new promotion programs, provide requested information, and buy specified food products.

Evaluating the Major Alternatives

Suppose a company has identified several channel alternatives and wants to select the one that will best satisfy its long-run objectives. Each alternative should be evaluated against economic, control, and adaptive criteria.

Using *economic criteria*, a company compares the likely profitability of different channel alternatives. It estimates the sales that each channel would produce and the costs of selling different volumes through each channel. The company must also consider *control issues*. Using intermediaries usually means giving them some control over the marketing of the product, and some intermediaries take more control than others. Other things being equal, the company prefers to keep as much control as possible. Finally, the company must apply *adaptive criteria*. Channels often involve long-term commitments to other firms, making it hard to adapt the channel to the changing marketing environment. The company wants to keep the channel as flexible as possible. Thus, to be considered, a channel involving long-term commitment should be greatly superior on economic and control grounds.

Designing International Distribution Channels

International marketers face many additional complexities in designing their channels. Each country has its own unique distribution system that has evolved over time and changes very slowly. These channel systems can vary widely from country to country. Thus, global marketers must usually adapt their channel strategies to the existing structures within each country. In some markets, the distribution system is complex and hard to penetrate, consisting of many layers and large numbers of intermediaries. Consider Japan:

The Japanese distribution system stems from the early seventeenth century when cottage industries and a [quickly growing] urban population spawned a merchant class....Despite Japan's economic achievements, the distribution system has remained remarkably faithful to its antique pattern....[It] encompasses a wide range of wholesalers and other agents, brokers, and retailers, differing more in number than in function from their American counterparts. There are myriad tiny retail shops. An even greater number of wholesalers supplies goods to them, layered tier upon tier, many more than most North American executives would think necessary. For example, soap may move through three wholesalers plus a sales company after it leaves the manufacturer before it ever reaches the retail outlet. A steak goes from rancher to consumers in a process that often involves a dozen middle agents....The distribution network...reflects the traditionally close ties among many Japanese companies...[and places] much greater emphasis on personal relationships with users....Although [these channels appear] inefficient and cumbersome, they seem to serve the Japanese customer well....Lacking much storage space in their small homes, most Japanese homemakers shop several times a week and prefer convenient [and more personal] neighborhood shops.[7]

Many Western firms have had great difficulty breaking into the closely knit, tradition-bound Japanese distribution network.

At the other extreme, distribution systems in developing countries may be scattered and inefficient, or altogether lacking. For example, China and India appear to be huge markets, each with populations in the hundreds of millions. In reality, however, these markets are much smaller than the population numbers suggest. Because of inadequate distribution systems in both countries, most companies can profitably access only a small portion of the population located in each country's most affluent cities.[8]

Thus, international marketers face a wide range of channel alternatives. Designing efficient and effective channel systems between and within country markets poses a difficult challenge. We discuss international distribution decisions further in Chapter 15.

The Japanese distribution system is remarkably traditional: A profusion of tiny retail shops is supplied by an even greater number of small wholesalers.

CHANNEL MANAGEMENT DECISIONS

Once the company has reviewed its channel alternatives and decided on the best channel design, it must implement and manage the chosen channel. Channel management calls for selecting and motivating individual channel members and evaluating their performance over time.

Selecting Channel Members

Producers vary in their ability to attract qualified marketing intermediaries. Some producers have no trouble signing up channel members. For example, when Toyota first introduced its Lexus line, it had no trouble attracting new dealers. In fact, it had to turn down many would-be resellers. In some cases, the promise of exclusive or selective distribution for a desirable product will draw plenty of applicants.

Nintendo Canada
www.nintendo.ca

At the other extreme are producers who have to work hard to line up enough qualified intermediaries. For example, in 1986 when distributors were approached about an unknown, new game called Nintendo, many refused to carry the product: They had recently been burned by the failure of Atari. But two Canadian distributors, Larry Wasser and Morey Chaplick, owners of Beamscope, accepted the product. Not a bad move considering that within one year of that decision, their sales went from next to nothing to $24 million![9]

When selecting intermediaries, the company should determine what characteristics distinguish the better ones. It will want to evaluate each channel member's years in business, other lines carried, growth and profit record, cooperativeness, and reputation. If the intermediaries are sales agents, the company will want to evaluate the number and character of other lines carried and the size and quality of the sales force. If the intermediary is a retail store that wants exclusive or selective distribution, the company will want to evaluate the store's customers, location, and future growth potential.

Motivating Channel Members

Once selected, channel members must be continuously motivated to do their best. The company must sell not only through the intermediaries but to them. Most companies see their intermediaries as first-line customers. Some use the carrot-and-stick approach: At times they offer *positive* motivators such as higher margins, special deals, premiums, cooperative advertising allowances, display allowances, and sales contests. At other times they use *negative* motivators, such as threatening to reduce margins, to slow down delivery, or to end the relationship altogether. A producer using this approach usually has not done a good job of studying the needs, problems, strengths, and weaknesses of its distributors.

More advanced companies try to forge long-term partnerships with their channel partners to create a marketing system that meets the needs of both the manufacturer and the partners. In managing its channels, a company must convince distributors that they can succeed better by working together as a part of a cohesive value delivery system.[10] Thus, Procter & Gamble and Wal-Mart work together to create superior value for final consumers. They jointly plan merchandising goals and strategies, inventory levels, and advertising and promotion plans. Similarly, GE Appliances works closely with its independent dealers to help them be successful in selling the company's products (see New Directions 11-2).

Many companies are now developing *partner relationship management (PRM)* systems to coordinate their whole-channel marketing efforts. Here's how Hewlett-Packard does it:

With more than 20 000 channel partners selling everything from pocket calculators to computer networks, Hewlett-Packard's small business group faces a staggering coordination challenge. Something as simple as distributing sales leads collected through various H-P marketing campaigns—everything from business cards dropped in fish bowls at trade shows to requests for product information from H-P's Internet site—can be a daunting task. To manage these tasks, H-P set up an integrating partner relationship management (PRM) system, which links H-P directly with its channel partners and helps coordinate channelwide marketing efforts. Using a secure Web site, H-P channel partners can log on at any time to obtain leads that have been generated for them. They can also use the Web site to order literature and sales support materials, obtain product specifications and pricing information, and check their co-op funding. The PRM system not only provides strong support for channel partners, it improves their collective effectiveness and provides assessment feedback to H-P. Under the old system, says an H-P manager, "We would generate a mass-mailing campaign, send it off to who knows where, out it would go, and we'd hope it would work. Now we can generate a targeted campaign, see when the opportunities start coming back, and...the channel partner tells us what happened....It's changing the way we do campaigns."[11]

Evaluating Channel Members

The producer must regularly check channel member performance against standards such as sales quotas, average inventory levels, customer delivery time, treatment of damaged and lost goods, cooperation in company promotion and training programs, and services to the customer. The company should recognize and reward intermediaries who are performing well and adding good value for consumers. Those who are performing poorly should be assisted or, as a last resort, replaced. A company may periodically "requalify" its intermediaries and prune the weaker ones.

Finally, manufacturers need to be sensitive to their dealers. Those who treat their dealers poorly risk not only losing dealer support, but also causing some legal problems. The next section describes various rights and duties pertaining to manufacturers and their channel members.

New Directions 11-2 >>   General Electric Adopts a "Virtual Inventory" System to Support Its Dealers

Before the late 1980s, General Electric worked at selling through its dealers rather than to them or with them. GE operated a traditional system of trying to load up the channel with GE appliances, on the premise that "loaded dealers are loyal dealers." Loaded dealers would have less space to feature other brands and would recommend GE appliances to reduce their high inventories. To load its dealers, GE would offer the lowest price when the dealer ordered a full-truck load of its appliances.

GE eventually realized that this approach created many problems, especially for smaller independent appliance dealers who could not afford to carry a large amount of stock. These dealers were hard-pressed to meet price competition from larger multibrand dealers. Rethinking its strategy from the point of view of creating dealer satisfaction and profitability, GE created an alternative distribution model called the Direct Connect system. Under this system, GE dealers carry only display models. They rely on a "virtual inventory" to fill orders. Dealers can access GE's order-processing system 24 hours a day, check on model availability, and place orders for next-day delivery. Using the Direct Connect system, dealers also can get GE's best price, financing from GE Credit, and no interest charges for the first 90 days.

Dealers benefit by having much lower inventory costs while still having a large virtual inventory available to satisfy their customers' needs. In exchange for this benefit, dealers must commit to selling nine major GE product categories, generating 50 percent of their sales from GE products, opening their books to GE for review, and

paying GE every month through electronic funds transfer.

As a result of Direct Connect, dealer profit margins have skyrocketed. GE also has benefited. Its dealers now are more committed to and dependent on GE, and the new order-entry system has saved GE substantial clerical costs. GE now knows the actual sales of its goods at the retail level, which helps it to schedule its production more accurately. It now can produce in response to demand rather than to meet inventory replenishment rules. And GE has been able to simplify its warehouse locations so as to be able to deliver appliances to 90 percent of its customers within 24 hours. Thus, by forging a partnership, GE has helped both its dealers and itself.

Source: See Michael Treacy and Fred Wiersema, "Customer Intimacy and Other Discipline Values," *Harvard Business Review,* January-February 1993, pp. 84–93.

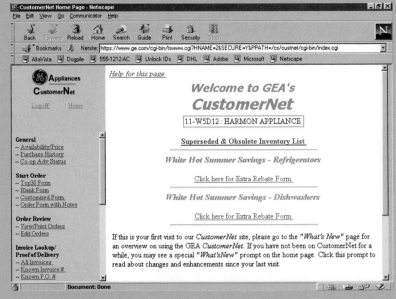

Using GE's Direct Connect system, dealers can access GE's order-processing system 24 hours a day, check on model availability, and place orders for next-day delivery.

Time for another rest stop. This time, compare the Caterpillar and GE Appliances channel systems.

- Diagram the Caterpillar and GE Appliances systems. How do they compare in terms of channel levels, types of intermediaries, channel member roles and responsibilities, and other characteristics. How well is each system designed?

- Assess how well Caterpillar and GE Appliances have managed and supported their channels. With what results?

PUBLIC POLICY AND DISTRIBUTION DECISIONS

For the most part, companies are legally free to develop whatever channel arrangements suit them. In fact, the laws affecting channels seek to prevent the exclusionary tactics of some companies that might keep another company from using a desired channel. Most channel law deals with the mutual rights and duties of the channel members once they have formed a relationship.

Many producers and wholesalers like to develop exclusive channels for their products. As you now know, when the seller allows only certain outlets to carry its products, this strategy is called exclusive distribution. When the seller requires that these dealers not handle competitors' products, its strategy is called *exclusive dealing*. Both parties can benefit from exclusive arrangements: The seller obtains more loyal and dependable outlets, and the dealers obtain a steady source of supply and stronger seller support. But exclusive arrangements also exclude other producers from selling to these dealers. This situation brings exclusive dealing contracts under the scope of the Competition Act. They are legal as long as they do not substantially lessen competition or create a monopoly and as long as both parties enter into the agreement voluntarily.

Exclusive dealing often includes *exclusive territorial agreements*. The producer may agree not to sell to other dealers in a given area, or the buyer may agree to sell only in its own territory. The first practice is normal under franchise systems as a way to increase dealer enthusiasm and commitment. It is also legal—a seller has no legal obligation to sell through more outlets than it wants. The second practice, whereby the producer tries to keep a dealer from selling outside its territory, has become a major legal issue.

Producers of a strong brand sometimes sell it to dealers only if the dealers will take some or all of the rest of the line. This is called full-line forcing. Such *tying agreements* are not necessarily illegal, but they do violate the Competition Act if they lessen competition substantially. The practice may prevent consumers from freely choosing among competing suppliers of these other brands.

Finally, producers are free to select their dealers, but their right to terminate dealers is somewhat restricted. In general, sellers can drop dealers "for cause." However, they cannot drop dealers if, for example, the dealers refuse to cooperate in a doubtful legal arrangement, such as exclusive dealing or tying agreements.[12]

MARKETING LOGISTICS AND SUPPLY CHAIN MANAGEMENT

In today's global marketplace, selling a product is sometimes easier than getting it to customers. Companies must decide on the best way to store, handle, and move their products and services so that they are available to customers in the right assortments, at the right time, and in the right place. Physical distribution and logistics effectiveness has a major impact on both customer satisfaction and company costs. Here we consider the nature and importance of logistics management in the supply chain, goals of the logistics system, major logistics functions, and the need for integrated supply chain management.

Nature and Importance of Marketing Logistics

To some managers, marketing logistics means only trucks and warehouses. But modern logistics is much more than this. **Marketing logistics**—also called **physical distribution**—involves planning, implementing, and controlling the physical flow of goods, services, and related information from points of origin to points of consumption to meet customer requirements at a profit. In short, it involves getting the right product to the right customer in the right place at the right time.

Traditional physical distribution typically started with products at the plant and then tried to find low-cost solutions to get them to customers. However, today's marketers prefer customer-centred logistics thinking, which starts with the marketplace and works backward to the factory, or even to sources of supply. Marketing logistics addresses not only *outbound distribution* (moving products from the factory to resellers and ultimately to customers) but also *inbound distribution* (moving products and materials from suppliers to the factory) and *reverse distribution* (moving broken, unwanted, or excess products returned by consumers or resellers). That is, it involves entire **supply chain management**—managing value-added flows of materials, final goods, and related information between suppliers, the company, resellers, and final users, as shown in Figure 11-5. Thus, the logistics manager's task is to coordinate activities of suppliers, purchasing agents, marketers, channel members, and customers. These activities include forecasting, information systems, purchasing, production planning, order processing, inventory, warehousing, and transportation planning.

Companies today place a lot of emphasis on logistics for several reasons. First, companies can gain a powerful competitive advantage by using improved logistics to give customers better service or lower prices. Second, improved logistics can yield tremendous cost savings to both the company and its customers. About 15

The Canadian Marketing Association
www.the-cma.org

Marketing logistics (physical distribution) The tasks involved in planning, implementing, and controlling the physical flow of materials, final goods, and related information from points of origin to points of consumption to meet customer requirements at a profit.

Supply chain management Managing value-added flows of materials, final goods, and related information between suppliers, the company, resellers, and final users.

Figure 11-5

Supply Chain Management

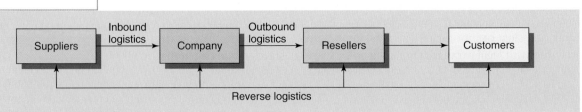

percent of an average product's price is accounted for by shipping and transport alone. Shaving off even a small fraction of these costs can mean substantial savings.

Third, the explosion in product variety has created a need for improved logistics management. For example, in 1911 the typical A&P grocery store carried only 270 items. The store manager could keep track of this inventory on about 10 pages of notebook paper stuffed in a shirt pocket. Today, the average A&P carries a bewildering stock of more than 16 700 items. Ordering, shipping, stocking, and controlling such a variety of products presents a sizable logistics challenge.

Finally, improvements in information technology have created opportunities for major gains in distribution efficiency. Using sophisticated supply chain management software, Web-based logistics systems, point-of-sale scanners, uniform product codes, satellite tracking, and electronic data interchange (EDI) and electronic funds transfer (EFT), companies can quickly and efficiently manage the flow of goods, information, and finances through the supply chain.

Goals of the Logistics System

Some companies state their logistics objective as providing maximum customer service at the least cost. Unfortunately, no logistics system can both maximize customer service and minimize distribution costs. Maximum customer service implies rapid delivery, large inventories, flexible assortments, liberal return policies, and other services—all of which raise distribution costs. In contrast, minimum distribution costs imply slower delivery, smaller inventories, and larger shipping lots— which represent a lower level of overall customer service.

The goal of marketing logistics should be to provide a targeted level of customer service at the least cost. A company must first research the importance of various distribution services to customers and then set desired service levels for each segment. The objective is to maximize profits, not sales. Therefore, the company must weigh the benefits of providing higher levels of service against the costs. Some companies offer less service than their competitors and charge a lower price. Other companies offer more service and charge higher prices to cover higher costs.

Major Logistics Functions

Given a set of logistics objectives, the company is ready to design a logistics system that will minimize the cost of attaining these objectives. The major logistics functions include order processing, warehousing, inventory management, and transportation.

Order Processing Orders can be submitted in many ways—through salespeople, by mail or telephone, via the Internet, or through electronic data interchange (EDI), the electronic exchange of data between companies. The company wants to design a simple, accessible, fast, and accurate process for capturing and processing orders. Both the company and its customers benefit when order processing is carried out quickly and efficiently.

In some cases, suppliers might actually be asked to generate orders and arrange deliveries for their customers. Many large retailers—such as Wal-Mart and Home Depot—work closely with major suppliers such as Procter & Gamble or Black &

Decker to set up *vendor-managed inventory (VMI) systems* (or collaborative planning, forecasting, and replenishment [CPFR] systems, if you're looking for an even fancier name).[13] Using VMI, the customer shares real-time data on sales and current inventory levels with the supplier. The supplier then takes full responsibility for managing inventories and deliveries. Some retailers even go so far as to shift inventory and delivery costs to the supplier. Such systems require close cooperation between the buyer and seller.

Warehousing Production and consumption cycles rarely match. So most companies must store their tangible goods while they wait to be sold. For example, Snapper, Toro, and other lawn mower manufacturers run their factories all year long and store up products for the heavy spring and summer buying seasons. The storage function overcomes differences in needed quantities and timing, ensuring that products are available when customers are ready to buy them.

A company must decide how many and what types of warehouses it needs and where they will be located. The company might use either storage warehouses or distribution centres. Storage warehouses store goods for moderate to long periods. **Distribution centres** are designed to move goods rather than just store them. They are large and highly automated warehouses designed to receive goods from various plants and suppliers, take orders, fill them efficiently, and deliver goods to customers as quickly as possible. For example, Wal-Mart operates a network of 62 huge U.S. distribution centres and another 37 around the globe. Almost 84 percent of the merchandise shipped to Wal-Mart stores is routed through one of its own distribution centres, giving Wal-Mart tremendous control over inventory management. One centre, which serves the daily needs of 165 Wal-Mart stores, contains some 11 hectares of space under a single roof. Laser scanners route as many as 190 000 cases of goods per day along 11 kilometres of conveyer belts, and the centre's 1000 workers load or unload 310 trucks daily.[14]

Like almost everything else, warehousing has seen dramatic changes in technology in recent years. Older, multi-storey warehouses with outdated materials-handling methods are steadily being replaced by newer, single-storey automated warehouses with advanced, computer-controlled materials-handling systems requiring few employees. Computers and scanners read orders and direct lift trucks, electric hoists, or robots to gather goods, move them to loading docks, and issue invoices.

Inventory Management Inventory levels also affect customer satisfaction. Here, managers must maintain the delicate balance between carrying too much inventory and carrying too little. Carrying too much inventory results in higher-than-necessary inventory-carrying costs and stock obsolescence. Carrying too little risks stock outs, causing customer dissatisfaction and costly emergency shipments or production. Thus, when managing inventory, firms must balance the costs of carrying larger inventories against resulting sales and profits.

Many companies have greatly reduced their inventories and related costs through *just-in-time* logistics systems. Through such systems, producers and retailers carry only small inventories of parts or merchandise, often only enough for a few days of operations. For example, Dell Computer, a master just-in-time produc-

Distribution centre A large, highly automated warehouse designed to receive goods from various plants and suppliers, take orders, fill them efficiently, and deliver goods to customers as quickly as possible

er, carries just 5 days of inventory, whereas competitors might carry 40 days or even 60.[15] New stock arrives exactly when needed, rather than being stored in inventory until being used. Just-in-time systems require accurate forecasting along with fast, frequent, and flexible delivery so that new supplies will be available when needed. However, these systems result in substantial savings in inventory-carrying and handling costs.

Transportation   Marketers need to take an interest in their company's transportation decisions. The choice of transportation carriers affects the pricing of products, delivery performance, and condition of the goods when they arrive—all of which will affect customer satisfaction. In shipping goods to its warehouses, dealers, and customers, the company can choose among five transportation modes: rail, truck, water, pipeline, and air.

Rail Because most of Canada's population is contained in a belt that is only 300 km wide but 6400 km long, rail still carries most of the country's freight. Railways are one of the most cost-effective modes for shipping large amounts of bulk products—coal, sand, minerals, farm and forest products—over long distances. In addition, railways recently have begun to increase their customer services. Both CN and CP have designed new equipment to handle special categories of goods, provided flatcars for carrying truck trailers by rail (piggyback), and provided in-transit services such as the diversion of shipped goods to other destinations en route and the processing of goods en route. Thus, after decades of losing out to truckers, railways appear ready for a comeback.[16]

Truck Trucks have increased their share of transportation steadily and now account for 25 percent of total cargo. They account for the largest portion of transportation *within* cities rather than *between* cities. Trucks are highly flexible in their routing and time schedules. They can move goods door to door, saving shippers the need to transfer goods from truck to rail and back again at a loss of time and risk of theft or damage. Trucks are efficient for short hauls of high-value merchandise. In many cases, their rates are competitive with railway rates, and trucks can usually offer faster service. Trucking firms have added many services in recent years. For example, Roadway Express now offers satellite tracking of shipments and sleeper tractors that move freight around the clock.

Roadway Express
www.roadway.com

Water Many goods are moved by ships and barges on coastal and inland waterways. On the one hand, the cost of water transportation is very low for shipping bulky, low-value, nonperishable products such as sand, coal, grain, oil, and metallic ores. On the other hand, water transportation is the slowest transportation mode and is sometimes affected by the weather. Thus, although many goods are shipped across the Great Lakes and through the St. Lawrence Seaway in the warmer months, these routes are impassable in the winter.

Pipeline Pipelines are used for shipping petroleum, natural gas, and chemicals from sources to markets. Pipeline shipment of petroleum products costs less than rail shipment but more than water shipment. Most pipelines are used by their owners to ship their own products.

Roadway and other trucking firms have added many services in recent years, such as satellite tracking of shipments and sleeper tractors that keep freight moving around the clock.

Information At The Speed Of Light

In today's business environment speed is critical.
Roadway Express moves your shipment around the clock
and communicates your shipment's location at the speed of light.
Continuously tracked by satellite, our new sleeper tractors
keep your shipment on the road and on time.
You get reliable service and reliable information.

*Just some of the ways we're changing to offer you
exceptional service...with no exceptions.*

ROADWAY
Roadway Express

Air Although air carriers transport less than 1 percent of the nation's goods, they are becoming more important as a transportation mode. Air-freight rates are much higher than rail or truck rates, but air freight is ideal when speed is needed or distant markets have to be reached. Among the most frequently air-freighted products are perishables (fresh fish, cut flowers) and high-value, low-bulk items (technical instruments, jewellery). Companies find that air freight also reduces inventory levels, packaging costs, and the number of warehouses needed.

Intermodal transportation Combining two or more modes of transportation

Increasingly, shippers are using **intermodal transportation**—combining two or more modes of transportation. *Piggyback* describes the use of rail and trucks; *fishyback,* water and trucks; *trainship,* water and rail; and *airtruck,* air and trucks. Combining modes provides advantages that no single mode can deliver. Each combination offers advantages to the shipper. For example, not only is piggyback cheaper than trucking alone, but it also provides flexibility and convenience.

In choosing a transportation mode for a product, shippers must balance many considerations: speed, dependability, availability, cost, and others. Thus, if a shipper needs speed, air and truck are the prime choices. If the goal is low cost, then water or pipeline might be best.

Integrated Supply Chain Management

Today, more and more companies are adopting the concept of **integrated supply chain management**. This concept recognizes that providing better customer service and trimming distribution costs requires teamwork, both inside the company and among all the marketing channel organizations. Inside, the company's various functional departments must work closely to maximize the company's own logistics performance. Outside, the company must integrate its logistics system with those of its suppliers and customers to maximize the performance of the entire distribution system.

Cross-Functional Teamwork Inside the Company In most companies, responsibility for various logistics activities is assigned to many different functional units—marketing, sales, finance, manufacturing, purchasing. Too often, each function tries to optimize its own logistics performance without regard for the activities of the other functions. However, transportation, inventory, warehousing, and order-processing activities interact, often in an inverse way. Lower inventory levels reduce inventory-carrying costs. But they may also reduce customer service and increase costs from stock outs, back orders, special production runs, and costly fast-freight shipments. Because distribution activities involve strong tradeoffs, decisions by different functions must be coordinated to achieve superior overall logistics performance.

The goal of integrated supply chain management is to harmonize all of the company's logistics decisions. Close working relationships among functions can be achieved in several ways. Some companies have created permanent logistics committees made up of managers responsible for different physical distribution activities. Companies can also create management positions that link the logistics activities of functional areas. For example, Procter & Gamble has created supply managers, who manage all of the supply chain activities for each of its product categories. Many companies have a vice president of logistics with cross-functional authority. Finally, companies can employ sophisticated, systemwide supply chain management software, now available from Oracle and other software providers.[17] The important thing is that the company coordinate its logistics and marketing activities to create high market satisfaction at a reasonable cost.

Building Channel Partnerships Companies must do more than improve their own logistics. They must also work with other channel members to improve whole-channel distribution. The members of a distribution channel are linked closely in delivering customer satisfaction and value. One company's distribution system is another company's supply system. The success of each channel member depends on the performance of the entire supply chain. For example, Zellers can charge the lowest prices at retail only if its entire supply chain—consisting of thousands of merchandise suppliers, transport companies, warehouses, and service providers—operates at maximum efficiency.

Smart companies coordinate their logistics strategies and forge strong partnerships with suppliers and customers to improve customer service and reduce channel costs. Many companies have created cross-functional, cross-company teams. For example, Procter & Gamble has a team of almost 100 people living in

Integrated supply chain management The logistics concept that emphasizes teamwork, both inside the company and among all the marketing channel organizations, to maximize the performance of the entire distribution system.

Bentonville, Arkansas, home of Wal-Mart. The P&Gers work jointly with their counterparts at Wal-Mart to find ways to squeeze costs out of their distribution system. Working together benefits not only P&G and Wal-Mart, but also their final customers. Other companies partner through shared projects. For example, many larger retailers are working closely with suppliers on in-store programs. Home Depot allows key suppliers to use its stores as a testing ground for new merchandising programs. The suppliers spend time at Home Depot stores watching how their product sells and how customers relate to it. They then create programs specially tailored to Home Depot and its customers.

Channel partnerships may also take the form of information sharing and continual inventory replenishment systems. Companies manage their supply chains through information. Suppliers link up with customers to share information and coordinate their logistics decisions. Here is an example:

Bailey Controls, a manufacturer of control systems for big factories, from steel and paper mills to chemical and pharmaceutical plants,...treats some of its suppliers almost like departments of its own plants. Bailey has plugged two of its main electronics suppliers into itself. Future Electronics is hooked in through an electronic data interchange system. Every week, Bailey electronically sends Future its latest forecasts of what materials it will need for the next six months so that Future can stock up in time. Bailey itself stocks only enough inventory for a few days of operation, as opposed to the three or four months' worth it used to carry. Whenever a bin of parts falls below a designated level, a Bailey employee passes a laser scanner over the bin's bar code, instantly alerting Future to send the parts at once. Arrow Electronics...is plugged in even more closely: It has a warehouse in Bailey's factory, stocked according to Bailey's twice-a-month forecasts. Bailey provides the space, Arrow the warehouseman and the $750 000 of inventory.[18]

Third-Party Logistics Most businesses perform their own logistics functions. However, a growing number of firms now outsource some or all of their logistics to **third-party logistics (3PL) providers** such as Ryder Systems, UPS Worldwide Logistics, FedEx Logistics, Roadway Logistics Services, or Emory Global Logistics. Such integrated logistics companies perform any or all of the functions required to get their clients' product to market. For example, Emory's Global Logistics unit provides clients with coordinated, single-source logistics services including supply chain management, customized information technology, inventory control, warehousing, transportation management, customer service and fulfillment, and freight auditing and control. "From sourcing raw materials to delivering finished products to stores," proclaims the Emery Web site, "our experts work with you to streamline and manage your entire supply chain and to keep you in control."

Companies use third-party logistics providers for several reasons. First, because getting the product to market is their main focus, these providers can often do it more efficiently and at lower cost. According to one study, outsourcing typically results in 15 percent to 30 percent cost savings.[19] Second, outsourcing logistics frees a company to focus more intensely on its core business. Finally, integrat-

Third-party logistics (3PL) provider An independent logistics provider that performs any or all of the functions required to get their clients' product to market.

ed logistics companies understand increasingly complex logistics environments. This can be especially helpful to companies attempting to expand their global market coverage. For example, companies distributing their products across Europe face a bewildering array of environmental restrictions that affect logistics, including packaging standards, truck size and weight limits, and noise and emissions pollution controls. By outsourcing its logistics, a company can gain a complete pan-European distribution system without incurring the costs, delays, and risks associated with setting up its own system.

<< Looking Back   < < < < < < < < <

So, what have you learned about distribution channels and integrated supply chain management? Marketing channel decisions are among the most important decisions that management faces. A company's channel decisions directly affect every other marketing decision. Each channel system creates a different level of revenues and costs and reaches a different segment of target consumers. Management must make channel decisions carefully, incorporating today's needs with tomorrow's likely selling environment. Some companies pay too little attention to their distribution channels, but others have used imaginative distribution systems to gain competitive advantage.

1. Explain why companies use distribution channels and discuss the functions these channels perform.

Most producers use intermediaries to bring their products to market. They try to forge a distribution channel—a set of interdependent organizations involved in the process of making a product or service available for use or consumption by the consumer or business user. Through their contacts, experience, specialization, and scale of operation, intermediaries usually offer the firm more than it can achieve on its own. Distribution channels perform many key functions. Some help complete transactions by gathering and distributing information needed for planning and aiding exchange; by developing and spreading persuasive communications about an offer; by performing contact work—finding and communicating with prospective buyers; by matching—shaping and fitting the offer to the buyer's needs; and by entering into negotiation to reach an agreement on price and other terms of the offer so that ownership can be transferred. Other functions help to fulfill the completed transactions by offering physical distribution—transporting and storing goods; financing—acquiring and using funds to cover the costs of the channel work; and risk taking—assuming the risks of carrying out the channel work.

2. Discuss how channel members interact and how they organize to perform the work of the channel.

The channel will be most effective when each member is assigned the tasks it can do best. Ideally, because the success of individual channel members depends on overall channel success, all channel firms should work together smoothly. They should understand and accept their roles, coordinate their goals and activities, and cooperate to attain overall channel goals. By cooperating, they can more effectively sense, serve, and satisfy the target market. In a large company, the formal organization structure assigns roles and provides needed leadership. But in a distribution channel made up of independent firms, leadership and power are not formally set. Traditionally, distribution channels have lacked the leadership needed to assign roles and manage conflict. Recently, however, new types of channel organizations have appeared that provide stronger leadership and improved performance.

3. **Identify the major channel alternatives open to a company.**

Each firm identifies alternative ways to reach its market. Available means vary from direct selling to using one, two, three, or more intermediary channel levels. Marketing channels face continuous and sometimes dramatic change. Three of the most important trends are the growth of vertical, horizontal, and hybrid marketing systems. These trends affect channel cooperation, conflict, and competition. Channel design begins with assessing customer channel service needs and company channel objectives and constraints. The company then identifies the major channel alternatives in terms of the types of intermediaries, the number of intermediaries, and the channel responsibilities of each. Each channel alternative must be evaluated according to economic, control, and adaptive criteria. Channel management calls for selecting qualified intermediaries and motivating them. Individual channel members must be evaluated regularly.

4. **Explain how companies select, motivate, and evaluate channel members.**

Producers vary in their ability to attract qualified marketing intermediaries. Some producers have no trouble signing up channel members. Others have to work hard to line up enough qualified intermediaries. When selecting intermediaries, the company should evaluate each channel member's qualifications and select those who best fit its channel objectives. Once selected, channel members must be continually motivated to do their best. The company must sell not only through the intermediaries, but also to them. It should work to forge long-term partnerships with their channel partners to create a marketing system that meets the needs of both the manufacturer and the partners. The company must also regularly check channel member performance against established performance standards, rewarding intermediaries who are performing well and assisting or replacing weaker ones.

5. **Discuss the nature and importance of marketing logistics and integrated supply chain management.**

Just as firms are giving the marketing concept increased recognition, more business firms are paying attention to marketing logistics (or physical distribution). Logistics is an area of potentially high cost savings and improved customer satisfaction. Marketing logistics addresses not only outbound distribution but also inbound distribution and reverse distribution. That is, it involves entire supply chain management—managing value-added flows between suppliers, the company, resellers, and final users. No logistics system can both maximize customer service and minimize distribution costs. Instead, the goal of logistics management is to provide a targeted level of service at the least cost. The major logistics functions include order processing, warehousing, inventory management, and transportation.

The integrated supply chain management concept recognizes that improved logistics requires teamwork in the form of close working relationships across functional areas inside the company and across various organizations in the supply chain. Companies can achieve logistics harmony among functions by creating cross-functional logistics teams, integrative supply manager positions, and senior-level logistics executives with cross-functional authority. Channel partnerships can take the form of cross-company teams, shared projects, and information sharing systems. Today, some companies are outsourcing their logistics functions to third-party logistics providers to save costs, increase efficiency, and gain faster and more effective access to global markets.

Navigating the Key Terms

Channel conflict, **p. 435**
Channel level, **p. 433**
Conventional distribution channel, **p. 436**
Direct marketing channel, **p. 433**
Disintermediation, **p. 439**
Distribution centre, **p. 454**
Distribution channel, **p. 431**
Exclusive distribution, **p. 445**
Horizontal marketing system, **p. 437**
Hybrid marketing channel, **p. 438**

Indirect marketing channel, **p. 433**
Integrated supply chain management, **p. 457**
Intensive distribution, **p. 445**
Intermodal transportation, **p. 456**
Marketing logistics (physical distribution), **p. 452**
Selective distribution, **p. 445**
Supply chain management, **p. 452**
Third-party logistics (3PL) provider, **p. 458**
Vertical marketing system (VMS), **p. 436**

Concept Check

Fill in the blanks and then check your answers.

1. A _____ is a set of interdependent organizations involved in the process of making a product or service available for use or consumption by the consumer or business user.

2. Members of the marketing channel perform many key functions. Chief among these are _____, _____, _____, _____, _____, physical distribution, financing, and risk taking.

3. A _____ marketing channel has no intermediary levels.

4. Disagreements over goals and roles generate channel conflict. McDonald's recently had a form of _____ conflict with some of its dealers when its aggressive expansion plans called for placing new stores in areas that took business from existing locations.

5. Three forms of vertical marketing systems (VMS) include _____, _____, and _____ VMS.

6. Changes in technology have caused traditional distribution to undergo changes such as _____, where more and more product and service producers are bypassing inter-

mediaries and going directly to final buyers, or that radically new types of channel intermediaries are emerging to displace traditional ones.

7. Companies must determine the number of channel members to use at each level. Producers of convenience products and common raw materials typically seek _____ distribution—a strategy in which they stock their products in as many outlets as possible.

8. Another term used to describe physical distribution is _____.

9. Managing value-added flows of materials, final goods, and related information between suppliers, the company, resellers, and final users is called _____ management.

10. The major logistics functions include _____, _____, _____, and _____.

11. With respect to common transportation modes, most of the country's freight is still moved by _____.

12. Given the growing popularity of outsourcing, _____ logistics providers such as Ryder Systems, UPS Worldwide Logistics, and FedEx Logistics are providing more services for customers than ever before.

Concept Check Answers: 1. distribution channel; 2. information, promotion, contact, matching, negotiation; 3. direct; 4. vertical; 5. corporate, contractual, administered; 6. disintermediation; 7. intensive; 8. marketing logistics; 9. supply chain management; 10. order processing, warehousing, inventory management, transportation; 11. rail; 12. third-party.

Discussing the Issues

1. List and briefly discuss the marketing channel functions that are involved in completing and fulfilling transactions. Which functions applies most in each of the following situations? (a) A retailer puts in a rush reorder for a needed holiday item that is in short supply. (b) An Internet marketer seeks ways to identify and contact its market. (c) A small retailer wants to expand its order size but does not currently have funds to pay for the expanded order. (d) A business buyer attends a large trade show looking for higher-quality products on a limited budget.

2. Give your own example of each of the three major forms of vertical marketing systems described in the chapter. What advantages do such systems have over traditional channel organizations? Where could problems occur? Explain and illustrate.

3. What is "disintermediation?" Give an example other than those discussed in the chapter. What opportunities and problems does disintermediation present for traditional retailers? Explain.

4. Which distribution strategy—intensive, selective, or exclusive—is used for the following products and why? (a) Piaget watches, (b) Acura automobiles, and (c) Snickers chocolate bars.

5. Regarding outsourcing: (a) Why would a company choose to outsource its distribution function? (b) What major factors contribute to a successful outsourcing relationship? What are the potential dangers of such a relationship? (c) Give an example of a company that could benefit from outsourcing its logistics and suggest some practical outsourcing alternatives for the company. (For additional information on outsourcing, see the Outsourcing Institute's Web site at **www.outsourcing.com**.)

 **Mastering Marketing**

Examine the distribution arrangements available to CanGo and then answer the following questions:

(a) How many intermediaries are used by the company?

(b) Diagram a potential vertical marketing system that might make the company more effective and efficient.

(c) Propose a new distribution network that might be beneficial for the company.

(d) How could channel members be better motivated to increase effectiveness and efficiency?

(e) Propose an integrated supply chain that would make the company and its distribution process more competitive.

(f) How can the company integrate the Internet into its distribution process?

 Check out the enclosed Video case CD-ROM, or our Companion Website at www.pearsoned.ca/armstrong, to view a video segment and case for this chapter.

MAP 11 Marketing Applications

You know about the Internet but have you ever heard of a "extranet"? An extranet occurs when a company opens its own internal network (or intranet) to selected business partners. Trusted suppliers, distributors, and other special users can then link into the company's network without having to go through traditional red-tape. The connecting company can use the Internet or virtual private networks for communication. Once inside the company's intranet, the outside company (or partner) can view whatever data the company makes available. What types of data? A supplier might analyze a customer's inventory needs: Boeing booked $100 million in spare parts from airline customers in one year. Partners might swap customer lists for interrelated products and services or share purchasing systems to gain savings through more efficient purchasing: General Electric claims that $500 million can be saved in purchasing costs by using an extranet. Imagine the strategic advantages that are created when "virtual" partners move information to one another in seconds about shifting supply and demand situations, customer requests and opportunities, and just-in-time inven-tory needs. Purchase processing times can be reduced from weeks to minutes at enormous cost savings that can be passed along to consumers.

Thinking Like a Marketing Manager

1. What role might an extranet play in distribution decisions for (a) retailers, (b) wholesalers, and (c) manufacturers?

2. What are the potential dangers of an extranet system?

3. What areas of a marketing organization's intranet would be most interesting to a partner using the extranet?

4. Assume that you are the marketing manager of Cisco Systems (investigate this master of e-commerce and networking at **www.cisco.com**). How could an extranet help you to better assist resellers? How could costs be saved by using an extranet? How does an extranet work with an outsourcing concept (if at all)? After examining the advantages and disadvantages of using an extranet, write a short position paper that outlines your thoughts on subject and its future in marketing commerce.

Digital Map
Visit our Web site at **www.pearsoned.ca/armstrong** for online quizzes, Internet exercises, and more!

CASE 11 ICON ACOUSTICS: BYPASSING TRADITION

The Dream

Like most entrepreneurs, Dave Fokos dreams a lot. He imagines customers eagerly phoning Icon Acoustics in Ottawa to order his latest, custom-made stereo speakers. He sees sales climbing, cash flowing, and hundreds of happy workers striving to produce top-quality products that delight Icon's customers.

Like most entrepreneurs, Dave has taken a long time to develop his dream. While majoring in electrical engineering at Queen's University, Dave discovered that he had a strong interest in audio engineering. Following graduation, Dave landed a job as a speaker designer with Conrad-Johnson, a high-end audio-equipment manufacturer. Within four years, Dave had designed 13 speaker models and decided to start his own company.

Dave identified a market niche that he felt other speaker firms had overlooked. The niche consisted of "audio addicts"—people who love to listen to music and appreciate first-rate stereo equipment. These affluent, well-educated customers are genuinely obsessed with their stereo equipment. "They'd rather buy a new set of speakers than eat," Dave observes.

Dave faced one major problem: how to distribute Icon's products. He had learned from experience at Conrad-Johnson that most manufacturers distribute their equipment primarily through stereo dealers. Dave did not hold a high opinion of most such dealers; he felt that they too often played hardball with manufacturers, forcing them to accept thin margins. Furthermore, the dealers concentrated on only a handful of well-known producers who provided mass-produced models. This kept firms that offered more customized products from gaining access to the market. Perhaps most disturbing, Dave felt that the established dealers often sold not what was best for customers, but whatever they had in inventory that month.

Dave dreamed of offering high-end stereo speakers directly to the audio-obsessed, bypassing the established dealer network. By going directly to the customers, Dave could avoid the dealer markups and offer top-quality products and service at reasonable prices.

The Plan

At age 28, Dave set out to turn his dreams into reality. Some customers who had come to know Dave's work became enthusiastic supporters of his dream and invested $189 000 in Icon. With their money and $10 000 of his own, Dave started Icon in a rented facility in an industrial park.

The Market. About 335 stereo-speaker makers compete for a $3 billion annual North American market for audio components. About 100 of these manufacturers sell to the low- and mid-range segments of the market, which account for 90 percent of the market's unit volume and about 50 percent of its value. In addition to competing with each other, U.S. manufacturers also compete with Japanese firms that offer products at affordable prices. The remaining 235 or so manufacturers compete for the remaining 10 percent of the market's unit volume and 50 percent of the value—the high end—where Dave hopes to find his customers.

Icon's Marketing Strategy. To serve the audio addicts segment, Dave offers only the highest-quality speakers. He has developed two models: the Lumen and the Parsec. The Lumen stands 45 cm high, weighs 11 kg, and is designed for stand mounting. The floor-standing Parsec is 1.2 m high and weighs 43 kg. Both models feature custom-made cabinets that come in natural, black oak, or walnut. Dave can build and ship two pairs of the Lumen speakers or one pair of the Parsec speakers per day by himself. To have an adequate parts inventory, he had to spend $50 000 of his capital on the expensive components.

Dave set the price of the Lumen and Parsec at $795 and $1795 per pair, respectively. He selected these prices to provide a 50 percent gross margin. He believes that traditional dealers would sell equivalent speakers at retail at twice those prices. Customers can call Icon on a toll-free number to order speakers or to get advice directly from Dave. Icon pays for shipping and any return freight via Federal Express—round-trip freight for a pair of Parsecs costs $486.

Dave offers to pay for the return freight because a key part of his promotional strategy is a 30-day, in-home, no-obligation trial. In his ads, Dave calls this "The 43 200 Minute, No Pressure Audition." This trial period allows customers to listen to the speakers in their actual listening environment. In a dealer's showroom, the customer must listen in an artificial environment and often feels pressure to make a quick decision.

Dave believes that typical high-end customers may buy speakers for "nonrational" reasons: They want a quality product and good sound, but they also want an image. Therefore, Dave has tried to create a unique image through the appearance of his speakers and to reflect that image in all of the company's marketing. He spent more than $40 000 on distinctive stationery, business cards, a brochure, and a single display ad. He also designed a laminated label he places just above the gold-plated input jack on each speaker. The label reads: "This loudspeaker was hand-crafted by [the technician's name who assembled the speaker goes here in his or her own handwriting]. Made in Canada by Icon Acoustics, Inc."

To get the word out, Dave concentrates on product reviews in trade magazines and on trade shows, such as the High End Hi-Fi show in New York. Attendees at the show cast ballots to select "The Best Sound at the Show." In the balloting, among 200 brands, Icon's Parsec speakers finished 15th. Among the top 10 brands, the least expensive was a pair priced at $2400, and six of the systems were priced from $8000 to $18 000. A reviewer in an issue of *Stereophile* magazine evaluated Icon's speakers and noted: "The overall sound was robust and dynamic, with a particularly potent low end. Parts and construction quality appeared to be first rate. Definitely a company to watch."

Dave made plans to invest in a slick, four-colour display ad in *Stereo Review,* the consumer stereo magazine with the highest circulation (600 000). He also expected another favourable review in *Stereophile* magazine.

The Reality

Dressed in jeans and a hooded sweatshirt, Dave pauses in the middle of assembling a cardboard shipping carton, pulls up a chair, and leans against the concrete-block wall of his manufacturing area. Reflecting on his experiences during his first year in business, Dave realizes he's learned a lot in jumping all the hurdles the typical entrepreneur faces. Dave experienced quality problems with the first cabinet supplier. Then, he ran short of a key component after a mix-up with a second supplier. Despite his desire to avoid debt, he had to borrow $50 000 from a bank. Prices for his cabinets and some components rose, and product returns were higher than expected (19 percent for the past six months). These price and cost increases put pressure on his margins, forcing Dave to raise his prices (from those quoted earlier). Despite the price increases, his margins remained below his 50 percent target.

Still, Dave feels good about his progress. The price increase does not seem to have affected demand. The few ads and word-of-mouth advertising appear to be working. Dave receives about five phone calls per day, with one in seven calls leading to a sale. Dave also feels the stress of the long hours and the low pay, however. He is not able to pay himself a high salary—just $9500 this year.

Dave reaches over and picks up his most recent financial projections from a workbench (see Table 11-1). He believes that this will be a break-even year—then he'll have it made. As Dave sets the projections back on the workbench, his mind drifts to his plans to introduce two exciting new speakers—the Micron ($2495 per pair) and the Millennium ($7995 per pair). He also wonders whether there is a foreign market for his speakers. Should he use his same direct marketing strategy for foreign markets, or should he consider distributors? The dream continues.

Questions

1. What functions do traditional stereo dealers perform?

2. Why has Dave Fokos decided to establish a direct channel? What objectives and constraints have shaped his decision?

3. What consumer service needs do Dave's customers have?

4. What problems will Dave face as a result of his channel decisions? What changes would you recommend in Dave's distribution strategy, if any? Will his strategy work in foreign markets?

5. What other changes would you recommend in Dave's marketing strategy? *Source:* Adapted from "Sound strategy," *INC.*, May 1991, pp. 46–56. © 1991 by Goldhirsh Group, Inc. Used with permission. Dave Fokos also provided information to support development of this case.

Table 11-1   Icon Acoustics' Pro-Forma Financials ($ in thousands)

	Year				
	1	2	3	4	5
Pairs of speakers sold	224	435	802	1256	1830
Total sales revenue	$303	$654	$1299	$2153	$3338
Cost of Sales					
Materials and packaging	$130	$281	$561	$931	$1445
Shipping	$43	$83	$157	$226	$322
Total cost of sales	$173	$364	$718	$1157	$1767
Gross profit	$130	$290	$581	$996	$1571
Gross margin	43%	44%	45%	46%	47%
Expenses					
New property and equipment	$3	$6	$12	$15	$18
Marketing	$13	$66	$70	$109	$135
General and administrative	$51	$110	$197	$308	$378
Loan repayment	$31	$31	$0	$0	$0
Outstanding payables	$30	$0	$0	$0	$0
Total expenses	$128	$213	$279	$432	$531
Pretax profit	$2	$77	$302	$564	$1040
Pretax margin	1%	12%	23%	26%	31%

12 >> Retailing and Wholesaling

Looking Ahead

In the previous chapter, you learned the basics of distribution channel design and management. Now, we'll look more deeply into the two major intermediary channel functions: retailing and wholesaling. You already know something about retailing—retailers of all shapes and sizes serve you every day. However, you probably know much less about the hoard of wholesalers that work behind the scenes. In this chapter, we'll navigate through the characteristics of different kinds of retailers and wholesalers, the marketing decisions they make, and trends for the future. You'll see that the retailing and wholesaling landscapes are changing rapidly to match explosive changes in markets and technology.

After studying this chapter, you should be able to

1. explain the roles of retailers and wholesalers in the distribution channel

2. describe the major types of retailers and give examples of each

3. identify the major types of wholesalers and give examples of each

4. explain the marketing decisions facing retailers and wholesalers

To start the tour, we'll look at Roots Canada, the highly successful leather goods company. Roots's success has resulted not just from excellent product selection, but also from outstanding service, stimulating retail environments, and reasonable prices.

"Take hard-as-nails consumers. Add murderous competition. What do you get? Some sizzling opportunities for radical retailers." There is no doubt that Canada has a turbulent retail environment: an environment marked by some dramatic failures—such as the bankruptcy of Eaton's and subsequent sale of the chain to Sears—but also some dramatic successes. Take Roots, for example, the little leather goods firm that has managed to become associated with what it means to be Canadian. Currently, Roots has more than 150 exclusive stores in Canada, the United States, Japan, Korea, and Taiwan.

Roots and other retailers that have thrived in this difficult era all share one distinguishing feature—the ability to anticipate what their customers want and provide that product or service before their competitors. But product selection alone isn't enough. Consumers also want outstanding service and stimulating retail environments, provided at a reasonable price. Retailing expert Dr. Len Berry puts it this way: Successful retailers are committed to "the creation of a compelling value for their target customers." Value is created by pricing products and services fairly, providing exciting merchandising, offering respectful service, saving customers' time and energy, and making shopping more fun. Creating stores that both entertain and provide goods and services is important, since "shopping is both a rational and an emotional experience." Retailers must understand how to stimulate consumers' senses to make shopping a more enjoyable and satisfying experience.

Even this may not be enough. One Toronto retailing analyst notes, "More specialty clothing stores are selling items that encompass an entire lifestyle." This is certainly what Roots Canada has done. New-style retailers, such as Roots, have been able to capture their customers' way of looking at the world. As the people at Roots note, "We don't want to just sell you clothes and athletic gear and shoes and bags—although it's obvi-ously important that we do. We want to help you embrace a lifestyle, a culture that will change the way you look at the world...and yourself."

It hasn't taken Canadians long to embrace such lifestyle marketers—Roots, Chateauworks, Club Monaco, and Urban Outfitters. These retailers sell an array of goods ranging from fashion items to perfume, furniture, housewares, stationery, cloth-ing, candy, makeup, and more in large, open-con-cept stores based around a single lifestyle theme. Club Monaco, for example, sells housewares and furniture that match its minimalist brand position-ing. Roots, describing itself as "eclectic," offers leather goods, casual clothing, perfume, house-hold goods, and furniture with what it calls "a retro feel" linked to its Canadian outdoor heritage.

Randy Scotland of the Retail Council of Canada believes the popularity of lifestyle stores "makes perfect marketing sense," especially if the retail-ers' product lines are in sync with the feel of the store and are "true to the feeling, ethics and cul-ture of brand." Alan Gee of Gee Jeffery & Partners Advertising agrees. He says that fashion retailers can be very successful at selling products for homes and lifestyles if they truly understand the meaning of their brand in consumers' lives. "Once you have brand understanding, you can leverage that code into [all] areas of a person's life." Today's powerful retailers realize that they are no longer distributors of manufacturers' brands: Instead, they are developing and posi-tioning their own brands and products that fit more diverse aspects of consumers' lives.

Years before it thought about lifestyle marketing, Roots worked long and hard to build its unique brand equity. Founders Michael Budman and Don Green, two Detroit-reared hippies who loved Canada and its outdoors, were among the first to understand the marketing potential of Canadiana. They founded more than a store; they built a brand using this theme. They brought it to life with sym-bols of pristine blue lakes, summer camps, blood red sunsets, towering green forests, and canoes. Thus, the Roots brand was born in the early 1970s with a single product—a negative-heel "earth" shoe. In the 1980s, it became identified even more with Canadian symbolism when Roots began to feature its beaver-logoed sweatshirts. Today Geoff Pevere, author of a book on Roots, describes the firm as the "quintessential Canadian success story.…It is successful but not overtly so, understated but immensely popular—in other words, good clean Canadian fun [yet a] high flyer of international fashion. The secret to their success? Hard work, an uncanny ability to predict and ride trends, quality products, and unabashed enthusiasm for that good ol' Canadian backwoods myth."

Building a brand is one thing. Successfully extending it without diluting its meaning for consumers is quite another. So far, Roots has managed to maintain its brand integrity. It has extended its brand from leather goods and casual clothing to fragrances. Roots offers *For Her* fragrance, a unisex product called *UniScent,* and *MiniScent,* a cologne for children. Forging ahead, Roots took advantage of the growing strength of its brand and expanded into the home furnishing market. It opened *Roots Home* in November 1998. In addition to furniture, these stores carry such items as pillows and bedding, luggage, jewellery, and desk accessories as well as "relaxed-style" clothing. We've had "a great response, [and] the furniture has done phenomenally," says Rima Biback, director of home operations. She describes the concept as "furniture for keeps." Roots also opened a lodge in British Columbia, which features Roots products as well as its lifestyle experience.

Some marketing analysts have started to wonder just how far Roots can extend its brand. When it announced "Roots Air" in June 2000, some wondered whether "The beaver could fly." Roots decided to partner with Skyservice Airlines to offer business travellers an alternative to Air Canada on routes between Toronto and Montreal, Calgary, Edmonton, and Winnipeg. This venture didn't last long and was discontinued.

Never a company to rest on its laurels, Roots works continually to build its brand. It has leapt beyond simply having Canadians wear its clothes to having Canadian Olympians sport them. Roots became a "Canadian brand" as our athletes stood in the global spotlight sporting their official red and white Roots gear, which became as tied to the country as it was to the company. Canadians weren't the only ones to notice the brand. Roots Canada gained worldwide recognition through its presence at the 1998 Nagano Winter Olympics. Not only did Roots Canada provide Canadian Olympians with distinctive uniforms, it "saw the power of television" as a tool to communicate its brand values and build a global presence. Using the theme, "these are my roots," a national television campaign featuring Canadian gold-medal-winning snowboarder and counter-culture icon Ross Rebagliati was launched across Canada and the United States. As Roots's strategists noted, however, "It's not just the advertising, it's the whole thing about sponsorship and the Olympics.…It's the constant overlapping of the brand into a wide range of categories that helps make the Roots brand name powerful and distinctive."

In addition to the brand value, lifestyle retailers like Roots offer their customers convenience. Linking together diverse products under a common brand theme simplifies consumer decision making. For those consumers who find time a key factor, lifestyle collections mean consumers no longer have to "go to 15 stores to find everything they want…they can do better things with their lives." To provide an even better response to the needs of time-pressed consumers, Roots was one of the first Canadian retailers to set up an e-commerce operation.

Like any vendor that takes its business online, Roots wanted to provide its customers with round-the-clock service availability—in other words, give consumers convenient access 24 hours a day, seven days a week. Roots knew it had a globally recognized brand name thanks in part to its Olympic sponsorships. It could fulfill orders through its two Canadian state-of-the-art manufacturing facilities. It sounded simple: set up an e-commerce site, have the inventory on hand, fulfill the orders, and voilà-happy customers!

Roots initially signed on with IBM's Global Merchant program to ensure secure real-time credit card processing, currency conversion, and order fulfilment on an international basis. However, in the spring of 2001, Roots ended the relationship with IBM's Global Merchant program and embarked on a new online strategy. In March 2001, the company opened a Roots Shop through the Sears.ca Web site. Canadian customers were offered many of the same styles as were available in the Sears catalogue. To support this initiative, Roots created a separate marketing site at roots.ca and roots.com to drive consumers to the new Sears site and to provide corporate and store information.

In January 2002, the second stage of the strategy was implemented. "Roots Direct" was opened as an online store to serve the United States market and to act as a platform for future expansion to Asia, South America, and Europe. The relationship with Sears.ca will continue, specifically for meeting Canadian domestic orders. To reinforce a dedicated approach to the various markets, Roots.ca and Roots.com were separated to reflect the different marketing strategies in Canada and the United States.

Although important, these features pale in comparison to other demands of online customers. Relationship management is the key, and Roots knew it had to care about the customers' total online experience just as it did in its bricks-and-mortar stores. As Ken Cassar, an analyst with Jupiter Communications' digital commerce strategy practice, warns, the "greatest challenge is living up to the expectations that consumers have toward their brands. Nailing the basics such as site performance, inventory, fulfillment management, and customer service becomes more crucial than ever."

Since ordering online involves more perceived risk, customers expect a confirmation e-mail within 15 minutes of placing their order. They also want to know they can contact a real person if they have a problem. Therefore, Roots provides a toll-free number as well as e-mail contact points. Finally, its developers stress that Root's Web site is more than a simple online store: "It's a coming together of strong brand and strong commerce."

Roots seems to have tapped one of the secrets to online success. "It's not the pure e-businesses, and it's not the bricks-and-mortar companies that will be successful. It will be the companies that combine both of them," an experienced e-business analyst notes. Even more important, Roots founder Michael Budman believes, "Web surfers from around the world will—whether they buy or not—get a great sense of who Canadians are and what our lifestyle is through this site." Have a look at Roots's Web site at www.roots.ca to see whether you agree.[1]

The Roots story provides many insights into the workings of one of Canada's most successful retailers. This chapter looks at retailing and wholesaling. In the first section of this chapter, we look at the nature and importance of retailing, major types of store and nonstore retailers, the decisions retailers make, and the future of retailing in Canada and abroad. In the second section, we discuss these same topics as they relate to wholesalers.

RETAILING

Retailing All activities involved in selling goods and services directly to consumers for their personal, nonbusiness use.

Retailer A business whose sales come primarily from retailing.

What is retailing? We all know that Wal-Mart, Sears, and The Bay are retailers, but so are Avon representatives, the local Holiday Inn, Internet marketers, and a doctor seeing patients. **Retailing** includes all the activities involved in selling goods or services directly to final consumers for their personal, nonbusiness use. Many institutions—manufacturers, wholesalers, and retailers—do retailing. But most retailing is done by **retailers**: businesses whose sales come *primarily* from retailing.

Although most retailing is done in retail stores, *nonstore retailing* has been growing much faster than has store retailing. Nonstore retailing includes selling to final consumers through direct mail, catalogues, telephone, home TV shopping shows, home and office parties, door-to-door contact, vending machines, online services and the Internet, and other direct retailing approaches. We discuss such direct marketing approaches in detail in Chapter 14. In this chapter, we focus on store retailing. Although we have separated the types of retailing, research has shown that customers who use multiple channels spend ten times more than shoppers who use a single channel. Specifically, Digitrends.net found that one retailer's Web-only customers spent $181 per year; those buying in stores spend $291 annually; while catalogue customers spent $438 yearly. However, customers who shopped all three channels spent $1575.[2]

Types of Retailers

Retail Council of Canada www.retailcouncil.org

Retail stores come in all shapes and sizes, and new retail types keep emerging. The most important types of retail stores are described in Table 12-1 and discussed in the following sections. They can be classified in terms of several characteristics, including the *amount of service* they offer, the breadth and depth of their *product lines,* the *relative prices* they charge, and how they are *organized.*

Amount of Service Different products require different amounts of service, and customer service preferences vary. Retailers may offer one of three levels of service—self-service, limited service, and full service.

Self-service retailers increased rapidly in Canada during the Great Depression of the 1930s. Customers were willing to perform their own "locate-compare-select" process to save money. Today, self-service is the basis of all discount operations and typically is used by sellers of convenience goods (such as supermarkets) and nationally branded, fast-moving shopping goods (such as the Future Shop).

Limited-service retailers, such as Sears or The Bay, provide more sales assistance because they carry more shopping goods about which customers need information. Their increased operating costs result in higher prices. In *full-service retailers,* such

Table 12-1 Major Types of Retailers

Type	Description	Examples
Specialty stores	Carry a narrow product line with a deep assortment within that line; apparel stores, sporting goods stores, furniture stores, florists, and bookstores. Specialty stores can be subclassified by the degree of narrowness in their product line. A clothing store would be a *single-line store;* a men's clothing store would be a *limited-line store;* and a men's custom-shirt store would be a *superspecialty store.*	Tall Men (tall men's clothing); The Limited (women's clothing); The Body Shop (cosmetics and bath supplies)
Department stores	Carry several product lines—typically clothing, home furnishings, and household goods—with each line operated as a separate department managed by specialist buyers or merchandisers.	Sears, The Bay
Supermarkets	Relatively large, low-cost, low-margin, high-volume, self-service operations designed to serve consumers' total needs for food, laundry, and household maintenance products.	Safeway Foods, A&P, Loblaws, Sobeys, Thrifty
Convenience stores	Relatively small stores that are located near residential areas, operate long hours seven days a week, and carry a limited line of high-turnover convenience products. Their long hours and their use by consumers mainly for "fill-in" purchases make them relatively high-price operations.	7-Eleven, Beckers, Mac's, Couche-Tard, Provi-Soir
Superstores	Larger stores that aim to meet consumers' total needs for routinely purchased food and non-food items. They include *supercentres,* combined supermarket and discount stores, which feature cross-merchandising. They also include *category killers* that carry a very deep assortment of a particular line. Another superstore variation is the *hypermarket,* a huge store that combines supermarket, discount, and warehouse retailing to sell routinely purchased goods as well as furniture, large and small appliances, clothing, and many other items.	*Supercentres:* Wal-Mart Supercentres; *Category killers:* Toys "R" Us (toys), Petsmart (pet supplies), Indigo (books), Home Depot (home improvement), Future Shop (consumer electronics); *Hyper-markets:* Carrefour (France); Pycra (Spain), Meijer's (Netherlands)
Discount stores	Sell standard merchandise at lower prices by accepting lower margins and selling higher volumes. A true discount store *regularly* sells its merchandise at lower prices, offering mostly national brands, not inferior goods. Discount retailers include both general merchandise and specialty merchandise stores.	*General discount stores:* Wal-Mart, Zellers; *Specialty discount stores:* Future Shop (electronics), Crown Bookstores (books)
Off-price retailers	Sell a changing and unstable collection of higher-quality merchandise, often leftover goods, overruns, and irregulars obtained at reduced prices from manufacturers or other retailers. They buy at less than regular wholesale prices and charge consumers less than retail. They include three main types:	T.J. Maxx, Winners

Type	Description	Examples
Independent off-price retailers	Owned and run by entrepreneurs or by divisions of larger retail corporations.	
Factory outlets	Owned and operated by manufacturers and normally carry the manufacturer's surplus, discontinued, or irregular goods. Such outlets increasingly group together in *factory outlet malls,* where dozens of outlet stores offer prices as much as 50 percent below retail on a broad range of items.	Dansk (dinnerware), Dexter (shoes), Ralph Lauren and Liz Claiborne (upscale apparel)
Warehouse (or wholesale) clubs	Sell a limited selection of brand name grocery items, appliances, clothing, and a hodgepodge of other goods at deep discounts to members who pay $25 to $50 annual membership fees. They serve small businesses and other club members out of huge, low-overhead, warehouse-like facilities and offer few frills or services.	Wal-Mart-owned Sam's Club, Max Clubs, Costco, BJ's Wholesale Club

as specialty stores and first-class department stores, salespeople assist customers in every phase of the shopping process. Full-service stores usually carry more specialty goods for which customers like to be "waited on." They provide more services resulting in much higher operating costs, which are passed along to customers as higher prices.

Product Line Retailers also can be classified by the length and breadth of their product assortments. Some retailers, such as **specialty stores**, carry narrow product lines with deep assortments within those lines. Today, specialty stores are flourishing. The increasing use of market segmentation, market targeting, and product specialization has resulted in a greater need for stores that focus on specific products and segments.

In contrast, **department stores** carry a wide variety of product lines. In recent years, department stores have been squeezed between more focused and flexible specialty stores on the one hand, and more efficient, lower-priced discounters on the other. In response, many have added "bargain basements" and promotional events to meet the discount threat. Others have set up store brand programs, "boutiques" and "designer shops" (such as Tommy Hilfiger or Polo shops within department stores), and other store formats that compete with specialty stores. Still others are trying mail-order, telephone, and Web site selling. Service remains the key differentiating factor.

Supermarkets are large, low-cost, low-margin, high-volume, self-service stores that carry a wide variety of food, laundry, and household products. Chains account for most of the supermarket sales in Canada, and this channel is rapidly consolidating. In 1998, Empire, owner of Atlantic Canada's Sobeys, purchased the Oshawa Group for $1.44 billion, adding banners like IGA and Price Chopper to its shopping cart. The purchase gave it roughly a 20 percent share of the Canadian grocery market. Rival Loblaw Companies countered by snapping up Provigo, boosting its share of the Canadian supermarket business to about 40 percent.[3] Despite ongoing con-

Specialty store A retail store that carries a narrow product line with a deep assortment within that line.

Department store A retail organization that carries a wide variety of product lines—typically clothing, home furnishings, and household goods; each line

Supermarket Large, low-cost, low-margin, high-volume, self-service store that carries a wide variety of food, laundry, and household products.

solidation, supermarkets continue to look for new ways to build their sales. Most chains now operate fewer but larger stores. They practise "scrambled merchandising," and carry many nonfood items—beauty aids, housewares, toys, prescriptions, appliances, video cassettes, sporting goods, garden supplies—hoping to find high-margin lines to improve profits. They also are improving their facilities and services to attract more customers. Many supermarkets are "moving upscale," providing "from-scratch" bakeries, gourmet deli counters, and fresh seafood departments. Others are cutting costs, establishing more efficient operations, and lowering prices to compete more effectively with food discounters.

Convenience stores are small stores that carry a limited line of high-turnover convenience goods. These stores are located near residential areas and are open long hours, seven days a week. When supermarkets won the right to open for business on Sundays, and drugstore chains and gas station boutiques began selling groceries and snack foods, convenience stores lost their monopoly on their key differentiating variable—*convenience.* The result has been a huge industry shakeout. Although many of the "mom-and-pop" stores that once dominated the industry are closing, others are being opened by the huge chains. For example, although Couche-Tard may not exactly be a household name, with 1600 outlets it is Canada's largest operator of convenience stores. It owns stores from Victoria, B.C., to Sept-Iles, Quebec—stores that operate under the Couche-Tard name as well as such banners as Mac's, Becker's, Mike's Mart, and Daisy Mart. The chain has been growing in both size and profitability at a time when convenience stores' share of Canadian food and grocery items fell from 2.1 to 1.7 percent. How has Couche-Tard done this? By positioning its stores as destination outlets. Whereas once these stores sold over-priced emergency goods, they now offer a wide range of convenience items that are competitively priced, as well as ATMs, fax machines, photocopiers, and stamp machines.

Moreover, 435 outlets have gas bars. Like their larger rivals, Couche-Tard convenience stores have started branding their own food items. They are investing heavily to redesign their stores to match the needs of their local neighbourhoods. Those in upscale areas offer such high-margin, mouth-watering, fresh-baked goods as croissants that customers can eat at in-store cafés. Those in areas frequented by male, blue-collar workers stock meat-laden Subway sandwiches. Like many savvy marketers, Couche-Tard also knows that employee ability and satisfaction is highly correlated with customer satisfaction. Therefore, it invests heavily in employee training so that its stores can offer the service and merchandising that rival their larger competitors.[4]

Superstores are much larger than regular supermarkets and carry a large assortment of routinely purchased food and nonfood items. "The Real Canadian Superstore," has locations from Thunder Bay, Ontario, west to Vancouver, B.C., with stores in all of Western Canada's major cities, including Whitehorse in the Yukon. These stores carry everything from telephones and children's apparel to fresh fruits and seafood and even provide access to President's Choice Financial Services that are located in-store.

Recent years have seen the advent of superstores that are actually giant specialty stores, the so-called **category killers**. These "big-box" retailers are the megastores

Convenience store A small store located near a residential area that is open long hours, seven days a week and carries a limited line of high-turnover convenience goods.

Superstore A store much larger than a regular supermarket that carries a large assortment of routinely purchased food and nonfood items and offers services such as dry cleaning, post offices, photo finishing, check cashing, bill paying, lunch counters, car care, and pet care.

Category killer Giant specialty store that carries a very deep assortment of a particular line and is staffed by knowledgeable employees.

that have crossed the border from the United States. As big as airplane hangars, the stores carry a wide assortment of a particular line and have a knowledgeable staff. Home Depot Canada, Indigo, Office Depot, The Sports Authority, and Michaels Arts and Crafts are among the many recent entrants into the Canadian marketplace.

Finally, for some retailers, the product line is actually a service. **Service retailers** include hotels and motels, banks, airlines, colleges, hospitals, movie theatres, tennis clubs, bowling alleys, restaurants, repair services, hair care shops, and dry cleaners. Service retailers in Canada are growing faster than product retailers.

Relative Prices Retailers can also be classified according to the prices they charge. Most retailers charge regular prices and offer normal-quality goods and customer service. Others offer higher-quality goods and service at higher prices. The retailers that feature low prices are discount stores and "off-price" retailers.

Discount Stores A **discount store** sells standard merchandise at lower prices by accepting lower margins and selling higher volume. The early discount stores cut expenses by offering few services and operating in warehouselike facilities in low-rent, heavily travelled districts. In recent years, facing intense competition from other discounters and department stores, many discount retailers have "traded up." They have improved decor, added new lines and services, and opened suburban branches, which have led to higher costs and prices.

Off-Price Retailers When the major discount stores traded up, a new wave of **off-price retailers** moved in to fill the low-price, high-volume gap. Ordinary discounters buy at regular wholesale prices and accept lower margins to keep prices down. In contrast, off-price retailers buy at less-than-regular wholesale prices and charge consumers less than retail. Off-price retailers can be found in all areas, from food, clothing, and electronics to no-frills banking and discount brokerages.

The three main types of off-price retailers are *independents, factory outlets,* and *warehouse clubs.* **Independent off-price retailers** either are owned and run by entrepreneurs or are divisions of larger retail corporations. Although many off-price operations are run by smaller independents, most large off-price retailer operations are owned by bigger retail chains. Examples include store retailers such Winners, which is owned by U.S.-based TJX.

Factory outlets sometimes group together in *factory outlet malls*, which have become one of the hottest growth areas in retailing. The malls now are moving upscale—and even dropping "factory" from their descriptions—narrowing the gap between factory outlet and more traditional forms of retailers. As the gap narrows, the discounts offered by outlets are getting smaller. However, a growing number of outlet malls now feature brands such as Arrow Shirts, Nike, and Danier Leather, causing department stores to protest to the manufacturers of these brands. Given their higher costs, the department stores have to charge more than the off-price outlets. Manufacturers counter that they send last year's merchandise and seconds to the factory outlet malls, not the new merchandise that they supply to the department stores. The malls are also located far from urban areas, making travel to them more difficult. Still, the department stores are concerned about the growing number of shoppers willing to make weekend trips to stock up on branded merchandise at substantial savings.[5]

Service retailers Retailers that sell services rather than products.

Discount store A retail institution that sells standard merchandise at lower prices by accepting lower margins and selling at higher volume.

Off-price retailer Retailer that buys at below wholesale prices and sells at less than retail. Examples are factory outlets, independents, and warehouse clubs.

Independent off-price retailer Off-price retailer that is either owned and run by entrepreneurs or is division of larger retail corporation.

Factory outlet Off-price retailing operation that is owned and operated by a manufacturer and that normally carries the manufacturer's surplus, discontinued, or irregular goods.

Warehouse clubs (or *wholesale clubs* or *membership warehouses*), such as Costco, operate in huge warehouselike facilities and offer few frills. Customers themselves must wrestle furniture, heavy appliances, and other large items to the checkout line. Such clubs make no home deliveries and often accept no credit cards. However, they do offer ultralow prices and surprise deals on selected branded merchandise. Warehouse clubs took the country by storm in the 1980s and early 1990s, but their growth has slowed considerably of late because of the emergence of Wal-Mart and strong competitive reactions by supermarket chains.

Retail Organizations Although many retail stores are independently owned, an increasing number are banding together under some form of corporate or contractual organization. The major types of retail organizations—*corporate chains, voluntary chains* and *retailer cooperatives, franchise organizations,* and *merchandising conglomerates*—are described in Table 12-2.

Chain stores are two or more outlets that are commonly owned and controlled. They have many advantages over independents. Their size allows them to buy in large quantities at lower prices. They can afford to hire corporate-level specialists to deal with areas such as pricing, promotion, merchandising, inventory control, and sales forecasting. And corporate chains gain promotional economies because their advertising costs are spread over many stores and over a large sales volume.

The great success of corporate chains caused many independents to band together in one of two forms of contractual associations. One is the **voluntary chain**—a wholesaler-sponsored group of independent retailers that engages in group buying and common merchandising. Examples include Western Auto and Independent Grocers Alliance (IGA). The other form of contractual association is

Warehouse club Off-price retailer that sells a limited selection of brand name grocery items, appliances, clothing, and a hodgepodge of other goods at deep discounts to members who pay annual membership fees.

Chain stores Two or more outlets that are owned and controlled in common, have central buying and merchandising, and sell similar lines of merchandise.

Voluntary chain A wholesale-sponsored group of independent retailers that engages in group buying and common merchandising.

Warehouse clubs such as Costco operate in huge ware-house-like facilities and offer few services. However, they do offer ultralow prices and surprise deals on selected branded merchandise.

Table 12-2 Major Types of Retail Organizations

Type	Description	Examples
Corporate chain stores	Two or more outlets that are commonly owned and controlled, employ central buying and merchandising, and sell similar lines of merchandise. Corporate chains appear in all types of retailing, but they are strongest in department stores, variety stores, drugstores, shoe stores, and women's clothing stores.	La Senza (lingerie), Sports Experts (sports goods), Loblaws (grocery)
Voluntary chains	Wholesaler-sponsored groups of independent retailers engaged in bulk buying and common merchandising.	Independent Grocers Alliance (IGA), Western Auto, True Value Hardware
Retailer cooperatives	Groups of independent retailers that set up a central buying organization and conduct joint promotion efforts.	Calgary Group (groceries), ACE (hardware), Mountain Equipment Co-op (outdoor goods)
Franchise organizations	Contractual association between a *franchiser*—a manufacturer, wholesaler, or organization—and *franchisees*-independent businesspeople who buy the right to own and operate one or more units in the franchise system. Franchise organizations are normally based on some unique product, service, or method of doing business, or on a trade name or patent, or on goodwill that the franchiser has developed.	McDonald's, Subway, Pizza Hut, Jiffy Lube, 7-Eleven, Yogen Früz
Merchandising conglomerates	A free-form corporation that combines several diversified retailing lines and forms under central ownership, along with some integration of their distribution and management functions.	The Venator Group (owner of Foot Locker, Lady Foot Locker, Northern Reflections, Northern Traditions)

Retailer cooperative Independent retailers that band together to set up a jointly owned central warehouse operation and conduct joint merchandising and promotion efforts.

Franchise A contractual association between a manufacturer, wholesaler, or service organization (a franchiser) and independent businesspeople (franchisees) who buy the right to own and operate one or more units in the franchise system.

the **retailer cooperative**—independent retailers that band together to set up a jointly owned, central wholesale operation and conduct joint merchandising and promotion efforts. True Value Hardware is an example. These organizations give independents the buying and promotion economies they need to meet the prices of corporate chains.

Another form of contractual retail organization is a **franchise**. The main difference between franchise organizations and other contractual systems (voluntary chains and retail cooperatives) is that franchise systems are normally based on some unique product or service; on a method of doing business; or on the trade name, goodwill, or patent that the franchiser has developed. Franchising has been prominent in fast-foods restaurants, video stores, health or fitness centres, haircutting, auto rentals, motels, travel agencies, real estate, and dozens of other product and service areas. Franchising is described in detail in New Directions 12-1.

Merchandising conglomerates are corporations that combine several retailing forms under central ownership and share some distribution and management functions. The Venator Group operates a number of specialty chains including Northern Reflections, Northern Traditions, Northern Elements, and Northern Getaway as well as Kinney Shoe Stores and Foot Locker (sports shoes). Diversified retailing, which provides superior management systems and economies that benefit all the separate retail operations, is likely to increase.

Canadian Franchise Association www.cfa.ca

New Directions 12-1 >> Franchise Fever

Once considered upstarts among independent businesses, 65 000 franchised businesses now operate in Canada, with a new Canadian franchise opening every hour and forty-five minutes. Generating more than $90 billion in sales, franchises account for 48 percent of all service and retail sales in Canada, compared with 35 percent in the United States. The franchise industry directly employs more than one million Canadians. According to Francon, Canada's sole franchise research company, Canadians have embraced franchising as a means of self-employment to a far greater extent than the populace of any other country. This isn't hard to believe in a society where it's nearly impossible to stroll down a city block or drive on a suburban thoroughfare without seeing a Tim Hortons, McDonald's, Midas Muffler, or 7-Eleven. In fact, you might be forgiven for thinking every possible corner in Canada is occupied by a Tim Hortons. The TDL Group Ltd., which operates the franchises, had 1700 locations in Canada and 100 in the United States in 2000, when sales for the chain topped $1.6 billion.

A number of Canadian franchise operations are also reaching beyond their domestic borders and trying to hook the world on the baked goods that have expanded our waistlines. Cinnaroll Bakeries Ltd., **www.cinnzeo.com**, which operates 25 Cinn-

zeo outlets in Western Canada selling decadent fresh-baked cinnamon buns, currently has 10 Cinnzeo franchises in the Philippines, with an additional 30 expected to open by 2002. Cinnaroll has ambitious international marketing plans and has its eye on further expansion into South America, Australia, Eastern Canada, and the United States. Says Cinnaroll president and CEO, Brian Latham: "We're not ruling out any area of the world." Similarly, The Great Canadian Bagel Co. of Markham, Ontario, founded in 1993, now operates nearly 160 stores across Canada, while its sister company, The Great American Bagel, has 58 outlets in the United States. Both are owned by the same Canadian family, the Flatleys. In 1997, it launched a new venture—The Great International Bagel. The division currently markets their particular brand of doughy goodness in both the United Kingdom and Russia.

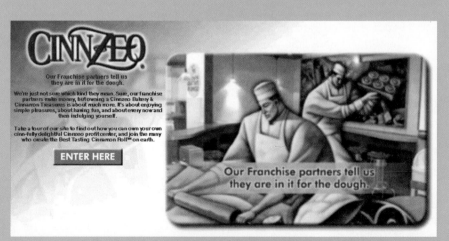

Canada's Cinnaroll Bakeries, which operates the Cinnzeo chain of outlets, has ambitious plans for overseas expansion.

How does a franchising system work? The individual franchises are a tightly knit group of enterprises whose systematic operations are planned, directed, and controlled by the operation's founder, called a *franchiser*. Generally, franchises are distinguished by three characteristics:

1. *The franchiser owns a trade or service mark and licenses it to franchisees in return for royalty payments.*

2. *The franchisee is required to pay for the right to be part of the system.* Yet this initial fee is only a small part of the total amount that franchisees invest when they sign a franchising contract. Start-up costs include rental and lease of equipment and fixtures, and sometimes a regular licence fee. McDonald's franchisees may invest as much as $864 000 in initial start-up costs. The franchisee then pays McDonald's a service fee and a rental charge that equal 11.5 percent of the franchisee's sales volume. Subway's success is partly due to its low start-up cost of $65 000 to $100 000, which is lower than 70 percent of other franchise system start-up costs.

3. *The franchiser provides its franchisees with a marketing and operations system for doing business.* McDonald's requires franchisees to attend its "Hamburger University" in Oak Brook, Illinois, for three weeks to learn how to manage the business. Franchisees must also adhere to certain procedures in buying materials.

In the best cases, franchising is mutually beneficial to both franchiser and franchisee. Franchisers can cover a new territory in little more than the time it takes the franchisee to sign a contract. They can achieve enormous purchasing power. (Consider the purchase order that Holiday Inn is likely to make for bed linens, for instance.) Franchisers also benefit from the franchisee's familiarity with local communities and conditions, and from the motivation and hard work of employees who are entrepreneurs rather than "hired hands." Similarly, franchisees benefit from buying into a proven business with a well-known and accepted brand name. And they receive ongoing support in areas ranging from marketing and advertising to site selection, staffing, and financing.

As a result of the franchise explosion in recent years, many types of franchisers are having difficulty.

John Lorinc, author of *Opportunity Knocks: The Truth about Canada's Franchise Industry,* says 35 percent of all franchises fail and 80 percent may only break even. Subway, in particular, has been criticized for misleading its franchisees by telling them that it has only a 2 percent failure rate when the reality is much different. Some franchisees also believe that they've been misled by exaggerated claims of support, only to feel abandoned after the contract is signed and $100 000 is invested. Difficulties may arise because of hidden costs imposed on franchisees or the signing up of people who lack the resources to get the business off the ground. The most common complaint: Franchisers focused on growth who "encroach" on existing franchisees' territory by bringing in another store. Or franchisees may object to parent-company marketing programs that may adversely affect their local operations. For instance, franchisees strongly resisted a McDonald's promotion in which the company reduced prices on Big Macs and Egg McMuffins in an effort to revive stagnant sales. Many franchisees believed that the promotion would cheapen McDonald's image and unnecessarily reduce their profit margins.

There will *always* be a conflict between the franchisers, who seek system-wide growth, and the franchisees, who want to earn a good living from their individual franchises. Some new directions that may deliver both franchiser growth and franchisee earnings are the following:

- *Strategic alliances, co-branding, and twinning.* The newest trend in franchising is the marriage between two independent franchises at a single location. Tim Hortons, for example, often shares facilities with Wendy's; Baskin-Robbins teams up with Dunkin Donuts; Second Cup partners with Harvey's. Since the largest costs borne by franchisees are for land and staff, forming an alliance with another franchisee to share a location makes economic sense and can draw a more broad-based market to the joint outlets.

- *Code of ethics.* Each member of the Canadian Franchise Association is bound by a code of ethics designed to overcome some areas of difficulty. The code stipulates these conditions: There will be a full and accurate written disclosure of all information considered material to the franchise relationship; the company selling the franchise will provide reasonable guidance, training, and supervision for franchisees; fairness shall characterize all dealings between the franchiser and its franchisees; and the franchiser shall make every effort to resolve complaints, grievances, and disputes through fair and reasonable negotiation.

- *Nontraditional site locations.* Franchises have opened in airports, sports stadiums, university campuses, hospitals, gambling casinos, theme parks, convention halls, and even river boats.

Franchise fever is unlikely to cool down soon. Canadian franchisers like Uniglobe Travel International, Speedy Muffler King, Priority Management Systems Inc., and Manchu Wok are not only growing in Canada, they are conquering international markets as well.

Sources: David North, "King Cruller," *Canadian Business,* 31 December 1999; David Todd, "Great Canadian Bagel Makes Slow but Sure Gains in Moscow," *Strategy,* 14 February 2000, p. 27; Norma Ramage, "Canadian Cinnamon Buns Savoured in Asia," *Marketing On-Line,* 19 June 2000; Norman D. Axelrad and Robert E. Weigand, "Franchising—A Marriage of System Members," in Sidney Levy, George Frerichs, and Howard Gordon, eds., *Marketing Managers Handbook,* 3rd ed., Chicago: Darnell, 1994, pp. 919–934; Lawrence S. Welch, "Developments in International Franchising," *Journal of Global Marketing,* 6(1–2), 1992, pp. 81–96; Andrew E. Serwer, "McDonald's Conquers the World," *Fortune,* 17 October 1994, pp. 103–116; "Trouble in Franchise Nation," *Fortune,* 6 March 1995, pp. 115–129; Robert Maynard, "The Decision to Franchise," *Nation's Business,* January 1997, p. 49–53; Cliff Edwards, "'Campaign 55' Flop Shows Growing Power of Franchisees," *Marketing News,* 7 July 1997, p. 9; "Canadian Franchise Association Code of Ethics," Advertising Supplement, *The Globe and Mail,* 18 September 1996, p. 6; Jennifer Lanthier, "How Franchises Seduce Those with the Most to Lose," *Financial Post,* 22 April 1997, p. 28, Susan Noakes, "Creating Marriages of Convenience," *Financial Post,* 14 February 1997, p. 16; Industry Canada "Canadian Capabilities: Key facts about Canadian Franchise Expertise," accessed online at **strategis.ic.gc.ca/SSG/dm01301e.html**, 7 November 2002; information accessed online at **www.cfa.ca**.

Slow down and think about all the different kinds of retailers you deal with regularly, many of which overlap in the products they carry.

- Pick a familiar product: a camera, microwave oven, hand tool, or something else. Shop for this product at two very different store types, say a discount store or category killer on the one hand, and a department store or smaller specialty store on the other. Compare the stores on product assortment, services, and prices. If you were going to buy the product, where would you buy it and why?

- What does your shopping trip suggest about the futures of the competing store formats that you sampled?

Retailer Marketing Decisions

Retailers are searching for new marketing strategies to attract and hold customers. In the past, retailers attracted customers with unique products, more or better services than their competitors offered, or credit cards. Today, national-brand manufacturers, in their drive for volume, have placed their branded goods everywhere. Thus, stores offer more similar assortments—national brands are found not only in department stores but also in mass-merchandise and off-price discount stores. As a result, stores are looking increasingly alike.

Service differentiation among retailers has also eroded. Many department stores have trimmed their services, whereas discounters have increased theirs. Customers have become smarter and more price sensitive. They see no reason to pay more for identical brands, especially when service differences are shrinking. For all these reasons, many retailers today are rethinking their marketing strategies.

As shown in Figure12-1, retailers face major marketing decisions about their *target market* and *positioning, product assortment and services, price, promotion,* and *place.*

Target Market and Positioning Decision Retailers first must define their target markets and then decide how they will position themselves in these markets. Should the store focus on upscale, midscale, or downscale shoppers? Do target shoppers want variety, depth of assortment, convenience, or low prices? Until they define and profile their markets, retailers cannot make consistent decisions about product assortment, services, pricing, advertising, store decor, or any of the other decisions that must support their positions.

Too many retailers fail to define their target markets and positions clearly. They try to have "something for everyone" and end up satisfying no market well. In contrast, successful retailers define their target markets well and position themselves strongly. For example, in 1963, Leslie H. Wexner borrowed $7000 from his aunt to create *The Limited,* which started as a single store targeted to young, fashion-conscious women. All aspects of the store—clothing assortment, fixtures, music, colours, personnel—were orchestrated to match the target consumer. He continued to open more stores, but a decade later his original customers were no longer in the "young" group. To catch the new "youngs," he started Express. Over the years, he has started or acquired other highly targeted store chains, including Lane Bryant, Victoria's Secret, Lerner, Structure, Bath & Body Works, and others to reach new segments. Today The Limited, Inc. operates more than 5300 stores in several different segments of the market, with sales of more than $23 billion.

Even large stores such as Wal-Mart, Sears, and The Bay must define their major target markets to design effective marketing strategies. In fact, in recent years, thanks to strong targeting and positioning, Wal-Mart has expanded to a point where its sales are almost equal to General Motors.

Product Assortment and Services Decision Retailers must decide on three major product variables: *product assortment, services mix,* and *store atmosphere.*

The retailer's *product assortment* should match target shoppers' expectations. In its quest to differentiate itself from competitors, a retailer can use any of several product-differentiation strategies. The retailer must determine both the product assortment's *width* and its *depth.* Thus, a restaurant can offer a narrow and shallow assortment (small lunch counter), a narrow and deep assortment (delicatessen), a wide and shallow assortment (cafeteria), or a wide and deep assortment (large

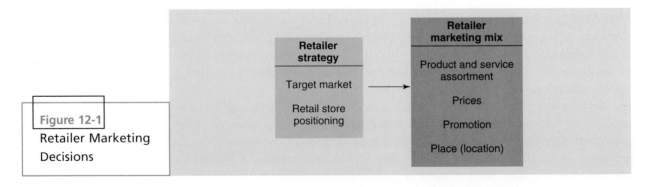

Figure 12-1
Retailer Marketing Decisions

restaurant). Another product assortment element is the *quality* of the goods: The customer is interested not only in the range of choice but also in the quality of the products available.

No matter what the store's product assortment and quality level, there always will be competitors with similar assortments and quality. Therefore, the retailer must find other ways to *differentiate* itself from similar competitors. It can use any of several product differentiation strategies. For one, it can offer merchandise that no other competitor carries—its own private brands or national brands on which it holds exclusives. Many of Canada's best-performing fashion retailers—Club Monaco, Roots Canada, and the Venator Group—not only stock their stores with their own brands of clothing, but also extend these brands into new lines of accessories and cosmetic products. Items such as jewellery, belts, backpacks, perfume, and toiletries are used to reinforce the store's brand image.[6] Second, the retailer can feature blockbuster merchandising events—Ben Moss Jewellers is known throughout Western Canada for their promotions involving celebrities. Finally, the retailer can differentiate itself by offering a highly targeted product assortment—Penningtons and Cotton Ginny Plus carry clothing for larger-sized women.

Retailers also must decide on a *services mix* to offer customers. The old mom-and-pop grocery stores offered home delivery, credit, and conversation—services that today's supermarkets ignore. The services mix is one of the key tools of nonprice competition for setting one store apart from another.

The store's *atmosphere* is another element in its product arsenal. Every store has a physical layout that makes moving around in it either hard or easy. Each store has a "feel"; one store is cluttered, another charming, a third plush, a fourth sombre. The store must have a planned atmosphere that suits the target market and moves customers to buy.

Virgin Megastore is the epitome of stores combining shopping and entertainment, with features including an in-store DJ booth, individual listening stations, booths for viewing movies, and a café.

Increasingly, retailers are turning their stores into theatres that transport customers into unusual, exciting shopping environments. Virgin Group (the company that includes Virgin Atlantic Airways, Virgin Hotels, Virgin Megastore, and Virgin Communications) has just entered retailing. The new music and entertainment Virgin Megastore in downtown Vancouver is the epitome of stores combining shopping and entertainment. The 12 000-square-metre facility has a wealth of interactive features including an in-store DJ booth, individual listening stations, booths for viewing movies, and a café where people can sip espresso. In-store performances encourage shoppers to spend more time and, of course, more money. Careful attention was paid to store design. Wide aisles, escalators, and careful signage allow for easy movement through the store. Metal and marble are used in some sections to give them a modern look; fresco-like murals are used in others to create a completely different atmosphere.[7]

Chapters/Indigo uses atmospherics to turn shopping for books into entertainment. It knows that shopping is a social activity for many consumers: People shop not only to make purchases, but also to mingle with others, see what's new, and treat themselves to something interesting or unexpected. Thus, Chapters/Indigo stores feature rich colours and wood accents. They hold special events and appearances by authors. They also offer plenty of space, where people can meet and feel at home.[8]

All this confirms that retail stores are much more than simply assortments of goods. They are environments to be experienced by the people who shop in them. Store atmospheres offer a powerful tool by which retailers can differentiate their stores from those of competitors.

Price Decision A retailer's price policy is a crucial positioning factor and must be decided in relation to its target market, its product and service assortment, and its competition. All retailers would like to charge high markups and achieve high volume, but the two seldom go together. Most retailers seek *either* high markups on lower volume (most specialty stores) *or* low markups on higher volume (mass merchandisers and discount stores). Thus, Winnipeg-based Hanford Drewitt prices men's suits starting at $1000 and shoes at $400—it sells a low volume but makes a hefty profit on each sale. At the other extreme, Winners sells brand-name clothing at discount prices, settling for a lower margin on each sale but selling at a much higher volume

Promotion Decision Retailers use the normal promotion tools—advertising, personal selling, sales promotion, public relations, and direct marketing—to reach consumers. They advertise in newspapers, magazines, radio, and television. Advertising may be supported by newspaper inserts and direct-mail pieces. Personal selling requires careful training of salespeople in how to greet customers, meet their needs, and handle their complaints. Sales promotions may include in-store demonstrations, displays, contests, and visiting celebrities. Public relations activities, such as press conferences and speeches, store openings, special events, newsletters, magazines, and public service activities, are always available to retailers. Most retailers also have Web sites, offering customers information and other features and often selling merchandise directly.

Place Decision Retailers often cite three critical factors in retailing success: *location, location,* and *location!* A retailer's location is key to its ability to attract customers. And the costs of building or leasing facilities have a major impact on the retailer's profits. Thus, site-location decisions are among the most important the retailer makes. Small retailers may have to settle for whatever locations they can find or afford. Large retailers usually employ specialists who select locations using advanced methods. One of the savviest location experts in recent years has been the toy-store giant Toys "R" Us. Most of their new locations are in rapidly growing areas where the population closely matches their customer base.

Most stores today cluster together to increase their customer pulling power and to give consumers the convenience of one-stop shopping. *Central business districts* were the main form of retail cluster until the 1950s. Every large city and town had a central business district with department stores, specialty stores, banks, and movie theatres. When people began to move to the suburbs, however, these central business districts, with their traffic, parking, and crime problems, began to lose business. Downtown merchants opened branches in suburban shopping centres, and the decline of the central business districts continued. In recent years, many cities have joined with merchants to try to revive downtown shopping areas by building malls and providing underground parking.

A **shopping centre** is a group of retail businesses planned, developed, owned, and managed as a unit. A *regional shopping centre,* the largest and most dramatic shopping centre, contains between 40 and 200 stores. It is like a covered miniature downtown and attracts customers from a wide area. A *community shopping centre* contains between 15 and 40 retail stores. It normally contains a branch of a department store or variety store, a supermarket, specialty stores, professional offices, and sometimes a bank. Most shopping centres are *neighbourhood shopping centres* or *strip malls* that generally contain between 5 and 15 stores. They are close and convenient for consumers. They usually contain a supermarket, perhaps a discount store, and several service stores—dry cleaner, self-service laundry, drugstore, video-rental outlet, barber or beauty shop, hardware store, or other stores.

> **Shopping centre** A group of retail businesses planned, developed, owned, and managed as a unit.

All shopping centres combined now account for about one third of all retail sales, but they may have reached their saturation point. Through the past decade, on average, consumers have been going to traditional malls less often, staying a shorter time, and visiting fewer stores. Why are people using shopping malls less? First, with more dual-income households, people have less time to shop. "You have two workers in every family and no one has time to go to the mall for four hours anymore," observes one industry analyst. "People who used to go to the mall 20 times a year now go two or three times."[9]

Second, a recent survey of B.C. shoppers revealed that 58 percent of consumers now find shopping more of a chore than they did in the past. Listed as the top three reasons for their frustration were long line-ups at checkouts, poor service, and lack of assistance in stores.[10]

Furthermore, shoppers appear to be tiring of traditional malls, which are too big, too crowded, and too much alike. Today's large malls offer great selection but are less comfortable and convenient. Finally, today's consumers have many alternatives to traditional malls, ranging from online shopping to *power centres,* which are presenting

Today's consumers have many alternatives to traditional malls, ranging from online shopping to power centres, which are presenting a new challenge to traditional malls.

a new challenge to traditional malls. These unenclosed shopping centres consist of a long strip of retail stores, including large, free-standing anchors such as Wal-Mart, Home Depot, Staples, Michaels, and Danier Leather Outlet. Each store has its own entrance with parking directly in front for shoppers who wish to visit only one store. Add to all this the emergence of Internet shopping, and you can see why some retail analysts believe the concept of the shopping mall is beginning to look dated.

The Future of Retailing

Retailers operate in a harsh and fast-changing environment, which offers threats as well as opportunities. For example, the industry suffers from chronic overcapacity, resulting in fierce competition for customer dollars. Consumer demographics, lifestyles, and shopping patterns are changing rapidly, as are retailing technologies. To be successful, then, retailers will have to choose target segments carefully and position themselves strongly. They will have to consider the following retailing developments as they plan and execute their competitive strategies.

New Retail Forms and Shortening Retail Life Cycles New retail forms continue to emerge to meet new situations and consumer needs, but the life cycle of new retail forms is getting shorter. Department stores took about 100 years to reach the mature stage of the life cycle; more recent forms, such as warehouse stores, reached maturity in about 10 years. In such an environment, seemingly solid retail positions can crumble quickly. One of Canada's most venerable retailers, Eaton's, knows this very well. The fall of the 127-year-old retailing veteran "serves as a stark reminder to mass-market retailers that past success means little in a fiercely competitive and rapidly changing industry."[11] Retailers can no longer sit back and rely on a once-successful formula—they must keep adapting.

Wheel of retailing concept A concept of retailing that states that new types of retailers usually begin as low-margin, low-price, low-status operations but later evolve into higher-priced, higher-service operations, eventually becoming like the conventional retailers they replaced

Many retailing innovations are partially explained by the **wheel of retailing concept**.[12] According to this concept, many new types of retailing forms begin as low-margin, low-price, low-status operations. They challenge established retailers that have become "fat" by letting their costs and margins increase. The new retailers' success leads them to upgrade their facilities and offer more services. In turn, their costs increase, forcing them to increase their prices. Eventually, the new retailers become like the conventional retailers they replaced. The cycle begins again when still newer types of retailers evolve with lower costs and prices. The wheel of retailing concept seems to explain the initial success and later troubles of department stores, supermarkets, and discount stores, and the recent success of off-price retailers.

Growth of Nonstore Retailing Although most retailing still takes place the old-fashioned way across countertops in stores, consumers now have an array of alternatives, including mail order, television, phone, and online shopping (see New Directions 12-2).

New Directions 12-2 >> E-Tailing: Alive, Well, and Growing

Most of us still make most of our purchases the old-fashioned way: We go to the store, find what we want, wait patiently in line to plunk down our cash or credit card, and bring home the goods. However, a growing number of retailers now provide an attractive alternative—one that lets us browse, select, order, and pay with little more effort than it takes to apply an index finger to a mouse button. They sell a rich variety of goods ranging from books, CDs, flowers, and food to stereo equipment, kitchen appliances, airplane tickets, auto parts, home mortgages, and bags of cement.

Only a few years ago, prospects for online retailing were soaring. Many experts predicted that—as more and more consumers flocked to the Web—a new breed of fast-moving e-tailers would quickly surpass stodgy "old economy" store retailers. Some even saw a day when we'd be doing almost all of our shopping via the Internet. However, the dot-com meltdown of 2000 dashed these overblown expectations, as many once-brash Web sellers such as eToys.com, Pets.com, Webvan.com, and Garden.com crashed and burned. In fact, after the shakeout of 2000, expectations reversed almost overnight. The experts now began to predict that no Web-only retailer could survive and that e-tailing was destined to be little more than a tag-on to in-store retailing.

Such doom-and-gloom scenarios, however, don't reflect the current state of Internet retailing. Although the pace has slowed and the playing ground is shifting,

today's e-tailing is alive, well, and growing. Projected online retail sales of $34 billion in 2001 are expected to grow to $130 billion by 2006. "The bubble may have burst, but this hasn't stopped millions of people from shopping online," says Toys "R" Us executive Ray Arthur. Bill Bass of Landsend.com often fields the same question from reporters, "How are you surviving the bloodbath?" He often retorts, "What bloodbath?" Sales on the Lands' End Web site have more than doubled during the past two years and now bring in 16 percent of the company's revenues.

Although the dramatic dot-com collapses have grabbed most of the headlines, some click-only retailers are now making it big on the Web. Heading this group is online auction site eBay, which has been consistently profitable since its inception—click-only competitors such as eBay and Amazon.com Auctions account for a lion's share of the online auctions business. Pure-play e-tailers account for a majority of online sales in several other categories as well, including books, music and video, foods and beverages, and collectibles. Business is also booming for online travel companies such as Travelocity.com and Expedia, which use the Web to sell airline tickets, hotel rooms, and discount travel packages to consumers. Thanks to these sites, online travel bookings grew 59 percent this year. In many ways, selling air travel on the Internet is a natural. Most air travel sold online uses e-tickets and e-confirmations, so no products need to be stored or shipped. "There are a bunch of businesses that don't make sense on the

Internet," says a Wall Street analyst. "Travel is the quintessential one that does."

Still, much of the anticipated growth in online sales will go to multichannel retailers—the click-and-brick marketers who can successfully merge the virtual and physical worlds. Toys "R" Us's Ray Arthur points out that Toysrus.com's initial online competitors, click-only operations such as eToys.com and Toysmart.com, have now closed their cyberdoors. In their place is a new lineup of click-and-brick competitors such as Walmart.com, Kbkids.com, and Kmart's BlueLight.com. In other categories as well, the true winners these days appear to be established brick-and-mortar companies that have added Web selling. It seems that almost every established retailer is now hanging out a shingle in Webland. Examples include Charles Schwab and Fidelity Investments (financial services), Dell and IBM (computers), Lands' End and L.L. Bean (apparel), and Staples and Office Depot (office supplies), to name just a few.

So, despite some serious setbacks and uncertainties, online retailing is anything but dead. Says one analyst about the recent successes of Travelocity.com and Expedia: "None of this guarantees that online travel won't crash someday like the rest of the dot-coms. But as the market takes off, these skies are looking downright friendly."

Sources: Based on Dennis K. Berman and Heather Green, "Cliff-Hanger Christmas," *Business Week,* 23 October 2000, pp. EB30–EB38; Molly Prior, "E-Commerce Alive and Well in the New Economy," *DSN Retailing Today,* 4 June 2001, p. 10; Wendy Zellner, "Where the Net Delivers: Travel," *Business Week,* 11 June 2001, pp. 142–144; Lewis Braham, "E-Tailers Are Clicking," *Business Week,* 23 July 2001, p. 73.

Despite all the talk about the Internet sounding the death knell of bricks-and-mortar retail operations, online shopping and retailing is still in its infancy and currently represents less than 3 percent of retail sales. Although Canadians are one of the most wired populations in the world, and declare themselves ready, willing, and able to shop online, they often find that there are few Canadian Web sites on which to make their purchases. Canadian retailers have been somewhat slow in entering the e-tailing race for a number of reasons. First, many don't see e-tailing as a significant competitive threat even though 63 percent of the dollars Canadian e-shoppers spend go to the United States. Other barriers to e-tailing development include lack of senior executive commitment, challenges of order fulfillment, lack of resources, and the complexity of measuring online performance.[13] However, e-tailing is expected to grow rapidly since Canadians have a history of being rapid adopters of new technologies and more and more Canadian retailers are starting to enter cyberspace using their sites to complement their store sales or provide consumers with product information.

Increasing Intertype Competition Today's retailers increasingly face competition from many different forms of retailers. For example, consumers can buy CDs at specialty music stores, discount music stores, electronics superstores, general merchandise discount stores, video-rental outlets, and through dozens of Web sites. They can buy books at stores ranging from independent local bookstores to discount stores such as Wal-Mart, superstores such as Chapters/Indigo, or Web sites such as Amazon.ca. And when it comes to brand name appliances, department stores, discount stores, off-price retailers, or electronics superstores all compete for the same customers. Industry experts note that there is a trend toward more cross-shopping—consumers buying one item at upscale retailers like Holt Renfrew and another from the Dollar Store.

The competition between chain superstores and smaller, independently owned stores has become particularly heated. Because of their bulk buying power and high sales volume, chains can buy at lower costs and thrive on smaller margins. The arrival of a superstore can quickly force nearby independents out of business. Yet the news is not all bad for smaller companies. Many small, independent retailers are thriving. Independents are finding that sheer size and marketing muscle are often no match for the personal touch small stores can provide or the specialty niches that small stores fill for a devoted customer base.

The Rise of Megaretailers The rise of huge mass merchandisers and specialty superstores, the formation of vertical marketing systems and buying alliances, and a rash of retail mergers and acquisitions have created a core of superpower megaretailers. Through their superior information systems and buying power, these giant retailers are able to offer better merchandise selections, good service, and strong price savings to consumers. As a result, they grow even larger by squeezing out their smaller, weaker competitors. The megaretailers also are shifting the balance of power between retailers and producers. A relative handful of retailers now controls access to enormous numbers of consumers, giving them the upper hand in their dealings with manufacturers. For example, Wal-Mart's revenues are more than five times those of Procter & Gamble, and Wal-Mart generates more than 20 percent of P&G's revenues. Wal-Mart can, and often does, use this power to wring concessions from P&G and other suppliers.[14]

The Growing Importance of Retail Technology Retail technologies are becoming critically important as competitive tools. Progressive retailers are using computers to produce better forecasts, control inventory costs, order electronically from suppliers, send e-mail among stores, and even sell to customers within stores. They are adopting checkout scanning systems, online transaction processing, electronic funds transfer, electronic data interchange, in-store television, and improved merchandise-handling systems.

Perhaps the most startling advances in retailing technology concern the ways in which today's retailers are connecting with customers:

In the past, life was simple. Retailers connected with their customers through stores, through their salespeople, through the brands and packages they sold, and through direct mail and advertising in the mass media. But today, life is more complex. There are dozens of new ways to attract and engage consumers....Indeed, even if one omits the obvious—the Web—retailers are still surrounded by technical innovations that promise to redefine the way they and manufacturers interact with customers. Consider, as just a sampling, touch screen kiosks, electronic shelf labels and signs, handheld shopping assistants, smart cards, self-scanning systems, virtual reality displays, and intelligent agents. So, if we ask the question, Will technology change the way [retailers] interface with customers in the future? the answer has got to be yes.[15]

The Global Expansion of Major Retailers Retailers with unique formats and strong brand positioning are increasingly moving into other countries. Many are expanding internationally to escape mature and saturated home markets. Over the years, several giant retailers—McDonald's, The Gap, Toys "R" Us—have become globally prominent because of their great marketing prowess. Others, such as Wal-Mart, are rapidly establishing a global presence. Wal-Mart, which now operates more than 1000 stores in nine countries abroad, sees exciting global potential. Its international division racked up fiscal 2001 sales of more than $32 billion, an increase of 41 percent over the previous year. Here's what happened when it opened two new stores in Shenzhen, China:

[Customers came] by the hundreds of thousands—up to 175,000 on Saturdays alone—to China's first Wal-Mart Supercenter and Sam's Club. They broke the display glass to snatch out chickens at one store and carted off all the big-screen TVs before the other store had been open an hour. The two out-lets...were packed on Day One and have been bustling ever since.[16]

However, U.S. retailers are still significantly behind Europe and Asia when it comes to global expansion. Only 18 percent of the top U.S. retailers operate glob-ally compared to 31 percent of Asian retailers and 40 percent of European retailers. Marks and Spencer, which started out as a penny bazaar in 1884, grew into a chain of variety stores over the decades and now has a thriving string of 150 franchised stores around the world, which sell mainly its private-label clothes, including Brooks Brothers. It also runs a major food business. IKEA's well-constructed but inexpensive furniture has proven very popular in Canada, where shoppers often spend an entire day in an IKEA store. And Carrefour, the world's second largest retailer after Wal-Mart, has embarked on an aggressive mission to extend its role as a leading international retailer:

Nowhere has that been more obvious than in its own backyards of France and Europe, where Carrefour operates 680 hypermarkets, 2260 supermarkets, and 3120 deep discount food stores. By purchasing or merging with a variety of retailers, Carrefour has accelerated its hold over the European market, where it now claims retail dominance in four leading markets: France, Spain, Belgium and Greece; it's the No. 2 retailer in Italy. But one of the retailer's greatest strengths is its market position outside of France and Europe. In South America, for instance, Carrefour is the market leader in Brazil and Argentina, where it operates more than 300 stores. By comparison, Wal-Mart has only 25 units in those two countries. In China, the land of more than a billion con-sumers, Carrefour operates 22 hypermarkets to Wal-Mart's five supercentres and one Sam's Club. In the Pacific rim, excluding China, Carrefour operates 33 hypermarkets in five countries to Wal-Mart's five units in South Korea alone. Carrefour is also on track to beat the competition into the Japanese market, the world's second largest nation in terms of consumption. In the all-important emerging markets of China, South America, and the Pacific rim, Carrefour outpaces Wal-Mart five-to-one in actual revenue. In short, Carrefour is bound-ing ahead of Wal-Mart in most markets outside North America. The only ques-tion: Can the French titan hold its lead? While no one retailer can rightly claim to be in the same league with Wal-Mart as an overall retail presence, Carrefour stands a better chance than most to dominate global retailing.[17]

Retail Stores as Communities or Hangouts With the rise in the number of people living alone, working at home, or living in isolated and sprawling suburbs has come a resurgence of establishments that, regardless of the product or service they offer, also provide a place for people to get together. These places include cafés, tea shops, juice bars, bookshops, superstores, children's play spaces, brew pubs, and urban greenmarkets. Brew pubs offer tastings and a place to pass the time. The Discovery Zone, a chain of children's play spaces, offers indoor spaces where kids can go wild without breaking anything and stressed-out parents can exchange stories. And today's bookstores have become part bookstore, part library, and part living room.

Welcome to today's bookstore. The one featuring not only shelves and cash registers but also cushy chairs and coffee bars. It's where backpack-toting high school students come to do homework, where retirees thumb through the gardening books and parents read aloud to their toddlers. If no one actually buys books, that's just fine, say bookstore owners and managers. They're offering something grander than ink and paper, anyway. They're selling comfort, relaxation, community.[18]

Brick-and-mortar retailers are not the only ones creating community. Others have also built virtual communities on the Internet.

Sony actively builds community among its Playstation customers. Its recent Playstation.com campaign created message boards where its game players could post messages to one another. The boards are incredibly active, discussing techie topics but also providing the opportunity for members, fiercely competitive and opinionated, to vote on lifestyle issues, such as music and personal taste, no matter how trivial. Although Sony is laissez-faire about the boards and does not feed them messages, the company sees the value in having its customers' adamant conversations occur directly on its site. "Our customers are our evangelists. They are a very vocal and loyal fan base," says a Sony spokesperson. "There are things we can learn from them."[19]

WHOLESALING

Wholesaling includes all activities involved in selling goods and services to those buying for resale or business use. We call **wholesalers** those firms engaged *primarily* in wholesaling activity.

Wholesalers buy mostly from producers and sell mostly to retailers, industrial consumers, and other wholesalers. But why are wholesalers used at all? For example, why would a producer use wholesalers rather than selling directly to retailers or consumers?

Wholesaling All activities involved in selling goods and services to those buying for resale or business use.

Wholesaler A firm engaged *primarily* in wholesaling activity.

Retailer communities: Sony Playstation.com Web site builds community among its customers. The site's message boards are incredibly active, discussing techie topics but also lifestyle issues, such as music and personal taste.

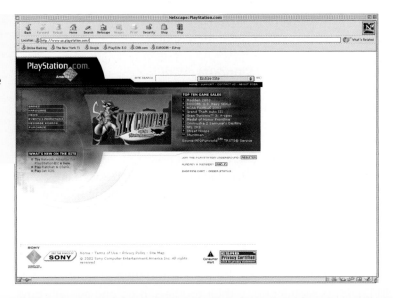

Time out! So-called experts have long predicted that nonstore retailing eventually will replace store retailing as our primary way to shop. What do you think?

• Shop for a good book at the Chapters/Indigo Web site at **www.chapters.indigo.ca**, taking time to browse the site and see what it has to offer. Next, shop at a nearby Chapters or Indigo, or other bookstore. Compare the two shopping experiences. Where would you rather shop? on what occasions? Why?

• Chapters/Indigo store creates an ideal community where people can hang out. How does its Web site compare on this dimension?

Quite simply, wholesalers are often better at performing one or more of the following channel functions:

• *Selling and promoting:* Wholesalers' sales forces help manufacturers reach many small customers at a low cost. The wholesaler has more contacts and is often more trusted by the buyer than the distant manufacturer.

• *Buying and assortment building:* Wholesalers can select items and build assortments needed by their customers, thereby saving the consumers much work.

• *Bulk breaking:* Wholesalers save their customers money by buying in carload lots and breaking bulk (breaking large lots into small quantities).

• *Warehousing:* Wholesalers hold inventories, thereby reducing the inventory costs and risks of suppliers and customers.

• *Transportation:* Wholesalers can provide quicker delivery to buyers because they are closer than the producers.

• *Financing:* Wholesalers finance their customers by giving credit, and they finance their suppliers by ordering early and paying bills on time.

• *Risk bearing:* Wholesalers absorb risk by taking title and bearing the cost of theft, damage, spoilage, and obsolescence.

- *Market information:* Wholesalers give information to suppliers and customers about competitors, new products, and price developments.

- *Management services and advice:* Wholesalers often help retailers train their salesclerks, improve store layouts and displays, and set up accounting and inventory control systems.

Types of Wholesalers

Wholesalers fall into three major groups (see Table 12-3): *merchant wholesalers, agents and brokers,* and *manufacturers' sales branches and offices.* **Merchant wholesalers** are the largest single group of wholesalers, accounting for roughly 50 percent of all wholesaling. Merchant wholesalers include two broad types: full-service wholesalers and limited-service wholesalers. *Full-service wholesalers* provide a full set of services, whereas the various *limited-service wholesalers* offer fewer services to their suppliers and customers. The several different types of limited-service wholesalers perform varied specialized functions in the distribution channel.

Brokers and *agents* differ from merchant wholesalers in two ways: They do not take title to goods, and they perform only a few functions. Like merchant wholesalers, they generally specialize by product line or customer type. A **broker** brings buyers and sellers together and assists in negotiation. **Agents** represent buyers or sellers on a more permanent basis. *Manufacturers' agents* (also called manufacturers' representatives) are the most common type of agent wholesaler. The third

Merchant wholesaler Independently owned business that takes title to the merchandise it handles.

Broker A wholesaler who does not take title to goods and whose function is to bring buyers and sellers together and assist in negotiation.

Agent A wholesaler who represents buyers or sellers on a relatively permanent basis, performs only a few functions, and does not take title to goods.

Manufacturers' sales branches and offices Wholesaling by sellers or buyers themselves rather than through independent wholesalers.

Table 12-3 Major Types of Wholesalers

Type	Description
Merchant Wholesalers	Independently owned businesses that take title to the merchandise they handle. In different trades, they are known as *jobbers, distributors,* or *mill supply houses.* Include full-service wholesalers and limited-service wholesalers:
Full-service wholesalers	Provide a full line of services: carrying stock, maintaining a sales force, offering credit, making deliveries, and providing management assistance. There are two types:
Wholesale merchants	Sell primarily to retailers and provide a full range of services. *General-merchandise wholesalers* carry several merchandise lines, while *general-line wholesalers* carry one or two lines in greater depth. *Specialty wholesalers* specialize in carrying only part of a line. (Examples: health-food wholesalers, seafood wholesalers.)
Industrial distributors	Sell to manufacturers rather than to retailers. Provide several services, such as carrying stock, offering credit, and providing delivery. May carry a broad range of merchandise, a general line, or a specialty line.
Limited-service wholesalers	Offer fewer services than full-service wholesalers. Limited-service wholesalers are of several types:

Type	Description
Cash-and-carry wholesalers	Carry a limited line of fast-moving goods and sell to small retailers for cash. Normally do not deliver. Example: A small fish store retailer may drive to a cash-and-carry fish wholesaler, buy fish for cash, and bring the merchandise back to the store.
Truck wholesalers (or truck jobbers)	Perform primarily a selling and delivery function. Carry a limited line of semi-perishable merchandise (such as milk, bread, snack foods), which they sell for cash as they make their rounds of supermarkets, small groceries, hospitals, restaurants, factory cafeterias, and hotels.
Drop shippers	Do not carry inventory or handle the product. Upon receiving an order, they select a manufacturer, who ships the merchandise directly to the customer. The drop shipper assumes title and risk from the time the order is accepted to its delivery to the customer. They operate in such bulk industries as coal, lumber, and heavy equipment.
Rack jobbers	Serve grocery and drug retailers, mostly in non-food items. They send delivery trucks to stores, where the delivery people set up toys, paperbacks, hardware items, health and beauty aids, or other items. They price the goods, keep them fresh, set up point-of-purchase displays, and keep inventory records. Rack jobbers retain title to the goods and bill the retailers only for the goods sold to consumers.
Producers' cooperatives	Owned by farmer members and assemble farm produce to sell in local markets. The co-op's profits are distributed to members at the end of the year. They often attempt to improve product quality and promote a co-op brand name, such as Sun Maid raisins, Sunkist oranges, or Diamond walnuts.
Mail-order wholesalers	Send catalogues to retail, industrial, and institutional customers featuring jewellery, cosmetics, specialty foods, and other small items. Maintain no outside sales force. Main customers are businesses in small outlying areas. Orders are filled and sent by mail, truck, or other transportation.
Brokers and Agents	Do not take title to goods. Main function is to facilitate buying and selling, for which they earn a commission on the selling price. Generally specialize by product line or customer types.
Brokers	Chief function is bringing buyers and sellers together and assisting in negotiation. They are paid by the party who hired them, and do not carry inventory, get involved in financing, or assume risk. Examples: food brokers, real estate brokers, insurance brokers, and security brokers.
Agents	Represent either buyers or sellers on a more permanent basis than brokers do. There are several types:
Manufacturers' agents	Represent two or more manufacturers of complementary lines. A formal written agreement with each manufacturer covers pricing, territories, order handling, delivery service and warranties, and commission rates. Often used in such lines as apparel, furniture, and electrical goods. Most manufacturers' agents are small businesses, with only a few skilled salespeople as employees. They are hired by small manufacturers who cannot afford their own field sales forces, and by large manufacturers who use agents to open new territories or to cover territories that cannot support full-time salespeople.

Type	Description
Selling agents	Have contractual authority to sell a manufacturer's entire output. The manufacturer either is not interested in the selling function or feels unqualified. The selling agent serves as a sales department and has significant influence over prices, terms, and conditions of sale. Found in such product areas as textiles, industrial machinery and equipment, coal and coke, chemicals, and metals.
Purchasing agents	Generally have a long-term relationship with buyers and make purchases for them, often receiving, inspecting, warehousing, and shipping the merchandise to the buyers. They provide helpful market information to clients and help them obtain the best goods and prices available.
Commission merchants	Take physical possession of products and negotiate sales. Normally, they are not employed on a long-term basis. Used most often in agricultural marketing by farmers who do not want to sell their own output and do not belong to producers' cooperatives. The commission merchant takes a truckload of commodities to a central market, sells it for the best price, deducts a commission and expenses, and remits the balance to the producer.
Manufacturers' and Retailers' Branches and Offices	Wholesaling operations conducted by sellers or buyers themselves rather than through independent wholesalers. Separate branches and offices can be dedicated to either sales or purchasing.
Sales branches and offices	Set up by manufacturers to improve inventory control, selling, and promotion. *Sales branches* carry inventory and are found in such industries as lumber and automotive equipment and parts. *Sales offices* do not carry inventory and are most prominent in dry goods and notions industries.
Purchasing offices	Perform a role similar to that of brokers or agents but are part of the buyer's organization. Many retailers set up purchasing offices in such major market centres as New York and Chicago.

major type of wholesaling is that done in **manufacturers' sales branches and offices** by sellers or buyers themselves rather than through independent wholesalers.

Wholesaler Marketing Decisions

Wholesalers have experienced growing competitive pressures in recent years. They have faced new sources of competition, more demanding customers, new technologies, and more direct-buying programs on the part of large industrial, institutional, and retail buyers. As a result, they have had to improve their strategic decisions on target markets and positioning, and on the marketing mix-product assortments and services, price, promotion, and place (see Figure 12-2).

Target Market and Positioning Decision Like retailers, wholesalers must define their target markets and position themselves effectively—they cannot serve everyone. They can choose a target group by size of customer (only large retailers), type of customer (convenience stores only), need for service (customers who need

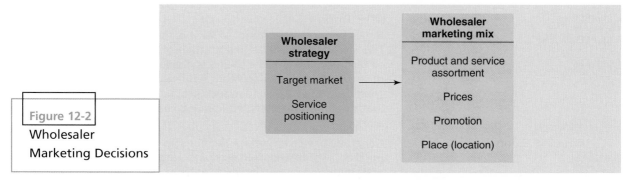

Figure 12-2
Wholesaler
Marketing Decisions

credit), or other factors. Within the target group, they can identify the more profitable customers, design stronger offers, and build better relationships with them. They can propose automatic reordering systems, set up management-training and advising systems, or even sponsor a voluntary chain. They can discourage less profitable customers by requiring larger orders or adding service charges to smaller ones.

Marketing Mix Decisions   Like retailers, wholesalers must decide on product assortment and services, prices, promotion, and place. The wholesaler's "product" is the assortment of *products and services* that it offers. Wholesalers are under great pressure to carry a full line and to stock enough for immediate delivery. But this practice can damage profits. Wholesalers today are cutting down on the number of lines they carry, choosing to carry only the more profitable ones. Wholesalers are also rethinking which services count most in building strong customer relationships and which should be dropped or charged for. The key is to find the mix of services most valued by their target customers.

Price is also an important wholesaler decision. Wholesalers usually mark up the cost of goods by a standard percentage—say, 20 percent. Expenses may run 17 percent of the gross margin, leaving a profit margin of 3 percent. In grocery wholesaling, the average profit margin is often lower than 2 percent. Wholesalers are trying new pricing approaches. They may cut their margin on some lines to win important new customers. They may ask suppliers for special price breaks when they can turn them into an increase in the supplier's sales.

Although *promotion* can be critical to wholesaler success, most wholesalers are not promotion minded. Their use of trade advertising, sales promotion, personal selling, and public relations is largely scattered and unplanned. Many are behind the times in personal selling—they still see selling as a single salesperson talking to a single customer instead of as a team effort to sell, build, and service major accounts. Wholesalers also need to adopt some of the nonpersonal promotion techniques used by retailers. They need to develop an overall promotion strategy and to make greater use of supplier promotion materials and programs.

Finally, *place* is important—wholesalers must choose their locations and facilities carefully. Wholesalers typically locate in low-rent, low-tax areas and tend to invest little money in their buildings, equipment, and systems. As a result, their materials-handling and order-processing systems are often outdated. Recently, however, large and progressive wholesalers have been reacting to rising costs by investing in automated warehouses and online ordering systems. Orders are fed from the retailer's system directly into the wholesaler's computer, and the items are picked up by mechanical devices and automatically taken to a shipping platform where they are assembled. Most large wholesalers use computers to carry out accounting, billing, inventory control, and forecasting. Modern wholesalers are adapting their services to the needs of target customers and finding cost-reducing methods of doing business.

Trends in Wholesaling

The thriving wholesaling industry faces considerable challenges. The industry remains vulnerable to one of the most enduring trends of the past decade—fierce resistance to price increases and the winnowing out of suppliers based on cost and quality. Progressive wholesalers constantly watch for better ways to meet the changing needs of their suppliers and target customers. They recognize that, in the long run, their only reason for existence comes from adding value by increasing the efficiency and effectiveness of the entire marketing channel. To achieve this goal, they must constantly improve their services and reduce their costs.

McKesson Canada, Canada's leading wholesaler of pharmaceuticals, health and beauty care, and home health care products, provides an example of progressive wholesaling. To survive, McKesson has to remain more cost effective than manufacturers' sales branches. Thus, the company has built efficient automated warehouses, established direct computer links with drug manufacturers, designed a computerized accounts-receivable program for pharmacists, and set up an extensive online supply management system by which customers can order, track, and manage their pharmaceutical and medical-surgical supplies. Retailers can even use the McKesson system to maintain medical profiles on their customers. According to McKesson, it adds value in the channel by "delivering unique supply and information management solutions that reduce costs and improve quality for its health care customers."[20]

One study predicts several developments in the wholesaling industry.[21] Geographic expansion will require that distributors learn how to compete effec-

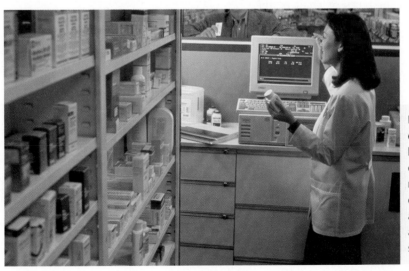

McKesson Canada has built efficient automated warehouses, established direct computer links with drug manufacturers, designed a computerized accounts-receivable program for pharmacists, and set up an extensive online supply management system.

tively over wider and more diverse areas. Consolidation will significantly reduce the number of wholesaling firms. Surviving wholesalers will grow larger, primarily through acquisition, merger, and geographic expansion. The trend toward vertical integration, in which manufacturers try to control their market share by owning the intermediaries that bring their goods to market, remains strong. In the health care sector, for instance, drug manufacturers have purchased drug distribution and pharmacy management companies. This trend began in 1993 when drug-industry giant Merck acquired Medco Containment Services, a drug-benefits manager and mail-order distributor. The surviving wholesaler-distributors in this sector and in others will be bigger and will provide more services for their customers.[22]

Wholesalers will continue to increase the services they provide to retailers—retail pricing, cooperative advertising, marketing and management information reports, accounting services, online transactions, and others. Rising costs on the one hand, and the demand for increased services on the other, will put the squeeze on wholesaler profits. Wholesalers who do not find efficient ways to deliver value to their customers will soon drop by the wayside. However, the increased use of computerized, automated, and Web-based systems will help wholesalers to contain the costs of ordering, shipping, and inventory holding, boosting their productivity.

Finally, facing slow growth in their domestic markets and such developments as the North American Free Trade Agreement, many large wholesalers are now going global. For example, in 1991, McKesson bought out its Canadian partner, Provigo. The company now receives about 3 percent of its total revenues from Canada.

<< Looking Back   < < < < < < < < <

Pull in here and reflect on this retailing and wholesaling chapter, the last of two chapters on distribution channels. In this chapter, we first looked at the nature and importance of retailing, major types of retailers, the decisions retailers make, and the future of retailing. We then examined these same topics for wholesalers. Although most retailing is conducted in retail stores, in recent years, nonstore retailing has increased rapidly. In addition, although many retail stores are independently owned, an increasing number are now banding together under some form of corporate or contractual organization. Wholesalers, too, have experienced recent environmental changes, most notably mounting competitive pressures. They have faced new sources of competition, more demanding customers, new technologies, and more direct-buying programs on the part of large industrial, institutional, and retail buyers.

1. Explain the roles of retailers and wholesalers in the distribution channel.

Retailing and wholesaling consist of many organizations bringing goods and services from the point of production to the point of use. *Retailing* includes all activities involved in selling goods or services directly to final consumers for their personal, nonbusiness use. *Wholesaling* includes all the activities involved in selling goods or services to those who are buying for the purpose of resale or for business use. Wholesalers perform many functions, including selling and promoting, buying and assortment building, bulk breaking, warehousing, transporting, financing, risk bearing, supplying market information, and providing management services and advice.

2. Describe the major types of retailers and give examples of each.

Retailers can be classified as *store retailers* and *nonstore retailers.* Although most goods and services are sold through stores, nonstore retailing has been growing much faster than has store retailing. Store retailers can be further classified by the *amount of service* they provide (self-service, limited service, or full service), *product line sold* (specialty stores, department stores, supermarkets, convenience stores, superstores, and service businesses), and *relative prices* (discount stores and off-price retailers). Today, many retailers are banding together in corporate and contractual *retail organizations* (corporate chains, voluntary chains and retailer cooperatives, franchise organizations, and merchandising conglomerates).

3. Identify the major types of wholesalers and give examples of each.

Wholesalers fall into three groups. First, *merchant wholesalers* take possession of the goods. They include *full-service wholesalers* (wholesale merchants, industrial distributors) and *limited-service wholesalers* (cash-and-carry wholesalers, truck wholesalers, drop shippers, rack jobbers, producers' cooperatives, and mail-order wholesalers). Second, *brokers* and *agents* do not take possession of the goods but are paid a commission for aiding buying and selling. Finally, *manufacturers' sales branches and offices* are wholesaling operations conducted by nonwholesalers to bypass the wholesalers.

4. Explain the marketing decisions facing retailers and wholesalers.

Each retailer must make decisions about its target markets and positioning, product assortment and services, price, promotion, and place. Retailers need to choose target markets carefully and position themselves strongly. Today, wholesaling is holding its own in the economy. Progressive wholesalers are adapting their services to the needs of target customers and are seeking cost-reducing methods of doing business. Faced with slow growth in their domestic markets and developments such as the North American Free Trade Association, many large wholesalers are also now going global.

Navigating the Key Terms

Concept Check

Fill in the blanks and then check your answers.

1. _____ includes all the activities involved in selling goods or services directly to final consumers for their personal, nonbusiness use.

2. Retailers can be classified by the length and breadth of their product assortments. _____ stores carry narrow product lines with deep assortments within those lines.

3. Recent years have seen the explosive growth of superstores that are actually giant specialty stores called _____. They feature stores the size of airplane hangers that carry a very deep assortment of a particular line with a knowledgeable staff.

4. The major types of retail organizations include corporate chains, _____ chains and _____ cooperatives, _____, and _____.

5. When establishing themselves, retailers must decide on three major product variables:_____, _____, and _____.

6. Retailers often cite three critical factors in retailing success: _____, _____, and _____!

7. According to the _____ concept, many new types of retailing forms begin as low-margin, low-price, low-status operations.

8. With the rise in the number of people _____, _____, or living in iso-lated and sprawling suburbs has come a resurgence of retail establishments that provide a place for people to get together.

9. _____ includes all activities involved in selling goods and services to those buying for resale or business use.

10. Typical functions performed by wholesalers include: (a) selling and promoting, (b) _____, (c) _____, (d) _____, (e) _____, (f) _____, (g) risk bearing, (h) market information, and (i) management services and advice.

11. _____ wholesalers are the largest single group of wholesalers, accounting for roughly 50 percent of all wholesaling.

12. According to Table 12-3, _____ wholesalers carry a limited line of semiperishable merchandise (such as milk or bread), which they sell for cash to customers (such as grocery stores).

Concept Checks Answers: 1. retailing; 2. specialty; 3. category killers; 4. voluntary (chains) and retailer (cooperatives), franchise organizations, merchandising conglomerates; 5. product assortment, services mix, store atmosphere; 6. location, location, location; 7. wheel of retailing; 8. living alone, working at home; 9. Wholesaling; 10. buying and assortment building, bulk-breaking, warehousing, transportation, financing; 11. Merchant; 12. truck (or truck jobbers).

Discussing the Issues

1. Giant superstores called category killers are an emerging trend. Answer the following questions: (a) How is a category killer different from other types of retailers? (b) Why has this form of retailing grown so rapidly? (c) What types of retailers are most threatened by category killers? Why? (d) How will online retailing affect category killers? Give an example of a category killer that has been affected by online marketing.

2. How has the growth of other types of large retailers affected the willingness of manufacturers to sell to off-price retailers at or below regular wholesale rates? What policy should Sony set for selling the following products to off-price retailers: (a) HDTV televisions, (b) big screen televisions, (c) regular televisions, (d) Walkman cassette players. Explain.

3. Compare the basic marketing decisions made by retailers and wholesalers to those made by manufacturers. Give examples that show the similarities and differences in marketing decisions made by these groups.

4. Use the "wheel of retailing" concept to assess the emergence and evolution of outlet malls. What do you predict will be the future of outlet malls? Explain.

5. List and describe each of the channel functions that have been traditionally assigned to wholesalers. How will wholesalers have to change to meet the threat of increasing competition from large retailers? What type of wholesaler seems best equipped to meet competition and change in the next decade? Explain.

Mastering Marketing

Examine the retailing and wholesaling relationships available to CanGo. Which of these seem strong? Which seem weak? Which need to be changed? What would you recommend to improve the company's retailing and wholesaling arrangements? What is the greatest distribution challenge that the company will face in the next few years? How would you solve this challenge? Explain.

Check out the enclosed Video case CD-ROM, or our Companion Website at www.pearsoned.ca/armstrong, to view a CBC video segment and case for this chapter.

MAP 12 Marketing Applications

If people had told you a few years ago that you would willingly stand in line to pay $2 for a cup of coffee, you would have thought they were nuts. Not so any more. Consumers do it everyday at the coffee counters of some 2000 Starbucks locations across the country. Daily espresso has become an expensive must for millions of Americans. However, as with all retailing trends, success may be fleeting without constant change. Starbucks success has drawn an explosion of competitors from "look-a-likes," to grocery stores (and their sophisticated coffee aisles), to ice cream distributors, and even restaurants. Starbucks is at a crossroads. How can it maintain its phenomenal 40 percent earnings growth rate? The company has decided on expansion as the best course of action. Current expansion strategies include new product development (juices, teas, and frozen drinks), expansion of past new product stars (Frappuccino—a cold-blended drink), joint ventures (partnering with PepsiCo for bottling Frappuccino and with Dreyer's Grand Ice Cream to package coffee ice cream). Also in the works are expansions in traditional retail endeavours (such as more stores and more partnerships with retail giants such as Barnes & Noble) and moves into untested waters (opening several Cafe Starbucks' and expansion into international markets).

Thinking Like a Marketing Manager

1. Assess Starbucks' retail strategy so far. Why has it been so successful? What appear to be its major strengths and weaknesses? (See **www. starbucks.com** for additional information.)

2. How dependent is Starbucks growth on direct retail sales? Do you see any potential problems with the company's aggressive expansion plans? Will cannibalization among stores and formats be a problem?

3. How might other fast-growing franchises that offer coffee products (such as Tim Hortons at

www.timhortons.com) be a threat to Starbucks? How should these challenges be met?

4. Assume that you are the marketing manager for Starbucks. Design a growth strategy for this company for the next two years. Look for new growth possibilities that will avoid cannibalism among existing outlets. What partnerships, alliances, and new product alternatives seem to be natural fits for the company? What forms of new competition do you think will emerge? How are competitors and other distribution forms likely to react to your plan? What will you do about this?

Digital Map

Visit our Web site at **www.pearsoned.ca/armstrong** for online quizzes, Internet exercises, and more!

CASE 12 DISCOUNT DAYS

It may be retailers, not politics and war, who eventually eliminate the traditional borders of countries. In Canada, we are familiar with how quickly large U.S. retailers such as Wal-Mart, Staples, and Home Depot have blended in with the retail landscape. In 2000, we also saw U.S.-based Best Buy acquire Future Shop. By contrast, we have also seen foreign retailers such as Marks and Spencer exit Canada. On an international level, many of the world's most powerful retailers are aggressively expanding: Royal Ahold, a Dutch supermarket chain, has purchased supermarkets in Poland, Spain, Argentina, and the United States. Tesco, Britain's largest food retailer, has expanded to South Korea and Taiwan, its tenth foreign market. It has also partnered with Safeway in the U.S. to jointly develop the GroceryWorks online retail concept. Carrefour, France's leading hypermarket and one of the largest retail organizations in the world, already competes in 20 markets including Chile, Colombia, Indonesia, Czech Republic, and Slovenia. The company has also been a significant shareholder in PETsMART Inc. in the U.S. since 1991, but recently sold off its shares to focus on its core retail food and allied businesses. Specialty retailers such as the Gap and Spain's Zara are opening new outlets in a new country every week. Zara has already opened in four markets in Canada (Montreal, Quebec City, Toronto, and Vancouver). In addition, over the last five years, at least another 15 U.S. retailers have entered Canada.

Many experts would argue that this massive expansion is generally doomed to failure. After all, retail is a 'local' business, with success being the result of catering to local tastes, culture, and consumer behaviour. International organizations have to recognize competition and develop a competitive strategy, they need to adapt to local real estate realities, municipal zoning regulations, suppliers, employability characteristics of the local population, distribution capabilities and changes in the weather. These expansion-minded retailers, however, will argue that these moves are basic strategies to gain market share, take advantage of global economies of scale, spread the rising costs of marketing and technology, and are necessary simply to remain competitive.

There have been some success stories, such as Wal-Mart, as well as some problems. For example, in spite of their global strength, Carrefour exited Hong Kong, unable to find enough large sites required for its hypermarket configuration. Marks and Spencer, the venerable British retailer, had difficulties and exited the Canadian market. It is also experiencing problems at home and in numerous other foreign markets, having reduced its exposure from 34 countries to 30 in the last three years. Toys R Us, present in 27 countries three years ago, is now placing more emphasis on online sales through its partnership with Amazon.com.

So why would Canada be attractive to these foreign retailers? Canada has a checkered history in retailing. The failure of Eaton's is well known. Then the attempt by Sears to resuscitate the brand on a selective store basis seemed to have merit. Yet, less than two years into the relaunch, in February 2002, the seven remaining Eaton's stores were converted to the Sears brand.

If we focus on the competitive environment for a moment, and do a competitive assessment, one of the unique aspects of the Canadian retail environment is the 'thrift' store. These are retail outlets that resell second-hand clothing and household articles, in some cases at as low as 5 percent of the original price.

One notable 'for profit' operator is Value Village, headquartered in New Westminster B.C., but operating 200 outlets in Canada, the U.S., and Australia (under 'The Savers' name). In addition to the corporate presence, there are 'not-for-profit' operators, notably Goodwill Industries, for decades a prime fund raising operation for charities through sales of donated second-hand goods. The other major player, operating over 200 stores in Canada, is the Salvation Army that resells discarded clothing and household effects. While these retail outlets are motivated not by profit, but by providing funds for 'good works', they are still a competitive factor. Another glaring example of the 'off-price' phenomena is the success of Winners, a division of U.S.-based TJX Companies. And while Winners may not be of Wal-Mart proportions yet, it is making gains. A report from Toronto-based NPD Group reveals that Winners has grown its market share of the apparel market to 2.8 percent, making it the fifth-largest clothing seller in Canada. That puts Winners behind only the four big department store players: Wal-Mart, The Bay, Zellers, and Sears. This is impressive growth, given that in 1997 it was only the eighth-largest clothing retailer in Canada with a 1.8 percent share.

So, it is becoming apparent that Canadians love a bargain. But have we become so price sensitive that upscale retailers will abandon the market? This is unlikely, but as an example of the strategic changes that may be necessary to remain competitive, Holt-Renfrew, one of Canada's premiere specialty retailers, is responding to the trend by expanding its lines of 'house brands', targeted to the 'mid-market' consumer.

There is a basic fact in Canadian society that is a significant contributor to these trends. Statistics Canada data indicates that over the last 10 years, Canadians' real incomes have fallen. By contrast, incomes in the U.S. have increased 18 percent over the same period. With less spending power, consumers will challenge marketers and retailers on price as never before.

Questions

1. What elements of the marketing mix will take precedence should you be in a position where you are charged with the responsibility of launching 'premium priced' new products through traditional retail channels in Canada?

2. What impact might these trends have on a decision to launch a 'bricks and mortar' operation versus an online only retail site?

3. Should Canadians start to experience growth in their incomes, providing for a potential of more discretionary spending, will consumers' price sensitivity be reduced? Why?

Source: This case was prepared by Peter Mitchell and is based on: "Discount Days", *Venture* #748. Evans W. and Barbiero P. (1999) "Foreign Retailers in Canada" **www.csca.ryerson.ca/publications**, accessed August 5, 2002, **www.holtrenfrew.com**, accessed August 5, 2002, **www.tjx.com**, accessed August 5, 2002, **www.valuevillage.com**, accessed August 5, 2002, Daniels, C. "Building an Off-Price Empire: Discount chain Winners-and its giant retail parent TJX-are giving Canadian bargain hunters something to shop about" *Marketing Magazine*, June 10, 2002.

13 >> Integrated Marketing Communications: Advertising, Sales Promotion, and Public Relations

Looking Ahead

We'll forge ahead now into the last of the marketing mix tools: promotion. You'll find that promotion is not a single tool but rather a mix of several tools. Ideally, under the concept of *integrated marketing communications,* the company will carefully coordinate these promotion elements to deliver a clear, consistent, and compelling message about the organization and its products. We'll begin by introducing you to the various promotion mix tools and to the importance of integrated marketing communications. Then, we'll look more carefully at three of the tools: advertising, sales promotion, and public relations. In the next chapter, we'll look at personal selling and direct marketing.

After reading this chapter, you should be able to

1. discuss the process and advantages of integrated marketing communications

2. define the five promotion tools and discuss the factors that must be considered in shaping the overall promotion mix

3. describe and discuss the major decisions involved in developing an advertising program

4. explain how sales promotion campaigns are developed and implemented

5. explain how companies use public relations to communicate with their publics

First stop: American Standard. Suppose you were a brand manager at American Standard and were assigned the task of preparing a promotion campaign for the company's line of toilets. That's right, toilets. Not an exciting prospect? As it turns out, the assignment offers some very interesting possibilities.

You probably haven't thought much about your bathroom—it's not something that most of us get very inspired about. But you probably have a relationship with your bathroom unlike that with any other room in your house. It's where you start and end your day, primp and preen and admire yourself, escape from the rigours of everyday life, and do some of your best thinking. The marketers at American Standard, the plumbing fixtures giant, understand this often-overlooked but special little room. A few years back they set out on a mission to help people design bathrooms worthy of their finest moments.

Working with its ad agency, Carmichael Lynch, American Standard created a wonderfully warm and highly effective but not-so-standard integrated marketing campaign. The campaign, called "We want you to love your bathroom," targeted men and women aged 25 to 54 from households planning to remodel bathrooms or replace fixtures. The campaign employed a carefully integrated mix of brand-image and direct-response media ads, direct mailings, and personal contacts to create a customer database, generate sales leads, gently coax customers into its retail showrooms, and build sales and market share.

The campaign began with a series of humorous, soft-sell brand-image ads in home and shelter magazines such as *Home, House Beautiful,* and *Country Living,* which reach a high percentage of readers undertaking remodelling projects. Featuring simple but artistic shots of ordinary bathroom fixtures and scenes, the ads positioned American Standard as a company that understands the special relationships we have with our bathrooms. For example, one ad showed a white toilet and a partially unwound roll of toilet paper, artfully arranged in a corner against plain blue-grey walls. "We're not in this business for the glory," proclaimed the headline. "Designing a toilet or sink may not be as glamorous as, say, designing a Maserati. But to us, it's every bit as important. After all, more people will be sitting on our seats than theirs."

Another ad showed the feet of a man standing on a white tile bathroom floor wearing his goofy-looking floppy-eared dog slippers. "The rest of the world thinks you're a genius," noted the ad. But "after a long day of being brilliant, witty, and charming, it's nice just to be comfortable. The right bathroom understands. And accepts you unconditionally." Each simple but engaging ad included a toll-free phone number and urged readers to call for a free guidebook "overflowing with products, ideas, and inspiration."

Whereas the brand-image ads positioned American Standard and its products, when it came to generating inquiries, the real workhorses were the one-third-page, couponlike direct-response ads that ran in the same magazines. One such ad noted, "You will spend seven years of your life in the bathroom. You will need a good book." Readers could obtain the free guidebook by mailing in the coupon or calling the toll-free number listed in the ad.

Consumers who responded found that they'd taken the first step in a carefully orchestrated relationship-building venture. First, they received the entertaining, highly informative, picture-filled 30-page guidebook *We Want You to Love Your Bathroom,* along with a folksy letter thanking them for their interest and noting the locations of nearby American Standard dealers. The guidebook's purpose was straightforward: "Walk into your bathroom, turn the knob and suddenly, for a moment or an hour, the world stops turning. You should love the place. If you don't, well, American Standard wants to further your relationship. Thumb through this book. In the bathroom, perhaps...." The guidebook was full of helpful tips on bathroom design, starting with answers to some simple questions: What kind of lavatory—what colour? The bathtub—how big? big enough for two? The toilet—sleek one-piece or familiar two-piece? The faucet? "You'll fumble for it every morning, so be particular about how it operates." To spice things up, the guidebook also contained loads of entertaining facts and trivia. An example: Did you know that "you will spend seven years in your bathroom...here's hoping your spouse doesn't sneak in first!" Another example: "During the Middle Ages, Christianity preached that to uncover your skin, even to bathe it, was an invitation to sin. Thank heavens for perfume. These days, we average about 4 baths or 7.5 showers a week." And, of course, the booklet contained plenty of information on American Standard products, along with a tear-out card that prospective customers could return to obtain more detailed guides and product catalogues.

In addition to the guidebook, customers received a carefully coordinated stream of communications from American Standard, starting with a series of "Bathroom Reading" bulletins, each containing information on specific bathroom design issues. For example, one issue contained information and tips on how to make a bathroom safer; another offered "10 neat ways to save water."

Meanwhile, information about prospective customers and their remodelling projects was collected by the 1-800 operator or from the coupon went into American Standard's customer database. The database generated leads for salespeople at American Standard's showrooms around the country. The company marketed the program to key distributors and kitchen and bath dealers, motivating them to follow up on leads and training them on how to do it effectively.

The key was to get customers who'd made inquiries to come into the showroom. Not long after making their inquiries, prospective customers typically received a handwritten postcard—or perhaps even a phone call—from a local dealer's showroom consultant, who extended a personal invitation to visit, see American

Standard products firsthand, and discuss bathroom designs. Thus, the integrated direct-marketing program built relationships not just with buyers but with dealers as well.

American Standard's integrated direct-marketing campaign did wonders for the company's positioning and performance. After the campaign began, American Standard's plumbing division experienced steady increases in sales and earnings. The campaign generated tens of thousands of qualified leads for local showrooms—more than a half million qualified leads in the first two years.

Research has confirmed significant shifts in consumer perceptions of American Standard and its products—from "boring and institutional" to well designed and loaded with "personal spirit." According to Bob Srenaski, group vice president of marketing at American Standard, the campaign "totally repositioned our company and established a momentum and winning spirit that is extraordinary." Says Joe Summary, an account manager at Carmichael Lynch, "the campaign was incredible. It gave American Standard and its products a more personal face, one that's helped us to build closer relationships with customers and dealers. From the first ad to the last contact with our dealers, the campaign was designed to help customers create bathrooms they'd love."

Modern marketing calls for more than just developing a good product, pricing it attractively, and making it available to target customers. Companies must also *communicate* with current and prospective customers, and what they communicate should not be left to chance.

THE MARKETING COMMUNICATIONS MIX

Marketing communications mix (promotion mix) The specific mix of advertising, personal selling, sales promotion, and public relations a company uses to pursue its advertising and marketing objectives.

A company's total **marketing communications mix**—also called its **promotion mix**—consists of the specific blend of advertising, sales promotion, public relations, personal selling, and direct-marketing tools that the company uses to pursue its advertising and marketing objectives:[1]

Advertising Any paid form of nonpersonal presentation and promotion of ideas, goods, or services by an identified sponsor.

- **Advertising:** Any paid form of nonpersonal presentation and promotion of ideas, goods, or services by an identified sponsor.

Sales promotion Short-term incentives to encourage the purchase or sale of a product or service.

- **Sales promotion:** Short-term incentives to encourage the purchase or sale of a product or service.

Public relations Building good relations with the company's various publics by obtaining favourable publicity, building a good corporate image, and handling or heading off unfavourable rumours, stories, and events. Major PR tools include press relations, product publicity, corporate communications, lobbying, and public service.

- **Public relations:** Building good relations with the company's various publics by obtaining favourable publicity, building a good corporate image, and handling or heading off unfavourable rumours, stories, and events.

Personal selling Personal presentation by the firm's sales force for the purpose of making sales and building customer relationships.

- **Personal selling:** Personal presentation by the firm's sales force for the purpose of making sales and building customer relationships.

Direct marketing Direct communications with carefully targeted individual consumers to obtain an immediate response.

- **Direct marketing:** Direct connections with carefully targeted individual consumers to both obtain an immediate response and cultivate lasting customer relationships—the use of telephone, mail, fax, e-mail, the Internet, and other tools to communicate directly with specific consumers.

Each category involves specific tools. For example, advertising includes print, broadcast, outdoor, and other forms. Sales promotion includes point-of-purchase displays, premiums, discounts, coupons, specialty advertising, and demonstrations. Public relations includes press releases and special events. Personal selling includes sales presentations, trade shows, and incentive programs. Direct marketing includes catalogues, telephone marketing, kiosks, the Internet, and more. Thanks to technological breakthroughs, people can now communicate through traditional media (newspapers, radio, telephone, television) as well as through newer media forms (fax, cell phones, and computers).

At the same time, communication goes beyond these specific promotion tools. The product's design, its price, the shape and colour of its package, and the stores that sell it *all* communicate something to buyers. Thus, although the promotion mix is the company's primary communication activity, the entire marketing mix—promotion *and* product, price, and place—must be coordinated for greatest communication impact.

In this chapter, we begin by examining the rapidly changing marketing communications environment and the concept of integrated marketing communications. Next, we discuss the factors that marketing communicators must consider in shaping an overall communication mix. Finally, we look at the first three promotion tools: advertising, sales promotion, and public relations. Chapter 14 examines the remaining promotion tools: personal selling and direct marketing.

INTEGRATED MARKETING COMMUNICATIONS

Companies around the world have perfected the art of mass marketing—selling highly standardized products to masses of customers. In the process, they have developed effective mass-media advertising techniques to support their mass-marketing strategies. These companies routinely invest millions of dollars in the mass media, reaching tens of millions of customers with a single ad. However, marketing managers now face some new marketing communications realities.

The Changing Communications Environment

Two major factors are changing marketing communications. First, as mass markets have fragmented, marketers are shifting away from mass marketing. Increasingly, they are developing focused marketing programs designed to build closer relationships with customers in more narrowly defined micromarkets. Second, vast improvements in information technology are speeding the movement toward segmented marketing. Today's information technology helps marketers to keep closer track of customer needs—more information about consumers at the individual and household levels is available than ever before. New technologies also provide new communications avenues for reaching smaller customer segments with more tailored messages.

The shift from mass marketing to segmented marketing has had a dramatic impact on marketing communications. Just as mass marketing gave rise to a new generation of mass-media communications, the shift toward one-to-one marketing is spawning a new generation of more specialized and highly targeted communications efforts.

Given this new communications environment, marketers must rethink the roles of various media and promotion mix tools. Mass-media advertising has long dominated the promotion mixes of consumer product companies. However, although television, magazines, and other mass media remain very important, their dominance is now declining. *Market* fragmentation has resulted in *media* fragmentation—in an explosion of more focused media that better match today's targeting

The new media environment: The shift toward one-to-one marketing has resulted in thousands of magazines targeting special-interest audiences, including online magazines such as Style.com.

strategies. Beyond the traditional mass-media channels, advertisers are making increased use of new, highly targeted media, ranging from highly focused specialty magazines and cable television channels, through CD catalogues and Web coupon promotions, to airport kiosks and floor decals in supermarket aisles. In all, companies are doing less *broadcasting* and more *narrowcasting.*

The Need for Integrated Marketing Communications

The shift from mass marketing to targeted marketing, and the corresponding use of a larger, richer mix of communication channels and promotion tools, poses a problem for marketers. Customers don't distinguish among message sources the way marketers do. In the consumer's mind, advertising messages from different media and different promotional approaches all become part of a single message about the company. Conflicting messages from these different sources can result in confused company images and brand positions.

All too often, companies fail to integrate their various communications channels. The result is a hodgepodge of communications to consumers. Mass-media advertisements say one thing, a price promotion sends a different signal, a product label creates still another message, company sales literature says something altogether different, and the company's Web site seems out of sync with everything else.

The problem is that these communications often come from different company sources. Advertising messages are planned and implemented by the advertising department or advertising agency. Personal selling communications are developed by sales management. Other functional specialists are responsible for public relations, sales promotion, direct marketing, Web sites, and other forms of marketing communications. Recently, such functional separation has been a major problem for many companies and their Internet communications activities, which are often split off into separate organizational units. "These new, forward-looking, high-tech functional groups, whether they exist as part of an established organization or as a separate new business operation, commonly are located in separate space, apart from the traditional operation," observes one IMC expert. "They generally are populated by young, enthusiastic, technologically proficient people with a burning desire to 'change the world,'" he adds, but "the separation and the lack of cooperation and cohesion" can be a *dis*integrating force in marketing communications (see New Directions 13-1).

In the past, no one person or department was responsible for thinking through the communication roles of the various promotion tools and coordinating the promotion mix. Today, however, more companies are adopting the concept of **integrated marketing communications** (IMC). Under this concept, as illustrated in Figure 13-1, the company carefully integrates and coordinates its many communications channels to deliver a clear, consistent, and compelling message about the organization and its products.[2] As one marketing executive puts it, "IMC builds a strong brand identity in the marketplace by tying together and reinforcing all your images and messages. IMC means that all your corporate messages, positioning and images, and identity are coordinated across all [marketing communications] venues. It means that your PR materials say the same thing as your direct mail campaign, and your advertising has the same 'look and feel' as your Web site."[3]

integrated marketing communications (IMC)
The concept under which a company carefully integrates and coordinates its many communications channels to deliver a clear, consistent, and compelling message about the organization and its products or services.

New Directions 13-1 >>   The Internet and Integrated Marketing Communications: *Dis*-Integrated Marketing Communications?

Ever had a day when you couldn't get a TV commercial out of your head? Or do ad lines and jingles from your childhood sometimes stick in your brain, such as "I'd like to buy the world a Coke," "Plop, plop, fizz, fizz. Oh, what a relief it is," or "Whassssupppppp?" Or do long lost words such as "Two all beef patties, special sauce, lettuce, cheese, pickles, onions, on a sesame seed bun" suddenly and inexplicably burst from your mouth? If you're like most people, you sop up more than a fair share of TV advertising.

Now, try to remember the last ad you saw while surfing the Internet. Drawing a blank? That's not surprising. The Web's ineffectiveness as a major brand-building tool is one of the today's hottest marketing issues. The problem? According to integrated marketing communication guru Don Schultz, all the special attention this new medium has gotten may have resulted in *dis*integrated marketing communications. Says Schultz:

> My mailbox has been filled with brochures, invitations, meetings, get-togethers, and debates all promising to explain interactivity, new media, e-commerce, and electronic media. Each…promises to give me the full picture of how to do the Internet, the Web, extranets, intranets, and all the other "nets" that are popping up everywhere. Not one has even suggested how all this new stuff might fit with, coordinate alongside, relate to, or be integrated with the existing media systems. Nothing on how to combine or bring together existing programs and existing customers with the brave new world of the twenty-first century.

Most troubling is that many firms have organized their new e-communications operations into separate groups or divisions, isolating them from mainstream marketing activities. "It is…the apartness that concerns me," Schultz observes. "We seem to be creating the same problems with new media, new marketing, and new commerce that we created years ago when we developed separate sales promotion groups, separate direct-marketing activities, separate public relations departments, separate events organ-

izations, and so on.…In my view, we are well on the way to *dis*integrating our marketing and communication programs and processes all over again."

However, whereas companies appear to be compartmentalizing the new communications tools, customers won't. According to Schultz:

> The truth is, most [consumers] won't compartmentalize their use of the new systems. They won't say, "Hey, I'm going off to do a bit of Net surfing. Burn my TV, throw out all my radios, cancel all my magazine subscriptions and, by the way, take out my telephone and don't deliver any mail anymore." It's not that kind of world for consumers, and it shouldn't be that kind of world for marketers either.

To be sure, the Internet promises exciting marketing communications potential. However, marketers trying to use the Web to build brands face many challenges. One limitation is that the Internet doesn't build mass brand awareness. Instead, it's like having millions of private conversations. The Web simply can't match the impact of the Super Bowl, where tens of millions of people see the same 30-second Nike or Hallmark ad at the same time. Using the Internet, it's hard to establish the universal meanings—such as "Just Do It!" or "When you care enough to send the very best"—that are at the heart of brand recognition and brand value. And whereas some advocates claim that the Web's interactivity and high involvement make it superior to an increasingly fragmented and cluttered television medium, others disagree:

> Some still think that the Web will replace TV as a major branding medium. I doubt it. Now, log on. Start clicking. Do you really believe that advertising-like solutions are going to work better on the Web than they do on CBS, ABC, NBC and the other 200 channels? There are millions—not hundreds—of places to go on the Web and everybody surfs with mouse in hand. Take a took at virtually any page—clutter galore: banners, icons, animated GIFs and Java applets are everywhere you look. [Thus], the new collective wisdom—branding on the Web will be built through experience, not [advertis-

ing].

Another Internet limitation is format and quality constraints. Web ads are still low in quality and impact. Large advertisers have been pushing to get Internet publishers to allow larger, more complex types of ads with high-quality sound and full-motion video. So far, however, ads on the Internet are all too ignorable. Even if advertisers could put larger, richer ads on the Web, they would likely face a consumer backlash. In the digital world, consumers control ad exposure. Many consumers who've grown up with the Internet are skeptical of ads in general and resentful of Web ads in particular. Internet advertisers face an uphill battle in getting such consumers to click onto their ads.

Facing such realities, most marketers opt for fuller promotion campaigns to build their brands. Even companies that rely primarily on e-commerce for sales are conducting most of their branding efforts offline. Business-to-business e-commerce star Cisco Systems spends ad money for full-page ads in the *Wall Street Journal* rather than on Web banners. Dell Computer, which now conducts 50 percent of all transactions online, is also one of the largest ad spenders in tech trade magazines and runs a $200 million-plus branding campaign almost entirely on TV.

Similarly, most traditional marketers have added the Web as an enhancement to their more traditional communication media. They wed the emotional pitch and impact of traditional brand marketing with the interactivity and real service offered online. For example, television ads for Saturn still offer the same old-fashioned humorous appeal. But now they point viewers to the company's Web site, which offers lots of help and very little hype. The site helps serious car buyers select a model, calculate payments, and find a dealer online. Even marketers that can't really sell their goods via the Web are using the Internet as an effective customer communication and relationship enhancer. For example, Procter & Gamble has turned Pampers.com into a one-stop centre for addressing the concerns of new or expectant parents. The site's research, learning, playing, and sharing centres offer information and advice on diapers and much more.

Thus, although the Internet offers good prospects for marketing communication, it can rarely stand alone as a brand-building tool. Moreover, if treated as a special case, it can disrupt an otherwise effective communications program. Instead, it must be carefully integrated into the broader marketing communications mix. Schultz makes this plea: "My cry is to integrate, not isolate. Yes, we need to explore and develop new media and new approaches, but we need to...integrate [them] with the old, melding e-commerce and across-the-counter commerce. There never has been a greater need for integration than there is today. Let's recognize and develop the new electronic forms on the basis of what they are—alternatives and perhaps enhancements for the existing approaches presently in place—and nothing more. Then again, they are nothing less, either."

Sources: Quotes and excerpts from Don E. Schultz, "New Media, Old Problem: Keep Marcom Integrated," *Marketing News,* 29 March 1999; and Robert C. Hacker, "The End of Brand Marketing on the Web?" *Target Marketing,* January 2000, pp. 42–44. Also see Al Ries and Laura Ries, *Immutable Laws of Internet Branding,* New York: HarperBusiness, 2000; Marc Braunstein, New Levine, and Edward H. Levine, *Deep Branding on the Internet: Applying Heat and Pressure Online to Ensure a Lasting Brand,* Roseville, CA: Prima Publishing, 2000; and Deborah Kania, *Branding.com: On-Line Branding for Marketing Success,* New York: NTC Publishing, 2001.

It's difficult to do major brand-building on the Web. Thus, e-commerce companies like Dell use off-line promotion to build their online business.

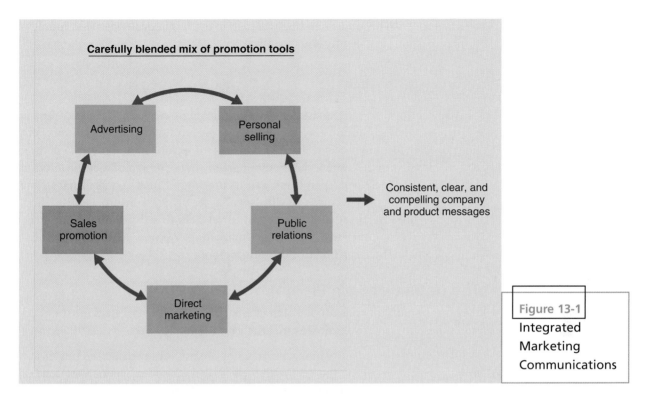

Figure 13-1

Integrated Marketing Communications

IMC calls for recognizing all contact points where the customer may encounter the company, its products, and its brands. Each *brand contact* will deliver a message, whether good, bad, or indifferent. The company must strive to deliver a consistent and positive message at all contact points.

A View of the Communication Process

Integrated marketing communications involves identifying the target audience and shaping a well-coordinated promotional program to elicit the desired audience response. Too often, marketing communications focus on overcoming immediate awareness, image, or preference problems in the target market. But this approach to communication is too shortsighted. Today, marketers are moving toward viewing communications as *managing the customer relationship over time,* during the pre-selling, selling, consuming, and postconsumption stages. Because customers differ, communications programs need to be developed for specific segments, niches, and even individuals. And, given the new interactive communications technologies, companies must ask not only, "How can we reach our customers?" but also, "How can we find ways to let our customers reach us?"

Thus, the communications process should start with an audit of all the potential contacts target customers may have with the company and its brands. For example, someone purchasing a new computer may talk to others, see television ads, read articles and ads in newspapers and magazines, visit various Web sites, and try out computers in one or more stores. The marketer needs to assess what influence each of these communications experiences will have at different stages of the buying process. This understanding will help marketers allocate their communication dollars more efficiently and effectively.

SETTING THE OVERALL COMMUNICATION MIX

The concept of integrated marketing communications suggests that the company must blend the promotion tools carefully into a coordinated *promotion mix*. But how does the company determine what mix of promotion tools it will use? Companies within the same industry differ greatly in the design of their promotion mixes. For example, Avon spends most of its promotion funds on personal selling and direct marketing, whereas Revlon spends heavily on consumer advertising. IBM relies on advertising and promotion to retailers to sell personal computers, whereas Dell Computer uses only direct marketing. We now look at factors that influence the marketer's choice of promotion tools.

The Nature of Each Promotion Tool

Each promotion tool has unique characteristics and costs. Marketers must understand these characteristics in selecting their mix of tools.

Institute of Canadian Advertising www.ica-ad.com

Advertising Advertising can reach masses of geographically dispersed buyers at a low cost per exposure, and it enables the seller to repeat a message many times. For example, television advertising can reach huge audiences. More than 131 million Americans and 3 million Canadians tuned in to at least part of the last Super Bowl, some 72 million people in North America watched at least part of the last Academy Awards broadcast, and nearly 52 million watched the final episode of the first *Survivor* series. "If you want to get to the mass audience," says a media services executive, "broadcast TV is where you have to be." He adds, "For anybody introducing anything who has to lasso audience in a hurry—a new product, a new campaign, a new movie—the networks are still the biggest show in town."[4]

Beyond its reach, large-scale advertising says something positive about the seller's size, popularity, and success. Because of advertising's public nature, consumers tend to view advertised products as more legitimate. Advertising is also very expressive—it allows the company to dramatize its products through the artful use of visuals, print, sound, and colour. On the one hand, advertising can be used to build up a long-term image for a product (such as Coca-Cola ads). On the other hand, advertising can trigger quick sales (as when Sears advertises a weekend sale).

Advertising also has some shortcomings. Although it reaches many people quickly, advertising is impersonal and cannot be as directly persuasive as can company salespeople. For the most part, advertising can carry on only a one-way communication with the audience, and the audience does not feel that it has to pay attention or respond. In addition, advertising can be very costly. Although some advertising forms, such as newspaper and radio advertising, can be done on smaller budgets, other forms, such as network TV advertising, require very large budgets.

Personal Selling Personal selling is the most effective tool at certain stages of the buying process, particularly in building buyers' preferences, convictions, and actions. It involves personal interaction between two or more people, so each per-

With personal selling, the customer feels a greater need to listen and respond, even if the response is a polite "no, thanks."

son can observe the other's needs and characteristics and make quick adjustments. Personal selling also allows all kinds of relationships to emerge, ranging from a matter-of-fact selling relationship to personal friendship. The effective salesperson uses a needs-based approach and attempts to meet customer needs with a product or service and to keep the customer's interests at heart to build a long-term relationship. Finally, with personal selling the buyer usually feels a greater need to listen and respond, even if the response is a polite "no thank you."

These unique qualities come at a cost, however. A sales force requires a longer-term commitment than does advertising—advertising can be turned on and off, but sales force size is harder to change. Personal selling is also the company's most expensive promotion tool, costing companies $270 on average per sales call.[5] North American firms spend up to three times as much on personal selling as they do on advertising.

Sales Promotion Sales promotion includes a wide assortment of tools—coupons, contests, cents-off deals, premiums, and others—all of which have many unique qualities. They attract consumer attention, offer strong incentives to purchase, and can be used to dramatize product offers and to boost sagging sales. Sales promotions invite and reward quick response—whereas advertising says, "Buy our product," sales promotion says, "Buy it now." Sales promotion effects are often short lived, however, and often are not as effective as advertising or personal selling in building long-run brand preference.

Public Relations Public relations is very believable—news stories, features, and events seem more real and believable to readers than ads do. Public relations can also reach many prospects who avoid salespeople and advertisements—the message gets to the buyers as "news" rather than as a sales-directed communication. And, as with advertising, public relations can dramatize a company or product. Marketers tend to underuse public relations or to use it as an afterthought. Yet a well-thought-out public relations campaign used with other promotion mix elements can be very effective and economical.

Direct Marketing Although there are many forms of direct marketing—telephone marketing, direct mail, online marketing, and others—they all share four distinctive characteristics:

1. Direct marketing is *nonpublic:* Messages are normally directed to a specific person.

2. Direct marketing is *immediate:* Messages can be prepared very quickly.

3. Direct marketing is *customized:* Messages can be tailored to appeal to specific consumers.

4. Direct marketing is *interactive:* It allows a dialogue between the marketing team and the consumer, and messages can be altered depending on the consumer's response.

Thus, direct marketing is well suited to highly targeted marketing efforts and to building one-to-one customer relationships.

Promotion Mix Strategies

Marketers can choose from two basic promotion mix strategies: *push* promotion or *pull* promotion. Figure 13-2 contrasts the two strategies. The relative emphasis on the specific promotion tools differs for push and pull strategies. A **push strategy** involves "pushing" the product through distribution channels to final consumers. The producer directs its marketing activities (primarily personal selling and trade promotion) to channel members to induce them to carry the product and to promote it to final consumers. Using a **pull strategy**, the producer directs its marketing activities (primarily advertising and consumer promotion) toward final consumers to induce them to buy the product. If the pull strategy is effective, consumers will then demand the product from channel members, who will in turn demand it from producers. Thus, under a pull strategy, consumer demand "pulls" the product through the channels.

Some industrial goods companies use only push strategies; some direct-marketing companies use only pull. However, most large companies use some combination of both. For example, Kraft uses mass-media advertising and consumer promotions to pull its products and a large sales force and trade promotions to push its products through the channels.

Companies consider many factors when designing their promotion mix strategies, including *type of product/market* and the *product life-cycle stage.* For example, the importance of different promotion tools varies between consumer and business markets. B2C companies usually "pull" more, putting more of their funds into advertising, followed by sales promotion, personal selling, and then public relations. In contrast, B2B marketers tend to "push" more, putting more of their funds into personal selling, followed by sales promotion, advertising, and public relations. Generally, personal selling is used more heavily with expensive and risky goods and in markets with fewer and larger sellers.

Push strategy A promotion strategy that calls for using the sales force and trade promotion to push the product through channels. The producer promotes the product to wholesalers, the wholesalers promote to retailers, and the retailers promote to consumers.

Pull strategy A promotion strategy that calls for spending a lot on advertising and consumer promotion to build consumer demand. If the strategy is successful, consumers will ask their retailers for the product, the retailers will ask the wholesalers, and the wholesalers will ask the producers.

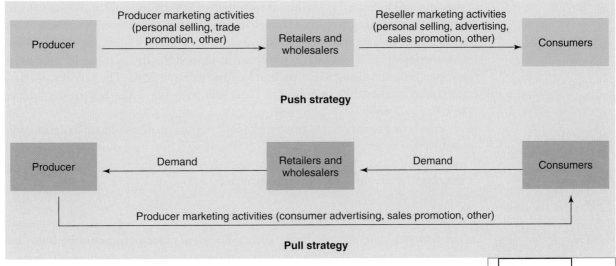

Push strategy

Pull strategy

Figure 13-2
Push Versus Pull Promotion Strategy

Now that we've examined the concept of integrated marketing communications and the factors that firms consider when shaping their promotion mixes, let's look more closely at the specific marketing communications tools.

ADVERTISING

Advertising can be traced back to the very beginnings of recorded history. Archaeologists working in the countries around the Mediterranean Sea have dug up signs announcing various events and offers. The Romans painted walls to announce gladiator fights, and the Phoenicians painted pictures promoting their wares on large rocks along parade routes. Modern advertising, however, is very different from these early efforts. According to a recent report commissioned by the Institute of Canadian Advertising, advertising is a significant industry in Canada. The advertising sector includes firms that create and support advertising (advertising services); the media that produce and carry advertising; and advertising-related work in industries whose output is not advertising (for example, animation firms). The industry accounts for about 212 000 jobs or 1.7 percent of all jobs in Canada. That's bigger than the insurance or real estate agent industry, or the accounting and legal services industry.[6] The aggregate expenditure of the Canadian advertising industry is $14.5 billion annually. U.S. advertisers spend $318 billion; worldwide ad spending exceeds $621 billion.

Although advertising is used mostly by business firms, it also is used by a wide range of nonprofit organizations, professionals, and social agencies that advertise their causes to various target publics.

The top three industries in terms of advertising expenditures in Canada, which account for 39 percent of all ad spending, are retail, automobile manufacturing, and business equipment and services. These categories are followed by food manufacturing, financial and insurance services, and entertainment. Despite the perception that beer ads are everywhere, brewers rank 12th in terms of ad spending. Although government advertising falls into 15th place, there has been a recent trend toward increased government spending on advertising both at the federal and provincial levels, as governments work to communicate directly with Canadians. In 1998 alone, Ottawa spent $89.1 million on advertising, a 43 percent increase over the previous year. The Ontario government topped the list in terms of provincial ad spending, allocating $50.6 million to advertising in 1998. The Quebec government also increased its spending to $39.2 million, while B.C.'s advertising budget rose to $31.2 million.[7]

Marketing management must make four important decisions when developing an advertising program (see Figure 13-3): *setting advertising objectives, setting the advertising budget, developing advertising strategy (message decisions* and *media decisions),* and *evaluating advertising campaigns.*

Setting Advertising Objectives

The first step is to set *advertising objectives.* These objectives should be based on past decisions about the target market, positioning, and the marketing mix, which define the job that advertising must do in the total marketing program.

An **advertising objective** is a specific communication *task* to be accomplished with a specific *target* audience during a specific *time.* Advertising objectives can be classified by primary purpose—whether the aim is to *inform, persuade,* or *remind.* Table 13-1 lists examples of each of these objectives.

Informative advertising is used heavily when introducing a new product category. In this case, the objective is to build primary demand. Thus, producers of DVD players must first inform consumers of the image quality and convenience benefits of the new product. *Persuasive advertising* becomes more important as competition increases. Here, the company's objective is to build selective demand. For example, once DVD players were established, Sony began trying to persuade consumers that *its* brand offers the best quality for their money.

Some persuasive advertising has become *comparative advertising,* in which a company directly or indirectly compares its brand with one or more other brands. Comparative advertising has been used for products ranging from soft drinks and computers to batteries, pain relievers, car rentals, and credit cards. For example, in

Advertising objective A specific communication task to be accomplished with a specific target audience during a specific time.

Figure 13-3

Major Advertising Decisions

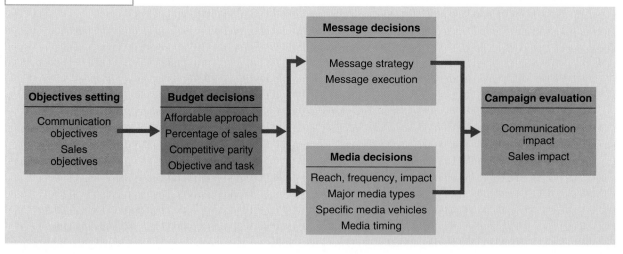

Table 13-1 Possible Advertising Objectives

Informative advertising

Telling the market about a new product	Describing available services
Suggesting new uses for a product	Correcting false impressions
Informing the market of a price change	Reducing consumers' fears
Explaining how the product works	Building a company image

Persuasive advertising

Building brand preference	Persuading customer to purchase now
Encouraging switching to your brand	Persuading customer to receive a sales call
Changing customer's perception of product attributes	

Reminder advertising

Reminding consumer that the product may be needed in the near future	Keeping the product in customer's mind during off-seasons
Reminding consumers where to buy the product	Maintaining its top-of-mind awareness

its classic comparative campaign, Avis positioned itself against market-leading Hertz by claiming, "We're number two, so we try harder." In its long-running comparative campaign, VISA has advertised, "American Express is offering you a new credit card, but you don't have to accept it. Heck, 7 million merchants don't." American Express has responded with ads bashing Visa, noting that AmEx's cards offer benefits not available with Visa's regular card, such as rapid replacement of lost cards and higher credit limits. As often happens with comparative advertising, both sides complain that the other's ads are misleading.

Reminder advertising is important for mature products—it keeps consumers thinking about the product. Expensive Coca-Cola television ads primarily remind people about Coca-Cola rather than informing or persuading them.

Setting the Advertising Budget

After determining its advertising objectives, the company next sets its *advertising budget* for each product and market. How does a company decide on its promotion budget? We look at four common methods used to set the total budget for advertising: the *affordable method*, the *percentage-of-sales method*, the *competitive-parity method*, and the *objective-and-task method*.

Affordable Method Some companies use the **affordable method**: They set the promotion budget at the level they think the company can afford. Small businesses often use this method, reasoning that the company cannot spend more on advertising than it has. They start with total revenues, deduct operating expenses and capital outlays, and then devote some portion of the remaining funds to advertising.

Unfortunately, this method of setting budgets completely ignores the effects of promotion on sales. It tends to place advertising last among spending priorities, even in situations in which advertising is critical to the firm's success. It leads to an

Affordable method
Setting the promotion budget at the level management thinks the company can afford.

uncertain annual promotion budget, which makes long-range market planning difficult. Although the affordable method can result in overspending on advertising, it more often results in underspending.

Percentage-of-sales method Setting the promotion budget at a certain percentage of current or forecasted sales or as a percentage of the unit sales price.

Percentage-of-Sales Method

Other companies use the **percentage-of-sales method**, setting their promotion budget at a certain percentage of current or forecasted sales. Or they budget a percentage of the unit sales price. The percentage-of-sales method has advantages: It is simple to use and helps management think about the relationships among promotion spending, selling price, and profit per unit.

Despite these claimed advantages, however, the percentage-of-sales method has little to justify it. It wrongly views sales as the *cause* of promotion rather than as the *result*. Studies often show positive correlations between advertising expenditures on a brand and brand performance. However, these findings may represent "effect and cause" rather than "cause and effect." Brands with higher sales can afford bigger advertising investments. Thus, the percentage of sales budget is based on availability of funds rather than on opportunities. It may prevent the increased spending sometimes needed to turn around falling sales. Because the budget varies with year-to-year sales, long-range planning is difficult. Finally, the method does not provide any basis for choosing a *specific* percentage, except what has been done in the past or what competitors are doing.

Competitive-parity method Setting the promotion budget to match competitors' outlays.

Competitive-Parity Method

Still other companies use the **competitive-parity method**, setting their promotion budgets to match competitors' outlays. They monitor competitors' advertising or get industry promotion spending estimates from publications or trade associations and then set their budgets based on the industry average.

Two arguments support this method. First, competitors' budgets represent the collective wisdom of the industry. Second, spending what competitors spend helps prevent promotion wars. Unfortunately, neither argument is valid. There are no grounds for believing that the competition has a better idea of what a company should be spending on promotion than does the company itself. Companies differ greatly, and each has its own special promotion needs. Finally, there is no evidence that budgets based on competitive parity prevent promotion wars.

Objective-and-task method Developing the promotion budget by (1) defining specific objectives, (2) determining the tasks that must be performed to achieve these objectives, and (3) estimating the costs of performing these tasks. The sum of these costs is the proposed promotion budget.

Objective-and-Task Method

The most logical budget-setting method is the **objective-and-task method**, whereby the company sets its promotion budget based on what it wants to accomplish with promotion. This budgeting method entails (1) defining specific promotion objectives, (2) determining the tasks needed to achieve these objectives, and (3) estimating the costs of performing these tasks. The sum of these costs is the proposed promotion budget.

The objective-and-task method forces management to spell out its assumptions about the relationship between dollars spent and promotion results. But it is also the most difficult method to use. Often, it is hard to figure out which specific tasks will achieve specific objectives. For example, suppose Sony wants 95 percent awareness for its latest DVD player during the six-month introductory period. What specific advertising messages and media schedules should Sony use to attain this objective? How much would these messages and media schedules cost? Sony management must consider such questions, even though they are hard to answer.

No matter which method is used, deciding how much to spend on advertising is one of the hardest marketing decisions facing a company. Measuring the results of advertising spending and "advertising return on investment" remains an inexact science. John Wanamaker, the department store magnate, once said, "I know that half of my advertising is wasted, but I don't know which half. I spent $2 million for advertising, and I don't know if that is half enough or twice too much." Thus, it is not surprising that companies vary widely in how much they spend on promotion. Even within a given industry, both low and high spenders can be found.[8]

Developing Advertising Strategy

Advertising strategy consists of two major elements: creating advertising *messages* and selecting advertising *media*. In the past, companies often viewed media planning as secondary to the message-creation process. The creative department first created good advertisements, then the media department selected the best media for carrying these advertisements to desired target audiences. This often caused friction between creatives and media planners.

Today, however, media fragmentation, soaring media costs, and more focused target marketing strategies have promoted the importance of the media-planning function. Increasingly, advertisers are orchestrating a closer harmony between their messages and the media that deliver them. In some cases, an advertising campaign

Media planners for Absolut Vodka work with creatives to design ads targeting to specific media audiences. "Absolut Bravo" appears in theatre playbills.

might start with a great message idea, followed by the choice of appropriate media. In other cases, however, a campaign might begin with a good media opportunity, followed by advertisements designed to take advantage of that opportunity. Among the more noteworthy ad campaigns based on tight media-creative partnerships is the pioneering campaign for Absolut vodka, marketed by Seagram.

For years, Seagrams Canada of Montreal has worked closely with a slew of magazines to set Absolut's media schedule. The schedule consists of up to 100 magazines, ranging from consumer and business magazines to theatre play-bills. The agency's creative department is charged with creating media-specific ads. The result is a wonderful assortment of very creative ads for Absolut, tightly targeted to audiences of the media in which they appear. For example, Seagrams has long been an avid supporter of the gay community, and it wanted to develop ads specifically geared to gays and lesbians. Working closely with niche publication *Xtra!* magazine staff, it developed the concept for "Absolut Pride," "Absolut Out" (aptly featuring a closet), and "Absolut Commitment" (showcasing two grooms on a wedding cake). Brand manager Holly Wyatt believed the partnership with *Xtra!* made sense because the magazine's staff were in tune with trends in the gay and lesbian community. "Absolut Pride," in particular, received a lot of extra media coverage including a feature on *Entertainment Tonight.* When asked why she targeted the gay and lesbian community, Wyatt noted that the market is the best representation of Absolut's target audience, regardless of sexual orientation. "They're young, sophisticated, somewhat upscale. And Absolut consumers do tend to swing towards the arts," she says. "It just makes sense for us." In all, Absolut has developed more than 500 ads for the almost two-decade-old campaign. At a time of soaring media costs and cluttered communication channels, a closer cooperation between creative and media people has paid off handsomely for Absolut. Largely as a result of its breakthrough advertising, Absolut now captures a 63 percent share of the imported vodka market in North America.[9]

Creating the Advertising Message   No matter how big the budget, advertising can succeed only if commercials gain attention and communicate well. Good advertising messages are especially important in today's costly and cluttered advertising environment.

About 99 percent of Canadian households are equipped with a television, and more than 77 percent of Canadians watch television at least once a day. However, the number of television channels beamed into Canadian homes has skyrocketed from 2 in the 1950s to more than 70 today: 1 national English channel, 1 national French channel, 18 regional channels, 39 specialty networks, and 12 pay TV offerings. Add to this the growing number of American signals that are picked up by Canadians who, in 2000, spent 24 percent of their viewing time watching U.S. stations. Canadian media options also include 910 radio stations, 108 daily newspapers, and 1600 magazines. The clutter is made worse by a continuous barrage of catalogues, direct-mail and online ads, and out-of-home media.[10]

If all this advertising clutter bothers some consumers, it also causes big problems for advertisers. Take the situation facing network television advertisers. They regularly pay $300 000 or more for 30 seconds of advertising time during a popular prime-time program, even more if it's an especially popular program such as *ER* ($946 000 per 30-second spot), *Friends* ($824 000), *Just Shoot Me* ($710 000), or a mega-event such as the Super Bowl (more than $2.4 million!).[11] Then, their ads are sandwiched in with a clutter of some 60 other commercials, announcements, and network promotions per hour.

Until recently, television viewers were a captive audience for advertisers. Viewers had only a few channels from which to choose. But with the growth in cable and satellite TV, VCRs, and remote-control units, today's viewers have many more options. They can avoid ads by watching commercial-free cable channels. They can "zap" commercials by pushing the fast-forward button during taped programs. With remote control, they can instantly turn off the sound during a commercial or "zip" around the channels to see what else is on. A recent study found that half of all television viewers now switch channels when the commercial break starts. And the new wave of digital video recorders (DVRs) and personal television services—such as TiVo, ReplayTV, and Microsoft's UltimateTV—have armed viewers with an arsenal of new-age zipping and zapping weapons.[12]

Just to gain and hold attention, today's advertising messages must be better planned, more imaginative, more entertaining, and more rewarding to consumers. "Today we have to entertain and not just sell, because if you try to sell directly and come off as boring or obnoxious, people are going to press the remote on you," points out one advertising executive. "When most TV viewers are armed with remote channel switchers, a commercial has to cut through the clutter and seize the viewers in one to three seconds, or they're gone," comments another.[13] Some advertisers even create intentionally controversial ads to break through the clutter and gain attention for their products.

Message Strategy The first step in creating effective advertising messages is to decide what general message will be communicated to consumers—to plan a *message strategy*. The purpose of advertising is to get consumers to think about or react to the product or company in a certain way. People will react only if they believe that they will benefit from doing so. Thus, developing an effective message strategy begins with identifying customer *benefits* that can be used as advertising appeals. Ideally, advertising message strategy will follow directly from the company's broader positioning strategy.

Message strategy statements tend to be plain, straightforward outlines of benefits and positioning points that the advertiser wants to stress. The advertiser must next develop a compelling *creative concept*—or *"big idea"*—that will bring the message strategy to life in a distinctive and memorable way. At this stage, simple message ideas become great ad campaigns. Usually, a copywriter and art director will team up to generate many creative concepts, hoping that one of these concepts will turn out to be the big idea. The creative concept may emerge as a visualization, a phrase, or a combination of the two.

The creative concept will guide the choice of specific appeals to be used in an advertising campaign. *Advertising appeals* should have three characteristics: First, they should be *meaningful*, pointing out benefits that make the product more desirable or interesting to consumers. Second, appeals must be *believable*—consumers must believe that the product or service will deliver the promised benefits. However, the most meaningful and believable benefits may not be the best ones to feature. Appeals should also be *distinctive*—they should tell how the product is better than the competing brands. For example, the most meaningful benefit of owning a wristwatch is that it keeps accurate time, yet few watch ads feature this benefit. Instead, based on the distinctive benefits they offer, watch advertisers might select any of a number of advertising themes. For years, Timex has been the affordable watch that "Takes a lickin' and keeps on tickin'." In contrast, Swatch has featured style and fashion, whereas Rolex stresses luxury and status.

Message Execution The advertiser now has to turn the big idea into an actual ad execution that will capture the target market's attention and interest. The creative people must find the best style, tone, words, and format for executing the message. Any message can be presented in different *execution styles,* such as the following:

- *Slice of life:* This style shows one or more "typical" people using the product in a normal setting. For example, two mothers at a picnic discuss the nutritional benefits of Jif peanut butter.

- *Lifestyle:* This style shows how a product fits in with a particular lifestyle. For example, an ad for Mongoose mountain bikes shows a serious biker traversing remote and rugged but beautiful terrain and states, "There are places that are so awesome and so killer that you'd like to tell the whole world about them. But please, *don't.*"

- *Fantasy:* This style creates a fantasy around the product or its use. For instance, many ads are built around dream themes. Gap even introduced a perfume named Dream. Ads show a woman sleeping blissfully and suggest that the scent is "the stuff that clouds are made of."

- *Mood or image:* This style builds a mood or image around the product, such as beauty, love, or serenity. No claim is made about the product except through suggestion. Bermuda tourism ads create such moods.

- *Musical:* This style shows one or more people or cartoon characters singing about the product. For example, one of the most famous ads in history was a Coca-Cola ad built around the song "I'd Like to Teach the World to Sing."

- *Personality symbol:* This style creates a character that represents the product. The character might be *animated* (the Jolly Green Giant, Cap'n Crunch, Garfield the Cat, the Pillsbury Doughboy) or *real* (the Marlboro man, Ol' Lonely, the Maytag repairman, or Brew, the Kokanee Beer Dog).

- *Technical expertise:* This style shows the company's expertise in making the product. Thus, Nabob shows one of its buyers carefully selecting coffee beans, and Titleist explains its ability to make a better golf ball.

- *Scientific evidence:* This style presents survey or scientific evidence that the brand is better or better liked than one or more other brands. For years, Crest toothpaste has used scientific evidence to convince buyers that Crest is better than other brands at fighting cavities.

- *Testimonial evidence or endorsement:* This style features a highly believable or likable source endorsing the product. It could be ordinary people saying how much they like a given product ("My doctor said Mylanta") or a celebrity presenting the product. Many companies use actors or sports celebrities as product endorsers.

The advertiser also must choose a *tone* for the ad. Procter & Gamble always uses a positive tone: Its ads say something very positive about its products. P&G usually avoids humour, which might take attention away from the message. In contrast, many advertisers now use edgy humour to break through the commercial clutter.

The advertiser must use memorable and attention-getting *words* in the ad. For example, rather than claiming simply that "a Volkswagen is a well-engineered automobile," Volkswagen uses more creative and higher-impact phrasing: "Drivers Wanted." London Life could promise prospective customers that it will help them plan for their retirement, but this would not have the impact of "Freedom 55."

Finally, *format* elements make a difference on an ad's impact as well as on its cost. A small change in ad design can make a big difference in its effect. The *illustration* is the first thing the reader notices—it must be strong enough to draw attention. Next, the *headline* must effectively entice the right people to read the copy. Finally, the *copy*—the main block of text in the ad—must be simple but strong and convincing. Moreover, these three elements must effectively work *together*.

Selecting Advertising Media

The major steps in media selection are (1) deciding on *reach, frequency,* and *impact,* (2) choosing among major *media types,* (3) selecting specific *media vehicles,* and (4) deciding on *media timing.*

Deciding on Reach, Frequency, and Impact To select media, the advertiser must decide what reach and frequency are needed to achieve advertising objectives. *Reach* is a measure of the *percentage* of people in the target market who are exposed to the ad campaign during a given period. For example, the advertiser might try to reach 70 percent of the target market during the first three months of the campaign. *Frequency* is a measure of how many *times* the average person in the target market is exposed to the message. For example, the advertiser might want an

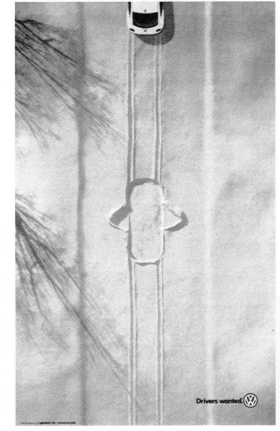

In an effective ad, like this award-winning Volkswagen ad, all the elements work together to attract attention and communicate the brand's personality and positioning.

average exposure frequency of three. The advertiser also must decide on the desired *media impact*-the *qualitative value* of a message exposure through a given medium. For example, for products that need to be demonstrated, messages on television may have more impact than messages on radio because television uses sight *and* sound. The same message in one magazine (say, *McLean's*) may be more believable than in another (say, *The National Enquirer*). Generally, the more reach, frequency, and impact the advertiser seeks, the higher the advertising budget will have to be.

Choosing Among Major Media Types The media planner has to know the reach, frequency, and impact of each of the major media types. As summarized in Table 13-2, the major media types are newspapers, television, direct mail, radio, magazines, outdoor, and the Internet. Each medium has advantages and limitations.

Media planners consider many factors when making their media choices. The *media habits of target consumers* will affect media choice—advertisers look for media that reach target consumers effectively. So will the *nature of the product*—for example, fashions are best advertised in colour magazines, and automobile performance is best demonstrated on television. Different *types of messages* may require different media. A message announcing a major sale tomorrow will require radio or newspapers; a message with a lot of technical data might require maga-

Table 13-2   Profiles of Major Media Types

Medium	Advantages	Limitations
Newspapers	Flexibility; timeliness; good local market coverage; broad acceptability; high believability	Short life; poor reproduction quality; small pass-along audience
Television	Good mass-market coverage; low cost per exposure; combines sight, sound, and motion; appealing to senses	High absolute costs; high clutter; fleeting exposure; less audience selectivity
Direct mail	High audience selectivity; flexibility; no ad competition within the same medium; allows personalization	Relatively high cost per exposure; "junk mail" image
Radio	Good local acceptance; high geographic and demographic selectivity; low cost	Audio only; fleeting exposure; low attention ("the half-heard" medium) fragmented audiences
Magazines	High geographic and demographic selectivity; credibility and prestige; high-quality reproduction; long life and good pass-along readership	Long ad-purchase lead time high cost; no guarantee of position
Outdoor	Flexibility; high repeat exposure; low cost; low message competition; good positional selectivity	Little audience selectivity creative limitations
Online	High selectivity; low cost; immediacy; interactive capabilities	Small audience; relatively low impact; audience controls exposure

zines, direct mailings, or an online ad and Web site. *Cost* is another major factor in media choice. For example, network television is very expensive, whereas newspaper or radio advertising costs much less but also reaches fewer consumers. The media planner looks both at the total cost of using a medium and at the cost per thousand exposures—the cost of reaching 1000 people using the medium.

Media impact and cost must be reexamined regularly. For a long time, television and magazines have dominated in the media mixes of national advertisers, with other media often neglected. Recently, however, the costs and clutter of these media have gone up, audiences have declined, and marketers are adopting strategies aimed at narrower segments. As a result, advertisers are increasingly turning to alternative media—ranging from cable TV and outdoor advertising to parking meters and elevators—that cost less and target more effectively (see New Directions 13-2).

New Directions 13-2 >> Advertisers Seek Alternative Media

As network television costs soar and audiences shrink, many advertisers are looking for new ways to reach consumers. The move toward micromarketing strategies, focused more narrowly on specific consumer groups, has also fuelled the search for alternative media to replace or supplement network television. Advertisers are shifting larger portions of their budgets to media that cost less and target more effectively.

Three media benefiting greatly from the shift are outdoor advertising, cable television, and digital satellite television systems. Billboards have undergone a resurgence in recent years. Gone are the ugly eyesores of the past; in their place we now see cleverly designed, colourful attention grabbers. Outdoor advertising provides an excellent way to reach important local consumer segments at a fraction of the cost per exposure of other major media. Cable television and digital satellite systems are also booming. Such systems allow narrow programming formats such as all sports, all news, nutrition, arts, gardening, cooking, travel, history, and others that target select groups. Advertisers can take advantage of such "narrowcasting" to "rifle in" on special market segments rather than use the "shotgun" approach offered by network broadcasting.

Outdoor, cable, and satellite media seem to make good sense. But, increasingly, ads are popping up in far less likely places. In their efforts to find less costly and more highly targeted ways to reach consumers, advertisers have discovered a dazzling collection of "alternative media." As consumers, we're used to ads on television, in magazines and newspapers, on the radio, and along the roadways. But these days, no matter where you go or what you do, you probably will run into some new form of advertising.

Tiny billboards attached to shopping carts, ads on shopping bags, and even advertising decals on supermarket floors urge you to buy Jell-O Pudding Pops or Pampers. Signs atop parking meters hawk everything from Jeeps to Minolta cameras to Recipe dog food. A city bus rolls by, fully wrapped for Trix cereal. You escape to the ballpark, only to find billboard-size video screens running Labatt Blue ads while a blimp with an electronic message board circles lazily overhead. How about a quiet trip in the country? Sorry—you find an enterprising farmer using his milk cows as four-legged billboards mounted with ads for Ben & Jerry's ice cream.

You pay to see a movie at your local theatre, but first you view a two-minute science fiction fantasy that turns out to be an ad for General Electric portable stereo boxes. Then the movie itself is full of not-so-subtle promotional plugs for Pepsi, Domino's Pizza, MasterCard, Fritos, BMWs, Ray Ban sunglasses, or any of a dozen other products. You head home for a little TV to find your favourite sitcom full of "virtual placements" of Coca-Cola, Sony, or M&M/Mars products digitally inserted into the program.

At the local rail station, it's the Commuter Channel. At the airport you're treated to the CNN

Marketers have discovered a dazzling array of "alternative media."

coffee as the familiar green-and-white Starbucks logo forms on the side. Sipping the brew, you slide on your Nikes to go grab the newspaper. The pressure sensitive shoes leave a temporary trail of swooshes behind them wherever you step. Walking outside, you pick up the Times and gaze at your lawn, where the fertilizer you put down last month time-releases ads for Scotts Turf Builder, Toro lawnmowers, Weber grills...

Even some of the current alternative media seem a bit far-fetched, and they sometimes irritate consumers who resent it all as "ad nauseam." But for many marketers, these media can save money and provide a way to hit selected consumers where they live, shop, work, and play. "We like to call it the captive pause," says an executive of an alternative media firm, where consumers "really have nothing else to do but either look at the person in front of them or look at some engaging content as well as 15-second commercials"—the average person waits in line about 30 minutes a day. Of course, this may leave you wondering whether there are any commercial-free havens remaining for ad-weary consumers. The backseat of a taxi, perhaps, or public elevators, or stalls in a public restroom? Forget it! Each has already been invaded by innovative marketers.

Airport Network while ads for Kenneth Cole baggage roll by on the luggage carousel conveyor belt. Boats cruise along public beaches flashing advertising messages for Sundown Sunscreen as sunbathers spread their towels over ads for Snapple pressed into the sand. Even church bulletins carry ads for Campbell's soup.

These days, you're likely to find ads—well, anywhere. Ad space is being sold on video cases, parking-lot tickets, golf scorecards, delivery trucks, gas pumps, ATMs, and municipal garbage cans. The following accounts takes a humorous look ahead at what might be in store for the future:

> Tomorrow your alarm clock will buzz at 6 A.M., as usual. Then the digital readout will morph into an ad for Burger King's breakfast special. Hungry for a Croissan'wich, you settle for a bagel that you plop into the toaster. The coils burn a Toastmaster brand onto the sides. Biting into your embossed bread, you pour a cup of

Sources: See Cara Beardi, "From Elevators to Gas Stations, Ads Multiplying," *Advertising Age,* 13 November 2000, pp. 40–42; Charles Pappas, "Ad Nauseam," *Advertising Age,* 10 July 2000, pp. 16–18; Beardi, "Airport Powerhouses Make Connection," *Advertising Age,* 2 October 2000, p. 8; and Wayne Friedman, "Eagle-Eye Marketers Find Right Spot," *Advertising Age,* 22 January 2001, pp. S2–S3.

Selecting Specific Media Vehicles The media planner now must choose the best *media vehicles*—specific media within each general media type. For example, television vehicles include *This Hour Has 22 Minutes, ER, Venture, Hockey Night in Canada.* Magazine vehicles include *McLean's, Chatelaine,* and *Western Living.*

Media planners must compute the cost per thousand persons reached by a vehicle. For example, if a full-page, four-colour advertisement in *McLean's* costs $30 563 and *McLean's* readership is 510 319 people, the cost of reaching each group of 1000 persons is about $60. The same advertisement in *Shift Magazine* may cost only $8125 but reach only 68 012 persons—at a cost per thousand of about $119. The media planner ranks each magazine by cost per thousand and favours those magazines with the lower cost per thousand for reaching target consumers.

The media planner must also consider the costs of producing ads for different media. Whereas newspaper ads may cost very little to produce, flashy television ads may cost millions. On average, advertisers pay $450 000 to produce a single 30-second television commercial. A few years ago, Nike paid $2.8 million to make a single ad called "The Wall."[14]

In selecting media vehicles, the media planner must balance media cost measures against several media impact factors. First, the planner should balance costs against the media vehicle's *audience quality*. For a baby lotion advertisement, for example, *New Mother* magazine would have a high-exposure value; *The Hockey News* would have a low-exposure value. Second, the media planner should consider *audience attention*. Readers of *Flare*, for example, typically pay more attention to ads than do *Economist* readers. Third, the planner should assess the vehicle's *editorial quality*—*McLean's* and *Canadian Business* are more believable and prestigious than *The National Enquirer*.

Deciding on Media Timing The advertiser must also decide how to schedule the advertising over a year. Suppose sales of a product peak in December and drop in March. The firm can vary its advertising to follow the seasonal pattern, to oppose the seasonal pattern, or to be the same all year. Most firms do some seasonal advertising. Some do *only* seasonal advertising: For example, Hallmark advertises its greeting cards only before major holidays.

Finally, the advertiser has to choose the pattern of the ads. *Continuity* means scheduling ads evenly within a given period. *Pulsing* means scheduling ads unevenly over a given period. Thus, 52 ads could either be scheduled at one per week during the year or pulsed in several bursts. The idea is to advertise heavily for a short period to build awareness that carries over to the next advertising period. Those who favour pulsing feel that it can be used to achieve the same impact as a steady schedule but at a much lower cost. However, some media planners believe that although pulsing achieves awareness, it sacrifices the depth of advertising communications.

Recent advances in technology have had a substantial impact on the media planning and buying functions. Today, for example, computer software applications called *optimizers* allow media planners to evaluate vast combinations of television programs and prices. Such programs help advertisers to make better decisions about which mix of networks, programs, and day parts will yield the highest reach per ad dollar.[15]

Evaluating Advertising

The advertising program should evaluate both the communication effects and the sales effects of advertising regularly. Measuring the *communication effects* of an ad—*copy testing*—tells whether the ad is communicating well. Copy testing can be done before or after an ad is printed or broadcast. Before the ad is placed, the advertiser can show it to consumers, ask how they like it, and measure recall or attitude changes resulting from it. After the ad is run, the advertiser can measure how the ad affected consumer recall or product awareness, knowledge, and preference.

But what *sales* are caused by an ad that increases brand awareness by 20 percent and brand preference by 10 percent? The *sales effects* of advertising are often harder to measure than the communication effects. Sales are affected by many factors besides advertising—such as product features, price, and availability. One way to measure the sales effect of advertising is to compare past sales with past advertising expenditures. Another way is through experiments. For example, to test the effects of different advertising spending levels, Coca-Cola could vary the amount it spends on advertising in different market areas and measure the differences in the resulting sales levels. It could spend the normal amount in one market area, half the normal amount in another area, and twice the normal amount in a third area. If the three market areas are similar, and if all other marketing efforts in the area are the same, then differences in sales in the three areas could be related to advertising level. More complex experiments could be designed to include other variables, such as difference in the ads or media used.

Other Advertising Considerations

In developing advertising strategies and programs, the company must address two additional questions. First, how will the company organize its advertising function—who will perform which advertising tasks? Second, how will the company adapt its advertising strategies and programs to the complexities of international markets?

Organizing for Advertising Different companies organize in different ways to handle advertising. In small companies, advertising might be handled by someone in the sales department. Large companies set up advertising departments whose job it is to set the advertising budget, work with the ad agency, and handle other advertising not done by the agency. Most large companies use outside advertising agencies because they offer several advantages.

Advertising agency A marketing services firm that assists companies in planning, preparing, implementing, and evaluating all or portions of their advertising programs.

How does an **advertising agency** work? Advertising agencies were started in the mid-to-late nineteenth century by salespeople and brokers who worked for the media and received a commission for selling advertising space to companies. As time passed, the salespeople began to help customers prepare their ads. Eventually, they formed agencies and grew closer to the advertisers than to the media. Today's agencies employ specialists who can often perform advertising tasks better than can the company's own staff. Agencies also bring an outside point of view to solving the company's problems, along with lots of experience from working with different clients and situations. Thus, today, even companies with strong advertising departments of their own use advertising agencies.

Some ad agencies are huge—the largest Canadian Agency, Cossette Communication Group, has annual gross income of $132 000 000. Recently, many agencies have grown by gobbling up other agencies, thus creating huge agency holding companies. The largest of these agency "megagroups," WPP Group, includes several large advertising, public relations, and promotion agencies with combined worldwide gross income of $8 billion on billings exceeding $67 billion.[16] Most large advertising agencies have the staff and resources to handle all phases of an advertising campaign for their clients, from creating a marketing plan to developing ad campaigns and preparing, placing, and evaluating ads.

Cossette Communication Group
www.cosette.com

International Advertising Decisions International advertisers face many complexities not encountered by domestic advertisers. The most basic issue concerns the degree to which global advertising should be adapted to the unique characteristics of various country markets. Some large advertisers have attempted to support their global brands with highly standardized worldwide advertising, with campaigns that work as well in Bangkok as they do in Barrie. For example, Jeep has created a worldwide brand image of ruggedness and reliability; Coca-Cola's Sprite brand uses standardized appeals to target the world's youth. Gillette's ads for its Sensor Excel for Women are almost identical worldwide, with only minor adjustments to suit the local culture. Ericsson, the Swedish telecommunications giant, spent $100 million on a standardized global television campaign with the tag line "make yourself heard," which features Agent 007, James Bond.

Standardization produces many benefits—lower advertising costs, greater global advertising coordination, and a more consistent worldwide image. But it also

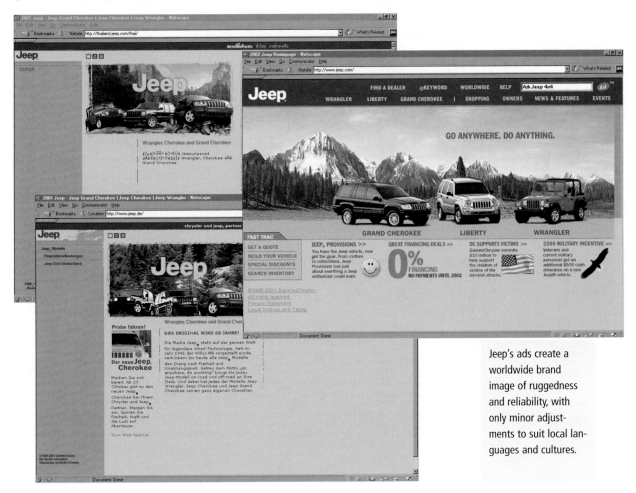

Jeep's ads create a worldwide brand image of ruggedness and reliability, with only minor adjustments to suit local languages and cultures.

has drawbacks. Most important, it ignores the fact that country markets differ greatly in their cultures, demographics, and economic conditions. Thus, most international advertisers "think globally but act locally." They develop global advertising *strategies* that make their worldwide advertising efforts more efficient and consistent. Then they adapt their advertising *programs* to make them more responsive to consumer needs and expectations within local markets.

For example, Coca-Cola has a pool of different commercials that can be used in or adapted to several different international markets. Some can be used with only minor changes—such as language—in several different countries. Local and regional managers decide which commercials work best for which markets. Recently, in a reverse of the usual order, a series of Coca-Cola commercials developed for the Russian market, using a talking bear and a man who transforms into a wolf, was shown in the United States. "This approach fits perfectly with the global nature of Coca-Cola," says the president of Coca-Cola's Nordic division. "[It] offers people a special look into a culture that is different from their own."[17]

Global advertisers face several special problems. For instance, advertising media costs and availability differ vastly from country to country. Countries also differ in the extent to which they regulate advertising practices. Many countries have extensive systems of laws restricting how much a company can spend on advertising, the media used, the nature of advertising claims, and other aspects of the advertising program. Such restrictions often require advertisers to adapt their campaigns from country to country.

For example, alcoholic products cannot be advertised or sold in Muslim countries. In many countries, Norway and Sweden, for example, no TV ads may be directed at children under 12. Moreover, Sweden is lobbying to extend that ban to all European Union member countries. To play it safe, McDonald's advertises itself as a family restaurant in Sweden. Comparative ads, while acceptable and even common in the United States and Canada, are less commonly used in the United Kingdom, unacceptable in Japan, and illegal in India and Brazil. China has restrictive censorship rules for TV and radio advertising; for example, the words *the best* are banned, as are ads that "violate social customs" or present women in "improper ways." Coca-Cola's Indian subsidiary was forced to end a promotion that offered prizes, such as a trip to Hollywood, because it violated India's established trade practices by encouraging customers to buy in order to "gamble."[18]

Thus, although advertisers may develop global strategies to guide their overall advertising efforts, specific advertising programs must usually be adapted to meet local cultures and customs, media characteristics, and advertising regulations.

Think about what goes on behind the scenes for the ads we see or hear.

- Pick a favourite print or television ad. Why do you like it? Do you think that it's effective? Can you think of an ad that people like that may not be effective?

- Dig a little deeper and learn about the campaign *behind* your ad. What are the campaign's objectives? What is its budget? Assess the campaign's message and media strategies. Looking beyond your own feelings about the ad, is the campaign likely to be effective?

SALES PROMOTION

Advertising and personal selling often work closely with another promotion tool, sales promotion. *Sales promotion* consists of short-term incentives to encourage purchase or sales of a product or service. Whereas advertising and personal selling offer reasons to buy a product or service, sales promotion offers reasons to buy *now*.

Examples of sales promotions are found everywhere. A freestanding insert in the Sunday newspaper contains a coupon offering $1 off Nabob coffee. An e-mail from Amazon.ca offers free shipping on your next purchase over $35. The end-of-the-aisle display in the local supermarket tempts impulse buyers with a wall of Coke cartons. An executive who buys a new Toshiba laptop gets a free carrying case, or a family buys a new Taurus and receives a rebate check for $500. A hardware store chain receives a 10 percent discount on selected Black & Decker portable power tools if it agrees to advertise them in local newspapers. Sales promotion includes a wide variety of promotion tools designed to stimulate earlier or stronger market response.

Rapid Growth of Sales Promotion

Sales promotion tools are used by most organizations, including manufacturers, distributors, retailers, trade associations, and nonprofit institutions. They are targeted toward final buyers *(consumer promotions)*, retailers and wholesalers *(trade promotions)*, business customers *(business promotions)*, and members of the sales force *(sales force promotions)*. Today, in the average consumer packaged-goods company, sales promotion accounts for 74 percent of all marketing expenditures.[19]

Several factors have contributed to the rapid growth of sales promotion, particularly in consumer markets. First, inside the company, product managers face greater pressures to increase short-term sales, and promotion is viewed as an effective short-run sales tool. Second, externally, the company faces more competition and competing brands are less differentiated. Increasingly, competitors are using sales promotion to help differentiate their offers. Third, advertising efficiency has declined because of rising costs, media clutter, and legal restraints. Fourth, consumers have become more deal oriented and ever-larger retailers are demanding more deals from manufacturers. Finally, the concentration of retail buying power in Canada, where the majority of sales of grocery products and health and beauty aids is dominated by a small number of large organizations, has resulted in a significant shift in marketing power to the retailer.

The growing use of sales promotion has resulted in *promotion clutter,* similar to advertising clutter. Consumers are increasingly tuning out promotions, weakening their ability to trigger immediate purchase. Manufacturers are now searching for ways to rise above the clutter, such as offering larger coupon values or creating more dramatic point-of-purchase displays.

In developing a sales promotion program, a company must first set sales promotion objectives and then select the best tools for accomplishing these objectives.

Sales Promotion Objectives

Sales promotion objectives vary widely. Sellers may use *consumer promotions* to increase short-term sales or to help build long-term market share. Objectives for *trade promotions* include getting retailers to carry new items and more inventory, getting them to advertise the product and give it more shelf space, and getting them to buy ahead. For the *sales force*, objectives include getting more sales force support for current or new products or getting salespeople to sign up new accounts. Sales promotions are usually used together with advertising, personal selling, or other promotion mix tools. Consumer promotions must usually be advertised and can add excitement and pulling power to ads. Trade and sales force promotions support the firm's personal selling process.

Generally, rather than creating only short-term sales or temporary brand switching, sales promotions should help to reinforce the product's position and build long-term *customer relationships.* Increasingly, marketers are avoiding "quick fix," price-only promotions in favour of promotions designed to build brand equity. Even price promotions can be designed to help build customer relationships. Examples include all the "frequency marketing programs" and clubs that have mushroomed in recent years. For example, The Book Company sponsors a Preferred Reader Program where the consumer pays $15 per year to receive mailings about new books, a discount on book purchases, and other services. The Royal Bank's Visa Gold loyalty program awards points each time the Visa card is used. These points are redeemable for merchandise. Sears has used the same concept for years through the Sears Club. By using your Sears' credit card on purchases, you earn points redeemable on future purchases. For example, if you spend $1000 and generate 1000 Club points, you are eligible for a certificate for $15 toward future purchases on your credit card in Sears stores. Norwegian Cruise Lines sponsors a loyalty program called Latitudes, a co-branding effort with Visa. The program includes a two-for-one cruise offer and a Latitudes Visa card that rewards users with points redeemable for discounts on NCL cruises. If properly designed, every sales promotion tool has the potential to build consumer relationships.

Major Sales Promotion Tools

Many tools can be used to accomplish sales promotion objectives. Descriptions of the main consumer, trade, and business promotion tools follow.

Consumer Promotion Tools The main *consumer promotion tools* include samples, coupons, cash refunds, price packs, premiums, advertising specialties, patronage rewards, point-of-purchase displays and demonstrations, and contests, sweepstakes, and games.

Samples are offers of a trial amount of a product. Sampling is the most effective—but most expensive—way to introduce a new product. Some samples are free; for others, the company charges a small amount to offset its cost. The sample might be delivered door-to-door, sent by mail, handed out in a store, attached to another product, or featured in an ad. Sometimes, samples are combined into sample packs, which can then be used to promote other products and services. Procter & Gamble has even distributed samples via the Internet:[20]

When Procter & Gamble decided to relaunch Pert Plus shampoo, it extended its $30 million ad campaign by constructing a new Web site (www.pertplus.com). P&G had three objectives for the Web site: to create awareness for reformulated Pert Plus, get consumers to try the product, and gather data about Web users. The site's first page invites visitors to place their heads against the computer screen in a mock attempt to measure the cleanliness of their hair. After "tabulating the results," the site tells visitors that they "need immediate help." The solution: "How about a free sample of new Pert Plus?" Visitors obtain the sample by filling out a short demographic form. The site offers other interesting features as well. For example, clicking "get a friend in a lather" produces a template that will send an e-mail to a friend with an invitation to visit the site and receive a free sample. How did the sampling promotion work out? Even P&G was shocked by the turnout. Within just two months of launching the site, 170 000 people visited and 83 000 requested samples. More surprising, given that the site is only 10 pages deep, the average person visited the site 1.9 times and spent a total of 7.5 minutes each visit.

Coupons are certificates that give buyers a saving when they purchase specified products. Most consumers love coupons: in Canada in 2001, marketers distributed 2.67 billion coupons, 6 percent more than in 2000, and consumers redeemed 122 million coupons valued at $128 million, up 7 percent from 2000.[21] However, as a result of coupon clutter, redemption rates have been declining in recent years. For example, in 1998, consumers redeemed about 130 million coupons. Thus, most major consumer goods companies are issuing fewer coupons and targeting them more carefully. They are also cultivating new outlets for distributing coupons, such as supermarket shelf dispensers, electronic point-of-sale coupon printers, or "paperless coupon systems." Some companies also offer coupons on their Web sites or through online coupon services such as Valpak.com and coupons.com. *Cash refund offers* (or *rebates*) are like coupons except that the price reduction occurs after the purchase rather than at the retail outlet. The consumer sends a "proof of purchase" to the manufacturer, who then refunds part of the purchase price by mail. For example, Toro ran a clever preseason promotion on some of its snowblower models, offering a rebate if the snowfall in the buyer's market area turned out to be below average. Competitors were not able to match this offer on such short notice, and the promotion was very successful.

Price packs (also called *cents-off deals*) offer consumers savings off the regular price of a product. Because retail price maintenance is illegal in Canada, the reduced prices are rarely marked directly on the label or package by the marketer. Instead, price packs can be single packages sold at a reduced price (such as two for the price of one), or two related products banded together (such as a toothbrush and toothpaste). This promotion is also referred to as "gift with purchase." Price packs are very effective—even more so than coupons—in stimulating short-term sales.

Premiums are goods offered either free or at low cost as an incentive to buy a product. If reusable, the package itself may serve as a premium—such as a decorative tin. Premiums are sometimes mailed to consumers who have sent in a proof of purchase, such as a box top. "Drink it. Get it." was the slogan for the Pepsi Stuff premium offer that one industry analyst called the "most successful promotion run in Canada in the last 40 years." Pepsi added value to a purchase of their product in a highly "youth-relevant" way by letting people redeem points of specially marked

Coupon Industry Association of Canada **www.couponscanada.org**

The Pepsi Stuff premium offer was called the "most successful promotion run in Canada in the last 40 years."

packages for "must-be-seen" merchandise from the Pepsi stuff catalogue. Eighty-one percent of soft-drink users were aware of the offer. The promotion increased Pepsi's market share by 7 percent. Although 53 percent of the gain came from people switching brands, the remainder came because heavy Pepsi drinkers consumed more product. Although the share gains are impressive, the program also improved consumer attitude and imagery measures of Pepsi.[22]

Advertising specialties are useful articles imprinted with an advertiser's name given as gifts to consumers. Typical items include pens, calendars, key rings, matches, shopping bags, T-shirts, caps, nail files, and coffee mugs. Such items can be very effective. In a recent study, 63 percent of all consumers surveyed were either carrying or wearing an ad specialty item. More than three quarters of those who had an item could recall the advertiser's name or message before showing the item to the interviewer.[23]

Patronage rewards are cash or other awards offered for the regular use of a certain company's products or services. For example, airlines offer frequent-flyer plans, awarding points for miles travelled that can be redeemed for free airline trips. Hotels have adopted honoured-guest plans that awards points to frequent users of their hotels. And supermarkets issue frequent shopper cards that dole out a wealth of discounts at the checkout.

Point-of-purchase (POP) promotions include displays and demonstrations that take place at the point of purchase or sale. Unfortunately, many retailers do not like to handle the hundreds of displays, signs, and posters they receive from manufacturers each year. Manufacturers have responded by offering better POP materials, tying them in with television or print messages, and offering to set them up.

Contests, sweepstakes, and *games* give consumers the chance to win something, such as cash, trips, or goods, by luck or through extra effort. A *contest* calls for consumers to submit an entry—a jingle, a guess, a suggestion—to be judged by a panel that will select the best entries. A *sweepstakes* calls for consumers to submit their names for a drawing. A *game* presents consumers with something—bingo numbers, missing letters—every time they buy, which may or may not help them win a prize. A *sales contest* urges dealers or the sales force to increase their efforts, with prizes going to the top performers.

Trade Promotion Tools Manufacturers direct more sales promotion dollars toward retailers and wholesalers (68 percent) than to consumers (32 percent). Trade promotion can persuade resellers to carry a brand, give it shelf space, promote it in advertising, and push it to consumers. Shelf space is so scarce these days that manufacturers often have to offer price-offs allowances, volume rebates, buy-back guarantees, or free goods to retailers and wholesalers to get products on the shelf and, once there, to stay on it.

Manufacturers use several trade promotion tools. Many of the tools used for consumer promotions—contests, premiums, displays—can also be used as trade promotions. Or the manufacturer may offer a straight *discount* off the list price on each case purchased during a stated period (also called a *price-off, off-invoice,* or *off-list*). Manufacturers also may offer an *allowance* (usually so much off per case) in return for the retailer's agreement to feature the manufacturer's products in some way. An *advertising allowance* compensates retailers for advertising the product. A *display allowance* compensates them for using special displays.

Manufacturers may offer *free goods,* which are extra cases of merchandise, to resellers who buy a certain quantity or who feature a certain flavour or size. They may offer *push money*—cash or gifts to dealers or their sales forces to "push" the manufacturer's goods. Manufacturers may give retailers free *specialty advertising items* that carry the company's name, such as pens, pencils, calendars, paperweights, matchbooks, memo pads, and yardsticks.

Business Promotion Tools Companies spend millions of dollars each year on promotion to industrial customers. These *business promotion tools* are used to generate business leads, stimulate purchases, reward customers, and motivate salespeople. Business promotion includes many of the same tools used for consumer or trade promotions. Here, we focus on two additional major business promotion tools: conventions and trade shows, and sales contests.

Many companies and trade associations organize *conventions and trade shows* to promote their products. Firms selling to the industry show their products at the trade show. More than 4300 trade shows take place every year, drawing as many as 85 million people. Vendors receive many benefits, such as opportunities to find new sales leads, contact customers, introduce new products, meet new customers, sell more to present customers, and educate customers with publications and audiovisual materials. Trade shows also help companies reach many prospects not reached through their sales forces. About 90 percent of a trade show's visitors see a company's salespeople for the first time at the show. Business marketers may spend as much as 35 percent of their annual promotion budgets on trade shows.[24]

A *sales contest* is a contest for salespeople or dealers to motivate them to increase their sales performance over a given period. Sales contests motivate and recognize good company performers, who may receive trips, cash prizes, or other gifts. Some companies award points for performance, which the receiver can redeem for any of a variety of prizes. Sales contests work best when they are tied to measurable and achievable sales objectives (such as finding new accounts, reviving old accounts, or increasing account profitability).

Developing the Sales Promotion Program

The marketer must make several other decisions to define the full sales promotion program. First, the marketer must decide on the *size of the incentive.* A certain minimum incentive is necessary if the promotion is to succeed; a larger incentive will produce more sales response. The marketer also must set *conditions for participation.* Incentives might be offered to everyone or only to select groups.

The marketer must then decide how to *promote and distribute the promotion* program itself. A 50-cents-off coupon could be given out in a package, at the store, by

More than 4300 trade shows take place every year, drawing as many as 85 million people, giving sellers chances to introduce new products and meet new customers. At this consumer electronics trade show, 2000 exhibitors attracted more than 91 000 professional visitors.

mail, or in an advertisement. Each distribution method involves a different level of reach and cost. Increasingly, marketers are blending several media into a total campaign concept. The *length of the promotion* is also important. If the sales promotion period is too short, many prospects (who may not be buying during that time) will miss it. If the promotion runs too long, the deal will lose some of its "act now" force.

Evaluation is also very important. Yet many companies fail to evaluate their sales promotion programs, and others evaluate them only superficially. The most common evaluation method is to compare sales before, during, and after a promotion. Suppose a company has a 6 percent market share before the promotion, which jumps to 10 percent during the promotion, falls to 5 percent right after, and rises to 7 percent later on. The promotion seems to have attracted new buyers and more buying from current customers. After the promotion, sales fell as consumers used up their inventories. The long-run rise to 7 percent means that the company gained some new users. If the brand's share had returned to the old level, then the promotion would have changed only the *timing* of demand rather than the *total* demand.

Consumer research would also show the kinds of people who responded to the promotion and what they did after it ended. *Surveys* can provide information on how many consumers recall the promotion, what they thought of it, how many took advantage of it, and how it affected their buying. Sales promotions also can be evaluated through *experiments* that vary factors such as incentive value, length, and distribution method.

Clearly, sales promotion plays an important role in the total promotion mix. To use it well, the marketer must define the sales promotion objectives, select the best tools, design the sales promotion program, implement the program, and evaluate the results. Moreover, sales promotion must be coordinated carefully with other promotion mix elements within the integrated marketing communications program.

PUBLIC RELATIONS

Another major mass-promotion tool is *public relations*—building good relations with the company's various publics by obtaining favourable publicity, building up a good corporate image, and handling or heading off unfavourable rumours, stories, and events. Public relations departments may perform any or all of the following functions:[25]

- *Press relations or press agentry:* Creating and placing newsworthy information in the news media to attract attention to a person, product, or service.

- *Product publicity:* Publicizing specific products.

- *Public affairs:* Building and maintaining national or local community relations.

- *Lobbying:* Building and maintaining relations with legislators and government officials to influence legislation and regulation.

- *Investor relations:* Maintaining relationships with shareholders and others in the financial community.

- *Development:* Public relations with donors or members of nonprofit organizations to gain financial or volunteer support.

Public relations is used to promote products, people, places, ideas, activities, organizations, and even nations. Trade associations have used public relations to rebuild interest in declining commodities such as eggs, apples, milk, and potatoes. Johnson & Johnson's masterly use of public relations played a major role in saving Tylenol from extinction after its product-tampering scare. Nations have used public relations to attract more tourists, foreign investment, and international support.

Public relations can have a strong impact on public awareness at a much lower cost than advertising can. The company does not pay for the space or time in the media. Rather, it pays a staff to develop and circulate information and to manage events. If the company develops an interesting story, it could be picked up by several different media, having the same effect as advertising that would cost millions of dollars. And it would have more credibility than advertising.

Public relations can also be used to help overcome corporate crisis. Whistler Mountain Resort Association faced such a crisis when its Quicksilver chair failed, detaching several chairs from the cable, injuring several skiers and killing one. Whistler's marketing director David Perry's first priority was to manage information flow and keep panic under control. He quickly informed parents waiting at the bottom of the hill that their kids were safe. Perry also opened up a media centre from which reporters could work. He recruited senior managers to call all the skiers who had been on the lift that day and arranged for counselling for employees affected by the stress of the accident. Whistler ran ads thanking the community for its support during the crisis and conducted technical investigations to prevent such a failure from occurring in the future. It also adjusted its PR policies based on this experience to ensure that they were even more effective.[26]

Despite its potential strengths, public relations is often described as a marketing stepchild because of its limited and scattered use. The public relations department is usually located at corporate headquarters. Its staff is so busy dealing with various publics—stockholders, employees, legislators, city officials—that public relations programs to support product marketing objectives may be ignored. Marketing managers and public relations practitioners do not always speak the same language. Many public relations practitioners see their job as simply communicating. In contrast, marketing managers tend to be much more interested in how advertising and public relations affect sales and profits.

This situation is changing, however. Many companies now want their public relations departments to manage all their activities with a view toward marketing the company and improving the bottom line. They know that good public relations can be a powerful brand-building tool. Two well-known marketing consultants provide the following advice, which points to the potential power of public relations as a first step in building brands:

Just because a heavy dose of advertising is associated with most major brands doesn't necessarily mean that advertising built the brands in the first place. The birth of a brand is usually accomplished with [public relations], not advertising. Our general rule is [PR] first, advertising second. [Public relations] is the nail, advertising the hammer. [PR] creates the credentials that provide the credibility for advertising....Anita Roddick built the Body Shop into a major brand with no advertising at all. Instead, she traveled the world on a relentless quest for publicity….Until recently, Starbucks Coffee Co. didn't spend a hill of beans on advertising, either. In 10 years, the company spent less than $10 million on advertising, a trivial amount for a brand that delivers annual sales of $1.3 billion. Wal-Mart Stores became the world's largest retailer…with very little advertising….In the toy field, Furby, Beanie Babies, and Tickle Me Elmo became highly successful…and on the Internet, Yahoo!, Amazon.com, and Excite became powerhouse brands, [all] with virtually no advertising.[27]

Thus, some companies are setting up special units called *marketing public relations* to support corporate and product promotion and image making directly. Many companies hire marketing public relations firms to handle their PR programs or to assist the company's public relations team.

Major Public Relations Tools

Public relations professionals use several tools. One of the major tools is *news*. PR professionals find or create favourable news about the company and its products or people. Sometimes news stories occur naturally, and sometimes the PR person can suggest events or activities that would create news. *Speeches* can also create product and company publicity. Increasingly, company executives must field questions from the media or give talks at trade associations or sales meetings, and these events can either build or hurt the company's image.

Another common PR tool is *special events,* ranging from news conferences, press tours, grand openings, and fireworks displays to laser shows, hot air balloon releases, multimedia presentations and star-studded spectaculars, or educational programs designed to reach and interest target publics.

Public relations people also prepare *written materials* to reach and influence their target markets. These materials include annual reports, brochures, articles, and company newsletters and magazines. *Audiovisual materials,* such as films, slide- and-sound programs, and video- and audiocassettes, are being used increasingly as communication tools. *Corporate identity materials* can also help create a corporate identity that the public immediately recognizes. Logos, stationery, brochures, signs, business forms, business cards, buildings, uniforms, and company cars and trucks—all become marketing tools when they are attractive, distinctive, and memorable. Finally, companies can improve public goodwill by contributing money and time to *public service activities.*

A company's Web site can be a good public relations vehicle. Consumers and members of other publics can visit the site for information and entertainment. Such sites can be extremely popular. For example, Butterball's site at **www.butterball.ca**, which features cooking and carving tips, received 550 000 visitors in one day during Thanksgiving week last year. Web sites can also be ideal for handling crises. For example, when several bottles of Odwalla apple juice sold on the West Coast were found to contain *E. coli* bacteria, Odwalla initiated a massive product recall. Within only three hours, it set up a Web site laden with information about the crisis and Odwalla's response. Company staffers also combed the Internet looking for newsgroups discussing Odwalla and posted links to the sites. In another

A company's Web site can be a good public relations vehicle. Butterball's site, which features cooking and carving tips, received 550 000 visits in one day during the Thanksgiving week.

example, American Home Products quickly set up a Web site to distribute accurate information and advice after a model died reportedly after inhaling its Primatene Mist. In all, notes one analyst, "Today, public relations is reshaping the Internet and the Internet, in turn, is redefining the practice of public relations." Says another, "People look to the Net for information, not salesmanship, and that's the real opportunity for public relations."[28]

As with the other promotion tools, in considering when and how to use product public relations, management should set PR objectives, choose the PR messages and vehicles, implement the PR plan, and evaluate the results. The firm's public relations should be blended smoothly with other promotion activities within the company's overall integrated marketing communications effort.

<< Looking Back < < < < < < < < <

In this chapter, you've learned about the concept of integrated marketing communications (IMC), defined the major marketing communications tools, and overviewed the general promotion mix strategies. We've also explored three of the specific communications mix elements—advertising, sales promotion, and public relations—more deeply. Before moving on to other promotion tools, let's review the important concepts.

Modern marketing calls for more than just developing a good product, pricing it attractively, and making it available to target customers. Companies also must *communicate* with current and prospective customers to inform them about product benefits and carefully position products in consumers' minds. To do this, they must blend five communication-mix tools, guided by a well-designed and well-implemented integrated marketing communications strategy.

1. Discuss the process and advantages of integrated marketing communications.

Recent shifts toward targeted or one-to-one marketing, coupled with advances in information technology, have had a dramatic impact on marketing communications. As marketing communicators adopt richer but more fragmented media and promotion mixes to reach their diverse markets, they risk creating a communications hodgepodge for consumers. To prevent this, more companies are adopting the concept of *integrated marketing communications (IMC)*. Guided by an overall IMC strategy, the company works out the roles that the various promotional tools will play and the extent to which each will be used. It carefully coordinates the promotional activities and the timing of major campaigns. Finally, to help implement its integrated marketing strategy, the company appoints a marketing communications director who has overall responsibility for the company's communications efforts.

2. Define the five promotion tools and discuss factors that must be considered in shaping the overall promotion mix.

A company's total *marketing communications mix*—also called its *promotion mix*—consists of the specific blend of *advertising, personal selling, sales promotion, public relations,* and *direct-marketing* tools that the company uses to pursue its advertising and marketing objectives. Advertising includes any paid form of nonpersonal presentation and promotion of ideas, goods, or services by an identified sponsor. In contrast, public relations focuses on building good relations with the company's various publics by obtaining favourable unpaid publicity. Personal selling is any form of personal presentation by the firm's sales force for the purpose of making sales and building customer relationships. Firms use sales promotion to provide short-term incentives to encourage the purchase or sale of a product or service. Finally, firms seeking immediate response from targeted individual customers use nonpersonal direct-marketing tools to communicate with customers.

The company wants to create an integrated *promotion mix*. It can pursue a *push* or a *pull* promotional strategy, or a combination of the two. The best specific blend of promotion tools depends on the type of product or market and the product life-cycle stage. People at all levels of the organization must be aware of the many legal and ethical issues surrounding marketing communications.

3. Describe and discuss the major decisions involved in developing an advertising program.

Advertising—the use of paid media by a seller to inform, persuade, and remind about its products or organization—is a strong promotion tool that takes many forms and has many uses. *Advertising decision making* involves decisions about the objectives, the budget, the message, the media, and, finally, the evaluation of results. Advertisers should set clear *objectives* as to whether the advertising is supposed to inform, persuade, or remind buyers. The advertising *budget* can be based on what is affordable, on sales, on competitors' spending, or on the objectives and tasks. The *message decision* calls for planning a message strategy and executing it effectively. The *media decision* involves defining reach, frequency, and impact goals; choosing major media types; selecting media vehicles; and deciding on media timing. Message and media decisions must be closely coordinated for maximum campaign effectiveness. Finally, *evaluation* calls for evaluating the communication and sales effects of advertising before, during, and after the advertising is placed.

4. Explain how sales promotion campaigns are developed and implemented.

Sales promotion covers a wide variety of short-term incentive tools—coupons, premiums, contests, buying allowances—designed to stimulate final and business consumers, the trade, and the company's own sales force. Sales promotion spending has been growing faster than advertising spending in recent years. A sales promotion campaign first calls for setting sales promotion objectives (in general, sales promotions should be *consumer relationship building*). It then calls for developing and implementing the sales promotion program by using consumer promotion tools (*samples, coupons, cash refunds* or *rebates, price packs, premiums, advertising specialties, patronage rewards,* and others); trade promotion tools *(discounts, allowances, free goods, push money)*; and business promotion tools *(conventions, trade shows, sales contests)*. The sales promotion effort should be coordinated carefully with the firm's other promotion efforts.

5. Explain how companies use public relations to communicate with their publics.

Public relations involves building good relations with the company's various publics. Its functions include *press agentry, product publicity, public affairs, lobbying, investor relations*, and *development*. Public relations can have a strong impact on public awareness at a much lower cost than advertising can, and public relations results can sometimes be spectacular.

Despite its potential strengths, however, public relations sometimes sees only limited and scattered use. Public relations tools include *news, speeches, special events, written materials, audiovisual materials, corporate identity materials,* and *public service activities.* A company's Web site can be a good public relations vehicle. In considering when and how to use product public relations, management should set PR objectives, choose the PR messages and vehicles, implement the PR plan, and evaluate the results. Public relations should be blended smoothly with other promotion activities within the company's overall integrated marketing communications effort.

Navigating the Key Terms

Advertising, **p. 508**

Advertising agency, **p. 530**

Advertising objective, **p. 518**

Affordable method, **p. 519**

Competitive-parity method, **p. 520**

Direct marketing, **p. 508**

Integrated marketing communications (IMC), **p. 510**

Marketing communications mix (promotion mix), **p. 508**

Objective-and-task method, **p. 520**

Percentage-of-sales method, **p. 520**

Personal selling, **p. 508**

Public relations, **p. 508**

Pull strategy, **p. 516**

Push strategy, **p. 516**

Sales promotion, **p. 508**

Concept Check

Fill in the blanks and then check your answers.

1. A company's marketing communications mix consists of a blend of _____, _____, _____, _____, _____, and tools.

2. _____ is any paid form of nonpersonal presentation and promotion of ideas, goods, or services by an identified sponsor.

3. _____ builds strong brand identity in the marketplace by tying together and reinforcing all your images and messages.

4. _____ can reach masses of geographically dispersed buyers at a low cost per exposure, and it enables the seller to repeat a message many times.

5. Using a _____ strategy, the producer directs its marketing activities (primarily advertising and consumer promotion) toward final consumers to induce them to buy the product.

6. Advertising objectives can be classified by primary purpose—whether the aim is to _____, _____, or _____.

7. There are four common methods used to set the total budget for advertising: the affordable method, the _____ method, the _____ method, and the _____ method.

8. Advertising appeals should have three characteristics: (1) _____; (2) _____; and, (3) _____.

9. _____ is a measure of how many times the average person in the target market is exposed to the message.

10. _____ consists of short-term incentives to encourage purchase or sales of a product or service.

11. The main consumer promotion tools include _____, _____, price packs, premiums, advertising specialties, patronage rewards, _____, and contests, sweepstakes, and _____.

12. Public relations departments perform many functions. Under the _____ function, the department conducts public relations with donors or members of nonprofit organizations to gain financial or volunteer support.

Concept Check Answers: 1. advertising, personal selling, sales promotion, public relations, and direct marketing; 2. Advertising; 3. Integrated marketing communications (IMC); 4. Advertising; 5. pull; 6. inform, persuade, or remind; 7. percentage-of-sales, competitive-parity, and objective-and-task; 8. meaningful, believable, distinctive; 9. Frequency; 10. Sales promotion; 11. samples, coupons, cash refunds, games; 12. development.

Discussing the Issues

1. The shift from mass marketing to targeted marketing, and the corresponding use of a richer mix of promotion tools and communication channels, poses problems for many marketers. Using all of the promotion-mix elements suggested in the chapter, propose a plan for integrating marketing communications for one of the following: (a) your university or college, (b) McDonald's, (c) Burton Snow Boards, and (d) a local zoo, museum, theatre, or civic event.

2. Advertising objectives can be classified by primary purpose: to inform, persuade, or remind. Using your local newspaper, find examples of ads that address each of these objectives. Using Table 13-1, discuss why your examples fit the chosen objective.

3. The chapter lists nine different execution styles that are often used by advertisers to meet advertising objectives. Which of these styles do you think is most commonly used? Explain. Pick any three styles and find an example of each. Critique each example selected on its content, effectiveness, and match to the selected target market.

4. Which of the sales promotion tools described in the chapter would be best for stimulating sales of the following products or services: (a) a dry cleaner wanting to emphasize low prices on washed and pressed dress shirts, (b) Gummy Bears new black cherry flavour, (c) Procter & Gamble's efforts to bundle laundry detergent and fabric softer together in a combined marketing effort, (d) a company that wants its customers to aid in developing a new jingle.

5. The latest public relations frontier is the Internet. Cyber-travellers can now post their problems with goods and services on electronic bulletin boards and in company chat rooms, putting pressure on companies to respond. Customers regularly share their experiences with product design flaws, service difficulties, prices, warranties, and other problems. What kinds of special public relations problems and opportunities does the Internet present to today's companies? How should companies change their company policies and Web sites to deal with these problems and opportunities? Find an example of a company that uses its Web site as a proactive public relations tool.

Mastering Marketing

After examining the communication and promotion function of CanGo, comment on the extent of the organization's ability to integrate these functions into an overall IMC effort. Comment on strengths and weaknesses. How can the weaknesses be corrected? Which of the promotional tools needs to be used more? Are current communication and promotion objectives sufficient? Comment, explain, and offer suggestions.

Check out the enclosed Video case CD-ROM, or our Companion Website at www.pearsoned.ca/armstrong, to view a CBC video segment and case for this chapter.

MAP 13 Marketing Applications

Is online advertising a boom or a bust? Even most critics still believe that advertising on the Internet has a bright future as long as its unique features are expanded and exploited. You can't treat an online advertisement as if it were just another television or magazine advertisement, they say, although in the beginning that's just what many advertisers did. Banners, pop-ups, sponsorships, vertical and horizontal space usage, and the ability to target unique (and interested) audiences will be strengths on which new and dynamic communication strategies can be built. In fact, most large advertising agencies now have online advertising divisions to ensure that this media form is used effectively and correctly. How is the medium doing? With about $7 billion in sales annually, it has already surpassed outdoor advertising and is close behind many forms of cable-TV advertising. Even though Web-based advertising is not designed to broadcast messages to the masses in the same way television advertising does, it can focus directly on particular upscale markets that are interesting to many sellers. To counter the Internet advertising problems of the past, advertisers are now spending more carefully and employing more carefully targeted messages. The new challenge in online advertising will be to determine not only how many times a consumer views an ad but who views it.

Although it may take a while, the medium may yet achieve superstar status.

Thinking Like a Marketing Manager

1. DoubleClick, one of the largest online advertising firms, specializes in targeted advertising. Visit the Web site at **www.doubleclick.com**. Look in the section targeted toward advertisers and describe how DoubleClick attempts to target ads using audience psychographics and buying behaviour.

2. When compared with television and magazine advertising, what are the advantages and disadvantages of online advertising?

3. How does online advertising monitor consumers' behaviour and capture data about them? Do other media forms do this? Comment.

4. Assume that you are the advertising manager for a large toy manufacturer that is considering a significant expenditure in online advertising for the upcoming holiday season. Visit NetRatings at **www.netratings.com** to examine the statistics on the top banner ads currently online. Then, design a banner ad that you think would be most effective for your company. Explain any assumptions you made about your company and its products when you designed your ad.

Digital Map

Visit our Web site at **www.pearsoned.ca/armstrong** for online quizzes, Internet exercises, and more!

CASE 13 FIERCE CREATURES: INSECTS, DOGS, AND OTHER AMIGOS WORK TO RING UP PCS SALES

In 1997, the sector that spent the most on advertising was the telecommunications industry. A record number of primetime ads were run as the telecommunications giants fought new market entrants. Canada's largest advertiser, BCE, parent of the Bell companies, spent a cool $99 million on advertising. Rogers Cantel dug deep and found $35.5 million for its communications budget. Sprint Canada splurged with another $17.6 million. AT&T budgeted $16.6 million. And Unitel coughed up an additional $13.8 million. Even the newest players had huge expenditures: Microcell and Clearnet spent $400 000 and $800 000, respectively.

Part of these expenditures went to support the launch of the industry's newest products—personal communications services or PCS—those funky little handsets that handle everything from e-mail to voice-mail to actual telephone calls. The fight for market share is being fought with a vengeance and, if this market follows the history of cell phones, it won't be an easy battle. Even after years on the market, cell phones have penetrated a meagre 12 to 15 percent of the Canadian market.

It may not be surprising that consumers have been so slow on the uptake. They have been barraged with ads and sales pitches, yet they find it impossible to compare prices and total costs of the services since most of the companies were subsidizing the cost of the phone by making consumers sign long-term service contracts and charging them premium per-minute usage rates. At least, that was the case until Clearnet, of Pickering, Ontario, entered the scene.

Clearnet is one of the four firms vying for share in this superheated market. While the telecommunications giants, Bell and Rogers Cantel, are marketing their PCS products to existing customers as upgrades for their current products, the upstarts, Clearnet and Microcell, want consumers to see PCS as a totally new product class that will give consumers control over their personal and business communications. Thus, Rogers Cantel used promotions that extended the Amigo brand into the PCS arena shouting, "Let's get digital!" and Bell used the same 12-year-old spokesperson for both its Bell Mobility and PCS spots to tie the two product lines together. Microcell built its strategy around faithful FIDO.

When planning its strategy, Clearnet believed it faced a three-fold challenge: Introduce a completely new technology; establish a unique brand identity for its product; and provide potential buyers with enough information so that they would be comfortable making a purchase decision.

Research conducted by Clearnet and its agency, TAXI Advertising and Design, showed that consumers were concerned about rampant technological change and the constant product variations it created. Therefore, the team knew that focusing on the technology itself would be a mistake. Unlike the other companies, Clearnet decided to offer national coverage from day one instead of rolling out its products on an area-by-area basis. It also decided to simultaneously aim its product at both the end-consumer and the business marketplaces. Unlike the other competitors, Clearnet's pricing strategy is simplicity itself. Consumers pay $149.99 for their PCS phone and sign up for one of two talk-time plans. George Cope, Clearnet president, says, "We've finally made wireless telephoning accessible and affordable. No more 60¢-a-minute charges." In addition to simplicity in pricing, Clearnet made its phones widely available. Customers can use one of over 600 outlets across Canada as well as such non-traditional phone sales outlets as Blockbuster Video, Business Depot, Future Shop, Grand & Toy, Battery Depot, and The Telephone Booth.

Given Clearnet's cross-country launch and non-traditional distribution channels, it needed a communications strategy that would be as meaningful in Amherstview as it was in the Okanagan. Moreover, Clearnet, a small player facing industry giants, had only a small communications budget to launch the product, $800 000 compared to the $10 million used by Bell to launch its PCS service. Therefore, Clearnet had to carefully integrate its efforts so that it could speak to consumers with one voice.

In the face of these daunting challenges, Clearnet decided to create a human face for its brand that would link all of the elements of their campaign. This thinking gave birth to Mike, the "buddy" who can handle all forms of communication including two-way radio. Mike is an unassuming guy meant to typify to potential users that the service is a practical way to save users both time and money. Clearnet put Mike everywhere. Clearnet decided it was important to use a shotgun approach, believing it could only reach key buyers with this type of campaign. Thus, Mike appeared in a teaser campaign placed in newspapers, on television, in direct-mail pieces, at special events, and in news releases.

Clearnet's initial campaign was aimed at generating awareness. Its next task was to provide potential buyers with more information to move them through the decision-making process. This is where newspaper advertising really came into its own. According to Rick Seifeddine, Clearnet's director of communications and advertising, "Newspapers allow you to touch a lot of people, but [they] give you a little more time to deliver a complex message."

The secondary objective of the campaign was to generate leads about people most interested in the product so that Clearnet could follow up with more personal, targeted sales methods. Being able to explore niche markets overlooked by the two big players is an important part of Clearnet's strategy. It plans to use a direct marketing program that will target small firms and home businesses in which internal and external communications is essential to getting their work done. As part of its direct marketing efforts, Clearnet will make use of the Web, telemarketing, direct mail, and direct television.

Clearnet's "Mike" campaign helped turn the company into the mouse that roared. It became the industry leader, selling 30 000 units and growing its staff from 11 employees to over 1600. To sustain this remarkable growth, Clearnet launched a second campaign late in 1997. All of the ads featured nature-based images-everything from dung beetles to fly-catching plants. Clearnet chose the images to convey its positioning as the "simple" choice-one that wouldn't ensnare customers in complex contracts. Ads contained the message that buying PCS technology was as hassle-free as buying a toaster.

Were the ads enough to help Clearnet reign supreme in the competitive jungle? They certainly turned the small firm into a force to be reckoned with. In October 2000, Clearnet was acquired by TELUS Corporation, western Canada's leading telecommunications company, and a new company, TELUS Mobility, was born. It has since moved quickly to the forefront of Canada's wireless marketplace.Go to the Clearnet website (**www.clearnet.com/english/pcs**) to learn more about its current advertising campaigns and the Telus merger.

Questions

1. When launching a new product based on a new technology, is competition a good or bad thing?

2. Which strategy do you think is most viable for the PCS product launch-the one followed by the big telecommunications companies that position their products as line extensions, or the one used by the upstart firms that position their products as break-through, new-to-the world offerings? Which one is easier to communicate to prospective customers? Which one offers the biggest payback?

3. Describe the unique selling proposition around which Clearnet's integrated communication program was built.

4. While Clearnet's shotgun approach may give the firm the volume it needs to cover the huge costs of launching the product, do you think this strategy is viable for the future?

5. The communications task facing marketers of the new PCS technology is complex. They have to convey messages to consumers that range from the benefits associated with the product to the capabilities of the new technologies. They must explain how PCS differs from cell phones and what the various price-points will be. The firms also have to move consumers step-by-step through the decision-making process. What media vehicles would you recommend for people at different decision-making stages? Can you use the same media for end-consumers and business customers?

6. The huge amount of ad spending in the telecommunications market may have caused considerable consumer confusion. Did Clearnet's advertising campaign differentiate the firm from its competition? Before you read this case, did you recall Clearnet's ads? Did you understand the benefits of its products?

7. As consumers become more comfortable with PCS technology, what communication challenges will Clearnet face in the future?

Sources: Quotes from Terence Belford, "Dial-up goes digital," *Financial Post,* 20 November 1997:P5; and David Bosworth, "Special report: Mike packs wallop with media splash," *Strategy,* 3 March 1997:30. Also see David Chilton, "Clearnet-Meet Mike," *Strategy,* 30 September 1996:5; Lesley Daw and Bobbi Bulmer, "The Telco barrage," *Marketing,* 20 October 1997:22-5; Mark De Wolf, "PCS products a natural for direct marketing," *Strategy,* 21 July 1997:DR1; Lara Mills, "Clearnet PCS adopts 'natural' strategy," *Marketing,* 6 October 1997:3; Patti Summerfield, "Bell Mobility launches PCS Plus," *Strategy,* 13 October 1997:2; **www.clearnet. com/.**

14 >> Integrated Marketing Communications: Personal Selling and Direct Marketing

Looking Ahead

In the previous chapter, you learned about integrated marketing communication (IMC) and three specific elements of the marketing communications mix: advertising, sales promotion, and publicity. In this chapter, we'll move down the road to learn about the final two IMC elements: personal selling and direct marketing. Personal selling is the interpersonal arm of marketing communications in which the sales force interacts with customers and prospects to make sales and build relationships. Direct marketing consists of direct connections with carefully targeted consumers to both obtain an immediate response and cultivate lasting customer relationships. Actually, direct marketing can be viewed as more than just a communications tool. In many ways, it constitutes an overall marketing *approach*—a blend of communications and distribution channels. As you read, remember that although this chapter examines personal selling and direct marketing as separate tools, they must be carefully coordinated with other elements of the marketing communication mix.

After studying this chapter, you should be able to

1. discuss the role of a company's salespeople in creating value for customers and building customer relationships
2. identify and explain the six major sales force management steps
3. discuss the personal selling process, distinguishing between transaction-oriented marketing and relationship marketing
4. define direct marketing and discuss its benefits for customers and companies
5. identify and discuss the major forms of direct marketing

We'll begin this leg of the journey with a look at Lear Corporation's sales force. Although you may never have heard of Lear, the chances are good that you've spent lots of time in one or more of the car interiors that it supplies to the world's major automotive manufacturers. Before you read on, close your eyes for a moment and envision a typical salesperson. If what you see is a stereotypical glad-hander out to lighten your wallet or purse by selling you something that you don't really need, you might be in for a surprise.

When someone says "salesperson," what image comes to mind? Perhaps it's the stereotypical "travelling salesperson"—the fast-talking, ever-smiling peddler who travels his or her territory foisting wares on reluctant customers. Such stereotypes, however, are out of date. Today, most professional salespeople are well-educated, well-trained men and women who work to build long-term, value-producing relationships with their customers. They succeed not by taking customers but by helping them, by assessing customer needs and solving customer problems.

Consider Lear Corporation, one of the largest, fastest-growing, and most successful automotive suppliers in the world. Each year, Lear produces more than $18 billion worth of automotive interiors—seat systems, instrument panels, door panels, floor and acoustic systems, overhead systems, and electronic and electrical distribution systems. Its customers include most of the world's leading automotive companies, from Ford, Daimler-Chrysler, General Motors, Fiat, Toyota, and Volvo to BMW, Ferrari, Rolls-Royce, and more than a dozen others. Lear now operates more than 300 facilities in 32 countries around the globe. During the past few years, Lear has achieved record-breaking sales and earnings growth. Lear's sales during the past five years have more than doubled, and its "average content per car" in North America has increased more than fourfold since 1990. It owns about a 30 percent share of the North American interior components market.

Lear Corporation owes its success to many factors, including a strong customer orientation and a commitment to continuous improvement, teamwork, and customer value. But perhaps more than any other part of the organization, it's Lear's outstanding 145-person sales force that makes the company's credo, "Consumer driven. Customer focused," ring true. Lear's sales force was recently rated by *Sales and Marketing Management* magazine as one of "America's Best Sales Forces." What makes this an outstanding sales force? Lear knows that good selling these days takes much more than just a sales rep covering a territory and convincing customers to buy the product. It takes teamwork, relationship building, and doing what's best for the customer. Lear's sales force excels at these tasks.

Lear's sales depend completely on the success of its customers. If the automakers don't sell cars, Lear doesn't sell interiors. So the Lear sales force strives to create not just sales, but also customer success. In fact, Lear salespeople aren't "sales reps," they're "account managers" who function more as consultants than as order getters. "Our salespeople don't really close deals," notes a senior marketing executive. "They consult and work with customers to learn exactly what's needed and when."

To more fully match customers' needs, Lear has diversified its product line to become a kind of "one-stop shopping" source. Until a few years ago, Lear supplied only seats; now it sells almost everything for a car's interior. Providing complete interior solutions for customers also benefits Lear. "It used to be that we'd build a partnership and then get only a limited amount of revenue from it," the executive says. "Now we can get as much as possible out of our customer relationships."

Lear is heavily customer focused, so much so that it's broken up into separate divisions dedicated to specific customers. For example, there's a Ford division and a General Motors division, and each operates as its own profit centre. Within each division, high-level "platform teams"—made up of salespeople, engineers, and program managers—work directly with their customer counterparts. These platform teams are closely supported by divisional manufacturing, finance, quality, and advanced technology groups. Lear's limited customer base, consisting of only a few dozen customers in all, allows Lear's sales teams to get very close to their customers. "Our teams don't call on purchasers; they're linked to customer operations at all levels," the marketer notes. "We try to put a system in place that creates continuous contact with customers." In fact, Lear often locates its sales offices in customers' plants. For example, the team that handles GM's light truck division works at GM's truck operation campus. "We can't just be there to give quotes and ask for orders," says the marketing executive. "We need to be involved with customers every step of the way—from vehicle concept through launch."

Lear's largest customers are worth billions of dollars in annual sales to the company. Maintaining

profitable relationships with such large customers takes much more than a nice smile and a firm handshake. And certainly there's no place for the "smoke and mirrors" or "flimflam" sometimes mistakenly associated with personal selling. Success in such a selling environment requires careful teamwork among well-trained, dedicated sales professionals who are bent on profitably taking care of their customers.[1]

In this chapter, we examine two more marketing communication and promotion tools—*personal selling* and *direct marketing*. Both involve direct connections with customers aimed toward building customer-unique value and lasting relationships.

PERSONAL SELLING

Robert Louis Stevenson once noted that "everyone lives by selling something." We are all familiar with the sales forces used by business organizations to sell products and services to customers around the world. But sales forces are also found in many other kinds of organizations. For example, universities use recruiters to attract new students, and churches use membership committees to attract new members. Hospitals and museums use fundraisers to contact donors and raise money. Even governments use sales forces. Canada Post, for instance, uses a sales force to sell direct-mail offerings, courier services, and other services to corporate customers. In the first part of this chapter, we examine the role of personal selling in the organization, sales force management decisions, and the personal selling process.

The Nature of Personal Selling

Selling is one of the oldest professions in the world. The people who do the selling go by many names: *salespeople, sales representatives, account executives, sales consultants, sales engineers, agents, district managers, marketing representatives,* and *account development reps,* to name just a few.

People hold many stereotypes of salespeople—including some unfavourable ones. "Salesperson" may bring to mind the image of Arthur Miller's pitiable Willy Loman in *Death of a Salesman*. Or you might think of Meredith Willson's cigar-smoking, backslapping, joke-telling Harold Hill in *The Music Man*. Both examples depict salespeople as loners, travelling their territories, trying to foist their wares on unsuspecting or unwilling buyers.

However, modern salespeople are very different from these unfortunate stereotypes. Today, most salespeople are well-educated, well-trained professionals who work to build and maintain long-term customer relationships by listening to their customers, assessing customer needs, and organizing the company's efforts to solve customer problems. Consider Boeing, the aerospace giant competing in the rough and tumble worldwide commercial aircraft market. It takes more than a warm smile to sell expensive airplanes:

Selling high-tech aircraft at $70–$90 million or more a copy is complex and challenging. A single big sale can easily run into billions of dollars. Boeing salespeople head up an extensive team of company specialists—sales and service technicians, financial analysts, planners, engineers—all dedicated to finding ways to satisfy airline customer needs. The salespeople begin by becoming experts on the airlines, much like Wall Street analysts would. They find out where each airline wants to grow, when it wants to replace planes, and details of its financial situation. The team runs Boeing and competing planes through computer systems, simulating the airline's routes, cost per seat, and other factors to show that their planes are most efficient. Then the high-level negotiations begin. The selling process is nerve-wrackingly slow—it can take two or three years from the first sales presentation to the day the sale is announced. Sometimes top executives from both the airline and Boeing are brought in to close the deal. After getting the order, salespeople then must stay in almost constant touch to keep track of the account's equipment needs and to make certain the customer stays satisfied. Success depends on building solid, long-term relationships with customers, based on performance and trust.[2]

Salesperson An individual acting for a company by performing one or more of the following activities: prospecting, communicating, servicing, and information gathering.

The term **salesperson** covers a wide range of positions. At one extreme, a salesperson might be largely an *order taker,* such as the department store salesperson standing behind the counter. At the other extreme are *order getters,* whose positions demand the *creative selling* of products and services ranging from appliances, industrial equipment, or airplanes to insurance, advertising, or consulting services. Here, we focus on the more creative types of selling and on the process of building and managing an effective sales force.

The Role of the Sales Force

Personal selling is the interpersonal arm of the promotion mix. Advertising consists of one-way, nonpersonal communication with target consumer groups. In contrast, personal selling involves two-way, personal communication between salespeople and individual customers—whether face to face, by telephone, through video or Web conferences, or by other means. Personal selling can be more effective than advertising in more complex selling situations. Salespeople can probe customers to learn more about their problems, then adjust the marketing offer to fit the special needs of each customer and negotiate terms of sale. They can build long-term personal relationships with key decision makers.

The role of personal selling varies from company to company. Some firms have no salespeople at all—for example, companies that sell only through mail-order catalogues or companies that sell through manufacturer's reps, sales agents, or brokers. In most firms, however, the sales force plays a major role. In companies that sell business products and services, such as Nortel, Bombardier, or Icon Office Systems, the company's salespeople work directly with customers. In consumer product companies such as Procter & Gamble or Wilson Sporting Goods that sell through intermediaries such as retailers, final consumers rarely meet salespeople or even know about them. Still, the sales force plays an important behind-the-scenes role. It works with wholesalers and retailers to gain their support and to help them be more effective in selling the company's products.

The sales force serves as a critical link between a company and its customers. In many cases, salespeople serve both masters—the seller and the buyer. First, they *represent the company to customers*. They find and develop new customers and communicate information about the company's products and services. They sell products by approaching customers, presenting their products, answering objections, negotiating prices and terms, and closing sales. In addition, salespeople provide customer service and carry out market research and intelligence work. At the same time, salespeople *represent customers to the company*, acting inside the firm as "champions" of customers' interests and managing the buyer-seller relationship. Salespeople relay customer concerns about company products and actions back inside to those who can handle them. They learn about customer needs and work with other marketing and nonmarketing people in the company to develop greater customer value. The old view was that salespeople should worry about sales and the company should worry about profit; The current view holds that salespeople should be concerned with more than just producing *sales*—they should work with others in the company to produce *customer satisfaction* and *company profit*.

MANAGING THE SALES FORCE

We define **sales force management** as the analysis, planning, implementation, and control of sales force activities. It includes designing sales force strategy and structure and recruiting, selecting, training, compensating, supervising, and evaluating the firm's salespeople. These major sales force management decisions are shown in Figure 14-1 and discussed in the following sections.

Sales force management
The analysis, planning, implementation, and control of sales force activities. It includes setting and designing sales force strategy; and recruiting, selecting, training, supervising, compensating, and evaluating the firm's salespeople.

The term "salesperson" covers a wide range of positions, from the clerk selling in a retail store to the engineering salesperson who consults with client companies.

Designing Sales Force Strategy and Structure

Marketing managers face several sales force strategy and design questions. How should salespeople and their tasks be structured? How big should the sales force be? Should salespeople sell alone or work in teams with other people in the company? Should they sell in the field or by telephone? We address these issues below.

Sales Force Structure   A company can divide sales responsibilities along any of several lines. The decision is simple if the company sells only one product line to one industry with customers in many locations. In that case, the company would use a *territorial sales force structure*. However, if the company sells many products to many types of customers, it might need a *product sales force structure,* a *customer sales force structure,* or a combination of the two.

Territorial sales force structure A sales force organization that assigns each salesperson to an exclusive geographic territory in which that salesperson sells the company's full line.

Territorial Sales Force Structure   In the **territorial sales force structure**, each salesperson is assigned to an exclusive geographic area and sells the company's full line of products or services to all customers in that territory. This organization clearly defines each salesperson's job and fixes accountability. It also increases the salesperson's desire to build local business relationships that, in turn, improve selling effectiveness. Finally, because each salesperson travels within a limited geographic area, travel expenses are relatively small.

A territorial sales organization is often supported by many levels of sales management positions. For example, Campbell Soup uses a territorial structure in which each salesperson is responsible for selling all Campbell Soup products. Starting at the bottom of the organization, *sales merchandisers* report to *sales representatives,* who report to *retail supervisors,* who report to *directors of retail sales operations,* who

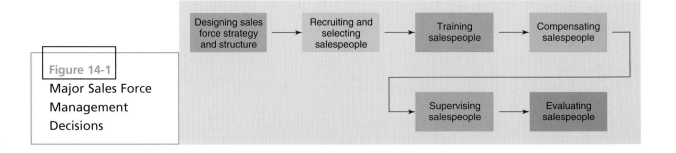

Figure 14-1

Major Sales Force Management Decisions

report to *regional sales managers*. Regional sales managers, in turn, report to *general sales managers*, who report to a *vice president* and *general sales manager*.

Product Sales Force Structure   Salespeople must know their products—especially when the products are numerous and complex. This need, together with the growth of product management, has led many companies to adopt a **product sales force structure**, in which the sales force sells along product lines. For example, Kodak uses different sales forces for its film products than for its industrial products. The film products sales force deals with simple products that are distributed intensively, whereas the industrial products sales force deals with complex products that require technical understanding.

The product structure can lead to problems, however, if a single large customer buys many different company products. For example, Allegiance Healthcare Corporation, a large health care products and services company, has several product divisions, each with a separate sales force. Several Allegiance salespeople might end up calling on the same hospital on the same day. This means that they travel over the same routes and wait to see the same customer's purchasing agents. These extra costs must be compared with the benefits of better product knowledge and attention to individual products.

Customer Sales Force Structure   More and more companies are now using a **customer sales force structure**, in which they organize the sales force along customer or industry lines. Separate sales forces may be set up for different industries, for serving current customers versus finding new ones, and for major accounts versus regular accounts.

Organizing the sales force around customers can help a company to become more customer focused and build closer relationships with important customers. For example, IBM shifted from a product-based structure to a customer-based one. Before the shift, droves of salespeople representing different IBM software, hardware, and services divisions might call on a single large client, creating confusion and frustration. Such large customers wanted a "single face," one point of contact for IBM's vast array of products and services. Following the restructuring, a single IBM "client executive" works with each large customer and manages a team of IBMers—product reps, systems engineers, consultants, and others—who work with the customer. The client executive becomes an expert in the customer's industry. Greg Buseman, a client executive in the distribution industry who spends most of his time working with a major consumer packaged-goods customer, describes his role this way: "I am the owner of the business relationship with the client. If the client has a problem, I'm the one who pulls together software or hardware specialists or consultants. At the customer I work most closely with, we usually have 15 to 20 projects going at once, and I have to manage them."[3] Such an intense focus on customers is widely credited for IBM's dramatic turnaround in recent years.

Complex Sales Force Structures   When a company sells a wide variety of products to many types of customers over a broad geographic area, it often combines several types of sales force structures. Salespeople can be specialized by customer and territory, by product and territory, by product and customer, or by territory, product, and customer. No single structure is best for all companies and situations. Each

Product sales force structure A sales force organization under which salespeople specialize in selling only a portion of the company's products or lines.

Customer sales force structure A sales force organization under which salespeople specialize in selling only to certain customers or industries.

company should select a sales force structure that best serves the needs of its customers and fits its overall marketing strategy.

Sales Force Size Once the company has set its structure, it is ready to consider *sales force size*. Salespeople constitute one of the company's most productive—and most expensive—assets. Therefore, increasing their number will increase both sales and costs.

Many companies use some form of *workload approach* to set sales force size. Using this approach, a company first groups accounts into different classes according to size, account status, or other factors related to the amount of effort required to maintain them. It then determines the number of salespeople needed to call on each class of accounts the desired number of times. The company might think as follows: Suppose we have 1000 Type-A accounts and 2000 Type-B accounts. Type-A accounts require 36 calls a year and Type-B accounts require 12 calls a year. In this case, the sales force's *workload*—the number of calls it must make per year—is 60 000 calls $[(1000 \times 36) + (2000 \times 12) = 36\,000 + 24\,000 = 60\,000]$. If an average salesperson can make 1000 calls a year, then the company needs 60 salespeople $(60\,000 \div 1000)$.

Other Sales Force Strategy and Structure Issues Sales management must also decide who will be involved in the selling effort and how various sales and sales support people will work together.

Outside and Inside Sales Forces The company may have an **outside sales force** (or *field sales force*), an **inside sales force**, or both. Outside salespeople travel to call on customers. Inside salespeople conduct business from their offices via telephone or visits from prospective buyers.

To reduce time demands on their outside sales forces, many companies have increased the size of their inside sales forces. Inside salespeople include technical support people, sales assistants, and telemarketers. *Technical support people* provide technical information and answers to customers' questions. *Sales assistants* provide clerical backup for outside salespeople. They call ahead and confirm appointments, conduct credit checks, follow up on deliveries, and answer customers' questions when outside salespeople cannot be reached. *Telemarketers* use the phone to find new leads and qualify prospects for the field sales force, or to sell and service accounts directly.

The inside sales force frees outside salespeople to spend more time selling to major accounts and finding major new prospects. Depending on the complexity of the product and customer, a telemarketer can make from 20 to 33 decision-maker contacts a day, compared with the average of 4 that an outside salesperson can make. And for many types of products and selling situations, telemarketing can be as effective as a personal call but much less expensive. Whereas the average personal sales call costs about $270, a routine industrial telemarketing call costs only about $7.50 and a complex call about $30.[4] Notes a DuPont telemarketer: "I'm more effective on the phone. [When you're in the field], if some guy's not in his office, you lose an hour. On the phone, you lose 15 seconds.…Through my phone calls, I'm in the field as much as the rep is." There are other advantages. "Customers can't throw things at you," quips the rep, "and you don't have to outrun dogs."[5]

Telephone marketing can be used successfully by both large and small companies:

Outside sales force (or field sales force) Outside salespeople who travel to call on customers.

Inside sales force Inside salespeople who conduct business from their offices via telephone or visits from prospective buyers.

Experienced telemarketers sell complex chemical products by telephone at DuPont's Customer telemarketing centre. Quips one, "I'm more effective on the phone…and [I] don't have to outrun dogs."

Kodak Canada recently began placing new emphasis on telemarketing. While it has always employed an inside sales staff to serve small or distant customers, it has now begun encouraging customers to call its telemarketers to receive faster service—whether it be improved inventory replenishment or updates on upcoming special offers and events. To retain the personal touch with customers using telemarketing services, Kodak has begun sending its customers photographs of its telesales reps along with flow charts so that customers can better understand how requests for service move through the company.

Similarly, Molson Breweries has hired six telesales people to manage inventory, promotions and merchandising for its smaller clients, allowing it to shrink its Ontario sales force from 125 salespeople to 70. Canadian telemarketing guru Jim Domanski stresses that telemarketing costs about one-tenth the rate for making a personal sales call and that a good telemarketer can reach as many companies in a day as a field sales rep can contact in a week.[6]

Climax Portable Machine Tools has proven that a small company can use telemarketing to save money and still lavish attention on buyers. Under the old system, Climax sales engineers spent one-third of their time on the road, training distributor salespeople and accompanying them on calls. They could make about 4 contacts a day. Now, each of 5 sales engineers on Climax's telemarketing team calls about 30 prospects a day, following up on leads generated by ads and direct mail. Because it takes about 5 calls to close a sale, the sales engineers update a prospect's computer file after each contact, noting the degree of commitment, requirements, next call date, and personal comments. "If anyone mentions he's going on a fishing trip, our sales engineer enters that in the computer and uses it to personalize the next phone call," says Climax's president, noting that's just one way to build good relations. Another is that the first mailing to a prospect includes the sales engineer's business card with his picture on it. Of course, it takes more than friendliness to sell $15 000 machine tools over the phone (special orders may run $200 000), but the telemarketing approach is working well. When Climax customers were asked, "Do you see the sales engineer often enough?" the response was overwhelmingly positive. Obviously, many people didn't realize that the only contact they'd had with Climax had been on the phone.[7]

Just as telemarketing is changing the way that many companies go to market, the Internet offers explosive potential for restructuring sales forces and conducting sales operations. More and more companies are now using the Internet to support their personal selling efforts—not just for selling, but also for everything from training salespeople to conducting sales meetings and servicing accounts (see New Directions 14-1).

New Directions14-1 >> Point, Click, and Sell: Welcome to the Web-Based Sales Force

There are few rules at Fisher Scientific International's sales training sessions. The chemical company's salespeople are allowed to show up for new workshops in their pyjamas. And no one flinches if they stroll in at midnight for their first class, take a dozen breaks to call clients, or invite the family cat to sleep in their laps while they take an exam. Sound unorthodox? It would be if Fisher's salespeople were trained in a regular classroom. But for the past year and a half, the company has been using the Internet to teach the majority of its salespeople in the privacy of their homes, cars, hotel rooms, or wherever else they bring their laptops.

To get updates on Fisher's pricing or refresh themselves on one of the company's highly technical products, all salespeople have to do is log onto the Web site and select from the lengthy index. Any time of the day or night, they can get information on a new product, take an exam, or post messages for product experts—all without ever entering a corporate classroom. Welcome to the new world of the Web-based sales force.

In the past few years, sales organizations around the world have begun saving money and time by using a host of new Web approaches to train reps, hold sales meetings, and even conduct live sales presentations. "Web-based technologies are becoming really hot in sales because they save salespeople's time," says technology consultant Tim Sloane. Web-based technologies help companies save time and travel costs while keeping reps up to speed on their company's new products and sales strategies. Fisher Scientific's reps can dial up the Web site at their leisure, and whereas newer reps might spend hours online going through each session in order, more seasoned sellers might just log on for a quick refresher on a specific product before a sales call. "It allows them to manage their time better, because they're only getting training when they need it, in the doses they need it in," says John Pavlik, director of the company's training department. If salespeople are spending less time on training, Pavlik says, they're able to spend more time on what they do best: selling.

Training is only one of the ways sales organizations are using the Internet. Many companies are using the Web to make sales presentations and service accounts. For example, Digital Equipment Corporation's salespeople used to spend a great deal of time travelling to the offices of clients and prospects. But since 1997, the company (now a division of Compaq) has been delivering sales pitches by combining teleconferences with Web presentations. For example, when Digital's account team in Connecticut needed to see what marketing manager Joe Batista and his team in Massachusetts had prepared for a client, Batista input his ideas into a PowerPoint presentation and uploaded it using Internet Conference Center, Web-based software provided by Contigo Software. The account team joined Batista via teleconference and used their own computers to log onto the Web site Batista specified.

Once everyone was logged on, Batista was able to take control of the browsers and lead the reps through the presentation in real time, highlighting and pointing out specific items as he went. The account reps added their comments, based on their more detailed knowledge of the client, and the revised presentation was then shown online to the client. The beauty of the whole process? It's so fast. "The use of [the Web] clearly helps shorten our sales cycle," Batista says. Presentations are created and delivered in less time—sometimes weeks less than the process would take face-to-face—and salespeople are able to close deals more quickly.

Other companies are using Web-based sales presentations to find new prospects. Oracle Corporation, the $8 billion software and information technology services company, conducts online, live product seminars for prospective clients. Prospects can scan the high-tech company's Web site to see which seminars they might want to attend, then dial in via modem and telephone at the appropriate time (Oracle pays for the cost of the phone call). The seminars, which usually consist of a live lecture describing the product's applications followed by a question-and-answer session, average about 125 prospective clients apiece. Once a seminar is completed, prospects are directed to another part of Oracle's Web site, from which they can order products. "It costs our clients nothing but time," says Oracle's manager of Internet marketing programs, "and we're reaching a much wider audience than we would if we were doing in-person seminars."

The Internet can also be a handy way to hold sales strategy meetings. Consider Cisco Systems, which provides networking solutions for the Internet. Sales meetings used to take an enormous bite out of Cisco's travel budget. Now the company saves about $1 million per month by conducting many of those sessions on the Web using PlaceWare virtual conference centre software. Whenever Cisco introduces a new product, it holds a Web meeting to update salespeople, in groups of 100 or more, on the product's marketing and sales strategy.

Usually led by the product manager or a vice president of sales, the meetings typically begin with a 10-minute slide presentation that spells out the planned strategy.

Internet selling support: Sales organizations around the world are now using a host of new Web approaches to train reps, hold sales meetings, and even conduct live sales presentations.

Then, salespeople spend the next 50 or so minutes asking questions via teleconference. The meeting's leader can direct attendees' browsers to competitors' Web sites or ask them to vote on certain issues by using the software's instant polling feature. "Our salespeople are actually meeting more online then they ever were face to face," says Mike Mitchell, Cisco's distance learning manager, adding that some salespeople who used to meet with other reps and managers only a few times a quarter are meeting online nearly every day. "That's very empowering for the sales force, because they're able to make suggestions at every step of the way about where we're going with our sales and marketing strategies."

Thus, Web-based technologies can produce big organizational benefits for sales forces. They help conserve salespeople's valuable time, save travel dollars, and give salespeople a new vehicle for selling and servicing accounts. But the technologies also have some drawbacks. For starters, they're not cheap. Setting up a Web-based system can cost several hundred thousand dollars. And such systems can intimidate low-tech salespeople or clients. "You must have a culture that is comfortable using computers," says one marketing communications man-ager. "As simple as it is, if your salespeople or clients aren't comfortable using the Web, you're wasting your money." Also, Web tools are susceptible to server crashes and other network difficulties, not a happy event when you're in the midst of an important sales meeting or presentation.

For these reasons, some high-tech experts recommend that sales executives use Web technologies for training, sales meetings, and preliminary client sales presentations, but resort to old-fashioned, face-to-face meetings when the time draws near to close the deal. "When push comes to shove, if you've got an account worth closing, you're still going to get on that plane and see the client in person," says sales consultant Sloane. "Your client is going to want to look you in the eye before buying anything from you, and that's still one thing you just can't do online."

Sources: Adapted from Melinda Ligos, "Point, Click, and Sell," *Sales and Marketing Management,* May 1999, pp. 51–55. Also see Chad Kaydo, "You've Got Sales," *Sales and Marketing Management,* October 1999, pp. 29–39; Ginger Conlon, "Ride the Wave," *Sales & Marketing Management,* December 2000, pp. 67–74; and Tom Reilly, "Technology and the Salesperson," *Industrial Distribution,* January 2001, p. 88.

Team selling Using teams of people from sales, marketing, engineering, finance, technical support, and even upper management to service large, complex accounts.

Team Selling As products become more complex, and as customers grow larger and more demanding, a single salesperson simply can't handle all of a large customer's needs. Instead, most companies now use **team selling** to service large, complex accounts. Companies are finding that sales teams can unearth problems, solutions, and sales opportunities that no individual salesperson could. Such teams might include experts from any area or level of the selling firm: sales, marketing, technical and support services, R&D, engineering, operations, finance, and others. In team selling situations, the salesperson shifts from "soloist" to "orchestrator."

In many cases, the move to team selling mirrors similar changes in customers' buying organizations. According to a recent study by *Purchasing* magazine, nearly 70 percent companies polled are using or are extremely interested in using multifunctional buying teams. Says the director of sales education at Dow Chemical, to sell effectively to such buying teams, "Our sellers…have to captain selling teams. There are no more lone wolves."[8]

Some companies, such as IBM, Xerox, and Procter & Gamble, have used teams for a long time. For example, Cutler-Hammer, which supplies circuit breakers, motor starters, and other electrical equipment to heavy industrial manufacturers such as Ford, recently developed "pods" of salespeople that focus on a specific geographical region, industry, or market. Each pod member contributes unique expertise and knowledge about a product or service that salespeople can leverage when selling to increasingly sophisticated buying teams.[9]

Team selling does have some pitfalls. For example, selling teams can confuse or overwhelm customers who are used to working with only one salesperson. Salespeople who are used to having customers all to themselves may have trouble learning to work with and trust others on a team. Finally, difficulties in evaluating individual contributions to the team selling effort can create some sticky compensation issues.

Recruiting and Selecting Salespeople

At the heart of any successful sales force operation is the recruitment and selection of good salespeople. The performance difference between an average salesperson and a top salesperson can be substantial. In a typical sales force, the top 30 percent of the salespeople might bring in 60 percent of the sales. Thus, careful salesperson selection can greatly increase overall sales force performance. Beyond the differences in sales performance, poor selection results in costly turnover. When a salesperson quits, the costs of finding and training a new salesperson—plus the costs of lost sales—can run as high as $75 000 to $125 000. Also, a sales force with many new people is less productive.[10]

What traits spell sure-fire sales success? One survey suggests that good salespeople have a lot of enthusiasm, persistence, initiative, self-confidence, and job commitment. They are committed to sales as a way of life and have a strong customer orientation. Another study suggests that good salespeople are independent, self-motivated, and excellent listeners. Still another study advises that salespeople should be a friend to the customer as well as persistent, enthusiastic, attentive, and—above all—honest. They must be internally motivated, disciplined, hardworking, and able to build strong relationships with customers. Finally, studies show that good salespeople are team players rather than loners (see New Directions 14-2).[11]

New Directions 14-2 >> Great Salespeople: Drive, Discipline, and Relationship-Building Skills

What sets great salespeople apart from all the rest? What separates the masterful from the merely mediocre? In an effort to profile top sales performers, Gallup Management Consulting Group, a division of the well-known Gallup polling organization, has interviewed as many as half a million salespeople. Its research suggests that the best salespeople possess four key talents: intrinsic motivation, disciplined work style, the ability to close a sale, and perhaps most important, the ability to build relationships with customers.

Intrinsic Motivation
"Different things drive different people—, happiness, money, you name it," says one expert. "But all

great salespeople have one thing in common: an unrelenting drive to excel." This strong, internal drive can be shaped and moulded, but it can't be taught. The source of the motivation varies—some are driven by money, some by hunger for recognition, some by a yearning to build relationships.

The Gallup research revealed four general personality types, all high performers, but all with different sources of motivation. *Competitors* are people who not only want to win but also crave the satisfaction of beating specific rivals—other companies *and* their fellow salespeople. They'll come right out and say to a colleague, "With all due respect, I know you were salesperson of the year, but I'm going after your title." The *ego driven* are salespeople who just want to experience the glory of winning. They want to be recognized as being the best, regardless of the competition. *Achievers* are a rare breed who are almost completely self-motivated. They like accomplishment and routinely set goals that are higher than what is expected of them. They often make the best sales managers because they don't mind seeing other people succeed, as long as the organization's goals are met. Finally, *service-oriented* salespeople are those whose strength lies in their ability to build and cultivate relationships. They are generous, caring, and empathetic. "These people are golden," says the national training manager of Minolta Corporation's business equipment division. "We need salespeople who will take the time to follow up on the 10 questions a customer might have, salespeople who love to stay in touch."

No one is purely a competitor, an achiever, ego driven, or service driven. There's at least some of each in most top performers. "A *competitor* with a strong sense of *service* will probably bring in a lot of business while doing a great job of taking care of customers," observes the managing director of the Gallup Management Consulting Group. "Who could ask for anything more?"

Disciplined Work Style

Whatever their motivation, if salespeople aren't organized and focused, and if they don't work hard, they can't meet the ever-increasing demands customers are making these days. Great salespeople are tenacious about laying out detailed, organized plans, then following through in a timely, disciplined way. There's no magic here, just solid organization and hard work. "Our best sales reps never let loose ends dangle," says the president of a small business equipment firm. "If they say they're going to make a follow-up call on a customer in six months, you can be sure that they'll be on the doorstep in six months." Top sellers rely on hard work, not luck or gimmicks. "Some people say it's all technique or luck," notes one sales trainer. "But luck happens to the best salespeople when they get up early, work late, stay up till two in the morning working on a proposal, or keep making calls when everyone is leaving at the end of the day."

The Ability to Close a Sale

Other skills mean little if a seller can't ask for the sale. No close, no sale. Period. So, what makes for a great closer? For one thing, an unyielding persistence, say managers and sales consultants. Claims one, "Great closers are like great athletes. They're not afraid to fail, and they don't give up until they close." Part of what makes the failure rate tolerable for top performers is their deep-seated belief in themselves and what they are selling. Great closers have a high level of self-confidence and believe that they are doing the right thing. And they have a burning need to make the sale happen—to do whatever it takes within legal and ethical standards to get the business.

The Ability to Build Relationships

Perhaps most important in today's relationship-marketing environment, top salespeople are customer problem solvers and relationship builders. They have an instinctive understanding of their customers' needs. Talk to sales executives and they'll describe top performers in these terms: empathetic, patient, caring, responsive, good listeners, *honest*. Top sellers can put themselves on the buyer's side of the desk and see the world through their customers' eyes. Today, customers are looking for business partners, not golf partners. "At the root of it all," says a Dallas sales consultant, "is an integrity of intent. High performers don't just want to be liked, they want to add value." High-performing salespeople, he adds, are "always thinking about the big picture, where the customer's organization is going, and how they can help them get there."

Sources: Adapted from Geoffrey Brewer, "Mind Reading: What Drives Top Salespeople to Greatness?" *Sales and Marketing Management,* May 1994, pp. 82–88. Also see Roberta Maynard, "Finding the Essence of Good Salespeople," *Nation's Business,* February 1998, p. 10; Jeanie Casison, "Closest Thing to Cloning," *Incentive,* June 1999, p. 7; Erika Rasmusson, "The 10 Traits of Top Salespeople," *Sales and Marketing Management,* August 1999, pp. 34–37; Kevin Dobbs, Jack Gordon, Kim Kiser, and David Stamps, "The Seven Secrets of Great Salespeople," *Training,* January 2000, p. 14; and Andy Cohen, "The Traits of Great Sales Forces," *Sales and Marketing Management,* October 2000, pp. 67–72.

When recruiting, companies should analyze the sales job itself and the characteristics of its most successful salespeople to identify the traits needed by a successful salesperson in their industry. Does the job require a lot of planning and paper-work? Does it call for much travel? Will the salesperson face many rejections? Will the salesperson be working with high-level buyers? The successful salesperson should be suited to these duties.

After management has decided on needed traits, it must *recruit* salespeople. The human resources department looks for applicants by getting names from current salespeople, using employment agencies, placing classified ads, searching the Web, and contacting postsecondary students. Another source is to attract top salespeople from other companies. Proven salespeople need less training and can be immediately productive.

Recruiting will attract many applicants from whom the company must select the best. The selection procedure can vary from a single informal interview to lengthy testing and interviewing. Many companies give formal tests to sales applicants. Tests typically measure sales aptitude, analytical and organizational skills, personality traits, and other characteristics. Test results count heavily in companies such as IBM, Investor's Group, Procter & Gamble, and Gillette. Gillette claims that tests have reduced turnover by 42 percent and that test scores have correlated well with the later performance of new salespeople. But test scores provide only one piece of information in a set that includes personal characteristics, references, past employment history, and interviewer reactions.[12]

Sales training: Today's new salespeople spend anywhere from a few weeks or months to a year or more in training.

Training Salespeople

Today's new salespeople, however, spend anywhere from a few weeks or months to a year or more in training. Rob Granby, vice president of sales at Cadbury Beverages Canada, believes that ongoing training and a supportive corporate culture are essential: "If your corporate culture isn't one that nourishes and helps salespeople flourish, then no matter what you layer on in terms of bonus programs and special incentives, it won't make a difference."[13]

Although training can be expensive, it can also yield dramatic returns on the training investment. Nabisco did an extensive analysis of the return on investment of its two-day professional selling program, which teaches sales reps how to plan for and make professional presentations to their retail customers. Although it cost about $1500 to put each sales rep through the program, the training resulted in additional sales of more than $183 000 per rep and yielded almost $31 000 of additional profit per rep.[14] Although some firms do their sales training in-house, others send their representatives to executive education programs or turn to the Canadian Professional Sales Association for help.

Today, many companies are adding Web-based training to their sales training programs. Such training may range from simple text-based product information to Internet-based sales exercises that build sales skills to sophisticated simulations that re-create the dynamics of real-life sales calls. IBM is learning that using the Internet to train salespeople offers many advantages.

With some 300,000 sales associates scattered in various locales, IBM is using the Internet to supplement on-the-job and other sales training approaches. The computer services giant uses online workshops to deliver increments of training when salespeople need updates on new products or customers. Salespeople dig into such training as deeply as their needs dictate, getting just enough information, just in time to complete the project at hand. The trainees are then encouraged to share and expand on what they've learned in informal discussions with others. "We're seeking greater efficiency, greater productivity, greater advantage," says Milt Hearne, IBM's vice president of worldwide high-performance selling. IBM hopes to move at least 35 percent of its training online. It expects the move to reduce days spent on formal training by a third and save upwards of $200 million on travel and hotel costs, time away from work, instructor salaries, and other expenses associated with formal training.[15]

Compensating Salespeople

To attract salespeople, a company must have an appealing compensation plan. Compensation is made up of several elements—a fixed amount, a variable amount, expenses, and fringe benefits. The fixed amount, usually a salary, gives the salesperson some stable income. The variable amount, which might be commissions or bonuses based on sales performance, rewards the salesperson for greater effort. Expense allowances, which repay salespeople for job-related expenses, let salespeople undertake needed and desirable selling efforts. Fringe benefits, such as paid vacations, sickness or accident benefits, pensions, and life insurance, provide job security and satisfaction.

Management must decide what *mix* of these compensation elements makes the most sense for each sales job. Different combinations of fixed and variable compensation give rise to four basic types of compensation plans: straight salary, straight commission, salary plus bonus, and salary plus commission. A study of sales force compensation plans showed that 70 percent of all companies surveyed use a combination of base salary and incentives. The average plan consisted of about 60 percent salary and 40 percent incentive pay.[16]

The sales force compensation plan can both motivate salespeople and direct their activities. Compensation should direct the sales force toward activities that are consistent with overall marketing objectives. Table 14-1 illustrates how a company's compensation plan should reflect its overall marketing strategy. For example, if the strategy is to grow rapidly and gain market share, the compensation plan might include a larger commission component coupled with a new-account bonus to encourage high sales performance and new-account development. In contrast, if the goal is to maximize current account profitability, the compensation plan might contain a larger base-salary component with additional incentives for current account sales or customer satisfaction. In fact, more and more companies are moving away from high commission plans that may drive salespeople to make short-term grabs for business. Notes one sales force expert, "The last thing you want is to have someone ruin a customer relationship because they're pushing too hard to close a deal." Instead, companies are designing compensation plans that reward salespeople for building customer relationships and growing the long-run value of each customer.[17]

Supervising Salespeople

New salespeople need more than a territory, compensation, and training—they need *supervision*. Through supervision, the company *directs* and *motivates* the sales force to do a better job.

Table 14-1   The Relationship Between Overall Marketing Strategy and Sales Force Compensation

	Strategic Goal		
	To Rapidly Gain Market Share	To Solidify Market Leadership	To Maximize Profitability
Ideal salesperson	• An independent self-starter	• A competitive problem solver	• A team player • A relationship manager
Sales focus	• Deal making • Sustained high effort	• Consultative selling	• Account penetration
Compensation role	• To capture accounts • To reward high performance	• To reward new and existing sales • To encourage team selling	• To manage the product mix • To reward account management

Source: Adapted from Sam T. Johnson, "Sales Compensation: In Search of a Better Solution," *Compensation & Benefits Review,* November–December 1993, pp. 53–60.

Companies vary in how closely they supervise their salespeople. Many help their salespeople in identifying customer targets and setting call norms. Some may also specify how much time the sales forces should spend prospecting for new accounts and set other time management priorities. One tool is the *annual call plan* that shows which customers and prospects to call on in which months and which activities to carry out. Activities include taking part in trade shows, attending sales meetings, and carrying out marketing research. Another tool is *time-and-duty analysis.* In addition to time spent selling, the salesperson spends time travelling, waiting, eating, taking breaks, and doing administrative chores.

Figure 14-2 shows how salespeople spend their time. On average, actual face-to-face selling time accounts for less than 30 percent of total working time! If selling time could be raised from 30 percent to 40 percent, this would be a 33 percent increase in the time spent selling. Companies always are looking for ways to save time-using phones instead of travelling, simplifying record-keeping forms, finding better call and routing plans, and supplying more and better customer information.

Many firms have adopted *sales force automation systems,* computerized sales force operations for more efficient order-entry transactions, improved customer service, and better salesperson decision-making support. Salespeople use laptops, handheld computing devices, and Web technologies, coupled with customer-contact software and customer relationship management (CRM) software, to profile customers and prospects, analyze and forecast sales, manage account relationships, schedule sales calls, make presentations, enter orders, check inventories and order status, prepare sales and expense reports, process correspondence, and carry out many other activities. Sales force automation not only lowers sales force costs and improves productivity, it also improves the quality of sales management decisions. Here is an example of successful sales force automation:[18]

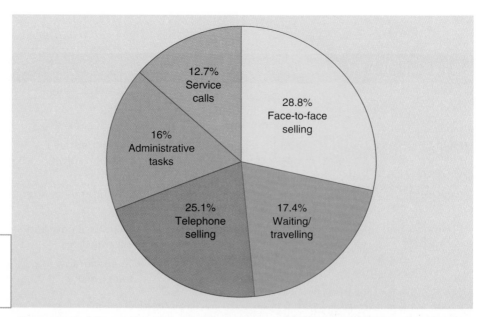

Figure 14-2

How Salespeople Spend Their Time

Source: Dartnell Corporation, *30th Sales Force Compensation Survey.* © 1998 Dartnell Corporation.

Owens-Corning has put its sales force online with FSA—its Field Sales Advantage system. FSA gives Owens-Corning salespeople a constant supply of information about their company and the people they're dealing with. Using laptop computers, each salesperson can access three types of programs. First, FSA gives them a set of *generic tools,* everything from word processing to fax and e-mail transmission to creating presentations online. Second, it provides *product information*—tech bulletins, customer specifications, pricing information, and other data that can help close a sale. Finally, it offers up a wealth of *customer information*—buying history, types of products ordered, and preferred payment terms. Before FSA, reps stored such information in loose-leaf books, calendars, and account cards. Now, FSA makes working directly with customers easier than ever. Salespeople can prime themselves on backgrounds of clients; call up prewritten sales letters; transmit orders and resolve customer-service issues on the spot during customer calls; and have samples, pamphlets, brochures, and other materials sent to clients with a few keystrokes. With FSA, "salespeople automatically become more empowered," says Charley Causey, regional general manager. "They become the real managers of their own business and their own territories."

Perhaps the fastest-growing sales force technology tool is the Internet. In a survey by Dartnell Corporation of 1000 salespeople, 61 percent reported using the Internet regularly in their daily selling activities. The most common uses include gathering competitive information, monitoring customer Web sites, and researching industries and specific customers. As more and more companies provide their salespeople with Web access, experts expect continued growth in sales force Internet usage.[19]

Beyond directing salespeople, sales managers must also motivate them. Some salespeople will do their best without any special urging from management. To

Owens-Corning's Field Sales Advantage system gives salespeople a constant supply of information about their company and the people with whom they're dealing.

them, selling may be the most fascinating job in the world. But selling can also be frustrating. Salespeople often work alone and they must sometimes travel away from home. They may face aggressive competing salespeople and difficult customers. Therefore, salespeople often need special encouragement to do their best.

Management can boost sales force morale and performance through its organizational climate, sales quotas, and positive incentives. *Organizational climate* describes the feeling that salespeople have about their opportunities, value, and rewards for a good performance. Some companies treat salespeople as if they were unimportant, and performance suffers accordingly. Other companies treat their salespeople as valued contributors and allow virtually unlimited opportunity for income and promotion. Not surprisingly, these companies enjoy higher sales force performance and less turnover.

Sales quota A standard that states the amount a sales person should sell and how sales should be divided among the company's products.

Many companies motivate their salespeople by setting **sales quotas**—standards stating the amount they should sell and how sales should be divided among the company's products. Compensation is often related to how well salespeople meet their quotas. Companies also use various *positive incentives* to increase sales force effort. *Sales meetings* provide social occasions, breaks from routine, chances to meet and talk with "company brass," and opportunities to air feelings and to identify with a larger group. Companies also sponsor *sales contests* to spur the sales force to make a selling effort above what would normally be expected. Other incentives include honours, merchandise and cash awards, trips, and profit-sharing plans.

Evaluating Salespeople

We have thus far described how management communicates what salespeople should be doing and how it motivates them to do it. This process requires good feedback. And good feedback means getting regular information about salespeople to evaluate their performance.

Management gets information about its salespeople in several ways. The most important source is *sales reports,* including weekly or monthly work plans and longer-term territory marketing plans. Salespeople also write up their completed activities on *call reports* and turn in *expense reports* for which they are partly or wholly repaid. Additional information comes from personal observation, customer surveys, and talks with other salespeople.

Using various sales force reports and other information, sales management evaluates members of the sales force. It evaluates salespeople on their ability to "plan their work and work their plan." Formal evaluation forces management to develop and communicate clear standards for judging performance. It also provides salespeople with constructive feedback and motivates them to perform well.

Take a break and reexamine your thoughts about salespeople and sales management.

• As you did at the start of the chapter, close your eyes and envision a typical salesperson. Have your perceptions of salespeople changed after what you've just read? How? Be specific.

• Apply each of the steps in sales force management shown in Figure 14-1 to the chapter-opening Lear Corporation example.

• Find and talk with someone employed in professional sales. Ask about and report on how this salesperson's company designs its sales force and recruits, selects, trains, compensates, supervises, and evaluates its salespeople. Would you like to work as a salesperson for this company?

The Personal Selling Process

We now turn from designing and managing a sales force to the actual personal selling process. The **selling process** consists of several steps that the salesperson must master (see Figure 14-3). These steps focus on the goal of getting new customers and obtaining orders from them. However, most salespeople spend much of their time maintaining existing accounts and building long-term customer *relationships*. We discuss the relationship aspect of the personal selling process in a later section.

Prospecting and Qualifying The first step in the selling process is **prospecting**—identifying qualified potential customers. Approaching the right potential customers is crucial to selling success. As one expert puts it: "If the sales force starts chasing anyone who is breathing and seems to have a budget, you risk accumulating a roster of expensive-to-serve, hard-to-satisfy customers who never respond to whatever value proposition you have." He continues, "The solution to this isn't rocket science. [You must] train salespeople to actively scout the right prospects. If necessary, create an incentive program to reward proper scouting."[20]

The salesperson must often approach many prospects to get just a few sales. Although the company supplies some leads, salespeople need skill in finding their own. They can ask current customers for referrals. They can cultivate referral sources, such as suppliers, dealers, noncompeting salespeople, and bankers. They can search for prospects in directories or on the Web and track down leads using the telephone and direct mail. Or they can drop in unannounced on various offices (a practice known as "cold calling").

Salespeople also need to know how to *qualify* leads—that is, how to identify the good ones and screen out the poor ones. Prospects can be qualified by looking at

Selling process The steps that the salesperson follows when selling, which include prospecting and qualifying, preapproach, approach, presentation and demonstration, handling objections, closing, and follow-up.

Prospecting The step in the selling process in which the salesperson identifies qualified potential customers.

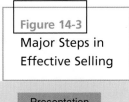

Figure 14-3

Major Steps in Effective Selling

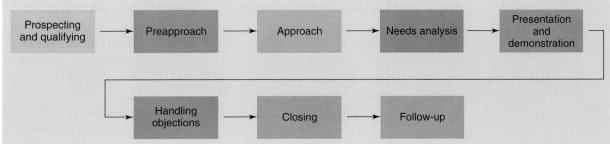

their financial ability, volume of business, special needs, location, and possibilities for growth.

Preapproach Before calling on a prospect, the salesperson should learn as much as possible about the organization (what it needs, who is involved in the buying) and its buyers (their characteristics and buying styles). This step is known as the **preapproach.** The salesperson can consult standard industry and online sources, acquaintances, and others to learn about the company. The salesperson should set *call objectives,* which may be to qualify the prospect, to gather information, or to make an immediate sale. Another task is to decide on the best approach, which might be a personal visit, a phone call, or a letter. The best timing should be considered carefully because many prospects are busiest at certain times. Finally, the salesperson should give thought to an overall sales strategy for the account.

Preapproach The step in the selling process in which the salesperson learns as much as possible about a prospective customer before making a sales call.

Approach During the **approach** step, the salesperson should know how to meet and greet the buyer and get the relationship off to a good start. This step involves the salesperson's appearance, opening lines, and the follow-up remarks. The opening lines should be positive to build goodwill from the beginning of the relationship. This opening might be followed by some key questions to learn more about the customer's needs or by showing a display or sample to attract the buyer's attention and curiosity. As in all stages of the selling process, listening to the customer is crucial.

Approach The step in the selling process in which the salesperson meets the customer for the first time.

Needs Analysis The needs analysis step is the root of needs-based selling. A needs analysis is a diagnosis of a buyer's needs accomplished through skillful questioning, listening, and observing. This precedes the recommendation or a demonstration of a seller's product or service. Questioning in this case focuses on customer benefits or results rather than on features of the product or service.

Needs analysis The process of determining a buyer's or prospect's needs before presenting or demonstrating a product or service.

This *need-satisfaction approach* calls for good listening and problem-solving skills. "I think of myself more as a...well, psychologist," notes one experienced salesperson. "I listen to customers. I listen to their wishes and needs and problems, and I try to figure out a solution. If you're not a good listener, you're not going to get the order." Another salesperson suggests, "It's no longer enough to have a good relationship with a client. You have to understand their problems. You have to feel their pain."[21]

Presentation and Demonstration During the **presentation** step of the selling process, the salesperson tells the product "story" to the buyer, presenting customer benefits and showing how the product meets the customers' needs that were identified in the needs analysis process. The problem-solver salesperson fits better with today's marketing concept than does a hard-sell salesperson or the glad-handing extrovert. Buyers today want solutions, not smiles; results, not razzle-dazzle. They want salespeople who listen to their concerns, understand their needs, and respond with the right products and services. The qualities that buyers *dislike most* in salespeople include being pushy, late, deceitful, unprepared, and disorganized. The qualities they *value most* include empathy, good listening skills, honesty, dependability, thoroughness, and follow-through. Great salespeople know how to sell, but more important, they know how to listen and to build strong customer relationships.[22]

Presentation The step in the selling process in which the salesperson tells the "product story" to the buyer, highlighting customer benefits.

Today, advanced presentation technologies allow for full multimedia presentations to only one or a few people. Audio- and videocassettes, laptop computers with presentation software, and online presentation technologies have replaced the flip

New sales presentation technologies: Advanced Sterilization Products, a Johnson & Johnson Company, provides its sales force with a presentation in which prospects don a helmet for a virtual reality tour of the inner workings of the Sterrad Sterilization System for medical devices and surgical instruments.

chart. Advanced Sterilization Products, a Johnson & Johnson company, even provides its sales force with a virtual reality presentation, called the STERRAD Experience. Originally designed for use at conferences, the presentation equipment has been redesigned for sales calls and consists of a small video player with five headsets, all easily transported in an ordinary-sized briefcase. Prospects don a helmet for a virtual reality tour of the inner workings of the Sterrad Sterilization System for medical devices and surgical instruments. The presentation provides more information in a more engaging way than could be done by displaying the actual machinery.[23]

Handling Objections   Customers usually have objections during the presentation or when asked to place an order. The problem can be either logical or psychological, and objections are often unspoken. In **handling objections**, the salesperson should use a positive approach, seek out hidden objections, ask the buyer to clarify any objections, take objections as opportunities to provide more information, and turn the objections into reasons for buying. Every salesperson needs training in the skills of handling objections.

Closing   After handling the prospect's objections, the salesperson now tries to close the sale. Some salespeople do not get around to **closing** or do not handle it well. They may lack confidence, feel guilty about asking for the order, or fail to recognize the right moment to close the sale. Salespeople should know how to recognize closing signals from the buyer, including physical actions, comments, and questions. For example, the customer might sit forward and nod approvingly or ask about prices and credit terms. Salespeople can use one of several closing techniques. They can ask for the order, review points of agreement, offer to help write up the order, ask whether the buyer wants this model or that one, or note that the buyer will lose out if the order is not placed now. The salesperson may offer the buyer special reasons to close, such as a lower price or an extra quantity at no charge.

Handling objections The step in the selling process in which the salesperson seeks out, clarifies, and overcomes customer objections to buying.

Closing The step in the selling process in which the salesperson asks the customer for an order.

Follow-up The last step in the selling process in which the salesperson follows up after the sale to ensure customer satisfaction and repeat business.

Follow-Up The last step in the selling process—**follow-up**—is necessary if the salesperson wants to ensure customer satisfaction and repeat business. Right after closing, the salesperson should complete any details on delivery time, purchase terms, and other matters. The salesperson then should schedule a follow-up call when the initial order is received to make sure there is proper installation, instruction, and servicing. This visit would reveal any problems, assure the buyer of the salesperson's interest, and reduce any buyer concerns that might have arisen since the sale.

Relationship Marketing

The principles of personal selling as just described are *transaction oriented*—their aim is to help salespeople close a specific sale with a customer. But in many cases, the company is not seeking simply a sale: It has targeted a major customer that it would like to win and keep. The company would like to show that it has the capabilities to serve the customer over the long haul in a mutually profitable *relationship*. **Relationship marketing** emphasizes maintaining profitable long-term relationships with customers by creating superior customer value and satisfaction.

> **Relationship marketing** The process of creating, maintaining, and enhancing strong, value-laden relationships with customers and other stakeholders.

Today's large customers favour suppliers who can sell and deliver a coordinated set of products and services to many locations and who can work closely with customer teams to improve products and processes. For these customers, the first sale is only the beginning of the relationship. Unfortunately, some companies ignore these new realities. They sell their products through separate sales forces, each working independently to close sales. Their technical people may not be willing to lend time to educate a customer. Their engineering, design, and manufacturing people may have the attitude that "it's our job to make good products and the salesperson's job to sell them to customers." Other companies, however, recognize that winning and keeping accounts requires more than making good products and directing the sales force to close lots of sales; it requires a carefully coordinated whole-company effort to create value-laden, satisfying relationships with important customers.

DIRECT MARKETING

Many of the marketing and promotion tools that we've examined in previous chapters were developed in the context of *mass marketing*: targeting broad markets with standardized messages and offers distributed through intermediaries. Today, however, with the trend toward more narrowly targeted or one-to-one marketing, many companies are adopting *direct marketing*, either as a primary marketing approach or as a supplement to other approaches. Increasingly, companies are using direct marketing to reach carefully targeted customers more efficiently and to build stronger, more personal, one-to-one relationships with them. In this section, we explore the exploding world of direct marketing.

> **Direct marketing** Direct connections with carefully targeted individual consumers to both obtain an immediate response and cultivate lasting customer relationships.

Direct marketing consists of direct connections with carefully targeted individual consumers to both obtain an immediate response and cultivate lasting customer relationships. Direct marketers communicate directly with customers, often on a one-to-one, interactive basis. Using detailed databases, they tailor their marketing offers and communications to the needs of narrowly defined segments or even individual buyers. Beyond brand and image building, they usually seek a direct, immediate, and measurable consumer response. For example, Dell Computer interacts directly with customers, by telephone or through its Web site, to design built-to-order systems that meet customers' individual needs. Buyers order directly from Dell, and Dell quickly and efficiently delivers the new computers to their homes or offices.

The New Direct-Marketing Model

Early direct marketers—catalogue companies, direct mailers, and telemarketers—gathered customer names and sold goods mainly by mail and telephone. Today, however, fired by rapid advances in database technologies and new marketing media—especially the Internet—direct marketing has undergone a dramatic transformation.

In previous chapters, we've discussed direct marketing as direct distribution—as marketing channels that contain no intermediaries. We also include direct marketing as one element of the marketing communications mix—as an approach for communicating directly with consumers. In actuality, direct marketing is both these things.

Most companies still use direct marketing as a supplementary channel or medium for marketing their goods. Thus, Lexus Canada markets mostly through mass-media advertising and its high-quality dealer network, but it supplements these channels with direct marketing. Its direct marketing includes promotional videos and other materials mailed directly to prospective buyers and a Web page that provides consumers with information about various models, competitive comparisons, financing, and dealer locations. Similarly, office-supply retailer Staples conducts most of its business through brick-and-mortar stores, but it also markets directly through its Web site.

Lexus Canada
www.lexus.ca

However, for many companies today, direct marketing is more than just a supplementary channel or medium. For these companies, direct marketing—especially in its newest transformation, Internet marketing and e-commerce—constitutes a new and complete model for doing business. "The Internet is not just another marketing channel; it's not just another advertising medium; it's not just a way to speed up transactions," says one strategist. "The Internet is the foundation for a new industrial order. [It] will change the relationship between consumers and producers in ways more profound than you can yet imagine."[24] This new *direct model* is rapidly changing the way companies think about building relationships with customers.

Dell Canada
www.dell.ca

Whereas most companies use direct marketing and the Internet as supplemental approaches, firms employing the direct model use it as the *only* approach. Some of these companies, such as Dell Computer, Amazon.ca, and eBay, began as only direct marketers. Other companies—such as Cisco Systems, eTrade Canada, IBM, and many others—are rapidly transforming themselves into direct-marketing superstars. The company that perhaps best exemplifies this new direct-marketing model is Dell Computer. Dell has built its entire approach to the marketplace around direct marketing. This direct model has proved highly successful, not just for Dell, but for the fast-growing number of other companies that employ it. Many strategists have hailed direct marketing as the new marketing model of this millennium.

Benefits and Growth of Direct Marketing

Whether employed as a complete business model or as a supplement to a broader integrated marketing mix, direct marketing brings many benefits to both buyers and sellers. As a result, direct marketing is growing very rapidly.

For buyers, direct marketing is convenient, easy to use, and private. From the comfort of their homes or offices, they can browse mail catalogues or company Web sites at any time of the day or night. Direct marketing gives buyers ready access to a wealth of products and information, at home and around the globe. Finally, direct marketing is immediate and interactive—buyers can interact with sellers by phone or on the seller's Web site to create exactly the configuration of information, products, or services they desire, then order them on the spot.

For sellers, direct marketing is a powerful tool for building customer relationships. Using database marketing, today's marketers can target small groups or individual consumers, tailor offers to individual needs, and promote these offers through personalized communications. Direct marketing can also be timed to reach prospects at just the right moment. Because of its one-to-one, interactive nature, the Internet is an especially potent direct-marketing tool. Direct marketing also gives sellers access to buyers that they could not reach through other channels. For example, the Internet provides access to *global* markets that might otherwise be out of reach.

Finally, direct marketing can offer sellers a low-cost, efficient alternative for reaching their markets. For example, direct marketing has grown rapidly in B2B marketing, partly in response to the ever-increasing costs of marketing through the sales force. When personal sales calls cost $270 per contact, they should be made only when necessary and to high-potential customers and prospects. Lower cost-per-contact media—such as telemarketing, direct mail, and company Web sites—often prove more cost effective in reaching and selling to more prospects and customers.

Because of these advantages to both buyers and sellers, direct marketing has become the fastest growing form of marketing. Sales through traditional direct-marketing channels (telephone marketing, direct mail, catalogues, direct-response television, and others) have been growing rapidly. Whereas retail sales over the past five years have grown at about 6 percent annually, direct-marketing sales grew at about 10 percent annually. According to the Canadian Marketing Association (formerly the Canadian Direct Marketing Association), the direct response industry generated $50 billion in sales in the year 2000 and is one of the top five industry sectors in the Canadian economy.[25]

Canadian Marketing Association www.the-cma.org

Customer Database and Direct Marketing

Effective direct marketing begins with a good customer database. A **customer database** is an organized collection of comprehensive data about individual customers or prospects, including geographic, demographic, psychographic, and behavioural data. The database can be used to locate good potential customers, tailor products and services to the special needs of targeted consumers, and maintain long-term customer relationships.

Many companies confuse a customer mailing list with a customer database. A customer mailing list is simply a set of names, addresses, and telephone numbers. A

Customer database An organized collection of comprehensive data about individual customers or prospects, including geographic, demographic, psychographic, and behavioural data.

customer database contains much more information. In B2B marketing, the salesperson's customer profile might contain the products and services the customer has bought; past volumes and prices; key contacts (and their ages, birthdays, hobbies, and favourite foods); competitive suppliers; status of current contracts; estimated customer spending for the next few years; and assessments of competitive strengths and weaknesses in selling and servicing the account. In consumer marketing, the customer database might contain a customer's demographics (age, income, family members, birthdays), psychographics (activities, interests, and opinions), buying behaviour (past purchases, buying preferences), and other relevant information. For example, the catalogue company Fingerhut maintains a database containing some 3000 pieces of information about each of 30 million households. Ritz-Carlton's database holds more than 500 000 individual customer preferences. Pizza Hut's database lets it track the purchases of more than 50 million customers. And Wal-Mart's data database contains more than 100 terabytes of data—that's 100 trillion bytes, equivalent to 16 000 bytes for every one of the world's 6 billion people.[26]

Armed with the information in their databases, these companies can identify small groups of customers to receive fine-tuned marketing offers and communications. Kraft Foods has amassed a list of more than 30 million users of its products who have responded to coupons or other Kraft promotions. Based on their interests, the company sends these customers tips on issues such as nutrition and exercise, as well as recipes and coupons for specific Kraft brands. FedEx uses its sophisticated database to create 100 highly targeted, customized direct-mail and telemarketing campaigns each year to its nearly 5 million customers shipping to 212 countries. By analyzing customers carefully and reaching the right customers at the right time with the right promotions, FedEx achieves response rates of 20 percent to 25 percent and earns an 8-to-1 return on its direct-marketing dollars.[27]

Smaller companies can also use database marketing:

HSBC faced just a small challenge—a new name, low brand awareness, and a budget significantly lower than that of other Canadian financial institutions targeting high-net-worth, educated, savvy investors during the cluttered RRSP period. Needless to say, it had to come up with a breakthrough campaign. Its solution—a teaser campaign promoting a fictional dot-com, **www.invest-the-world.com**. Knowing sophisticated investors took pride in knowing each and every investment opportunity, HBSC bet that an unknown site would spark investors' fear of missing out on a great opportunity. Using its customer database, HSBC sent a direct mail piece to 95 400 potential investors that directed them to the site. Once there, HSBC's RRSP products were presented along with the chance to win a free trip for two anywhere in the world HSBC mutual funds were managed. The direct mailing was cleverly supported by print, outdoor, online banner ads, newspaper wraps, and even Post-it notes that also grabbed attention. The campaign not only won awards, it resulted in a flood of new clients who opened up new accounts in one of the worst RRSP seasons in more than a decade.[28]

Companies use their databases in many ways. They can use a database to identify prospects and generate sales leads by advertising products or offers. Or they can use the database to profile customers based on previous purchasing and to decide which customers should receive particular offers. Databases can help the company to deepen customer loyalty—companies can build customers' interest and enthusiasm by remembering buyer preferences and by sending appropriate information, gifts, or other materials.

For example, Masterfoods, a market leader in pet food as well as candy, maintains a significant pet database. The company has the website mypetstop.com, which is the #1 petcare website globally live in specific versions in countries such as Argentina, Puerto Rico, the United States, the United Kingdom, France, Germany, Austria, Switzerland, Russia, Japan, and Australia. In Germany, for example, the database holds a significant amount of data on German families that are cat owners. The information is obtained with the permission of the owners as they participate in on line surveys and marketing programs. Mypetstop.com is used in conjunction with various brands such as Whiskas®, Sheba®, and Catsan®. All of the brands offer various consumer relationship marketing programs, such as, the birthday card program which forwards a card (via mail or electronically) every year to the those participating cats who have a birth date recorded in the database. The result is a lasting relationship with the cat's owner.

The database can help a company make attractive offers of product replacements, upgrades, or complementary products, just when customers might be ready to act. For example, a General Electric appliance customer database contains each customer's demographic and psychographic characteristics along with an appliance purchasing history. Using this database, GE marketers assess how long specific customers have owned their current appliances and which past customers might be ready to purchase again. They can determine which customers need a new GE range, refrigerator, clothes washer, or something else to go with other recently purchased products. Or they can identify the best past GE purchasers and send them gift certificates or other promotions to apply against their next GE purchases. A rich customer database allows GE to build profitable new business by locating good

Databases can help a company deepen customer loyalty. The petfood division of Masterfoods located in Germany sends birthday cards to the cats, whose dates of birth have been captured in their database as part of a consumer marketing program.

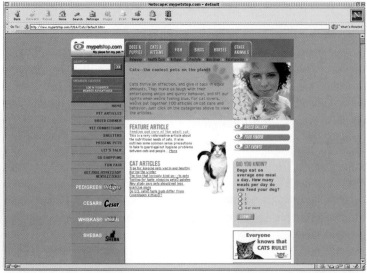

Webpage © Mars, Incorporated. 2001

prospects, anticipating customer needs, cross-selling products and services, and rewarding loyal customers.

Like many other marketing tools, database marketing requires a special investment. Companies must invest in computer hardware, database software, analytical programs, communication links, and skilled personnel. The database system must be user-friendly and available to various marketing groups, including those in product and brand management, new-product development, advertising and promotion, direct mail, telemarketing, Web marketing, field sales, order fulfillment, and customer service. A well-managed database should lead to sales gains that will more than cover its costs.

Forms of Direct Marketing

The major forms of direct marketing—as shown in Figure 14-4—include *personal selling, telephone marketing, direct-mail marketing, catalogue marketing, direct-response television marketing, kiosk marketing,* and *online marketing.* We examined personal selling in depth earlier in this chapter and looked closely at online marketing in Chapter 3. Here, we examine the other direct-marketing forms.

Telephone Marketing **Telephone marketing**—using the telephone to sell directly to consumers—has become the major direct-marketing communication tool. Telephone marketing now accounts for more than 38 percent of all direct-marketing media expenditures and 36 percent of direct-marketing sales. We're all familiar with telephone marketing directed toward consumers, but B2B marketers also use telephone marketing extensively, accounting for 58 percent of all telephone marketing sales.[29]

Marketers use *outbound* telephone marketing to sell directly to consumers and businesses. *Inbound* toll-free 800 numbers are used to receive orders from television and radio ads, direct mail, or catalogues. The use of 800 numbers has taken off in recent years as more and more companies have begun using them, and as current

Telephone marketing
Using the telephone to sell directly to customers.

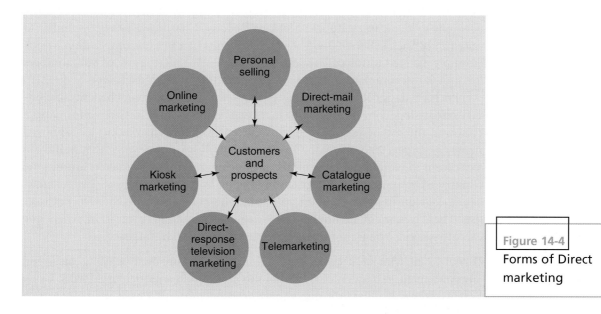

Figure 14-4
Forms of Direct marketing

RMHC® provides comfort and care to children and their families in neighborhoods throughout the world by making grants to not-for-profit organizations and by providing support to over 180 Ronald McDonald Houses in 14 countries.

The Ronald McDonald House® Program, the cornerstone program of Ronald McDonald House Charities®, has provided a "home-away from home" for nearly two million family members since its inception in 1974.

As we move towards the 21st century, RMHC is committed to ensuring that children around the world benefit from: strong bodies, strong minds, safe supportive places to grow, and caring communities.

In 1997, Ronald McDonald House Charities rose to Colin Powell's Challenge at the President's Summit for America's Future, and announced a five-year commitment of $100 million to help children.

MAILING COMPLIMENTS OF AT&T

Support the Children who need you now.

Ronald McDonald House Charities® provides comfort and care to children and their families.

1-900-CALL-RMHC®
(225-5764)

Call now to help the children of Ronald McDonald House Charities.

Each call contributes $15.00 which will appear on your monthly telephone bill.

Each call to 900-CALL-RMHC results in a $15 contribution to Ronald McDonald House Charities, which is simply charged to the caller's local phone bill.

users have added new features such as toll-free fax numbers. Residential use has also grown. To accommodate this rapid growth, new toll-free area codes (888, 877, 866) have been added. After the 800 area code was established in 1967, it took almost 30 years before its 8 million numbers were used up. In contrast, the 888 area code numbers, established in 1996, were used up in only 2 years.[30]

Other marketers use 900 numbers to sell consumers' information, entertainment, or the opportunity to voice an opinion on a pay-per-call basis. For example, for a charge, consumers can obtain weather forecasts from American Express (900-WEATHER—75 cents a minute); pet care information from Quaker Oats (900-990-PETS—95 cents a minute); and golf lessons from *Golf Digest* (900-454-3288—95 cents a minute). In addition to its 800 number and Internet site, Nintendo offers a 900 number, for $1.50 per minute, for game players wanting assistance with the company's video games. Ronald McDonald House Charities uses a 900 number to raise funds. Each call to 900-CALL-RMHC results in a $15.00 contribution, which is simply charged to the caller's local phone bill. Overall, the use of 900 numbers has grown by more than 10 percent a year over the past five years.[31]

Properly designed and targeted telemarketing provides many benefits, including purchasing convenience and increased product and service information. However, the recent explosion in unsolicited telephone marketing has annoyed many consumers who object to the almost daily "junk phone calls" that pull them away from the dinner table or fill the answering machine. Lawmakers around the country are responding with legislation ranging from banning unsolicited telemarketing calls during certain hours to letting households sign up for "Do not call" lists. These lists are maintained by the Canadian Marketing Association, where one executive notes, "We want to target people who want to be targeted."

Direct-Mail Marketing **Direct-mail marketing** involves sending an offer, announcement, reminder, or other item to a person at a particular address. Using highly selective mailing lists, direct marketers send out millions of mail pieces each

Direct-mail marketing
Direct marketing through single mailings that include letters, ads, samples, foldouts, and other "salespeople with wings" sent to prospects on mailing lists.

year—letters, ads, brochures, samples, video- and audiotapes, CDs, and other "salespeople with wings." Direct mail accounts for more than 23 percent of all direct-marketing media expenditures and 31 percent of direct-marketing sales. Together, telemarketing and direct-mail marketing account for more than 60 percent of direct-marketing expenditures and 66 percent of direct-marketing sales.[32]

Direct mail is well suited to direct, one-to-one communication. It permits high target-market selectivity, can be personalized, is flexible, and allows easy measurement of results. Although the cost per thousand people reached is higher than with mass media such as television or magazines, the people who are reached are much better prospects. Direct mail has proven successful in promoting all kinds of products, from books, magazine subscriptions, and insurance to gift items, clothing, gourmet foods, and industrial products. Direct mail is also used heavily by charities to raise billions of dollars each year.

The direct-mail industry constantly seeks new methods and approaches. For example, videotapes and CDs are now among the fastest-growing direct-mail media. For instance, to introduce its Donkey Kong Country video game, Nintendo created a 13-minute MTV-style video and sent 2 million copies to avid video game players. This direct-mail video helped Nintendo sell 6.1 million units of the game in only 45 days, making it the fastest-selling game in industry history. America Online has mailed out CDs by the hundreds of millions in one of the most successful direct-mail campaigns in history. Now other marketers, especially those in technology or e-commerce, are using CDs in their direct-mail offers. Used in conjunction with the Internet, CDs offer an affordable way to drive traffic to Web pages personalized for a specific market segment or a specific promotion. They can also be useful for demonstrations of computer-related products. For example, Sony recently sent out a CD that allowed PC users to demo its new VAIO portable notebook on their own computers.[33]

Until recently, all mail was paper based and handled by Canada Post or delivery services such as Purolater, FedEx, or DHL. Recently, however, three new forms of mail delivery have become popular: fax mail, e-mail, and voicemail.

1. *Fax mail:* Marketers now routinely send fax mail announcing special offers, sales, and other events to prospects and customers with fax machines. Fax mail messages can be sent and received almost instantaneously. However, some prospects and customers resent receiving unsolicited fax mail, which ties up their machines and consumes their paper.

2. *E-mail:* Many marketers now send sales announcements, offers, product information, and other messages to e-mail addresses—sometimes to a few individuals, sometimes to large groups. As discussed in Chapter 3, today's e-mail messages have moved far beyond the drab text-only messages of old. The new breed of e-mail ad uses glitzy features such as animation, interactive links, streaming video, and personalized audio messages to reach out and grab attention. However, as people receive more and more e-mail, they resent the intrusion of unrequested messages. Smart marketers are using permission-based programs, sending e-mail ads only to those who want to receive them.

3. *Voicemail:* Voicemail is a system for receiving and storing oral messages at a telephone address. Some marketers have set up automated programs that exclusively target voice mail boxes and answering machines with recorded messages. These systems target homes between 10 A.M. and 4 P.M. and businesses between 7 P.M. and 9 P.M. when people are least likely to answer. If the automated dialler hears a live voice, it disconnects. Such systems thwart hang-ups by annoyed potential customers. However, they can also create substantial ill will.[34]

These new forms deliver direct mail at incredible speeds compared with the post office's "snail mail" pace. Yet, much like mail delivered through traditional channels, they may be resented as "junk mail" if sent to people who have no interest in them. For this reason, marketers must carefully identify appropriate targets so as not waste their money and recipients' time.

Catalogue Marketing Advances in technology, along with the move toward personalized, one-to-one marketing have resulted in exciting changes in **catalogue marketing**. *Catalog Age* magazine used to define a *catalogue* as "a printed, bound piece of at least eight pages, selling multiple products, and offering a direct ordering mechanism." Today, only a few years later, this definition is out of date. With the stampede to the Internet, more and more catalogues are going electronic. Many traditional print cataloguers have added Web-based catalogues to their marketing mixes and a variety of new Web-only cataloguers have emerged. However, the Internet has not yet killed off printed catalogues—far from it. Printed catalogues remain the primary medium and many former Web-only companies have created printed catalogues to expand their business.

Catalogue marketing has grown explosively during the past 25 years. Annual catalogue sales (both print and electronic) grew from $120 billion in 2000 to more than $160 billion by 2002.[35] Some huge general-merchandise retailers—such as Canadian Tire and Sears—sell a full line of merchandise through catalogues. In recent years, these giants have been challenged by thousands of specialty catalogues that serve highly specialized market niches. Consumers can buy just about anything from a catalogue. Sharper Image sells $3600 jet-propelled surfboards. IKEA Canada can help you furnish almost any living space or office with style. Harry Rosen can dress you for any occasion; although customers get the catalogue (which combines feature articles and fashion advice) free, others can buy it on newsstands for $6. Tilley Endurables and Mountain Equipment Co-op feature everything you need to go hiking in the rainforest or the Sahara.

Specialty department stores, such as Holt-Renfrew, Ashley China, and Nieman Marcus use catalogues to cultivate upper-middle-class markets for high-priced, often exotic merchandise. Walt Disney Company mails out more than 6 million catalogues each year featuring videos, stuffed animals, and other Disney items.

More than three quarters of all catalogue companies now present merchandise and take orders over the Internet. For example, the Lands' End Web site, which debuted in 1995, greeted 28 million visitors last year. Its Web-based sales have more than doubled in the past two years, now accounting for 16 percent of total sales. During the hectic Christmas season, the site handled a record of 15 000 visitors in just one hour.[36]

Catalogue marketing
Direct marketing through print, video, or electronic catalogues that are mailed to a select customers, made available in stores, or presented online.

Along with the benefits, Web-based catalogues present challenges. Whereas a print catalogue is intrusive and creates its own attention, Web catalogues are passive and must be marketed. "Attracting new customers is much more difficult to do with a Web catalogue," says an industry consultant. "You have to use advertising, linkage, and other means to drive traffic to it." Kevin Bartus, president of Blue*Spark, a Toronto-based Web development firm, says, "Retailers are learning an online business is not, in most cases, big enough to support a complete business offering. Retailers are turning to a tri-channel: bricks and mortar, catalogue, and Web."[37] Take the case of La Senza, the Montreal-based lingerie retailer. It first launched a Web site featuring a separate line of merchandise to avoid cannibalizing store sales, but finally had to relaunch the site as an arm of its existing business. To further integrate, customers can return items bought online in stores and sign up for the e-mail club there as well. Thus, even cataloguers who are sold on the Web are not likely to abandon their print catalogues completely.

Direct-Response Television Marketing **Direct-response television marketing** takes one of two major forms. The first is *direct-response advertising.* Direct marketers air television spots, often 60 or 120 seconds long, that persuasively describe a product and give customers a toll-free number for ordering. Television viewers often encounter 30-minute advertising programs, or *infomercials,* for a single product.

Some successful direct-response ads run for years and become classics. For example, Dial Media's ads for Ginsu knives ran for seven years and sold almost 3 million sets of knives worth more than $40 million in sales; its Armourcote cookware ads generated more than twice that much. And over the past 40 years, infomercial czar Ron Popeil's company, Ronco, has sold more than $1 billion worth of TV-marketed gadgets, including the original Veg-O-Matic, The Pocket Fisherman, Mr. Microphone, the Giant Food Dehydrator and Beef Jerky Machine, and the Showtime Rotisserie & BBQ.[38] The current infomercial champ:

Direct-response television marketing Television spots that persuasively describe a product and give customers a toll-free number for ordering.

The current infomercial champion? Direct-response TV ads helped George Foreman's Lean Mean Fat-Reducing Grilling Machines notch $400 million in sales last year.

It's three o'clock in the morning. Plagued with insomnia, you grab the remote and flip around until a grinning blonde in an apron catches your attention: "I'm going to show you something you won't believe! Juicy meals in minutes! Something else you won't believe...George Foreman!" The studio roars, and boxing's elder statesman, in a red apron, shows off his Lean Mean Fat-Reducing Grilling Machine and highlights the grease caught in the pan below. "Eew!" the audience screams. It can be yours for three easy payments of $19.95 (plus shipping and handling). Don't laugh. Such infomercials helped the Foreman grills product line notch almost $400 million in sales last year.[39]

For years, infomercials have been associated with somewhat questionable pitches for juicers and other kitchen gadgets, get-rich-quick schemes, and nifty ways to stay in shape without working very hard at it. Recently, however, a number of large companies—GTE, Johnson & Johnson, MCA Universal, Sears, Procter & Gamble, Revlon, Apple Computer, Cadillac, Volvo, Land Rover, and Anheuser-Busch—have begun using infomercials to sell their wares over the phone, refer customers to retailers, or send out coupons and product information.[40]

Home shopping channels, another form of direct-response television marketing, are television programs or entire channels dedicated to selling goods and services. Some home shopping channels, such as The Shopping Channel, broadcast 24 hours a day. The program's hosts offer bargain prices on such products as jewellery, lamps, collectible dolls, clothing, power tools, and consumer electronics—usually obtained by the home shopping channel at closeout prices. The Shopping Channel's savvy customer-centred marketers didn't take long to add the Web to their marketing mix. Long accustomed to providing consumers with the convenience of shopping at any time, day or night, in the medium of their choice, they launched in May 1999. The site presents browsers with a full selection of all of its products, spanning nine product categories—jewellery, health and beauty, fashions, fitness, at home, electronics, toys, crafts, and collectibles. The site allowed the television retailer to break free of the limitations inherent in using TV, which can focus on only one product at a time. TV did not allow shoppers to browse through the channel's full offerings. TSC's online customers can now have access to a full assortment of its products at any time without having to wait for the information on these products to appear in shows on television. TSC's best customers, those with higher income and education, have naturally gravitated to TSC.ca, but, more important, the site has attracted a significant number of new customers. Moreover, the average order value is 27 percent higher than that of television-only users. View and click obviously makes a dynamic marketing option.[41]

Kiosk Marketing Some companies place information and ordering machines—called *kiosks* (in contrast to vending machines, which dispense actual products)—in stores, airports, and other locations. Hallmark and American Greetings use kiosks to help customers create and purchase personalized greeting cards.

Lee jeans stores use a kiosk called Fit Finder to provide women with a quick way to determine the size and style of Lee jeans that fit their personal preference. Toyota Canada used kiosks to target younger buyers. The Liquor Control Board of Ontario installed interactive kiosks to run advertisements for featured products

The Shopping Channel
www.tsc.ca

and to enhance customer service. IKEA Canada allows UNICEF to set up fundraising kiosks in its stores.[42]

Business marketers also use kiosks. Investment Canada placed a kiosk at an Atlanta trade show to introduce Canadian telecommunications and computer products to international buyers. Dow Plastics places kiosks at trade shows to collect sales leads and to provide information on its 700 products. The kiosk system reads customer data from encoded registration badges and produces technical data sheets, which can be printed at the kiosk or faxed or mailed to the customer. The system has resulted in a 400-percent increase in qualified sales leads.[43]

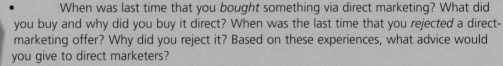

Stop a moment and think about the impact of direct marketing on your life.

- When was last time that you *bought* something via direct marketing? What did you buy and why did you buy it direct? When was the last time that you *rejected* a direct-marketing offer? Why did you reject it? Based on these experiences, what advice would you give to direct marketers?

- For the next week, keep track of all the direct-marketing offers that come your way via direct mail and catalogues, telephone, and direct-response television. Then analyze the offers by type, source, and what you liked or disliked about each offer and the way it was delivered. Which offer best hit its target (you)? Which missed by the widest margin?

Integrated Direct Marketing

Too often, a company's individual direct-marketing efforts are not well integrated with one another or with other elements of its marketing and promotion mixes. For example, a firm's media advertising may be handled by the advertising department working with a traditional advertising agency. Meanwhile, its direct-mail and catalogue business may be handled by direct-marketing specialists while its Web site is developed and operated by an outside Internet firm. Even within a given direct-marketing campaign, too many companies use only a "one-shot" effort to reach and sell a prospect or a single vehicle in multiple stages to trigger purchases.

A more powerful approach is **integrated direct marketing**, which involves using carefully coordinated multimedia, multistage campaigns. Such campaigns can greatly improve response. Whereas a direct-mail piece alone might generate a 2 percent response, adding a Web site and toll-free phone number might raise the response rate by 50 percent. Then, a well-designed outbound telemarketing effort might lift response by an additional 500 percent. Suddenly, a 2 percent response has grown to 15 percent or more by adding interactive marketing channels to a regular mailing.

More elaborate integrated direct-marketing campaigns can be used. Consider the multimedia, multistage campaign shown in Figure 14-5. Here, the paid ad creates product awareness and stimulates inquiries. The company immediately sends direct mail to those who inquire. Within a few days, the company follows up with

Integrated direct marketing Direct-marketing campaigns that use multiple vehicles and multiple stages to improve response rates and profits.

Figure 14-5

An Integrated Direct-Marketing Campaign

a phone call seeking an order. Some prospects will order by phone; others might request a face-to-face sales call. In such a campaign, the marketer seeks to improve response rates and profits by adding media and stages that contribute more to additional sales than to additional costs.

Public Policy and Ethical Issues in Direct Marketing

Direct marketers and their customers usually enjoy mutually rewarding relationships. Occasionally, however, a darker side emerges. The aggressive and sometimes shady tactics of a few direct marketers can bother or harm consumers, giving the entire industry a black eye. Abuses range from simple excesses that irritate consumers to instances of unfair practices or even outright deception and fraud. The direct-marketing industry has also faced growing concerns about invasion-of-privacy issues.

Irritation, Unfairness, Deception, and Fraud Direct-marketing excesses sometimes annoy or offend consumers. Most of us dislike direct-response TV commercials that are too loud, too long, and too insistent. Especially bothersome are dinnertime or late-night phone calls. Beyond irritating consumers, some direct marketers have been accused of taking unfair advantage of impulsive or less sophisticated buyers. TV shopping shows and program-long "infomercials" seem to be the worst culprits. They feature smooth-talking hosts, elaborately staged demonstrations, claims of drastic price reductions, "while they last" time limitations, and unequalled ease of purchase to inflame buyers who have low sales resistance.

Worse yet, so-called heat merchants design mailers and write copy intended to mislead buyers. Even well-known direct mailers have been accused of deceiving consumers. Sweepstakes promoter Publishers Clearing House recently paid $52 million to settle accusations that its high-pressure mailings confused or misled consumers, especially the elderly, into believing that they had won prizes or would win if they bought the company's magazines.[44]

Other direct marketers pretend to be conducting research surveys when they are actually asking leading questions to screen or persuade consumers. Fraudulent schemes, such as investment scams or phony collections for charity, have also multiplied in recent years. Crooked direct marketers can be hard to catch: Direct-marketing customers often respond quickly, do not interact personally with the seller, and usually expect to wait for delivery. By the time buyers realize that they have been bilked, the thieves are usually somewhere else plotting new schemes.

Invasion of Privacy Invasion of privacy is perhaps the toughest public policy issue now confronting the direct-marketing industry. These days, it seems that almost every time consumers enter a sweepstakes, apply for a credit card, take out a magazine subscription, or order products by mail, telephone, or the Internet, their names are entered into some company's already bulging database. Using sophisticated computer technologies, direct marketers can use these databases to "microtarget" their selling efforts.

Consumers often benefit from such database marketing—they receive more offers that are closely matched to their interests. However, many critics worry that marketers may know *too* much about consumers' lives and that they may use this knowledge to take unfair advantage of consumers. At some point, they claim, the extensive use of databases intrudes on consumer privacy.

For example, they ask, should Bell or Telus or SaskTel be allowed to sell marketers the names of customers who frequently call the 800 numbers of catalogue companies? Should a company such as American Express be allowed to make data on cardholders available to merchants who accept AmEx cards? Is it right for credit bureaus to compile and sell lists of people who have recently applied for credit cards—people who are considered prime direct-marketing targets because of their spending behaviour? Or is it right for provinces to sell the names and addresses of driver's licence holders? In one survey of consumers, 79 percent said they were concerned about threats to their personal privacy. In their drives to build databases, companies sometimes get carried away. For example, when first introduced, Intel's Pentium III chip contained an embedded serial number that allowed the company to trace users' equipment. When privacy advocates screamed, Intel disabled the feature. Similarly, Microsoft caused substantial privacy concerns when it introduced its Windows 95 software. It used a "Registration Wizard," which allowed users to register their new software online. However, when users went online to register, without their knowledge, Microsoft "read" the configurations of their PCs to learn about the major software products running on each customer's system. When users learned of this invasion, they protested loudly and Microsoft abandoned the practice. Such actions have spawned a quiet but determined "privacy revolt" among consumers and public policymakers.[45]

In a survey of Internet users, 71 percent of respondents said there should be laws to protect Web privacy and a full 84 percent objected to firms selling information about users to other companies.

Governments around the world have been exploring the question of whether to institute privacy legislation. The first major step was taken by the European Union. In 1995, it issued a directive on the protection of personal data, which provides a framework for collecting and processing personal data. Predictably, the United States and Canada have responded to the whole privacy issue differently. While the United States opted for industry self-regulation, Canadian governments believed more controls were needed. Until recently, Quebec was the only province with legislation dealing with the privacy of personal information. On 1 January 2001, the Canadian *Personal Information Protection and Electronic Documents Act* (formerly Bill C6) came into effect. For full details on the Act, visit the Privacy Commissioner of Canada Web site. The privacy act governs all federally regulated industries and businesses that operate interprovincially. Provinces have until 2004 to develop their own legislation to regulate businesses that operate solely within their boundaries. The new legislation uses several guiding principles to protect consumers and control how firms gather and use their personal information:

- *Consumer consent:* Knowledge and consent must be obtained from consumers before a firm can collect, use, or disclose consumers' personal information.

- *Limitations:* A firm may collect only the information appropriate for the purposes for which it is being gathered. For example, if it needs to mail you something, the firm can ask for your home mailing address, but not any additional, unnecessary information beyond what it needs to address the mailing.

Privacy Commissioner of Canada
www.privcom.gc.ca

Furthermore, a firm may use the information only for the purpose for which it was gathered. To make additional use of the information, a company must get permission from the individual. Finally, a firm may not transfer the information to a third party without the permission of the individual.

- *Accuracy:* A firm must ensure that the information it gathers is recorded accurately, and it must appoint an employee to be responsible for this. For example, to comply with this portion of the legislation, Peter Cullen was recently designated as the new corporate privacy officer at the Royal Bank of Canada.

- *Right to access:* Individuals have the right to know what information is being held about them. They can also demand that errors in their personal information be rectified and may request that their personal information be withdrawn from a firm's database.

The direct marketing industry is addressing issues of ethics and public policy. Direct marketers know that, left untended, such problems will lead to increasingly negative consumer attitudes, lower response rates, and calls for more restrictive provincial and federal legislation. Most direct marketers want the same things that consumers want: honest and well-designed marketing offers targeted only toward consumers who will appreciate and respond to them. Direct marketing is just too expensive to waste on consumers who don't want it.

<< Looking Back   < < < < < < < < <

Pull over and revisit this chapter's key concepts. The chapter is the second of two chapters covering the final marketing mix element—promotion. The previous chapter dealt with advertising, sales promotion, and public relations. This one investigates personal selling and direct marketing.

Personal selling and direct marketing are both direct tools for communicating with and persuading current and prospective customers. Selling is the interpersonal arm of the communications mix. To be successful in personal selling, a company must first build and then manage an effective sales force. Firms must also be good at direct marketing, the process of forming one-to-one connections with customers. Today, many companies are turning to direct marketing in an effort to reach carefully targeted customers more efficiently and to build stronger, more personal, one-to-one relationships with them.

1. **Discuss the role of a company's salespeople in creating value for customers and building customer relationships.**

Most companies use salespeople, and many companies assign them an important role in the marketing mix. For companies selling business products, the firm's salespeople work directly with customers. Often, the sales force is the customer's only direct contact with the company and therefore may be viewed by customers as representing the company itself. In contrast, for consumer product companies that sell through intermediaries, consumers usually do not meet salespeople or even know about them. The sales force works behind the scenes, dealing with wholesalers and retailers to obtain their support and helping them become effective in selling the firm's products.

As an element of the promotion mix, the sales force is very effective in achieving certain marketing objectives and carrying out such activities as prospecting, communicating, selling and servicing, and information gathering. But with companies becoming more market oriented, a market-focused sales force also works to produce both *customer sat-*

isfaction and *company profit*. To accomplish these goals, the sales force needs skills in marketing analysis and planning in addition to the traditional selling skills.

2. Identify and explain the six major sales force management steps.

High sales force costs necessitate an effective *sales management process* consisting of six steps: *designing sales force strategy and structure, recruiting and selecting, training, compensating, supervising,* and *evaluating* salespeople.

In designing a sales force, sales management must address issues such as what type of sales force structure will work best (territorial, product, customer, or complex structure); how large the sales force should be; who will be involved in the selling effort; and how its various sales and sales support people will work together (inside or outside sales forces and team selling).

To hold down the high costs of hiring the wrong people, salespeople must be *recruited* and *selected* carefully. In recruiting salespeople, a company may look to job duties and the characteristics of its most successful salespeople to suggest the traits it wants in its salespeople and then look for applicants through recommendations of current salespeople, employment agencies, classified ads, and the Internet, and by contacting postsecondary students. In the selection process, the procedure can vary from a single informal interview to lengthy testing and interviewing. After the selection process is complete, *training* programs familiarize new salespeople not only with the art of selling but also with the company's history, its products and policies, and the characteristics of its market and competitors.

The sales force *compensation* system helps to reward, motivate, and direct salespeople. In compensating salespeople, companies try to have an appealing plan, usually close to the going rate for the type of sales job and needed skills. In addition to compensation, all salespeople need *supervision*, and many need continuous encouragement because they must make many decisions and face many frustra-tions. Periodically, the company must *evaluate* their performance to help them do a better job. In evaluating salespeople, the company relies on getting regular information gathered through sales reports, personal observations, customers' letters and complaints, customer surveys, and conversations with other salespeople.

3. Discuss the personal selling process, distinguishing between transaction-oriented marketing and relationship marketing.

The art of selling involves a eight-step *selling process: prospecting and qualifying, preapproach, approach, needs analysis, presentation and demonstration, handling objections, closing,* and *follow-up*. These steps help marketers close a specific sale and as such are *transaction oriented*. However, a seller's dealings with customers should be guided by the larger concept of *relationship marketing*. The company's sales force should help to orchestrate a whole-company effort to develop profitable long-term relationships with key customers based on superior customer value and satisfaction.

4. Define direct marketing and discuss its benefits for customers and companies.

Direct marketing consists of direct connections with carefully targeted individual consumers to both obtain an immediate response and cultivate lasting customer relationships. Using detailed databases, direct marketers tailor their offers and communications to the needs of narrowly defined segments or even individual buyers.

For buyers, direct marketing is convenient, easy to use, and private. It gives them ready access to a wealth of products and information, at home and around the globe. Direct marketing is also immediate and interactive, allowing buyers to create exactly the configuration of information, products, or services they desire, then order them on the spot. For sellers, direct marketing is a powerful tool for building customer relationships. Using database marketing, today's marketers can target small groups or individual consumers, tailor offers to individual needs, and promote these offers through personalized communications. It also offers them a low-cost, efficient alternative for reaching their markets. Because of these advantages for both buyers and sellers, direct marketing has become the fastest growing form of marketing.

5. Identify and discuss the major forms of direct marketing.

The main forms of direct marketing include *personal selling, telephone marketing, direct-mail marketing, catalogue marketing, direct-response television marketing, kiosk marketing,* and *online marketing.* We discuss personal selling in the first part of this chapter and examined online marketing in detail in Chapter 3. *Telephone marketing* consists of using the telephone to sell directly to consumers. *Direct-mail marketing* consists of the company sending an offer, announcement, reminder, or other item to a person at a specific address. Recently, three new forms of mail delivery have become popular—*fax mail, e-mail,* and *voice-mail.* Some marketers rely on *catalogue marketing,* or selling through catalogues mailed to a select list of customers or made available in stores. *Direct-response television marketing* has two forms: *direct-response advertising* or *infomercials* and *home shopping channels. Kiosks* are information and ordering machines that direct marketers place in stores, airports, and other locations. *Online marketing,* discussed in Chapter 3, involves online channels and e-commerce, which electronically link consumers with sellers.

Navigating the Key Terms

Approach, **p. 572**
Catalogue marketing, **p. 582**
Closing, **p. 573**
Customer database, **p. 576**
Customer sales force structure, **p. 557**
Direct-mail marketing, **p. 580**
Direct marketing, **p. 574**
Direct-response television marketing, **p. 583**
Follow-up, **p. 573**
Handling objections, **p. 573**
Inside sales force, **p. 558**
Integrated direct marketing, **p. 585**
Needs analysis, **p. 572**

Outside sales force (or field sales force), **p. 558**
Preapproach, **p. 572**
Presentation, **p. 572**
Product sales force structure, **p. 557**
Prospecting, **p. 571**
Relationship marketing, **p. 574**
Sales force management, **p. 555**
Sales quota, **p. 570**
Salesperson, **p. 554**
Selling process, **p. 571**
Team selling, **p. 562**
Telephone marketing, **p. 579**
Territorial sales force structure, **p. 556**

Concept Check

Fill in the blanks and then check your answers.

1. Robert Louis Stevenson once noted that "everyone lives by _____ something."

2. In the _____ structure, each salesperson is assigned to an exclusive geographic area and sells the company's full line of products or services to all customers in that geographic area.

3. Compensation of salespeople is made up of several elements: a _____ amount, a

_____ amount, _____, and _____.

4. If the strategic goal were to maximize profitability, the ideal salesperson would be a _____ and a _____ manager.

5. According to Figure 14-3, the selling process consists of the following steps: _____ and qualifying, _____, approach, needs analysis, presentation and demonstration, _____, _____, and follow-up.

6. Many companies today are moving away from _____ marketing with its emphasis on making a sale, and are moving toward _____ marketing, which emphasizes maintaining profitable long-term relationships with customers by creating superior customer value and satisfaction.

7. _____ consists of direct connections with carefully targeted individual consumers to obtain an immediate response and cultivate lasting customer relationships.

8. A _____ is an organized collection of comprehensive data about individual customers or prospects, including geographic, demographic, psychographic, and behavioural data.

9. Companies use their databases in many ways: they can use a database to _____ and generate sales leads, profile customers based on previous purchasing, or deepen_____.

10. According to Figure 14-4, the major forms of direct marketing include: personal selling, _____ _____, _____, _____, direct-response television marketing, _____, and online marketing.

11. _____ marketing involves sending an offer, announcement, reminder, or other item to a person at a particular address.

12. In the past, too many companies used a "one-shot" effort to reach and sell a prospect. A more powerful approach is _____ marketing, which involves using carefully coordinated multimedia, multistage campaigns.

Concept Check Answers: 1. selling; 2. territorial sales force; 3. fixed, variable, expenses, fringe benefits; 4. team player, relationship; 5. prospecting, preapproach, handling objections, closing; 6. transaction, relationship; 7. Direct marketing; 8. customer database; 9. identify prospects, customer loyalty; 10. telephone marketing, direct-mail marketing, catalogue marketing, kiosk marketing; 11. Direct-mail; 12. integrated direct.

Discussing the Issues

1. What did Robert Louis Stevenson mean when he said "everyone lives by selling something"? Describe all the various positions and roles the modern salesperson might be required to fill or play.

2. One of the most pressing issues that sales managers face is how to structure salespeople and their tasks. Evaluate the methods described in the text. For each method, provide (a) a brief description of its chief characteristics, (b) an example of how it's used, and (c) a critique of its effectiveness.

3. List and briefly describe the steps in the personal selling process. Which step do you think is the most difficult for the average salesperson? Which step is the most critical to successful selling? Which step do you think is usually done most correctly?

4. Explain the meaning of relationship marketing. Describe how relationship marketing might be used in (a) selling a personal computer to a final consumer, (b) selling a new car, (c) providing a student with a college education, and (d) selling season tickets for a local drama theatre.

5. Contact one of the personal computer direct marketers (such as Dell Computer at **www.dell.ca** or Gateway at **www.gateway. com**). (a) How does the company make it easy to order its products? (b) What differentiates this company from traditional retailers or manufac-

turers? (c) What are the company's chief advantages and disadvantages? (d) How does it provide security for customers (or not)? (e) Based on this experience, what is your opinion of online marketers?

 ## Mastering Marketing

After examining the sales function of CanGo, devise a plan where the company could alter its sales force strategy and structure to better serve the needs of present and future customers. Be specific with your comments. Next, devise a plan where CanGo could implement a program of direct marketing. Specify why this might be a good idea, how a customer data base could be used, and what the anticipated results of this effort might be.

 Check out the enclosed Video case CD-ROM, or our Companion Website at www.pearsoned.ca/armstrong, to view a CBC video segment and case for this chapter.

MAP 14 Marketing Applications

Jonathan Ellermann was excited about his new job as a personal communication consultant for Nokia (see **www.nokia.ca**), the giant phone producer that captures a quarter of the global market and half the profits. Rivals such as Ericsson (at **www.ericsson.ca**), Vodafone (at **www.vodaphone.com**), Panasonic (at **www.panasonic.ca**), and Motorola (at **www.motorola.ca**) have vowed to make things tougher for Nokia in the coming year. They've developed new designs, communications applications, and strategic alliances between hardware and software makers in an effort to lure fickle consumers away from Nokia.

Thinking Like a Marketing Manager

1. Ellermann is seeking to sell Nokia's latest model personal communication device to Shell Oil's Houston branch (approximately 5000 phones). What sales strategy and plan should Ellermann recommend? In your answer, consider the advantages and disadvantages of Nokia's product.

2. Would you recommend that Nokia employ individual selling or team selling? Explain.

3. Which step of the sales process do you think will be most critical to Ellermann's success?

4. What could Ellermann do to establish a strong relationship with local Shell representatives?

 ### Digital Map
Visit our Web site at **www.pearsoned.ca/armstrong** for online quizzes, Internet exercises, and more!

CASE 14 CARS DIRECT.COM: SHAKING UP THE COMPETITION

Not long ago, buying a car was an onerous task. When consumers visited a dealership, they were at a disadvantage. Not only did they have little information, they also couldn't negotiate. Because consumers buy cars infrequently, few develop strong negotiation skills and most forget what they learned the last time.

Even consumers who took the time and effort to gather information and who were skillful negotiators found the process long and tedious. They visited the car lot, haggled with the salesperson, and then haggled more with the business manager over financing. The process could take hours, even days. At the end, many consumers believed that they had been taken advantage of by the dealer, who had all the power.

Along Came the Internet The Internet let consumer-oriented organizations distribute information easily. Consumer Reports at **www.consumerreports.org**, AutoSite at **www.autosite.com**, Car and Driver at **www.caranddriver.com**, Kelley Blue Book at **www.kbb.com**, and Edmund's at **www.edmunds.com** quickly set up Web sites offering consumers performance, pricing, and dealer information. Carforums. com at **www.carforums.com** even offered model-specific chat rooms so that consumers could talk with one another about their cars and car problems.

Although helping consumers get more information was fine, savvy e-commerce entrepreneurs saw that the Internet offered a way to begin to change the car-buying process itself. Autobytel at **www.autobytel.ca** was one of the first companies to offer car-buying assistance. Other companies, such as Cost Finder Canada at **www.costfindercanada.com**, AutoConnect at **www.autoconnect.com**, AutoWeb at **www.autoweb.com**, and AutoVantage at **www.autovantage.com** quickly followed. In fact, analysts estimated that there were soon more than 100 automotive Web sites offering some type of car-shopping help. Autobytel and similar services signed up dealers who agreed to participate and pay fees for referrals. The sites helped consumers identify dealers in their areas who had the cars they were seeking. The services would either notify the dealer about an interested consumer or simply let the consumer know where to find the dealer. Some sites allowed consumers to submit electronic, "no-haggle" bids to dealers. Using these services, however, the consumer still had to visit the dealer to conclude the negotiations and take possession of the car.

Cars Delivered Fresh Daily It was only a matter of time before some bold entrepreneur took the next logical step. As a result of having gone through the traditional car-buying process himself, Internet entrepreneur Bill Gross realized there had to be a better way. Gross had previously founded the Pasadena, California-based Internet incubator Idealab!, which had already spawned such companies as eToys, GoTo.com, and Free-PC. Gross and other investors, including Michael Dell of Dell Computer, established CarsDirect.com at **www.carsdirect.com**.

Rather than just serving as an electronic intermediary, CarsDirect actually closes the sale and delivers the car to the consumer. A consumer visiting the CarsDirect Web site finds a simple, three-step process to follow. First, the site guides the consumer through the process of selecting the vehicle. Using information and guidance that the site provides, consumers can choose from a complete selection of production vehicles available in the United States. Consumers who want a specialty vehicle, such as a Ferrari, or who don't find the vehicle they are seeking, can e-mail the company directly. A service advisor contacts them within 24 hours.

Once a consumer selects a car, CarsDirect negotiates with the 1700 dealers in its network to find it. CarsDirect tries to set a price for the consumer that is in the bottom 10 percent of the market price range for the particular vehicle. Its substantial buying power allows CarsDirect to get the vehicle from the dealer at an even lower price, then make a profit on the difference between what it pays the dealer and what it charges the consumer. One dealer reported selling 53 cars to CarsDirect in three months. Selling to CarsDirect lowers the dealer's costs because the dealer doesn't have to pay the sales commission it would normally pay to salespeople.

Having found a car and set a price, CarsDirect offers the car to the consumer. Consumers can lock in the price by making a fully refundable $50 deposit. They can pay cash; use their own financing, such as through a local bank; or select a lease or loan package that CarsDirect.com offers. Consumers who want to use a CarsDirect financing package can fill out an application online.

Finally, the consumer decides how to take delivery. The company offers consumers the option of going to a local CarsDirect Priority Dealer to pick up the vehicle. Or, depending on where they live and the vehicle purchased, CarsDirect will deliver the vehicle to a consumer's home or office. (In Los Angeles, CarsDirect delivery trucks display the slogan, "Cars Delivered Fresh Daily.") No matter which option consumers select, they will be able to inspect their vehicles, find out about service options, and ask questions.

CarsDirect was the first company to offer the consumer the opportunity to purchase a vehicle, finance the purchase, and take delivery without ever leaving home.

Will This Work? Based on the initial success of the concept, CarSmart. Com opened up a used channel in late 2001 to sell high-quality used vehicles through a selective dealer network.

In mid-2002 CarSmart.com was identified by *Time* magazine as one of their 50 Best Web Sites, and *Forbes Magazine* recognized CarSmart.com as Forbes' Favorite for online car buying. Notwithstanding the accolades, as in many industries, consolidation has become a survival strategy and the online car business is not immune to the pressures of he e-commerce marketplace. CarsDirect.com is now a unit of Autobytel Inc., the organization that now owns and operates the major automobile sales sites on the Internet, namely, Autobytel.com, Autoweb.cam, Carsmart.com and A.I.C (Automotive Information Centre), a provider of automotive marketing data and technology for manufacturers and dealerships. Combined, these sites are responsible for $17 billion in sales (approximately 4 percent of total North American new car sales), represent 8900 dealers, and attract 3.5 million unique visitors.

We could surmise then that in the short term, the online concept is working. But where are the manufacturers in this? Although Ford and DaimlerChrysler allow you to custom build and price your new car, the Web sites continue to refer buyers to dealers.

However, several companies are experimenting with e-commerce car-buying strategies in foreign markets. GM is testing strategies in Taiwan, where it already sells 10 percent of its vehicles via the Internet. It began building cars to order in 2000. Ford has set up a seamless e-commerce system in the Philippines that links consumers, dealers, Ford, and its suppliers. Meanwhile, Autobytel has moved into Europe. There, European Union laws enable manufacturers to restrict new car sales to captive dealers. Such laws have led to inflated prices in many markets, as much as 25 percent higher on average than in the United States. When this exemption expires in 2002, Autobytel hopes to be able to offer direct sales over the Internet.

Where to from Here? Where will this lead? No one's sure. An analyst for one company argues that, "All [CarsDirect has] is motivated salespeople in a call centre" who try to get dealers to sell cars for less than CarsDirect's customer is paying. Other analysts note that online advertising impressions grew 136 percent from May 2001 to May 2002 and that 94 percent of consumers who started looking for a car in March 2002 went online for price quotes, dealer locations, and model information. However, CarsDirect and other online vehicle retailers face restrictive state franchise laws, some of which ban Internet sales. They also face political and legal actions by some of the 20 000 established dealers and complicated ordering systems by which automakers require dealers to take unwanted cars to get hot-selling models.

Finally, CarsDirect has proven that some consumers will make a five-figure purchase over the Internet without having seen the car. However, some analysts still wonder: Are there enough such consumers out there for CarsDirect to become profitable?

Questions

1. How do customers and CarsDirect each benefit from online marketing?

2. Outline CarsDirect's marketing strategy. What problems do you see with its strategy?

3. What marketing recommendations would you make to CarsDirect? Specifically, how can CarsDirect get more people to visit its site and purchase cars using its service?

4. What advantages or disadvantages will CarsDirect and its competitors face in foreign markets? How are Canadian auto dealers preparing for the entry of firms like CarsDirect?

5. What ethical issues does CarsDirect face? How should it deal with those issues?

Sources: CarsDirect.com home page, accessed online at **www.carsdirect.com** Edward Harris, "Web Car-Shopping Puts Buyers in Driver's Seat," *The Wall Street Journal,* 15 April 1999, p. B10; Daniel Taub, "Firm Proves People Are Ready to Buy Cars on the Web," *Los Angeles Business Journal,* 23 August 1999, p. 5; John Couretas, "CarsDirect Tops Online Buying List from Gomez," *Automotive News,* 20 September 1999, p. 10; Fara Warner, "Internet Auto Retailer CarOrder.com Receives Funds to Acquire Dealerships," *The Wall Street Journal,* 29 September 1999, p. B2; Tim Burt, "Autobytel to Push Online Car Sales in Europe," *Financial Times,* 8 October 1999, p. 30; Fara Warner, "New Tactics Shake up Online Auto Retailing," *The Wall Street Journal,* 18 October 1999, p. B1; and Fara Warner, "GM Tests E-Commerce Plans in Emerging Markets," *The Wall Street Journal,* 25 October 1999, p. B6, eMarketer Daily, Issue 110, 2002.

15 >> The Global Marketplace

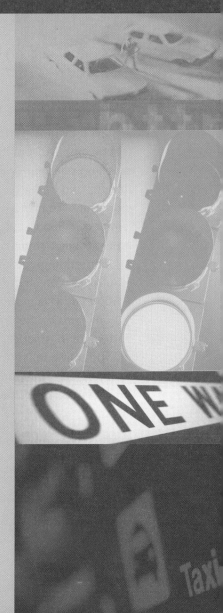

Looking Ahead

You've come a long way on your marketing journey. You've now learned the fundamentals of how companies develop marketing strategies and marketing mixes to build lasting customer relationships by creating superior customer value. In the final two chapters, we'll extend these fundamentals to two special areas: global marketing, and social responsibility and marketing ethics. Although we've visited these topics in each previous chapter, because of their special importance, we will focus exclusively on them here at the end of your journey. We'll look first at special considerations in global marketing. Advances in communication, transportation, and other technologies have made the world a much smaller place. Today, almost every firm, large or small, faces international marketing issues. In this chapter, we will examine six major decisions marketers make in going global.

After studying this chapter, you should be able to

1. discuss how the international trade system, economic, politico-legal, and cultural environments affect a company's international marketing decisions.

2. describe three key approaches to entering international markets.

3. explain how companies adapt their marketing mixes for international markets.

4. identify the three major forms of international marketing organization.

Buckle up and let's get going! Our first stop is the NBA, an organization that has taken a North American game global. The NBA's success abroad is primarily a result of the league's strong marketing efforts.

Basketball, a quintessential North American game, is rapidly becoming a worldwide craze. A *New York Times* survey of more than 45 000 teenagers on five continents asked: "What are your favourite entertainment pursuits?" The top two answers were watching television and basketball. If you ask Canadian teenagers aged 12 to 17 to name their favourite athletes, Wayne Gretzky loses out to Kobe Bryant, Michael Jordan, Shaquille O'Neal, and Vince Carter. And no organization is doing more to promote basketball worldwide than the National Basketball Association (NBA), a truly global marketing enterprise. NBA games are televised around the world, and the league, with its partners, sells millions of dollars worth of NBA-licensed basketballs, backboards, T-shirts, and other merchandise both inside and outside North America every year. The NBA is now a powerful worldwide brand. A recent *Fortune* article summarizes:

> Deployed by global sponsors Coca-Cola, Reebok, and McDonald's, these well-paid travelling salesmen will hawk soda, sneakers, burgers, and basketball to legions of mostly young fans. That they are recognized from Santiago to Seoul says a lot about the soaring worldwide appeal of hoops—and about the marketing juggernaut known as the NBA. After watching their favorite stars swoop in and slam-dunk on their local TV stations, fans of the league now cheer the mate in Latin America, the trofsla in Iceland, and the smash in France. Care to guess the most popular basketball team in China? Why, it's the "Red Oxen" from Chicago, of course.

Like many other businesses, the NBA's primary motive for going global is growth. In the United States, the league now sells out most of its games, and licensing revenues have flattened in recent years. According to NBA commissioner David Sterns, "There are just so many seats in an arena and so many hours of television programming, period. The domestic business is becoming mature. That's why we're moving internationally." Compared with the NBA's overall yearly revenues of $3 billion, current international revenues are modest—estimated at a little more than $90 million from TV rights fees, sponsorships, and the league's share of licensing sales. But worldwide potential is huge, and the league is investing heavily to build its popularity and business abroad.

The NBA's success abroad is primarily a result of the league's strong marketing efforts. Entry into the Canadian market was a natural for the NBA since basketball, originally invented by a Canadian, was already a popular sport. Examining how the NBA built its Canadian fan base is a case study on the tactics the organization has used around the world. The NBA rolled out a marketing machine that's been fine-tuned for a decade in the United States. Television programming leads the way—not just broadcasts of games but also an array of NBA-produced programs, mostly targeting children and teenagers, which promote the league and its players. But given the popularity of hockey in Canada, getting Canadian television coverage was a major challenge. Ken Derrett, managing director of NBA Canada Inc., notes: "Providing access to NBA games on television is an essential foundation for growth."

Before the Toronto Raptors and Vancouver Grizzlies (relocated to Memphis at beginning of the 2001–02 season) began playing in the league in 1995, broadcast coverage of the NBA in Canada was sparse. Since NBA basketball is as much about spectacle and entertainment as it is about sport, having televised games is only one part of the mix. NBA-based programs were also used to promote the league and its players: *NBA in the Paint* and YTV's *Dunk Street,* a half-hour hoop show with a Canadian slant, for example, drew an average of 204 000 weekly viewers. NBA Canada also ran two advertising spots "I love this game," designed to further educate Canadians about basketball, and "I love this stuff," focused on promoting merchandise sales. The ads ran on TV shows popular among young fans, like Much Music. And the tactics worked. After one year, research revealed that 57 percent of NBA fans in English Canada were more interested in the NBA than they had been previously.

Once television has pried open the new foreign market, the NBA and its partners move in with an array of live events, attractions, and grassroots activities. For example, McDonald's and the NBA sponsor a program called 2Ball that teaches basic basketball skills to thousands of kids in its international marketplaces. Coca-Cola, meanwhile, targets basketball-crazed teenagers by putting NBA and team logos on Sprite soft-drink cans sold in 30 countries. "We're using the NBA and their players to help sell Sprite, but at the same time it does a lot for the NBA," says Coca-Cola's director for worldwide sports.

Since live fans are important to the excitement of the game, the NBA and its Canadian sponsors knew they had to draw teens to the games. However, how do you make the game more accessible and exciting, given the limited income of most teens? Raptors-sponsor Sprite found one key when it created the Sprite Zone at the Air Canada Centre. The Sprite Zone is a special section of 1442 seats where tickets cost only $10 (less than half the regular $24 ticket price). The Zone is also a fun, dynamic place for Sprite's teen target audience to watch the game, spurred on by six "Sprite Zone leaders," theme nights, and chances to win Raptor merchandise or upgraded courtside tickets.

Merchandise sales and corporate sponsorships are the final tactics used in new international markets to help build loyalty and generate revenues for the teams' coffers. For example, NBA Canada has issued more than 60 licences to date. Air Canada, Shoppers Drug Mart, and Nestlé Canada were quick to jump on board. Kellogg Canada was another eager partner, putting the phone number for season tickets on its boxes of Rice Krispies. Kellogg's Joanne Doyle, manager of product communications, went with NBA sponsorship because "the demographics of the [NBA] broadcasts also show a good female viewership, important to us since most grocery shoppers are women." Despite skillful marketing, however, the NBA's success in Canada is far from assured.

Similar tactics to those used in Canada were used to "slam-dunk" the European and Asian marketplaces, where amateur basketball had been thriving since the 1936 Olympics. To help build the market for professional basketball in these areas, the NBA also leveraged the Internet. The NBA's Web site offers materials in several languages and draws almost a third of its visitors from outside North America. A survey of 28 000 teenagers in 45 countries by a global ad agency found that Jordan was the world's favourite athlete by far. In China, which has its own professional basketball leagues, boys on the streets of Beijing and Shanghai wear Bulls gear because they want to be like Mike.

The NBA recently encountered a rash of problems—the end of the Chicago Bulls dynasty, negative publicity surrounding several high-profile players, and a prolonged players' strike that cut the 1998-1999 season in half. These and other events present fresh challenges to the league's marketing prowess. Still, the future looks bright. The NBA emerged from the potentially disastrous players' strike nearly unscathed, and although TV ratings for the NBA finals dipped, games still top the Nielsen ratings. Most experts expect more high flying from the NBA as it continues to extend its international reach. One sustaining factor in the NBA's global appeal is the continuing presence of foreign-born players. Almost every team roster includes one: Toni Kukoc from Croatia, Luc Longley from Australia, and Canada's own Steve Nash. Such players attract large followings in their home countries. As *Fortune* concludes:

Imagine, then, the impact in China if a promising 18-year-old, seven-foot-one centre named Wong Zhizhi, who played for that country's...Olympic team, develops into an NBA star. Basketball's popularity is already exploding in China, one of the very few nations where the NBA gives away its TV programming because [it] is determined to make inroads there. Nearly all of China's 250 million TV households get the *NBA Action* highlights show and a game of the week on Saturday mornings; this year China Central TV broadcast the NBA all-star game live for the first time. Winning the loyalty of two billion Chinese won't be a *kou qui*—a slam-dunk—but Stern is, well, bullish. "The upside is tremendous," he says. Can Ping-Pong survive an NBA invasion? Stay tuned.[1]

Toronto Raptors
www.nba.com/raptors

NBA
www.NBA.com

Given our small domestic marketplace, the ability to trade internationally has long been important to Canadian citizens and businesses. For example, Canadian exports in 2000 were more than 45 percent of gross domestic product (GDP), higher than any other G-8 countries, and well above the United States' 25 percent. Trade means imports as well as exports bringing in technology and materials needed to create exports while offering Canadians a wider range of purchase choices for everything from oranges to cars to medication. It encourages competitive pricing, creates jobs, stimulates technological advances, and promotes ever-increasing knowledge and skills. It can't be denied, however, that trade, like any opportunity, involves risk, especially in today's highly complex, globally competitive marketplace.2

GLOBAL MARKETING IN THE TWENTY-FIRST CENTURY

The world is shrinking rapidly with the advent of faster communication, transportation, and financial flows. Products developed in one country—Gucci purses, Mont Blanc pens, McDonald's hamburgers, Japanese sushi, Pierre Cardin suits, German BMWs—are finding enthusiastic acceptance in other countries. We would not be surprised to hear about a German businessperson wearing an Italian suit and meeting an English friend at a Japanese restaurant and who later returns home to drink Russian vodka and watch Canada's *The Air Farce* on television.

International trade is booming. Since 1969, the number of multinational corporations in the world's 14 richest countries has more than tripled, from 7000 to 24 000. Experts predict that, by 2005, world exports of goods and services will reach 28 percent of world gross domestic product, up from only 9 percent 20 years ago. With $412 billion in exports of goods and services in 1999, Canada is one of the world's leading trading nations and the most export-oriented of the G–8 industrialized economies. In fact, one in three jobs in Canada is tied to trade. We export more, proportionally, than the United States or Japan. More than 43 percent of Canada's GDP is linked to trade. With the projected increase in exports, soon half of Canada's

International trade is booming. British Columbia's Blitz Design Corp. markets its mints to more than 15 countries around the world.

output will be sent overseas. Compare these figures with those of the United States, where international trade now accounts for a quarter of GDP. Although Canadian companies have long been criticized for depending excessively on the easily accessible U.S. market, more firms are broadening their trade horizons. Companies exporting to both the U.S. *and* other countries increased by 53 percent in 2000.[3]

True, many companies have been carrying on international activities for decades: Nortel, Bell, McCain, Bata, Coca-Cola, IBM, Kodak, Nestlé, Shell, Bayer, Nokia, Sony, and other companies are familiar to most consumers around the world. But global competition is intensifying. Foreign firms are expanding aggressively into new international markets, and domestic companies that never thought about foreign competitors suddenly find these competitors in their own backyards. The firm that stays at home to play it safe may not only lose its chance to enter other markets, but also risk losing its home market.

In North America, such names as Sony, Toyota, Nestlé, Norelco, Mercedes, and Panasonic have become household words. Products and services that appear to be domestic really are produced or owned by foreign companies: Bantam books, Cadbury chocolate, Baskin-Robbins ice cream, GE and RCA televisions, Firestone tires, Kiwi shoe polish, Lipton tea, Carnation milk, and Pillsbury products, to name a few. North America also has attracted huge foreign investments in such basic industries as steel, petroleum, tires, and chemicals, and in tourist and real estate ventures, illustrated by Japanese land purchases in British Columbia and California. Few North American industries are now safe from foreign competition.

In an era of free trade, firms must learn how to enter foreign markets and increase their global competitiveness. Many Canadian companies have been successful at international marketing: Fairmont Hotels, Nortel, Mosaid, Corel, IMAX, Bombardier, CAE, Labatt, Moosehead, Northern Reflections, Alcan, Magna International, Barrick Gold Corp., Nova Corp., Newbridge Networks, and Atco, to name a few. Order some French fries in Thailand, Russia, Costa Rica, Tunisia, Vietnam, or Syria, and chances are you will be biting into a product manufactured by McCain International Inc. of Florenceville, New Brunswick. But you don't have to be an industry giant to venture into overseas markets. Blitz Design Corp. of Langley, British Columbia, developed and markets sugar-free breath mints to more than 15 countries around the world. Its largest market is the United States, where it is among the top 10 in sales—not a bad accomplishment, considering it took on such giant brands as Breathsavers, Tic Tac, Certs, and Clorets.[4]

Canadian Export Development Corp.
www.edc-see.ca

Department of Foreign Affairs and International Trade
www.dfait-maeci.gc.ca

Many firms are still hesitant about testing foreign waters. However, the federal government and its "Team Canada" approach, the Canadian Export Development Corp., and the Department of Foreign Affairs and International Trade are helping Canadian businesses, both large and small, make inroads in overseas markets.

The longer companies delay taking steps toward internationalizing, the more they risk being shut out of growing markets in Western Europe, Eastern Europe, the Pacific Rim, and elsewhere. All companies first have to answer some basic questions: What market position should we try to establish in our country, in our economic region, and globally? Who will our global competitors be and what are their strategies and resources? Where should we produce or source our products? What strategic alliances should we form with other firms around the world?

Although the need for companies to go abroad is great, so are the risks. Companies that go global confront several major problems. High debt, inflation, and unemployment in many countries have resulted in highly unstable governments and currencies, which limits trade and exposes global firms to many risks. For example, in 1998 Russia created a global economic crisis when it devalued the ruble, effectively defaulting on its global debts. A more widespread Asian economic downturn had a far-reaching impact on Western firms with significant markets or investments there.

Governments are placing more regulations on foreign firms, such as requiring joint ownership with domestic partners, mandating the hiring of nationals, and limiting profits that can be taken from the country. Moreover, foreign governments often impose high tariffs or trade barriers to protect their own industries. Finally, corruption is an increasing problem: Officials in several countries often award business not to the best bidder but to the highest briber.

Still, companies selling in global industries have no choice but to internationalize their operations. A **global industry** is one in which the competitive positions of firms in given local or national markets are affected by their global positions. A **global firm** is one that, by operating in more than one country, gains marketing, production, R&D, and financial advantages that are not available to purely domestic competitors. The global company sees the world as one market. It minimizes the importance of national boundaries and raises capital, obtains materials and components, and manufactures and markets its goods wherever it can do the best job. Global firms gain advantages by planning, operating, and coordinating their activities worldwide. For example, Ford's "world truck" sports a cab made in Europe and a chassis built in Canada; it is assembled in Brazil and imported to the United States for sale. Otis Elevator gets its elevator-door systems from France, small geared parts from Spain, electronics from Germany, and special motor drives from Japan. It uses the United States only for systems integration.

Because firms around the world are going global at a rapid rate, domestic firms in global industries must act quickly before the window closes. This does not mean that small and medium-sized firms must operate in a dozen countries to succeed; these firms can practise global niching. In fact, companies marketing on the Internet may find themselves going global whether they intend it or not (see New Directions 15-1). But the world is shrinking, and every company operating in a global industry-whether large or small-must assess and establish its place in world markets.

As Figure 15-1 shows, a company faces six major decisions in international marketing. Each decision will be discussed in detail in this chapter.

Global industry An industry in which the strategic positions of competitors in given geographic or national markets are affected by their overall global positions.

Global firm A firm that, by operating in more than one country, gains R&D, production, marketing, and financial advantages that are not available to purely domestic competitors.

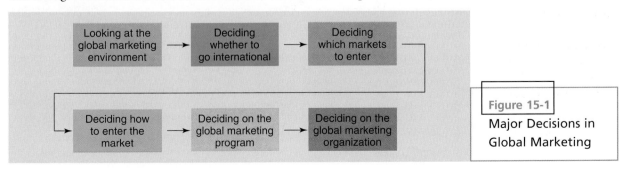

Figure 15-1

Major Decisions in Global Marketing

New Directions 15-1 >>   WWW: The World Is Your Oyster.com

As the Internet and online services attract more users around the world, many marketers are taking advantage of the Internet's global reach. Major global marketers already on the Net range from automakers (General Motors) to publishers who put their magazines online (Brunico Inc.), to retailers who put catalogues online (J. Crew), to global wine shippers (Virtual Vineyards), to compact disc marketers (CDNow), to banks (ING). All are taking advantage of cyberspace's making national boundaries trivial.

Companies that sell or promote on the Internet have the whole world for a market. For some of these companies, the global market has largely been a haphazard affair. They present their content in English for the North American market; and, if any international users stumble across it and end up buying something, so much the better.

Other marketers have made a strategic decision to enter the global market. They're using the Web and online services to reach new customers outside their home countries, support existing customers who reside abroad, and build global brand awareness.

Many companies have adapted their Web sites to provide country-specific content and services to their best potential international markets, often in the local language. For example, in an attempt to increase brand awareness in individual European markets, Reebok has launched a multilingual European Web site—available in English, French, Italian, Spanish, Greek, and Turkish. The site at **www.Europe.reebok.com** targets sports and fitness enthusiasts and includes local events in each market. Similarly, Dell Computer offers dozens of country-specific, local-language Web sites for such markets as France, Germany, Belgium, China, Japan, and Brunei.

For the most part, marketers have zeroed in on the countries or regions with the largest potential online populations. Europe and Japan are prime targets. Although European and Japanese online usage has lagged behind that in North America, it is catching up quickly. Online subscribers are expected to grow from 7 percent of Europe's population in 1998 to 13 percent in 2001. The Japanese Internet user population was expected to double by the year 2001, with e-commerce jumping from $2.5 billion in 1998 to $12.5 billion.

Despite encouraging e-commerce developments in Europe and Asia, Internet marketers sometimes overstate seemingly sure-fire global opportunities. The reality of the global Internet market depends on each country's economic, technical, cultural, political, and regional dynamics. Technological challenges abound. Although telecommunications channels, the backbone of the Internet, are ubiquitous in Canada and the United States, response times overseas can be dismal. Many countries remain technologically underdeveloped and have a low-income citizenry lacking PCs or even phone connections. Other countries have acceptable phone and PC penetration, but high subscription and connection costs sharply restrict such casual uses as surfing on the Internet. For example, in Europe, net subscriptions typically run $105 a month, more than triple North American rates. In the United Kingdom, connection rates can run over $5 per hour, with long-distance calling and data surcharges in rural areas running as high as $24 per hour.

In addition, the global marketer may run up against governmental or cultural restrictions. France, for instance, has laws against providing encrypted content. In Germany, a vendor can't accept payment via credit card until two weeks after an order has been sent. Privacy regulations also vary. Europe and Canada have strict codes limiting direct marketing firms from gathering certain types of data. Furthermore, underdeveloped banking systems limit credit card usage in many countries. The issue of who pays taxes and duties on global e-commerce is even murkier. Therefore, marketers outside North America sometimes have to find alternative marketing and collection approaches.

Businesses need to realize that the Web does not offer complete solutions for transacting global business—and it probably never will. Most companies will always find it difficult to complete a big business-to-business deal via e-mail. The Internet will not overcome customs red tape or local regulations regarding import or export of certain goods. The

named the 2000 Exporter of the Year by the Department of Foreign Affairs and International Trade, which has given the Canada Export Awards for the past 17 years to Canadian companies that demonstrate excellence in competing internationally. SMART uses the Internet to promote sales of its Canadian-made products to more than 50 countries. Visit its Web site and click on the "Where to buy" button, and you will find a list of SMART's international distributors.

SMART Technologies, a winner of the 2000 Canada Export Awards, uses its Web site to serve both domestic and international clients.

Web can't guarantee that goods will arrive in perfect condition. Despite the barriers, however, global Internet enterprise is growing rapidly. In fact, 83 percent of managers surveyed recently by consulting firm KPMG Peat Marwick said that e-commerce would be a major export vehicle beyond the year 2000. For companies that want to go global, the Internet and online services can represent an easy way to get started or to reinforce other efforts.

For larger companies, casting an international web is natural. For example, Hewlett-Packard uses a Web site to deal with its resellers Europe-wide, offering information in many languages. Nestlé's Web site links to company sites for Taiwan, Australia, Brazil, Chile, New Zealand, Switzerland, Spain, Germany, France, Japan, Sweden, Greece, and the United Kingdom. Texas Instruments' European Semiconductor group uses a "TI & Me" site to sell and support its signal processors, logic devices, and other chips across Europe.

But small companies can also market globally on the Web. Calgary's SMART Technologies Inc. was

Upscale retailer and cataloguer The Sharper Image now gets 25 percent of its online business from overseas customers. Online music marketer CDNow, which stumbled onto global markets almost by accident, now actively develops its global business. So get online and see if the world can be your oyster.

Sources: Peter Krasilovsky, "A Whole New World," *Marketing Tools Supplement, American Demographics,* May 1996, pp. 22–25; "2000 Canada Export Awards," *Canadian Business,* 5 February 2001, p. 61; Richard N. Miller, "The Year Ahead," *Direct Marketing,* January 1997, pp. 42–44; Jack Gee, "Parlez-Vous Inter-Net?" *Industry Week,* 21 April 1997, pp. 78–79; Michelle V. Rafter, "Multilingual Sites Give Companies Access to Global Revenue Sources," *Business Section, Chicago Tribune,* 11 May 1998, p. 9; "Reebok Targets Its New Web Site at Euro Markets," *Marketing,* 1 October 1998, p. 16; Shannon Oberndorf, "Europe Jumps Online," *Catalog Age,* June 1999, p. 10; Bill Spindle, "E-commerce (A Special Report)," *The Wall Street Journal,* 12 July 1999, p. R22; Erika Rasmusson, "E-commerce Around the World," *Sales and Marketing Management,* February 2000, p. 94.

LOOKING AT THE GLOBAL MARKETING ENVIRONMENT

Before deciding whether to operate internationally, a company must thoroughly understand the international marketing environment. That environment has changed a great deal over the past two decades, creating both new opportunities and new problems. The world economy has globalized. World trade and investment have grown rapidly, with many attractive markets opening up in Western and Eastern Europe, China, India, the Pacific Rim, Russia, and elsewhere. Global brands have grown in automobiles, food, clothing, electronics, and many other categories. The international financial system has become more complex and fragile, and North American companies face increasing trade barriers erected to protect domestic markets from outside competition.

The International Trade System

Tariff A tax levied by a government against certain imported products to either raise revenue or protect domestic firms.

A company looking abroad must first understand the international *trade system.* When selling to another country, the firm faces various trade restrictions. The most common is the **tariff**, which is a tax levied by a foreign government against certain imported products. The tariff may be designed either to raise revenue or to protect domestic firms. The exporter also may face a **quota**, which sets limits on the amount of goods the importing country will accept in certain product categories. The purpose of the quota is to conserve on foreign exchange and to protect local industry and employment. An **embargo**, or boycott, bans an import.

Quota A limit on the amount of goods that an importing country will accept in certain product categories to conserve on foreign exchange and to protect local industry and employment.

Firms may face **exchange controls**, which limit the amount of foreign exchange and the exchange rate against other currencies. They also may encounter **nontariff trade barriers,** such as biases against bids or restrictive product standards that go against North American product features. The Japanese have found a clever way to keep foreign manufacturers out of their domestic market: They plead "uniqueness." Japanese skin is different, the government argues, so foreign cosmetics companies must test their products in Japan before selling there. The Japanese say their stomachs are small and have room for only the *mikan,* the local tangerine, so imports of U.S. oranges are limited. Now the Japanese have come up with what may be the flakiest argument yet: Their snow is different, so ski equipment should be too.[5] At the same time, certain forces *help* trade between nations. Examples are the General Agreement on Tariffs and Trade and various regional free trade agreements.

Embargo A ban on the import of a certain product.

Exchange controls Government limits on the amount of its foreign exchange with other countries and on its exchange rate against other currencies.

Nontariff trade barriers Nonmonetary barriers to foreign products, such as biases against a foreign company's bids or product standards that go against a foreign company's product features.

The World Trade Organization and GATT The World Trade Organization (WTO) is a global organization that deals with the rules of trade between nations. As of January 2002, the WTO had 144 member countries that account for more than 90 percent of world trade. Other countries are negotiating membership. The WTO works to ensure that trade among the world's nations flows as smoothly and freely as possible. It administers trade agreements, provides a forum for trade negotiations, and handles trade disputes. The WTO was established on 1 January 1995 as the successor to the General Agreement on Tariffs and Trade (GATT), which had been in effect since 1948.

World Trade Organization www.wto.org

The GATT set up the basis for a multilateral trading system that was designed to promote world trade by reducing tariffs and other international trade barriers. Since the signing of GATT, world trade has grown significantly. Member nations have met in eight rounds of GATT negotiations, designed to reassess trade barriers and set new rules for international trade. The first seven rounds of negotiations reduced the average worldwide tariffs on manufactured goods from 45 to 5 percent. The most recently completed GATT negotiations, dubbed the Uruguay Round, dragged on for seven long years, from 1986 to 1994. The benefits of the Uruguay Round will be felt for many years, as the accord promotes long-term global trade growth. It reduced the world's remaining merchandise tariffs by 30 percent. The new agreement also extended GATT to cover trade in agriculture and a wide range of services and it toughened international protection of copyrights, patents, trademarks, and other intellectual property. The Uruguay Round established the WTO to enforce GATT rules.[6]

Negotiations to further liberalize world trade continued after the end of the Uruguay Round. In 1997, agreement was reached on further liberalization measures for trading telecommunication services, information technology products, banking, insurance, securities, and financial information. In 1998, WTO members agreed to study trade issues arising from global electronic commerce. In 2000, talks focused again on agriculture and services. The WTO also works with other organizations on a number of special issues. For example, in early 2001, it participated in a joint workshop with the World Health Organization to discuss how to improve poor countries' access to essential drugs.

Regional Free Trade Zones Some countries have formed *free trade zones* or **economic communities**—groups of nations organized to work toward common goals in the regulation of international trade. One community is the *European Union (EU)*. Formed in 1957, the European Union—then called the Common Market—set out to create a single European market by reducing barriers to the free flow of products, services, finances, and labour among member countries and

Economic community A group of nations organized to work toward common goals in the regulation of international trade.

The Department of Foreign Affairs and International Trade and its trade commissioners help Canadian businesses penetrate world markets.

developing policies on trade with nonmember nations. Today, the European Union represents one of the world's single largest markets. Its 15 member countries—Belgium, Germany, France, Italy, Luxembourg, the Netherlands, Denmark, Ireland, the United Kingdom, Greece, Spain, Portugal, Austria, Finland, and Sweden—contain more than 376 million consumers and account for 20 percent of the world's exports. As more European nations seek admission, the EU could contain as many as 450 million people in 28 countries. The EU imports $15.6 billion of goods and services from Canada—4.71 percent of our export trade. However, we import almost twice as many goods and services from Europe as we export ($31.8 billion).

European unification offers tremendous trade opportunities for North America and other non-European firms. However, it also poses threats. Because of increased unification, European companies will grow bigger and more competitive. Perhaps an even greater concern is that lower barriers inside Europe will only create thicker outside walls. Some observers envision a "Fortress Europe" that heaps favours on firms from EU countries but hinders outsiders by imposing such obstacles as stiffer import quotas, local content requirements, and other nontariff barriers.

Progress toward European unification has been slow; many doubt that complete unification will ever be achieved. However, on 1 January 1999, 11 of the 15 member nations took a significant step toward unification by adopting the Euro as a common currency. In January 2001, Greece became the 12th member nation to adopt the Euro. Currencies of the individual countries with the exception of Britain were phased out gradually until 1 January 2002, when the Euro became the only currency. Adoption of the Euro will decrease much of the currency risk associated with doing business in Europe, making member countries with previously weak currencies more attractive markets. In addition, by removing currency conversion hurdles, the switch will likely increase cross-border trade and highlight differences in pricing and marketing from country to country.[7]

Even with the adoption of the Euro as a standard currency, from a marketing viewpoint, creating an economic community will not create a homogeneous market. As one international analyst suggests, "Even though you have fiscal harmonization, you can't go against 2000 years of tradition."[8] With 14 languages and distinctive national customs, it is unlikely that the EU will ever become one unified whole. Although economic and political boundaries may fall, social and cultural differences will remain, and companies marketing in Europe will face a daunting mass of local rules. Still, even if only partly successful, European unification will make a more efficient and competitive Europe a global force with which to reckon.[9]

In North America, the United States and Canada phased out trade barriers in 1989. In January 1994, the *North American Free Trade Agreement (NAFTA)* established a free trade zone among the United States, Mexico, and Canada. The agreement created a single market of 360 million people producing and consuming $10 trillion worth of goods and services. Within its first 15 years, NAFTA will eliminate all trade barrier and investment restrictions among the three countries.

Canada is also a member of APEC—the Asia-Pacific Economic Cooperation. The 21 member economies began their association in 1989. The other APEC members are Australia, Brunei, Chile, China, Hong Kong, Indonesia, Korea, Japan, Malaysia, Mexico, New Zealand, Peru, the Philippines, Papua New Guinea, Russia,

**NAFTA Secretariat
www.nafta-sec-alena.
org**

**APEC Secretariat
www.apecsec.org.sg**

Singapore, Taiwan, Thailand, the United States, and Vietnam. As part of Canada's celebration of the year of Asia-Pacific, these economies met in Vancouver in 1997. The association hopes to foster free trade in a region that now accounts for 45 percent of world trade. Although the more developed countries want to set a timeline for the implementation of tariff reductions, less developed countries, such as Indonesia, Malaysia, and Thailand, have been more cautious, fearing that such actions will harm industries just in their infancy.[10]

Other free trade areas are forming in Latin America. MERCOSUR links four charter members—Argentina, Brazil, Paraguay, and Uruguay—and associate members—Bolivia, Chile, and Peru. With a population of more than 200 million and a combined economy of over $1.5 trillion a year, these countries make up the largest trading bloc after NAFTA and the EU. There is talk of a free trade agreement between the EU and MERCOSUR.[11]

Although the recent trend toward free trade zones has caused great excitement and new market opportunities, it also raises some concerns. For example, many North American unions fear that NAFTA will lead to the further exodus of manufacturing jobs to Mexico, where wage rates are much lower than in Canada and the United States. Environmentalists also worry that companies that are unwilling to play by the strict environmental protection rules will relocate in Mexico where pollution regulation has been lax.

Whether conducting business in North America or venturing further afield, Canadian businesspeople must realize that each nation has unique features that must be understood. A nation's readiness for different products and services and its attractiveness as a market to foreign firms depend on its economic, politico-legal, ethical, and cultural environments.

Economic Environment

The international marketer must study each target country's economy. Two economic factors reflect the country's attractiveness as a market—the country's industrial structure and its income distribution. The country's *industrial structure* shapes its product and service needs, income levels, and employment levels. The four types of industrial structures are:

- *Subsistence economies.* In a subsistence economy, the vast majority of people engage in simple agriculture. They consume most of their output and barter the rest for simple goods and services. They offer few market opportunities.

- *Raw-material-exporting economies.* These economies are rich in one or more natural resources but poor in other ways. Much of their revenue comes from exporting resources. Examples are Chile (tin and copper), Zaire (copper, cobalt, and coffee), and Saudi Arabia (oil). Canada's "old economy" is as a major exporter of raw materials of softwood lumber, paper, petroleum, coal, and fish. These countries are good markets for large equipment, tools and supplies, and trucks. If there are many foreign residents and a wealthy upper class, they are also a market for luxury goods. For example, the Canadian firm Crystal Fountains has received orders of about $1 million from the United Arab Emirates, where people are willing to pay $150 000 to $200 000 for fountains.

- *Industrializing economies.* In an industrializing economy, manufacturing accounts for 10 to 20 percent of the country's economy. Examples include Egypt, the Philippines, India, and Brazil. As manufacturing increases, the country needs more imports of raw textile materials, steel, and heavy machinery, and fewer imports of finished textiles, paper products, and automobiles.

- *Industrial economies.* Industrial economies are major exporters of manufactured goods and investment funds. They trade goods among themselves and also export them to other types of economies for raw materials and semifinished goods. The varied manufacturing activities of these industrial nations and their large middle class make them rich markets for all sorts of goods. Canada's "new economy" is made up of manufacturing, service, and high-tech firms, which export a large portion of their output. The transportation-equipment industry (autos, railway equipment, aircraft) accounts for 26 percent of our exports. The communications sector, led by such giants as Nortel and BCE, also accounts for much of our international trade. Canada is also an exporter of many services. SNC-Lavalin, located in Montreal, is one of the world's largest consulting engineering firms. Our banks are heavily involved in international markets. When Canadian Pacific Hotels & Resorts bought a majority interest in the U.S.-based Fairmont Hotels chain in 1999, it became a dominant player in the luxury hotel market, with 36 properties and more than 18 000 rooms in the United States, Canada, Mexico, and the Caribbean.[12]

The second economic factor is the country's *income distribution.* Countries with subsistence economies may consist mostly of households with very low family incomes. In contrast, industrialized nations may have low-, medium-, and high-income households. Still other countries may have only households with either very low or very high incomes. However, marketers must not form stereotypes based on average income alone. Even people in low-income countries may find ways to buy products that are important to them:[13]

Philosophy professor Nina Gladziuk thinks carefully before shelling out her hard-earned zlotys for Poland's dazzling array of consumer goods. But spend she certainly does. Although she earns just $750 a month from two academic jobs, Gladziuk, 41, enjoys making purchases: They are changing her lifestyle after years of deprivation under communism. In the past year, she has furnished a new apartment in a popular neighborhood near Warsaw's Kabaty Forest, splurged on foreign-made beauty products, and spent a weekend in Paris before attending a seminar financed by her university....Meet Central Europe's fast-rising consumer class. From white-collar workers like Gladziuk to factory workers in Budapest to hip young professionals in Prague, incomes are rising and confidence surging as a result of four years of economic growth. In the region's leading economies—the Czech Republic, Hungary, and Poland—the new class of buyers is growing not only in numbers but also in sophistication....In Hungary, ad agency Young & Rubicam labels 11 percent of the country as "aspirers," with dreams of the good life and buying habits to match. Nearly one-third of all Czechs, Hungarians, and Poles—some 17 million people—

Developing economies: In Central Europe, companies are catering to the new class of buyers who are eager to snatch up everything from Western consumer goods to high fashions and the latest cellular phones.

are under 30 years old, eager to snap up everything from the latest fashions to compact discs.

Thus, international marketers face many challenges in understanding how the economic environment affects decisions about which global markets to enter and how.

Politico-Legal and Environment

Nations differ greatly in their politico-legal environments. A company must consider at least four politico-legal factors in deciding whether to do business in a given country: attitudes toward international buying, government bureaucracy, political stability, and monetary regulations.

In their attitudes toward international buying, some nations are quite receptive to foreign firms, but others are quite hostile. For example, India has import quotas, currency restrictions, and limits on the percentage of the management team that can be non-nationals in foreign firms. As a result, many North American companies left India. In contrast, such neighbouring Asian countries as Singapore, Thailand, Malaysia, and the Philippines woo foreign investors and shower them with incentives and favourable operating conditions.

A second factor is *government bureaucracy*—the extent to which the host government runs an efficient system for helping foreign companies: efficient customs handling, good market information, and other factors that support conducting business. North Americans are often shocked by demands for bribes to make these trade barriers disappear even though such demands are illegal and unethical. These issues are discussed in New Directions 15-2.

Political stability is another issue. Governments change hands, sometimes violently. Even without a change, a government may decide to respond to new popular feelings. The foreign company's property may be taken, its currency holdings may be blocked, or import quotas or new duties may be set. International marketers may find it profitable to do business in an unstable country, but the unsteady situation will affect how they handle business and financial matters.

New Directions 15-2 >>   The Grey Zone: International Marketing Ethics

Well-known business ethics scholar Richard De George wrote: "Business ethics is as national, international, or global as business itself, and no arbitrary geographical boundaries limit it." International business ethics is increasingly becoming front-page news, but the topic isn't a new one or even one born in modern times. For centuries, trade has brought people and cultures into direct conflict. The exploitation of numerous countries in the colonial periods of France, England, and Spain illustrate extreme cases of unethical marketing practice. Exchanges in which worthless beads were traded for gold and silver make some scandals presented in the modern press pale in comparison.

Marketing has long been associated with questions of ethics, both nationally and internationally. Marketing and ethics are closely aligned since the element of trust is inherent in the creation of the ongoing exchange relationships that lie at the heart of marketing. It cannot be denied that firms operating in international markets face a growing number of ethical issues. Business is increasingly global in nature: Firms operate in multiple national markets and they seek to raise capital from multiple international sources. Moreover, since foreign market growth outpaced North American market growth, the mandate for understanding how to manage international ethical behaviour is growing.

Decisions that marketers must make while working within the context of any corporation are complex and are often fraught with conflicts of values. Such conflicts are at the heart of many ethical dilemmas even in national business enterprises. They become seemingly insurmountable problems in the arena of international businesses, where people from different cultures, political systems, economies, value systems, and ethical standards must interact. In other words, ethical concerns involve more than black-and-white decisions; they involve many shades of grey, where the values of people from one country conflict with those from another. For example, in some countries, giving and receiving gifts is customary at the close of business transactions. However, for many North American firms, acceptance of gifts, other than mere tokens of appreciation such as chocolates or flowers, is viewed as unethical and may even be illegal.

Ethical issues arise in all the functional areas of international business and centre on such business strategy questions as market-entry decisions, bribery and gift giving, contract negotiations, human resource issues, crisis management situations, product policy, advertising practices, pricing and transfer pricing, information systems management and privacy, grey markets, environmental concerns, accounting, finance and taxation, and production. Many of these areas are of specific concern to marketers. International advertising, for example, often raises ethical concerns. Although many European countries use nudity and sexual innuendo in their advertising, some North Americans find this offensive. In some countries, such as India, even showing people kissing is objectionable.

Offering certain products for sale in some countries has also raised ethical criticism. North American companies have been criticized for marketing harmful chemicals overseas, chemicals that are banned from use in their home markets. Avon has been criticized for selling cosmetics to people in countries where many people cannot afford enough food. Even though a product itself may not be inherently harmful, ethical criticism has been directed at companies that did not take measures to prevent harm arising to consumers who incorrectly used products (like baby formula, drugs, or pesticides) because of high rates of illiteracy and inability to understand instructions. There are also ethical issues associated with packaging in international markets. In some countries, such as Germany, manufacturers must recycle all packaging. In others, because of a lack of disposal facilities, packaging adds to pollution problems.

Pricing raises yet another set of ethical concerns. Sometimes, higher prices must be charged due to the increased costs of marketing overseas, but when overly high prices are levied just because a firm has a monopoly in a foreign country, ethical questions have to be asked. Ethical criticism has been levied at firms for their refusal to send female sales representatives or managers into countries with adverse gender stereotypes even though this hampers women's chances for advancement or higher earnings.

Bribery is always a thorny issue in international markets. Although it is undeniable that in some countries it is viewed as a "normal" way of doing business, this is not universally the case. Marketers should be aware that in most countries, bribery is an illegal practice. And because North Americans hold the stereotypical belief that bribes are expected overseas, we often make the mistake of offering such a payment when we perceive the slightest hesitation in signing a business deal. Rather than expecting a bribe, the foreign official may just be risk averse or want more information. The offering of a bribe, in these cases, will not only cause offence but will often terminate the relationship.

When discussing international business ethics, North Americans believe that we take the moral highroad. We've all read reports of companies being blocked from doing business in South America because of rigged bidding systems, or losing sales in China or Korea because firms cannot legally pay the bribes necessary to get the business. However, we have to be aware that some countries may have higher moral standards than we do. For example, one survey showed that fewer Japanese executives will cheat on their expense sheets than will a comparable group of North American executives. Other surveys of Canadian businesspeople have shown that most ethical problems arise not in doing business in exotic locales, but rather in dealing with our closest neighbour, the United States. Although this may be because we do more business with the United States than with any other country, problems such as industrial espionage, product safety concerns, sales practices, and hiring practices have been areas of growing ethical concern.

Despite the number of ethical issues marketers face, they often have few guidelines to help them come to terms with those issues. International marketers must be aware, however, that they have multiple responsibilities to the firms and their customers. They must avoid knowingly harming any of their constituents. They must sell safe products, ensure truthful advertising, and charge fair prices. As a minimum, marketers working for Canadian companies must abide by the laws of the countries in which they operate. However, being an ethical marketer often means going beyond the mere provisions of a legal system. Marketers also must consider what is right or wrong. Such considerations involve respecting the human rights of people, no matter what country they reside in. It involves avoiding the exploitation of individuals or their environment.

Many companies, such as Imperial Oil and Warner-Lambert, have developed codes of ethics to guide their employees' decisions. A 1995 survey of the CEOs of the top 500 companies in Canada revealed that 80 percent of these firms had codes of ethics. Many of these firms require that the principles outlined in the code be applied wherever the firm is operating. In other words, the rules that apply to conducting business in Canada also apply to subsidiaries of the business operating overseas.

In Canada, top levels of management are responsible for setting ethics policy and ensuring its implementation throughout the firm. Leading scholars in the field of marketing ethics emphasize that planning for ethical behaviour must begin at the same time as the rest of the strategic international market planning effort. Ethics cannot be an afterthought. This type of planning includes making such decisions as which international markets to enter, since some areas are known for their inherent ethical challenges. For example, does the firm want to enter markets dominated by totalitarian and military regimes, or those known for their record of human rights violations or ongoing environmental damage? Other questions include what types of products to market. The marketing of pesticides, tobacco, liquor, and pharmaceuticals, for example, all have unique ethical questions associated with them.

In addition to having a code of ethics, a firm must actively train its employees to be more sensitive to ethical issues, especially as it sends them overseas. Although fewer than 40 percent of firms offer ethics training, surveys indicate that employees want this type of training, that it has a positive effect in reducing unethical behaviour, and that it heightens ethical issue recognition and sensitivity.

In the end, although international marketing can be one of the most exciting and rewarding areas of the profession, be aware that it also presents some of the most difficult ethical problems and issues.

Source: This material is based on Peggy Cunningham's article "Managing Marketing Ethics in International Business: Literature Review and Directions for Future Research," published in the Proceedings of the ASAC Conference, Windsor, June 1995.

Finally, companies must consider a country's *monetary regulations*. Sellers want to take their profits in a currency of value to them. Ideally, the buyer can pay in the seller's currency or in other world currencies. Short of this, sellers may accept a blocked currency—one whose removal from the country is restricted by the buyer's government—if they can buy other goods in that country that they need themselves or can sell elsewhere for a needed currency. Besides currency limits, a changing exchange rate also creates high risks for the seller.

Cultural Environment

Each country has its own folkways, norms, and taboos. The seller must examine the way consumers in different countries think about and use certain products before planning a marketing program. There are often surprises. For example, the average French man uses almost twice as many cosmetics and beauty aids as his wife. The Germans and the French eat more packaged, branded spaghetti than do Italians. Italian children like to eat chocolate bars between slices of bread as a snack. Japanese people will not eat chocolate and peanuts together because they believe that it will cause nose bleeds. Companies that ignore such differences can make some very expensive and embarrassing mistakes:[14]

McDonald's and Coca-Cola managed to offend the entire Muslim world by putting the Saudi Arabian flag on their packaging. The flag's design includes a

Overlooking cultural differences can result in embarrassing mistakes. When Muslims objected to a stylized "Air" logo on Nike shoes that resembled "Allah" in Arabic script, Nike apologized for the mistake and pulled the shoes from distribution.

passage from the Koran (the sacred text of Islam), and Muslims feel very strongly that their Holy Writ should never be wadded up and tossed in the garbage. Nike faced a similar situation in Arab countries when Muslims objected to a stylized "Air" logo on its shoes that resembled "Allah" in Arabic script. Nike apologized for the mistake and pulled the shoes from distribution.

Business norms and behaviour also vary among countries. Business executives need to be briefed on these factors before conducting business in another country. These are some examples of differing global business behaviour:

- South Americans like to sit or stand very close to each other when they talk business; in fact, almost nose to nose. The North American business executive tends to keep backing away as the South American moves closer. Both may end up being offended.

- In face-to-face communications, Japanese business executives rarely say no, leaving North Americans frustrated and not knowing where they stand. However, when North Americans come to the point quickly, Japanese business executives may find this behaviour pushy and offensive.

- In France, wholesalers don't want to promote a product. They ask their retailers what they want and deliver it. If a company builds its strategy around the French wholesaler's cooperation in promotions, it is likely to fail.

- When North American executives exchange business cards, each usually gives the other's card a cursory glance and stuffs it in a pocket for later reference. In Asia, however, executives dutifully study each other's cards during a greeting, carefully noting company affiliation and rank. They use both hands to give their card to the most important person first.

Therefore, marketers must study the cultural traditions, preferences, and behaviours of each country and region they want to enter. An understanding of key differences in consumer and distributor behaviour kept Vogue Pools, located in LaSalle, Quebec, from falling off the deep end:[15]

Vogue Pools sells backyard swimming pools-virtually the same products around the world. However, the firm realized that it needed very different product and distribution strategies to meet the needs of customers in different countries. For example, in Canada, 90 percent of pools are sold through specialized pool retailers, which offer their customers installation service. In Europe, however, just the opposite is true. Ninety percent of people buying pools do their own installation. Therefore, Vogue realized, these consumers would need help. Since Vogue representatives couldn't join buyers in their backyards to offer a helping hand, they did the next best thing. Pools were redesigned to simplify the installation process. In fact, Vogue took the "IKEA approach." Customers must still dig a hole, but they can use a single tool to assemble their Vogue pool and no longer need to use a confusing array of nuts and bolts. Differences in behaviour didn't stop with customers. Distributors had unique perspectives as well. Gilles Lebuis, VP of marketing, notes, "A distributor in France will know his market much better...than someone from Switzerland...." Thus, even though it might have been cheaper to use a single European distributor, Vogue chose different distributors for each country. It sells through major do-it-yourself chains in France and pool distributors in Belgium, Switzerland, Germany, and Austria. Sales have topped $11 million using these strategies, keeping Vogue stroking along.

DECIDING WHETHER TO GO INTERNATIONAL

Although many firms view themselves as local businesses serving their immediate communities, they must become aware of the globalization of competition even if they never plan to go overseas themselves. Too many companies have recognized the dangers too late and have gone out of business when faced with new competitors such as the category killers from the United States or abroad. Companies that operate in global industries, where their strategic positions in specific markets are affected strongly by their overall global positions, have no choice but to think and act globally. Thus, Nortel must organize globally if it is to gain purchasing, manufacturing, financial, and marketing advantages. Firms in a global industry must be able to compete worldwide if they are to succeed.

Several factors may draw a company into the international arena. Global competitors may attack the company's domestic market by offering better products or lower prices. The company may want to counterattack these competitors in their home markets to tie up their resources. Or it may discover foreign markets that present higher profit opportunities than the domestic market does. The company's domestic market may be shrinking, or the company may need a larger customer base to achieve economies of scale. Or it may want to reduce its dependence on any one market to reduce its risk. Finally, the company's customers may be expanding abroad and require international servicing.

Before going abroad, the company must weigh the risks and assess its ability to operate globally. Can the company learn to understand the preferences and buyer behaviour of consumers in other countries? Can it offer competitively attractive products? Will it be able to adapt to other countries' business cultures and deal effectively with foreign nationals? Do the company's managers have the necessary international experience? Has management considered the impact of regulations and the political environments of other countries?

Because of the risks and difficulties of entering international markets, most companies do not act until some situation or event thrusts them into the global arena. Someone—a domestic exporter, a foreign importer, a foreign government—may ask the company to sell abroad. Or the company may be saddled with overcapacity and must find additional markets for its goods.

DECIDING WHICH MARKETS TO ENTER

Before going abroad, the company must set its international *marketing objectives and policies*. First, it must decide what *volume* of foreign sales it wants. Most companies start small when they go abroad. Some plan to stay small, seeing international sales as a small part of their business. Other companies have bigger plans, seeing international business as equal to or even more important than their domestic business.

The company must choose *how many* countries it wants to market in. Generally, it makes sense to operate in fewer countries with deeper commitment and penetration in each. The Bulova Watch Company decided to operate in many international markets and expanded into more than 100 countries; unfortunately, it had spread itself too thin, made profits in only two countries, and lost around $55 million.

In contrast, although consumer-product company Amway is now breaking into markets at a furious pace, it is doing so only after decades of gradually building up its overseas presence. Known for its neighbour-to-neighbour direct-selling networks, Amway expanded into Australia in 1971, a country far away but similar to its North American market. Then, in the 1980s, Amway expanded into 10 more countries, and the pace increased rapidly from then on. By 1994, Amway was firmly established in 60 countries, including Hungary, Poland, and the Czech Republic. Following its substantial success in Japan, China, and other Asian countries, the company entered India in 1998. International proceeds account for more than 70 percent of the company's overall sales.[16]

Next, the company must decide on the *types* of countries to enter. A country's attractiveness depends on the product, geographical factors, income and population, political climate, and other factors. The seller may prefer certain country groups or parts of the world. In recent years, many major markets have emerged, offering both substantial opportunities and daunting challenges.

After listing possible international markets, the company must screen and rank each one. Consider this example:[17]

Many mass marketers dream of selling to China's more than 1.3 billion people. For example, Colgate is waging a pitched battle in China, seeking control of the world's largest toothpaste market. Yet, this country of infrequent brushers offers great potential. Only 20 percent of China's rural dwellers brush daily, so Colgate and its competitors are aggressively pursuing promotional and educational programs, from massive ad campaigns to visits to local schools to sponsoring oral care research. Through such efforts, in this $350 million market dominated by local brands, Colgate has expanded its market share from seven percent in 1995 to 24 percent today.

Colgate's decision to enter the Chinese market seems straightforward: China is a huge market without established competition. Given the low rate of brushing, this already huge market can grow even larger. Yet we still can question whether market size *alone* is reason enough for selecting China. Colgate must also consider other factors. Will the Chinese government remain stable and supportive? Does China provide for the production and distribution technologies needed to produce and market Colgate's products profitably? Will Colgate be able to overcome cultural barriers and convince Chinese consumers to brush their teeth regularly? Can Colgate compete effectively with dozens of local competitors? Colgate's current success in China suggests that it could answer yes to all of these questions. Still, the company's future in China is filled with uncertainties.

A company should rank possible global markets on several factors, including market size, market growth, cost of doing business, competitive advantage, and risk level. It can use indicators like those shown in Table 15-1 to determine the potential of each market, and then decide which ones offer the greatest long-run return on investment.

General Electric's appliance division sells more than 12 million appliances each year in 150 world markets under the GE Profile, GE, Hotpoint, and RCA brand names. This experienced global marketer uses what it calls a "smart bomb" strategy for selecting global markets to enter. GE Appliances' executives examine each potential country in detail, measuring factors such as strength of local competitors, market growth potential, and availability of skilled labour. Then they target only markets in which they can earn more than 20 percent on their investment. The goal: "To generate the best returns possible on the smallest investment possible." Once targets are selected, GE Appliances zeros in with marketing smart bombs—products and programs tailored to yield the best performance in each market. Because of this strategy, GE is trouncing competitors Whirlpool and Maytag in Asian markets.[18]

Table 15-1 Indicators of Market Potential

1. **Demographic characteristics**
   Size of population
   Rate of population growth
   Degree of urbanization
   Population density
   Age structure and composition of the population
2. **Geographic characteristics**
   Physical size of a country
   Topographical characteristics
   Climate conditions
3. **Economic factors**
   GNP per capita
   Income distribution
   Rate of growth of GNP
   Ratio of investment to GNP
4. **Technological factors**
   Level of technological skill
   Existing production technology
   Existing consumption technology
   Education levels
5. **Sociocultural factors**
   Dominant values
   Lifestyle patterns
   Ethnic groups
   Linguistic fragmentation
6. **National goals and plans**
   Industry priorities
   Infrastructure investment plans

Source: Susan P. Douglas, C. Samuel Craig, and Warren Keegan, "Approaches to assessing international marketing opportunities for small and medium-sized businesses," *Columbia Journal of World Business,* Fall 1982:26–32, © 1982, 1999,Columbia Journal of World Business, reprinted with permission. Also see Tamer S. Cavusil, "Measuring the Potential of Emerging Markets: An Indexing Approach," *Business Horizons,* January–February 1997, pp. 87–91.

Slow down, stretch your legs, and think for a minute about the difficulties of assessing and selecting international markets.

- Assess China as a market for McDonald's. What factors make it attractive? What factors make it less than attractive?
- Assess Canada as a market for McDonald's. In what ways is Canada more attractive than China? In what ways is it less attractive?
- If McDonald's could operate in only one of these countries, which one would you choose and why?

DECIDING HOW TO ENTER THE MARKET

Once a company has decided to sell in a foreign country, it must determine the best mode of entry. Figure 15-2 shows three market-entry strategies—*exporting, joint venturing,* and *direct investment*—along with the options each one offers. As the figure shows, each succeeding strategy involves more commitment and risk, but also more control and potential profits.

Exporting

The simplest way to enter a foreign market is through **exporting**. The company can passively export its surpluses periodically, or it can make an active commitment to expand exports to a particular market. In either case, the company produces all its goods in its home country, possibly modifying them for the export market. Exporting involves the least change in the company's product lines, organization, investments, or mission.

Companies typically start with *indirect exporting,* working through independent international marketing intermediaries. Indirect exporting involves less investment because the firm does not require an overseas sales force or set of contacts. It also involves less risk. International marketing intermediaries—domestic-based export merchants or agents, cooperative organizations, and export-management companies—bring know-how and services to the relationship, so the seller normally makes fewer mistakes.

Sellers may eventually move into *direct exporting* and handle their own exports. The investment and risk are somewhat greater in this strategy, but so is the potential return. A company can conduct direct exporting in several ways. It can set up a

Exporting Entering a foreign market by sending products and selling them through international marketing intermediaries (indirect exporting) or through the company's own department, branch, or sales representatives or agents (direct exporting).

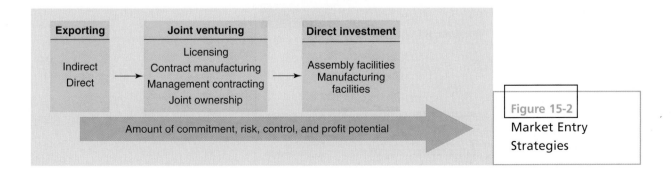

Exporting	Joint venturing	Direct investment
Indirect Direct	Licensing Contract manufacturing Management contracting Joint ownership	Assembly facilities Manufacturing facilities

Amount of commitment, risk, control, and profit potential →

Figure 15-2

Market Entry Strategies

domestic export department that carries out export activities. It can set up an overseas sales branch that handles sales, distribution, and perhaps promotion; the sales branch gives the seller more presence and program control in the foreign market and often serves as a display centre and customer service centre. The company also can send home-based salespeople abroad at certain times to find business. Finally, the company can do its exporting either through foreign-based distributors who buy and own the goods or through foreign-based agents who sell the goods on behalf of the company.

Joint Venturing

Joint venturing Entering foreign markets by joining with foreign companies to produce or market a product or service.

A second method of entering a foreign market is **joint venturing**—joining with domestic or foreign companies to produce or market products or services. Joint venturing differs from exporting in that the company joins with a partner to manufacture or market abroad. It differs from direct investment in that an association is formed with someone in the foreign country. The four types of joint ventures are licensing, contract manufacturing, management contracting, and joint ownership.

Licensing A method of entering a foreign market in which the company enters into an agreement with a licensee in the foreign market, offering the right to use a manufacturing process, trademark, patent, trade secret, or other item of value for a fee or royalty.

Licensing   **Licensing** is a simple way for a manufacturer to enter international marketing. The company forms an agreement with a licensee in the foreign market. For a fee or royalty, the licensee buys the right to use the company's manufacturing process, trademark, patent, trade secret, or other item of value. The company gains entry into the market at little risk; the licensee gains production expertise or a well-known product or name without having to start from scratch.

Coca-Cola markets internationally by licensing bottlers around the world and supplying them with the syrup needed to produce the product. Molson Breweries ditched its longtime partner, Anheuser-Busch, and licensed its beers to Coors. Tokyo Disneyland is owned and operated by Oriental Land Company under licence

Licensing: Tokyo Disneyland is owned and operated by Oriental Land Company under licence from the Walt Disney Company.

from the Walt Disney Company: The 45-year licence gives Disney licensing fees plus 10 percent of admissions and 5 percent of food and merchandise sales. And in an effort to bring online retail investing to people abroad, online brokerage E*Trade has launched E*Trade-branded Web sites outside North America, initially forming licensing agreements and launching sites in Australia, New Zealand, France, and Scandinavia. In addition, E*Trade established joint ventures and launched Web sites in the United Kingdom and Japan.[19]

Licensing has potential disadvantages, however. The firm has less control over the licensee than it would over its own production facilities. If the licensee is very successful, the firm has given up these profits, and when the contract ends, it may find it has created a competitor.

Contract Manufacturing With **contract manufacturing**, the company contracts with manufacturers in the foreign market to produce its product or provide its service. Sears used this method in opening up department stores in Mexico and Spain, where it found qualified local manufacturers to produce many of the products it sells. The drawbacks of contract manufacturing are the decreased control over the manufacturing process and the loss of potential profits on manufacturing. The benefits are the chance to start faster, with less risk, and the later opportunity either to form a partnership with or to buy out the local manufacturer.

Contract manufacturing A joint venture in which a company contracts with manufacturers in a foreign market to produce the product.

Management Contracting Under **management contracting**, the domestic firm supplies management expertise to a foreign company that supplies the capital. The domestic firm exports management services rather than products. Canada's 2000 trade mission to Russia resulted several management contracts, including the $220-million deal signed between Moscow-based Aeroflot and Montreal-based engineering giant SNC-Lavalin to build a rapid transit system linking Sheremetyevo Airport with downtown Moscow.[20]

Management contracting A joint venture in which the domestic firm supplies the management expertise to a foreign company that supplies the capital; the domestic firm exports management services rather than products.

Management contracting is a low-risk method of getting into a foreign market, and it yields income from the beginning. The arrangement is even more attractive if the contracting firm has an option to buy some share in the managed company later on. The arrangement is not sensible, however, if the company can put its scarce management talent to better uses or if it can make greater profits by undertaking the whole venture. Management contracting also prevents the company from setting up its own operations for a time.

Joint Ownership **Joint ownership** ventures consist of one company joining forces with foreign investors to create a local business in which they share ownership and control. A company can buy an interest in a local firm, or the two parties can form a new business venture. Magna International, the Canadian auto parts manufacturer, acquired much of U.K. firm Marley PLC to expand its business into the European Union.[21] Joint ownership may be needed for economic or political reasons. The firm may lack the financial, physical, or managerial resources to undertake the venture alone, or a foreign government may require joint ownership as a condition for entry.

Joint ownership A joint venture in which a company joins investors in a foreign market to create a local business in which the company shares joint ownership and control.

Joint ownership has drawbacks. The partners may disagree over investment, marketing, or other policies. Whereas many Canadian firms like to reinvest earnings for growth, local firms often like to take out these earnings; whereas Canadian firms emphasize the role of marketing, local investors may rely on selling.

Direct Investment

Direct investment
Entering a foreign market by developing foreign-based assembly or manufacturing facilities.

The greatest involvement in a foreign market comes through **direct investment**— the development of foreign-based assembly or manufacturing facilities. If a company has gained experience in exporting and if the foreign market is large enough, foreign production facilities offer many advantages. The firm may have lower costs in the form of cheaper labour or raw materials, foreign government investment incentives, and freight savings. The firm may improve its image in the host country because it creates jobs. Generally, a firm develops a deeper relationship with government, customers, local suppliers, and distributors, allowing it to better adapt its products to the local market. Finally, the firm keeps full control over the investment and can, therefore, develop manufacturing and marketing policies that serve its long-term international objectives.

The main disadvantage of direct investment is the many risks: restricted or devalued currencies, falling markets, or government takeovers. In some cases, a firm has no choice but to accept these risks if it wants to operate in the host country. These lessons were very clear when Toronto-based Bata Shoes decided to return to its Czech homeland and begin operations through the route of direct investment. The route, however, wasn't an easy one. Negotiations with government officials to reestablish the family shoe business took years of wrangling. Legal and political hurdles represented only half the battle, as marketing manager Jeanne Milne quickly learned. She faced problems ranging from lack of customer research to redesigning window displays. She discovered that offering sales didn't work since consumers in the Czech Republic equate discounts with inferior quality. Service providers had to be trained since providing service had become a foreign concept. As one Czech employee complained, "Why should I smile at customers? They don't smile at me." Even customers had to be reeducated. When employees went to the stockroom to search for correct sizes, customers followed them, believing that shoe clerks were going elsewhere to avoid serving them. The struggle has been worth it. Bata is held up as an exemplar of one of the few truly successful privatization efforts in Eastern Europe.

DECIDING ON THE GLOBAL MARKETING PROGRAM

Standardized marketing mix An international marketing strategy for using basically the same product, advertising, distribution channels, and other elements of the marketing mix in all of the company's international markets.

Adapted marketing mix
An international marketing strategy for adjusting the marketing mix elements to each international target market, bearing more costs but hoping for a larger market share and return.

Companies that operate in one or more foreign markets must decide how much, if at all, to adapt their marketing mixes to local conditions. At one extreme, some global companies use a **standardized marketing mix**, primarily selling the same products and using the same marketing approaches worldwide. At the other extreme, some companies use an **adapted marketing mix**, adjusting the marketing mix elements to each target market, bearing more costs but hoping for a larger market share and return.

How does a firm choose whether to adapt or standardize the marketing mix? The marketing concept holds that marketing programs will be more effective if tailored to the unique needs of each targeted customer group. If this concept applies within a country, it should apply even more in international markets. Consumers in different countries have widely varied cultural backgrounds, needs and wants, spending power, product preferences, and shopping patterns. Because these differences are hard to change, most marketers adapt their products, prices, channels, and promotions to fit consumer desires in each country.

However, some global marketers are bothered by what they see as too much adaptation, which raises costs and dilutes global brand power. As a result, many companies have created so-called world brands—more or less the same product sold the same way to all consumers worldwide. Marketers at these companies believe that advances in communication, transportation, and travel are turning the world into a common marketplace. These marketers claim that people around the world want the same products and lifestyles. Despite what consumers say they want, all consumers want good products at low prices.

Such arguments ring true. The development of the Internet, the rapid spread of cable and satellite television around the world, and the creation of telecommunications networks linking previously remote places have all made the world a smaller place. American TV programming beamed into homes in the developing world has sparked a convergence of consumer appetites, particularly among youth. One economist calls these emerging consumers the "global MTV generation": "They prefer Coke to tea, Nikes to sandals, Chicken McNuggets to rice, and credit cards to cash," he says.[22] Fashion trends spread almost instantly, propelled by TV and Internet chat groups. Around the world, news and comment on almost any topic or product is available at the click of a mouse or twist of a dial. The resulting convergence of needs and wants has created global markets for standardized products, particularly among the young middle class.

Proponents of global standardization claim that international marketers should adapt products and marketing programs only when local wants cannot be changed or avoided. Standardization results in lower production, distribution, marketing, and management costs, and thus lets the company offer consumers higher quality and more reliable products at lower prices. In fact, some companies have successfully marketed global products formats—for example, Coca-Cola soft drinks, McDonald's hamburgers, Black & Decker tools, and Sony Walkmans.

However, even for these "global" brands, companies make some adaptations. Moreover, the assertion that global standardization leads to lower costs and prices, causing more goods to be snapped up by price-sensitive consumers, is questionable. Consider these cases in which the incremental revenues from adapting products far exceeded the incremental costs:[23]

Mattel Toys had sold its Barbie doll successfully in dozens of countries without modification. But in Japan, it did not sell well. Takara, Mattel's Japanese licensee, surveyed eighth-grade Japanese girls and their parents and found that they thought the doll's breasts were too big and that its legs were too long. Mattel, however, was reluctant to modify the doll because this would require additional production, packaging, and advertising costs. Finally, Takara won out, and Mattel made a special Japanese Barbie. Within two years, Takara had sold more than two million of the modified dolls.

Even MTV, with its largely global programming, has retrenched along more local lines. Pummeled by dozens of local music channels in Europe, such as Germany's Viva, Holland's The Music Factory, and Scandinavia's ZTV, MTV Europe has had to drop its pan-European programming, which featured a large amount of American and British pop along with local European favourites. In its place, the division created regional channels broadcast by four separate MTV stations—MTV: UK & Ireland, MTV: Northern Europe, MTV: Central Europe, and MTV: Southern Europe. Each of the four channels shows programs tailored to music tastes of its local market, along with more traditional pan-European pop selections. Within each region, MTV further subdivides its programming. For example, within the United Kingdom, MTV offers sister stations M2 and VH-1, along with three new digital channels: MTV Extra, MTV Base, and VH-1 Classic. Says the head of MTV Europe, "We hope to offer every MTV fan something he or she will like to watch any time of the day."

Which approach is best—global standardization or adaptation? Clearly, global standardization is not an all-or-nothing proposition but rather a matter of degree. Companies should look for more standardization to help keep down costs and prices and to build greater global brand power. But they must not replace long-run marketing thinking with short-run financial thinking. Although standardization saves money, marketers must make certain that they offer consumers in each country what they want.[24]

Many possibilities exist between the extremes of standardization and complete adaptation. For example, although Whirlpool ovens, refrigerators, clothes washers, and other major appliances share the same interiors worldwide, their outer styling and features are designed to meet the preferences of consumers in different countries. Coca-Cola sells virtually the same Coke beverage worldwide and pulls advertisements for specific markets from a common pool of ads designed to have cross-cultural appeal. However, Coca-Cola is less sweet or less carbonated in some countries. The company also sells a variety of other beverages created specifically for the taste buds of local markets and modifies its distribution channels according to local conditions.

Similarly, McDonald's uses the same basic operating formula in its restaurants around the world but adapts its menu to local tastes. For example, it uses chili sauce instead of ketchup on its hamburgers in Mexico. In India, where cows are considered sacred, McDonald's serves chicken, fish, vegetable burgers, and the Maharaja Mac—two all-mutton patties, special sauce, lettuce, cheese, pickles, onions on a sesame-seed bun. In Vienna, its restaurants include "McCafes," which offer coffee blended to local tastes, and in Korea, it sells roast pork on a bun with a garlicky soy sauce.[25]

Some international marketers suggest that companies should "think globally but act locally." They advocate a "glocal" strategy in which the firm standardizes certain core marketing elements and localizes others.[26] The corporate level gives strategic direction; local units focus on the individual consumer differences. They conclude: global marketing, yes; global standardization, not necessarily.

Marketing mix adaptation: In India, McDonald's serves chicken, fish, vegetable burgers, and the Maharaja Mac—two all-mutton patties, special sauce, lettuce, cheese, pickles, onions on a sesame-seed bun.

Product

Figure 15-3 shows the five strategies for adapting products and promotions to a foreign market.[27] We first discuss the three product strategies and then turn to the two promotion strategies.

Straight product extension is marketing a product in a foreign market without any change. Top management tells its marketing people: "Take the product as is and find customers for it." The first step, however, should be to find out whether foreign consumers use that product and what form they prefer.

Straight extension has been successful in some cases and disastrous in others. Coca-Cola, Kellogg cereals, Heineken beer, and Black & Decker tools are all sold successfully in about the same form around the world. But General Foods introduced its standard powdered Jell-O in the British market only to find that British consumers prefer a solid-wafer or cake form. Straight extension is tempting because it involves no additional product development costs, manufacturing changes, or new promotion. But it can be costly in the long run if products fail to satisfy foreign consumers.

Product adaptation involves changing the product to meet local conditions or wants. For example, Procter & Gamble's Vidal Sassoon shampoos contain a single

Straight product extension Marketing a product in a foreign market without any change.

Product adaptation Adapting a product to meet local conditions or wants in foreign markets.

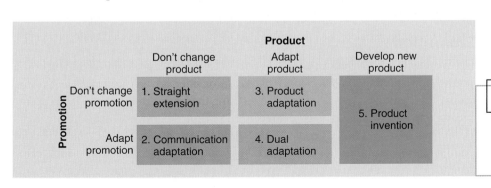

	Product		
Promotion	Don't change product	Adapt product	Develop new product
Don't change promotion	1. Straight extension	3. Product adaptation	5. Product invention
Adapt promotion	2. Communication adaptation	4. Dual adaptation	

Figure 15-3

Five International Product and Promotion Strategies

fragrance worldwide, but the amount of scent varies by country—less in Japan, where subtle scents are preferred, and more in Europe. Gerber serves the Japanese baby food fare that might turn the stomachs of many Western consumers: Local favourites include flounder and spinach stew, cod roe spaghetti, mugwort casserole, and sardines ground up in white radish sauce. Finnish cellular phone superstar Nokia customized its 6100 series phone for every major market. Developers built in rudimentary voice recognition for Asia where keyboards are a problem and raised the ring volume so the phone could be heard on crowded Asian streets.[28]

In some instances, products must also be adapted to local superstitions or spiritual beliefs. In Asia, the supernatural world often relates directly to sales. Hyatt Hotels' experience with feng shui is a good example:[29]

A practice widely followed in China, Hong Kong, and Singapore (and which has spread to Japan, Vietnam, and Korea), feng shui means "wind and water." Practitioners of feng shui, or geomancers, will recommend the most favorable conditions for any venture, particularly the placement of office buildings and the arrangement of desks, doors, and other items within. To have good feng shui, a building should face the water and be flanked by mountains. However, it should not block the view of the mountain spirits. The Hyatt Hotel in Singapore was designed without feng shui in mind and, as a result, had to be redesigned to boost business. Originally the front desk was parallel to the doors and road, and this was thought to lead to wealth flowing out. Furthermore, the doors were facing northwest, which easily let undesirable spirits in. The geomancer recommended design alterations so that wealth could be retained and undesirable spirits kept out.

Product invention
Creating new products or services for foreign markets.

The **product invention** strategy, creating something new for the foreign market, can take two forms. It may mean reintroducing earlier product forms that happen to be well adapted to the needs of a given country. For example, the National Cash Register Company reintroduced its crank-operated cash register at half the price of a modern cash register and sold large numbers in Asia, Latin America, and Spain. Or a company can create a new product to meet a need in another country. For example, an enormous need exists for low-cost, high-protein foods in less developed countries. Companies such as Maple Leaf Foods, McCain, Quaker Oats, Swift, and Monsanto are researching the nutrition needs of these countries, creating new foods, and developing advertising campaigns to gain product trial and acceptance. Product invention can be costly, but the payoffs are worthwhile.

Promotion

Companies can either adopt the same promotion strategy they use in their home market or change it for each local market. Consider advertising messages: Some global companies use a standardized advertising theme around the world. For example, to help communicate its global reach, IBM Global Services runs virtually identical "People Who Think. People Who Do. People Who Get It." ads in dozens of countries around the world. However, even in highly standardized promotion campaigns, some small changes may be required to adjust for language and minor cul-

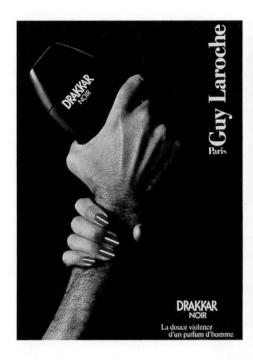

Some companies standardize their advertising around the world, adapting only to meet cultural differences. Guy Laroche uses similar ads in Europe (left) and Arab countries (right), but tones down the sensuality in the Arab version—the man is clothed and the woman barely touches him.

tural differences. For instance, when Heinz Pet Food introduced its 9 Lives cat food in Russia, it used its standardized advertising featuring Morris the Cat. It turns out, however, that Morris needed a makeover. Russian consumers prefer a fatter-looking spokeskitty—it's considered healthier—so Heinz put a beefier Morris on the package.[30]

Companies must also change colours sometimes to avoid taboos in some countries: Purple is associated with death in most of Latin America; white is a mourning colour in Japan; and green is associated with jungle sickness in Malaysia. Even names must be changed: In Sweden, Helene Curtis changed the name of its Every Night Shampoo to Every Day because Swedes usually wash their hair in the morning; Kellogg had to rename Bran Buds cereal in Sweden, where the name roughly translates as "burned farmer."

Other companies follow a strategy of **communication adaptation**, fully adapting their advertising messages to local markets. Kellogg ads in North America promote the taste and nutrition of Kellogg's cereals over competitors' brands. In France, where consumers drink little milk and eat little for breakfast, Kellogg's ads must convince consumers that cereals are a tasty and healthful breakfast.

Media also need to be adapted internationally because their availability varies from country to country. Television advertising time is very limited in Europe, for instance, ranging from four hours a day in France to none in Scandinavian countries. Advertisers must buy time months in advance, and they have little control over airtimes. Magazines also vary in effectiveness. For example, magazines are a major medium in Italy and a minor one in Austria. Newspapers are national in the United Kingdom but are only local in Spain.

The Institute of Canadian Advertising, which represents most of Canada's major agencies, launched a 1997 marketing initiative aimed at achieving better

Communication adaptation A global communication strategy of fully adapting advertising messages to local markets.

The Institute of Canadian Advertising
www.ica-ad.com

recognition of the strong track record and worldwide capabilities of Canadian agencies. In an effort that integrated public relations, ads in trade publications, direct marketing, a Web site, and the 126-page book *Canadian Advertising, Push the Boundaries,* the institute worked to convey the message that Canadian-produced advertising travels well beyond Canada's borders. The campaign featured work done by Canadian agencies such as a promotion for Visa ads that helped to reinforce the leadership position of the card in Canada and South America.[31]

Price

Companies face many problems in setting their international prices. For example, how might Black & Decker price its power tools globally? It could set a uniform price all around the world, but this amount would be too high a price in poor countries and not high enough in rich ones. It could charge what consumers in each country would bear, but this strategy ignores differences in the actual costs from country to country. Finally, the company could use a standard markup of its costs everywhere, but this approach might price Black & Decker out of the market in some countries where costs are high.

Regardless of how companies go about pricing their products, their foreign prices probably will be higher than their domestic prices. Makers of Feathercraft kayaks discovered the problem of price escalation as they market in Japan. Even though the kayaks cost the Japanese consumer twice as much as they do Canadian purchasers, the firm makes its lowest margins on Japanese sales. The problem results from Japan's multilevel distribution system. A kayak may have to pass through five intermediaries before reaching the consumer, and each intermediary gets a cut of the price pie.

Another problem involves setting a price for goods that a company ships to its foreign subsidiaries. If the company charges a foreign subsidiary too much, it may end up paying higher tariff duties even while paying lower income taxes in that country. If the company charges its subsidiary too little, it can be charged with *dumping*—charging less than the good costs or less than it charges in its home market. Harley-Davidson accused Honda and Kawasaki of dumping motorcycles on the U.S. market.[32] Canadian farmers have been charged with dumping wheat on the U.S. market. The U.S. International Trade Commission also ruled recently that Japan was dumping computer memory chips in the United States and laid stiff duties on future imports. Various governments are always watching for dumping abuses, and often force companies to set the price charged by other competitors for the same or similar products.

Recent economic and technological changes have had an impact on global pricing. In the European Union, the transition by 11 countries to a single currency, the Euro, will certainly reduce the amount of price differentiation. In 1998, for instance, a bottle of Gatorade cost 3.5 European currency units (ECU) in Germany but only about 0.9 in Spain. Once consumers recognize price differentiation by country, companies will be forced to harmonize prices throughout the countries that have adopted the single currency. The Internet also makes global price differences more obvious. When firms sell their wares over the Internet, customers can see how much products sell for in different countries. They may even be able to order a product directly from the company location or dealer offering the lowest price. This will force companies to standardize international pricing.[33]

Distribution Channels

The international company must take a **whole-channel view** of distributing products to final consumers. Figure 15-4 shows the three major links between the seller and the final buyer. The first link, the *seller's headquarters organization*, supervises the channels and is part of the channel itself. The second link, *channels between nations*, moves the products to the borders of the foreign nations. The third link, *channels within nations*, moves the products from their foreign entry point to the final consumers. Some North American manufacturers may think their job is done once the product leaves their hands, but they would do well to pay attention to its handling within foreign countries.

Channels of distribution within countries vary greatly from nation to nation. First, there are the large differences in the *numbers and types of intermediaries* serving each foreign market. For example, a Canadian company marketing in China must operate through a frustrating maze of state-controlled wholesalers and retailers. Chinese distributors often carry competitors' products and frequently refuse to share even basic sales and marketing information with their suppliers. Hustling for sales is an alien concept to Chinese distributors, who are used to selling all they can obtain. Working with or getting around this system sometimes requires substantial time and investment.

Whole-channel view
Designing international channels that take into account all the necessary links in distributing the seller's products to final buyers, including the seller's headquarters organization, channels between nations, and channels within nations.

Figure 15-4

Whole-Channel Concept for International Marketing

Seller → Seller's headquarters organization for international marketing → Channels between nations → Channels within nations → Final user or buyer

A "neighbourhood committee" member sells Coke in Shanghai.

Another difference lies in the *size and character of retail units* abroad. Whereas large-scale retail chains dominate in North America, much retailing in other countries is done by many small independent retailers. In India, millions of retailers operate tiny shops or sell in open markets. Their markups are high, but the actual price is lowered through price haggling. Supermarkets could offer lower prices, but supermarkets are difficult to build and open because of many economic and cultural barriers. Incomes are low, and people who lack refrigeration prefer to shop daily for small amounts rather than weekly for large amounts. Packaging is not well developed because it would add too much to the cost. These factors have kept large-scale retailing from spreading rapidly in developing countries.

Slow down here and think again about McDonald's global marketing issues.

- To what extent can McDonald's standardize for the Chinese market? What marketing strategy and program elements can be similar to those used in the United States and other parts of the Western world? Which ones must be adapted? Be specific.
- To what extent can McDonald's standardize its products and programs for the Canadian market? What elements can be standardized and which must be adapted?

DECIDING ON THE GLOBAL MARKETING ORGANIZATION

Companies can manage their international marketing activities in at least three different ways. Most companies first organize an export department, then create an international division, and finally become a global organization.

Many companies become involved in several international markets and ventures. A company can export to one country, license to another, have a joint ownership venture in a third, and own a subsidiary in a fourth. Eventually, it will create an *international division* or subsidiary to handle all of its international activity.

Several firms have passed beyond the international division stage and become truly *global organizations*. They stop thinking of themselves as national marketers who sell abroad and start thinking of themselves as global marketers. The top corporate management and staff plan worldwide manufacturing facilities, marketing policies, financial flows, and logistical systems. The global operating units report directly to the chief executive or executive committee of the organization, not to the head of an international division. Executives are trained in worldwide operations, not just domestic *or* international. The company recruits management from many countries, buys components and supplies where they cost the least, and invests where the expected returns are greatest.

Consider the history of Nortel Networks, Canada's premium high-tech manufacturer. In the early 1970s, it sold most of its production to another member of the BCE family, Bell Canada. By the 1980s, with its state-of-the-art digital switching technology, it was making more than 50 percent of its sales to the United States, and 5 percent to other world markets. By 1994, however, 32 percent of Nortel's $8.9 billion in revenue came from global markets. Today, it operates in more than 150 countries and has offices and facilities in Canada, Europe, Asia-Pacific, the Caribbean and Latin America, the Middle East, Africa, and the United States.

Major companies must become more global if they hope to compete. As foreign companies successfully invade their domestic markets, companies must move more aggressively into foreign markets. They will have to change from companies that treat their international operations as secondary concerns to companies that view the entire world as a single borderless market.[34]

<< Looking Back < < < < < < < < <

Companies today can no longer afford to focus only on their domestic market, regardless of its size. Many industries are global, and firms that operate globally achieve lower costs and higher brand awareness. At the same time, global marketing is risky because of variable exchange rates, unstable governments, protectionist tariffs and trade barriers, and several other factors. Given the potential gains and risks of international marketing, companies need a systematic way to make their international marketing decisions.

1. Discuss how the international trade system, economic, politico-legal, and cultural environments affect a company's international marketing decisions.

A company must understand the global marketing environment, especially the international trade system. It must assess each foreign market's economic, politico-legal, and cultural characteristics. The company must then decide on the volume of international sales it wants, how many countries it wants to market in, and which specific markets it wants to enter. This last decision calls for weighing the probable rate of return on investment against the level of risk.

2. Describe three key approaches to entering international markets.

The company must decide how to enter each chosen market—whether through exporting, joint venturing, or direct investment. Many companies start as exporters, move to joint ventures, and finally make a direct investment in foreign markets. In exporting, the company enters a foreign market by sending and selling products through international marketing intermediaries (indirect exporting) or the company's own department, branch, or sales representative or agent (direct exporting). When establishing a joint venture, a company enters foreign markets by joining with foreign companies to produce or market a product or service. In licensing, the company enters a foreign market by contracting with a licensee in the foreign market, offering the right to use a manufacturing process, trademark, patent, trade secret, or other item of value for a fee or royalty.

3. Explain how companies adapt their marketing mixes for international markets.

Companies must decide how much their products, promotion, price, and channels should be adapted for each foreign market. At one extreme, some global companies use a standardized marketing mix worldwide. At the other, some use an adapted marketing mix, in which they adjust the marketing mix to each target market, bearing more costs but hoping for a larger market share and return.

4. Identify the three major forms of international marketing organization.

The company must develop an effective organization for international marketing. Most firms start with an export department and graduate to an international division. A few become global organizations, with worldwide marketing planned and managed by the top officers of the company. Global organizations view the entire world as a single, borderless market.

Navigating the Key Terms

Adapted marketing mix, **p. 622**

Communication adaptation, **p. 627**

Contract manufacturing, **p. 621**

Direct investment, **p. 622**

Economic community, **p. 607**

Embargo, **p. 606**

Exchange controls, **p. 606**

Exporting, **p. 619**

Global firm, **p. 603**

Global industry, **p. 603**

Joint ownership, **p. 621**

Joint venturing, **p. 620**

Licensing, **p. 620**

Management contracting, **p. 621**

Non-tariff trade barriers, **p. 606**

Product adaptation, **p. 625**

Product invention, **p. 626**

Quota, **p. 606**

Standardized marketing mix, **p. 622**

Straight product extension, **p. 625**

Tariff, **p. 606**

Whole-channel view, **p. 629**

Concept Check

Fill in the blanks and then check your answers.

1. A _____ is one that, by operating in more than one country, gains marketing, production, R&D, and financial advantages that are not available to purely domestic competitors. This type of firm sees the world as one market.

2. The most common trade restriction is the _____, which is a tax levied by a foreign government against certain imported products.

3. The purpose of a _____, as a form of trade restriction, is to conserve on foreign exchange and to protect local industry and employment.

4. The _____ treaty is a 50-year old treaty designed to promote world trade by reducing tariffs and other international trade barriers. The most recent meeting was the Uruguay Round.

5. The _____, as a form of an economic community, represents one of the world's single largest markets with 15 member countries, more than 374 million consumers, and 20 percent of the world's exports.

6. The four types of industrial structures are as follows: _____, _____, _____,

and industrial economies.

7. In _____, the company contracts with manufacturers in the foreign market to produce its product or provide its service.

8. Once a company has decided to sell in a foreign country, it must decide the best mode of entry. Its choices are _____, _____, and _____.

9. When a company pays a fee or royalty in order to use another company's manufacturing process, trademark, patent, trade secret, or other item of value, the company is using _____ as a means to enter an international market.

10. Coca-Cola uses the same product, pricing, communication, and distribution system worldwide. This is called a _____ marketing mix.

11. _____ involves changing the product to meet local conditions or wants.

12. Problems often occur in international marketing when a company ships to its foreign subsidiaries. _____ occurs when a company either charges less than its costs or less than it charges in its home market.

Concept Check Answers: 1. global firm; 2. tariff; 3. quota; 4. General Agreement on Tariffs and Trade (GATT); 5. European Union; 6. subsistence economies, raw material exporting economies, industrializing economies; 7. contract manufacturing; 8. exporting, joint venturing, direct investment; 9. licensing; 10. standardized; 11. product adaptation; 12. dumping.

Discussing the Issues

1. When exporting goods to a foreign country, a marketer may face various trade restrictions. Discuss the effects that each of these restrictions might have on an exporter's marketing mix: (a) tariffs, (b) quotas, and (c) embargoes.

2. A country's industrial structure shapes its product and service needs, income levels, and employment levels. Discuss examples of countries exhibiting each of the major types of industrial structures.

3. Once a company has decided to sell in a foreign country, it must determine the best mode of entry. Assume that you are the marketing manager for Mountain Dew and must devise a plan for marketing your product in China. Pick a mode of entry, explain your marketing strategy, and comment on possible difficulties you might encounter.

4. "Dumping" leads to price savings to the consumer. Determine why governments make dumping illegal. What are the *disadvantages* to the consumer of dumping by foreign firms?

5. Which type of international marketing organization would you suggest for the following companies: (a) a new division of Beanie Babies sold by Ty (see **www.ty.com**) that intends to sell the stuffed animals exclusively online worldwide, (b) a European perfume firm that plans to expand into the United States, and (c) Daimler-Chrysler planning to sell its full line of products in the Middle East.

 **Mastering Marketing**

After examining the expansion strategies of CanGo, devise a plan where the company could expand into the international marketplace beyond any existing efforts. Choose at least one foreign market that would be a good candidate for your expansion strategy. Pick a mode of entry into that market. Discuss any difficulties that might be present in an attempt to enter this market. Evaluate your chances of success.

Check out the enclosed Video case CD-ROM, or our Companion Website at www.pearsoned.ca/armstrong, to view a video segment and case for this chapter.

ON LOCATION

MAP 15 Marketing Applications

Nowhere is international competition more apparent than in the digital camera market. Overnight, the advent of digital cameras has changed the way many photographers view their equipment. Digital cameras offer opportunities for reproduction and Internet viewing unmatched by more traditional products. However, the market is also uncharted, chaotic, and increasingly crowded, with more than 20 manufacturers worldwide. A recent entrant is film giant Fuji, **www.fujifilm.ca**. As the world's number two producer, Fuji now plans to meet or beat Kodak, **www.kodak.ca**; Sony, **www.sony.ca**; Olympus **www.olympus.com**, and Konica **www.konica.ca** in digital camera products. Fuji introduced its first digital cameras in its own backyard—Japan, which is also a Sony stronghold. One factor motivating the move into digital cameras was its inability to erode Kodak's worldwide share of the film market. If the wave of the future turns out to be digital, Fuji plans to ride the wave's crest for as long as it can.

Thinking Like a Marketing Manager

1. Analyze Fuji's strategy of entering the digital camera market. What challenges will Fuji most likely face? How can Fuji's traditional strengths in film aid its efforts in the new digital camera market?

2. What world markets should Fuji consider after Japan? Explain.

3. If you were the marketing manager of Fuji, what advertising strategy would you suggest for Fuji's new product venture? What distribution strategy?

4. What actions will Kodak, Olympus, Konica, and Sony probably take to counter Fuji's entry?

Digital Map
Visit our Web site at **www.pearsoned.ca/armstrong** for online quizzes, Internet exercises, and more!

CASE 15 WAL-MART: PILING 'EM HIGH AND SELLING 'EM CHEAP AROUND THE GLOBE

The internal point of view: "Wal-Mart employees who do not think globally are working for the wrong company."—David Glass, chief executive, Wal-Mart

The external point of view: "Wal-Mart must think and act as if it's a global company. Otherwise, it can't grow enough in North America to maintain its stock price. It needs to be in South America. It needs to be in Asia. It needs to be in Europe."—George Rosenbaum, Leo J. Shapiro Associates

When a major retailer like Wal-Mart sets its mind and cash to global expansion, it's amazing what it can do. At the end of the 1980s, Wal-Mart was a mostly U.S. phenomenon; by the end of the 1990s, it was a global presence, poised to become the world's dominant retailer. From a base of about 2200 U.S. stores and sales of less than $125 billion in the early 1990s, Wal-Mart expanded to more than 3600 stores worldwide, with sales of $205 billion and a net income of $6.64 billion.

Not bad for a company that began its international expansion in 1993 with the purchase of 122 Woolco stores in Canada.

Spurred on by NAFTA, Wal-Mart quickly moved into Mexico using joint ventures to end the decade with more than 400 Mexican stores. In Hong Kong, through a joint venture with Ek Chor Distribution System Co. Ltd., Wal-Mart established several Value Clubs, which became stepping stones to mainland China, the most populous country in the world and a market with an emerging middle class. Because Ek Chor is actually owned by CP Pokphand of Bangkok, Wal-Mart also entered Thailand, and then Indonesia. In 1995, the retailing giant once again looked south, moving into South America with stores in Brazil, Argentina, and Chile.

Most of these countries appear to be good markets for Wal-Mart, as each constitutes a heavily populated emerging market. Although not high in discretionary income, each of these markets exhibits growing income, giving people more money to shop while retaining their price sensitivity. Wal-Mart's inventory of discounted brand-name merchandise offers consumers in these markets the quality they desire at prices they can afford.

Initially, Wal-Mart's moves into emerging markets matched the expectations of industry analysts. Most experts predicted that Wal-Mart's next move would be into Eastern Europe, where the populace still sought discount prices rather than high-end goods. But in 1998, Wal-Mart confounded the experts by buying the 21-unit Wertkauf chain in Germany. In 1999, it purchased a second German retailer, the 74-unit Interspar hypermarkets chain. Within only one and a half years, Wal-Mart moved from having no presence in Germany to being the country's number four retailer.

Why was this move into Germany so surprising? The Germany countryside is littered with the carcasses of other retailers, such as Toys "R" Us, which tried and failed to penetrate the market. Although Germany is the third largest market in the world (behind the United States and Japan), it is an especially tough market. First, zoning laws, scarcity of land, and high real estate prices make it almost impossible to find affordable space for new supercentres or hypermarkets. Second, German retailing is dominated by a few large chains, such as Metro, Rewe, and Edeka. As a result, the market is characterized by excessive price competition and extremely narrow margins—2 percent or less.

Third, Germany has very strong unions, and German workers are among the most highly paid in the world. Wal-Mart will find it very difficult to make these workers gather early in the morning as they do in the United States to do the Wal-Mart cheer ("Give me a W!" "W!" "Give me an A!" "A!") Fourth, German laws governing retailing severely limit store hours. No retailers (except for bakeries and gas stations) are open on Sunday. And until recently, all stores closed at noon on Saturday (now, it's 4 p.m.) and stayed open late (until 8 p.m.) only one night a week—not an appealing policy for a company that keeps many of its North American stores open 24 hours a day.

Fifth, in attempting to apply the same low-price strategy in Europe as in North America, Wal-Mart would conflict with some manufacturers' marketing strategies.

For example, many clothing brands that are positioned more as commodities and sold in many stores at discount prices (such as Levis) are positioned as more high-end products in Europe. Thus, selling in Wal-Mart as a discount item would under-cut such brands' positioning and damage international profits. Sixth, sales in Germany had been flat for the past four years, and no increases were expected given the country's high level of unemployment. Finally, consumers in Western Europe are considered more sophisticated and more demanding than North American consumers—not the kinds of buyers likely to be swayed by a greeter at the door who asks, "How are you today?" (or, rather, "*Wie geht's?*").

So, who was wrong here—Wal-Mart or the analysts? With so much seemingly going against it, how could Wal-Mart expect to be successful in Germany? What did it have to offer that established retailers didn't? The answer—service. In a country full of surly store clerks, sometimes described as having perfected "service with a snarl," customers might respond well to service with a smile. They might like to shop where their patronage is valued—where store clerks are trained when asked, "Who's number one?" to respond, "The customer!" and where customers' purchas-es are bagged for them instead of by them.

In a country where it's difficult to get to the store because of its limited hours, Wal-Mart has pushed its store hours to the legal limit. It opens at 7 a.m. (the earli-est allowed) despite the customary 8 a.m. or 9 a.m. opening times. Customers who work might appreciate the extra hour of time to shop. Also, Wal-Mart helps shop-pers reduce shopping time by using common North American practices, such as locating steak sauce or seasoning packets near the meats and salad dressings near the produce so that shoppers don't have to walk back and forth in the store to find complementary goods.

To make shopping more pleasant, Wal-Mart has begun to renovate its German stores, many of which were badly run down. It has created wider aisles, refurbished fixtures, piled the goods higher, and renamed its stores Wal-Mart. Most important, in a land of *pfennig* pinchers, Wal-Mart has introduced everyday low pricing, or EDLP. "*Jeden Tag Tiefpriese*" signs throughout its stores proclaim drastically slashed prices on over 4000 items. Wal-Mart's EDLP/JTT strategy has worked so well that other German retailers, who previously relied on specials and sales to reduce prices, have been forced to reduce their daily prices.

In a sense, low prices have pulled customers into Wal-Mart's German stores while other attributes, such as friendly clerks and wider aisles, have made shopping more pleasant. What allows Wal-Mart to out-discount the European discounters? The answer lies in its 101-terabyte computer system. Wal-Mart is the country's most sophisticated retailer in terms of using information systems. Every second, data from around the globe are transmitted via satellite to the Wal-Mart computer. Store managers can point handheld scanners at a product on their shelves and find out how much of the product the store has sold today at what price and profit con-tribution, what its inventory levels are (by colour, size, and other characteristics), and whether more is on order. Analysts pore over thousands of pages of output to track sales everywhere. If a product is moving slowly in one store, it's shipped to another rather than being cleared through reduced prices. Very few goods sit in inventory for very long, which reduces costs. Orders and reorders are placed strictly on the basis of sales. Wal-Mart knows faster than any other retailer what's selling and what's not.

In addition, Wal-Mart's sophisticated distribution system backs up this information system. Wal-Mart has applied for and obtained several free-trade-zone distribution centres in Arizona and Georgia. Goods pour into these centres, where they are repackaged, marked, labelled, and reshipped. While goods remain in the zone, Wal-Mart pays no duty on them: Duties are paid only when goods are shipped. Each zone saves Wal-Mart more than $750 000 annually. Such close attention to distribution costs saves Wal-Mart money and supports rapid shipment of goods.

The analysts expected that, following its move into Germany, Wal-Mart would expand next into France. However, the company confounded the experts once again by buying ASDA, the third largest chain in the United Kingdom. Why? U.K. retailing has the highest margins in Europe—ranging from 5 percent to 7 percent. If Wal-Mart can survive on less than 2 percent in Germany, it can do very well with the higher margins in the United Kingdom.

Wal-Mart now poses a serious threat to European retailers. With the purchase of one more major European chain next year, Wal-Mart will become the largest retailer in Europe, irrevocably changing the face of European retailing. And it will have accomplished this feat in only four years.

How are European retailers retaliating? Wal-Mart's entry spawned a series of mergers, which can result only in a concentration of retailers worldwide. Carrefour and Promodes in France have merged to become the largest retailer in five European countries: France, Spain, Belgium, Portugal, and Greece. Through its holdings in other firms, it will have significant shares of the Argentine, Brazilian, Taiwanese, and Indonesian markets. Metro, the largest retailer in Germany, bought the Allkauf chain and Kriegbaum-Unternemensgruppe in southwest Germany to consolidate its lead in Germany. Ahold, the major Dutch retailer, bought up several chains in Spain.

Questions

1. Describe Wal-Mart's global strategy. What tactics has it used to become a major global retailer?

2. Can Wal-Mart sustain its competitive advantage in global retailing?

3. Explain the importance to the Wal-Mart strategy of selling only brand-name merchandise.

4. Choosing markets to enter is of major importance in global expansion. If you were in charge of Wal-Mart, what European country would you enter next? Why? Would entering this country require adaptation of Wal-Mart's marketing strategy and tactics? If so, how?

5. If you were running Wal-Mart, what non-European country in the world would you enter next? Why? Would entering this country require adaptation of Wal-Mart's marketing? If so, how?

Sources: "A Foothold in Europe's Heartland," *Discount Store,* October 1999, p. 77; "Europe Seen As Tough, While Asia's a Natural on Wal-Mart's Globe," *WWD,* 23 August 1994, p. 1; "How is Wal-Mart Doing in Germany?" *Eurofood,* 1 July 1999, p. 11; "Wal-Mart Doubles Its Size in Europe," *Eurofood,* 17 December 1998, p. 11; Stephen Armstrong, "Wal-Mart Goes Shopping in Europe," *European,* 2 March 1998, p. 23; Carol Emert, "Wal-Mart Sets up to Enter Europe, Central America," *WWD,* 22 August 1994, p. 8; Richard Halverson, "Wal-Mart 'Walks the Walk' of a Global Retailer; Eyes All Corners of the Globe," *Discount Store News,* 5 December 1994, p. 95; Samer Iskander, "Retailers Plan Biggest Store Chain in Europe," *Financial Times,* 30 August 1999, p. 1; Tony Lisanti, "Europe's Abuzz over Wal-Mart," *Discount Store News,* 3 May 1999, p. 11; David Moin, "Wal-Mart to Enter Europe with Buy of German Chain," *WWD,* 19 December 1997, p. 2; Elliot Zwiebach, "Europe: In Wal-Mart's Wake," *Supermarket News,* 20 September 1999, p. 40.

16 >> Marketing and Society: Social Responsibility and Marketing Ethics

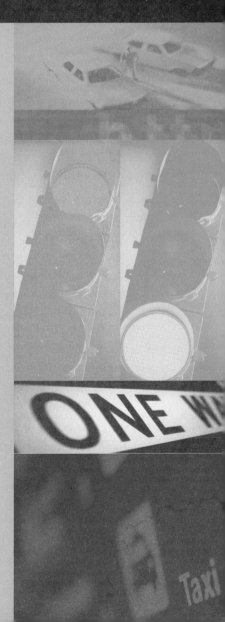

Looking Ahead

You've almost completed your introductory marketing travels. In this final chapter, we'll focus on marketing as a social institution. First, we'll look at some common criticisms of marketing as it affects individual consumers, other businesses, and society. Then, we'll examine consumerism, environmentalism, and other citizen and public actions to keep marketing in check. Finally, we'll see how companies themselves can benefit from proactively pursuing socially responsible and ethical practices. You'll see that social responsibility and ethical actions are more than just the right thing to do; they're also good for business.

After studying this chapter, you should be able to

1. identify the major social criticisms of marketing
2. define consumerism and environmentalism and explain how they affect marketing strategies
3. describe the principles of socially responsible marketing
4. explain the role of ethics in marketing

To begin the final leg of the journey, we'll visit the concept of social responsibility in business. Companies are embracing the idea of "values-led business" or "caring capitalism." But can a company dedicating to doing good still do well?

"New models of philanthropy are emerging [that emphasize] a far closer relationship among business, individuals, and communities. Corporations are not just giving donations to charity but are entering partnerships that exemplify the best creative approaches to meeting community needs." These words, uttered by Courtney Pratt, former CEO of Noranda, are the hallmark of an era in which corporations are redefining what it means to act in a socially responsible manner. It wasn't long ago that moral philosophers such as Milton Friedman stated that the only social responsibility of a firm was to create wealth for its stockholders while acting within the bounds of the law and the moral dictate of society. But Environics International's Millennium Poll on Corporate Social Responsibility revealed that just being profitable isn't enough in today's world. Consumers from North America to Australia want businesses that not only make profits and create jobs, but also help build a better society. In fact, the poll revealed that 88 percent of Canadians want companies to contribute to broader social goals.

Firms that are sensitive to the demands of the public and consumers are starting to define social responsibility as the "triple bottom line." Not only are they working to be economically responsible, but they are also being environmentally and socially responsible. In other words, rather than just focusing on business problems and their shareholders, many firms are taking a stakeholder perspective, realizing that they need to further and respect the rights of their customers, their employees, their suppliers, their communities, and even their competitors.

Rather than just spouting words about this mandate, many companies are actively working not just to be profitable, but also to improve the quality of life in their communities. They contribute the time and energy of their employees; they share their expertise and knowledge; they donate their products, services, and money to resolve many social dilemmas. These efforts range from cause-related marketing programs, in which firms donate a portion of the sales revenue from a product to a specific cause, to social alliances in which firms join with nonprofit organizations in an effort to resolve complex, long-term social issues.

The list of firms undertaking these types of efforts is growing daily. Firms come from every sector of the Canadian economy, and their efforts are as varied as the social needs themselves. On the list of socially active firms is Bell Canada, which donates 1 percent of pretax profits to charities, is a financial and moral supporter of The Boys and Girls Clubs of Canada, and is a long-time sponsor of the Kids Help Phone (**kidshelp.sympatico.ca**), which receives more than 4000 calls a day. Bell has recently launched a Kids Help Phone Web site. The site receives 12 000 visits per day and provides counselling for lonely and vulnerable youth on a range of issues from suicide to eating disorders. Compaq Canada's Go for Green environmental program includes an extraordinary Web site that lets the world know about the thousands of hiking trails that Canada has to offer (**www.trail-paq.ca**). Compaq believes that anyone who hikes a trail will have a heightened sense of the need to protect the fragile environment.

Molson Breweries also takes a leading place with its long history of social marketing. Molson and its co-sponsors have raised millions of dollars for AIDS research. In addition, Molson is active in local communities through their Local Heroes program, which provides funding to upgrade community recreational facilities. McDonald's Restaurants of Canada is well known for its long-standing Ronald McDonald's Children's Charities and Ronald McDonald House programs. Procter & Gamble supports the Canadian Breast Cancer Foundation, while Nissan Canada partners with Meals on Wheels to deliver hot lunches to the elderly and shut-ins. Nortel Networks works diligently to support the Childhood Cancer Foundation, while Sears Canada joined forces with Industry Canada to provide more than 100 000 refurbished computers to classrooms and libraries across Canada in its Computers for Schools program. For the past 10 years, Telus has sponsored an annual golf tournament, The Telus Skins Game, that raises funds for Big Brothers and Big Sisters of Canada.

And it's not just large companies that are responding to calls for help. SaskEnergy's employees collaborated with the United Way and collected more than 200 000 sweaters to be distributed to the needy throughout Saskatchewan, while Winnipeg's Assiniboine Credit Union collected used cars to raise funds for kidney disease research.

Let's look at one case in detail. Altamira Financial Services Ltd. (**www.altamira.com**) won the 1999 Imagine New Spirit of Community award in recognition of its ongoing charitable efforts. As its award submission noted: "Sharing and caring is part of the Altamira way of life. That is why the Altamira Foundation reaches out to charitable organizations and communities that are most in need. Our corporate giving program is focused on areas in which we believe we can make a difference." The Altamira Foundation, established in 1995, "invests in Canada's most precious and critical future resource—its children." Altamira believes that children have the right to grow up in a safe environment, the right to an education, and the right to become productive citizens. To foster these rights, Altamira donates at least 1 percent of its pretax profits and sponsors a range of events that support specific programs.

Altamira undertakes a number of initiatives to accomplish its goals. Since 1997, Altamira and its corporate partners, such as Kellogg Canada, Birks, and Nike, have convinced some of the world's best golfers to donate their time and skills to raising money for children's charities. These efforts resulted in the Altamira Charity Golf Challenge, the largest one-day event of its kind in Canada. The event has raised more than $3.5 million and supports several children's charities including the Toronto Star Fresh Air Fund, the Hospital for Sick Children, the Kids Help Foundation, Sheena's Place, a home for children with eating disorders, and The Learning Partnership. Working with the Canadian Opera Company, Altamira sponsored the No Load Opera Concerts and Opera Summer Camps for Children. The $135 000 raised has been donated to various community-based groups, such as the Canadian Feed the Children Fund, which funds breakfast and lunch programs for hungry children throughout the country and across the globe, giving them a better opportunity to learn.

Although undoubtedly important, raising money isn't enough. Through the Altamira Homework Club, more than 40 Altamira staff members have volunteered their time to tutor and mentor students and promote literacy in communities across Canada. Each week during the school year, grade eight students from a local school visit Altamira for help in reading, writing, and doing their homework.

Why are companies taking on these expanded roles and responsibilities? Many businesses see social marketing as a means of reaching their target customers and enhancing the value of their brands. They align themselves with nonprofit organizations to break through the clutter of traditional advertising and add distinctiveness and value to their offerings. Molson believes its program helps build stronger relationships with customers, enhances its corporate image, and creates a sense of pride among its employees. Sears believes it is reinforcing its position as Canada's family store and its reputation as a company that supports communities. Other firms want to create lifestyle associations between themselves and the causes they support. They develop social marketing programs to address corporate or brand image problems, to build brand loyalty, and to address issues of employee morale and productivity.

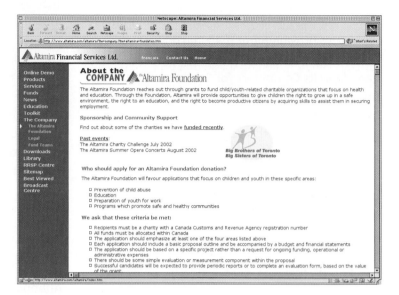

Although a business-related mandate may form part of the motivation behind these efforts, it must be stressed that the marketers involved in these programs are sincerely involved in the causes they choose to support. These firms are leaders—not just market leaders, but leaders in their communities. They take on the full breadth of challenges community membership presents. These firms work diligently with their nonprofit partners to resolve social issues. Social marketing appears to be here to stay, according to 82 percent of Canadian executives recently surveyed: Almost two thirds of companies polled use some form of social marketing, and many plan to expand these efforts.[1]

Responsible marketers discover what consumers want and respond with the right products, priced to give good value to buyers and profit to the producer. The *marketing concept* is a philosophy of customer service and mutual gain.

Not all marketers follow the marketing concept, however. In fact, some companies use questionable marketing practices, and some marketing actions that seem innocent in themselves strongly affect society. Consider the sale of cigarettes. Theoretically, companies should be free to sell cigarettes, and smokers should be free to buy them. But this transaction affects the public interest. First, smokers may be shortening their own lives. Second, smoking places a health care burden on smokers' families and on society. Third, people around smokers may suffer discomfort and harm from second-hand smoke. Thus, private transactions may involve larger questions of public policy.

This chapter examines the social effects of marketing practices. We examine several questions: What are the most frequent social criticisms of marketing? What steps have private citizens taken to curb marketing ills? What steps have legislators and government agencies taken to curb marketing ills? What steps have enlightened companies taken to carry out socially responsible and ethical marketing? We examine how marketing affects and is affected by each of these issues.

Social Criticisms of Marketing

Marketing is often criticized. Some of the criticism is justified; much is not. Social critics claim that certain marketing practices hurt individual consumers, society as a whole, and other business firms.

Marketing's Impact on Individual Consumers

Consumers have many concerns about how well the marketing system serves their interests. Surveys usually show that consumers hold mixed or even slightly unfavourable attitudes toward marketing practices. Consumers, consumer advocates, government agencies, and other critics have accused marketing of harming consumers through high prices, deceptive practices, high-pressure selling, shoddy or unsafe products, planned obsolescence, and poor service to disadvantaged consumers.

High Prices Many critics charge that the marketing system causes prices to be higher than they would be under more "sensible" systems. They point to three factors: *high costs of distribution, high advertising and promotion costs,* and *excessive markups.*

High Costs of Distribution A long-standing charge is that greedy intermediaries mark up prices beyond the value of their services. Critics allege either that there are too many intermediaries or that intermediaries are inefficient and poorly run, that they provide unnecessary or duplicate services, and that they practise poor management and planning. As a result, distribution costs too much, and consumers pay for these excessive costs in the form of higher prices.

How do retailers answer these charges? First, intermediaries do work that would otherwise have to be done by manufacturers or consumers. Second, markups reflect services that consumers themselves want—more convenience, larger stores and assortment, longer store hours, return privileges, and others. Third, the costs of operating stores keep rising, forcing retailers to raise their prices. Fourth, retail competition is so intense that margins are actually quite low. For example, after taxes, supermarket chains are typically left with 1 percent to 3 percent profit on their sales. If some resellers try to charge too much relative to the value they add, other resellers will step in with lower prices. Low-price stores such as the Dollar Store, Zellers, and Wal-Mart pressure their competitors to operate efficiently and keep their prices down. In addition, the expanding use of the Internet by consumers doing research before major purchases are made adds to the downward pressure on prices.

High Advertising and Promotion Costs Modern marketing is accused of pushing up prices because of heavy advertising and sales promotion. For example, a dozen tablets of a heavily promoted brand of pain reliever sell for the same price as 100 tablets of less promoted brands. Differentiated products—cosmetics, detergents, toiletries—include promotion and packaging costs that can amount to 40 percent or more of the manufacturer's price to the retailer. Critics charge that much of the packaging and promotion adds only psychological value to the product rather than functional value. Retailers use additional promotions—advertising, displays, and sweepstakes—that add several cents to retail prices.

Marketers answer these charges in several ways. First, consumers want more than the merely functional qualities of products. They also want psychological ben-

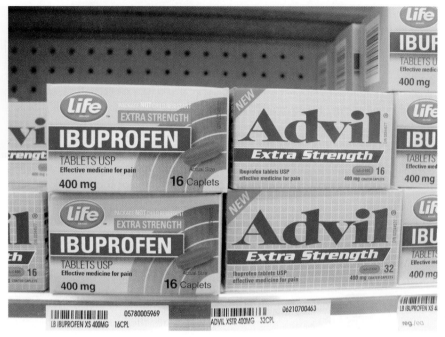

Critics charge that much of the packaging and promotion adds only psychological value to the product rather than functional value. Heavily promoted brands often sell for much more than a generic or store-brand product.

efits—they want to feel wealthy, beautiful, or special. Consumers usually can buy functional versions or products at lower prices but are often willing to pay more for products that also provide desired psychological benefits. Second, branding gives buyers confidence. A brand name implies a certain quality, and consumers are willing to pay for well-known brands even if they cost a little more. Third, heavy advertising is needed to inform millions of potential buyers of the merits of a brand. If consumers want to know what is available on the market, they must expect manufacturers to spend large sums of money on advertising. Fourth, heavy advertising and promotion may be necessary for a firm to match competitors' efforts. The business would lose "share of mind" if it did not match competitive spending. At the same time, companies are cost-conscious about promotion and try to spend their money wisely. Finally, heavy sales promotion is needed at times because goods are produced ahead of demand in a mass-production economy, and special incentives must be offered to sell inventories.

Excessive Markups Critics charge that some companies mark up goods excessively. They point to the drug industry, where a pill costing 5 cents to make may cost the consumer 40 cents to buy. They point to the pricing tactics of funeral homes that prey on the emotions of bereaved relatives and to the high charges for television and auto repair.

Marketers respond that most businesses try to deal fairly with consumers because they want repeat business. Most consumer abuses are unintentional. When shady marketers take advantage of consumers, they should be reported to the police, Better Business Bureau, and the provincial ministry of consumer and commercial relations. Marketers also respond that consumers often don't understand the reason for high markups. For example, pharmaceutical markups must cover the costs of purchasing, promoting, and distributing existing medicines and the high research and development costs of finding new medicines.

Deceptive Practices Marketers are sometimes accused of deceptive practices that lead consumers to believe that they will get more value than they actually do. Deceptive practices fall into three groups: deceptive pricing, promotion, and packaging. *Deceptive pricing* includes such practices as falsely advertising "factory" or "wholesale" prices or a large price reduction from a phony high retail list price. The Competition Bureau has taken action against merchants who advertise false values, sell old merchandise as new, or charge too much for credit. For example, in 1995 the Competition Bureau fined Montreal-based Suzy Shier Ltd., which operates 375 outlets across Canada, $300 000 after it was found to be double-tagging merchandise. Although this practice of placing a sales ticket showing an original price and another ticket showing a sales price on a piece of clothing is not illegal, Suzy Shier violated the law because it had not sold a substantial volume of goods at the original price. In fact, much of the double tagging was done at the factory.[2]

Deceptive promotion includes such practices as overstating the product's features or performance, luring the customer to the store for a bargain that is out of stock, or running rigged contests. *Deceptive packaging* includes exaggerating package contents through subtle design, not filling the package to the top, using misleading labelling, or describing size in misleading terms.

Phone fraud has become a significant deceptive practice. According to PhoneBusters, the national reporting centre for telemarketing fraud, Canadians have lost about $40 million through this activity since 1995. Criminals use telecommunications to prey on innocent victims, especially those most vulnerable, such as senior citizens. The Canadian Marketing Association (CMA) has partnered with government to develop initiatives aimed at preventing and combating this crime. Bill C-20 has equipped enforcement agencies with stronger investigative tools and imposed more restrictions on telemarketers. Information on Bill C-20 is available on the CMA's Web site.

Canadian Marketing Association
www.the-cma.org

Since deceptive practices hurt the reputation of all marketers, the CMA works to develop codes of ethics and standards of good practice so that industry can regulate itself better. It works with policymakers to strengthen the Competition Act. In the case of telemarketing fraud, it joined the Deceptive Telemarketing Prevention Forum to launch a public education campaign designed to help consumers avoid becoming victims of telephone fraud. The campaign, "Stop Phone Fraud, It's a Trap!" consists of posters, pamphlets, public service announcements, an upgraded Web site for PhoneBusters, and educational materials to help consumers learn how to tell the difference between an honest telemarketer and a scam artist. Training videos are also made available to volunteer groups that work with seniors.[3]

Deceptive practices have led to industry self-regulation standards as well as legislation and other consumer protection actions. The Competition Act forbids many of the practices. Advertising Standards Canada has published several guidelines listing deceptive practices. The toughest problem is defining what is "deceptive."

High-Pressure Selling Salespeople are sometimes accused of high-pressure selling to persuade people to buy goods they had no intention of buying. It is often said

Telemarketing fraud hurts consumers and the marketing profession. The Deceptive Telemarketing Prevention Forum launched a campaign to help consumers avoid becoming victims of phone fraud.

that encyclopedias, insurance, real estate, cars, and jewellery are *sold*, not *bought*. Some salespeople are trained to deliver smooth, canned talks to entice purchase. They sell hard because sales contests promise big prizes to those who sell the most.

Marketers know that buyers often can be talked into buying unwanted or unneeded things. Laws require door-to-door salespeople to announce that they are selling a product. Sellers in most provinces require a licence to sell door-to-door and buyers in most provinces have a three-day cooling-off period in which they can cancel a contract after rethinking it. In addition, when they feel that undue selling pressure has been applied, consumers can complain to the Better Business Bureau or to their provincial ministry regulating commerce.

Shoddy or Unsafe Products Another criticism is that products lack the quality they should have. Consumers often complain that many products are not made well or that services did not perform well. Such complaints have been lodged against such products as home appliances, automobiles, and clothing, and such services as home and auto repair.

A second complaint is that many products deliver little benefit. For example, some consumers are surprised to learn that many of the "healthy" foods being marketed today—from cholesterol-free salad dressings and low-fat frozen dinners to high-fibre bran cereals—may have little nutritional value. In fact, they may even be harmful:[4]

[Despite] sincere efforts on the part of most marketers to provide healthier products,...many promises emblazoned on packages and used as ad slogans continue to confuse nutritionally uninformed consumers and...may actually be harmful to that group.... [Many consumers] incorrectly assume the product is "safe" and eat greater amounts than are good for them.... For example, General Foods'..."low-cholesterol, low-calorie" cherry coffee cake...may confuse some consumers who shouldn't eat much of it. While each serving is only 90 calories, not everyone realizes that the suggested serving is tiny [1/13 of the small cake]. Although eating half a...cake may be better than eating half a dozen Tim Horton's Donuts...neither should be eaten in great amounts by people on restrictive diets.

A third complaint concerns product safety. Product safety has been a problem for several reasons, including manufacturer indifference, increased production complexity, poorly trained labour, and poor quality control. For years, Consumers Union—the organization that publishes *Consumer Reports*—has reported hazards in tested products: electrical dangers in appliances, carbon-monoxide poisoning from room heaters, injury risks from lawn mowers, and faulty automobile design, among many others. The organization's testing and other activities have helped consumers make better buying decision and encouraged businesses to eliminate product flaws.

However, most manufacturers *want* to produce quality goods. The way a company deals with product quality and safety problems can damage or help its reputation. Companies selling poor-quality or unsafe products risk damaging conflicts with consumer groups and regulators. Moreover, unsafe products can result in product liability suits and large awards for damages. More fundamentally, consumers who are unhappy with a firm's products may avoid future purchases and talk other consumers into doing the same. Consider what happened to Bridgestone/Firestone following its recent recall of 6.5 million flawed Firestone tires. Product liability and safety concerns have driven the company to the edge of bankruptcy:

Profits have disappeared, and both customers and tire dealers alike are fleeing the Firestone make. Ford, the tire maker's biggest customer, recently announced plans to replace another 13 million Firestone tires that it believes are unsafe. "You have a serious risk of the Firestone brand imploding," warns an industry analyst. How bad will the financial hit get? Cutting ties with Ford will cost the company 4 percent of its $7.5 billion in revenues—about 40 percent of its sales to car companies. Mounting damages awards from rollover suits and legal bills could easily top the company's $463 million legal reserve. And if the National Highway Traffic & Safety Administration supports Ford's latest recall, Firestone could find itself liable for much of the $3 billion cost.[5]

Thus, quality missteps can have severe consequences. Today's marketers know that customer-driven quality results in customer satisfaction, which in turn creates profitable customer relationships.

Planned Obsolescence Critics have charged that some producers follow a program of planned obsolescence, causing their products to become obsolete before they actually should need replacement. Critics charge that some producers continually change consumer concepts of acceptable styles to encourage more and earlier buying; an example is constantly changing clothing fashions. Other producers are accused of holding back attractive functional features, then introducing them later to make older models obsolete; critics claim that this occurs in the consumer electronics and computer industries. Still other producers are accused of using materials and components that will break, wear, rust, or rot sooner than they should.

Marketers respond that consumers *like* style changes: They get tired of the old goods and want a new look in fashion or a new design in cars. No one has to buy the new look and, if too few people like it, it will simply fail. Companies frequently withhold new features when they are not fully tested, when they add more cost to the product than consumers are willing to pay, and for other good reasons. But they do so at the risk that a competitor will introduce the new feature and steal the market. Moreover, companies often put in new materials to lower their costs and prices. They do not design their products to break down earlier, because they do not want to lose customers to other brands. Instead, they implement total quality programs to ensure that products will consistently meet to exceed customer expectations. Thus, much of so-called planned obsolescence is the working of the competitive and technological forces in a free society—forces that lead to ever-improving goods and services.

Poor Service to Disadvantaged Consumers Finally, the marketing system has been accused of poorly serving disadvantaged consumers. Critics claim that the urban poor often have to shop in smaller stores that carry inferior goods and charge higher prices. A recent Consumers Union study compared the food shopping habits of low-income consumers and the prices they pay relative to middle-income consumers in the same city. The study found that the poor pay more for inferior goods. The results suggested that the presence of large national chain stores in low-income neighbourhoods made a big difference in keeping prices down. However, the study also found evidence of "redlining," a type of economic discrimination in which major chain retailers avoid placing stores in disadvantaged neighbourhoods. Similar redlining charges have been levelled at the home insurance, consumer lending, and banking industries.[6] When disadvantaged consumers are identified and discriminated against in the online environment, the practice is called weblining.

As never before, the Internet lets companies identify (or "profile") high- and low-value customers, so firms can decide which product deals, prices, and services it will offer. For the most valued customers, this can mean better information and discounts. Low-value customers may pay the most for the least and sometimes get left behind. In lending, old-style redlining is unacceptable because it is based on geographic stereotypes, not concrete evidence that specific individuals are poor credit risks. Webliners may claim to have more evidence against the people they snub. But their classifications could also be based on irrelevant profiling data that marketing companies and others collect on the Web. How important to your mortgage status, say, is your taste in paperbacks, political discussion groups, or clothing? Yet all these far-flung threads are getting sewn into online profiles, where they are increasingly intertwined with data on your health, your education loans, and your credit history.[7]

Clearly, better marketing systems must be built in low-income areas—one hope is to get large retailers to open outlets in low-income areas. Moreover, low-income people and other vulnerable groups clearly need consumer protection.

Time for a break. Few marketers *want* to abuse or anger consumers—it's simply not good business. Instead, as you know well by now, most marketers work to build long-term relationships with customers based on real value and caring. Yet, some marketing abuses do occur.

• Think back over the past three months or so and list the instances in which you've suffered a marketing abuse such as those just discussed. Analyze your list. What kinds of companies were involved? Were the abuses intentional? What did the situations have in common?

• Pick one of the instances you listed and describe it in detail. How might you go about righting this wrong? Write out an action plan, then do something to remedy the abuse. If we all took such actions when wronged, there would be far fewer wrongs to right!

Marketing's Impact on Society as a Whole

The marketing system has been accused of adding to several "evils" in society. Advertising has been a special target—so much so that the American Association of Advertising Agencies launched a campaign to defend advertising against what it felt to be common but untrue criticisms.

False Wants and Too Much Materialism

Critics, led by Professor Rick Pollay of the University of British Columbia, have charged that the marketing system urges too much interest in material possessions. Pollay wrote an article in the *Journal of Marketing* that outlined the unintended consequences of advertising. The article documented the work of a range of social critics who claim that advertising promotes materialism, undermines family values, reinforces negative stereotypes, and creates a class of perpetually dissatisfied consumers.[8] People are judged by what they *own* rather than by who they *are*.

Such critics as Adbusters do not view this interest in material things as a natural state of mind, but rather as a matter of false wants created by marketing. Businesses hire advertisers to stimulate people's desires for goods, and advertisers use the mass media to create materialistic models of the good life. People work harder to earn the necessary money. Their purchases increase the output of North American industry, and industry in turn uses advertisers to stimulate more desire for the industrial output. Thus, marketing is seen as creating false wants that benefit industry more than they benefit consumers.

Others believe that these criticisms overstate the power of business to create needs. People have strong defences against advertising and other marketing tools. Marketers are most effective when they appeal to existing wants rather than when they attempt to create new ones. Furthermore, people seek information when making important purchases and often do not rely on single sources. Even minor purchases that can be affected by advertising messages lead to repeat purchases only if

Adbusters Magazine
www.adbusters.org/
home

Social critics, like Adbusters, decry the materialism they claim advertising creates.

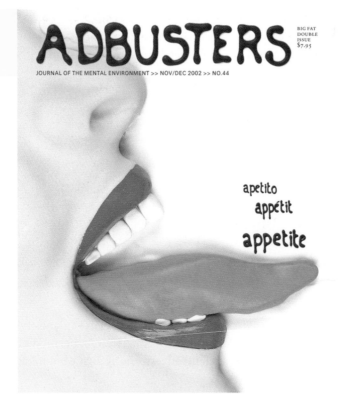

the product performs as promised. Finally, the high failure rate of new products shows that companies are not able to control demand.

On a deeper level, our wants and values are influenced not only by marketers, but also by family, peer groups, religion, ethnic background, and education. If North Americans are highly materialistic, these values arose out of basic socialization processes that go much deeper than business and mass media alone could produce.

Too Few Social Goods Business has been accused of overselling private goods at the expense of public goods. As private goods increase, they require more public services that are usually not forthcoming. For example, an increase in automobile ownership (private good) requires more highways, traffic controls, parking spaces, and police services (public goods). The overselling of private goods results in "social costs." For cars, the social costs include traffic congestion, air pollution, and deaths and injuries from car accidents.

A way must be found to restore a balance between private and public goods. One option is to make producers bear the full social costs of their operations. For example, the government could require automobile manufacturers to build cars with more safety features and better pollution-control systems. Automakers would then raise their prices to cover extra costs. If buyers found the price of some cars too high, however, the producers of these cars would disappear, and demand would move to those producers that could support the sum of the private and social costs.

Cultural Pollution Critics charge the marketing system with creating *cultural pollution*. Our senses are being assaulted constantly by advertising. Commercials interrupt serious programs; pages of ads obscure printed matter; billboards mar beautiful scenery. Vancouver, for example, has placed a moratorium on new billboards in the city as have most surrounding municipalities. These interruptions continually pollute people's minds with messages of materialism, sex, power, or status. Although most people do not find advertising overly annoying (some even think it is the best part of television programming), critics call for sweeping changes.

Marketers answer the charges of "commercial noise" with these arguments. First, they hope that their ads reach primarily the target audience; but, because of mass-communication channels, some ads are bound to reach people who have no interest in the product and, therefore, become annoyed. People who buy magazines addressed to their interests—such as *Garden's West* or *Canadian Business*—rarely complain about the ads because the magazines advertise products of interest. Second, ads make it possible for consumers to receive commercial television and radio free and keep down the costs of magazines and newspapers. Many people think commercials are a small price to pay for these benefits.

Too Much Political Power Another criticism is that business wields too much political power. Oil, tobacco, auto, and pharmaceutical firms lobby governments to promote their interests against the public interest. Advertisers are accused of holding too much power over the mass media, limiting their freedom to report independently and objectively. One critic has asked: "How can *Life*…and *Reader's Digest* afford to tell the truth about the scandalously low nutritional value of most packaged foods…when these magazines are being subsidized by such advertisers as General Foods, Kellogg's, Nabisco, and General Mills?…The answer is *they cannot and do not.*"[9]

North American industries promote and protect their interests. They have a right to representation in Parliament and the mass media, although their influence can become too great. Fortunately, many powerful business interests once thought to be untouchable have been tamed in the public interest. For example, Petro-Canada was formed to give Canadians greater control over the oil industry. Ralph Nader created legislation that forced the automobile industry to build more safety into its cars. Amendments to the Tobacco Products Control Act made it necessary for cigarette manufacturers to place stronger warnings on their packages about the dangers of smoking. Warnings, and pictorial representations of the harmful effects of smoking, must appear on the face of the package. They include such messages as "Cigarettes cause strokes and heart disease" and "Tobacco can make you impotent." Because the media receive advertising revenues from many advertisers, it is easier to resist the influence of one or a few of them. Too much business power tends to result in counterforces that check and offset these powerful interests.

Marketing's Impact on Other Businesses

Critics charge that a company's marketing practices can harm other companies and reduce competition. Three problems are involved: acquisitions of competitors, marketing practices that create barriers to entry, and unfair competitive marketing practices.

Critics claim that firms are harmed and competition reduced when companies expand by acquiring competitors rather than by developing their own new products. During the past decade, Corel bought WordPerfect; Interbrew SA, a Belgian company, acquired Labatt in a $2.7 billion takeover in the summer of 1995; Procter & Gamble gobbled up Richardson-Vicks, Noxell, and parts of Revlon. Acquisition is a complex subject. Acquisitions can sometimes be good for society. The acquiring company may gain economies of scale that lead to lower costs and lower prices. A well-managed company may take over a poorly managed company and improve its efficiency. An industry that was not very competitive may become more competitive after the acquisition. But acquisitions also can be harmful and, therefore, are regulated by the government.

Critics have charged that marketing practices bar new companies from entering an industry. Large marketing companies can use patents and heavy promotional spending, and can tie up suppliers or dealers to keep out or drive out competitors. Nowhere are these issues more apparent than in Canada's pharmaceutical industry. In 1993, Canada revised the regulations dealing with patent protection for drugs. Patent protection was extended from 17 to 20 years. Manufacturers of branded drugs claimed that this increased protection has made the Canadian pharmaceutical industry more competitive internationally. The report is hotly disputed, however. The generic manufacturers want patent protection reduced to 10 years. They claim that the branch of the pharmaceutical industry comprising branded drug firms has actually cut jobs since being granted extended protection.

Finally, some firms have used unfair competitive marketing practices with the intention of hurting or destroying other firms. They may set their prices below costs, threaten to stop doing business with suppliers, or discourage the buying of a competitor's products. Various laws work to prevent such predatory competition. It is difficult, however, to prove that the intent or action was predatory. In recent years, Wal-Mart, Air Canada, Intel, and Microsoft have all been accused of predatory practices:[10]

Microsoft's…reach extends beyond the PC into everything from computerized toys and TV set-top boxes to selling cars and airline tickets over the Internet. In its zeal to become a leader not just in operating systems but also on the Internet, the company bundled its Internet Explorer browser into its Windows software. This move sparked an antitrust suit by the government, much to the delight of Microsoft's rivals. After all, Web-browsing innovator Netscape has seen its market share plummet as it tries to sell what Microsoft gives away for free.

Although competitors and the government charge that Microsoft's actions are predatory, the question is whether this is unfair competition or the healthy competition of a more efficient company against the less efficient.

CITIZEN AND PUBLIC ACTIONS TO REGULATE MARKETING

Because some people view business as the cause of many economic and social ills, grassroots movements have arisen from time to time to keep business in line. The two major movements are *consumerism* and *environmentalism*.

Consumers' Association of Canada
www.consumer.ca

Consumerism

The first consumer movements took place in the early 1900s and in the mid-1930s. Both were sparked by an upturn in consumer prices. Another movement began in the 1960s. Consumers had become better educated; products had become more complex and hazardous; and people were questioning the status quo. Many accused big business of wasteful and unethical practices. Since then, many consumer groups have been organized, and several consumer laws have been passed. The consumer movement has spread beyond North America and is especially strong in Europe.

But what is the consumer movement? **Consumerism** is an organized movement of citizens and government agencies to improve the rights and power of buyers in relation to sellers. The Consumers' Association of Canada (CAC) has acted as a consumer advocate and has provided information to Canadian consumers for more than 50 years. It is a volunteer-based, nongovernmental organization dedicated to representing the interests of Canadian consumers. Founded in 1947, it is the only nationally organized group of consumers in Canada and has offices in every province. The association lobbies government to secure consumer rights in areas of food, health care, environment, consumer products and services, regulated industries (phone, electricity, telecommunications, cable), financial institutions, taxation, trade, and any other issue of concern to Canadians facing complex buying decisions. The association establishes annual priorities. Recent issues include health care reform, the information highway, interprovincial trade barriers, consumer education and purchasing literacy, GST reform, price visibility, package downsizing, and environmental rights and responsibilities. The association has also outlined the following as fundamental consumer rights:[11]

Consumerism An organized movement of citizens and government agencies to improve the rights and power of buyers in relation to sellers.

- *The right to safety.* Consumers have the right to be protected against the marketing of goods that are hazardous to health or life.

- *The right to be informed.* Consumers must be protected against fraudulent, deceitful, or grossly misleading information, advertising, labelling, or other practices. They are to be given the facts needed to make an informed choice.

- *The right to choose.* Consumers have the right to choose, wherever possible, among a variety of products and services at competitive prices. In industries where competition is not workable and government regulation is substituted, consumers must be assured of satisfactory quality and service at fair prices.

- *The right to be heard.* It is important that consumers' voices be heard. Thus, they must receive full and sympathetic consideration in the formulation of government policy, and fair and expeditious treatment in its administrative tribunals.

- *The right to redress against damage.* Consumers have the right to seek redress from a supplier of goods and services for any loss or damage suffered because

Consumer desire for more information led to putting ingredients and nutrition and dating information on product labels.

of bad information, or faulty products or performance, and should have easy and inexpensive access to settlement of small claims.

- *The right to consumer education.* Canadian consumers have the right to be educated as children so that they will be able to act as informed consumers through their lives. Adults also have the right to consumer education.

Each proposed right has led to more specific proposals by consumerists. The right to be informed includes the right to know the true interest on a loan (truth in lending), the true cost per unit of a brand (unit pricing), the ingredients in a product (ingredient labelling), the nutrition in foods (nutritional labelling), product freshness (open dating), and the true benefits of a product (truth in advertising). Proposals related to consumer protection include strengthening consumer rights in cases of business fraud, requiring greater product safety, and giving more power to government agencies. Proposals relating to the quality of life include controlling the ingredients that go into certain products (detergents) and packaging (soft-drink containers), reducing the level of advertising "noise," and appointing consumer representatives to company boards to protect consumer interests.

In addition to the CAC, some better business bureaus offer tips to consumers to protect themselves from fraud or shady business practices. The one for mainland British Columbia, for example, provides information on the dangers of advertisements that promise consumers easy ways of earning money at home, explains the rules about the cooling-off periods, tells how to differentiate between legitimate and fraudulent requests for charitable contributions, and discusses the legality of pyramid schemes.

Consumers have not only the *right* but also the *responsibility* to protect themselves instead of leaving this function to someone else. Consumers who believe they got a bad deal have several remedies available, including writing to the company president or to the media; contacting federal, provincial, or local agencies; and going to small claims court.

Environmentalism

Environmentalism is an organized movement of concerned citizens, businesses, and government agencies to protect and improve people's living environment. Environmentalists are not against marketing and consumption; they simply want people and organizations to operate with more care for the environment. The marketing system's goal should not be to maximize consumption, consumer choice, or consumer satisfaction, but rather to maximize life quality. And "life quality" means not only the quantity and quality of consumer goods and services, but also the quality of the environment. Environmentalists want environmental costs included in both producer and consumer decision making.

In response to these concerns, the Canadian government has undertaken a number of initiatives to improve the environment. It froze production levels of chlorofluorocarbons (CFCs), the major cause of ozone layer depletion, at 1986 levels and committed itself to reducing production by a further 50 percent by the year 2000. In December 1999, environmental ministers from around the world met in Beijing and agreed to even stronger controls. Canada was one of the first countries to agree to a freeze of ozone-depleting chemicals. Subsequently, Canada's Ozone-Depleting Substances (ODS) Regulations, 1998 were revised to enable Canada to accept what became known as the Beijing Amendment, which came into force on 1 January 2001.[12]

Canada's environment ministers established a voluntary program intended to reduce excessive packaging by 50 percent by the year 2000. Patterning itself after the successful Blue Angel program in West Germany, the Canadian government developed an environmentally friendly labelling program and endorsed the goal of sustainable development put forward by the World Commission on Environment and Development. The Canadian Environmental Assessment Act is one piece of legislation developed to promote its goal of improving the environment.

Marketers cannot ignore the urgency of environmental issues or ignore the fact that governments are increasingly willing to take action and pass regulations restricting marketing practices. All parts of the marketing mix are affected. Advertisers are accused of adding to the solid waste problem when they use direct mail or newspaper inserts. Manufacturers are criticized for making products that incorporate materials that increase pollution or cannot be recycled.[13] Distribution systems have been cited for adding to air pollution as trucks move products from the factory to the store. Critics claim that even when environmentally friendly products are available, they are priced too high for many consumers to afford.

Buying behaviour has changed as sensitivity to this issue has grown. The late 1980s saw the birth of a new product attribute: environmentally friendly. A recent survey conducted by the Grocery Product Manufacturers of Canada found that 80 percent of respondents said they would be willing to pay more for "green" products. Companies began to respond to these changes in demand. Wal-Mart has asked its suppliers to provide more of these products. Loblaws has developed an entire line of products under its "green" President's Choice label. Governments are demanding that newsprint be made with a high proportion of recycled paper. The City of Toronto has stated it will favour products that are "green."

Environmentalism An organized movement of concerned citizens and government agencies to protect and improve people's living environment.

Members of the National Packaging Association of Canada have worked to reduce the amount of packaging going into landfills and have gained international marketing opportunities in return.

Some people claim that "green marketing" is dead. If you think that is true, just consider some of the initiatives by the Canadian packaging industry:[14]

Canada's packaging industry has been working diligently to meet the goals established by the National Packaging Protocol, a voluntary agreement formulated to reduce the amount of packaging sent to landfills by 50 percent relative to what was sent to the trash in 1988. Thus, in the early 1990s, when Canada's major laundry detergent manufacturers introduced concentrated powders to the market, they not only reduced the amount of detergent that people used, they also resulted in a 40 percent reduction in packaging materials. This is only part of the commitment of the packaging industry, which has invested more than $2 billion in infrastructure to reduce, reuse, and recycle its packaging. Compared to a decade ago, there is almost no packaging produced in Canada that hasn't been improved from an environmental perspective. For example, the average glass container has a 34 percent recycled content. Weights of containers have been reduced by at least 10 percent, saving fuel and shipping costs. Because the Canadian packaging industry had a jump on almost every other country in the world in designing better environmental packaging, there is strong export demand for Canadian packaging, especially in the U.S. It's a good initiative when you can sell more by using less.

The first wave of modern environmentalism was driven by environmental groups and concerned consumers; the second wave was driven by government, which passed laws and regulations governing industrial practices affecting the environment. Today, the first two environmentalism waves are merging into a third and stronger wave in which more companies are accepting responsibility for doing no harm to the environment. They are shifting from protest to prevention and from regulation to responsibility. Companies are adopting policies of **environmental sustainability**—developing strategies that both sustain the environment and produce

Environmental sustainability A management approach that involves developing strategies that both sustain the environment and produce profits for the company.

profits for the company. According to one strategist, "The challenge is to develop a sustainable global economy: an economy that the planet is capable of supporting indefinitely.... [It's] an enormous challenge—and an enormous opportunity."[15]

Figure 16-1 shows a grid that companies can use to gauge their progress toward environmental sustainability. At the most basic level, a company can practise pollution prevention. This involves more than pollution control—cleaning up waste after it has been created. Pollution prevention means eliminating or minimizing waste before it is created. Companies have developed ecologically safer products, recyclable and biodegradable packaging, better pollution controls, and more energy-efficient operations (see New Directions 16-1). They are finding that they can be both green and competitive. Consider how the Dutch flower industry has responded to its environmental problems:[16]

Intense cultivation of flowers in small areas was contaminating the soil and groundwater with pesticides, herbicides, and fertilizers. Facing increasingly strict regulation,...the Dutch understood that the only effective way to address the problem would be to develop a closed-loop system. In advanced Dutch greenhouses, flowers now grow in recirculated water and rock wool, not in soil. This lowers the risk of infestation, and reduces the need for fertilizers and pesticides. The...closed-loop system also reduces variation in growing conditions, thus improving product quality. Handling costs have also gone down.... The net result is not only dramatically lower environmental impact but also lower costs, better product quality, and enhanced global competitiveness.

	Internal	External
Tomorrow	**New environmental technology** Is the environmental performance of our products limited by our existing technology base? Is there potential to realize major improvements through new technology?	**Sustainability vision** Does our corporate vision direct us toward the solution of social and environmental problems? Does our vision guide the development of new technologies, markets, products, and processes?
Today	**Pollution prevention** Where are the most significant waste and emission streams from our current operations? Can we lower costs and risks by eliminating waste at the source or by using it as useful input?	**Product stewardship** What are the implications for product design and development if we assume responsibility for a product's entire life cycle? Can we add value or lower costs while simultaneously reducing the impact of our products?

Source: Reprinted by permission of *Harvard Business Review*. From "Beyond Greening: Strategies for a Sustainable World," by Stuart L. Hart, January–February 1997, p. 74. Copyright © 1997 by the President and Fellows of Harvard College; all rights reserved.

Figure 16-1
The Environmental Sustainability Grid

New Directions 16-1 >>   The New Environmentalism and Green Marketing

On Earth Day 1970, a newly emerging environmentalism movement made its first large-scale effort to educate people about the dangers of pollution. This was a tough task: At the time, most folks weren't very interested in environmental problems. By 1990, however, Earth Day had become an important day across North America, marked by articles in major magazines and newspapers, prime-time television extravaganzas, and countless events. It turned out to be just the start of an entire "Earth Decade" in which environmentalism became a massive worldwide force.

These days, environmentalism has broad public support. People hear and read daily about a growing list of environmental problems—global warming, acid rain, depletion of the ozone layer, air and water pollution, hazardous waste disposal, the buildup of solid wastes—and they are calling for solutions. The new environmentalism is causing many consumers to rethink what products they buy and from whom. These changing consumer attitudes have sparked a major new marketing thrust—*green marketing,* the movement by companies to develop and market environmentally responsible products. Committed "green" companies pursue not only environmental cleanup but also pollution prevention. True "green" work requires companies to practise the three Rs of waste management: reducing, reusing, and recycling waste.

Nortel has developed a program in which the company examines all the components it designs into products to help ensure that they are made from more environmentally responsible materials and that finished products can be recycled once their life cycle is complete. Spencer Francey Group, a Toronto-based communications firm, is developing more environmentally friendly media kits, trade-show displays, and information packages. In developing more environmentally friendly advertising and promotion materials for its clients, the firm reduced the amount of materials used, incorporated recycled materials whenever possible, and reduced inclusion of superfluous information. Not only did the company improve the environmental sensitivity of its products, but it also found that it produced clearer, more concise, and more memorable messages in the process. One of the

firm's programs was so successful that *Time* named it one of the best designs of the year.

Specialized products and services have been developed to meet the demands of green consumers. Such products are even being offered on the financial market. Ethical Funds, the largest family of "green funds" in Canada, invests only in firms that pass an ethical screening process that includes such criteria as records of good labour relations and charitable giving, as well as sound environmental policies.

McDonald's provides another example of green marketing. It used to purchase Coca-Cola syrup in plastic bags encased in cardboard, but now the syrup is delivered as gasoline is, pumped directly from tank trucks into storage vats at restaurants. The change saved 34 million kilograms of packaging a year. All napkins, bags, and tray liners in McDonald's restaurants are made from recycled paper, as are its carryout drink trays and even the stationery used at headquarters. For a company the size of McDonald's, even small changes can make a big difference. For example, just making its drinking straws

Changing consumer attitudes have sparked a major new marketing thrust— *green marketing,* the movement by companies to develop and market environmentally responsible products.

A positive sign.

McDonald's Earth Effort

20 percent lighter saved the company 500 000 kilograms of waste per year. Beyond turning its own products green, McDonald's purchases recycled materials for building and remodelling its restaurants, and it challenges its suppliers to furnish and use recycled products.

Producers in a range of industries are responding to environmental concerns. For example, 3M runs a Pollution Prevention Pays program, which has led to substantial pollution and cost reduction. Dow built a new ethylene plant in Alberta that uses 40 percent less energy and releases 97 percent less waste water than its previous plant.

During the early phase of the new environmentalism, promoting environmentally improved products and actions ballooned into a big business. In fact, environmentalists and regulators became concerned that companies were going overboard with their use of terms like *recyclable, biodegradable,* and *environmentally responsible.* Perhaps of equal concern was that, as more marketers used green marketing claims, more consumers would view them as mere gimmicks.

Responsible green marketing is not an easy task and is full of many contradictions. Even companies like The Body Shop, while admired for increasing awareness of such issues as degradation of the rain forests and the use of animal testing, are criticized for exaggerating their progressive practices. However, environmentalism appears to be moving into a more mature phase. Gone are the hastily prepared environmental pitches and products designed to capitalize on, or even exploit, growing public concern. The new environmentalism is now going mainstream—broader, deeper, and more sophisticated. In the words of one analyst:

Dressing up ads with pictures of eagles and trees will no longer woo an environmentally sophisticated audience. People want to know that companies are incorporating environmental values into their manufacturing processes, products, packaging, and the very fabric of their corporate cultures. They…want to know that companies will not compromise the ability of future generations to enjoy the quality of life that we enjoy today…. As a result, we're seeing the marriage of performance benefits and environmental benefits…one reinforces the other. Some companies have responded to consumer environmental concerns by doing only what is required to avert new regulations or to keep environmentalists quiet. Others have rushed to make money by catering to the public's mounting concern for the environment. But enlightened companies are taking action not because someone is forcing them to or to reap short-run profits, but because it is the right thing to do. They believe that environmental far-sightedness today will pay off tomorrow—for both the customer and the company.

Sources: Quote from Robert Rehak, "Green Marketing Awash in Third Wave," *Advertising Age,* 22 November 1993, p. 22. Also see Joe Schwartz, "Earth Day Today," *American Demographics,* April 1990, pp. 40–41; Eric Wieffering, "Wal-Mart Turns Green in Kansas," *American Demographics,* December 1993, p. 23; David Woodruff, "Herman Miller: How Green Is My Factory," *Business Week,* 16 September 1991, pp. 54–56; Jacquelyn Ottman, "Environmentalism Will Be the Trend of the '90s," *Marketing News,* 7 December 1992, p. 13; Peter Stisser, "A Deeper Shade of Green," *American Demographics,* March 1994, pp. 24–30; Jon Entine, "In Search of Saintly Stock Picks," *Report on Business,* October 1995, p. 45; and Carolyn Leitch, "PR Firm Delivers Fewer Pounds in the Ruff, in the Aid of Less Waste," *Report on Environmental Protection, The Globe and Mail,* 27 February 1990, p. C1.

At the next level, companies can practise *product stewardship*—minimizing not only pollution from production, but all environmental impacts throughout the full product life cycle. Many companies, such as Nortel, are adopting *design for environment* (DFE) practices, which involve thinking ahead in the design stage to create products that are easier to recover, reuse, or recycle. DFE practices not only help to sustain the environment, but also can be highly profitable:[17]

Consider Xerox Corporation's Asset Recycle Management (ARM) program. A well-developed [process] for taking back leased copiers combined with a sophisticated remanufacturing process allows components to be reconditioned, tested, and then reassembled into "new" machines. Xerox estimates that ARM savings in raw materials, labour, and waste disposal in 1995 alone were in the $400 million to $500 million range.... Xerox has discovered a way to add value and lower costs. It can continually provide lease customers with the latest product upgrades, giving them state-of-the-art functionality with minimum environmental impact.

At the third level of environmental sustainability, companies look to the future and plan for *new environmental technologies.* Although many organizations have made significant headway in pollution prevention and product stewardship, they are limited by existing technologies and need to develop new technologies. Monsanto, for example, is tackling this problem with biotechnology. By controlling plant growth and pest resistance through bioengineering rather than through the application of pesticides or fertilizers, it hopes to find an environmentally sustainable path to increased agricultural yields.[18]

Finally, companies can develop a *sustainability vision,* which serves as a guide to the future. It shows how the company's products and services, processes, and policies must evolve and what new technologies must be developed to get there. This vision of sustainability provides a framework for pollution control, product stewardship, and environmental technology.

Most companies today invest in pollution prevention. Some forward-looking companies practise product stewardship and are developing new environmental technologies. Few companies have well-defined sustainability visions. However, emphasizing only one or a few cells in the environmental sustainability grid in Figure 16-1 can be short-sighted. Although investing only in the bottom half of the grid puts a company in a good position today, it will be vulnerable in the future. In contrast, undue emphasis on the top half suggests good environmental vision, but not the skills needed to implement it. Therefore, companies should work at developing all four dimensions of environmental sustainability.

Environmentalism creates some special challenges for global marketers. As international trade barriers come down and global markets expand, environmental issues are having a growing impact on international trade. Countries in North America, Western Europe, and other developed regions are developing stringent environmental standards. A side accord to the North American Free Trade Agreement (NAFTA) set up a commission for resolving environmental matters. And the European Union's Eco-Management and Audit Regulation provides guidelines for environmental self-regulation.[19]

However, environmental policies vary widely from country to country, and uniform worldwide standards are not expected for many years. Although countries such as Canada, Denmark, Germany, Japan, and the United States have fully developed environmental policies and high public expectations, major countries such as China, India, Brazil, and Russia are only in the early stages of developing such policies. Moreover, environmental factors that motivate consumers in one country may have no impact on consumers in another. For example, PVC soft-drink bottles cannot be used in Switzerland or Germany. However, they are preferred in France, which has an extensive recycling process for them. Thus, international companies are finding it difficult to develop standard environmental practices that work around the world. Instead, they are creating general policies and then translating these into tailored programs to meet local regulations and expectations.

Public Actions to Regulate Marketing

Citizen concerns about marketing practices usually will lead to public attention and legislative proposals. New bills will be debated—many will be defeated, others will be modified, and a few will become workable laws. Many of the laws that affect marketing are listed in Chapter 3. The task is to translate these laws into the language that marketing executives understand as they make decisions about competitive relations, products, price, promotion, and channels of distribution. Figure 16-2 illustrates the major legal and ethical issues facing marketing management.

BUSINESS ACTIONS TOWARD SOCIALLY RESPONSIBLE MARKETING

At first, many companies opposed consumerism and environmentalism: They thought the criticisms were either unfair or unimportant. However, most compan-

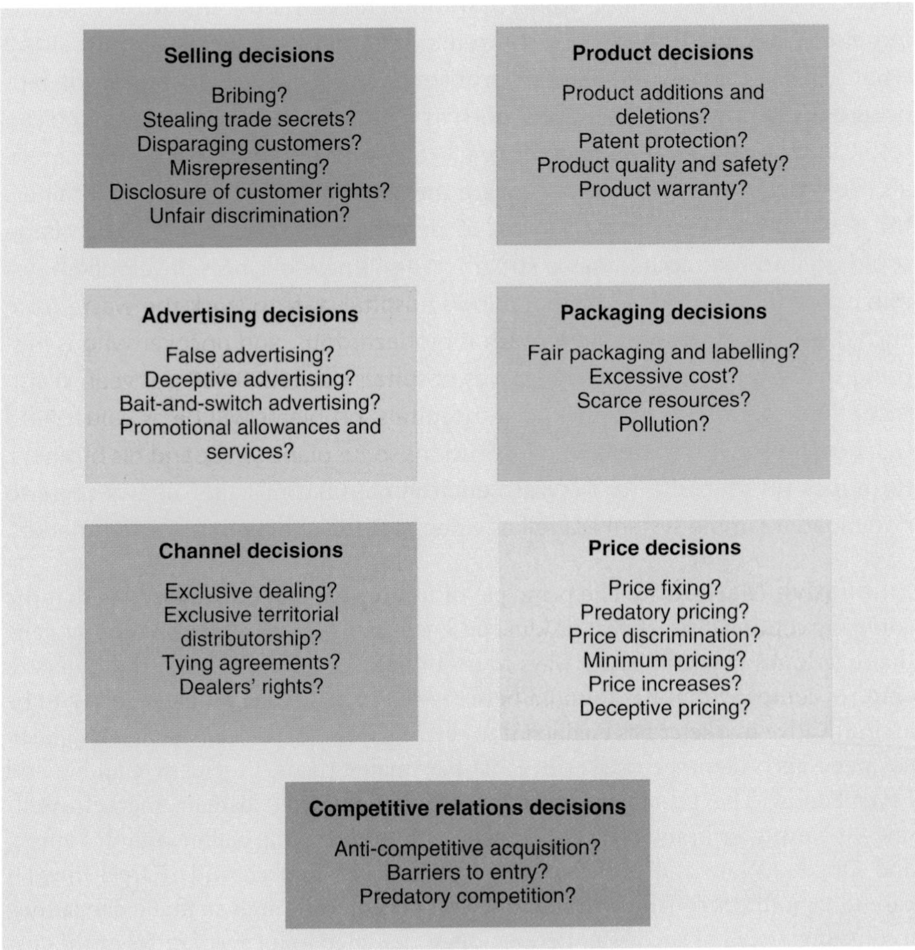

Selling decisions

Bribing?
Stealing trade secrets?
Disparaging customers?
Misrepresenting?
Disclosure of customer rights?
Unfair discrimination?

Product decisions

Product additions and deletions?
Patent protection?
Product quality and safety?
Product warranty?

Advertising decisions

False advertising?
Deceptive advertising?
Bait-and-switch advertising?
Promotional allowances and services?

Packaging decisions

Fair packaging and labelling?
Excessive cost?
Scarce resources?
Pollution?

Channel decisions

Exclusive dealing?
Exclusive territorial distributorship?
Tying agreements?
Dealers' rights?

Price decisions

Price fixing?
Predatory pricing?
Price discrimination?
Minimum pricing?
Price increases?
Deceptive pricing?

Competitive relations decisions

Anti-competitive acquisition?
Barriers to entry?
Predatory competition?

Figure 16-2

Legal Issues Facing Marketing Management

Enlightened marketing A marketing philosophy holding that a company's marketing should support the best long-run performance of the marketing system; its five principles are consumer-oriented marketing, innovative marketing, value marketing, sense-of-mission marketing, and societal marketing.

ies have grown to accept the new consumer rights, at least in principle. They may oppose certain pieces of legislation as inappropriate for solving certain consumer problems, but they recognize the consumer's right to information and protection. Many companies have responded positively to consumerism and environmentalism to serve consumer needs better.

Enlightened Marketing

The philosophy of **enlightened marketing** holds that a company's marketing should support the best long-run performance of the marketing system. Enlightened marketing consists of five principles: *consumer-oriented marketing, innovative marketing, value marketing, sense-of-mission marketing,* and *societal marketing.*

Consumer-oriented mar-keting A principle of enlightened marketing that holds that a company should view and organize its marketing activities from the consumer's point of view.

Consumer-Oriented Marketing **Consumer-oriented marketing** means that the company should view and organize its marketing activities from the consumer's point of view. It should work hard to sense, serve, and satisfy the needs of a defined group of customer. Consider this example:[20]

Montreal-based Walsh Integrated Environmental Systems Inc. focused on solving the waste management problems of hospitals. The owner, David Walsh, fresh out of business school, wanted to found his own business. After conducting a 12-week waste audit at Montreal's Royal Victoria Hospital, he realized what a huge waste management problem hospitals faced. Disposing of biohazardous waste costs 20 times as much as getting rid of regular waste and can result in bills of over $450 000 per year. Yet Walsh also saw that other materials, from pop cans to newspapers, were thrown in the biohazardous containers the hospital was using. In fact, about 65 percent of the material in the garbage could go into the regular waste stream. Walsh's new business developed a system called the Waste Tracker that allows hospital staff to track the waste from each department, identify how much is biohazardous, and uncover who is misusing the system. His system now saves hospitals over $200 000 per year. Walsh is confident that his focus on solving hospitals' problems will be as valuable to U.S. hospitals as it is to Canadian institutions so he plans to expand his business. He hopes his Web site (**www.walshenvironmental.com/**) that allows users to download a sample system as well as video material will help crack this market.

Innovative marketing A principle of enlightened marketing that requires that a company seek real product and marketing improvements.

Innovative Marketing The principle of **innovative marketing** requires that the company continually seek real product and marketing improvements. The company that overlooks new and better ways to do things will eventually lose customers to another company that has found a better way. Cosmair Canada Inc.'s ability to be an innovative marketer has enabled it to retain its lead in the $2.5 billion Canadian cosmetic and fragrance market over its two major rivals, Procter & Gamble and Lever-Ponds. The Canadian subsidiary of Paris-based Cosmair markets well-known consumer brands L'Oréal, Lancôme, Biotherm, Maybelline, Ralph Lauren, and Drakkar Noir, and professional products in its Redken and L'Oréal lines. It carefully monitors consumer trends and competitors' offerings so that it can launch a constant stream of successful new products designed to fill every niche of the cosmetic and fragrance marketplace. It dominates the channels of distribution, and spends more than $20 million annually on advertising.[21]

Value Marketing According to the principle of **value marketing**, a company should put most of its resources into marketing investments that build long-run consumer loyalty by continually improving the value that consumers receive from the firm's marketing offer. Lowering costs and prices, making services more convenient, and improving product quality are some value-adding strategies. The value-adding strategy of Canada's Forrec Limited has made it a leader in international theme park design. Although the company name isn't exactly a household word, Forrec has been responsible for creating Canada's Wonderland north of Toronto and the casino in Niagara Falls. It also brought a South Pacific beach to the middle of Edmonton, created the streets of San Francisco in the heart of Florida, added a rooftop water park to the Bangkok horizon, built a theme park at the edge of the Pyramids of Giza, and is developing an aquarium in Shanghai. Steve Moorehead reveals the secret of his company's success: "We make the site a place where people want to be, and provide a sense of enjoyment, where they know that they're not being ripped off, and we entice them to come back again and again."[22]

> **Value marketing** A principle of enlightened marketing that holds that a company should put most of its resources into value-building marketing investments.

Sense-of-Mission Marketing **Sense-of-mission marketing** means that the company should define its mission in broad *social* terms rather than narrow *product* terms. When a company defines a social mission, employees feel better about their work and have a clearer sense of direction. For example, defined in narrow product terms, ice-cream marketer Ben & Jerry's mission might be "to sell ice cream and frozen yogurt." However, on its Web page, the company states its mission more broadly as one of "linked prosperity":[23]

> **Sense-of-mission marketing** A principle of enlightened marketing that holds that a company should define its mission in broad social terms rather than narrow product terms.

Ben & Jerry's is dedicated to the creation and demonstration of a new corporate concept of linked prosperity. Our mission consists of three interrelated parts....

Product To make, distribute and sell the finest quality all natural ice cream and related products in a wide variety of innovative flavors made from Vermont dairy products.

Economic To operate the Company on a sound financial basis of profitable growth, increasing value for our shareholders, and creating career opportunities and financial rewards for our employees.

Social To operate the Company in a way that actively recognizes the central role that business plays in the structure of society by initiating innovative ways to improve the quality of life of a broad community-local, national, and international.

Underlying the mission of Ben & Jerry's is the determination to seek new and creative ways of addressing all three parts, while holding a deep respect for individuals inside and outside the Company and for the communities of which they are a part.

Reshaping the basic task of selling consumer products into the larger mission of serving the interests of consumers, employees, and others in the company's various "communities" has allowed the firm to grow and prosper while simultaneously

New Directions 16-2 >> Mission: Social Responsibility

In a recent poll, 92 percent of consumers said they believe it's important for marketers to be good corporate citizens. More than three quarters said that they would switch brands and retailers when price and quality are equal for a product associated with a good cause. Companies have responded to this call for social responsibility with actions ranging from supporting worthwhile causes to writing social responsibility into their underlying mission statements.

Today, acts of good corporate citizenship abound. For example, American Express's Charge against Hunger program—through which the company donates three cents from every transaction made during the holiday season—has raised more than $30 million for hunger relief. Maxwell House, a division of Kraft Foods, recently created a partnership with Habitat for Humanity to build 100 homes in as many days, while working to raise awareness for the organization. Post Cereal celebrated its 100th anniversary by donating to Second Harvest—one of the largest networks of hunger-relief charities—enough cereal to feed more than one million people. In addition, Post partnered with grocery retailers to sponsor a 100-day food drive supported by national and local ads to increase hunger awareness and to encourage consumer participation in the drive.

It seems that almost every company has a pet cause. Alarm company ADT gives away personal security systems to battered women. Avon Products helps fund the fight against breast cancer. Dow donates employees' time and home construction materials to Habitat for Humanity. Coca-Cola sponsors local Boys and Girls Clubs, Petro-Canada funds the Canadian Cancer Society's Information Service, while RBC Dominion Securities works with Raising the Roof.

In the chapter opener example, we examined the socially responsible mission of some of Canada's firms that have won awards for their efforts. Here are two more examples of companies working to better their communities:

Saturn. From its inception, Saturn Corporation has worked to distinguish itself as a "different" car company. As its slogan states, Saturn is "A different kind of company. A different kind of car." The company claims to focus more on its employees, customers, and communities than on revenues and bottom lines. Saturn president and chair Don Hudler notes that "a part of Saturn's business philosophy is to meet the needs of our neighbours." An example of this philosophy in action is Saturn Playgrounds, a company program for employee involvement and community betterment. The goal of the program is to provide young children in poor communities with a safe, fun environment during nonschool hours as an alternative to gangs, drugs, and crime. Backed by Saturn retail facility dollars, local Saturn employees and customers join with community members to build a community playground in a single day. So far, Saturn and its customers have built over 50 playgrounds in towns across Canada. When Saturn dedicated the new playground built on the grounds of the Toronto Zoo, 6700 owners and their families participated. But playgrounds aren't the only things needed by communities. Saturn retailers are the eyes and ears of the company, and when a community

Backed by Saturn retail facility dollars, local Saturn employees and customers join with community members to build a community playground in a single day.

need arises, Saturn tries to respond. Saturn planted trees in areas hard hit by the 1997 ice storm. In North Bay, it provided funds for a new heart-monitoring unit. As a member of one local United Auto Workers union commented: "The Saturn Playgrounds project is a perfect example of the partnership we've built at Saturn. Working together can bring powerful results, not just in our jobs, but in our communities."

The Body Shop: In 1976, Anita Roddick opened The Body Shop in Brighton, England, a tiny storefront selling beauty products out of specimen bottles. Now the company and its franchisees operate nearly 1600 stores in 47 countries. Fundamental to this rapid growth, Roddick advocates including social responsibility alongside financial performance as a measure of company success. The Body Shop's mission is "to dedicate our business to the pursuit of social and environmental change." In keeping with that mission, the company manufactures and sells natural-ingredient-based cosmetics in simple and appealing recyclable packaging. All the products are formulated without any animal testing, and supplies are often sourced from developing countries. Each franchise is required to participate in annual projects designed to better its community. In addition to these projects, The Body Shop is committed to continual activism. For example, to promote AIDS awareness, the company has handed out condoms and pamphlets about safe sex. The Body Shop also donates a percentage of profits each year to animal-

rights groups, homeless shelters, Amnesty International, Save the Rain Forest, and other social causes. As The Body Shop grows, however, it appears to be moving from rebel to mainstream. As other retailers not shackled by The Body Shop's "principles before profits" mission invade its markets, the retailer's sales growth and profits are flattening. Still, says Roddick, "Business innovation is no longer just about product [and profits]. It's about the very role of business itself."

Sources: Quotes from Anat Arkin, "Open Business Is Good for Business," *People Management,* January 1996, pp. 24–27; David Lennon, "Roddick Isn't Finished Yet," *Europe,* March 1997, pp. 39-40; "Saturn Dealers Build Six New Playgrounds in One Weekend," *PR Newswire,* 4 June 1997; and The Body Shop Web site, accessed online at **www.bodyshop.com**, January 2000. Information also provided by Chuck Novak, Saturn brand manager Saturn Canada in an interview with Peggy Cunningham, 21 July 1999. Also see David Bosworth, "GM Attracts Site Seers," *Strategy,* 22 June 1998, p. D1; Sinclair Steward, "Putting the Customer First," *Strategy,* 9 November 1998, p. 21; Daniel Kadlec, "The New World of Giving," *Time,* 5 May 1997, pp. 62–64; Heather Salerno, "From Selling Cars to Building Playgrounds," *Washington Post,* 9 June 1997, p. F11; "Can Doing Good Be Good for Business?" *Fortune,* 2 February 1998, pp. 148G–148J; Ernest Beck, "Body Shop Founder Roddick Steps Aside as CEO," *The Wall Street Journal,* 13 May 1998, p. B14; and Cathy Hartman and Caryn Beck-Dudley, "Marketing Strategies and the Search for Virtue: A Case Analysis of The Body Shop, International," *Journal of Business Ethics,* July 1999, pp. 249-263.

accomplishing a social agenda. Many companies today are undertaking socially responsible actions or even building social responsibility into their underlying missions (see New Directions 16-2).

Many nonprofit and special interest organizations also use mission marketing. Vancouver ad agency Lanyon Phillips Partners helped Friends of Animals, a New York-based group opposed to the wearing of fur for fashion, when it developed an award-winning 1995 campaign. Vickers and Benson's "Little Girl" ad showing a little girl talking to the audience was another recent award winner. The dialogue, "I went out last night and got totally hammered. Beer. Shooters, I puked my guts out. I don't even know how I got home...." dramatically brought attention to the problems of youth alcohol abuse.

Societal Marketing Following the principle of **societal marketing**, an enlightened company makes marketing decisions by considering consumers' wants and interests, the company's requirements, and society's long-run interests. The company is aware that neglecting consumer and societal long-run interests is a disservice to consumers and society. Alert companies view societal problems as opportunities.

Societal marketing A principle of enlightened marketing that holds that a company should make marketing decisions by considering consumers' and society's long-run interests.

Alcohol and Drug Concerns Inc. used mission marketing to dramatically bring attention to the problem of youth alcohol abuse.

Hewlett-Packard Canada is proud of its commitment to the local communities in which it operates. In fact, it points out that citizenship is one of its seven corporate objectives. The company articulates this belief as follows: "HP Canada sees its contribution to societal needs as creating better places for Canadians to live, including HP employees and our customers." This sense of citizenship is more than corporate public relations. The company works to translate its words into practice. It actively works to protect the environment by carefully following the three Rs (reduce, recycle, reuse), and it supports important causes such as education and health care since it believes "that the betterment of our society is not a job to be left to a few; it is a responsibility to be shared by all."[24]

A societally oriented marketer wants to design products that are not only pleasing but also beneficial. The difference is shown in Figure 16-3. Products can be classified according to their degree of immediate consumer satisfaction and long-run consumer benefit. **Deficient products**, such as bad-tasting and ineffective medicine, have neither immediate appeal nor long-run benefits. **Pleasing products** give high immediate satisfaction but may hurt consumers in the long run: An example is cigarettes. **Salutary products** have low appeal but benefit consumers in the long run: Insurance is a salutary product. **Desirable products** give both high immediate satisfaction and high long-run benefits. President's Choice "Too Good to Be True" soup mixes have been cited as healthful products. Developed for people with special dietary needs, they have been welcomed by a range of consumers who want good-tasting, high-fibre, low-fat, easy-to-prepare, healthful food. Another example of a desirable product is Herman Miller's Avian office chair, which is not just attractive and functional but also environmentally responsible:[25]

Herman Miller, one of the world's largest office furniture makers, has received numerous awards for environmentally responsible products and business practices. In 1994, the company formed an earth friendly design task force respon-

Deficient products Products that have neither immediate appeal nor long-run benefits.

Pleasing products Products that give high immediate satisfaction but may hurt consumers in the long run.

Salutary products Products that have low appeal but may benefit consumers in the long run.

Desirable products Products that give both high immediate satisfaction and high long-run benefits.

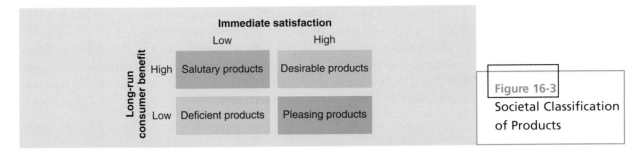

Immediate satisfaction

	Low	High
High	Salutary products	Desirable products
Low	Deficient products	Pleasing products

Long-run consumer benefit

Figure 16-3

Societal Classification of Products

sible for infusing the company's design process with its environmental values. The task force carries out life cycle analyses on the company's products, including everything from how much of a product can be made from recycled materials to how much of the product itself can be recycled at the end of its useful life. For example, the company's Avian chair is designed for the lowest possible ecological impact and 100 percent recyclability. Herman Miller reduced material used in the chair by using gas-assist injection molding for the frame, which resulted in hollow frame members (like the bones of birds, hence the chair's name). The frame needs no paint or other finish. All materials are recyclable. No ozone-depleting materials are used. The chair is shipped partially assembled, thus reducing the packaging and energy needed to ship it. Finally, a materials schematic is embedded in the bottom of the seat to help recycle the chair at the end of its life. This is truly a desirable product—it's won awards for design and function and for environmental responsibility.

Herman Miller's earth-friendly design task force infuses the company's design process with environmental values. It designed the Avian chair for the lowest possible ecological impact and 100 percent recyclability.

The challenge posed by pleasing products is that they sell very well but may end up hurting the consumer. The product opportunity, therefore, is to add long-run benefits without reducing the product's pleasing qualities. For example, Sears developed a phosphate-free laundry detergent that was also very effective. The challenge posed by salutary products is to add some pleasing qualities so that they will become more desirable in the consumers' minds.

Pause here, and look back on the Societal Marketing Concept section in Chapter 1.

- How does Figure 1-4 apply to the Enlightened Marketing section in this chapter?
- Use the five principles of socially responsible marketing to assess the actions of a company that you believe exemplifies socially responsible marketing (if you can't think of one, look at Mountain Equipment Co-op or one of the companies discussed in this chapter).
- Use the principles of enlightened marketing to assess the actions of a company that you believe falls short of socially responsible marketing. (A hint: Look at toy sites for kids or Labatt's or Molson's Web sites to determine whether these companies could be perceived as promoting underage drinking.)

Marketing Ethics

Conscientious marketers face many moral dilemmas. The best thing to do is often unclear. Because not all managers have fine moral sensitivity, companies need to develop *corporate marketing ethics policies*—broad guidelines that everyone in the organization must follow. These policies should cover distributor relations, advertising standards, customer service, pricing, product development, and general ethical standards.

The finest guidelines cannot resolve all the ethical situations the marketer faces. Table 16-1 lists some difficult ethical situations that marketers could face during their careers. If marketers choose immediate sales-producing actions in all these cases, their marketing behaviour may well be described as immoral or even amoral. If they refuse to go along with *any* of the actions, they may be ineffective as marketing managers and unhappy because of the constant moral tension. Managers need a set of principles that will help them to determine the moral importance of each situation and decide how far they can go in good conscience.

But *what* principle should guide companies and marketing managers on issues of ethics and social responsibility? One philosophy is that such issues are decided by the free market and legal system. Under this principle, companies and their managers are not responsible for making moral judgments. Companies can in good conscience do whatever the system legally allows.

A second philosophy puts responsibility not in the system but in the hands of individual companies and managers. This more enlightened philosophy suggests that a company should have a "social conscience." Companies and managers should apply high standards of ethics and morality when making corporate decisions, regardless of "what the system allows." History provides an endless list of examples of company actions that were legal and allowed but were highly irresponsible. Consider this example:[26]

Table 16-1   Some Morally Difficult Situations in Marketing

1.	You work for a cigarette company and up until now have not been convinced that cigarettes cause cancer. A report comes across your desk that clearly shows the link between smoking and cancer. What do you do?
2.	Your R&D department has changed one of your products slightly. It is not really "new and improved," but you know that putting this statement on the package and in advertising will increase sales. What do you do?
3.	You have been asked to add a stripped-down model to your line that could be advertised to attract customers to the store. The product won't be very good, but salespeople will be able to switch buyers up to higher-priced units. You are asked to give the green light for this stripped-down version. What do you do?
4.	You are considering hiring a product manager who just left a competitor's company. She would be more than happy to tell you all the competitor's plans for the coming year. What do you do?
5.	One of your top dealers in an important territory has recently had family troubles, and his sales have slipped. It looks like it will take him some time to straighten out his family trouble. Meanwhile, you are losing many sales. Legally, you can terminate the dealer's franchise and replace him. What do you do?
6.	You have a chance to win a big account that will mean a lot to you and your company. The purchasing agent hints that a "gift" would influence the decision. Your assistant recommends sending a fine colour television set to the buyer's home. What do you do?
7.	You have heard that a competitor has a new product feature that will make a big difference in sales. The competitor will demonstrate the feature in a private dealer meeting at the annual trade show. You can easily send a snoop to this meeting to learn about the new feature. What do you do?
8.	You have to choose between three ad campaigns outlined by your agency. *A* is a soft-sell, honest information campaign. *B* uses sex-loaded emotional appeals and exaggerates the product's benefits. *C* involves a noisy, irritating commercial that is sure to gain audience attention. Pretests show that the campaigns are effective in the following order: C, B, and A. What do you do?
9.	You are interviewing a capable female applicant for a job as a salesperson. She is better qualified than the men just interviewed. Nevertheless, you know that some of your important customers prefer dealing with men, and you will lose some sales if you hire her. What do you do?
10.	You are a sales manager in an encyclopedia company. Your competitor's salespeople are getting into homes by pretending to take a research survey. After they finish the survey, they switch to their sales pitch. This technique seems to be very effective. What do you do?

Prior to the [U.S.] Pure Food and Drug Act, the advertising for a diet pill promised that a person taking this pill could eat virtually anything at any time and still lose weight. Too good to be true? Actually the claim was quite true; the product lived up to its billing with frightening efficiency. It seems that the primary active ingredient in this "diet pill" was tapeworm larvae. These larvae would develop in the intestinal tract and, of course, be well fed; the pill taker would in time, quite literally, starve to death.

Each company and marketing manager must work out a philosophy of socially responsible and ethical behaviour. Under the social marketing concept, companies and managers must look beyond what is legal and allowed and develop standards based on personal integrity, corporate conscience, and long-run consumer welfare. According to a survey of the CEOs of Canada's top 500 companies, 84 percent agreed that there was a good understanding of ethics in their companies, and 90 percent said that ethics was a priority for senior managers. Many Canadian companies (80 percent) have developed codes of ethics to help their managers make better decisions. Even more important, 70 percent of the codes were written to develop standards that go beyond mere legal compliance. However, only 27 percent of the firms surveyed offered ethics training programs, and only 25 percent have ethics compliance officers. Nonetheless, 75 percent of the companies studied reported that employees of their firms had been disciplined because of lack of ethical behaviour.[27]

The issue of ethics provides special challenges for international marketers. Business standards and laws vary widely from one country to the next. For example, while Levi Strauss, Nike, and Gap have forward-thinking human relations policies in North America, these firms have been accused of exploiting workers working for their subcontractors in Latin America and Southeast Asia. Like many other international firms, Nike has responded by developing a code of ethics that applies to their international businesses as well as to their domestic operations.

Gift giving, always a thorny issue in international business negotiations, is often covered under these codes. Some firms, such as General Motors and Bata Industries Ltd., have very strict codes that forbid the acceptance of gifts, entertainment, or other gratuity. The codes rule out acceptance of any token including tickets to a football game, birthday presents from suppliers, or even a watch sent through the mail. GM realizes that in some countries, like China, where gift giving is part of the business culture, refusal to accept a gift would have significant negative implications. Therefore, GM's representatives working there can accept a gift as long as they do it in the name of the company and turn it over for display on the company premises. Bata believes that such a strict policy is necessary because it is impossible to differentiate between a gift and a bribe. Either can lead a decision maker into a conflict of interest and an inability to make a purchase decision that represents the best value for the company.[28]

When firms go beyond gift giving to influence decisions into the realm of bribery—giving a covert payment to a government official to obtain a concession—they are no longer just committing an unethical act, they are committing an illegal one violating the Corruption of Foreign Public Officials Act tabled by the Canadian government in 1998.

Many professional associations and firms have developed codes of ethics to better manage ethical issues related to marketing. For example, the American Marketing Association, an international association of marketing managers and scholars with many Canadian members, developed the code of ethics shown in Table 16-2. Companies are also developing programs to teach managers about important ethics issues and help them find the proper responses. They hold ethics workshops and seminars and set up ethics committees.

Canadian Marketing Association
www.the-cma.org

The Canadian Marketing Association has established codes of practice for its 750 member companies. These ethical standards acknowledge that marketers have a responsibility to the public necessary to winning and maintaining public confidence. The CMA code is comprehensive and includes standards of practice for such topics as consumer offers and fulfillment, media related standards, product safety, privacy protection and advertising to children. For more information, go to the CMA's Web site.

Some organizations, such as The Royal Bank and Imperial Oil, have appointed high-level ethics officers to champion ethics issues and to help resolve ethics problems and concerns facing employees. Nynex created a new position of vice president of ethics, supported by a dozen full-time staff and a million-dollar budget. Since 1991, the ethics department has trained some 95 000 employees. This train-

Table 16-2   American Marketing Association Code of Ethics

Members of the American Marketing Association are committed to ethical, professional conduct. They have joined together in subscribing to this Code of Ethics embracing the following topics:

Responsibilities of the Marketer

Marketers must accept responsibility for the consequences of their activities and make every effort to ensure that their decisions, recommendations, and actions function to identify, serve, and satisfy all relevant publics: customers, organizations, and society.

Marketers' professional conduct must be guided by:

1. The basic rule of professional ethics: not knowingly to do harm;
2. The adherence to all applicable laws and regulations;
3. The accurate representation of their education, training, and experience; and
4. The active support, practice, and promotion of this Code of Ethics.

Honesty and Fairness

Marketers shall uphold and advance the integrity, honor, and dignity of the marketing profession by:

1. Being honest in serving consumers, clients, employees, suppliers, distributors, and the public;
2. Not knowingly participating in conflict of interest without prior notice to all parties involved; and
3. Establishing equitable fee schedules including the payment or receipt of usual, customary, and/or legal compensation for marketing exchanges.

Rights and Duties of Parties in the Marketing Exchange Process

Participants in the marketing exchange process should be able to expect that:

1. Products and services offered are safe and fit for their intended uses;
2. Communications about offered products and services are not deceptive;
3. All parties intend to discharge their obligations, financial and otherwise, in good faith; and
4. Appropriate internal methods exist for equitable adjustment and/or redress of grievances concerning purchases.

It is understood that the above would include, but is not limited to, the following responsibilities of the marketer:

In the area of product development and management,

- disclosure of all substantial risks associated with product or service usage;
- identification of any product component substitution that might materially change the product or impact on the buyer's purchase decision;
- identification of extra cost-added features.

In the area of promotions,

- avoidance of false and misleading advertising;
- rejection of high-pressure manipulations, or misleading sales tactics;
- avoidance of sales promotions that use deceptions or manipulation.

In the area of distribution,

- not manipulating the availability of a product for purpose of exploitation;
- not using coercion in the marketing channel;

- not exerting undue influence over the reseller's choice to handle a product.

In the area of pricing,

- not engaging in price fixing;
- not practicing predatory pricing;
- disclosing the full price associated with any purchase.

In the area of marketing research,

- prohibiting selling or fundraising under the guise of conducting research;
- maintaining research integrity by avoiding misrepresentation and omission of pertinent research data;
- treating outside clients and suppliers fairly.

Organizational Relationships

Marketers should be aware of how their behavior may influence or impact on the behavior of others in organizational relationships. They should not demand, encourage, or apply coercion to obtain unethical behavior in their relationships with others, such as employees, suppliers, or customers.

1. Apply confidentiality and anonymity in professional relationships with regard to privileged information;
2. Meet their obligations and responsibilities in contracts and mutual agreements in a timely manner;
3. Avoid taking the work of others, in whole, or in part, and represent this work as their own or directly benefit from it without compensation or consent of the originator or owner;
4. Avoid manipulation to take advantage of situations to maximize personal welfare in a way that unfairly deprives or damages the organization of others.

Any AMA member found to be in violation of any provision of this Code of Ethics may have his or her Association membership suspended or revoked.

ing includes sending 22 000 managers to full-day workshops that include case studies on ethical actions in marketing, finance, and other business functions.[29]

Many companies have developed innovative ways to educate employees about ethics:[30]

Citicorp has developed an ethics board game, which teams of employees use to solve hypothetical quandaries. General Electric employees can tap into specially designed software on their personal computers to get answers to ethical questions. At Texas Instruments, employees are treated to a weekly column on ethics over an electronic news service. One popular feature: a kind of "Dear Abby" mailbag, answers provided by the company's ethics officer,…that deals with the troublesome issues employees face most often.

Still, written codes and ethics programs do not ensure ethical behaviour. Ethics and social responsibility require a total corporate commitment. They must be a component of the overall corporate culture. According to David R. Whitman, chairman of the board of Whirlpool Corporation:

In the final analysis, "ethical behavior" must be an integral part of the organization, a way of life that is deeply ingrained in the collective corporate body.…In any business enterprise, ethical behavior must be a tradition, a way of conducting one's affairs that is passed from generation to generation of employees at all levels of the organization. It is the responsibility of management, starting at the very top, to both set the example by personal conduct and create an environment that not only encourages and rewards ethical behavior, but [that] also makes anything less totally unacceptable.[31]

Canada's 74 000 charities and nonprofit organizations are not immune to questions of ethics. Although few question the importance of these worthy causes, there has been growing criticism about some of the fundraising methods they use. Two major concerns have surfaced. More charities are using lotteries to raise funds. These not only add to the pressures on people to gamble, they may often jeopardize the welfare of the nonprofit. Use of professional telemarketers is another source of ethical concern. They raise funds on the part of nonprofit organizations, but the charity may only see a small portion of the money raised. In the face of growing public scrutiny, nonprofits have to be as ethically aware and socially responsible as their for-profit counterparts.

The future holds many challenges and opportunities for marketing managers. Technological advances in solar energy, personal computers, interactive television, modern medicine, and new forms of transportation, recreation, and communication provide abundant marketing opportunities. However, forces in the socioeconomic, cultural, and natural environments increase the limits under which marketing can be carried out. Companies that are able to create new values in a socially responsible way will have a world to conquer.

<< Looking Back   < < < < < < < < <

Well—here you are at the end of your introductory marketing travels! In this chapter, we've closed with many important concepts involving marketing's sweeping impact on individual consumers, other businesses, and society as a whole. You learned that responsible marketers discover what consumers want and respond with the right products, priced to give good value to buyers and profit to the producer. A marketing system should sense, serve, and satisfy consumer needs and improve the quality of consumers' lives. In working to meet consumer needs, marketers may take some actions that are not to everyone's liking or benefit. Marketing managers should be aware of the main *criticisms of marketing*.

1. Identify the major social criticisms of marketing.

Marketing's *impact on individual consumer welfare* has been criticized for its high prices, deceptive practices, high-pressure selling, shoddy or unsafe products, planned obsolescence, and poor service to disadvantaged consumers. Marketing's *impact on society* has been criticized for creating false wants and too much materialism, too few social goods, cultural pollution, and too much political power. Critics have also criticized marketing's *impact on other businesses* for harming competitors and reducing competition through acquisitions, practices that create barriers to entry, and unfair competitive marketing practices.

2. Define consumerism and environmentalism and explain how they affect marketing strategies.

Concerns about the marketing system have led to *citizen action movements. Consumerism* is an organized social movement intended to strengthen the rights and power of consumers relative to sellers. Alert marketers view it as an opportunity to serve consumers better by providing more consumer information, education, and protection. *Environmentalism* is an organized social movement seeking to minimize the harm done to the environment and quality of life by marketing practices. The first wave of modern environmentalism was driven by environmental groups and concerned consumers, whereas the second wave was driven by government, which passed laws and regulations governing industrial practices affecting the environment. Today, the first two environmentalism waves are merging into a third and stronger wave in which companies are accepting responsibility for doing no environmental harm. Companies now are adopting policies of *environmental sustainability*—developing strategies that both sustain the environment and produce profits for the company.

3. **Describe the principles of socially responsible marketing.**

Many companies originally opposed these social movements and laws, but most of them now recognize a need for positive consumer information, education, and protection. Some companies have followed a policy of *enlightened marketing*, which holds that a company's marketing should support the best long-run performance of the marketing system. Enlightened marketing consists of five principles: *consumer-oriented marketing, innovative marketing, value marketing, sense-of-mission marketing,* and *societal marketing.*

4. **Explain the role of ethics in marketing.**

Increasingly, companies are responding to the need to provide company policies and guidelines to help

their managers deal with questions of *marketing ethics.* Of course, even the best guidelines cannot resolve all the difficult ethical decisions that individuals and firms must make. But there are some principles that marketers can choose among. One principle states that such issues should be decided by the free market and legal system. A second, and more enlightened principle, puts responsibility not in the system but in the hands of individual companies and managers. Each firm and marketing manager must work out a philosophy of socially responsible and ethical behavior. Under the societal marketing concept, managers must look beyond what is legal and allowable and develop standards based on personal integrity, corporate conscience, and long-term consumer welfare.

Because business standards and practices vary from country to country, the issue of ethics poses special challenges for international marketers. The growing consensus among today's marketers is that it is important to make a commitment to a common set of shared standards worldwide.

Navigating the Key Terms

Consumerism, **p. 653**
Consumer-oriented marketing, **p. 662**
Deficient products, **p. 666**
Desirable products, **p. 666**
Enlightened marketing, **p. 662**
Environmentalism, **p. 655**
Environmental sustainability, **p. 656**

Innovative marketing, **p. 662**
Pleasing products, **p. 666**
Salutary products, **p. 666**
Sense-of-mission marketing, **p. 663**
Societal marketing, **p. 665**
Value marketing, **p. 663**

Concept Check

Fill in the blanks and then check your answers.

1. Consumers, consumer advocates, government agencies, and other critics have accused marketing of harming consumers through high prices, deceptive practices, _____, _____, _____, and poor service to disadvantaged consumers.

2. Many critics charge that the North American marketing system causes prices to be higher than they would be under more "sensible" systems. Three factors contribute to the high price perception: _____, _____, and _____.

3. The _____ _____ _____ Act is one piece of legislation developed to promote the World Commission on Environment and Development's goal of improving the environment.

4. Critics have charged that some producers follow a program of _____, causing their products to become obsolete before they actually should need replacement.

5. Common criticisms against modern advertising practice include indictments that advertising has, creates, or contributes to _____, _____, _____, and too much political power.

6. _____ is an organized movement of citizens and government agencies to improve the rights and power of buyers in relation to sellers.

7. Traditional *buyer's rights* include the right to not buy a product that is offered for sale; the right to expect _____; the right to expect _____.

8. _____ is an organized movement of concerned citizens, businesses, and government agencies to protect and improve people's living environment.

9. The environmental sustainability grid consists of four cells new environmental technology, _____, _____, and _____.

10. Enlightened marketing consists of five principles: consumer-oriented marketing, _____, _____, _____, and societal marketing.

11. _____ marketing means that the company should define its mission in broad social terms rather than narrow product terms.

12. Products can be classified according to their degree of immediate consumer satisfaction and long-run consumer benefit. _____ products such as seat belts and air bags have low appeal but benefit consumers in the long run.

Concept Check Answers: 1. high-pressure selling, shoddy or unsafe products, planned obsolescence; 2. high costs of distribution, high advertising and promotion costs, excessive markups; 3. Canadian Environmental Assessment; 4. planned obsolescence; 5. false wants and too much materialism, too few social goods, cultural pollution; 6. Consumerism; 7. the product to be safe; the product to perform as claimed; 8. Environmentalism; 9. pollution prevention, sustainability vision, product stewardship; 10. innovative marketing, value marketing, sense-of-mission marketing; 11. sense-of-mission; 12. salutary.

Discussing the Issues

1. You have been invited to appear along with an economist on a panel assessing marketing practices in the soft-drink beverage industry. You are somewhat surprised when the economist opens the discussion with a long list of criticisms, especially focusing on unnecessarily high marketing costs and deceptive promotional practices. Abandoning your prepared comments, you feel

the need to defend marketing in general and in the beverage industry in particular. How would you respond to the economist's attack?

2. Comment on the state of consumers' rights on the Internet and in e-commerce. Design a Bill of Rights that would protect consumers while they shop for products and services on the Internet. Consider such issues as government regulation, ease and convenience of use, solicitation, privacy, and cost-efficient commerce.

3. Comment on how a modern firm can establish and implement a strategy of environmental sustainability. Using a corporate example of your own choosing, match your example to Figure 16-1. How would your organization pay for such a program?

4. Compare the marketing concept with the principle of societal marketing. Should all marketers adopt the societal marketing concept? Why or why not?

5. You are the marketing manager for a small kitchen appliance firm. While conducting field tests, you discover a design flaw in one of your most popular appliances that could potentially be harmful to a small number of customers. However, a product recall would likely bankrupt your company and cause all the employees (including yourself) to lose their jobs. What would you do? Explain.

 **Mastering Marketing**

After examining the marketing strategies and practices of CanGo, evaluate those strategies and practices against the ethical guidelines proposed by the American Marketing Association in Table 16-2.

Comment on strategies or practices that seem to be out-of-alignment. How would you remedy the situation(s)?

 Check out the enclosed Video case CD-ROM, or our Companion Website at www.pearsoned.ca/armstrong, to view a CBC video segment and case for this chapter.

 Marketing Applications

Are you fed up with products and services that do not work in the promised way? What can you do about it? Will complaining do any good? If you were to complain, to whom would you complain? You could go straight to a store manager or to the offending company to air your gripes. However, you may find that you are just one consumer trying to take on the "establishment." Now, a new day has dawned for the disgruntled consumer. The Internet is changing the way consumers can complain. Because of the Internet, your complaint is joined by thousands of others. Many, many consumers now have the chance to see your complaint via chat rooms, Web boards,

and complaint Web sites. When thousands of people see something wrong, that something often gets fixed. Visit the following Web sites: **www.planetfeedback.com** and **www.bbbonline.org**.

Thinking Like a Marketing Manager

1. As a consumer, think about problems you have had in the past with products or services. Make a complaint online to one of the Web sites mentioned.

2. What response did you receive to your complaint? Did anyone contact you? Did you get further information? Did you find others that had a similar complaint?

3. Critique the future of complaint Web sites. Will these sites effectively police the Internet? Are these sites a good alternative to federal or provincial regulation?

4. How can complaint Web sites be misused or harm honest merchants? Find one example in which you think this has happened.

5. Assume that you are the marketing manager for a newly established Internet company. Design a complaint policy that will ensure quick response, accuracy of complaint reporting, accountability, fairness, and genuine concern for the consumer. How would you promote this policy?

Digital Map

Visit our Web site at **www.pearsoned.ca/armstrong** for online quizzes, Internet exercises, and more!

CASE 16 DYING TO BE THIN

In 1995, Ann Gilmore just wanted to lose a little weight. Her doctor prescribed a diet pill in the hope that losing weight would help relieve her chronic back pain. Gilmore lost some weight, but not much, so she quit taking the medication after only three months. About a month later, she underwent a series of tests and was diagnosed with primary pulmonary hypertension, or PPH, a rare and deadly lung condition that kills most of its victims within two years. Too late for Gilmore, research revealed that diet drugs containing fenfluramine and dexfenfluramine increased the chance of developing PPH by 23 times. In Canada, the drugs went under the names of Ponderal and Redux.

Although some Canadians such as Gilmore seek to lose weight for medical reasons, others diet to improve their appearance. North Americans spend almost $60 billion a year trying to stay thin. A recent survey found that 90 percent of respondents believe that they weigh too much, even though only 25 percent were deemed medically overweight. Even more troubling is the fact that this number includes underweight women who still view themselves as fat.

No one denies that being medically overweight is a serious problem. The medical community considers obesity to be the second greatest health hazard, right behind smoking. But there is a difference between people who are actually overweight and those who perceive themselves to be in this category even though they are well within their recommended weight limits.

Perceptions of obesity may make people susceptible to unscrupulous marketing tactics. They may purchase premium-priced products with dubious benefits. For example, products sold by Weight Watchers or Jenny Craig are priced significantly higher than other food items in the same product category, yet people purchasing these diet foods keep cash registers humming. Millions join expensive health clubs and get no more benefit than they would by going for a daily walk. Although these products and services may eat up consumers' dollars, they probably don't result in significant long-term harm.

That wasn't the case for the more than 150 000 Canadians who took diet drugs. Twelve have developed PPH and recent Health Canada documents show that two people have died. Dozens more have developed heart and lung problems. These people, including Gilmore, have launched a class action suit against the French drug manufacturer and the Canadian distributor, Servier Canada. Seeking $750 million in damages, they're hopeful of a quick victory since a U.S. firm has already agreed to pay up to $4.5 billion in damages to people who took the drugs. Many people wonder why Health Canada didn't ban these drugs sooner given the growing number of research studies that pointed to the drugs' dangers.

Redux was first launched in North America after receiving approval by the U.S. Federal Drug Administration (FDA). In just five years, after a major promotional program, annual sales of Redux soared to an estimated $1.4 billion. It wasn't long, however, before serious questions were raised about Redux. The prestigious *New England Journal of Medicine* published a study linking the main ingredient in Redux to a rare but fatal lung disorder. Even though sales declined and Redux was withdrawn from the market, it was already too late for consumers who had suffered and died from taking a seemingly harmless item—diet pills.

Why do such tragedies occur? Are consumers to blame for their obsession with being thin? Certainly this obsession has driven sales of diet soft drinks to a level of $25 billion a year. Health clubs rake in an additional $14 billion; exercise-equipment manufacturers have sales of $6 billion a year; and commercial weight-loss programs, such as Weight Watchers, earn more than $3 billion a year. Not only is this a large market, but it has also been experiencing considerable growth potential. If nothing else, it is almost guaranteed repeat business. Almost all the North Americans who shed kilograms each year put them back on eventually, and the dieting-exercising cycle starts again.

Dieting and exercising require effort and time. People must forgo what they want most—lots of tasty food—and suffer the pain and discomfort of exercise to lose only a kilogram a week. Doctors and public health officials frequently caution against losing too much weight too quickly. Consequently, the deprivation and suffering can go on for a long time. No wonder diet pills look so good. Taking pills is easy, requires no immediate or obvious pain, and doesn't force you to give up what you want.

Redux was a prescription drug, but word of mouth had its effect, and taking a pill is easier than exercising. Moreover, Redux succeeded in curbing people's appetites. Users found that they would sit down to a normal meal but never finish it. They felt satisfied before eating everything on their plate. As a result, they ate less. Some users lost up to 18 kg in just two months—instant success with little effort or pain. Given news of the product's success, it's not surprising that overweight North Americans flooded doctors' offices seeking prescriptions for the product.

But why would medical practitioners concerned with people's health recommend or prescribe such a product? Some of the blame can be placed at the door of manufacturers, who were overly zealous in their attempts to sell the product. Pharmaceutical salespeople pitched the drug to family physicians, psychiatrists, cardiologists, interns, and even gynecologists—people who are less likely to be familiar with the drug or treatment of obesity. According to one analysis, Redux salespeople logged 140 000 doctor visits in the first three months alone—making it one of the largest drug launches in 1996. Doctors received patient starter kits that contained coupons for joining Weight Watchers and Jenny Craig diet centres. Consultants believed that receipt of the kits encouraged doctors to prescribe the drug without monitoring a patient's weight loss.

Although some health risks were known at the time of the launch, some salespeople either were unaware of them or neglected to mention them during their sales calls. Physician Dr. Gary Huber says that the salesperson who called on him touted Redux as safe for lifetime use—even though the company's own brochures admit that the drug had been tested for only one year—and hardly addressed the lung disease risk. "I was amazed at how little the salesman knew," Dr. Huber said. Thus, poorly prepared or overly aggressive salespeople were calling on doctors who might be unfamiliar with either weight-loss methods or drugs, and who in turn might prescribe the product to people whose weight loss they did not monitor.

Although many doctors believe that an approved drug is a safe drug, Redux was initially approved with a caveat. Doctors were to prescribe it only for use by obese patients—individuals who were at least 7 kg to 10 kg overweight. The FDA knew that pulmonary hypertension, a constriction of blood vessels near the heart that can lead to heart failure, was associated with Redux. An international study indicated that use of Redux could lead to the death of as many as 46 people per million when taken for just three months. However, ordinary Aspirin can kill more individuals per million than Redux. For obese persons, the risk of death or debilitation from Redux was acceptable precisely because the risk of death or debilitation from obesity is higher. Consequently, some of the risk associated with Redux was known to the FDA and was considered acceptable under certain conditions.

The major problem, however, was not with medically obese people who were closely supervised by their doctors. Rather, it was with the millions of individuals who wanted Redux to shed a kilogram or two so that they would look better. For these people, Redux raised the risks of death to unacceptable levels. Some knew the risks and wanted the drug anyway, but others did not. Again, the obsession with being thin, coupled with the willingness of doctors to prescribe a heavily marketed drug, led to use of Redux by the wrong market segment.

When one reads of cases such as Redux, one wonders who is to blame for such tragedies. Was it government regulators who approved a drug with known side effects? Was it salespeople who were motivated to earn their commissions regardless of the consequences for final consumers? Was it harried doctors who were too busy to follow up with their patients? Or was it consumers themselves who pursue an elusive body image that few can actually attain?

Questions

1. Consider the buyers' and sellers' rights listed in this chapter. Which rights were violated in the Redux case?

2. The Redux case is an example of a product that caused extreme harm. Although the outcomes may be less severe, do other products with diet positionings—labelled as "lite," cholesterol free, or calorie reduced—exploit consumers in the same way?

3. Many critics blame advertising for people's obsession with thinness. Are these criticisms valid? Can you find specific ads that help support your claim? What is the effect of campaigns like the one by The Body Shop showing a model with a rounded figure, or Special K's efforts to make women more aware of the need for a healthy diet? Although women are most often viewed as the victims of poor body images, do men feel pressured by images of slim, muscular male models in ads?

4. If you were the marketing manager for a firm marketing a diet pill, what methods could you develop that would prevent a case like Redux from repeating itself? What would a code of ethics for such a firm look like?

Sources: L. Davis, A. Gardiner, D. Greene, K. Harness, and S. Mickle, "The Ethics of the Diet Industry," case written for Comm 338, Queen's University; Robert Langreth, "Is Marketing of Diet Pill Too Aggressive?" *The Wall Street Journal,* 21 November 1996, p. B1; Robert Langreth, "Diet-Drug Mix May Damage Heart Valves," *The Wall Street Journal,* 9 July 1997, p. B1; Robert Langreth, "Eminent Journal Urges Moratorium on Diet-Drug Use," *The Wall Street Journal,* 28 August 1997, p. B1; Jay Palmer, "Hey, Fatso!" *Barron's,* 1 July 1996, p. 25–29; Michael D. Lemonick, "The Miracle Drug?" *Time,* 23 September 1996, available online at **www.pathfinder.com/time/magazine/domestic/1996/960923/ test.html**; Timothy Sawa, "Dying to Be Thin," *CBC Radio News In-Depth,* 9 May 2001, available online at **http://cbc.ca/consumers/indepth/dietdrug**.

COMPREHENSIVE CASE: TAXIGUY

You've been out celebrating with some friends. A great dinner, a few clubs, a few drinks. It's time to head home, and you realize that you've all had enough to drink that no one should be driving. Apart from the danger, the police road checks are aggressively checking suspected drinkers and drivers.

Getting home safely has never been easier: just call 1-888-TAXIGUY, from anywhere in Canada, and a taxi will be dispatched to your location. No hassling with the yellow pages or finding a cab company that will pick you up at 2:00 a.m.; just one phone number and a quick call. In fact, three options are available to access the service: a traditional telephone; a payphone—a toll free call; or a cell phone. For land-line calls, Automatic Number Identifier (ANI) software identifies the originating city and transfers the call directly to a TAXIGUY-authorized local cab company. With a cell phone, you will be asked to enter the first three letters of the city you are in. It's that easy.

This new service, conceived and created by Justin Raymond and backed by Molson Canada, has handled 260 000 calls in its first three and a half years, with call volume doubling each month!

THE BIRTH OF TAXIGUY

1·888·TAXIGUY™

Justin Raymond is an Ottawa native who holds a Master's Degree in Education with a concentration on Sports Marketing and Administration. He began his career handling sponsorship and marketing for the McCall's LPGA Classic Golf Tournament. He then moved to an associative event marketing company, where he worked on sponsorship-based retail promotions for Coca-Cola and allied brands, with tie-ins to various sports organizations within the United States Olympic Committee. During this time, he entertained the executive bodies of these sport groups, retail executives, Coca-Cola bottlers, and other groups associated with Coke's promotions.

Justin noticed that every event he organized included the consumption of alcohol, and that clients and business contacts were driving after the event as it was difficult to coordinate simple alternatives. He also noted the increasing use of 1-800 numbers for a broad range of services from plumbers to florists; after extensive research, he concluded that the concept had viability for the taxicab industry as well. Justin researched possible telecommunications solutions by "nagging engineers at AT&T," wrote a business plan, quit his job, and returned to Canada to try out the concept.

After recruiting five cab companies in the Greater Toronto area to become 1-888-TAXIGUY Network Partners, Justin still needed expansion capital to develop a telecommunications infrastructure that would allow him to expand the concept beyond the initial market area. He was aware that companies in the beverage alcohol industry had budgets for "responsible use," but he needed some help determining which organization to approach first.

Justin's first stop was the Brewer's Association of Canada (BAC), which is active in the development of partnerships and programs to promote responsible beer consumption. The BAC recommended that Justin directly approach a brewery, and it helped set up his first appointment with the Senior Vice-President of Corporate Affairs at Molson.

When asked why he had chosen Molson instead of other brewers, Justin explained: "Molson kept popping into my head; maybe it was their tie-in with hockey, their tie-in to music, the fact that they are a truly Canadian company, or maybe their 'Take Care' responsible use campaign. I wasn't sure and still don't question it … it just felt right."

Molson immediately saw the potential for the 1-888-TAXIGUY concept and agreed to provide the funds for further development in return for becoming the exclusive "malt-beverage" sponsor. It saw in the concept a revolutionary drinking and driving countermeasure and a method of raising awareness of the hazards of drinking and driving. The service also provides Molson with a powerful consumer communication tool and an excellent public relations platform, all combined with a program that brings tangible results—260 000 calls since it began.

Armed with the necessary capital to expand, 1-888-TAXIGUY was rolled out region by region and has become a national network of taxicab company partners. Taxicab companies were recruited in stages, beginning in Ontario, then Quebec, then the rest of Canada. When asked how he was able to attract new partners, Justin responded: "By growing region by region, we were able to snowball the success story to new territories. Brochure strategies focused heavily on (1) Molson Canada marketing and advertising support; (2) competitive advantage for partners; and (3) long-term possibility of TAXIGUY becoming a household name."

While a highly detailed brochure was developed and used as the primary communications tool to tell the 1-888-TAXIGUY success story in partner recruitment efforts, much of the recruitment of taxicab partners was done person to person. Justin commented that he "concentrated on building the relationships and building respect for the business."

There is an obvious consumer need for this service and Molson offers a unique communications tool—but how does 1-888-TAXIGUY, as a company, generate revenues? It sells marketing kits to Network Partners across Canada. These kits contain TAXIGUY brand identification in the form of magnets, phone stickers, wallet cards, window decals, and placards. The taxicab business is highly competitive, and cab companies are continually looking for ways to differentiate themselves in the mind of the consumer. The 1-888-TAXIGUY material provides a credibility boost for the cab company and provides another portal to their dispatch.

TAXIGUY AND SOCIAL RESPONSIBILITY MARKETING

The TAXIGUY concept is not only innovative; it is also timely. One of the hot issues in the hospitality industry in Canada is "alcohol liability." In recent court rulings, proprietors and servers have been found liable for allowing intoxicated patrons to drive after leaving a bar or pub and have been subject to legal action where death or injury has occurred to either the drinker or to others involved in accidents caused by a drinking driver. The result has been an increase in bar, pub, and restaurant liability insurance, placing a substantial cost burden on many of these businesses.

TAXIGUY is the ideal concept for licensed establishments faced with the responsibility of overseeing their customers' behaviour when consuming alcoholic beverages. Justin recently developed a program called "Smart Call" after extensive research in both the hospitality and insurance industries. In Ontario, the legislative program "Smart Serve" requires staff training, including tactics for observing drinkers, and TAXIGUY is developing programs to tie-in with these initiatives. In its simplest form, the involvement could be TAXIGUY-branded material extensively displayed throughout licensed establishments by way of tent cards, posters, and phone placards.

In addition, TAXIGUY has developed a formal relationship with the Shoeless Joe's restaurant chain and its insurance broker to implement an extensive program in all 28 of the chain's restaurants. This formal agreement followed a successful test market in a small number of Shoeless Joe's establishments, in which the placement of these promotional materials resulted in 20 to 30 calls per month.

TAXIGUY truly reinforces the concept of "responsible use." Extensive initiatives in this area have been in place in Canada for many years. For example, the Association of Canadian Distillers and other national and regional organizations have developed or supported programs as diverse as the "Downtown Designated Driver" program in Halifax, the well-known "Don't Drink and Drive" campaigns, and the Fetal Alcohol Syndrome/Fetal Alcohol Effects Information Service.

THE MOLSON PERSPECTIVE

From an outsider's viewpoint, there may appear to be a constant tension between what could be considered opposing strategies—between beer sales and responsible use. However, Nathalie Masse, a spokesperson for Molson, captures their unified strategy succinctly: "At Molson, brand advertising and responsible use go hand in hand: there is no conflict between them." As the leader in this area, Molson was one of the first brewers in Canada to include a responsible use program in its marketing and communications strategy. Today, this program combines advertising with other initiatives to promote the responsible use of, and attitude towards, alcohol. As far back as 1989, Molson launched a national advertising campaign under the tag line "Take Care." In 1999, the program was refocused to respond to address drinking and driving. Today, the program runs under the tag line "Don't Drink and Drive."

As a result of this new direction, Molson decided to add a component that could further enhance its social responsibility role. In 1999, it formed the partnership with TAXIGUY that has now become a key part of its responsible use program.

This partnership provides the program with an "action trigger" that allows people to plan ahead and reinforces the "Don't Drink and Drive" message.

There is no question that Molson's main aim is to sell beer. However, it readily accepts its social responsibility to raise awareness around the dangers of drinking and driving, and the responsible use program is an integral component of its sales campaigns and is promoted by its sales representatives. Molson views this program much like its brand awareness campaigns: it is a tool that further differentiates it from its competitors and contributes to building a favourable disposition towards the company and its products.

Moving Forward

Justin Raymond was counting on Molson's continued commitment to the responsible use program when, in April 2001, TAXIGUY started planning its pitch to convince Molson to renew their partnership contract. Since all the executives who had supported his initial pitch had left Molson, he had to build new relationships and resell the TAXIGUY concept. The "Operation Ossifer" campaign was a well-planned marketing effort that focused on securing Molson's continued support. On the following pages, you can read the marketing plan and find out what the result was.

Questions

1. Go to the Molson (www.molson.ca), Labatt (www.labatt.com), and Sleeman's Brewery (www.sleeman.ca) Web sites. Look for references to "Responsible Use" on each of these Web sites. Of these three brewers, which ones demonstrate a clear commitment to a responsible use strategy? Support your answer.

2. Molson is a large organization with money and expertise. Why would an organization such as Molson choose to partner with a small, highly focused, entrepreneurial organization like TAXIGUY? While we know that TAXIGUY benefits from Molson's financial and corporate support, what other organizational benefits does Molson gain from this partnership apart from the obvious link to this unique concept?

3. There are other industries that employ a similar strategy of encouraging responsible use of their products. Auto manufacturers, for example, take a similar view. While they highlight the speed and power of their vehicles, they also stress the safety features and the need to have safe driving habits. Go to three well-known auto manufacturers' Web sites and reflect on the balance of information available to a consumer in terms of the "speed/power" selling features vs. the "safe driving habits/safety" features. Which of these attributes is more obvious—speed, power, looks, or safety features? Can you see any synergy between the features of these cars and the overall communications strategy?

4. Beer and other alcoholic beverages can legally be sold to consumers over a certain age. Yet, because a minority of people misuse the product, industry associations and the government put pressure on the manufacturers to promote

moderation in the use of these products. Cigarette packages carry cancerous images of various body parts and explicit warnings about the hazards of smoking. Can we expect that McDonald's hamburgers and fries will soon come with a warning stating: "May contribute to a high fat diet that has been linked to obesity, and obesity has been linked to diabetes and heart conditions"? Where does society draw the line as to what requires warning against misuse? Who do we as marketers need to recognize as prime movers in any initiatives to regulate usage of our products?

5. How effective is advertising for a beer company that includes having a good time but using the product in a responsible manner? Do consumers see the company as positively and socially responsible, or are consumers so jaded that they view this as just another public relations gimmick?

6. To this point, Justin Raymond has not taken the TAXIGUY concept past Molson. What possible expansion opportunities can you see for other product categories? Does the TAXIGUY concept work only in situations where responsible use is the primary strategy, or are there other possible applications?

MARKETING PLAN
1-888-TAXIGUY

"OPERATION OSSIFER"

The executive summary is one to two pages in length. It should provide an overview of the most critical information within the marketing plan. This is the first impression the reader will have of the plan and will often determine if the plan will receive budget approval.

A. Executive Summary

TAXIGUY provides consumers with toll-free access to taxi services across Canada. The company has been growing rapidly over the past two and a half years. This growth is largely due to the financial support from Molson Canada, which entered into a three-year agreement with TAXIGUY as part of its "Responsible Use" program. The contract is expiring in the next eight months.

TAXIGUY's target market is primarily taxicab companies in Canada. TAXIGUY has been able to develop a strong customer base across the country, but this base has to grow. Although TAXIGUY faces no competition, continued support from Molson is necessary to grow the base.

TAXIGUY has to secure another contract with Molson, increase general consumer awareness of the toll-free number, and grow the number of taxicab customers. The competitive taxicab industry and changing social trends make it possible for TAXIGUY to achieve these objectives.

B. Situation Analysis

This overview provides the reader with a summary of the company history and current product offering.

1. Company and Service Overview

TAXIGUY was formed in 1998 to offer a toll-free number to order a taxi anywhere in Canada. The company originated in Toronto and has expanded to provide coverage across Canada. To date, TAXIGUY has handled over 260 000 phone calls and has a network of 400+ taxicab companies.

TAXIGUY recruits Canadian taxicab companies as Network Partners. The partners are sold marketing kits containing promotional material with the 1-888-TAXIGUY toll-free number. Taxicab companies want to be associated with the toll-free number because it increases their revenues. TAXIGUY has developed strong relationships with these Network Partners.

The success of TAXIGUY is directly dependent on its strategic alliance with Molson Canada. This relationship is critical to the future success of TAXIGUY, as Molson is a key provider of funding for business development. Molson also gives the program credibility along with market awareness.

A company overview may also include the mission/vision statement and resources.

This marketing plan focuses on securing continued sponsorship from Molson. It is necessary to provide an overview of the customers of this service, to fully understand the marketing issues related to the plan targeting Molson.

2. Market Overview

Corporate Target Markets:
a. Liquor producers based in Canada.
b. Taxicab companies in Canada.

Market Analysis—Liquor Producers: The trend towards responsible drinking and driving has encouraged liquor companies to seek alternatives that promote responsible consumption. TAXIGUY has a service that is consistent with these efforts, providing liquor companies with an avenue to promote themselves as participants in a positive social movement.

Market Analysis—Taxicab Companies: TAXIGUY's marketing opportunity is attributable to:
a. A competitive taxicab industry
b. The trend towards more responsible drinking and driving habits
c. Increased insurance premiums for the hospitality industry because of "alcohol liability"

The taxicab industry has traditionally been a very competitive industry due to low barriers to entry, numerous options for transportation, and regulated pricing. Taxicab companies across the country are looking for ways to increase their revenues, and the toll-free number provides an additional portal for customers to contact the taxicab company. The TAXIGUY partnership also allows taxicab companies to differentiate themselves from their competitors.

The number of groups raising awareness around this issue shows the trend towards more responsible drinking and driving. The TAXIGUY service supports these efforts.

The hospitality industry is facing increased risk and insurance premiums because of "alcohol liability." Alcohol liability refers to recent court rulings that have held proprietors and servers liable for the actions of intoxicated patrons. Governments have started to introduce legislation for training programs, and TAXIGUY has started to develop programs that tie in with these legislated initiatives.

3. Competitive Environment

Currently, TAXIGUY does not have any direct competitors, although sponsorship funding is at risk from substitute programs promoting responsible alcohol consumption.

The market overview often includes information about the company, customers, competition, and opportunities.

Target markets are not limited to customers but can also include key sources of funding.

A marketing plan should provide background market information because the plan is read by many people inside and outside the company. Groups outside the company could include ad agencies or strategic partners.

The ability to articulate the opportunity succinctly is critical because the message has to be repeatable by the reader.

A marketing plan should address competition, even if there is none, because of the impact competition can have on the company.

4. SWOT

Strengths	Weaknesses
Molson sponsorship Strong relationships with Network Partners Successful service launch Network Partners across Canada	Dependent on one company, Molson, for funding of growth opportunities Limited financial resources Success dependent on broad awareness of service
Opportunities	**Threats**
Trend towards responsible drinking and driving Molson's sponsorship exclusive for only "malt-beverage" companies—other liquor producers could be approached for funding Service that differentiates customers (taxicabs) from their competitors Hospitality industry's need for programs that help reduce "alcohol liability" Access to key communication channels towards Molson executives Ability to secure an ad agency to do the creative development for free No competition	Agreement with Molson up for renewal Key Molson executive supporters of the original agreement no longer with the company Taxicab companies' satisfaction dependent on continuing to increase the number of toll-free phone calls

C. Target Market

1. Molson Canada
2. Public and private sectors of society

D. Value Proposition

The efforts by Molson and TAXIGUY to develop the 1-888-TAXIGUY toll-free phone number is significantly contributing to supporting responsible drinking and driving. This brings positive recognition to Molson.

SWOT analysis provides an overview of Strengths, Weaknesses, Opportunities, and Threats. This information informs decisions made in the marketing plan.

Strengths and Weaknesses are usually internally focused, and Opportunities and Threats are external to the company.

An effective marketing plan has a clearly defined target market on which the activities within the plan are focused. A poorly defined target market often leads to poor results.

The value proposition will clearly specify why the customer will want the product or service.

E. Marketing Objectives

1. To raise the overall awareness level for 1-888-TAXIGUY inside the walls of relevant institutions in both the private and public sectors of society during the contract renewal period with Molson Canada.

2. To bring positive recognition and praise to our key partner Molson Canada for their vision and support of the 1-888-TAXIGUY program.

3. To illustrate some of the many highly creative advertising angles that the 1-888-TAXIGUY Responsible Use program provides to its partners.

The objectives specify what the company is trying to achieve. Objectives are usually quantified, but don't always have to be.

F. Marketing Strategies

1. Utilize a network of public relations contacts and advisors to consult on and oversee the development of a detailed PR/communication plan.

2. Recruit a Toronto-based advertising firm to develop the creative program in exchange for rights to enter the creative work in advertising award shows.

The marketing strategy section will outline the marketing mix—the 4 Ps.

G. Marketing Tactics

1. Initiate a letter-writing campaign inside important Molson Canada key relationship areas of Government (all levels), Customers (key accounts), NFP Sector (not-for-profit groups).

   a. Letter to congratulate Molson Canada on their decision to believe in and support the 1-888-TAXIGUY vision
   b. Letter to acknowledge the 200 000+ taxicab rides facilitated to date
   c. Letter to be sent between April 1, 2001, and June 1, 2001

2. Secure billboard location at corner of Bloor and Church (across from Molson National Office) from June 1, 2001, through July 1, 2001.

3. Erect billboard and distribute Molson Executive thank-you piece on June 1, 2001.

4. Send media kit (briefing letter, miniature billboard, and thank-you piece) to three select media outlets (National Post, Globe and Mail, and Marketing Magazine).

This section provides a list of specific, time-related activities that will fulfil the Marketing Objectives.

All marketing plans will include information about forecasts and budget estimates.

H. Financial Data

Financial Objectives:

The overall financial objective of this campaign is to successfully negotiate a renewal of the first sponsorship contract. The goal is to raise Molson's awareness of the success of TAXIGUY during the term of the first agreement, and thereby obtain both a new agreement and more favourable financial terms.

Budget: $10,000

Timeline: Two months

A marketing plan will have clearly stated objectives that are often quantified. These objectives are usually unit sales, revenue, or growth targets. In this section of the marketing plan, the manager will clarify when the financial objectives will be achieved. The manager will also state the budget for the marketing plan for control purposes. This specific marketing plan for TAXIGUY is primarily focused upon one client. As the goal is to secure continued funding, the financial target is the equivalent of the value of the total contract.

The manager will monitor spending and performance against goals to ensure the marketing plan is working. If variances occur between the budgeted amount or the financial targets, then the manager will often make adjustments to the marketing plan to ensure success.

Digital Map

Visit our Web site at **www.pearsoned.ca/armstrong** for access to more marketing plans.

Results of Operation Ossifer

1. Letter-writing campaign participants:

- *Government*: Transport Canada, Ontario Premier's Office, Ontario Ministry of Transportation, Ontario Ministry of Education, Ontario Progressive Conservative Party, RCMP (multiple districts), Ontario Provincial Police, Eastern Ontario Courts (multiple judges), and the MPPs for London, Hamilton, St. Catharines, Peterborough, and Kingston

- *Key accounts (customers)*: Montana Restaurant, Woodbine Entertainment Group, Shoeless Joe's Restaurants, and Gabby's Restaurants

- *Not-for-profit groups*: Ontario Community Council on Impaired Driving (OCCID), Students Against Drinking and Driving (SADD), Student Life Education Company, and Bacchus Canada

2. Billboard Execution

The billboard was up for the calendar month of June 2001, during which time the Toronto Pride Parade took place. The billboard received excellent feedback and went on to be a nominee in the prestigious Marketing Magazine Advertising Awards, as well as a finalist at the International Advertising Awards in London, England.

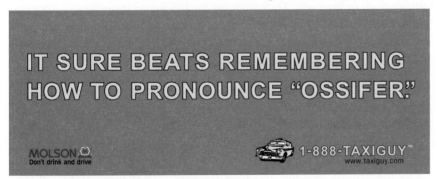

The Operation Ossifer billboard

3. The Executive Thank-You Piece

This piece was distributed to the 25 highest-ranked officers at Molson Canada. It was hand-delivered on the day that the billboard was erected across the street from their offices. Apparently, the pieces still adorn many of the bookshelves inside Molson Canada. The front cover of the box reads: "Three years ago, a company decided to make it in the back seat of a cab." On the inside of the box, just below a cast-iron mini taxicab, is the note: "Thank you Molson, for opening the door." Below this, the message reads: "When Molson wanted to take their Don't Drink and Drive program somewhere, TAXIGUY said 'where to?' 200,000 rides later in 700 cities and towns, what we're saying is 'where to next?'"

The thank-you piece given to Molson executives

4. The Marketing Magazine Article

The quest for an article was successful. The very popular "Street Talk" column in Marketing Magazine wrote an article about TAXIGUY's marketing plan and included an image of the billboard.

Summary

In the end, TAXIGUY ended up getting the attention of the key people inside Molson Canada. They will never know for sure what would have happened if they didn't go through with the plan, but they could not afford to let complacency govern the future of their business. They went on to sign a new multi-year agreement with Molson Canada and strengthened their corporate relationship.

Looking Back: Justin Raymond's View

I look back on the "Operation Ossifer" marketing plan as an excellent example of resource utilization and detailed execution. The theoretical plan is exactly that—only a theory—the execution of that theory is everything. The marketing components used in our plan were complementary and synergistic. In my opinion, it was for this reason that the plan was so successful. The big splash of the billboard followed by the unique personal touch of the executive thank-you gift set the table for everything else. The letter-writing campaign generated a consistent flow of praise and recognition to all the key contact people at Molson Canada. The final component (public relations) fell into place as a result of the execution up to that point. It all came together inside of a tight timeline and right on budget.

APPENDIX II   MARKETING ARITHMETIC

One aspect of marketing not discussed within the text is marketing arithmetic. The calculation of sales, costs, and certain ratios is important for many marketing decisions. This appendix describes three major areas of marketing arithmetic: the *operating statement, analytic ratios,* and *markups, margins, and markdowns.*

OPERATING STATEMENT

The operating statement and the balance sheet are the two main financial statements used by companies. The **balance sheet** shows the assets, liabilities, and net worth of a company at a given time. The **operating statement** (also called **profit-and-loss statement** or **income statement**) is the more important of the two for marketing information. It shows company sales, cost of goods sold, and expenses during a specified period. By comparing the operating statement from one time period to the next, the firm can spot favourable or unfavourable trends and take appropriate action.

Table AII-1 shows the 2003 operating statement for Dale Parsons Men's Wear, a specialty store in the Prairies. This statement is for a retailer; the operating statement for a manufacturer would be different. Specifically, the section on purchases within the "cost of goods sold" area would be replaced by "cost of goods manufactured."

The outline of the operating statement follows a logical series of steps to arrive at the firm's $25 000 net profit figure:

Net sales	$300 000
Cost of goods sold	−175 000
Gross margin	$125 000
Expenses	−100 000
Net profit	$ 25 000

The first part details the amount that Parsons received for the goods sold during the year. The sales figures consist of three items: *gross sales, returns and allowances,* and *net sales.* **Gross sales** is the total amount charged to customers during the year for merchandise purchased in Parsons's store. As expected, some customers returned merchandise because of damage or a change of mind. If the customer gets a full refund or full credit on another purchase, we call this a *return.* Or the customer may decide to keep the item if Parsons will reduce the price. This is called an *allowance.* By subtracting returns and allowances from gross sales, we arrive at net sales— what Parsons earned in revenue from a year of selling merchandise:

Gross sales	$325 000
Returns and allowances	− 25 000
Net sales	$300 000

The second major part of the operating statement calculates the amount of sales revenue Dale Parsons retains after paying the costs of the merchandise. We start with the inventory in the store at the beginning of the year. During the year, Parsons bought $165 000 worth of suits, slacks, shirts, ties, jeans, and other goods. Suppliers gave the store discounts totaling $15 000, so that net purchases were $150 000. Because the store is located away from regular shipping routes, Parsons had to pay an additional $10 000 to get the products delivered, giving the firm a net cost of $160 000. Adding the beginning inventory, the cost of goods available for sale amounted to $220 000. The $45 000 ending inventory of clothes in the store on 31 December is then subtracted to come up with the $175 000 **cost of goods sold.** Here again we have followed a logical series of steps to figure out the cost of goods sold:

Amount Parsons started with (beginning inventory)	$ 60 000
Net amount purchased	1 150 000
Any added costs to obtain these purchases	110 000
Total cost of goods Parsons had available for sale during year	$220 000
Amount Parsons had left over (ending inventory)	245 000
Cost of goods actually sold	$175 000

The difference between what Parsons paid for the merchandise ($175 000) and what he sold it for ($300 000) is called the **gross margin** ($125 000).

To show the profit Parsons "cleared" at the end of the year, we must subtract from the gross margin the *expenses* incurred while doing business. *Selling expenses* included two sales employees, local newspaper and radio advertising, and the cost of delivering merchandise to customers after alterations. Selling expenses totalled $50 000 for the year. *Administrative expenses* included the salary for an office manager, office supplies such as stationery and business cards, and miscellaneous expenses including an administrative audit conducted by an outside consultant. Administrative expenses totalled $30 000 in 2003. Finally, the general expenses of rent, utilities, insurance, and depreciation came to $20 000. Total expenses were therefore $100 000 for the year. By

Table AII-1   Operating Statement: Dale Parsons Men's Wear Year ending 31 December, 2003

Gross Sales			$325 000
Less: Sales returns and allowances			25 000
Net sales			$300 000
Cost of goods sold			
Beginning inventory, January 1, at cost		$ 60 000	
Gross purchases	$165 000		
Less: Purchase discounts	15 000		
Net Purchases	$150 000		
Plus: Freight-in	10 000		
Net cost of delivered purchases		$160 000	
Cost of goods available for sale		$220 000	
Less: Ending inventory, December 31, at cost		$ 45 000	
Cost of goods sold			$175 000
Gross margin			$125 000
Expenses			
Selling expenses			
Sales, salaries, and commissions	$ 40 000		
Advertising	5 000		
Delivery	5 000		
Total selling expenses		$ 50 000	
Administrative expenses			
Office salaries	$ 20 000		
Office supplies	5 000		
Miscellaneous (outside consultant)	5 000		
Total administrative expenses		$ 30 000	
General expenses			
Rent	$ 10 000		
Heat, light, telephone	5 000		
Miscellaneous (insurance, depreciation)	5 000		
Total general expenses		$ 20 000	
Total expenses			$100 000
Net profit			$ 25 000

subtracting expenses ($100 000) from the gross margin ($125 000), we arrive at the net profit of $25 000 for Parsons during 2003.

ANALYTIC RATIOS

The operating statement provides the figures needed to compute some crucial ratios. Typically these ratios are called **operating ratios**—the ratio of selected operating statement items to net sales. They let marketers compare the firm's performance in one year to that in previous years (or with industry standards and competitors in the same year). The most commonly used operating ratios are the *gross margin percentage,* the *net profit percentage,* the *operating expense percentage,* and the *returns and allowances percentage.*

Another useful ratio is the *stockturn rate* (also called *inventory turnover rate*). The stockturn rate is the number of times an inventory turns over or is sold during a specified period (often one year). It may be computed on a cost, selling price, or units basis. Thus, the formula can be

$$\text{Stockturn rate} = \frac{\text{cost of goods sold}}{\text{average inventory at cost}}$$

or

$$\text{Stockturn rate} = \frac{\text{selling price of goods sold}}{\text{average selling price of inventory}}$$

or

$$\text{Stockturn rate} = \frac{\text{sales in units}}{\text{average inventory in units}}$$

We will use the first formula to calculate the stockturn rate for Dale Parsons Men's Wear:

$$\frac{\$175\ 000}{(\$60\ 000 + \$45\ 000)/2} = \frac{\$175\ 000}{\$52\ 500} = 3.3$$

That is, Parsons's inventory turned over 3.3 times in 2003. Normally, the higher the stockturn rate, the higher the management efficiency and company profitability.

Return on investment (ROI) is frequently used to measure managerial effectiveness. It uses figures from the firm's operating statement and balance sheet. A commonly used formula for computing ROI is

$$\text{ROI} = \frac{\text{net profit}}{\text{sales}} \times \frac{\text{sales}}{\text{investment}}$$

You may have two questions about this formula: Why use a two-step process when ROI could be computed simply as net profit divided by investment? And what exactly is "investment"?

To answer these questions, let's look at how each component of the formula can affect the ROI. Suppose Dale Parsons Men's Wear has a total investment of $150 000. Then ROI can be computed as follows:

Ratio	Formula	Computation from Table AII-1
Gross margin percentage	$= \dfrac{\text{gross margin}}{\text{net sales}}$	$= \dfrac{\$125\ 000}{\$300\ 000} = 42\%$
Net profit percentage	$= \dfrac{\text{net profit}}{\text{net sales}}$	$= \dfrac{\$25\ 000}{\$300\ 000} = 8\%$

Ratio	Formula	Computation from Table AII-1
Operating expense percentage	$= \dfrac{\text{total expenses}}{\text{net sales}}$	$= \dfrac{\$100\ 000}{\$300\ 000} = 33\%$
Returns and allowances percentage	$= \dfrac{\text{returns and allowances}}{\text{net sales}}$	$= \dfrac{\$25\ 000}{\$300\ 000} = 8\%$

$$ROI = \frac{\$25\ 000\text{(net profit)}}{\$300\ 000\text{(sales)}} \times \frac{\$300\ 000\text{(sales)}}{\$150\ 000\text{(investment)}}$$

$$= 8.3\% \times 2 = 16.6\%$$

Now suppose that Parsons had worked to increase his share of market. He could have had the same ROI if his sales had doubled while dollar profit and investment stayed the same (accepting a lower profit ratio to get higher turnover and market share):

$$ROI = \frac{\$25\ 000\text{(net profit)}}{\$600\ 000\text{(sales)}} \times \frac{\$600\ 000\text{(sales)}}{\$150\ 000\text{(investment)}}$$

$$= 4.16\% \times 4 = 16.6\%$$

Parsons might have increased its ROI by increasing net profit through more cost cutting and more efficient marketing:

$$ROI = \frac{\$50\ 000\text{(net profit)}}{\$300\ 000\text{(sales)}} \times \frac{\$300\ 000\text{(sales)}}{\$150\ 000\text{(investment)}}$$

$$= 16.6\% \times 2 = 33.2\%$$

Another way to increase ROI is to find some way to get the same levels of sales and profits while decreasing investment (perhaps by cutting the size of Parsons's average inventory):

$$ROI = \frac{\$25\ 000\text{(net profit)}}{\$300\ 000\text{(sales)}} \times \frac{\$300\ 000\text{(sales)}}{\$75\ 000\text{(investment)}}$$

$$= 8.3\% \times 4 = 33.2\%$$

What is "investment" in the ROI formula? *Investment* is often defined as the total assets of the firm. But many analysts now use other measures of return to assess performance. These measures include *return on net assets (RONA), return on stockholders' equity (ROE),* or *return on assets managed (ROAM).* Because investment is measured at a point in time, we usually compute ROI as the average investment between two time periods (say, January 1 and December 31 of the same year). We can also compute ROI as an "internal rate of return" by using discounted cash flow analysis (see any finance textbook for more on this technique). The objective in using any of these measures is to determine how well the company has been using its resources. As inflation, competitive pressures, and cost of capital increase, such measures become increasingly important indicators of marketing and company performance.

MARKUPS, MARGIN, AND MARKDOWNS

Retailers and wholesalers must understand the concepts of **markups, margins** and **markdowns.** They must make a profit to stay in business, and the markup percentage affects profits. Markups and markdowns are expressed as percentages.

There are two different ways to compute markups—on *cost* or on *selling price:*

$$\text{Markup} = \frac{\text{dollar markup}}{\text{cost}}$$

$$\text{Margin} = \frac{\text{dollar markup}}{\text{selling price}}$$

Dale Parsons must decide which formula to use. If Parsons bought shirts for $15 and wanted to mark them up $10 to a price of $25, his markup percentage on cost would be $10/$15 = 67.7%. If Parsons wanted to calculate margin, the percentage would be $10/$25 = 40%.

Suppose Parsons knew his cost ($12) and desired markup on price (25%) for a man's tie, and wanted to compute the selling price. The formula is

$$\text{Selling price} = \frac{\text{cost}}{1 - \text{markup}}$$

$$\text{Selling price} = \frac{\$12}{0.75} = \$16$$

As a product moves through the channel of distribution, each channel member adds a markup before selling the product to the next member. This "markup chain" is shown for a suit purchased by a Parsons customer for $200:

		$ Amount	% of Selling Price
Manufacturer	Cost	$108	90%
	Markup	12	10
	Selling price	120	100
Wholesaler	Cost	120	80
	Markup	30	20
	Selling price	150	100
Retailer	Cost	150	75
	Markup	50	25
	Selling price	200	100

The retailer whose markup is 25 percent does not necessarily enjoy more profit than a manufacturer whose markup is 10 percent. Profit also depends on how many items with that profit margin can be sold (stock-turn rate) and on operating efficiency (expenses).

Sometimes a retailer wants to convert margins to markups, and vice versa. The formulas are

$$\text{Margin} = \frac{\text{markup}}{100\% + \text{markup}}$$

$$\text{Markup} = \frac{\text{margin}}{100\% - \text{margin}}$$

Suppose Parsons found that his competitor was using a markup of 30 percent based on cost and wanted to know what this would be as a percentage of selling price. The calculation would be:

$$\frac{30\%}{100\% + 30\%} = \frac{30\%}{130\%} = 23\%$$

Because Parsons was using a 25 percent markup on suits, he felt that his markup was suitable compared with that of the competitor.

Near the end of the summer Parsons still had an inventory of summer slacks in stock. Therefore, he decided to use a *markdown,* a reduction from the original selling price. Before the summer he had purchased 20 pairs at $10 each, and he had since sold 10 pairs at $20 each. He marked down the other pairs to $15 and sold 5 pairs. We compute his *markdown ratio* as follows:

$$\text{Markdown percentage} = \frac{\text{dollar markdown}}{\text{total net sales in dollars}}$$

The dollar markdown is $25 (5 pairs at $5 each) and total net sales are $275 (10 pairs at $20 + 5 pairs at $15). The ratio, then, is $25/$275 = 9%.

Larger retailers usually compute markdown ratios for each department rather than for individual items. The ratios provide a measure of relative marketing performance for each department and can be calculated and compared over time. Markdown ratios can also be used to compare the performance of different buyers and salespeople in a store's various departments.

Key Terms

Balance Sheet
Cost of goods sold
Gross margin
Gross sales
Margin
Markdown
Operating ratios
Operating statement (for profit-and-loss
  statement or income statement)
Return on investment (ROI)

Notes

Chapter 1

1. MEC Corporate Web site at **www.mec.ca**, and Eve Lazarus, "MEC facing marketing challenges," *Marketing Magazine*, 19 June 2000, p. 2

2. There are numerous other definitions. As one example, the American Marketing Association offers this: "Marketing is the process of planning, and executing the conception, pricing, promotion and distributing of ideas, goods and services to create exchanges that satisfy individual or organizational objectives."

3. Vicky Sanderson, "In the Aisles: Housewares—Little Guy vs. *Mass Merchant*," Hardware Merchandising, 1 February 2002.

4. Ibid.

5. See B. Joseph Pine II and James Gilmore, "Welcome to the Experience Economy," *Harvard Business Review*, July-August 1998, p. 99.

6. See Theodore Levitt's classic article "Marketing Myopia," *Harvard Business Review*, July-August 1960, pp. 45-46.

7. For more detailed information on delighting customers, see *The Customer Delight Principle: Exceeding Customer Expectations for Bottom-Line Success*, by Timothy Keiningham and Terry Vavra, Chicago: McGraw-Hill, 2001.

8. Lois Therrien, "Motorola and NEC: Going for Glory," *Business Week*, 1991, pp. 60-61 (special issue on quality).

9. National Quality Institute Web site at **www.nqi.ca**. For a broader perspective, see the American Society for Quality's Web site at **www.asq.org** and the Customer Care Institute at **www.customercare.com**.

10. Edwin McDowell, "Ritz-Carleton's Keys to Good Service," *New York Times*, 31 March 1993, p. 1.

11. Chuck Novak, Saturn Canada brand manager, in an interview with Peggy Cunningham, 21 July 1999.

12. Tom Smith, "Dell Ties E-Storefront to Buyer Processes," *Internet Week*, 17 May 1999, p. 6; and Michael Dell, "Twenty-First-Century Commerce," *Executive Excellence*, December 1999, pp. 3-4.

13. For more discussion on demand states, see Philip Kotler, *Marketing Management: Analysis, Planning, Implementation and Control*, 10th ed., Upper Saddle River, NJ: Prentice-Hall, 2000, Chapter 1.

14. Douglas Pruden, "Retention Marketing Gains Spotlight," *Brandweek*, 6 February 1995, p. 15.

15. For more on assessing customer value, see Gordon A. Wyner, "Customer Valuation: Linking Behaviors and Economics," *Marketing Research*, Summer 1996, pp. 36-38.

16. Barry Farber and Joyce Wycoff, "Customer Service: Evolution and Revolution," *Sales and Marketing Management*, May 1991, p. 47.

17. "Mind the Gap," *Venture*, 7 November 2000.

18. Ralph Waldo Emerson offered this advice: "If a man…makes a better mousetrap…the world will beat a path to his door." Several companies have built better mousetraps, yet failed. One was a laser mousetrap costing $1500. Contrary to Emerson's quote, people do not automatically learn about new products, believe a company's claims, or willingly pay higher prices.

19. Howard Schlossberg "Customer Satisfaction: Not a Fad, but a Way of Life," *Marketing News*, 10 June 1991, p. 18.

20. See "Leaders of the Most Admired," *Fortune*, 29 January 1990, pp. 40-54; and Thomas A. Stewart, "America's Most Admired Companies" *Fortune*, March 2002.

21. Speech by Barbara J. Hedjuk, President Imperial Oil Charitable Foundation, Social Marketing for Business Conference, Toronto, 9 November 1995.

22. NFO CFgroup, *Canadian Netizens*, March 2002.

23. Robert D. Hof, "The 'Click Here Economy,'" *Business Week*, 22 June 1998, pp. 122-128.

24. Wallys W. Conhaim, "E-commerce," *Link Up*, March/April 1998, pp. 8-10.

25. Statistics Canada, "Electronic Commerce and Technology," *The Daily*, 2 April 2002, accessed online at **www.statcan.ca/Daily/English/020402/d020402a.htm**, 20 April 2002.

26. Ibid.

27. Mark de Wolf, "Non-Profits Take on Private Sector Marketing Tactics," *Strategy: The Canadian Marketing Report*, 12 April 1999, p. D20.

Chapter 2

1. Note that the airline industry in North America uses "available seat mile (ASM)" as a standard measurement. It is not expressed in kilometres.

2. Sources include the WestJet Web site at **http://c0dsp.westjet.com/internet/sky/about/index.jsp**, accessed 20 May 2002; *WestJet Annual Information Form 2001*; Norma Ramage, "WestJet Revels in Rival's Shadow," *Marketing Magazine* (Online edition), 6 May 2002; Norma Ramage, "Clive's Flight Plan," *Marketing Magazine* (Online edition), 10 September 2001; Sarah Smith, "Flying Cluttered Skies," *Marketing Magazine* (Online edition), 9 April 2001; Peter Fitzpatrick, "Canadian Considers No-Frills Flying," *Financial Post*, 12 April 1999, p. C3. Mathew Ingram, "WestJet on the Right Flight Path," *The Globe and Mail*, 8 September 1998, p. B2.

3. See Philip Kotler, *Kotler on Marketing,* New York: Free Press, 1999, pp. 165-166.

4. Ibid., pp. 165-166.

5. For a more detailed discussion of corporate- and business-level strategic planning as they apply to marketing, see Philip Kotler, *Marketing Management: Analysis, Planning, Implementation, and Control,* 11th ed., Upper Saddle River, NJ: Prentice Hall, 2003, Chapter 3.

6. Leslie Brokaw, "The Secrets of Great Planning," *Inc.,* October 1992, p. 152.

7. Leslie Brokaw, "The Secrets of Great Planning," *Inc.,* October 1992, p. 152; and Kotler, *Marketing Management,* Chapter 3.

8. For these and other examples, see Romauld A. Stone, "Mission Statements Revisited," *SAM Advanced Management Journal,* Winter 1996, pp. 31-37; Orit Gadiesh and James L. Gilbert, "Frontline Action," *Harvard Business Review,* May 2001; and "eBay Community," accessed online at **www.ebay.com/community/aboutebay/community/index. html**, June 2001.

9. Digby Anderson, "Is This the Perfect Mission Statement?" *Across the Board,* May-June 2001, p. 16.

10. Stone, "Mission Statements Revisited," p. 33. For more on mission statements, see Bradley Johnson, "Bill Gates' Vision of Microsoft in Every Home," *Advertising Age,* 19 December 1994, pp. 14-15; J. W. Graham and W. C. Havlick, *Mission Statements: A Guide to the Corporate and Nonprofit Sectors,* New York: Garland Publishing, 1994; P. Jones and L. Kahaner, *Say It and Live It: The 50 Corporate Mission Statements That Hit the Mark,* New York: Doubleday, 1995; Thomas A. Stewart, "A Refreshing Change: Vision Statements That Make Sense," *Fortune,* 30 September 1996, pp. 195-196; and Christopher K. Bart, "Making Mission Statements Count," *CA Magazine,* March 1999, pp. 37-38.

11. Andyne Computing Limited, *1996 Annual Report*, p. 2.

12. See Gary Hamel, "Reinvent Your Company," *Fortune,* 20 June 2000, pp. 98-112; and "Fortune 500," *Fortune,* 16 April 2001, pp. F1-F2.

13. H. Igor Ansoff, "Strategies for Diversification," *Harvard Business Review,* September-October 1957, pp. 113-124. Also see Philip Kotler, *Kotler on Marketing,* New York: Free Press, 1999, pp. 46-48.

14. Michael E. Porter, *Competitive Advantage: Creating and Sustaining Superior Performance,* New York: Free Press, 1985; and Michel E. Porter, "What Is Strategy?" *Harvard Business Review,* November-December 1996, pp. 61-78. Also see Jim Webb and Chas Gile, "Reversing the Value Chain," *Journal of Business Strategy,* March-April 2001, pp. 13-17.

15. John C. Narver and Stanley F. Slater, "The Effect of a Market Orientation on Business Profitability," *Journal of Marketing,* 1990, pp. 20-35. Also see Susan Foreman, "Interdepartmental Dynamics and Market Orientation," *Manager Update,* Winter 1997, pp. 10-19; and Philip Kotler, *Kotler on Marketing,* New York: Free Press, 1999, pp. 20-22.

16. For more detailed information on Magna International, visit the corporate Web site at **www.magnasteyr.com**.

17. John Southerst, "Customer Crunching," *Canadian Business,* September 1993, pp. 28-35.

18. The four Ps classification was first suggested by E. Jerome McCarthy, *Basic Marketing: A Managerial Approach,* Homewood, IL: Irwin, 1960. For more discussion of this classification scheme, see Walter van Waterschoot and Christophe Van den Bulte, "The 4P Classification of the Marketing Mix Revisited," *Journal of Marketing,* October 1992, pp. 83-93; Michael G. Harvey, Robert F. Lusch, and Branko Cavarkapo, "A Marketing Mix for the Twenty-First Century," *Journal of Marketing Theory and Practice,* Fall 1996, pp. 1-15; and Don E. Schultz, "Marketers: Bid Farewell to Strategy Based on Old 4 Ps," *Marketing News,* 12 February 2001, p. 7.

19. Robert Lauterborn, "New Marketing Litany: 4Ps Passé; C-Words Take Over," *Advertising Age,* 1 October 1990, pp. 26. Also see Kotler, *Marketing Management,* Chapter 1.

20. For a good discussion of gaining advantage through implementation effectiveness versus strategic differentiation, see Michael E. Porter, "What Is Strategy?" *Harvard Business Review,* November-December 1996, pp. 61-78. Also see Charles H. Noble and Michael P. Mokwa, "Implementing Marketing Strategies: Developing and Testing a Managerial Theory," *Journal of Marketing,* October 1999, pp. 57-73.

21. Brian Dumaine, "Why Great Companies Last," *Business Week,* 16 January 1995, p. 129. See James C. Collins and Jerry I. Porras, *Built to Last: Successful Habits of Visionary Companies,* New York: HarperBusiness, 1995; Geoffrey Brewer, "Firing Line: What Separates Visionary Companies from All the Rest?" *Performance,* June 1995, pp. 12-17; and Rob Goffee and Gareth Jones, *The Character of a Corporation: How Your Company's Culture Can Make or Break Your Business,* New York: HarperBusiness, 1998.

22. Joseph Winski, "One Brand, One Manager," *Advertising Age,* 20 August 1987, p. 86. Also see Jack Neff, "P&G Redefines the Brand Manager," *Advertising Age,* 13 October 1997, pp. 1, 18; Alan J. Bergstrom, "Brand Management Poised for Change," *Marketing News,* 7 July 1997, p. 5; James Bell, "Brand Management for the Next Millennium," *The Journal of Business Strategy,* March-April 1998, p. 7; and Jack Neff, "The New Brand Management," *Advertising Age,* 8 November 1999, pp. S2, S18.

23. See Roland T. Rust, Valarie A. Zeithaml, and Katherine N. Lemon, *Driving Customer Equity: How Lifetime Customer Value Is Reshaping Corporate Strategy,* New York: Free Press, 2000.

24. For details, see Philip Kotler, *Marketing Management,* Chapter 20.

Chapter 3

1. Jerry Wind and Arvid Rangaswamy, "Customerization: The Next Revolution in Mass Customization," *Journal of Interactive Marketing,* Winter 2001, pp. 13-32.

2. John A. Byrne, "Management by the Web," *Business Week,* 28 August 2000, pp. 84-96.

3. Ian Mitchell, "Internet Zoo Spawns New Business Models," *Marketing Week,* 21 January 1999, pp. 24-25.

4. Paola Hjelt, "Flying on the Web in a Turbulent Economy," *Business Week,* 30 April 2001, pp. 142-148.

5. Global eXchange Services, "About Us," accessed online at **www.gegxs.com/gxs/aboutus**, 6 October 2002.

6. Deloitte Consulting, *Collaborative Commerce: Going Private to Get Results,* p. 2, accessed online at **www.dc.com/obx/library/pdf/collab_commerce.pdf**, 6 October 2002.

7. Gary Hamel and Jeff Sampler, "The E-Corporation: More than Just Web-Based, It's Building a New Industrial Order," *Fortune,* 7 December 1998, p. 82.

8. Frederick F. Reichheld and Phil Schefter, "E-Loyalty: Your Secret Weapon on the Web," *Harvard Business Review,* July-August 2000, pp. 105-113.

9. "E-commerce Trudges Through Current Slowdown," accessed online at **www.cyberatlas.com**, 22 May 2001.

10. "Blue Collar Occupations Moving Online," accessed online at **www.cyberatlas.internet.com**, 12 April 2001.

11. Roger O. Crockett, "A Web That Looks Like the World," *Business Week,* 22 March 1999, pp. EB46-EB47. Also see "True Colors," *American Demographics,* April 2001, pp. 14-15.

12. RBC Financial Group/Ipsos-Reid study, *Canadian Families and the Internet,* accessed online at

www.rbc.com/newsroom/20020123canfamnet.html, 10 October 2002.

13. Michael J. Weiss, "Online America," *American Demographics,* March 2001, pp. 53-60.

14. Statistics Canada, "Household Internet Use Survey," *The Daily,* accessed online at **www.statcan.ca/Daily/English/ 010726/d010726a.htm**, 10 October 2002.

15. Steve Hamm, "E-Biz: Down but Hardly Out," *Business Week,* 26 March 2001, pp. 126-130.

16. Statistics Canada, "Household Internet Use Survey," *The Daily*, accessed online at **www.statcan.ca/Daily/English/ 020402/d020402a.htm**, 10 October 2002.

17. Darnell Little, "Let's Keep This Exchange to Ourselves," *Business Week,* 4 December 2000, p. 48.

18. Cathy Bowen, "Behind the Spree in Payments for C2C," *Credit Card Management,* April 2000, pp. 28-34.

19. Heather Green, "How to Reach John Q. Public," *Business Week,* 26 March 2001, pp. 132-134.

20. Bradley Johnson, "Out-of-Sight Spending Collides with Reality," *Advertising Age,* 7 August 2000, pp. S4-S8.

21. Gary Hamel, "Is This All You Can Build with the Net? Think Bigger," *Fortune,* 30 April 2001, pp. 134-138.

22. See Ann Weintraub, "For Online Pet Stores, It's Dog-Eat-Dog," *Business Week,* 6 March 2000, pp. 78-80; "Death of a Spokespup," *Adweek,* 11 December 2000, pp. 44-46; and Jacques R. Chevron, "Name Least of Pet.com's Woes," *Advertising Age,* 22 January 2001, p. 24.

23. Quoted in Gary Armstrong and Philip Kotler, *Marketing: An Introduction,* 6th ed., Upper Saddle River, NJ: Prentice Hall, 2003.

24. Hamm, "E-Biz: Down but Hardly Out," p. 127.

25. See Chuck Martin, *Net Future,* New York: McGraw-Hill, 1999, p. 33.

26. "E-commerce Trudges Through Current Slowdown," accessed online at **www.cyberatlas.internet.com**, May 22, 2001.

27. Laurie Freeman, "Why Internet Brands Take Offline Avenues," *Marketing News,* July 1999, p. 4; and Paul C. Judge, "The Name's the Thing," *Business Week,* 15 November 1999, pp. 35-39.

28. John Deighton, "The Future of Interactive Marketing," *Harvard Business Review,* November-December 1996, p. 154.

29. Adapted from information found in Don Peppers and Martha Rogers, "Opening the Door to Consumers," *Sales and Marketing Management,* October 1998, pp. 22-29; and

Mike Beirne, "Marketers of the NextGeneration: Silvio Bonvini," *Brandweek*, 8 November 1999, p. 64.

30. Jeffrey F. Rayport and Bernard J. Jaworski, *e-Commerce*, New York: McGraw Hill, 2001, p. 116.

31. Lisa Bertagnoli, "Getting Satisfaction," *Marketing News*, 7 May 2001, p. 11.

32. Eilene Zimmerman, "Catch the Bug," *Sales and Marketing Management*, February 2001, pp. 78-82. Also see Ellen Neuborne, "Viral Marketing Alert," *Business Week*, 19 March 2001, p. EB8.

33. Devin Leonard, "Madison Ave. Fights Back," *Fortune*, 5 February 2001, pp. 150-154.

34. Rob Norton, "The Bright Future of Web Advertising," *Ecompany Now*, June 2001, pp. 50-60.

35. Dennis Callaghan, "Brands to Watch: Paul Allen: MyFamily.com," *MC Technology Marketing Intelligence*, February 2000, pp. 44-46; and "MyFamily.com Fact Sheet," accessed online at **www.MyFamily.com**, 30 May 2001.

36. See Thane Peterson, "E-I-E-I-E-Farming," *Business Week*, 1 May 2000, p. 202; and **www.@griculture.com**.

37. Arlene Weintraub, "When E-Mail Ads Aren't Spam," *Business Week*, 16 October 2000, pp. 112-113.

38. Erika Rasmusson, "Tracking Down Sales," *Sales and Marketing Management*, June 1998, p. 19.

39. See Robert Sales, "IFN Launches Infogate, Targets Online Equities Market Data Users," *Wall Street and Technology*, May 2000, p. 84.

40. Amy Cortese, "It's Called Webcasting, and It Promises to Deliver the Info You Want, Straight to Your PC," *Business Week*, 24 February 1997, pp. 95-104. Also see Amy Borrus, "Angry About Junk E-Mail? Congress Is Listening," *Business Week*, 23 April 2001, p. 53.

41. Elizabeth Corcoran, "The E Gang," *Fortune*, 24 July 2000, p. 145.

42. Michael Porter, "Strategy and the Internet," *Harvard Business Review*, March 2001, pp. 63-78.

43. A more detailed review of this legislation can be accessed at online at **www.privcom.gc.ca**.

44. See "Digital Divide Persists in the U.S.," accessed online at **www.cyberatlas.com**, 8 July 1999; Heather Green, Mike France, Narcia Stepanek, and Amy Borrus, "It's Time for Rules in Wonderland," *Business Week*, 20 March 2000, pp. 83-94; and Steve Jarvis, "Maybe This Year," *Marketing News*, 23 April 2001, pp. 1, 13.

Chapter 4

1. Quotes from James R. Rosenfield, "Millennial Fever," *American Demographics*, December 1997, pp. 47-51; Keith Naughton and Bill Vlasic, "The Nostalgia Boom: Why the Old Is New Again," *Business Week*, 23 March 1998, pp. 58-64; and "New Beetles: Drivers Wanted," accessed online at **www.vw.com/cars/newbeetle/main.html**, 11 August 1998. Also see Greg Farrell, "Getting the Bugs Out," *Brandweek*, 6 April 1998, pp. 30-40; "Beetle Mania," *Adweek*, 13 July 1998, p. 24; Volkswagen Press Release, "Volkswagen's New Beetle Selected 1999 North American Car of the Year," accessed online at **www.vw.com**, 4 January 1999; remarks by Jens Neumann at the 1999 North American International Auto Show, accessed online at **www.vw.com**, 4 January 1999; and Judann Pollack, "Heinz Waxes Nostalgic over Revived Glass Bottle," *Advertising Age*, 3 May 1999, p. 17.

2. Jennifer Lach, "Dateline America: May 1, 2025," *American Demographics*, May 1999, pp. 19-20.

3. Jim McElgunn, "Foot Puts the Boot to Current 'Life-Cycle' Trends," *Marketing*, 15 June 1992, p. 1; Daniel Stoffman, "Completely Predictable People," *Report on Business*, November 1990, pp. 78-84; "Boomers Slowing Pace of Leisure," *Toronto Star*, 20 June 1993, p. G3.

4. Elizabeth Church, "Birth Bulge Breeds Its Own Industry," *Globe and Mail*, 24 September 1996, p. B12.

5. Jane Gadd, "Commitment to Healthy Diet Declines," *The Globe and Mail*, 11 November 1997, p. A10.

6. Patti Summerfield, "RMB Rolls out National Study," *Strategy*, 24 April 2000, p. 18.

7. Statistics Canada, *Population and Dwelling Counts, for Canada, Provinces and Territories, 2001 and 1996 Censuses*, accessed online at **www12.statcan.ca/english/census01/ products/standard/popdwell/Table-PR.cfm**, 11 October 2002.

8. See the world population clock, which gives daily estimates of the world population, online at **www.census.gov/main/www/popclock.html**. Many of the global statistical data in this chapter are drawn from the *World Almanac and Book of Facts*, 1993.

9. Sally D. Goll, "Marketing: China's (Only) Children Get the Royal Treatment," *Wall Street Journal*, 8 February 1995, pp. B1, B2.

10. John Kettle, "Kettle's Future: Canada Shows Its Age," *The Globe and Mail*, 17 January 1997, p. B11.

11. Daniel Stoffman, "Completely Predictable People," *Report on Business*, November 1990, pp. 78-84.

12. See Thomas Exter, "And Baby Makes 20 Million," *American Demographics*, July 1991, p. 55; Joseph Spiers, "The Baby Boomlet Is for Real," *Fortune*, 10 February 1992, pp.

101-104; Joe Schwartz, "Is the Baby Boomlet Ending?" *American Demographics,* May 1992, p. 9; and Christopher Farrell, "The Baby Boomlet May Kick in a Little Growth," *Business Week,* 10 January 1994, p. 66.

13. See Diane Crispell and William H. Frey, "American Maturity," *American Demographics,* March 1993, pp. 31-42; Charles F. Longino, "Myths of an Aging America," *American Demographics,* August 1994, pp. 36-43; Melissa Campanelli, "Selling to Seniors: A Waiting Game," *Sales & Marketing Management,* June 1994, p. 69.

14. Marina Strauss, "Seniors Grasp for Friendlier Packaging," *The Globe and Mail,* 7 October 1993, p. B4; *Today's Seniors,* October 1995, pp. 3-9; "The Countdown to the Twenty-First Century," *Vision 2000,* The Royal Bank.

15. Statistics Canada, "1996 Census: Marital Status, Common-Law Unions and Families," 14 October 1997; "Women in Canada," *The Daily,* accessed online at **www.statcan.ca/Daily/English/ 000914/d000914c.htm**, 14 September 2000.

16. Statistics Canada, "Demographic Statistics, First Quarter 2000 (Preliminary)," *The Daily,* accessed online at **www.statcan.ca**, 20 June 2000,

17. Statistics Canada, "Migration 1998/99," *The Daily,* accessed online at **www.statcan.ca**, 26 September 2000.

18. Barbara Smith, "Special Feature: Gay and Lesbian Marketing: Market Becoming More Accessible," *Strategy,* 18 September 1995, p. 35.

19. James W. Hughes, "Understanding the Squeezed Consumer," *American Demographics,* July 1991, p. 44-50. Also see Patricia Sellers, "Winning over the New Consumer," *Fortune,* 29 July 1991, pp. 113-25; and Brian O'Reilly, "Preparing for Leaner Times," *Fortune,* 27 January 1992, pp. 40-47.

20. Mark MacKinnon, "High-Income Neighbourhoods," *The Globe and Mail,* 1 March 1999, p. B1; Mark MacKinnon, "The Lowest Incomes in Canada Are Found on Native Reserves," *The Globe and Mail,* 1 March 1999, p. B2.

21. David Leonhardt, "Two-Tier Marketing," *Business Week,* 17 March 1997, pp. 82-90.

22. Margot Bigg-Clark, "Juggling Jobs a '90s Necessity," *The Globe and Mail,* 28 July 1997, pp. B1, B3; Harvey Schachter, "Slaves of the New Economy," *Canadian Business,* April 1996, pp. 86-92.

23. Nancy DeHart, "Clocking In," *Kingston Whig-Standard,* 26 May 1997, p. 15.

24. Zena Olijnyk, "Loblaw Takes a Run at Time-Starved Diners," *Financial Post,* 11 November 1997, p. 10.

25. For more discussion, see Philip Kotler, Gary Armstrong, and Peggy H. Cunningham, *Principles of Marketing,* 5th Cdn ed., Toronto: Pearson Education, 2002, the "Environmentalism" section in Chapter 18. Also see Patrick Carson and Julia Moulden, *Green Is Gold,* Toronto: Harper Business Press, 1991; Michael E. Porter and Claas van der Linde, "Green and Competitive: Ending the Stalemate," *Harvard Business Review,* September-October 1995, pp. 120-134; Stuart L. Hart, "Beyond Greening: Strategies for a Sustainable World," *Harvard Business Review,* January-February 1997, pp. 67-76; Jacquelyn Ottman, "Environment Winners Show Sustainable Strategies," *Marketing News,* 27 April 1998, p. 6; Lisa E. Phillips, "Green Attitude," *American Demographics,* April 1999, pp. 46-74; and Forest L. Reinhardt, "Bringing the Environment Down to Earth," *Harvard Business Review,* July-August 1999, pp. 149-157.

26. "13-year-old Bids Over $3m for Items in eBay Auctions," *USA Today,* 30 April 1999, p. 10B.

27. Rajiv Chandrasekaran, "AOL Settles Marketing Complaints," *Washington Post,* 29 May 1998, p. F1.

28. See Cyndee Miller, "Trendspotters: 'Dark Ages' Ending; So Is Cocooning," *Marketing News,* 3 February 1997, pp. 1, 16.

29. Philip Kotler, *Kotler on Marketing,* New York: Free Press, 1999, p. 3.

30. See Carl Zeithaml and Valerie A. Zeithaml, "Environmental Management: Revising the Marketing Perspective," *Journal of Marketing,* Spring 1984, pp. 46-53.

Chapter 5

1. See "Coke 'Family' Sales Fly as New Coke Stumbles," *Advertising Age,* 17 January 1986, p. 1; Jack Honomichl, "Missing Ingredients in 'New' Coke's Research," *Advertising Age,* 22 July 1985, p. 1; Leah Rickard, "Remembering New Coke," *Advertising Age,* 17 April 1995, p. 6; Rick Wise, "Why Things Go Better with Coke," *The Journal of Business Strategy,* January-February 1999, pp. 15-19; and Sean Mehegan, "Soft Drinks," *Adweek,* 23 April 2001, p. SR24.

2. See Philip Kotler, *Kotler on Marketing,* New York: Free Press, 1999, p. 73.

3. Christina Le Beau, "Mountains to Mine," *American Demographics,* August 2000, pp. 40-44. Also see Joseph M. Winski, "Gentle Rain Turns into Torrent," *Advertising Age,* 3 June 1991, p. 34; David Shenk, *Data Smog: Surviving the Information Glut,* San Francisco: HarperSanFrancisco, 1997; Diane Trommer, "Information Overload-Study Finds Intranet Users Overwhelmed with Data," *Electronic Buyers' News,* 20 April 1998, p. 98; and Stewart Deck, "Data Storm Ahead," *CIO,* 15 April 2001, p. 97.

4. Alice LaPlante, "Still Drowning!" *Computer World,* 10 March 1997, pp. 69-70.

5. Philip Kotler, Gary Armstrong, and Peggy H. Cunningham, *Principles of Marketing*, 5th Cdn ed., Toronto: Pearson Education, 2002.

6. Stan Crock, "They Snoop to Conquer," *Business Week,* 28 October 1996, p. 172.

7. See Suzie Amer, "Masters of Intelligence," *Forbes*, 5 April 1999, p. 18.

8. Kotler et al., *Principles of Marketing*, 5th Cdn ed.

9. For more on marketing and competitive intelligence, see David B. Montgomery and Charles Weinberg, "Toward Strategic Intelligence Systems," *Marketing Management,* Winter 1998, pp. 44-52; Morris C. Attaway Sr., "A Review of Issues Related to Gathering and Assessing Competitive Intelligence," *American Business Review,* January 1998, pp. 25-35; and Conor Vibert, "Secrets of Online Sleuthing," *Journal of Business Strategy,* May-June 2001, pp. 39-42.

10. ACNielsen, Retail Measurement Services, *MarketTrack-Understanding Product Performance & Market Dynamics,* accessed online at **www.acnielsen.ca/sect_retailmes/retail_en.htm**, 14 October 2002.

11. Justin Martin, "Ignore Your Customer," *Fortune,* 1 May 1995, p. 126

12. Rebecca Piirto Heather, "Future Focus Groups," *American Demographics*, January 1994, p. 6. For more on focus groups, see Holly Edmunds, *The Focus Group Research Handbook,* Lincolnwood, IL: NTC Business Books, 1999.

13. Sarah Schafer, "Communications: Getting a Line on Customers," *Inc. Technology*, 1996, p. 102. Also see Judith Langer, "15 Myths of Qualitative Research: It's Conventional, But Is It Wisdom?" *Marketing News,* 1 March 1999, pp. 13-14; and Alison Stein Wellner, "I've Asked You Here Because…," *Business Week,* 14 August 2000, p. F14.

14. Janet McFarland, "YOUtv Captures Customer Feedback," *The Globe and Mail,* 19 November 1996, p. B15

15. Lesley Daw, "Customer Polling Takes to the Net," *Marketing,* 27 January 1997, p. 3.

16. Gail El Baroudi, "Bank Survey Is a Hit," *The Globe and Mail,* 7 October 1997, p. C5.

17. Diane Crispell, "People Talk, Computers Listen," *American Demographics,* October 1989, p. 8; and Peter J. DePaulo and Rick Weitzer, "Interactive Phones Technology Delivers Survey Data Quickly," *Marketing News,* 6 June 1994, pp. 33-34.

18. Marc L. Songini, "FedEx Expects CRM System to Deliver," *Computerworld,* 6 November 2000, p. 10.

19. Kevin Fogarty, "Is CRM a Faint Hope?" *Computerworld,* 4 June 2001, p. 50.

20. Robert McLuhan, "How to Reap the Benefits of CRM," *Marketing,* 24 May 2001, p. 35.

21. See Nancy Levenburg and Tom Dandridge, "Can't Afford Research? Try Miniresearch," *Marketing News,* 31 March 1997, p. 19; and Nancy Levenburg, "Research Resources Exist for Small Businesses," *Marketing News,* 4 January 1999, p. 19.

22. Many of the examples in this section, along with others, are found in Subhash C. Jain, *International Marketing Management*, 3rd ed., Boston: PWS-Kent, 1990, pp. 334-339. Also see Jack Honomichl, "Research Cultures Are Different in Mexico, Canada," *Marketing News*, 5 May 1993, pp. 12-13; Naghi Namakforoosh, "Data Collection Methods Hold Key to Research in Mexico," *Marketing News*, 29 August 1994, p. 28; Ken Gofton, "Going Global with Research," *Marketing,* 15 April 1999, p. 35; and Jack Edmonston, "U.S., Overseas Differences Abound," *Advertising Age's Business Marketing,* January 1998, p. 32.

23. Jain, *International Marketing Management*, p. 338.

24. David Chilton, "Canadians Don't Mind Being Surveyed," *Strategy,* 1 April 1996, p. 5.

25. David Eggleston, "Canadians Condemn DoubleClick Profiling Plans," *Strategy,* 13 March 2000, p. 2.

26. Susan Vogt, "Online Privacy Laws All over the Map," *Strategy,* 11 September 2000, p. 12.

27. Cynthia Crossen, "Studies Galore Support Products and Positions, but Are They Reliable?" *Wall Street Journal,* 14 November 1991, pp. A1, A9.

Chapter 6

1. Quotes from Richard A. Melcher, "Tune-up Time for Harley," *Business Week*, 8 April 1997, pp. 90–94; Ian P. Murphy, "Aided by Research, Harley Goes Whole Hog," *Marketing News*, 2 December 1996, pp. 16, 17; and Dyan Machan, "Is the Hog Going Soft?" *Forbes,* 10 March 1997, pp. 114–119. Also see "Hot Stuff," *Money,* April 1997, p. 174.

2. Allan R. Gregg, "Coming of Age: After a Rough Ride, Canada's Mood Has Returned to the Confident Outlook Found in 1984's First Year-End Poll," Bruce Wallace, "What Makes a Canadian? We're Certain We're Unique, but We Don't Seem to Know Precisely What Sets us Apart from Others," *Maclean's,* 20 December 1999: Cover Story; Robert Sheppard, "We Are Canadian," *Maclean's,* 25 December 2000: Cover; accessed online at **www.macleans.ca/2000/12/25/cover/ 45320.shtml**.

3. Ministry of Supply and Services Canada, *Shared Values: The Canadian Identity,* 1991, p. 1; Craig McKie and Keith Thompson, *Canadian Social Trends,* Toronto: Thompson Educational Publishing, Inc.

4. Statistics Canada, "1996 Census: Mother tongue, Home Language and Knowledge of Languages," *The Daily,* 2 December 1997.

5. Jo Marney, "Counting Ethnic Canadians In," *Marketing Magazine* (Online edition), 4 June 2001; *Top 25 Ethnic Origins in Canada* (1) 1996 Census, Statistics Canada, available online at **www.statcan.ca/english.census96/ feb17/eolcan.htm**, accessed 24 May 2002; Malcolm Dunlop and Christine Comi, "Multicultural Explosion," *Strategy Magazine,* 11 February 2002, p. 25; Astrid Van Den Broek, "Fighting Cultural Fade," *Strategy Magazine,* 2 February 2002, p. 21.

6. Carey Toane, "Veering off from the Mainstream: Marketers Are Finding Divergent Ways beyond Traditional Advertising to Reach Ethnic Consumers," *Marketing On-Line,* 5 June 2000; Patrick Lejtenyi, "Underlying Differences: Market Researchers Must Be Diligent about Identifying Subcultures within Ethnic Groups," *Marketing On-Line,* 5 June 2000.

7. Sinclair Stewart, "Special report: Multicultural Marketing: A Long and Winding Road: While the Numbers Suggest Canada's Ethnic Communities Are Well Worth Wooing, National Advertisers Are Still Reluctant to Embark on a Multicultural Mission," *Strategy,* 17 August 1998, p. 20.

8. Carey Toane, "Veering off from the Mainstream: Marketers Are Finding Divergent Ways beyond Traditional Advertising to Reach Ethnic Consumers," *Marketing On-Line,* 5 June 2000.

9. Jennifer Lynn, "Approaching Diversity," *Marketing,* 30 July 1995, p. 15; David Menzies, "TD Bank Opens a Branch in Cyberspace," *Marketing,* 19 June 1995, p. 11; James Pollock, "Opening Doors of Opportunity," *Marketing,* 18 September 1995; Isabel Vincent, "Chasing after the Ethnic Consumer," *The Globe and Mail,* 18 September 1995; Craig McKie and Keith Thompson, *Canadian Social Trends.*

10. Keith McArthur, "Internet Has Transformed Life!" *The Globe and Mail,* 22 March 2000, p. B11.

11. Nielsen/NetRatings, "Canadian Internet Users Spend More Time Online than U.S. Web Surfers," *Reports on Internet Usage in Canada,* Average Web Usage, February 2002.

12. Industry Canada, "Internet Usage Statistics and User Characteristics: Demographic Characteristics of Internet Users," *Canadian Internet Retailing Report,* 23 October 1998, Chapter 3.1, available online at **strategis.ic.gc.ca/SSG/ir01621e.html**, accessed 28 October 2002.

13. Steve Ferley, "PMB '97 Reveals That Canadian Internet Usage Patterns Fall along Both Language and Demographic Lines," *Print Measurement Bureau, 1997 Study,* p. 16.

14. "Lifestyles of the Rich," *National Post,* 22 April 2000, p. E11.

15. Courteny Kane, "Advertising: TBWA/Chiat Day Brings 'Street Culture' to a Campaign for Levi-Strauss Silver Tab Clothing," *New York Times,* 14 August 1998, p. D8.

16. Debra Goldman, "Spotlight Men," *Adweek,* 13 August 1990, pp. M1–M6; Dennis Rodkin, "A Manly Sport: Building Loyalty," *Advertising Age,* 15 April 1991, pp. S1, S12; Nancy Ten Kate, "Who Buys the Pants in the Family?" *American Demographics,* January 1992, p. 12; and Laura Zinn, "Real Men Buy Paper Towels, Too," *Business Week,* 9 November 1992, pp. 75–76.

17. Jeffery Zbar, "Hardware Builds Awareness among Women," *Advertising Age,* 11 July 1994, p. 18.

18. David Leonhardt, "Hey Kids, Buy This," *Business Week,* 30 June 1997, pp. 62–67. Also see Chankon Kim and Hanjoon Lee, "Development of Family Triadic Measures for Children's Purchase Influence," *Journal of Marketing Research,* August 1997, pp. 307–321; Judann Pollack, "Food Targeting Children Aren't Just Child's Play," *Advertising Age,* 1 March 1999, p. 16; Carolyn M. Edy, "Babies Mean Business," *American Demographics,* May 1999, pp. 46–47; and Paul Sensbach, "Don't Kid Around with Kid Packaging," *Marketing News,* 20 November 2000, p. 14.

19. See Paul C. Judge, "Are Tech Buyers Different?" *Business Week,* 26 January 1998, pp. 64–65, 68; Josh Bernoff, Shelley Morrisette, and Kenneth Clemmer, *The Forrester Report,* Forrester Research, Inc., 1998; and the Forrester Web site at **www.forrester.com**, July 2001.

20. Salem Alaton, "Look Who's Going Cellular," *The Globe and Mail,* 5 December 1995, p. C1.

21. Myron Magnet, "Let's Go for Growth," *Fortune,* 7 March 1994, p. 70.

22. David Todd, "Quebec Milk Producers Play on Emotional Ties," *Strategy,* 1 March 1999, p. 31; Stephanie Whittaker, "Milk Grows Up," *Marketing On-Line,* 9 August 1999.

23. See Leon Festinger, *A Theory of Cognitive Dissonance,* Stanford, CA: Stanford University Press, 1957; Leon G. Schiffman and Leslie L. Kanuk, *Consumer Behavior,* pp. 6th ed., Upper Saddle River, NJ: Prentice Hall, 1997, pp. 271–272; Jeff Stone, "A Radical New Look at Cognitive Dissonance," *American Journal of Psychology,* Summer 1998, pp. 319–326; Thomas R. Schultz, Elene Leveille, and Mark R. Lepper, "Free Choice and Cognitive Dissonance Revisited: Choosing 'Lesser Evils' versus 'Greater Goods,'" *Personality and Social Psychology Bulletin,* January 1999, pp. 40–48; and Jillian C. Sweeney, Douglas Hausknecht, and Geoffrey N. Soutar, "Cognitive Dissonance After Purchase: A Multidimensional Scale," *Psychology and Marketing,* May 2000, pp. 369–385.

24. See Frank Rose, "Now Quality Means Service Too," *Fortune,* 22 April 1991, pp. 97–108; Chip Walker, "Word of Mouth," *American Demographics,* July 1995, p. 40; Thomas O. Jones and W. Earl Sasser Jr., "Why Satisfied Customers Defect," *Harvard Business Review,* November–December 1995, pp. 88–99; and Roger Sant, "Did He Jump or Was He Pushed?" *Marketing News,* 12 May 1997, pp. 2, 21.

25. The following discussion draws heavily from Everett M. Rogers, *Diffusion of Innovations,* 3rd ed., New York: Free Press, 1983. Also see Hubert Gatignon and Thomas S. Robertson, "A Propositional Inventory for New Diffusion Research," *Journal of Consumer Research,* March 1985, pp. 849–867; Rogers, *Diffusion of Innovations,* 4th ed., New York: Free Press, 1995; and Marnik G. Dekiple, Philip M. Parker, and Milos Sarvary, "Global Diffusion of Technological Innovations: A Coupled-Hazard Approach," *Journal of Marketing Research,* February 2000, pp. 47–59.

26. Sarah Lorge, "Purchasing Power," *Sales and Marketing Management,* June 1998, pp. 43–46.

27. Patrick J. Robinson, Charles W. Faris, and Yoram Wind, *Industrial Buying Behavior and Creative Marketing,* Boston: Allyn & Bacon, 1967. Also see Erin Anderson, Weyien Chu, and Barton Weitz, "Industrial Purchasing: An Empirical Exploration of the Buyclass Framework," *Journal of Marketing,* July 1987, pp. 71–86; Cynthia Webster, "Buying Involvement in Purchasing Success," *Industrial Marketing Management,* August 1993, p. 199; and Edward G. Brierty, Robert W. Eckles, and Robert R. Reeder, *Business Marketing,* 3rd ed., Upper Saddle River, NJ: Prentice Hall, 1998, pp. 74–82.

28. Frederick E. Webster Jr. and Yoram Wind, *Organizational Buying Behavior,* Upper Saddle River, NJ: Prentice Hall, 1972, pp. 33–37. Also see Brierty, Eckles, and Reeder, *Business Marketing,* Chap. 3.

29. Thomas V. Bonoma, "Major Sales: Who Really Does the Buying," *Harvard Business Review,* May–June 1982, p. 114. Also see Ajay Kohli, "Determinants of Influence in Organizational Buying: A Contingency Approach," *Journal of Marketing,* July 1989, pp. 50–65; and Jeffrey E. Lewin, "The Effects of Downsizing on Organizational Buying Behavior: An Empirical Investigation," *Academy of Marketing Science,* Spring 2001, pp. 151–164.

30. Patrick J. Robinson, Charles W. Faris, and Yoram Wind, *Industrial Buying Behavior and Creative Marketing,* Boston: Allyn & Bacon, 1967, p. 14.

31. John H. Sheridan, "Buying Globally Made Easier," *Industry Week,* 2 February 1998, pp. 63–64; information accessed online at **www.wiznet.net**, September 1999; and John Evan Frook, "Catalog Management Race Begins," *B to B,* 19 March 2001, p. 20.

32. See Andy Reinhardt, "Extranets: Log on, Link up, Save Big," *Business Week,* 22 June 1998, p. 134; "To Byte the Hand That Feeds," *The Economist,* 17 January 1998, pp. 61–62; Ken Brack, "Source of the Future," *Industrial Distribution,* October 1998, pp. 76–80; James Carbone, "Internet Buying on the Rise," *Purchasing,* 25 March 1998, pp. 51–56; ad "E-Procurement: Certain Value in Changing Times," *Fortune,* 30 April 2001, pp. S2–S3.

Chapter 7

1. See Steve Jarvis, "P&G's Challenge," *Marketing News,* 28 August 2000, pp. 1, 13; Robert Berner, "Can P&G Clean up Its Act?" *Business Week,* 12 March 2001, pp. 80-83; and information accessed online at **www.pg.com** and **www.tide.com**, July 2001.

2. Arlene Weintraub, "Chairman of the Board," *Business Week,* 28 May 2001, p. 94.

3. Nelson D. Schwartz, "What's in the Cards for AmEx?" *Fortune,* 22 January 2001, pp. 58-70.

4. Laurel Cutler, quoted in "Stars of the 1980s Cast Their Light," *Fortune,* 3 July 1989, p. 76; and Robert E. Linneman and John L. Stanton Jr., *Making Niche Marketing Work: How to Grow Bigger by Acting Smaller,* New York: McGraw-Hill, 1991. Also see Arlene Weintraub, "Little Niches That Grew," *Business Week,* 18 June 2001, p. 100.

5. For a collection of articles on one-to-one marketing and mass customization, see James H. Gilmore and B. Joseph Pine, *Markets of One: Creating Customer-Unique Value through Mass Customization,* Boston: Harvard Business School Press, 2001.

6. Quoted in Phillip Kotler, Gary Armstrong, and Peggy Cunningham, *Principles of Marketing,* 5th Cdn ed., Toronto: Pearson Education Canada, 2002.

7. "Absolut East," *Marketing,* 18 September 1995, p. 2.

8. Edward Caffyn, "Just Try to Sell Me," *Marketing,* 4 August 1997, pp. 13-14.

9. Gregory Skinner, "Youth Marketing: Calvin's the Dude Who Rocks the Nation," *Strategy,* 20 January 1997, p. 13.

10. See "Automakers Learn Better Roads to Women's Market," *Marketing News,* October 12, 1992, p. 2; Alan Alder, "Purchasing Power Women's Buying Muscle Shops up in Car Design, Marketing," *Chicago Tribune,* 29 September, 1996, p. 21A; Jean Halliday, "GM Taps Harris to Help Lure Women," *Advertising Age,* 17 February 1997, pp. 1, 37; and Mary Louis Quinlin, "Women: We've Come a Long Way, Maybe," *Advertising Age,* 13 February 1999, p. 46.

11. Raymond Serafin, "I Am Woman, Hear Me Roar…in My Car," *Advertising Age,* 7 November 1994, pp. 1, 8.

12. Deborah Read, "The Young and the Jobless," *Report on Business,* April 1996, pp. 117-118.

13. Astrid Van Den Broek, "Targeting Yourself," *Marketing,* 2 August 1999, p. 9.

14. For a detailed discussion of personality and buyer behaviour, see Leon G. Schiffman and Leslie Lazar Kanuk, *Consumer Behavior,* 5th ed., Englewood Cliffs, NJ: Prentice Hall, 1994, Chapter 5.

15. Bobbi Bulmer, "Nokia Aims 'Fashionable' Phones at Women," *Marketing,* 22 September 1997, p. 3.

16. "RadioShack Giving E-Gifts This Holiday Season," *Adnews On-Line Daily,* 13 November 2000, available online at **www.adnews.com**.

17. Helena Lazar, "Creating New Habits: Well-Targeted Ads Encourage Light Users to Pour on the Sauce," *Marketing On-line,* 20 September 1999; Warren Thayer, "Target Heavy Buyers!" *Frozen Food Age,* March 1998, pp. 22-24.

18. See Thomas V. Bonoma and Benson P. Shapiro, *Segmenting the Industrial Market,* Lexington, MA: Lexington Books, 1983. For examples of segmenting business markets, see Kate Bertrand, "Market Segmentation: Divide and Conquer," *Business Marketing,* October 1989, pp. 48-44.

19. Daniel S. Levine, "Justice Served," *Sales & Marketing Management,* May 1995, pp. 63-71.

20. For more on segmenting business markets, see John Berrigan and Carl Finkbeiner, *Segmentation Marketing: New Methods for Capturing Business,* New York: HarperBusiness, 1992; Rodney L. Griffith and Louis G. Pol, "Segmenting Industrial Markets," *Industrial Marketing Management,* 23, 1994, pp. 39-46; Stavros P. Kalafatis and Vicki Cheston, "Normative Models and Practical Applications of Segmentation in Business Markets," *Industrial Marketing Management,* November 1997, pp. 519-30; and James C. Anderson and James A. Narus, *Business Market Management,* Upper Saddle River, NJ: Prentice Hall, 1999, pp. 44-47.

21. Cyndee Miller, "Teens Seen as the First Truly Global Consumers," *Advertising Age,* 27 March 1995, p. 9.

22. Shawn Tully, "Teens: The Most Global Market of All," *Fortune,* 16 May 1994, pp. 90-97; "MTV Hits 100 Million in Asia," *New Media Markets,* 28 January 1999, p. 12; and Brett Pulley and Andrew Tanzer, "Sumner's Gemstone," *Forbes,* 21 February 2000, pp. 106-111. For more on international segmentation, see V. Kumar and Anish Nagpal, "Segmenting Global Markets: Look Before You Leap," *Marketing Research,* Spring 2001, pp. 8-13.

23. See Michael Porter, *Competitive Advantage,* New York: Free Press, 1985, pp. 4-8. 234-236.

24. Paul Davidson, "Entrepreneurs Reap Riches from Net Niches," *USA Today,* 20 April 1999, p. B3; and information accessed online at **www.ostrichesonline.com**, February 2000.

25. "Raking in the Chips," *Report on Business,* April 1992, pp. 39-40.

26. Chris Cobb, "Toying with Children's Minds," *Kingston Whig-Standard,* 18 December 1993, p. 2; Michael Wilke, "Toy Companies Take up Diversity Banner," *Advertising Age,* 27 February 1995, pp. 1, 8.

27. "Selling Sin to Blacks," *Fortune,* 21 October 1991, p. 100; Dorothy J. Gaiter, "Black-Owned Firms Are Catching an Afrocentric Wave," *The Wall Street Journal,* 8 January 1992, p. B2.

28. Marina Strauss, "Labatt Targeted Youth, Consultant Says," *The Globe and Mail,* 21 July 1995, p. B3.

29. "Are auto dealers biased?" *Business Week,* 14 August 1995, p. 26.

30. Bruce Little, "Poor Left Behind in Computer Revolution," *The Globe and Mail,* 15 January 1996, p. B11.

31. Cyndee Miller, "The Ultimate taboo," *Marketing News,* 29(17), pp. 1, 18.

32. Jim McElgunn, "Money, Marketing and Gender," *Marketing,* 30 January 1995, pp. 11-13.

33. Cyndee Miller, "Cosmetics Firms Finally Discover the Ethnic Market," *Marketing News,* 30 August 1993, p. 2.

34. For an interesting discussion of finding ways to differentiate marketing offers, see Ian C. MacMillan and Rita Gunther McGrath, "Discovering New Points of Differentiation," *Harvard Business Review,* July-August 1997, pp. 133-145.

35. Anne Dimon, "The Concierge Can Turn out to Be Your Best Friend in Need," *The Globe and Mail Report on Business Travel,* 13 February 1996, C9; Jeremy Ferguson, "Where Rescue Operations Are Routine," *The Globe and Mail, Report on Business Travel,* 13 February 1996, C9.

36. Marina Strauss, "Zellers Returns to Pitching Prices," *The Globe and Mail,* 13 March 2000, pp. B1, B3; Fawzia Sheikh, "Zellers Plans to Expand Its Brands," *Marketing On-line,* 17 May 1999.

37. See Philip Kotler, *Kotler on Marketing,* Upper Saddle River, NJ: Prentice Hall, 1999:59-63.

Chapter 8

1. Intrawest, *1997 Annual Report,* Vancouver, BC.

2. Intrawest, *1997 Annual Report,* Vancouver, BC.

3. Ann Gibbon, "Big Seen As Best for Ski Resorts," *The Globe and Mail*, 17 September 1996, pp. B1, B4; Patti Summerfield, "Special Report: Top Database Marketers: Top in Hotels and Tourism: Intrawest Delivers Multi-Resort Message," *Strategy*, 21 July 1997, p. DR12; Steve Threndyle, "Turning the Corner: Canada's Ski Industry Grows for the Future," *Supplement to the Financial Post Magazine*, October 1996, pp. 1-8; Konrad Yarabuski, "Intrawest Plans Peak Success," *The Globe and Mail*, 29 September 1997, pp. B1, B11; Erica Zlomislic, "Whistler Targets American Skiers," *Strategy*, 18 August 1997, p. 8.

4. Mark Hyman, "The Yin and Yang of the Tiger Effect," *Business Week*, 16 October 2000, p. 110; and "Finance and Economics: A Tiger Economy," *The Economist*, 14 April 2001, p. 70.

5. See Philip Kotler, Irving J. Rein, and Donald Haider, *Marketing Places: Attracting Investment, Industry, and Tourism to Cities, States, and Nations,* New York: Free Press, 1993, pp. 202, 273. Additional information accessed online at **www.ireland.travel.ie** and **www.ida.ie**, August 2001.

6. Accessed online at **www.social-marketing.org/aboutus.html**, August 2001.

7. See V. Rangan Kasturi, Sohel Katin, and Sheryl K. Sandberg, "Do Better at Doing Good," *Harvard Business Review*, May-June 1996, pp. 42-54; Alan R. Andreasen, *Marketing Social Change: Changing Behavior to Promote Health, Social Development, and the Environment,* San Francisco: Jossey-Bass, 1995; Alan R. Andreasen, Rob Gould, and Karen Gutierrez, "Social Marketing Has a New Champion," *Advertising Age*, 7 February 2000, p. 38; information also accessed online at **www.adcouncil.org**, February 2000.

8. See Lois Therrien, "Motorola and NEC: Going for Glory," *Business Week*, special issue on quality, 1991, pp. 60-61. For more on quality, see Roland T. Rust, Anthony J. Zahorik, and Timothy L. Keiningham, "Return on Quality (ROQ): Making Service Quality Financially Accountable," *Journal of Marketing*, April 1995, pp. 58-70; John Dalrymple and Eileen Drew, "Quality: On the Threshold or the Brink?" *Total Quality Management,* July 2000, pp. S697-S703; and Thomas J. Douglas and William Q. Judge, "Total Quality Management Implementation and Competitive Advantage," *Academy of Management Journal,* February 2001, pp. 158-169.

9. Philip Kotler, *Kotler on Marketing,* New York: Free Press, 1999, p. 17.

10. See "Hot R.I.P.: The Floppy Disk," *Rolling Stone*, 20 August 1998, p. 86; Owen Edwards, "Beauty and the Box," *Forbes*, 5 October 1998, p. 131; Bob Woods, "iMac Drives Apple's Q2 Results," *Computer Dealer News*, 30 April 1999, p. 39; and Pui-Wing Tam, "Designing Duo Helps Shape Apple's Fortunes," *The Wall Street Journal,* 18 July 2001, p. B1.

11. Alice Rawsthorn, "The World's Top 50 Logos," *Report on Business Magazine,* November 2000, pp. 84-100.

12. Gerry Khermouch, "The Best Global Brands," *Business Week,* 6 August 2001, pp. 50-64.

13. See Roland T. Rust, Katherine N. Lemon, and Valerie A. Zeithaml, *Driving Customer Equity: How Lifetime Customer Value Is Reshaping Corporate Strategy,* New York: Free Press, 2000; and Katherine N. Lemon, Roland T. Rust, and Valerie A. Zeithaml, "What Drives Customer Equity," *Marketing Management,* Spring 2001, pp. 20-25.

14. Warren Thayer, "Loblaws Exec Predicts: Private Labels to Surge," *Frozen Food Age*, May 1996, p. 1; "President's Choice Continues Brisk Pace," *Frozen Food Age*, March 1998, pp. 17-18; David Dunne and Chakravarthi Narasimhan, "The New Appeal of Private Labels," *Harvard Business Review*, May-June 1999, pp. 41-52; **www.sendpc.com**; and "New Private Label Alternatives Bring Changes to Supercenters, Clubs," *DSN Retailing Today,* 5 February 2001, p. 66.

15. Marina Strauss, "Oshawa Group Plans to Fire up Private-Label War," *The Globe and Mail,* 3 June 1994, pp. B1-B2.

16. Fawzia Sheikh, "Zellers Aims for $200M in Truly Sales," *Marketing On-line*, 8 March 1999; Bud Jorgensen, "Cott Cashes in, Makes Enemies," *The Globe and Mail,* 8 January 1994, pp. B1, B6.

17. See Patrick Oster, "The Eurosion of Brand Loyalty," *Business Week*, 19 July 1993, p. 22; Marcia Mogelonsky, "When Stores Become Brands," *American Demographics,* February 1995, pp. 32-38; John A. Quelch and David Harding, "Brands versus Private Labels: Fighting to Win," *Harvard Business Review,* January-February 1996, pp. 99-109; Stephanie Thompson, "Private Label Marketers Getting Savvier to Consumption Trends," *Brandweek*, 24 November 1997, p. 9; and David Dunne and Chakravarthi Narasimham, "The New Appeal of Private Labels," *Harvard Business Review,* May-June 1999, pp. 41-52.

18. Jan Wong, "Putting Your Own Stamp on Snail Mail," *The Globe and Mail,* 2 May 2000, pp. A1, A6; Wendy Stueck, "Thirsty? Get Your Personalized Pop On-Line," *The Globe and Mail,* 16 March 2000, pp. B1, B4.

19. See Silvia Sansoni, "Gucci, Armani, and…John Paul II?" *Business Week,* 13 May 1996, p. 61; Bart A. Lazar, "Licensing Gives Known Brands New Life," *Advertising Age*, 16 February 16, 1998, p. 8; Laura Petrecca, "'Corporate Brands' Put Licensing in the Spotlight," *Advertising Age,* 14 June 1999, p. 1; and Rachel Miller, "How Licensing Can Invigorate Brands," *Marketing*, 22 March 2001, pp. 29-30.

20. See Wendy Cuthbert, "Biscuits Leclerc Scores Major Licensing Coup: Signs Deal with Warner Bros. for Right to Use Looney Tunes Characters," *Strategy*, 5 July 1999, p. 25; Terry Lefton, "Warner Brothers' Not Very Looney Path to

Licensing Gold," *Brandweek,* 14 February 1994, pp. 36-37; Robert Scally, "Warner Builds Brand Presence, Strengthens 'Tunes' Franchise," *Discount Store News,* 6 April 1998, p. 33; and Adrienne Mand, "Comet Cursors Bring WB Characters to Web," *Adweek,* 19 April 1999, p. 113. Silvia Sansoni, "Gucci, Armani, and... John Paul II?" *Business Week,* 13 May 1996, p. 61; Bart A. Lazar, "Licensing Gives Known Brands New Life," *Advertising Age,* 16 February 1998, p. 8; Robert Oas, "Licensed Merchandise Sales Decrease, but Corporate Merchandise Is on the Rise," *Potentials,* April 1999, p. 8; and Laura Petrecca, "'Corporate Brands' Put Licensing in the Spotlight," *Advertising Age,* 14 June 1999, p. 1.

21. David Eggleston, "Patriot Flexes Muscle for Barbie: Canadian Computer Firm Joins with Mattel to Market Licensed PCs," Strategy, 16 August 1999, p. 1; Jean Gaudreau, "The Principles of Online Branding," Strategy, 13 September 1999, p. 29.

22. Phil Carpenter, "Some Cobranding Caveats to Obey," *Marketing News,* 7 November 1994, p. 4; and Gabrielle Solomon, "Co-Branding Alliances: Arranged Marriages Made by Marketers," *Fortune,* 12 October 1998, p. 188.

23. See David Aaker, "Should You Take Your Brand to Where the Action Is?" *Harvard Business Review,* September-October 1997, pp. 135-145; Zeynep Gurhan-Canli and Durairaj Maheswaran, "The Effects of Extensions on Brand Name Dilution and Enhancement," *Journal of Marketing,* November 1998, pp. 464-473; and Lauren Goldstein, "Barbie's Secret Plan for World Domination," *Fortune,* 23 November 1998, pp. 38-39.

24. For more on the use of line and brand extensions and consumer attitudes toward them, see Deborah Roedder John, Barbara Loken, and Christopher Joiner, "The Negative Impact of Extensions: Can Flagship Brands Be Eroded?" *Journal of Marketing,* January 1998, pp. 19-32; Zeynep Gurrhan-Canli and Durairaj Maheswaran, "The Effects of Extensions on Brand Name Dilution and Enhancement," *Journal of Marketing,* November 1998, pp. 464-473; Daniel A. Sheinin, "The Effects of Experience with Brand Extensions on Parent Brand Knowledge," *Journal of Business Research,* July 2000, pp. 47-55; and Chung K. Kim, Anne M. Lavack, and Margo Smith, "Consumer Evaluation of Vertical Extensions and Core Brands," *Journal of Business Research,* June 2001, pp. 211-222.

25. See Joan Holleran, "Packaging Speaks Volumes," *Beverage Industry,* February 1998, p. 30; and "Packaging—A Silent Salesman," *Retail World,* 28 August-8 September 2000, p. 23.

26. Robert M. McMath, "Chock Full of (Pea)nuts," *American Demographics,* April 1997, p. 60.

27. Bro Uttal, "Companies That Serve You Best," *Fortune,* 7 December 1987, p. 116. For an excellent discussion of sup-

port services, see James C. Anderson and James A. Narus, "Capturing the Value of Supplementary Services," *Harvard Business Review,* January-February 1995, pp. 75-83.

28. See Industry Canada's Web site at **www.ic.gc.ca**; and Ronald Henkoff, "Service Is Everybody's Business," *Fortune,* 27 June 1994, pp. 48-60.

29. See Ronald Henkoff, "Service Is Everybody's Business," *Fortune,* 27 June 1994, pp. 48-60; Valerie Zeithaml and Mary Jo Bitner, *Services Marketing,* New York: McGraw-Hill, 1999, pp. 8-9; Allen Sinai, "Services in the U.S. Economy," accessed online at **http://usinfor.state.gov/journals/ites/0496/ijee/ej10.htm**; and News Release, "Gross Domestic Product," U.S. Bureau of Economic Analysis, accessed online at **www.bea.gov/bea/newsrel/gdp101f.htm**, 29 June 2001.

30. See James L. Heskett, Thomas O. Jones, Gary W. Loveman, W. Earl Sasser Jr., and Leonard A. Schlesinger, "Putting the Service-Profit Chain to Work," *Harvard Business Review*, March-April 1994, pp. 164-174; and James L. Heskett, W. Earl Sasser Jr., and Leonard A. Schlesinger, *The Service Profit Chain: How Leading Companies Link Profit and Growth to Loyalty, Satisfaction, and Value,* New York: Free Press, 1997. Also see Anthony J. Rucci, Steven P. Kirn, and Richard T. Quinn, "The Employee-Customer-Profit Chain at Sears," *Harvard Business Review,* January-February 1998, pp. 83-97; and Eugene W. Anderson and Vikas Mittal, "Strengthening the Satisfaction-Profit Chain," *Journal of Service Research,* November 2000, pp. 107-120.

31. For excellent discussions of service quality, see A. Parasuraman, Valerie A. Zeithaml, and Leonard L. Berry, "A Conceptual Model of Service Quality and Its Implications for Future Research," *Journal of Marketing*, Fall 1985, pp. 41-50; A. Parasuraman, Valerie A. Zeithaml, and Leonard L. Berry, "Reassessment of Expectations as a Comparison Standard in Measuring Service Quality: Implications for Further Research," *Journal of Marketing*, January 1994, pp. 111-124; Valerie A. Zeithaml, Leonard L. Berry, and A. Parasuraman, "The Behavioral Consequences of Service Quality," *Journal of Marketing,* April 1996, pp. 31-46; and Valerie Zeithaml, "Service Quality, Profitability, and the Economic Worth of Customers: What We Know and What We Need to Learn," *Academy of Marketing Science Journal,* Winter 2000, pp. 67-85.

32. See Erika Rasmusson, "Winning Back Angry Customers," *Sales and Marketing Management,* October 1997, p. 131; and Stephen S. Tax, Stephen W. Brown, and Murali Chandrashekaran, "Customer Evaluations of Service Complaint Experiences: Implications for Relationship Marketing," *Journal of Marketing,* April 1998, pp. 60-76; and Stephen W. Brown, "Practicing Best-in-Class Service Recovery," *Marketing Management,* Summer 2000, pp. 8-9.

33. See Philip Cateora, *International Marketing*, 8th ed., Homewood, IL: Irwin, 1993, p. 270.

Chapter 9

1. Quotes from Wendy Cuthbert, "Gillette scores with Cavalcade of Sports," *Strategy*, 22 May 2000, p. 21; Lawrence Ingrassia, "Taming the Monster: How Big Companies Can Change," *The Wall Street Journal*, 10 December 1992, pp. A1, A6; William H. Miller, "Gillette's Secret to Sharpness," *Industry Week*, 3 January 1994, pp. 24-30; Linda Grant, "Gillette Knows Shaving—And How to Turn out Hot New Products," *Fortune*, 14 October 1996, pp. 207-210; and Dana Canedy, "Gillette's Strengths in Razors Undone by Troubles Abroad," *The New York Times*, 19 June 1999, p. 3. Also see William C. Symonds, "Would You Spend $1.50 for a Razor Blade?" *Business Week*, 27 April 1998, p. 46; James Heckman, "Razor Sharp: Adding Value, Making Noise with Mach3 Intro," *Marketing News*, 29 March 1999, pp. E4, E13; and William C. Symonds, "The Big Trim at Gillette," *Business Week*, 8 November 1999, p. 42.

2. Neff, J. "Ads to Hype Improvements to Mach 3 and Venus Razors", Advertising Age, 25 February 2002.

3. "Bright Ideas," *Royal Bank Reporter*, Fall 1992, pp. 6-15.

4. See Philip Kotler, *Kotler on Marketing*, New York: Free Press, 1999, p. 51; Martha Wirth Fellman, "Number of New Products Keeps Rising," *Marketing News*, 29 March 1999, p. 3; Sarah Theodore, "Heads or Tails?" *Beverage Industry*, September 2000, p. NP4; and Eric Berggreb and Thomas Nacher, "Why Good Ideas Go Bust," *Management Review*, February 2000, pp. 32-36.

5. Gary Hamel, "Innovation's New Math," *Fortune*, 9 July 2001, pp. 130-131.

6. See Tim Stevens, "Idea Dollars," *Industry Week*, 16 February 16, 1998, pp. 47-49; and William E. Coyne, "How 3M Innovates for Long-Term Growth," *Research Technology Management*, March-April 2001, pp. 21-24.

7. Paul Lukas, "Marketing: The Color of Money and Ketchup," *Fortune*, 18 September 2000, p. 38.

8. Pam Weisz, "Avon's Skin-So-Soft Bugs Out," *Brandweek*, 6 June 1994, p. 4; and information accessed online at **www.avon.com**, August 2001.

9. Kotler, *Kotler on Marketing*, pp. 43-44. For more on developing new product ideas, see Andrew Hargadon and Robert I. Sutton, "Building an Innovation Factory," *Harvard Business Review*, May-June 2000, pp. 157-166.

10. Brian O'Reilly, "New Ideas, New Products," *Fortune*, 3 March 1997, pp. 61-64. Also see Michael Schrage, "Getting Beyond the Innovation Fetish," *Fortune*, 13 November 2000, pp. 225-232.

11. See John McCormick, "The Future Is Not Quite Now," *Automotive Manufacturing and Production*, August 2000, pp. 22-24; "DaimlerChrysler Unveils NECAR 5 Methanol-Powered Fuel Cell Vehicle," *Chemical Market Reporter*, 13 November 2000, p. 5; Dale Buss, "Green Cars," *American Demographics*, January 2001, pp. 57-61; and Catherine Greenman, "Fuel Cells: Clean, Reliable (and Pricey) Electricity," *New York Times*, 10 May 2001, p. G8.

12. See Raymond R. Burke, "Virtual Reality Shopping: Breakthrough in Marketing Research," *Harvard Business Review*, March-April 1996, pp. 120-131; Mike Hoffman, "Virtual Shopping," *Inc.*, July 1998, p. 88; and Christopher Ryan, "Virtual Reality in Marketing," *Direct Marketing*, April 2001, pp. 57-62.

13. See Faye Rice, "Secrets of Product Testing," *Fortune*, 28 November 1994, pp. 172-174.

14. Judann Pollack, "Baked Lays," *Advertising Age*, 24 June 1996, p. S2; and Jack Neff and Suzanne Bidlake, "P&G, Unilever Aim to Take Consumers to the Cleaners," *Advertising Age*, 12 February 2001, pp. 1, 2.

15. See Robert McMath, "To Test or Not to Test," *Advertising Age*, June 1998, p. 64.

16. Emily Nelson, "Colgate's Net Rose 10% in Period, New Products Helped Boost Sales," *Wall Street Journal*, 2 February 2001, p. B6.

17. Laurie Freeman, "Study: Leading Brands Aren't Always Enduring," *Advertising Age*, 28 February 2000, p. 26.

18. See David Stipp, "The Theory of Fads," *Fortune*, 14 October 1996, pp. 49-52; "Fads vs. Trends," *The Futurist*, March-April 2000, p. 67; Irma Zandl, "How to Separate Trends from Fads," *Brandweek*, 23 October 2000, pp. 30-33; and "Scooter Fad Fades, as Warehouses Fill and Profits Fall," *The Wall Street Journal*, 14 June 2001, p. B4.

19. For an interesting discussion of how brand performance is affected by the product life-cycle stage at which the brand enters the market, see Venkatesh Shankar, Gregory S. Carpenter, and Lekshman Krishnamurthi, "The Advantages of Entry in the Growth Stage of the Product Life Cycle: An Empirical Analysis," *Journal of Marketing Research*, May 1999, pp. 269-276.

20. Mark McMaster, "Putting a New Spin on Old Products," *Sales and Marketing Management*, April 2001, p. 20.

21. Michael Hartnett, "Cracker Jack: Chris Neugent," *Advertising Age*, 26 June 2000, p. S22.

Chapter 10

1. Thomas Nagle and Reed K. Holden, *The Strategy and Tactics of Pricing*, 2nd ed., Upper Saddle River, NJ: Prentice-

Hall, 1995, p. 1. Also see Philip Kotler, *Kotler on Marketing,* New York: Free Press, 1999, pp. 142-148.

2. See Lara Mills, "Cereal Sales Buck Soggy U.S. Trend," *Marketing On-Line,* 18 January 1999; Peter Vamos, "Top Client, Food & Beverage: Kellogg Keeping Its Cereal Fresh," *Strategy,* 31 July 2000, p. B11; John Greenwald, "Cereal Showdown," *Time,* 29 April 1996, p. 60; "Cereal Thriller," *Economist,* 15 June 1996, p. 59; Gretchen Morgenson, "Denial in Battle Creek," *Forbes,* 7 October 1996, p. 44; Judann Pollack, "Post's Price Play Rocked Category, but Did It Work?" *Advertising Age,* 1 December 1997, p. 24; Carleen Hawn, "General Mills Tests Limits," *Forbes,* 6 April 1998, p. 48; Judann Pollack, "Price Cuts Unsettling to Cereal Business," *Advertising Age,* 28 September 1998, p. S10; Rekha Balu, "Kellogg Increases Prices on Majority of Cereal Brands," *The Wall Street Journal,* 15 December 1998, p. B23; Susan Pulliam, "Kellogg, Long Treated as Stale by Wall Street, Shows Signs of Putting Some Snap in its Walk," *The Wall Street Journal,* 16 February 1999, pp. C2,C3; Terril Yue Jones, "Outside the Box," *Forbes,* 14 June 1999, pp. 52-53; and Amy Kover, "Why the Cereal Business Is Soggy," *Fortune,* 6 March 2000.

3. See Amy E. Cortese, "Good-Bye to Fixed Pricing?" *Business Week,* 4 May 1998, pp. 71-84; Robert D. Hof, "The Buyer Always Wins," *Business Week,* 22 March 1999, pp. EB26-EB28; Robert D. Hof, "Going, Going, Gone," *Business Week,* 12 April 1999, pp. 30-32; and Michael Vizard, Ed Scannell, and Dan Neel, "Suppliers Toy with Dynamic Pricing," *InfoWorld,* 14 May 2001, p. 28.

4. Paul Hunt, "Pricing for Profit," *Marketing On-Line,* 26 April 1999.

5. For an excellent discussion of factors affecting pricing decisions, see Nagle and Holden, *The Strategy and Tactics of Pricing,* Chap. 1.

6. See Steve Gelsi, "Spin-Cycle Doctor," *Brandweek,* 10 March 1997, pp. 38-40. Tim Stevens, "From Reliable to 'Wow,'" *Industry Week,* 22 June 1998, pp. 22-26; and William C. Symonds, "'Build a Better Mousetrap' Is No Claptrap," *Business Week,* 1 February 1999, p. 47.

7. See Timothy M. Laseter, "Supply Chain Management: The Ins and Outs of Target Costing," *Purchasing,* 12 March 1998, pp. 22-25; and John K. Shank and Joseph Fisher, "Case Study: Target Costing as a Strategic Tool," *Sloan Management Review,* Fall 1999, pp. 73-82. Also see the Swatch Web page at **www.swatch.com**.

8. Brian Dumaine, "Closing the Innovation Gap," *Fortune,* 2 December 1991, pp. 56-62.

9. Joshua Rosenbaum, "Guitar Maker Looks for a New Key," *The Wall Street Journal,* 11 February 1998, p. B1; and information accessed online at **www.gibson.com**, September 1999.

10. See Nagle and Holden, *The Strategy and Tactics of Pricing,* Chap. 4.

11. Judy Waytiuk, "No Haggle, No Hassle," *Marketing On-Line,* 28 August 2000.

12. Melissa Campanelli, "The Price to Pay," *Sales and Marketing Management,* September 1994, pp. 96-102. Also see Corinna C. Petry, "The State of the Plate," October 2000, pp. 28-38; and "Nucor Ranks No. 1 with Customers," *Purchasing,* 2 September 1999, p. 32B26.

13. See Kotler, *Kotler on Marketing,* p. 54.

14. See Darren McDermott, "Cost-Consciousness Beats 'Pricing Power,'" *The Wall Street Journal,* 3 May 1999, p. A1. Also see Thomas J. Winninger, "Competing on Value," *Executive Excellence,* September 2000, p. 13; and Robert B. Tucker, "Adding Value Profitably," *The American Salesman,* April 2000, pp. 17-20.

15. See John Bell, "Sam Walton (1918-1992): Everyday Low Prices Pay Off," *Journal of Business Strategy,* September-October 1999, pp. 36-38.

16. For a comprehensive discussion of pricing strategies, see Nagle and Holden, *The Strategy and Dynamics of Pricing,* Also see Robert J. Dolan and Hermann Simon, *Power Pricing: How Managing Price Transforms the Bottom Line* (New York: Free Press, 1997).

17. See Edward F. Moltzen, "Intel Cuts Chip Pricing, Again," *CRN,* 4 June 2001, p. 12.

18. Seanna Browder, "Nintendo: At the Top of Its Game," *Business Week,* 9 June 1997, pp. 72-73; Orit Gadiesh and James L. Gilbert, "Profit Pools: A Fresh Look at Strategy," *Harvard Business Review,* May-June 1999, p. 140; and N'Gai Croal, "Game Wars 5.0," *Newsweek,* 28 May 2001, pp. 65-66.

19. Susan Krafft, "Love, Love Me Doo," *American Demographics,* June 1994, pp. 15-16; Damon Darlin, "Zoo Doo," *Forbes,* 22 May 1995, p. 92; and information from the Zoo Doo Web site, accessed online at **www.zoodoo.com**, July 2001.

20. See Nagle and Holden, *The Strategy and Tactics of Pricing,* pp. 225-228; and Manjit S. Yadav and Kent B. Monroe, "How Buyers Perceive Savings in a Bundle Price: An Examination of a Bundle's Transaction Value," *Journal of Marketing Research,* August 1993, pp. 350-358.

21. For more reading on reference prices and psychological pricing, see Richard A. Briesch, Lakshman Krishnamurthi, Tridib Mazumdar, and S. P. Raj, "A Comparative Analysis of Reference Price Models," *Journal of Consumer Research,* September 1997, pp. 202-214; John Huston and Nipoli Kamdar, "$9.99: Can 'Just-Below' Pricing Be Reconciled with Rationality?" *Eastern Economic Journal,* Spring 1996, pp.

137-145; Robert M. Schindler and Patrick N. Kirby, "Patterns of Right—Most Digits Used in Advertised Prices: Implications for Nine-Ending Effects," *Journal of Consumer Research,* September 1997, pp. 192-201; Dhruv Grewal, Kent B. Monroe, Chris Janiszewski, and Donald R. Lichtenstein, "A Range Theory of Price Perception," *Journal of Consumer Research,* March 1999, pp. 353-368; Tridib Mazumdar and Purushottam Papatla, "An Investigation of Reference Price Segments," *Journal of Marketing Research,* May 2000, pp. 246-258; and Indrajit Sinha and Michael Smith, "Consumers' Perceptions of Promotional Framing of Price," *Psychology and Marketing*, March 2000, pp. 257-271.

22. Tim Ambler, "Kicking Price Promotion Habit Is Like Getting off Heroin—Hard," *Marketing,* 27 May 1999, p. 24.

23. Jack Trout, "Prices: Simple Guidelines to Get Them Right," *Journal of Business Strategy*, November-December 1998, pp. 13-16.

24. For an interesting discussion of buyer perceptions of price increases, see Margaret C. Campbell, "Perceptions of Price Unfairness: Antecedents and Consequences," *Journal of Marketing Research*, May 1999, pp. 187-199.

25. For an excellent discussion of these issues, see Dhruv Grewal and Larry D. Compeau, "Pricing and Public Policy: A Research Agenda and Overview of Special Issue," *Journal of Marketing and Public Policy*, Spring 1999, pp. 3-10.

26. Mike France, "Does Predatory Pricing Make Microsoft a Predator?" *Business Week,* 23 November 1998, pp. 130-132.

27. Grewel and Compeau, "Pricing and Public Policy: A Research Agenda and Overview of Special Issue," p. 8.

28. For more on public policy and pricing, see Louis W. Stern and Thomas L. Eovaldi, *Legal Aspects of Marketing Strategy,* Upper Saddle River, NJ: Prentice Hall, 1984, Chap 5; Robert J. Posch, *The Complete Guide to Marketing and the Law,* Upper Saddle River, NJ: Prentice Hall, 1988, Chap. 28; Nagle and Holden, *The Strategy and Tactics of Pricing,* Chap. 14; Joseph P. Guiltinan and Gregory Gunlach, "Aggressive and Predatory Pricing: A Framework for Analysis," *Journal of Marketing,* July 1996, pp. 87-102; Bruce Upbin, "Vindication," *Forbes,* 17 November 1997, pp. 52-56; and Grewel and Compeau, "Pricing and Public Policy: A Research Agenda and Overview of Special Issue," pp. 3-10.

Chapter 11

1. Quotes from Donald V. Fites, "Make Your Dealers Your Partners," *Harvard Business Review,* March-April 1996, pp. 84-95; and De'Ann Weimer, "A New Cat on the Hot Seat," *Business Week,* March 1998, pp. 56-62. Also see Peter Elstrom, "This Cat Keeps on Purring," *Business Week,* 20 January 1997, pp. 82-84; Press Release, "Caterpillar CEO Optimistic about Company's Future," accessed online at **www.cat.com**, 14 April 1999; and "Best Sales Forces: Caterpillar," *Sales & Marketing Management,* July 1999, p. 64.

2. For definitions and a complete discussion of distribution channel topics, see Anne T. Coughlin, Erin Anderson, Louis W. Stern, and Adel El-Ansary, *Marketing Channels,* 6th ed., Upper Saddle River, NJ: Prentice Hall, 2001, pp. 2-3.

3. Ian Jack, "Dealers Declare War on Ford Canada," *Financial Post,* 31 March 2000, pp. C1, C5; Greg Keenan, "Ford Targets Bigger Stake in Dealerships," *The Globe and Mail,* 18 November 1998, pp. B1, B16.

4. See Richard C. Hoffman and John F. Preble, "Franchising into the Twenty-First Century," *Business Horizons,* November-December 1993, pp. 35-43; "Canada's Largest Franchise-Only Show Returns," advertising supplement, *The Globe and Mail,* 24 September 1997, p. 1; and Industry Canada's franchising Web site at **strategis.ic.gc.ca/SSG/dm01179e.html**.

5. Peter Fitzpatrick, "Airlines of the World—Unite," *Financial Post,* 22 November 1997, p. 8.

6. Rochelle Garner, "Mad as Hell," *Sales & Marketing Management,* June 1999, pp. 55-61.

7. Subhash C. Jain, *International Marketing Management,* 3rd ed., Boston: PWS-Kent Publishing, 1990, pp. 489-491. Also see Emily Thronton, "Revolution in Japanese Retailing," *Fortune,* 7 February 1994, pp. 143-147.

8. For examples, see Philip Cateora, *International Marketing,* 7th ed., Homewood, IL: Irwin, 1990, pp. 570-571; Dexter Roberts, "Blazing Away at Foreign Brands," *Business Week,* 12 May 1997, p. 58; and "Taking on Distribution," *Business China,* 5 June 2000, p. 2.

9. Jennifer Wells, "We Can Get It for You Wholesale," *Report on Business,* March 1995, pp. 52-62.

10. For more on channel relationships, see James A. Narus and James C. Anderson, "Rethinking Distribution," *Harvard Business Review*, July-August 1996, pp. 112-120; James C. Anderson and James A. Narus, *Business Market Management,* Upper Saddle River, NJ: Prentice Hall, 1999, pp. 276-288; and Jonathon D. Hibbard, Nirmalya Kumar, and Louis W. Stern, "Examining the Impact of Destructive Acts in Marketing Channel Relationships," *Journal of Marketing Research,* February 2001, pp. 45-61.

11. Pat Curry, "Channel Changes," *Industry Week,* April 2, 2001, pp. 45-48.

12. For a full discussion of laws affecting marketing channels, see Coughlin, Anderson, Stern, and El-Ansary, *Marketing Channels*, Chap. 12.

13. See Robert E. Danielson, "CPFR: Improving Your Business without Being Limited by Technology," *Apparel*

Industry Magazine, February 2000, pp. 56-57; and Ben A. Chaouch, "Stock Levels and Delivery Rates in Vendor-Managed Inventory Programs," *Production and Operations Management,* Spring 2001, pp. 31-44.

14. John Huey, "Wal-Mart: Will It Take over the World?" *Fortune,* 30 January 1989, pp. 52-64; and Mike Troy, "Wal-Mart: Behind the Scenes Efficiency Keeps Growth Curve on Course," *DSN Retailing Today,* 4 June 2001, pp. 80, 91.

15. J. William Gurley, "Why Dell's War Isn't Dumb," *Fortune,* 9 July 2001, pp. 134-136.

16. Shawn Tully, "Comeback Ahead for Railroads," *Fortune,* 17 June 1991, pp. 107-113.

17. See Lara L. Sowinski, "Supply Chain Management and Logistics Software," *World Trade,* February 2001, pp. 34-36; Keith Schultz, "Supply Chain Management Tools," *Internetweek,* 25 June 2001, pp. PG25-PG34; and Karen Lundegaard, "E-Commerce (A Special Report)—Bumpy Ride: Supply-Chain Management Sounds Beautiful in Theory; In Real Life, It's a Daunting Task," *The Wall Street Journal,* 21 May 2001, p. R21.

18. Myron Magnet, "The New Golden Rule of Business," *Fortune,* 21 February 1994, pp. 60-64. For a related example, see Justin Martin, "Are You as Good as You Think You Are?" *Fortune,* September 1996, pp. 145-146.

19. "Is Third Party Logistics in Your Future?" *Modern Materials Handling,* December 2000, pp. S3-S15.

Chapter 12

1. Quotes taken from Sonja Rasula, "Beyond Clothes: Fashion Retailers Are Evolving into Lifestyle Merchandisers—Clothing the Home as Well as the Body," *Marketing On-Line,* 10 May 1999; David Eggleston, "New Web Site Gets to Roots of E-Commerce," *Strategy,* 3 January 2000, p. D14; and Natalie Bahadur, "Roots Rolls out Inaugural Television Campaign," *Strategy,* 12 October 1998, p. 10. Also see Natalie Bahadur, "Roots Extends to Home Furnishings," *Strategy,* 9 November 1998, p. 9; Julie McCann, "Tip of the Hat to the Roots Boys," *Marketing On-Line,* 21/28 December 1998; information accessed online at **www.Roots.com**.

2. Nathan Rudyk, "Multi-Channel Customers Spend 10 Times More," *Strategy,* 6 November 2000, p. D6.

3. Sinclair Stewart, "Sobeys Shops for Agency: Grocer Preparing to Fend off Aggressive Foes," *Strategy,* 6 December 1999, p. 1.

4. Brian Dunn, "The King of Bread, Butts and Beer," *Marketing,* 25 October 1999, p. 23; Anita Lahey, "Cornered Stores," *Marketing,* 4 August 1997, pp. 10-11; Luis Millan, "King of the Corner Store," *Canadian Business,* 26 September 1997, pp. 101-103.

5. See Ray A. Smith, "Outlet Centers Go Upmarket with Amenities," *The Wall Street Journal,* 6 June 2001, p. B12.

6. Mariam Mesbah, "Special Report: Fashion Retailers Branch into Cosmetics," *Strategy,* 20 January 1997, p. 20.

7. Erica Zlomislic, "Special Report: Store-Level Marketing: Virgin's Megahit," *Strategy,* 26 May 1997, p. 24.

8. Laura Campbell, "Ending Not Yet Written in Cutthroat Bookstore War," *Financial Post,* 7 October 1997, p. 10; Myron Magnet, "Let's Go for Growth," *Fortune,* 7 March 1994, pp. 60-72; Val Ross, "Indigo Books Stakes out Kingston," *The Globe and Mail,* 7 February 1997, p. C3. Also see Deirdre Donahue, "Bookstores: A Haven for the Intellect," *USA Today,* 10 July 1997, pp. D1, D2.

9. Steven Bergsman, "Slow Times at Sherman Oaks: What's Ailing the Big Malls of America?" *Barron's,* 17 May 1999, p. 39.

10. See Joanna Dale, "Consumer Attitudes towards Retail in BC," Retail Council of Canada, accessed online at **www.retailcouncil.org/research/bcretail/sld026.htm**, 21 September 2000; Bergsman, "Slow Times at Sherman Oaks," p. 39.

11. Amy Barrett, "A Retailing Pacesetter Pulls up Lame," *Business Week,* 12 July 1993, pp. 122-123.

12. See Malcolm P. McNair and Eleanor G. May, "The Next Revolution of the Retailing Wheel," *Harvard Business Review,* September-October 1978, pp. 81-91; Stephen Brown, "The Wheel of Retailing: Past and Future," *Journal of Retailing,* Summer 1990, pp. 143-147; Stephen Brown, "Variations on a Marketing Enigma: The Wheel of Retailing Theory," *Journal of Marketing Management,* 7, no. 2, 1991, pp. 131-155; Stanley C. Hollander, "The Wheel of Retailing," reprinted in *Marketing Management,* Summer 1996, pp. 63-66; and Jennifer Negley, "Retrenching, Reinventing and Remaining Relevant," *Discount Store News,* 5 April 1999.

13. IBM and the Retail Council of Canada, *E-Retail: The Race Is On,* June 1999, pp. 3-7.

14. See "The Fortune 500," *Fortune,* 16 April, 2001, p. F1.

15. Regina Fazio Maruca, "Retailing: Confronting the Challenges that Face Bricks-and-Mortar Stores," *Harvard Business Review,* July-August 1999, pp. 159-168. Also see Marshall L. Fisher, Ananth Raman, and Anna Sheen McClelland, "Rocket Science Retailing Is Almost Here: Are You Ready?" *Harvard Business Review,* July-August 2000, pp. 115-124.

16. James Cox, "Red-Letter Day as East Meets West in the Aisles," *USA Today,* September 11, 1996, p. B1; "Wal-Mart Around the World," Wal-Mart 2001 Annual Report, accessed online at **www.Wal-Mart.com/corporate/annual_2001/p8.html**.

17. Tim Craig, "Carrefour: At the Intersection of Global," *DSN Retailing Today,* September 18, 2000, p. 16. Also see Richard Tomlinson, "Who's Afraid of Wal-Mart?" *Fortune,* June 26, 2000, pp. 186-196.

18. Christina Nifong, "Beyond Browsing," *Raleigh News and Observer,* 25 May 1999, p. E1.

19. Kathleen Cholewka, "Standing Out Online: The 5 Best E-Marketing Campaigns," *Sales and Marketing Management,* January 2001, pp. 51-58.

20. "McKesson: Online Annual Report 2001," accessed online at **www.mckesson.com/wt/ar_2001.php**, August 2001.

21. See Arthur Andersen & Co., *Facing the Forces of Change: Beyond Future Trends in Wholesale Distribution,* Washington, DC: Distribution and Education Foundation, 1987:7; Joseph Weber, "It's 'Like Somebody Had Shot the Postman,'" *Business Week,* 13 January 1992, p. 82; and Michael Mandel, "Don't Cut out the Middleman," *Business Week,* 16 September 1996, p. 30.

22. Richard A. Melcher, "The Middlemen Stay on the March," *Business Week,* 9 January 1995, p. 87.

Chapter 13

1. The first four of these definitions are adapted from Peter D. Bennett, *Dictionary of Marketing Terms,* Chicago: American Marketing Association, 1995.

2. See Don E. Schultz, Stanley I. Tannenbaum, and Robert F. Lauterborn, *Integrated Marketing Communication,* Chicago, IL: NTC, 1992, Chap. 3 and 4. Also see James R. Ogdan, *Developing a Creative and Innovative Integrated Marketing Communications Plan,* Upper Saddle River, NJ: Prentice Hall, 1998; and David Picton and Amanda Broderick, *Integrated Marketing Communications,* New York: Financial Times Management, 1999.

3. P. Griffith Lindell, "You Need Integrated Attitude to Develop IMC," *Marketing News,* 26 May 1997, p. 6. For more discussion of integrated marketing communications, see J. P. Cornelissen and Andrew L. Lock, "Theoretical Concept of Management Fashion: Examining the Significance of IMC," *Journal of Advertising Research,* September-October 2000, pp. 7-15; Stephen J. Gould, "The State of IMC Research and Applications," *Journal of Advertising Research,* September-October 2000, pp. 22-23; and Kim Bartel Sheehan and Caitlin Doherty, "Re-Weaving the Web: Integrating Print and Online Communications," *Journal of Interactive Marketing,* Spring 2001, pp. 47-59.

4. Stuart Elliott, "Fewer Viewers, More Commercials," *New York Times,* 8 June 1999, p. 1; Bill Carter, "After Super Bowl, 'Survivor' Is the Season's Top Hit on TV," *New York Times,* 30 January 2001, p. C8; and Joe Flint, "Oscar Ratings Fall, but the Program Finishes on Time," *The Wall Street Journal,* 27 March 2001, p. B8.

5. Michele Marchetti, "What a Sales Call Costs," *Sales and Marketing Management,* September 2000, p. 80. The Dollar figure was changed to the equivalent Canadian funds.

6. The Institute of Canadian Advertising, *Economic Impact Report 1998,* accessed online at **www.ica-ad.com**.

7. Jim McElgunn, "Canada's Top 25 Advertising Categories," *Marketing On-Line,* 27 September 1999; Astrid Van Den Broek, "Government Ad Spends Soared in '98," *Marketing On-Line,* 19 April 1999.

8. For more on advertising budgets, see Andrew Ehrenberg, Neil Barnard, and John Scriven, "Justifying Our Advertising Budgets," *Marketing and Research Today,* February 1997, pp. 38-44; Dana W. Hayman and Don E. Schultz, "How Much Should You Spend on Advertising?" *Advertising Age,* 26 April 1999, p. 32; and Laura Q. Hughes, "Measuring Up," *Advertising Age,* 5 February 2001, pp. 1, 34.

9. Rosalind Stefanac, "Corporate Ads in Rainbow Colours: Big Mainstream Marketers Are Crafting Innovative Advertising Strategies in a Bid to Get Closer to Gay and Lesbian Consumers," *Marketing On-Line,* 1 May 2000; Gary Levin, "'Meddling' in Creative More Welcome," *Advertising Age,* 9 April 1990, pp. S4, S8; Eleftheria Parpis, "TBWA: Absolut," *Adweek,* 9 November 1998, p. 172; Sarah Theodore, "Absolut Secrets," *Beverage Industry,* July 2000, p. 50; and the Q & A section of the Absolut Web site, accessed online at **www.absolut.com**, July 2001.

10. *1999-2000 Media Digest,* Canadian Media Directors' Council.

11. Joe Mandese, "'ER' Tops Price Charts," *Advertising Age,* 2 October 2000, pp. 1.

12. Larry Armstrong, "Smart TV Get Even Smarter," *Business Week,* 16 April 2001, pp. 132-134; and Jeff Howe, "Total Control," *American Demographics,* July 2001, pp. 28-32.

13. Edward A. Robinson, "Frogs, Bears, and Orgasms: Think Zany If You Want to Reach Today's Consumers," *Fortune,* 9 June 1997, pp. 153-156. Also see Chuck Ross, "MBC Blasts Beyond the 15-Minute Barrier," *Advertising Age,* 7 August 2000, p. 3.

14. New Release, *"AAAA's TV Commercial Production Survey Shows Largest Cost Increase in 13 Years,"* American Association of Advertising Agencies, accessed online at **www.aaaa.org**, 16 November 2000.

15. See Gary Schroeder, "Behavioral Optimization," *American Demographics,* August 1998, pp. 34-36; Erwin Ephron, "Ad World Was Ripe for Its Conversion to Optimizers," *Advertising Age,* 22 February 1999, p. S16; and

Steven J. Stark, "A New and Improved Tool," *Broadcasting and Cable,* 28 February 2000, pp. 30-32.

16. Information on advertising agency income and billings from AdAge.com, accessed online at **http://adage.com/dataplace/archieves/dp514.html**, July 2001.

17. Patti Bond, "Today's Topic: From Russia with Fizz, Coke Imports Ads," *Atlanta Journal and Constitution,* 4 April 1998, pp. E2.

18. See "U.K. Tobacco Ad Ban Will Include Sports Sponsorship," *AdAgeInternational.com,* May 1997; "Coca-Cola Rapped for Running Competition in India," *AdAgeInternational.com,* February 1997; Naveen Donthu, "A Cross Country Investigation of Recall of and Attitude Toward Comparative Advertising," *Journal of Advertising,* 27, 22 June 1998, pp. 111; and John Shannon, "Comparative Ads Call for Prudence," *Marketing Week,* 6 May 1999, p. 32.

19. "Promotion Practices Condensed," *Potentials,* November 1998, p. 6. Also see Jack Neff, "Trade Promotion Rises," *Advertising Age,* 3 April 2000, p. 24.

20. Debra Aho Williamson, "P&G's Reformulated Pert Plus Builds Consumer Relationships," *Advertising Age,* 28 June 1999, p. 52.

21. NCH Promotional Services Ltd., information accessed online at **www.wattsgroup.com/nch/SR102.htm**.

22. Jeff Lobb, "Stuff-ing It to Coke," *Marketing Magazine,* 27 January 1997, p. 15.

23. See "Power to the Key Ring and T-Shirt," *Sales and Marketing Management,* December 1989, p. 14; and Chad Kaydo, "Your Logo Here," *Sales and Marketing Management,* April 1998, pp. 65-70.

24. See Richard Szathmary, "Trade Shows," *Sales and Marketing Management,* May 1992, pp. 83-84; Srinath Gopalakrishna, Gary L. Lilien, Jerome D. Williams, and Ian Sequeira, "Do Trade Shows Pay Off?" *Journal of Marketing,* July 1995, pp. 75-83; Peter Jenkins, "Making the Most of Trade Shows," *Nation's Business,* June 1999, p. 8; and Ben Chapman, "The Trade Show Must Go On," *Sales and Marketing Management,* June 2001, p. 22.

25. Adapted from Scott Cutlip, Allen Center, and Glen Broom, *Effective Public Relations,* 8th ed., Upper Saddle River, NJ: Prentice Hall, 1999, Chap. 1.

26. Gail Chiasson, "PR in Action: When the Media Come Calling," *Marketing Magazine,* 12 February 1996, p. 23.

27. Al Ries and Laura Ries, "First Do Some Publicity," *Advertising Age,* 8 February 1999, p. 42.

28. See Mark Gleason, "Edelman Sees Niche in Web Public Relations," *Advertising Age,* 20 January 1997, p. 30; Michael

Krauss, "Good PR Critical to Growth on the Net," *Marketing News,* 18 January 1999, p. 8; Steve Jarvis, "How the Internet Is Changing Fundamentals of Publicity," *Marketing News,* 17 July 2000, p. 6; and Don Middleberg, *Winning PR in the Wired World: Powerful Communications Strategies or the Noisy Digital Space,* New York: McGraw-Hill Professional Publishing, 2000.

Chapter 14

1. Quotes from Andy Cohen, "Top of the Charts: Lear Corporation," *Sales and Marketing Management,* July 1998, p. 40. Also see "Lear Corporation," *Sales and Marketing Management,* July 1999, p. 62; Fara Warner, "Lear Won't Take a Back Seat," *Fast Company,* June 2001, pp. 178-185; and "This Is Lear," accessed online at **www.lear.com**, July 2001.

2. See Bill Kelley, "How to Sell Airplanes, Boeing-Style," *Sales and Marketing Management,* 9 December 1985, pp. 32-34; Andy Cohen, "Boeing," *Sales and Marketing Management,* October 1997, p. 68; and Stanley Holmes, "Rumble Over Tokyo," *Business Week,* 2 April 2001, pp. 80-81.

3. Geoffrey Brewer, "Love the Ones You're With," *Sales and Marketing Management,* February 1997, pp. 38-45.

4. Michele Marchetti, "What a Sales Call Costs," *Sales and Marketing Management,* September 2000, p. 80.

5. See Martin Everett, "Selling by Telephone," *Sales and Marketing Management,* December 1993, pp. 75-79.

6. Mark Stevenson, "The Lean, Mean Sales Machine," *Canadian Business,* January 1994, pp. 34, 36.

7. See "A Phone Is Better Than a Face," *Sales and Marketing Management,* October 1987, p. 29; Brett A. Boyle, "The Importance of the Industrial Inside Sales Force: A Case Study," *Industrial Marketing Management,* September 1996, pp. 339-348; Victoria Fraza, "Upgrading Inside Sales," *Industrial Distribution,* December 1997, pp. 44-49; and Michele Marchetti, "Look Who's Calling," *Sales and Marketing Management,* May 1998, pp. 43-46.

8. Rick Mullin, "From Lone Wolves to Team Players," *Chemical Week,* 14 January 1998, pp. 33-34; and James P. Morgan, "Cross-Functional Buying: Why Teams Are Hot," *Purchasing,* 5 April 2001, pp. 27-32.

9. Robert Hiebeler, Thomas B. Kelly, and Charles Ketteman, *Best Practices: Building Your Business with Customer-Focused Solutions,* New York: Arthur Andersen/Simon & Schuster, 1998, pp. 122-124. Also see Mark A. Moon and Susan Forquer Gupta, "Examining the Formation of Selling Centers: A Conceptual Framework," *Journal of Personal Selling and Sales Management,* Spring 1997, pp. 31-41; Donald W. Jackson Jr., Scott M. Widmier, Ralph Giacobbe, Janet E. Keith, "Examining the Use of Team Selling by

Manufacturers' Representatives: A Situational Approach," *Industrial Marketing Management*, March 1999, pp. 155-164; and Henry Canaday, "Flyaway Sales," *Selling Power*, October 2000, pp. 104-113.

10. See George H. Lucas Jr., A. Parasuraman, Robert A. Davis, and Ben M. Enis, "An Empirical Study of Sales Force Turnover," *Journal of Marketing*, July 1987, pp. 34-59; Thomas R. Wotruba and Pradeep K. Tyagi, "Met Expectations and Turnover in Direct Selling," *Journal of Marketing*, July 1991, pp. 24-35; Chad Kaydo, "Overturning Turnover," *Sales and Marketing Management*, November 1997, pp. 50-60, and Marchetti, "What a Sales Call Costs," p. 80.

11. See Geoffrey Brewer, "Mind Reading: What Drives Top Salespeople to Greatness?" *Sales and Marketing Management*, May 1994, pp. 82-88; Barry J. Farber, "Success Stories for Salespeople," *Sales and Marketing Management*, May 1995, pp. 30-31; Roberta Maynard, "Finding the Essence of Good Salespeople," *Nation's Business*, February 1998, p. 10; and Jeanie Casison, "Closest Thing to Cloning," *Incentive*, June 1999, p. 7.

12. See "To Test or Not to Test," *Sales and Marketing Management*, May 1994, p. 86; and Elena Harris, "Reduce Recruiting Risks," *Sales and Marketing Management*, May 2000, p. 18.

13. Mark De Wolf, "Special Report: Motivating the Sales Force," *Strategy*, 18 August 1997, p. 19.

14. Robert Klein, "Nabisco Sales Soar After Sales Training," *Marketing News*, 6 January 1997, p. 23. Also see Malcolm Fleschner, "Training: How to Find the Best Training Solutions for Your Sales Team," *Selling Power*, June 2001, pp. 93-97.

15. Kevin Dobbs, "Training on the Fly," *Sales and Marketing Management*, November 2000, pp. 93-98. Also see Malcolm Fleschner, "Training: Easy Does It," *Selling Power*, March 2001, pp. 118-122.

16. Christen P. Heide, "All Levels of Sales Reps Post Impressive Earnings," press release, accessed online at **www.dartnell.com**, 5 May 1997; and *Dartnell's 30th Sales Force Compensation Survey*, Dartnell Corporation, August 1998.

17. Geoffrey Brewer, "Brain Power," *Sales and Marketing Management*, May 1997, pp. 39-48; Don Peppers and Martha Rogers, "The Price of Customer Service," *Sales and Marketing Management*, April 1999, pp. 20-21; and Michelle Marchetti, "Pay Changes Are on the Way," *Sales and Marketing Management*, August 2000, p. 101.

18. David Prater, "The Third Time's the Charm," *Sales and Marketing Management*, September 2000, pp. 101-104.

19. Melinda Ligos, "Point, Click, and Sell," *Sales and Marketing Management*, May 1999, pp. 51-56; Tim Wilson, "Salespeople Leverage the Net," *Internetweek*, 4 June 2001, pp. PG11, PG13; and Amy J. Morgan and Scott A. Inks, "Technology and the Sales Force: Increasing Acceptance of Sales Force Automation," *Industrial Marketing Management*, July 2001, pp. 463-472.

20. Bob Donath, "Delivering Value Starts with Proper Prospecting," *Marketing News*, 10 November 1997, p. 5. Also see Sarah Lorge, "The Best Way to Prospect," *Sales and Marketing Management*, January 1998, p. 80; "Skills Workshop: Prospecting," *Selling Power*, October 2000, pp. 54-56.

21. David Stamps, "Training for a New Sales Game," *Training*, July 1997, pp. 46-52; and Erin Stout, "Throwing the Right Pitch," *Sales and Marketing Management*, April 2001, pp. 61-63.

22. Betsey Cummings, "Do Customers Hate Salespeople?" *Sales and Marketing Management*, June 2001, pp. 44-51; and Don Chambers, "Draw Them In," *Selling Power*, March 2001, pp. 51-52.

23. "Briefcase Full of Views: Johnson & Johnson Uses Virtual Reality to Give Prospects an Inside Look at Its Products," *American Demographics*, April 1997.

24. Gary Hamel and Jeff Sampler, "The E-Corporation: More Than Just Web-Based, It's Building a New Industrial Order," *Fortune*, 7 December 1998, pp. 80-92.

25. David Eggleston, "Technology Takes Spotlight at CMA Summit," *Strategy*, 22 May 2000, p. D1.

26. Carol Krol, "Pizza Hut's Database Makes Its Couponing More Efficient," *Advertising Age*, 30 November 1998, p. 27; and Dana Blakenhorn, "Marketers Hone Targeting," *Advertising Age*, 18 June 2001, p. T16.

27. For these and other examples, see Jonathan Berry, "A Potent New Tool for Selling: Database Marketing," *Business Week*, 4 September 1994, pp. 56-62; Weld F. Royal, "Do Databases Really Work?" *Sales and Marketing Management*, October 1995, pp. 66-74; Daniel Hill, "Love My Brand," *Brandweek*, 19 January 1998, pp. 26-29; "FedEx Taps into Data Warehousing," *Advertising Age's Business Marketing*, January 1999, p. 25; and Harriet Marsh, "Dig Deeper into the Database Goldmine," *Marketing*, 11 January 2001, pp. 29-30.

28. "The 2000 RSVP Awards: Winners by Category— Financial Services and Insurance Wealth Management," *Strategy*, 24 November 2000, p. 34.

29. *Economic Impact: U.S. Direct Marketing Today Executive Summary*, Direct Marketing Association, 2001.

30. Matthew L. Wald, "Third Area Code Is Added in the Land of the Toll-Free," *New York Times*, 4 April 1998, p. 10.

31. Kevin R. Hopkins, "Dialing in to the Future," *Business Week*, 28 July 1997, p. 90; and Holly McCord, "1-900-CALL-AN-RD," *Prevention*, August 1997, p. 54.

32. *Economic Impact: U.S. Direct Marketing Today Executive survey*, Direct Marketing Association, 2001.

33. Hallie Mummert, "The Year's Best Bells and Whistles," *Target Marketing*, November 2000, pp. TM3-TM5; and Susan Reda, "Software Package Seeks to Revive CD-ROMs as Consumer Marketing Technology," *Stores*, November 2000, pp. 66-70.

34. Kruti Trivedi, "Telemarketers Don't Want You, Just Your Answering Machine," *The Wall Street Journal*, 6 August 1999, p. B1; Karen E. Nussel, "Voice Mail Offers Opportunities," *Advertising Age's Business Marketing*, August 1999, p. 16; and Stuart Elliot, "ABC Backs Away from Using Voice Mail to Promote Lineup," *New York Times*, 22 July 2000. p. B1.

35. *Economic Impact: U.S. Direct Marketing Today Executive Summary*, Direct Marketing Association, 2001.

36. Molly Prior, "Lands' End Crosses Threshold of Internet Retailing Excellence," *DSN Retailing Today*, 6 November 2000, pp. 6, 52; and Carol Sliwa, "Clothing Retailer Finds Worldwide Business on the Web," *Computerworld*, 30 April 2001, p. 40.

37. Andrea Zoe Aster, "Deciphering the New E-Retail," *Marketing On-Line*, 20 November 2000.

38. Ron Donoho, "One-Man Show," *Sales and Marketing Management*, June 2001, pp. 36-42.

39. Erika Brown, "Ooh! Aah!" *Forbes*, 8 March 1999, p. 56; and Shirley Leung, "Grill Sales Slow but Big Payouts Flow to Foreman," *The Wall Street Journal*, 2 February 2001, p. B1.

40. See Jacqueline M. Graves, "The Fortune 500 Opt for Infomercials," *Fortune*, 6 March 1995, p. 20; "Infomercials," *Advertising Age*, 8 September 1997, pp. A1-A2; Carol Krol, "Navy Infomercial Aims at Prospective Recruits," *Advertising Age*, 31 May 1999, p. 12; Dave Guilford, "Cadillac Takes New Route for Sevill STS: Infomercial," *Advertising Age*, 23 August 1999, p. 8; Jean Halliday, "Volvo Ready to Act on Leads After Infomercial Success," *Advertising Age*, 25 January 1999, p. 61; and Alison Stein Wellner, "Hot Wheels," *American Demographics*, August 2000, pp. 48-49.

41. Jim Auchmute, "But Wait, There's More!" *Advertising Age*, 17 October 1985, p. 18; Kathy Haley, "Infomercials Lure More Top Marketers," *Advertising Age*, 9 May 1994, pp. IN2, IN8; Chad Rubel, "Infomercials Evolve as Major Firms Join Successful Format," *Marketing News*, 2 January 1995, pp. 1, 36; Jacqueline M. Graves, "The Fortune 500 Opt for Infomercials," *Fortune*, 6 March 1995, p. 20.

42. M. R. Kropko, "Card Markers Struggling with Computer Kiosks," *Marketing News*, 3 June 1996, p. 6; David Chilton, "LCBO Installs Interactive Kiosks," *Strategy*, 24 January 1997, p. 13; Wendy Cuthbert, "Cineplex Gets Ad Kiosks," *Strategy*, 31 March 1997, p. 4; "For the Record: UNICEF Kiosks at IKEA," *Strategy*, 24 November 1997, p. 15.

43. "Interactive: Ad Age Names Finalists," *Advertising Age*, 27 February 1995, pp. 12-14.

44. "Sweepstakes Groups Settles with States," *The New York Times*, 27 June 2001, p. A14; and "Business Brief—Publishers Clearing House: Payment of $34 Million Set to Settle with 26 States," *The Wall Street Journal*, 27 June 2001, p. B8.

45. John Hagel III and Jeffrey F. Rayport, "The Coming Battle for Customer Information," *Harvard Business Review*, January-February 1997, pp. 53-65; Bruce Horovitz, "AmEx Kills Database Deal After Privacy Outrage," *USA Today*, 15 July 1998, p. B1; and Carol Krol, "Consumers Reach the Boiling Point," *Advertising Age*, 29 March 1999, p. 22.

Chapter 15

1. Extracts and quotes from Ken Derrett, "NBA Canada Grabs a Rebound," *Marketing On-Line*, 22 February 1999; Stuart Foxman, "Sponsored Supplement: The NBA in Canada: Celebrating Season II," *Strategy*, 6 January 1997, p. 31; Marc Gunther, "They All Want to Be Like Mike," *Fortune*, 21 July 1997, pp. 51-53: ©1997 Time, Inc.; and Warren Cohen, "Slam-Dunk Diplomacy," *U.S. News & World Report*, 8 June 1998, p. 7. Also see Tracy Atkinson, "The Teen Fun Zone," *Marketing On-Line*, 2 August 1999; Astrid Van Den Broek, "NBA Deal Shoots for Higher Ratings," *Marketing On-Line*, 10 April 2000; Stefan Fatsis, "NBA Bravely Plans for Post-Jordan Era," *The Wall Street Journal*, 6 February 1998, p. B1; "NBA Will Face Difficult Recovery from Lockout," *Greensboro News Record*, 24 December 1998, p. C2; Mark Hyman, "Another Ruined Season That Wasn't," *Business Week*, 7 June 1999, p. 40; David Bauder, "Mike Takes the Air out of NBA Ratings," *Raleigh News & Observer*, 24 June 1999, p. E7; "Worldwide TV Coverage of the 1999 NBA Finals," accessed online at **www.nba.com**, September 1999; and Daniel Roth, "The NBA's Next Shot," *Fortune*, 21 February 2000, pp. 207-215.

2. Department of Foreign Affairs and International Trade, "Trade and the Canadian Economy: Why Trade Matters," accessed online at **www.dfait-maeci.gc.ca/tna-nac/text-e.asp**, 14 November 2002; and New Release No. 133, "Pettigrew Announces Names of Winners of the Canada Export Awards," Department of Foreign Affairs and International Trade, 24 September 2001; World Trade Organization, "International trade statistics 2002," Table III.16: Merchandise Trade of Canada by Region and Economy, 2001, accessed online at **www.wto.org/english/res_e/statis_e/its2002_e/section3_e/iii16.xls**, 14 November 2002.

3. Bruce Little, "Who Exports Canada's Goods to the World?" *The Globe and Mail,* 29 January 2001, p. B10; Press Release No. 172, "Pettigrew Announces Finalists for 2000 Canada Export Awards," Department of Foreign Affairs and International Trade, 4 July 2000; Press Release, "International Trade Minister Pettigrew—Talking Trade," Department of Foreign Affairs and International Trade, accessed online at **www.dfait-maeci.gc.ca/trade/ canadexport/docs/active/vol.%2018,%20no%209@33- e.htm**, 14 November 2002; John Alden, "What in the World Drives UPS?" *International Business,* April 1998, pp. 6-7; Karen Pennar, "Two Steps Forward, One Step Back," *Business Week,* 31 August 1998, p. 116; Michelle Wirth Fellman, "A New World for Marketers," *Marketing News,* 10 May 1999, p. 13.

4. Department of Foreign Affairs and International Trade, "1997 Canada Exports Awards," *Report on Business Magazine,* July 1997.

5. "The Unique Japanese," *Fortune,* 24 November 1986, p. 8. For more on nontariff and other barriers, see Warren J. Keegan and Mark C. Green, *Principles of Global Marketing,* Upper Saddle River, NJ: Prentice Hall, 1997, pp. 200-203.

6. Douglas Harbrecht and Owen Ullmann, "Finally GATT May Fly," *Business Week,* 29 December 1993, pp. 36-37; Ping Deng, "Impact of GATT Uruguay Round on Various Industries," *American Business Review,* June 1998, pp. 22-29. Also see Charles W. L. Hill, *International Business,* Chicago: Richard A. Irwin, 1997, pp. 165-168; "Special Article: World Trade: Fifty Years On," *The Economist,* 16 May 1998, pp. 21- 23; and Helene Cooper, "The Millennium—Trade & Commerce: Trading Blocks," *The Wall Street Journal,* 11 January 1999, p. R50; information accessed online at **www.wto.org/index.htm.**

7. Stanley Reed, "We Have Liftoff! The strong launch of the euro is hailed around the world," *Business Week,* 18 January 1999: 34-7.

8. James Welsh, "Enter the Euro," *World Trade,* January 1999, pp. 34-38.

9. For more on the European Union, see "Around Europe in 40 years," *The Economist,* 31 May 1997, p. S4; "European Union to Begin Expansion," *The New York Times,* 30 March 1998, p. A5; Joan Warner, "Mix Us Culturally? It's Impossible," *Business Week,* 27 April 1998, p. 108; Paul J. Deveney, "World Watch," *The Wall Street Journal,* 20 May 1999, p. A12; and information accessed online at **www.dfait-maeci.gc.ca/english/geo/europe/EU/ fact-eur.htm.**

10. Alan Freeman, "Leaders Aim for Free Trade at APEC Forum," *The Globe and Mail,* 12 November 1994, p. B3; "The Vancouver Summit," *The Globe and Mail,* 19 November 1997, pp. D1-D4.

11. Larry Rohter, "Latin America and Europe to Talk Trade," *New York Times,* 26 June 1999, p. 2.

12. Bruce Little, "Who Exports Canada's Goods to the World?" *The Globe and Mail,* 29 January 2001, p. B10; Peter Vamos, "Fairmont Hotels Puts on Ad Blitz," *Strategy,* 29 January 2001, p. 6.

13. David Woodruff, "Ready to Shop Until They Drop," *Business Week;* 22 June 1998, pp. 104-108.

14. Rebecca Piirto Heath, "Think Globally," *Marketing Tools,* October 1996, pp. 49-54.

15. Adam Pletsch, "Vogue Pool Products Dives into Europe," *Maclean Hunter Publishing Limited,* 1999, accessed online at **www.plant.ca/Content/1999/990118/pla01189904.html.**

16. Charles A. Coulombe, "Global Expansion: The Unstoppable Crusade," *Success,* September 1994, pp. 18-20; "Amway Hopes to Set up Sales Network in India," *The Wall Street Journal,* 17 February 1998, p. B8; Gerald S. Couzens, "Dick Devos," *Success,* November 1998, pp. 52-57.

17. See "Crest, Colgate Bare Teeth in Competition for China," *Advertising Age International,* November 1996, p. I3; Mark L. Clifford, "How You Can Win in China," *Business Week,* 26 May 1997, pp. 66-68; and Ben Davies, "The Biggest Market Retains Its Luster," *Asia Money,* January 1998, pp. 47-49.

18. Linda Grant, "GE's 'Smart Bomb' Strategy," *Fortune,* 21 July 1997, pp. 109-110; Richard J. Babyak, "GE Appliances: The Polar Approach," *Appliance Manufacturer,* February 1997, p. G22; Joe Jancsurak, "Asia to Drive World Appliance Growth," *Appliance Manufacturer,* February 1999, pp. G3- G6; and Jim Rohwer, "GE Digs into Asia," *Fortune,* 2 October 2000, pp. 165-178.

19. Robert Neff, "In Japan, They're Goofy About Disney," *Business Week,* 12 March 1990, p. 64; "In Brief: E*Trade Licensing Deal Gives It an Israeli Link," *American Banker,* 11 May 1998.

20. Press Release, "Pettigrew's Trade Mission to Russia Continues to Bear Fruit: SNC-Lavalin Signs Deal with New Russian Partner," Department of Foreign Affairs and International Trade, 18 December 2000.

21. Greg Keenan, "Magna Buys U.K. Business," *The Globe and Mail,* 21 March 1996, p. B1.

22. Lawrence Donegan, "Heavy Job Rotation: MTV Europe Sacks 80 Employees in the Name of 'Regionalisation,'" *Guardian,* 21 November 1997, p. 19.

23. Cyndee Miller, "Chasing Global Dreams," *Marketing News,* 2 December 1996, pp. 1, 2; Christian Lorenz, "MTV Europe Launches Channels," *Billboard,* 27 February 1999, p. 48.

24. See Theodore Levitt, "The Globalization of Markets," *Harvard Business Review,* May-June 1983, pp. 92-102; David M. Szymanski, Sundar G. Bharadwaj, and Rajan Varadarajan, "Standardization Versus Adaptation of International Marketing Strategy: An Empirical Investigation," *Journal of Marketing,* October 1993, pp. 1-17; Ashish Banerjee, "Global Campaigns Don't Work; Multinationals Do," *Advertising Age,* 18 April 1994, p. 23; Miller, "Chasing Global Dreams;" Jeryl Whitelock and Carole Pimblett, "The Standardization Debate in International Marketing," *Journal of Global Marketing,* 1997, p. 22; and David A. Aaker and Ericj Joachimsthaler, "The Lure of Global Branding," *Harvard Business Review,* November-December 1999, pp. 137-144.

25. See "In India, Beef-Free Mickie D," *Business Week,* 7 April 1995, p. 52; Jeff Walters, "Have Brand Will Travel," *Brandweek,* 6 October 1997, pp. 22-26; and David Barboza, "From Abroad, McDonald's Finds Value in Local Control," *New York Times,* 12 February 1999, p. 1.

26. See Martha M. Hamilton, "Going Global: A World of Difference," *Washington Post,* 10 May 1998, p. H1.

27. See Warren J. Keegan, *Global Marketing Management,* 4th ed., Upper Saddle River, NJ: Prentice Hall, 1989, pp. 378-381; and Keegan and Green, *Principles of Global Marketing,* pp. 294-298.

28. For these and other examples, see Andrew Kupfer, "How to be a Global Manager," *Fortune,* 14 March 1988, pp. 52-58; Maria Shao, "For Levi's: A Flattering Fit Overseas," *Business Week,* 5 November 1990, pp. 76-77; Joseph Weber, "Campbell: Now It's M-M-Global," *Business Week,* 15 March 1993, pp. 52-53; Zachary Schiller, "Make It Simple," *Business Week,* 9 September 1996, p. 102; Chester Dawson, "Gerber Feeding Booming Japanese Baby Food Market," *Durham Herald-Sun,* 21 February 1998, p. C10; and Jack Neff, "Test It in Paris, France, Launch It in Paris, Texas," *Advertising Age,* 31 May 1999, p. 28.

29. J. S. Perry Hobson, "Feng Shui: Its Impacts on the Asian Hospitality Industry," *International Journal of Contemporary Hospitality Management* 6(6), 1994, pp. 21-26; Bernd H. Schmitt and Yigang Pan, "In Asia, the Supernatural Means Sales," *New York Times,* 19 February 1995, pp. 3, 11; Sally Taylor, "Tackling the Curse of Bad Feng Shui," *Publishers Weekly,* 27 April 1998, p. 24.

30. Erika Rasmusson, "Global Warning," *Sales and Marketing Management,* November 1998, p. 17; Bradley Johnson, "IBM Talks Global Clout, in Foreign Languages," *Advertising Age,* 7 June 1999, p. 10.

31. "The Showcase," *Marketing Magazine,* 20 October 1997, pp. 14-19.

32. See Michael Oneal, "Harley-Davidson: Ready to Hit the Road Again," *Business Week,* 21 July 1986, p. 70; and "EU Proposes Dumping Change," *East European Markets,* 14 February 1997, pp. 2-3.

33. Ram Charan, "The Rules Have Changed," *Fortune,* 16 March 1998, pp. 159-162.

34. See Kenichi Ohmae, "Managing in a Borderless World," *Harvard Business Review,* May-June 1989, pp. 152-161; William J. Holstein, "The Stateless Corporation," *Business Week,* 14 May 1990, pp. 98-105; and John A. Byrne and Kathleen Kerwin, "Borderless Management," *Business Week,* 23 May 1994, pp. 24-26.

Chapter 16

1. Quotes From Canadian Centre for Philanthropy, Press Release, "1999 Imagine New Spirit of Community, Mutual Fund Industry Corporate Industry Award Presented to Altamira Investments Services Inc." available online at **www.ccp.ca**; Canadian Centre for Philanthropy, Press Release, "'Tis the Season for Some Good News," Toronto, 15 December 2000; and Bruce Pope, CEO Molson Breweries, Queen's University, School of Business, 27 March 1996. Also See Press Release, "Consumers Worldwide Expect Businesses to Achieve Social as Well as Economic Goals," Environics, *The Millennium Poll on Corporate Social Responsibility,* 20 September 1999, available online at **www.environics.net/eil/millennium/press**; Janet MacPhail, "Event Marketing: Social Marketing a Process, Not a Program," *Strategy,* 29 September 1997, p. 20; David Menzies, "All For a Good Cause," *Marketing,* 26 September 1994, pp. 13-15; Erica Zlomislic, "Sears Backs PC Donation Effort," *Strategy,* 24 November 1997, p. 1; "And the Winners Are," *Inter Sector: A Newsletter for Imagine's Community Partners,* 3(6), p. 1; Bell Canada Web Site at **www.bell.ca**.

2. Barrie McKenna, "Suzy Shier Fined $300,000," *The Globe And Mail,* 18 July 1994, p. B7.

3. John Gustavson, "The New Fraud Busters," *Marketing On-Line,* 16 August 1999.

4. Sandra Pesmen, "How Low Is Low? How Free Is Free?" *Advertising Age,* 7 May 1990, p. S10; Karolyn Schuster, "The Dark Side of Nutrition," *Food Management,* June 1999, pp. 34-39.

5. David Welch, "Firestone: Is This Brand Beyond Repair?" *Business Week,* 11 June 2001, p. 48.

6. See Judith Bell and Bonnie Maria Burlin, "In Urban Areas, Many More Still Pay More for Food," *Journal of Public Policy And Marketing,* Fall 1993, pp. 268-270; Alan R. Andreasen, "Revisiting the Disadvantaged: Old Lesson and New Problems," *Journal of Public Policy and Marketing,* Fall 1993, pp. 270-275; Tony Attrino, "Nationwide Settles Redlining Suit in Ohio," *National Underwriter,* 27 April 1998, p. 4; Angelo B. Henderson, "First Chicago Unit Agrees to Lend $3

Billion in Detroit," *The Wall Street Journal,* 26 June 1998; and Kathryn Graddy and Diana C. Robertson, "Fairness of Pricing Decisions," *Business Ethics Quarterly,* April 1999, pp. 225-243.

7. Marcia Stepanek, "Weblining," *Business Week,* April 3, 2000, pp. EB26-EB43. Also See Karin Helperin, "Wells Fargo Online Service Accused of Redlining," *Bank Systems and Technology,* September 2000, p. 19.

8. Richard W. Pollay, "The Distorted Mirror: Reflections on the Unintended Consequences of Advertising," *Journal Of Marketing,* April 1986, pp. 18-36.

9. From an advertisement for *Fact* magazine, which does not carry advertisements.

10. Steve Hamm, "Microsoft's Future," *Business Week,* 19 January 1998, pp. 58-68; and Ronald. A. Cass, "Microsoft, Running Scared," *New York Times,* 28 June 1999, p. 17.

11. Consumers' Association of Canada, 404-267 O'Connor Street, Ottawa, ON K2P 1V3; **www.consumer.ca.**

12. Press Release, "Canada Shows Continued Leadership on Protecting the Ozone Layer," Government of Canada, Ottawa, 18 December 2000, accessed online at **www.ec.gc.ca/press/001219_n_e.htm**, 17 November 2002.

13. Ken MacQueen, "Ministers Declare War on Excess Packaging," *Whig-Standard,* 22 March 1990, p. 11.

14. Alan M. Robinson, "It's Easy Being Green: Environmentalism Isn't Dead," *Marketing On-Line,* 11 October 1999.

15. Stuart L. Hart, "Beyond Greening: Strategies for a Sustainable World," *Harvard Business Review,* January-February 1997, pp. 66-76. Also See Jacquelyn Ottman, "What Sustainability Means to Marketers," *Marketing News,* 21 July 1997, p. 4; And James L. Kolar, "Environmental Sustainability: Balancing Pollution Control with Economic Growth," *Environmental Quality Management,* Spring 1999, pp. 1-10.

16. Michael E. Porter and Claas van Derlinde, "Green and Competitive: Ending The Stalemate," *Harvard Business Review,* September-October 1995, pp. 120-134.

17. Hart, "Beyond Greening," p. 72. For other examples, see Jacquelyn Ottman, "Environmental Winners Show Sustainable Strategies," *Marketing News,* 27 April 1998, p. 6.

18. Hart, "Beyond Greening," p. 73; Linda Grant, "Monsanto's Bet: There's Gold in Going Green," *Fortune,* 14 April 1997, pp. 116-118; Carl Pope, "Billboards of the Garden Wall," *Sierra,* January-February 1999, pp. 12-13.

19. See John Audley, *Green Politics and Global Trade: NAFTA and the Future of Environmental Politics,* Georgetown:

Georgetown University Press, 1997; Lars K. Hallstrom, "Industry Versus Ecology: Environment in the New Europe," *Futures,* February 1999, pp. 25-38; Joe McKinney, "NAFTA: Four Years down the Road," *Baylor Business Review,* Spring 1999, pp. 22-23; Andreas Diekmann And Axel Franzen, "The Wealth of Nations and Environmental Concern," *Environment and Behavior,* July 1999, pp. 540-549.

20. Linda Sutherland, "Brothers Find Focus in Waste," *The Globe and Mail,* 6 January 1997, p. B8.

21. Louise Gagnon, "Cosmetic Changes," *Marketing Magazine,* 21/28 July 1997, p. 18.

22. Ian Cruikshand, "Fun Factory," *Report on Business Magazine,* August 1997, pp. 30-34.

23. Ben and Jerry's mission statement, accessed online at **www.benjerry.com/mission.html**, 17 November 2002.

24. "Getting Involved in the Community: The HP Way," Supplement Sponsored by Hewlett-Packard (Canada) Ltd., *Report on Business,* April 1996, p. 30.

25. Information accessed online at **www.hermanmiller.com/company/environment/conservation.html**, January 2000.

26. Dan R. Dalton And Richard A. Cosier, "The Four Faces of Social Responsibility," *Business Horizons,* May-June 1982:19-27.

27. Survey data collected by Peggy Cunningham and Derek Gent, Queen's University, 1995.

28. Janet McFarland, "When Is a Gift a Bribe?" *The Globe and Mail,* 15 January 1996; "GM's Gift Policy Covers the Bases," *The Globe and Mail,* 11 September 1997, p. B17.

29. Mark Hendricks, "Ethics in Action," *Management Review,* January 1995, pp. 53-55.

30. Kenneth Labich, "The New Crisis in Business Management," *Fortune,* 20 April 1992, pp. 167-176.

31. From "Ethics as a Practical Matter," A Message from David R. Whitman, Chairman of the Board of Whirlpool Corporation, reprinted in Ricky E. Griffin and Ronald J. Ebert, *Business,* Upper Saddle River, NJ: Prentice Hall, 1989, pp. 578-579. For more on marketing ethics, see Lynn Sharp Paine, "Managing for Organizational Integrity," *Harvard Business Review,* March-April 1994, pp. 106-117; Tom McInerney, "Double Trouble: Combining Business and Ethics," *Business Ethics Quarterly,* January 1998, pp. 187-189; John F. Gaski, "Does Marketing Ethics Really Have Anything to Say?" *Journal of Business Ethics,* February 1999, pp. 315-334; and Thomas W. Dunfee, N. Craig Smith, and William T. Ross, "Social Contracts and Marketing Ethics," *Journal of Marketing,* July 1999, pp. 14-32.

GLOSSARY

Actual product A product's parts, quality level, features, design, brand name, packaging, and other attributes that combine to deliver core product benefits. *306*

Adapted marketing mix An international marketing strategy for adjusting the marketing mix elements to each international target market, bearing more costs but hoping for a larger market share and return. *622*

Adoption process The mental process through which an individual passes from first hearing about an innovation to final adoption. *231*

Advertising Any paid form of nonpersonal presentation and promotion of ideas, goods, or services by an identified sponsor. *508*

Advertising agency A marketing services firm that assists companies in planning, preparing, implementing, and evaluating all or portions of their advertising programs. *530*

Affordable method Setting the promotion budget at the level management thinks the company can afford. *519*

Age and life-cycle segmentation Offering different products to or using different marketing approaches for different age and life-cycle groups. *266*

Agent A wholesaler who represents buyers or sellers on a relatively permanent basis, performs only a few functions, and does not take title to goods. *493*

Allowance Promotional money paid by manufacturers to retailers in return for an agreement to feature the manufacturer's products in some way. *405*

Approach The step in the selling process in which the salesperson meets the customer for the first time. *572*

Attitude A person's consistently favourable or unfavourable evaluations, feelings, and tendencies toward an object or idea. *224*

Augmented product Additional consumer services and benefits built around the core and actual products. *306*

B2B (business-to-business) e-commerce Using B2B trading networks, auction sites, spot exchanges, online product catalogues, barter sites, and other online resources to reach new customers, serve current customers more effectively, and obtain buying efficiencies and better prices. *92*

B2C (business to consumer) e-commerce The online selling of goods and services to final consumers. *90*

Baby boom The major increase in the annual birth rate following World War II and lasting until the early 1960s. The "baby boomers," now moving into middle age, are a prime target for marketers. *133*

Behavioural segmentation Dividing a market into groups based on consumer knowledge, attitude, use, or response to a product. Occasion segmentation Dividing the market into groups according to occasions when buyers get the idea to buy, actually make their purchase, or use the purchased item. *269*

Belief A descriptive thought that a person holds about something. *223*

Benefit segmentation Dividing the market into groups according to the different benefits that consumers seek from the product. *270*

Brand equity The value of a brand, based on the extent to which it has high brand loyalty, name awareness, perceived quality, strong brand associations, and other assets such as patents, trademarks, and channel relationships. *315*

Brand extension Using a successful brand name to launch a new or modified product in a new category. *320*

Brand A name, term, sign, symbol, design, or a combination of these intended to identify the goods or services of one seller or group of sellers and to differentiate them from those of competitors. *314*

Break-even pricing (target profit pricing) Setting price to break even on the costs of making and marketing a product, or setting price to make a target profit. *396*

Broker A wholesaler who does not take title to goods and whose function is to bring buyers and sellers together and assist in negotiation. *493*

Business analysis A review of the sales, costs, and profit projections for a new product to find out whether these factors satisfy the company's objectives. *356*

Business buyer behaviour The buying behaviour of organizations that buy goods and services for use in the production of other products and services that are sold, rented, or supplied to others. *235*

Business portfolio The collection of businesses and products that compose the company. *53*

Business product A product bought by individuals and organizations for further processing or for use in conducting a business. *309*

Business unit strategy Strategy that determines how the unit will compete in its given business and how it will position itself among its competitors. *47*

Buying centre All the individuals and units that participate in the business buying-decision process. *238*

By-product pricing Setting a price for by-products to make the main product's price more competitive. *404*

C2B (consumer-to-business) e-commerce Online exchanges in which consumers search out sellers, learn about their offers, and initiate purchases, sometimes even driving transaction terms. *95*

C2C (consumer-to-consumer) e-commerce Online exchanges of goods and information between final consumers. *94*

Captive-product pricing Setting a price for products that must be used along with a main product, such as blades for a razor and film for a camera. *403*

Catalogue marketing Direct marketing through print, video, or electronic catalogues that are mailed to select customers, made available in stores, or presented online. *582*

Category killer Giant specialty store that carries a very deep assortment of a particular line and is staffed by knowledgeable employees. *475*

Causal research Marketing research to test hypotheses about cause-and-effect relationships. *172*

Chain stores Two or more outlets that are owned and controlled in common, have central buying and merchandising, and sell similar lines of merchandise. *477*

Channel conflict Disagreement among marketing channel members on goals and roles–who should do what and for what rewards *435*

Channel level A layer of intermediaries that performs some work in bringing the product and its ownership closer to the final buyer. *433*

Click-and-mortar companies Traditional brick-and-mortar companies that have added e-marketing to their operations. *98*

Click-only companies The so-called dot-coms, which operate only online, without any brick-and-mortar market presence. *96*

Closing The step in the selling process in which the salesperson asks the customer for an order. *573*

Co-branding The practice of using the established brand names of two different companies on the same product. *319*

Cognitive dissonance Buyer discomfort caused by postpurchase conflict. *228*

Commercialization Introducing a new product into the market. *358*

Communication adaptation A global communication strategy of fully adapting advertising messages to local markets. *627*

Competition-based pricing Setting prices based on the prices that competitors charge for similar products. *400*

Competitive-parity method Setting the promotion budget to match competitors' outlays. *520*

Competitive advantage An advantage over competitors gained by offering consumers greater value, either through lower prices or by providing more benefits that justify higher prices. *283*

Concentrated marketing A market-coverage strategy in which a firm goes after a large share of one or a few submarkets *278*

Concept development Expanding the new product idea into various alternative forms. *353*

Concept testing Testing new product concepts with a group of target consumers to find out whether the concepts have strong consumer appeal *354*

Consumer buyer behaviour The buying behaviour of final consumers–individuals and households who buy goods and services for personal consumption. *207*

Consumer market All the individuals and households who buy or acquire goods and services for personal consumption. *207*

Consumer-oriented marketing A principle of enlightened marketing that holds that a company should view and organize its marketing activities from the consumer's point of view. *662*

Consumer product Product bought by final consumer for personal consumption. *308*

Consumerism An organized movement of citizens and government agencies to improve the rights and power of buyers in relation to sellers. *653*

Contract manufacturing A joint venture in which a company contracts with manufacturers in a foreign market to produce the product.

Convenience product A consumer product that the customer usually buys frequently, immediately, and with a minimum of comparison and buying effort. *308*

Convenience store A small store located near a residential area that is open long hours, seven days a week and carries a limited line of high-turnover convenience goods. *475*

Conventional distribution channel A channel consisting of one or more independent producers, wholesalers, and retailers, each a separate business seeking to maximize its own profits even at the expense of profits for the system as a whole. *436*

Core product The problem-solving services or core benefits that consumers are really buying when they purchase a product. *303*

Corporate strategic planning Setting the mission for a firm as a whole. *47*

Corporate Web site A Web site designed to build customer goodwill and to supplement other sales channels, rather than to sell the company's products directly. *101*

Cost-plus pricing Adding a standard markup to the cost of the product. *395*

Cultural environment Institutions and other forces that affect society's basic values, perceptions, preferences, and behaviours. *151*

Culture The set of basic values, perceptions, wants, and behaviours learned by a member of society from family and other important institutions. *208*

Customer database An organized collection of comprehensive data about individual customers or prospects, including geographic, demographic, psychographic, and behavioural data. *576*

Customer relationship management (CRM) Sophisticated software and analytical tools that integrate customer information from all sources, analyze it in depth, and use the results to build stronger customer relationships. *188*

Customer sales force structure A sales force organization under which salespeople specialize in selling only to certain customers or industries. *557*

Customer satisfaction The extent to which a product's perceived performance in delivering value matches a buyer's expectations. *11*

Customer value The difference between the values the customer gains from owning and using a product and the costs of obtaining the product. *10*

Decline stage The product life-cycle stage in which a product's sales decline. *369*

Deficient products Products that have neither immediate appeal nor long-run benefits. *666*

Demand curve A curve that shows the number of units the market will buy in a given period at different prices that might be charged. *392*

Demands Human wants that are backed by buying power. *6*

Demarketing Marketing to reduce demand temporarily or permanently –the aim is not to destroy demand, but to reduce or shift it. *16*

Demographic segmentation Dividing the market into groups based on demographic variables such as age, sex, family size, family life cycle, income, occupation, education, religion, race, and nationality. *266*

Demography The study of human populations in terms of size, density, location, age, sex, race, occupation, and other statistics. *131*

Department store A retail organization that carries a wide variety of product lines–typically clothing, home furnishings, and household goods; each line is operated as a separate department managed by specialist buyers or merchandisers. *474*

Desirable products Products that give both high immediate satisfaction and high long-run benefits. *666*

Derived demand Business demand that ultimately comes from (derives from) the demand for consumer goods. *235*

Descriptive research Marketing research to better describe marketing problems, situations, or markets, such as the market potential for a product or the demographics and attitudes of consumers who buy the product. *172*

Differentiated marketing A market-coverage strategy in which a firm decides to target several market segments and designs separate offers for each *278*

Direct-mail marketing Direct marketing through single mailings that include letters, ads, samples, foldouts, and other "salespeople with wings" sent to prospects on mailing lists. *580*

Direct marketing Direct communications with carefully targeted individual consumers to obtain an immediate response. *508*

Direct-response television marketing Television spots that persuasively describe a product and give customers a toll-free number for ordering. *583*

Direct investment Entering a foreign market by developing foreign-based assembly or manufacturing facilities. *622*

Direct marketing Direct connections with carefully targeted individual consumers to both obtain an immediate response and cultivate lasting customer relationships. *574*

Direct marketing channel A marketing channel that has no intermediary levels. *433*

Discount store A retail institution that sells standard merchandise at lower prices by accepting lower margins and selling at higher volume. *476*

Discount A straight reduction in price on purchases during a stated period. *405*

Disintermediation The displacement of traditional resellers from a marketing channel by radical new types of intermediaries or by product and service producers going directly to final buyers. *439*

Distribution centre A large, highly automated warehouse designed to receive goods from various plants and suppliers, take orders, fill them efficiently, and deliver goods to customers as quickly as possible *454*

Diversification A strategy for company growth by starting up or acquiring businesses outside the company's current products and markets. *59*

Distribution channel A set of interdependent organizations involved in the process of making a product or service available for use or consumption by the consumer or business user. *431*

Dynamic pricing The practice of charging different prices depending on individual customers and situations. *383*

E-business The use of electronic platforms—intranets, extranets, and the Internet—to conduct a company's business. *86*

E-commerce Buying and selling processes supported by electronic means, primarily the Internet. *86*

E-marketing The "e-selling" side of e-commerce, including company efforts to communicate about, promote, and sell products and services over the Internet. *86*

Economic community A group of nations organized to work toward common goals in the regulation of international trade. *607*

Economic environment Factors that affect consumer buying power and spending patterns. *143*

Embargo A ban on the import of a certain product. *606*

Engel's laws Differences noted more than a century ago by Ernst Engel in how people shift their spending across food, housing, transportation, health care, and other goods and services categories as family income rises. *145*

Enlightened marketing A marketing philosophy holding that a company's marketing should support the best long-run performance of the marketing system; its five principles are consumer-oriented marketing, innovative marketing, value marketing, sense-of-mission marketing, and societal marketing. *662*

Environmental management perspective A management perspective in which the firm takes aggressive action to affect the publics and forces in its marketing environment rather than simply watching and reacting to them. *154*

Environmental sustainability A management approach that involves developing strategies that both sustain the environment and produce profits for the company. *656*

Environmentalism An organized movement of concerned citizens and government agencies to protect and improve people's living environment. *655*

Exchange The act of obtaining a desired object from someone by offering something in return. *12*

Exchange controls Government limits on the amount of its foreign exchange with other countries and on its exchange rate against other currencies. *606*

Exclusive distribution Giving a limited number of dealers the exclusive right to distribute the company's products in their territories. *445*

Experimental research The gathering of primary data by selecting matched groups of subjects, giving them different treatments, controlling unrelated factors, and checking for differences in group responses. *180*

Exploratory research Marketing research to gather preliminary information that will help define problems and suggest hypotheses. *171*

Exporting Entering a foreign market by sending products and selling them through international marketing intermediaries (indirect exporting) or through the company's own department, branch, or sales representatives or agents (direct exporting). *619*

Extranet A network that connects a company with its suppliers and distributors. *83*

f.o.b origin pricing A geographic pricing strategy in which goods are placed free on board a carrier and the customer pays the freight from the originating point to the required destination. *410*

Factory outlet Off-price retailing operation that is owned and operated by a manufacturer and that normally carries the manufacturer's surplus, discontinued, or irregular goods. *476*

Fads Fashions that enter quickly, are adopted with great zeal, peak early, and decline very quickly. *363*

Fashion A currently accepted or popular style in a given field. *363*

Focus group interviewing Personal interviewing of a small group of people invited to gather for a few hours with a trained interviewer to discuss a product, service, or organization. The interviewer focuses the group discussion on important issues. *181*

Follow-up The last step in the selling process in which the salesperson follows up after the sale to ensure customer satisfaction and repeat business. *573*

Franchise A contractual association between a manufacturer, wholesaler, or service organization (a franchiser) and independent businesspeople (franchisees) who buy the right to own and operate one or more units in the franchise system. *478*

Functional strategy Strategy that deals with questions of how the function can best support the business unit strategy. *48*

Gender segmentation Dividing a market into different groups based on sex. *267*

Geographic segmentation Dividing a market into different geographical units such as nations, states, regions, counties, cities, or neighbourhoods. *266*

Global firm A firm that, by operating in more than one country, gains R&D, production, marketing, and financial advantages that are not available to purely domestic competitors. *603*

Global industry An industry in which the strategic positions of competitors in given geographic or national markets are affected by their overall global positions. *603*

Group Two or more people who interact to accomplish individual or mutual goals. *215*

Growth-share matrix A portfolio-planning method that evaluates a company's strategic business units in terms of their market growth rate and relative market share. SBUs are classified as stars, cash cows, question marks, or dogs. *55*

Growth stage The product life-cycle stage in which a product's sales start climbing quickly. *364*

Handling objections The step in the selling process in which the salesperson seeks out, clarifies, and overcomes customer objections to buying. *573*

Horizontal marketing system A channel arrangement in which two or more companies at one level join together to follow a new marketing opportunity *437*

Hybrid marketing channel Multichannel distribution system in which a single firm sets up two or more marketing channels to reach one or more customer segments *438*

Idea generation The systematic search for new product ideas. *350*

Idea screening Screening new product ideas to spot good ideas and drop poor ones as soon as possible. *353*

Income segmentation Dividing a market into different income groups. *268*

Independent off-price retailer Off-price retailer that is either owned and run by entrepreneurs or is division of larger retail corporation. *476*

Indirect marketing channel Channel containing one or more intermediary levels. *433*

Individual marketing Tailoring products and marketing programs to the needs and preferences of individual customers. *261*

Innovative marketing A principle of enlightened marketing that requires that a company seek real product and marketing improvements. *662*

Inside sales force Inside salespeople who conduct business from their offices via telephone or visits from prospective buyers. *558*

Integrated direct marketing Direct-marketing campaigns that use multiple vehicles and multiple stages to improve response rates and profits. *585*

Integrated marketing communications (IMC) The concept under which a company carefully integrates and coordinates its many communications channels to deliver a clear, consistent, and compelling message about the organization and its products or services. *510*

Integrated supply chain management The logistics concept that emphasizes teamwork, both inside the company and among all the marketing channel organizations, to maximize the performance of the entire distribution system. *457*

Intensive distribution Stocking the product in as many outlets as possible. *445*

Intermarket segmentation Forming segments of consumers who have similar needs and buying behaviour even though they are located in different countries *274*

Intermodal transportation Combining two or more modes of transportation *456*

Internal databases Electronic collections of information obtained from data sources within the company. *168*

Internet A vast public web of computer networks that connects users of all types all around the world to each other and to a large information repository. The Internet is an information highway that can dispatch bits at incredible speeds from one location to another. *83*

Intranet A network that connects people within a company to each other and to the company network. *83*

Introduction stage The product life-cycle stage in which the new product is first distributed and made available for purchase. *364*

Joint ownership A joint venture in which a company joins investors in a foreign market to create a local business in which the company shares joint ownership and control. *621*

Joint venturing Entering foreign markets by joining with foreign companies to produce or market a product or service. *620*

Learning Changes in an individual's behaviour arising from experience. *223*

Licensing A method of entering a foreign market in which the company enters into

an agreement with a licensee in the foreign market, offering the right to use a manufacturing process, trademark, patent, trade secret, or other item of value for a fee or royalty. *620*

Lifestyle A person's pattern of living as expressed in his or her activities, interests, and opinions. *218*

Line extension Using a successful brand name to introduce additional items in a given product category under the same brand name, such as new flavours, forms, colours, added ingredients, or package sizes. *320*

Local marketing Tailoring brands and promotions to the needs and wants of local customer groups–cities, neighbourhoods, and even specific stores. *261*

Macroenvironment The larger societal forces that affect the microenvironment–demographic, economic, natural, technological, political, and cultural forces. *127*

Management contracting A joint venture in which the domestic firm supplies the management expertise to a foreign company that supplies the capital; the domestic firm exports management services rather than products. *621*

Manufacturers' sales branches and offices Wholesaling by sellers or buyers themselves rather than through independent wholesalers. *493*

Market development A strategy for company growth by identifying and developing new market segments for current company products. *59*

Market-penetration pricing Setting a low price for a new product to attract a large number of buyers and a large market share. *401*

Market-skimming pricing Setting a high price for a new product to skim maximum revenues layer by layer from the segments willing to pay the high price; the company makes fewer but more profitable sales. *401*

Market penetration A strategy for company growth by increasing sales of current products to current market segments without changing the product. *58*

Market positioning Arranging for a product to occupy a clear, distinctive, and desirable place relative to competing products in the minds of target consumers. *64*

Market segment A group of consumers who respond in a similar way to a given set of marketing efforts. *63*

Market segmentation Dividing a market into smaller groups of buyers with distinct needs, characteristics, or behaviours who might require separate products or marketing mixes. *258*

Market targeting The process of evaluating each market segment's attractiveness and selecting one or more segments to enter. *63*

Market The set of all actual and potential buyers of a product or service. *14*

Marketing audit A comprehensive, systematic, independent, and periodic examination of a company's environment, objectives, strategies, and activities to determine problem areas and opportunities and to recommend a plan of action to improve the company's marketing performance. *71*

Marketing communications mix (promotion mix) The specific mix of advertising, personal selling, sales promotion, and public relations a company uses to pursue its advertising and marketing objectives.

Marketing concept The marketing management philosophy that holds that achieving organizational goals depends on determining the needs and wants of target markets and delivering the desired satisfactions more effectively and efficiently than competitors do. *21*

Marketing control The process of measuring and evaluating the results of marketing strategies and plans, and taking corrective action to ensure that objectives are achieved. *71*

Marketing environment The factors and forces outside marketing's direct control that affect marketing management's ability to develop and maintain successful transactions with target customers. *126*

Marketing implementation The process that turns marketing strategies and plans into marketing actions to accomplish strategic marketing objectives. *69*

Marketing information system (MIS) The people, equipment, and procedures needed to gather, sort, analyze, evaluate, and distribute needed, timely, and accurate information to marketing decision makers. *166*

Marketing intelligence A systematic collection and analysis of publicly available information about competitors and developments in the marketing environment. *169*

Marketing intermediaries Firms that help the company to promote, sell, and distribute its goods to final buyers; they include resellers, physical distribution firms, marketing services agencies, and financial intermediaries. *128*

Marketing logistics (physical distribution) The tasks involved in planning, implementing, and controlling the physical flow of materials, final goods, and related information from points of origin to points of consumption to meet customer requirements at a profit. *452*

Marketing management The analysis, planning, implementation, and control of programs designed to create, build, and maintain beneficial exchanges with target buyers so as to achieve organizational objectives. *15*

Marketing mix The set of controllable tactical marketing tools–product, price, place, and promotion–that the firm blends to produce the response it wants in the target market. *64*

Marketing process The process of (1) analyzing marketing opportunities, (2) selecting target markets, (3) developing the marketing mix, and (4) managing the marketing effort. *61*

Marketing research The systematic design, collection, analysis, and reporting of data relevant to a specific marketing situation facing an organization. *171*

Marketing strategy development Designing an initial marketing strategy for a new product based on the product concept. *355*

Marketing strategy The marketing logic by which the business unit hopes to achieve its marketing objectives. *68*

Marketing Web site A Web site that engages consumers in interactions that will move them closer to a direct purchase or other marketing outcome. *101*

Marketing A social and managerial process by which individuals and groups obtain what they need and want through creating and exchanging products and value with others. *5*

Maturity stage The stage in the product life cycle in which sales growth slows or levels off *365*

Merchant wholesaler Independently owned business that takes title to the merchandise it handles. *493*

Microenvironment The forces close to the company that affect its ability to serve its customers–the company, suppliers, marketing channel firms, customer markets, competitors, and publics. *127*

Micromarketing The practice of tailoring products and marketing programs to the needs and wants of specific individuals and local customer groups–includes local marketing and individual marketing. *261*

Mission statement A statement of the organization's purpose–what it wants to accomplish in the larger environment. *51*

Modified rebuy A business buying situation in which the buyer wants to modify product specifications, prices, terms, or suppliers. *238*

Motive (drive) A need that is sufficiently pressing to direct the person to seek satisfaction of the need. *221*

Natural environment The natural resources needed as inputs by marketers or affected by marketing activities. *145*

Need A state of felt deprivation. *5*

Needs analysis The process of determining a buyer's or prospect's needs before presenting or demonstrating a product or service. *572*

New product development The development of original products, product improvements, product modifications, and new brands through the firm's own R&D efforts. *349*

New product A good, service, or idea that is perceived by some potential customers as new. *231*

New task A business buying situation in which the buyer purchases a product or service for the first time. *238*

Niche marketing Focusing on subsegments or niches with distinctive traits that may seek a special combination of benefits. *260*

Nontariff trade barriers Nonmonetary barriers to foreign products, such as biases against a foreign company's bids or product standards that go against a foreign company's product features. *606*

Objective-and-task method Developing the promotion budget by (1) defining specific objectives, (2) determining the tasks that must be performed to achieve these objectives, and (3) estimating the costs of performing these tasks. The sum of these costs is the proposed promotion budget. *520*

Observational research The gathering of primary data by observing relevant people, actions, and situations. *176*

Off-price retailer Retailer that buys at below wholesale prices and sells at less than retail. Examples are factory outlets, independents, and warehouse clubs. *476*

Online (Internet) marketing research Collecting primary data through Internet surveys and online focus groups. *182*

Online advertising Advertising that appears while consumers are surfing the Web, including banner and ticker ads, interstitials, skyscrapers, and other forms. *105*

Online databases Computerized collections of information available from online commercial sources or via the Internet. *176*

Open trading networks Huge e-marketspaces in which B2B buyers and sellers find each other online, share information, and complete transactions efficiently. *93*

Opinion leader A person within a reference group who, because of special skills, knowledge, personality, or other characteristics, exerts influence on others. *215*

Optional-product pricing The pricing of optional or accessory products along with a main product. *402*

Outside sales force (or field sales force) Outside salespeople who travel to call on customers. *558*

Packaging The activities of designing and producing the container or wrapper for a product. *322*

Percentage-of-sales method Setting the promotion budget at a certain percentage of current or forecasted sales or as a percentage of the unit sales price. *520*

Perception The process by which people select, organize, and interpret information to form a meaningful picture of the world. *222*

Personal selling Personal presentation by the firm's sales force for the purpose of making sales and building customer relationships. *508*

Pleasing products Products that give high immediate satisfaction but may hurt consumers in the long run. *666*

Political environment Laws, government agencies, and pressure groups that influence and limit various organizations and individuals in a given society. *148*

Portfolio analysis A tool management uses to identify and evaluate the businesses that compose the company. *54*

Preapproach The step in the selling process in which the salesperson learns as much as possible about a prospective customer before making a sales call. *572*

Presentation The step in the selling process in which the salesperson tells the "product story" to the buyer, highlighting customer benefits. *572*

Price elasticity A measure of the sensitivity of demand to changes in price. *393*

Price The amount of money charged for a product or service, or the sum of the values that consumers exchange for the benefits of having or using the product or service. *383*

Primary data Information collected for the specific purpose at hand. *173*

Private brand (or store brand) A brand created and owned by a reseller of a product or service. *317*

Private trading networks (PTNs) B2B trading networks that link a particular seller with its own trading partners. *93*

Product adaptation Adapting a product to meet local conditions or wants in foreign markets. *625*

Product bundle pricing Combining several products and offering the bundle at a reduced price. *404*

Product concept A detailed version of the new product concept stated in meaningful consumer terms. *353*

Product concept The idea that consumers will favour products that offer the most quality, performance, and features and that the organization should therefore devote its energy to making continual product improvements. *21*

Product development Developing the product concept into a physical product to ensure that the product idea can be turned into a workable product. *356*

Product invention Creating new products or services for foreign markets. *626*

Product life cycle (PLC) The course of a product's sales and profits over its lifetime. It involves five distinct stages: product development, introduction, growth, maturity, and decline. *362*

Product line pricing Setting the price steps among various products in a product line based on cost differences among the products, customer evaluations of different features, and competitors' prices. *402*

Product line A group of products that are closely related because they function in a similar manner, are sold to the same consumer groups, are marketed through the same types of outlets, or fall within given price ranges. *327*

Product mix (or product assortment) The set of all product lines and items that a particular seller offers for sale. *328*

Product position The way the product is defined by consumers on important attributes–the place the product occupies in consumers' minds relative to competing products. *282*

Product quality The ability of a product to perform its functions; it includes the product's overall durability, reliability, precision, ease of operation and repair, and other valued attributes. *312*

Product sales force structure A sales force organization under which salespeople specialize in selling only a portion of the company's products or lines. *557*

Product support services Services that augment actual products. *325*

Product—market expansion grid A portfolio-planning tool for identifying company growth opportunities through market penetration, market development, product development, or diversification. *57*

Product Anything that can be offered to a market for attention, acquisition, use or consumption and that might satisfy a want or a need. *303*

Production concept The idea that consumers will favour products that are available and highly affordable and that management should therefore focus on improving production and distribution efficiency. *20*

Products Anything that can be offered to a market for attention, acquisition, use, or consumption that might satisfy a want or need. They include physical objects, services, persons, places, organizations, and ideas. *6*

Promotional pricing Temporarily pricing products below the list price, and sometimes even below cost, to increase short-run sales. *409*

Prospecting The step in the selling process in which the salesperson identifies qualified potential customers. *571*

Psychographic segmentation Dividing a market into different groups based on social class, lifestyle, or personality characteristics *269*

Psychological pricing A pricing approach that considers the psychology of prices and not simply the economics; the price is used to say something about the product. *406*

Public Any group that has an actual or potential interest in or impact on an organization's ability to achieve its objectives. *130*

Public relations Building good relations with the company's various publics by obtaining favourable publicity, building a good corporate image, and handling or heading off unfavourable rumours, stories, and events. Major PR tools include press relations, product publicity, corporate communications, lobbying, and public service. *508*

Pull strategy A promotion strategy that calls for spending a lot on advertising and consumer promotion to build consumer demand. If the strategy is successful, consumers will ask their retailers for the product, the retailers will ask the wholesalers, and the wholesalers will ask the producers. *516*

Push strategy A promotion strategy that calls for using the sales force and trade promotion to push the product through channels. The producer promotes the product to wholesalers, the wholesalers promote to retailers, and the retailers promote to consumers. *516*

Quota A limit on the amount of goods that an importing country will accept in certain product categories to conserve on foreign exchange and to protect local industry and employment. *606*

Reference prices Prices that buyers carry in their minds and refer to when they look at a given product. *406*

Relationship marketing The process of creating, maintaining, and enhancing strong, value-laden relationships with customers and other stakeholders. *12*

Retailer cooperative Independent retailers that band together to set up a jointly owned central warehouse operation and conduct joint merchandising and promotion efforts. *478*

Retailer A business whose sales come primarily from retailing. *472*

Retailing All activities involved in selling goods and services directly to consumers for their personal, nonbusiness use. *472*

Sales force management The analysis, planning, implementation, and control of sales force activities. It includes setting and designing sales force strategy; and recruiting, selecting, training, supervising, compensating, and evaluating the firm's salespeople. *555*

Sales promotion Short-term incentives to encourage the purchase or sale of a product or service. *508*

Sales quota A standard that states the amount a sales person should sell and how sales should be divided among the company's products. *570*

Salesperson An individual acting for a company by performing one or more of the following activities: prospecting, communicating, servicing, and information gathering. *554*

Salutary products Products that have low appeal but may benefit consumers in the long run. *666*

Sample A segment of the population selected to represent the population as a whole *185*

Secondary data Information that already exists somewhere, having been collected for another purpose. *173*

Segment marketing Isolating broad segments that make up a market and adapting the marketing to match the needs of one or more segment *259*

Segmented pricing Selling a product or service at two or more prices, where the difference in prices is not based on differences in costs. *406*

Selective distribution The use of more than one, but fewer than all, of the intermediaries who are willing to carry the company's products. *445*

Selling concept The idea that consumers will not buy enough of the organization's products unless the organization undertakes a large-scale selling and promotion effort. *21*

Selling process The steps that the salesperson follows when selling, which include prospecting and qualifying, preapproach, approach, presentation and demonstration, handling objections, closing, and follow-up. *571*

Sense-of-mission marketing A principle of enlightened marketing that holds that a company should define its mission in broad social terms rather than narrow product terms. *663*

Service-profit chain The chain that links service firm profits with employee and customer satisfaction. *331*

Service inseparability A major characteristic of services–they are produced and consumed at the same time and cannot be separated from their providers, whether the providers are people or machines. *330*

Service intangibility A major characteristic of services–they cannot be seen, tasted, felt, heard, or smelled before they are bought. *330*

Service perishability A major characteristic of services–they cannot be stored for later sale or use. *331*

Service retailers Retailers that sell services rather than products. *476*

Service variability A major characteristic of services–their quality may vary greatly, depending on who provides them and when, where, and how. *330*

Services Any activities or benefits that one party can offer to another that are essentially intangible and do not result in the ownership of anything. Examples include banking, airlines, hotels, tax preparation, and home repair services. *7*

Shopping centre A group of retail businesses planned, developed, owned, and managed as a unit. *485*

Shopping product A consumer good that the customer, in the process of selection and purchase, characteristically compares on such bases as suitability, quality, price, and style. *308*

Single-source data systems Electronic monitoring systems link consumers' exposure to television advertising and promotion (using television meters) with what they buy in stores (measured using store check scanner data). *179*

Slotting fees Payments demanded by retailers before they will accept new products and place them on shelves. *317*

Social classes Relatively permanent and ordered divisions in a society whose members share similar values, interests, and behaviours. *214*

Social marketing The design, implementation, and control of programs that seek to increase the acceptability of a social idea, cause, or practice among a target group. *311*

Societal marketing concept The idea that the organization should determine the needs, wants, and interests of target markets and deliver the desired satisfaction more effectively and efficiently than do competitors in a way that maintains or improves the consumer's and society's well-being. *23*

Societal marketing A principle of enlightened marketing that holds that a company should make marketing decisions by considering consumers' and society's long-run interests. *665*

Specialty product A consumer product with unique characteristics or brand identification for which a significant group of buyers is willing to make a special purchase effort. *309*

Specialty store A retail store that carries a narrow product line with a deep assortment within that line. *474*

Standardized marketing mix An international marketing strategy for using basically the same product, advertising, distribution channels, and other elements of the marketing mix in all of the company's international markets. *622*

Straight product extension Marketing a product in a foreign market without any change. *625*

Straight rebuy A business buying situation in which the buyer routinely reorders something without any modifications. *237*

Strategic business unit (SBU) An identifiable unit within a larger company with its own profit and loss responsibility; it may have one or more divisions and product lines. *47*

Strategic planning The process of developing and maintaining a strategic fit between the organization's goals and capabilities and its changing marketing opportunities. *47*

Style A basic and distinctive mode of expression. *363*

Subculture A group of people with shared value systems based on common life experiences and situations *209*

Supermarket Large, low-cost, low-margin, high-volume, self-service store that carries a wide variety of food, laundry, and household products. *474*

Superstore A store much larger than a regular supermarket that carries a large assortment of routinely purchased food and nonfood items and offers services such as dry cleaning, post offices, photo finishing, check cashing, bill paying, lunch counters, car care, and pet care. *475*

Supply chain management Managing value-added flows of materials, final goods, and related information between suppliers, the company, resellers, and final users. *452*

Survey research The gathering of primary data by asking people questions about their knowledge, attitudes, preferences, and buying behaviour. *179*

Systems selling Buying a packaged solution to a problem from a single seller, thus avoiding all the separate decisions involved in a complex buying situation. *238*

Target costing Pricing that starts with an ideal selling price, then targets costs that will ensure that the price is met. *388*

Target market A set of buyers sharing common needs or characteristics that the company decides to serve. *277*

Tariff A tax levied by a government against certain imported products to either raise revenue or protect domestic firms. *606*

Team selling Using teams of people from sales, marketing, engineering, finance, technical support, and even upper management to service large, complex accounts. *562*

Technological environment Forces that create new technologies, in turn creating new product and market opportunities. *147*

Telephone marketing Using the telephone to sell directly to customers. *579*

Territorial sales force structure A sales force organization that assigns each salesperson to an exclusive geographic territory in which that salesperson sells the company's full line. *556*

Test marketing The stage of new product development in which the product and marketing program are tested in more realistic market settings. *357*

Third-party logistics (3PL) provider An independent logistics provider that performs any or all of the functions required to get their clients' product to market. *458*

Transaction A trade between two parties that involves at least two things of value, agreed-on conditions, a time of agreement, and a place of agreement. *12*

Undifferentiated marketing A market-coverage strategy in which a firm decides to ignore market segment differences and go after the whole market with one offer. *277*

Uniform delivered pricing A geographic pricing strategy in which the company charges the same price plus freight to all customers, regardless of location *410*

Unsought product A consumer product that the consumer either does not know about or knows about but does not normally think of buying. *309*

Value-based pricing Setting price based on buyers' perceptions of value rather than on the seller's cost. *397*

Value analysis An approach to cost reduction in which components are studied carefully to determine whether they can be redesigned, standardized, or made by less costly methods of production. *243*

Value chain The series of departments that carry out value-creating activities to design, produce, market, deliver, and support a firm's products. *59*

Value delivery network The network made up of the company, suppliers, distributors, and ultimately customers who partner with one another to improve the performance of the entire system. *60*

Value marketing A principle of enlightened marketing that holds that a company should put most of its resources into value-building marketing investments. *663*

Value proposition The full positioning of a brand–the full mix of benefits on which it is positioned *287*

Vertical marketing system (VMS) A distribution channel structure in which producers, wholesalers, and retailers act as a unified system. One channel member owns the others, has contracts with them, or has so much power that they all cooperate. *436*

Viral marketing The Internet version of word-of-mouth marketing–the creation of e-mail messages or other marketing events that are so infectious that customers will want to pass them along to their friends. *106*

Voluntary chain A wholesale-sponsored group of independent retailers that engages in group buying and common merchandising. *477*

Want The form taken by a human need as shaped by culture and individual personality. *6*

Warehouse club Off-price retailer that sells a limited selection of brand name grocery items, appliances, clothing, and a hodgepodge of other goods at deep discounts to members who pay annual membership fees. *477*

Web communities Web sites on which members can congregate online and exchange views on issues of common interest. *108*

Webcasting The automatic downloading of customized information to recipients' computers, creating an attractive channel for delivering Internet advertising or other information. *111*

Wheel of retailing concept A concept of retailing that states that new types of retailers usually begin as low-margin, low-price, low-status operations but later evolve into higher-priced, higher-service operations, eventually becoming like the conventional retailers they replaced *486*

Whole-channel view Designing international channels that take into account all the necessary links in distributing the seller's products to final buyers, including the seller's headquarters organization, channels between nations, and channels within nations. *629*

Zone pricing A geographic pricing strategy in which the company sets up two or more zones. All customers within a zone pay the same total price: the more distant the zone, the higher the price. *411*

CREDITS

Chapter 1

2 Courtesy of Mountain Equipment Co-op and Solstice Photography; 7 Reprinted with permission of State of Health Products; 9 © David Young-Wolff, PhotoEdit; 14 © General Motors Media Archives; 17 Courtesy of BC Hydro; 18 Gage Rob/FPG International LLC; 22 L.L. Bean; 26 Photodisc; 31 Kraft Canada Inc.; 33 © 2001 Dell Computer Corporation and Microsoft Corporation.

Chapter 2

46 Courtesy of WestJet; 50 Courtesy of Sabian; 51 © 3M. All rights reserved. Reprinted with permission; 53 Courtesy of Norco; 54 Courtesy of General Electric Corporation; 57 Alene M. McNeill; 60 Courtesy of Wal-Mart, Inc./Bill Cornett Photography; 63 Courtesy of Rolls Royce & Bentley Motor Cars, Inc.; © Toyota Corporation. All rights reserved; 67 Courtesy of Bruce Ayres/Getty Images Inc.

Chapter 3

81 Dick Hemingway; 85 (Both) Courtesy of Reflect.com; 88 © Jose Luis Pelaez Inc./Corbis/Stock Market; 92 Courtesy of 24hourflowerpower; 93 PMC-Sierra; 94 These materials have been reproduced with the permission of eBay Inc. COPYRIGHT © EBAY INC. ALL RIGHTS RESERVED; 100 James Leysner/CORBIS SABA/MAGMA; 102 Sony Style Canada; 104 © Burpee; 107 © 2001 Mypoints.com, Inc. Used with permission; 109 iVillage.com.

Chapter 4

124 (Both) Volkswagen of America, Inc.; 131 Courtesy of Wal-Mart; 135 Reprinted with permission of Houston Effler Herstek Favat; 139 © Index Stock Imagery, Inc.; 141 Courtesy of Air Canada; 144 Reprinted with permission of Business Week; 147 Courtesy of Sally Wiener Grotta/Corbis/Stock Market; 154 "Whale," a commercial produced by the Canadian Heritage Commission for its "The World Needs More Canada" campaign, reprinted with permission of Canadian Tourism Commission.

Chapter 5

165 Courtesy of Roger Ressmeyer/Corbis; 166 © Tom, DeeAnn McCarthy/Corbis/Stock Market; 175 © The Dialog Corporation. Used with permission; 177 © Getty Images, Inc./Photodisc Inc.; 182 © 2001 Active Group; 184 © Greenfield Online, 2001; 187 (Both) Twin Vision Productions, Inc.; 189 Courtesy of SPSS Smarter CRM; 192 Strategis Web site (http://strategis.gc.ca/engdoc/main.html), Industry Canada, 2002. Reproduced with the permission of the Minister of Public Works and Government Services, 2002; 194 © Roper Starchworldwide.

Chapter 6

206 © Harley-Davidson Motor Company. Reprinted with permission; 211 CIBC Aboriginal Banking; 212 Courtesy of Air Canada and Hamazaki Wong; 217 © Warner Bros. Courtesy of Chevrolet and Warner Bros.; 219 © Bachmann/PhotoEdit; 225 Photographer: Dominique Malaterre (Ad agency: PNMD); 226 Bell Sports; 229 Photo Courtesy of Gerber Products Company; 236 Courtesy of Intel Corporation; 239 © 1998 Volvo Trucks North America, Inc.; 241 L.D. Gordon/Getty Images, Inc.

Chapter 7

256 © The Procter & Gamble Company. Used by permission; 260 © 2001 Vans, Inc.; 262 Courtesy of Ford Motor Company of Canada Ltd.; 266 Courtesy of Seagram Canada; 268 © Neiman Marcus; 270 Courtesy of Leo Burnett; 275 © MTV, a division of Viacom; 279 © Oshkosh Truck; 282 Reprinted with permission of Altimira Investment Services Inc.; 284 © Volvo corporation; 288 Courtesy of Pillsbury Europe; 290 Courtesy of WestJet.

Chapter 8

305 (Both) Metereon is a registered trademark of KTMA Inc., a business unit of Sony Corporation of America © Sony Corp; 307 © Sony Corp.; 311 Courtesy of Parallel Strategies; 313 Courtesy of Apple iMac; 314 By permission of Lanyon Phillips Partners; 318 Loblaw Brands Limited; 321 © Simon & Schuster; 324 Tetra Pak, Inc. 328 © Mercedes-Benz of North America, Inc.; 332 The Ritz-Carleton Hotel Company; 337 Munshi Ahmed Photography.

Chapter 9

348 Brooks Kraft/Corbis Sygma Photo News; 351 © Avon Corporation; 354 © Liason Agency, Inc., DaimlerChrysler Corporation; 357 Shaw Industries, Inc.; 360 Reproduced with permission of Elumens Corporation; 362 Courtesy of Hershey'®s; 366 Kraft Canada Inc.; 370 © (Left) AP/Wide World Photos, (Right) FritoLay, Inc.

Chapter 10

383 © The Terry Wild Studio, Inc.; **384** Reprinted with permission from CNET, Inc.; © Swatch; **391** © Kinko's Inc.; **394** © 2001, Gibson Guitar Corp. All Rights Reserved; **399** © D. Young-Wolff/PhotoEdit; **403** Images courtesy of Nintendo of America, Inc.; **407** Blair Seitz/Photo Researchers, Inc.; **409** Dick Hemingway; **411** Charles Gupton/Stock Boston; **416** Reprinted with permission of Leo Burnett Company, Inc. and Procter & Gamble Company

Chapter 11

430 (Both) Reprinted Courtesy of Caterpillar Inc.; **437** Dick Hemingway; **439** Reproduced by permission from www.can.ibm.com/store. Copyright 2002 by IBM Canada Ltd.; **444** (Left) Lee Lockwood/Black Star, (Right) © Michael Rizza/Stock Boston; **445** Courtesy of Bentley Motors Ltd.; **447** Charles Gupton/Stock Boston; **450** Courtesy of General Electric Corporation; **456** Courtesy of Roadway Express, Inc.

Chapter 12

471 Roots Canada Ltd.; **477** Courtesy of Costco; **479** Courtesy of Cinnzeo/A division of Cinnaroll Bakeries Limited; **483** Courtesy of Virgin Megastore, Vancouver; **486** Dick Hemingway; **492** © Playstation.com; **497** Courtesy of McKesson Corporation.

Chapter 13

507 Courtesy of American Standard; **509** STYLE.com© 2002 CondeNet, Inc. All rights reserved. Reprinted with permission; **512** © Dell Computer Corporation; **515** © Jon Feingersh/Stock Boston; **521** Reprinted with Permission of TBWA; **525** Used with permission of Volkswagen of America; **528** Michael J. Treola/AP/Wide World Photos; **531** Jeep® is a registered trademark of DaimlerChrysler Corporation; **536** By permission of Pepsi-Cola Canada Ltd.; **538** © Jeff Scheid/Gamma-Liason, Inc.; **542** © Butterball a division of ConAgra Foods.

Chapter 14

553 © Lear Corporation; **556** (Left) © John Henley/Stock Market, (Right) © Gabe Palmer/Stock Market; **559** Courtesy of DuPont & Company; **561** © Dan Bosler/Getty Images Inc.; **565** © Jon Coletti/Stock Boston; **569** © Rob Nelson/Black Star; **573** Courtesy of Advanced Sterilizations Products, a division of Ethum, Inc.; **578** Courtesy of Mars Incorporated; **580** © McDonald's Corporation; **583** © Karen Leitza/Karin Leitza.

Chapter 15

600 Kevin Frayer/Canadian Press; **601** (Left) Courtesy of feathercraft products Ltd., (Right) Courtesy of Blitz Design & Graphic Garage; **605** © SMART Technologies Inc.; **607** Used by permission of Canada Department Foreign Affairs and International Trade; **611** © Joseph Polleross/Regina Maria Anzenberger; **614** © Cary S Wolinsky/Cary Sol Wolinsky/Trillium Studios; **620** © Walt Disney Attractions Japan, Ltd.; **625** © Douglas E. Curran/Agence France-Presse; **627** (Both) Prestige & Collections; **629** © Fritz Hoffmann/Fritz Hoffmann.

Chapter 16

642 Courtesy of Altamira; **644** Dick Hemingway; **646** Courtesy of PhoneBusters; **650** Courtesy www.adbusters.org; **654** Courtesy of Campbell Soup Company Ltd.; **656** Courtesy of the Packaging Association of Canada; **658** Reprinted with permission of McDonald's Corporation; **664** Copyright 2003 General Motors Corp. Used with permission of GM Media Archives; **666** Courtesy of Concerns Canada; © Herman Miller, Inc.

INDEX

Company Index

Subject Index

System Requirements

PC

Pentium®-based PC or compatible processor
At least 32 MB of RAM
(64 MB for Windows® NT)
Windows® 95 or higher;
Windows®2000; Windows® ME;
Windows® NT 4.0 or higher
Sound Blaster or compatible sound card with speakers or headphones
4x or faster CD-ROM drive
Internet connection
QuickTime 4 or higher
Netscape 4.7 or Microsoft Internet
Explorer 4.01sp2 or later versions
Monitor with 800x600 resolution

Macintosh

PowerPC Processor-based Macintosh
At least 32 MB of RAM
Mac OS 7.6 or later
4x or faster CD-ROM drive
Internet connection
QuickTime 4 or higher
Netscape 4.7 or Microsoft Internet
Explorer 5 or later versions
Monitor with 800x600 resolution

Setup Instructions

FOR WINDOWS® USERS:

1. Start your computer.
2. Insert the Mastering Marketing CD into the CD-ROM drive.
3. If Mastering Marketing does not automatically start, double click the My Computer icon on your desktop.
4. Double click on the CD-ROM drive.
5. Double click the MasteringMarketing.html file.
6. Follow the instructions on the screen.
7. If you encounter any problems, see the readme file on the CD-ROM.

FOR MAC USERS:

1. Start your computer.
2. Insert the Mastering Marketing CD into the CD-ROM drive.
3. Double click on the Mastering Marketing icon on the desktop.
4. Double click the MasteringMarketing.html file.
5. Follow the instructions on the screen.
6. If you encounter any problems, see the readme file on the CD-ROM.